S0-BJM-477

A course in microeconomic theory

A course in

microeconomic theory

David M. Kreps

PRINCETON UNIVERSITY PRESS

Copyright © 1990 by David M. Kreps
Published by Princeton University Press, 41 William Street, Princeton, New Jersey 08540

All rights reserved

Library of Congress Cataloging-in-Publication Data
Kreps, David M.
A course in microeconomic theory / David M. Kreps.
p.   cm.
Includes bibliographical references.
ISBN 0-691-04264-0 (alk. paper)
1. Microeconomics. I. Title.
HB172.K74 1990
338.5–dc20   89-27619

This book has been composed in Palatino and Computer Modern typefaces.

Princeton University Press books are printed on acid-free paper, and meet the guidelines for permanence and durability of the Committee on Publication Guidelines for Book Longevity of the Council on Library Resources

Printed in the United States of America by Princeton University Press, Princeton, New Jersey

10 9 8 7 6 5 4 3 2 1

Figures from Chapter 20 have been adapted with permission of The Free Press, a Division of Macmillan, Inc. from THE ECONOMIC INSTITUTIONS OF CAPITALISM by Oliver E. Williamson. Copyright © 1985 by Oliver E. Williamson.

for Anat

contents

part I: Individual and social choice

chapter four: Dynamic choice   133

chapter five: Social choice and efficiency   149

part II: The price mechanism

chapter six: Pure exchange and general equilibrium   187

chapter seven: The neoclassical firm   233

appendix two: Dynamic programming   791

index   817

preface

This book provides an introduction to the content and methods of microeconomic theory. The primary target for this book is a first-year graduate student who is looking for an introduction to microeconomic theory that goes beyond the traditional models of the consumer, the firm, and the market. It could also be used by undergraduate majors who seek an "advanced theory" course following traditional intermediate micro. And, for relatively mathematically sophisticated students, it could be used as a nontraditional intermediate micro course. The book presumes, however, that the reader has survived the standard intermediate microeconomics course, and the student who has not gone through such a course may find it helpful on occasion to consult a traditional intermediate text. There are many excellent books around; four that I have recommended to students are Friedman, *Price Theory* (South-Western Publishing, 1986), Hirshleifer, *Price Theory and Applications* (4th edition, Prentice Hall, 1988), Nicholson, *Microeconomic Theory — Basic Principles and Extensions* (3d edition, Dryden Press, 1985), and Pindyck and Rubinfeld, *Microeconomics* (Macmillan, 1989).

The distinguishing feature of this book is that although it treats the traditional models (in parts I and II) it emphasizes more recent variations, with special emphases on the use of noncooperative game theory to model competitive interactions (part III), transactions in which private information plays a role (part IV), and the theory of firms and other nonmarket institutions (part V).

For the most part, the formal mathematical requirements of this book are mild. The reader will have to be able to do constrained optimization problems with inequality constraints, using Lagrange multipliers and the complementary slackness conditions. A cookbook recipe for this technique and an example are presented in an appendix. The reader can trust that for any problem in this book, with exceptions as noted, any solution to the first-order conditions and the complementary slackness conditions is a global optimum. That is, with a few exceptions, only "convex" problems are considered. The reader is expected to know basic probability theory.

For the sake of completeness, I sometimes delve into "optional" topics that either require a significant amount of mathematics or deal with somewhat advanced and/or esoteric topics. This material is presented both in footnotes and in slightly smaller typesize in the text. For the most part, it is up to the reader to supply the necessary mathematical background. The one exception concerns dynamic programming; a second appendix gives just enough background in the techniques of d.p. to get through its uses in this book. I apologize for any frustration the more technical material may cause. I have tried to make the book comprehensible even if the reader skips all this material.

The level of mathematical sophistication required (as opposed to the number of mathematical tools) rises as the book progresses. I have written this book with a first-year graduate student in mind, and I expect that the tolerence of such students for abstract arguments will rise as their first year of study unfolds.

The general style of the book is informal, and the number of theorems and proofs is relatively low. This book is meant to be a skeleton survey of microeconomic theory or, more precisely, of some of the topics and techniques of microeconomic theory; students and instructors will wish to supplement what is here according to their own tastes and interests. I try at the end of each chapter to indicate where the reader should go for more advanced and complete coverage of the topics under discussion.[1] The text is relatively more complete and formal in part III, the introduction to noncooperative game theory, because there are fewer good advanced treatments of that material other than the original papers.

Two caveats are called for by the style I employ. Despite the very impressive number of pages in this book, the number of ideas per page is low relative to a standard text. I prefer, and I think students prefer, books that are relatively chatty. Be that as it may, *this* book is relatively chatty. (This is my excuse for calling this *A Course in* .... Perhaps it would have been better to have called this *Lectures in* ....) I hope that readers who know some of the material aren't put off by this but can get to what they don't know without much delay. Second, I've tried to write a good textbook, which is not to my mind the same thing as a good reference book. The reader who goes back to this book to find something specific may find the exercise somewhat trying. In particular, many important concepts are discussed only in the context of specific problems, with the reader left to think through the general structure. I think this makes for a good textbook; but it doesn't make for a good reference book. Besides not always giving general formulations of concepts, I never give exhaustive surveys of the

----

[1] These reading lists are products of convenience, which means that they emphasize my own work and the work of close colleagues; there is certainly a Stanford and then American bias to these lists. They are not intended to be exhaustive; they certainly are not intended to establish precedence. It is inevitable that I have omitted many excellent and important citations, and apologies are hereby tendered to anyone offended.

range of applications that can be found in the literature; I hope that the reader, having digested my one example in one context, will be prepared to study other examples and contexts encountered outside this book. And I have not tried to diversify among topics. Some economy is achieved by using related examples (many of which I draw from the literature on industrial organization), and a book this long should economize whenever and wherever possible.

Owing to the limitations of time (and, less importantly, space), I didn't get to a few topics that I would have liked to have included. These fall primarily in the areas of parts IV and V and include: rational expectations with differential information; search; coordination failures; micromodels of market institutions, including auctions; models of political institutions. If ever there is a second edition, perhaps it will be longer still!

Insofar as a textbook can have a plot or a story or a message, I believe that this book does; this is not simply a compendium of many interesting and somewhat connected models. It is traditional, I believe, to give a précis of the "message" in the preface. But I have instead moved this to the end of chapter 1 in the hope that more readers will see it there than would see it here.

Concerning the ordering of topics, I am greatly undecided on one point (and instructors using this book may wish to undo the decision I settled on). To show applications of game theory as the techniques are developed, it may be sensible to interleave parts III and IV. After finishing chapter 12, go on to the earlier sections of chapter 16. Then take up chapter 17 and, when the game theoretic treatment of signaling is encountered, return to chapter 13. The disadvantage is that this breaks up the "oligopoly story" that runs through part III; my own experience is that the oligopoly story generates sufficient interest for a first pass through the techniques, and then parts IV and V provide good opportunities to review the techniques of part III. More generally, the book is filled with material that various instructors may find peripheral or too detailed for a first course; the course that I have taught, which formed the basis for this book, went from the first page to the last in ten weeks, but covered perhaps a third to a half of what fits between.

Most of the chapters come with a set of problems at the end. The serious student should do as many as possible. There are fewer problems per topic than one normally finds in textbooks, and the problems tend to be longer than most textbook problems because they often develop variations on the basic themes that the text doesn't cover. Variations are left to the problems on the principle that "doing" a model is a much better way to learn than reading about the model. A few of these problems require mathematical skills substantially beyond those needed to read the text of the book; the student who completes all the problems will have done extraordinarily well.

In teaching a course based on this book, I've supplemented the material here with reading in other, more traditional, texts, and (as importantly) with discussion of a few case studies from the Harvard Business School. I have found particularly valuable: *The Oil Tanker Shipping Industry in 1983* (Case #9-384-034) for discussion of perfect competition; *GE vs. Westinghouse in Large Turbine Generators (A), (B), and (C)* (#9-380-128,129,130) for discussion of implicit collusion in a noisy environment; *The Lincoln Electric Company* (#376-028) for discussion of incentives, screening, and nonneoclassical models of the firm; and *The Washington Post (A) and (B)* (#667-076,077) for discussion of internal organization, implicit contracts, transaction cost economics, and so forth.

I am grateful to a number of colleagues (some of whom were anonymous reviewers) and students who made helpful comments and suggestions on drafts of this book.[2] It would be impossible to give a comprehensive list, but Dilip Abreu, Anat Admati, David Baron, Elchanan Ben Porath, Ken Binmore, Don Brown, Drew Fudenberg, Oliver Hart, Bengt Holmstrom, David Levine, Nachum Melumad, Andrew McLennan, Paul Milgrom, Barry Nalebuff, John Pencavel, Stefan Reichelstein, Peter Reiss, John Roberts, Ariel Rubinstein, José Scheinkman, Jean Tirole, Guy Weyns, Jin Whang, Bob Wilson, Mark Wolfson, and especially Alex Benos, Marco Li Calzi, and Janet Spitz deserve special mention. I am also grateful to Virginia Barker, who copy-edited the book with skill and grace, and to Jack Repcheck of the Princeton University Press for his unflagging efforts in the preparation of this book and for his confidence in it, even when confronted with the possibility of yet another unexpected hundred pages.

It goes without saying that most of what is contained here I learned from and with many teachers, colleagues, and students. The list of such individuals is much too long to give here, so I will refrain except to note my obvious debt to Robert Wilson and to thank him and all of the rest of you.

---

[2] Many of the reviewers will be unhappy that I didn't more directly address their criticisms. But let me take this opportunity to assure them that I took those criticisms to heart, and I think they all helped make this a far better book.

A course in microeconomic theory

chapter one

An overview

This opening chapter sets out some basic concepts and philosophy for the rest of the book. In particular, we address four questions: What are the basic categories in microeconomic theory? What are the purposes of microeconomic theory? How does one's purpose influence the levels of scope, detail, and emphasis in one's model? How will the development of the theory proceed in this book?

1.1. The basic categories: Actors, behavior, institutions, and equilibrium

Microeconomic theory concerns the behavior of individual economic actors and the aggregation of their actions in different institutional frameworks. This one-sentence description introduces four categories: The individual *actor*, traditionally either a consumer or a firm; the *behavior* of the actor, traditionally utility maximization by consumers and profit maximization by firms; an *institutional framework*, which describes what options the individual actors have and what outcomes they receive as a function of the actions of others, traditionally the price mechanism in an impersonal marketplace; and the mode of analysis for modeling how the various actors' behaviors will aggregate within a given framework, traditionally *equilibrium* analysis.

The actors

In the standard treatment of microeconomics, the two types of actors are the individual *consumer* and the *firm*. We will follow the standard approach by regarding the consumer as an actor. For the firm, we will follow the standard approach for a while by treating the firm as an actor. But firms can also be thought of as institutions within which the behavior of various sorts of constituent consumers (workers, managers, suppliers, customers) are aggregated. From this alternative perspective, what a firm does results from the varying desires and behavior of its constituent consumers, the institutional framework the firm provides, and the equilibrium that is attained among the constituent consumers within that institutional framework. Much recent work in microeconomics has been directed towards treating the firm in this fashion, and we will take up this approach in the final part of the book.

Behavior

In the standard approach, behavior always takes the form of constrained maximization. The actor chooses from some specified set of options, selecting the option that maximizes some objective function. In orthodox theory, consumers have *preferences* that are represented by a *utility function*, and they choose in a way that maximizes their utility subject to a *budget constraint*. Firms, on the other hand, are modeled as *maximizing profits* subject to the constraints imposed by their *technological production possibilities set*.

These models of consumer and firm behavior typically strike people as fairly obnoxious. We don't find consumers strolling down the aisles of supermarkets consulting a utility function to maximize when making their choices, nor do we typically think of business executives being guided completely and solely (or even mainly) by the effect of their decisions on business profits. Nonetheless, we will use the standard model of consumer behavior throughout, and we will use the standard model of the firm for most of the book. It behooves us, then, to say why we think such models are useful.

Three rationales are often given. First, our models don't presume that consumers actively maximize some tangible utility function; the presumption is that consumers act *as if* this is what they do. Hence an important part of the theory of individual behavior concerns *testable restrictions* of the models we use: What behavior, if observed, would clearly falsify our models? If the models are not falsified by our observations, then our models are good positive models — perhaps not descriptive as to *why* things happen, but good in describing *what* happens.

Unhappily, rather a lot of data has been collected, especially experimentally, which falsifies the models we will employ. At this we fall back to our second line of defense by saying that such violations may be minor and not amount to much. That is, the standard models may be good approximations of individual behavior, and the conclusions of models built from such approximations may thus be approximately valid. This requires a leap of faith, but it is still a leap that has some intuitive appeal. In fact, we can take this a step further: In many (but not all) of our models, the behavior of the individual is unimportant; instead the aggregate behavior of many individuals matters. If we believe that violations of our models tend to exhibit no particular biases and cancel out at the level of aggregate behavior, then the models may work well. If all we care about are the implications of our models for aggregate behavior, then we will be content to look for testable implications (and falsifications) of our models at the level of aggregate behavior.

The third line of defense is the most subtle. Even if we know that there are systematic violations of our models by individuals, violations that do not cancel out, we can still gain insight into questions of interest by studying models where we assume away those violations. This line of defense is delicate because it requires the theorist to have a deep understanding of which assumptions drive the conclusions that are generated by the theory; we will return to this in the next two sections.

The institutional framework

The actions taken by any individual depend on the opportunities that are presented to the individual. Those opportunities, in turn, often depend upon the collective actions of others. And the consequences for an individual of that individual's actions usually depend on what others have chosen to do. The term *institutional framework* is used throughout to refer to those parts of a model that describe (a) the general nature of options that an individual has, and (b) the options available to and outcomes ensuing for each individual, as a function of other individuals' actions.

In the traditional models of microeconomics, *prices in an impersonal marketplace* constitute the institutional framework; consumers can choose any bundle they can afford, where what is affordable is determined by prices. The market is impersonal in the sense that all consumers face the same array of prices. And the precise choices available to one consumer depend on the consumption choices of all consumers (and the production choices of firms) through these prices.

As we will discuss at length, the workings of the price mechanism are quite fuzzy and ambiguous. Where do prices come from? How are they set, and how do they reflect the actions of individual consumers? Note also the potential of circularity in this; prices constrain the choices of individual consumers, and those choices simultaneously determine prices.

Spurred by these questions, we will look at more concrete and detailed institutional frameworks that are more precise about the connection between the choices of some individuals and the options available to and outcomes resulting for other individuals. An example of a more concrete mechanism, which in some sense leads to the establishment of a "price," is the institution of a sealed bid, first price auction: Anyone who wishes to may submit a bid for an object, with the high bidder winning the object and paying his or her bid. A different institutional framework for the same purpose is a progressive oral auction — an auction where bids are made openly, and each new bid must beat the previous high bid by some minimal amount.

Predicting the outcome: Equilibrium analysis

Having modeled the behavior of individuals, the nature of the choices they have, and the ways in which their actions affect each other, we are left with the task of saying just what the product of these things will be, that is, predicting what actions will be selected and what results will ensue. We will use various forms of *equilibrium analysis* to address this task. Generally speaking, an equilibrium is a situation in which each individual agent is doing as well as it can for itself, given the array of actions taken by others and given the institutional framework that defines the options of individuals and links their actions.

Although it is not quite how we will conduct business, you might think of this as a feedback system; individuals make individual choices, and the institutional framework aggregates those actions into an aggregate outcome which then determines constraints that individuals face and outcomes they receive. If individuals take a "trial shot" at an action, after the aggregation is accomplished and the feedback is fed back, they may learn that their actions are incompatible or didn't have quite the consequences they foresaw. This leads individuals to change their individual actions, which changes the feedback, and so on. An equilibrium is a collection of individual choices whereby the feedback process would lead to no subsequent change in behavior.

You might suppose that instead of studying only the equilibria of such a system, we will dive in and look at the dynamics of the feedback, change in behavior, change in feedback, ..., cycle, that is, the *disequilibrium dynamics* for the institutions we pose. We will do something like this in a few cases. But when we do, we will turn it into a study of *equilibrium dynamics*, where the institutional framework is expanded to include the feedback loops that are entailed and where individuals' behaviors are dynamically in equilibrium — each individual doing as well as possible given the institutional framework and the dynamic behaviors of others.

Our use of equilibrium analysis raises the question: Why are equilibria germane? Put another way, why do we think that what happens corresponds to an equilibrium? *We make no such blanket assumption.* As we will make especially clear in chapter 12, we rely on intuition and experience to say when this sort of analysis is germane, and while we will sketch a variety of reasons that equilibria might be achieved and equilibrium analysis might be relevant, we try never to *presume* in a particular application that this is so.

1.2. *The purpose of microeconomic theory*

Having set out the basic categories of microeconomic theory (at least as practiced in this book), we come to the question: What do we intend to get out of the theory? The simple answer is a better understanding of economic activity and outcomes.

Why do we seek a better understanding? One reason that needs no explanation is simple intellectual curiosity. But beyond that, a better understanding of economic activity can be useful in at least two ways. First, as a participant in the economic system, better understanding can lead to better outcomes for oneself. That is why budding business executives (are told to) study microeconomics; a better understanding of the ways in which markets work will allow them to make markets work better for themselves. And second, part of the study of microeconomics concerns the efficiency and specific inefficiencies in various institutional frameworks with a view towards policy. One tries to see whether a particular institution can, by tinkering or by drastic change, be made to yield a socially better outcome; the vague presumption is that changes that improve the social weal might be made via social and political processes. In this book, we will touch on the efficiency of various institutions, although this will be relatively deemphasized.

What constitutes better understanding? Put differently, how does one know when one has learned something from an exercise in microeconomic theory? The standard acid test is that the theory should be (a) testable and (b) tested empirically, either in the real world or in the lab.[1] But many of the models and theories given in this book have not been subjected to a rigorous empirical test, and some of them may never be. Yet, I maintain, models untested rigorously may still lead to better understanding, through a process that combines casual empiricism and intuition.

By casual empiricism joined with intuition I mean that the reader should look at any given model or idea and ask: Based on personal experience and intuition about how things are, does this make sense? Does it help put into perspective things that have been observed? Does it help organize thoughts about a number of "facts?" When and if so, the exercise of theory construction has been useful.

---

[1] See chapters 3, 6, and 15 if the concept of a laboratory test of an economic theory is new to you.

Imagine that you are trying to explain a particular phenomenon with one of two competing theories. Neither fits the data perfectly, but the first does a somewhat better job according to standard statistical measures. At the same time, the first theory is built on some hypotheses about behavior by individuals that are entirely ad hoc, whereas the second is based on a model of behavior that appeals to your intuition about how people act in this sort of situation. I assert that trying to decide which model does a better job of "explaining" is *not* simply a matter of looking at which fits better statistically. The second model should gain credence because of its greater face validity, which brings to bear, in an informal sense, other data.[2]

Needless to say, one's intuition is a personal thing. Judging models on the basis of their level of intuitive credibility is a risky business. One can be misled by models, especially when one is the creator of the model, and one is more prone to be misled the more complex the model is. Empirical verification should be more than an ideal to which one pays lip service; one should try honestly to construct (and even test) testable models. But intuition honestly applied is not worthless and should not be completely abandoned. Moreover, exercises can be performed to see what drives the conclusions of a model; examine how robust the results are to changes in specification and precise assumptions.

There is something of a "market test" here: one's ability to convince others of one's personal intuitive insights arising from specific models. Microeconomic theorists have a tendency to overresearch "fashionable" topics; insofar as they can be convinced by something because it is fashionable and not because it rings true, they are less than ideal for this market test. But less theoretically and more empirically inclined colleagues (and, sometimes even better, practitioners) are typically good and sceptical judges of the value of a particular model. Attempts to convince them, while sometimes frustrating, are usually helpful both to understand and improve upon a model.

The usefulness of falsified models

To push this even further, I would argue that sometimes a model whose predictions are clearly falsified is still useful. This can happen in at least three ways. First, insofar as one understands how the assumptions led to the falsified conclusions, one understands which assumptions *don't*

---

[2] Readers who know about Bayesian inference should think of this as a case in which the likelihood of the first model is greater, but the second has higher prior probability. Which has a greater posterior probability is then unclear and depends on the relative strengths of the priors and likelihoods.

lead to the "truth." Knowing what doesn't work is often a good place to begin to figure out what does.

Second, theory building is a cumulative process. Under the presumption that most economic contexts share some fundamental characteristics, there is value in having models that conform to "generally accepted principles" that have served well in other contexts. Compared with a model that is radically different from standard models, a model that conforms to standard assumptions and principles will be better understood, both by the theory creator and by the audience. Moreover, unification of theory is valuable for its own sake to gain a better understanding of the shared characteristics. Of course, not all contexts are the same, and sometimes what economists think of as "generally acceptable and universally applicable principles" are pushed too far. Economists are well-known among social scientists as imperialists in the sense that economists attempt to reduce everything to economic notions and paradigms. But a real case still can be made for tradition and conservatism in the development of economic (and other) theory.

Granting this, when looking at an economic phenomenon that is poorly understood, economic theorists will attempt to build models that fit into the general rules of the discipline. Such attempts are rarely successful on the first trial. But insofar as first trials do lead to second and third trials, each of which gets one closer, the first trial is of value, and learning about another's first trial may help you construct the second and third.[3]

Economists tell a parable about theory and theorists that relates to this. An economic theorist lost his wallet in a field by a road and proceeded to search futilely for the wallet in the road under the illumination of a street light on the grounds that "that is where the light is." So, the folktale goes, it is with using theoretically "correct" but otherwise inappropriate theory. But an amendment to this tale is suggested by José Scheinkman: Without defending the actions of this particular theorist, perhaps one could try to construct a string of lights that begins in the road and that will eventually reach the field, on the grounds that the road is where electricity presently is found.

Third, and perhaps most subtly, models that fail to predict because they lack certain realistic features can still help clarify the analyst's thinking about the features they do encompass, as long as the analyst is able to combine intuitively and informally what has been omitted from the model

---

[3] That said, I cannot help but note that the journals contain many more papers that begin "This paper takes a first step in..." than papers that take second or third steps. Not every attempt at widening the scope of economic theory is successful!

with what has been learned from it. Of course, everything else held equal, it is "better" to have a model that captures formally more of the salient aspects of the situation than to have one that omits important features. But all else is rarely equal, and one shouldn't preclude building intuition with models that make somewhat falsified assumptions or give somewhat falsified conclusions, as long as one can understand and integrate informally what is missing formally.

1.3. *Scope, detail, emphasis, and complexity*

This leads to a third point about the theories and models that will be encountered in this book: their levels of scope, detail, emphasis, and complexity.

On scope, chapter 8 presents an excellent illustration. Chapter 8 concerns the theory of perfect competition. It begins with the analysis of a market for a single good — the theory of perfect competition that will be familiar to you from intermediate microeconomics. You may recall from intermediate micro that the industry supply curve is the horizontal sum of the individual supply curves of firms, and the supply curves of firms are their marginal cost curves. (If you don't recall this or never heard of it before, just read on for the flow of what I'm about to say.) This would lead to inaccurate predictions of, say, how price will move with shifts in demand, if one factor of production of the good in question comes from a market that itself has an upward sloping supply curve. To illustrate this, we move in chapter 8 from the traditional model of a single market to consideration of two linked markets, both of which are perfectly competitive. But why stop with two markets? Why not consider all markets together? At the end of chapter 8, under the assumption that all markets are perfectly competitive, we will see what can be said about such a (so-called) general equilibrium.

So what is the appropriate scope for a given model? There is a natural inclination to say that larger scope is better. But there are drawbacks to larger scope. The larger the scope, the more intractable the model, and the harder it is to draw out sharp and/or intuitively comprehensible results. One might feel relatively comfortable making strong assumptions in a model with a narrow scope about how the "outside" affects what is inside the model, assumptions that are (or seem) likely to be true and hence good modeling assumptions but that cannot easily be deduced generally in a model with an expanded scope.

For level of detail, consider how one should treat the family unit in a model of consumer demand. The standard model of consumer demand envisions a single individual who maximizes his or her utility subject to a budget constraint. Almost anyone who has lived in a family will recognize that family expenditure decisions are a bit more involved than this. Individual members of the family, presumably, have their own tastes. But they recognize a strong interdependence in their personal consumption decisions. (Family members may like, or dislike, taking their vacations in the same location, for example.) And they often pool resources, so that their individual budget constraints get mixed together. Should we treat the family unit as a single consumer or attempt to build a more detailed model about interactions among family members? The answer will depend on what phenomena we are trying to explain. In most models, families are treated "coarsely," as consuming units, each family conforming to the standard model of the consumer. But for models of the labor supply decisions of families, for example, the detailed modeling of family interaction is sometimes crucial to what is being explained and so is included within the formal model. In general, one pays a cost in tractability and comprehension for increased detail. But in some contexts, greater detail is essential to get at the point in question.

Emphasis is meant to connote something like scope and like detail that isn't quite either. When looking at a particular phenomenon, the analyst may wish to emphasize certain aspects. To do this, the model may become unbalanced — heavy on one aspect of detail, or wide in one aspect of scope, but simple and narrow in all others. Especially when building a model to develop intuition concerning one facet of a larger problem, and where one will rely on less formal methods to integrate in other facets, models that (over)emphasize the facet of immediate interest are warranted.

This discussion is meant to alert the reader to a crucial aspect of microeconomic models and a crucial skill for microeconomists: Building a model is a matter of selecting the appropriate scope, level of detail, and matters to emphasize. There is no set formula to do this, because the appropriate levels of each depend on what the model seeks to accomplish. When "proving" the efficiency of the market system (see chapters 6 and 8), a wide scope is appropriate because overall efficiency is an economy-wide phenomenon. To demonstrate the *possibility* of a particular form of inefficiency in a particular form of market, narrower scope and greater emphasis on a few crucial details are called for. In this book you will see a wide variety of models that vary in their levels of scope, detail, and emphasis, and it is hoped that you will both get a taste for the variety of "types" of models that are used by microeconomic theorists and get a sense of the strengths and weaknesses of those types.

Let me add two further considerations, using the general notion of the level of complexity of one's models. Complexity combines scope and detail, but has other aspects as well, such as the level of mathematics required. Insofar as the model is meant to generate insights and to build intuition, too great a level of complexity in any form is usually bad. Insights and intuition are built from understanding — recognizing (in the model) which assumptions are crucial and what leads to what. The more complex a model is, the harder it is to achieve that sort of understanding. At the same time, simple models too often lead to flawed insights, because the conclusions depend too heavily on the simple setting that is assumed. Lessons that seem obvious from models of single markets in isolation are too easily overturned when one examines the interaction between markets. Balancing these considerations is not easy.

By the same token, building models to explain one's own insights to others requires a balance between complexity and simplicity. Recall that the proposed "market test" was whether you could convince an economist or practitioner who is perhaps not up-to-date with the latest fashion in economic theory but who instead has a well-developed intuitive understanding of how things are. Very complex models that require either a lot of knowledge about the latest techniques or incredible patience to work through mathematical detail will not pass this test. But, at the same time, a lot of the more complex techniques in microeconomic theory are there to check the *consistency* of models; however appealing the conclusions are, a model that is predicated on assumptions that are logically inconsistent or inconsistent with most standard theory is unsatisfactory. The best theories and models are those that pass (possibly complex) tests of consistency or validity and, at the same time, provide insights that are clear and intuitive and don't depend on some mathematical sleight-of-hand. Not all the theories and models that are presented here will pass this dual test. All will pass the consistency test (I hope), so you can anticipate that those that fail will fail on grounds of being too complex to be intuitive.[4] And those that do fail on grounds of complexity are, by virtue of that failure, somewhat of second (or lower) quality.

1.4. A précis of the plot

This book may be thought of as a collection of somewhat interconnected models that are interesting in their own right. But, at the same

---

[4] Put an X in the margin by this sentence. When we get to analysis of the centipede game in chapter 14, I will remind you that I gave fair warning.

time, the book has been written to convey the strengths and weaknesses of the tools that microeconomic theory has at its disposal. You should have little problem seeing the individual pieces from the table of contents, but it may be helpful to discuss the more global development that I intend.

First, insofar as one can split the subject of microeconomic theory into (1) actors and their behavior and (2) institutions and equilibrium, this is a book that stresses institutions and equilibrium. I don't mean to disparage the theories of individual behavior that are a cornerstone of microeconomic theory. I've even written a different book on one aspect of that subject. But I believe that *detailed* study of this topic can wait until one studies institutions and equilibrium, and the latter subject is of greater immediate interest and appeal. Still, it is necessary to understand the basics of the standard models of consumer (and firm) behavior before you can understand models of equilibrium, and part I and chapter 7 in part II provide the necessary background. Some readers of this book will have already taken a course that stressed the standard theories of the consumer and the firm. Such readers will probably find a light skim of chapters 2 and 7 adequate, but chapters 3, 4, and 5 present important background for the rest of the book that is treated here in greater depth than is typical in the traditional first course in microeconomics.

Part II takes up the classic "mechanism" by which individuals' diverse desires are meant to be brought into equilibrium: the price mechanism. We progress from situations of perfect competition in which, except for ambiguity about how prices are set, the price mechanism works both clearly and well, to monopoly and oligopoly, where it is less clear that prices alone are doing the equilibrating. By the time we reach the end of oligopoly, we see rather large holes in our understanding of how prices work, and we tentatively attribute those holes to a lack of specification of what precisely is "the price mechanism."

In part III we look at techniques that are meant to help us fill in those holes, techniques from noncooperative game theory. Game theoretic analyses have been extremely fashionable in microeconomic theory since the mid-1970s because such analyses are quite precise concerning institutional framework and because they help us see how institutions matter. Indeed, we will see cases in which, according to the theory, the institutional framework seems to matter too much. But we develop at the same time two weaknesses in such analyses. One, in many important cases, the theory is not determinative — many "equilibria" are possible, and which equilibrium if any arises depends on conjectures that are not provided for by the theory. Two, insofar as institutions matter, one has to wonder where existing institutions come from. Game theoretic analyses take the institutions as exogenously given. Until we understand where institutions come from and how they evolve, an important part of the puzzle is left unsolved.

Part IV exhibits some of the most important achievements of microeconomic theory in the 1970s and 1980s, developments in the so-called *economics of information.* You are meant to come away from part IV impressed by the insights that can be gleaned by the close analysis of market institutions, both with and without the techniques of noncooperative game theory. To be sure, the problems with our techniques that are discussed throughout part III are not resolved here, and many important questions are left unanswered. But insofar as microeconomic theory has made progress on substantial questions over the past twenty years, this is an area of progress.

In part V we take up the theory of the firm. In standard microeconomic theory firms are actors very much like consumers. We will criticize this classical view and consider instead a view of the firm as something in the category of a market — an institution within which diverse desires of consumers of various sorts are equilibrated. We are able to shed some light on what role firms and other nonmarket institutions play, but we will see that matters crucially important to this subject do not seem amenable to study with the tools at our disposal. In a sense we will come back full circle to individual behavior. The argument will be that we cannot do an adequate job studying firms and other institutions, and especially the origins and evolution of these institutions, unless and until we reformulate and refine the models we have of individual behavior.

All this is, presumably, a bit hard to fathom without a lot of fleshing out. But that's the point of the next eight hundred-odd pages.

part I

Individual and social choice

chapter two

The theory of consumer choice and demand

Prologue to part I

The central figure in microeconomic theory is the consumer, and the first step is almost always to provide a model of the consumer's *behavior*. This model may be substantially implied (see the discussion in 8.1 on demand curves), but it is there at some level. We usually think of the consumer as an entity who *chooses* from some given set of feasible options, and so our first order of business, which takes up most of part I, is to provide models of consumer choice.

You will recall from intermediate micro (and even most principles courses) the representation of consumer choice given in figure 2.1. We imagine a consumer who consumes two goods, say wine, denominated in numbers of bottles, and beer, denominated in numbers of cans. Imagine that this consumer has $1,000 to spend, the price of beer is $1 per can, and the price of wine is $10 per bottle. Then our consumer can purchase any combination of beer and wine in the shaded area in figure 2.1.

The consumer has preferences over combinations of beer and wine represented by *indifference curves*; these are the curves in figure 2.1. All

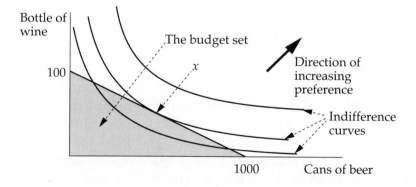

Figure 2.1. The usual picture for consumer demand.

points along a given curve are bundles of beer and wine that the consumer rates as being equally good (so she is *indifferent* among them), and the consumer prefers to be "further out," in the direction of the heavy arrow. Hence this consumer selects the point marked x, the point on the highest indifference curve that still is affordable given prices and the consumer's level of income.

With this picture, you and your teacher probably went on to consider how the consumer reacts as his level of income changes, the price of wine decreases, an excise tax is imposed on one good or the other, and so on. This picture encapsulates a simple model of consumer choice, viz., the consumer chooses from the feasible set some point that is on the highest available indifference curve. In this chapter, we explore the foundations for this picture (and more complex generalizations of it) by considering choice and preference in the abstract and we consider the fundamental application of this theory in microeconomics, *Marshallian demand*. In chapter 3, we consider choice where the objects from which choice is made have uncertain prizes. In chapter 4, we look at how to model choices that are made through time instead of all at once.

In most situations, when there is more than one consumer the choices the various consumers wish to make are somewhat in conflict. The rest of the book (chapter 7 excepted) concerns the resolution of such conflicts. We will, by and large, imagine that the conflicts are resolved by particular institutional arrangements (such as the price mechanism); we will go on to model specific institutions and study how the conflicts are resolved. But to close part I, we will look briefly at the problem of *social choice* in the abstract, studying principles that might be used to characterize particular resolutions and even to dictate a specific resolution.

To begin then, keep figure 2.1 firmly in mind as we ask, Where do these indifference curves come from and what do they represent?

2.1. Preferences and choices

The objects of choice

We are interested here in the behavior of an individual, called *the consumer*, who is faced with the problem of choosing from among a set of objects. To begin, we formalize the set from which the choice is to be made. Let X represent some set of *objects*. It is quite typical in economic applications to think of X as a space of consumption bundles, modeled as a subset of R^K, where R is the real line and K is the number of commodities. In an economy with three commodities, say beer, wine and whisky, $K = 3$, and a typical consumption bundle is a three-vector,

$x = (x_1, x_2, x_3)$, representing x_1 cans of beer, x_2 bottles of wine, and x_3 shots of whisky. The units — cans, bottles, shots — are arbitrary; we choose any convenient units.

A favorite game of economists is to make simple, basic constructions work in ever wider and wilder circumstances; while you think of commodities such as cans of beer, also think of commodities such as cans of beer next week, as distinct from cans of beer today or in two weeks time; the services of a bottle opener next week; the services of a bartender to draw a beer next week, if the temperature tomorrow gets over seventy degrees and then falls to sixty-five sometime in the next four days. These, and things even stranger, are shoehorned into the basic framework. For now, think of beer, wine, whisky (or, when we draw two-dimensional pictures as in figure 2.1, drop the whisky). But bear in mind that economic theory is often a shell game that seeks to convince you with simple, concrete examples and then gets you to extrapolate without thinking too much about more problematic settings.

The basic preference relation

The standard way to model the consumer is with a preference relation. Imagine that we present the consumer with pairs of alternatives, x and y, and ask how they compare. Our question is, Is either x or y better than the other in your eyes? If the consumer says that x is in fact better than y, we write $x \succ y$ and we say that x is *strictly preferred* to y.

For each pair x and y, we can imagine four possible responses to our question: (1) The consumer may say that x is better than y, but not the reverse. (2) She may say that y is better than x, but not the reverse. (3) She may say that neither seems better to her; she is unwilling to commit to a judgment. (4) She may say that x is better than y *and* y is better than x. Right away we wish to preclude the fourth possibility. It is logically possible for a consumer to state that each alternative is better than the other, but this stretches the meaning of the language too far and, more to the point, it would be very inconvenient for later purposes. Hence we assume

Assumption 1. *Preferences are* **asymmetric:** *There is no pair x and y from X such that $x \succ y$ and $y \succ x$.*

But before you conclude that this is obvious, consider two problems with our entire story that bear on this assumption. First, we have said nothing about when our consumer is making these judgments. Our story sounds as if these judgments are made at some single point in time, in which case assumption 1 seems reasonable. But when we apply models that are based on assumption 1, we will sometimes assume that the judgments expressed by our consumer at one point in time remain valid at subsequent times. You might not find so reasonable an assumption that, if a consumer decides she will prefer x to y a week from now, four days hence she will necessarily continue to prefer x to y after three further days. But in some contexts, when consumers are making choices at a number of distinct dates, by making assumption 1 and applying the standard model as usual, we will be assuming that this is so. (For more on this see chapter 4.)

A second reason to wonder about assumption 1 concerns the framing of a particular choice. It is easiest to illustrate this with an example taken from Kahneman and Tversky (1979):

> As a doctor in a position of authority in the national government, you've been informed that a new flu epidemic will hit your country next winter and that this epidemic will result in the deaths of 600 people. (Either death or complete recovery is the outcome in each case.) There are two possible vaccination programs that you can undertake, and doing one precludes doing the other. The first will save 400 people with certainty. The second will save no one with probability 1/3 and 600 with probability 2/3. Which do you prefer?

Formulate an answer to this question, and then try:

> As a doctor in a position of authority in the national govenment, you've been informed that a new flu epidemic will hit your country next winter. To fight this epidemic, one of two possible vaccination programs is to be chosen, and undertaking one program precludes attempting the other. In the first program, 200 people will die with certainty. In the second, there is a 2/3 chance that no one will die, and a 1/3 chance that 600 will die. Which do you prefer?

These questions are complicated by the fact that they involve some uncertainty, the topic of chapter 3. But they make the point very well. Asked of medical professionals, the modal responses to this pair of questions were preferences for the first program in the first question and for the second program in the second question. The point is that the questions are identical in terms of outcomes — the only difference is in the way that the questions have been framed or phrased. In the first question, those 600 are dead, and most people choose to bring some of them back to life with certainty. In the second question, no one is dead yet, and it seems rather callous to consign 200 people to certain death.[1] Framing can affect comparative judgments like the ones we are asking our consumer, especially when the items under consideration are complex. When items are complex, the cognitive process that underpins an eventual rank ordering can involve focusing on certain aspects, and the way in which the alternatives are framed can affect what is focused upon and, therefore, what is chosen. Given a particular framing of alternatives, we might not hear $x \succ y$ and $y \succ x$ in the same breath, but the pause between breaths in which these two "contradictory" judgments are made may be short indeed.

Despite these objections, assumption 1 is made in virtually every model of consumer choice in economics. Joined to it is a second assumption, which says that if a consumer makes the judgment $x \succ y$, she is able to place any other option z somewhere on the ordinal scale set by these two: better than y, or worse than x (or both). Formally:

Assumption 2. *Preferences are* **negatively transitive***: If* $x \succ y$*, then for any third element* z*, either* $x \succ z$*, or* $z \succ y$*, or both.*

(The term *negative transitivity* will remain mysterious if you don't do problem 1.) The content of this assumption can best be illustrated by an example that is intended to cast doubt on it. Suppose that objects like x and y are bundles of cans of beer and bottles of wine: vectors (x_1, x_2), where the first component is the number of cans of beer and the second is the number of bottles of wine. Our consumer might have no problem comparing the two bundles $(20, 8)$ and $(21, 9)$. Presumably (assuming a lack of temperance), $(21, 9) \succ (20, 8)$. But let $x = (21, 9)$, $y = (20, 8)$, and $z = (40, 2)$ in assumption 2. Since $x \succ y$, the assumption maintains that either $x \succ z$, or $z \succ y$, or both; that is, either $(21, 9) \succ (40, 2)$, or $(40, 2) \succ (20, 8)$, or both. Our consumer, however, may claim that she can rank the two bundles $(21, 9)$ and $(20, 8)$, but comparing either with $(40, 2)$ is too hard, and our consumer refuses to commit to either ranking. It is this that assumption 2 rules out.

Beyond assumptions 1 and 2, other properties seem natural for strict preference. Three natural properties are:

(1) *Irreflexivity*: For no x is $x \succ x$.

(2) *Transitivity*: If $x \succ y$ and $y \succ z$, then $x \succ z$.

---

[1] If you care to see how even one word makes a difference, reread the first question with the word *all* inserted just before the 600 in the next-to-last sentence.

(3) *Acyclicity*: If, for a given finite integer n, $x_1 \succ x_2, x_2 \succ x_3, \ldots, x_{n-1} \succ x_n$, then $x_n \neq x_1$.

All three of these properties are implied by assumptions 1 and 2. We state this as a proposition:

Proposition 2.1. *If $\succ$ is asymmetric and negatively transitive, then $\succ$ is irreflexive, transitive and acyclic.*

We leave almost all the proofs of propositions in this section to you, but this one is so easy that we will give it. First, irreflexivity is directly implied by asymmetry: If $x \succ x$, then $\succ$ would not be asymmetric. (Note that in the definition of asymmetry, we did not say that $x \neq y$.) For transitivity, suppose that $x \succ y$ and $y \succ z$. By negative transitivity and $x \succ y$, we know that either $x \succ z$ or $z \succ y$. But since $y \succ z$, asymmetry forbids $z \succ y$. Hence $x \succ z$. And, for acyclicity, if $x_1 \succ x_2$, $x_2 \succ x_3$, $\ldots$, $x_{n-1} \succ x_n$, then transitivity implies that $x_1 \succ x_n$. And then asymmetry implies that $x_1 \neq x_n$.

That is all there is to the basic standard model of preference in microeconomics: The consumer makes rank order judgments between pairs of alternatives that satisfy assumptions 1 and 2. From this point there are four paths to follow: First, from expressed strict preference $\succ$, economists create associated weak preference and indifference relations. Second, this model of rank ordering pairs of alternatives is related to choices made by the consumer, when she has more than two alternatives at her disposal. Third, for reasons of analytical convenience, we seek a numerical representation for preferences. And fourth, we seek additional assumptions that will make the model of individual preference (and resulting choice) more amenable to analysis, so, for example, we get pictures like that shown in figure 2.1, with "nicely" shaped indifference curves, where "nice" remains to be defined. We consider each of these in turn.

Weak preference and indifference

Suppose our consumer's preferences are given by the relation $\succ$. From this we can define two further relations among pairs of alternatives in X:

Definitions. *For x and y in X, write $x \succeq y$, which is read x is **weakly preferred** to y, if it is not the case that $y \succ x$. And write $x \sim y$, read as x is **indifferent** to y, if it is not the case that either $x \succ y$ or $y \succ x$.*

Note carefully what has been done here: Weak preference is defined as the absence of strict preference "the other way," and indifference is defined as the absence of strict preference "in either direction." Does this accord with one's intuitive sense of what weak preference and indifference mean? Not entirely, insofar as there are judgments that are hard for the individual to make. Our consumer who is choosing cans of beer and bottles of wine may feel unable to say either $(40, 2) \succ (20, 8)$ or $(20, 8) \succ (40, 2)$, but this doesn't make her positively indifferent between these two. Or if it did, indifference would be a strange animal: If this implies $(20, 8) \sim (40, 2)$, and if a similar inability to rank $(21, 9)$ and $(40, 2)$ implies $(21, 9) \sim (40, 2)$, then two bundles $((20, 8)$ and $(21, 9))$, one of which is strictly preferred to another, would both be indifferent to a third.

> (*As promised in the preface, certain esoteric matters in this book will be relegated to paragraphs such as this one: tighter spacing, smaller type, and slight indentation. This material isn't required for most of what follows, and the reader may find it less confusing to skip these paragraphs on a first reading and then return to them later.*) In view of such concerns, we might be happier to define weak preference and indifference as follows: In addition to expressing strict preference $\succ$, the consumer expresses positive indifference $\sim$, and weak preference is defined as the conjunction of the two: $x \succeq y$ if either $x \succ y$ or $x \sim y$. We would probably want to insist that $x \sim y$ is incompatible with either $x \succ y$ or $y \succ x$, so by assumption 1, at most one of these three possibilities would be true for any pair x and y. But we do not preclude a fourth possibility, namely that x and y are simply incomparable. This is an interesting but nonstandard way to proceed, and we will not pursue it in depth here; see Fishburn (1970).

Despite such concerns, weak preference and indifference are usually defined from strict preference in the fashion of the definition given above. And if one has assumptions 1 and 2 in hand, the associated weak preference and indifference relationships are well behaved.

Proposition 2.2. *If strict preference $\succ$ is asymmetric and negatively transitive, and weak preference and indifference are defined from strict preference according to the definitions given above, then:*

*(a) Weak preference $\succeq$ is **complete**: For every pair x and y, either $x \succeq y$ or $y \succeq x$ or both.*

*(b) Weak preference $\succeq$ is **transitive**: If $x \succeq y$ and $y \succeq z$, then $x \succeq z$.*

*(c) Indifference $\sim$ is **reflexive**, $x \sim x$ for all x, **symmetric**, $x \sim y$ implies $y \sim x$, and **transitive**, $x \sim y$ and $y \sim z$ implies $x \sim z$.*[a]

---

[a] (*And sometimes mathematical esoterica is found in footnotes. Footnotes that are labeled with letters are more technical. Footnotes labeled with numbers should be read by all.*) A binary relation that is reflexive, symmetric and transitive is called an *equivalence* relation in mathematical jargon. So we can paraphrase part (c) as: given our two assumptions concerning $\succ$, indifference is an equivalence relation. See problem 2 for more on this.

(d) If $w \sim x, x \succ y$, and $y \sim z$, then $w \succ y$ and $x \succ z$.

There is one thing left to say about strict and weak preference. We have taken strict preference as primitive (what the consumer expresses) and defined weak preference from it. Most books begin with weak preference and induce strict preference. I prefer beginning with strict preference because it makes it easier to discuss noncomparability possibilities. Most authors prefer weak preference, I suspect, because negative transitivity is hard to wrap one's head around. But in the standard treatment, these two approaches are completely equivalent. Suppose you started with weak preference $\succeq$ and then defined strict preference $\succ$ by $x \succ y$ if it is not the case that $y \succeq x$ and defined indifference by $x \sim y$ if both $x \succeq y$ and $y \succeq x$. Then there would be no difference between beginning with $\succ$ or with $\succeq$. Moreover, if you began with $\succeq$, which is complete and transitive, the relation $\succ$ obtained would be asymmetric and negatively transitive. So for the standard treatment, it makes no difference whether you begin with asymmetric and negatively transitive strict preference $\succ$ or with complete and transitive weak preference $\succeq$, as long as you define the other as above.[b]

> When we discussed negative transitivity of $\succ$, we illustrated what could go wrong with an example suggested by an inability to compare bundles. If we had begun our discussion of preferences with $\succeq$, it would have been natural to use a similar example to show what goes wrong with an assumption that $\succeq$ is complete. You may conclude from this that negative transitivity of $\succ$ corresponds in some way to completeness of $\succeq$. Yet if you do problem 1, you will see that this is wrong; negative transitivity of $\succ$ corresponds to transitivity of $\succeq$, while asymmetry of $\succ$ corresponds to completeness of $\succeq$. The reason for this apparent conundrum is that we define $x \succeq y$ if it is not the case that $y \succ x$ (and vice versa). In this definition, when we start with $\succ$, we include in $\succeq$ any cases of noncomparability. Put differently, if we admitted the possibility of incomparable pairs and so defined separately from $\succ$ a relation $\sim$ that expresses positive indifference, and we then defined $\succeq$ not by $x \succeq y$ if not $y \succ x$, but instead by $x \succeq y$ if $x \succ y$ or $x \sim y$, the relationship between negative transitivity of $\succ$ and completeness of $\succeq$ would be more in line with our intuition. (You will probably make sense of all this only if you take the time to hunt down a treatment of preference in which there is a formal difference between positive indifference and noncomparability.)

From preference to choice

So far our consumer has given her rank ordering between pairs of alternatives out of X. In typical situations, she will be choosing out of a

---

[b] When authors begin with $\succeq$, they sometimes add a third assumption, namely that $\succeq$ is reflexive, or $x \succeq x$ for all x. This is implied by completeness and so is redundant.

set with more than two members. So how do we relate her preferences and her choice behavior? It is typical to assume that *choice* is induced from *preference* according to the following formal definition.

Definition. *Given a preference relation $\succ$ on a set of objects X and a nonempty subset A of X, the **set of acceptable alternatives** from A according to $\succ$ is defined to be*

$$c(A; \succ) = \{x \in A : \text{there is no } y \in A \text{ such that } y \succ x\}.$$

The content of this definition is that the consumer is happy to choose anything that isn't bettered by something else that is available. Note several things concerning this:

(1) The set $c(A; \succ)$ is, by definition, a subset of A. Anything else wouldn't make sense given our interpretation.

(2) The set $c(A; \succ)$ may contain more than one element. When $c(A; \succ)$ contains more than one element, the interpretation is that the consumer is willing to take any one of those elements; she isn't particular about which one she gets.[2]

(3) In some cases, the set $c(A; \succ)$ may contain no elements at all. For example, suppose that $X = [0, \infty)$ with $x \in X$ representing x dollars. And suppose A is the subset $\{1, 2, 3, \ldots\}$. If you always prefer more money to less, or $x \succ y$ whenever $x > y$, $c(A; \succ)$ will be empty. No matter how much money you might take, some amount of money in A is greater, hence better. Or suppose, in the same context, that $A = [0, 10)$. For those of you unused to this notation, this means that A consists of all dollar amounts up to *but not including* 10. Then if money is divisible into arbitrarily fine units, there is no element of A that isn't bettered by some other.[c]

---

[2] Students will sometimes get a bit confused at this point, so let me be very pedantic. In most applications, an alternative x is a bundle of goods — a vector representing so many bottles of wine, so many cans of tuna fish, etc. If $c(A; \succ)$ has two elements, say x and x', we do not interpret this as saying that the individual chooses to take both x and x' together. If having both these bundles together was a possibility, then the vector sum $x + x'$ would be an element of A. Instead, $c(A; \succ) = \{x, x'\}$ means that the individual is happy with *either* x or x'.

[c] You may object that (a) there isn't an infinite amount of money to be had and (b) money isn't divisible past the penny or the mill, so that both examples are unrealistic. In this case, let me pose one further example. I will flip a coin N times, where N is a positive integer. On the first occurrence of heads, I will give you $10. If there are N tails in a row, you get nothing. You must choose N from the set $\{1, 2, \ldots\}$. Now you might claim that you are indifferent between $N = 10^{100}$ and anything larger. But if you always prefer N to be larger, then you will have no best choice.

(4) In the examples just given, $c(A; \succ)$ is empty because A is too large or "not nice." In the next section, we will see how to avoid this problem (by restricting the range of sets A to which $c(\cdot; \succ)$ is applied). But we could also get empty choice sets if $\succ$ is badly behaved; suppose $X = \{x, y, z, w\}$, and $x \succ y$, $y \succ z$, and $z \succ x$. Then $c(\{x, y, z\}; \succ) = \emptyset$.

(5) On an entirely different plane of objections to this approach, you might expect that what our consumer chooses out of a set of alternatives A depends on such things as the time of day, the way the choices are framed, or even the range of choices offered; she chooses apple pie over cherry, unless she can alternatively have banana, in which case cherry is chosen. All these sorts of choice behaviors are observed in real life, and they are *not* modelable given our preference-based definition of choice. We will return to this.

We haven't yet said anything about the consequences for choice of assuming that $\succ$ conforms to the standard assumptions. We can add that to the stew at this point:

Proposition 2.3. *Suppose that $\succ$ is asymmetric and negatively transitive. Then*

(a) For every finite set A, $c(A; \succ)$ is nonempty.

(b) Suppose that both x and y are in both A and B, and $x \in c(A; \succ)$ and $y \in c(B; \succ)$. Then $x \in c(B; \succ)$ and $y \in c(A; \succ)$.

You are asked to provide a proof in problem 3. This proposition leaves open the question about choice from infinite sets A. We will deal with this to some extent below.

From choice to preference

A quick review of the plot so far is: We started with strict preferences and saw connections with weak preference and indifference. Then we discussed how choice behavior might be induced from preferences. But from the viewpoint of descriptive theory (where one tries to build a model that matches what is observed), one would naturally proceed the other way around. Unless we provide our consumer with a questionnaire or otherwise directly enquire as to her preferences, the only signs we will see of her preferences are the choices she makes. Put another way, saying that the consumer has preferences that explain choice according to the formula given in the previous subsection is our *model* of her behavior, and it would make more sense to take her behavior as primitive and ask, When are her choices consistent with our preference-based model of choice?

In an abstract and not entirely satisfactory sense, we take up this question next. The approach is not entirely satisfactory because of the primitive we use; we assume that we have our hands on the consumer's entire *choice function*. Consider the following formal definition.

Definition. *A **choice function** on X is a function c whose domain is the set of all nonempty subsets of X, whose range is the set of all subsets of X, and that satisfies $c(A) \subseteq A$ for all $A \subseteq X$.*

To repeat, the interpretation is that the consumer, given her choice out of A, is content to take any one element of $c(A)$. Compare this definition with the definition of $c(\cdot, \succ)$ that was given for a preference relation $\succ$. Viewed as a mathematical object, $c(\cdot, \succ)$ is a choice function for fixed $\succ$. That is, in the previous subsection we constructed a choice function (according to the definition just given) from a primitive preference relation. In this subsection, the choice function is the primitive object.

We can raise objections to this approach similar to those raised concerning $\succ$; taking choice as a primitive in this fashion doesn't pay heed to the possibility that choice will change with changes in the timing of choice or the framing of alternatives. As before, economists for the most part ignore these possibilities. And they go on, usually, to make the following two assumptions about c (which you should be comparing with the two parts of proposition 2.3).

Assumption 3. *The choice function c is nonempty valued: $c(A) \neq \emptyset$ for all A.*

Assumption 4. *The choice function c satisfies **Houthakker's axiom of revealed preference**: If x and y are both contained in both A and B and if $x \in c(A)$ and $y \in c(B)$, then $x \in c(B)$ and $y \in c(A)$.*

Assumption 3 has already been discussed in the context of $c(\cdot, \succ)$ for a given $\succ$, but let us say a bit more about it. The problems encountered when a set A is infinite remain, and so we restrict attention for the time being to the case of finite X. Even granting this assumption, when choice is primitive, we can once again wonder about our consumer's actions when faced with a difficult decision. Consider our consumer choosing cans of beer and bottles of wine, and suppose she is given her choice out of $\{(40, 2), (20, 9)\}$. If she has difficulty comparing these two bundles, she might freeze up and be unable to choose. This is precluded by assumption 3. We don't rule out the possibility that she chooses "both"; that is, $c(\{(40, 2), (20, 9)\}) = \{(40, 2), (20, 9)\}$, which means that she would be happy with either of the two bundles. But we would interpret this as a definite expression of indifference between the two bundles.

Next examine assumption 4. It bears the following interpretation. Under the conditions that x and y are both in A and $x \in c(A)$, our consumer *reveals* by this that x is (weakly) preferred to y. Now if $y \in c(B)$ and $x \in B$, since x is no worse than y, x should also be among the most preferred things in B. (And by a symmetric argument, $y \in c(A)$ must hold as well.) Once again, the easiest way to grasp what this is saying is to consider a case in which it would fail. Suppose that x represents a wonderful meal at a classical French restaurant, while y represents an equally wonderful meal at a classical Japanese restaurant. The choice is a difficult one, but our consumer, given the choice out of $A = \{x, y\}$, decides that she prefers x. That is, $c(\{x, y\}) = \{x\}$. Now imagine that z is a meal at a somewhat lesser French restaurant, one at which our consumer had the misfortune recently to dine and which caused her an upset stomach from all the rich food. Suppose that $B = \{x, y, z\}$. Now if we give our consumer her choice out of B, the presence of z among the alternatives may remind her of all the butter and cream that goes into classical French cooking and that didn't agree with her when she dined at z. This, in turn, colors her evaluation of x; perhaps she prefers Japanese cuisine after all. This might lead to behavior given by $c(B) = \{y\}$, which together with $c(A) = \{x\}$ constitutes a violation of assumption 4. This is something like a framing effect; the presence of other alternatives may change how one regards a given alternative and thus change one's choices. It is this that assumption 4 rules out.

An interesting interplay existing between properties of nonemptiness and revealed preference is worth mentioning. By assuming nonemptiness, we rule out the possibility that the consumer, faced with a set A, is unable to choose. We could reduce this to a tautology by saying that choosing not to choose is a choice; that is, append to the set A one more element, "make no choice," and then whenever choice is too hard to make, interpret it as a choice of this "make no choice" element. If we did proceed by allowing "make no choice" to be a possible item, we would run into two problems. First, c is supposed to be defined on all subsets of X, and we've just assumed that it is defined only on subsets that contain this "make no choice" option. But we can deal with c defined only on some subsets of X; cf. problem 4(c). Second, and more substantively, if nonemptiness is really a problem, we are probably going to run afoul of the axiom of revealed preference by this dodge. Suppose that x and y are so hard to rank that the consumer freezes when given a choice out of $\{x, y\}$. We would, in our tautologizing, interpret this as saying that $c(\{x, y, \text{"make no choice"}\}) = \{\text{"make no choice"}\}$. But one assumes that $c(\{x, \text{"make no choice"}\}) = \{x\}$; if x is the only thing really on offer, it is taken, at least if it is not noxious. This, then, would constitute a violation of the axiom of revealed preference.

On the same point, imagine an indecisive consumer who wishes to obey assumption 3. This consumer, when faced with a difficult choice, gets past her indecision by volunteering to take any option that she can't disqualify. Our wine-and-beer-drinking friend will illustrate the point. She has a hard time comparing the two bundles $(40,2)$ and $(20,8)$, so her choice function specifies $c(\{(40,2), (20,8)\}) = \{(40,2), (20,8)\}$. And she has a hard time comparing the two bundles $(40,2)$ and $(21,9)$, so her choice function specifies $c(\{(40,2), (21,9)\}) = \{(40,2), (21,9)\}$. But then imagine giving her a choice out of the threesome $\{(40,2), (21,9), (20,8)\}$. Presumably she chooses either of the first two of these three — the bundle $(20,8)$ is excluded because $(21,9)$ is surely better. But if this is her choice function evaluated on the threesome, she has run afoul of Houthakker's axiom. (Prove this!) Salvation for an indecisive consumer is not possible according to the standard model.

We have already seen in proposition 2.3 that if our consumer has strict preferences given by an asymmetric and negatively transitive relation $\succ$, and if we define a choice function $c(\cdot; \succ)$ from $\succ$ (on a finite set X), then this choice function satisfies assumptions 3 and 4. The converse is also true, in the following sense: Given a choice function c, define an induced strict preference relation $\succ_c$ by $x \succ_c y$ if for any $A \subseteq X$ with $x, y \in X$, $x \in c(A)$ and $y \notin c(A)$. In words, $x \succ_c y$ if in any instance when both x and y are available, x is chosen and y isn't. Or, put succinctly, $x \succ_c y$ if choice ever reveals an instance where x seems to be strictly preferred to y.

Proposition 2.4. *Given a choice function c that satisfies assumptions 3 and 4, the relation $\succ_c$ defined from c as above is asymmetric and negatively transitive. Moreover, if you begin with c satisfying assumptions 3 and 4, induce $\succ_c$, and then define $c(\cdot; \succ_c)$, you will be back where you started: $c(\cdot; \succ_c) \equiv c$. And if you begin with $\succ$, induce $c(\cdot; \succ)$, and then induce from this $\succ_{c(\cdot; \succ)}$, you will again be back where you started.*

That is, taking as primitive $\succ$ that is asymmetric and negatively transitive is equivalent to taking as primitive a choice function c that is nonempty valued and satisfies Houthakker's axiom of revealed preference. The proof is left as an exercise.

There are two remarks to make here. First, proposition 2.4 is true under the maintained hypothesis that X is finite. Extensions to infinite X can be developed, but then one has to be careful about nonemptiness of the choice function. Except for brief remarks in the next section, we won't take up this subject here, leaving it for the interested reader to explore in more advanced treatments of the subject. (Look for references to abstract revealed preference theory.) Second, proposition 2.3 can be viewed as providing the testable restriction of the standard model of choice arising from preference; one needs to look either for a violation of nonemptiness or of Houthakker's axiom of revealed preference. As long as the data are consistent with a choice function that satisfies these two assumptions, they are consistent with the standard preference-based theory of consumer behavior. (But see problem 4 for more on this point.)

We will return to revealed preference interpreted as *the* testable restriction of the standard model of consumer behavior in the next section, when we get to the specific application of consumer demand.

Utility representations

Our third excursion from the starting point of consumer preferences concerns *numerical representations*. We need a definition.

Definition. *Given preferences $\succ$ on a set X, a **numerical representation** for those preferences is any function U with domain X and range the real line such that*

$$x \succ y \quad \text{if and only if} \quad U(x) > U(y).$$

That is, U measures all the objects of choice on a numerical scale, and a higher measure on the scale means the consumer likes the object more. It is typical to refer to such a function U as a *utility function* for the consumer (or for her preferences).

Why would we want to know whether $\succ$ has a numerical representation? Essentially, it is convenient in applications to work with utility functions. As we will see in later sections of this chapter and in the problems, it is relatively easy to specify a consumer's preferences by writing down a utility function. And then we can turn a choice problem into a numerical maximization problem. That is, if $\succ$ has numerical representation U, then the "best" alternatives out of a set $A \subseteq X$ according to $\succ$ are precisely those elements of A that have maximum utility. If we are lucky enough to know that the utility function U and the set A from which choice is made are "nicely behaved" (e.g., U is differentiable and A is a convex, compact set), then we can think of applying the techniques of optimization theory to solve this choice problem.

All sorts of nice things might flow from a numerical representation of preference. So we want to know: For a given set of preferences $\succ$, when do these preferences admit a numerical representation?

Proposition 2.5. *For $\succ$ to admit a numerical representation, it is necessary that $\succ$ is asymmetric and negatively transitive.*

But these two properties are not quite sufficient; you need as well that either the set X is "small" or that preferences are well behaved.[d] We will give the two simplest and most useful "converses" to proposition 2.5, although the second requires that you know a bit of mathematics and so is treated as optional reading. You should have no problem proving both propositions 2.5 and 2.6. Consult a good book on choice and utility theory for a proof of 2.7 and for variants on 2.7.

Proposition 2.6. *If the set X on which $\succ$ is defined is finite, then $\succ$ admits a numerical representation if and only if it is asymmetric and negatively transitive.[e]*

As for the second converse to proposition 2.5, we will specialize to the case where the objects being chosen are consumption bundles: elements of R^K, for some K. We assume that negative consumption levels are not possible, so X is the positive orthant in R^K.[3] In this setting, we say that preferences given by $\succ$ are *continuous*

(a) if $\{x^n\}$ is a sequence of consumption bundles with limit x, and if $x \succ y$, then, for all n sufficiently large, $x^n \succ y$

(b) and if $\{x^n\}$ is a sequence of consumption bundles with limit x, and if $y \succ x$, then, for all n sufficiently large, $y \succ x^n$

Proposition 2.7. *In this setting, if $\succ$ is asymmetric, negatively transitive, and continuous, then $\succ$ can be represented by a continuous function U. Moreover, if $\succ$ is represented by a continuous function U, then $\succ$ must be continuous as well as asymmetric and negatively transitive.*

The restriction to X being the positive orthant in R^K for some K isn't really important to this result. We do need some of the topological properties that this setting provides, but the result generalizes substantially. See Fishburn (1970). Or if you prefer reading original sources, see Debreu (1954).

Suppose that $\succ$ has a numerical representation U. What can we say about other possible numerical representations? Suppose that $f : R \to R$ is a strictly increasing function (some examples: $f(r) = r^3 + 3r^5$; $f(r) = e^r$; $f(r) = -e^{-r^3}$). Then defining a function $V : X \to R$ by $V(x) = f(U(x))$ gives another numerical representation for $\succ$. This is easy to see: $V(x) > V(y)$ if and only if $U(x) > U(y)$. Since V and U induce the same order on X, whatever U represents (ordinally) is represented just as well by V.

---

[d] See problem 5 for an example of what can go wrong.

[e] In fact, this is true as long as X is countably infinite.

[3] We will try to be careful and distinguish between numbers that are *strictly positive* and those that are *nonnegative*. But much of conventional language blurs these distinctions; in particular, the *positive* orthant of R^K is used when referring to vectors that can have zeros as components. We will signal the other cases in which following conventional language leads to this sort of ambiguity.

The converse to this isn't true: That is, if V and U both represent $\succ$, there is not necessarily a strictly increasing function $f : R \rightarrow R$ with $V(x) = f(U(x))$ for all x. But almost this is true. There is always a function $f : R \rightarrow R$ that is nondecreasing and strictly increasing on the set $\{r \in R : r = U(x) \text{ for some } x \in X\}$ such that $V(\cdot) \equiv f(U(\cdot)).^{f}$ A rough paraphrase of the situation is

Numerical representations for $\succ$ are unique only up to strictly increasing rescalings.

The point is that the units in a utility scale, or even the size of relative differences, have no particular meaning. We can't, in looking at a change from x to y, say that the consumer is better off by the amount $U(y) - U(x)$ or by anything like this. At this point (it will be different when we get to uncertainty in chapter 3), the utility function is introduced as an analytical convenience. It has no particular cardinal significance. In particular, the "level of utility" is unobservable, and anything that requires us to know the "level of utility" will be untestable. This is important as we go through demand theory; we'll want to be careful to note which of the many constructions we make are based on observables, and which are things that exist (if at all) only in the mind of the economist.

Properties of preferences for consumption bundles

When (momentarily) we go off into the subject of consumer demand, we will be making all manner of assumptions about the utility function that represents our consumer's preferences. We might ask, for example, exactly what it takes to get pictures as "nice" as in figure 2.1.

Since our interest attaches specifically to the problem of consumer demand, we will specialize throughout this subsection to the case that X is the positive orthant of R^K for some integer K. That is, there are K commodities, and preferences are defined over bundles of those commodities where the amount of each commodity in any bundle is required to be nonnegative.[g] We assume throughout that preferences $\succ$ for some consumer are given, and these preferences are asymmetric and negatively transitive.

We can, with this alone, begin to offer some interpretation of figure 2.1. For each $x \in X$, we define the *indifference class* of x, denoted

---

[f] If you are good at mathematics, proving this should be easy.

[g] For those readers who know some real analysis, extensions to linear spaces for X should not prove difficult.

Indiff(x), by Indiff(x) = $\{y \in X : y \sim x\}$. Since $\sim$ is reflexive, symmetric, and transitive, we can show that the family of indifference classes, or the various Indiff(x) ranging over x, partition X. That is, every $y \in X$ is in one and only one Indiff(x). You are asked to prove this in problem 2. The indifference curves of figure 2.1 are then indifference classes for some implicit preference ordering of the consumer under investigation.

The questions we wish to address in this context are: What further properties might we think reasonable to suppose of $\succ$? And how do those properties translate into properties of numerical representations for $\succ$ and into pictures such as figure 2.1?

Monotonicity and local insatiability. In many cases, it is reasonable to assume that consumers prefer more to less. Or at least they do not strictly prefer less to more. We have the following definitions and results:

*Definitions. Preferences $\succ$ are **monotone** if for any two bundles x and y such that $x \geq y$, $x \succeq y$. (By $x \geq y$, we mean that each component of x is at least as large as the corresponding component of y.) And preferences $\succ$ are **strictly monotone** if for any two bundles x and y such that $x \geq y$ and $x \neq y$, $x \succ y$.*

*A function $U : X \to R$ is **nondecreasing** if for any two bundles x and y such that $x \geq y$, $U(x) \geq U(y)$. And U is **strictly increasing** if for any two bundles x and y such that $x \geq y$ and $x \neq y$, $U(x) > U(y)$.*

Proposition 2.8. *If U represents preferences $\succ$, these preferences are monotone if and only if U is nondecreasing, and these preferences are strictly monotone if and only if U is strictly increasing.*

The proof of this proposition is virtually a matter of comparing definitions.

One might wish somewhat less of some goods; week-old fish and contaminated water come to mind. For others some of the good is desirable, but past a certain point any additional amounts are undesirable; any extremely rich or sweet food would be a natural example. One doesn't value more of many goods; while I would not mind having around more hydrochloric acid or rolled steel, I do not strictly prefer more of these goods to less. The first two sorts of examples cast doubt on an assumption that preferences are monotone, while the last example questions strict monotonicity. Neither assumption is necessary for much of what we do subsequently. But for later purposes we need the assumption that arbitrarily close to any bundle x is another that is strictly preferred to x. This property is called *local insatiability*.

Definition. *Preferences* $\succ$ *are* **locally insatiable** *if for every* $x = (x_1, \ldots, x_K) \in$ X *and for every number* $\epsilon > 0$ *there is another bundle* $y = (y_1, \ldots, y_K) \in X$ *such that* (a) $|x_j - y_j| < \epsilon$ *for every* $j = 1, \ldots, K$, *and* (b) $y \succ x$.[h]

The interested reader can translate this property into the corresponding statement about a numerical representation of $\succ$.

   Convexity. The next property that we consider is *convexity* of preferences.

Definitions. (a) *Preferences* $\succ$ *are* **convex** *if for every pair* x *and* y *from* X *with* $x \succeq y$ *and for every number* $a \in [0, 1]$, *the bundle* $ax + (1 - a)y \succeq y$.

(b) *Preferences* $\succ$ *are* **strictly convex** *if for every such* x *and* y, $x \neq y$, *and for every* $a \in (0, 1)$, $ax + (1 - a)y \succ y$.

(c) *Preferences* $\succ$ *are* **semi-strictly convex** *if for every pair* x *and* y *with* $x \succ y$ *and for every* $a \in (0, 1)$, $ax + (1 - a)y \succ y$.

By $ax + (1 - a)y$, we mean the component-by-component convex combination of the two bundles.

   Why would one ever think that preferences are or should be convex? The story, such as it is, is related to the notion of diminishing marginal utility or the classic ideal of "moderation in all things." Under the assumption $x \succeq y$, we know that in moving along the line segment from y to x we will reach a point (x) at least as good as the point (y) from which we started. The various forms of convexity are variations on the general notion that at each step along this path, we are never worse off than where we began. That, precisely, is convexity. Semi-strict convexity maintains that if $x \succ y$, so we will be better off at the end of the journey, then we are strictly better off at each step. And strict convexity holds that even if $x \sim y$, if we are strictly between the two we are better off than at the extremes.

   You will sometimes see convexity of preferences defined a bit differently. For each point $x \in X$, define the set $\text{AsGood}(x) = \{y \in X : y \succeq x\}$. Recall that a set $Z \subseteq R^k$ is *convex* if for every x and y from Z and every number $a \in [0, 1]$, $ax + (1 - a)y \in Z$. (If you have never seen or heard of

---

[h] Note that becoming satiated in one commodity, say baklava, does not necessarily pose problems for local insatiability; all that is needed is that, from any consumption bundle, the consumer would prefer a small increase (or decrease) in *some* of the commodities.

the definition of a convex set before, get someone who has seen it to draw a few pictures for you.) Then:

Proposition 2.9. *Preferences $\succ$ are convex if and only if for every point x, the set AsGood(x) is convex.*

The proof of this proposition is left as an exercise.

As for the consequences of convexity of preferences for numerical representations, we must give some definitions from mathematics. These definitions are used throughout this book, so pay attention if they are new to you:

Definitions. *Let Z be a convex subset of R^K for some integer K and let f be a function with domain Z and range R.*

*The function f is **concave** if for all $x, y \in Z$ and $a \in [0,1]$, $f(ax + (1-a)y) \geq af(x) + (1-a)f(y)$. This function is **strictly concave** if for all such x and y, $x \neq y$, and for all $a \in (0,1)$, $f(ax + (1-a)y) > af(x) + (1-a)f(y)$.*

*The function f is **convex** if for all $x, y \in Z$ and $a \in [0,1]$, $f(ax + (1-a)y) \leq af(x) + (1-a)f(y)$. This function is **strictly convex** if for all such x and y, $x \neq y$, and for all $a \in (0,1)$, $f(ax + (1-a)y) < af(x) + (1-a)f(y)$.*

*The function f is **quasi-concave** if for all $x, y \in Z$ such that $f(x) \geq f(y)$ and for all $a \in [0,1]$, $f(ax + (1-a)y) \geq f(y)$. This function is **strictly quasi-concave** if for such x and y, $x \neq y$, and for $a \in (0,1)$, $f(ax+(1-a)y) > f(y)$. And f is **semi-strictly quasi-concave** if for all x and y with $f(x) > f(y)$ and for all $a \in (0,1)$, $f(ax + (1-a)y) > f(y)$.*

*The function f is **quasi-convex** if for all $x, y \in Z$ such that $f(x) \geq f(y)$ and for all $a \in [0,1]$, $f(ax + (1-a)y) \leq f(x)$. This function is **strictly quasi-convex** if for such x and y, $x \neq y$, and for $a \in (0,1)$, $f(ax + (1-a)y) < f(x)$.[i]*

Proposition 2.10. *(a) If preferences $\succ$ are represented by a concave function U, then preferences are convex. If they are represented by a strictly concave function U, then they are strictly convex.*

(b) Suppose that U is a numerical representation of preferences $\succ$. Then U is quasi-concave if and only if preferences $\succ$ are convex; U is strictly quasi-

---

[i] We have no need of semi-strictly quasi-convex functions. We also didn't define semi-strict concavity for functions. Try to draw a concave function that isn't semi-strictly quasi-concave and you'll see why.

concave if and only if preferences $\succ$ are strictly convex; and U is semi-strictly quasi-concave if and only if preferences $\succ$ are semi-strictly convex.[4]

Once again, the proofs are left to you. Note that part (a) runs in one direction only; if preferences have a concave representation, they are convex. But convex preferences can have numerical representations that are not concave. We can demonstrate this quite simply: Suppose that U is a concave function that represents $\succ$. We know from the discussion following propositions 2.5 and 2.6 that if $f : R \rightarrow R$ is a strictly increasing function, then the function V defined by $V(x) = f(U(x))$ is another numerical representation of $\succ$. But it is quite easy to construct, for a given concave function U, a strictly increasing function f such that $f(U(\cdot))$ is not concave. Create such an example if this isn't obvious to you. The idea is to make f "more convex" than U is concave.

In contrast, part (b) says that every representation of convex preferences $\succ$ is quasi-concave. Hence we conclude that if U is a quasi-concave function and f is strictly increasing, $f(U(\cdot))$ is also quasi-concave. (It is equally clear that similar statements hold for strict and semi-strict quasi-concavity.) You may find it helpful to prove this directly, although you should be sure that you understand the indirect path of logic that got us to this conclusion.

This leaves open one question. We know (or, rather, you know if you constructed an example two paragraphs ago) that convex preferences can have numerical representations that are not concave functions. But this doesn't mean that we can't show: *If preferences $\succ$ are convex, they admit at least one concave numerical representation.* But, in fact, we can't show this; it is quite false. On this point, see problem 7.[j]

Continuity. We have already mentioned the property of continuous preferences. It was used previously as a way to guarantee that preferences have a numerical representation when the set X is not finite, and in fact we claimed that it guaranteed the existence of a *continuous* numerical representation. We don't need continuity of preferences to guarantee the existence of a numerical representation. But, at the same time, continuity has intuitive appeal in its own right. N.B., continuous preferences always admit a continuous

---

[4] You are entitled to a bit of displeasure concerning the fact that con*vex* preferences go together with (quasi-)con*cave* utility functions. This would all be easier to remember if we called the property of preferences concavity. But, as you will see in chapter 6, convexity of the AsGood sets plays the crucial mathematical role, and for this reason preferences with convex AsGood sets are said to be convex, even though they have (quasi-)concave representations.

[j] In chapter 3, we will be able to give an intuitive property about the consumer's preferences that ensures these preferences admit a concave numerical representation.

numerical representation. But not every numerical representation of continuous preferences is continuous.

About figure 2.1. The preferences that are implicitly identified by the very standard picture in figure 2.1 are strictly monotone and strictly convex. You can see the strict convexity from the fact that the indifference curves are strictly convex to the origin; if we take any two points and the line segment between them, this segment will be everywhere above the indifference curve of the "lower" of the two points. Strict monotonicity is implicit from the fact that the curves run down and to the right, never flattening out to be completely horizontal or vertical, so that from any point, any second point above and/or to the right is on a strictly "higher" indifference curve.

> And the preferences represented in figure 2.1 are continuous. We see this because the "weakly better than" and "weakly worse than" sets for each point x are all closed; you can check that this is equivalent to the definition of continuity of preferences that we gave.
>
> The technically astute reader may wish to investigate the extent to which figure 2.1 is *the* picture for preferences that are continuous, strictly convex and strictly monotone. The reader may also wish to investigate how the picture might change if we drop strict convexity or even convexity altogether, or if we drop (strict) monotonicity. On this general question, see the alternative pictures appearing later in this chapter.

2.2. Marshallian demand without derivatives

The prototypical application of the general model of choice that we have developed is *Marshallian demand*. The theory of Marshallian (consumer) demand has played a central role in the development of microeconomic theory; it is traditionally viewed as among the most important subjects to study in microeconomics, and the results obtained are useful in many applied contexts.

A complete and precise treatment of Marshallian demand takes many pages and much time. Because Marshallian demand plays a very limited role in the remainder of this book and the literature provides many very good textbook treatments (see the bibliographic notes at the end of this chapter), we will give this subject relatively short shrift here. The discussion will be more than adequate to acquaint you with some of the basic categories of questions addressed and answers given. But it does not provide the depth of treatment or precision that you will find elsewhere, and students not already acquainted with this subject will do well someday to study it more intensively and extensively.

We divide our treatment of the subject between two sections. In this section we take no derivatives. In the following section, we take derivatives without end.

The consumer's problem

The theory of Marshallian demand concerns a consumer with preferences as described in section 2.1, who seeks to buy a bundle of goods for consumption. We assume that the space of consumption bundles, X, is the positive orthant of R^K for some positive integer K, with the usual interpretation that K is the number of commodities. Stated in words, then, the *consumer's problem* is

Choose the consumption bundle x that is best according to preferences, subject to the constraint that total cost of x is no greater than the consumer's income.

We can express the constraint part of this fairly easily. We use p from R^K to denote the price vector; that is, $p = (p_1, \ldots, p_K)$, where p_j is the price of one unit of good j. We assume that the consumer has a fixed amount of money to spend on his[5] consumption bundle: Let Y denote the consumer's *income*. Then we write the constraint as $\sum_{j=1}^{K} p_j x_j \leq Y$, or, for short, $p \cdot x \leq Y$, where $\cdot$ is the dot or scalar product.[6]

It is implicit in this formulation that the consumer's choice of amounts to consume does not change unit prices of the goods; the consumer faces a *linear price schedule* (no quantity discounts, no increases in price as he tries to buy more, etc.). This is a standard assumption in microeconomics. Quantity discounts are ruled out because, if they were significant, a consumer could buy a lot of the good at a discount and then resell it to other consumers. (But what if resale were impossible? We'll discuss this sort of thing in chapter 9.) And the rationale for the assumption that prices do not increase with increased demand by the single consumer is that the consumer's demand is only a small part of all the demand for the good. This assumption of linear prices is not necessary for a lot of the theory, but it is convenient, and we'll hold to it throughout this chapter.

---

[5] Generic consumers in this book will change gender occasionally — not so much, I hope, that confusion is created, but often enough so that I am somewhat evenhanded. In particular, later in the book when we have numbered individuals, all odd numbered individuals will be women and all even numbered individuals will be men.

[6] The use of the term "income" is traditional, although "wealth" or "resources" might, for some applications, give more appropriate connotations. The use of an uppercase Y is meant to prevent confusion with consumption bundles; we will sometimes use y as an alternative to x.

That takes care of representing the budget constraint. We can rewrite the consumer's problem as

Choose that consumption bundle x that is best according to preferences, subject to $p \cdot x \leq Y$.

Not bad, but still not great. We still have the objective ("best according to preferences") with which to contend. But reaching back to the previous section, we assume that our consumer has preferences that are asymmetric, negatively transitive, and continuous. This implies that there is a continuous numerical representation U for the consumer's preferences,[7] and we can write the consumer's problem as

$$\text{Choose } x \text{ to maximize } \quad U(x) \text{ subject to } \quad p \cdot x \leq Y \text{ and } x \geq 0. \qquad \text{(CP)}$$

(The $x \geq 0$ part comes from our assumption that the set of feasible consumption bundles, or X, is the positive orthant in R^K.) If we assume that U is well behaved, concave, say, and differentiable, we can even begin creating Lagrangians, differentiating, and so on.

Before making any further assumptions, however, we will see what we can get out of the assumptions that the consumer's preferences are asymmetric, negatively transitive and continuous or, equivalently, that there is a continuous function U that represents preferences.

Right away, we have to wonder whether (CP) has a solution at all.

Proposition 2.11. *If preferences are asymmetric, negatively transitive, and continuous, or equivalently if they are represented by a continuous function U, then:*

(a) The problem (CP) has at least one solution for all strictly positive prices and nonnegative levels of income.

(b) If x is a solution of (CP) for given p and Y, then x is also a solution for $(\lambda p, \lambda Y)$, for any positive scalar λ.

(c) If in addition to our basic three assumptions on preferences, we assume as well that preferences are convex, then the set of solutions to (CP) for given p and Y is a convex set. If preferences are strictly convex, then (CP) has a unique solution.

(d) If in addition (to the original three assumptions) preferences are locally insatiable and if x is a solution to (CP) at (p, Y), then $p \cdot x = Y$.

Let us comment on these four assertions in turn. Before doing so, we give one very useful piece of terminology: For prices p and income Y, the

---

[7] For those readers who skip the smaller type, take my word for it.

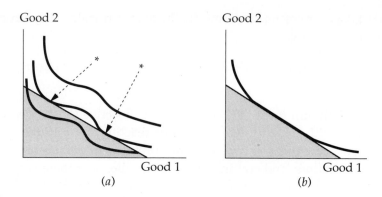

Figure 2.2. Two examples of multiple solutions of (CP).

set of points $\{x \in R^K : p \cdot x \leq Y, x \geq 0\}$ is called the *budget set* for the consumer.

First, the proof of (a) requires a bit of mathematics: You need to know that a continuous function on a compact set achieves a maximum. And then you must show that if prices are strictly positive and income is nonnegative, the budget set is compact. If you know about compact sets, this will be obvious; otherwise, you will have to take (a) on faith.[k]

Part (a) says that (CP) has at least one solution for every p and Y, but there is no reason to suppose that (CP) doesn't have many solutions. In figure 2.2 we show a shaded budget set and preferences by means of the usual indifference curve diagram. In figure 2.2(a) we have nonconvex preferences and two solutions to (CP) marked with stars. In figure 2.2(b) we have convex preferences that are not strictly convex, and we see an entire line segment of solutions.[l]

Part (b) should be immediately obvious because the budget set is unchanged if prices and wealth are scaled up or down proportionately. If (CP) has a unique solution, and we wrote this solution as $x(p, Y)$, then part (b) could be written: $x(p, Y) = x(\lambda p, \lambda Y)$, for $\lambda > 0$. That is, *Marshallian demand* (the function $x(p, Y)$) *is homogeneous of degree zero.*

---

[k] If you know about compact sets, you may also know that it would be enough for U to be upper semi-continuous. In fact, one can define upper semi-continuous preferences and use this assumption in place of our assumption of continuous preferences in most of the development to come. Also, we will not worry here about what happens when prices of individual goods can be zero, but see the attention we pay this issue in chapter 6.

[l] The preferences represented in 2.2(b) are semi-strictly convex, so that property won't help with multiple solutions. Note also that in figure 2.2 we show only monotone preferences. Draw pictures with preferences that aren't monotone and, especially for part (d) of the proposition, with preferences that aren't locally insatiable.

Part (c) of the proposition is easy to prove: Budget sets are convex: If x and x' are two solutions of (CP) for given p and Y, then $ax+(1-a)x'$ for $a \in [0,1]$ is in the budget set. And if preferences are convex, $ax + (1-a)x'$ is at least as good as the worser of x and x'. Since these are (presumed to be) both solutions of (CP), they are equally good and as good as anything in the budget set. But then $ax + (1-a)x'$ is a solution of (CP) as well. And if preferences are strictly convex and there are two distinct solutions x and x', $.5x+.5x'$ would be both strictly better than x and x' and would still be in the budget set, a contradiction.

Turning to (d), we begin by noting that if x is any solution to (CP), then $p \cdot x \leq Y$. The content of (d) lies in the assertion that this weak inequality is in fact an equality. The inequality $p \cdot x \leq Y$ is known as *Walras' law*, whereas the equation $p \cdot x = Y$ is called *Walras' law with equality*: Hence we can paraphrase (d) as: *If the consumer is locally insatiable, Walras' law holds with equality.*[8] The proof runs as follows. If some x that solved (CP) for given p and Y satisfied $p \cdot x < Y$, then the consumer can afford any bundle x' that is in some small neighborhood of x, where the size of the neighborhood has to do with how much slack is in the budget constraint and how large the largest price is. But by local insatiability, in every neighborhood of any point x something is strictly preferred to x. Hence x could not solve (CP).[m]

GARP

The set of solutions of (CP) plays, in the specific context of consumer demand, the role that the choice function c plays in abstract choice theory: It is the observable element of choice. Just as we asked before whether a choice function c was consistent with choice according to some underlying preferences, we ask now: *Is observed demand consistent with preference maximization for some set of preferences?* Note two changes from before: The sets A out of which choice is being made are now budget sets and so are infinite. And even if we know all the solutions of (CP) for all prices p and incomes Y, we don't know choice out of all subsets of X; we only know

---

[8] The term *Walras' law* is sometimes used only for aggregate demand. So you may encounter treatments of the theory of demand where (d) would be paraphased: The consumer's *budget constraint* is satisfied with equality.

[m] Mathematically inclined readers should supply the formal details. Readers sometimes worry about the possibility of getting stuck along an axis in this proof; while the budget constraint may be slack, perhaps it is one of the nonnegativity constraints that binds and keeps the consumer from attaining higher utility. But note carefully that local insatiability is defined relative to the nonnegativity constraints. It says that *within X* and near to every x is something that is strictly better than x. So we can't get stuck along one of the axes.

choice out of budget sets. Since we don't know "c" for all subsets, it may be harder to answer the question posed above.

But, since much of economics is built on the assumption that consumers act as in the problem (CP), it is natural to look at the observed demand and devise and run tests that could lead us to reject this model. That is, it is natural to try to answer the question above. This has been the object of much attention in the theory of the consumer, and two different sorts of answers come out. We give the first here; the second, which is very different in style, will be given at the end of the next section (2.3).

For the balance of this subsection, the assumption is that we observe a finite set of demand data. That is, for a finite collection of prices and income levels $(p^1, Y^1), (p^2, Y^2), \ldots, (p^n, Y^n)$, we observe corresponding demands $x^1, \ldots, x^n$ by our consumer. We do *not* preclude the possibility that at prices p^i and income Y^i there are solutions to (CP) other than x^i. And we set out to answer the question: Given this finite set of data, are the choices we observe consistent with the standard model of some locally insatiable consumer solving (CP)?

The answer is somewhat like the revealed preference axiom we discussed in section 2.1. First, if x is chosen at (p, Y) and $p \cdot x' \leq Y$, then we would have to conclude that $x \succeq x'$ because x is chosen when x' is available. Assuming local insatiability, if the same were true with $p \cdot x' < Y$, then we would know that $x \succ x'$, because otherwise something close to x' would be strictly better than x' and still feasible at prices p with income Y, and x was chosen over this. We can draw pictures of this. In figure 2.3, we show the budget set defined by $p \cdot x \leq Y$ and $x \geq 0$. Suppose the point marked x is chosen. Since everything in the budget set (the shaded

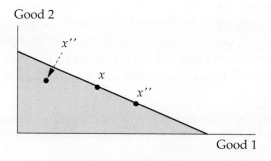

Figure 2.3. Revealed preference from demand data.
If the point x is demanded from the shaded budget set, then x is revealed to be at least as good as points such as x' and, assuming the consumer is locally insatiable, strictly better than points such as x''.

region) was feasible, x must be at least as good as those. In particular, x must be at least as good as x'. And if the consumer is locally insatiable, x must be strictly better than the point marked x''.

Now suppose that this sort of consideration "revealed" that $x^1 \succ x^2 \succeq x^3 \succeq x^4 \succeq x^1$ for some chain of bundles x^1, x^2, x^3, and x^4. We would clearly be unable to rationalize this with preferences that had the properties we've been assuming; a numerical representation would be impossible since we would need to have $U(x^1) > U(x^2) \geq U(x^3) \geq U(x^4) \geq U(x^1)$. This leads to the so-called *Generalized Axiom of Revealed Preference* or GARP, as follows:

Definitions. *Take any finite set of demand data: x^1 chosen at (p^1, Y^1), x^2 chosen at (p^2, Y^2), ..., and x^n chosen at (p^n, Y^n). If $p^j \cdot x^i \leq Y^j$, the data are said to reveal that x^j is **weakly preferred to** x^i, written $x^j \succeq x^i$. And the data reveal that x^j is **strictly preferred to** x^i, written $x^j \succ x^i$, if $p^j \cdot x^i < Y^j$. The data are said to satisfy **GARP** if, for preferences (weak or strong) that the data reveal, you cannot construct a cycle $x^{n_1} \succeq x^{n_2} \succeq \ldots \succeq x^{n_1}$, where one or more of the $\succeq$s is a $\succ$.*

Proposition 2.12. *A finite set of demand data satisfies GARP if and only if these data are consistent with maximization of locally insatiable preferences.*

The argument just sketched shows that satisfaction of GARP is necessary for there to be underlying well-behaved preferences. Sufficiency of GARP is harder to show and is perhaps surprising, but nonetheless, for a finite collection of demand data, if GARP is satisfied, you cannot reject the model of the consumer we have posed.[n]

This is all quite abstract, so let's have an example. Suppose our consumer lives in a three-commodity world.

When prices are $(10, 10, 10)$ and income is 300, the consumer chooses the consumption bundle $(10, 10, 10)$.

When prices are $(10, 1, 2)$ and income is 130, the consumer chooses the consumption bundle $(9, 25, 7.5)$.

When prices are $(1, 1, 10)$ and income is 110, the consumer chooses the consumption bundle $(15, 5, 9)$.

---

[n] If you are so minded, try a proof. Can you show that these preferences can be assumed to be continuous? Can you show that these preferences can be assumed to be convex? That is, are more testable restrictions generated from the assumptions that preferences are continuous and/or convex? What about strict convexity? If you try this, compare whatever you get with problem 4.

	Bundles		
	(10,10,10)	(9,25,7.5)	(15,5,9)
(10,10,10)	300	415	290
(10,1,2)	130	130	173
(1,1,10)	120	109	110

Table 2.1. Cost of three bundles at three sets of prices.

From these data, we calculate the cost of each bundle that is selected at each of the three sets of prices. This is done for you in table 2.1. In each case, the bundle selected exhausts the income of the consumer; this is as it should be, given local insatiability. The important things to note are:

When $(10, 10, 10)$ was chosen (at prices $(10, 10, 10)$ and income 300), the bundle $(15, 5, 9)$ could have been purchased with some money left over. Apparently, this consumer strictly prefers $(10, 10, 10)$ to $(15, 5, 9)$.

At the second set of prices $(10, 1, 2)$, since $(10, 10, 10)$ and $(9, 25, 7.5)$ both cost 130 and $(9, 25, 7.5)$ was selected, the latter must be at least as good as $(10, 10, 10)$.

And at the third set of prices $(1, 1, 10)$, the bundle $(9, 25, 7.5)$ costs 109, while $(15, 5, 9)$ costs 110. And we are told that with income 110, the consumer chose $(15, 5, 9)$. Hence $(15, 5, 9) \succ (9, 25, 7.5)$.

Oops! The data tell us that $(10, 10, 10) \succ (15, 5, 9) \succ (9, 25, 7.5) \succeq (10, 10, 10)$. Hence these data are inconsistent with consumer behavior based on the standard preference-maximization model. On the other hand, suppose the third piece of data that we have wasn't as above, but was instead:

At prices $(1, 2, 10)$ and income 115, the bundle selected is $(15, 5, 9)$.

Then we would come to no negative conclusions. At the first set of prices and income, the bundles $(10, 10, 10)$ and $(15, 5, 9)$ are affordable, and as the first bundle is selected, it is revealed (strictly) preferred to the second. At the second set of prices and income level, $(10, 10, 10)$ and $(9, 25, 7.5)$ are affordable and the second is selected, so it is revealed to be (weakly) preferred to the first. This is just as before. But now, at the third set of prices and income level, only $(15, 5, 9)$ (of the three bundles) is affordable. Knowing that it is selected tells us nothing about how it ranks compared to the other two; it could well come at the bottom of the heap. And we know from the result claimed above, because we observe no violations of GARP in these data, the data can indeed be reconciled with a preference ranking of the usual sort on all bundles.

The indirect utility function

We write $\nu(p, Y)$ for the *value of the problem* (CP). That is,

$$\nu(p, Y) = \max\{U(x) : p \cdot x \leq Y \text{ and } x \geq 0\}.$$

In words, the function ν, which is called the *indirect utility function*, says how much utility the consumer receives at his optimal choice(s) at prices p and income Y. Of course the definition of ν does not depend on (CP) having a unique solution. Note also that the units of ν depend on the specific numerical representation U that is used. If we rescale U, say by replacing U with $V(\cdot) \equiv f(U(\cdot))$, then we transform ν by the same rescaling function f. Put another way, we can never observe ν, since its range is something entirely arbitrary and intangible.

Proposition 2.13. *Assume that U is a continuous function that represents locally insatiable preferences. The indirect utility function ν is*

(a) homogeneous of degree zero in p and Y;

(b) continuous in p and Y (for $p > 0$ and $Y \geq 0$);

(c) strictly increasing in Y and nonincreasing in p; and

(d) quasi-convex in (p, Y).

> **Parts of the proof.** Part (a) should be obvious. The technique of proof used for part (b) reappears frequently in microeconomic theory; so if you know enough of the required mathematics, pay close attention. We take two steps:
>
> *Step 1.* Suppose that (p^n, Y^n) is a sequence with (bounded) limit (p, Y) such that $p > 0$. Let x^n be a solution of (CP) at (p^n, Y^n) so that $\nu(p^n, Y^n) = U(x^n)$, and let n' be a subsequence along which $\lim_{n'} U(x^{n'}) = \limsup_n \nu(p^n, Y^n)$. Since $p > 0$, one can show that (for large enough n') the union of the budget sets defined by the $(p^{n'}, Y^{n'})$ and (p, Y) is bounded. Thus the sequence $x^{n'}$ lives in a compact space and has some limit point — call it x. Since $p^{n'} \cdot x^{n'} \leq Y^{n'}$, by continuity we know that $p \cdot x \leq Y$. Thus $\nu(p, Y) \geq U(x) = \lim_{n'} U(x^{n'}) = \limsup_n \nu(p^n, Y^n)$.
>
> *Step 2.* Now let x represent a solution of (CP) for (p, Y), so that $\nu(p, Y) = U(x)$. We know from local insatiability that $p \cdot x = Y$. Let a^n be the scalar

$Y^n/(p^n \cdot x)$. By continuity, $\lim_n a^n = Y/(p \cdot x) = 1$. Thus by continuity of U, $\lim_n U(a^n x) = U(x)$. At the same time, $p^n \cdot a^n x = Y^n$, so that $a^n x$ is feasible for the problem defined by (p^n, Y^n). Hence $\nu(p^n, Y^n) \geq U(a^n x)$, and $\liminf_n \nu(p^n, Y^n) \geq \lim_n U(a^n x) = U(x) = \nu(p, Y)$.

Now combining steps 1 and 2 we see that $\liminf_n \nu(p^n, Y^n) \geq \nu(p, Y) \geq \limsup_n \nu(p^n, Y^n)$, which establishes that $\lim_n \nu(p^n, Y^n)$ exists and is equal to $\nu(p, Y)$.

Part (c) is left for you to do. For the first half of part (c), remember that our consumer is assumed to be locally insatiable. (What would it take to get the conclusion that ν is strictly decreasing in p?)

For part (d), fix some (p^i, Y^i) for $i = 1, 2$ and some $a \in [0, 1]$. Let x be a solution of (CP) at $(ap^1 + (1 - a)p^2, aY^1 + (1 - a)Y^2)$. We claim that x is feasible for either (p^1, Y^1) or for (p^2, Y^2) (or both); nonnegativity constraints can't be a problem, and if $p^1 \cdot x > Y^1$ and $p^2 \cdot x > Y^2$, then $(ap^1 + (1 - a)p^2) \cdot x > aY^1 + (1 - a)Y^2$, which contradicts the assumption that x is a solution at $(ap^1 + (1 - a)p^2, aY^1 + (1 - a)Y^2)$. If x is feasible at (p^1, Y^1), then $\nu(ap^1 + (1 - a)p^2, aY^1 + (1 - a)Y^2) = U(x) \leq \nu(p^1, Y^1)$, while if x is feasible at (p^2, Y^2), we would conclude that $\nu(ap^1 + (1 - a)p^2, aY^1 + (1 - a)Y^2) \leq \nu(p^2, Y^2)$. One or the other must be true, so that

$$\nu(ap^1 + (1 - a)p^2, aY^1 + (1 - a)Y^2) \leq \max\{\nu(p^1, Y^1), \nu(p^2, Y^2)\},$$

which is quasi-convexity.

You may be asking: So what? But we will get something out of the definition of ν and all this work in the next section and in the next chapter.

The dual consumer problem and the expenditure function

To continue preparations for the next section (while continuing to refrain from taking derivatives), we examine the following optimization problem for given utility function $U(\cdot)$, prices p and real number u:

$$\textit{minimize} \quad p \cdot x \quad \textit{subject to} \quad U(x) \geq u, x \geq 0. \qquad \text{(DCP)}$$

In words, we seek the minimum amount the consumer must spend at prices p to get for himself utility level u. The appropriate picture is in figure 2.4. The shaded area is the set of bundles x satisfying $U(x) \geq u$; this is the set of points along and above the $U(x) = u$ indifference curve. Iso-expense lines are drawn in; these are lines of the form $p \cdot x = \text{constant}$, for various constants. Note that the closer these lines are to the origin, the

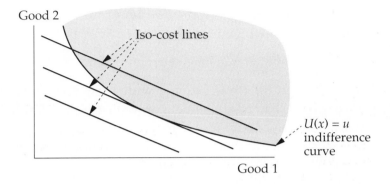

Figure 2.4. The picture for the problem (DCP).

less the constant expense they represent. And the point marked x in the figure is the solution of the problem (DCP).[o]

The problem (DCP) is parametrized by prices p and the utility level u that is to be achieved. (It is also parametrized by the utility function $U(\cdot)$, but we will hold that fixed throughout all our discussions.) As we vary p and u, we get other solutions. We will write $e(p, u)$ for the value of the problem as a function of (p, u); that is,

$$e(p, u) = \min\{p \cdot x : U(x) \geq u, x \geq 0\},$$

and we will call the function e the *expenditure function*.

In parallel with propositions 2.11 and 2.13, we have

Proposition 2.14. *Suppose that p is strictly positive and u is a level of utility that is achievable and greater or equal the utility of consuming the zero vector; that is, $u = U(x)$ for some $x \geq 0$, and $u \geq U(0)$. Then,*

(a) The problem (DCP) has a solution at (p, u). If x solves (DCP) for (p, u), then $U(x) = u$. If U represents convex preferences, the set of solutions to (DCP) is convex. If U represents strictly convex preferences, (DCP) has a single solution for each (p, u). If x solves (DCP) for (p, u), then x is a solution of (DCP) for $(\lambda p, u)$, where λ is any strictly positive scalar.

(b) The expenditure function $e(p, u)$ is homogeneous of degree one in p, or

---

[o] For reasons we will not explain in this book, this problem is called the *dual consumer problem* (giving the mnemonic [DCP]), because it is dual to the problem (CP) in a precise mathematical sense.

$e(\lambda p, u) = \lambda e(p, u)$ *for* $\lambda > 0$. *The expenditure function is strictly increasing in* u *and nonincreasing in* p.

(c) The expenditure function is concave in p.

Proofs of parts (a) and (b) are left to you with a few remarks and hints. Recall that we needed local insatiability to prove that Walras' law held with equality at any solution of (CP). But here we don't need local insatiability to show that $U(x) = u$ at a solution x. (In fact, we don't need to assume local insatiability in this proposition at all! But we do assume that U is a continuous function.) So how does the argument go? Suppose that x solves (DCP) for (p, u) with $U(x) > u$. If $u > U(0)$, our consumer is spending something at x to achieve u. But then consider bundles of the form αx for α a bit less than one. These bundles cost proportionately less than x and, by continuity of U, for α close enough to one they give more utility than u (since $U(x) > u$). This would contradict the assumption that x solves (DCP). And if $u = U(0)$, the solution to (DCP) at (p, u) is clearly $x = 0$.[p]

   Part (c) of the proposition is crucial to later events, so we give the proof here. Let x solve (DCP) for $(ap + (1 - a)p', u)$, so that $e(ap + (1 - a)p', u) = (ap + (1 - a)p') \cdot x$. Since $U(x) = u$, the bundle x is always a feasible way to achieve utility level u, although it may not be the cheapest way at prices other than $ap + (1 - a)p'$. Accordingly,

$$e(p, u) \leq p \cdot x \text{ and } e(p', u) \leq p' \cdot x.$$

Combining these two inequalities gives

$$ae(p, u) + (1 - a)e(p', u) \leq ap \cdot x + (1 - a)p' \cdot x$$
$$= (ap + (1 - a)p') \cdot x = e(ap + (1 - a)p', u).$$

That does it.

Comparative statics

   We are almost ready to start taking derivatives, but before doing so, we take one further excursion into definitions and basic concepts.

   A standard exercise in the theory of consumer demand is to ask how demand responds to changes in various parameters such as prices and

---

[p] What would happen if $u < U(0)$?

income. When (CP) has more than one solution this exercise is a bit hard to interpret, so we assume for the balance of this subsection that (CP) has a unique solution.[9] We write $x(p, Y) = (x_1(p, Y), \ldots, x_K(p, Y))$ for the solution; that is, $x_j(p, Y)$ is the amount of good j purchased by our consumer when he faces prices p and has income Y to spend.

We are interested in how $x(p, Y)$ (and its constituent components) change with changes in the various p_i and in Y.

(a) For example, how does $x_j(p, Y)$ change with changes in p_j? If good j becomes more expensive, we "expect" that less j will be demanded; in fact, we expect this so much that a good for which this is true is called a *normal* good. When the demand for good j rises with increases in the price of good j, we say that good j is a *Giffen good*. We will return briefly to normal and Giffen goods and this general subject of *own price effects* in the next section (2.3).

(b) How does $x_j(p, Y)$ change with changes in p_i for $i \neq j$, holding fixed the prices of other goods and income? This depends in the first place on the relationship between goods i and j. If good i, say, is popcorn and j is popcorn poppers, a rise in the price of i will probably cause the demand for good j to fall. If good i is popcorn and j is peanuts, demand for j will probably rise with a rise in the price of i. We will have a little to say about this subject of *cross-price effects* in section 2.3, as well.

(c) How does $x_j(p, Y)$ change with changes in income Y? If we think of two goods, 1 and 2, we get pictures like those in figure 2.5; the heavy curve in each case shows how demand shifts with shifts in Y. These curves are called *income expansion paths* or *Engle curves*. In most cases, we expect that x_j will rise with increasing income, but it is possible that demand for j falls with increases in Y; goods j such that x_j falls as Y increases are called *inferior* goods. An example might be potatoes, insofar as an increase in income means the consumer can afford to substitute more expensive, higher "quality" food such as meat for potatoes. Good 1 in figure 2.5(a) is an example of an inferior good, at least for a range of Y. In case x_j increases with increasing Y, we become interested in whether x_j increases

---

[9] A sufficient condition for this is that preferences are strictly convex; see proposition 2.11. But strict convexity is unpalatable in some cases. For example, I have no use whatsoever for hydrochloric acid. My preferences are completely unaffected by the amount of hydrochloric acid in my consumption bundle. Hence my preferences are not strictly convex along the dimension of hydrochloric acid. On the other hand, this doesn't affect the uniqueness of a solution to (CP) for me, since at positive prices for hydrochloric acid I will buy no hydrochloric acid at all. On this point, see problem 10.

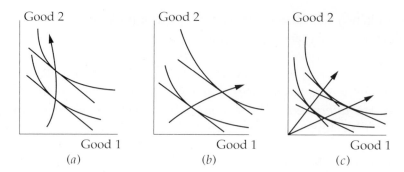

Figure 2.5. Various income expansion paths or Engle curves.
In (a), good 1 is an inferior good over a range of Y. In (b), good 1
is a luxury good and good 2 is a necessary good. In (c), demand is
homothetic.

more or less proportionately with Y. When $x_j(p, Y)/Y$ increases (a higher
fraction of income is spent on j with increases in Y), j is called a *luxury* good; when $x_j(p, Y)/Y$ decreases with increases in Y, j is called
a *necessary* good. In figure 2.5(b), good 1 is a luxury good and good 2
is a necessary good. When $x_j(p, Y)/Y$ doesn't change with changes in
Y for all j, the consumer's preferences are said to be *homothetic*, as in
figure 2.5(c).

These are examples of *comparative statics* exercises of the simplest kind
— asking how consumer behavior changes with changes in underlying
parameters. The term "statics" is used because it is assumed that the consumer fully adjusts to the changes in the parameters. Indeed, we might
better phrase the question: What differences would be observed if we observed two different but identical consumers placed in two different circumstances? More difficult comparative statics exercises, built from these
simple exercises, ask how consumer behavior shifts with shifts in other
"parameters" of the model. How does demand for cigarettes change if
we impose an excise tax on cigarettes? How does demand for cigarettes
change if we impose an income tax on consumers?

We should stress that each of the exercises involves shifts in demand
as one parameter changes, the others being held fixed. If we assumed
that the demand function $x(p, Y)$ were differentiable, we would be asking
questions about the partial derivatives of x. In a moment we will assume
that $x(p, Y)$ is differentiable, and so when we return to these questions,
they will be phrased in terms of partial derivatives. You may find it helpful
to recast the terms just given in the language of partial derivatives before
reading ahead.

2.3. *Marshallian demand with derivatives*

The first-order conditions for (CP)

How do we solve the problem (CP)? The standard approach is to assume that the utility function U is differentiable; form a Lagrangian; and look at the combined first-order conditions and complementary slackness conditions. (Consult appendix 1 immediately if you have no idea what this means, or if you need a quick review.) Letting λ be the multiplier on the budget constraint $p \cdot x \leq Y$ and μ_j (for $j = 1, \ldots, K$) the multiplier on the constraint $x_j \geq 0$, the Lagrangian is

$$U(x) + \lambda \left(Y - \sum_{j=1}^{K} p_j x_j \right) + \sum_{j=1}^{K} \mu_j x_j,$$

and the first-order conditions read

$$\frac{\partial U}{\partial x_j} = \lambda p_j - \mu_j.$$

The multipliers are all constrained to be nonnegative and, of course, the solution must obey the original constraints $p \cdot x \leq Y$ and $x \geq 0$. The complementary slackness conditions must also hold:

$$\lambda(Y - p \cdot x) = 0 \quad \text{and} \quad \mu_j x_j = 0 \text{ for } j = 1, \ldots, K.$$

We can rewrite this as follows: Since the μ_j are nonnegative, these multipliers can be eliminated and the first-order condition for x_j and the complementary slackness condition for μ_j can be combined succinctly as

$$\frac{\partial U}{\partial x_j} \leq \lambda p_j, \text{ with equality if } x_j > 0.$$

(Be absolutely certain that you see why this is equivalent to the combined first-order condition with the μ_j included and the complementary slackness condition on μ_j.) Assuming prices are all strictly positive (which we do throughout this chapter), we can rewrite again as

$$\frac{1}{p_j} \frac{\partial U}{\partial x_j} \leq \lambda, \text{ with equality if } x_j > 0.$$

Or in words, for goods that are consumed in positive levels, the ratios of the marginal utility of the goods to their respective prices must be equal, and these ratios are greater than the corresponding ratios for goods that are not consumed.

If we know that $\lambda > 0$, we can rewrite in yet another form that you may recall from intermediate micro or even from principles courses. For two goods i and j that are consumed in positive amounts at the optimum,

$$\frac{\partial U}{\partial x_i} \bigg/ \frac{\partial U}{\partial x_j} = p_i/p_j.$$

Or, in words, the ratio of marginal utilities equals the ratio of prices. You may recall this stated as *the marginal rate of substitution of good i for good j (along an indifference curve) equals the ratio of their prices.* In fact, even if $\lambda = 0$ we have this relationship, as long as we recognize that when $\lambda = 0$, the first-order conditions read that $\partial U/\partial x_i = 0$ for goods that are consumed in positive amounts, and we interpret $0/0$ as being any number we wish.

> But is $\lambda > 0$? Because we will assume that it is throughout the remainder of this section, some justification should be given. Recall that the indirect utility function $\nu(p, Y)$ gives the value of the problem (CP) as a function of the parameters p and Y. If you have a good background in constrained optimization, you will note immediately that λ is $\partial \nu/\partial Y$. (Assume that ν is differentiable for the time being; we'll discuss this later.) Proposition 2.13 shows that ν is strictly increasing in Y, assuming local insatiability, so things look good. But there are strictly increasing, differentiable functions whose derivatives are zero at isolated points. And so it is with $\partial \nu/\partial Y$ and λ; depending on the representation U of preferences that we use, we can produce examples where the multiplier is sometimes zero. This is true even if U represents convex preferences, as long as we only insist on U being quasi-concave; there are strictly increasing and quasi-concave functions whose derivatives go to zero at points. Now if U is a concave function, we are certainly in business. Then we can show that $\nu(p, Y)$ is concave in Y, and a strictly increasing, concave function can never have zero derivative. But assuming concavity of U is hard to do on first principles (until next chapter). Conclusions: In any application where you specify a concave function U, you can freely assume and will always find that the multiplier λ is strictly positive. But if you assume that U is quasi-concave based on an assumption of even strictly increasing and strictly convex preferences, it takes a little more to be sure that the multiplier is strictly positive.

We have all this from writing down the first-order and complementary slackness conditions. But what is their standing in relation to the problem (CP)? If you find a solution to (CP), must these conditions hold (for some multipliers)? If you find a solution to the first-order conditions and the complementary slackness conditions (that satisfies the sign constraints on the multipliers and the various feasibility constraints on the variables x_i), will it be a solution to (CP)? Those readers who have studied constrained optimization will know that for this problem, *if U is concave, these conditions are necessary and sufficient for a solution.* Those readers who have not studied constrained optimization now have a bit more incentive to do so.

> But what is the status of an assumption that U is concave? And all this is predicated on the assumption that U is differentiable; can that assumption be grounded in some assumption on preferences $\succ$? I do not know of any natural conditions on $\succ$ that would guarantee that $\succ$ admits a differentiable representation. Note well the way this was put. We have no hope whatsoever that every representation of a given $\succ$ will be differentiable, since we already saw that some representations of $\succ$ will not be continuous. It is the same, as we've noted, for concavity. Concavity of U will not necessarily be preserved by monotonic transformations, so we can't say anything that will make every representation of $\succ$ concave. As we saw at the end of section 2.1, the "natural" notion of convexity of $\succ$ will only guarantee that $\succ$ has a quasi-concave representation. And if you are able to do problem 7, you will discover that otherwise well-behaved convex preferences may admit no concave representations at all. So, granting differentiability, we can still ask for the status of the first-order and complementary slackness conditions for a quasi-concave U. These are necessary, but not quite sufficient for optimality; those of you who have studied constrained optimization now have an incentive to go back and review those chapters at the end of your old textbook about quasi-concavity (or -convexity).

Assumptions galore

Now we make some serious assumptions. We henceforth assume that both (CP) and (DCP) have unique solutions for every (p, Y) and (p, u). As noted, strict convexity of preferences suffices for this but is not an innocuous assumption. We write $x(p, Y)$ for the solution of (CP) as a function of (p, Y) and $h(p, u)$ for the solution of (DCP) as a function of (p, u). The function $x(p, Y)$ is called the *Marshallian* demand function, and $h(p, u)$ is called the *Hicksian* demand function.

We further assume that Marshallian demand, Hicksian demand, the indirect utility function and the expenditure function are all continuously differentiable functions of all their arguments.

What justification can there be for these assumptions? If you followed the proof of proposition 2.13(b) (continuity of the indirect utility function), you should be able to use that technique with the assumptions that (CP) and (DCP) have unique solutions to show that the four functions are all continuous. But differentiability is quite a bit more. We do not provide justification here. In more advanced treatments of the subject, you will find that, in essence, one requires that U is twice-continuously differentiable (and well behaved along axes.) And as we had no reason to suppose from first principles concerning $\succ$ that U is differentiable, we have even less reason to assume that it is twice differentiable. You can also ask how much of what follows can be extended to cases where our assumptions of differentiability are not met. All these matters we simply sweep under the rug, and they constitute one of the principal reasons that the treatment of demand theory here is just a sketch.

Hicksian demand and the expenditure function

Proposition 2.15. *The expenditure function and the Hicksian demand function are related as follows:*

$$h_i(p, u) = \frac{\partial e(p, u)}{\partial p_i}.$$

Proof. We give a very slick graphical proof of this result first. Fix the utility argument u^* and all the prices p_j^* except for p_i, and graph the function

$$p_i \to e((p_1^*, \dots, p_{i-1}^*, p_i, p_{i+1}^*, \dots, p_K^*), u^*).$$

We are assuming that this function is differentiable.[q] Now at the value $p_i = p_i^*$, what is its derivative? Since we know that we can get utility u^* from the bundle $h(p^*, u^*)$, we know that

$$e((p_1^*, \dots, p_{i-1}^*, p_i, p_{i+1}^*, \dots, p_K^*), u^*) \leq p_i h_i(p^*, u^*) + \sum_{j \neq i} p_j^* h_j(p^*, u^*).$$

The function on the right-hand side, therefore, is everywhere above the function $e(p, u^*)$, and it touches at p^*, so it must be tangent as shown in figure 2.6. But it is a linear function of p_i, and its slope (in the p_i direction) is $h_i(p^*, u^*)$. Done.[r]

---

[q] In fact, we know from proposition 2.14 that this is a concave function, which almost, but not quite, gives differentiability; see the fn. following.

[r] (1) What if we didn't assume that $e(p, u)$ is differentiable? It is still concave in p_i, so we would get a similar picture, except that we might find that e has a kink at p_i^*. We would then get a statement about how $h_i(p^*, u^*)$ lies between the right- and left-hand partial derivatives of e, where their existence is guaranteed by concavity. (2) Suppose that we assume that e is differentiable, but we don't assume directly that (DCP) has a unique solution. What does the proposition tell us?

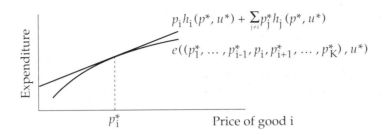

Figure 2.6. Connecting Hicksian demand and the expenditure function.

This proof is so slick that you may be unable to replicate it in other situations. So we will give a more dreary algebraic proof, which illustrates a technique that is much used in this branch of microeconomics. As a first step, differentiate both sides of the accounting identity $e(p, u) = p \cdot h(p, u)$ with respect to p_i. This gives

$$\frac{\partial e}{\partial p_i} = h_i(p, u) + \sum_{j=1}^{k} p_j \frac{\partial h_j}{\partial p_i}.$$

In words, if we raise the price of good i, then the resulting change in expenditure needed to reach utility level u comes from two terms. First, the amount h_i of good i that we were buying before is more expensive; expenditure rises at precisely the rate $h_i(p, u)$. And, second, we'll probably buy less i and more or less of other things; the sum term above gives the "cost" of changes in the optimal bundle to buy. The result we are supposed to be heading for says that the summation term is identically zero.

To see why this is, recall that $h(p, u)$ is the solution of (DCP), or

$$\min_{x} p \cdot x \quad \text{subject to} \quad U(x) \geq u.$$

If we make η the Lagrange multiplier on the constraint, the first-order condition (for x_i) reads

$$p_i = \eta \frac{\partial U}{\partial x_i},$$

evaluated, of course, at the optimum, which is $h(p, u)$. (We ignore nonnegativity constraints on x here; the diligent reader may wish to replicate our argument with that additional complication.) This has a partial of U with respect to x_i, whereas we are interested in getting rid of a sum involving partials of h with respect to p_i; so we aren't quite there yet. But now a little sleight of hand comes into play. First write the accounting identity

$$U(h(p, u)) = u.$$

Implicitly partially differentiate both sides with respect to p_i, and you get

$$\sum_{j=1}^{K} \frac{\partial U}{\partial x_j} \frac{\partial h_j}{\partial p_i} = 0.$$

We can push our first-order conditions into this, and get

$$(1/\eta) \sum_{j=1}^{K} p_j \frac{\partial h_j}{\partial p_i} = 0.$$

This is just what we want, as long as the Lagrange multiplier η isn't zero or infinite. There are ways to ensure this. See the discussion above concerning the multiplier on the budget constraint in (CP).

Roughly put, our technique here is to substitute into one equation a first-order condition for something that is optimal in a constrained optimization problem. This technique is closely connected to the picture we drew: In essence, we are trading on the fact that, at the optimum, when the price of p_i changes, we have the same marginal impact on expenditure by "absorbing" all the change into good i as we would by fully reoptimizing. If we fully reoptimized our consumption bundle, we would do better than by absorbing the change into good i alone; this is why the expenditure function lies everywhere below the line in figure 2.6. But because, at a solution of (DCP), the ratios of marginal utilities to prices of the goods are equal, the difference on the margin between fully reoptimizing and using good i alone is of second order (assuming differentiability of the expenditure function and ignoring nonnegativity constraints, which are left for you to handle). This technique is formalized in general in *the envelope theorem*, so-called because the expenditure function is the lower envelope of linear functions like the one we have drawn. If you have not already studied the envelope theorem in general, you may wish to do so (elsewhere).

Roy's identity

Taking the partial derivative of the expenditure function with respect to the ith price gave us Hicksian demand for the ith good. Can we get anything nice by taking partial derivatives of the indirect utility function? An affirmative answer is given by *Roy's identity*.

Proposition 2.16. *Marshallian demand and the indirect utility function are related as follows:*

$$x_i(p, Y) = -\frac{\partial \nu}{\partial p_i} \Big/ \frac{\partial \nu}{\partial Y}.$$

Proof. Suppose that $x^* = x(p, Y)$. Let $u^* = U(x^*)$. Then we claim that $x^* = h(p, u^*)$, and $Y = e(p, u^*)$. (This step is left to you. Remember that we are assuming that [CP] and [DCP] have unique solutions.) Thus $u^* \equiv \nu(p, e(p, u^*))$ for fixed u^* and all p. Differentiate this with respect to p_i and you get

$$0 = \frac{\partial \nu}{\partial p_i} + \frac{\partial \nu}{\partial Y} \frac{\partial e}{\partial p_i}.$$

Use proposition 2.15 to replace $\partial e / \partial p_i$ with $h_i(p, u^*) = x_i^* = x_i(p, Y)$ and rearrange terms.

Roy's identity may seem a bit mysterious, but it has a fairly intuitive explanation which requires that you know that $\partial \nu / \partial Y$ is the multiplier λ in (CP). Assuming $x_i(p, Y) > 0$, the first-order condition for x_i in (CP) can be written

$$\frac{1}{p_i} \frac{\partial U}{\partial x_i} = \lambda.$$

Roy's identity can be written

$$-\frac{\partial \nu}{\partial p_i} = \frac{\partial \nu}{\partial Y} x_i,$$

so substituting λ for $\partial \nu / \partial Y$ and combining, we get

$$-\frac{\partial \nu}{\partial p_i} = \lambda x_i = \frac{x_i}{p_i} \frac{\partial U}{\partial x_i}. \qquad (\spadesuit)$$

(What happens if $x_i = 0$?) What does this mean? Imagine that the price of good i decreases by a penny. How much extra utility can our consumer obtain? The consumer with income Y to spend, if he buys the bundle he was buying before, has x_i pennies left over because good i is cheaper. He can use this "extra" income naively, spending all of it on good i. If he does this, he can buy (approximately) one penny times x_i/p_i more of good i, which raises his utility by one penny times $(x_i/p_i)(\partial U/\partial x_i)$. Now this is a naive response to a decrease in the price of good i; our consumer will probably do some further substituting among the various goods. But, what

Roy's identity shows, these substitutions will *not* have a first-order effect on the consumer's utility; the main effect is captured by naively spending his "windfall" entirely on good i. (You should complement this discussion by obtaining (♠) in two related ways: drawing a picture like figure 2.6 and by constructing an argument where some first-order condition is used as in the previous subsection.)

The Slutsky equation: Connecting Marshallian and Hicksian demand

What happens to Marshallian demand for commodity j starting at prices p and income Y if the price of commodity i rises? Two things: First, in real terms the consumer is a bit poorer; the general "price index" has risen. Roughly, since the consumer was buying $x_i(p, Y)$ of good i, his "real income" falls at approximately the rate $x_i(p, Y)$ (a penny rise in the price of i means $x_i(p, Y)$ pennies less to spend). This will cause our consumer to change his demand for j, at a rate (roughly) $-(\partial x_j/\partial Y)x_i(p, Y)$. That is, we multiply the rate of change in consumption of j per unit change in income times the rate of change in real income that we just computed.

Second, good i no longer looks so attractive — its relative price has risen. So the consumer will (probably) consume less of i. And, depending on the relationship between i and j, this may cause the consumer to take more of j or less. In any event, there is a "cross-substitution" effect on the consumption of j. We want to isolate this substitution effect from the change in consumption of j due to the change in real income, so we look for some sort of compensated demand function — change the price of good i, compensate the consumer so that his real income stays the same, and see how the change in p_i affects the compensated demand for j.

There are two obvious ways to compensate our consumer. We could raise Y enough so that the consumer could afford the bundle that he was previously buying — Slutsky compensation. Or we could give the consumer sufficient income so that, after he optimizes, he is as well off in terms of his preferences as before — Hicks compensation. If you took intermediate micro, or even a good principles course, you probably will remember something like this.

Our friend the Hicksian demand function is based on Hicksian compensation. Actually making Hicksian compensation is not going to be possible because it depends on the unobservable utility function; it is meant solely as a theoretical construct. Despite this, since we have this demand function defined, let's adopt Hicksian compensation. The Hicks compensated substitution term is simply $\partial h_j/\partial p_i$. (Slutsky compensation makes a nice homework problem.)

So we expect that the change in Marshallian demand of j as p_i changes is the sum of the income effect and the compensated substitution effect. Let us record our expectations in the form of a proposition.

Proposition 2.17. *Marshallian demand and Hicksian demand are related as follows:*

$$\frac{\partial x_j}{\partial p_i} = \frac{\partial h_j}{\partial p_i} - \frac{\partial x_j}{\partial Y} x_i, \qquad (\star)$$

where we evaluate, for given prices p and income level Y, the Marshallian demand at those prices and that income, and, for the Hicksian demand function, the utility level achieved at that Marshallian demand point.

Expecting that this equation holds and proving it are two different things. Our verbal argument above is loose in two places: We don't know that Hicksian compensation is correct, and our income adjustment x_i is not quite correct because of the substitution out of x_i. But a formal proof is relatively painless. Write the identity $x_j(p, e(p, u)) \equiv h_j(p, u)$ and differentiate both sides with respect to p_i. We get

$$\frac{\partial x_j}{\partial p_i} + \frac{\partial x_j}{\partial Y}\frac{\partial e}{\partial p_i} = \frac{\partial h_j}{\partial p_i}.$$

Since $\partial e / \partial p_i$ is $h_i(p, u) = x_i(p, e(p, u))$, this reads

$$\frac{\partial x_j}{\partial p_i} + \frac{\partial x_j}{\partial Y} x_i(p, e(p, u)) = \frac{\partial h_j}{\partial p_i},$$

which, once we make right substitutions for dummy variables, is equation $(\star)$. Equation $(\star)$ is known as the *Slutsky equation*.

About differentiable concave functions

(You may be wondering where all this is headed. We are certainly taking lots of derivatives, and it isn't at all clear to what end we are doing so. Some results are coming, but we need a bit more setting-up to get them. Please be patient.)

To motivate what comes next, think of a twice-continuously differentiable concave function of one variable. A concave function (of one variable) is a function whose derivative is nonincreasing; hence it is a function whose second derivative is nonpositive.

For concave functions of several variables this generalizes as follows: For a given twice-continuously differentiable function $f : R^K \to R$ and any point $z \in R^K$, let $H(z)$ be $K \times K$ matrix whose (i, j)th element is the term

$$\left. \frac{\partial^2 f}{\partial z_i \partial z_j} \right|_z .$$

That is, $H(z)$ is the matrix of mixed second partials of f, evaluated at z. This matrix is called the *Hessian matrix* of f. Note that a Hessian matrix is automatically symmetric; the mixed second partial of f with respect to z_i and z_j is the same as the second partial of f with respect to z_j and z_i.

Definition. *A $k \times k$ matrix H is **negative semi-definite** if for all $\zeta \in R^K$, $\zeta H \zeta \leq 0$.*

(By $\zeta H \zeta$, we mean $\zeta^T H \zeta$, where the superscript T denotes transpose, and we think of ζ as a $K \times 1$ column vector.)

Corollary of the definition. *If H is a negative semi-definite $K \times K$ matrix, then $H_{ii} \leq 0$ for $i = 1, \ldots, K$.*

The corollary follows immediately from the definition, if we take for ζ a vector with 1 in the ith position and 0 in all others.

Mathematical fact. *A twice-continuously differentiable function $f : R^K \to R$ is concave if and only if its Hessian matrix (evaluated at each point in the domain of f) is negative semi-definite.*[s]

The main result, with applications to comparative statics

We can now connect all the pieces and obtain some results. We state the conclusion first, and then give the chain of logic that yields it.

Proposition 2.18. *If $x(p, Y)$ is a Marshallian demand function, then the $K \times K$ matrix whose ijth term is*

$$\frac{\partial x_i(p, Y)}{\partial p_j} + \frac{\partial x_i(p, Y)}{\partial Y} x_j(p, Y),$$

*which is called the matrix of **substitution terms**, is symmetric and negative semi-definite.*

---

[s] This is true as well if f is defined on an open domain within R^K, which in fact is how we will use it.

This conclusion is reached as follows. By the Slutsky equation, the i, jth term of our matrix is $\partial h_i(p, u)/\partial p_j$, evaluated at $(p, U(x(p, Y)))$. This, according to proposition 2.15, is $\partial^2 e/(\partial p_i \partial p_j)$. So the matrix of substitution terms is the Hessian matrix of the expenditure function. The expenditure function is concave in p by proposition 2.14(c). So the result follows from properties of Hessian matrices of concave functions.

Of what use is this? We return to the comparative statics exercises sketched at the end of the last section. Good j is inferior if $\partial x_j/\partial Y < 0$; it is a necessary good if $0 \leq \partial x_j/\partial Y < x_j/Y$; and it is a luxury good if $x_j/Y \leq \partial x_j/\partial Y$. It is a normal good if $\partial x_j/\partial p_j < 0$, and it is a Giffen good if $\partial x_j/\partial p_j > 0$.

Consider the possibility of a Giffen good. By the Slutsky equation,

$$\frac{\partial x_j}{\partial p_j} = \frac{\partial h_j}{\partial p_j} - \frac{\partial x_j}{\partial Y} x_j.$$

We know by the corollary from the previous subsection and proposition 2.18 that $\partial h_j/\partial p_j < 0$; that is, the own-price substitution term is always nonpositive. So the only way that a good could be a Giffen good is if it is an inferior good. It has to be sufficiently inferior so that the income effect term $-(\partial x_j/\partial Y)x_j$ overcomes the substitution term $\partial h_j/\partial p_j$. And, roughly speaking, an inferior good stands a better chance of being a Giffen good if it looms larger in the consumer's consumption bundle; note that $\partial x_j/\partial Y$ is multiplied by x_j. So if one is ever to find a Giffen good (and it isn't clear that one has ever been identified) the place to look is at inferior goods that make up a large part of the consumer's consumption bundle.

Or consider cross-price effects, that is, things like $\partial x_j/\partial p_i$. In informal economics, the term *substitutes* is used to describe pairs of goods where an increase in the price of one good causes an increase in the demand of the second, and *complements* is used when an increase in the price of one good causes a decrease in the demand of the other. If we attempt to formalize this in terms of the signs of $\partial x_j/\partial p_i$, we run into the unhappy possibility that $\partial x_j/\partial p_i < 0$ and, at the same time, $\partial x_i/\partial p_j > 0$. The symmetry of the substitution terms precludes this unhappy possibility when, instead, we define substitute and complement pairs of goods in terms of the sign of $\partial h_j/\partial p_i$. And so it has become common to use this definition, thereby admitting the possibility that, say, $\partial x_i/\partial p_j < 0$ even when i and j are formally substitutes, because the income effect term might outweigh the substitution term.

In general, the Slutsky equation allows us to view comparative statics in prices as the sum of an income effect and a substitution effect, where the latter is given by the partial derivatives (in prices) of Hicksian demand. And our proposition gives us some information about the nature of these substitution effects.

Integrability

The big payoff to all our labors comes when we ask the question: Given a function $x(p, Y)$ that is claimed to be a Marshallian demand function, is some locally insatiable, preference-maximizing consumer behind it?

Why would anyone ever ask such a question? In applied (econometric) work, it is sometimes useful to have parametric functional specifications for a consumer's demand function. Now we could write down nice closed form parametrizations for the utility function U, and then solve (CP) to derive Marshallian demand. But for most analytically tractable specifications of U, the Marshallian demand function that results is a mess. It is often more convenient to specify a parametric form for Marshallian demand directly, being sure that this parametrization is analytically tractable. But then, to be sure that one's parametrization plays by the rules of microeconomic theory, one would want to know that the question asked in the previous paragraph is answered affirmatively.

We assume that we have a functional specification of an entire Marshallian demand function which is differentiable. From easy first principles, we know that Marshallian demand should be homogeneous of degree zero and should obey Walras' law with equality. And we now also know that the matrix of substitution terms (which are functions of Marshallian demand) must be symmetric and negative semi-definite. Subject to some technical caveats, these things are *sufficient* as well: Assuming that Marshallian demand obeys Walras' law with equality and that it is homogeneous of degree zero, if the matrix of substitution terms is symmetric and negative semi-definite, then it can be "integrated up" to get the indirect utility function, from which a representative of the direct utility function can be constructed. We won't even attempt to sketch the proof here; serious students will wish to consult a standard text on demand theory to see how it's done.

2.4. Aggregate demand

One further subject will come into play in later developments in this book and should be mentioned — *aggregate consumer demand*.

Until now, we have been considering demand by a single consumer. But in much of this book, we will be interested instead in demand by a host of consumers, which, at prices p, will be the sum of their individual demands given their individual incomes. Our interest will be strong especially because it is hard (not impossible) to obtain data on the demand by a single consumer.

Of course, total demand will shift about as a function of how individual incomes are distributed, even holding total (societal) income fixed. So it makes no sense to speak of aggregate demand as a function of prices and social income.

Even with this caveat, results analogous to the Slutsky restrictions (proposition 2.18) or GARP do not necessarily hold for aggregate demand. Think of GARP for a moment. Imagine a two-person, two-commodity economy in which we fix each person's income at 1,000. At prices $(10, 10)$, we might have one person choose $(25, 75)$ and the second choose $(75, 25)$. Hence aggregate demand is $(100, 100)$. Suppose that at prices $(15, 5)$, the first chooses $(40, 80)$ and the second $(64, 8)$. Neither individual violates GARP; the first can't afford $(40, 80)$ at prices $(10, 10)$, so we imagine that he has to settle for $(25, 75)$ at those prices. And the second can't purchase $(75, 25)$ at the prices $(15, 5)$, so we imagine that she must settle for the worse bundle $(64, 8)$ at the second set of prices.

But aggregate demand is $(100, 100)$ in the first case, which is affordable at both sets of prices, and $(104, 88)$ in the second case, which is both affordable at both sets of prices and inside the "social budget set" at the prices where it isn't chosen. Society doesn't obey GARP, even though both individuals do.

So what can we say about aggregate demand, based on the hypothesis that individuals are preference/utility maximizers? Unless we are willing to make strong assumptions about the distribution of preferences or income throughout the economy (everyone has the same homothetic preferences, for example), there is little we can say. Aggregate demand will be homogeneous of degree zero in prices and (everyone's) income. And if all consumers are locally insatiable, Walras' law will hold with equality for the entire economy. But beyond that, almost anything is possible for aggregate demand. In the advanced literature of demand theory, this result is stated and proved formally.

2.5. Bibliographic notes

The material in section 2.1, on preferences, choice, and numerical representations, belongs to the subject of abstract choice theory. For a fairly complete treatment of this subject, see Fishburn (1970). Less complete (and, in particular, lacking the proof that a continuous preference relation admits a continuous numerical representation) but perhaps a bit more readable is Kreps (1988).

We mentioned in section 2.1 problems with the standard models of choice concerning framing. If you are interested, a good place to begin is the brief introductory article by Kahneman and Tversky (1984). For a broader treatment and some applications, see the *Journal of Business* symposium issue of 1987. We also mentioned "time of day" problems; this will be further discussed in chapter 4, and references will be given there.

As for standard references in demand theory, Deaton and Muellbauer (1980) and Varian (1984) are good sources for many of the details and topics omitted here. In particular, both cover functional separability of preferences, which is very important to econometric applications. Katzner (1970) is a good source for seeing how to think about differentiability and other mathematical niceties.

References

Deaton, A., and J. Muellbauer. 1980. *Economics and Consumer Behavior.* Cambridge: Cambridge University Press.

Debreu, G. 1954. "Representation of a Preference Ordering by a Numerical Function." In *Decision Processes*, R. Thrall, C. Coombs, and R. Davis, eds. New York: John Wiley and Sons.

Fishburn, P. [1970] 1979. *Utility Theory for Decision Making.* New York: John Wiley and Sons. Reprint. Huntington, N.Y.: R. E. Krieger Publishing.

Kahneman, D., and A. Tversky. 1979. "Prospect Theory: An Analysis of Decision Under Risk." *Econometrica* 47:263–91.

————. 1984. "Choices, Values, and Frames." *American Psychologist* 39:341–50.

Kannai, Y. 1977. "Concavifiability and Constructions of Concave Utility Functions." *Journal of Mathematical Economics* 4:1–56.

Katzner, D. 1970. *Static Demand Theory.* New York: Macmillan.

Kreps, D. 1988. *Notes on the Theory of Choice.* Boulder, Colo.: Westview Press.

Varian, H. 1984. *Microeconomic Analysis.* 2d edition. New York: W. W. Norton.

2.6. Problems

■ 1. Let $\succ$ be a binary relation on a set X, and define $\succeq$ as in section 2.1; $x \succeq y$ if it is not the case that $y \succ x$. Show that $\succ$ is asymmetric if and only if $\succeq$ is complete. Show that $\succ$ is negatively transitive if and only if $\succeq$ is transitive. (Hint: For the second part, it may help to know that the statements "A implies B" and "not B implies not A" are logical equivalents. The latter is called the *contrapositive* of the former. We gave negative transitivity in the form *if* $x \succ y$, *then* for any z, either $x \succ z$ or $z \succ y$. What is the contrapositive of this if–then? Now do you see why it is called negative transitivity?)

■ 2. Show that if $\succ$ is asymmetric and negatively transitive, then $\sim$ defined as in the text is reflexive, symmetric, and transitive. Then for each $x \in X$, recall that $\text{Indiff}(x) = \{y \in X : y \sim x\}$. Show that the sets $\text{Indiff}(x)$, ranging over $x \in X$, partition the set X. That is, show that each $x \in X$ is in at least one $\text{Indiff}(y)$ and that for any pair x and y, either $\text{Indiff}(x) = \text{Indiff}(y)$ or $\text{Indiff}(x) \cap \text{Indiff}(y) = \emptyset$.

■ 3. Prove proposition 2.3. (Hint: Use proposition 2.1.)

■ 4. (a) Prove proposition 2.4.

A "problem" with proposition 2.4 is that it assumes that we have the entire function c. If we are trying to test the basic preference-based choice model on observed data, we will have less data than all of c in two respects. First, for sets $A \subseteq X$ where $c(A)$ contains more than one element, we are apt to observe only one of the elements. And we will not see $c(A)$ for all subsets $A \subseteq X$, but only for some of the subsets of X.

(b) Show that the first of these problems is virtually unresolvable. Assume that when we see $x \in A$ chosen from A, this doesn't preclude the possibility that one or more $y \in A$ with $y \neq x$ is just as good as x. Prove that in this case, no data that we see ever contradict the preference-based choice model of section 2.1. (Hint: This is a trick question. If you see the trick, it takes about two lines.)

By virtue of (b), we either will need to assume that we see all of $c(A)$ for those subsets A where we observe choice, or we otherwise need something like local insatiability to tell us when something not chosen is revealed strictly worse than what is chosen.

(c) Suppose that, for some (but not all) subsets $A \subseteq X$, we observe $c(A)$. Show that these partial data about the function c may satisfy Houthakker's axiom and still be inconsistent with the standard preference-based choice model. Formulate a condition on these data such that if the data satisfy this condition, the data are not inconsistent with the standard model. If it helps, you may assume that X is a finite set. (Hint: Proposition 2.12 may help give you the right idea.)

■ 5. Consider the following preferences: $X = [0, 1] \times [0, 1]$, and $(x_1, x_2) \succ (x_1', x_2')$ if either $x_1 > x_1'$ or if $x_1 = x_1'$ and $x_2 > x_2'$. These are called *lexicographic* preferences, because they work something like alphabetical order; to rank any two objects, the first component (letter) of each is compared, and if those first components agree, the second components are considered. Show that this preference relation is asymmetric and negatively transitive but does not have a numerical representation. (Hint: You should have no problem with the first part of the statement, but the second is more difficult and requires that you know about countable and uncountable sets. This example will appear in almost every book on choice theory, so if you get badly stuck, you can look it up.)

■ 6. Prove proposition 2.9.

■ 7. *Part (a) is not too hard if you know the required mathematics. Part (b) is extremely difficult; see Kannai (1977) if you can't do it and are insatiably curious.*

(a) Consider the following two utility functions defined on the positive orthant in R^2:

$$U_1(x_1, x_2) = \begin{cases} x_1 x_2 & \text{if } x_1 x_2 < 4, \\ 4 & \text{if } 4 \le x_1 x_2 \le 8, \text{ and} \\ x_1 x_2 & \text{if } 8 \le x_1 x_2. \end{cases}$$

$$U_2(x_1, x_2) = \begin{cases} x_1 x_2 & \text{if } x_1 x_2 < 4, \\ 4 & \text{if } x_1 x_2 = 4 \text{ and } x_1 \ge x_2, \\ 5 & \text{if } x_1 x_2 = 4 \text{ and } x_1 < x_2, \text{ and} \\ x_1 x_2 + 1 & \text{if } x_1 x_2 > 4. \end{cases}$$

Show that the corresponding two preferences are both convex. Show that neither could be represented by a concave utility function. Are either or both of the corresponding preferences semi-strictly convex? Are either or both of the corresponding preferences continuous?

(b) There are preferences that are both semi-strictly convex and continuous but that don't admit any concave numerical representations. One such utility function is

$$U_3(x_1, x_2) = \begin{cases} \frac{2(1+x_2)}{2-x_1} - 1 & \text{if } x_1 + x_2 \leq 1, \text{ and} \\ x_1 + x_2 & \text{if } x_1 + x_2 \geq 1. \end{cases}$$

Prove that preferences given by this utility function cannot be represented by any concave function.

■ 8. We assumed local insatiability throughout our discussion of Marshallian demand. One way to obtain this property indirectly is to assume that (a) preferences are semi-strictly convex, (b) preferences are globally insatiable — for all $x \in X$ there exists some $y \in X$ with $y \succ x$, and (c) the consumption set X is convex. Prove that (a), (b), and (c) imply that preferences are locally insatiable.

■ 9. Marshallian demand must be homogeneous of degree zero in prices and income and, as long as preferences are locally insatiable, must satisfy Walras' law with equality. Proposition 2.12 maintains that a finite set of demand data is consistent with maximization of locally insatiable preferences if and only if the data satisfy GARP. Hence satisfaction of GARP must preclude demand that is not homogeneous of degree zero or that fails to satisfy Walras' law with equality. If you like mathematical puzzles, work out why this is. How is it that satisfaction of GARP rules these things out? (Hint: In the definition of revealed preference preceding proposition 2.12, what relation is presumed about the superscripts i and j?)

■ 10. Suppose that in a world with K goods, a particular consumer's preferences $\succ$ have the following property. Her preferences are strictly convex in the first j goods. That is, if x^1 and x^2 are two distinct bundles of goods with $x^1 \succeq x^2$ and $x_i^1 = x_i^2$ for all $i = j+1, j+2, \ldots, K$, and if $a \in (0,1)$, then $ax^1 + ax^2 \succ x^2$. And she has no use whatsoever for the goods with index above j. If x^1 and x^2 are two bundles of goods with $x_i^1 = x_i^2$ for $i = 1, 2, \ldots, j$, then $x^1 \sim x^2$. Show that if prices are strictly positive, this consumer's solution to (CP) is unique.

■ 11. A particular consumer has Marshallian demand for two commodities given as follows

$$x_1(p_1, p_2, Y) = \frac{Y}{p_1 + 2p_2} \quad \text{and} \quad x_2(p_1, p_2, Y) = \frac{2Y}{p_1 + 2p_2}.$$

This is valid for all price and income levels that are strictly positive. This consumer assures me, by the way, that at prices (p_1, p_2) and income Y, his Marshallian demand is strictly better for him than anything else he can afford.

Does this consumer conform to the model of the consumer used in this chapter? That is, is there some set of preferences, given by a utility function, such that maximization of that utility subject to the budget constraint gives rise to this demand function?

If the answer to the first part of the question is yes, how much about the consumer's utility function and/or preferences can you tell me? Can you nail down the consumer's utility function precisely? (If you answer this yes, and if you've ever played the board game Monopoly, "go directly to jail.") Can you nail down precisely the consumer's preferences over consumption bundles? If not, how much can you say about the consumer's preferences?

■ 12. The purpose of compensated demand functions is to try to isolate the substitution and income effects on demand arising from a change in price. Hicksian compensation holds the consumer to a given level of utility, so that we have the Hicksian demand function, $h(p, u)$, as a function of the level of prices p and the level of utility u to which we wish to hold the consumer. An alternative is *Slutsky* compensation, where we hold the consumer to the income needed to purchase a given bundle of goods. Formally, define $s(p, x)$ as the demand of the consumer at prices p if the consumer is given just enough income to purchase the bundle x at the prices p.

We learned that the matrix of Hicksian substitution terms, whose (i, j)th element is $\partial h_i / \partial p_j$, is symmetric and negative semi-definite. Suppose we looked at the matrix of Slutsky substitution terms, whose (i, j)th entry is $\partial s_i / \partial p_j$. This matrix is also symmetric and negative semi-definite. Prove this. (Hint: Express $s(p, x)$ in terms of the Marshallian demand function. Then see what this tells you about the matrix of Slutsky substitution terms.)

■ 13. In a three-good world, a consumer has the Marshallian demands given in table 2.2. Are these choices consistent with the usual model of a locally insatiable, utility-maximizing consumer?

prices			income	demand		
p_1	p_2	p_3	y	x_1	x_2	x_3
1	1	1	20	10	5	5
3	1	1	20	3	5	6
1	2	2	25	13	3	3
1	1	2	20	15	3	1

Table 2.2 Four values of Marshallian demand.

■ 14. Let Σ denote the substitution matrix of some given Marshallian demand system. That is,

$$\Sigma_{ij} = \frac{\partial x_i(p, Y)}{\partial p_j} + \frac{\partial x_i(p, Y)}{\partial Y} x_j(p, Y).$$

Prove that $p\Sigma = 0$, where p is to be thought of as a $1 \times K$ vector, Σ as a $K \times K$ matrix, and 0 as a $1 \times K$ vector. (Hint: Try showing first that $\Sigma p' = 0$, where p' is the transpose of p.)

■ 15. Construct a Marshallian demand function in which one good is a Giffen good. Construct a demand function in which two goods i and j are substitutes but $\partial x_i/\partial p_j < 0$. Be sure that you have given a Marshallian demand function!

chapter three

Choice under uncertainty

Up to this point, we've been thinking of the bundles or objects among which our consumer has been choosing as "sure things" — so many bottles of wine, so many cans of beer, so many shots of whisky. Many important consumption decisions concern choices the consequences of which are uncertain at the time the choice is made. For example, when you choose to buy a car (new or used), you aren't sure what the quality is. When you choose an education, you aren't sure about your abilities, later opportunities, the skills of your instructors, etc. Both in financial and real markets, commodities of risky or uncertain character are traded all the time.

Nothing in the theory up to this point precludes such commodities. A can of Olympia beer is a definite thing — a share of GM is another — and we could simply proceed by taking as given the consumer's preferences for bundles that contain so many cans of beer, so many shares of GM, and so on. But *because* there is special structure to the commodity *a share of GM* (or, rather, because we can model it as having a special structure), we are able to (a) make further assumptions about the nature of our consumer's preferences for such things and, thereby, (b) get out something more concrete about the consumer's demand for these kinds of commodities. This is the basic plot of this chapter.

We begin in section 3.1 with the theory of von Neumann–Morgenstern expected utility. In this theory, uncertain prospects are modeled as probability distributions over a given set of prizes. That is, the probabilities of various prizes are given as part of the description of the object — probabilities are *objective*. Section 3.2 takes up the special case where the prizes in section 3.1 are amounts of money; then one is able to say a bit more about the nature of the utility function that represents preferences. In section 3.3, we briefly discuss a few applications of this theory to the topic of market demand. In section 3.4, we turn to a richer theory, where uncertain prospects are functions from "states of nature" to prizes, and where probabilities arise (if at all) *subjectively*, as part of the representation of a consumer's preferences. In section 3.5 we will explore theoretical and empirical problems with these models. Finally, we will turn briefly to a normative (re)interpretation of this development. While our emphasis is on the use of these models as descriptive models of choice, they are also used as normative guides to aid consumers who must make choices. This is sketched in section 3.6.

3.1. Von Neumann–Morgenstern expected utility

Setup

To begin, think of a basic set of "prizes" X — these are just like our commodity bundles from before — and then a larger set of *probability distributions* over the prizes. Let P denote the set of probability distributions with prizes in X. For the time being, we will assume that P consists only of probability distributions that have a finite number of possible outcomes — such probability distributions are called *simple*. Formally,

Definition. *A **simple probability distibution** p on X is specified by*

*(a) a finite subset of X, called the **support** of p and denoted by* $\mathrm{supp}(p)$*, and*

(b) for each $x \in \mathrm{supp}(p)$ a number $p(x) > 0$, with $\sum_{x \in \mathrm{supp}(p)} p(x) = 1$.

The set of simple probability distributions on X will be denoted by P.

To take an example, suppose that X is the positive orthant in R^2, where $x = (x_1, x_2)$ represents x_1 cans of beer and x_2 bottles of wine. A typical simple probability distribution is one with support $\{(10, 2), (4, 4)\}$, $p((10, 2)) = 1/3$, and $p((4, 4)) = 2/3$. This represents a one-third chance of receiving 10 cans of beer and 2 bottles of wine and a two-thirds chance of getting 4 cans and 4 bottles. We will depict simple probability distributions by *chance nodes*; the example just given is depicted in figure 3.1. Note that the numbers on branches are the probabilities, with the prizes written out at the end of the branches.

Some terminology goes along with this; members x of X will be called *prizes* or *outcomes*. Members p of P will be called *lotteries*, *gambles*,

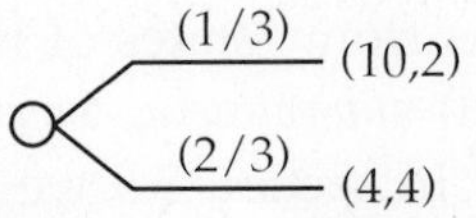

Figure 3.1. A simple probability distribution.

and *probability distributions*, all interchangeably.[a]

And some notation follows: The lottery that gives the prize x with probability one will be written δ_x.

How does this do as a model of the commodity space that we imagine is "out there?" We can say three things here: First, if you thought of commodity bundles as so many cans of beer, so many shares of GM, etc., then you might have thought in terms of a vector of probability distributions instead of a probability distribution on vectors. That is, in terms of our example, we would write a typical commodity bundle as a vector (p_1, p_2) where p_1 is a probability distribution over the number of cans of beer and p_2 is a probability distribution over the number of bottles of wine. But the way we are doing things is superior. You will learn why this is in section 3.3, but for now (if it makes sense) note that if you have a vector of probability distributions, you won't know about any correlations in the prizes they give. A probability distribution over vector prizes tells you not only the marginal distribution on each component but also all conditional and joint probabilities.

Second, the assumption that every distribution has finite support may seem rather limiting. For one thing, we can't in this framework represent a gamble constructed as follows: I flip a coin until the first time it is tails and give you as many dollars as times I flipped the coin, which would give you $1 with probability $1/2$, $2 with probability $1/4$, and so on. Or if the prize space X was R, representing an amount of money, and it was analytically convenient to have Normal probability distributions, our formalism wouldn't be adequate. We will address this shortcoming at the end of this section.

Third, the probabilities all come as part of the description of the object — probabilities are "objective" instead of "subjective." But in real world applications, there may be no objective probability for a random event. For example, suppose an entrepreneur is considering a venture that will earn her a given amount of money if a certain technique for gene splicing works. To use our model in describing her choice problem, we need to know the probability that this technique will work, something about which well-informed individuals might disagree. We'll deal with subjective probabilities in section 3.4.

To complete the setup, we need one more concept. Suppose we have two simple probability distributions p and q and a number α that lies

---

[a] For readers who know the terminology of probability theory, we tend to use *lotteries* and *gambles* when the term *random variable* is appropriate, while *probability distribution* is used when that is appropriate.

between zero and one, inclusive. Then we can form a new probability distribution, written $\alpha p + (1 - \alpha)q$, in two steps:

(a) The support of this new probability distribution is the union of the supports of p and q

(b) If x is some member of this union, then the probability given by $\alpha p + (1 - \alpha)q$ to x is $\alpha p(x) + (1 - \alpha)q(x)$, where $p(x)$ is understood to be zero if x is not in the support of p, and similarly for q

An example may help. Suppose p gives probabilities .3, .1, and .6 to prizes x, y, and z, respectively, and q gives probabilities .6 and .4 to prizes x and w, respectively. We form, say, $(1/3)p + (2/3)q$ as follows: The support of $(1/3)p + (2/3)q$ is $\{x, y, z, w\}$, and the probabilities it gives to its four possible prizes are, respectively,

for x, $(1/3)(.3) + (2/3)(.6) = .5$
for y, $(1/3)(.1) + (2/3)(0) = .0333\ldots$
for z, $(1/3)(.6) + (2/3)(0) = .2$
for w, $(1/3)(0) + (2/3)(.4) = .26666\ldots$

When we depict probability distributions such as $(1/3)p + (2/3)q$ in the example just given, we sometimes will draw a *compound lottery*. For example, in figure 3.2(a), we show $(1/3)p + (2/3)q$ as a compound lottery: a lottery whose outcomes are the lotteries p and q. In figure 3.2(b), we depict the one-stage lottery to which this compound lottery reduces. *In our setup, if not our pictures, 3.2(a) and (b) depict precisely the same thing.* In a minute, we will assume that we are given some individual's preferences over all simple lotteries, and it is implicit that *if* the individual doesn't regard 3.2(a) and (b) as precisely the same object, then at least she is indifferent between them. As we will discuss in section 3.5, this is somewhat counterfactual. Individuals, faced with choices that involve the sorts of pictures in figure 3.2, sometimes do make different choices depending on whether the "picture" is 3.2(a) or (b). The standard theory that we are about to develop does not permit this.

Axioms for preference

Now assume that our consumer has preferences over the set P of all simple probability distributions on X, given, as before, by a relation $\succ$ that expresses *strict preference*. We insist on two properties immediately.

Assumption 1. $\succ$ must be **asymmetric and negatively transitive.**

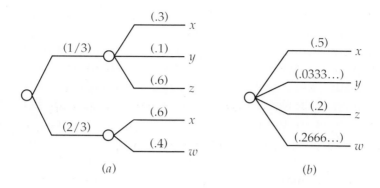

Figure 3.2. Compound and reduced lotteries.
The compound lottery (a) reduces to the single-stage lottery (b) by the
laws of probability theory. In our theory, the consumer either *identifies*
these two as being the same object or, at least, is indifferent between
them.

This is just as before. Also as before, we construct from $\succ$ a *weak preference*
relation $\succeq$ and an *indifference* relation $\sim$.

We add to these two properties some properties that exploit the fact
that our objects of choice are probability distributions. Consider first

Assumption 2. *Suppose p and q are two probability distributions such that
$p \succ q$. Suppose α is a number from the open interval $(0, 1)$, and r is some other
probability distribution. Then $\alpha p + (1 - \alpha)r \succ \alpha q + (1 - \alpha)r$.*

This is called the *substitution axiom*. The idea is that in both of the two final
probability distributions, the consumer is getting r with probability $1 - \alpha$,
hence this "same part" won't affect the consumer's preferences. Overall
preference depends on how the consumer feels about the differences between the two, that is, on p vs. q. Since we suppose that the consumer
prefers p to q, and since $\alpha > 0$ implies that there is some chance that this
difference matters, we conclude that the consumer prefers $\alpha p + (1 - \alpha)r$ to
$\alpha q + (1 - \alpha)r$.

Assumption 3. *Suppose that p, q, and r are three probability distributions
such that $p \succ q \succ r$. Then numbers α and β exist, both from the open interval
$(0, 1)$, such that $\alpha p + (1 - \alpha)r \succ q \succ \beta p + (1 - \beta)r$.*

This is called (for obscure reasons) the *Archimedean axiom*. Think of it this
way: Since p is strictly better than q, then no matter how bad r is, we
can find some "mixture" of p and r, which we'll write $\alpha p + (1 - \alpha)r$,
with weight on p close enough to one so this mixture is better than q.

And, similarly, no matter how much better p is than q, we can find a β sufficiently close to zero so $\beta p + (1 - \beta)r$ is worse than q. To help you understand this, consider an example in which you might think it is false. Suppose p gives you $100 for sure, q gives you $10 for sure, and r consists of your death. You might then say that r is so much worse than q that no probability α however close to one makes $\alpha p + (1 - \alpha)r$ better than q. But if you think so, think again. Imagine that you are told that you can have $10 right now or, if you choose to drive to some nearby location, a check for $100 is waiting for you. If you are like most people, you will probably get into your car to get the $100. But this, to a minute degree, increases the chances of your death.

The representation

Does consumer choice conform to these axioms? A lot of experimental evidence suggests that the answer to this is no; see section 3.5 below. Despite this, vast quantities of economic theory are based on the assumption that consumer choice does conform to these axioms, which leads to the following representation of preferences:

Proposition 3.1. *A preference relation $\succ$ on the set P of simple probability distributions on a space X satisfies assumptions 1, 2, and 3 above if and only if there is a function $u : X \to R$ such that*

$$p \succ q \quad \text{if and only if} \quad \sum_{x \in \text{supp}(p)} u(x)p(x) > \sum_{x \in \text{supp}(q)} u(x)q(x).$$

Moreover, if u provides a representation of $\succ$ in this sense, then v does as well if and only if constants $a > 0$ and b exist such that $v(\cdot) \equiv au(\cdot) + b$.

In words, $\succ$ has an *expected utility* representation. Each possible prize has a corresponding utility level, and the value of a probability distribution is measured by the expected level of utility that it provides. Moreover, this utility function is unique up to a positive affine transformation (which is a fancy way of putting the last statement).

This is sometimes called a von Neumann–Morgenstern expected utility representation, since one of the original modern developments of this theory appears in von Neumann and Morgenstern's *Theory of Games and Economic Behavior*. But the form goes back a good deal further, to the eighteenth century and Daniel Bernoulli.

Note that the proposition establishes the existence of a numerical representation for preferences on p. That is, there is a function $U : P \to R$

such that $p \succ q$ if and only if $U(p) > U(q)$. The proposition establishes a good deal more than this. It also establishes that we can assume that this function U takes the form of expected utility of prizes: $U(p) = \sum_{x \in \text{supp}(p)} u(x)p(x)$, for some $u : X \to R$.

Numerical representations, you will recall, are unique up to strictly increasing rescalings. That is, if $U : X \to R$ gives a numerical representation of $\succ$, then so will $V(\cdot) \equiv f(U(\cdot))$ for any strictly increasing f. But if U has the form of expected utility, so that $U(p) = \sum_{x \in \text{supp}(p)} u(x)p(x)$, for some $u : X \to R$, and if f is an arbitrary increasing function, then the function V that results from composing U with f may not have the form of expected utility. You can be sure that V will be another expected utility representation if and only if f is an increasing affine function, or $f(r) = ar + b$ for $a > 0$, in which case the $v : X \to R$ that goes with V will be $v(\cdot) \equiv au(\cdot) + b$.

Continuing on this general point, recall that we said in the previous chapter that there is no cardinal significance in utility differences. That is, if $U(x) - U(x'') = 2(U(x') - U(x'')) > 0$ (where U is defined on X), this doesn't mean anything like x is twice better than x'' than is x'. It just means that $x \succ x' \succ x''$. But in the context of expected utility, if $u(x) - u(x'') = 2(u(x') - u(x'')) > 0$ where u gives an expected utility representation on P, this has cardinal significance. It means that a lottery that gives either x or x'', each with probability $1/2$, is indifferent to x' for sure.

How is proposition 3.1 proven? We will sketch the proof here; if you are ambitious and know a bit of real analysis, problem 1 will give you a few hints on how to fill in the details. (It isn't very hard.) First, we'll add one assumption (to be taken away in problem 1): In X are a best prize b and a worst prize w; the consumer in question at least weakly prefers b for sure to any other probability distribution over X, and any other probability distribution over X is a least as good as w for sure. If the consumer is indifferent between b for sure and w for sure, then the representation is trivial, so we'll assume as well that $\delta_b \succ \delta_w$. Now we can use assumptions 1, 2, and 3 to obtain three lemmas.

Lemma 1. *For any numbers α and β, both from the interval $[0,1]$, $\alpha\delta_b + (1 - \alpha)\delta_w \succ \beta\delta_b + (1 - \beta)\delta_w$ if and only if $\alpha > \beta$.*

Or, in words, if we look at lotteries involving only the two prizes b and w, the consumer always (strictly) prefers a higher probability of winning the better prize.

Lemma 2. *For any lottery $p \in P$, there is a number $\alpha \in [0,1]$ such that $p \sim \alpha\delta_b + (1 - \alpha)\delta_w$.*

This result, which is sometimes simply assumed, is called the *calibration* property. It says that we can *calibrate* the consumer's preference for any lottery in terms of a lottery that involves only the best and worst prizes. Note that by virtue of lemma 1, we know that there is exactly one value α that will do in lemma 2; if p were indifferent to two different mixtures of the best and worst prizes, it would be indifferent to two things, one of which is strictly preferred to the other.

Lemma 3. *If $p \sim q$, r is any third lottery, and α is any number from the closed interval $[0, 1]$, then $\alpha p + (1 - \alpha)r \sim \alpha q + (1 - \alpha)r$.*

This is just like the substitution axiom, except that $\succ$ is replaced by $\sim$ here. This is sometimes assumed as an axiom, and it itself is then sometimes called the substitution axiom.

The rest is very easy. For every prize x, define $u(x)$ as that number between zero and one (inclusive) such that

$$\delta_x \sim u(x)\delta_b + (1 - u(x))\delta_w.$$

This number $u(x)$ will be the utility of the prize x. We know that one such number exists by lemma 2, and this number is unique by lemma 1. Take any lottery p:

Lemma 4. *For $u : X \to R$ defined as above, any lottery p is indifferent to the lottery that gives prize b with probability $\sum u(x)p(x)$ and w with the complementary probability, where the sum is over all x in the support of p.*

Once we have this result, we can use lemma 1 to finish the main part of the proof: Compare any two lotteries, p and q. The lottery p is indifferent to the lottery that gives b with probability $\sum u(x)p(x)$ and w with the complementary probability, and q is indifferent to the lottery that gives b with probability $\sum u(x)q(x)$ and w with the complementary probability. We know by lemma 1 how to compare the two lotteries over b and w: Whichever gives a higher probability of b is better. But this is precisely the representation.

Proving lemma 4 is fairly simple in concept but rather cumbersome notationally. The idea is that we take each prize x in the support of p and substitute for it the lottery that gives b with probability $u(x)$ and w with probability $1 - u(x)$. By lemma 3, each time we make such a substitution we will have a new lottery that is indifferent to p. And when we are done with all these substitutions, we will have the lottery that gives prize b with probability $\sum u(x)p(x)$ and w with probability

$1 - \sum u(x)p(x)$. Figure 3.3 shows how this works for a particular lottery: We begin with p, which has prizes x, x', and x'' with probabilities $1/2$, $1/3$, and $1/6$, respectively. This is shown in 3.3(a). In 3.3(b) we replace the prize x'' with a lottery giving prize b with probability $u(x'')$ and w with probability $1 - u(x'')$; this is the lottery p_1, which we show both as a "compound" lottery and as a "one-stage" lottery. We claim that $p \sim p_1$ by lemma 3: Write p as $(5/6)[(3/5)\delta_x + (2/5)\delta_{x'}] + (1/6)\delta_{x''}$; by lemma 3 this is indifferent to $(5/6)[(3/5)\delta_x + (2/5)\delta_{x'}] + (1/6)[u(x'')\delta_b + (1 - u(x''))\delta_w]$, which is p_1. Continuing in this fashion, from p_1 we create p_2, which substitutes for x' in p_1 the lottery that gives b with probability $u(x')$ and w with probability $1 - u(x')$; we know that $p_1 \sim p_2$. And then we create p_3 from p_2, substituting for x in p_2. Once again, lemma 3 tells us that $p_2 \sim p_3$. But then $p \sim p_1 \sim p_2 \sim p_3$, and by transitivity of indifference, $p \sim p_3$, which (for the lottery p) is just what lemma 4 claims.

Of course, this is only a demonstration of lemma 4 on a particular example; it is not a proof. The exact proof is left as an exercise (problem 1(d)); if you try this, you should use induction on the size of the support of p.

All this was based on our added assumption that there was a best and worst prize. But this assumption can be done away with; you can either consult one of the standard reference books or try your hand at problem 1(e).

To complete the proof of the proposition, we need to show that if preferences have an expected utility numerical representation, then those preferences satisfy assumptions 1 through 3, and we need to show that a representing utility function u is unique up to positive affine transformations. (That is, any other function v that gives an expected utility representation for fixed preferences $\succ$ satisfies $v \equiv au + b$ for constants $a > 0$ and b.) These parts of the proof are left to you.

To summarize: We began by taking a choice space that had some special structure — a set of probability distributions. We used that structure to pose some axioms for the consumer's preferences that exploited this structure. Then, using those axioms, we showed that a numerical representation for consumer preferences can be created that exploits this structure; viz., the representing function U on P takes the form of expected utility for some function u defined on X. We continue this in the next section, by making further assumptions about X and $\succ$.

But first we address a concern voiced earlier: In this development we only got the representation for probability distributions with finite support. Can this sort of representation be extended to probability distributions such as, say, the Normal distribution? Yes, it certainly can be. We sketch one

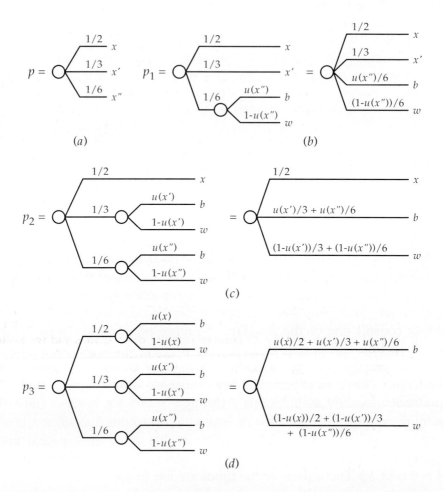

Figure 3.3. Lemma 3 in action.

In the figure above, we successively replace each prize in the lottery p with the lottery between b and w that is just indifferent to that prize. Lemma 3 ensures that, at each step, the lottery replaced is indifferent to the lottery that replaces it. So, in the end, we have a lottery between b and w that is just indifferent to the original lottery. This final lottery gives prize b with probability $\sum_x u(x)p(x)$, and since (by lemma 1) we know that lotteries over b and w are ranked by the probability with which they give b, we know that all lotteries are ranked by their expected utility.

way to proceed, which requires that you know some advanced probability theory. Assume that X is R^k or the positive orthant of R^k. (If you know enough math, take X to be a compact subset of a complete separable metric space.) Let P be the space of all Borel measures on X and assume that preferences are continuous in the weak topology on measures. If assumptions 1, 2, and 3 hold for all probability distributions in P, they hold for the subspace of simple probability distributions, so we produce an expected utility representation for some function $u : X \rightarrow R$ that works for simple probability distributions. We can then use the continuity assumption to show that u must be bounded. (If u were unbounded [say] above, we could find a sequence of prizes $\{x_n\}$ with $u(x_n) > 2^n$. Construct the lottery that gives prize x_n with probability $1/2^n$. This has "expected utility" infinity. If you are clever, you should be able to show that this poses real problems for the Archimedean axiom and weak continuity.) And then use the fact that simple probability distributions are dense in the Borel probabilities in the weak topology to extend the expected utility representation to all of P. You can go on to show that u must be continuous (on X) as well as bounded.

The boundedness of u is somewhat limiting in applications. For example, for reasons to be explored later, a very nice utility function in applications is exponential, or $u(x) = -e^{-\lambda x}$, where X is the real line. This utility function is unbounded below. So we would want a way to obtain an expected utility representation for more than simple probability distributions that didn't require bounded u. This can be done as well. Essentially, we obtained bounded u because we took P to be all Borel probability distributions and we assume continuity over all of P. If one restricts P, say to distributions that meet certain tail conditions, then the set of compatible utility functions becomes those u that don't grow "too quickly" relative to the assumed rate at which tail probabilities must die off. For further details, see Fishburn (1970) or Kreps (1988).

3.2. On utility for money

Now we specialize even further to the case where the prizes are dollar values. That is, X is the real line, or some interval thereof. We'll continue to refer to the probability distributions p as lotteries, and we'll continue to restrict attention to simple probability distributions. Throughout, we assume that we have the three assumptions of the previous section and, therefore, an expected utility representation.

In this case, it seems reasonable to suppose that our consumer prefers more money to less. This has a straightforward consequence for the representation, which you should have no difficulty proving.

Proposition 3.2. *Suppose that for all x and y in X such that $x > y$, $\delta_x \succ \delta_y$. This is so if and only if the function u is strictly increasing.*

Risk aversion

More subtle is the property of *risk aversion*. First we need a piece of notation. For a lottery p, let Ep represent the expected value of p, or $Ep = \sum_x xp(x)$.[b]

Proposition 3.3. *Suppose that for all lotteries p, $\delta_{Ep} \succeq p$. This is true if and only if the utility function u is concave.*

A consumer who prefers to get the expected value of a gamble for sure instead of taking the risky gamble, (and whose utility function, in consequence, is concave) is said to be *risk averse*. We could also define a *risk-seeking* consumer as one for whom $p \succeq \delta_{Ep}$ for all p; this sort of behavior goes with a convex utility function u. And a consumer is *risk neutral* if $p \sim \delta_{Ep}$, which goes with a linear utility function. In economic theory, risk aversion, which includes risk neutrality as a special case, is typically assumed.

The proof of proposition 3.3 is left as an exercise. We draw a picture that indicates what is going on. Consider figure 3.4. We have graphed there a concave utility function u, and we've joined by a line segment two points $(x, u(x))$ and $(x', u(x'))$. Take any $\alpha \in (0,1)$, say $\alpha = 2/3$, and consider the lottery $p = \alpha\delta_x + (1 - \alpha)\delta_{x'}$; that is, an α chance at x and a $1 - \alpha$ chance at x'. The expected value of p is precisely $x'' = \alpha x + (1-\alpha)x'$.[1] Which does our consumer prefer, $\delta_{x''}$ or the lottery p? We can answer this by comparing the expected utilities of the two. For $\delta_{x''}$, we have utility $u(\alpha x + (1 - \alpha)x')$, while the expected utility of p is $\alpha u(x) + (1 - \alpha)u(x')$. By concavity, the former is at least as large as the latter, which is what we want. Of course, the property of risk aversion is meant to hold for all lotteries and not just those with supports of size two. But concavity of u is just what is needed, in general.

> We have defined risk aversion in terms of comparisons of a lottery with its expected value. We can generalize this sort of thing as follows. It is possible to partially order lotteries according to their riskiness. That is, for *some* pairs of lotteries p and p', it makes sense to say that p is *riskier than* p'. For example, suppose that p' gives prizes 10 and 20 with probabilities 2/3 and 1/3, and p gives prizes 5, 15, and 30 with probabilities 1/3, 5/9, and

---

[b] We later will write $E\theta$ for the expected value of a random variable θ. No confusion should result.

[1] Careful! The lottery $p = \alpha\delta_x + (1 - \alpha)\delta_{x'}$ denotes a probability distribution with two possible outcomes, whereas the number $x'' = \alpha x + (1-\alpha)x'$ is the convex combination of two numbers. And, appearing momentarily, $\delta_{x''}$ is a probability distribution with one possible outcome, namely x''.

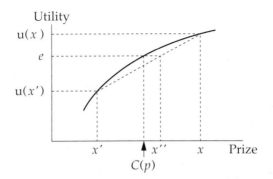

Figure 3.4. Concavity, risk aversion and certainty equivalents.
For a lottery p that gives prize x with probability 2/3 and x' with probability 1/3, we mark the expected value of the lottery as x'', the expected utility of the lottery as e, and the certainty equivalent of the lottery as $C(p)$.

1/9, respectively. I claim that p is riskier than p'. Among the many ways to justify this claim, one is that p is p' "plus noise." Imagine conducting p'. If the outcome is 10, then either take 5 away (leaving 5) or give 5 more (leaving 15), each with probability 1/2. If the outcome is 20, either take away 5 with probability 2/3 (leaving 15) or give 10 more with probability 1/3. Think of this as a compound lottery, and you will see that first I do p' and then, conditional on the outcome, I conduct a lottery with expected value zero. But this compound lottery reduces to p. Since p is gotten from p' in this fashion, if a consumer was risk averse, she would (weakly) prefer p' to p. (Why?) In general, if p and p' are related in this fashion (p is p' plus zero-conditional-mean noise), then any risk averse decision maker will (weakly) prefer p' to p. This will be true also if p is p_1 plus zero-conditional-mean noise, p_1 is p_2 plus such noise, ..., and p' is p_n plus such noise.

As something of a converse, we can define "riskier than" by p is riskier than p' if p and p' have the same expected value and *every* risk averse consumer (weakly) prefers p' to p. Then an interesting question is, What is the relationship between this definition of "riskier than" and the characterizations that involve zero-conditional-mean noise? The general notion of more or less risky gambles is an important one in the literature of the economics of uncertainty, although we will not develop it here; see Rothschild and Stiglitz (1970, 1971, 1973), Diamond and Stiglitz (1974), or Machina (forthcoming).

Certainty equivalents

Because the utility function u in figure 3.4 is continuous, we know (from the intermediate value theorem of calculus) that for every $\alpha \in [0, 1]$ there is some value x^* with $u(x^*) = \alpha u(x) + (1 - \alpha)u(x')$. For any such x^*, we know from the expected utility representation that $\delta_{x^*} \sim p$. Such an x^* is called a *certainty equivalent* of p. In general,

Definition. *A **certainty equivalent** for a lottery p is any prize x such that $\delta_x \sim p$.*

Proposition 3.3. *If X is an interval of R and u is continuous, then every lottery p has at least one certainty equivalent. If u is strictly increasing, every p has at most one certainty equivalent.*

(The proof is left as an exercise.) We henceforth assume that the utility function under consideration is continuous, strictly increasing, and concave, the latter two reflecting increasing and risk averse preferences. Hence every p has a unique certainty equivalent, which we denote $C(p)$. Note that risk aversion, in this setting, can be characterized by $C(p) \leq Ep$.

> What right have we to assume that u is continuous? It turns out that concavity of u implies that u is continuous on the interior of the interval X, although perhaps not at any endpoints of the interval. (Can you show this? Does the assumption that u is strictly increasing help about the endpoints in any way?) But we will want u to be continuous even at the endpoints, and we might want u to be continuous even if u didn't represent risk averse preferences. One can prove that u must be continuous if and only if preferences are continuous in the weak topology, relative to the space of simple probability distributions. So if you know about the (relative) weak topology, you know what is necessary and sufficient for this often very useful assumption about u.

Absolute (and relative) risk aversion

Assume henceforth that any von Neumann–Morgenstern utility function u we consider is strictly increasing, concave, and has at least two continuous derivatives.[c] This implies, of course, that u is continuous, and so each lottery p has a unique certainty equivalent $C(p)$ that is less than or equal to Ep. We will call the difference $Ep - C(p)$ the *risk premium* of p, written $R(p)$.

Now consider a lottery p and a (dollar) amount z. Write $p \oplus z$ for the lottery that gives prize $x + z$ with probability $p(x)$. That is, $p \oplus z$ is just the

---

[c] What justification is there for the assumption that u is twice differentiable? We can justify continuity and concavity. This then implies that u will have left- and right-hand derivatives everywhere. The properties of nondecreasing or nonincreasing risk aversion are then sufficient to show that u is continuously differentiable. (This makes a good homework exercise.) Concavity again implies that u' is decreasing, and we could, by complicating matters substantially, get away without assuming a continuous second derivative. But unless one is being very much more exact about this than we are, it isn't worth the difficulty entailed.

lottery constructed from p by increasing each prize of p by the amount z. By thinking of these prizes as the "after the gamble" wealth level of our consumer, as we increase z in $p \oplus z$, we increase the consumer's general wealth level. It seems somewhat natural to suppose that as someone becomes richer, she cares less and less about risks that she takes in given gambles. In symbols, this would say that as z increases, $R(p \oplus z)$ should not increase; the consumer's risk premium for a fixed gamble should not increase as the consumer becomes wealthier. We formalize this notion and two related to it as follows:

Definition. *For a fixed consumer with utility function u, if $R(p \oplus z)$ is nonincreasing in z, the consumer is said to be **nonincreasingly risk averse**.[d] If $R(p \oplus z)$ is constant in z, we say that the consumer has **constant risk aversion**. If $R(p \oplus z)$ is nondecreasing in z, then we say the consumer is **nondecreasingly risk averse**.*

Our assertion about what seems "somewhat natural" is that consumers are nonincreasingly or perhaps constantly risk averse.

What does all this portend for the utility function u? We give a definition and then the result.

Definition. *Given a (twice continuously differentiable, concave, strictly increasing) utility function u, let $\lambda(x) = -u''(x)/u'(x)$, and call the function λ the **coefficient of absolute risk aversion** for the consumer.*

Since u is concave and strictly increasing, $\lambda(x) \geq 0$.

Proposition 3.4. *A consumer is nonincreasingly risk averse if and only if λ (defined from her von Neumann–Morgenstern utility function u) is a nonincreasing function of x. The consumer is nondecreasingly risk averse if and only if λ is a nondecreasing function of x. And the consumer has constant risk aversion if and only if λ is a constant function, in which case the utility function u is a positive affine translate of the utility function $-e^{-\lambda x}$. (If λ is the constant zero, then $u(x)$ is a positive affine translate of the function x; the consumer is risk neutral.)*

We do not attempt to prove this or the subsequent proposition in this subsection. References will be supplied at the end of the chapter.

---

[d] Sloppy terminology is sometimes used, and this property is called decreasing risk aversion.

We can use this general concept of the coefficient of risk aversion to compare the risk averseness of two different consumers. Imagine we have two consumers who conform to the model we are investigating. Let u be the first consumer's von Neumann–Morgenstern utility function, with $\lambda(x) = -u''(x)/u(x)$, and let v be the second consumer's von Neumann–Morgenstern utility function, with $\eta(x) = -v''(x)/v'(x)$. We wish to capture formally the idea that the first consumer is *at least as risk averse* as the second. A natural definition[e] is:

Definition. *The first consumer is at **least as risk averse** as the second if, for every lottery p and sure thing x such that the first consumer weakly prefers the lottery p to x for sure, the second consumer prefers the lottery as well.*

Put another way, any time the at-least-as-risk-averse consumer is willing to take the risk, so is the at-most-as-risk-averse consumer.

Proposition 3.5. *The first consumer is at least as risk averse as the second if and only if $\lambda(x) \geq \eta(x)$ for every x, which is equivalent to the statement that $v(\cdot) \equiv f(u(\cdot))$ for some strictly increasing, concave function f.*

Another variation sometimes played on this theme concerns how a single consumer responds to proportional gambles with her wealth. We suppose, for purposes of this discussion, that $X = (0, \infty)$, and the consumer's von Neumann–Morgenstern utility function u is concave, strictly increasing, and twice continuously differentiable. We imagine that the consumer has at her disposal an amount of wealth x, all of which she stakes in a gamble that pays a random *gross return*. Such a random gross return is specified by a simple probability distribution p with domain X, where our consumer's wealth after the gamble is θx (for $\theta \in \text{supp}(p)$) with probability $p(\theta)$. We can define a *certainty equivalent rate of return*, $CRR(p; x)$, which is that number $\hat{\theta}$ such that our consumer is indifferent between staking her wealth according to the gross return distribution p or taking $\hat{\theta}x$ for sure. And we can ask how $CRR(p; x)$ changes with changes in the consumer's initial level of wealth x. It is generally considered somewhat natural to suppose that $CRR(p; x)$ is nonincreasing in x — the richer our consumer is, the more conservative she becomes in staking all of her wealth. If we define $\mu(x) = -xu''(x)/u'(x)$, we can get results such as $CRR(p; x)$ is nonincreasing in x if and only if $\mu(x)$ is nonincreasing in x. The function μ is called the *coefficient of **relative** risk aversion*, as distinguished from $\lambda \equiv -u''/u'$, the coefficient of *absolute* risk aversion. For more on this, consult one of the references at the end of the chapter.

---

[e] But see Ross (1981) for a critique of this definition.

3.3. *Applications to market demand*

Many applications can be given for the model developed above, and many books are filled with those applications. What follows is a very haphazard selection of a few applications. The first is intended to tie up a loose end from the previous section; the second two are there to whet your appetite for more.

Induced preferences for income

In section 3.2 we looked at the special case where the prize space X is single dimensional. The obvious application is to the case of money prizes. But consumers don't eat money — money is useful for the commodities one can buy with it. So a fairly obvious question is: If a consumer has von Neumann–Morgenstern preferences for consumption bundles and if her preferences for money arise entirely from the purchasing power of that money, what conditions on her preferences for consumption bundles will translate into the sorts of properties we discussed in section 3.2?

To explore this question, we take the following setting. There are k commodities, and the consumption space X for our consumer is the positive orthant in R^k. We assume that the consumer, considering simple lotteries over the consumption bundles x that she might consume, conforms to the three assumptions of section 3.1. Thus there is a function $u : X \to R$, which is her von Neumann–Morgenstern utility function for simple lotteries on X. Note well, u is a perfectly good ordinal representation for our consumer's preferences on sure-thing consumption bundles. That is, u could be used in all of the developments of chapter 2; in particular, corresponding to u is an indirect utility function $v(p, Y)$ which gives the amount of utility (on the scale of u) our consumer derives from income Y at prices p. But u is more than just any ordinal numerical representation for preferences on X. We can use u (and positive affine transformations of u) to compute expected utilities for simple lotteries on X to rank-order our consumer's preferences for those simple lotteries.

We also assume for the time being that prices are fixed and given by some price vector p. (We will explore uncertain prices later.)

The notation we used earlier in this chapter conflicts with the notation from chapter 2, and we will proceed conforming to the notation in chapter 2. We will use Y to denote a level of income, so that simple lotteries on income have prizes denoted by Y. The space of income levels will be taken to be $[0, \infty)$. A simple probability distribution or lottery on the space of possible income levels will be denoted by π.

Now we pose the basic issue: Suppose our consumer attempts to compare two simple probability distributions on her income, say π and π'. *Suppose that our consumer learns how much income she has to spend before she makes any purchases of consumption bundles. Then it is natural to assume that, if she has income Y to spend, she purchases $x(p, Y)$ (her Marshallian demand) which gives her utility $\nu(p, Y)$. Accordingly, the expected utility she achieves from π is*

$$\sum_{Y \in \text{supp}(\pi)} \nu(p, Y)\pi(Y),$$

so that $\pi \succ \pi'$ if and only if

$$\sum_{Y \in \text{supp}(\pi)} \nu(p, Y)\pi(Y) > \sum_{Y \in \text{supp}(\pi')} \nu(p, Y)\pi'(Y).$$

That is to say, $\nu(p, Y)$, viewed as a function of Y for the fixed prices p, is a von Neumann–Morgenstern utility function for our consumer when she examines her preferences for lotteries over levels of income.[f]

The italic in the previous paragraph is there because what is asserted is more subtle than may be apparent. In the first place, the assumption that all uncertainty about income resolves before any consumption decisions are made is crucial. See the remarks about temporal resolution of uncertainty in section 3.5. Secondly, here, for the first time in this book, is a dynamic structure to choice. The consumer is (presumably) choosing some lottery on income that she will spend for consumption purposes. That uncertainty resolves, and *then* she chooses how to spend that income. The phrase *it is natural* in the previous paragraph assumes that when our consumer chooses her income lottery, she thinks ahead to how she will spend the income she might have available, and her tastes over income levels today are completely consonant with her later tastes for consumption bundles. All of chapter 4 is given over to exploring just how natural this really is. You should grant that this is natural for the sake of argument now, but don't be too convinced by it at least until after finishing chapter 4.

So questions about properties of the consumer's utility function for income become questions about properties of the indirect utility function.

---

[f] We have used the Marshallian demand function $x(p, Y)$ for purposes of exposition only. It should be clear that we don't require the consumer's problem (CP) to have a unique solution.

We give a few basic results in the following proposition. We begin by summarizing the basic state of affairs.

Proposition 3.6. *Suppose the consumer has preferences over lotteries of consumption bundles that satisfy the three assumptions of section 3.1. Let u be the resulting von Neumann–Morgenstern utility function on consumption bundles and let ν(p, Y) be the corresponding indirect utility function. Then the consumer's preferences over lotteries pertaining to income satisfy the three von Neumann–Morgenstern assumptions, and Y → ν(p, Y) is a von Neumann–Morgenstern utility function for income. Moreover:*

(a) Assuming the consumer is locally insatiable, ν(p, Y) is strictly increasing in Y. If u is continuous, ν(p, Y) is continuous in Y.

(b) If u is a concave function, then ν(p, Y) is a concave function in Y; that is, our consumer is risk averse.

Proof. To begin, note that the preamble asserts that the consumer's preferences on income lotteries satisfy the three von Neumann–Morgenstern assumptions. We know this *because* her preferences over income lotteries have an expected utility representation; note that proposition 3.1 states that the three assumptions are necessary and sufficient for expected utility. Part (a) follows from proposition 2.13(b,c). As for (b), take any two income levels Y and Y' and $a \in (0,1)$. Let x solve (CP) for (p, Y), and let x' solve (CP) for (p, Y'). Then $ax + (1-a)x'$ is feasible at prices p with income $aY + (1-a)Y'$, and

$$a\nu(p, Y) + (1-a)\nu(p, Y') = au(x) + (1-a)u(x')$$
$$\leq u(ax + (1-a)x') \leq \nu(p, aY + (1-a)Y'),$$

where the first inequality follows from the concavity of u, and the second follows from the definition of ν as the most utility that can be obtained at prices p with a given income level.

We had rather a lot to say in chapter 2 about concavity of utility functions on consumption bundles; essentially we said there is no particular fundamental reason to think it is a valid assumption. Now it would seem we need this assumption. But now we can motivate this assumption by considerations that were not available to us in chapter 2. Now we can ask our consumer: For any two bundles x and x', would you rather have the bundle $.5x + .5x'$ (where we are taking the convex combination of the bundles) or a lottery where you get x with probability 1/2 and x' with probability 1/2? If our consumer always (weakly) prefers the sure thing, and if she conforms to the assumptions of the von Neumann–Morgenstern theory, then her von Neumann–Morgenstern utility function, which is a perfectly good representation of her (ordinal) preferences on X, will be concave. [9]

We leave for the reader the interesting task of exploring what conditions on u give properties such as constant absolute risk aversion for lotteries in Y.

> In the derivation above, we assume that prices are certain, given by a fixed p. What if there is uncertainty about prices? Specifically, imagine that our consumer enters into a lottery that determines her income Y, and at the same time prices are determined by a lottery ρ. All uncertainty resolves, and then our consumer chooses what to consume.
>
> If we want to speak of the consumer's preferences over lotteries in her income in this setting, we must assume that the uncertainty affecting her income is statistically independent of the uncertainty affecting prices. A simple example will illustrate the point. Consider a consumer who is evaluating an income lottery that gives her \$10,000 with probability 1/2 and \$20,000 with probability 1/2. Suppose that prices will be either p or $2p$, each with probability 1/2. If our consumer's income level is perfectly positively correlated with the price level, she faces no real uncertainty; her real purchasing power is unchanged. If, on the other hand, her income level is perfectly negatively correlated with the price level, she faces rather a lot of uncertainty in her purchasing power. It will be a rare consumer indeed who is indifferent between these two situations, even though in terms of the lotteries on (nominal) income, the two situations are identical. Either we must consider how the consumer feels about lotteries jointly on prices and income (in which case all the developments of section 3.2, which depend on one-dimensional prizes, go by the board), or we have to make some assumption that prevents this sort of problem. Independence is one such assumption.
>
> Assuming the price and income level are independent and letting ρ be the probability distribution on prices, the induced expected utility our consumer obtains from the probability distribution π on Y is given by
>
> $$\sum_{Y \in \mathrm{supp}(\pi)} \sum_{p \in \mathrm{supp}(\rho)} \nu(p, Y)\rho(p)\pi(Y).$$
>
> Thus the consumer's von Neumann–Morgenstern utility function for income, which we will now write $v(Y)$, is
>
> $$v(Y) = \sum_{p \in \mathrm{supp}(\rho)} \nu(p, Y)\rho(p).$$

---

[9] Assume that her preferences are continuous in the weak topology, so checking for 50-50 convex combinations is sufficient to obtain concavity. Alternatively, ask the question for general $a \in (0, 1)$.

You can quickly check that in this setting proposition 3.6 holds without any change except for this redefinition of the utility function on income.

We can ask here a different question. How does the consumer respond to uncertainty in the price level? Imagine that we fix the consumer's income Y and we let the consumer select the economy in which to buy, where different economies have different distributions over prices. To put it simply, imagine we ask this consumer: Given two price vectors p and p', would you rather be in an economy where prices are certain to be given by $.5p + .5p'$ or in an economy where prices are either p or p', each with probability $1/2$? There is no clear answer to this question; see problem 3.

Demand for insurance

One of the most important markets in which uncertainty plays a role is the insurance market. We will return to this market in part IV of the book, when we examine some advanced issues pertaining to insurance. But for now, let us establish some simple basic properties about the demand for insurance.

Imagine a consumer whose income level is subject to some uncertainty. Specifically, her income will be Y with probability π and Y' with probability $1 - \pi$, where $Y > Y'$. Think of the difference $\Delta = Y - Y'$ as some loss the consumer might sustain, either because of an accident, or ill health, or theft, or some other misfortune. An insurance company is willing to insure against this loss; if the consumer will pay a premium of δ, the insurance company is prepared to pay Δ back to the consumer if she sustains this loss. The consumer may buy partial coverage; if she pays $a\delta$, she gets back $a\Delta$ if she sustains the loss. We do not restrict a to $[0,1]$. There are good reasons why such a restriction or one even more severe might be in place, but they have to do with matters we take up later in the book.

We assume that this consumer satisfies the three assumptions of the von Neumann–Morgenstern theory concerning lotteries in her final level of income, net of any payments to/from the insurance company, and her utility function v is strictly increasing, concave, and differentiable. Then the consumer's problem concerning how much insurance to buy can be written

$$\max_{a} \pi v(Y - a\delta) + (1 - \pi)v(Y' + a\Delta - a\delta).$$

Rewrite $Y' + a\Delta$ as $Y - (1 - a)\Delta$, and the first-order condition on this problem becomes

$$\pi\delta v'(Y - a\delta) = (1 - \pi)(\Delta - \delta)v'(Y - (1 - a)\Delta - a\delta).$$

Note that since u is concave and a is unconstrained, the first-order condition is necessary and sufficient for a solution.

The insurance contract is said to be *actuarially fair* if the expected payout $(1 - \pi)\Delta$ equals the premium δ. This equality can be rewritten as $\pi\delta = (1 - \pi)(\Delta - \delta)$; so if the contract is actuarially fair, the first-order condition becomes

$$v'(Y - a\delta) = v'(Y - (1 - a)\Delta - a\delta),$$

and we see that this equation holds when $a = 1$.

The contract is *actuarially unfair* if the expected payout is less than the premium. Let $\beta = \pi\delta/((1 - \pi)(\Delta - \delta))$, so that for an actuarially unfair contract, $\beta > 1$. The first-order conditions can be written

$$\beta v'(Y - a\delta) = v'(Y - (1 - a)\Delta - a\delta),$$

so at any solution to the first-order equation, we will need

$$v'(Y - a\delta) < v'(Y - (1 - a)\Delta - a\delta).$$

Since v is assumed to be concave, its derivative is decreasing, and so we will find a solution to the first-order equation at a point where

$$Y - a\delta > Y - (1 - a)\Delta - a\delta,$$

which is at some $a < 1$.

We conclude that *if the insurance contract is actuarially fair, the consumer will purchase full insurance. If the insurance contract is actuarially unfair, the consumer will purchase only partial insurance.* (If the contract were actuarially *over*fair, the consumer would overinsure.) These are somewhat rough statements because we need to worry about whether the first-order condition and the problem have a solution at all.[2] And we must worry whether this problem has multiple solutions.[3] But except for these worries, these are precise statements, and they can be generalized substantially. The basic idea is that insofar as insurance insures dollar for dollar against a loss, consumers will wish to smooth their income. If the insurance is actuarially

---

[2] What would happen if the consumer was risk neutral and the contract was actuarially unfair? What would happen if we added in the constraint that $a \geq 0$?

[3] Suppose the consumer is risk neutral and the contract is actuarially fair. What is the set of all solutions?

unfair, there is a cost to do this, and consumers do not completely smooth their income. Instead, in this case they choose to bear *some* of the risk. (But see problems 4 and 5.)

Demand for financial assets

Imagine a consumer who will do all her consuming one year hence. This consumer has W dollars to invest, and the income out of which she will consume next year will consist of the proceeds from her investments. Letting Y denote the proceeds from her investments, we assume that her preferences over lotteries on Y satisfy the von Neumann–Morgenstern assumptions, with v her von Neumann–Morgenstern utility function on Y, which is strictly increasing, concave, and differentiable.

Assume that our consumer can invest her money in one of two assets. The first of these is a riskless asset — for every dollar invested, our consumer gets back $r > 1$ dollars next year. The second asset is risky. Its gross return, denoted by θ, has a simple probability distribution π, so that $\pi(\theta)$ represents the probability that the risky asset has a gross return of θ. By gross return we mean a dollar invested in the risky asset returns θ dollars next year.

The consumer's problem, then, is to decide how much money to invest in each of the two assets. Since every dollar invested in the second asset is precisely one dollar less invested in the first, we can write her decision problem as a problem in one variable α, the amount of money she invests in the second, risky asset. Now if θ is the gross return on the risky asset, investing α in this asset means she will have

$$Y = \theta\alpha + r(W - \alpha) = \alpha(\theta - r) + rW$$

dollars to spend on consumption next period. So her problem is to

$$\max_{\alpha} \sum_{\theta \in \mathrm{supp}(\pi)} v(\alpha(\theta - r) + rW)\pi(\theta).$$

Should we constrain α? That depends on the ability of the consumer to *short-sell* either or both of the assets. If she can borrow as much money as she pleases at the riskless rate of r to invest in the risky asset, then we would not constrain α above. (If, as is more realistic, she can borrow money but at a rate of interest exceeding what she may lend at, the problem becomes more difficult but not intractable.) If she can short-sell the risky asset, which means she is given the purchase price of the asset today (to invest in the riskless asset) but must make good on the return of the asset in a year, then we would not constrain α below. We will proceed assuming that she cannot short-sell the asset but that she can borrow money at the riskless rate; you may wish to try other variations on your own.

Hence we add to this problem the constraint that $\alpha \geq 0$. Since v is concave, we find the solution to the problem by looking for a solution to the first-order condition

$$\sum_{\theta \in \text{supp}(\pi)} (\theta - r)v'(\alpha(\theta - r) + rW)\pi(\theta) \leq 0,$$

where the inequality must be an equality if $\alpha > 0$.

What can we say about solutions to this problem? A few obvious remarks are

(a) If $\theta > r$ for all $\theta \in \text{supp}(\pi)$, then there can be no solution. This is so mathematically because v' is always strictly positive. (That is, v is strictly increasing.) The economic intuition behind this is straightforward. If $\theta > r$ for all possible values of θ, then the consumer can make money for sure by borrowing money (selling the riskless asset) and buying the risky asset. Since we have not constrained borrowing, the consumer will wish to do this on an infinite scale, reaping infinite profits. Such a thing is called an *arbitrage opportunity*, and one presumes that arbitrage opportunities are rarely to be found. (Note that if $\theta \geq r$ with strict inequality for at least one $\theta \in \text{supp}(\pi)$, we have exactly the same problem.)

(b) Suppose the consumer is risk neutral. That is, $v(Y) = aY + b$ for $a > 0$. The first-order condition is then $\sum_{\theta \in \text{supp}(\pi)} (\theta - r)a\pi(\theta) \leq 0$. If we write $E\theta$ for the expected gross return on the risky asset, or $E\theta = \sum_{\theta \in \text{supp}(\pi)} \theta\pi(\theta)$, the first-order condition becomes $E\theta \leq r$, with equality if $\alpha > 0$. Since α is entirely removed from the first-order condition, there are three possibilities: If $E\theta < r$, the consumer chooses $\alpha = 0$. If $E\theta = r$, any α is a solution. And if $E\theta > r$, there is no solution. The economic intuition is: If the consumer is risk neutral, she compares assets according to their expected gross return only. If the expected gross return on the risky asset equals that of the riskless asset (the middle case), she is happy to invest in any fashion. If the expected gross return on the risky asset exceeds that of the riskless asset, she wishes to borrow at the riskless rate in infinite amounts and invest in the risky asset. If the expected gross return on the risky asset is less than that of the riskless asset, she wants none of the risky asset and, in fact, she would wish to short-sell the risky asset in infinite amounts if she were allowed to do so.

(c) Now return to the case where the consumer is strictly risk averse. Assume that there is a solution to the first-order conditions. (See problem 6 for a case in which this can be guaranteed.) Suppose that $E\theta < r$. Then we assert that the only possible solution of the first-order conditions is $\alpha = 0$. That is, if the expected return of the risky asset is less than that of the riskless asset, a risk averse consumer will necessarily buy none of it.[h] Constructing a precise and detailed argument that this is so is left as an exercise. But the basic idea is easily sketched. Recall that if v is concave, v' will be decreasing. Suppose that $\alpha > 0$. In the first-order condition, we multiply $(\theta - r)$ by $v'(\cdot\cdot\cdot)\pi(\theta)$. The stuff inside the v' increases with increasing θ and so multiplying by v' (which decreases as the stuff inside increases) puts relatively more weight on $(\theta - r)$ for smaller values of θ. But if we look at the weighted sum of $\theta - r$ weighted by the probabilities $\pi(\theta)$ alone, we would get something strictly negative. Putting more weight on the smaller terms makes the weighted sum even smaller, so for any $\alpha > 0$, the sum is strictly negative. Only $\alpha = 0$ can be a solution.[i]

(d) Finally, suppose that $E\theta > r$. Then the only solutions of the first-order conditions have $\alpha > 0$. It is easy to see this mathematically; plug $\alpha = 0$ into the first-order condition, and you will find that the sum term is $v'(Wr)(E\theta - r)$. In terms of economic intuition, for the first little bit of the risky asset the consumer buys, she is approximately risk neutral. If $E\theta > r$, the risky asset is a good deal for a risk neutral investor. It is only when the scale of her investment in the risky asset grows to some significant size that her risk aversion begins to take over, and then she may find that, on the margin, it is no longer worth purchasing still more of the risky asset.

In fact, the intuition of this problem is entirely captured by the previous sentence. Think of beginning in a position where the investor has none of the risky asset. Then for small changes in her holdings, she is risk neutral, and the direction she wishes to move in depends on the sign of $E\theta - r$. If this sign is positive and she increases her holdings of the risky asset, the marginal impact on her expected utility of still more risky asset is given by the sum term in the first-order conditions. As noted above, this puts more and more relative weight on the smaller values of $\theta - r$ as

---

[h] Before getting too excited about this, see later discussion concerning more than one risky asset.

[i] We can shortcut this argument if we assume that v is strictly concave. Using the strict concavity, we can prove rather simply that the problem has a unique solution in α as long as the risky asset is risky. And verifying that the first-order conditions are satisfied at $\alpha = 0$ is easy.

α grows. Now if all the terms are positive, there is no end to this process (which is [a]). And if the shift in weight is never sufficient to make the marginal impact on her expected utility nonpositive, this process never stops (which includes [b]). Of course, if we start out with the sign being negative, we never get started at all (which is [c]). And if the sign is positive, we will have to move some distance away from $\alpha = 0$ before coming to the level where the marginal value of the risky asset is zero (which is [d]). Once you understand intuitively why the sum term is the marginal value of the risky asset and you understand how, when u is concave, the relative weights shift as they do as a function of α, the intuition of this situation should be crystal clear.

Conclusions (c) and (d) are no longer valid when there is more than one risky asset, unless the returns on risky assets are statistically independent of one another. We will illustrate the basic problem in a setting with two risky assets. As before, we imagine that there is a riskless asset with gross rate of return r. The two risky assets will be indexed by $i = 1, 2$, with θ^i representing the gross return on asset i. We do not assume that the two assets returns are statistically independent; instead we take as given the joint distribution of their gross returns. This is given by a probability distribution π which, for a finite number of two dimensional vectors (θ^1, θ^2), specifies that $\pi(\theta^1, \theta^2)$ is the joint probability that the first asset has gross return θ^1 and the second has gross return θ^2. (You will recall, I hope, that the two random returns are statistically independent if and only if there are one-dimensional probability distributions π^1 and π^2 such that $\pi(\theta^1, \theta^2) = \pi^1(\theta^1)\pi^2(\theta^2)$.) The expected values of the two assets' gross returns will be written $E\theta^i$ for $i = 1$, 2.

Our consumer's problem is to decide how much to invest in each of the two risky assets, with anything left over going into the riskless asset. We let α^i be the amount invested in asset i. As in the previous subsection, we work with the case in which the risky assets can't be sold short but the riskless asset can be (that is, the consumer can borrow at the riskless rate), so the consumer's problem is

$$\max_{\alpha^1, \alpha^2} \sum_{(\theta^1, \theta^2)} v\left(\alpha^1(\theta^1 - r) + \alpha^2(\theta^2 - r) + Wr\right)\pi(\theta^1, \theta^2)$$

subject to $\alpha^1 \geq 0, \alpha^2 \geq 0$. (I will be sloppy about the supports of distributions throughout this discussion, on the presumption that, if you've survived this far, you can stand the sloppiness.) The first-order condition for α^i is

$$\sum_{(\theta^1, \theta^2)} (\theta^i - r)v'\left(\alpha^1(\theta^1 - r) + \alpha^2(\theta^2 - r) + Wr\right)\pi(\theta^1, \theta^2) \leq 0,$$

with equality if $\alpha^i > 0$.

It shouldn't be hard to see that these first-order conditions can have no solution if either (a') $\theta^i > r$ with probability one for one of the two assets, or (b') the consumer is risk neutral and $E\theta^i > r$ for one of the two assets. Those conclusions carry over intact. In fact, we can sharpen (a') a bit: It must not be possible to find nonnegative β^1 and β^2 such that $\beta^1 + \beta^2 = 1$ and $\beta^1\theta^1 + \beta^2\theta^2 \geq r$ with probability one, with a strict inequality with positive probability. If we could find such β^1 and β^2, then arbitrage would be possible. (Prove this!)

However, in contrast to the case of one risky asset, we assert that it is possible that (c') $\alpha^1 > 0$ when $E\theta^1 < r$, and (d') $\alpha^1 = 0$ when $E\theta^1 > r$.[j] The "problem" is that we don't know, at a particular α^1 and α^2, how the term $v'(\cdots)$ is shifting weight on the $\theta^1 - r$ terms. For example, if both α^1 and α^2 are positive and θ^1 and θ^2 are negatively correlated, then at "large" values of θ^1 the stuff inside v' could tend to be small because of the $\alpha^2(\theta^2 - r)$ part, which would make v' *large* when θ^1 is large. This, then, could give (c'). Alternatively, if the two assets' gross returns are positively correlated, even at $\alpha^1 = 0$, we get from the $\alpha^2(\theta^2 - r)$ term some relative shift of weight towards lower values of θ^1, which would permit (d').

That, to be sure, is a fairly opaque way of demonstrating the possibilities suggested in (c') and (d'). In fact, this is no demonstration at all. A proper demonstration would consist of a pair of concrete (and, one hopes, simple) examples. This task is left to you; see problem 8 for some hints. Moreover, we asserted at the outset that, if assets 1 and 2 had gross return distributions that were statistically independent, everything would work as in the previous subsection. This is left to you as well.

The first-order conditions in our problem with two risky assets tell us that the marginal effect of putting money into risky asset i when one is holding a particular portfolio of assets depends upon how the return of asset i "covaries" with the marginal utility of consumption at the given portfolio. Very roughly put, the smaller the "covariance," the worse it is for putting additional funds into asset i, since this means weight is shifted to the smaller terms in the first-order conditions. The intuition behind this is not too difficult. If asset i pays off relatively well when times are good (when the marginal utility of consumption is low) and relatively poorly when times are bad, holding more of asset i compounds the risk the investor faces. But if asset i pays off well when times are bad and (relatively) poorly when times are good overall, then asset i serves as insurance against the other assets being held. And as we saw in the subsection on insurance, one may be willing to take up some insurance, even if it is actuarially unfair.

Moreover, since the marginal utility of consumption at a given portfolio is a decreasing function of the overall return on one's portfolio, this intuition suggests that the "marginal value" of an asset in a given portfolio has to do with the "covariance" between the returns of the asset and the returns of the portfolio; everything else held equal, the marginal value of an asset is smaller the larger is its "covariance" with the overall return on the portfolio.

---

[j] Assertion (c') shouldn't come as a complete surprise. Remember that there can be demand for insurance, even when the insurance is actuarially unfair. But the point is a bit more subtle here, since the risk against which one buys insurance is given exogenously, and here all risks that the consumer faces are chosen by her.

   This intuition can be made quite precise (which is to say, we can remove the quote marks from the word covariance) if we assume that our consumer evaluates her possible portfolios in terms of the portfolios' means and variances. Holding variance fixed, a higher mean return is better, and holding mean fixed, a lower variance is better. *If* our consumer's preferences over portfolios could be reduced to something this simple, then we would have available a very nice theory. Looking at any finite set of risky assets (and, for simplicity, one riskless asset), all we would need to compute the mean and variance of a given portfolio of assets is the vector of expected returns and the variance-covariance matrix of those returns.

   We will not develop the theory of mean-variance efficient portfolios here; this is one of the starting points of the modern theory of finance, and you may consult one of the many textbooks on the subject. (See the end of this chapter for one recommendation.) But I did wish to suggest this last step and to make one comment which good textbooks in finance will amplify.

   Moving from von Neumann–Morgenstern preferences to mean-variance driven preferences is not a trivial step. A consumer who maximizes the expectation of some utility function v defined on the gross income from her investments does not, in general, have preferences that can be reduced to a comparison of the mean–variance pairs of various portfolios she might hold. *If* her utility function is quadratic, $v(Y) = a + bY - cY^2$ (for $b, c > 0$), then this works. (Why?) But quadratic utility functions are not so nice; they are concave, but for $Y \geq b/(2c)$ they are decreasing. Alternatively, we could restrict attention to assets whose distributions are such that risk averse expected utility maximizers always prefer higher expected returns holding variance constant and lower variance holding expected return constant. For example, if assets have a joint Normal (multivariate) distribution, then any portfolio of the assets has a Normal distribution. And for any risk averse expected utility maximizer (whose utility function is increasing), two Normal distributions with the same variance are ranked according to their means (higher is better), and two Normal distributions with the same mean are ranked according to their variances (lower is better). The reader who knows a bit of mathematics and who knows about multivariate Normals may wish to construct a proof.

3.4. States of nature and subjective probability

   In the preceding development, the objects of choice were probability distributions over prizes. That is, the probabilities — numerical expressions of likelihood — were given exogenously. As discussed in section 3.1, this would be inadequate for modeling certain situations. In some contexts, the odds of various outcomes are not at all clear, and what a consumer chooses depends very critically on what she subjectively assesses as the odds of the outcomes. To take a very simple example, imagine you are offered your choice of two bets: In the first, you win \$100 if a Latin American team wins the next World Cup soccer tournament, and zero otherwise. In the second, you win \$100 if a European team wins the next World Cup. If we tried to apply the von Neumann–Morgenstern model to this problem, things would be very trivial. The von Neumann–Morgenstern model would regard the two gambles as lotteries with objectively specified probabilities. And then our consumer would pick whichever has the better chance of getting for her the $100 prize. Any (reasonable) consumer would bet the same way. But what makes this sort of bet interesting are the odds one consumer or another assesses. We don't expect all consumers to bet the same way on this (although see the final subsection of this section). And so we need a model of choice under uncertainty that develops within itself the *subjective* probabilities that are assessed by a consumer faced with this sort of uncertainty. (To distinguish between situations where the probabilities are objective and those where probabilities are subjective, one sometimes encounters the following terminology: The former situations are cases where there is *risk*, while the latter are cases of *uncertainty*.)

The framework

The classic formal treatment of choice where there is subjective uncertainty is that of Savage (1954). The framework employed by Savage runs as follows. We have a set of prizes X, just as before. And we have a set of *states of nature*, S. Each $s \in S$ is a description of the resolution of any (relevant) uncertainty. The states in S should be mutually exclusive and exhaustive. You might think in terms of a horse race (or, if you prefer, the next World Cup competition). Each s will describe the order of finish of all the horses in the race, and S will be the set of all such orders of finish.

Since the formality may be a bit forbidding, let us carry along a simple example. Imagine a two-horse race between horses named Secretariat and Kelso. There are three possible outcomes of the race: Kelso wins, Secretariat wins, or the race is a dead heat. We will label these three s_1, s_2 and s_3, respectively.

We next form from X and S the set of all *horse race lotteries*, H. A horse race lottery h will describe for each state s a prize x that is won if s is the outcome of the race. Formally, H is the set of all functions from S to X; in very formal notation, $H = X^S$. We write $h(s)$ for the prize won at the horse race lottery h if the state is s.

So, for example, imagine that for $2 you can purchase a betting ticket that pays off $3.85 if Secretariat wins the race and $0 if Kelso wins. If the race is a dead heat, then you get your $2 back. Net of the cost of the ticket, this gamble is represented by the function h, which is given

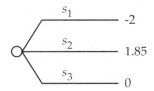

Figure 3.5. A horse race chance node.

by $h(s_1) = -2$, $h(s_2) = 1.85$, and $h(s_3) = 0$. We will depict horse race gambles by "chance nodes"; in figure 3.5, you see this particular horse race gamble.

If we were being less fanciful — thinking of S as the set of all states of the world, and X as a space of commodity bundles — then standard terminology would style H as the set of *state contingent commodity bundles* or *state contingent claims*.

In the classic theory due to Savage, H is the set of objects of choice. (He calls them *acts* instead of horse race lotteries.) The consumer's preferences are given by $\succ$ defined on H; certain properties of $\succ$ are assumed and a representation of $\succ$ is derived.

The representation and a weaker alternative

What sort of representation is sought? Savage seeks (and most economists employ) a representation of the following form. There exist a probability distribution π over S and a utility function $u : X \to R$ such that

$$h \succ h' \text{ if and only if } \sum_{s \in S} u(h(s))\pi(s) > \sum_{s \in S} u(h'(s))\pi(s). \qquad (\star)$$

(This representation has been written under the presumption that S is a finite set. In fact, Savage's treatment requires that S be infinite, and the summations just given become appropriately defined integrals.) This is just like von Neumann–Morgenstern expected utility, except that the probabilities of the various prizes are obtained by a two-step process: Probabilities are *subjectively* assessed for the various states of nature. The probability of getting a particular prize x if horse race lottery h is chosen is just the sum of the probabilities of those states $s \in S$ such that $h(s) = x$.

If we are able to obtain representation $(\star)$, we have done quite well. To understand how well, consider the following two cases in which $(\star)$ is inappropriate:

(1) Imagine you are marketing a particular product and trying to decide how much advertising to do. To keep things simple, imagine that the

product will either sell 1,000 units or 10,000. If it sells 1,000, you will lose $1,000, not including the cost of advertising. If it sells 10,000, you will make $3,000. You can either advertise a lot or not at all. Not advertising costs you nothing, while advertising a lot costs you $1,000.

Create the following model. The prize is your net profit. Possible values are $-2,000$, $-1,000$, $2,000$, and $3,000$, so these four dollar amounts constitute X. The states are your level of sales: You sell 1,000 units (state s_1) or 10,000 (state s_2). Hence there are two states in S. The two acts you can consider are: "advertise," which we denote by h, where $h(s_1) = \$ - 2,000$ and $h(s_2) = \$2,000$; and "don't advertise," which we denote by h', where $h'(s_1) = \$ - 1,000$ and $h'(s_2) = \$3,000$.

As long as your utility function u is increasing in increasing profits, if the representation $(\star)$ holds you never choose to advertise. Whatever probabilities you assess for s_1 and s_2, h' always gives a better outcome (by the $1,000 cost of advertising) in both states. The problem is that your choice of an act presumably influences how many units you sell. *In Savage's representation $(\star)$, the probabilities of the states do not depend on the act chosen.* That is, we don't write $\pi(s; h)$ or anything like that. So in cases where acts influence state probabilities, we couldn't expect $(\star)$ to hold.

(In this example, a cure is very simple. The problem is that our state space is deficient. We really need three states: s_1, which is the state that the product sells 1,000 units whether you advertise or not; s_2, which is the state that the product sells 1,000 units if you don't advertise and 10,000 units if you do; and s_3, which is the state that the product sells 10,000 whether you advertise or not.[4] The question of whether to advertise becomes one of how likely is the state s_2, in which you increase your profits by $3,000 if you do advertise, compared to the "lost" $1,000 in advertising fees in states s_1 and s_3.)

(2) Imagine that you are thinking of undertaking one of two gambles. In the first, you will win $100 if the yen:dollar exchange rate (i.e., the number of yen that can be bought with $1) increases over the next month and otherwise you lose $100. In the second, you win $100 if the yen:dollar ratio doesn't increase and lose $100 if it does. We create a model where the states of natures ($s \in S$) are the various possible yen:dollar exchange rates and where the prizes ($x \in X$) are -100 and $100. It should be easy for you to see (given today's yen:dollar exchange rate) how to model the lotteries from which you are meant to choose.

---

[4] If there is a chance that advertising will anger potential customers, we would add a fourth state.

Do we expect the representation (⋆) to hold in this case? Probably not. *In the representation (⋆) the value of any prize u(x) is independent of the state of nature in which the prize is won.* But winning $100 when the yen:dollar exchange rate is low is worse than winning $100 when the yen:dollar exchange rate is high. This should be very clear if you live in Japan. But, if you think about it, it is probably true if you live in some country other than Japan.[5] Put another way, suppose, for the sake of argument, that you think it as likely that the yen:dollar ratio will go up as that it will go down. Then according to the representation (⋆), you should be indifferent between the two gambles. But because $100 is worth more when the yen:dollar ratio is high and less when the ratio is low, the first of these two gambles is (pretty clearly) the better of the two.

What can we do to salvage the representation (⋆) in cases such as this? One thing to try is to redefine prizes X in a way that makes the value of a given prize independent of the state in which it is won. Instead of making the prize a dollar amount, we might consider recording prizes in terms of the purchasing power the prize represents, using some standard market bundle of goods. But this can get very messy, very quickly. And so, as an alternative, we might consider giving up on (⋆) and trying for a weaker representation. We might ask for a probability distribution π on S and a "state-dependent utility function" $u : X \times S \to R$ such that

$$h \succ h' \text{ if and only if } \sum_{s \in S} u(h(s), s)\pi(s) > \sum_{s \in S} u(h'(s), s)\pi(s).$$

If this is what we are after, we can simplify one level further. Given π and u, define $v : X \times S \to R$ by $v(x, s) = u(x, s)\pi(s)$. Then the representation just given becomes

$$h \succ h' \text{ if and only if } \sum_{s \in S} v(h(s), s) > \sum_{s \in S} v(h'(s), s). \qquad (\star\star)$$

Since this form conveys what is important in this weaker type of representation, we will use it. Whereas representation (⋆) is styled as a *subjective expected utility* representation, the weaker alternative (⋆⋆) is styled as an *additive across states* representation.[k]

---

[5] Suppose you live in the United States. The "market bundle" of goods that $100 will buy at 150 yen to the dollar is better than the bundle that $100 will buy at 125 yen to the dollar, insofar as the lower exchange rate means that Japanese goods in the market bundle are more expensive.

[k] Does the probability distribution π convey any information if we allow u to be state dependent? See problem 10 for more on this.

Savage's sure thing principle

Now that we know what sort of representation we are after, we can see how it might be obtained. The classic derivation of the representation $(\star)$, as we said before, is due to Savage (1954). Savage begins with preferences $\succ$ defined on H and develops a number of properties of $\succ$ that lead to the representation $(\star)$. Some of the properties are those you've seen before; $\succ$ is asymmetric and negatively transitive.[l] Other properties exploit the particular structure we have here. Although we won't go through the Savage treatment here, it may help (to give a flavor of the subject) to give the "most important" of the other properties that he invokes, which is called the *independence axiom* or the *sure thing principle*. (This comes the closest to our substitution axiom in the theory of section 2.1.) It runs as follows:

Savage's sure thing principle. *Suppose we are comparing two horse race lotteries h and g. Suppose moreover that the set of states S contains a subset T on which h and g are identical; for every $s \in T$, $h(s) = g(s)$. Then how the consumer feels about h compared to g depends only on how h and g compare on states that are not in T. Formally, if $h \succ g$, and if h' and g' are two other horse race lotteries such that (a) h is identical with h' and g is identical with g' on $S \setminus T$, and (b) h' and g' are identical on T, then $h' \succ g'$ must follow.*

This is easier than it seems. The idea is that the ranking of h and g doesn't depend on the specific way that they agree on T — that they agree is enough. Figure 3.6 shows this idea in pictorial form.

You should have little difficulty seeing that Savage's sure thing principle is implied by the representation $(\star)$ and even by the representation $(\star\star)$. If we write, in the spirit of $(\star\star)$, $U(h) = \sum_{s \in S} v(h(s), s) = \sum_{s \in T} v(h(s), s) + \sum_{s \in S \setminus T} v(h(s), s)$, and write a similar expression for g, then as $h(s) = g(s)$ for $s \in T$, a comparison of $U(h)$ and $U(g)$ depends on how $\sum_{s \in S \setminus T} v(h(s), s)$ compares with $\sum_{s \in S \setminus T} v(g(s), s)$. This comparison is entirely independent of what h and g are on T.

The theory of Anscombe and Aumann

Savage's treatment goes on from the sure thing principle to other assumptions that are more complex, and then develops these assumptions mathematically in very complex fashion. His treatment is a bit hard for

---

[l] These would have to be entailed, since we obtain a numerical representation.

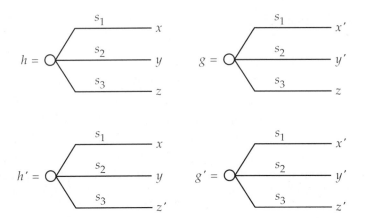

Figure 3.6. Savage's independence axiom in action.
Since h and g give the same prize in s_3, a comparison between them
depends only on what they give on the other states. The prize they give
on s_3 is irrelevant to the comparison. Hence, however h and g are
ranked, h' and g' rank the same way.

a first pass on this subject, so we will continue with a different, easier
formalization, taken from Anscombe and Aumann (1963).

Anscombe and Aumann avoid the complexities that Savage encounters by enriching the space over which preferences are defined. Like Savage, they take as given a prize space X and a state space S. We will
assume that S is a finite set.

Their innovation comes at this point. Let P denote the set of all simple probability distributions on X, and redefine H so that it is the set of all
functions from S to P. In comparison, Savage has H as the set of functions
from S to X. A story that might be told about the Anscombe–Aumann
construction runs as follows: Imagine that we have at our disposal a set
of "objective" randomizing devices — coins we can flip, dice we can roll,
roulette wheels we can spin — that allow us to construct any "objective"
probability distribution that we wish. That is, given any $p \in P$, we can use
the devices at our disposal to stage the gamble p in a way such that every
consumer we might meet agrees to the objective probabilities in p. For
example, if we wish to create a lottery that gives the prize \$10 with prob-
ability 4/5 and \$0 with probability 1/5, we might roll a symmetrical die,
paying \$10 if it comes up with one through four spots up, paying \$0 if it
comes up with five spots up, and rolling again (until we get an outcome between one and five) if it comes up with six spots up. It is assumed that every consumer we might encounter regards this as an objective probability
lottery with prizes \$10 and \$0 and probabilities 4/5 and 1/5, respectively.

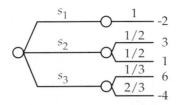

Figure 3.7. A horse race lottery with roulette wheel lotteries for prizes.

We'll call such objective gambles *roulette wheel gambles* or *lotteries*. The next step is to construct the set H of all functions from S to P. In words, an h from this H is a betting ticket that specifies, for each possible outcome of the horse race, a roulette wheel lottery that is won by the holder of the betting ticket. Embedded in this new, fancy H is the old (Savage) H, where the prize contingent on each state s is a degenerate roulette wheel lottery that gives some prize in X for sure. But this new H is bigger, because the set of possible prizes is larger; a prize in the horse race lottery is now a roulette lottery.

To give an example, imagine a (very complex) betting ticket that pays the following: In state s_1 (Kelso wins), you get $\$-2$ for sure. (That is, you lose \$2 for sure.) In state s_2 (Secretariat wins), you get \$3 with probability 1/2 and \$1 with probability 1/2. In state s_3 (a dead heat), you get \$6 with probability 1/3 and you lose \$4 with probability 2/3. This sort of creature is depicted by a compound chance node, as in figure 3.7, where the compounding is now an important part of the mathematical formalism.

And (the punchline) Anscombe and Aumann (and we) will assume that the consumer has preferences given by $\succ$ defined on this fancy H.

Before talking about those preferences, we introduce a bit of notation. First, if $h \in H$ is a horse race lottery in the new, expanded sense, we write $h(\cdot|s)$ for that element of P that is the prize under h in state s, and we write $h(x|s)$ for the objective probability of winning $x \in X$ under h, contingent or conditional on the state s. Second, suppose h and g are two horse race lotteries (in the new, expanded sense), and α is a number between zero and one. Define a new horse race lottery, denoted $\alpha h + (1-\alpha)g$, as follows: For each state s, the new horse race lottery gives as prize the roulette wheel lottery $\alpha h(\cdot|s) + (1-\alpha)g(\cdot|s)$, where this last object is defined as in section 3.1. Figure 3.8 gives an example of this sort of operation.

Now we can start suggesting properties for the consumer's preferences $\succ$.

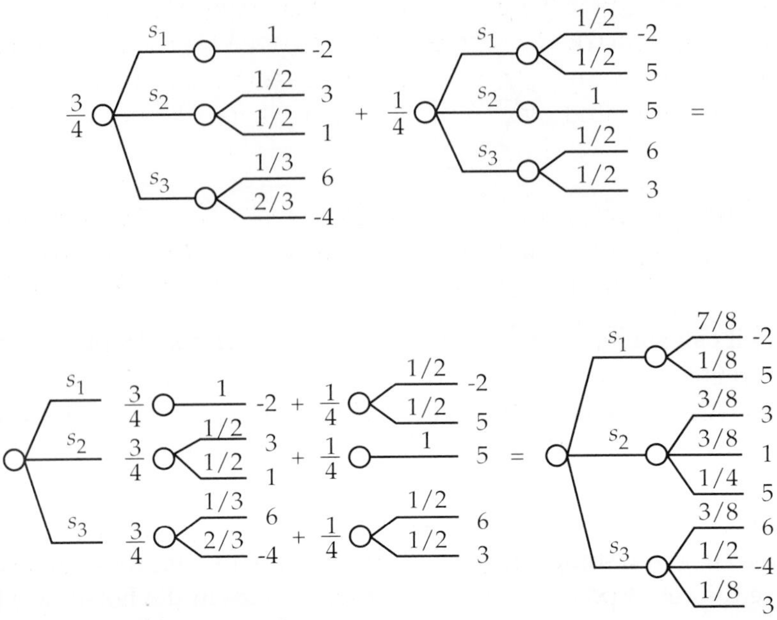

Figure 3.8. Taking mixtures of horse race lotteries.
When mixing horse race lotteries, you mix the prizes for each outcome
of the horse race.

Assumption 4. *(a)* $\succ$ *is asymmetric.*

(b) $\succ$ *is negatively transitive.*

(c) $\succ$ *satisfies the substitution axiom of section 3.1.*

(d) $\succ$ *satisfies the Archimedean axiom of section 3.1.*

The first two parts of this assumption should come as no surprise, but
the latter two properties may take some explanation. Look back at the
substitution and Archimedean axioms in section 3.1. They don't depend
on the fact that p, q, and r are probability distributions — only that
convex combinations of the objects of choice can be taken.[m] And in the
preceding paragraph you were told how to take convex combinations of
horse race lotteries. So the latter two properties make mathematical sense.

Do they make sense as properties of consumer choice? That is a
harder question to answer, of course. This is left to your own judgment

---

[m] In more advanced texts these properties are stated for algebraic objects called *mixture spaces,* and the conclusions of these properties for general mixture spaces, which is something just short of the von Neumann–Morgenstern expected utility representation, is given by the so-called *Mixture Space Theorem.* See any of the advanced texts referenced in section 3.7.

(although read section 3.5 if you are too optimistic or too pessimistic) with the (obvious) remark that buying these properties in this setting takes somewhat more courage than buying them in the context of section 3.1.

Whether you find them sensible or not, they do produce a rather nice result.

Proposition 3.7. *Suppose that S is finite. Then the four properties in assumption 4 are necessary and sufficient for $\succ$ to have a numerical representation U of the following form. There exists for each state s a function u_s from X to the real line such that for $h \in H$,*

$$U(h) = \sum_{s \in S} \sum_x u_s(x)h(x|s).$$

Some hard staring is required to comprehend this result. Of course, when we say that U is a numerical representation of $\succ$, we mean that

$$h \succ g \quad \text{if and only if} \quad U(h) > U(g).$$

The result here establishes the existence of such a numerical representation *and* tells us something about the structure we can assume for the function U: For each state, there is a state-dependent utility function u_s. To evaluate h, first, for each state s, compute the expected utility of the roulette gamble $h(\cdot|s)$ using the utility function for state s. This is the term $\sum_x u_s(x)h(x|s)$. Then sum these expected utilities, summing over the states s.

Example: Suppose that your utility functions, depending on the outcome of the horse race, are: In state s_1, $u_{s_1}(x) = x/2$; in state s_2, $u_{s_2}(x) = -2e^{-.2x}$; in state s_3, $u_{s_3}(x) = -.01e^{-.1x}$. Then the overall utility of the gamble depicted in figure 3.7 is computed as follows. In state s_1, you have \$$-2$ for sure, so your state-dependent expected utility in state s_1 is $-2/2 = -1$. In state s_2, your state-dependent expected utility is $(1/2)(-2e^{-.2\times3}) + (1/2)(-2e^{-.2\times1}) = -1.3675$. And in state s_3, your state-dependent expected utility is $(1/3)(-.01e^{-.1\times6})+(2/3)(-.01e^{-.1\times-4}) = -.0118$. Hence the overall index (utility) of this gamble is $(-1) + (-1.3675) + (-.0118) = -2.3793$.

What is nice here is that (a) we get additive separability over outcomes of the horse race and (b) for each outcome of the horse race, we compute expected utility as in section 3.1. What is less nice is that we only get additive separability over horse race outcomes; the state-dependent utility functions needn't bear any particular relationship to one another. Put

another way, this representation is very much like the representation (⋆⋆),
where the state dependent utility function $v(h(\cdot|s), s)$ defined on $P \times S$ has
the form, for each s, of von Neumann–Morgenstern expected utility. Now
we could stop here (and go on to see what consequences this representation
has for demand behavior — the consequences are substantial); or we could
add properties for each state-dependent utility function (such as decreasing
risk aversion, etc., if the prizes are money amounts). But instead we will
add another property for $\succ$ that will tie together the various u_s.

This requires a bit of notation. For $p \in P$ (a roulette lottery), write p
as an element of H (a horse race lottery) meaning the horse race lottery
that gives, regardless of the outcome of the horse race, the prize p. With
this, we can give the new property:

Assumption 5. *Fix any p and q from P. Fix any state s^*. Construct horse
race lotteries h and g as follows: Pick (arbitrarily) any $r \in P$, and let $h(s) = r$
if $s \neq s^*$, $h(s^*) = p$, $g(s) = r$ if $s \neq s^*$, and $g(s^*) = q$. Then $p \succ q$ if and only
if $h \succ g$.*

What does this mean? First, understand what h and g are. Both h and
g give prize r if the horse race outcome is anything other than s^*; h has
prize p if the outcome is s^*; and g has prize q if the outcome is s^*. Note
that as long as the other four properties hold, the choice of r is (therefore)
irrelevant to the preference relation between h and g; the difference in
$U(h)$ and $U(g)$ is the difference between

$$\sum_x u_{s^*}(x)p(x) \quad \text{and} \quad \sum_x u_{s^*}(x)q(x).$$

With this, we can reinterpret the property given: It says that the sign of the
difference between the two terms in the display just above is independent
of the particular state s^*. If the difference runs one way for one s^*, it runs
the same way for all. (This isn't quite what the property says, but you
should be able to convince yourself that it is equivalent.) In other words,
the preference that the consumer has between a pair of roulette lotteries
is independent of the state in which the two are compared. See figure 3.9
for an illustration.

And the consequence is

Proposition 3.8. *For finite S, $\succ$ satisfies assumptions 4 and 5 if and only if we
have a representation U of the following type. There is a function $u : X \to R$*

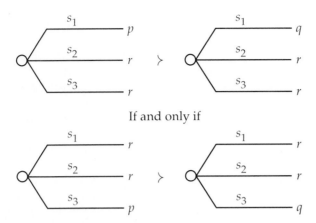

Figure 3.9. An equivalent formulation of the extra property.
The extra property is equivalent to the assumption that the consumer's preference over roulette wheel lotteries at any given outcome of the horse race doesn't depend on outcome. (We find preference over roulette wheel lotteries at a given outcome by holding constant the prizes won at all other outcomes.)

and a strictly positive probability distribution π on S such that

$$U(h) = \sum_{s \in S} \pi(s) \sum_x u(x) h(x|s).$$

In this representation, π is unique and u is unique up to positive affine transformations.

The interpretation is that our consumer assesses subjective probability $\pi(s)$ that the outcome of the horse race will be s, and he has a utility function for prizes u that is (otherwise) independent of the state. In words, a horse race gamble is as good as its *subjective expected utility*. Except for the objective lottery part of these gambles, we have Savage's representation $(\star)$.

For example, in our horse race example, a "typical" representation might be that $u(x) = -e^{-x}$, $\pi(s_1) = .6$, $\pi(s_2) = .399$, and $\pi(s_3) = .001$. We would interpret this as *the consumer has constant absolute risk aversion* (recall the previous section) *and assesses probability .6 that Kelso will win, probability .399 that Secretariat will win, and probability .001 that the race will end in a dead heat.*

If you like a challenge, you should be able to prove this proposition from earlier propositions without difficulty; remember the uniqueness part of the proposition in section 3.1. In this version we require that the subjective probability of every state s is strictly positive. This we did for convenience; it is easy to dispense with. Finally, all this requires a finite state space S. Infinite state spaces are significantly harder to handle.

The Anscombe–Aumann treatment, and especially the result of proposition 3.7, is more subtle than it may seem at first. Let me support that contention with one that is more concrete: It is *crucial* for this theory that the horses run before the roulette wheel is spun. That is, one could imagine beginning with $H = X^S$, as in Savage's treatment, and then letting $\succ$ be defined on all simple probability distributions on H. Posing assumption 4 on this space, where, more or less, we build compound lotteries with the objective uncertainty coming first, would lead to a result far weaker than the representation in proposition 3.7. Until you understand why this is, you miss an implicit assumption that is crucial to the Anscombe–Aumann representation. I will not attempt to explain this here but send you instead to Kreps (1988,105-8).

The Harsanyi doctrine

There is a final philosophical point to make about subjective expected utility and subjective probability. In economics, one usually takes the tastes and preferences of the consumer as exogenous data. This isn't to say, for example, that you can't present a consumer with information that will cause the consumer to realize a particular product is a good or one he will enjoy; but, in the end, there is no arguing about tastes. Is the same true of subjective probability assessments? Are subjective probability assessments as subjective and personal as tastes?

To be very pedantic about this, return to the question of betting on the next World Cup. We will look at gambles whose outcomes depend only on whether the winner of the next Cup comes from Europe (including the Soviet Union) or from Latin America or from the rest of the world, so we take a three-element state space $S = \{s_1, s_2, s_3\}$ where s_1 is the state that a European team wins the next World Cup, s_2 is the state that a Latin American team wins, and s_3 is the state that some other team wins. We will take the prize space X to be $[0, 100]$, with numerical amounts representing dollars won. Now imagine that we give some consumer her choice of the three gambles (from the Anscombe–Aumann version of H) depicted in figure 3.10. Suppose she ranks the three as $h \succ h' \succ h''$. Then if her preferences conform to the Anscombe–Aumann axioms (and if she prefers more money to less), we interpret this as: Our consumer assesses probability greater than .48 that a Latin American team will win and probability less than .48 that a European team will win. Indeed, by varying the probability in h' and looking for a value where she is

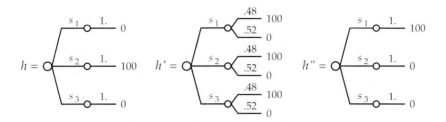

Figure 3.10. Three compound lotteries.

indifferent between h and h' (as modified), we will find the subjective probability that she assesses that a Latin American team will win. All this talk about subjective probabilities that she assesses is entirely a construct of the representation that is guaranteed by the Anscombe–Aumann axioms, and it arises entirely from our consumer's preferences for lotteries like those shown. A different consumer might express the preferences $h'' \succ h' \succ h$, and we would, therefore, know that these consumers' preferences are represented by different subjective assessments over the state space S, if each set of preferences satisfies the Anscombe–Aumann axioms.

Economists (of a neoclassical stripe) would rarely if ever insist that consumers have the same ordinal preferences over bundles of goods or the same levels of risk aversion or risk tolerance. Individual consumers are allowed to have individual preferences. Seemingly then, one would allow subjective probabilities, as another part of the expression of personal preferences, to vary across individuals. If this seems so to you, and it certainly does to me, you are forewarned that, amongst many microeconomists, it is dogma (philosophy?) that two individuals *having access to the same information* will necessarily come up with the same subjective probability assessments. Any difference in subjective probability assessments must be the result of differences in information. Our two consumers might express the preferences given above, but only if they have been exposed to different pieces of information about the qualities of the various teams, etc. This assumption has very substantial implications for exchange among agents; we will encounter some of these later in the book. I leave it to others to defend this assumption — see, for example, Aumann (1987, section 5) — as I cannot do so. But the reader should be alerted to this modeling assumption, which plays an important role in parts of modern microeconomic theory; it is called both the *common prior assumption* and the *Harsanyi doctrine.*

3.5. *Problems with these models*

The von Neumann–Morgenstern model, where probabilities are objective, and the Savage (or Anscombe–Aumann) model, where probabilities are subjective, are the chief models of consumer choice under uncertainty in microeconomics. Indeed, "chief" is an understatement; "predominant" is better, but still not strong enough. One wonders, then: (a) Are there theoretical reasons to distrust these models? (b) How good are they empirically? (c) If there are problems with the models, what are the alternatives? In this section we begin to answer these questions.

Theoretical problems

There are a number of theoretical reasons for distrusting these models. These reasons often arise from the way the models are used in applications; only a limited portion of the consumer's overall decision problem is modeled, and it is assumed that the consumer's choice behavior on the limited problem conforms to this sort of model. *Even though the consumer's overall choice behavior might conform to this sort of model, choice behavior can fail to conform on pieces examined in isolation.* Two of the most important reasons for this have to do with portfolio effects and the temporal resolution of uncertainty.

Portfolio effects are, in spirit, the same as complement/substitute effects in the usual theory of consumer choice under certainty. If we wished to model the demand for, say, wheat, it would be important to realize that the price of corn is a key variable. We (probably) wouldn't try to analyze the wheat market in isolation. Or, rather, when we do try to analyze the wheat market in isolation, there is a lot of incanting of ceteris paribus (or, everything else, and in particular the price of corn, held equal). With lotteries, something similar but even more sinister takes place. Suppose we asked the consumer how he felt about lotteries posed by taking positions in the stock of General Motors. According to these models, we would describe the lotteries by probability distributions over the dollar returns from the positions (possibly having the consumer give his subjective assessment of those distributions), and we would expect the consumer's preferences concerning the gambles are given by the expected utilities they engender. But if this consumer already has a position in the stock of General Motors, or a position in the stock of, say, Ford, we would expect his preferences to be affected. Put another way, given the consumer has an initial position in Ford, if we had two gambles with the exact same probability distribution, but one involved the stock of General Motors and the other involved the stock of General Mills, *because of differences in the correlations in returns between Ford and General Motors and between Ford and General Mills,* we expect the consumer to feel differently about them. We would see this if we modeled the entire portfolio choice problem of the individual — including in one model all the separate gambles that make up the one grand lottery that this individual faces. But we cannot look at preferences between gambles involving the stock of General Motors and the stock of General Mills in isolation and expect the model to work. And we can't incant ceteris paribus here with much conviction — holding fixed the consumer's net position in Ford isn't the issue. The issue is instead the differences in correlation between the gambles being investigated and the gambles left out of the model. The (marginal) probability distributions of the gambles under consideration are not sufficient descriptions of the objects under choice; two gambles with the same marginal distributions (but different joint distributions with the consumer's unmodeled portfolio) would rank differently.[n]

As for temporal resolution of uncertainty, the easiest way to introduce this is with an example. Suppose a coin will be flipped (independent of everything else in the world). If it comes up heads, you'll be given a check for $10,000$; if it comes up tails, you'll get nothing. Or you can have a check for $3,000$. (You may wish to supply a number in place of the $3,000$, so that you just slightly prefer the gamble.) One complication arises; the money will be given to you next September 1. This isn't so complicated that we can't gear up the models of choice from the previous sections. Assuming it is a fair coin, this sounds like a gamble with probability .5 of $10,000$ and .5 of nothing, against a sure thing of $3,000$.

But consider a real complication. We have in mind three gambles that you might be given. The first is just as above, a coin flip gamble, where the coin is flipped today *and you are told the result today.* The second is just as above, a coin flip gamble, where the coin is flipped next September 1 *and you are told the result at that date.* And in the third, we have the same coin flip, flipped today, *and you will be told the result next September 1.* How do you rank these three?

If you conformed to the models above when applied to this choice problem in isolation, then you would rank them identically. They all have the same probability distribution on prizes. (Note also, they are independent of other gambles you may be facing; this isn't a portfolio problem.) But if you are like most people, you like the first gamble better

---

[n] Readers who followed our earlier discussion of demand for assets with more than one risky asset will recognize that discussion as a more precise version of what has been described here.

than the second two, and you are indifferent between the second two. Two things are at work here:

(a) Getting the information sooner is valuable to you

(b) The important time is when the uncertainty resolves for you, the decision maker, and not when the uncertainty is "physically" resolved

These two statements follow from things we leave out of the model when we think of these gambles simply as probability distributions over some income you might receive. For example, between now and next September 1 you have a number of consumption choices to make — how much to spend on an apartment, on food, on a vacation. What you will do between now and then depends, at least in part, on the resources you have now and the resources you think you will have later. If the uncertainty in this gamble is resolved for you now, you can use that information better to fit your consumption choices between now and September 1 to your (now better-known) resources. If the uncertainty resolves for you next September 1, you will have to temporize in the meantime. Note well that what drives this is the presence of (consumption) decisions you must make that are not analyzed if we look at the gambles in isolation. It is a problem, as before, of a partial or incomplete model of your overall choice problem. (This is why in our discussion of induced preferences for income, induced from preferences for consumption, we said that it was important that the uncertainty about income resolved before any consumption decisions had to be made.)

This shows that timing of resolution of uncertainty can matter.[6] When viewing these gambles in isolation, it isn't enough to describe the possible prizes and their probabilities. What is less obvious (but still true) is that we mightn't expect the usual sort of model to hold in comparing gambles, if we fix all gambles to resolve at a specified later date. (Problem 11 will confirm this.)

What do we do in the face of these problems? One solution is to include in our models all the relevant portions of the consumer's overall choice problem. This is fairly unpalatable; putting everything in makes the model unwieldy and, often, intractable. Or you could restrict attention

---

[6] The timing of resolution of uncertainty can be important for "psychological" reasons as well, even if the consumer has no particular use for the information in the sense that it could change some decisions he must make. Pending/hanging uncertainty can, in itself, be a good or a bad. The commonplace view is that hanging uncertainty when there is a small chance of very good news and no chance of bad news is typically good, while any hanging uncertainty about a possible bad is in itself a bad. These are important effects, worthy of attention. But they are different from the effects that concern us here.

only to those pieces for which the standard models do apply. This is unpalatable because the conditions required for the standard models to apply are quite stringent (see the next paragraph). A better alternative is to look for models of choice that are correct for pieces of a bigger model. Such models will necessarily have less structure than the standard von Neumann–Morgenstern or Savage models but can still have enough structure to permit some analysis. For example, in dealing with portfolio effects, if you choose a "states of the world" model, then you can have additive separability across states and (even) some comparability of the various state-dependent utility functions. In dealing with problems in temporal resolution of uncertainty, you can have preferences that are "locally linear in probabilities"; recent work by Machina (1982, 1984) shows that this is enough to get back some of the standard results in the economics of uncertainty.

Empirical evidence in simple settings

For the two reasons above (and others besides), one worries about the application of these models of choice to contexts that study an isolated piece of the consumer's overall choice problem. It can be shown, though, that isolating a piece is okay if the consumer obeys the model of choice overall and if the piece has the simplest possible structure; the risk in the gambles is independent of other risks the decision maker might face, and the uncertainty in the gambles resolves immediately. But we can (and do) still wonder how these models perform as *descriptive* models of individual choice under uncertainty, even in settings with this ultra-simple structure.

The typical method for investigating this question is to run experiments on subject populations. The caricature subject population consists of college sophomores who are told in their introductory psych courses that they need to take part in a certain number of such experiments to pass the course. The subjects are asked hypothetical questions: How would you pick if offered a choice between _____ and _____; between _____ and _____; etc.? And we look for violations of the usual models of choice. Such studies are often criticized as being artificial: The subject population isn't used to dealing with the sort of question asked; the subjects aren't given appropriate incentives to take the question seriously (the questions are hypothetical); it isn't clear that the experiments have anything to say about choices made in economically important contexts, and so on. (Since these studies draw so much fire, you can already guess what they will say.) But experimental economists and psychologists have dealt within their limited budgets with these criticisms, and these experiments continue to give over and over a few results that are not in keeping with the models above and that make it incumbent on economists to offer excuses for themselves and their models.

We will discuss three of the most important "effects" suggested by the experimental literature. They all have to do with choice under uncertainty. This isn't to say that the models of choice under certainty haven't been scrutinized in like manner — they have been — and problems arise there as well, along with very nice perceptual and cognitive models concerning how individuals do make choices.

(a) The Allais Paradox. The most famous violation of the von Neumann–Morgenstern expected utility model is named after its discoverer, Maurice Allais. One variation on this runs as follows:

> Choose between two gambles. The first gives a .33 chance of $27,500, a .66 chance of $24,000, and a .01 chance of nothing. The second gives $24,000 for sure.

> Choose between two gambles. The first gives a .33 chance of $27,500 and a .67 chance of nothing. The second gives a .34 chance of $24,000 and a .66 chance of nothing.

The typical (modal) response pattern is to take the sure thing in the first case, and the first gamble in the second. This particular response pattern violates the substitution axiom.[7]

A number of explanations have been hypothesized for this. The spirit of most of them is that individuals rescale probabilities, with more weight (proportionately) given to small probability events.

(b) The Ellsberg Paradox. Due to Daniel Ellsberg, this runs as follows:

> An urn contains 300 colored marbles; 100 of the marbles are red, and 200 are some mixture of blue and green. We will reach into this urn and select a marble at random:

> You receive $1,000 if the marble selected is of a specified color. Would you rather that color be red or blue?

> You receive $1,000 if the marble selected is not of a specified color. Would you rather that color be blue or red?

The modal responses are red in the first case and red in the second. And the preferences are strict.

---

[7] Try to prove this yourself, or see the discussion on framing. Alternatively, you can show that no expected utility maximizer could express the two choices above.

This violates the Savage or Anscombe–Aumann axioms. If those axioms are satisfied, then the decision maker chooses as if he assessed subjective probabilities that the marble selected is red, blue, and green. (It seems natural to assess probability 1/3 for red, and it seems natural to me at least to assess 1/3 each for blue and green as well. But the assessment is up to the consumer.) If the consumer strictly prefers red in the first case, he must assess a higher probability for red than for blue. But then he should assess a higher probability for the event *the marble is not blue* than for the event that *the marble is not red*. Hence he should, if he conforms to the model, strictly prefer to answer blue in the second question.

Ellsberg (and others both before and after him) use this sort of behavior to claim that there is a real distinction to be made between situations where there is risk (objective uncertainty) and situations with uncertainty (subjective uncertainty). The story goes: People dislike the ambiguity that comes with choice under uncertainty; they dislike the possibility that they may have the odds wrong and so make a wrong choice. Hence in this example in each case they go with the gamble where they know the odds — betting for or against red.

(c) Framing. Early in chapter 2, we discussed the effect that framing can have on choice. In fact, the example given there about various vaccination programs was an example of choice under uncertainty. In that example, the two different ways of framing the options amounted to a shift of the "status quo" — are the six hundred still alive or already dead? — and experimenters have shown that, in general, choices made under uncertainty can be powerfully influenced by the decision maker's perception of the status quo. (See Kahneman and Tversky, 1979.)

There are many interesting aspects of framing and its impact on choice, many more than we can describe here. But one aspect of framing is especially relevant to our earlier discussion. Consider the two compound gambles in figure 3.11(a) and (b). Which would you choose?

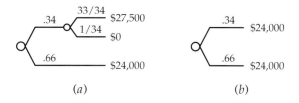

(a)   (b)

Figure 3.11. Two compound lotteries.

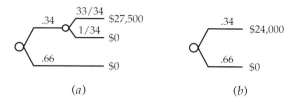

Figure 3.12. Two more compound lotteries.

And how would you choose between the two compound lotteries in figure 3.12?

These gambles are drawn so that the decision maker naturally focuses on the "differences" between the two in each pair — a 33/34 chance of $27,500 (and a 1/34 chance of nothing) in (a) against $24,000 for sure in (b). The incidence of "consistent choices," that is, (a) in both cases or (b) in both cases, is higher than in the Allais paradox.[8] But these compound gambles "are" precisely the gambles of the Allais paradox; that is, they reduce to the single-stage gambles of the Allais paradox if the rules of probability theory are applied.[9] Insofar as framing these gambles as compound lotteries changes choice from when the gambles are framed as single-stage lotteries, the entire structure on which the standard theory is built begins to shake.

Rather a lot of work has been done recently on recasting von Neumann–Morgenstern expected utility theory in ways that allow preferences to accommodate the Allais paradox. Somewhat less, but still some, work has been done on modifying the standard Savage and Anscombe–Aumann models to allow for Ellsberg paradox-like preferences. Machina (forthcoming) contains a good survey of this material, together with an exposition of the standard models and the experimental evidence that is available. Very little indeed has been done (at least, in the literature of economics) to confront generally problems of framing. This is a very important frontier in choice theory.

Validity of the models in complex settings

Another reason to disbelieve these models of choice, especially in how they are applied in economic contexts, concerns the complexity of the decision problems in which they are employed. They are used, for

---

[8] See, for example, Tversky and Kahneman (1986).

[9] This indicates, of course, how it is that the Allais paradox is a violation of the von Neumann–Morgenstern substitution axiom.

example, to model the consumption-investment budgeting problems of an individual, over the individual's entire life. They are used to model individuals who are assumed to be solving statistical inference problems that the economist who is writing down the model cannot solve. They are used to model extraordinarily complex interactions between individuals, where each individual is (correctly) assessing what others will be doing in response to information that they have, even though the person writing down the model can't make that assessment, and so on. (Lest you think I am sneering at such silly applications, which are quite common among microeconomic theorists, the three sins listed above are my own.)

This problem is sometimes described as one of assumed *unlimited rationality* on the part of individuals in economic models. Individuals are assumed to understand to an amazing extent the environment within which they act, and it is assumed they can perform fantastic calculations to find their own best course of actions at no cost and taking no time. This is, of course, ridiculous. Faced with complexity, individuals resort to rules of thumb, to "back of the envelope" calculations, to satisficing behavior (taking the first "satisfactory" alternative that arises), and the like. It seems patent that such *limitedly rational* behavior would, when placed in a complex economic context, have important implications.

We hinted in chapter 1 at the excuses that are typically made. There is the "positive economics" defense: It is only necessary that behavior is "as if" these calculations were performed. For example (this line of defense often goes), the calculations necessary when driving a car and determining whether it is safe to pass someone ahead are incredibly complex. Yet we see individuals, even those without the benefit of a high school education, succeed in such calculations every day. (We also see them fail occasionally, but there is some chance of a bad outcome any time there is uncertainty.) One might retort that such choices are made, but they are done heuristically, and (probably) with a greater than optimal margin of safety built in. The defender of the faith would respond that this is "as if" the individual were optimizing with a more risk averse utility function.

Moreover (the defender of the faith will say) small variations from the theory on the individual level are not important if they cancel out in aggregate. Of course, this presumes that it is the aggregate outcomes that are of consequence. And it presumes no systematic bias in the deviations in behavior from that which is posited. Any systematic bias would (probably) have aggregate consequences that are important.

The defender of the faith has yet another line of defense that was not mentioned in chapter 1: There are no palatable alternatives. Most alternatives that have been proposed have been criticized as being ad hoc and without any testable restrictions: If we allow any behavior at all, or if the behavior that is allowed is at the whim of the modeler, predictive power is lost. But this rejoinder is something of a non sequitur. *If* the alternatives so far developed are ad hoc (and I don't mean to prejudge this issue at all), this doesn't mean that acceptable alternatives cannot be developed. One always hopes that some good and generally accepted models of limitedly rational behavior will come along. (And there are, occasionally, some attempts in this direction. Indeed, as this is being written, there is rather more activity in this direction than usual.) But until they do....

Finally (and this is the line of defense with which I am personally the most comfortable), you should not rule out the possibility that you can learn things of value by making such heroic assumptions about powers of economic actors. This isn't to say that you can't be misled, or that you can't learn other things with more reasonable assumptions. But neither of these precludes insight coming from models of behavior that are somewhat incredible along this dimension.

3.6. *Normative applications of the theory*

Another way to view the models of this chapter is to interpret them as normative rather than descriptive theory. The normative view runs:

(0) Suppose you are in a situation in which you must make a particular, fairly complex choice. The choice in question might involve random events without "objective" probabilities, many different outcomes, and so on.

(1) Ask yourself: Can this situation be embedded within a general choice situation that has the structure of one of the models above?

(2) If the answer to the first question is yes, do the "properties of preference" that we have discussed seem sensible in this situation? In other words, is it reasonable to take a choice based on preferences that conform to these properties?

(3) If the answer is yes again, then we know that you want your choice to be based on the sort of criteria that is implied by the particular framework and properties — expected utility maximization or subjective expected utility maximization.

(4) And (the punchline to this) it may be possible to get the data needed for the representation by asking yourself about less complex specific choices and about general properties of your preferences. This will give you the

data for the representation — then with that data you *compute* the best option in the complex situation.

For example, suppose you are offered a gamble in which the prizes are $1,000, $700, $470, $225, $32, $ − 87, $ − 385, $ − 642, and $ − 745. The probabilities depend on the exact closing level of the Dow Jones Industrial Average next Friday afternoon. For example, the gamble might specify that you get $1,000 if the DJIA is 100 points above its current level, $700 if it is between 100 and 80 points over its current level, and so on.

(1) Can we formulate this in terms of one of the models above? Quite definitely — the Anscombe–Aumann model applies, where the states of the world are various levels of the DJIA.

(2) Do you subscribe to the appropriate axioms? In this case, you might. The uncertainty resolves quite soon, and you may not have significant asset holdings that are correlated with this uncertainty. (If you did, a more complex normative model could be used.)

(3) Hence your choice whether to take this gamble or not should be made according to the representation of the Anscombe–Aumann framework. We need to get your subjective probability assessment for the future level of the DJIA, and we need to get your utility function for money.

So far, nothing useful has come out of this exercise. Indeed, in (1) and (2) you were asked some hard questions, which (one hopes) you thought hard about. But now:

(4a) Consider first your subjective assessment for the DJIA. A number of procedures help to do this. Some, involving inference from past data, are probably already familiar to you. Others involve framing questions for yourself in a way that is easy to perceive and that eliminates systematic biases. In the end, you will still have to give your subjective assessment, but there are ways to increase your confidence in the "validity" of the assessment you make.

(4b) It is somewhat easier to describe how to simplify getting your utility function. First, it is probably safe to assume that your preferences are increasing in money; your utility function is monotone. Second, as long as you can "afford" to lose the $745, you can probably be convinced that you are risk averse; your utility function will be concave. Kahneman and Tversky (and others before them) tell us to be careful around the level of zero — you may exhibit a "zero illusion" — putting more significance into the difference between gains and losses on this gamble than you would want, once this is pointed out to you.[o] We need your utility function for a range of $1,000 to $ − 745, and we can get this, at least roughly, by asking you relatively simple questions such as: What is your certainty equivalent for a coin flip gamble where the prizes are $1,000 and $ − 800? Note what we're doing here. We ask the simplest possible certainty equivalent question, involving a coin flip gamble. With the answers to such relatively easy questions, we can build your utility function for the entire range, and we can put you through consistency checks of the answers you give.

And more besides. Now you know about increasing and decreasing and constant risk aversion. It is likely that you can be convinced in general that you wish to be (weakly) nonincreasingly risk averse. And if the range of prizes isn't too significant for you, as might be the case for this particular problem, then you may even be able to be convinced that you wish to exhibit virtually constant absolute risk aversion over this range. If you accept this, then we are really in business; we have the determination of your utility function down to finding a single constant, which we determine by a single question about a coin flip gamble (although we'll ask several, as a consistency check). The greater is the number of qualitative properties to which you are willing to ascribe in this particular problem (and constant risk aversion over this range of prizes is an easy-to-understand and incredibly powerful property), the easier it is to carry out probability and utility function *assessment*. Once we have your subjective probability assessments and your utility function, we can quickly grind through the complex gamble given to see if you "want" to take it.

3.7. Bibliographic notes

The material of this chapter combines a lot of the theory of choice under uncertainty and a bit of the economics of uncertainty. On the subject of choice under uncertainty, you are directed to three text/reference books: Fishburn (1970), Kreps (1988), and Machina (forthcoming). For getting all the details of the standard model, Fishburn is highly recommended. Kreps (1988) omits some of the details of proofs, but is perhaps more immediately accessible than Fishburn. Machina (forthcoming), besides providing a complete treatment of the standard theory, gives the

---

[o] One approach is to frame the same gamble several different ways. For example, we ask you for your certainty equivalent for a coin flip gamble where the prizes are $ − 1,000 and $0, and then we ask you for your certainty equivalent for a coin flip gamble where the prizes are $0 and $1,000, where you first must pay $1,000. These are the "same" questions in terms of the final balance of your bank account, and, upon reflection, you are likely to decide that you want to give the same net answer.

reader an up-to-date account of recent developments in choice theory that are intended to address Allais and Ellsberg style paradoxes. If you like to consult original sources, see von Neumann and Morgenstern (1944), Savage (1954), and Anscombe and Aumann (1963).

The material on utility functions for money (and especially absolute and relative risk aversion) is further developed (in varying degrees) in the three books listed above. The classic references are Arrow (1974) and Pratt (1964) (the coefficient of absolute risk aversion is sometimes called the Arrow-Pratt measure of risk aversion in consequence). We touched very briefly (in smaller type) on the subject of more and less risky gambles; Machina (forthcoming) gives a particularly good treatment of this.

The economics of uncertainty (demand for insurance, demand for risky assets) is developed in many different places. Borch (1968) provides a very readable introduction and Arrow (1974) contains a number of classic developments. Matters concerned with asset markets quickly merge in the academic discipline of finance; a good text on this subject is Huang and Litzenberger (1988).

The papers cited concerning the empirical problems with these models are Allais (1953), Ellsberg (1961), and Kahneman and Tversky (1979). Machina (forthcoming) provides an overview of much of this, with recent theoretical developments that are intended to respond to Allais and Ellsberg style paradoxes.

References

Allais, M. 1953. "Le Comportement de l'Homme Rationnel devant le Risque, Critique des Postulates et Axiomes de l'École Americaine." *Econometrica* 21:503–46.

Anscombe, F., and R. Aumann. 1963. "A Definition of Subjective Probability." *Annals of Mathematical Statistics* 34:199–205.

Arrow, K. 1974. *Essays in the Theory of Risk Bearing.* Amsterdam: North Holland.

Aumann, R. 1987. "Correlated Equilibrium as an Expression of Bayesian Rationality." *Econometrica* 55:1–18.

Borch, K. 1968. *The Economics of Uncertainty.* Princeton, N.J.: Princeton University Press.

Diamond, P., and J. Stiglitz. 1974. "Increases in Risk and in Risk Aversion." *Journal of Economic Theory* 8:337–60.

Ellsberg, D. 1961. "Risk, Ambiguity, and the Savage Axioms." *Quarterly Journal of Economics* 75:643–69.

Fishburn, P. [1970] 1979.   *Utility Theory for Decision Making.* New York: John Wiley and Sons. Reprint. Huntington, N.Y.: R. E. Krieger Publishing.

Huang, C-f., and R. Litzenberger. 1988. *Foundations for Financial Economics.* New York: Elsevier Science Publishing Company.

Kahneman, D., and A. Tversky. 1979. "Prospect Theory: An Analysis of Decision Under Risk." *Econometrica* 47:263–91.

Kreps, D. 1988. *Notes on the Theory of Choice.* Boulder, Colo.: Westview Press.

Machina, M. 1982. "'Expected Utility' Analysis without the Independence Axiom." *Econometrica* 50:277–323.

————. 1984. "Temporal Risk and the Nature of Induced Preferences." *Journal of Economic Theory* 33:199–231.

————. (Forthcoming). *The Economic Theory of Individual Choice Under Uncertainty: Theory, Evidence, and New Directions.* Cambridge: Cambridge University Press.

Pratt, J. 1964. "Risk Aversion in the Small and in the Large." *Econometrica* 32:122–36.

Ross, S. 1981. "Some Stronger Measures of Risk Aversion in the Small and in the Large with Applications." *Econometrica* 49:621–38.

Rothschild, M., and J. Stiglitz. 1970. "Increasing Risk. I: A Definition." *Journal of Economic Theory* 2:225–43.

————. 1971. "Increasing Risk. II: Its Economic Consequences." *Journal of Economic Theory* 3:66–84.

————. 1973. "Addendum to Increasing Risk." *Journal of Economic Theory* 5:306.

Savage, L. 1954. *The Foundations of Statistics.* New York: John Wiley and Sons. Rev. and enl. ed. New York: Dover Publications, 1972.

Tversky, A., and D. Kahneman. 1986. "Rational Choice and the Framing of Decisions." *Journal of Business* 59:S251–78.

Von Neumann, J., and O. Morgenstern. 1944. *Theory of Games and Economic Behavior.* Princeton, N.J.: Princeton University Press. (2d edition 1947; 3d edition 1953).

3.8. Problems

■ 1. (a) Prove lemma 1. (Assumption 2 should figure prominently in your proof. Begin with the case $\alpha = 1$.)

(b) Prove lemma 2. (Deal with the cases $p \sim \delta_b$ and $p \sim \delta_w$ first. Then define $\alpha = \inf\{\beta : \beta\delta_b + (1 - \beta)\delta_w \succ p\}$. Use the Archimedean property to show that $\alpha\delta_b + (1 - \alpha)\delta_w \sim p$.)

(c) Prove lemma 3. (This is harder than lemmas 1 and 2 and is left as something of a challenge. Consider three cases: $p \sim q \sim s$ for all $s \in P$; there is some $s \in P$ with $s \succ p$; and then there is some $s \in P$ with $p \succ s$.)

(d) Give a formal proof of lemma 4. (Use induction on the size of the support of p. Recall here that we assume that all probability distributions in question have finite support.)

(e) Extend the proof of lemma 4 to cases without best and worst prizes. (Suppose there are two prizes with $\delta_b \succ \delta_w$. Arbitrarily set $u(b) = 1$ and $u(0) = 0$. If $\delta_b \succeq \delta_x \succeq \delta_w$, define $u(x)$ as in lemma 2. If $\delta_x \succ \delta_b$, use lemma 2 to show that there is a unique α such that $\alpha\delta_x + (1 - \alpha)\delta_w \sim \delta_b$ and define $u(x) = 1/\alpha$. If $\delta_w \succ \delta_x$, use lemma 2 to show that there is a unique α such that $\alpha\delta_b + (1 - \alpha)\delta_x \sim \delta_w$, and define $u(x) = -\alpha/(1 - \alpha)$. Then show that this u works. Everything should be clear, if a bit tedious, once you figure out why this gives the right definition for u.)

(f) Prove the "uniqueness" part of proposition 3.1. (Hint: Begin your proof as follows. Suppose u and v (with domain X) both give expected utility representations for $\succ$. Suppose it is not the case that $v(\cdot) \equiv au(\cdot) + b$ for constants $a > 0$ and b. Then there exist three members of X such that....)

■ 2. Let p' be a probability distribution giving prizes \$10 and \$20 with probabilities 2/3 and 1/3, respectively, and let p be a probability distribution giving prizes \$5, \$15, and \$30 with probabilities 1/3, 5/9 and 1/9, respectively. Show that any risk averse expected utility maximizer will (weakly) prefer p' to p. (Hint: Construct p as a compound lottery as discussed at the end of the subsection on risk aversion.) Can you supply a general statement of the principle at work in this specific example?

■ 3. At the end of the first subsection of section 3.3, we asked the question: Fix a consumer with von Neumann–Morgenstern preferences over lotteries for consumption bundles, and fix this consumer's income at some level Y. Given two price vectors p and p', would the consumer rather be in an economy where prices are either p or p', each probability 1/2, or in an economy where the prices are sure to be $.5p + .5p'$? We asserted that there is no clear answer to that question. In this problem, you are asked to develop two examples that indicate what can happen along these lines.

(a) Imagine that there are two goods, and the consumer's *ordinal* preferences are given by $U(x_1, x_2) = x_1 + x_2$. That is, the consumer's von Neumann–Morgenstern utility function is $u(x_1, x_2) = f(x_1 + x_2)$ for some strictly increasing function f on the real line. Suppose that $p = (1, 3)$ and $p' = (3, 1)$. Show that *regardless of what the function f is*, this consumer prefers to take her chances with the risky prices.

(b) Imagine that there are two goods and the consumer's von Neumann–Morgenstern utility function is $u(x_1, x_2) = f(\min\{x_1, x_2\})$ for some concave, strictly increasing function f on the real line. Assume that $f(0)$ is finite. Now suppose that the risk in prices is entirely risk in the overall price level: $p = (\gamma, \gamma)$ and $p' = (1/\gamma, 1/\gamma)$ for some scalar $\gamma > 1$. Prove that for fixed γ you can always find a function f such that the consumer prefers the certain prices $.5p + .5p'$ to the risky prices. And prove that for every concave, strictly increasing function f with $f(0)$ finite there is a γ sufficiently large so the consumer prefers the risky prices to the certain prices.

▪ 4. Recall the analysis of an insurance buying consumer in section 3.3. Suppose this consumer has a concave utility function for net income that is not necessarily differentiable. What changes does this cause for the results given in our discussion?

▪ 5. Suppose that an insurance policy compensates a victim for loss, but does so somewhat imperfectly. That is, imagine that in the story given about the insurance buying consumer our consumer's income prior to any insurance is $Y - \Delta$, where Δ is a simple lottery whose support includes 0 and some strictly positive amounts. The available insurance policy pays a flat amount B in the event of any loss, that is, in the event that Δ exceeds zero. The premium is still δ. Let π be the probability that the consumer sustains a loss. The contract is actuarially fair if $\delta = \pi B$. Suppose this is so and that B is the expected amount of the loss, if there is a loss. If the consumer has a concave, differentiable utility function, will she buy full insurance? (Use a simple parameterized example if you can't do this in general.)

Questions 6 through 9 all concern the discussion in section 3.3 of demand for risky assets.

▪ 6. Consider the following specialization of the discussion in section 3.3: The consumer has \$$W$ to invest, which he must allocate between two possible investments. The first is a sure thing — put in \$1, and get \$$r > \$1$ back. The second is risky — for every \$1 invested, it returns a random amount $\$\theta$, where θ is a simple lottery on $(0, \infty)$ with distribution π. We assume that the expected value of θ is strictly greater than r but that there is positive probability that θ takes on some value that is strictly less than r. We allow this investor to *sell short* the riskless asset but not the risky asset. And we do not worry about the net payoff being negative; the consumer's utility function will be defined for negative arguments.

This investor evaluates his initial choice of portfolio according to the expected utility the portfolio produces for his net payoff. Moreover, this consumer has a constant coefficient of absolute risk aversion $\lambda > 0$. That is, he chooses the amount of his wealth to invest in the risky asset (with the residual invested in the safe asset) to maximize the expectation of $-e^{-\lambda Y}$, where Y is his (random) net payoff from the portfolio he picks. Let us write $\alpha(W, \lambda)$ for the optimal amount of money to invest in the risky asset, as a function of the consumer's initial wealth W and coefficient of risk aversion λ.

(a) Prove that $\alpha(W, \lambda)$ is finite for all W and α. That is, the consumer's investment problem has a well-defined solution.

Even if you can't do part (a), assume its result and go on to parts (b) and (c).

(b) Prove that $\alpha(W, \lambda)$ is independent of W; no matter what his initial wealth, the consumer invests the same amount in the risky asset.

(c) Prove that $\alpha(W, \lambda)$ is nonincreasing in λ; the more risk averse the individual, the less he invests in the risky asset.

■ 7. Consider the general formulation of the consumer's problem with one risky asset. Show that if the risky asset is genuinely risky — that is, it has non-zero variance — and if the consumer's von Neumann–Morgenstern utility function is strictly concave, then the consumer's problem, if it has any solution at all, must have a unique solution.

■ 8. Recall that in the discussion of demand for risky assets with more than one risky asset, we asserted that it was possible that an asset could have an expected return less than r and still be demanded and that an asset could have an expected return greater than r and not be demanded at all. (Recall that we are not allowing short-sales of risky assets.) Produce examples to support these claims. (Hints: For the first example, recall that you want negative correlation between the returns on the two risky assets. Imagine that each asset returns either $\theta = 1$ or $\theta = 5$ and that $r = 2$. You should be able to construct an example from this. The second example is even easier. What happens if θ^1 and θ^2 are perfectly positively correlated and θ^2 always exceeds θ^1?)

■ 9. Prove that if we have two risky assets with independent return distributions, all the results obtained in the text for the case of one risky asset extend.

■ 10. With regard to the *additive across states* representation (★★) in section 3.4, we might wonder whether there is any value in obtaining the representation with subjective probabilities over the states, so that the representation becomes one of *subjective **state dependent** expected utility*. Prove the following: If we have a representation (★★), then for *any* strictly positive probability distribution π on S, there is a state-dependent utility function $u : X \times S \to R$ such that subjective state-dependent expected utility, using this probability distribution π and the utility function u, represents $\succ$. (Since π is completely arbitrary here, up to being strictly positive, the answer to the question posed at the start of this question is there is apparently very little value. Which is why we don't include subjective probabilities in (★★).)

■ 11. Consider a consumer who will live today and tomorrow. On each date, this consumer consumes a single good (manna), whose price on each date is $100 per unit. We write c_0 for the amount of manna this consumer consumes today and c_1 for the amount he consumes tomorrow. This consumer faces some uncertainty in how much manna he will be able to afford (to be explained in the next paragraph), and his preferences over uncertain consumption pairs (c_0, c_1) are given by the expectation of the von Neumann–Morgenstern utility function $u(c_0, c_1) = \ln(c_0) + \ln(c_1)$, where ln is the logarithm to the base e.

This consumer currently possesses $100 of wealth. He can spend it all today, or he can put some of it in the bank to take out and use to buy manna tomorrow. This bank pays no interest and has no deposit or withdrawal charges — $1 put in today will mean $1 taken out tomorrow. In addition to any savings that he carries forward, the consumer has a random amount of extra income, which he will receive tomorrow. If there is any uncertainty about this income, that uncertainty doesn't resolve until tomorrow — until after today's levels of consumption and savings must be fixed.

(a) Suppose the consumer is sure to receive an extra $34 tomorrow. What consumption level does he choose today, and what is his overall expected utility?

(b) Suppose that, tomorrow, the consumer will receive an extra $100 with probability 1/2, and nothing more with probability 1/2. What consumption level does he choose today, and what is his overall expected utility? (To solve this analytically, you will have to solve a quadratic equation.)

(c) Suppose that, tomorrow, the consumer will receive nothing with probability 1/4, $34 with probability 1/2, and $100 with probability 1/4. What consumption level does he choose today, and what is his overall expected utility? (A good approximate answer is acceptable here, because to get the exact solution you have to solve a cubic equation. You will need to be quite accurate in your calculations; the third significant digit is important.)

(d) Assuming you get this far, what strikes you about the answers to parts (a), (b), and (c)? In particular, if we asked for this consumer's preferences over lotteries in the "extra income," where it is understood that all uncertainty resolves tomorrow, would this consumer satisfy the von Neumann–Morgenstern axioms?

■ 12. Kahneman and Tversky (1979) give the following example of a violation of von Neumann–Morgenstern theory. Ninety-five subjects were asked:

> Suppose you consider the possibility of insuring some property against damage, e.g., fire or theft. After examining the risks and the premium you find that you have no clear preference between the options of purchasing insurance or leaving the property uninsured.

> It is then called to your attention that the insurance company offers a new program called *probabilistic insurance*. In this program you pay half of the regular premium. In case of damage, there is a 50 percent chance that you pay the other half of the premium and the insurance company covers all the losses, and there is a 50 percent chance that you get back your insurance payment and suffer all the losses.…

> Recall that the premium is such that you find this insurance is barely worth its cost.

> Under these circumstances, would you purchase probabilistic insurance?

And 80 percent of the subjects said they wouldn't.

Ignore the "time value of money."[10] Does this provide a violation of the

---

[10] Because the insurance company gets the premium now, or half now and half later, the interest that the premium might earn can be consequential. I want you to ignore such effects.

von Neumann–Morgenstern model, if we assume (as we usually do) that all expected utility maximizers are risk neutral or risk averse? Is someone who definitely turns down probabilistic insurance exhibiting behavior that is inconsistent with the model (with risk aversion/neutrality a maintained assumption)? You will have gotten the problem half right if you show rigorously that the answer to this question is yes. But you will be getting the entire point of this problem if you can provide a reason why I, an utterly consistent von Neumann–Morgenstern expected utility maximizer, would say no to probabilistic insurance. (Hint: See problem 11.)

■ 13. We earlier showed that the Ellsberg paradox is a violation of the Savage–Anscombe–Aumann theories by referring to their representations of preference. Demonstrate directly that the Ellsberg paradox is a violation of their axioms; that is, show (by example) a specific axiom that is being violated. You may choose either the Savage axioms or the Anscombe–Aumann axioms — only one of the two is necessary. (In the case of Savage, you only know three of the axioms — preference is asymmetric, negatively transitive, and the sure thing principle. One of these three is violated by the Ellsberg example. There are five axioms in Anscombe–Aumann to choose from, so it might be easier to work with the three Savage axioms, which are fewer.)

■ 14. The following bit of nonsense is often heard:

Suppose I offered you, absolutely for free, a gamble where with probability .4 you win $1,000 and with probability .6 you lose $500. You might well choose not to take this gamble (if the alternative is zero) if you are risk averse; although this gamble has a positive expected value $((.4)(1000) + (.6)(−500) = \$100)$, it also has substantial risk. But if I offered you, say, 100 independent trials of this gamble, then you would certainly wish to take them; the law of large numbers says that you will wind up ahead. That is, risk aversion is perhaps sensible when a single gamble is being contemplated. But it is senseless when we are looking at many independent copies of the same gamble; then the only sensible thing is to go with the long-run averages.

Is this nonsense? Can you produce a particular "consumer" who is rational according to the von Neumann–Morgenstern axioms, and who would

---

To do this, you could assume that if the insurance company does insure you, the second half of the premium must be increased to account for the interest the company has foregone. While if they do not, when they return the first half premium, they must return it with the interest it has earned. But it is easiest to simply ignore these complications altogether.

turn down all independent copies of this gamble, no matter how many were offered? Or would any von Neumann–Morgenstern expected utility maximizer take these gambles if offered enough independent copies? (Hints: Either answer can be correct, depending on how you interpret the phrase "enough copies of the gamble." The problem is easiest if we read this phrase as: We offer the consumer a number of copies, fixed in advance, but very large. Then you should be able to produce a consumer who will not take any of the gambles. If you are worried about bankruptcy of this consumer, you may take your pick: [1] This consumer is never bankrupt — his utility function is defined for all monetary levels, however positive or negative; [2] this consumer is bankrupt if his wealth, which begins at a level of $2,000, ever reaches $0; and we will stop gambling with this consumer the moment he becomes bankrupt. Interpretation [1] is the easier to work with, but either is okay.)

And, if you like challenges, try to prove the following: Suppose that we play according to rule (2): The consumer is offered "up to N gambles" with the proviso that we stop gambling if ever the consumer's wealth falls to $0. Assume that the consumer has a utility function for final wealth that is strictly increasing and that is finite at zero. (a) If the consumer's utility function is unbounded, then there is an N sufficiently large so that, offered N gambles or more, the consumer will take them. (b) While if the consumer's utility function is bounded above, the result can go either way: The consumer might turn down the gambles, for all sufficiently large N; or the consumer might accept the gambles, for all sufficiently large N. If you can further characterize the two cases in (b), that would be better still.

■ 15. A particular consumer that I know must choose between (1) a sure payment of $200; (2) a gamble with prizes $0, $200, $450, and $1,000, with respective probabilities .5, .3, .1, and .1; (3) a gamble with prizes $0, $100, $200, and $520, each with probability 1/4. This consumer, in the context of these choices, subscribes to the von Neumann–Morgenstern axioms. Moreover, this consumer, upon reflection, is willing to state that her preferences exhibit constant absolute risk aversion over this range of prizes, and her certainty equivalent for a gamble with prizes $1,000 and $0, each equally likely, is $470. Which of the three gambles given is best for this consumer (granting the validity of all her judgments)?

chapter four

Dynamic choice

Many important choices made in economic contexts are made through time. The consumer takes some action today, knowing that subsequent choices will be required tomorrow and the day following and so on. And today's choice has impact on either how the consumer views later choices or what choices will later be available or both. We refer to this as a situation of *dynamic choice*, and in this short chapter we discuss how economists model the process of dynamic choice.

Actually, there are two theoretically distinct issues here. When a consumer makes choices today, she presumably does so with some notion of what further choices she plans to be making in the future. We can ask how those plans affect the choice currently being made. That is, what are the consequences for *static choice* of the fact that static choice is part of a larger dynamic choice problem? Then tomorrow comes, and our consumer makes a subsequent choice. We ask how choice on subsequent dates knits together with choice on earlier dates. That is, what is the structure of *dynamic choice*?

In microeconomics, the issue of dynamic choice is usually dealt with by reducing dynamic choice to the static choice of an *optimal dynamic strategy* which is then carried out. We will discuss this standard approach by means of an example in section 4.1. (We have already seen examples in chapter 3, but here we will be more explicit about what is going on.) Then in section 4.2 we will discuss in the context of a different example both the standard approach and a pair of alternatives. General discussion follows in section 4.3.

4.1. Optimal dynamic strategies

A simple example

Imagine a consumer faced with the following problem. This consumer will live for two periods, consuming in each. She consumes only two things: artichokes and broccoli. Hence a full consumption bundle for her is a four-tuple $x = (a_0, b_0, a_1, b_1)$ where a_t is the amount of artichoke she consumes at date t and b_t is the amount of broccoli she consumes at date t, for $t = 0, 1$. We will refer to date zero as *today* and date one as *tomorrow*.

This consumer's preferences over vector consumption bundles x are given by some ordinal utility function $U(a_0, b_0, a_1, b_1)$. (We do not consider her preferences over lotteries of consumption for a while.)

We could imagine that at date zero markets are open in which this consumer can purchase any bundle x that she wishes (and can afford); that is, she can *forward contract* for artichoke and broccoli delivery tomorrow. This would make the choice problem that she faces a simple static problem in the style of chapter 2, and no complications would be encountered. But instead we imagine that today markets are open for current artichokes and broccoli; tomorrow new markets will open for then current artichokes and broccoli; and today the consumer has the ability to save (or borrow) money at a bank that she can withdraw (repay) tomorrow for purposes of subsequent consumption.[a] Using, say, dollars as the unit of account, we assume this consumer has $\$Y_0$ to spend or save today, and she will receive an additional $\$Y_1$ in income tomorrow, to which will be added any savings she may bring forward and from which will be subtracted any loans she must repay. We assume that the dollar prices of artichoke and broccoli are p_0^a and p_0^b today, the prices will be p_1^a and p_1^b tomorrow, and the bank with which our consumer deals will return r dollars tomorrow for every dollar invested today (or will give a dollar today in return for a promise to repay r dollars tomorrow).

Our consumer, knowing all this, thinks things through strategically.

(1) She must decide today how much artichoke and broccoli to consume today and how much to borrow from or lend to the bank. We use a_0 and b_0 for the first two decision variables, and we use z for her net position at the bank today, where $z > 0$ means that she loans z to the bank today and $z < 0$ means that she borrows $-z$ from the bank. We assume that she can consume only nonnegative amounts of vegetables, and so a_0 and b_0 are constrained to be nonnegative. And she has to finance all her purchases and banking activities with her current income Y_0; she faces the budget constraint

$$p_0^a a_0 + p_0^b b_0 + z \leq Y_0. \tag{BC1}$$

Note carefully the appearance of z in the budget constraint; if $z > 0$, she is saving money for tomorrow, and this increases her "expenditures" today,

---

[a] To keep matters simple, we assume that vegetables spoil very quickly, so any vegetables bought today must be consumed today; they cannot be left for consumption tomorrow.

whereas if $z < 0$, she has extra money to spend today, which loosens her budget constraint on vegetables.

(2) Tomorrow she must decide how much artichoke and how much broccoli to consume. Her resources for doing so will consist of her income tomorrow Y_1 and her net proceeds from the bank, rz. So tomorrow she anticipates she will choose a_1 and b_1 subject to the budget constraint

$$p_1^a a_1 + p_1^b b_1 \leq Y_1 + rz. \tag{BC2}$$

Note again that the sign of z is correct; if $z > 0$, she saved money in the first period, giving her more money to spend on vegetables tomorrow, whereas if $z < 0$, she borrowed, giving her less.

(3) Anticipating all this, our consumer recognizes that she can choose any bundle $x = (a_0, b_0, a_1, b_1)$ that she wishes, subject to the single budget constraint

$$p_0^a a_0 + p_0^b b_0 + (p_1^a / r) a_1 + (p_1^b / r) b_1 \leq Y_0 + (Y_1 / r). \tag{BC}$$

We obtain this single, combined budget constraint by moving the z to the right-hand side in (BC1), dividing (BC2) by r, and then adding the two.

The point is that we have turned the consumer's dynamic choice problem into a static choice problem of the sort discussed in chapter 2. We *presume* that our consumer will choose x subject to (BC) (and the implicit nonnegativity constraints) to maximize her utility from consumption. Once we obtain a solution to this static overall choice problem, we can work out how much the consumer has to save or borrow to implement the solution; that is, given the optimal levels of a_0 and b_0, the consumer will set $z = Y_0 - p_0^a a_0 - p_0^b b_0$ today.

This example illustrates the basic approach that is typically taken to dynamic choice. One imagines that the consumer looks ahead to all decisions that she will be called upon to make and considers her choice today as part of an overall strategy for choice. She works out what the consequences of each strategy will be in terms of an overall outcome; she considers her preferences over the possible overall outcomes; and she evaluates strategies accordingly. She chooses the optimal stategy according to her preferences and proceeds to carry out this strategy. The key implicit assumptions are that her preferences are for overall outcomes; these preferences on overall outcomes conform to a standard model of choice of the sort we explored in chapters 2 and 3, and they are stable through time. And the consumer is blessed with a farsighted strategic sense: She can foresee what her options will be in the future; how current decisions will affect later choices; what overall strategies she has available; and what the consequences of her strategic choices will be.

The example complicated with uncertainty

One should not be misled by the example into believing that the consumer's farsighted strategic sense implies that she possesses perfect foresight. There may be things about which she is uncertain, including the consequences of some of her actions. But she accommodates those with a model with uncertainty in the style of chapter 3. We can adapt our basic example to illustrate how this works.

Imagine that the consumer in our example can place her money not only in the bank but also in a risky asset that pays either $\bar{\theta}$ or $\underline{\theta}$ next period, each with probability $1/2$. (We assume $\bar{\theta} > r > \underline{\theta}$.) She cannot sell this risky asset short, although she can borrow money from the bank. Imagine as well that the consumer is uncertain about the price of artichokes tomorrow; the price will be $\bar{p}_1^a$ with probability $1/3$ and $\underline{p}_1^a$ with probability $2/3$. (We assume, to keep the example simple, that there is no uncertainty about the price of broccoli tomorrow.) Finally, the return on the risky asset and the price of artichokes are correlated: The joint probability that the price of artichokes will be $\bar{p}_1^a$ and the return on the risky asset will be $\bar{\theta}$ is $1/4$.

Since there is now uncertainty, we assume that our consumer's preferences over lotteries of consumption bundles x satisfy the assumptions of von Neumann-Morgenstern expected utility theory, and $u(x)$ is the consumer's von Neumann-Morgenstern utility function.

As in the simple example, our consumer thinks through her choice problem strategically.

(1) Today she must decide how much to consume, how much to invest in the risky asset, and how much to borrow or lend to the bank. We denote her consumption decision variables by a_0 and b_0 as before, and we let ζ be the amount of money she invests in the risky asset. All these must be nonnegative. Since our consumer always likes more to eat, we can safely

assume that she will satisfy her budget constraint today with equality. The amount she lends to the bank is, therefore,

$$z = Y_0 - \zeta - p_0^a a_0 - p_0^b b_0.$$

(Note that if $z < 0$, she is borrowing.)

(2) Next period both her assets and the prices of the consumption goods are random. Four "states" are possible: She has at her disposal $Y_1 + rz + \zeta\overline{\theta}$ and the price of artichokes is $\overline{p}_1^a$ with probability $1/4$; she has at her disposal $Y_1 + rz + \zeta\overline{\theta}$ and the price of artichokes is $\underline{p}_1^a$ with probability $1/4$; she has $Y_1 + rz + \zeta\underline{\theta}$ to spend and the price of artichokes is $\overline{p}_1^a$ with probability $1/12$; and she has $Y_1 + rz + \zeta\underline{\theta}$ and the price of artichokes is $\underline{p}_1^a$ with probability $5/12$.[1]

We assume that our consumer will know which of these four situations prevails when she must decide how to allocate her resources between artichokes and broccoli tomorrow. Thus she has eight decision variables tomorrow: How much artichoke and how much broccoli to consume in the first state (as a function of her decisions today, since they determine the resources she has to spend on vegetables tomorrow); how much to consume in the second state; and so on. Since she always likes more vegetable to less, we can reduce the problem to four decision variables for tomorrow. Given the amount of artichoke she purchases in the first state a_1^1, where the subscript pertains to time and the superscript to state one, it can be assumed that her broccoli consumption will be

$$b_1^1 = \frac{Y_1 + rz + \zeta\overline{\theta} - a_1^1\overline{p}_1^a}{p_1^b},$$

and so on for states 2, 3, and 4, making the appropriate substitutions for $\overline{\theta}$ and for $\overline{p}_1^a$.[b]

(3) So we have her decision problem down to a seven variable problem: a_0, b_0, ζ, and a_1^n for $n = 1, 2, 3, 4$. Given values for these seven decision

---

[1] Where did these probabilities come from? This is the first time in the book that we have a two-by-two outcome space and you are given the two marginal distributions and one joint probability, but it is very far from the last. If you have any problems replicating these probabilities from the data given a couple of paragraphs ago, seek assistance immediately!

[b] Of course, when we eliminate the decision variables b_1^n in this fashion, the nonnegativity constraints on these variables must be incorporated as more constraints on the decision variables that we leave in the problem. For example, the constraint $b_1^1 \geq 0$, which is $[Y_1 + rz + \zeta\overline{\theta} - a_1^1\overline{p}_1^a]/p_1^b \geq 0$, is reexpressed as $Y_1 + rz + \zeta\overline{\theta} \geq a_1^1\overline{p}_1^a$.

variables, we can work out our consumer's expected utility of consumption; just for the record, this is a sum of four terms, the first of which (for the first state) is

$$\frac{1}{4}u\left(a_0, b_0, a_1^1, \frac{Y_1 + r[Y_0 - \zeta - p_0^a a_0 - p_0^b b_0] + \zeta\overline{\theta} - a_1^1 \overline{p}_1^a}{p_1^b}\right).$$

(This is the probability $1/4$ of the first state times our consumer's von Neumann-Morgenstern utility of consumption in the first state, as a function of her decisions. Be sure you could have come up with this term and you know what the other three are.) We have nonnegativity constraints to watch for, and the nonnegativity constraints on tomorrow's broccoli consumption in each of the four states become nonnegativity constraints on the fourth argument of u above and its mates. But given all this, if we have u, we have a perfectly well-posed static optimization problem to solve. This isn't as simple a problem as in the first example; in particular, we aren't able to reduce the problem to a problem with a single budget constraint. But it is still an optimization problem that can be solved without much difficulty.

As in the simpler version of the problem, we are following the basic pattern of reducing the dynamic problem to a static problem of finding an optimal strategy. A strategy here is a seven-tuple (subject to some constraints); for each strategy we know how to evaluate its consequences in terms of overall expected utility; and we assume that our consumer selects what to consume and how to invest today and tomorrow in a way that is consistent with the optimal overall strategy so determined. This is the standard approach to dynamic choice in microeconomic theory.

At this point we can take two paths in further developments and discussion. The usual path is to begin to think about how we might effectively solve optimization problems such as the one just posed. The mathematical technique of *dynamic programming* is especially useful here. An unusual path is to wonder about alternatives to the standard way of modeling dynamic choice. We will proceed in this chapter along the unusual path, on the assumption that you have either already followed or will follow the former. Appendix 2 gives a brief summary of the parts of dynamic programming that are important in this book; all readers should know about finite horizon dynamic programming, which is discussed in the first two sections of appendix 2. And readers who consume all the small type will need to know a bit about solving problems with infinite horizons, which is covered in the second two sections of appendix 2. In case you wish to test your knowledge of these topics, problem 3 provides the appropriate diagnostic.

4.2. Menus and meals

A context

Rather than work with the dynamic consumption budgeting problem of the previous section, we will work with a simpler, discrete setting. As in the previous section, we look at a two-period problem, with dates $t = 0$ (today) and $t = 1$ (tomorrow). Tomorrow the consumer will find herself at a restaurant, and she will select some meal from the menu that restaurant offers. Today the consumer selects the restaurant, which (effectively) comes down to choosing the menu from which choice will be made tomorrow. To keep matters simple, we will assume that menu items are completely described by the entrée served, and the same entrée at two different restaurants is the same meal. Atmosphere, the chef's skills, etc., all come to naught; the only difference between menus/restaurants is in the menus of meals that they offer.

Formally, we suppose that the set of all possible entrées is given by some finite set X, and the set of all possible menus is the set of all nonempty subsets of X, which we denote by M. Today our consumer has her choice from some subset of M; we write M' for this set of feasible menus. And if she chooses $m \in M'$ today, then tomorrow she chooses some x from m.

This is, to be sure, a very stylized example. But for the examples we wish to present, it captures the salient aspect of dynamic choice: Choice today constrains the *opportunity set* from which one subsequently chooses. (Another aspect of how choice today affects subsequent choice is by changing one's later tastes. This is something we will miss in our examples but which you will see briefly in problem 5.) If the reader's imagination is fired by the toy examples we give next, more realistic applications will not be hard to imagine.

The standard, strategic approach

To develop alternatives to the standard approach, we first see what the standard approach would look like in this context. It is quite simple. We assume that the consumer has preferences defined on the space of "final consumption" X. These preferences will be assumed to satisfy the standard properties and (since X is finite) to be represented by some (ordinal) utility function $U : X \to R$. The consumer, looking at all the menus in M', considers that a strategy for dynamic choice is to choose first an $m \in M'$ and then some $x \in m$, which has consequences x. Thus she has available to herself any meal $x \in X' = \bigcup_{m \in M'} m$. If we let x^* be the meal in X' that has the greatest utility (according to the index U), our consumer plans to choose x^*, and she begins carrying out this plan by choosing any $m \in M'$ that contains x^*. As we said, this is simplicity itself.

We can take a step in this context that we didn't take in the first section and ask what consequences this model of dynamic choice has for our consumer's static choice behavior today. The consumer's choice behavior today is represented quite simply: Comparing any two menus m and m', she strictly prefers m to m' if and only if the U-best meal in m is strictly better than the U-best meal in m'. That is, if we define a function $V : M \to R$ from U by

$$V(m) = \max_{x \in m} U(x),$$

then V is a numerical representation of our consumer's static preferences over menus.

Note that V so defined has the property that if $V(m) \geq V(m')$, then $V(m \cup m') = V(m)$. In words, if m is at least as good as m', then $m \cup m'$ is indifferent to m. Or, in symbols, if we let $\succ$ denote preferences *defined on* M according to V (and we use $\succeq$ for weak preferences and $\sim$ for indifference), we have

$$m \succeq m' \text{ implies } m \sim m \cup m'. \tag{$\clubsuit$}$$

Note well, $\succ$ is preferences defined on M; other, closely related preferences are defined on X and represented by U.

Revealed preference and the standard model

Now we can turn the questions we've been asking somewhat on their heads. Following the standard approach to dynamic choice, we've looked at the problem from the point of view of the consumer; what should she do today and subsequently in view of her overall objectives (where it is a maintained assumption that she has overall objectives). Suppose we observe a consumer making choices today and we ask: Does this choice behavior *reveal* that she is acting according to the standard model, or does it refute that model?

Suppose that we are in the enviable position of having quite a lot of data with which to answer this question. Specifically, suppose we know the consumer's preferences $\succ$ defined on M. Since, in the standard model, $\succ$ has a numerical representation V, we know that it is necessary (if the standard model is to apply) that the consumer's preferences are asymmetric and negatively transitive. Moreover, the previous discussion indicates that ($\clubsuit$) is a necessary condition for the standard model. In fact, these conditions are sufficient.

Proposition 4.1. *A consumer's preferences $\succ$ on M are asymmetric, negatively transitive, and satisfy ($\clubsuit$) if and only if the consumer's preferences arise from some function $U : X \to R$ according to the standard model (as sketched in the previous subsection).*[c]

Our statement of this proposition is no model of mathematical elegance, but its meaning should be clear. The standard model generates very specific "testable restrictions" on static choice behavior on M. When we observe individuals who choose today in ways that are inconsistent with those restrictions, we have individuals whose choice behavior is inconsistent with the standard model.

The weak-willed dieter

With this as prologue, we can give our first example of choice behavior that is inconsistent with the standard model. Imagine that X consists of precisely two meals, *fish* and *pasta*. Hence M contains three elements: $\{fish, pasta\}$, $\{fish\}$, and $\{pasta\}$. Consider a consumer whose static choice behavior is given by the preferences

$$\{fish\} \succ \{fish, pasta\} \sim \{pasta\}.$$

This consumer's preferences (on M) satisfy the standard assumptions on M; that is, her strict preferences are asymmetric and negatively transitive. But she strictly prefers the *fish* only menu to the menu that gives her a choice of *fish* or *pasta*. It is obvious that this doesn't conform to ($\clubsuit$), so the standard model doesn't apply.

But our consumer has a very simple explanation: She is on a diet and is weak-willed. Today, as she chooses the menu from which she will later choose a meal, her will is strong and she knows that she should avoid *pasta*. And she knows that when it comes to the event and she must choose a meal, her will will weaken; if *pasta* is available, she will choose it. Hence

---

[c] You are asked to prove this in problem 4. It isn't hard.

she prefers to choose today in a way that eliminates the opportunity to choose *pasta* tomorrow.

This is an example of what is called *sophisticated choice when a change in tastes is anticipated*. References to the literature in which this sort of model is developed are given in the next section, but it is hard to resist giving an early example. Odysseus, when sailing past the Isle of the Sirens, wishing to hear their song but at the same time wishing not to give in to their spell, had himself lashed to the mast. This behavior, which showed a clear preference for smaller opportunity sets, cannot be explained by the standard model of dynamic choice in economics.

Uncertain future tastes and maintained flexibility

Our second example concerns a case in which three meals are possible, $X = \{chicken, fish, pasta\}$, and a consumer whose immediate preferences over M are given by

$$\{chicken, fish, pasta\} \succ \{chicken, fish\} \sim \{chicken, pasta\}$$
$$\sim \{fish, pasta\} \succ \{chicken\}$$
$$\succ \{fish\} \succ \{pasta\}.$$

Again we have static (strict) preferences that are asymmetric and negatively transitive. And again we find (♣) violated; $\{chicken\} \succ \{fish\}$, and so if (♣) were to hold, we would require that $\{chicken\} \sim \{chicken, fish\}$. Indeed, if (♣) holds, then some single-element set would necessarily be indifferent to the menu containing all the options. And that certainly doesn't hold here.

The explanation offered by our consumer in this case is again a simple story. She is uncertain what her tastes will be when she sits down to dine tomorrow. Perhaps she will like *chicken* most of all, then *fish*, and then *pasta*. But perhaps her preferences will be *fish*, then *chicken*, and then *pasta*. And perhaps they will be *pasta*, then *chicken*, and then *fish*. She believes that each of these is as likely as any other and she evaluates a menu as follows: Given the menu and her (then) preferences, she gets three utils if her first choice is available, two utils if her second choice is the best available, and only one if all she can have is her third choice. If you compute "expected utils" by this scheme, you will come to the preferences above.

The reader is entitled to object that we are introducing uncertainty into the story surreptitiously. Had we mentioned this uncertainty about future preferences at the start, we wouldn't have expected (♣) to be necessary and sufficient for the standard model. This objection is accepted, but then let us turn the question around: Which preference relations $\succ$ on M can we explain by the "standard model" where we allow the endogenous incorporation of this sort of uncertainty?

Proposition 4.2. *Assume X is finite. A (strict) preference relation $\succ$ on M is asymmetric and negatively transitive and, for the associated weak preference and indifference relations $\succeq$ and $\sim$, satisfies*

$$m \supseteq m' \text{ implies } m \succeq m', \text{ and} \tag{$\star$}$$

$$m \supseteq m' \text{ and } m \sim m' \text{ implies } m \cup m'' \sim m' \cup m'' \text{ for all } m'', \tag{$\star\star$}$$

if and only if there is a finite set S and a function $u : S \times X \to R$ such that

$$m \succ m' \text{ if and only if } \sum_{s \in S} \max_{x \in m} u(s, x) > \sum_{s \in S} \max_{x \in m'} u(s, x).$$

We won't attempt to prove this here; it is here only for purposes of illustration and doesn't reappear later in the book.[2] But let us interpret it. We start with preferences $\succ$ on menus that, when you think of menus as the basic objects, satisfy the standard assumptions of chapter 2. In addition, our consumer always (at least weakly) prefers to leave herself with more choices (which is ($\star$)). And if more choices are of no value in some situation, adding more options "to both sides" doesn't make those original extra options valuable. (This is a rough description of ($\star\star$).) Then (and only then) can we justify this consumer's preferences over menus by a model with preferences over meals that depend on some implicit "states of future preferences" and where preferences for menus are obtained by adding up the utility of the "best" meal the menu provides in each state.

4.3. Bibliographic notes and discussion

To repeat from before, the standard approach to dynamic choice consists of reducing dynamic choice to a problem of static choice of an optimal strategy under the presumptions that (1) the consumer at each point in time has coherent preferences over overall outcomes; (2) she believes at each point in time that these preferences will not shift with time or circumstances; (3) she is smart enough to work out the consequences of her

---

[2] For a proof, see Kreps (1979).

choices, so she can find an optimal strategy according to the preferences assumed in (1); and (4) the second presumption is correct in the sense that the consumer subsequently carries out the optimal strategy she is assumed to find. This approach is ingrained in almost all microeconomic theory, so much so that it is often employed in textbooks without any discussion whatsoever. This is something of a retreat from the careful consideration given to these issues in seminal work on the theory of choice; see, for example, the discussion and justification of the standard approach given by Savage (1972, 15-17).

It is probably safe to assume that, for at least some consumers, tastes and desires shift as time passes; (4) is likely to be false. Grant for the moment that a consumer for whom this is so has coherent preferences at each point in time. That is, grant (1). And grant that she can work out the consequences of her actions, or (3). Granting (1) and (3), one can wonder whether she acts under the "false" presumption of (2) or not. If she assumes (2) and acts accordingly, then her static behavior at each point in time will look sensible according to the standard approach to dynamic choice, but her dynamic actions will be inconsistent. On the other hand, if she is sophisticated enough to deny (2), and if her current tastes govern her actions, she may act as does our weak-willed dieter, so that her static choice does not conform to the standard model. These sorts of issues are discussed and attacked generally in the literature on changing tastes. A sampler of this literature (taking various positions on the value of such models) would include Strotz (1955-56), Peleg and Yaari (1973), Hammond (1976), Stigler and Becker (1977), and Thaler (1980).

Suppose that we rejected assumption (3) of the standard approach — that individuals are able to foresee all the consequences of their actions. How then can we possibly model dynamic choice behavior? Consider the following general scheme: (a) Model choice at each given point of time according to the basic models of choice of chapters 2 and 3, with strict preferences that are asymmetric and negatively transitive, and so on. But model choice at a given point in time as choice over things that are chosen *at that time only* so that, for example, one incorporates in the description of an item chosen the opportunities that current choice leaves for later choice. When doing this, (b) pay attention to how the individual's bounded rationality might affect what static choices she does make, especially if she is aware of her own limitations. And then, (c) consider how choice behavior at different points in time might or might not fit together.

Our second nonstandard example is somewhat of this character. We can imagine that our consumer, choosing a menu, can't conceive of all the consequences of her choice of menu. But still, at the level of selecting a menu, she has "standard preferences." That is, she satisfies (a). Because of her inability to conceive of all the consequences of her choice of menu, she generally prefers to leave herself with more flexibility. That is, her preferences over menus satisfy (⋆) of proposition 4.2, as an example of what we intend for (b). Then if her static preferences conform as well to (⋆⋆), we have from the proposition a fairly nice (and quite standard looking) representation of her preferences over menus, a representation that was originally suggested by Koopmans (1964). And we could imagine considering how her static preferences at different points of time might evolve.

If we admit the possibility that the consumer is limitedly rational in the sense the she cannot foresee all the consequences of her current decisions, this in itself might lead us to reject the approach just sketched on grounds that *even* her static choice behavior might fail to conform to the usual assumptions; her inability to work out strategic plans in a complex, dynamic environment leads her immediate choice by rules of thumb (or serendipity) that cannot be represented by a single numerical index. Even at this level one can pursue interesting models of static (and then dynamic) choice: For example, Bewley (1986) suggests a model where once a consumer has chosen a strategic plan of action, she will deviate from that plan (as unexpected options arise) only if some alternative seems substantially better than the status quo plan. Bewley formalizes this with a model where static weak preferences are not complete and with an "inertia" assumption that gives precedence to the status quo, and he considers how this would affect dynamic choice behavior.

Having mentioned these possible alternatives to the standard approach to dynamic choice, we will follow the standard approach until the end of the book. This discussion is meant to accomplish two things: To make you aware of the strong assumptions that go into the standard approach; and to indicate that interesting alternatives to the standard approach are possible. These alternatives are, at the time that I write this, very far from mainstream microeconomic theory. But when we delve later in the book into the serious deficiences of the techniques of the current mainstream theory, we will return to issues in dynamic choice and to the very strong assumptions of the standard approach.

References

Bewley, T. 1986. "Knightian Decision Theory: Part I." Cowles Foundation discussion paper no. 807, Yale University. Mimeo.

Hammond, P. 1976. "Changing Tastes and Coherent Dynamic Choice." *Review of Economic Studies* 43:159–73.

Koopmans, T. 1964. "On the Flexibility of Future Preferences." In *Human Judgments and Optimality*, M. Shelly and G. Bryan, eds. New York: John Wiley and Sons.

Kreps, D. 1979. "A Representation Theorem for Preference for Flexibility." *Econometrica* 47:565–77.

Peleg, B., and M. Yaari. 1973. "On the Existence of a Consistent Course of Action when Tastes Are Changing." *Review of Economic Studies* 40:391–401.

Savage, L. [1954] 1972. *The Foundations of Statistics*. New York: John Wiley and Sons. Rev. and enl. ed. New York: Dover Publications.

Stigler, G., and G. Becker. 1977. "De Gustibus Non Est Disputandum." *American Economic Review* 67:76–90.

Strotz, R. 1955–1956. "Myopia and Inconsistency in Dynamic Utility Maximization." *Review of Economic Studies* 23:165–80.

Thaler, R. 1980. "Toward a Positive Theory of Consumer Choice." *Journal of Economic Behavior and Organization* 1:39–60.

4.4. Problems

■ 1. (a) Consider the first example, in which the consumer must decide how much artichoke and broccoli to consume today and tomorrow and how much to save (or borrow) today, where there is no uncertainty. Suppose the consumer's preferences are given by the utility function

$$U(a_0, b_0, a_1, b_1) = \ln(a_0) + .9\ln(b_0) + .8\ln(a_1) + .7\ln(b_1).$$

Solve this consumer's dynamic consumption–savings problem, as a function of prices p_0^a, p_0^b, p_1^a, and p_1^b, the gross return r on loans to/from the bank, and the consumer's incomes Y_0 and Y_1. Recall that we assume that the consumer can borrow or lend at gross return r.

(b) Suppose we assumed that the consumer could only lend money at rate r but cannot borrow at all. What is the solution in this case?

■ 2. Suppose in the problem described in problem 1(a) that the consumer is able to store vegetables from today to tomorrow. Assume there is no spoilage or anything like that — vegetable put in the refrigerator today and taken out for consumption tomorrow is just as good as vegetable bought fresh tomorrow. What is the solution to the consumer's dynamic consumption-savings problem?

■ 3. *Part (a) tests your knowledge of finite horizon dynamic programming. If you cannot do this problem using the techniques of dynamic programming, consult the first two sections of appendix 2. (The analysis of this problem is given there in detail, so try the problem before looking at the appendix.) Part (b) tests your knowledge of infinite horizon dynamic programming. This is a good deal more difficult, and you will only need the skills required to solve this for some optional material in later chapters. But if you are curious, this problem is worked out in detail in the second two sections of appendix 2.*

(a) A consumer lives for three periods, denoted by $t = 0, 1, 2$, and consumes artichoke and broccoli on each day. We let a_t be the amount of artichoke consumed on day t and b_t be the amount of broccoli. This consumer has preferences over lotteries on consumption bundles (where a consumption bundle is a six-tuple $(a_0, b_0, a_1, b_1, a_2, b_2)$), which satisfy the von Neumann-Morgenstern axioms and are represented by the von Neumann-Morgenstern utility function

$$U(a_0, b_0, a_1, b_1, a_2, b_2) = (a_0 b_0)^{.25} + .9(a_1 b_1)^{.25} + .8(a_2 b_2)^{.25}.$$

This consumer can buy artichoke and broccoli in the marketplace each day. Because both vegetables spoil rapidly, what he buys on any given day is his consumption for that day. (He is constrained to consume nonnegative amounts of each vegetable.) The price of artichoke is $1 per unit on each and every day. The price of broccoli is more complex: It begins as $1 per unit of broccoli at $t = 0$. But at $t = 1$, it is either $1.10 or $.90, each of these being equally likely. And at $t = 2$, the price of broccoli is again random and depends on the price the day before: If its price was $1.10 at $t = 1$, then it is either $1.20 or $1.00, with each equally likely. If its price was $.90 at $t = 1$, then at $t = 2$ it is either $.98 or $.80, each equally likely. At date $t = 0$, the consumer has no information (beyond what is given above) about subsequent prices of broccoli. At date $t = 1$, he knows the current price of broccoli and no more. At date $t = 2$, he knows the current price.

This consumer has $300 to spend on artichoke and broccoli over the three days, which he can divide any way he wishes. Any money he doesn't spend on a given day sits in his pocket where it earns zero interest.

(b) Imagine that our consumer eats at times $t = 0, 1, 2, \ldots$. At each date, he consumes both artichoke and broccoli. His utility function, defined for an infinite stream of consumption $(a_0, b_0, a_1, b_1, \ldots)$ is

$$U(a_0, b_0, a_1, b_1, \ldots) = \sum_{t=0}^{\infty} (.95)^t (a_t b_t)^{.25}.$$

This consumer starts out with wealth $1,000, which he can spend on vegetable or can deposit in his local bank. Any funds deposited at the bank earn interest at a rate of 2% per period, so that $1 deposited at time t turns into $1.02 at time $t+1$.

The price of artichoke is fixed at $1. The price of broccoli is random. It begins at $1. Then, in each period, it either increases or decreases. Being very specific, if the price of broccoli at date t is p_t,

$$p_{t+1} = \begin{cases} 1.1 p_t & \text{with probability .5, and} \\ .9 p_t & \text{with probability .5.} \end{cases}$$

The consumer wishes to manage his initial wealth $1,000 in a way that maximizes his expected utility. How should he do this?

■ 4. Prove proposition 4.1.

■ 5. Consider the consumer in the first example of this chapter, where we specialize to the case in which $p_0^a = p_0^b = p_1^a = p_1^b = r = 1$, and $Y_0 = Y_1 = 3$. Suppose that this consumer is a standard sort of consumer (in microeconomic theory), with preferences given by the utility function

$$U(a_0, b_0, a_1, b_1) = \ln(a_0) + \ln(b_0) + \ln(a_1) + \ln(b_1).$$

(a) What is the solution to this consumer's consumption-savings problem, under the assumption that she is a completely normal consumer?

But this is not a normal consumer. She is quite abnormal, in that she is susceptible to becoming addicted to broccoli! Specifically, if she eats (a_0, b_0) today, then tomorrow when she goes to purchase vegetables, she chooses according to the utility function

$$U^1(a_1, b_1; a_0, b_0) = \ln(a_1) + b_0 \ln(b_1).$$

Note well what is going on here; the more broccoli she consumes today, the more she values broccoli consumption tomorrow.

(b) Assume that this consumer seeks to consume and save today in a fashion that will maximize her U-utility over the consumption bundle x that she chooses dynamically, and she realizes that tomorrow she will spend her resources in a way that maximizes her U^1-utility. What does she (optimally) consume and save today, and what is the overall outcome that she achieves?

chapter five

Social choice and efficiency

So far we have discussed the choice behavior of a single consumer, both in general and in market settings. For the rest of this book, we are interested in what happens when many consumers are choosing simultaneously. Each consumer will come with the sorts of preferences we described in chapters 2 and 3, and each attempts to choose in an optimal fashion given those preferences. It will typically happen that the diverse preferences of consumers will be in conflict with each other. (For example, each consumer typically wants "more" at the expense of the consumption of his fellow consumers.) We will be looking at various *institutional arrangements* by which those conflicts are meant to be resolved. But before moving to institutional arrangements, we look briefly at the abstract *theory of social choice*.

The theory of social choice is concerned with the selection of some *social outcome* that affects a number of individuals, when those individuals have diverse and conflicting preferences. We try to characterize desirable properties of the outcome that is to be selected, properties that usually involve (and blend) notions of *efficiency* and *equity*. In some cases, those properties are insufficient to fix on a single social outcome, but instead restrict attention to some subset of the feasible outcomes. Adding more properties can sometimes pin down a single social outcome that has all the desired attributes. And in some contexts we find that there is no way to satisfy simultaneously all the properties thought to be desirable.

We will not do justice to this very broad topic here. In this chapter we will acquaint you with a few of the basic notions, with emphasis on the concept of efficiency, and we will give a smattering of the classic results. But we only scratch the surface.

5.1. The problem

We begin by formulating the problem in a very general setting. A finite number of individual consumers, indexed by $i = 1, 2, \ldots, I$, make up a society. Each member x of a set X of *social outcomes* describes how every member of this society is treated. Each consumer has preferences over the possible social outcomes. We assume that these preferences can be represented numerically, and we let $V_i : X \to R$ represent i's preferences.

We are interested, ultimately, in answering the question: For each subset $X' \subset X$ of *feasible social outcomes*, which social outcome(s) should be selected? Following our general approach to choice, along the way we will be making binary comparisons — trying to say when one outcome is better than another. [a]

Utility imputations

Fixing specific numerical representations for the preferences of each consumer, to each social outcome x there corresponds a vector of utilities $v = (V_1(x), V_2(x), \ldots, V_I(x)) \in R^I$ for the I consumers. We call such a vector of utility levels a *utility imputation*. Given a set X' of feasible social outcomes, there is a corresponding set of feasible utility imputations. For each social outcome x, we write $V(x)$ for the I-dimensional vector $(V_1(x), V_2(x), \ldots, V_I(x))$, and for a set X' of feasible social outcomes, we will write $V(X')$ for the set of *feasible utility imputations*:

$$V(X') = \{v \in R^I \ : \ v = V(x) \text{ for some } x \in X'\}.$$

Pictures of feasible utility imputations for the case of two consumers will be used below, so we give a couple of examples in figure 5.1. In 5.1(a) the

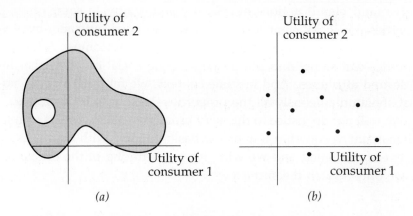

Figure 5.1. Feasible utility imputations for two-consumer societies.

---

[a] Be a bit sceptical here. Just because individual choice is typically modeled as being driven by such binary comparisons is no reason to suppose that when it comes to social choice this approach ought to be taken. We will discuss this point.

shaded area gives one typical picture, while the finite collection of points in figure 5.1(b) corresponds to a case in which the set X' is finite. Of course, these pictures are all relative to specific numerical representations of the preferences of individual consumers; as we change those representations, we make corresponding changes in pictures such as those in figure 5.1.

Exchange of commodities

The general problem just described may be a bit too abstract to think about, so let us sketch a more concrete setting. Imagine K commodities; write Z for the positive orthant in R^K; and assume that each consumer i consumes some bundle $z \in Z$. Exactly as in chapter 2, imagine that consumer i has preferences for his own levels of consumption, given by a utility function $U_i : Z \to R$.

A social outcome, in this case, is a vector $x = (z_1, \ldots, z_I) \in X = Z^I$, which specifies the bundle z_1 that consumer 1 consumes, the bundle z_2 that consumer 2 consumes, and so on. Note that each z_i is itself a (nonnegative) K-dimensional vector.

The preferences of consumer i over social outcomes x in this case are represented by the function V_i, with domain X, defined by

$$V_i(x) = U_i(z_i), \text{ where } x = (z_1, \ldots, z_I).$$

Note well, in this specialization the preferences of consumer i depend by assumption only on what consumer i consumes; consumer i's preferences do not depend on what is consumed by anyone else. In our general formulation of the problem this assumption is not imposed, and it may seem to you a pretty silly assumption (unless you have taken economics courses before and so are properly socialized into the discipline). But this is an assumption that will play a critical role in developments in chapter 6.

As for the set of feasible social outcomes in this specification, it is typical to imagine that society has at its disposal a given stack of consumption goods, called the *social endowment* and represented by an element $e \in Z$, which can be divided among the I consumers. So the set of feasible social outcomes, in this context called the set of *feasible allocations* (of society's resources), is

$$Z' = \{x = (z_1, \ldots, z_I) \in Z^I \ : \ z_1 + \ldots + z_I \leq e\}.$$

Note that the sum of what is allocated to the consumers is required to be *less or equal to* the social endowment; if one or more of the goods is noxious and we can't dispose freely of this good, then we might wish to replace the inequality with an equality.

The Edgeworth box

For the case of two consumers and two goods, a standard picture of this situation is drawn, known as an *Edgeworth box*. We label the two consumers 1 and 2 and the two goods a and b, and we write $x = ((z_{1a}, z_{1b}), (z_{2a}, z_{2b}))$. Consider figure 5.2. In figure 5.2(a), we represent the preferences of consumer 1 by the usual indifference curve diagram. Note the heavy dot; this is meant to be the location of the social endowment $e = (e_a, e_b)$.

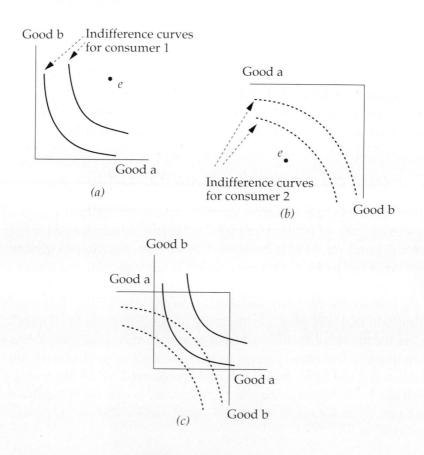

Figure 5.2. Edgeworth boxes.
Figures 5.2(a) and (b) give the two sets of data that make up an *Edgeworth box*: the social endowment and the indifference curves of the two parties, in (a) for consumer 1 and in (b) for 2. In figure 5.2(c) the indifference curves are superimposed.

In figure 5.2(b) the preferences of consumer 2 are represented by the usual indifference curve diagram, except that we have rotated the usual picture by 180 degrees and have put the origin "up" at the level of e in figure 5.2(a), so the social endowment e in this picture is down at the level of the origin in figure 5.2(a).

Given e, what are the feasible allocations? They are all allocations x such that $z_{1a} + z_{2a} \leq e_a$ and $z_{1b} + z_{2b} \leq e_b$. Since (according to figure 5.2) our consumers always prefer more of either good to less, let us restrict attention to allocations where none of the social endowment is wasted — where the two inequalities above are equalities. Then given z_{1a} and z_{1b} (and holding e fixed), we know that $z_{2a} = e_a - z_{1a}$ and $z_{2b} = e_b - z_{1b}$.

In figure 5.2(c), we have all this recorded very neatly and compactly. First, note that we have superimposed figures 5.2(a) and (b), locating the origin of consumer 2's coordinate system at the point e in consumer 1's coordinate system so that e in 2's coordinates is the origin in 1's coordinate system. Then the box formed by the two sets of axes represents all the feasible allocations of e (assuming no wastage of the social endowment); each point (z_{1a}, z_{1b}) in 1's coordinate system is at the same time the point $(e_a - z_{1a}, e_b - z_{1b})$ in 2's coordinate system.

5.2. Pareto efficiency and optimality: Definitions

Return to the general setting of the first part of section 5.1. That is, there is a set X of social outcomes and I consumers whose preferences over the social outcomes are represented by functions V_i. We begin with pairwise comparisons of two social outcomes x and x'.

Definitions. *Outcome x is said to be **Pareto superior** to outcome x' if $V_i(x) \geq V_i(x')$ for every consumer i, with a strict inequality for at least one i. Outcome x is said to be **strictly Pareto superior** to x' if $V_i(x) > V_i(x')$ for all i.*

Or, in words, one outcome is Pareto superior to another if no consumer finds the first any worse than the second and at least one consumer finds the first strictly better. And the first is strictly Pareto superior to the second if every consumer strictly prefers the first. In such cases, we also say that the second outcome is (strictly) Pareto *inferior* to the first.

It should be carefully noted that Pareto superiority is a *partial ordering* of social outcomes, in general. That is, we might have two social outcomes x and x' such that some consumers strictly prefer x to x' and others strictly prefer x' to x. In such cases, we would say that x and x' are Pareto *incomparable*.

It is easy to see Pareto superiority and inferiority in pictures of utility imputations for two consumers such as figure 5.1. The outcome x is Pareto superior to x' if the corresponding utility imputation $V(x)$ is above and/or to the right of $V(x')$. And x is strictly Pareto superior to x' if $V(x)$ is above *and* to the right of $V(x')$.

Definitions. *Given a set X' of feasible social outcomes, an outcome $x \in X'$ is said to be **Pareto efficient** or Pareto optimal in X' if no other feasible outcome $x' \in X'$ is Pareto superior to x. The subset of Pareto efficient outcomes in X' is called the **Pareto frontier** of X'.*

In the definition of Pareto efficiency, a fine point arises concerning whether Pareto inferiority or strict Pareto inferiority should be the criterion by which a point is disqualified. That is, suppose we have a point x which is Pareto dominated by some other feasible point x', but which is not strictly Pareto inferior to any feasible point. Should we say that x' is Pareto efficient? In the definition we have given, we do not. But in other treatments of this subject, such a point would be included. This is a place where you have to watch carefully the definitions that are made.

Pareto efficiency is easy to see in pictures of utility imputations. Consider the sets of feasible utility imputations in figure 5.3. These are just the same as in figure 5.1. In both 5.3(a) and (b) we show a utility imputation marked v', which is not Pareto efficient, and another marked v, which

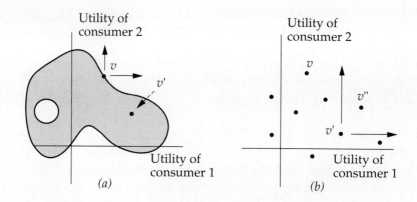

Figure 5.3. Pareto efficiency in the space of utility imputations.
In each figure, the point marked v is Pareto efficient and the point marked v' is not.

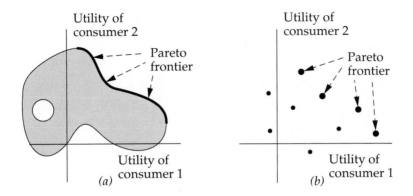

Figure 5.4. *Pareto frontiers in the space of utility imputations.*
In (a), the Pareto frontier is the heavy curve. In (b), points on the Pareto
frontier are the heavier dots.

is.[1]   In each case there is a simple test.   From any utility imputation,
say v in 5.3(a), draw a "positive orthant" with origin at v. If no feasible
utility imputation falls in this orthant (including its edges), then v is Pareto
efficient.   In figure 5.3(b) we do the same thing for v', and we see, by
virtue of the point v'', which is Pareto superior to v', that v' is not Pareto
efficient.   In figure 5.4 we draw in (with a heavy curve in [a], and with
heavier dots in [b]), the two Pareto frontiers.

Pareto efficiency and the Edgeworth box

To illustrate these notions, consider the Edgeworth box depicted in
figure 5.5(a).   Consider in particular the points x and x' marked there.
From the point x', it is possible to find points that give more utility to
each of the two consumers — the set of points for which this is true is the
set of points in the shaded lens-shaped area. On the other hand, the point
x, which lies at a point of tangency of the two consumer's indifference
curves, is Pareto efficient. To make one consumer better off (staying along
or above the consumer's indifference curve through x), you must go into a
region that is below the indifference curve of the other consumer through
x. Thus x is Pareto efficient and x' is not.

We draw the corresponding pictures of utility imputations in figure
5.5(b). We show both $v' = V(x')$ and $v = V(x)$. Note that v is on the Pareto
frontier and v' is not. (Test your understanding of this picture by answer-

---

[1] We will work simultaneously with social states and their utility imputations. And we
will abuse the language and use terms such as *Pareto efficiency, Pareto superiority*, and *Pareto
frontier* both for social states and for their utility imputations.

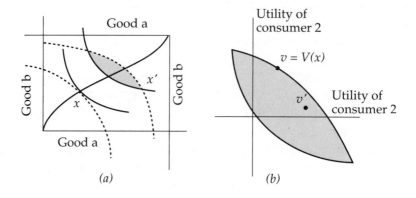

Figure 5.5. Pareto efficiency and Edgeworth boxes.
In (a), we show a Pareto efficient point x, an inefficient point x', and (the heavy line) the Pareto frontier or contract curve. The points v and v' in utility imputation space corresponding to x and x' are shown in (b).

ing: Where in figure 5.5[b] do you find utility imputations corresponding to the shaded lens shaped area in figure 5.5[a]?)

Finally, returning to figure 5.5(a), note the heavy line passing through x. This is the set of points at which the indifference curves of the two consumers are tangent; hence this is the Pareto frontier for this Edgeworth box. When dealing with Edgeworth boxes, the Pareto frontier is often called the *contract curve*.

> One variation on the picture in 5.5(a) should be mentioned. We have characterized the contract curve as the set of points in the Edgeworth box for which the two indifference curves through the points are tangent. You should try to draw a picture where this characterization doesn't work, because the point in question is against a boundary of the box, corresponding to a non-negativity constraint for the consumption of some good by some consumer. In general, the contract curve is defined to be those points that are Pareto efficient in the box; the "tangent indifference curves" characterization is only used informally.

5.3. Benevolent social dictators and social welfare functionals

Imagine that you, an outsider (not one of the consumers), have been appointed dictator for a given society; it is up to you to select a social outcome from among those feasible. We will suppose that you wish to be a benevolent dictator, and we explore what might be said about how you should choose.

An obvious first question is whether we should expect that your choice can be rationalized by some (asymmetric and negatively transitive) preference relation $\succ$ on the set X of social outcomes. To see why this might not be such a reasonable thing, suppose there are three individuals in this society and two feasible outcomes: $X' = \{x, x'\}$. Suppose that two of the consumers strictly prefer x to x' and one strictly prefers x' to x. You might worry about the relative strengths of these strict preferences, but such interpersonal comparisons may be difficult to make, and so you might reasonably suppose that you should select x. But now imagine that a third option is available, x''. The first two consumers rank $x \succ x' \succ x''$ while the third ranks $x' \succ x'' \succ x$. Since everyone prefers x' to x'', it seems unreasonable that you would select x''.[2] But is it now reasonable to suppose that you will take x over x'? The outcome x' is no worse than the second choice of each individual, whereas x is the third consumer's worst alternative. It certainly isn't clear that x' should be chosen in this case, but neither is it clear that x should be chosen; it is certainly less clear that x should be chosen than it was when only x and x' were available.[3]

Nonetheless, if your choice behavior (as benevolent dictator) can be rationalized by a preference relation, a choice of x in the first instance necessarily implies a choice of x (assuming x'' isn't chosen) in the second; this is an easy consequence of Houthakker's axiom of revealed preference.

Objections concerning our discussion of this example are easy. Perhaps you find x the obvious choice in the second case, and (what I personally find more compelling) perhaps x is not so obvious a choice in the first instance; as a benevolent social dictator, you (perhaps) feel that you must somehow consider intensity of preferences. Nonetheless, we proceed on the basis of the following assumption, although you may wonder if this assumption is at all sensible in this context.

Assumption 1. *The social dictator's choice behavior can be rationalized by an asymmetric and negatively transitive strict preference relation $\succ$ on X. Moreover, $\succ$ is sufficiently well behaved so that it admits a numerical representation $V^* : X \to R$.*

---

[2] We'll formalize this restriction on your choice behavior in just a moment; for now we are only dealing with an example.

[3] Your intuition might be that x should be prefered to x' in both cases because x is preferred to x' in both cases by a majority of society. We will discuss majority rule below.

The last part of assumption 1 follows immediately if X is a finite set. But if X is infinite, we may need something more, such as continuity of $\succ$.[b]

   To this we add two assumptions that relate your preferences as social dictator to those of the members of the society.

Assumption 2. *If x is Pareto superior to x', then $x \succ x'$ or, equivalently, $V^*(x) > V^*(x')$.*

Assumption 3. *If $V_i(x) = V_i(x')$ for all $i = 1, 2, \ldots, I$, then $V^*(x) = V^*(x')$.*

Assumption 2 is virtually an "axiom" of benevolence, *if* you are willing to accept that members of society are entitled to their own tastes. Given this, how could one argue with the assertion that if one social outcome is Pareto superior to a second — if everyone in society at least weakly prefers the first, and some strictly prefer it — then the dictator, if she is benevolent, should prefer the first? We could imagine a slightly weaker assumption, where it is necessary that x is strictly Pareto superior to x' before we conclude $x \succ x'$, but assumption 2 as stated seems pretty reasonable.

   Assumption 3, in a sense, pushes assumption 2 to a "limit."[c] If everyone is indifferent between x and x', then what business does a benevolent social dictator have in choosing between them? One might retort: If every consumer is indifferent between x and x', then no one will mind if the dictator chooses according to whim or her own tastes. But we will proceed assuming this as well.

Proposition 5.1. *Fix numerical representations of the consumers' preferences V_i. Then the social dictator's preferences satisfy assumptions 1, 2, and 3 if and only if the social dictator's preferences are represented by a function $V^* : X \rightarrow R$ that takes the form*

$$V^*(x) = W(V(x))$$

for some function $W : R^I \rightarrow R$ that is strictly increasing on the range of the vector function $V = (V_1, \ldots, V_I) : X \rightarrow R^I$.[4]

---

   [b] We won't spend time on continuity of the preferences of the social dictator, but you might think about whether this is reasonable if the preferences of the consumers in this society are not continuous.

   [c] Suppose that social outcomes come from some convex subset of a finite dimensional Euclidean space, and for each x and $\epsilon > 0$, there is some $\hat{x}$ that is Pareto superior to x and within ϵ of x. This would hold, for example, if social outcomes are consumption allocations, individual's preferences depend only on what they consume, and at least one consumer is locally insatiable. Suppose, moreover, that the dictator's preferences are continuous. Then assumption 3 follows from assumption 2 (and continuity) in precisely the sense of a limit.

   [4] Recall that $V(x)$ is shorthand for the vector $(V_1(x), \ldots, V_I(x))$.

The bit about "strictly increasing..." is less ferocious than it may seem. The idea is that if we have x and x' from X such that $V_i(x) \geq V_i(x')$ for all i, with a strict inequality for at least one i, then $W(V(x)) > W(V(x'))$.

> Proving one direction of this proposition is easy. Suppose that for some given W with the postulated properties we define V^* by $V^*(x) = W(V(x))$ and then we define the dictator's preferences from V^*. Showing that these social preferences satisfy assumptions 1, 2, and 3 is a simple matter of comparing definitions. The other direction (going from the assumptions to the existence of such a W) is a bit harder, but only a bit. Assumption 1 guarantees that some V^* represents $\succ$. For each vector $r \in R^I$ such that $r = V(x)$ for some $x \in X$, define $W(r)$ to be $V^*(x)$. Then W is well-defined by assumption 3, and it is strictly increasing on the range of V by assumption 2. One can extend W to all of R^I in any way you please. One might wish W to be extended to be increasing or even strictly increasing on all of R^I, and the mathematically adept reader might find it interesting to consider whether either or both of these wishes can be fulfilled in general.

Note well that the function W defined on R^I depends crucially on the particular V_i that are chosen to represent the preferences of individual consumers. We could, for example, replace V_1 with a function V_1' given by $V_1'(x) = (V_1(x) + 1000)^3$ (which is a strictly increasing transformation), and then we would have to change how W responds to its first argument. Still, the notion is simple. Fixing representations of our consumer's preferences, every "reasonable" benevolent social dictator has preferences given by a strictly increasing function W on the space of utility imputations, and every such function W defines a "reasonable" benevolent social dictator, where the definition of reasonable is that the dictator conforms to assumptions 1, 2, and 3.

Functions W of this sort are sometimes referred to as *social welfare functionals*. Standard examples are

(a) $W(r_1, \ldots, r_I) = \sum_{i=1}^{I} r_i$, the so-called *utilitarian* social welfare functional

(b) $W(r_1, \ldots, r_I) = \sum_{i=1}^{I} \alpha_i r_i$ for a set of strictly positive weights $\{\alpha_i\}$, the so-called *weighted utilitarian* social welfare functional. This class of functions is also referred to as the class of *Bergsonian social welfare functionals*. They will reappear later.

In example (a), all members of society are given equal weight.[d] In example (b), we may possibly weight consumers differently. We might agree, for example, that it would be sensible to give the utility of professors ten

---

[d] Of course, this statement is not quite sensible, since this is all relative to some fixed numerical representation of consumer's preferences.

times the weight given to the utility of undergraduates, who in turn get ten times the weight given to the utility of graduate students.[5]

As an alternative way to weight utilities, you might consider making the weight given to a consumer depend on the relative utility the consumer receives.

(c) Let $\alpha_1 \geq \alpha_2 \geq \ldots \geq \alpha_I \geq 0$ be a nonincreasing sequence of positive weights, and for any vector $(r_1, \ldots, r_I)$, let $r_{[i]}$ be the ith smallest number in the set $\{r_1, \ldots, r_I\}$. (That is, if $I = 4$ and $r = (4, 5, 4, 3)$, then we have $r_{[1]} = 3, r_{[2]} = r_{[3]} = 4$, and $r_{[4]} = 5$.) And set $W(r_1, \ldots, r_I) = \sum_{i=1}^{I} \alpha_i r_{[i]}$. This gives relatively more weight to the "worse off" members of society.

(d) To take an extreme case of (c), let $W(r_1, \cdots, r_I) = \min\{r_i : i = 1, \ldots, I\}$. That is, the worst off member of the society gets all the weight. This isn't quite going to give a social welfare functional as we've defined the term, since it isn't strictly increasing. (It gives rise to a benevolent social dictator for whom assumption 2 is replaced by the weaker assumption: If x strictly Pareto dominates x', then $x \succ x'$.) This (almost-) social welfare functional is sometimes called a *Rawlsian social welfare functional*.

The range of possible choices of a social welfare functional

What are we to make of these social welfare functionals? Put another way, what conclusions can we draw if we believe that social choice is determined by some preference ordering that satisfies assumptions 1, 2, and 3?

Proposition 5.2. *Suppose that choice out of any set X' of feasible social states is made by maximization of a function $W(V_1(x), \ldots, V_I(x))$, where W is strictly increasing in each argument. Then the chosen social state will always be Pareto efficient (in X').*

There is almost nothing to this; it is virtually a matter of comparing definitions. So we can rephrase the question: Are there any Pareto efficient outcomes that are not selected by some suitably chosen social welfare functional? For all practical purposes the answer to this question is no. In fact, we can, under certain conditions, get a virtually negative answer if we restrict attention to Bergsonian social welfare functionals.

To see how this works, we need the mathematical notion of the *convex hull* of a set. For any set of points A of R^K (for any integer K), the convex hull of A is the set of all points $z \in R^K$ such that $z = \sum_{n=1}^{N} \alpha_n z_n$ for some integer N, some selection of points $z_n \in A$, and some selection of scalars

---

[5] You may decide how much weight is appropriate for assistant professors.

$\alpha_n > 0$ such that $\sum_{n=1}^{N} \alpha_n = 1$. Don't be put off by the symbols; the convex hull of any set is just the smallest convex set that contains the original set. It is obtained by "filling in" any holes or concave pieces in the set.[6]

Proposition 5.3. *Suppose x^* is Pareto efficient in some set X' and the utility imputation corresponding to x^*, or $V(x^*)$, is Pareto efficient in the convex hull of $V(X')$.[7] Then for some selection of **nonnegative** weights $\{\alpha_i\}_{i=1,\ldots,I}$, at least one of which is positive, x^* maximizes $\sum_{i=1}^{I} \alpha_i V_i(x)$ over the set X'.*

(We will sketch the proof in a bit.)

Note two things about this proposition: first, this ugly condition about $V(x^*)$ being Pareto efficient in the convex hull of $V(X')$. Since x^* is Pareto efficient in X', we know that $V(x^*)$ is Pareto efficient in $V(X')$ itself. So, for example, if we know that $V(X')$ is a convex set, then this added condition is unnecessary. It is a little too much to hope that $V(X')$ will be convex, but still we can eliminate the ugly condition by some quite standard assumptions.

Proposition 5.4. *Suppose X' is a convex set and each $V_i : X \to R$ is concave. Then if x^* is Pareto efficient in X', the utility imputation $V(x^*)$ is Pareto efficient in the convex hull of $V(X')$.*

(The proof is left as a homework exercise.) Consider, for example, the specific application of division of some endowment of commodities among I consumers, where each consumer cares only about how much he consumes. Then X' is convex, and all we need is an assumption that the utility functions of the consumers are concave. We discussed at some length the reasonableness of such an assumption on consumer's utility, and we do not repeat that discussion here. But this assumption is met in many applications.[e]

The second remark to make about proposition 5.3 is that the weights in the sum of utilities are only nonnegative; we don't guarantee that they are strictly positive. If one or more of the weights is zero, then we don't have a social welfare functional as we've defined the term, because the

---

[6] If you've never seen this notion before, get someone who has to draw a few pictures for you.

[7] Recall that $V(X') = \{v \in R^I : v = V(x) \text{ for some } x \in X'\}$.

[e] What if the ugly condition is not met? Can one still guarantee that every Pareto efficient point is selected for some legitimate social welfare functional, albeit not a Bergsonian social welfare functional? The answer is virtually yes, where one waffles a bit for the same reason that we permit zero weights in proposition 5.3. Untangling this statement is left to the more mathematically inclined reader.

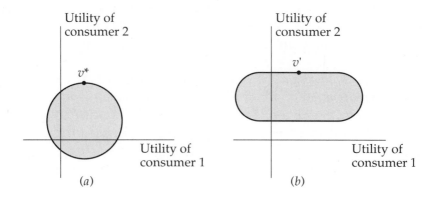

Figure 5.6. Why zero weights are needed in the proof of proposition 5.3.

function is not strictly increasing in the utility of consumers who have zero weight in the sum. Allowing for zero weight is necessary if we are to get all the Pareto efficient points. Consider, in this regard, figure 5.6(a). We have here the set $V(X')$ for a two-person society, and we imagine that $V(X')$ is a circle. Since the slope of the Pareto frontier at the point marked v^* is zero, if we put any (positive) weight on consumer 1's utility in a weighted sum, we will not choose v^* as a maximizing point. But if we allow zero weights, and if $V(X')$ is as in 5.6(b), then points such as v' might be selected as maximizing social outcomes. In terms of our definitions, such points are not strictly Pareto dominated by any other (as long as one of the weights is strictly positive, we could never select a point that is strictly Pareto dominated), but they are not Pareto efficient either. One can either give up guarantees that points such as v^* are obtained as maxima, or allow the possibility that points such as v' are; both these "solutions" to the problem of zero weights can be found in the literature.

Now we give a proof of proposition 5.3. This will be in small type and so is optional material, but all readers are urged to persevere. We are about to introduce the separating hyperplane theorem, a very important tool in economic theory.

We begin by stating the separating hyperplane theorem. Suppose A and B are nonintersecting convex sets in R^2. By drawing pictures, you should be able to convince yourself that it is always possible to draw a line between them, with all the points from A lying on one side of the line and all the points from B lying on the other. If you are really clever in your pictures, you will be able to draw a situation in which points from one or both of the two sets must lie on the line, so we will permit this. The mathematical result that formalizes your ability always to draw such a line or, in higher dimensions, to draw the appropriate analogue to a line, is

The Separating Hyperplane Theorem. *If A and B are convex sets in R^K that don't intersect, then there is a vector $\alpha = (\alpha_1, \ldots, \alpha_K) \in R^K$, not identically zero, and a scalar β, such that $\alpha \cdot a \leq \beta$ for all $a \in A$ and $\alpha \cdot b \geq \beta$ for all $b \in B$, where $\cdot$ means the dot or inner product.*

With this it is easy to prove proposition 5.3. Take any Pareto efficient point x^* that satisfies the hypothesis of the proposition. Consider the following two convex sets in R^I. Let A = the convex hull of $V(X')$; and let $B = \{v \in R^I : v > V(x^*)\}$. In the definition of B, the strict inequality (which is between two I-dimensional vectors) should be read v is greater or equal to $V(x^*)$ in every component and strictly greater in at least one. Because x^* is Pareto efficient in the convex hull of $V(X')$ and B is the set of utility vectors that Pareto dominate the utility imputation associated with x^*, A and B do not intersect. The set A is convex by definition; it shouldn't take you too long to prove that B is convex. Hence there exists a vector $\alpha = (\alpha_1, \ldots, \alpha_I)$ and a scalar β such that $\alpha \cdot a \leq \beta$ for all $a \in A$ and $\alpha \cdot b \geq \beta$ for all $b \in B$. Since $V(x^*)$ is "almost" in B, $\alpha \cdot V(x^*) = \beta$. (To be precise, use continuity.) Hence $V(x^*)$ maximizes the function $\alpha \cdot v$ over v in A, hence over $v \in V(X')$. And hence x^* maximizes the function $\sum_{i=1}^{I} \alpha_i V_i(x)$ over $x \in X'$. We are done as soon as we show that each $\alpha_i \geq 0$. For this we use our definition of the set B. Suppose that $\alpha_i < 0$ for some i. For each integer N, let

$$v^N = (V_1(x^*), \ldots, V_{i-1}(x^*), V_i(x^*) + N, V_{i+1}(x^*), \ldots, V_I(x^*)).$$

That is, we look at the utility imputation resulting from x^*, and we give consumer i an increase of N in his utility. Then $v^N \in B$ by definition. And if $\alpha_i < 0$, then by making N very large, we can make $\alpha \cdot v^N$ as small as we wish, in particular smaller than β, which would contradict the defining property of α and β.

If you get lost in this mathematical proof, simply consider the picture in figure 5.7. We've drawn the set $V(X')$ here as a finite collection of points, presumably resulting from a finite set X'. We then shade in both the convex hull of $V(X')$ and the set of utility vectors that Pareto dominate the utility imputation $v^* = V(x^*)$ for some $x^* \in X'$. We can separate these two by a line that necessarily passes through $V(x^*)$. Using this line and lines parallel to it to define "iso-social welfare" lines, we see that for some linear social welfare functional, x^* is socially optimal. Since the separating line has to stay outside the interior of the set B, it can't have positive slope. Note also the point v', which is Pareto efficient in $V(X')$ but *not* in the convex hull of $V(X')$. We can't, therefore, obtain v' as the choice of a Bergsonian social welfare functional. Finally, draw the corresponding picture for the point v^* in figure 5.6. This should show you again why we sometimes need zero weights.

Apparently, then, assumptions 1, 2, and 3 don't do a lot to pin down social choice. They do tell us how to restrict social choice to the Pareto

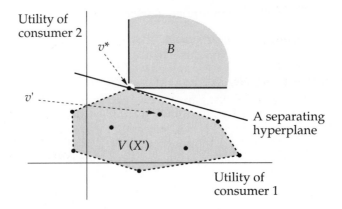

*Figure 5.7. Separating feasible utility vectors from Pareto
dominating vectors in the proof of proposition 5.4.*

frontier, but (following propositions 5.3 and 5.4) in many cases of interest
even Bergsonian social welfare functions allow us to get almost the entire
Pareto frontier as "socially optimal." So how should we proceed?

We might try to say more about how social choice should be determined in general from arrays of consumer preferences. That is, we might
deal not with a single array of consumer preferences but instead with
a family of them, discussing how social preferences should change with
changes in the array of consumer preferences. This approach is discussed
in section 5.5 with the most famous result along these lines, *Arrow's possibility theorem.*

5.4. Characterizing efficient social outcomes

But before doing this, we illustrate how social welfare functionals can
be used as a tool of analysis. Their usefulness analytically springs from
precisely their weakness in normative choice theory: They can be used to
find the entire Pareto frontier as the solution to a parametric optimization
problem. That is, suppose we have a social choice problem in which (for
simplicity) proposition 5.4 applies. Then we know that every point on the
Pareto frontier is the solution to maximizing social welfare using a Bergsonian social welfare functional for some selection of weights. As we vary
the weights, we trace the entire Pareto frontier. It might be interesting to
see what conditions must hold at an efficient outcome in a particular setting, which thus comes down to the conditions that must hold at solutions
of maximizing a weighted sum of individuals' utilities.

To illustrate this technique, we develop three examples that will be used to some extent in the rest of the book.

The production and allocation of private goods

Our first example takes place in the context of production and allocation of commodities. We imagine a situation with K commodities and I individuals. We write Z for the positive orthant in R^K, and we write $x = (z_1, z_2, \ldots, z_I)$ for a social outcome — an allocation of commodities to the individuals. Each z_i is an element of Z, a nonnegative K-dimensional vector, and we write z_{ik} for the amount of good k allocated to individual i.

We restrict attention for now to the case in which these are *private goods*, meaning that the preferences of individual i concerning the social outcome x depend only on i's own bundle of commodities. More precisely, if $V_i : X \to R$ represents i's preferences over X, then V_i can be written as $V_i(z_1, \ldots, z_I) = U_i(z_i)$ for some function $U_i : Z \to R$. We assume that U_i is concave and continuously differentiable; the usual remarks about these assumptions are taken as read. We also assume that none of the commodities are noxious, so that each U_i is nondecreasing.

So far everything is as in section 5.1. But now we add one complication. Instead of supposing that a social endowment bundle is to be distributed, we imagine that this society is endowed at the outset with a supply of some $K + 1$ good that no one wishes to consume but which can be transformed into various bundles of the K goods individuals wish to consume.[f] We assume that this society has at its disposal a production or transformation technology that is characterized by a function $\phi : Z \to [0, \infty)$ with the following interpretation: For each bundle $z \in Z$, the amount of the $K + 1$ good needed to produce z is $\phi(z)$. We assume that society has at its disposal an amount e_0 of this $K + 1$ good, so the social choice problem is to (a) choose a bundle from Z to produce from society's supply e_0 of the $K + 1$ good and then (b) divide the bundle produced among the I individuals. That is, the space of feasible social outcomes X' is

$$X' = \{x \in X : x = (z_1, \ldots, z_I), \ \phi(\sum_{i=1}^{I} z_i) \le e_0\}.$$

Let us be clear: $\sum_{i=1}^{I} z_i$ is the vector sum of the commodity bundles allocated to the individuals; it is a K-dimensional vector. So the constraint reads that it must be feasible to produce from e_0 what is to be allocated.

---

[f] This $K + 1$ good is simply an expository device. Readers who know a bit about modeling technologies will see that we could dispense with it.

We assume that the function ϕ is strictly increasing (it always takes more to make more), continuously differentiable, and quasi-convex. Differentiability of ϕ is assumed for ease of exposition,[9] but quasi-convexity of ϕ is essential for what follows. Quasi-convexity basically says that if z and z' can both be produced from e_0 units of the $K + 1$ good, then so can any convex combination of z and z'.[8] The reason for the assumption is so that we obtain: *The set X' defined above is convex, hence proposition 5.4 applies.* We leave this to the reader to prove. We go on to harvest the consequences, which are that every efficient social outcome can be found as the solution of the following maximization problem:

$$\text{Maximize } \sum_{i=1}^{I} \alpha_i U_i(z_i) \text{ subject to } \phi(\sum_{i=1}^{I} z_i) \leq e_0,$$

for nonnegative weights (α_i).

To keep matters simple, we will assume that the weights α_i are all strictly positive, that solutions to the problem above are characterized by the first-order conditions, that at those solutions relevant multipliers and partial derivatives are strictly positive, and that the only constraint that binds is the social feasibility constraint, or $\phi(\sum_{i=1}^{I} z_i) \leq e_0$. The first of these three assumptions can, at the cost of some analysis, be dispensed with. The second is fairly innocuous (and is completely innocuous if the function ϕ is convex). The third takes some work, but for most applications it will hold.[h] But the fourth assumption is quite strong. Essentially we are characterizing efficient allocations where every consumer is allocated a positive amount of each of the K consumption goods. The diligent reader may wish to redo our analysis without this assumption.

The characterization is now easy to derive. Letting λ be the multiplier on the social feasibility constraint, the first-order condition for z_{ik}, the amount of good k allocated to consumer i is

$$\alpha_i \frac{\partial U_i}{\partial z_{ik}} = \lambda \frac{\partial \phi}{\partial z_k},$$

where partial derivatives are, of course, evaluated at the optimal solution. We should be careful about one thing in this first-order condition. When

---

[9] The mathematically well-versed reader can try to do without it.

[8] For more on this assumption, which is essentially an assumption that the production technology is convex, see chapter 7.

[h] It involves an implicit assumption that each consumer's utility rises in increases in each good, at least for some levels of the good's consumption.

reading $\partial\phi/\partial z_k$ on the right-hand side, remember that ϕ is a function of K variables; we mean here the partial derivative of ϕ taken with respect to the total social production of commodity k.

Take any two goods k and k', and take the two first-order conditions for z_{ik} and $z_{ik'}$. With all the assumptions we have made, we can divide one by the other, cancel the α_is on one side and the λs on the other, and obtain

$$\frac{\partial U_i}{\partial z_{ik}} \bigg/ \frac{\partial U_i}{\partial z_{ik'}} = \frac{\partial\phi}{\partial z_k} \bigg/ \frac{\partial\phi}{\partial z_{k'}}.$$

The ratio on the left-hand side is called the *marginal rate of substitution for individual i of good k for k'*, whereas the ratio on the right-hand side is called the *marginal rate of technical substitution of k for k'*, and we have the result; at an efficient social outcome these ratios should be equal for each consumer for each pair of goods. Moreover, since the right-hand side is independent of the consumer i, we see that the marginal rates of substitution of each pair of goods should be equal for each pair of consumers.

These characterizations of efficient social production and allocation are easy enough to explain. First, suppose that for two consumers, i and i', their marginal rates of substitution of k for k' were different; suppose the marginal rate for i was larger. Then we could take a bit of k' away from i, compensating her with just enough k so she is indifferent, and give the k' to i' in return for the k we gave to i. The ratio of k to k' that makes i indifferent will, because of the presumed difference in the ratios, strictly benefit i'. Hence we didn't have a socially efficient allocation. Next, suppose that for consumer i the marginal rate of substitution of k for k' is not the same as the marginal rate of technological substitution. Suppose her ratio is larger. Then we can make a bit less k' and a bit more k in a ratio that is technologically feasible and give the extra k to i in exchange for the k' we need to make the extra. Given our assumptions on her rate of marginal substitution relative to the rate of technological substitution, this makes her strictly better off, and we were not efficient in terms of our choice of production plan.[i]

---

[i] Note that it has to be possible to take k from the second consumer and k' from the first to make these variations. This is where our assumption that nonnegativity constraints don't bind come into play, and it is where we would have to modify these simple characterizations if nonnegativity constraints did bind.

The production and allocation of private and public goods

If you have had a course in intermediate microeconomics, you probably already knew all that, at least at some level. But now we consider a variation that you may not have seen before. We suppose that of our K commodities, the first is a *public good*. A public good is one where the consumption of the good by one individual in no way prevents others from consuming the good or diminishes their enjoyment of it. Classical examples of public goods include clean air and national defence. Parks and highways have some of the character of a public good, but they don't quite qualify — the more people consume Yellowstone Park or the Pennsylvania Turnpike, the less utility each takes from it.[j]

We formalize this situation as follows. Now a social outcome is a $1 + I(K - 1)$ vector,

$$x = (y, (z_{12}, \ldots, z_{1K}), \ldots, (z_{I2}, \ldots, z_{IK})),$$

where y is the amount of the public good, $z_1 = (z_{12}, \ldots, z_{1K})$ is the amount of the private goods consumed by individual 1, and so on. The preferences of individual i over social states are given by a utility function U_i defined on the space of vectors $(y, z_1) = (y, (z_{12}, \ldots, z_{1K}))$. Otherwise, the formulation of the technological possibilities for this society remains the same, so now the space of feasible social outcomes is

$$X' = \{x = (y, z_1, \ldots, z_I) \in R^{1+I(K-1)} : \phi(y, \sum_{i=1}^{I} z_i) \le e_0\}.$$

Convexity of X' is unaffected, and if we make assumptions similar to those made in the previous subsection, to characterize efficient social outcomes in this setting we have to solve the problem

$$\text{maximize} \sum_{i=1}^{I} \alpha_i U_i(y, z_i) \text{ subject to } \phi(y, \sum_{i=1}^{I} z_i) \le e_0.$$

---

[j] Public goods are extreme examples of goods with externalities, which we discuss in the next chapter. A useful exercise, once you've read the discussion given in the next chapter on externalities, is to characterize the efficient allocation of goods in the style of this section in cases with general externalities.

First-order equations on the z_{ik} for $i = 1, \ldots, I$ and $k = 2, \ldots, K$ are just as before, but for the public good we get the first-order condition

$$\sum_{i=1}^{I} \alpha_i \frac{\partial U_i}{\partial y} = \lambda \frac{\partial \phi}{\partial y}.$$

Now consider any one of the private goods, say good #2. By manipulating the first-order condition for z_{i2}, we obtain

$$\alpha_i = \lambda \frac{\partial \phi}{\partial z_2} \bigg/ \frac{\partial U_i}{\partial z_{i2}}.$$

Substituting for α_i in the first-order condition for y gives

$$\sum_{i=1}^{I} \left[\lambda \frac{\partial \phi}{\partial z_2} \bigg/ \frac{\partial U_i}{\partial z_{i2}} \right] \frac{\partial U_i}{\partial y} = \lambda \frac{\partial \phi}{\partial y},$$

and dividing through by $\lambda (\partial \phi / \partial z_2)$ on both sides, we get

$$\sum_{i=1}^{I} \left[\frac{\partial U_i}{\partial y} \bigg/ \frac{\partial U_i}{\partial z_{i2}} \right] = \frac{\partial \phi}{\partial y} \bigg/ \frac{\partial \phi}{\partial z_2}.$$

Or, in words, the marginal rate of technological substitution of the public good for any of the private goods (the right-hand side) should equal the *sum* of the marginal rates of substitutions of the public good for the private good summed over consumers.

Syndicate theory

Our third illustration of this technique, *syndicate theory* (Wilson, 1968), comes from the economics of uncertainty. There are I consumers who jointly own a gamble that pays off different amounts of money in N different states of nature. The N states of nature are written $\{s_1, \ldots, s_N\}$, and in state s_n the gamble pays off $\$Y_n$. A "social outcome" consists of a sharing rule for dividing the payoff of the gamble in each state. We write y_{in} for the amount of money received by consumer i in state s_n, so the set of all feasible social outcomes is the set of all vectors $(y_{in})_{i=1,\ldots,I;n=1,\ldots,N} \in R^{IN}$ such that for each n, $\sum_{i=1}^{I} y_{in} = Y_n$. The last constraint is the "adding up" constraint; the consumers can't divide among themselves more than they have to divide. (Thus, in the notation of the general formulation, all vectors (y_{in}) that meet this constraint make up the set X' of feasible social outcomes.) Note that we don't restrict the y_{in} to be nonnegative; we will permit consumers in some states to *contribute* funds.

Each consumer (or member of the syndicate) cares only about what he receives. Each evaluates his part of any division $(y_{in})_{n=1,...,N}$ using an expected utility calculation with probabilities $\{\pi_n\}$ and with utility function u_i. That is, the utility to i of the sharing rule (y_{in}) is given by

$$\sum_{n=1}^{N} \pi_n u_i(y_{in}).$$

Note carefully: We are assuming that the different consumers all have the same probability distribution over the N states. You may wish to consider how what follows will change if we imagine that different consumers have different subjective assessments concerning the likelihoods of the various states. We are also assuming that the individual consumers evaluate their shares in this gamble without regard to any other risky assets they might hold; this (presumably) makes sense only if this risk is independent of any other risks they might face. We assume that the consumers are all risk averse (including risk neutrality as a limit case); that is, the functions u_i are all concave. And for technical reasons we assume that the functions u_i are all continuously differentiable.

Now we pose the question in which we are interested. *Which sharing rules are Pareto efficient?*

The set of feasible sharing rules is clearly convex. And the utility functions of the individuals viewed as functions on the sharing rules are concave because each of the utility functions u_i is concave.[k] So proposition 5.4 applies; and then according to proposition 5.3, we can find all the efficient division rules by maximizing various weighted averages of the consumers' expected utilities.

That is, if we let $(\alpha_i)_{i=1,...,I}$ be a vector of nonnegative weights, then the solution to

$$\max \sum_{i=1}^{I} \alpha_i \left[\sum_{n=1}^{N} \pi_n u_i(y_{in}) \right] \text{ subject to } \sum_{i=1}^{I} y_{in} = Y_n \text{ for each } n$$

is a Pareto efficient sharing rule, and as we vary the weights α_i, we get all the Pareto efficient sharing rules.

---

[k] The technically astute reader will see that the concavity of u_i is not quite the same as concavity of the "V_i" functions, but it quickly implies concavity of the "V_i." If this is gibberish, don't worry about it.

What happens if some of the weights are zero? Suppose $\alpha_i = 0$. Then we put no weight on the expected utility of consumer i. And since we haven't restricted shares to be nonnegative, the "solution" to the maximization problem just given is to make y_{in} extremely large negative, distributing this "tax" on i among those consumers that have positive weight. More precisely, the maximization problem given has no solution at all.[l] So we can restrict attention to strictly positive weights.[m]

Now let us rewrite the objective function in the maximization problem by interchanging the order of summations. That is,

$$\sum_{i=1}^{I} \alpha_i \left[\sum_{n=1}^{N} \pi_n u_i(y_{in}) \right] = \sum_{n=1}^{N} \pi_n \left[\sum_{i=1}^{I} \alpha_i u_i(y_{in}) \right],$$

so we can rewrite the problem above as

$$\max \sum_{n=1}^{N} \pi_n \left[\sum_{i=1}^{I} \alpha_i u_i(y_{in}) \right] \text{ subject to } \sum_{i=1}^{I} y_{in} = Y_n \text{ for each } n.$$

If you stare hard at this reformulation of the problem, you will see that we solve it by looking at each state separately; if we solve separately, for each state n,

$$\max \sum_{i=1}^{I} \alpha_i u_i(y_{in}) \text{ subject to } \sum_{i=1}^{I} y_{in} = Y_n,$$

then we have the solution to the grand problem. Let us record this and other "facts" we encounter as we go along:

Fact 1. Efficient sharing among members of the syndicate is done on a state-by-state basis. The probabilities assessed for the various states play no role in this sharing. All that matters to the sharing rule in a particular state is the total

---

[l] If u_i is not defined for negative arguments, then trying to figure out what the maximization problem means is an interesting mathematical puzzle. We'll avoid this puzzle by restricting attention to strictly positive weights and by assuming that the problem given has a solution constrained only by the adding up constraint within the domain of definition of the u_i.

[m] Even if the weights are all strictly positive, we cannot guarantee that the maximization problem has a solution. We will proceed assuming that there is a solution, and then, since we have not constrained the y_{in}, this solution is given by simultaneous solution of the first-order conditions. But this assumption is unwarranted for some parameterizations, and we leave it to the careful reader to put in place the necessary caveats.

payoff in that state (and the weights given to the consumers, which are held fixed in any efficient sharing rule). That is, in an efficient sharing rule, one doesn't reward Peter in one state and compensate Paul in another.[n]

So how do we share in state s_n? Letting μ_n be the multiplier on the adding up constraint for state s_n, we get as first-order conditions

$$\alpha_i u_i'(y_{in}) = \mu_n \text{ for } i = 1, \ldots, I.$$

Assume for the time being that each u_i is strictly concave (so that u_i' is a strictly decreasing function). Then for each fixed value of the multiplier μ_n, the equation $\alpha_i u_i'(y) = \mu_n$ has a unique solution in y.[9][o] Let us write that solution as a function $y_i(\mu_n)$ of the multiplier μ_n. Because u_i' is strictly decreasing, the value of $y_i(\mu_n)$ is strictly decreasing in μ_n. Because we assumed that u_i is continuously differentiable, the solution is continuous in μ_n. Hence the function $\sum_{i=1}^{I} y_i(\mu_n)$ is strictly decreasing and continuous in μ_n. At the value of μ_n for which the sum equals Y_n, we have the unique solution to the first-order conditions for state s_n.

Fact 2. *If all the consumers are strictly risk averse (that is, if all the u_i are strictly concave), the first-order conditions have a unique solution for each state of nature. There is a unique efficient sharing rule (for the fixed weights).*

Consider next how the shares of consumer i vary across various states. Consider two states s_n and $s_{n'}$ such that $Y_n > Y_{n'}$. The solution for state n will be where $\sum_{i=1}^{I} y_i(\mu_n) = Y_n$. The solution for state n' will be where $\sum_{i=1}^{I} y_i(\mu_{n'}) = Y_{n'}$. Since the functions $y_i(\cdot)$ are strictly decreasing, $\mu_n < \mu_{n'}$. Hence the share for each consumer i in state n, $y_{in} = y_i(\mu_n)$, will be strictly larger than his share in state n'.

Fact 3. *If all the consumers are strictly risk averse, then the share of any consumer in a state is strictly increasing in the overall payoff in that state.*

So far we've considered efficient division when all the consumers are strictly risk averse. Now let us consider what happens when one of the consumers is risk neutral and the others are (strictly) risk averse. For our

---

[n] The reader who is thinking about how this would change if the consumers assessed different probabilities for the different states should think hard about this first fact!

[9] The weights α_i are held fixed throughout this discussion. As they shift, we shift the point on the Pareto frontier that we are investigating, a comparative statics exercise that is left for the reader.

[o] We might get $+\infty$ or $-\infty$ as the solution, and the careful reader can worry about what happens then.

risk neutral consumer, say consumer number 1, we have $u_1' \equiv c$ for some constant c. Hence the first-order condition for this consumer in state s_n is $\alpha_1 c = \mu_n$. But the left-hand side of this first-order condition doesn't depend on n. So we conclude that the multipliers μ_n for the various states n must all be the same; they must all be $\alpha_1 c$. Thus the share y_{in} of consumer $i = 2, \ldots, I$ in state n must be the (unique) solution of $\alpha_i u_i'(y) = \alpha_1 c$. Since we have assumed that all the consumers other than number 1 are strictly risk averse, the equation for i has a unique solution. Thus the shares of consumers other than number 1 are constant; consumer 1 bears all the risk.

Fact 4. *If one consumer is risk neutral and the others are strictly risk averse, then the consumers who are risk averse receive, in any efficient division, a payoff that is constant among the various states. The risk neutral consumer bears all the risk; his payoff in state s_n is Y_n plus or minus some constant (that doesn't depend on n).*

This fact will become important in chapter 16.

Now, just to show how far one could take this sort of thing, we move to a very specific parameterization. We assume that each consumer is strictly risk averse and has constant absolute risk aversion, or $u_i(y) = -e^{-\lambda_i y}$ for some $\lambda_i > 0$. Recall that λ_i is called consumer i's coefficient of (absolute) risk aversion. The reciprocal of λ_i, which we write τ_i, is conventionally called i's *coefficient of risk tolerance*; it will be more convenient to work with risk tolerances than with risk aversions, so we rewrite $u_i(y) = -e^{-y/\tau_i}$. It is also conventional to refer to $\sum_{i=1}^{I} \tau_i$ as *society's risk tolerance*; we will use this term and the symbol T to represent this sum. We have the following result:

Fact 5. *If all the consumers have constant absolute risk tolerance, then the efficient divisions take the form*

$$y_{in} = \frac{\tau_i}{T} Y_n + k_i, \ i = 1, \ldots, I$$

where the constant k_i is a constant that depends on all the parameters of the maximization problem, including the weights (α_i).

We leave this for you to prove in problem 6; some hints are given there. But note how remarkable this is. In this very special case, in any efficient sharing rule consumer i receives a proportional share of the total pie plus a constant payment (which may well be a tax). The size of his proportional share is given by the ratio of his risk tolerance to society's risk tolerance.

We shift around on the Pareto frontier solely by adjusting the constant payments; efficient sharing always involves the same "risky parts" in the efficient sharing rule.

5.5. Social choice rules and Arrow's possibility theorem

Now we return to the problem of normative social choice. In section 5.3, we looked at a single array of consumer preferences, given by an array of numerical rankings $(V_i)_{i=1,...,I}$ on the set of social outcomes X, and we attempted to characterize "reasonable" social preferences. We might get further along in the general program of normative social choice if we expand the scope of our analysis. Specifically, we might consider a *family* of possible arrays of consumer preferences and characterize reasonable social preferences for each array in the family. The point is that this expanded scope allows us to pose conditions concerning how social preferences respond to changes in the array of consumer preferences.

For example, we might pose the following property:

Positive Social Responsiveness. *Suppose that for a given array of consumer preferences the resulting social preferences rank x as better than x'. Suppose that the array of consumer preferences changes so that x falls in no one's ranking and x' rises in no one's ranking. Then the social ranking should continue to rank x better than x'.*

We aren't being very precise in this definition because we haven't set a context for the problem. But the reader can probably glean from this the spirit of what we will try to do.

We will use the following terminology. A map or function from some given family of arrays of consumer preferences to resulting social preferences will be called a *social choice rule*.

A setting and three examples

We begin by looking at this general program in the following setting. Assume we are given a finite set X of social outcomes, a finite collection of consumers indexed by $i = 1, \ldots, I$, and for each consumer, an asymmetric and negatively transitive strict preference relation $\succ_i$ on X. From $\succ_i$ we define weak preference $\succeq_i$ and indifference $\sim_i$ in the usual fashion. We will work directly with the preference relations $\succ_i$; specific numerical representations for these preferences will play no role for the time being. In this setting, an array of consumer preferences is then an I-dimensional vector of preference orders, $(\succ_1, \ldots, \succ_I)$, where each preference order is asymmetric and negatively transitive. One might put restrictions on the possible arrays of consumer preferences under consideration; we, however, will assume that any vector of asymmetric and negatively transitive orderings of X is permitted.

A *social choice rule* takes an array $(\succ_1, \ldots, \succ_I)$ as input and produces social preferences as output; we assume that the output is in the form of a binary relation $\succ^*$.[p]

Consider the following examples of social choice rules in this setting.

Example 1. The Pareto rule. *In the Pareto rule, $x \succ^* x'$ if and only if x Pareto dominates x'. (Or we could insist on x strictly Pareto dominating x'.)*

The Pareto rule produces social preferences that are not negatively transitive. That is, we might find two outcomes x and x' where x Pareto dominates x', hence $x \succ^* x'$, yet both x and x' are Pareto incomparable with a third x'', hence neither $x'' \succ^* x'$ nor $x \succ^* x''$. You can easily construct specific examples from our discussion of negative transitivity in chapter 2.

Example 2. Majority rule and variations. *For each pair of social outcomes x and x', let $P(x, x')$ be the number of individuals i who express $x \succ_i x'$. In **simple majority rule**, we define $x \succ^* x'$ if $P(x, x') > I/2$. Variations include plurality rule, or $x \succ^* x'$ if $P(x, x') > P(x', x)$; and α-majority rule, for $\alpha > 1/2$, in which $x \succ^* x'$ if $P(x, x') > \alpha I$.*

We could also have α-plurality rules, and so on. And we could have weighted majority rules, where different members of society have different numbers of votes they are allowed to cast.

The problem with majority rule is that preference cycles are possible. Specifically, imagine that we have three outcomes in X, call then x, y, and z, and we have three consumers. The first consumer ranks $x \succ_1 y \succ_1 z$. The second ranks $y \succ_2 z \succ_2 x$. The third ranks $z \succ_3 x \succ_3 y$. Then $x \succ^* y$ by majority rule. (Consumers 1 and 3 feel this way.) And $y \succ^* z$ by majority rule (according to consumers 1 and 2). And $z \succ^* x$ by majority rule (according to consumers 2 and 3). This isn't so good, especially when it comes to choosing from $\{x, y, z\}$.[q]

---

[p] If we were being formal, we would write $\succ^*$ as a function of $(\succ_1, \ldots, \succ_I)$. We will not indulge in such formal notation; I hope no confusion results in consequence. We could instead think of the output of the social choice rule coming in some other form — say a choice function that doesn't necessarily derive from any binary preference relation. On this point, see the next footnote.

[q] If we allowed the social choice rule to prescribe for an array of consumer preferences a choice rule instead of binary preferences, we might define it as follows: For any pair

Example 3. The Borda rule. *Suppose there are* N *social outcomes. For each consumer* i *construct a numerical ranking for the* N *outcomes from* $\succ_i$ *as follows: If there is some single best social outcome* x *according to* $\succ_i$, *let* $U_i(x) = N$. *More generally, suppose* i *ranks* m *social outcomes* $x_1, x_2, \ldots, x_m$ *as being equally good and all better than anything else. Then set* $U_i(x_1) = \ldots = U_i(x_m) = [N + (N-1) + \ldots + (N - m + 1)]/m$. *In general, the* nth *best social outcome is given numerical ranking* n, *where ties average their rankings. Then define* $U^*(x) = \sum_{i=1}^{I} U_i(x)$, *and define* $\succ^*$ *to be in accord with* U^*.

Readers who follow American college sports (and, for all I know, others) will know something like this system in the rankings of college football and basketball teams. Sportswriters or coaches rank the top twenty teams, giving 20 points to the best, 19 to the second best, and so on, and then these points are summed to get the "consensus" rankings. (It isn't clear that the rankers are allowed to express ties, and to be the classic Borda rule, the rankers would have to rank all the teams.)

What's wrong with the Borda rule? We leave this for you to discover for homework.

Four properties and Arrow's theorem

Consider the following four properties for a social choice rule in the setting of the previous subsection.

Property 1. *The social choice rule should prescribe an asymmetric and negatively transitive ordering* $\succ^*$ *over social outcomes* X *for every array of individual preferences* $(\succ_i)$.

There are two parts to this property. First, the output of the social choice rule should itself be an asymmetric and negatively transitive order on the social outcomes. As we discussed in section 5.3, this is not entirely non-controversial. Second, the social choice rule is meant to operate no matter what profile of individual preferences is specified. This is sometimes called the *universal domain* property; the domain of definition of the social choice rule should be all conceivable arrays of individual preferences.

$x, y \in X$, let $m(x, y)$ be the number of consumers who strictly prefer y to x. Then given a set X' from which choice must be made, for each $x \in X$, let $M(x, X') = \max_{y \in X'} m(x, y)$. The choice out of X' is defined to be those $x \in X'$ that minimize $M(x, X')$. In words, we choose outcomes against which there is the least "opposition" in any pairwise comparison. For an analysis that begins in roughly this fashion (and for references to antecedents), see Caplin and Nalebuff (1988).

Property 2. Pareto efficiency. *If $x \succ_i x'$ for all i, then $x \succ^* x'$.*

This is something like assumption 2 from section 5.3, except that we require that x strictly Pareto dominate x' in order to conclude that $x \succ^* x'$.

Properties 1 and 2 concern how the social choice rule works at a given array of consumer preferences. Properties 3 and 4, on the other hand, concern the workings of the rule as we vary the array of consumer preferences.

Property 3. Independence of irrelevant alternatives. *Take any two x and x' from X. The social ranking of x and x' does not change with changes in the array of consumer rankings of other social outcomes. That is, if $(\succ_i)$ and $(\succ'_i)$ are arrays of consumer rankings that satisfy $x \succ_i x'$ if and only if $x \succ'_i x'$ for all i, then the social ranking of x and x' is the same in these two situations.*

This property is meant to capture the notion that all that ought to matter in our social choice rule is the relative rankings of pairs of alternatives: There are no interpersonal comparisons of "intensity" of ranking. To get a sense of this, consider a three-person society with three outcomes. Consider an array of individual preferences where the first two consumers rank $x \succ_i x' \succ_i x''$ and the third ranks $x' \succ_i x \succ_i x''$. In this case, it seems "natural" to expect that $x \succ^* x'$. Now consider an array of individual preferences in which the first two consumers continue to rank $x \succ_i x' \succ_i x''$ and the third ranks $x' \succ_i x'' \succ_i x$. Property 3 would guarantee that society should still prefer x and x'. We argued at the start of section 5.3 this is no longer so obvious *if* we think that since x is consumer 3's worst alternative in the second array we ought to give more consideration to x' as the social choice. But how are we to judge how bad 3's worst outcome is for him (instead of his best outcome) relative to how good 1's and 2's first best outcomes are for them (instead of their second bests)? If we actively forebear from making such comparisons, then property 3 seems sensible.

Property 4. Absence of a dictator. *No single consumer i is a dictator in the sense that $x \succ_i x'$ implies $x \succ^* x'$ no matter what the preferences of the other consumers are.*

This seems sensible as long as there are more than two consumers; suppose that one consumer prefers x to x' and all the others prefer x' to x. We might be uncomfortable if society then chose x over x'. We'd be even more uncomfortable if society did this for any pair x and x', for a single consumer. Note carefully that someone is a dictator even if he doesn't impose his will in matters of indifference. That is, we allow $x \sim_i x'$ and $x \succ^* x'$ without disqualifying i as a dictator. (See problem 9.)

And now for the punchline:

Arrow's Possibility Theorem. *Suppose there are at least three social outcomes. Then no social choice rule simultaneously satisfies properties 1, 2, 3, and 4.*

The theorem stated is Arrow's theorem 2 (1963, 97). There are in the literature many variations on this basic result, in which the four properties are changed and/or weakened in various ways, sometimes at the cost of changing the result slightly. (A good example of the latter sort of treatment is Wilson [1972] who eliminates the Pareto property, but in consequence replaces the absence of a dictator with something a bit weaker.) In all these variations, the same basic result appears; no social choice rule satisfies four properties of roughly the character of the four properties we've given.

So to keep alive the possibility of a "reasonable" social choice rule, some one (or more) of the four properties will have to go. Doing away with the first part of property 1 removes the whole point of the exercise, unless we find some reasonable way to weaken this part of property 1 without losing its entire content. Getting rid of Pareto efficiency doesn't seem appealing (and doesn't really solve anything; see Wilson [1972]). So we must consider whether we wish to give up having a social choice rule that gives well-behaved social preferences or give up on the universal domain part of property 1, or property 3, or property 4. Since dictators are somewhat out of fashion, the universal domain part of property 1 and property 3 get the most attention in the literature. The references listed in section 5.5 will lead you into this rich literature.

> We proceed to sketch the proof of the version of Arrow's theorem given above. (We roughly follow Arrow [1963, 97ff].) Assume we have a social choice rule that satisfies properties 1, 2, and 3. (We will demonstrate that there is a dictator.)
>
> *Step 1.*   For any pair of outcomes x and y, all that matters to the social ranking of x and y for a given array of consumer preferences are the sets of individuals such that $x \succ_i y$, $x \sim_i y$, and $y \succ_i x$. That is, for any two arrays of consumer preferences that have the same partition of I into these three sets, x and y will be ranked similarly socially. This is simply a restatement of the independence of irrelevant alternatives.
>
> *Step 2.*   For any distinct pair of outcomes x and y, we say that a subset $J \subseteq I$ is *decisive* for x over y if, when $x \succ_i y$ for all $i \in J$ and $y \succ_i x$ for all $i \notin J$, $x \succ^* y$. We assert that there exists some pair of outcomes x and y and some single individual i such that $\{i\}$ is decisive for x over y.

The proof of this assertion runs as follows. Look over all pairs of distinct outcomes x and y and all the sets of consumers that are decisive for x over y. Note that by Pareto efficiency I is decisive for every x over every y, so we are looking over a nonempty collection of pairs and sets. Since I is a finite set, some smallest (measured by number of members) set of consumers is decisive for some pair x and y. (We are taking the smallest decisive set, ranging over all pairs and all decisive sets at once.) Let J be this smallest set. Suppose that J has more than one element. Partition J into any two nontrivial subsets, called J' and J''. Pick any third element z. (There is a third element by assumption.) Consider any array of social preferences where x, y, and z are ranked as follows:

For $i \in J'$, $z \succ_i x \succ_i y$
For $i \in J''$, $x \succ_i y \succ_i z$
For $i \notin J$, $y \succ_i z \succ_i x$

Since J is decisive for x over y, at this profile $x \succ^* y$. Since social preference is negatively transitive, either $x \succ^* z$ or $z \succ^* y$ (or both). But if $x \succ^* z$, then J'' is decisive for x over z. And if $z \succ^* y$, J' is decisive for z over x. In either case, we have a pair of outcomes and a decisive set for those outcomes that is strictly smaller than the smallest decisive set, a contradiction. Hence the smallest decisive set must contain a single element.

Step 3. Let i be decisive for some pair x and y. Then i is a dictator.
  To show this involves looking at numerous cases.

(1) We will show that for any array of consumer preferences where $x \succ_i z$, it follows that $x \succ^* z$. First consider the case where $z \neq y$. For any array where $x \succ_i z$ rearrange (using universal domain) the relative rankings of y as follows: For i, rank $x \succ_i y \succ_i z$, and for everyone else, rank $y \succ_j x$ and $y \succ_j z$. Since $y \succ_j z$ for all $j \in I$, $y \succ^* z$ by Pareto efficiency. Since i is decisive for x over y, $x \succ^* y$. So by transitivity of $\succ^*$, $x \succ^* z$. This leaves the case $z = y$. But in this case, take any third element w. We just showed that i is decisive for x over w (and more), so repeating the argument above with y replacing z and w replacing y covers $z = y$.

(2) We claim that if $z \succ_i y$ for any z in some array of consumer preferences, then $z \succ^* y$. If $z \neq x$, construct a preference array that preserves the original rankings of z and y and that has $z \succ_i x \succ_i y$ and, for $j \neq i$, $z, y \succ_j x$. By Pareto efficiency, $z \succ^* x$. Because i is decisive for x over y, $x \succ^* y$. Hence $z \succ^* y$. If $z = x$, take any third element w. What was just shown establishes that i is decisive for w over y, hence reapplication of the argument leads to the conclusion that $x \succ^* y$.

(3) We claim that if $z \succ_i x$ for any z in some array of consumer preferences, then $z \succ^* x$. To see this, for any third outcome $w \neq x, y$ set up an array of consumer preferences in which $w \succ_i y \succ_i x$ and, for $j \neq i$ $y \succ_j x \succ_j w$. By Pareto efficiency, $y \succ^* x$. By (2), $w \succ^* y$. Hence i is decisive for w over x and applying (2) again (with x in place of y) leads to the desired conclusion.

(4) Now suppose we have any two outcomes w and z such that $w \succ_i z$. If $w = x$, we conclude from (1) that $w \succ^* z$. If $z = x$, we conclude from (3)

that $w \succ^* z$. While if neither w nor z is x, we can without changing the relative rankings of w and z, arrange matters so that $w \succ_i x \succ_i z$ for i. By (1), $x \succ^* z$. By (3), $w \succ^* x$. So by transitivity $w \succ^* z$.

This finishes step 3 and completes the proof.

Social choice rules with interpersonal comparisons of intensity of preference

One way to try to avoid the negative conclusion of Arrow's theorem is to get into the business of making interpersonal comparisons concerning intensity of preference, at least to some degree. One approach to this concerns what are known as *Nash social choice rules*, which are adaptations of the *Nash bargaining solution* from cooperative game theory (Nash, 1953). We will not give anything like a complete treatment of this subject here; this is not mainstream microeconomic theory. But a few remarks on how the problem is set up may give the diligent reader a sense of at least one direction that can be taken. What follows is loosely transcribed from the treatment given in Kaneko and Nakamura (1979).

The setting in this case begins with a finite set X of social outcomes, as before, and a finite set I of consumers. Three special assumptions are made.

We allow feasible social outcomes to include probability distributions over social outcomes out of X. That is, if X' enumerates the feasible social outcomes, we consider choosing a probability distribution with support X'. We use $P(X')$ to denote the set of probability distributions over X'.

Each individual consumer's preferences over $P(X)$ satisfy the von Neumann-Morgenstern axioms, and so are represented by expected utility. We let u_i denote i's von Neumann-Morgenstern utility function on X.

There is a distinguished social outcome, x_0, such that every other social outcome is strictly preferred by every consumer to x_0.

You can think of x_0 as being "everyone dies," or "no one gets anything to eat."

Having von Neumann-Morgenstern preferences and this distinguished social outcome gives us a "scale" on which intensity of preferences can be measured. Suppose one consumer prefers x to y and another y to x, where neither x nor y is x_0. We can think of measuring which of these two likes their preferred outcome "more" by asking: For the first consumer, what number α satisfies $\alpha \delta_x + (1 - \alpha)\delta_{x_0} \sim \delta_y$; for the second consumer, what number β satisfies $\beta \delta_y + (1 - \beta)\delta_{x_0} \sim \delta_x$? (Here as in chapter 3, δ_x means the lottery that gives prize x with certainty.) If $\alpha > \beta$, then there is a sense in which it matters more to the second consumer to have y instead of x than it does to the first consumer to have x instead of y. In other words, we can use the *cardinal* aspect of von Neumann-Morgenstern preferences and the distinguished reference point x_0 to calibrate intensity of preference, at least in some sense.

The domain for a social choice rule can now be taken to be all arrays of I von Neumann-Morgenstern utility functions $(u_1, \ldots, u_I)$ on X, where we insist that x_0 is worst for everyone in every utility function. And we can then try to pose properties on a social choice rule with this domain that makes use of the stucture provided. The interested reader can consult Kaneko and Nakamura (1979) to see this carried out in at least one fashion. (For the insatiably curious, they give properties that lead to the conclusion: Social choice out of $P(X')$ should be that lottery p that maximizes $\prod_{i=1}^{I}(u_i(p) - u_i(x_0))$, where $u_i(p)$ is shorthand for the expected utility of p computed with respect to u_i.) All we wish to show here is a way in which interpersonal comparison of "intensity of preference" might be incorporated into a theory; you shouldn't conclude that this is impossible.

The rest of the book

We will not explore abstract social choice theory any further. The books and articles listed below will give you a good entrée into this enormous subject. (We will briefly revisit the subject of social choice in chapter 18 under conditions where we mightn't know the preferences of individuals and so must elicit those preferences.) Instead, the remainder of this book takes for the most part a very different tack. Rather than thinking normatively about desirable properties for social choice, we regard "social choice" as the product of individuals interacting in various institutional environments. We describe those institutions and predict the outcome of individual actions within those institutions. Especially in chapters 6 and 8, we will say a bit in the spirit of this chapter about the efficiency of the "social outcomes" that are so selected. But our approach is that of taking the institutions as given exogenously and describing (to the best of our abilities) what "social choices" will be made.

5.6. Bibliographic notes

The classic reference in the theory of social choice is Arrow (1963). Many other excellent books on the subject that follow Arrow; you might in particular wish to consult Sen (1970). To get a taste of more recent developments, a number of survey articles could be consulted; I recommend Sen (1986) and for a shorter treatment Sen (1988). Either of the later pieces by Sen will provide an exhaustive bibliography.

The analysis of syndicate theory, used here to illustrate how to "find" the Pareto frontier in applications, is drawn from Wilson (1968), who draws out many further consequences of the analysis.

References

Arrow, K. 1963. *Social Choice and Individual Values*, 2d ed. New Haven: Cowles Foundation.

Caplin, A., and B. Nalebuff. 1988. "On 64% Majority Rule." *Econometrica* 56:787–815.

Kaneko, M., and K. Nakamura. 1979. "The Nash Social Welfare Function." *Econometrica* 47:423–36.

Nash, J. 1953. "Two-person Cooperative Games." *Econometrica* 21:128–40.

Sen, A. 1970. *Collective Choice and Social Welfare.* San Francisco: Holden-Day.

———. 1986. "Social Choice Theory." In *Handbook of Mathematical Economics*, vol. 3, K. Arrow and M. Intrilligator, eds. Amsterdam: North Holland.

———. 1988. "Social Choice." In *The New Palgrave*, vol. 4, J. Eatwell, M. Milgate, and P. Newman, eds. London: Macmillan.

Wilson, R. 1968. "The Theory of Syndicates." *Econometrica* 36:119–32.

———. 1972. "The Game-Theoretic Structure of Arrow's General Possibility Theorem." *Journal of Economic Theory* 5:14–20.

5.7. *Problems*

■ 1. Suppose that we have numerical representations $(V_1, \ldots, V_I)$ for the preferences $(\succ_i)$ of our I consumers, and we are using a weighted utilitarian social welfare functional for some given collection of weights (α_i) to make social choices. Show that we can change to the (equal-weighted) utilitarian social welfare functional without changing the choices that are made by changing at the same time the numerical representations of the preferences $(\succ_i)$.

■ 2. Consider the following social choice problem in the setting of consumption of two goods by two consumers. The two goods are called tillip and quillip and the two consumers are called 1 and 2. Consumer 1 has utility function $U_1(t, q) = 6 + .4\ln(t) + .6\ln(q)$ (where t is the amount of tillip 1 consumes and q is the amount of quillip). Consumer 2 has utility function $U_2(t, q) = 8 + \ln(t) + \ln(q)$. The social endowment consists of 15 units of tillip and 20 units of quillip.

(a) Suppose that a social dictator has social welfare functional of the following form: Social welfare, as a function of (u^1, u^2) is a weighted sum with weight 2 on the lesser of u^1 and u^2 and weight 1 on the greater of the two. What will be the welfare optimum plan chosen by this social planner?

(b) What is the set of all feasible, Pareto efficient allocations of the consumption good for this society?

■ 3. Prove proposition 5.4.

■ 4. Construct two nonintersecting convex sets in R^2 such that the only separating hyperplane between them necessarily intersects each of the sets.

■ 5. Suppose that in the setting of syndicate theory we have one risk neutral consumer and $I-1$ who are strictly risk averse. As in the text, let the risk neutral consumer have index 1. We know (from fact 4) that the risk averse consumers' parts of any efficient sharing rule consist of a constant payment regardless of the state. The size of these payments depend, of course, on all the data in the problem; in particular, they depend on the weights of the consumers in the Bergsonian social welfare functional. Holding fixed everything else (that is, the utility functions of the consumers and the payoffs in each state of nature), write $y_i(\alpha_1, \ldots, \alpha_I)$ for the payment to consumer i (for $i \geq 2$) as a function of the vector of weights. What can you say about how the function y_i changes as we change any of the individual weights?

■ 6. Prove the fifth fact from the subsection on syndicate theory. The key is to find out the right values for the constants k_i. The k_i are defined so that the first-order conditions all hold and the adding up condition holds. There are $I+N$ unknowns (each value of k_i and each multiplier μ_n) and $IN+1$ equations (IN first-order conditions and one adding up constraint), so you can see that some of the equations must be redundant, which is why this is such a special case.

■ 7. In the context of the fifth fact concerning syndicate theory, suppose the syndicate has available a number of gambles that it might undertake. Specifically, for $m = 1, \ldots, M$ the syndicate might undertake a project whose payoff in state s_n is Y_{mn}. The syndicate can undertake only one of these M alternative projects, it must undertake one, and the decision which to undertake must be made before any uncertainty concerning the state of nature resolves. In this case, the set of feasible social outcomes consists of sharing rules (y_{in}) such that for some $m = 1, \ldots, M$, $\sum_{i=1}^{I} y_{in} = Y_{mn}$ for all n. What now is the set of efficient sharing rules? (Because of the discrete nature of the variable m, you seemingly cannot solve this problem just with calculus techniques. But consider expanding the range of feasible social outcomes still further to include the possibility that the choice of gamble to take may be made randomly.)

■ 8. For each of the three examples of social choice rules given in section 5.4 (that is, the Pareto rule, majority rule, and the Borda rule), which of the four properties in Arrow's theorem does the rule obey, and which does it violate.

■ 9. Suppose that we changed the definition of a dictator in property 4 to be: i is a dictator (in a given social choice rule) if $\succ_i \equiv \succ^*$ for any array of consumer preferences. That is, we add to the definition: When i is indifferent, society is indifferent. Prove that if property 4 is changed in this fashion, it is possible to find a social choice rule that satisfies the four properties. (If you like a challenge: How precisely can you categorize all social choice rules that obey the first three properties? We know there must be a dictator in the sense of the original property 4. But what can you say about cases in which this dictator is indifferent between two outcomes?)

part II

The price mechanism

chapter six

Pure exchange and general equilibrium

Prologue to part II

Part II of this book concerns the classic models of price-mediated exchange in markets. We begin in this chapter with situations of *pure exchange*, where consumers wish to exchange bundles of goods they hold at the outset for other bundles they will subsequently consume. We will use this setting to introduce the reader to the theory of *price-mediated market transactions* and, more particularly, the theory of *general equilibrium*, in which all markets in all goods are considered simultaneously. Then, for the rest of part II, *firms* are brought into the story. Chapter 7 will give some of the fundamental concepts of the classical theory of the firm, which is very much parallel to the theory of the consumer from chapter 2. Chapter 8 will consider, both in settings of partial and general equilibrium, models of competitive firms and markets. In chapter 9 we will introduce monopoly and in chapter 10 oligopoly.

Beyond treating these fundamental pieces of classical microeconomics, we will return throughout to a particular message: Price-mediated exchange in the marketplace and, in particular, the equilibrium notions that we use are "reduced forms" for some unspecified institutional mechanisms of exchange. Especially as we encounter the models of imperfectly competitive markets in chapters 9 and 10, questions will arise about why (and whether) these are appropriate "reduced forms," questions that seemingly can be resolved only if we are more specific about the institutional mechanisms involved.

6.1. Pure exchange and price equilibrium

The problem

We imagine a world with a finite number I of *consumers*. The I consumers will be indexed $i = 1, \ldots, I$. These consumers will all (shortly) sit

down to a grand feast at which they will do all their consuming. There
are *K commodities*, indexed by $k = 1, \ldots, K$, that the consumers might
consume in varying amounts. Thus a consumption bundle for any of the
I consumers is a vector x from R^K. We will assume that consumers cannot consume negative amounts of any of the commodities, but they can
consume any nonnegative vector x from R^K, so we restrict attention to
consumption bundles from the positive orthant of R^K, which we denote
by X. Each of our *I* consumers has preferences over what she will consume; the preferences of consumer i are assumed to be represented (in the
style of chapter 2) by the utility function $U_i : X \to R$. We assume that the
consumers are all *locally insatiable* and that none of the goods is noxious,
so that preferences (and the utility functions U_i) are nondecreasing. We
assume that each consumer has continuous preferences.

We also imagine that these consumers come with *endowments* in the
form of a commodity bundle from X. We let $e^i \in X$ represent the endowment of consumer i.[1]

Our consumers could simply sit down and consume their endowments. But one consumer might, for example, be endowed with a lot of
some good that she is not particularly fond of. She may wish to exchange
some of that good for something that she likes more. So we wonder,
Which exchanges will take place? What will each consumer wind up
consuming?

The problem is one of *pure exchange* because everything that is eventually consumed comes from someone's endowment. If we write $e = \sum_{i=1}^{I} e^i$,
then e is the total endowment of all the consumers in this society, and what
consumers wind up consuming cannot exceed e in sum.

In the case of two consumers, we can use an Edgeworth box to depict
the situation. Create an Edgeworth box as in the last chapter, where the
origin of consumer 2's coordinate system is placed at the point $e = e^1 + e^2$
of consumer 1's coordinate system. If we mark point e^1 in 1's coordinate
system (which is also point e^2 in 2's coordinate system), we get the picture in figure 6.1. Note in particular the shaded "lens" and the heavily
marked portion of the contract curve. The lens represents all reallocations
of the social endowment between the two consumers in a fashion that
leaves them both at least as well off as if they consume their respective
endowments. And the shaded portion of the contract curve represents all
the Pareto efficient points that make one or the other or both better off
than at their respective endowments.

---

[1] We use a superscript i so that we can write things like e_k^i for the amount of good k
with which consumer i is endowed.

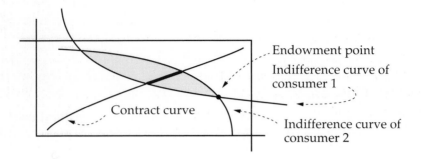

Figure 6.1. The Edgeworth box with endowments.
We show here an Edgeworth box with the endowment point of the two consumers marked. The shaded lens gives all reallocations of the social endowment (that are nonwasteful) that give each consumer at least as much utility as she obtains at her original endowment. And the heavy part of the contract curve represents all efficient reallocations with this property.

We call a collection of the objects above — a list of consumption goods, a list of consumers, and utility functions and endowments for each consumer — a *pure exchange* economy.

Price equilibrium

Now imagine that these goods are traded in markets, where p_k is the price of good k, and $p = (p_1, \ldots, p_K)$ is used to denote the *price vector*. Imagine that each of our I consumers is aware of the prices given by p, and each believes that she cannot by her actions affect any of these prices. Then consumer i has at her disposal wealth $Y^i = p \cdot e^i$. That is, she can take her endowment to each market and sell it. She will receive $p_k e^i_k$ for her endowment of good k; summing over all the k yields Y^i. She can then spend this wealth buying whatever bundle x^i maximizes her utility, subject to her budget constraint $p \cdot x^i \leq Y^i$. Of course, if she wishes to save on the number of trips she has to make, she can do the whole thing in one go-round. Having worked out which bundle she wishes to consume, she first sells commodities for which her endowment exceeds her desired consumption and then buys more of the goods for which her endowment is less than desired.

However we imagine this happening, we have the following *problem of consumer i at prices p*:

$$\text{maximize } U_i(x) \text{ subject to } x \in X \text{ and } p \cdot x \leq p \cdot e^i. \qquad \text{CP}(i,p)$$

Definition.   *A* **general equilibrium***, also called a* **Walrasian equilibrium***, for a given pure exchange economy consists of a price vector* p *and consumption bundles* x^i *for each consumer such that*

(1) at prices p, x^i *solves the problem* $CP(i, p)$

(2) markets clear: $\sum_{i=1}^{I} x^i \leq \sum_{i=1}^{I} e^i$

The array of final consumption vectors (x^i) *is referred to as the* **final consumption allocation** *in the equilibrium.*

Following in the footsteps of generations of classical microeconomists, we make the rather heroic assertion that *in many situations of pure exchange consumers will wind up at the consumption allocation part of some Walrasian equilibrium for the economy, and insofar as there are markets in these goods, prices will correspond to equilibrium prices.*

If you weren't before, perhaps you are finally rather impressed with the chutzpah of generations of microeconomists. If so, understand that no one is asserting that in *every* situation of pure exchange the outcome will resemble constituent pieces of a Walrasian equilibrium. For example, with two consumers, the case of the Edgeworth box, we might assert (or at least hope) that the two would find their way to the contract curve, and we'd be rather surprised if one or the other wound up worse off than where she had started. But we wouldn't necessarily expect the outcome to correspond to a Walrasian equilibrium. The sense of most economists who believe in Walrasian equilibrium is that it takes "many" consumers, no one (or few) of whom hold monopoly positions in one or more of the goods, to believe that the previously made assertion is apt to be correct, and it takes an institutional framework in which something like prices appear — something that establishes the "rates" at which one commodity can be exchanged for another.

We will discuss in the next section (a) reasons to believe this assertion, (b) reasons given sometimes that do not inspire belief, and (c) some reasons for doubt. But first, we give a few simple technical notes.

(1) If we multiply all prices in a Walrasian equilibrium by a positive scalar, the solutions to the consumer's problems don't change, and so we still have an equilibrium. In other words, if $(p, (x^i))$ is a Walrasian equilibrium, so is $(\lambda p, (x^i))$, for any (strictly) positive scalar λ. Put still differently, what is important in a Walrasian equilibrium are the relative prices — the rates at which one commodity can be exchanged for another.

(2) We have assumed that consumers' preferences are nondecreasing. We can conclude from this assumption that every price p_k must be nonneg-

ative at any equilibrium. This is so because if $p_k < 0$, then a consumer could "buy" lots of good k at no decrease in her utility and "buying" a good with a negative price means more resources to buy other goods. We assume consumers are locally insatiable, so if some price were negative, consumers would never find an optimal solution to their consumption problem, and we certainly wouldn't find markets clearing in this good.[a]

(3) Since we have assumed that consumers are locally insatiable, they are sure to spend all their wealth at any solution to CP(i, p); that is, $p \cdot x^i = p \cdot e^i$. By summing over all consumers' budget constraints, we conclude that

$$\sum_i p \cdot x^i = \sum_i p \cdot e^i.$$

Yet we only require that $\sum_i x^i \leq \sum_i e^i$. By virtue of (2) we know that prices are nonnegative, so we conclude that the only goods k for which $\sum_i x_k^i < \sum_i e_k^i$ is possible are goods whose price p_k is zero. (Be sure you see why this follows from [2].)

(4) We could never have a Walrasian equilibrium where all prices are zero, as long as consumers (or even just one consumer) are locally insatiable.

(5) While we don't take quite seriously the notion of a Walrasian equilibrium in a two-person economy, nonetheless it may be instructive to see what these equilibria look like in an Edgeworth box. Refer to figure 6.2(a). We have put a negatively sloped line through the endowment point; the slope of this line represents a particular set of relative prices for the two goods, and the shaded triangle represents the set of budget-feasible consumption bundles for consumer 1 at these relative prices. Hence consumer 1, solving her problem at these relative prices, would select the point marked with a star. The crucial thing is that at these relative prices, the same "budget line" works for consumer 2 in his coordinate system. It should take you a moment's reflection to see why this is true. To help you see this, we have drawn the relative prices in figure 6.2(a,b,c) so that the price of good 1 is half that of good 2. Hence consumer 2's budget feasible set is the shaded region in figure 6.2(b), and he chooses the point marked

---

[a] To come to this conclusion it would suffice to have one consumer who is locally insatiable and has nondecreasing preferences, since it is implicit in the definition of an equilibrium that every consumer's problem has a finite solution. For some goods, such as pollution, it may not be sensible to assume that preferences are nondecreasing. To allow for such goods, one must allow for negative prices and replace the inequality in the "markets clear" relationship with an equality. You will find this variation discussed in most books that study general equilibrium in detail.

with the box. If we superimpose the two, as we do in figure 6.2(c), we see that we don't have an equilibrium at these relative prices; consumers 1 and 2 together want more of the first good than is available.

In figure 6.2(d) we show what things look like at an equilibrium. At the relative prices shown there, both consumers choose the point marked with the star, although this star represents different bundles in the two different coordinate systems. Note carefully that each consumer's indifference curve through the point ⋆ is tangent to the budget line at that point, *and hence the two indifference curves are tangent to each other at* ⋆. That is, the Walrasian equilibrium allocation lies along the contract curve; it is Pareto efficient. This is a "proof in a picture" of a very general fact that we will prove in section 6.3.

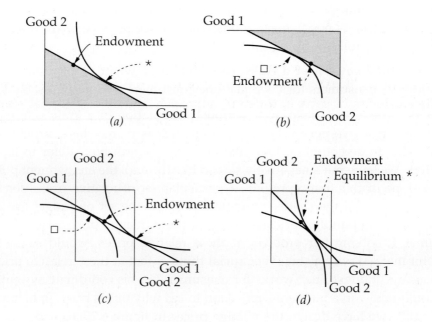

Figure 6.2. Walrasian equilibrium and the Edgeworth box.
In (a), we show the demand of consumer 1 at a particular set of relative prices, and in (b), we see consumer 2's demand at those prices. Superimposing the two in (c), we see that these demands are inconsistent; this is not a Walrasian equilibrium. In (d) we see the picture of a Walrasian equilibrium, and in particular we see that a Walrasian equilibrium lies along the contract curve.

6.2. Why (not) believe in Walrasian equilibrium?

Why should anyone believe that the outcome of exchange will look like a Walrasian equilibrium? Or, rather, in what situations would it be sensible to believe this assertion? One thinks first of a free-market economy in which goods do sell at some prices, where consumers know those prices, and where consumers can buy and sell commodities in whatever quantities they wish at the prevailing prices. If we ever found consumers in such a situation, then we would have consumers who are aware of the relative rates of exchange of each commodity for every other. If all consumers take these rates of exchange as given, if all consumers face the same rates of exchange, if all maximize their utility as in chapter 2, and if all consumers are in the end happy with the exchanges they have made, then we would necessarily have a Walrasian equilibrium. Let us make a list of some things this suggests we might worry about.

(1) Each consumer must be aware of all the prices for every good. In reality, some goods trade at more than one price in different locations. There are reasons that this could persist which are consistent with every consumer knowing all the prices at all locations, (such as buying a good at a particular location bundles together the purchase of the good with different levels of service, different ambiance, and so on). But it seems unrealistic to suppose that all consumers know all prices in all locations; anyone who has ever shopped for a new car (at least, in the United States) will know this. As soon as consumers face different prices, the assertion is in trouble (unless we modify the definition to allow for prices that change with the individual consumer).

Another aspect concerns dynamic choice in an uncertain world. Insofar as some of the exchanges made today depend on exchanges the consumer hopes she will be able to make later, today's choices depend on forecasts of later prices and market opportunities. (Consider, for example, buying a particular car based on a hypothesis about the price of gasoline that will later prevail.) Do consumers accurately forecast all subsequent prices? And what if, a priori, there is uncertainty about the future that will later resolve, the resolution of which affects later prices? (For example, the price of gasoline three years hence may depend on the political situation in various parts of the world, oil reserves found or not found in particular locations, and so on.) Economists adapt the model of Walrasian equilibrium to situations where time and/or uncertainty play a role. These adaptations will be discussed briefly in section 6.5; until then (and, perhaps, even after), scepticism about how well the basic assertion will do when time and/or uncertainty plays a role seems warranted.

(2) Consumers must be able to buy or sell as much or as little as they want at the going prices. There are (at least) two reasons to doubt this. First, consumers might wish to transact in such large amounts that they affect the prices they face. J. D. Rockefeller, seeking to sell all the oil he owned, would probably have found that an attempt to do so would have changed the price of oil. The second reason for doubt is at a more pedestrian level. In many economies rationing and stock-outs are not unknown. In some economies, a consumer may wish to buy a leg of lamb and may know the "price" of lamb that is supposed to be charged, but there is no guarantee that any lamb will be in stock at the butcher shop.

(3) Consumers may not act rationally; that is, in the fashion of chapter 2. Little is left to say about this that we haven't already said.

(4) In most economies where we might hope to meet all the conditions mentioned, the economy is not one where agents simply exchange their endowments. In most economies production also takes place. If all the good candidate economies have production, then the foregoing definition, which involves pure exchange, may be descriptive of almost nothing.

>   We will introduce production in the context of private enterprise economies in the next few chapters, but for now let us mention a variation on the basic definition of a Walrasian equilibrium that will go at least partway toward meeting this source of worry. We imagine an economy with K commodities, I consumers, and a "productive sector" — either a sector of firms or a government enterprise sector or some mix. We can think of the total effect of this productive sector as: a certain vector of commodities z^I is bought as input and another vector z^O is sold as output. Then,
>
>   **Definition.** *A **Walrasian equilibrium** for a given pure exchange economy **with fixed total production input** z^I **and output** z^O consists of a price vector p and consumption bundles x^i for each consumer such that the following hold:*
>
>   *(1) for each i, at prices p, x^i solves the problem $CP(i,p)$ and*
>
>   *(2) markets clear:* $z^I + \sum_{i=1}^{I} x^i \leq z^O + \sum_{i=1}^{I} e^i$.
>
>   In other words, we take the production plans as exogenously given and look at the "consumer exchange" part of the economy. In later chapters we will move the production plans into the category of things endogenously chosen. But we could, with the definition above, at least study consumer exchange for each fixed production plan.[b]

---

[b] At the risk of being overly pedantic and confusing the reader, a caution should be entered here when you think of the productive sector as a state enterprise. In such cases, some of the inputs to production may result from taxation of consumers' initial endowments, or from taxes on the sale and purchase of particular items, especially labor services. The consumer's problem would have to be changed to reflect any such taxation.

For each of the reasons given above and others besides, you might not think that the results of trading, even in a well-functioning market economy, would result in a Walrasian equilibrium. To deal with these criticisms, many variations on the basic model have been created. For example, there is an enormous literature (to which you will shortly be introduced) about price equilibrium in markets where time and/or uncertainty play a role. There are attempts to model equilibrium price dispersion (caused by lack of perfect information). There is analysis of situations where some consumers can change prices with their actions (although it is far more typical to think that firms have this sort of power; we will see such models in chapters 9 and 10). There is a literature on equilibrium where consumers can be rationed. All these are variations on the theme of Walrasian equilibrium as defined above. So both to understand situations where these qualifications aren't needed and to set a benchmark against which such variations can be measured, we proceed with our study of Walrasian equilibrium.

Mechanisms behind Walrasian equilibrium

While we may look at market economies for cases in which Walrasian equilibrium is a reasonable solution concept, one thing that the concept of a Walrasian equilibrium doesn't provide is any sense of *how* markets operate. There is no model here of who sets prices, or what gets exchanged for what, when, and where. One thing that we see in most market economies and that is completely missing from the story is *money*. (Prices have to be measured in some numeraire but, as we have already seen, in the theory it is only relative prices of commodities that matter.) Because of this, a Walrasian equilibrium is a *reduced form* solution concept; it describes what we imagine will be the outcome of some underlying and unmodeled process. It seems natural to think that we could increase (or decrease) our faith in the concept of a Walrasian equilibrium if we had some sense of how markets really do operate. And economists have studied specific models of market/exchange mechanisms, attempting to see whether those mechanisms confirm Walrasian equilibrium as an appropriate reduced form solution concept.

A fairly unrealistic mechanism, which nonetheless populates some of the literature on general equilibrium, concerns an individual known as the *Walrasian auctioneer*. This individual stands up in front of the entire population of an economy and calls out a price vector p. Every consumer consults her preferences and determines what she would want to buy and sell at these prices; we will write $z^i(p) = x^i(p) - e^i$ for the *net trade* that consumer i desires at prices p. Each consumer reports back to the auctioneer what net trade she wishes, and the auctioneer adds them up; if $\sum_{i=1}^{I} z^i(p) \le 0$, everyone breathes a sigh of relief and the net trades are executed. But if markets don't clear at prices p, then the auctioneer tries a different price vector p', and so on. One can pose various rules that the auctioneer might employ in determining what prices p' to quote if p doesn't work — say he raises the price of goods that are overdemanded (that is, any good k for which $\sum_{i=1}^{I} z_k^i(p) > 0$) and lowers the price of those that are underdemanded. We may wonder whether this scheme of price adjustment will lead to an equilibrium. You can find discussion of this in the literature; look for references to the *tatonnement* adjustment process. (We won't carry further on this subject because Walrasian auctioneers are not usually found in real economies.)

A second unrealistic mechanism involves each consumer simply reporting to the central authorities her desired excess demands at *every* price p. (In cases where at a price vector p the consumer is indifferent between several excess demand vectors, we will allow her to submit all the alternatives she would be happy to take.) The authorities (who previously employed the Walrasian auctioneer) examine all these submissions and look for one or more prices p where markets clear. (We won't say what they do if the excess demand functions submitted are not consistent with market clearing at any price.)

A major reason why the two previous mechanisms seem unrealistic is that they involve equilibration of all markets for all consumers at once. It is more realistic to think of institutions and mechanisms where either each market operates separately or trades are made between pairs of individuals.

For example, we can imagine consumers wandering around a large market square, with all their possessions on their backs. They have chance meetings with each other, and when two consumers meet, they examine what each has offer, to see if they can arrange a mutually agreeable trade.[2] To be very precise, we might imagine that at every chance meeting of this sort the two flip a coin and depending on the outcome one is allowed to propose an exchange, which the other must either accept or reject. If an exchange is made, the two swap goods and wander around in search of more advantageous trades made at chance meetings. The rule is that you can't eat until you leave the market square, so consumers wait until they are satisfied with what they possess and then leave to have a picnic in the adjacent park. In this story, a smart consumer who hates

---

[2] For those readers who follow American baseball, think of general managers trading players, but on a larger scale.

apples may nonetheless give up some of her pears for someone else's apples if the apples are offered on good terms, in the speculative hope that she will later be able to trade the apples for the cherries that she really wants.[3]

Or we can imagine models in which it is imagined that markets in the various goods operate independently. One might imagine a model with market makers — individuals who specialize in a particular commodity or related commodities. Over in one corner of the market square is the cheese vendor who is happy to buy or sell cheese (for money or for some standard good, such as wheat or gold), in another corner is a specialist in corn, and so on. We might imagine that the cheese vendor posts prices at his stall, in which case we might want to have a few cheese vendors with stalls adjacent to each other to provide some competition, or we might imagine more traditional bargaining between anyone who comes up to the cheese stand and the cheese vendor. The point is that all transactions in cheese go via the cheese vendor; if consumer 1 is endowed with too much cheese and consumer 2 with too little, consumer 1 sells her excess cheese to the cheese vendor, who then resells some of this to consumer 2.

Or we could organize the cheese market without a specialist cheese vendor. Making, say, wheat the medium of exchange, we might imagine that at 10:05 A.M., it is time to auction off Stilton cheese. Anyone with Stilton to sell is allowed to post an "asking price"; this person will sell a standardized amount of Stilton for so many bushels of wheat. At the same time, those interested in buying Stilton are allowed to post "bids" — so many bushels of wheat for a piece of Stilton. At any point in time, a consumer can "take" any offer that is currently posted: Consumers can post new offers (on either side of the market), they can improve offers they already have posted, and they can retract offers they previously have made. The posting of offers can be done by open outcry or by some fancy electronic posting service. (Consumers all sit at CRT terminals and can enter bids or asks; the CRT always displays the current "best" bids and asks; and one can take the best posted offer at the touch of a particular key on the keyboard.) All this takes place from 10:05 until 10:20, after which it is time for Camembert, and so on.

The exploration of more realistic models of markets is in relative infancy. A large part of this literature appears in the monetary economics (the economic theory of money) and is concerned first and foremost with the use of money in these types of markets. The analysis of the "random

---

[3] Fans of baseball may recall the occasional trade based on this sort of calculation.

meetings" marketplace has been quite popular recently, and the analysis that has been done offers *qualified* support for the Walrasian equilibrium notion. Analysis of markets in a single commodity, both of the market-maker and two-sided auction variety (as well as one-sided auctions) can be found as well, although little of this work has extended from the case of a single market to issues associated with general equilibrium. References will be provided in section 6.6, although in general you will need to get through part III of this book before this literature will be accessible.

Experimental evidence

If you consult these references, you will find that the analysis is hard and the conclusions require consumers who are extraordinarily sophisticated. You might worry, in consequence, that the results derived in support of the concept of Walrasian equilibrium are not very credible. To assuage these worries, you should consult the literature on experimental economics. A number of researchers have attempted to see whether markets perform under controlled conditions in the way economists assume they do. In the typical experiment, different subjects are induced to have different valuations for some good, relative to a numeraire good (money). Some of the subjects who are initially endowed with the good put a relatively low value on it; others who do not have it put a relatively high value on it. From the data of the experimental conditions, one can compute what the "equilibrium price" for the good should be (if standard microeconomic theory is correct). The subjects are then put into an exchange environment, to see whether they make exchanges the way the theory says they will. The CRT-terminal-mediated double "oral" auction market mechanism is often used.

The results obtained are usually striking in their support of Walrasian equilibrium. Subjects are not given the data needed to calculate a priori what the equilibrium prices "ought" to be. So the first time the market operates, some trades are made far from the theoretical equilibrium. But if the market is repeated (endowments are restored), subjects typically learn extremely quickly what the market clearing price for the good will be, and they trade in a way that is quite close to what theory predicts.

These experiments do not quite get to the level of generality of a Walrasian equilibrium for a general equilibrium with many interdependent markets. But the repertory of experiments is growing quickly and, except for a few special cases, those experiments that have been run are consistent with the notion of Walrasian equilibrium. All in all, they make Walrasian equilibrium look quite good.

6.3. The efficiency of a general equilibrium

We now turn to properties of Walrasian equilibrium. We return to the setting of section 6.1 with K commodities and I consumers who exchange those commodities. We suppose that a Walrasian equilibrium is achieved. And we ask: Is this Walrasian equilibrium a *good* way to allocate resources in this economy? Putting it in slightly melodramatic and ideological terms, can we confiscate everyone's endowment, reallocate goods, and in so doing obtain an allocation better than that achieved in a Walrasian equilibrium?

Of course, to answer this question we need a sense of what we mean by "better." Following developments from the last chapter, we use the concept of Pareto efficiency.

The two theorems of welfare economics

Having chosen Pareto efficiency as our criterion, we can recall a remark made in section 6.1 about the Edgeworth box: In a two-person, two-good economy, the allocation part of a Walrasian equilibrium is Pareto efficient (that is, lies along the contract curve). This result generalizes very neatly.

Theorem. The First Theorem of Welfare Economics. *A Walrasian equilibrium always yields a Pareto efficient allocation of the social endowment.*[4]

The proof is quite simple. Suppose that $(p, (\hat{x}^i))$ is a Walrasian equilibrium and $(\check{x}^i)$ is a Pareto superior allocation of the social endowment. We will derive a contradiction.

Since $(\check{x}^i)$ is a reallocation of the social endowment $e = \sum_{i=1}^{I} e^i$, we have $\sum_{i=1}^{I} \check{x}^i \leq e$. Since equilibrium prices are nonnegative, this implies

$$\sum_{i=1}^{I} p \cdot \check{x}^i \leq p \cdot e. \qquad (\star)$$

Since preferences are locally insatiable, Walras' law holds with equality for each consumer and summing these equations yields

$$\sum_{i=1}^{I} p \cdot \hat{x}^i = p \cdot e. \qquad (\star\star)$$

---

[4] We maintain here the earlier hypotheses that consumers are all locally insatiable and have nondecreasing preferences. We wouldn't need to assume nondecreasing preferences if we posed the "markets clear" conditions in the definitions of an equilibrium and a feasible allocation as equalities.

By assumption, each consumer i likes $\breve{x}^i$ as much as $\hat{x}^i$, and some one (or more) consumer likes $\breve{x}^i$ more. Consider consumer i. Since this consumer at least weakly prefers $\breve{x}^i$ to $\hat{x}^i$, it must be that $p{\cdot}\breve{x}^i \geq p{\cdot}\hat{x}^i = p{\cdot}e^i$. For if $p \cdot \breve{x}^i < p \cdot \hat{x}^i$, then by local insatiability i could afford something strictly better than $\breve{x}^i$ at prices p, which would be strictly better than $\hat{x}^i$, which would then contradict the supposed optimality of $\hat{x}^i$ for i at prices p. Similarly (in fact, even more simply), for any consumer i such that $\breve{x}^i$ is strictly better than $\hat{x}^i$, we must have $p{\cdot}\breve{x}^i > p{\cdot}\hat{x}^i = p{\cdot}e^i$. This must hold for at least one consumer since we assume $(\breve{x}^i)$ Pareto dominates $(\hat{x}^i)$, and so by summing up these weak and strict inequalities we obtain

$$\sum_{i=1}^{I} p \cdot \breve{x}^i > \sum_{i=1}^{I} p \cdot \hat{x}^i.$$

Comparing this inequality with $(\star)$ and $(\star\star)$ gives us the desired contradiction and completes the proof.

You should now be hearing choirs of angels and choruses of trumpets. The "invisible hand" of the price mechanism produces equilibria that cannot be improved upon.

Of course, one can wonder whether the price mechanism produces any equilibrium at all; the result above is predicated on the existence of a Walrasian equilibrium. We will attend to questions about the existence of equilibrium in the next section. But granting existence, it should still be noted that "improved upon" in the previous paragraph refers to Pareto improvements. There is no reason to suppose that the equilibrium allocation is not vastly inequitable, giving lots of utility to some consumers and very little to others. In response to this consideration, we have the following result.

Theorem. The Second Theorem of Welfare Economics. *Assume that preferences are convex, continuous, nondecreasing, and locally insatiable. Let $(\hat{x}^i)$ be a Pareto efficient allocation of the social endowment that is strictly positive: $\hat{x}_k^i > 0$ for all i and k. Then $(\hat{x}^i)$ is the allocation part of a Walrasian equilibrium, if we first appropriately redistribute endowments among the consumers.*

In other words, if one imagines that it would be difficult for a social dictator to find an equitable and efficient allocation of the social endowment, and if the economy has well-functioning markets, the dictator might choose to reallocate initial endowments in an equitable fashion and then let the market take over. If you wonder how the social dictator could decide a priori on an equitable initial redistribution of the social endowment, see problem 3 for at least one idea.

Here is a sketch of the proof. Suppose $(\hat{x}^i)$ is the Pareto efficient allocation of the social allocation e that we wish to obtain as a Walrasian equilibrium. Let $\hat{e} = \sum_{i=1}^{I} \hat{x}^i$. Note that $\hat{e} \leq e$; a strict inequality is possible for some components. (We will have to work around this possibility.)
Define

$$X^* = \{x \in X : x \text{ can be allocated among the } I$$

$$\text{consumers in a way that strictly Pareto dominates } (\hat{x}^i)\}.$$

We assert (and you can prove for homework) that the set X^* is convex because preferences are convex. Let

$$X^\dagger = \{x \in R^K : x \leq e\}.$$

This is obviously a convex set.

The supposed Pareto efficiency of the "hat" allocation ensures that X^* and $X^\dagger$ do not intersect. Thus there is a *separating hyperplane* between them — a nonzero K-dimensional vector $p = (p_1, \ldots, p_K)$ and a scalar β such that $p \cdot x \leq \beta$ for all $x \in X^\dagger$ and $p \cdot x \geq \beta$ for all $x \in X^*$. By local insatiability and continuity, we can show that $\hat{e}$, which is in $X^\dagger$, is on the boundary of X^*, and so $p \cdot \hat{e} = \beta$. We assert that $p \geq 0$; the proof is left to you. (Use the shape of the set $X^\dagger$.) We assert that $p \cdot e = \beta$ as well; since preferences are nondecreasing we can take any goods left over from the social endowment in the allocation (x^i) and allocate them among the consumers and then repeat the argument using local insatiability and continuity. Thus we know that if $\hat{e}_k < e_k$ for some good k, then $p_k = 0$.

Let $\hat{e}^i$ be any allocation of the social endowment e such that $p \cdot \hat{e}^i = p \cdot \hat{x}^i$. We know that such allocations exist because the goods not fully used up in the allocation (x^i) must have zero price.

We claim that $(p, (\hat{x}^i))$ is a Walrasian equilibrium for the economy if consumers start out with the endowments $(\hat{e}^i)$. To see this, suppose it is not a Walrasian equilibrium. Partition the set of consumers into two subsets: those for whom $\hat{x}^i$ is the best they can afford at prices p with endowment $\hat{e}^i$ and those for whom there is something better they can afford. Since by assumption $(p, (\hat{x}^i))$ is not a Walrasian equilibrium, the second set in this partition is nonempty.

For each i from the second set in the partition, let x^i be any bundle which i strictly prefers to $\hat{x}^i$ and that is affordable at prices p with endowment $\hat{e}^i$. By continuity of preferences, for some positive scalar $\alpha^i < 1$, the bundle $\alpha^i x^i$ is strictly preferred to $\hat{x}^i$ and satisfies $p \cdot \alpha x^i < p \cdot x^i \leq p \cdot \hat{e}^i$.[c]

---

[c] This implicitly assumes that $p \cdot x^i > 0$. But if $p \cdot x^i = 0$, since x^i is strictly positive, $p \cdot \hat{e}^i = p \cdot \hat{x}^i > 0$. And then $p \cdot x^i < p \cdot \hat{e}^i$, which is what we really need.

Define $\check{x}^i = \alpha x^i$. Let $s = \sum p \cdot (\hat{e}^i - \check{x}^i)$ where this sum is over the second set of consumers. By construction $s > 0$. Using this "budget surplus" and the local insatiability of preferences, it is possible to find bundles $\check{x}^i$ for the consumers i in the first group such that $\check{x}^i$ is strictly preferred by i to $\hat{x}^i$ and such that $\sum_{i=1}^{I} p \cdot \check{x}^i < \sum_{i=1}^{I} p \cdot \hat{x}^i = \beta$. But since $(\check{x}^i)$ is strictly Pareto superior to $(\hat{x}^i)$, $\sum_{i=1}^{I} \check{x}^i \in X^*$. And for all $x \in X^*$, $p \cdot x \geq \beta$. This gives the desired contradiction, completing the proof.

There are two remarks to make about this theorem and proof. First, the assumption that $(\hat{x}^i)$ is a strictly positive allocation is much too strong. There are, presumably, goods that one consumer doesn't like at all; these goods don't lower her utility (we're assuming nondecreasing preferences), but they do nothing to raise her utility. If these goods are appreciated by others, then strict positivity of the allocation is inconsistent with Pareto efficiency! To repair this catastrophe, there are numerous ways to proceed. One of the simplest is to say that a good is *desirable* if everyone's preferences are strictly increasing in that good. Then we could replace the assumption that $(\hat{x}^i)$ is strictly positive with the much less obnoxious assumption that every consumer is given, in the allocation $(\hat{x}^i)$, a positive amount of at least one desirable good. You are asked in problem 4(c) to show that this will be enough to get the result of the second welfare theorem.

Second, we used a separating hyperplane argument in the previous chapter to prove proposition 5.2, and it may be useful to highlight the differences. Here, we are separating two convex sets in the space of commodity bundles, R^K. Separating hyperplanes in this space have the right dimensionality to be prices. In proposition 5.2, we were separating convex sets in the space of utility imputations, R^I, and the hyperplane gave us "weights" to put on the utilities of the various consumers. Note also that in proposition 5.2, we obtained convexity of one of the two separated sets from an assumption that the utility functions were concave functions. (To be precise, in the proof of proposition 5.2, we assumed convexity by fiat, by looking at the convex hull of $V(X')$. But we justified this approach in proposition 5.3 by assuming that utility functions were concave.) Here we are making the weaker assumption that preferences are convex; we don't need to assume that they have a concave numerical representation.

Externalities

Do you hear the angels and trumpets now? There are good reasons still not to hear them having to do with all the hidden assumptions made in the story of Walrasian equilibrium. We will discuss one of these, *externalities*, in some detail here.

In the model of an exchange economy posed above, each consumer is an "island" given prices. In particular, the utility of each consumer is unaffected by the consumption decisions of other consumers, if prices are held fixed.

In reality, matters may be more complex. Consumer i may enjoy filling his front yard with junk or may wish to add to the traffic of a particular highway, which will depress the utility of neighbor i' and fellow driver i''. On the other hand, consumer j may take good care of her garden, which raises the utility level of neighbor j'.

These are simple examples of *externalities*, situations where the consumption of some good(s) by one consumer affects the utility of another. In the first two cases, consumer i is generating negative externalities for i' and for i''. In the third case, consumer j is providing positive externalities for j'. When there are externalities, we can't speak of the utility of consumer i as being represented by a function $U_i : X \to R$; now the domain for i's utility function will potentially be the *entire* vector of consumption $x = (x^1, x^2, \ldots, x^I) \in X^I$. Following the notation of chapter 5, we will use V_i to represent the preferences of consumer i over entire consumption allocations.

What do we mean by a Walrasian equilibrium when there are externalities? To see why there is a question here, imagine that consumer 1 attaches greater value to keeping her yard in good shape if her neighbor, consumer 2, keeps his yard clean. (To be precise, assume that the marginal utility consumer 1 attaches to keeping her yard neat increases with increases in the neatness of 2's yard.) Then at any prices, the amount of money consumer 1 will wish to spend on her yard depends on how neatly she believes her neighbor will keep his. If she believes that he will keep his yard in good shape, she will wish to spend more than if she believes that he will keep his yard in poor shape. We can't tell how much she will wish to spend if we don't know what he will spend on his yard. And, assuming the externality works in both directions, we can't say what he will spend until we know what she is going to spend. There is a simultaneity problem involving the two utility maximizations.

It is typical when modeling general equilibrium with externalities to come to grips with this by supposing that each consumer chooses her own consumption levels taking as given the *equilibrium* consumption levels of her fellow consumers. We define:

Definition. *A **Walrasian equilibrium with externalities** consists of prices p and a consumption vector $\hat{x} = (\hat{x}^1, \ldots, \hat{x}^I)$ such that*

(a) For each consumer i, $\hat{x}^i$ is the solution in the variable x^i to the problem

$$\text{maximize } V_i(\hat{x}^1, \ldots, \hat{x}^{i-1}, x^i, \hat{x}^{i+1}, \ldots, \hat{x}^I)$$
$$\text{subject to } x^i \in X \text{ and } p \cdot x^i \leq p \cdot e^i.$$

(b) Markets clear: $\sum_{i=1}^{I} x^i \leq \sum_{i=1}^{I} e^i$.

We might wonder whether this is the appropriate definition: Will consumers in an exchange economy in which there are externalities find their way to a Walrasian equilibrium?[5] Setting that question aside, we can ask if Walrasian equilibria in this setting will be efficient.

The answer is in general no. If there are externalities, our proof of the first welfare theorem will not work. Specifically, the proof breaks down at the step where we say that if $(\check{x}^i)$ is Pareto superior to $(\hat{x}^i)$, then $p \cdot \check{x}^i \geq p \cdot \hat{x}^i$, with strict inequality for some consumers i. Before, $(\check{x}^i)$ being Pareto superior to $(\hat{x}^i)$ meant that consumer i would be at least as well off consuming $\check{x}^i$ as $\hat{x}^i$, *no matter what her fellow consumers did*, because her utility only depended on her own consumption. But to say that $(\check{x}^i)$ is better for i than $(\hat{x}^i)$ does not imply that

$$ V_i(\hat{x}^1, \ldots, \hat{x}^{i-1}, \check{x}^i, \hat{x}^{i+1}, \ldots, \hat{x}^I) > V_i(\hat{x}^1, \ldots, \hat{x}^{i-1}, \hat{x}^i, \hat{x}^{i+1}, \ldots, \hat{x}^I). $$

That is, consumer i cannot necessarily do better (staying within her budget set) by changing only her own level of consumption. The components of $(\check{x}^i)$ might all be affordable, and $(\check{x}^i)$ might be Pareto superior, and still the components of $(\hat{x}^i)$ might solve the individual consumers' maximization problems *given* other consumers are choosing their parts of $(\hat{x}^i)$.

Establishing that the proof breaks down is not the same thing as showing that equilibrium allocations will be inefficient. We will offer a loose argument in a particular setting that every equilibrium allocation will be inefficient owing to externalities.[6] Since this argument applies to every equilibrium allocation, it shows that both the first and second theorems aren't valid when there are externalities. (The loose argument that follows requires that you have at least a sense of Taylor series expansions. If this sort of thing is entirely foreign to you, then skip the next paragraph.)

Imagine a three-person economy in which the first commodity is "gardening services," the consumption of which makes one's yard more beautiful. Imagine that two of the consumers in this society live in adjacent houses, while the third lives on the other side of a particularly large mountain. Consumption by the third consumer of gardening services generates no externality for the other consumers, but each of the others generates

---

[5] Thinking ahead to part III of the book, we can suggest why they might not, at least in some cases. Suppose that in equilibrium i and i' spend very little on their respective yards, and suppose each would happily spend more if the other spent more. Then we might imagine a neighborhood conference where each promises to spend more on condition that the other spends more. We have to worry about how this would be enforced; but in chapter 14 we will see one quite natural enforcement mechanism for this sort of agreement.

[6] In problem 5 you are asked to provide a precise example to go with this argument, and in problem 6 you are given another concrete example to work through.

a positive externality for her neighbor through the consumption of gardening services. At any prices p, each consumer chooses the level of gardening services to consume in a way that equates the ratio of marginal utilities of gardening services to the marginal utility of consumption of other goods to the ratio of their prices. That is, each sets

$$\frac{\partial V_i}{\partial x_1^i} \bigg/ \frac{\partial V_i}{\partial x_2^i} = \frac{p_1}{p_2},$$

where x_1^i is the level of consumption of gardening services by i, and x_2^i is i's level of consumption of some other good that doesn't generate any externalities. Thus if we increase the amount of gardening services that, say, consumer 1 consumes by some small amount δ and lower the amount of good 2 that she consumes by $(p_1/p_2)\delta$, the marginal impact on her utility is approximately

$$\frac{\partial V_1}{\partial x_1^1}\delta - \frac{\partial V_1}{\partial x_2^1}\frac{p_1}{p_2}\delta = 0.$$

Similarly, if we simultaneously decrease the amount of gardening services that consumer 3 consumes by δ and raise the amount of good 2 that he consumes by $(p_1/p_2)\delta$, the impact on his utility is approximately zero. So this small reallocation doesn't change the utilities of either consumer 1 or consumer 3. But because of the positive externality that raising the level of gardening services consumed by consumer 1 has on the utility of consumer 2, this small reallocation improves the utility of consumer 2. Thus this small reallocation is Pareto improving, showing that a Walrasian equilibrium will not be Pareto efficient.

We will return to externalities in chapter 8; there are other interesting examples to discuss, but they require an economy with a productive sector. For now, we simply note that externalities give one reason to doubt that markets lead to efficient allocations. There are other reasons to doubt the conclusions of the two theorems; we put off discussion of one of them (taxes) also to chapter 8.

6.4. *Existence and the number of equilibria*

We turn next to a brief discussion of two highly mathematical points concerning Walrasian equilibrium. Because the second point especially is very important to one of the central messages of the book, I urge you to pay attention at least to the discussion in regular-sized type.

Existence

So far, we have discussed properties of Walrasian equilibria for exchange economies under the supposition that at least one equilibrium exists. It is, of course, interesting to know whether these results have any relevance: For a given exchange economy, are there Walrasian equilibria?[d] In general the answer will be no, so the question really becomes: *Under what conditions on an exchange economy can we guarantee the existence of at least one Walrasian equilibrium?*

To see ways to answer this question, consider an economy with two goods. We continue to maintain all assumptions made earlier: Consumer's preferences are continuous, locally insatiable and nondecreasing. For a two-good economy, this means we can draw some very simple pictures, constructed from the following considerations:

(1) We already know that if (p_1, p_2) is an equilibrium price vector, so is $(\lambda p_1, \lambda p_2)$ for any positive constant λ. Since preferences are nondecreasing, we know that equilibrium prices will be nonnegative, and since equilibrium prices are certainly nonzero, we know that at any equilibrium $p_1 + p_2 > 0$. Putting these facts together, if (p_1', p_2') are equilibrium prices, so are $p_1 = p_1'/(p_1' + p_2')$ and $p_2 = p_2'/(p_1' + p_2')$, and of course $p_1 + p_2 = 1$. In other words, we can restrict attention to prices (p_1, p_2) such that $p_1 + p_2 = 1$.

(2) Fix prices p_1 and $p_2 = 1 - p_1$ such that $p_2 > 0$. Suppose that for a given consumer i, x_1^i is part of a solution to the consumer's utility maximization problem at these prices. Since local insatiability implies that the consumer satisfies her budget constraint with equality at any solution, we know that the corresponding x_2^i must be

$$x_2^i = \frac{p_1 e_1^i + p_2 e_2^i - p_1 x_1^i}{p_2}.$$

(3) Continue to hold fixed a pair of prices p_1 and $p_2 = 1 - p_1 > 0$. Suppose that for each consumer i, x_1^i is part of a solution to consumer i's utility maximization problem at these prices and suppose that markets clear in good 1 precisely: $\sum_{i=1}^{I} x_1^i = \sum_{i=1}^{I} e_1^i$. *We assert that this guarantees that we*

---

[d] If you pay attention to the more technical material, you know that in the proof of the second theorem of welfare economics we established that Walrasian equilibria exist for at least some initial allocations of the social endowment. For comparison with later discussion in this section, note that this theorem assumed that all consumers have convex preferences.

have an equilibrium. All that is missing is knowledge that the market in good 2 clears. But

$$\sum_{i=1}^{I} x_2^i = \sum_{i=1}^{I} \frac{p_1 e_1^i + p_2 e_2^i - p_1 x_1^i}{p_2}$$

$$= \frac{1}{p_2}\left[p_1 \sum_{i=1}^{I}(e_1^i - x_1^i) + p_2 \sum_{i=1}^{I} e_2^i\right] = \frac{1}{p_2}\left[p_2 \sum_{i=1}^{I} e_2^i\right] = \sum_{i=1}^{I} e_2^i.$$

The key equality in this string is the next to last, where we use the fact that markets clear in good 1.

We are ready to draw pictures when we make one more assumption:

Assumption 1. *For every pair of strictly positive prices p_1 and p_2, and for each consumer i, the consumer's utility maximization problem has a unique solution.*

There are two parts to this assumption. First, this assumption entails the existence of a solution to each consumer's utility maximization problem for every set of strictly positive prices. If you look back to proposition 2.11(a) (and we assume that endowments are nonnegative), you will see that we already have made enough assumptions for this. The second part of the assumption is that the solution is unique. This is more problematic, but proposition 2.11(c) tells us that this is guaranteed if we add strict convexity to our assumptions about the consumer's preferences.

With this assumption, we can write $x_1^i(p_1)$ for the first-commodity part of the unique solution to i's utility maximization problem at prices p_1 and $p_2 = 1 - p_1$ such that $0 < p_1 < 1$. Note carefully that we only make p_1 an argument of this function, since, by (1), we can restrict attention to prices that sum to one. Also, $x_1^i(p_1)$ explicitly gives demand for the first commodity only; but the demand for the second commodity is implicit, by (2).

Now let $X_1(p_1) = \sum_{i=1}^{I} x_1^i(p_1)$. This gives the *aggregate demand* for the first commodity at prices p_1 (and $p_2 = 1 - p_1$). This is what we graph; in figure 6.3, you see the function $p_1 \to X_1(p_1)$ graphed for arguments p_1 between zero and one. Also in figure 6.3, you see in each picture a horizontal line drawn at the height $e_1 = \sum_{i=1}^{I} e_1^i$, that is, at the level of the social endowment in good 1. *By virtue of (3), at any price $p_1 < 1$ such that $X_1(p_1) = e_1$, we have a Walrasian equilibrium.*

Suppose the following two assumptions hold:

Assumption 2. *For some (small) value of $p_1 > 0$, $X_1(p_1) \geq e_1$, and for some (large) value of $p_1 < 1$, $X_1(p_1) \leq e_1$.*

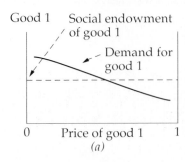

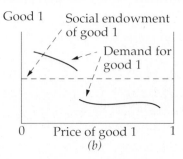

(a)   (b)

Figure 6.3. Existence of Walrasian equilibrium for the case of two goods.
We have a Walrasian equilibrium at any price p_1 between zero and one
(and $p_2 = 1 - p_1$) where $X_1(p_1) = e_1$; that is, where markets clear in
good 1 and hence clear in good 2. In (a), we see a case where there is a
Walrasian equilibrium, while in (b) we see a case without. Note that, in
accordance with assumption 2, we draw in each case aggregate demand
that satisfies $X_1(p_1) \geq e_1$ for sufficiently small $p_1 > 0$ and $X_1(p_1) \leq e_1$
for sufficiently large $p_1 < 1$.

Assumption 3. *The function $X_1(p_1)$ is continuous in p_1 for $0 < p_1 < 1$.*

Under these two assumptions, the intermediate value theorem of calculus
would guarantee the existence of a Walrasian equilibrium; a continuous
function can't get from a level above e_1 to a level below e_1 without at
some point being precisely equal to e_1.

So are these two assumptions sensible? Begin with the first part of
assumption 2. We would like to conclude that for small p_1 the demand for
good 1 is no smaller than the social endowment. Consider the indifference
curve diagrams in figure 6.4. In (a), we have a consumer with the usual
sort of indifference curves. We see there that for low enough prices of the
first good — a typical such budget line is sketched in — the consumer
will necessarily choose to consume no less than her endowment in the
first good. This is clearly the case because all the points that give her
at least as much utility as her endowment and that are affordable (the
shaded half-lens area) lie to the right of her endowment. If we had this
sort of picture for every consumer, then every consumer (for low enough
p_1) would demand at least her endowment in the first good, justifying the
assumption that $X_1(p_1) \geq e_1$.

But what if the picture for one of the consumers was as in figure 6.4(b).
This consumer's indifference curve through her endowment has slope zero
at the endowment point. (If you find this an odd case, try drawing the

picture for a consumer whose endowment of the second good is zero.) For this consumer, we wouldn't know that $x^i(p_1) \geq e_1^i$ for all sufficiently small p_1, and so we wouldn't necessarily have the first part of assumption 2. In essence, the first part of assumption 2 rules out this sort of picture holding for all the consumers; if the price of good 1 gets low enough, someone likes it sufficiently to want (and can afford) enough so that aggregate demand exceeds the social endowment.

For the other half of assumption 2, we consider budget lines that have very steep slope, corresponding to prices p_1 close to one (and hence p_2 close to zero). You may draw the pictures; the basic intuition is the same.

As for assumption 3, if preferences are continuous and demand is single valued (assumption 1), then using techniques similar to the proof of proposition 2.13(b), you can show that demand will be continuous for strictly positive prices.[e] So this assumption is entailed by earlier assumptions we made.

To generalize this result, there are essentially three things to think about. First, assumption 1 is too strong. We want to weaken this, but in a way that preserves the "sense" of assumption 3. Second, assumption 2, which can be paraphrased "aggregate demand is well behaved at extreme prices" requires attention. Third, it is clearly desirable to extend beyond the case of only two goods: We'll have to do with something other than the intermediate value theorem.

We will *not* persevere in detail on this subject but instead offer a quick

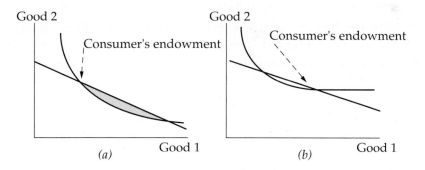

Figure 6.4. Justifying assumption 2.

---

[e] The more mathematically inclined reader can give this a shot, if you didn't already do so when challenged in chapter 2. Or wait a bit for proposition 6.1, where we will generalize this result a step further.

"executive summary." In the references given below and elsewhere, the following happens:

(1) Assumption 1 is simply dropped. Consumers are allowed to have preferences that admit more than one solution at given prices. We redefine $X_1(p_1)$ to be the *set* of all possible aggregate demands for the first good as a function of p_1 (and, implicitly, $p_2 = 1 - p_1$); that is, $x \in X_1(p_1)$ if $x = \sum_{i=1}^{I} x_1^i$ where x_1^i is the first component of some solution of i's utility maximization problem at prices $(p_1, 1 - p_1)$. A function that takes on values that are sets is generally called a *correspondence*; when you hear economic theorists chattering about the *aggregate demand correspondence*, this is what they have in mind.

Not every aggregate demand correspondence will give equilibria. Once we give up uniqueness of the solution to the consumers' problems, we give up automatic continuity, and we need something in place of assumption 3. To see that this is needed, consider first figure 6.5(a). Here we show a consumer's problem where at the prices shown there will be precisely two solutions. It isn't hard to imagine filling in indifference curves so that at other prices, there are unique solutions to the consumer's problem and so that, moreover, demand for good 1 is (except at these relative prices) decreasing in the relative price for good 1. This sort of demand by the individual will lead to aggregate demand as in figure 6.5(b); think of this as aggregate demand for three consumers whose indifference curves look like those in 6.5(a), but with relative prices at which we have two solutions different for the three. With such aggregate demand, there will be no guarantee of an equilibrium, just as depicted in figure 6.5(b).

It turns out that in place of a continuous aggregate demand function we need aggregate demand that is *upper semi-continuous and convex valued.*[f] Moreover, we have the following proposition:

Proposition 6.1. *If consumer preferences are continuous, aggregate demand is upper semi-continuous. If consumer preferences are convex, aggregate demand is convex valued.*[g]

---

[f] A correspondence $X(p_1)$ is upper semi-continuous if the graph of the correspondence — the set of all points (p_1, x) such that $x \in X(p_1)$ — is a closed set. The term *upper hemi-continuous* is sometimes used instead, reserving *semi-* for functions. And the correspondence is convex valued if for every p_1 the set $X(p_1)$ is convex.

[g] Both assertions are for strictly positive prices, since we don't know that aggregate demand is well defined for zero prices. For more mathematically inclined readers, this proposition is a useful result to try to prove.

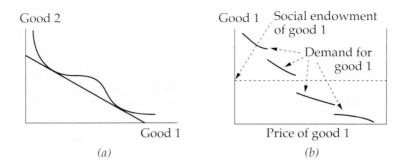

*Figure 6.5. Nonexistence of Walrasian equilibrium
with demand correspondences.*

In (a), we show a consumer whose demand for good 1 takes on two
values at a critical price. This can lead to the sorts of discontinuities in
aggregate demand shown in (b), which in turn can imply that there is
no equilibrium.

So in many general treatments of the existence question, one finds an
assumption that preferences are continuous and convex.[h]

(2) The problem of well-behaved aggregate demand for extreme prices (or
as prices become extreme) is handled in a number of ways. These problems
become a bit more involved when there are more than two goods, because
then we need to worry about demand when one good has a zero price,
when two have zero price, and so on, up to one less than the total number
of goods. This matter gets fairly technical fairly quickly, so we leave it for
you to read about elsewhere.

(3) When there are more than two commodities, we won't be able to employ the intermediate value theorem so neatly. What then? The mathematical hammer that is used in place of the intermediate value theorem is
a *fixed point theorem*. (If you don't persevere through the small type, then
at least you should know that when economic theorists are discussing
fixed point theorems, the odds are good that they are discussing general
equilibrium existence results.)

---

[h] In the higher reaches of mathematical economics, you will find ways even to dispense
with convexity of consumer preferences. Without going into detail, the idea is that what we
require is aggregate demand that is upper semi-continuous and convex valued. We can get
the convex-valued property for aggregate demand even if individual demand is not convex
valued, *if* we have "many" consumers of like characteristics.

There are many fixed point theorems. For our purposes, the two relevant ones are

Brouwer's Fixed Point Theorem. Two things are given: a nonempty, compact, convex set Z (a subset of some Euclidean space, say), and a continuous function $\phi : Z \to Z$. In this setting the theorem asserts that the function has a fixed point; there is a point $z \in Z$ such that $\phi(z) = z$.

Kakutani's Fixed Point Theorem. The function ϕ in Brouwer's theorem is replaced by a correspondence that associates to each point $z \in Z$ a nonempty subset $\phi(z) \subseteq Z$. This theorem asserts that if ϕ is upper semi-continuous and convex valued, then ϕ has a fixed point — a point z for which $z \in \phi(z)$.

These are fairly heavy mathematical results, but if you know some mathematical programming, some very beautiful algorithmic proofs can be given; see Scarf (1973).

Of what use are these? Suppose there are K commodities. Let Π be the space of all nonnegative price vectors in R^K that sum to one: $p = (p_1, \ldots, p_K) \in \Pi$ if $\sum_k p_k = 1$. Let us retreat to the world of assumption 1; the solution of each consumer's problem at any set of prices is unique. In fact, since this is just an "executive briefing," we'll assume this is true for all nonnegative, nonzero prices. (This is clearly a noxious assumption, since one might expect that as the price of some good goes to zero, demand for that good rises to infinity. But this is only an executive briefing.) We can therefore write for each consumer i and commodity k, $x_k^i(p)$ for the demand for good k by consumer i at prices p. Write $X_k(p) = \sum_{i=1}^{I} x_k^i(p)$ for the aggregate demand for good k.

Assume that $X_k(p)$ is continuous for each k. (Let us say again that this is now for all price vectors, including those where some of the goods have zero price, so this is an overly strong assumption, made only for purposes of illustration.) Consider the following vector function $\phi = (\phi_1, \ldots, \phi_K)$ from Π into Π:

$$\phi_k(p) = \frac{p_k + \max(0, X_k(p) - e_k)}{\sum_{k'=1}^{K} [p_{k'} + \max(0, X_{k'}(p) - e_{k'})]}.$$

Don't panic — this isn't as bad as it looks. Take the numerator first. We add to the old price p_k a positive amount *if* there is excess demand for good k at prices p. (That makes sense; raise the prices of goods for which there is too much demand.) Then the denominator takes these new relative prices and rescales them so they sum to one again.

This is clearly a function from Π to Π. And we claim that if each $X_k(p)$ is continuous, then so is each ϕ_k, hence so is ϕ. This takes a bit of a proof, but readers with mathematical background shouldn't have a problem with it. Hence by Brouwer's fixed point theorem, this function ϕ has a fixed point.

We claim that if p is a fixed point of ϕ, then p gives Walrasian prices. To see this, note that at a fixed point of ϕ,

$$p_k = \frac{p_k + \max(0, X_k(p) - e_k)}{\sum_{k'=1}^{K} \left[p_{k'} + \max(0, X_{k'}(p) - e_{k'}) \right]}.$$

Note that $\sum_{k'=1}^{K} p_{k'} = 1$, so if we multiply on both sides of the equation by the denominator, we get

$$p_k \left[1 + \sum_{k'=1}^{K} \max(0, X_{k'}(p) - e_{k'}) \right] = p_k + \max(0, X_k(p) - e_k).$$

Cancel the common term p_k from both sides, and you get

$$p_k \sum_{k'=1}^{K} \max(0, X_{k'}(p) - e_{k'}) = \max(0, X_k(p) - e_k),$$

for each k. Multiply both sides of this equation by $X_k(p) - e_k$ and sum over K, and we get

$$\left[\sum_{k=1}^{K} p_k (X_k - e_k) \right] \left[\sum_{k'=1}^{K} \max(0, X_{k'}(p) - e_{k'}) \right]$$
$$= \sum_{k=1}^{K} (X_k - e_k) \max(0, X_k(p) - e_k).$$

Since Walras' law holds with equality for every consumer, it holds with equality for aggregate demand, which means that the left-hand side of this equation must be zero. Each term in the sum on the right-hand side is nonnegative, so the only way that sum could be zero is if each term is zero, which can only be true if $X_k(p) \leq e_k$ for each k, which is the condition for an equilibrium.

Don't be too taken with this "general" proof. We are back to assuming that the consumers' maximization problems have unique solutions; the proof would be better if we dealt in demand correspondences (which is where Kakutani's fixed point theorem comes in). And, more importantly, our assumption that $X_k(p)$ is well defined and continuous around the edges of Π is really quite outrageous; a better general proof would work quite hard to avoid this.

Nonetheless, the "style" of the proof should be clear. We create a map from the set of prices into itself such that any fixed points are Walrasian equilibria, and then we make assumptions sufficient to guarantee that the map has a fixed point, enlisting a general fixed point theorem along the way.

Finiteness and local uniqueness

So now we know that a Walrasian equilibrium will exist for "well-behaved" exchange economies. We worry next about the other extreme possibility; for a given economy there are so many equilibria that we learn little (except that the equilibrium allocation is Pareto efficient) about what is the outcome of the market process. Have a look at the Edgeworth box in figure 6.6, for example. We've drawn things so that three equilibria are shown, and nothing prevents us from continuing to draw indifference curves shaped so that *every* point along the contract curve between the points marked x and x' are Walrasian equilibrium allocations for the initial endowment shown.

But, if we did that, it would only be for this endowment point that we have so many equilibria. For any other endowment point (nearby this endowment point), there would be only a single equilibrium. (Convince yourself of this on the drawing before reading on.) So, in some sense, it would be quite a remarkable "coincidence" if there were so many equilibria for a given exchange economy with a "randomly selected" initial endowment.

This picture is suggestive of some very deep results about the number of equilibria that a "randomly selected" exchange economy may have. One must define what it means for an economy to be randomly selected (and

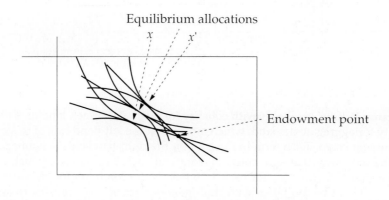

Figure 6.6. Too many equilibria.
From the endowment point marked, three equilibria are shown. We could continue to draw in indifference curves so that from this endowment point, *every* point along the contract curve between x and x' is a Walrasian equilibrium allocation. Note that if we do this, then for any other point "close" to the marked endowment point, there is only a single Walrasian equilibrium.

the mathematical methods for doing this are themselves very advanced), but this can be done. And then it is possible to obtain results along the following lines:

Theorem. *A "randomly selected" exchange economy will have a finite, and indeed odd, number of equilibria.*

To prove this takes methods of differential topology; we won't even try to explain how this is done here. But we will try to say why this sort of result is of economic (as opposed to mathematical) interest.

Ideally, we would like each exchange economy with which we deal to have a unique Walrasian equilibrium. If this were true, then the theory that a Walrasian equilibrium obtains would make a very definite and precise prediction; we would have enormous scope for testing the theory empirically. We might even be able to go on to economy-wide comparative statics exercises — for example, how does a single consumer's consumption of a given good change if we increase that consumer's endowment of the good, or if we increase some other consumer's endowment of the good? If we could trace how a change in endowment translates into changes in *unique* equilibrium prices and allocations, it would be possible (potentially) to answer this question.

On the other hand, if economies generally have infinite numbers of equilibria, the proposition that an equilibrium will be attained would help us very little. At some given endowment, we might find ourselves at a particular equilibrium. But then if we perturb that endowment, say by giving a fixed consumer more of a particular good, we would have little notion concerning which new equilibrium would pertain. At least, knowing that some equilibrium will pertain would not help us much in predicting how this individual's consumption would react to this perturbation in her endowment.

The point is that for the sake of definite predictions, having a single equilibrium for every set of initial data is ideal and having an infinite number of equilibria for each set of initial data is terrible.

Unhappily, it is simply unreasonable to suppose that there will be a unique Walrasian equilibrium for a general exchange economy. Conditions on the economy can be given that guarantee uniqueness, but they are very strong.[7] What the theorem outlined above says is that while the ideal of a unique equilibrium may be unreasonable, we have the "next best" situation of a finite number of equilibria. Moreover, the theorem sketched

---

[7] If you go looking for such results, the key words are *gross substitutes*.

can be extended as follows: For most economies, picking any one of its (finitely many) Walrasian equilibria, as we perturb slightly the data of the economy one and only one equilibrium for the perturbed economy will be "close" to the originally selected equilibrium. If we believe that small perturbations of the data of the economy will be met (if possible) by small shifts in the equilibrium, then we can still do local comparative statics for "randomly selected" economies.

To understand this probably takes a more complete discussion than we have given. But an important point is buried here that will return in chapter 14 and at the end of the book in the criticisms that will be given to the application of game theoretic methods. If the preceding discussion is somewhat opaque now, don't worry; you will be returning to this subsection after a while, at which point (I hope and expect) this will make a lot more sense.

6.5. Time, uncertainty, and general equilibrium

As we have already noted, the model of general equilibrium is not clearly relevant to situations where choices will be made through time and under conditions of uncertainty. What does the theory of general equilibrium tell us about choice in a dynamic and uncertain environment?

One approach works within the limited context of choices that are made at any single point in time.

This isn't to say that the future doesn't matter to such choices. The value to the consumer of some of the commodities that are bought or sold at a given point in time is strongly connected to anticipated future prices. For example, preferences over engine size in cars presumably relate to expectations about future gasoline prices. Indeed, some current "commodities" derive value entirely from future considerations. For example, any form of savings or financial investment gives utility only because of the presumed value those savings or investments will have later.

Even so, consumer preferences at a single point in time over current commodities, including financial securities and consumer durables such as cars, can be assumed to conform to the basic models of chapters 2 and 3. If the currently traded commodities have prices, nothing prevents us from analyzing choice in currently open markets according to the methods discussed above.[i]

---

[i] There are a few differences: One can borrow money or, in some cases, short sell securities. This would be modeled formally as "consumption" of a negative amount of those

This approach is taken in some of the literature of microeconomics. Work along these lines tends to take a bit more out of the structure of financial assets and the like to put a bit more into the model about preferences for these things. And it tends to work not simply with choice at one point in time, but with choices made serially, where each choice is of the sort analyzed in this chapter, focusing on the connections between choices made at one date and choices made at others. But the basic model of market choice at any single time is just what we have above, where durable and financial assets are treated as commodities. This line of research goes by the general rubric of *temporary general equilibrium.*

But in line with the general tendency to regard dynamic choice as the static choice of an overall strategy, the temporary general equilibrium approach is followed much less frequently than approaches that look at *all* market choices at once.

Arrow-Debreu contingent claims markets

The easiest way to think of looking at all market choices at once is to imagine that all market choices are in fact made at once. A fictional marketplace, known as the market in *Arrow-Debreu contingent claims*, is the central modeling device used here.

We begin by setting the stage. We imagine a finite list of K commodities, each of which can be consumed at any one of a finite number of *dates*, indexed by $t = 0, 1, \ldots, T$. Moreover, we imagine that there is uncertainty, which will resolve as time passes. Before consumption at date T takes place, consumers will know which state s from a finite state space S prevails. Between time 0 and time T, uncertainty about the true state s may resolve. This is modeled by a sequence of nondecreasingly finer partitions of S, denoted $F_0, F_1, \ldots, F_T$, where $F_0 = \{S\}$ and F_T is the fine partition, where each state is in a set by itself.

For the reader who is unused to the mathematical terminology, a *partition* of S is a set of subsets of S with the properties that each $s \in S$ is in one and only one of the subsets. The members of a given partition are called the *cells* of the partition. A sequence of partitions is nondecreasingly finer if for any two consecutive dates t and $t + 1$, if f is a cell for date $t + 1$ (that is, if $f \in F_{t+1}$), then for some date t cell $f' \in F_t$, $f \subseteq f'$.

The interpretation is as follows. At date t, consumers all know that one of the cells in F_t prevails, and no one knows anything more. An

---

"commodities." Hence we would have to work in a setting that allowed for negative levels of consumption of some goods. This can pose a number of special problems, especially for questions of the existence of equilibrium.

example may help. Suppose that S has five elements, $\{s_1, \ldots, s_5\}$. Suppose that $T = 3$. Then we can imagine that

$$F_0 = \{\{s_1, s_2, s_3, s_4, s_5\}\};$$
$$F_1 = \{\{s_1, s_2\}, \{s_3, s_4, s_5\}\};$$
$$F_2 = \{\{s_1, s_2\}, \{s_3\}, \{s_4, s_5\}\}; \text{ and}$$
$$F_3 = \{\{s_1\}, \{s_2\}, \{s_3\}, \{s_4\}, \{s_5\}\}.$$

This means at date zero, consumers have no idea which state prevails. At date one, they learn that either the state is one of the first two or one of the last three. At date two, if the state is one of the first two, they learn nothing new. And if the state is one of the last three, they learn that either the state is s_3 or one of the last two. Finally, at date three consumers learn whatever is left to learn about which state prevails.

We could depict this example (and any example of this type) with a tree diagram, as in figure 6.7. Time moves from left to right, and at each date, the tree branches reflect information accumulated to that point. So, for example, at the level of the tree corresponding to date 2, the tree has split already into three pieces, one of which (at the next date) branches into s_1 or s_2, the second of which leads to s_3, and the third of which branches (at the next date) into s_4 and s_5.

We stress that we are assuming that at each date t, all consumers have access to precisely the same information. This model does not allow one consumer to have better information about the state of nature than another. Extensions of this basic model do permit consumers to have

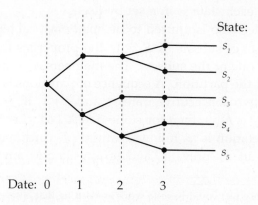

Figure 6.7. Depicting the resolution of uncertainty with a tree.

private information (extensions we won't get to in this book), but the basic model forbids this.

We now add a bit of notation and terminology. For a given date t and a cell $f \in F_t$, we refer to the pair (t, f) as a *date-event* pair. The set of all date-event pairs for date t, which is just $\{t\} \times F_t$ is denoted $\mathcal{E}_t$. And the union over all the dates $t = 1, \ldots, T$ of all the date-event pairs is denoted $\mathcal{E}$, which is just $\bigcup_{t=1}^{T} \mathcal{E}_t$. Don't be put off by the formalisms here; in our example, $\mathcal{E}_0$ has one element, $\mathcal{E}_1$ has two, $\mathcal{E}_2$ has three, and $\mathcal{E}_3$ has five, so $\mathcal{E}$ has eleven elements corresponding to the eleven heavy dots in the tree shown in figure 6.7.

With all this, the consumption space for consumers is the space of all vectors x in the positive orthant X of $(R^K)^{\mathcal{E}}$. This may look horrible but it isn't. The idea is that the consumer consumes at each date t, and the consumer can change what she consumes according to information she has received at that time. Hence at date 0, she consumes some vector in R^K; this follows from the fact that F_0 contains a single element. At date 1, she consumes some vector in R^K *contingent upon* which of the two cells in F_1 prevails; this is a vector in the space $(R^K)^{\mathcal{E}_1}$, and so on. A full consumption vector for her is a listing of what she consumes in every date-event pair that she may find herself in, which is $(R^K)^{\mathcal{E}}$.

For example, suppose in the example there are two goods. Then a consumption bundle for the consumer says how much of each she consumes at date zero, how much she consumes at date 1 if one of the first two states prevails, how much she consumes at date 1 if one of the last three states prevails, and so on. Since there are eleven date-event pairs in the tree in figure 6.7, a consumption bundle for a consumer in this economy would be a point in the positive orthant of R^{22} (or $(R^2)^{11}$).

We assume that each consumer has the usual sort of preferences over X so defined. It is entirely natural to think that since there is uncertainty in this story, we might be able to use the methods of chapter 3 to pin down the nature of the consumer's preferences somewhat. And this is done in most applications. But we will proceed assuming that the consumer has general preferences over X given by a utility function $U_i : X \to R$.

Finally we come to the most heroic assumption of all. Imagine that prior to date zero consumption there are markets in every good deliverable at every date in every "recognizable" contingency. That is, suppose in our example the two goods are artichokes and broccoli. Then prior to date zero consumption, a consumer can buy or sell artichokes and broccoli for immediate delivery. (The term *spot market* is used for markets in immediately delivered commodities.) But the consumer can buy and sell much more. The consumer can buy and sell, for example, broccoli to be delivered at date 2 in the event $\{s_1, s_2\}$. This good, which is called an *Arrow-Debreu contingent claim* to broccoli, should be regarded with care. The story is that if you buy ten units of these, when date 2 rolls around, if the state is one of the first two, someone will hand you ten units of broccoli. But if one of the other three states prevails, this claim entitles you to nothing. If you sell one of these claims, you must make it good at date 2 if the state is one of the first two.

Note that we don't imagine markets in date 2–state s_1 broccoli. When date 2 rolls around, consumers are assumed to be unable to tell whether the prevailing state is s_1 or s_2. Hence we couldn't know whether to make good on a claim against date 2 broccoli contingent on the state being s_1.

You may recall that way back at the start of choice and demand theory, you were warned that eventually you would be asked to consider commodities of the form — a pint of beer three years from today if the temperature next July 4 is more than ten degrees (Farenheit) hotter than the temperature the following June 30. This "commodity" is just a bundle of Arrow-Debreu contingent claims. It's a bundle because it isn't contingent on all the uncertainty that will resolve between now and three years hence. But it is a claim to future consumption contingent on some of the uncertainty that will resolve.

That, essentially, is it. If we imagine that there are, at the outset, markets in every Arrow-Debreu contingent claim, and if preferences are defined on the space X (and endowments lie in the space X), then the theory described early in this chapter can be applied without problem. In earlier developments, we never said what the character of a commodity had to be; so we just apply the theory to the case where commodities include all manner of these contingent claims. Time and uncertainty are fully handled within general equilibrium theory!

Securities and spot markets

Nonsense, you are probably saying. All this is based on the presumption that, before any consumption takes place, there is a complete set of Arrow-Debreu contingent claims markets. Now there are, in the real world, some futures markets where you can contract to receive (or sell) pork bellies or iced broilers at a fixed later date. But you can't buy a pork belly for delivery a year hence contingent on the weather in August. And even the number of futures markets is somewhat limited. There is no futures market whatsoever in broccoli.

General equilibrium theorists have a neat response to this. Suppose that, in our example, the prices of artichokes and broccoli were denominated in dollars. (What's a dollar? Where did this money come from?

These are nontrivial questions that arise in this theory, and I will simply shrug them off here. This isn't to say that these aren't questions that are crucial to this entire story. They are crucial. But this is only going to be an introduction to the subject.) And suppose that, at date zero, there are both spot markets in artichokes and broccoli and markets in claims to $1 in each date-event pair in the tree. That is, at date zero, for a given price, you can purchase a claim to $1 in, say, date 2 if the state is either s_1 or s_2. Note that there are ten date-event pairs other than the date zero pair, so this means twelve markets are open — two spot and ten "financial." Suppose that, moreover, there will be spot markets in the two vegetables at every date, whatever the contingency.

If the assumptions made so far aren't heroic enough, we offer a really big one next: Suppose that, sitting back at time zero, each consumer can precisely and accurately forecast what will be the prices of artichokes and broccoli in their spot markets for each date-event pair. To take an example, suppose consumers know that at date 2 in the event $\{s_1, s_2\}$ the spot price of broccoli will be $.75 per unit. Suppose as well that at time zero, the price of a claim to $1 at date 2 contingent on the event $\{s_1, s_2\}$ is $.40. Then if a consumer wishes to purchase at time zero a unit of date 2–event $\{s_1, s_2\}$ broccoli, she can do so by implementing the following plan: Buy three-quarters of a $1 date 2–event $\{s_1, s_2\}$ financial contingent claim, which costs $.30. If at date 2 the event realized is $\{s_1, s_2\}$, this provides her with $.75. And with this $.75 she buys her unit of broccoli in the spot market. On the other hand, if she is well endowed with broccoli in this date-event pair and wishes to sell some of it, she can sell date 2–event $\{s_1, s_2\}$ financial contingent claims at date zero, and if at date 2 this event rolls around, she can sell off broccoli to meet her financial obligations.

The point is that if consumers know in advance all the future spot market prices, and if there is a full array of financial contingent claims, consumers can trade from any endowment point $e \in X$ to any desired (and affordable) consumption point $x \in X$ by designing an appropriate dynamic strategy. Money is transferred between date–event pairs using the financial contingent claims, and that money is allocated between consumption goods subsequently in the spot markets. This then implies that all the methods of general equilibrium discussed earlier apply.

Note how strongly we use the assumption that consumers accurately anticipate all future spot market prices. And we assume that consumers follow the standard pattern of chapter 4 in reducing a dynamic choice problem to a static problem of choosing an optimal strategy for dynamic action. In other words, we assume consumers are *hyperrational*, both in their predictive powers and in their planning abilities. These are very strong assumptions. You will have to judge for yourself whether these assumptions are too strong. (Wait to see applications, which we don't provide here, before making this judgment. These are strong assumptions, but depending on how they influence the conclusions that are drawn in a particular application, you might find them palatable.)

You may still object that even granting hyperrational agents this isn't a realistic model, because these financial contingent claims don't exist. (Where can you buy a claim to $1 next August, payable only if the amount of rain in July in New York exceeds the amount of rain in Philadelphia by less than one inch?)

We don't need to have all the financial contingent claims traded at the outset. Suppose, in our example, at date zero a pair of financial contingent claims are traded, one that pays $1 at date one in the event $\{s_1, s_2\}$ and a second that pays $1 at date one in the event $\{s_3, s_4, s_5\}$. In date 1–event $\{s_1, s_2\}$, there is a market in a contingent financial claim that pays $1 at date 2; and in date 1–event $\{s_3, s_4, s_5\}$, there are two financial claims, one that pays $1 at date 2 in the contingency $\{s_3\}$, and the other paying $1 at date 2 in the contingency $\{s_4, s_5\}$, and so on. The idea is that at each date in each contingency for that date, there are claims that pay at the next date in every possible following contingency.

Suppose as well that consumers at the outset know what will be the equilibrium prices of these claims as well as the equilibrium prices of spot vegetables. Then a consumer could do just as well as if there were a full array of contingent claims markets. For example, suppose that

At date zero, a claim paying $1 at date 1 in event $\{s_3, s_4, s_5\}$ costs $.50.

At date 1 in event $\{s_3, s_4, s_5\}$, a claim paying $1 at date 2 in event $\{s_4, s_5\}$ will cost $.60.

At date 2 in event $\{s_4, s_5\}$, a claim paying $1 at date 3 in event $\{s_4\}$ will cost $.40.

Broccoli at date zero costs $2.00 per unit.

Artichokes at date 3 in event $\{s_4\}$ will cost $\frac{2}{3}$ per unit.

Then a consumer, knowing all this, can "trade" date zero broccoli for date 3–event $\{s_4\}$ artichokes as follows: For every unit of date zero broccoli sold (realizing $2), he buys four claims to date 1–event $\{s_3, s_4, s_5\}$ dollars. At date 1, if the event is $\{s_3, s_4, s_5\}$, he plans to use the $4 to buy $6\frac{2}{3}$ claims for $1 at date 2 in event $\{s_4, s_5\}$. At date 2, if the event is $\{s_4, s_5\}$, he plans to use the $6\frac{2}{3}$ to buy $16\frac{2}{3}$ claims for $1 at date 3 in event $\{s_4\}$. And if at date 3 the event is $\{s_4\}$, he plans to use the $16\frac{2}{3}$ to buy 25 units of artichoke. That is, the consumer, by buying and selling, can exchange immediate broccoli for date 3–event $\{s_4\}$ artichokes at a ratio of 1:25. If we gave all the prices for all the marketed goods (both vegetable and financial), you (and, presumably, our very smart consumers) could work out the exchange rates for vegetables in any two date-event pairs. (See problem 9 for a harder example than the one above.)

So all we need are spot markets in vegetables and in financial claims for contingent money at the "next date" and in every possible "next contingency." (We also need very smart consumers.)

You may still be dissatisfied. There are no financial claims around of the type described that pay $1 in one event and nothing at any other time. There are plenty of financial claims being traded: equity in companies, debt instruments, options on common stock, and so on. But none of it has this simple form. The avid general equilibrium theorist responds to this objection with a still further elaboration: In some (not all) cases, by trading cleverly in the sort of financial instruments just listed, a consumer can manufacture the types of financial claims assumed two paragraphs ago. What is required is that consumers know what prices existing financial instruments will command in every date–event pair, and that there are "enough" of those financial instruments. (The meaning of "enough" is made precise in the literature.)

We will leave you here, with further readings suggested in the bibliographic notes. The basic message to be taken away is that by means of increasingly elaborate constructions, economic theorists extend the reach of the basic model of general equilibrium to cases where time and uncertainty play a part. But often this involves consumers who are both extremely knowledgeable about the future and who are extremely good at planning.

6.6. Bibliographic notes

The classic treatments of general equilibrium theory are Debreu (1959) and Arrow and Hahn (1971). Debreu's monograph gives the essential details, while Arrow and Hahn give a more complete treatment of many of the issues touched on here (and other issues not mentioned here at all). Scarf (1973) presents algorithms for computing Walrasian equilibria, and Scarf and Shoven (1984) show how these computational techniques can be applied. For treatment of issues such as local uniqueness of equilibria for "randomly selected" economies, Mas Colell (1985), can be consulted by the reader who is very well trained mathematically. (The key tools come from differential topology.) Work on general equilibrium theory is ongoing, for example dealing with economies that have infinitely many commodities and/or infinitely many consumers; a recent "state of the art" treatment of the case of infinitely many commodities is Aliprantis, Brown and Burkinshaw (1989).

Theoretical work on the institutional foundations of general equilibrium belongs for the most part to the journal literature, hence references given here are apt to be superseded rather quickly. With this in mind, I would recommend Osborne and Rubinstein (forthcoming) for bargaining theoretic foundations.

Experimental work that supports, in limited contexts, the notion of a Walrasian equilibrium is also scattered among the journals. A good starting point is the review article by Plott (1986).

Extending the notions of general equilibrium to models where time and uncertainty play a role takes place in the literatures of both microeconomics and theoretical finance. The notion of a contingent claim is due to Arrow and to Debreu (hence the name Arrow-Debreu contingent claim); some exposition can be found in both Debreu (1959) and Arrow and Hahn (1971). The use of financial claims and "planning" originated in an article by Arrow that is published in English as Arrow (1964). The use of general financial claims and the basic equilibrium concept is formalized in Radner (1972). Since Arrow's and Radner's seminal contributions, there has been a very large literature on the subject; Huang and Litzenberger (1988, chaps. 7, 8) is an accessible introduction. This sort of model becomes especially powerful when trading in securities can take place continuously in time. The theory requires substantial mathematical sophistication, but the reader can get a taste of what goes on in Kreps (1982) and a systematic exposition in Duffie (1988).

References

Aliprantis, C., D. Brown, and O. Burkinshaw. 1989. *Existence and Optimality of Competitive Equilibria*. Berlin: Springer-Verlag.

Arrow, K. 1964. "The Role of Securities in the Optimal Allocation of Risk-Bearing." *Quarterly Journal of Economics* 31:91–96.

Arrow, K., and F. Hahn. 1971. *General Competitive Analysis*. San Francisco: Holden-Day.

Debreu, G. 1959. *Theory of Value*. New Haven: Cowles Foundation.

Duffie, D. 1988. *Securities Markets: Stochastic Models*. Boston: Academic Press.

Huang, C-f., and R. Litzenberger. 1988. *Foundations for Financial Economics*. Amsterdam: North Holland.

Kreps, D. 1982. "Multiperiod Securities and the Efficient Allocation of Risk: A Comment on the Black-Scholes Option Pricing Model." In *The Economics of Information and Uncertainty*, J. McCall, ed. Chicago: University of Chicago Press. Pp.203–32.

Mas Colell, A. 1985. *The Theory of General Equilibrium; A Differentiable Approach*. Cambridge: Cambridge University Press.

Osborne, M., and A. Rubinstein. Forthcoming. *Bargaining and Markets.* Boston: Academic Press.

Plott, C. 1986. "Rational Choice in Experimental Markets." *Journal of Business* 59:S301–27.

Radner, R. 1972. "Existence of Equilibrium of Plans, Prices, and Price Expectations." *Econometrica* 40:289–303.

Scarf, H. (in collaboration with T. Hansen). 1973. *The Computation of Economic Equilibrium.* New Haven: Cowles Foundation.

Scarf, H., and J. Shoven. 1984. *Applied General Equilibrium Analysis.* Cambridge: Cambridge University Press.

6.7. Problems

■ 1. Return to the picture of price equilibrium in the two-consumer, two-good case. For each set of relative prices, we can mark the point that consumer 1 would demand. (Assume that consumers have strictly convex preferences so their maximization problems always have unique solutions.) As we vary the relative prices of the goods, we trace out a curve — the so-called *offer curve* of consumer 1. This is shown for you in figure 6.8.

We can create a similar offer curve for consumer 2, and rotating the picture for consumer 2 by 180 degrees and putting his origin at the location of the social endowment in her (consumer 1's) coordinate system, we get the Edgeworth box with two offer curves. Consider the assertion: *Walrasian equilibrium allocations correspond to points where the two offer curves intersect.* This is not quite correct as it stands. Why not? If you see why not, try to repair the assertion.

■ 2. Consider the following exchange economy. There are two goods and two consumers. The two goods are called tillip and quillip and the two

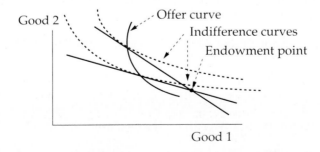

Figure 6.8. The offer curve of a consumer in a two-commodity world.

consumers are called 1 and 2. Consumer 1 has utility function $U_1(t,q) = .4\ln(t) + .6\ln(q)$ (where t is the amount of tillip 1 consumes, and q is the amount of quillip). Consumer 2 has utility function $U_2(t,q) = .5\ln(t) + .5\ln(q)$. Consumer 1 is endowed with 10 units each of quillip and tillip. Consumer 2 is endowed with 10 units of quillip and 5 units of tillip.

(a) What is the Walrasian equilibrium of this economy? (If there is more than one equilibrium, give them all.)

(b) Suppose a social dictator wished to implement an allocation that makes $U_1(t,q) + U_2(t,q)$ as large as possible at the equilibrium. Give *all* the possible reallocations of the endowment that give the dictator's optimal endowment as a Walrasian equilibrium.

■ 3. A particular social planner I know is very big on mellow consumers. Specifically, she hopes to prevent her consumers from envying each other. To this end, she defines an *envy-free* allocation of resources as one in which no consumer would rather have the consumption bundle assigned to another consumer instead of his or her own. Our social planner wishes to implement an envy-free allocation. She also wishes the allocation to be efficient.

This social planner is also lazy. She isn't willing to figure out the utility functions of her consumers. (She does have a good list of all their endowments.) She is blessed with an economy that functions well as an exchange economy; however she reassigns endowments, the economy finds a Walrasian equilibrium.

Can you help out this social planner? Specifically, describe how to reallocate endowments and shares so that the resulting Walrasian equilibrium is guaranteed to be both efficient and envy free. (Hint: the trick is to find some way to redistribute endowments and shareholdings so that, *at every set of prices*, consumers all begin with the same level of wealth to spend on consumption. There is a way to redistribute endowments and shareholdings so this is true: What is it?)

■ 4. (a) In the proof of the second theorem of welfare economics, it is claimed that the set

$$X^* = \{x \in X : x \text{ can be allocated among the } I$$
$$\text{consumers in a way that strictly Pareto dominates } (\hat{x}^i)\}$$

is convex if preferences are convex. Prove this.

(b) Later in that proof it is asserted that the separating hyperplane vector p is nonnegative. Provide a proof of this assertion.

(c) The remarks after the proof assert that we can replace the assumption that the allocation $(\hat{x}^i)$ is strictly positive with an assumption that each consumer is given a positive amount of at least one desirable good. Show that this assumption will suffice. (Hint: First show that the price of any desirable good must be strictly positive. Although it isn't necessary, to carry out this step you may assume that there is at least one more good and it is in positive supply in the social endowment.)

■ 5. Imagine a three-person economy in which the first commodity is gardening services, the consumption of which makes one's yard more beautiful, and the second good is food. Imagine that two of the consumers in this society live in adjacent houses, while the third lives on the other side of a particularly large mountain. Consumption by the third consumer of gardening services generates no externality for the other consumers, but each of the others generates a positive externality for her neighbor through the consumption of gardening services. To be precise, imagine that consumers 1 and 2 have utility functions of the form

$$V^i(x) = w(x_1^i) + w(x_1^2) + x_2^i$$

where $w : [0, \infty) \to R$ is a strictly increasing, strictly concave, and differentiable function. Note well that consumers 1 and 2 get just as much utility out of their neighbor's yard as they do out of their own, and their utility for food is linear. (You were warned that this is a very special setting.) Also imagine that consumer 3 has a utility function of the form $V^3(x) = w(x_1^3) + x_2^3$. There is a social endowment of gardening services and food.

(a) Suppose the social endowment is initially allocated evenly among the three consumers. What will be the corresponding Walrasian equilibrium (with externalities)?

(b) Characterize the set of Pareto efficient allocations of the social endowment. Is the equilibrium allocation in (a) Pareto efficient?

■ 6. In a two-person, two-commodity economy, the two commodities are labeled x and y and the two consumers are called A and B. Let x_A, for example, denote the amount of consumption of good x by person A. Each of the two individuals has initial endowments of one unit of each good apiece. The preferences of a are given by the utility function

$$u_A(x_A, y_A) = \frac{1}{3} \log x_A + \frac{2}{3} \log y_A.$$

The preferences of B are a bit stranger than this. They are given by

$$u_B(x_B, y_B, x_A) = \log x_B + \log y_B + \log(2 - x_A).$$

That is, B gets "disutility" out of A's consumption of the first good. You may assume throughout that both individuals are locally insatiable (and indeed they are), and you can assume that any solution of first-order conditions and complementary slackness is a global maximium.

(a) What is the Walrasian equilibrium (or equilibria) for this economy? (This is an economy with externalities, so use the definition given in the section on externalities.) You will find that matters are fairly simple if you normalize the prices of the two goods so that they sum to one. Let p be the price of good x so $1 - p$ is the price of good y.

(b) Is the equilibrium allocation in part (a) Pareto optimal? If so, why? (That is, how do you know that it is?) If it is not, how do you know that?

(c) Whether the equilibrium allocation in part (a) is Pareto optimal or not, Mr. B registers the complaint that Ms. A is consuming all too much x for his tastes. Accordingly, a social planner named Lindahl proposes to change the economy as follows. Instead of two prices (for x and y), there will be six. These will be p and $1 - p$ as before, and also q_A, q_B, r_A and r_B. These last four are "transfer prices"; for every unit of x that A consumes, she must transfer q_A units of account (money) to B. For every unit of x that B consumes, he must transfer q_B units of account to A. If A consumes y_A units of good y, she must transfer $r_A y_A$ to B, and r_B gives the transfer price from B to A for B's consumption of y. The prices $q_A, q_B, r_A,$ and r_B may be positive, zero, or even negative.

Now the economy works as follows. Taking prices $p, 1-p, q_A, q_B, r_A,$ and r_B as given (the usual price-taking assumption), A chooses a complete allocation (x_A, y_A, x_B, y_B) for the economy, subject to a single constraint: The net inflow of units of account to A should equal or exceed the net outflow of units from her. That is,

$$px_A + (1 - p)y_A + q_A x_A + r_A y_A \le p1 + (1 - p)1 + q_B x_B + r_B y_B.$$

(Recall that A's endowment is one unit of each of the two goods apiece. This explains the two ones on the right-hand side.) Ms. A chooses the complete allocation to maximize her utility subject only to this constraint; she is under no obligation to make her chosen allocation feasible. Mr. B also chooses a complete allocation, subject to the analogous constraint for him.

An equilibrium for the economy is a set of six prices and a single social allocation such that (1) both consumers faced with those prices independently choose that allocation, and (2) the allocation is socially feasible. In cases where one consumer is indifferent among many different levels in the optimization problem and the second consumer strictly prefers one of those levels, we count this as an agreement in terms of requirement (1).

Find an equilibrium of this economy, for the sort of equilibrium defined above.

(d) Is the equilibrium you computed in part (c) Pareto efficient? If so, how do you know this? If not, how do you know this?

(e) How do the utilities of Ms. A compare in the two equilibria, one from part (a) and one from part (c)? If Ms. A complains to Mr. Lindahl that she, A, is being treated unfairly in this new form of economy, what could Mr. Lindahl do to rectify matters?

(f) If we let Mr. Lindahl loose on the economy of problem 5, what would happen?

■ 7. *Parts of this problem may not make sense until chapter 8 is completed.* Grapple Synthetics of Boonton (GSB), Inc., has a problem concerning its computer facilities. Its computer facility services 600 identical users with two computers, one of which has a bit more software support than the other, but is more liable to congestion. Specifically, if one of the users uses the first computer and the total number of users of that computer is n, the individual user is able to increase her productivity by an amount $\$(30 - n/10)$. And if one of the users uses the second computer and the total number of users of that computer is m, the user increases her daily productivity by the amount $\$(10 - m/30)$. Assume throughout that these 600 users are all there are; no new ones will appear. The marginal cost of servicing a user is zero. And don't worry if your answers don't come out in even integers; fractional users will be okay, for purposes of this problem.

(a) Until now, GSB has not tried at all to regulate use of its computers. Each user has allocated herself to one of the two computers, choosing so as to maximize her individual productivity gain from the computer under the assumption that other users will stick with the computers they have chosen. Assuming that this is so, what is the equilibrium allocation of users to the two computers? How many are using computer 1; How many are using computer 2; and How many are using neither?

(b) The head of the computer center at GSB is concerned that the current, unregulated method of allocating individuals to computers is not maximizing the total contribution possible for GSB. He suggests the following scheme of transfer prices: A "price per day" will be named for the services of the computers, and users should be told to make use of either computer only if the productivity gain they attain in so doing exceeds this "transfer price." What (single) price per day should GSB name, assuming that its computer users will honestly allocate themselves between computers (or no use) to maximize individual productivity gain less transfer price? What will be the resulting usage for the two computers? (Hint: If you have trouble getting started, try to discover what would happen if the single price of $5 per day were charged [for each computer].)

(c) The head of the accounting department at GSB thinks that this transfer price scheme is a good idea, but she suggests a more complex scheme in which a different price per day will be charged for each of the two computers. What is the optimal scheme of this sort? What is the resulting pattern of usage for the two computers?

(d) The head of the economic analysis department at GSB is quite confused by the answers you obtained in parts (b) and (c). He says that he recalls from his old days as a microeconomist something called the second theorem of welfare economics, in which it was claimed that efficient allocations of resources should follow the dictates of a (Walrasian) market mechanism. He points out that if the computer services were served by competitive outside vendors (that is, users would actually pay a market price for the services they used), then the competitive price would equal marginal cost, which is zero. Thus zero transfer price should lead to an efficient solution. He suggests that you recheck your algebra in part (b) and (c). In no more than 200 words, explain to this individual why he should, instead, check his economics textbook.

■ 8. With regard to proposition 6.1:

(a) Prove that if consumer preferences are convex, aggregate demand is convex valued. This should be rather easy.

(b) Prove that if consumer preferences are continuous, aggregate demand is upper semi-continuous. This is done by mimicking the argument made for proposition 2.13(b).

(c) Use (b) to give a fast proof that if consumer preferences are continuous and single-valued, aggregate demand is given by a continuous function.

In all parts of this problem, we are dealing with strictly positive prices only.

▪ 9. Consider the set of date-event pairs depicted in figure 6.7. Recall the following data given before:

At date zero, a claim paying $1 at date 1 in event $\{s_3, s_4, s_5\}$ costs $.50

At date 1 in event $\{s_3, s_4, s_5\}$, a claim paying $1 at date 2 in event $\{s_4, s_5\}$ will cost $.60

At date 2 in event $\{s_4, s_5\}$, a claim paying $1 at date 3 in event $\{s_4\}$ will cost $.40

Broccoli at date zero costs $2.00 per unit

Artichokes at date 3 in event $\{s_4\}$ will cost $.67 per unit

Add to this the following addition data:

At date zero, a claim paying $1 at date 1 in event $\{s_1, s_2\}$ costs $.40

At date 1 in event $\{s_1, s_2\}$, a claim paying $1 at date 2 in event $\{s_1, s_2\}$ will cost $.90

At date 2 in event $\{s_1, s_2\}$, a claim paying $1 at date 3 in event $\{s_1\}$ will cost $.40

At date 3 in event $\{s_1\}$, artichokes will cost $1.33

Suppose a consumer wished to sell some date 3–event $\{s_1\}$ artichokes with which she is endowed and use the proceeds to buy date 3–event $\{s_4\}$ artichokes. For every unit of date 3–event $\{s_1\}$ artichokes she sells, how many units of date 3–event $\{s_4\}$ artichokes can she purchase? What is the strategy she follows for affecting such a trade? (This strategy should involve changing her "position" in vegetables at these two date-event pairs only. The key is the first step. She sells date 1–event $\{s_1, s_2\}$ dollars and uses the proceeds from that sale to buy date 1–event $\{s_3, s_4, s_5\}$ dollars.)

chapter seven

The neoclassical firm

In neoclassical economic theory, the firm is an entity, just like the consumer. The consumer has an objective function, utility, that is maximized subject to a budget constraint and any constraints on feasible consumption. The firm has an objective function, profit, that it maximizes subject to constraints imposed by its technological capabilities.

In chapter 2 we spent a lot of time on the consumer's objective function, talking about preferences, choices, and finally utility functions. The budget set constraint was not discussed much. For the neoclassical firm, the reverse is typically true. There is a lot of discussion about how to represent the technological capabilities of the firm and very little about profit maximization.

For the time being, we will keep to this tradition. In this chapter we will describe ways to model the firm's technological capabilities (section 7.1), and then we will discuss the firm's behavior, assuming it chooses inputs and outputs to maximize its profits (sections 7.2 and 7.3). We don't try to explain or justify profit maximization; that discussion is left to much later in the book (chapter 19) on the grounds that we will have little good to say about profit maximization, and only then will we be in a position to give alternatives.

The reader may justifiably wonder, If bad things will be said about profit maximization later in the book, why spend so much time now (and for the next three chapters) using that assumption? There are two reasons: First, this is the traditional model of the firm in microeconomic theory, and more modern developments can best be understood if you understand these classical antecedents. Second, our objections to profit maximization will be on "theoretical grounds" — that is, we don't see a good argument that firms necessarily will or ought to maximize their profits. But that doesn't mean that profit maximization isn't a good positive model. Only the data can speak to that, and then only after we see the implications of profit maximization for observable behavior.

7.1. Models of the firm's technological capabilities

The production possibility set

Firms are presumed to possess productive capabilities. That is, firms are able to transform arrays of commodities into different arrays.

The standard general model is set as usual in a world where there are K commodities. Some of these commodities may be inputs to the firm, some may be outputs of the firm, and some may be either inputs or outputs. Still others may have nothing at all to do with the firm. The firm's productive capabilities are modeled by a set of *netput* vectors in R^K. The term *netput* is used as a generalization of *in*put and *out*put: For each commodity, we record the firm's production or usage of this commodity, using negative numbers for net inputs and positive numbers for net outputs. For example, suppose there are five commodities: labor (number 1), steel wire (number 2), straight pins (number 3), safety pins (number 4), and wheat (number 5). A typical netput vector for a firm (that makes two types of pins) would be $(-5, -8, 10, 3, 0)$. Interpret this: This firm can take 5 units of labor (say, hours of work), and 8 units (feet?) of steel wire, and make of them 10 units of straight pins and 3 units of safety pins. Another feasible netput vector for this firm might be $(-79, -120, 200, 0, 0)$; with 79 units of labor and 120 units of steel wire, it can make 200 straight pins and no safety pins. Or suppose we had a firm that used inputs one and two to make intermediate product three, and then used more input one and intermediate product three to make product four. In this case, its netput vectors could be either $(-, -, -, +, 0)$ or $(-, -, +, +, 0)$. The first would be appropriate if, in addition to the amount of intermediate good it produced, the firm bought more from the outside. Then it would be a net consumer of the intermediate product, and we would record its net consumption as a negative number. If, however, it sold some of the intermediate good, it would be a net supplier, and the second set of "signs" would be correct. Of course, if it used precisely the amount of the intermediate product that it produced, its netput vector would look like $(-, -, 0, +, 0)$.

The firm's technological capabilities are, then, the set of all the netput vectors of which it is capable. We denote this set of all *feasible* netput vectors for a firm by Z, a subset of R^K. The set Z is called the *production possibility set* or the *technology set* for the firm. Elements $z \in Z$ are called netput vectors or *production plans*.

When $K = 2$, we can draw pictures. Suppose this firm has one input, x (the abscissa component) and one output, y (the ordinate). The picture for Z would be as in figure 7.1.

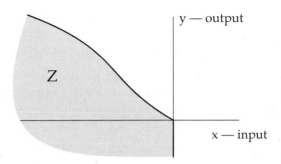

Figure 7.1. A typical production possibilities set.

We sometimes think of the firm's capabilities as varying with the amount of time over which the firm is operating. It is typically assumed that the firm has greater flexibility in what it can do in the long run, so some netput vectors are feasible in the long run but not in the short run. When we wish to make such a distinction, we write Z^l for the firm's long-run production possibility set and Z^s for its short-run production possibilities; the assumption that the firm can do more in the long run than in the short is then written as $Z^s \subseteq Z^l$.

Among the properties that a production set Z might have are:

Convexity: *If z and z' are both possible for the firm, then so is $\alpha z + (1-\alpha)z'$ for each α between zero and one.* It is often hard to believe that this assumption is realistic (see nonincreasing returns below), but it is a standard assumption in economics.

Free disposal: *If $z \in Z$ and $z' \le z$, then $z' \in Z$.* This is a dumpster theory of production; the firm can always throw out stuff it doesn't want. If one of the outputs of the firm were an effluent, we might doubt this assumption. But as long as more of a commodity is better for someone, better enough so that this someone will come and haul the stuff away, it isn't so bad.

The ability to shut down: *$0 \in Z$, where 0 means the commodity vector of all zeros.* This seems reasonable if we are thinking of Z as a long-run production possibility set and is less reasonable in the short run. (In the short run, the firm may have contractual obligations to buy inputs, for example.)

Nonincreasing returns to scale: *If $z \in Z$ and $0 \le \alpha \le 1$, then $\alpha z \in Z$.* In words, if U.S. Steel can make steel in a big blast furnace, it can do so as well in scaled-down blast furnaces. This assumption is implied by convexity and $0 \in Z$, since it consists of taking a convex combination of z and 0.[1] The name might seem a bit hard to put with the property; it might better be called "nondecreasing returns to scaling down." (The name will make more sense when we get to production functions.) People will sometimes say decreasing returns to scale and mean nonincreasing returns. Since a minimum efficient scale in blast furnace technology exists (a blast furnace with the capacity for making one pound of steel per day is not likely to be very efficient), this seems a dubious assumption. Nonetheless, it is typically assumed.

Nondecreasing returns to scale: *If $z \in Z$ and $\alpha \geq 1$, then $\alpha z \in Z$.* Or, if U.S. Steel can run a big blast furnace, they can run two, or three, or five and a quarter of them. This property is sometimes called increasing returns to scale.

Constant returns to scale: *If $z \in Z$ and $\alpha \geq 0$, then $\alpha z \in Z$.* This is just a conjunction of the previous two properties.

For the one-input, one-output case, the appropriate pictures of increasing, decreasing, and constant returns to scale are easy to draw. If the pictures don't appear instantly in your head, draw them.

Other assumptions are usually added to this list — assumptions of a technical nature that guarantee that the firm's maximization problem (soon to be posed) has a solution. We will wait until such assumptions are necessary before giving the one we will use.

Inputs and outputs: Input requirement sets and iso-quants

In many applications, the commodities that are inputs to the firm are clearly divided from those that are potential outputs. Suppose that we index the K commodities so that commodities 1 through N are inputs, $N+1$ through $N+M$ are outputs, and $N+M+1$ through K have nothing whatsoever to do with the firm. In terms of the firm's production possibility set Z, this division of commodities translates into: If $z = (z_1, \ldots, z_K) \in Z$, then $z_k = 0$ for $k = N + M + 1, \ldots, K$, and $z_k \leq 0$ for $k = 1, \ldots, N$. Note that we don't preclude the possibility that the firm has a negative level of its "outputs"; it could buy some of its potential outputs and throw them away or, more realistically, outputs could be potential inputs to later stages of production. This division, then, really binds only on inputs and "noputs." We might wish to add one further assumption: If $z_k > 0$ for some $k = N + 1, \ldots, N + M$, then $z_k < 0$ for at least one k between 1 and N.

---

[1] But is it equivalent to the two? Draw a picture to see that the answer is no.

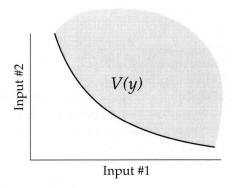

Figure 7.2. A typical input requirement set.

That is, a positive level of any of the outputs requires some nonzero amount of inputs.

When commodities are divided in this fashion into inputs, outputs, and "no-puts," we will change notation slightly. We'll write $x = (x_1, \ldots, x_N)$ for the input vector, where now the levels of the inputs are recorded as positive numbers, and $y = (y_1, \ldots, y_M)$ for the levels of the outputs. That is, $(x, y) \in R^{N+M}$ is a feasible input-output combination for the firm if

$$z = (-x_1, \ldots, -x_N, y_1, \ldots, y_M, 0, \ldots, 0) \in Z.$$

For a fixed level $y = (y_1, \ldots, y_M)$ of outputs, we can ask if y is a feasible level of outputs for the firm: Is there some feasible netput vector $z \in Z$ that gives this vector of outputs? That is, is there some vector of inputs x such that $z = (-x, y, 0) \in Z$? If so, we can go on to ask which vectors of input x satisfy $(-x, y, 0) \in Z$. Call the set of such $x \in R^N$ the *input requirement set* for making the output vector y and denote it by $V(y)$.[2]

For the case of two inputs, a typical input requirement set is depicted in figure 7.2. It is typical because it satisfies the following two properties:

Comprehensive Upwards: This is a fancy way to say that *if $x \in V(y)$ and $x' \geq x$, then $x' \in V(y)$*. This is something like the free disposal assumption on Z, but it is a bit weaker. (Can you draw a picture to show that this is a weaker assumption?)

---

[2] Formally, $V(y) = \{x \in R^N : (-x, y, 0) \in Z\}$, with $V(y) = \emptyset$ if it is infeasible for the firm to produce output vector y.

Convex: This is the obvious property. Convexity of each $V(y)$ is implied by, but does not imply, convexity of Z. (Can you provide a proof?)

This all concerns the input requirement set for one vector y of outputs. We may want to discuss the input requirements for several levels at once, in which case it is natural to suppose (and free disposal guarantees) a *nesting* property: If $y \geq y'$, then $V(y) \subseteq V(y')$; i.e., it takes more to make more. (If all input requirement sets are comprehensive upwards, and if they nest in this sense, is free disposal implied?)

When we have this nesting property, the "frontier" of the input requirement set is called the y-output *iso-quant.*[a] In intermediate textbooks, production possibility sets are often depicted by the iso-quants, which look rather a lot like indifference curves.

The case of one output: Production functions

We can specialize still further in the case where the firm has a single output, or $M = 1$. (Some of what follows will work for more than one output, but it is rather a mess to draw and explain, so we'll restrict attention to one-output firms.)

In this case, it is natural to suppose that from a given selection of inputs $x = (x_1, \ldots, x_N)$ the firm will make as much output y as it can. Hence we have what is called the *production function*, $f(x)$, which gives this greatest amount. Formally, $f(x) = \max\{y : x \in V(y)\}$. Properties of Z translate into properties of f as follows:

Free disposal implies that f is nondecreasing; you can make as much if you have more.

Convexity of Z implies that f is quasi-concave; with a convex combination of inputs, you can make (at least) the lesser of the two levels of output. Alternatively, if each $V(y)$ is convex and if the $V(y)$ nest, then f is quasi-concave. (We'll often go whole hog and assume that f is concave.)

Nondecreasing returns to scale in Z is the same as $f(\alpha x) \geq \alpha f(x)$ for $\alpha > 1$. If an author is fairly careful, the term "increasing" returns to scale will mean that $f(\alpha x) > \alpha f(x)$ for $\alpha > 1$. But some authors will be sloppy and say "increasing" returns to scale when they mean only a weak inequality.

Nonincreasing returns to scale in Z is the same as $f(\alpha x) \leq \alpha f(x)$ for $\alpha > 1$. (Equivalently, we could say $f(\beta x) \geq \beta f(x)$ for $0 \leq \beta < 1$. And remarks

---

[a] Being very formal, this frontier is the set $V(y) \setminus \bigcup_{y' > y} V(y')$.

similar to those in the preceding property apply to the term "decreasing returns.")

Constant returns to scale in Z is the same as $f(\alpha x) = \alpha f(x)$, or f is homogeneous of degree 1.

7.2. The profit function

Profits and competitive firms

Having described the firm's technological capabilities, we ask which production plan the firm will adopt. As noted previously, we conform for now to the standard assumption that the firm seeks to maximize its profits.

How do we formulate this objective? Begin with the general model of a firm characterized by the production possibility set Z. We might be very general about things and write $\Pi(z)$ for some function $\Pi : Z \to R$ as the profits accrued at production plan z. But we can be more specific: Profits are revenues less the costs. If the prices of the K goods are given by the vector $p = (p_1, \ldots, p_K)$, then the firm's profits at netput vector z are $\sum_{k=1}^{K} p_k z_k = p \cdot z$. Note that the sign convention in a netput vector is correct for this formula. Inputs are recorded as negative components in z; if k is an input, so that $z_k < 0$, the "contribution" to profits $p_k z_k$ is negative (assuming prices are positive).

Writing profits as $\Pi(z) = p \cdot z$ involves an implicit assumption: The firm, by its choice of activities, doesn't change the prices that it faces. We made a similar assumption when we analyzed the consumer, namely that a consumer's choice of consumption bundle didn't change the prices she faced. Our excuse was that, excluding individuals such as J. D. Rockefeller, it is unlikely that any single consumer can change the price of a good by anything worth caring about simply by changing her own demand. Here that excuse doesn't work quite as well. General Motors certainly changes the price of Chevrolets when it changes the number of Chevrolets that it produces. And it probably buys enough steel to have a noticeable effect on the price of steel when it changes its production levels. So for large firms that do affect the prices they face, we might write $p_k(z)$ for the price of commodity k as a function of the production plan the firm selects, and so write the firm's profits as $\Pi(z) = \sum_{k=1}^{K} p_k(z)z_k = p(z) \cdot z$.

We will rarely be quite this general. We will want, in some places, to consider cases where the firm does change prices of commodities by what it does. But we will almost always be concerned with cases in which the firm's effect on the price of commodity k depends only on the firm's level of input or output of commodity k. That is, we will suppose that $p_k(z)$ can be written as $p_k(z_k)$, so that $\Pi(z) = \sum_{k=1}^{K} p_k(z_k) z_k$.

We will use the following terminology. When the firm's level of activities has no effect on the price of commodity k, we will say that the firm is a *price taker* for commodity k, or that the firm is *competitive* in the market for commodity k. When a firm is a price taker in all markets (so that its profits are written very simply as $p \cdot z$ for the market prices p), we will say that the firm is *competitive*.

Pictures from intermediate micro

In general, then, the firm solves the following problem:

$$\text{Maximize } p(z) \cdot z \text{ subject to } z \in Z.$$

We can depict this problem rather easily.

Consider first the case where the firm is competitive, so that the firm's problem simplifies to $\max_{z \in Z} p \cdot z$ for some fixed p. Figure 7.3(a) gives the usual picture for the one-input, one-output case. *Iso-profit* lines are given: lines of the form $p \cdot z$ equal to some constant. Profits increase up and to the right, and the firm picks the point in Z that is furthest up on this scale. This looks quite similar to the consumer's problem except that for the consumer the feasibility set had a simple shape (it was a budget set, with a flat surface), and the iso-objective curves, which are straight lines here, were iso-utility curves, which are typically curved.

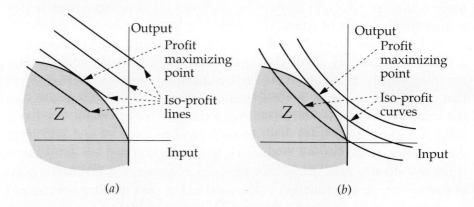

Figure 7.3. The firm's profit-maximization
problem for the one-input, one-output case.
In (a), we have a firm with no market power, whereas (b) gives the picture for a firm with market power.

The picture for the firm is a bit more complex if the firm isn't a price taker. Now prices p will depend (by assumption) on the level of the firm's activities z. Iso-profit lines become iso-profit curves — curves along which $p(z) \cdot z$ is constant. In figure 7.3(b) we've drawn the typical picture. Note the convexity of the iso-profit curves. This can be justified by various assumptions about the firm's market power, to which you will not be subjected here. Now the firm looks more complex than the consumer; both the feasible set and the iso-objective curves are curved. But if we considered a consumer who had market power, this consumer would have a convex budget set (under the right assumptions), and the two sorts of problems would be identical mathematically.[b] The point is that at this level the mathematics of the firm's and the consumer's problems are extraordinarily similar.

Analysis from intermediate micro

Besides drawing pictures, intermediate microeconomics texts (or, at least, those that use calculus) carry on with some basic analysis of the firm's problem, at least for the case of a firm that produces a single output and so is described by a production function f. Given a production function f and assuming that the firm is competitive, we can write the firm's problem as

$$\max_{x=(x_1,\dots,x_N)\geq 0} pf(x) - \sum_{n=1}^{N} w_n x_n,$$

where p is the price of the output good and w_n is the price of input factor n. Assuming f is differentiable and the solution is at an interior point,[3] the first-order condition for factor n is

$$p\frac{\partial f}{\partial x_n} = w_n.$$

This, in turn, is read according to the verbal formula: *The value of the marginal product* of factor n should equal the price of that factor.

Suppose the firm is competitive in its factor markets but not in its product market. For simplicity, assume that the price of the firm's output

---

[b] Except that in the case of the firm we have to worry whether its set of feasible plans is sufficiently "compact" to guarantee the existence of a solution, something we don't need to worry about in the analysis of the consumer. See also the discussion following the proof of Shephard's lemma.

[3] Supply the changes required if one or more of the nonnegativity constraints is binding.

depends only on the level of that output and not (otherwise) on the levels of inputs chosen, so we can write $p(f(x))$ for the price of the output good. The firm's problem becomes

$$\max_{x=(x_1,\ldots,x_N)\geq 0} p(f(x))f(x) - \sum_{n=1}^{N} w_n x_n,$$

which (assuming p is differentiable and we have an interior maximum) gives us the first-order condition (for x_n):

$$[p'(f(x))f(x) + p(f(x))]\left(\frac{\partial f}{\partial x_n}\right) = w_n.$$

This is turned into the verbal formula: *The price of each factor should equal the **marginal revenue product** of the factor.*

We could go on to cases where the firm has market power in some of the factor markets. If we assume that the price of factor n depends only on the amount of factor n used by the firm, so we can write $w_n(x_n)$, the firm's problem is

$$\max_{x=(x_1,\ldots,x_N)\geq 0} p(f(x))f(x) - \sum_{n=1}^{N} w_n(x_n)x_n,$$

and the first-order condition for factor n (at an interior solution) is

$$[p'(f(x))f(x) + p(f(x))]\left(\frac{\partial f}{\partial x_n}\right) = w'(x_n)x_n + w_n(x_n).$$

We can call the right-hand side of this equation the *marginal factor cost* of factor n, and then the first-order condition is verbally rendered: *The marginal factor cost of each factor should equal the marginal revenue product of the factor.*

The profit function for a competitive firm

Suppose we are given a competitive firm, described by a production possibility set Z. At prices (which by assumption do not depend on the z chosen by the firm) given by p, the firm is assumed to pick z to solve the problem

$$\text{maximize } p \cdot z \text{ subject to } z \in Z. \qquad\qquad \text{FP}(p)$$

When this problem has a solution for given prices p, we write $\pi(p)$ for the value of the objective function. This function π is called the *profit function* of the firm. [c]

Does the problem FP(p) have a solution for every vector of prices p, or even for every strictly positive vector of prices? The answer is no, in general. If, for example, a firm has a constant returns to scale technology, where it can convert n units of a single input (commodity k) into αn units of a single output (commodity k') for any n, and if $p_k < (1/\alpha)p_{k'}$, then our fortunate firm can make infinite profits. Our first order of business, then, is to provide conditions under which we are assured that FP(p) has a solution.

We make a very strong (and inelegant) assumption. For any two sets A and B in R^K, when we write $A + B$ we mean the set

$$\{x \in R^K : x = a + b \text{ for some } a \in A \text{ and } b \in B\}.$$

We write R_-^K for the negative orthant in R^K; that is, the set of points $x \in R^K$ all of whose components are nonpositive.

Assumption. *There is a compact set Z' such that $Z' \subseteq Z \subseteq Z' + R_-^K$.*

Note that if Z itself is compact, it meets this assumption. On the other hand, it is quite possible for Z to have the free disposal property and meet this assumption. But increasing or constant returns to scale (for any nontrivial set Z) would violate the assumption. This is not unexpected; we just saw an example where constant returns led to difficulties.

This assumption gets the result we want, which we state somewhat more generally than we need.

Proposition 7.1. *Suppose that Z satisfies the assumption just given, and that $\Pi : Z \to R$ is a continuous and nondecreasing function. (Nondecreasing means that $\Pi(z) \geq \Pi(z')$ if $z \geq z'$.) Then the problem*

$$maximize\ \Pi(z)\ subject\ to\ z \in Z$$

has a solution, and (moreover) solutions may be found in Z'. In particular, if $\Pi(z) = p \cdot z$ for some nonnegative price vector p, then Π is continuous and nondecreasing, hence FP(p) has a solution.

The proof is rather easy if you know the relevant mathematics, so easy that we don't even bother to give it as a problem.

This is not the weakest assumption possible to arrive at the desired conclusions. You will find other, weaker assumptions in the literature. Some of

---

[c] Please note that we use Π for profits as a function of the production plan z, whereas π gives maximal profits as a function of (parametric) prices. Do not confuse the two.

the development to follow can be extended to give partial results if no assumption of the form above is made; instead the statements of subsequent results are qualified with clumsy formulae such as: "If FP(p) has a solution..."; or "...for prices where π is defined." You are invited to provide such extensions.

If you skipped the technical excursions, we just guaranteed that FP(p) has a solution for all nonnegative prices p. And with this we can proceed to some results:

Proposition 7.2. Properties of the profit function.

(a) The profit function π is homogeneous of degree one in prices.

(b) The profit function is continuous in p.

(c) The profit function is convex in p.

Part (a) is proved fairly easily. Suppose that z^* solves FP(p). Then at prices λp for λ a positive scalar, z^* gives profits $\lambda p \cdot z^* = \lambda \pi(p)$, hence $\pi(\lambda p) \geq \lambda \pi(p)$. And if $z^\dagger$ solves FP(λp), then at prices p, $z^\dagger$ gives profits $p \cdot z^\dagger$, so that $\pi(p) \geq p \cdot z^\dagger = (1/\lambda)\lambda p z^\dagger = (1/\lambda)\pi(\lambda p)$, or $\lambda \pi(p) \geq \pi(\lambda p)$. Combining these two inequalities does it.

The proof of part (b) is a little bit technical. Let $p^n \to p$. Let z^n be a solution of FP(p^n) so that $\pi(p^n) = p^n \cdot z^n$. By proposition 7.1 we can assume that z^n is drawn from the compact set Z', hence any subsequence of $\{z^n\}$ has a convergent subsubsequence with limit in Z. Look along a subsequence n' in n such that $\lim_{n'} \pi(p^{n'}) = \limsup_n \pi(p^n)$. Then looking along a subsubsequence n'' of the subsequence n' where $z^{n''}$ converges to some $z^0 \in Z$, we have by continuity of the dot product that $\limsup_n \pi(p^n) = \lim_{n''} \pi(p^{n''}) = \lim_{n''} p^{n''} \cdot z^{n''} = p \cdot z^0 \leq \pi(p)$. Conversely, if z solves FP(p), then $\liminf_n \pi(p^n) \geq \lim_n p^n \cdot z = p \cdot z = \pi(p)$. That does it.

The proof of (c) is quite simple. Take any two prices p and p', and any scalar $\alpha \in [0,1]$, and let $p'' = \alpha p + (1-\alpha)p'$. Let $z \in Z$ solve FP(p''), so that $\pi(p'') = p'' \cdot z$. Of course, since z remains feasible at prices p and p', $\pi(p) \geq p \cdot z$ and $\pi(p') \geq p' \cdot z$. Hence

$$\pi(p'') = p'' \cdot z = (\alpha p + (1-\alpha)p') \cdot z$$
$$= \alpha p \cdot z + (1-\alpha)p' \cdot z \leq \alpha \pi(p) + (1-\alpha)\pi(p').$$

We go on to properties of solutions of FP(p):

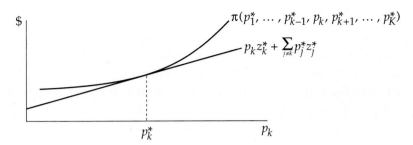

$$\pi(p_1^*, \ldots, p_{k-1}^*, p_k, p_{k+1}^*, \ldots, p_K^*)$$

$$p_k z_k^* + \sum_{j \neq k} p_j^* z_j^*$$

Figure 7.4. Proving Hotelling's lemma.

Proposition 7.3. *(a) If z^* is a solution of FP(p), then for any positive scalar λ, z^* is a solution of FP(λp).*

(b) If Z is convex, the set of solutions of FP(p) is convex for each p.

Both of these are left for you as easy exercises.[d]

Finally, we have a result that has a name. In fact, it has two names:

Proposition 7.4. The Derivative Property, or Hotelling's Lemma. *Suppose that the profit function π is continuously differentiable at price vector p^*. Let z^* be any solution of FP(p^*). Then for every $k = 1, \ldots, K$,*

$$\left. \frac{\partial \pi}{\partial p_k} \right|_{p^*} = z_k^*.$$

If you think about this for a moment, you'll see that this implies that if π is continuously differentiable at p, then FP(p) has a unique solution.[e]

The proof can be provided by a simple picture. (If you remember our proof that the derivatives of the expenditure function equal Hicksian demands, you should have no trouble doing this without reading any further.) If z^* is a solution to FP(p^*), then $p^* \cdot z^* = \pi(p^*)$. Since z^* is feasible at any prices p, $p \cdot z^* \leq \pi(p)$. Fix k. In figure 7.4 we graph the functions

$$p_k \to \pi(p_1^*, \ldots, p_{k-1}^*, p_k, p_{k+1}^*, \ldots, p_K^*) \text{ and } p_k \to p_k z_k^* + \sum_{j \neq k} p_j^* z_j^*.$$

---

[d] If you are mathemcatically inclined, you may wish to continue with more properties of solutions of FP(p). In particular, we will later wonder what ensures that FP(p) has a unique solution. See problems 4 and 5.

[e] Math whizzes: Is the converse true?

We have seen that the second of these functions, which is linear, is everywhere below or touching the first, and it touches at $p_k = p_k^*$. By assumption, π is differentiable at p^*, so the derivatives of the two functions must be equal. And the derivative of the linear function is z_k^*.

Or, in words, suppose the price of commodity k changes. We expect that the firm will adjust its production plans. But if the change is small, the difference (beginning from a profit-maximizing position) of staying at the plan z^* or moving to the new optimum is of second order relative to the change in profits overall.

You can also proof this result algebraically, using first-order conditions from the firm's profit-maximization problem.

Of what use is this? Combining this result with the earlier result on the convexity of π gives us some comparative statics results similar to those in chapter 2. To begin, we record a mathematical fact.

Fact. *If* $\phi : R^K \to R$ *is a convex function and* ϕ *is twice continuously differentiable at the argument* x^*, *then the* $K \times K$ *matrix of second partial derivatives of* ϕ, *whose* (k, j)th *element is* $[\partial^2\phi/(\partial x_k \partial x_j)]|_{x^*}$ *is positive semi-definite; if* $M(x^*)$ *is this matrix, then* $xM(x^*)x \geq 0$ *for all* $x \in R^k$. *In particular, the diagonal terms of this matrix are nonnegative. Of course, this matrix is also symmetric.*

Corollary. *Suppose a firm's profit function* π *is differentiable at prices* p^*. *Suppose as well that, for all points* p *in a neighborhood of* p^*, *FP(p) has a unique solution* $z^*(p)$ *which, moreover, is continuously differentiable in* p. *Then the* $K \times K$ *matrix whose* (k, j)th *element is* $\partial z_j^*/\partial p_k$ *is symmetric and positive semi-definite. In particular:*

(a) $\partial z_j^*/\partial p_k = \partial z_k^*/\partial p_j$ *for all* j *and* k; *and*

(b) $\partial z_k^*/\partial p_k \geq 0$ *for all* k.

If you followed developments in chapter 2, you should have no trouble seeing how this follows immediately. Parts (a) and (b) deserve verbal restatements. Part (a) is a bit surprising; it says that the firm's reaction to a penny change in the price of k in terms of netput level z_j equals its reaction in z_k to a penny change in the price of j. You can consider cases where both k and j are inputs, or where both are outputs, but it may be most instructive to think through the case where k is an output and j an input. If the price of output good k rises by a penny, we expect the firm to increase its output and, therefore, to increase the level of its inputs. Increasing the level of input j means that z_j will become more negative, so in this case we expect $\partial z_j^*/\partial p_k < 0$. And if the price of input j rises by a penny, we expect the firm to cut its output; this is the straightforward $\partial z_k^*/\partial p_j < 0$. Of course, (a) says more than this; it not only says that the signs of the two partial derivatives agree, but also that the two agree precisely in level. (This part is surprising.)

Part (b) is fairly clear. If k is an output and its price rises, we expect the firm will increase its level of that output. Whereas if k is an input and its price rises, we expect that the firm will decrease the amount that it uses of that input, which means that z_k (which is negative) will get closer to zero, which is again a positive partial derivative.

You may rightfully wonder about the status of our assumption that FP(p) has a unique and continuously differentiable solution in a neighborhood of p^*. We will not attempt to justify the differentiability part. But for continuity and uniqueness of the solution, see problems 4 and 5.

Testable restrictions

In our study of the theory of the consumer, we posed the question: What conditions on a finite set of demand data are implied by the model of the consumer as a utility maximizer? We can ask a similar question here. Suppose we see a finite amount of data about the production decisions of a firm. These data are assumed to take the form: At prices p^i, the firm's netput vector is z^i, for $i = 1, \ldots, I$. When are these data consistent with our model?

The answer is very simple to give if we maintain the hypothesis that the firm is competitive and that its production possibility set Z hasn't changed over the time frame for which we've gathered these data.[f] Suppose $p^j z^i > p^j z^j$ for some $j \neq i$. Then we have a problem. We know that z^i is feasible for the firm. And from the given inequality, we know that, at prices p^j, z^i gives higher profits than z^j. So why was z^j chosen when prices were p^j?

This consideration gives all the restrictions of the model:

Proposition 7.5. *Suppose you are given a finite set of data of the form: At prices p^i, the firm chose netput vector z^i, for $i = 1, \ldots, I$. These data are consistent with the profit-maximizing model of a competitive firm (whose production possibility set isn't changing) if and only if for no pair i, j is it the case that $p^j z^i > p^j z^j$.*

---

[f] If the firm isn't competitive, the exercise gets quite complicated. Who is setting the prices we observe, and with what objective? After chapters 9 and 10, you could take a run at this sort of analysis with firms that aren't competitive. If we think that the firm's production capabilities may be changing with changing prices or over the time that the data are observed, then there is little we can say. But see problem 6.

The proof is trivial. If there are no obvious violations of profit maximization in the sense of the proposition, then one can take $Z = \{z^1, \ldots, z^I\}$.
That is, the firm is capable of precisely the I observed netput vectors and
no more. (Why does this prove the proposition?) Of course, this is a very
odd looking production possibilities set, but we can fill in all the "holes."
If we take Z to be the convex hull of the observed netput vectors, or
Z to be all netput vectors that are less or equal to points in the convex
hull (assuming all prices are nonnegative), we have Zs consistent with
the data. In fact, we might ask what is the largest candidate Z consistent
with the data? This is easy to give. For each i, let H_i be the half-plane
$\{z \in R^K : p^i \cdot z \le p^i \cdot z^i\}$. Then any Z that contains all the observed z^i
and that is contained within $\bigcap_{i=1}^{I} H_i$ is consistent with the observations.

It may help to give an example for the two-commodity case and draw
some pictures. Suppose the first commodity is the firm's input, and the
second is its output. Suppose that

    (a) At prices $(1, 1)$, the firm's netput vector is $(-3, 5)$

    (b) At prices $(1, 2)$, the firm's netput vector is $(-6, 7)$

    (c) At prices $(2, 1)$, the firm's netput vector is $(0, 0)$

First check that these data are consistent with the model. At prices $(1, 1)$,
the firm chooses a netput vector that yields profits 2; the other two netputs
we know to be feasible give (at these prices) profits 1 and 0. So far, so
good. At prices $(1, 2)$, the firm chooses $(-6, 7)$, which gives profits 8; the
other two netputs we know to be feasible give profits 7 and 0. Okay again.
And at prices $(2, 1)$, the firm chooses a production plan that gives profits
0; at these prices the other two known-to-be-feasible production plans give
losses of 1 and 5, respectively. So these data are consistent with the model.

Now we draw pictures. Consider the first piece of data. In figure
7.5(a), we put in the point $(-3, 5)$ (as a heavy dot) and through it we drew
the iso-profit line corresponding to prices $(1, 1)$. We also put in the two
other production plans we saw from the firm as open dots. It is important
that they lie below and to the left of the iso-profit line drawn in. We also
put in (as dashed lines) the iso-profit lines corresponding to prices $(2, 1)$
and $(1, 2)$ through the production plans selected at those prices. Note once
again that in each case the "other" two points lie below and to the left of
the iso-profit lines.

What can we say about the production possibility set consistent with
these three pieces of data and the model? The set Z must, of course, contain the three production plans that we observed. If Z is convex, it must
contain all the points in the heavily shaded region in figure 7.5(b) — the

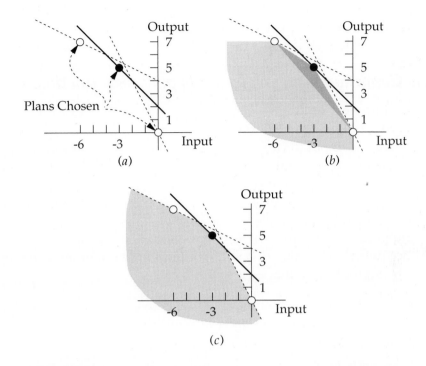

Figure 7.5. Testable restrictions in the model of the firm.
In (a), we show three pieces of data consistent with the standard model
of the firm. Each piece of data consists of a production plan and prices
at which that plan was chosen. Those prices are used to create iso-profit
lines for the plan chosen at those prices. And the data are consistent with
the model because all points chosen at some set of prices lie on or below
the iso-profit lines so created. In (b), we show the minimal possible Z
consistent with the model and these three data points if Z is convex
(the heavier shading) and Z is convex and has free disposal (the lighter
shading). In (c) we show the largest Z consistent with the model and
these three data points: Z must be contained within the intersection of
the half-planes lying below and to the left of the iso-profit lines drawn
in (a).

convex hull of the three points. If Z is convex and has free disposal, it
must contain all the points in the lightly shaded region in figure 7.5(b).

And in figure 7.5(c) we show the greatest possible extent of this production possibility set, consistent with the data and the model. If any point
in Z lies above one of the three iso-profit lines through the respective selected plans, that point would have been selected by a profit-maximizing
firm instead of the plan supposedly selected. Hence points in Z must lie

below these three iso-profit lines. The shaded region in 7.5(c) is just the intersection of the half-planes referred to previously.

7.3. Conditional factor demands and cost functions

We turn next to the model of the firm with N identified inputs and M outputs. We use the notation developed in section 7.1: The vector x will denote an input vector; y will denote an output vector; $V(y)$ will denote the input requirement set for obtaining outputs at the levels given by y; and, assuming the firm is competitive in factor markets (which we do throughout this section), $w = (w_1, \ldots, w_N) \in R^N$ will denote the prices of the various inputs or factors of production.

Suppose the firm, for whatever reason, fixes on the idea that it must produce outputs at levels y. It still will pick inputs in order to minimize its costs of production; that is, it will solve

$$\text{minimize } w \cdot x \text{ subject to } x \in V(y). \qquad \text{FCMP}(w,y)$$

Here, FCMP are the initials of the firm's cost-minimization problem.

> We have fewer worries about the problem than we do about FP(p). In particular, existence of a solution is much less a problem. Assuming $V(y)$ is nonempty and closed, if the factor prices w are strictly positive, then we are guaranteed a solution: Take any point $x \in V(y)$. Since x is one feasible way to produce y, costing $w \cdot x$, the optimal solution costs no more. That is, the optimal solution must come from the set $\{x' \in V(y) : w \cdot x' \leq w \cdot x; x' \geq 0\}$. If $V(y)$ is closed, this set is compact, ensuring the existence of a solution.

We write $c(w,y)$ for the value of this cost-minimization problem, as a function of the two sets of parameters, prices w and output level desired y. This function c is called the *cost function*.

For the case of two inputs, we can give a very revealing depiction of FCMP(w,y). (If you have taken a course in intermediate micro, you are sure to have seen this picture.) In figure 7.6, *iso-cost* lines are parallel straight lines, and the firm will select that point in $V(y)$ that is as far down in terms of cost as possible. This picture should remind you of figure 2.4, the picture for the Dual Consumption Problem that defines the expenditure function and Hicksian demand. Instead of a production iso-quant for a given level of production, we had there an indifference curve for a given level of utility. Instead of minimizing cost, we were minimizing

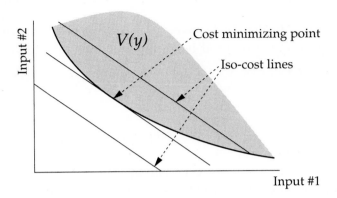

Figure 7.6. *Finding the cost function in the two-input case.*

expenditure. But the pictures are the same, and so, it turns out, are the mathematics.

Proposition 7.6. Properties of the cost function.

(a) The cost function is homogeneous of degree one in w for each fixed y.

(b) The cost function is nondecreasing in w for each fixed y.

(c) The cost function is concave in w for each fixed y.

Parts (a) and (b) are left for you to prove. The proof of (c) should be old hat by now, but let us give it a final time. Choose any two factor price vectors w and w' and some $\alpha \in [0,1]$, and let $w'' = \alpha w + (1 - \alpha)w'$. Let x be any solution of FCMP(w'', y). Then $x \in V(y)$, and x could be used to produce y at prices w and at prices w'. Of course, at these two sets of factor prices something might be better than x, so that $c(w, y) \leq w \cdot x$ and $c(w', y) \leq w' \cdot x$. And thus $\alpha c(w, y) + (1 - \alpha)c(w', y) \leq \alpha w \cdot x + (1 - \alpha)w' \cdot x = w'' \cdot x = c(w'', y)$.

Solutions of FCMP(w, y) are called *conditional factor demands*, where "conditional" refers to the fact that the output vector y is fixed.

Proposition 7.7. Properties of solutions of FCMP(w, y).

(a) If x solves FCMP(w, y), then x solves FCMP$(\lambda w, y)$ for all strictly positive scalars λ.

(b) If $V(y)$ is convex, then the set of solutions of FCMP(w, y) is convex.[9]

---

[9] See problems 4 and 5 for more and, in particular, for conditions sufficient to guarantee

The proofs are left to you. You should have no problems by now.

Proposition 7.8. Shephard's Lemma. *Suppose that $c(w, y)$ is continuously differentiable in w (for fixed y) at price vector w^*. Let x^* be any solution of FCMP(w^*, y). Then*

$$\left. \frac{\partial c(w, y)}{\partial w_n} \right|_{(w^*, y)} = x_n^*.$$

As noted immediately following Hotelling's lemma, this implies that if $c(w, y)$ is continuously differentiable in w at w^*, then FCMP(w^*, y) necessarily has a unique solution.[h]

This should be compared to proposition 2.15. It is essentially the same result, although we're a bit fancier here by noting that FCMP(w^*, y) must have a unique solution if c is continuously differentiable in w rather than assuming uniqueness of the solution. In any event, the proof is precisely the same; use the same picture as figure 2.6, although the names of the various objects change.

> Time for a really technical aside. We have four applications of the "envelope theorem," namely proposition 2.15, Roy's identity (proposition 2.16), Hotelling's lemma (proposition 7.4), and now Shephard's lemma. Of the four, all but Roy's identity were extremely easy, whereas Roy's identity was only easy. A difference between Roy's identity and the other three explains why the three were easier. In proposition 2.15, Hotelling's lemma, and Shephard's lemma, prices, as they change, change the objective function in the optimization problem being studied. But the feasible set stays the same. In Roy's identity, as prices change, the objective function (utility) stays and the feasible set (the consumer's budget set) changes. The latter is simply a bit harder. You can't just sit at the old optimal solution and see what its value is at the new prices; to remain feasible you have to move a bit from the old optimal solution. If you can make sense of all this, think through: What would be the analogous result for the following (quite daft) problem for a firm with one output? Given a fixed budget to be spent on inputs, maximize the amount of output you can produce, as parameterized by the prices of the inputs.

Suppose that for fixed output y, FCMP(w, y) has a unique solution for each w in some neighborhood, and suppose, moreover, that these solutions, viewed as a function $w \to x_n^*(w, y)$, are continuously differentiable. By virtue of proposition 7.6(c) and 7.8, we can now start developing results of the usual sort based on the observation that the $N \times N$ matrix whose

---

that FCMP(w, y) has a unique solution.

[h] Same challenge as before: What is the status of the converse?

(ℓ, n)th term is $\partial x_\ell^* / \partial w_n$ is a symmetric, negative semi-definite matrix. You ought to be capable of discerning the implications of this by now.

7.4. From profit or cost functions to technology sets

(This entire section is in small type for the technical reader.) In chapter 2, we posed the question: Given a set of alleged Marshallian demand functions, are the given functions in fact demand functions for some consumer conforming to the standard model? The reason for asking this question, we said, was to build tractable models. It is hard to get closed form demand functions from utility functions that give the sorts of parametric flexibility we might like. But if we have an answer to the question, then we can start with demand functions that have the desired parametric features and check that they are in keeping with the standard model.

For the same reason, we wish to be able to answer the question: Given a profit function π, or given a cost function c, under what conditions are we certain that these arise from profit-maximizing behavior by a competitive firm? We are interested in these questions because it might be convenient to start with a profit function or a cost function instead of with a production possibility set or a collection of input requirement sets.

We could, as well, put the question: Are given conditional demand functions x^* (whose arguments are pairs (w, y)) consistent with profit maximization by a competitive firm? And although we didn't introduce the terminology previously, we can ask: Suppose we are given *supply/demand* functions z^* (with domain the space of prices R_+^K and range the space of netputs R^K) that are alleged solutions of FP(p) for some competitive firm. Are they in fact consistent with the standard model?

We will give answers here for the profit and supply/demand functions. We will assume that these given functions are smooth; the profit function (if that is what we are given) is twice continuously differentiable, and the supply/demand functions (if that is what we are given) are continuously differentiable. You may wish to adapt our results and analysis to cost functions and conditional factor demand functions and (what is harder) to less smooth candidate profit and supply/demand functions.

Proposition 7.9. *(a) If a candidate profit function π is homogeneous of degree one and convex, and if we define supply/demand functions z^* from π by $z_k^*(p) = \partial \pi / \partial p_k$, then these supply/demand functions are homogeneous of degree zero, and the $K \times K$ matrix of terms $\partial z_j^* / \partial p_k$ for $j, k = 1, \ldots, K$ is symmetric and positive semi-definite.*

(b) If candidate supply/demand functions z^* are homogeneous of degree zero, and the $K \times K$ matrix of terms $\partial z_j^* / \partial p_k$ for $j, k = 1, \ldots, K$ is symmetric and positive semi-definite, then the profit function π defined by $\pi(p) = p \cdot z^*(p)$ is homogeneous of degree one and convex.

(c) In either case (a) or (b), if we define from π the set Z given by

$$Z = \{z \in R^k : p \cdot z \le \pi(p) \text{ for all } p \ge 0\},$$

then π and z^* correspond to a competitive firm that has production possibility set Z.

To prove this we need to know:

(1) Euler's law: If $\phi : R^K \rightarrow R$ is a differentiable function that is homogenous of degree one, then $\phi(x) = \sum_{k=1}^{K} x_k (\partial \phi / \partial x_k)$.

(2) If ϕ is homogeneous of degree one, the functions $\partial \phi / \partial x_k$ are all homogeneous of degree zero.

(3) If ϕ is homogeneous of degree zero, $\sum_{k=1}^{K} x_k (\partial \phi / \partial x_k) = 0$.

These are easy to prove: Differentiate the identity $\phi(\lambda x) = \lambda \phi(x)$ first with respect to λ for (1) and then with respect to x_k for (2). And for (3), differentiate the identity $\phi(\lambda x) = \phi(x)$ with respect to λ.

Thus if π is homogeneous of degree one, the supply/demand functions defined in (a) are homogeneous of degree zero. And the convexity of ϕ gives the corresponding properties on the matrix of mixed partials of z^*. This is (a).

Conversely, if we have supply/demand functions that are homogeneous of degree zero, defining π from them as in (b) clearly gives us a function homogeneous of degree one. For this π,

$$\left. \frac{\partial \pi}{\partial p_k} \right|_p = z_k^*(p) + \sum_{k'=1}^{K} p_{k'} \frac{\partial z_{k'}^*}{p_k}$$

$$= z_k^*(p) + \sum_{k'=1}^{K} p_{k'} \frac{\partial z_k^*}{p_{k'}} = z_k^*(p),$$

where the next to last equality follows from the presumed symmetry, and the last equality follows from (3). And then the positive semi-definiteness of the matrix of mixed partials of z^* implies that π is convex. This gives (b).

Finally, for (c), we need to show that for every p, $z^*(p)$ is the solution to the profit-maximization problem at prices p where choice is out of Z as defined. It is immediately clear that no alternative production plan from Z will give higher profits than $z^*(p)$, since Z is defined precisely so this is so. The key is to show that $z^*(p)$ is in Z as defined, which means that $p' \cdot z^*(p) \leq \pi(p')$ for all $p' \geq 0$. This can be shown as follows: Since π is convex, we can show that

$$\pi(p') \geq (p' - p) \cdot \mathbf{D}\pi(p) + \pi(p) = p' \cdot \mathbf{D}\pi(p) - p \cdot \mathbf{D}\pi(p) + \pi(p),$$

where $\mathbf{D}\pi(p) = (\partial \pi / \partial p_1, \ldots, \partial \pi / \partial p_K)|_p$. (Consult a good book about convex functions for this result.) But by (1), $p \cdot \mathbf{D}\pi(p) = \pi(p)$, so this inequality simplifies to $\pi(p') \geq p' \cdot \mathbf{D}\pi(p)$. And $\mathbf{D}\pi(p) = z^*(p)$, so the inequality is $\pi(p') \geq p' \cdot z^*(p)$, which is just what we want.

Besides giving us useful test conditions for when a profit function or set of supply/demand functions corresponds to a competitive profit-maximizing firm, this result, or rather its proof, illustrates how one recovers the "relevant technology" of a firm from profit functions and/or supply/demand functions. The definition of Z given in the proposition is the key. Recall that in the subsection on testable restrictions, we said that the largest possible production possibility set consistent with a given set of data was the intersection of half-planes given by those data. If you look at the definition of Z that is given, you will see that it is nothing more than the intersection of the infinitely many half-planes given to us by the supply/demand function! And then the real magic in the proof is the demonstration that $z^*(p)$ for each p is in that intersection, which is where the convexity of π comes in.

7.5. Cost functions and -runs

In section 7.3, we investigated properties of the cost function in factor prices for fixed output level y. Now we suppose that w is fixed (as a function of x) and look at the cost function as a function of output levels y. We will deal throughout with the case of a one-output firm.[i]

Assume we have a one-output firm, and assume the technology of the firm is described by the production function $f(x)$. Fix factor prices w, which we will allow to depend on the levels of the factor inputs. Define, for each production level y,

$$TC(y) = \min\{w(x) \cdot x : y = f(x)\}.$$

That is, $TC(y)$ gives the cost of the least-cost combination of factor inputs from which y can be produced. TC stands for *total cost*; we append the T because we will shortly deal with other modifiers (average, marginal). Note that we do not require that the firm is competitive in factor markets; compare with our treatment of cost functions in section 7.3.

Assuming we have the cost function TC, the firm's problem is to maximize $p(y)y - TC(y)$. The first-order condition is $p'(y)y + p(y) = TC'(y)$, or *marginal revenue equals marginal cost*. The term $\epsilon(y) = p(y)/yp'(y)$ is called (for various reasons) the elasticity of demand facing the firm; with this definition, we can rewrite this first-order condition as

$$p(y)\left(1 + \frac{1}{\epsilon(y)}\right) = TC'(y).$$

[i] Everything that follows concerning total and marginal costs would work easily for multiproduct firms. But what we will say about average costs doesn't extend at all easily; if you have ever been involved in the allocation of joint costs among several products, you will see why immediately.

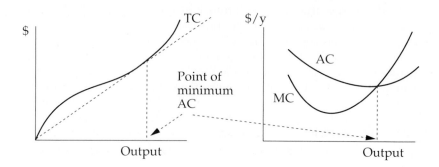

Figure 7.7. Total cost, average cost, and marginal cost curves.

If the firm has no market power in the product market, so that $p'(y) = 0$ and $1/\epsilon(y) = 0$ (the firm faces a perfectly elastic demand curve), the first-order condition simplifies to $p(y) = TC'(y)$, or *price equals marginal cost.*[4]

As for the geometry of the cost function, it is typical to define the average cost function by $AC(y) = TC(y)/y$ and marginal cost by $MC(y) = TC'(y)$, obtaining the picture in figure 7.7. Average costs always will be falling when marginal cost is less than average cost, and average costs are rising when marginal cost is greater than average cost: To see this differentiate $AC(y)$ to get $AC'(y) = TC'(y)/y - TC(y)/y^2 = (1/y)[MC(y) - AC(y)]$. Hence whenever $MC(y) = AC(y)$, we are at a local minimum or maximum (or, if we want to list all the cases, some other critical point) of AC.

Suppose our technology exhibits increasing returns to scale over some region. Then AC will be falling (or, at least, not rising), hence $MC \leq AC$. This takes a proof, which you are asked to supply in problem 10. You are also asked in problem 10 to show that the converse is not necessarily correct. But when there are constant returns to scale, AC will be flat, which means that $AC = MC$.

Fixed and variable costs as long- and short-run costs

In a number of models, the distinction between what a firm can do in the long and short runs is modeled by supposing that there are certain inputs whose levels cannot be shifted at all in the short run but that are freely variable in the long run. In terms of the general formulation in which a firm's technology is described by Z, we would begin with a

---

[4] If the "equation" $1/\epsilon = 0$ when $\epsilon = k/0$ bothers you, just use the first-order condition $p'(y)y + p(y) = TC'(y)$.

long-run production possibility set Z^l; there would be commodities, say $k = 1,\ldots,K'$, which are fixed in the short run, and for levels $(\hat{z}_1,\ldots,\hat{z}_{K'})$ of those short-run fixed levels of netput, the short-run production possibility set of the firm would be

$$Z^s = \{z \in Z^l : z_k = \hat{z}_k \text{ for } k = 1,\ldots,K'\}.$$

Note that we should index this set Z^s by $(\hat{z}_1,\ldots,\hat{z}_{K'})$; as those levels change, so does Z^s. Note also that this accommodates short-run fixed levels of factor inputs *and* short-run fixed levels of required outputs. This isn't entirely general: If the firm has short-run commitments that it must meet but can exceed (say, it must supply $\hat{z}_K$ of good K), then it would make more sense to define Z^s where the restriction on the level of z_K is $z_K \geq \hat{z}_K$.

Now consider the special case of a one-output firm whose technology is given by a production function formulation and that is competitive in its factor markets. The short-run restrictions are that levels of some of the factor inputs are set. As usual, we index factor inputs by $1,2,\ldots,N$, and we let $1,\ldots,N'$ index those that are fixed in the short run, and $N'+1,\ldots,N$ index those that are freely variable in the short run. In the short run, then, we are stuck at some level of factor inputs $(\hat{x}_1,\ldots,\hat{x}_{N'})$, paying a bill $\sum_{n=1}^{N'} w_n \hat{x}_n$ for them.[5] If we wish to produce y units of output, we minimize short-run costs by solving

$$\min_{x_{N'+1},\ldots,x_N} \left\{ \sum_{n=N'+1}^{N} w_n x_n : y = f(\hat{x}_1,\ldots,\hat{x}_{N'},x_{N'+1},\ldots,x_N) \right\}. \qquad (\star)$$

The cost of the fixed factors, $\sum_{n=1}^{N'} w_n \hat{x}_n$, is called the *fixed cost*, or FC. The minimum cost of the variable factors, given by $(\star)$, is called the (short-run, total) *variable costs*, or $TVC(y)$. (Implicitly, this function depends on the levels of the fixed factors.) Of course, only TVC depends on y. Finally, total costs are $TC(y) = FC + TVC(y)$.

At this point, we can define average variable costs, average fixed costs, average fixed-plus-variable costs, and marginal costs. The pictures are as in figure 7.8. Since the variable costs, average variable costs, average total

---

[5] For the remainder of this section, we will assume that the firm is a price taker in its factor markets. You might ponder what changes if (1) w_n is a function of x_n or (2) w_n is a function of the entire vector x. In (2), consider in particular what happens if w_n for some $n \leq N'$ depends on $x_{n'}$ for some $n' > N'$.

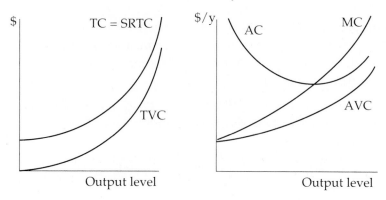

Figure 7.8. *Short-run cost curves.*

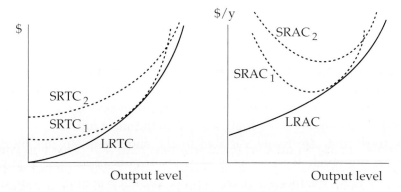

Figure 7.9. *Short- and long-run cost curves.*

(fixed-plus-variable) costs, and marginal costs all are based on the short-run consideration that some of the factors can't be varied, they are also sometimes called short-run variable, short-run average variable, short-run average fixed-plus-variable, and short-run marginal costs.

And, to conclude, we can in the long run vary all the factor inputs to give us long-run total, average, and marginal costs. As we change the quantities of the fixed factors, we trace out all the possible short-run cost curves. Long-run cost curves (of the total and average variety) are the lower envelopes of the various short-run cost curves. See figure 7.9. Note that, in figure 7.9, some short-run average cost curves lie everywhere above the long-run average cost curve. *A SRAC curve is tangent to the LRAC curve only if the fixed amounts of the short-run fixed factors are optimum overall for some level of output.* If (because, e.g., factor prices changed unexpectedly) the firm is "stuck" with fixed factor amounts that are not optimal for any long-run level of production, then the firm will have SRTC and SRAC curves that are everywhere strictly above the LRTC and LRAC curves.

7.6. *Bibliographic notes*

Varian (1984) covers a number of topics not covered here, including remarks on the geometry of cost functions, conditional factor demand functions, and input requirement sets. (If an iso-quant is flat, what does that mean for conditional factor demands? If an iso-quant is kinked, what are the implications?) He also introduces the problems of empirical estimation of production and cost functions.

We have been very loose in our treatment of technical issues such as differentiability of demand/supply and conditional factor demand functions. All this can be done rigorously; see Sonnenschein (1987) for the gory details.

References

Sonnenschein, H. 1987. *Lecture Notes in Microeconomic Theory*. Princeton University. Mimeo.

Varian, H. 1984. *Microeconomic Analysis*, 2d ed. New York: W. W. Norton.

7.7. *Problems*

■ 1. Below are six production functions for a firm that turns two variable factors of production, capital k and labor l, into a single output y. Labor is freely variable in the short and the long run. Capital is fixed in the short run, but can be varied in the long run. Assume that the firm is a price taker in the factor markets, that the price of capital is r, and the price of labor is w. For each of these six production functions, what is the firm's long-run total (variable) cost function? What is the firm's short-run total (variable) cost function (given a level k of capital)? In the short and in the long run, does the firm exhibit increasing, decreasing, or constant returns to scale?

(a) $f(k,l) = k^\alpha l^\beta$ for $\alpha > 0, \beta > 0$, and $\alpha + \beta < 1$.

(b) Same as part (a), but $\alpha + \beta = 1$.

(c) How about $\alpha + \beta > 1$?

(d) $f(k,l) = \left(\min\left[k/\alpha, l/\beta\right]\right)^\gamma$, where $\alpha > 0$, $\beta > 0$, and $0 < \gamma < 1$.

(e) Same as (d), but $\gamma = 1$.

(f) $f(k,l) = \alpha k + (1 - \alpha)l$.

■ 2. (a) Show that if, for a given firm, Z has free disposal, then $V(y)$ is comprehensive upwards for every y. (Assume the firm has N inputs and M outputs.) Show by example that the converse is false. If each $V(y)$ is comprehensive upwards and the nesting property holds (if $y \geq y'$, then $V(y) \subseteq V(y')$), does the corresponding set Z have free disposal?

(b) Show that if Z is convex, then each $V(y)$ is convex. Show by example that the converse is false.

■ 3. Suppose a one-output firm is described by a production function $f(x)$. Show that if the firm has free disposal, then f is nondecreasing. Show that convexity of Z implies that f is quasi-concave. Show that nondecreasing returns to scale in Z is the same as $f(\alpha x) \geq \alpha f(x)$ for $\alpha > 1$.

■ 4. Let $Z^*(p)$ be the set of all solutions of FP(p) for a firm whose production possibility set Z is closed. Show that the correspondence $p \to Z^*(p)$ is upper semi-continuous. Show that if FP(p) has a unique solution for all prices in some region, then the function $z^*(p)$ defined over that region is continuous. State and prove parallel results for the correspondence $p \to X^*(p)$ of solutions of FCMP(w, y).

■ 5. For a given production possibility set Z, we say that $z \in Z$ is *efficient* if there is no $z' \in Z$ such that $z' \geq z$ and $z' \neq z$. Suppose that Z is convex and has the property that if z and z' are both in Z and $\alpha \in (0, 1)$, then $\alpha z + (1 - \alpha)z'$ is not efficient. Show that this implies that, for a competitive firm facing strictly positive prices p, the solution to FP(p) is unique. Construct a parallel definition for input requirement sets $V(y)$ and give a parallel result concerning the uniqueness of solutions for FCMP(w, y).

■ 6. Suppose that we have obtained a sequence of observations of the production plans adopted by a firm for a sequence of prices. Specifically, we observe at one time that, at prices p^1, the firm chooses production plan z^1; at a later time, at prices p^2, the firm chooses plan z^2; and so on, with the last observation being that at prices p^I the firm chooses plan z^I. The model we have is that the firm is competitive and chooses a profit-maximizing plan from its production possibility set at each point in time, but that the production possibility set may, because of technological advances, be growing through time. That is, at the time of the first choice, the firm has production possibility set Z^1; at the second time, the firm has a production possibility set Z^2 with $Z^1 \subseteq Z^2$, and so on. In the spirit of proposition 7.5, give necessary and sufficient conditions on the sequence of observations being consistent with this sort of model.

■ 7. Suppose that for some reason we were interested in studying solutions to the following problem: A firm produces a single output y from N inputs $x = (x_1, \ldots, x_N)$. The firm is given a certain budget that it can spend on inputs, and the firm produces as much output as it can given that budget. Letting B be the budget and supposing the firm is described by a production function $f(x)$ and that the firm is competitive and faces factor prices w, we can define

$$y^*(w, B) = \max\{f(x) : w \cdot x \leq B\}.$$

Devise a theory concerning this problem in the spirit of the results we have given concerning partial derivatives of y^* and solutions to the problem just posed.

■ 8. Carry out the proofs of (1), (2), and (3) that are used in the proof of proposition 7.9.

■ 9. Give results in the spirit of proposition 7.9 for the cost and conditional factor demand functions. If it makes things easier, you may restrict attention to the case of a single output. (If you can do this, you may want the further challenge of giving a proof of the "integrability" result for Marshallian demand.)

■ 10. Show that if the technology of a one-output firm has nondecreasing returns to scale, then average costs for the firm (as a function of the amount of output) will be nonincreasing. Show that if the technology has constant returns to scale, then average costs are constant. Show by example that the technology of a one-output firm may have nonincreasing returns to scale and yet average costs for the firm fall with scale of the output, at least for some levels of output. (All of these are for fixed factor prices and a competitive firm.)

■ 11. Consider the model of the competitive firm with N inputs, one output, and production function f. We say that the firm has *homothetic conditional factor demands* if, for fixed factor prices w, the optimal conditional factor demands do not change proportions as we change the scale of output; that is, if x^* solves FCMP$(w, 1)$, then for every $y > 0$ there is an $\alpha(y) > 0$ such that $\alpha(y)x^*$ is a solution of FCMP(w, y).

(a) Show that the firm has homothetic conditional factor demands if $f(x)$ takes the form $\phi(F(x))$ for a function $F : R_+^N \to R$ that is homogeneous of degree one and $\phi : R \to R$ is strictly increasing.

(b) Which of the production functions in problem 1 give homothetic conditional factor demands?

(c) If a firm has homothetic conditional factor demands and nonincreasing returns to scale, what can you say about the behavior of average costs as scale increases (for fixed factor prices)?

(d) Give an example of a firm without homothetic conditional factor demands.

chapter eight

The competitive firm and perfect competition

Now that we have a way to model firms, we can include them in models of price-mediated, market equilibrium. In this chapter we will consider market equilibria for competitive firms, firms that act as price takers.

We move immediately to a caveat: In all the models of this chapter, there will be a finite number of firms and (at least implicitly) a finite number of consumers. Prices will change if there are changes in the aggregate supply and demand decisions of firms and consumers, so it *cannot* be correct that all firms and all consumers do not affect prices by their actions. If there are many firms and consumers, each individual firm and consumer may have very small effect on prices, but the effect is not zero. The theory we develop is not based on a hypothesis that firms and consumers have no effect on prices. Instead it is based on the hypothesis that they *act* as if they have no effect; consumers choose what to consume and firms choose their production plans in the belief that the prices they see are unaffected by their decisions. Consumers and firms, then, act on an incorrect supposition. But if, the story is meant to go, there are many consumers and firms, and if no single consumer is a J. D. Rockefeller and no firm is a General Motors, then these suppositions are only a little incorrect.

There are two ways to proceed in the theory. We could continue analysis of general equilibrium in the style of chapter 6, but with firms added to the story. Or we can undertake *partial equilibrium* analysis — analysis of the market in a single good (or in a few related goods), holding fixed what goes on outside our limited frame of view. We will do both of these, and in doing so we begin an important transition in the style of this book. After the general equilibrium parts of this chapter, we will generally tend to look at quite small pieces of a larger economic picture; our attention hereafter will usually be very focused.

This is not to say that general equilibrium is completely broad and all-encompassing. Even if we have a model that incorporates all markets, market behavior is still embedded in a larger social and political environment, which general equilibrium takes as given. The difference between our partial equilibrium analyses and general equilibrium analyses is one of degree and not of type. But, as you will see, the difference in degree is substantial.

We begin with the classic partial equilibrium analysis of perfect competition. We then develop an example that shows how a partial equilibrium perspective can be misleading, and with that as stimulus, we briefly discuss general equilibrium with firms.

8.1. A perfectly competitive market

In the standard partial equilibrium analysis of perfect competition, we imagine a number of firms, all of whom can produce a single good, which is sold to consumers in exchange for some "numeraire" good, money. The market operates under the following qualitative conditions.

(a) The consumers of the good in question are happy to have the good from any of the many producers/vendors of the good. No vendor of the good has any particular advantage in selling to any consumer; no consumer would knowingly pay a higher price to one vendor if the good can be had from another vendor at a lower price. In jargon, the good is *undifferentiated* and/or is a *commodity*.

(b) The consumers have perfect information about the prices being charged by the various vendors of the good.

(c) Vendors of the good are willing to sell to any buyer, and they wish to get as high a price as they can. They have perfect information about prices being paid by consumers elsewhere, and they have the ability to "undercut" competitors if it is worth their while.

(d) Resale of the good in question cannot be controlled, and both sale and resale are costless.

These four conditions are taken to imply that *all exchanges will take place at some single price for the good*. These conditions are also taken to imply that *prices are **linear**; there is a single unit price for the good, and if a consumer wishes to purchase n units of the good, he or she pays n times whatever unit price the good commands*.

To justify formally that there will be a single price and prices will be linear, we would need to flesh out a precise model of the market institutions. We would have to say what the forum for these exchanges is, how prices are set, and so on. In the theory of perfect competition, this specification is not done. Rather, the italicized "conclusions" just given are really the assumptions of the theory, and the four things listed as "conditions" are our excuses for these real assumptions. It is held that in real markets where the four conditions and the others that follow hold to some degree of approximation, the conclusions listed above and others that follow will be borne out. This, of course, is an empirical question. For some industries this is true, and for others it is not.[1]

> We could alternatively imagine that the good in question can be sold at nonlinear prices, in the sense that quantity discounts or premia can be charged to individual consumers and consumers shop for the best price schedule. For this sort of thing to work, it must be possible to control resale of the good. A possible example of this would be telephone services in the United States, where phone services are not offered by a (government or other) monopoly; AT&T, MCI, Sprint, etc., might offer quantity discounts, where "resale" of phone services is not possible if the service is tied to a particular phone in a particular location. Even if resale is not possible, if there is really very good information about the prices the various carriers charge and if consumers don't mind from which carrier they buy phone services, then we can imagine perfect competition in this industry without linear prices. But we won't try that on a first pass through the subject.

To continue with informal conditions:

(e) Each individual consumer takes price as given. No consumer believes that he or she could in any way change the price paid per item by changing his or her level of demand for the item.

(f) The producers/vendors of the item in question (which will hereafter be called the firms) also take as given the market price for the good in question. They believe that they can sell as much of the item as they wish at the going price, and they can sell none at all at a higher price.

So we are led to the following:

Definition. *Equilibrium in a perfectly competitive market is given by a price p for the good, an amount purchased by each consumer, and an amount supplied by each firm, such that at the given price each consumer is purchasing*

---

[1] If you wish to see an industry where the assumptions and predictions of perfect competition can be tested, read about the *Oil Tanker Shipping Industry*, as described in the Harvard Business School Case #9-384-034. (This case is reprinted in Porter [1983], which contains a number of other cases that provide interesting illustrations of concepts discussed in this book.) If you do this, be forewarned that this is an industry in which the model of perfect competition both works and doesn't work. We'll say a bit more about this epigram in a later footnote.

her preferred amount and each producer is maximizing profits, and the sum of the amounts purchased equals the sum of the amounts supplied.

The reader is more than entitled to some befuddlement at this definition. How can we say what a consumer will demand as a function of the price of this one good? How can we say what a firm will supply? Presumably we will use the model of the consumer from chapter 2, but then we need to know what the other prices are and what form the consumer's wealth takes: perhaps an amount of the numeraire good, as in the stories of Marshallian demand in chapter 2; or some endowment bundle, as in chapter 6. As for firms, presumably they will all be described by one of the methods explored in the last chapter. But we will need to say something about the entire array of prices they face.

The consumer side: Demand curves

In most treatments of partial equilibrium analysis, the consumer side of the market is pretty much ignored. In the back of our minds are consumers as in chapter 2 and an assumption that prices of other goods that the consumers might consume are fixed.[2] And so in the back of our minds is an assumption that we can write, for each price p that the good in question might command, the total amount the consumer side of the market will demand, denoted $D(p)$. All these things stay in the back of our minds, and we simply take as given a demand curve $D(p)$. Moreover, it is typically assumed that this demand curve is downward sloping — more is demanded the lower the price of the good.

Nothing stops us from bringing all this up to the front of our minds. We could present a detailed model of the consumer side of the market. Later, when we look at "competitive" markets in which the goods aren't quite commodities and we become interested in the shape and character of aggregate demand, we will do just this. And we will do this when, for various reasons, we become interested in a more detailed look at market institutions.[a]

But the focus in the classic partial equilibrium analysis of perfect competition is on firm behavior, so it is typical to simplify the consumer side and simply posit the existence of a downward sloping demand function.

---

[2] But see section 8.3.

[a] If you wish to see a bit of this, look ahead to problem 3 in chapter 10. The issue there is one of rationing a limited supply among a number of consumers. Specifically, we ask how the rationing scheme employed for one good affects demand for a "second" good. Since rationing schemes work at the level of individual consumers, we have to disaggregate market demand and consider the preferences of individual consumers and how those preferences and different rationing schemes lead to amounts demanded for the second good.

We will follow this tradition until we get to general equilibrium later in this chapter.

Firms: The supply function

We attend to firms in greater detail. We will assume that each firm produces only the good in question from some array of factors of production. There will be J firms, indexed $j = 1, \ldots, J$, and firm j will be described for now by a total cost function $TC_j(y)$. Since firm j acts competitively in the product market, if the equilibrium price of the good is p, firm j supplies the amount $y_j(p)$ that solves

$$MC_j(y_j(p)) = p.$$

And total supply at price p is $S(p) = \sum_{j=1}^{J} y_j(p)$.

It is typical to assume that total costs are convex, so that marginal costs are nondecreasing and the first-order condition $MC_j(y) = p$ gives an optimal level of production. If total costs are strictly convex, marginal costs are strictly increasing, and the supply of the firm at price p, $y_j(p)$ is uniquely defined and increasing in p.

If this holds for all firms, $S(p)$, hereafter called *industry supply*, is strictly increasing. And now putting together the unmodeled demand side of the market specified by the demand function $D(p)$ and the slightly modeled supply side characterized by the supply function $S(p)$, we have an equilibrium at the price p where $D(p) = S(p)$. One has the standard pictures from intermediate and even principles textbooks shown in figure 8.1. Note well one graphical characterization developed there: The industry supply curve is the horizontal sum of individual firms' marginal cost curves.

8.2. Perfect competition and -runs

The short and intermediate runs

If the story stopped there, we wouldn't have much of a story. So we proceed to elaborate the supply side story.

(1) We imagine that the firms are characterized by production functions plus a fixed cost. If firm j is in the business of producing this good, it must pay a fixed cost K_j. It must pay this cost even if chooses to produce zero output; this cost is avoided only if the firm leaves the industry, an option firms will not be given for now. And if the firm is in business, it produces output from various combinations of N factor inputs, where

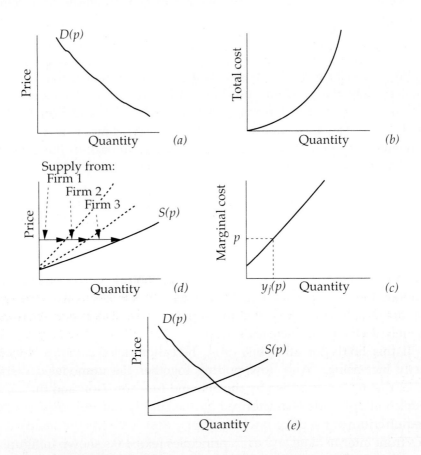

Figure 8.1. Equilibrium in a perfectly competitive market.
Demand is given in the form of a downward sloping demand curve, as
depicted in (a). Each firm has a total cost curve as in (b) and a corresponding marginal cost curve as in (c). At each price p, firm j supplies
the amount $y_j(p)$ that equates marginal cost with price (shown in [c]).
Industry supply is obtained as the horizontal sum of individual firms'
supply functions, which is just the horizontal sum of individual firms'
marginal cost functions (shown in [d]). Equilibrium is where supply
(computed in [d]) intersects demand (given in [a]). Superimposing (a)
and (d), we get (e) and the equilibrium price and quantity.

$f_j(x_1, \ldots, x_N)$ denotes the production function, the amount of output derived from factor inputs $(x_1, \ldots, x_N)$. Note well: The total costs of firm j
if j uses the factor inputs $(x_1, \ldots, x_N)$ is the sum of costs of those inputs
plus the fixed cost K_j.

(2) We imagine that the firms are price takers not only in the market for

their output but also in the factor markets, and we let $w = (w_1, \ldots, w_N)$ be the vector of factor prices, which is taken as fixed throughout our analysis.

(3) We imagine that firms begin with some initial levels of the factor inputs, some of which can be adjusted in the "short run," while others can only be adjusted in the "intermediate run."

Breaking time in this fashion, into a short run and an intermediate run and then partitioning the factor inputs into those that are short-run adjustable and others that are intermediate-run adjustable is hardly realistic. It would be more realistic to suppose that some of the firms can change the levels of all their factor inputs quickly, while others may be able to change very little until a lot of time has elapsed. Still, we explore what will happen in this market in the short and in the intermediate run, assuming that these time frames are meaningful and apply to all firms in the industry, and assuming that what is fixed in the short run for one firm is fixed in the short run for all.

We assume that factor inputs $n = 1, \ldots, N'$ are fixed in the short run and variable in the intermediate run, and factor inputs $n = N' + 1, \ldots, N$ are variable in both the short and the intermediate run. We also assume that the industry starts off at a point where firm j has been using factor inputs at the levels $(\hat{x}_1^j, \ldots, \hat{x}_N^j)$.

What, then, does industry supply look like in the short run? In the short run, the total variable cost function of firm j, written $SRTVC_j(y)$ is

$$\min_{(x_{N'+1}, \ldots, x_N)} \left\{ \sum_{n=N'+1}^{N} w_n x_n : y = f_j(\hat{x}_1^j, \ldots, \hat{x}_{N'}^j, x_{N'+1}, \ldots, x_N) \right\},$$

and the short-run total cost function is

$$SRTC_j(y) = SRTVC_j(y) + \sum_{n=1}^{N'} w_n \hat{x}_n^j + K_j.$$

The short-run marginal cost of firm j is the derivative of the short-run total cost (which is the same as the derivative of the short-run total variable cost), and short-run industry supply is the horizontal sum of the firms' short-run marginal cost curves, just as in the previous section.

What does it take for $SRTC$ to be strictly convex?

Proposition 8.1. *If the production function f is strictly concave, then the total cost function (for fixed factor prices, for any run as long as some of the factors are variable) is strictly convex.*

This is left for homework.

In the intermediate run, the total variable cost function of firm j is

$$IRTC_j(y) = \min_{(x_1,\dots,x_N)} \left\{ \sum_{n=1}^{N} w_n x_n : y = f_j(x_1,\dots,x_N) \right\} + K_j.$$

This gives intermediate-run marginal cost curves, and the intermediate-run industry supply curve is the horizontal sum of these marginal cost curves.

How will short-run and intermediate-run supply curves compare? The easiest way to think about this is to begin with the relevant short- and intermediate-run total cost curves. In the short run, where the firm can adjust only variable factors of production, the total cost of production will be everywhere at least as much as intermediate-run total cost. As long as the short-run fixed factors of production are at an optimal level for some level of output, the two total cost curves will touch at that level of output. We're assuming rising marginal costs, so total costs are convex; the picture is as in figure 8.2(a). And now marginal cost is the slope

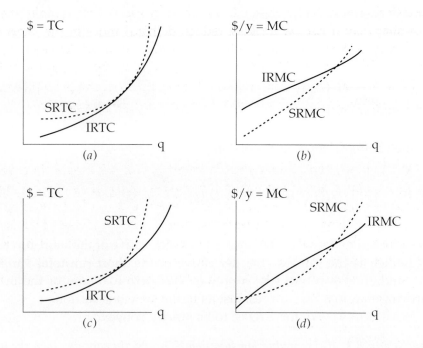

*Figure 8.2. Short- and intermediate-run total
cost curves and marginal cost curves.*

of total cost, so that the two marginal cost curves are as in figure 8.2(b). Note well: This has been drawn so that short-run marginal cost is lower than intermediate-run marginal cost for all low levels of output and higher for all high levels of output. But this particular drawing of the two isn't necessarily implied by figure 8.2(a). In figures 8.2(c) and (d) another case is given. What is implied in general is that short-run marginal cost is lower than intermediate-run marginal cost for quantities just below the point where the two total costs are tangent and is higher at quantities just above.[3]

This tells us how supply changes from the short to the intermediate run. What about demand? There are certainly good reasons to think that demand in the short-run will be different from demand in a longer intermediate-run time frame. If, to take one case, the good in question is a variable factor of production in some downstream production process, then short-run demand for it will be based on calculations that do not allow producers to substitute it for (or substitute for it) more-fixed factors in downstream production. In the intermediate run, substitution of/for more fixed factors may come into play. We'd expect demand to shift according to the run in such cases.[4] Even if the good in question is a final consumption good, we can think of reasons that short- and intermediate-run demand will be different. If the good is somewhat durable, then a price shift, say a rise, will likely reduce demand more in the short run than it will in the longer run. (Why?) If the good is an addictive good, the reverse is true. (Why?) Despite these examples, it is typical in the theory to work with the case where market demand doesn't change with changes in the time frame, and we will henceforth make that assumption.

The long run

We continue to elaborate the theory by adding a long-run time frame. We begin with J firms producing the good in question. But we imagine that these J firms are not committed forever to continue producing the good, and we imagine that there are many potential producers of the good in question. In the long run, firms can enter and/or leave this industry: Firms that are in the industry are assumed to depart if at equilibrium prices they are sustaining losses. And firms will enter the industry if at equilibrium prices they can make strictly positive profits.

---

[3] Can you prove this?

[4] Admittedly, this is "cheating" a bit, since we didn't mention in our discussion of the demand side of the market the possibility that demanders are other firms. But there are certainly markets in which this case would pertain.

Note well: Firms that can at best make zero profits are just on the cusp of the entry/exit decision. A firm that is producing and makes zero profits will be willing to remain, whereas a firm that is not producing and would make zero profits at the going equilibrium price is assumed to stay out.[b]

We formalize this elaboration as follows. We imagine that many firms could be in this business, indexed by $j = 1, \ldots, J^*$ for a very large J^*. Each firm is characterized by a production function f_j and a fixed cost K_j, as stated. Then,

Definition. *A **long-run equilibrium in a perfectly competitive market** consists of (a) a price p for the good, (b) a list of active firms taken from the list of all potentially active firms, and (c) for each active firm, a production plan such that*

(d) Each active firm is maximizing its profits, taking prices as given, at the production plan prescribed in (c)

(e) Each active firm is making nonnegative profits with its production plan

(f) Each inactive firm would make nonpositive profits at best, taking prices as given, if it became active

(g) The total supply from the active firms, gotten by summing their output levels as specified by their production plans, equals market demand at the equilibrium price p

Note that this is just a specialization of our general definition of equilibrium in a perfectly competitive market, if we think that the long-run total costs for each firm are zero at zero level of production and rise to K_j if any production at all is undertaken.

It does seem rather a mess, but we make a fair bit of progress in clearing up this mess if we add one final assumption.

Assumption ⋆. *For every firm that is potentially active in this business, there are "many" other potentially active firms that have precisely the same production function and fixed costs.*

---

[b] Recall the earlier epigrammatic comment about the model of perfect competition holding and not holding in the oil tanker shipping industry. With regard to this, note that firms might behave in the way the theory says they do in the short and intermediate run, and at the same time behave quite crazily from the perspective of the theory in the long run. Then short- and intermediate-run predictions of the theory could be borne out, while long-run predictions, which we are about to develop, would fail.

Informal Proposition. *If assumption* ⋆ *holds, then in any long-run equilibrium, all active firms make precisely zero profits.*

We call this an informal proposition because it is based on the very informal "many" in the assumption. The logic runs as follows: For any active firm in a long-run equilibrium let π be its level of profits. If there are "many" firms like this one, some of those will be inactive. *This is the sense of "many"; it must be that for every active firm at least one firm identical to it is inactive.* In a long-run equilibrium, all inactive firms must be capable of making zero profits at best. Since there is an inactive firm identical to our active firm, it could (if it entered) make profits π. So π must be nonnegative, if the active firm is to stay active. And π must be nonpositive, if the inactive firm is to remain inactive, which implies that π must be zero.

Suppose that an active firm is, in fact, making zero profits at the equilibrium price p. Consider where it is producing along its long-run average cost curve. *It must be producing at its point of minimum long-run average cost, and this minimum level of long-run average cost must be the equilibrium price.* To see this, first note the accounting identity

$$\text{Profit} = [\text{Price} - \text{LRAC(Quantity)}] \times \text{Quantity},$$

where LRAC is the long-run average cost function. Now if price exceeds the minimum level of LRAC, the firm, by producing at the level of minimum LRAC, would make positive profits. If price is less than the minimum level of long-run average costs, the firm cannot make nonnegative profits at any level of output. The only way that a profit-maximizing, competitive firm can make zero profits is if price equals minimum LRAC. And the firm then makes zero profits only by producing at a quantity that minimizes LRAC.

This discussion leads immediately to the following corollary to the informal proposition.

Informal corollary. *If assumption* ⋆ *holds, then in any long-run equilibrium every firm is producing at* **efficient scale**, *where efficient scale is any scale that minimizes the average costs of the firm.*

Assumption ⋆ is often made part of the defining characteristics of a perfectly competitive industry. The justification for it is that in a competitive industry, no firm has a technological advantage over any other — whatever technologies there are will be freely available to anyone who cares to use them. Hence we always will have potential entrants identical to anyone who is active in the business.

And once we have assumption $\star$, we arrive at the conclusion: In a long-run equilibrium, firms make zero profits and produce at efficient scale.

Of course, the rest of the assumptions of the theory hang together very nicely if we don't make assumption $\star$. Think, for example, of the wheat farming industry. We might well consider wheat to be a commodity good with a single, well-known price, which all wheat farmers and wheat buyers take as given. Still, some wheat farmers are lucky enough to own land that is especially good for growing wheat; these farmer-firms have a "technology" that is superior to the technology owned by farmer-firms who farm less fertile land. So we expect those farmers to make strictly positive profits.

When we don't make assumption $\star$, so it is possible that firms can make positive profits in a long-run equilibrium, we also don't expect those firms to be producing at efficient scale. In fact, they won't do so; these firms will always produce at larger-than-efficient scale. You are asked to prove this in problem 2.

In such cases, one can (and some authors do) define things so that, even though assumption $\star$ is not made, profits still equal zero in a long-run equilibrium. This is done by saying that what a firm with a "productive advantage" earns are not profits, but rather *rents* to its advantaged production capabilities. These rents come off the top as costs to be paid for the advantaged technology, so that the firm is back to making zero profits. (If you like this sort of proof-by-definition, consider why this means that the firm now is producing at the point of minimal LRAC.)

An example

To clarify some of the points made, consider the following simple example. The numbers in this example are selected because they give relatively clean and simple answers; they are not meant to be at all realistic.

In a particular economy, a product called *pfillip*, which is a nonnarcotic stimulant, is produced by a competitive industry. Each firm in this competitive industry has the same production technology, given by the production function

$$y = k^{1/6}l^{1/3},$$

where y is the amount of pfillip produced, k is the amount of *kapitose* (a specialty chemical) used in production, and l is the amount of *legume* (a common vegetable) used in production. Firms also incur fixed costs of $1/6.

Legumes are traded in a competitive market, and the price of a unit of legume is a fixed \$1, regardless of the amount of legume demanded for the production of pfillip. The level of legume can be freely varied in the short run. Kapitose is traded in a competitive market, at price \$1/2. The amount of kapitose used by any firm in production cannot be varied in the short run but can be adjusted in the intermediate run.

Many firms could enter this industry in the long run, and firms are free to depart. All firms, both those in the industry and potential entrants, have the technology and cost structure just described.

Demand is given by the demand function $D(p) = 400 - 100p$, where p is the price of pfillip and $D(p)$ is the amount demanded at this price.[5]

What is the long-run equilibrium in this perfectly competitive market?

As a first step, let us compute the total cost function of each firm in this industry, where we assume that the firm can vary both its level of kapitose and legume inputs.

The cost-minimizing way to produce y units of output is the solution of

$$\min_{k,l} \frac{k}{2} + l, \text{ subject to } k^{1/6}l^{1/3} \geq y.$$

It is clear that the solution will have the constraint binding. (We should put in nonnegativity constraints, although they will not bind and so we've left them out.) Since the constraint will bind, we can solve for k in terms of l to obtain $k = y^6/l^2$, and so the problem becomes

$$\min_{l} \frac{y^6}{2l^2} + l.$$

The first-order condition is

$$\frac{y^6}{l^3} = 1, \quad \text{or} \quad l = y^2 \text{ and } k = y^2,$$

---

[5] We will use models with linear demand throughout this book, and it should always be understood that demand is nonnegative; that is, $D(p)$ is really $\max\{400 - 100p, 0\}$ in this example. We also should be careful about demand at a price of zero; what is important is that revenue at a price of zero is zero.

so that the long-run total cost for producing y is

$$TC(y) = \frac{3}{2}y^2 + \frac{1}{6}.$$

From this we can easily find the long-run equilibrium price: It must be the minimum value of average cost. Average costs are given by $AC(y) = (3/2)y + 1/(6y)$, which is minimized at $3/2 = 1/(6y^2)$, or $y = 1/3$. That is, producing $1/3$ of a unit is the efficient scale for firms in this industry. And when firms produce $1/3$ of a unit, they have average costs of $1. So the long-run equilibrium price is $1.

At this price, demand is $400 - 100(1) = 300$, so total industry demand is 300. And since each firm will be producing $1/3$ of a unit, there will have to be 900 active firms.

To summarize, at a long-run equilibrium 900 firms will be active, each producing 1/3 of a unit, for a total industry supply of 300 units. The equilibrium price will be $1, and each firm will be making zero profits. Each of the 900 firms will be utilizing 1/9 unit each of legume and kapitose.

Now suppose the demand curve suddenly shifts, becoming $D(p) = 750 - 150p$. What will be the industry response in the short run, in the long run, and in the intermediate run?

We will take the short run first. In the short run, there are 900 firms, each of whom is fixed at $1/9$ units of kapitose. If any of these firms wishes to have output level y, they must employ enough legume l so that

$$(1/9)^{1/6}l^{1/3} = y \text{ or } (1/9)l^2 = y^6 \text{ or } l = 3y^3.$$

This gives total variable costs of $3y^3$. Hence the short-run marginal cost function of the firm is $MC(y) = 9y^2$. And so, at price p, a single firm supplies the amount $y(p)$ that solves $9y(p)^2 = p$ or $y(p) = \sqrt{p}/3$. Since there are 900 identical firms, industry supply at price p is 900 times this, or $S(p) = 300\sqrt{p}$. The short-run equilibrium price is where short-run supply equals demand:

$$300\sqrt{p} = 750 - 150p.$$

If you solve this equation for p, you get (approximately) $p = 2.1$.

The short-run equilibrium price is $2.10. At this price, total industry demand is 750 − 150(2.1) = 435, which is divided among the 900 firms so that each firm produces approximately .483 units. This requires each firm to employ approximately .338 units of legume. Each firm must also pay the cost of the fixed 1/9 unit of kapitose and the 1/6 fixed cost, for total costs of .338 + (1/9)(1/2) + 1/6 = .56 against which each firm makes revenue of (2.1)(.483) = 1.014, for a profit per firm of .454.

Moving to the intermediate run, we still have 900 firms active, but now each has total cost function $(3/2)y^2 + 1/6$, or marginal costs $MC(y) = 3y$. Hence at price p, each firm supplies (in the intermediate run) $p/3$ units, and the intermediate-run industry supply curve is $300p$. Intermediate-run equilibrium is where $300p = 750 - 150p$ or $p = 5/3 = 1.667$. So we conclude:

The intermediate-run equilibrium price is $1.667. At this price, total industry demand and supply equal 500 units, and each firm produces 5/9 of a unit. This costs the firm $(3/2)(5/9)^2 + 1/6 = 34/54$, against revenues of $(5/3)(5/9) = 25/27$, for a net profit of $16/54 = $.296$. (We leave it to you to work out kapitose and legume utilization per firm.)

And the long run is easiest of all. We already know that at the long-run equilibrium price must be $1 and each firm must produce 1/3 of a unit. So,

The long-run equilibrium price is $1, which means that industry demand is for 600 units. Each firm produces 1/3 of a unit, so the number of firms doubles to 1,800. Each firm makes zero profits, and each firm utilizes 1/9 unit each of legume and kapitose.

We draw these "dynamics" in figure 8.3. We show there the original demand curve and the long-run supply curve in solid lines. Note that the long-run supply curve is horizontal as it must be in this sort of industry. The short-run and intermediate-run supply curves beginning from the initial equilibrium position are drawn in as dashed lines; note that the short-run supply curve has the steepest slope. We also draw in the "new" demand curve as a dashed line, and we mark the stages of industry response to the shift in demand: (1) marks the original equilibrium, (2) the new short-run equilibrium, (3) the new intermediate-run equilibrium, and (4) the new long-run equilibrium. Note that equilibrium quantities rise at each stage, and prices jump way up and then move down. Also note (not from the picture) the pattern of kapitose and legume usage by one of the originally active 900 firms. In the short run legume usage rises, then

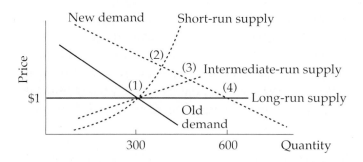

Figure 8.3. Equilibrium "dynamics" for a perfectly competitive industry.

it falls in the intermediate and long runs. Kapitose usage per firm stays constant in the short run (as it is constrained to do), then rises, and then falls.

The qualitative features of this simple example generalize substantially: In an industry where assumption ⋆ concerning potential entrants holds (and factor prices don't change with the scale of industry output; cf. the next section), long-run supply will necessarily be perfectly elastic (flat), so shifts in demand will not change the long-run equilibrium price for the good. Moreover, as asserted in section 8.2, short-run supply will generally be more inelastic than intermediate-run supply, at least for small changes in quantity, for a fixed number of firms. Hence the qualitative features of figure 8.3 can be expected to hold generally (if the story about all these runs is correct); an upwards shift in demand will be met in the short run by a small increase in quantity and a large increase in price, in the intermediate run by a further increase in quantity and a decrease in price (still above the original level), and in the long run with price retreating to the original level and output (and the number of firms) expanded to meet this increased demand.

Other changes can lead to other dynamics. For example, in problem 6 you are asked to sketch out what happens if one of the factor prices suddenly changes. Those dynamics can also be generalized beyond simple parametric examples, at least in cases where cost and demand curves are assumed to be "typical."

Such exercises illustrate the formidable power of partial equilibrium analysis in general and partial equilibrium analysis of perfect competition in particular. If cost and demand curves are "typical," which is to say demand is downward sloping and supply is nondecreasing, then the theory predicts a unique equilibrium. (Compare with general equilibrium. And, when we get to it, compare this with the predictions made using the methods of part III.) Insofar as we can empirically estimate demand functions and cost functions, we can construct the theoretical industry supply curve and get very good tests of the theory. Moreover, this runs version of the theory makes very definite predictions about how equilibrium prices and quantities will respond dynamically to shifts in parameters of the model, again giving us a lot of empirical leverage. While our example is only an example, it indicates how powerful the theory can be.

8.3. *What's wrong with partial equilibrium analysis?*

At the same time, the theory is predicated on a number of assumptions that may not prove true, particularly assumptions that are required by the narrow focus of a partial equilibrium model.

For example, in a partial equilibrium analysis of the sort we have been conducting, we hold "fixed" various things left out of the model. It is typical in a partial equilibrium analysis of the market in a single product to say that one is holding fixed the prices of all commodities not in the market. For example, if we were more explicit about the demand side of our markets, we would look at consumer demand functions in the spirit of chapter 2. And it would be typical to analyze how demand for the commodity in question changes, holding fixed the price of other commodities and holding fixed the incomes the consumers have to spend. Rendered in symbols, if $x_k^i(p_1, \ldots, p_K, Y^i)$ is the demand function of consumer i for good k as a function of all prices and the consumer's income Y^i, the usual practice is to think of the industry demand curve as arising from fixing all prices except p_k, say at levels $\hat{p}_{k'}$, fixing all the Y^i, and then, for each price p_k for good k, saying that

$$D(p_k) = \sum_{i=1}^{I} x_k^i(\hat{p}_1, \ldots, \hat{p}_{k-1}, p_k, \hat{p}_{k+1}, \ldots, \hat{p}_K, Y^i),$$

where $i = 1, \ldots, I$ in the sum indexes the set of consumers.

In many applications, this would be the wrong thing to do, if you were really interested in industry demand. Suppose the commodity being considered is wheat. Of course, the demand for wheat depends on other factors, such as the price of corn. Should we write down the demand curve for wheat, holding fixed the price of corn? This is what is typically done and what the scheme above advises. But is it the right thing to do? As the price of wheat changes, the level of demand for corn will change. It is natural to expect that demand for corn rises as the price of wheat rises. Unless the supply of corn is perfectly elastic (is perfectly flat), the price of corn shifts. And this then will change how much wheat will be demanded. In the short run at least, it makes little sense to suppose that the supply of corn is perfectly elastic. And so it makes little sense to suppose that the demand curve for wheat, at least in the short run, should be computed on the basis of an unchanging price of corn. *Changes in the price of wheat will, through the workings of markets, change the price of corn, which then affects the demand for wheat.* Predictions on the demand for wheat (as the price of wheat changes) that are based on a fixed price of corn will, therefore, be wrong.

If you are analyzing the market in a commodity where changes in its price (and the corresponding level of demands) won't much change the prices of other goods, then a demand curve computed under the hypothesis that other prices don't change at all won't be too far wrong. But unless this condition holds for the commodity you are interested in, you will want to think about whether there might be other prices that move substantially as the price of the good in question moves, with feedback to the demand for the good in question. If other prices can reasonably be expected to move with movements in the price of the good in question, then you must analyze more than the single market, if reasonable predictions are to emerge.

The same sort of consideration arises on the supply side of the market. Our analysis in section 8.2, for example, was predicated on an assumption that the prices of factors of production don't change. We might think to justify this assumption by appealing to the notion that many firms are in the industry, and so each is a price taker in all the factor markets. But this is no justification at all. As we change industry supply levels, we aren't looking at changes in demand for a given factor caused by a single firm; instead we are looking at changes in demand for the factor caused by changes in the activities of many firms in the industry. If this factor of production is used by many firms in the industry, if demand for this factor by firms in the industry is a large part of the demand for the factor, and if supply of the factor is not perfectly elastic, then it is wrong to build *industry* supply curves based on the supposition that the prices of the factors don't change with changes in the level of *industry* supply.

An elaborate example

Let us illustrate by continuing with the example from the previous section. We will continue to suppose that the price of legume is $1 per unit, no matter how many units of legume are bought by producers in the pfillip industry. But we suppose that the price of kapitose changes with changes in pfillip industry demand for kapitose. In particular, we suppose that if the pfillip industry demands K units of kapitose, the price per unit that kapitose will command is $K/200$.

Why might this happen? We might suppose that kapitose is produced by an industry of perfectly competitive firms, but entry to this industry is blocked on legal grounds — say only a given set of firms are licensed to produce kapitose. If entry to the industry is restricted for this or any other reason, then even when firms in the industry are price takers, the industry supply curve may be rising; see problem 4. Or the kapitose industry might be perfectly competitive and with free entry, but potential entrants have progressively less efficient technologies for producing kapitose; see problem 5.[6]

When kapitose was assumed to trade at \$.50 per unit regardless of demand for kapitose from pfillip producers, the long-run supply curve of pfillip was perfectly elastic at price \$1. We now proceed to compute the long-run supply curve of pfillip under the newly presumed conditions. This gets a bit involved, but try to persevere.

Suppose the price of kapitose is q at some point. Each individual pfillip producer is (assumed to be) a price taker, so each computes long-run total costs of producing y units, given this factor price, as

$$\min_{k,l} qk + l + \frac{1}{6} \text{ subject to } k^{1/6}l^{1/3} \geq y.$$

If you work through the math, you will find that this leads to a total cost function

$$TC(y) = \frac{3}{2}(2q)^{1/3}y^2 + \frac{1}{6},$$

and an average cost function

$$AC(y) = \frac{3}{2}(2q)^{1/3}y + \frac{1}{6y}.$$

Efficient scale for a firm with these average costs is the solution of $(3/2)(2q)^{1/3} = 1/(6y^2)$; if you manipulate the algebra, you will find that this is

$$y^e(q) = \frac{1}{3(2q)^{1/6}},$$

where the superscript e stands for *efficient*. At this efficient scale, the level of average costs is

$$AC^e(q) = \frac{3}{2}(2q)^{1/3}\frac{1}{3(2q)^{1/6}} + \frac{1}{6/[3(2q)^{1/6}]} = (2q)^{1/6}.$$

---

[6] Yet another possibility is that the kapitose industry is not competitive at all. In the problems at the end of chapter 9, you will be asked to consider the case of a monopoly kapitose producer. This situation is harder to deal with because the notion of a kapitose supply curve is not well defined in a monopoly situation.

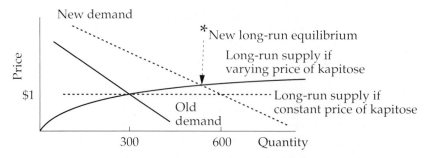

Figure 8.4. Supply and long-run equilibrium in the pfillip market when the price of kapitose rises with increasing demand for kapitose by pfillip producers.

(Don't be lazy; go through all the steps in these math derivations!) Hence if q is the long-run equilibrium price of kapitose, $(2q)^{1/6}$ is the long-run equilibrium price of pfillip. Turning this around, if p is the long-run price of pfillip, the equilibrium price of kapitose must be $q(p) = p^6/2$.

At the same time, if $q = p^6/2$ is the price of kapitose and if each firm in the pfillip industry is producing optimally at the efficient scale of $y^e = 1/[3(2q)^{1/6}] = 1/(3p)$, each firm is using $k^e = y^2/(2q)^{2/3} = 1/(18q) = 1/(9p^6)$ units of kapitose. (You need to work out the solution to the cost minimization problem above to see how we did this.)

This may seem counterintuitive to you. We have found that the level of production of the single firm is a *decreasing* function of the price of pfillip! But this is not counterintuitive as long as you remember that we are speaking here of equilibrium values. The only way the price of pfillip could be higher in a long-run equilibrium is if the price of kapitose is higher. And a higher price of kapitose lowers the efficient scale of all the firms.

Suppose long-run industry supply of pfillip is S when the price of pfillip is p. Since each firm is producing $1/(3p)$, this means we have $J = 3pS$ firms. Each of these firms uses $1/(9p^6)$ units of kapitose, so total kapitose utilization by the pfillip industry firms is

$$K = \frac{J}{9p^6} = \frac{3pS}{9p^6} = \frac{S}{3p^5}.$$

This causes the price of kapitose to be

$$\frac{p^6}{2} = q = \frac{K}{200} = \frac{S}{200(3p^5)}.$$

Solving for S in terms of p yields

$$S(p) = 300p^{11}.$$

This is the long-run equilibrium supply curve for pfillip.

In figure 8.4 we've drawn what we've discovered. The two demand curves are the two curves from the previous example: the original $D(p) = 400 - 100p$; and the shifted demand curve $D(p) = 750 - 150p$. We've dashed in the long-run supply curve of pfillip under the conditions that the price of kapitose is always $.50; this is perfectly elastic supply at $p = 1$ since, if the price of kapitose never changes, the long-run average cost curves of firms are always the same (at any scale of industry production), and so minimum average cost is always $1. And we've drawn in the long-run industry supply curve for the case where the price of kapitose rises with kapitose demand; this is the curve $S(p)$ derived above.

Note that the two supply curves intersect at $p = 1$, at the level $S(p) = 300$, which just happens to be the equilibrium quantity for both with the original demand curve. This is no coincidence; the numbers were picked so this would happen. [c] The point is that at higher levels of long-run equilibrium price, the long-run industry supply of pfillip is less than when kapitose costs a flat $.50. Hence if demand shifts in the fashion of the example and the price of kapitose rises with kapitose usage, the new long-run equilibrium, marked with a $\star$ in the figure, has a price higher than $1 and an equilibrium quantity less than the 600 we had before. (It is left to you to compute the new long-run equilibrium prices and quantities. Since this involves an eleventh degree polynomial, you will probably have to resort to numerical approximation!)

This derivation may seem quite involved to you. It is. But it has to be. We are solving for equilibria in two markets at once. We can't tell what the price of kapitose will be until we know how much is demanded by the pfillip producers. But we can't tell how much is demanded by pfillip producers until we know the price of kapitose. And we are relying on the pfillip market being in a long-run equilibrium. Putting all that together is not an easy exercise. (Now try problem 3.)

One point should be stressed about the example. The individual firm is always acting as a price taker. When we solved the individual firm's cost minimization problem, we took the price of kapitose to be an unchanging q. As we noted at the start of the chapter, this isn't quite right. As even a single firm increases its demand for kapitose, the price of kapitose rises. But this is no worse than what happens in the individual firm's profit-maximization problem, given price p. Given downward sloping demand, as a single firm raises its level of output, it depresses the market price however slightly, something else our price-taking firms are ignoring.

8.4. *General equilibrium with firms*

Since perfectly competitive markets may be tied together as in the previous section, we might try to put competitive firms into a general equilibrium analysis.

---

[c] It wasn't hard to do. Knowing that the first equilibrium has $p = 1$, $q = .5$, $Y = 300$, and industry kapitose utilization of $K = 100$, a supply curve for kapitose was selected so that at $K = 100$, q would be .5.

This is not an obvious thing to do if you are doing it to study the behavior of the economy we inhabit. A model of general equilibrium in which *all* firms are price takers is not all that realistic. Some firms, and some industries, may be perfectly competitive (or may be nearly so), but we might be sceptical if it is asserted that all are. That is one of the virtues of partial equilibrium analysis; if one makes an assumption such as firms are competitive, the assumption doesn't have to apply to every firm, but only to those currently under examination.

At the same time, we have the problems of partial equilibrium analysis highlighted in the previous section to contend with. We can do as we did in the example: Try to cobble together a model of all the markets that are relatively strongly connected, without bringing into the picture absolutely every market there is. Or, if we are really interested in studying the general equilibrium, we can "hold out" the production plans of firms that are not competitive. Recall the definition we gave in section 6.2 of an exchange equilibrium with fixed production. We could try a similar trick here: Take as exogenously given the production plans of firms that are not price takers (and, if it exists, any government or quasi-government production), and endogenously model the production decisions of competitive firms, along the lines to be sketched below.

We will not give a lot of details here, but instead give a quick overview of what goes on in general equilibrium with firms.

The economy

An economy is specified by:

(a) A finite number K of *commodities*.

(b) A finite number J of *firms*. Each firm j is specified by a production possibility set $Z^j \subseteq R^K$.

(c) A finite number I of *consumers*. We assume that each consumer can consume any nonnegative bundle of the K goods, so the consumer's preferences are defined on the positive orthant of R^K, denoted X. These preferences are assumed to be representable by a utility function $U_i : X \to R$. We assume throughout that preferences are continuous and are locally insatiable. Each consumer comes with an endowment $e^i \in X$. Each consumer also comes with an entitlement to share in the profits of the firms. (This is a strictly capitalist economy.) Consumer i is entitled to the share s^{ij} of the profits of firm j. These shares will be assumed to be nonnegative and to satisfy $\sum_{i=1}^{I} s^{ij} = 1$ for each j; that is, consumers taken together are entitled to all the profits generated by each firm (and no more).

An ensemble of the items listed above is called a (general equilibrium) *economy*.

Walrasian equilibrium

Definition. *A* **Walrasian equilibrium** *for a given economy consists of a price vector $p \in R^K$, an array of production plans (z^j), one for each firm j, and an array of consumption plans (x^i), one for each consumer i, such that*

(a) For each firm j, $z^j \in Z^j$ (the production plan of j is feasible), and z^j solves the problem

$$\text{maximize } p \cdot z \text{ subject to } z \in Z^j.$$

(b) For each consumer i, $x^i \in X$, and x^i solves the problem

$$\text{maximize } U_i(x) \text{ subject to } x \in X, \ p \cdot x \leq p \cdot e^i + \sum_{j=1}^{J} s^{ij} p \cdot z^j.$$

(c) Markets clear: $\sum_{i=1}^{I} x^i \leq \sum_{i=1}^{I} e^i + \sum_{j=1}^{J} z^j$.

Or in words, firms are maximizing profits, consumers are maximizing their utility given their budget constraints, and demand is less than supply for all commodities. Note especially the budget constraint for the consumer; the consumer derives wealth from her endowment and from the profits paid out by firms.[d]

Three technical remarks are in order:

(1) It should be obvious that if $(p, (z^j), (x^i))$ is a Walrasian equilibrium, so is $(\lambda p, (z^j), (x^i))$, for any scalar $\lambda > 0$.

(2) We will want (for reasons of ease of exposition) to conclude that equilibrium prices are nonnegative. In chapter 6 we obtained this conclusion by assuming that preferences are nondecreasing. That will work quite well here. But we can equally well assume that at least one firm has access to a free disposal technology. (The proof is left to you.) We hereafter will assume that equilibrium prices are always nonnegative, by virtue of one of these two reasons. Of course, local insatiability implies that equilibrium prices could not be identically zero.

---

[d] It has not been assumed that profits are nonnegative; consumers are assumed to make up the losses incurred by a firm in proportion to their shareholdings. But by adding an assumption that $0 \in Z^j$ for each j, this unhappy possibility is avoided.

(3) Since consumers are locally insatiable, we know that in any equilibrium they will spend their entire budget, or $p \cdot x^i = p \cdot e^i + \sum_{j=1}^{J} s^{ij} p \cdot z^j$. Sum this over i using the fact that $\sum_{i=1}^{I} s^{ij} = 1$ and you will conclude that

$$p \sum_{i=1}^{I} x^i = p \cdot e + p \cdot \sum_{j=1}^{J} z^j,$$

where $e = \sum_{i=1}^{I} e^i$ is the social endowment. By virtue of (2) then, any good in excess supply in equilibrium must have zero price.

Everything we said in chapter 6 about the credibility of this reduced form solution concept extends to a setting with firms. We haven't specified a trading mechanism or trading institutions, so this is a reduced form solution concept. There are many realistic reasons to doubt that the outcome of economic activity in an economy would approximate a Walrasian equilibrium. But there is experimental evidence to support the concept, at least in very carefully controlled conditions.

The welfare theorems

When considering the efficiency of a Walrasian equilibrium, we are concerned only with the preferences of the consumers. Accordingly, for a fixed general equilibrium economy, the following definitions are made:

*Definitions. (a) A **plan** for the economy consists of an array of production plans (z^j), one for each firm, and an array of consumption plans (x^i), one for each consumer. A plan $((z^j), (x^i))$ is called **feasible** if $z^j \in Z^j$ for each j, $x^i \in X$ for each i, and $\sum_{i=1}^{I} x^i \le \sum_{i=1}^{I} e^i + \sum_{j=1}^{J} z^j$.*

*(b) A feasible plan $((z^j), (x^i))$ is **Pareto efficient** if there is no other feasible plan $((\hat{z}^j), (\hat{x}^i))$ such that the allocation $(\hat{x}^i)$ Pareto dominates (x^i).*

*Theorem. **The First Theorem of Welfare Economics.** If $(p, (z^j), (x^i))$ is a Walrasian equilibrium, then $((z^j), (x^i))$ is a Pareto efficient plan.*

The proof is not much different from the proof for a pure exchange economy. Assume that $(p, (z^j), (x^i))$ is a Walrasian equilibrium and that there is some feasible plan $((\hat{z}^j), (\hat{x}^i))$ such that the allocation $(\hat{x}^i)$ Pareto dominates (x^i). Since the hat plan is feasible, $\sum_{i=1}^{I} \hat{x}^i \le \sum_{i=1}^{I} e^i + \sum_{j=1}^{J} \hat{z}^j$. Since prices p are nonnegative, we can premultiply this vector inequality with p and keep the inequality:

$$\sum_{i=1}^{I} p \cdot \hat{x}^i \le \sum_{i=1}^{I} p \cdot e^i + \sum_{j=1}^{J} p \cdot \hat{z}^j.$$

As noted above, since consumers are locally insatiable,

$$\sum_{i=1}^{I} p \cdot x^i = \sum_{i=1}^{I} p \cdot e^i + \sum_{j=1}^{J} p \cdot z^j.$$

By the argument from chapter 6, we know that $p \cdot x^i \leq p \cdot \hat{x}^i$ for every i, with a strict inequality for at least one consumer i. So

$$\sum_{i=1}^{I} p \cdot e^i + \sum_{j=1}^{J} p \cdot z^j = \sum_{i=1}^{I} p \cdot x^i < \sum_{i=1}^{I} p \cdot \hat{x}^i \leq \sum_{i=1}^{I} p \cdot e^i + \sum_{j=1}^{J} p \cdot \hat{z}^j.$$

Look at the two extreme terms and cancel the common term $\sum_{i=1}^{I} p \cdot e^i$. This leaves

$$\sum_{j=1}^{J} p \cdot z^j < \sum_{j=1}^{J} p \cdot \hat{z}^j.$$

Thus for at least one j, $p \cdot z^j < p \cdot \hat{z}^j$. But this would say that z^j is not a profit-maximizing plan for this firm j at prices p, a contradiction to the definition of a Walrasian equilibrium.

Theorem. The Second Theorem of Welfare Economics. *Assume that preferences are convex, continuous, nondecreasing and locally insatiable, and production sets are convex. Let $((z^j), (x^i))$ be a Pareto efficient plan such that x^i_k is strictly postive for all i and k. Then the plan $((z^j), (x^i))$ is the plan part of a Walrasian equilibrium, if we first redistribute endowments and shareholdings among consumers.*

We will not go into the details of the proof. The proof used in chapter 6 works quite well, except that you have to modify the definition of $X^\dagger$; let

$$X^\dagger = \{x \in R^K : x = \sum_{i=1}^{I} x^i \text{ for some feasible plan } ((z^j),(x^i))\}.$$

As we noted in chapter 6, the assumption that the allocation part (x^i) of the plan is strictly positive is much too strong, and serious renditions of this result will weaken this assumption.

At the risk of confusing you, we add a remark about efficiency. We suggested earlier that when some firms in a competitive industry have access to a "better" technology than others do, the better firms will (a) make profits and

(b) operate at larger than efficient scale. (You will prove that [a] implies [b] in problem 2.) The same thing can happen if there is a limit to the number of firms that can enter a perfectly competitive industry; i.e., firms in the industry can be making positive profits and, therefore, be producing at larger than efficient scale. (See problem 4 for an example.) How do these "inefficiencies" square with the result of the first welfare theorem? Is there an implicit assumption in the theorem (which guarantees that a Walrasian equilibrium is efficient) that for any production technology Z possessed by any firm, there will always be a queue of potential entrants possessing this technology? Is it implied that firms in a Walrasian equilibrium always make zero profits?

The answers to the last two questions are resounding noes. Any confusion on this point arises because "efficiency" is being used in two different ways. Efficiency in the welfare theorems pertains to efficiency relative to the productive capacities of the economy, which are determined (in part) by the number of firms possessing each technology. If, in an equilibrium, a firm is making positive profits and producing at larger than efficient scale, then we would be able to improve (in the sense of Pareto) on the equilibrium plan if we could create more firms with this technology. But this isn't how efficiency is defined in the welfare theorems; efficiency in those theorems is relative to the firms that are present in the given economy.

We can read this distinction in two ways. On the one hand, earlier discussion of firms producing at larger than efficient scale shouldn't be taken to mean that the market system (with price-taking firms) leads to correctable inefficiencies; the market system will be doing as well as it can given the economy's technology. On the other hand, even if all firms in an economy are competitive, one can potentially "improve" on the allocation of goods achieved in a Walrasian equilibrium when there are profit-making firms by transferring the technology of the profit-making firms to others. (This last recommendation is not a serious policy recommendation. One has to worry about the supply by innovators of profitable innovations. If the government immediately transfers any profitable innovation from the innovator to many competitors, there wouldn't be much incentive to innovate. Because these issues are well beyond us at this point, they are left for the interested reader to pursue.)

Externalities, taxes, and efficiency

As we noted in chapter 6, externalities can overthrow the conclusions of the two welfare theorems. That remains as true here as in the pure exchange context, if not more so. In chapter 6 we considered consumption externalities; firms add to the potential for consumption externalities, as anyone who has lived next to an oil refinery or chemical plant can testify.[7]

---

[7] We should note that insofar as effluents and noxious odors from refineries and chemical plants are modeled as commodities, we will have to redo a lot of the theory we've presented; these are goods for which preferences are not nondecreasing, and they are not freely disposable by firms. If you read on in general equilibrium theory, you will see how to model noxious commodities like these.

But the presence of firms gives us a new category of externalities to worry about, namely production externalities.

The idea in a production externality is that a firm, by its choice of production plan (or, for that matter, a consumer by her choice of consumption bundle) changes the feasible set of production plans for other firms. A chemical plant sited on a river can certainly change the feasible technology of its downriver neighbor, a soft-drink manufacturer. A firm that extracts oil from one plot of land can affect the ease with which a neighboring firm can extract oil, when the oil comes from a common underground pool. A firm that raises sheep by grazing the sheep on the village green affects the prospects for its neighbor who wishes to graze its goats on the same village green.

When production externalities of these sorts exist, the welfare theorems once again go awry. We will point out where the proof of the first welfare theorem would break down, leaving you the (harder) task of showing that, in such cases, a Walrasian equilibrium can most certainly be inefficient. The theorem breaks down right at the end. Recall that we supposed a feasible plan $((\hat{z}^j), (\hat{x}^i))$ that was Pareto superior to the Walrasian equilibrium plan $((z^j), (x^i))$. We concluded (and would, absent problems of consumption externalities, continue to conclude) that in this case it would have to be that

$$\sum_{j=1}^{J} p \cdot \hat{z}^j > \sum_{j=1}^{J} p \cdot z^j,$$

where p are the Walrasian equilibrium prices. From this we concluded that for at least one firm, $p \cdot \hat{z}^j > p \cdot z^j$, which was taken to imply that z^j was not profit maximizing for firm j at prices p. But when there are production externalities, this last step doesn't quite work. When there are production externalities, what firm j can do depends on the production plans selected by other firms; we would write something like $Z^j((z^{j'}), (x^i))$ for the production possibility set of firm j. And then it might be possible that $\hat{z}^j \notin Z^j((z^{j'}), (x^i))$ while $\hat{z}^j \in Z^j((\hat{z}^{j'}), (\hat{x}^i))$. That is, $\hat{z}^j$ would give better profits for firm j, but isn't feasible given that other firms and consumers are following the plan $((z^{j'}), (x^i))$.

Taxes give further grounds for scepticism about the two welfare theorems. This statement may seem rather perverse, since you might have read the second welfare theorem as saying that to change the distribution of utility among consumers, you should reallocate endowments through a system of taxes and subsidies and then let the market go to work to achieve efficiency. But you need to be very careful in interpreting the second welfare theorem and the sort of "taxes and subsidies" that go along with it.

In the second welfare theorem, people begin with endowments, and a redistribution of endowments is supposed to be accomplished before any economic activity is undertaken. In contrast, redistributive taxes and transfers in the real economy are undertaken by taxes on the product/outcome of economic activity. You trade leisure, part of your endowment, for wages with which to buy consumption goods, and the chief form of tax in the U.S. economy, an income tax, takes away part of those wages. Hence when you decide how much leisure to trade for wages, you make a marginal calculation based on your after-tax income. Your employer, in deciding how much labor to purchase, calculates on the basis of pretax wages. (Actually, the employer looks at the effect of wages on her post-tax earnings, which compounds many tax effects.) The point is that in the welfare theorems, it is crucial to the results that all consumers and firms face the same set of prices — the same set of marginal tradeoffs. Reallocating endowments at the start doesn't cause problems, as this sort of reallocation doesn't affect the (equilibrium) marginal trade-offs that an individual faces; in particular, all face the same margins. But when we tax wages or impose excise or sales taxes on goods, the prices that the buyer and seller face are forced apart, and there is no particular reason to think that efficiency will result.

Where would this cause the proof of the first welfare theorem to break down? Recall that the proof began with the supposition that $(p, (z^j), (x^i))$ is a Walrasian equilibrium, and $((\hat{z}^j), (\hat{x}^i))$ is a Pareto superior, feasible plan. Using the feasibility constraints and the fact that prices are nonnegative, we premultiplied each side of the feasibility constraints by the equilibrium prices to get a "value" inequality for the hat plan and (using local insatiability) a value equation for the equilibrium plan. From there, by comparing the values of bundles and production plans consumer-by-consumer and firm-by-firm we proceeded to derive a contradiction.

What are we to do when different actors in the economy face different prices for the same good? We can still make the firm-by-firm and consumer-by-consumer comparisons using the prices that the firm and consumer face. But we can't use different sets of prices in going from the feasibility inequalities to the value equation/inequality. The entire method of proof breaks down.

There are good reasons to have taxes on endogenous economic variables such as income that are simply missed by the general equilibrium model. Take as given the position that it is equitable to redistribute somewhat from the more fortunate in terms of ability or luck to the less, even, if necessary, at the cost of some loss in efficiency. The second welfare theorem says that, ideally, you don't need to suffer any efficiency loss; figure out in advance who is among the more fortunate and transfer some of their endowment to the less. But this scheme presumes that the more and less fortunate can be identified at the outset. Endowments and shares in the firms are publicly available data; someone fortunate in these things cannot "hide" her fortune in order to avoid the tax man. In reality, we cannot tell who is more fortunate and who is less — who will be lucky, who has more ability, and so on. The clues we will get will be based on observed market data such as income levels. And, therefore, equitable redistribution may well have to come at the cost of some efficiency loss.

We might try to make the efficiency loss as small as possible, by manipulating the form of taxes we impose. This is taken up in the literature of public finance. Your attention is called especially to the literature on optimal taxation; here a social welfare function is given and, subject to informational constraints that more nearly approximate a realistic setting, the analyst uses the methods of chapter 5 to find an optimal tax system, one which balances the gains from a more equitable distribution of income, which comes out of the social welfare function, with the losses in efficiency, captured by the extent to which the constraints bind.

Existence and local uniqueness

Finally, questions arise about the number of Walrasian equilibria for economies with firms. Recall that in chapter 6, we discussed results along the lines of every exchange equilibrium that meets certain conditions has at least one equilibrium, and "most" exchange economies have only finitely many. Similar results can be obtained for economies with competitive firms. The results on "most" economies having finitely many equilibria involve mathematics that are completely beyond the scope of this book, and we do not comment further, but for readers who read through the subsection on the existence of equilibria in exchange economies, we include some brief technical remarks:

> The sort of fixed point techniques sketched in chapter 6 are adapted to the context of economies with competitive firms to prove existence. Besides looking at consumer demand at given prices, we also must look at the firms' profit-maximizing choice of netput vectors. These choices will have to be well behaved mathematically, just as consumers' demand choices are required to be well behaved. But we have already seen that this can be done: If Z is convex, then the set of solutions to the firm's profit-maximization problem at a given set of prices is convex (proposition 7.3[b]); and if Z is closed, the correspondence that associates to each price vector the set of solutions is upper semi-continuous (problem 4 in chapter 7). Actually, a lot of the work that goes on in general equilibrium with firms is done in an attempt to

avoid very strong assumptions on Z that guarantee a solution to the firm's profit-maximization problem for any prices. In particular, general equilibrium theorists like to get existence results even when production technologies have constant returns to scale, where part of the existence proof will be that prices where the firms can make infinite profits will be avoided.

8.5. Bibliographic notes

Virtually every text presents the partial equilibrium analysis of perfectly competitive markets a bit differently from every other text, so you may wish to reinforce the material on partial equilibrium by looking at other treatments. I strongly recommend as well looking at some examples of presumably perfectly competitive industries; as noted in the text, the *Oil Tanker Shipping Industry* case is an example with enough things going on to make the comparison with the theory very interesting.

As for general equilibrium with firms, the standard references given at the end of chapter 6, namely Debreu (1959) and Arrow and Hahn (1971), remain the best places to go.

One of the unsatisfactory things about models of perfect competition is that firms' conjectures are usually wrong; firms assume they have no market power when in fact they have a little bit. One might hope for formal results showing that perfect competition is appropriate as an approximate model of economies where firms have (and realize they have) a small amount of market power. There is a literature on this subject which, if you are very ambitious, you may wish to tackle. You probably should complete part III of this book before looking at this literature. But, if ever and whenever you are ready, a good place to start is with the *Journal of Economic Theory* symposium issue of April 1980.

References

Arrow, K., and F. Hahn. 1971. *General Competitive Analysis*. San Francisco: Holden-Day.

Debreu, G. 1959. *Theory of Value*. New Haven: Cowles Foundation.

Porter, M. 1983. *Cases in Competitive Strategy*. New York: Free Press.

8.6. Problems

■ 1. Prove proposition 8.1.

■ 2. (a) Prove that it is inconsistent with the theory of perfect competition that a firm in a long-run equilibrium would ever produce a (positive) quantity at which its long-run average costs are declining. What are the implications of this for an industry in which all firms have average costs that are perpertually declining?

(b) Prove that in any long-run equilibrium, firms produce at efficient scale or larger, and if a firm is making positive profits, it must be producing at larger than efficient scale. (You may assume that average and marginal cost curves are all continuous.)

Endless variations on the example given in section 8.2 and 8.3 can be played. Problem 3 is quite difficult; in it you consider the "equilibrium dynamics" in the second example from the text. In problem 4, you see what happens if there is limited entry into a competitive industry; in problem 5 we consider a case in which firms possess a number of different technologies; and in problem 6 you work through "equilibrium dynamics" when a factor price changes.

■ 3. (a) In the analysis of the example in section 8.3, we worked through the long-run equilibrium supply curve of pfillip for the case where the price of kapitose depends on kapitose demand by pfillip consumers: The price q of kapitose is $K/200$, where K is pfillip industry demand for kapitose as a factor of production. Suppose demand for pfillip is given by $D(p) = 400 - 100p$. What is the long-run equilibrium? (This should be very easy.)

(b) Suppose demand for pfillip is given by $D(p) = 750 - 150p$. What is the long-run equilibrium? (You will probably need to resort to numerical calculations, both here and throughout the rest of the problem.)

(c) Suppose demand for kapitose begins at $D(p) = 400 - 100p$, and the long-run equilibrium you computed in (a) is reached. Then, suddenly, demand for pfillip changes to $D(p) = 750 - 150p$. What is the new short-run equilibrium, where in the short run firms cannot enter or leave the industry and cannot change their levels of kapitose utilization. (Once again, this is very easy, given what is in the text.)

(d) Continuing from (c), what is the equilibrium in the intermediate run, where in the intermediate run firms cannot enter or leave the industry but can change their levels of kapitose and legume utilization. (Good luck!)

■ 4. Imagine that for some reason there can be only 300 firms producing kapitose; only these 300 firms have licenses, say. In the long run, these 300 firms can exit the market (and later reenter, if conditions warrant), and they can vary the amount of legume and kapitose they use. In the intermediate run, firms cannot leave (or enter), but they vary their factor usage. In the short run, firms can only change their levels of legume usage. Assume the price of kapitose is $q = \$.50$, no matter how much kapitose is used by pfillip producers. (That is, we are back in the setting of section 8.2.)

(a) Suppose demand is given by $D(p) = 400 - 100p$. What is the long-run equilibrium in this industry?

(b) Suppose the equilibrium computed in part (a) is reached, and then demand suddenly shifts to $D(p) = 750 - 150p$. What is the short-run equilibrium position? What is the intermediate-run equilibrium position? What is the new, long-run equilibrium position?

(c) What is the long-run industry supply curve?

■ 5. Suppose there are two production processes for making pfillip. In the first, the production function is $y = k^{1/6}l^{1/3}$ and fixed costs are $1/6$. In the second, the production function is $y = k^{1/9}l^{2/9}$ and fixed costs are $1/4$. One hundred firms have access to the first technology, but only those hundred can use this technology. An unlimited number of firms have access to the second technology. Assume that the price of kapitose is $\$.50$ no matter how much kapitose is utilized by pfillip producers.

(a) What is the long-run industry supply curve for this industry?

(b) Suppose demand is given by $D(p) = 400 - 100p$. What is the long-run equilibrium for this industry?

(c) Suppose demand suddenly shifts to $D(p) = 750 - 150p$. Work out the short-run, intermediate-run, and new long-run equilibria.

■ 6. In the production of psillip, a nonnarcotic relaxant, there are three factors of production: legume, kapitose, and jehosa fat. Letting l be the amount of legume, k the amount of kapitose, and j the amount of jehosa fat, the production function is

$$y = f(j, k, l) = j^{1/6}k^{1/6}l^{1/6}.$$

The price of legume is a fixed $1 per unit; kapitose costs $4 per unit, and, at the start of this problem, jehosa fat costs $2 per unit. Many firms could enter this industry, all of whom have access to this technology, and each of whom, if active, must pay a fixed cost (in addition to the costs of any factor inputs) of $216. Demand for psillip is given by $D(p) = 1440 - 10p$, where p is the price of psillip.

(a) Assuming conditions of free entry and exit and assuming all firms are price takers in all markets, what is the long-run equilibrium in the psillip market under these conditions? Give: equilibrium price, quantity, number of firms, output per firm, amount of factors used by each firm, profit per firm. (Hint: The equilibrium price is 72.)

(b) Suddenly the jehosa crop fails, and the price of jehosa fat jumps to $4 per unit. In the very short run, firms can vary the amount of legume they input to production, but the levels of jehosa fat and kapitose are fixed and the number of firms is fixed. In the medium short run, firms can vary the amounts of legume and jehosa fat they use, but the level of kapitose is fixed and the number of firms is fixed. In the medium run, kapitose joins legume and jehosa fat as a variable factor of production, but the number of firms is fixed. And in the long run, there is free entry and exit from this industry. Solve for the very short-run, medium short-run, medium-run and long-run equilibria in this industry, beginning from the equilibrium position of part (a). When you solve for the long-run equilibrium, do not worry about fractional numbers of firms.

The next problem shifts a factor price in the setting of two linked markets.

■ 7. The manufacture of rhillip, a nonnarcotic nutrient, takes two stages. In the first stage, legume and kapitose are used to produce rhipigume. In the second stage, rhipigume and further amounts of kapitose are used to make rhillip. Rhipigume has no uses other than for the manufacture of rhillip; as you know full well by now, legume and kapitose are the bases for many speciality chemicals.

For purposes of this problem, suppose that legume and kapitose are traded in perfectly competitive markets. The price of kapitose is $1, and the price of legume is $4 (for the time being).

Rhipigume is produced in a perfectly competitive industry that is filled with many identical firms, each of which has production function

$$r = k^{1/4}l^{1/4},$$

where r is the amount of rhipigume produced from k units of kapitose and l units of legume. Each firm in this industry faces fixed costs of $16 (per firm) as well. There is completely free entry and exit to and from this industry.

Rhillip is produced in another perfectly competitive industry. (For legal reasons, no firm can produce both rhillip and rhipigume.) There are many firms in this industry as well, each of whom has production function

$$R = k^{1/4}r^{1/4},$$

where R is the amount of rhillip produced from k units of kapitose and r units of rhipigume. Each firm in this industry has fixed costs of $72 (per firm). There is completely free entry and exit to and from this industry. Industry demand for Rhillip is given by the equation

$$P = 96 - R/10,$$

where P is the price of rhillip and R is the total quantity of rhillip brought to market.

(a) What is the long-run equilibrium in these two industries? I want to know prices for the two goods, numbers of firms in each industry, output supply and factor demands of each firm, profits per firm, and total industry supply and factor demands.

In the short run, firms in both industries can vary the amounts of kapitose they use in production, but not the amounts of legume or rhipigume. In the intermediate run, firms can vary the amounts of their factor inputs, but entry to or exit from either industry is not possible. In the long run, entry and exit becomes possible.

(b) Beginning from the position you computed in part (a), the price of legume suddenly falls to $.25. What will happen in these two industries in the short run? In the intermediate run? And in the long run? (For the long run, don't worry about fractional numbers of firms.)

The next problem works through what happens when there are constant returns to scale.

■ 8. Suppose that the production function of a single firm in an industry that produces zipple, a nonnarcotic pain killer, out of kapitose and legume is $f(k, l) = k^{1/3}l^{2/3}$. In this case, firms have no fixed costs. Suppose that the price of kapitose is given by $q = 1/2$ and the price of legume is $1. Suppose there are precisely 100 firms in the industry; they can leave if they are unprofitable, but no one else can enter.

(a) If demand for zipple is given by $D(p) = 400 - 100p$, what is the long-run equilibrium? Are there parts of the long-run equilibrium that are indeterminate? (Yes!)

(b) Demand shifts to $D(p) = 750 - 150p$. What is the new short-run equilibrium where the firms can vary their usage of legumes but not their usage of kapitose? Does the indeterminacy you found in part (a) affect your answer to this part?

Next we have an easy finger exercise, which will come back to haunt you in Chapter 19.

■ 9. Imagine that there is an industry for a particular product where the demand for this product is given by $P = 100 - X$. There are two factors of production, capital K and labor L; the price of each will be $1 throughout. The firms all have identical technology, which is given by a *fixed coefficients* production function:

$$Y = \left(\min \left(\frac{K}{\alpha}, \frac{L}{1-\alpha} \right) \right)^{1/2},$$

where Y is the level of output and α is some constant from $(0, 1)$. Each firm has fixed costs of 16.

(a) Suppose there are precisely six firms in this industry; they can exit if they are unprofitable, but no firms can enter. What is the long-run equilibrium in this case? (Even though there are only six firms, they all entertain competitive conjectures about their effect on various prices.)

(b) Suppose there is free entry into this industry. What is the long-run equilibrium?

■ 10. Suppose one firm in a general equilibrium economy has a technology with free disposal. Prove that Walrasian equilibrium prices are nonnegative.

■ 11. Consider the following economy: There are three goods, legume, tillip and quillip, two consumers (called 1 and 2), and two firms (called x and y). Firm x is owned entirely by consumer 1 and makes tillip out of legume according to the simple linear production technology $t \leq 3l$. That is, for every unit of legume input, this firm produces three times as many (or less) units of tillip. Firm y is owned entirely by consumer 2 and makes quillip out of legume according to the production technology $q = 4l$. Each consumer initially owns 5 units of legume. Consumer 1 has utility function $u_1(t, q) = 6 + .4 \ln(t) + .6 \ln(q)$. Consumer 2 has utility function $u_2(t, q) = 8 + \ln(t) + \ln(q)$.

(a) What is the general equilibrium of this economy? Assume that firms take prices as given and are profit maximizers, and consumers take prices as given. When you give prices, normalize them so the price of legume is $1. What would be the general equilibrium if the shareholdings were reversed? If each consumer held a half-share in each firm?

(b) What is the set of all feasible, Pareto efficient allocations for this economy?

chapter nine

Monopoly

The theory of monopoly is, on the face of things, very simple and straight-forward. But behind this simple and straightforward theory lie some deep and interesting questions. We won't be able to answer most of these questions here, but we can pose the questions and give a rough idea what the answers might look like. And later in the book we will see some of the answers that have been developed.

9.1. The standard theory

In a monopoly market, we imagine many buyers and a single vendor of a good. This single vendor is called the *monopoly*.[1] Buyers are assumed to be price takers, and their demand as a function of price is given, as in the case of perfect competition, by an aggregate demand function. We will write $D(p)$ for the level of demand at price p, and we will also write $P(d)$ for the *inverse demand function*; that is, $P(D(p)) = p$. To guarantee a well-defined inverse demand function exists, we must make certain assumptions about demand. But we make those without qualms: We assume that demand is downward sloping. In fact, to keep the mathematics simple, we assume that D is a continuously differentiable function whose derivative is strictly negative (and finite) at any argument $p > 0$ such that $D(p) > 0$. To cover "corner cases," we assume that the monopoly can sell as much of the good in question as desired, if the price of the good is set at 0. We do not require that the demand function is continuous at the price of zero; that is, there may be a finite upper bound on the amount demanded at any positive price. And we do not require strictly positive demand at every price; demand may be zero at some finite price (and at all higher prices).

The monopoly is assumed to be characterized by a total cost function $TC(x)$, where x is the level of the monopoly's output. Then, the standard

---

[1] This is a firm, so we will use the impersonal pronoun *it*. Although it is sometimes awkward, we will refer to the monopoly as if it were making decisions; we should be referring to the monopoly's manager, but that becomes too tortured.

theory runs, the monopoly sets the quantity of output x to maximize its profits:

$$\max_{x} P(x)x - TC(x),$$

which gives first-order conditions

$$P'(x)x + P(x) = MC(x).$$

That is, we have the slogan that *marginal revenue equals marginal cost.*[a] Note here that the monopoly's conjectures about how the price of its product will change with changes in the level of output (or, alternatively, how the level of demand will change with changes in the price he charges) are correct; they are given by the actual market demand curve. Compare this with the perfect competitors of chapter 8, whose conjectures were slightly wrong.

Recall from chapter 7 that we can rewrite marginal revenue as $P(x)(1 + 1/\epsilon(x))$, where $\epsilon(x) = P(x)/(xP'(x))$ is the elasticity of demand. Since $P(x)$ is decreasing (by assumption), ϵ is a negative function. When $-\epsilon(x) < 1$, demand is said to be *inelastic*; when $-\epsilon(x) > 1$, demand is said to be *elastic*; and when $-\epsilon(x) = 1$, demand is said to have *unit elasticity*. From the formula given above for marginal revenue, we see that this means that the monopoly's marginal revenue is negative when demand is inelastic; it is zero when demand has unit elasticity; and it is positive when demand is elastic. Note that whenever marginal revenue is negative, the monopoly increases *revenues* by decreasing quantity sold. Since, it is normally presumed, marginal costs are always positive (or, at least, nonnegative), this implies that a monopoly would never produce a quantity at which demand is inelastic. If marginal costs are everywhere strictly positive, then production would never be at a level where demand has unit elasticity.

We can also think of the monopoly choosing an optimal price p. In this case, the monopoly's problem would be written

$$\max_{p} D(p)p - TC(D(p)).$$

---

[a] We are sloppy and assume a solution to the monopoly's problem at some finite level of output x. The easiest way to justify this assumption is to assume price is zero beyond some finite level of supply and, as supply goes to zero, prices stay bounded. But we do not restrict attention to this sort of case in examples, and the careful reader will no doubt check us as we proceed. Moreover, we don't check second-order conditions in the marginal revenue equals marginal cost equation. But in examples, TC will be convex and TR will be concave, so we'll always be okay.

The first-order conditions are

$$D'(p)p + D(p) = MC(D(p))D'(p).$$

If you remember the formula for the derivative of the inverse of a function $f(x)$ is $df^{-1}(y)/dy|_{y^0} = 1/(df/dx)|_{x^0=f^{-1}(y^0)}$, you will see that this is the same first-order equation as before.

There is no presumption that the monopoly will produce at an efficient scale (that is, at a scale where average costs are minimum). In figure 9.1(a), we see a case where the monopoly will produce at an inefficiently large scale, and in figure 9.1(b) a case where the monopoly will produce at an inefficiently small scale.

How do we know this? The problem is to find the position of the marginal revenue curve. You are given a geometrical procedure for doing this in figure 9.2; if you use this procedure, you remember the relative positions of marginal and average cost, and you remember that the monopoly equates marginal revenue to marginal cost, you should have no problem with these conclusions. But this leaves the question: Why is this geometrical procedure correct? Problem 1 asks for a proof.

That's it. That's all there is to the standard theory of monopoly. We think of the monopoly being able to select the quantity it will supply or, equivalently, the price it will charge, and the resulting equilibrium price or quantity is read off the demand curve. But this simple classic theory is subject to a lot of questions, caveats, variations, and elaborations. In the next few sections, a few of these are sketched.

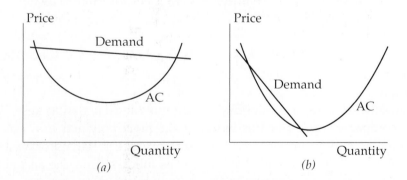

Figure 9.1. The optimal scale of a monopoly.
The optimal scale of a monopoly is inefficiently large in (a) and inefficiently small in (b).

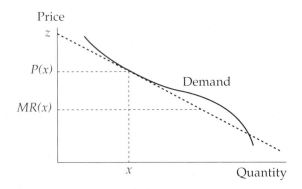

Figure 9.2. Computing the value of marginal revenue.
At any point x along the quantity axis, draw the tangent to the inverse demand demand curve $P(x)$ back to the p-axis. Measure the distance from the point z where this tangent intersects the p-axis to $P(x)$ and move an equal amount on the other side from $P(x)$. This is $MR(x)$. That is, $MR(x) = P(x) - (z - P(x))$.

9.2. *Maintaining monopoly*

You might wonder, for example, how the monopoly came to be a monopoly, and why it stays that way. If the monopoly is making a profit, why doesn't the industry attract entrants? It may be that legal barriers impede entry. The monopoly might hold a patent on a particular production process or on a particular product. Or it might be illegal for any competitors to enter the market. This is especially likely to happen where the production technology favors one very large company — where average costs are falling at all levels of output. (The case where average costs are decreasing at every level of output is sometimes referred to as the case of a "natural monopoly.") In cases such as this, the monopoly is apt to be subject to regulation; it can't charge any price it wishes, but instead must obtain approval of some regulatory body for the prices it sets. There is a very large literature on the economics of regulation that looks at this situation.

Another reason we might find a monopoly industry is because, while other companies *can* enter this industry, the monopoly acts in a way that forestalls potential competitors. A classic story of this sort associated with the names of Bain and Sylos-Labini runs as follows: Imagine an industry in which there is a constant variable cost of production, say $1 per unit and a fixed cost for any firm in the industry amounting to $2.25. (These are convenient, not realistic, numbers.) This production technology is available to one and all. Demand in this industry is given by $D(p) = 9 - p$. There is, at the time being, a single firm in this industry (seemingly a monopoly). Note that the standard theory of monopoly suggests that this monopoly will equate marginal cost, which is 1, with marginal revenue, which is $9 - 2x$ at output level x. (Total Revenue $= 9x - x^2$. Differentiate.) This gives $x = (9-1)/2 = 4$, $P = 5$, and monopoly profits of $4(5-1) - 2.25 = 13.75$.

But despite this prediction of the standard theory, it is discovered upon inspection that the monopoly has set the quantity of output equal to 5, thus realizing a profit of $5(4 - 1) - 2.25 = 12.75$. When asked why, the monopoly responds:

> Out there are many people who would enter this industry and take away my profits if they thought that they themselves could make a profit. So put yourself in their shoes. Here am I (the monopoly) with an output of 5. If you enter and have an output of x', assuming that I keep my output level at 5, the price would be $9 - 5 - x' = 4 - x'$, so your margin (gross of your fixed costs) would be $3 - x'$. You will then (optimally) set $x' = 1.5$ so your gross profits will be 2.25. That is, at best, you will only just cover your fixed costs. Since you won't make a positive profit, you won't enter, and I'll stay a monopoly. On the other hand, if I were producing 4 units, and potential entrants believed that I would hold to this level of output, then they would be able to cover their fixed costs, and they would enter. My choice of an output level of 5 may look silly in the short run, but if it keeps you (and other potential entrants) out of my market, it is a good strategy to employ.

The general idea is that the monopoly's choice of quantity and/or price may be based on a strategy for keeping the monopoly, rather than for maximizing short-term profits.

Now rather a lot is wrong with the story just told, primarily concerning the supposed follow-on if you, as a potential entrant, choose to enter: Why would you suppose that after you enter the monopoly will maintain its quantity of output at 5 units? Why wouldn't it accommodate to your entry? What will it do if you enter? We aren't in a position just yet to talk about such things (since, for one thing, they involve what happens in a duopoly). And so we will leave this simple story of *entry deterrence* as it stands for now, returning to it in chapter 13. But the point remains: If monopoly power isn't granted by law, then monopolies may take actions that are directed towards the maintenance of monopoly power, which may be very different from short-run profit maximization. Hence, in trying to analyze what a monopoly will do in its market, it is essential to have answers to the questions: Where does the monopoly come from? What (if anything) must be done to maintain it?

Although this may be beating the subject to death, it should also be noted that even when the monopoly results from legal protection, say by a patent, considerations like those just mentioned may intrude. Suppose that a manufacturer does hold an unbreakable patent on a particular product. The scope of patent protection does not always extend to protection against close substitutes for the patented product. If substitute products are produced and sold, they restrain the monopoly's market power by flattening and shifting-in the monopoly's demand curve. That is, as the monopoly raises the price charged, many of its customers will move to the substitute good, and it will see a dramatic fall in the quantity it can sell. In this situation, what is observed will be in accord with the standard theory; it is just that the monopoly will face fairly elastic demand.

But (and this is the reason for introducing this now) suppose those substitute goods are not being produced and sold. Then the monopoly may act in a way to impede the entry of producers of those substitute goods. The story is one degree more complex than the story of entry deterrence sketched above, but the same basic notions apply. What we anticipate seeing in the short run, according to the standard theory, may not be observed, insofar as the monopoly is setting its price to keep substitute products from being placed on the market.

9.3. Multigood monopoly

The idea of substitutes for a monopoly product comes up in another context — that of multigood monopolies. Suppose a monopoly has monopoly rights on two different products that are substitutes. By raising the price of one, demand is stimulated for the other and vice versa. Hence we might well see prices for two substitute goods that are higher than the prices we would expect if we analyzed in isolation the market for either.

An extreme form of this, which combines aspects of the sort of entry deterrence discussed above, involves what are called "sleeping patents." Suppose a firm holds a monopoly in a certain product, and it knows on its own or learns of the existence of a close substitute that is not yet on the market but which may be produced. The monopoly may then seek to patent (or buy exclusive rights to manufacture and sell) the substitute. And then, once it holds exclusive right to manufacture the substitute, it may produce none at all. Especially when there are large fixed costs in production, the monopoly may maximize its profits by producing only one of several close substitutes. Hence it gains the patent to prevent anyone else from manufacturing the substitute, and then it puts the patent "to sleep" to maximize its overall profits.

A third issue on substitute goods and monopolies concerns the range of product variety. A monopoly often offers a number of varieties of the basic product it produces. In the offering of many varieties, the monopoly is competing with itself; red and blue widgets are probably close substitutes, and insofar as the monopoly is selling red widgets, by offering them in blue it cuts into its own market. There is no real problem if no extra fixed cost is associated with offering multiple colors (or, in general, different varieties). But where there are increased fixed costs, either in manufacture or distribution, then the monopoly must decide how many (and which) varieties to offer. We leave these vague ideas here, although problems 9, 10, and 11 will give you some ideas about how to model and analyze this issue.

On the other hand, a monopoly might hold monopolies in two complementary goods. Lowering the price of one stimulates demand for the other. Hence we might expect to see prices lower than those we would predict from analyzing in isolation the market for either. For example, imagine a firm that produces both cameras and film for a particular sort of photographic process for which it has no rivals. (Think of a case where conventional photography is a substitute but not a perfect substitute.) It isn't hard to imagine that this firm might sell cameras suited for its film at a relatively low price to stimulate demand for its film.

Even more interesting are cases where a monopoly in one product can also participate in a second market in which it doesn't hold a monopoly. Suppose, for example, that there are potential entrants ready and willing to serve the second market. And suppose that the products involved are very strong complements. Then the monopoly may be able to use its monopoly in the first product to gain power in the second; we have what is called an *extending monopoly*. For example, a firm that holds a monopoly on a particular sort of computer might bundle sale of the computer with servicing (which, for the sake of argument, we assume anyone could perform). The company might even go to the extreme of refusing to sell its computers at all — it will only lease them — so that it can control forever who services the machines.

9.4. Nonlinear pricing

The standard theory presumes that the monopoly must charge linear prices. That is, the monopoly sets a price per unit, and customers can buy as many/few units as they wish at that price. The usual justification for this assumption is that the good is bought anonymously and can be resold. If the monopoly were, say, to give a quantity discount, then someone would buy a large amount (at a discount) and resell it in smaller lots to consumers who don't want quite as many. If the monopoly were to try to mark up the price for larger lots, then the consumer desiring a large lot would buy a number of small lots (or have her friends buy small lots and resell them to her). But for many sorts of commodities this justification for linear prices doesn't hold water. The resale of electricity, or telephone services, or education (or just about any sort of service) is difficult if not impossible, and the purchase of electricity or telephone services (at least) is not anonymous. When resale is impossible and/or the purchase of the item is not done anonymously, the monopoly may wish to consider using nonlinear prices to increase its profits.

This is not only true for monopolies. The same sort of consideration might intrude in the case of oligopolists, or even in a competitive industry. But analyses of nonlinear pricing have, for the most part, been devoted to the context of monopoly, because nonlinear pricing is hard enough without introducing considerations of competition.

The absolutely best position for a monopoly to be in is (a) to know the precise utility function of every consumer, (b) to be able to tailor a "price schedule" for each individual consumer, and (c) to be able to control absolutely any resale of the good being sold. Then the monopoly can make a "take-or-leave" offer to each individual consumer, which extracts from the consumer all the surplus that this consumer would otherwise obtain from consumption of the good in question. That is, suppose that our consumer's preferences can be represented by a utility function $u(x, y)$, where x is the amount of the good produced by this monopoly that the consumer consumes, and y is the income that this consumer has to make other purchases. All other prices are being held fixed. Note that this function u is something like an indirect utility function, and it should be parameterized by those fixed other prices. We suppose that this consumer has total income (or wealth) y^0, so if the consumer consumes none of the monopoly's product, the consumer will have utility $u^0 = u(0, y^0)$. Now imagine that the monopoly makes a take-or-leave offer to the consumer; the consumer may take x^* units of the good, for a payment of z^* in total. Note well: The consumer isn't being given the option of taking as much or as little as he desires at a price per unit of z^*/x^*. The consumer may have x^* or none, and that is it. The consumer, then, will take this offer if it gives him utility greater than u^0; that is, if $u(x^*, y^0 - z^*) > u^0$. We can see that the monopoly, if it makes a take-or-leave offer with x^* the amount of the good offered, will set the payment z^* as high as possible while keeping to the constraint $u(x^*, y^0 - z^*) > u^0$. (In mathematical analysis of the problem, we'll have trouble with this strict inequality. So it is typical in economics to rewrite the constraint as $u(x^*, y^0 - z^*) \geq u^0$, and either assume that the consumer, if indifferent, will buy, or later fudge things by assuming that the monopoly charges, say, a nickel less than z^*.)

This is for a single consumer. If we look over all consumers, indexing them by the subscript i, we find that this lucky monopoly is seeking to solve the problem

$$\max \sum_i z_i^* - TC \left(\sum_i x_i^* \right) \text{ subject to } u_i(x_i^*, y_i^0 - z_i^*) \geq u_i^0 \text{ for all } i,$$

where TC is the monopoly's total cost function. Letting λ_i be the multiplier on the utility constraint of consumer i, the first-order conditions on z_i^* and x_i^* are

$$1 = \lambda_i \frac{\partial u_i}{\partial y} \bigg|_{(x_i^*, z_i^*)} \quad \text{and} \quad MC \left(\sum_i x_i^* \right) = \lambda_i \frac{\partial u_i}{\partial x} \bigg|_{(x_i^*, z_i^*)}.$$

Combining these two, we see that our monopoly will set each consumer's marginal rate of substitution of the good for money to be equal to its own "marginal rate of substitution," which is just its marginal cost. In other words, the monopoly will make available to every consumer enough of the good so the consumer's marginal value (in terms of dollars of other consumption) for the good is just equal to the monopoly's marginal cost. (How does this compare with the strategy of a monopoly that is using linear prices?) Then the monopoly extracts all the utility gains that the consumer gets by setting the fixed take-or-leave price at the most the consumer is willing to pay. It takes a little more algebra, but it can be demonstrated that, short of coercion, there is no way the monopoly can do better than this.

Of course, the assumptions that underpin this analysis are extreme. The monopoly is assumed to be able to deal with each consumer individually. It knows the utility function of each. It can tailor its prices to each; one consumer might be asked to pay $100 for 100 units of the good, whereas a second, who gets greater utility from the consumption of 50 units, might be asked to pay $500 for those 50. (For these two to be part of an optimal scheme, the marginal valuation of the first consumer for the 101st unit must equal the marginal valuation of the second for the 51st, and each of these must equal the monopoly's marginal cost for producing another unit.)

In fact, it seems unlikely that a monopoly would have this much knowledge and power. Even if the monopoly knows the utility function of each individual consumer, it may be compelled by law to offer to any consumer any deal that it offers to a second. (In which case our second consumer above would, it seems likely, prefer to pay $100 for 100 units, and forego paying $500 for 50.) Of course, if the monopoly doesn't know which consumer has which utility function, then it is forced to offer to each one the same set of deals and leave it to them to select which they wish to accept.

Still, even if the same set of deals must be offered to all consumers (allowing them to pick which they want), nonlinear prices may come in handy. We might imagine the monopoly trying linear prices but with a fixed charge to each consumer; you can buy as much as you wish (as a consumer) at a set price p per unit, but if you buy any, you must pay k up front. Or we might imagine a scheme where consumers can buy up to n_1 units at a price of p_1 per unit, and further units cost p_2 apiece. Will p_1 be greater or less than p_2? It depends, in part, on how well the monopoly can control to whom it sells how much. You are probably familiar, on the one hand, with quantity discounts for telephone service. On the other hand, the rate of interest on a loan will typically increase with the size of the loan.

Actually solving for the optimal nonlinear pricing scheme can be quite an involved problem. But the basic method is easy to state. One supposes that the population of consumers has a given distribution of utility functions, levels of wealth, and so on. Then, for each pricing scheme, one can work out how each type of consumer will react, hence how consumer reactions will be distributed across the population. From this, one obtains profits for the given scheme. If the scheme is characterized by only a few parameters (e.g., a price plus fixed fee system has two parameters, namely k and p; a two-part linear tariff system has three, namely p_1, n_1 and p_2), one might be able to solve analytically for the optimal scheme. Or one could at least conduct a numerical search over values of the parameters. For the optimal nonlinear price scheme in general, somewhat more advanced techniques (the calculus of variations or control theory) may be needed, but the same basic method is employed.

An example: A monopoly selling to monopolies

To illustrate some of these notions of nonlinear pricing and price discrimination, consider the following example. A manufacturing monopoly can produce a particular item, called a poiuyt, at a constant unit cost of c per unit. For some reason this manufacturer cannot engage in the retailing of this item. Instead, it must work through a system of retailers, each of whom holds a monopoly on the retail business in a particular geographical region. More specifically, in each of I regions, indexed by $i = 1, ..., I$, one firm is allowed to engage in the retail sale of poiuyts. We will assume that retailing is a simple business — so simple that it involves no cost at all, except for the cost incurred by the retailer in buying the units from the manufacturer. Demand for poiuyts at the retail level in region i is given by the demand curve $x_i = (A - p_i)/B_i$ or, equivalently, $p_i = A - B_i x_i$, where p_i is the retail price in region i, and x_i is the level of units sold in region i; A and B_i are positive constants.[2] We will assume that the manufacturer sets price(s) for the retailers, who then set prices p_i for the retail trade in each region. To keep matters simple, we'll assume that there is no possibility of customers in one region buying from the retailer or some middleman in another, so there is no need to insist that $p_i = p_j$ in equilibrium. Moreover, we'll assume that, in the retail markets, only linear prices can be charged and no discrimination is possible. We will, however, not *insist* on these requirements for the wholesale markets. Instead, we'll make a series of different assumptions about the wholesale market to see how things change with those assumptions.

To begin, we'll assume that the manufacturer, whom we will call M hereafter (using pronouns she and her, to distinguish from the retailers for whom we use he and him), must use linear prices, but is allowed to discriminate among the various retailers. That is, each retailer i is quoted a wholesale price P_i, which this retailer must pay per unit bought at wholesale. The retailer is allowed to choose how many units he wishes to buy and resell (or, equivalently, what retail price p_i he will charge *his* customers). Retailer i, facing wholesale price P_i, will treat P_i as his marginal cost and will set p_i to

$$\max_{p_i} \frac{(p_i - P_i)(A - p_i)}{B_i}.$$

---

[2] We assume throughout that $A > c$. The fact that the same constant A applies to all regions is an enormous convenience analytically. If you wish to, try replicating the analysis to follow for the case where A_i changes from region to region. If you do, be prepared to do a lot of algebra.

Since this is nearly the first time we've worked with linear demand and imperfect competition, and it is far from the last, let us solve this in gruesome detail. First, since demand is given by $p_i = A - B_i x_i$, total revenue at sales level x_i is $TR(x_i) = Ax_i - B_i x_i^2$. Marginal revenue is thus $A - 2B_i x_i$. Marginal revenue equals marginal costs (of P_i) at $A - 2B_i x_i = P_i$, or $x_i = (A - P_i)/2B_i$, which gives $p_i = (A + P_i)/2$, and profits $\pi_i = (A - P_i)^2/4B_i$. We depict all this in figure 9.3. Demand is given by the solid line. Marginal revenue is the dashed line; note that it has the same intercept on the price axis, and its slope is twice as great as the slope of demand.[3] Marginal costs are given by the horizontal line $MC = P_i$, so we get x_i where this line hits marginal revenue. The retailer marks up the price of the good to p_i, and the retailer's profits equal the area of light shading. The area of darker shading will be explained momentarily.

So how should M set P_i? If she sets the wholesale price at P_i, the retailer will purchase $(A - P_i)/2B_i$. Hence her profits will be $(P_i - c)(A - P_i)/2B_i$. In figure 9.3, this is the more darkly shaded region. She picks P_i to maximize these profits, which leads to $P_i = (A + c)/2$, hence (see

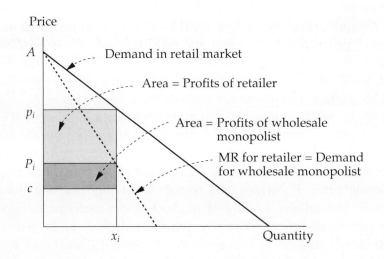

Figure 9.3. Retailer demand and mark up at price P_i.
Given the manufacturer charges retailer i the per-unit price P_i, the retailer purchases $(A - P_i)/2B_i = x_i$ units and marks the price up to $(A + P_i)/2 = p_i$. The more lightly shaded region gives the retailer's profits, and the more darkly shaded region gives the manufacturer's profits.

---

[3] Does this square with the geometrical formula given in figure 9.2?

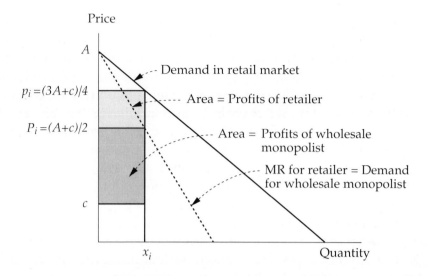

Figure 9.4. The optimal value of P_i is $(A+c)/2$.

figure 9.4) $p_i = (3A + c)/4$, $x_i = (A - c)/4B_i$, $\pi_i = (A - c)^2/(16B_i)$, and $\Pi_i = (A - c)^2/(8B_i)$, where π_i is the retailer's profits and Π_i is M's profits from this particular part of her operations.

Note two things here. First, we assumed that M could charge a different unit price to the various retailers. Because the intercept A is the same in all the regions, she doesn't use that power of discrimination; she charges $P_i = (A+c)/2$ regardless of i. Second, if M engaged directly in the retail business in region i, she would set the retail price p_i to maximize her profits $(p_i - c)(A - p_i)/B_i$, which gives $p_i = (A + c)/2$. That is, if M sold the good directly, more would be sold at a lower price than when M must go through a (monopoly) retailer.

Now consider nonlinear prices. In particular, imagine that M, recognizing that she is the only person who can produce poiuyts, decides to charge the retailers a *per unit* price P_i and a *franchise fee* F_i. Of course, she can't compel the retailers to pay this fee, but she can (and does) insist that they pay the fee if they want to purchase any poiuyts from her. Note that we've subscripted both the per unit price and the franchise fee. We'll assume for now that she can perfectly discriminate.

So what are the optimal P_i and F_i to set? Retailer i will face the total cost function $TC(x_i) = F_i + P_i x_i$ (for $x_i > 0$), so this retailer's marginal costs will be P_i, and, assuming he buys any at all, he will purchase $(A - P_i)/2B_i$, mark them up in price to $(A + P_i)/2$, and realize gross profits (gross of the franchise fee) of $(A - P_i)^2/4B_i$, just as before. In fact, he'll do all this if his net profits $(A - P_i)^2/4B_i - F_i$ are nonnegative. (We'll assume that if he just breaks even, he'll still buy and sell poiuyts. If this is wrong, then the analysis to follow changes a bit; F_i should be set just a bit below what we derive below, leaving retailer i with a small net profit, so that he'll stay in business.) So, pretty clearly, M wants to set the franchise fee F_i at $(A - P_i)^2/4B_i$, leaving retailer i with precisely zero profits. Of course, as she raises P_i, she decreases the franchise fee she can set. But she'll make more on the per unit sales. Where is the optimum? It comes as the solution to

$$\max_{P_i} (P_i - c)\left(\frac{A - P_i}{2B_i}\right) + \frac{(A - P_i)^2}{4B_i},$$

where the first term represents her profit from per unit sales, and the second is the franchise fee she'll collect. To find the optimum, we set the derivative of the expression above equal to zero, which is

$$\frac{A - P_i}{2B_i} - \frac{P_i - c}{2B_i} - \frac{2(A - P_i)}{4B_i} = 0.$$

The first and third terms cancel out, and we are left with $(P_i - c)/2B_i = 0$, or $P_i = c$.

This simple answer may surprise you a bit at first, but it really is very intuitive. M is going to set F_i at retailer i's gross profits. Thus, in the end, M is going to wind up with profits equal to the *two* shaded areas in figure 9.3, so P_i should be set to maximize those two areas together. But the two areas together are just the profits that M would make charging p_i in the retail market, if M marketed the product directly. We know that the optimal p_i for direct retailing by M is $(A+c)/2$. So M wants to set P_i so that retailer i will charge that price, which is what $P_i = c$ accomplishes.

Note that while P_i is independent of i, F_i is not. If B_i is larger than B_j, market i is *smaller* than market j. Thus retailer i will make smaller gross profits than will retailer j, and the franchise fee set for i can't be set as large as the franchise fee for j. Our manufacturer M is certainly using her powers of discrimination here. This, by the way, is not an outrageous use of the powers of discrimination. One generally thinks that price discrimination won't work in cases where the good can be resold by one customer who is charged a lower price to another who would be charged a higher price. But the franchise to sell a product is not something that can be resold so easily (or, at least, the contract that gives the franchise can be written so that the franchise would be hard to resell). And it is not altogether ridiculous to think that, say, a McDonald's franchisee in a potentially very large market will have to pay a higher fee than a McDonald's franchisee in a potentially small market.

Nonetheless, let us consider what would happen if M were forced by law or by circumstances to charge the same franchise fee and per unit cost to all the retailers. It doesn't quite make sense in this setting, but if M is unable to tell which retailers have which B_i but knows the distribution of B_i within the population, this restriction on her behavior would be natural; she would have to charge the same (nonlinear) prices to all her customers, and let them, by their actions, identify themselves in terms of their characteristics. That is to say, the sort of analysis we will take on at this point is the appropriate form of analysis for cases where a monopoly uses nonlinear prices to discriminate among a heterogeneous population, but where the monopoly is unable to tell a priori which sort of customer is any given customer.

We'll be very specific at this point. Suppose that $A = 12$, $c = 0$, and there are eight retailers: three have $B_i = 9$ and five have $B_i = 6$.[4] How should M set P and F (without subscripts) now? In particular, will $P = c = 0$ be the solution?

Suppose that P is set at zero. Then the gross profits of the three retailers with $B_i = 9$ are $A^2/4B_i = 144/36 = 4$, while the five with $B_i = 6$ will have gross profits of 6. Our manufacturer will consider only two possible values for F. She can set $F = 4$, so that all eight retailers will sign up. This will net her profits of 32 (and will leave 2 for each of the five retailers in the relatively large markets). Or she can set $F = 6$. This will cause the three retailers with the smaller markets to refuse to buy franchises, but will net 6 each from the five larger markets, for a net of 30. The point is that $F < 4$ is silly, since raising F up to 4 will simply increase her profits. And once $F > 4$, she may as well push F all the way up to 6. So, with $P = 0$, the best thing to do is to set $F = 4$, giving her profits of 32.

Let us try $P = 1$ next. Now the gross profits of the two types of retailers will be 3.3611, on unit sales of .6111 for the three smaller retailers, and 5.042, on unit sales of .91666 for the five larger retailers. (Be sure that you can replicate these numbers.) If M sets $F = 5.041$, she'll get the five larger retailers to participate, netting $5.041 + .91666 = 5.957666$ from each (the sum of the franchise fee plus the net of unit sales), for a total profit of 29.78 (approximately). No surprise there — we know that if she is going to deal with the five larger retailers only, she can (without discriminating) charge the best combination of F and P for them, namely $F = 6$ and

---

[4] If $c = 0$ bothers you, set $A = 13$ and $c = 1$, and you'll get the same answers.

$P = 0$. So setting $P = 1$ and then charging whatever F will get these five only must be suboptimal.

But she could also try $F = 3.3611$ in conjunction with $P = 1$. Then all eight retailers will deal with her. Her net profits will be approximately

$$8 \times 3.3611 + 5 \times 1 \times .91666 + 3 \times 1 \times .61111 = 33.3.$$

Note that this is eight franchise fees, plus .91666 sold to five clients at a price of 1 apiece, plus .6111 sold to three clients at a price of 1 apiece. And, sure enough, this gives greater profits than the best scheme with $P = 0$. What is happening here is that, since M can't extract all the profits from the five larger retailers (without losing the three smaller ones), she is forced back in the direction of the scheme where she can't charge a franchise fee at all, where P is not zero.

So the optimal P won't be 0. What will it be? You can work this out if you wish, although you may find it more challenging to try problem 3, where you are asked to work out a slightly more complex version of this problem.

9.5. *Monopoly power?*

In all of the previous discussion, it was assumed that the monopoly could name its price (or, equivalently, the quantity that it would sell) or could make a take-or-leave offer to potential consumers. You might wonder just why this is supposed to be true. Consider, for example, our "fortunate" monopoly, which can make a different take-or-leave offer to every consumer and which knows the characteristics of each consumer. Suppose it makes this take-or-leave offer to consumer X, who says "no thanks," and then comes back with a take-or-leave offer of her own. For example, consumer X might offer to take n units off the hands of the monopoly, at (being generous) \$1 above the monopoly's marginal cost for producing the n units. Wouldn't the monopoly take this deal, if it really believed it was the best deal it could get? And, if so, how do we determine who, in this sort of situation, does have the bargaining power? Why did we assume implicitly that the monopoly had all this power (which we most certainly did when we said that consumers were price takers)?[5]

___
[5] For those of you who remember back to a principles or intermediate micro course, another way to think of this is to consider that the monopoly dealing separately with a single consumer is in a position of *bilateral monopoly* which, you will recall, is meant to have an indeterminate solution.

Standard stories, if given at all, get very fuzzy at this point. Hands start to wave, hems give way to haws, and way is quickly given to the next subject. The handwaving typically involves something about how there is one monopoly and many consumers, and it can do without any one of them, but they can't do without it. Somehow (and this is never made precise), the monopoly's advantage in numbers gives it a credibility about setting and sticking to a price or in sticking to its take-or-leave offer.

An important variation on this basic theme explores the extent to which the monopoly is its own worst enemy when it comes to sticking credibly to a price. Imagine a monopoly that is able to produce a particular good at a cost of $1 per good. Demand for this good is given by the demand function $D(p) = 25 - p$. If you solve the monopoly's problem, you'll find that the optimal solution is for it to set $p = 13$ and to produce 12 units of the good. So suppose it does this — it sells the 12 units at $13 apiece. Once those twelve units are sold, why doesn't our monopoly decide to sell a few more at, say, $8 apiece? At $8, there is unsatisfied demand, and our monopoly will net $7 for every additional unit it sells. After selling what it can at $8 apiece, why not cut the price again, to say, $4, and so on?

The problem with this is that if you are a consumer who values the good highly (you are willing to pay $13, or even $24, if it comes to that) and if you think that the monopoly is going to cut the price after it sells off a few at a high price, then you will wish to wait for the price to drop. If all consumers rationally anticipate the drop in price, then no one will buy at $13.

Note well that the monopoly itself is the real problem here. Once it makes some sales at $13, if it makes any (and even if not), it is in its own best interests ex post to drop prices and sell more. It won't be in its own best interests ex ante to be perceived in this fashion. But if everyone understands that, ex post, this will be in its interests and this is what it will do, then there isn't much it can do to convince people that it won't drop price.

The problem we are alluding to here is variously known in the litera-ture as the Coase conjecture and the problem of a durable goods monopoly. (The relevance of durability comes from the notions that (a) the market isn't continually regenerating itself, as is, for example, the market in wheat, and (b) if the good is durable, waiting for price to drop won't hurt a consumer too much.) The Coase conjecture, stated a bit more baldly than normal, is that a monopoly doesn't have monopoly power. It won't be able to keep itself from dropping the price ex post, and so everyone expects to see prices drop. But then no one will buy at a high price. And (so the argument goes, when worked out fairly rigorously) a monopoly can't get anyone to buy above the price at which it is just willing to sell — its marginal costs.[6]

Once again, the problem is one of credibility. Before we were asking how the monopoly credibly maintains that it won't haggle with an individual customer. Now, how does the monopoly credibly maintain that it won't drop the price it charges as time passes?

It may well be that the monopoly can make credible commitments not to haggle and not to lower its price. We don't need to know why and how such commitments can be made credibly if we are testing the theory empirically; if, in a particular market, a monopoly acts the way the theory suggests, then we suppose that somehow or other the firm has this credibility. But a more precise analysis of why and how it has this sort of credibility would help refine any empirical investigation that we conduct.

What would a more precise analysis look like? Let us give two rough examples:

(1) Certain forms of art, lithographs and castings, can be made cheaply in multiple copies. So a common practice of artists who make lithographs and castings is to "break the mold" after making a given number of prints/casts. This practice is clearly directed towards the durable goods problem; the artist would otherwise always have an incentive to produce and sell more (down to the marginal cost of production, which is very low). More generally, a monopoly seeking to commit to produce a certain quantity and no more might try to commit itself to a production technology where the marginal cost of production rises precipitously past the level it wishes to produce. With such a technology, the monopoly could credibly refuse to haggle on grounds that the marginal cost of producing an additional unit (beyond the monopoly quantity) is prohibitive.

(2) The monopoly, in a fit of "largesse," could offer all its customers "most favored customer" guarantees. Such a guarantee might state, for example, that if the monopoly ever sells the good in question at a price below that which a particular customer pays, then the customer is entitled to a rebate of the difference (with accrued interest, say). The effect of this is dramatic. To conduct a precise analysis takes techniques that we don't have at our disposal yet, but the following assertions are likely to appeal to your

---

[6] More precisely, the extent to which a monopoly can exploit its monopoly power depends on two factors: the extent to which the monopoly can limit its own ability to drop the price it quotes and the impatience of customers. If, for example, the monopoly cannot change its price more than once a month, and if some customers are unwilling to wait a month for a somewhat lower price, then the monopoly can "exploit" those customers.

intuition. If some single customer attempts to haggle with the monopoly, the monopoly will point out the dire consequences to it of lowering the price for even one customer (namely, it means lowering the price for all). Similarly, lowering the price as time passes is no longer attractive. Note that insofar as the monopoly's credibility problems prevent it from otherwise charging monopoly prices, it is in the interests of customers to have a *general* prohibition against such guarantees. But each customer sees it in her personal interest to take such a guarantee if offered, so we can imagine that such guarantees might be given and taken, if conditions would permit them to be enforced effectively.[b] For such a guarantee to be enforceable, each customer would have to be able to observe all the deals the monopoly makes. It is, therefore, in the interest of monopoly and against the collective interests of customers to arrange matters so that all sales are a matter of public record, so that the guarantees will be effective.

These are only two examples. There are other sources of the type of credibility that the monopoly would like to have. In particular, in chapter 14 we will explore models in which the monopoly's *reputation* could provide the backbone needed to name and stick to a price.

Our point for now is primarily methodological: In the two examples sketched (and, it will turn out, when we look at models of reputation), we address the monopoly's ability to commit to a price by examining the institutions of production and exchange. As long as we avoid these institutional details, it is hard to say much about whether a monopoly can muster the credibility required. More generally, many of the questions posed (but not answered) in this chapter arise from the lack of specification of the institutional environment. To investigate these questions, it would seem useful to get more deeply involved with the details of the monopoly's environment. We will pick up on this theme even more strongly in the next chapter.

9.6. Bibliographic notes

The objective of this chapter has been to raise some issues that we hope will lead you to conclude that rather a lot is interesting to resolve concerning monopoly; certainly there is more to the subject than recitation of $MR = MC$. Some of these issues will be resolved when we get to the appropriate tools in later parts of the book. But for the most part, you will have to read elsewhere for the resolution of these questions. An

---

[b] That is, we are seeing here a reason why it might matter that there is one monopoly and many customers; viz., the many customers may by their numbers be unable to act collectively.

excellent treatment of all manner of material that has been touched on in this chapter (and much that has not) is given by Tirole (1988). Part I of Tirole covers the basic theory of monopoly and a host of topics including the Coase conjecture, multigood monopolies, nonlinear pricing, the problem of a manufacturing monopoly selling to retailing monopolies, product selection, and advertising. His chapters 8 and 9 give treatments of entry deterrence. (You will have a much easier time with these two chapters after completing part III of this book.)

On the subject of nonlinear pricing and price discrimination, also highly recommended are Phlips (1983) and Wilson (forthcoming).

References

Phlips, L. 1983. *The Economics of Price Discrimination*. Cambridge: Cambridge University Press.

Tirole, J. 1988. *The Theory of Industrial Organization*. Cambridge, Mass.: MIT Press.

Wilson, R. Forthcoming. *Nonlinear Pricing*. Palo Alto, Cal.: Electric Power Research Institute.

9.7. Problems

■ 1. Why is the geometrical procedure for finding the value of marginal revenue at a quantity x given in figure 9.2 correct? Why do we know that a monopoly (which maximizes profits in the traditional way) will produce at larger than efficient scale in figure 9.1(a) and smaller than efficient scale in figure 9.1(b)?

■ 2. What is wrong with the picture in figure 9.5, which is meant to describe the situation of a monopoly I know?

■ 3. Recall that in section 9.4 we considered a large manufacturing monopoly selling to individual retailing monopolies. There were eight retailers, three of whom face demand of the form $p = 12 - 9x$, and five of whom face demand of the form $p = 12 - 6x$. Well, it turns out that there are actually ten retailers — the eight described above and two more who face demand of the form $p = 12 - 2x$. Costs of production and sales are zero. The retailers are price takers in their dealings with the manufacturer. The manufacturer can set a fixed fee F and a per unit charge P; the retailers take these as given and decide (a) whether to participate at all, and (b) if so, how many units to purchase. The fixed fee and per unit charge must be the same for all the retailers; no discrimination is allowed.

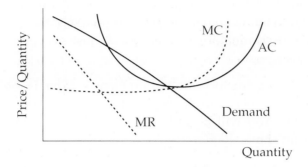

Figure 9.5. Picture for problem 2.

(a) What is the optimal fixed fee to charge if P is set at zero?

(b) What is the optimal fixed fee to charge if $P = 1$?

(c) What is the optimal fixed fee and per-unit charge?

■ 4. In problem 3(c), you found the optimal nondiscriminatory fixed fee-per unit charge pricing scheme for the manufacturer to employ. Now consider general nondiscriminatory schemes. Imagine that the manufacturer is able to publish any sort of price scheme she wants. Being formal about it, the manufacturer picks a function $\Phi : (0, \infty) \rightarrow [0, \infty]$ with the following interpretation: A retailer can purchase quantity x from the manufacturer at a total cost of $\Phi(x)$. We allow $\Phi(x) = \infty$ for some quantities x, with the interpretation that the manufacturer is unwilling to sell that quantity. The manufacturer is able to control resale of this good, so each retailer must live with the scheme Φ; given Φ, each retailer chooses that level x to buy such that its revenues selling x less its costs $\Phi(x)$ are as large as possible. But the manufacturer is unable to discriminate among the retailers; the manufacturer must set a single cost schedule Φ and allow the different retailers each to choose his own preferred point.

(a) Prove that the best the manufacturer can do with such a general nondiscriminatory scheme is strictly worse than what she can do if she is allowed to discriminate (and use general schemes).

(b) To what extent does your proof in part (a) depend on the exact numbers and parameterization in problem 3? Specifically, suppose that we looked at an example in which there were a number of different retailers, all of whom faced demand with the same B but with different A_i.

Would your proof work in this case? And what if both the A_i and B_i varied? Would your proof still work in all cases? Would it only work in some? If the latter, can you characterize precisely those circumstances in which a nondiscriminatory scheme can do just as well as the optimal discriminatory scheme?

(c) Go back to the parameterization of problem 3. What is the best general nondiscriminatory scheme from the point of view of the manufacturer? (This is difficult. You will be in better shape to tackle this part of this problem after finishing chapter 18.)

■ 5. Recall from chapter 8 all the problems about the pfillip industry. In particular, recall that you solved in problem 3 for the market equilibria (in pfillip and kapitose) when the kapitose supply function was given by $q = K/200$ and the demand for pfillip was given by $D(p) = 750 - 150p$. Now consider what will happen in these two industries if the supply of kapitose is controlled by a monopoly whose marginal costs for producing K units of kapitose are $K/200$. (You may well need to resort to numerical solutions.)

We did nothing in this chapter in the way of deriving testable propositions from the standard model. Just so you don't get away without at least a taste of this:

■ 6. Consider a monopoly that faces a downward sloping demand curve $X = D(P)$ and constant unit costs c. We are interested in how this monopoly will adjust the price it charges as c changes.

(a) If demand is linear $X = A - P$, show that less than the full change in costs is passed on to the customers. (That is, if we think of $p(c)$ as the monopoly price, given as a function of cost c, then $dp(c)/dc < 1$.)

(b) Suppose that demand takes the form $X = P^{-\alpha}$ for $\alpha > 1$. Show that the monopoly passes on more than the full cost increase to consumers. (That is, $dp(c)/dc > 1$.)

(c) For which demand functions (if any) will the monopoly precisely pass on to consumers any cost increase? (That is, for which demand functions will $dp(c)/dc = 1$?) You should give demand functions for which this works at every level of c. (Hint: If you begin by drawing the obvious picture in part [a], it may help you see what to do in part [c].)

Since we introduced linear demand in the last two chapters, it might be a good idea to say something about where it comes from. So:

■ 7. In an economy that I know, there are many consumers. One of the goods consumed in this economy is phiffle, a nonnarcotic relaxant. It turns out (for reasons that needn't concern you) that we can represent the preferences of every consumer in this economy as follows: If the consumer consumes x units of phiffle and has $\$z$ left to spend on all other commodities, whose prices are held fixed throughout this problem, the consumer's utility has the form

$$u_i(x) + k_i z,$$

where the subscript i refers to the consumer's index, u_i is a given function, and k_i is a given positive constant. This consumer must consume a nonnegative amount of phiffle and cannot spend more money on phiffle than he has in total, but is otherwise unconstrained.

(a) Suppose the consumer has $\$w$ to spend in total, and the price of phiffle is $\$p$ per unit. Set up, as a constrained maximization problem, the problem of the consumer (who is a price taker) in deciding how much phiffle to consume. Give first-order conditions and (if relevant) complementary slackness conditions.

(b) Suppose in this economy there are ten consumers. Each of these consumers has $u_i(x) = \sqrt{x}$. Three of the consumers have $k_i = 4$; four have $k_i = 3$; and three have $k_i = 2$. Each consumer has $\$1,000$ to spend. What is the market demand curve for phiffle in this case?

(c) Continue to suppose the data from part (b). Imagine that the production of phiffle was controlled by a monopoly with rising marginal costs given by $MC(x) = x$. What will be the price and quantity delivered by this monopoly?

(d) Now we suppose in this economy there are 100 consumers. Each of these consumers has $k_i = 1$, and each has $u_i(x) = x - c_i x^2$ for $x \leq 1/(2c_i)$ and $u_i(x) = 1/(4c_i)$ for $x \geq 1/(2c_i)$. Moreover, the 100 consumers are indexed by $i = 1, \ldots, 100$ and for consumer number i, $c_i = i$. All the consumers in this industry have initial wealth of (at least) 2. What is the market demand curve for phiffle in this case?

(e) Suppose in a somewhat larger economy there are 10,000,000 consumers. This economy is broken into four regions. In region 1, are 4,000,000 consumers; in region 2 are 3,000,000; in region 3 are 2,000,000; and in region 4 are 1,000,000. Inside each region, the consumers are a scaled-up replica of the 100 consumer economy of part (d). That is, in region 2 (say) are 30,000 consumers with $c_i = 1$, 30,000 with $c_i = 2$, etc. What are the demand functions for phiffle in each of these regions?

■ 8. Suppose a monopoly facing the sort of credibility problem sketched in section 9.5 decided to be generous to its customers and offer each one a "most favored customer" contract as outlined there. Create and analyze a formal model that supports some (or, if you can, all) of the intuitive assertions we made. You may ignore the time value of money, to keep the analysis relatively simple. You may wish to return to continue your analysis after you have completed part III of the book.

In the next three problems, you are introduced to ways of modeling demand for differentiated goods and to the problem of a monopoly deciding how many "varieties" of a good to provide. We look at a particularly simple case of this problem; see Tirole (1988, chap. 2) for a much more complete discussion.

■ 9. Imagine a single consumer with the following very strange pattern of demand for a particular good. This good, which we will call a griffle, can come in any number of varieties. Specifically, any griffle is of a type t for some $t \in [0, 1]$. Our consumer is interested in purchasing at most one and precisely one griffle; he will do so *if* there is a griffle whose price and type meet a hurdle that he sets. His preferences and demand behavior for griffles are characterized by a function $r : [0, 1] \rightarrow (0, \infty)$ as follows. Suppose N types of griffles are for sale, types $t_1, t_2, \ldots, t_N$. Suppose that $p(t_n)$ is the price of a griffle of type t_n. Then if for each n, $p(t_n) > r(t_n)$, our consumer will not purchase any griffle. On the other hand, if for some t_n, $p(t_n) \leq r(t_n)$, then our consumer will purchase precisely one unit of some type n that maximizes the difference $r(t_n) - p(t_n)$. Note well: If more than one type n maximizes this difference, our consumer will purchase precisely one unit of some one of the maximands; it is indeterminate which he will purchase. [c]

(a) Suppose that our consumer's demand behavior is characterized by the function $r(t) = r_0 + k|t - t_0|$ for some constants r_0, k, and $t_0 \in [0, 1]$. Being very specific, suppose that $r_0 = 5$, $k = 1$, and $t_0 = .6$. Suppose three types of griffle are being sold: types .3, .5, and .7 at prices 3, 3.3, and 4, respectively. What will our consumer do (in terms of purchasing griffle) in these circumstances?

(b) Fix the prices of types .3 and .7 at 3 and 4, respectively. Draw this

---

[c] You may worry that this sort of demand doesn't conform to our models of consumer preference and demand in chapter 2. But except for an unhappy lack of continuity, this demand behavior can be rationalized by preferences that are representable with a utility function. If you like a real challenge, give one such utility function.

consumer's demand curve for griffle of type .5 as a function of the price of this type of griffle.

You may wonder how to interpret these types of good. One interpretation appropriate for the particular function $r(t)$ given in problem 9 is that there is really only one type of griffle, but the different types refer to locations at which griffle is sold. More precisely, imagine that consumers live along a 100-mile-long highway. Our consumer lives at milepost 60. Our consumer is willing to pay 5 for a unit of griffle, as long as that griffle is delivered to her door. But there is no griffle delivery service. Instead, there are stores along the highway where griffle is sold. Specifically, there are stores at mileposts 30, 50, and 70. It costs our consumer .05 to drive one mile, and she counts this against the purchase cost of griffle. So if griffle is being sold for 3 at the store at milepost 50, she figures this means a roundtrip of 20 miles and an "effective" price to her of $3 + (.05)(20) = 4$. She is willing to buy a unit of griffle if it is sold somewhere at an effective price of 5 or less, and if it is sold at this reservation price or less, she buys it from wherever the effective price is lowest.

■ 10. Now suppose there are many consumers, all of whom have demand of the sort described in problem 9, but with different values of r_0, k, and t_0. We imagine, in fact, there is a "mass" of consumers given by a density function $\phi(r, k, t)$ defined on the space $[0, 10] \times [0, 10] \times [0, 1]$. That is, for any subset $\Lambda \subseteq [0, 10] \times [0, 10] \times [0, 1]$, the number of consumers whose characteristics (r_0, k, t_0) lie within the set Λ is $\int_\Lambda \phi(r, k, t) dr dk dt$.[d]
If ϕ is a uniform density, what does the aggregate demand function for griffle of type .5 look like, if griffle of types .3 and .7 are for sale at prices 3 and 4, respectively. (If you find this too hard, assume that all consumers have $r_0 = 5$, $k = 1$, and t_0 distributed uniformly on the interval $[0, 1]$.)

■ 11. Assume consumers are distributed according to a uniform density ϕ as in problem 10. (If that is too difficult, answer both parts of this question assuming that only t_0 is distributed among the population, with uniform distribution on $[0, 1]$.) Suppose a monopoly manufactures and sells griffle. This monopoly has a constant marginal cost technology, with marginal cost equal to 1.

(a) If the monopoly may sell only one variety of griffle, what variety of griffle will the monopoly sell and at what price?

(b) Suppose the monopoly may sell as many varieties of griffle as it chooses, but it must pay a fixed cost of 1 for every variety of griffle it

---

[d] If you know measure theory, generalize suitably.

chooses to offer. Suppose that the total mass of consumers is 100; that is, $\phi(r, k, t) \equiv 1$ for all $(r, k, t) \in [0, 10] \times [0, 10] \times [0, 1]$. How many varieties of griffle will the monopoly offer? What varieties will be offered? What price will be charged for each?

chapter ten

Imperfect competition

We move next to models of imperfect competition. Firms in these models have rivals, and the actions of their rivals affect how well they do. But at the same time firms are not price takers; when they optimize, they take into account how their actions affect the prices they face both directly and, through possible reactions of their rivals, indirectly.

We will give only a bare introduction to the subject. As in chapter 9, we will cover the rudiments, in this case the classic models of duopoly with undifferentiated goods: Cournot, von Stackelberg, Bertrand, and kinked demand. Then we will discuss informally and briefly some of the many important issues that impinge on the basic models. (The problems present the opportunity to move beyond informal discussion.)

10.1. The classic models of duopoly

We imagine an industry with two vendors/firms, each producing and selling a single good. Consumers don't care from which firm they purchase the good. Demand, as in the theories of perfect competition and monopoly, is given by a demand curve. We'll take a very concrete and simple case of linear demand: $X = A - P$, where P is price, X is total quantity demanded, and A is a constant. We'll assume that the two firms are identical, with constant marginal costs of production k and no fixed costs. (We assume that $A > k$.)

Just to set the stage, we recall the competitive and monopolistic outcomes in this setting. In a competitive industry, price (in the long run) would equal minimum average cost, which in this very simple setting is marginal cost k. So quantity sold would be $X_c = A - k$. If the industry were a monopoly, the monopolist would equate marginal cost k with marginal revenue $A - 2X$, giving equilibrium price $P_m = (A + k)/2$ and equilibrium quantity $X_m = (A - k)/2$.

What differentiates the various models of duopoly are the *conjectures* that each industry participant makes concerning the actions and reactions of its rival. In the typical model, one makes assumptions about those conjectures and then finds the corresponding equilibrium outcome, where an equilibrium is a point at which neither firm in the pursuit of maximal profits wishes to change its own action, given the (re)actions that it *supposes* others will take if it changes its own action.

Cournot equilibrium

In the first model we consider, each firm has *Cournot conjectures* about the actions of its rival: Each of the two firms assumes that the other firm will act in a way to keep fixed the quantity that it sells.

If we suppose that each firm has these conjectures about the other, we can compute what is called the *reaction function* of each to the quantity choice of the other. Suppose that firm 2 has output at level x_2. Firm 1, since it has Cournot conjectures, supposes that firm 2 will not change this level of output. So firm 1 conjectures that as a function of its level of output x_1, price is $A - x_2 - x_1$. The profits of firm 1 as a function of x_1 will be $(A - x_2 - x_1)x_1 - kx_1$. This is maximized (as long as $x_2 \leq A - k$) at

$$x_1^*(x_2) = (A - k - x_2)/2.$$

(To see this, simply differentiate the profit function of firm 1.) This reaction function of firm 1 to firm 2 says how firm 1 reacts (optimally) to the quantity choice of firm 2, based on firm 1's Cournot conjectures about firm 2. Similarly, firm 2's reaction function to firm 1's choice of quantity x_1 is given by

$$x_2^*(x_1) = (A - k - x_1)/2.$$

We are at an *equilibrium* in this industry when neither firm wants to change what it is doing, given how it believes the other firm will react to any change. Here the assumed reaction is to keep the same level of output. So we are at an equilibrium when we are at quantity levels $(\hat{x}_1, \hat{x}_2)$, which are on the two (optimal) reaction functions. That is, $(\hat{x}_1, \hat{x}_2)$ should satisfy $\hat{x}_1 = x_1^*(\hat{x}_2)$ and $\hat{x}_2 = x_2^*(\hat{x}_1)$. Since we have these two reaction functions, we can solve these two equations (in two unknowns) and find that the unique solution is $\hat{x}_1 = \hat{x}_2 = (A - k)/3$. Alternatively, we can graph the two reaction functions in (x_1, x_2) space and find this intersection point graphically; this is done for you in figures 10.1 and 10.2. In figure 10.1, we graph the reaction function of firm 1 to firm 2, with iso-profit curves

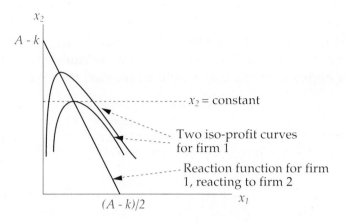

Figure 10.1. A Cournot reaction function and the iso-profit curves from which it is built.

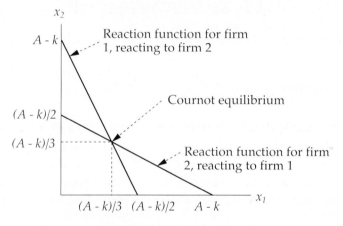

Figure 10.2. The Cournot equilibrium.

for firm 1.[1] Note that the reaction function for firm 1 is the locus of points where its iso-profit curves are tangent to lines of the form x_2 = constant. In figure 10.2, we superimpose the reaction functions of the two firms. Where they intersect is the Cournot equilibrium.

At this *Cournot equilibrium*, total output is the sum of the two equilibrium quantity choices, or $X_C = 2(A - k)/3$, and price is $P_C = A - X_C = A/3 + 2k/3$. Note that the Cournot equilibrium price is higher than the competitive price but lower than the monopoly price. Prices aren't

---

[1] An iso-profit curve for firm 1 is a locus of points (x_1, x_2) that give the same level of profit to firm 1; that is, for a given constant C, the C-iso-profit curve is the set of points such that $(A - x_1 - x_2 - k)x_1 = C$.

competitive, because each firm takes into account that it depresses price when it raises output. (That is, firms are not price takers.) But firms, by raising quantity, don't feel the full brunt of the depressed price; their competitor feels some of this as well. Hence the equilibrium is at a lower price and higher quantity than would be the case for a monopoly.

In the analysis above, we took as the decision variable the quantity chosen by each firm. We could, with greater algebraic difficulty, have made price the decision variable. At the risk of confusing matters, let us go through this exercise: Suppose firm 2 is producing a quantity x_2. Firm 1 can choose the optimal equilibrium price P for itself under the Cournot conjectures that x_2 will remain the output of firm 2. Of course, not every price P is available to firm 1; it can't have a price $P > A - x_2$, since such a price would be inconsistent with firm 2 selling x_2. And, we can presume, it won't want to choose a price P lower than zero. In fact, it won't want to choose a price P lower than k, since its average costs will be k. So suppose it chooses a price P from $[k, A - x_2]$. Under its Cournot conjectures, it will sell a quantity $x_1 = A - x_2 - P$ for a profit of $(P - k)(A - x_2 - P)$. The optimal choice of P as a function of x_2 is $P^*(x_2) = (A - x_2 + k)/2$. Similarly, as a function of x_1, firm 2 will want the market price to be $P^*(x_1) = (A - x_1 + k)/2$. We solve for the equilibrium with the conditions that at the equilibrium price and quantities the price that each side desires should be equal to each other and to the equilibrium price. That is,

$$P^*(\hat{x}_2) = P^*(\hat{x}_1) = A - \hat{x}_1 - \hat{x}_2, \quad \text{or}$$

$$(A - \hat{x}_2 + k)/2 = (A - \hat{x}_1 + k)/2 = A - \hat{x}_1 - \hat{x}_2,$$

which simplifies to the equilibrium we computed before: $\hat{x}_1 = \hat{x}_2 = (A - k)/3$. Why go through this algebra when we already had the answer? We wish to stress that to say that firms have Cournot conjectures is not to say they take quantity (and not price) to be their decision variable. Rather, Cournot conjectures are conjectures about the response of the other firm, namely that the other firm will (re)act in a way to keep the quantity that it sells fixed. [a]

Von Stackelberg equilibrium

Continue to suppose that firm 2 has Cournot conjectures about the actions of firm 1, so that firm 2's reaction as a function of the quantity choice x_1 of firm 1 is $x_2^*(x_1) = (A - x_1 - k)/2$. But suppose that firm 1 does not have Cournot conjectures. Instead, firm 1 believes (correctly, as

---

[a] Although it will seem cryptic to most readers, a further comment is in order for those of you who have read about Cournot equilibrium elsewhere. The statements just made do not contradict an assertion we will make at the end of this chapter and more coherently in chapter 12, namely that one reason to suppose that firms have Cournot conjectures is that quantity output is the decision variable of each firm. For those of you to whom this is hopelessly cryptic, wait until the end of chapter 12 before panicking.

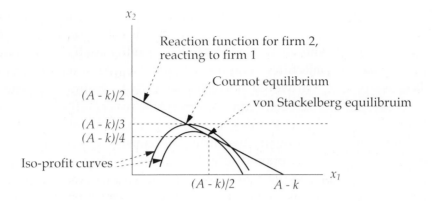

Figure 10.3. The von Stackelberg equilibrium.

it turns out) that firm 2 will react to firm 1's choice of quantity in Cournot fashion. That is, firm 1 believes that firm 2 will be influenced by x_1; firm 2 will set $x_2 = x_2^*(x_1)$. In this case, firm 1 selects x_1 to

$$\max_{x_1}[(A - x_1 - x_2^*(x_1))x_1 - kx_1].$$

Substituting for $x_2^*(x_1)$ and differentiating with respect to x_1, this yields an optimal quantity choice for firm 1 of $\hat{x}_1 = (A-k)/2$, which in turn leads to a choice by firm 2 of $\hat{x}_2 = x_2^*((A - k)/2) = (A - k)/4$, total quantity of $3(A - k)/4$, and equilibrium price of $A/4 + 3k/4$.

This is known as the *von Stackelberg* model of duopoly, with firm 1 the so-called von Stackelberg *leader* and firm 2 the *follower*. To be more precise, we should call this the Cournot-von Stackelberg model, since it is assumed that the follower has Cournot conjectures, and the leader knows (and uses) this fact.

The "picture" for this equilibrium is given in figure 10.3. We see here the reaction function of firm 2, and iso-profit curves for firm 1. Firm 1 is choosing from the reaction function of firm 2 that point which maximizes its own profits.

Two von Stackelberg leaders and consistency of conjectures at the equilibrium

Suppose that both firms had the conjectures of firm 1 above. That is, firm 1 conjectures that firm 2 will respond to x_1 with $x_2^*(x_1)$ and firm 2 conjectures that firm 1 will respond to x_2 with $x_1^*(x_2)$. What would be the equilibrium in this case?

Presumably, the only possibility for an equilibrium is where both firms produce $(A - k)/2$. But is this an equilibrium? If firm 1 sees firm 2 producing $(A - k)/2$ when it is producing this quantity itself, it will surely recognize that its conjectures about firm 2 are false, and similarly for firm 2. Because of this, we would not call this an equilibrium. In general, we will say that we have an equilibrium when two conditions are met: Neither firm, given its conjectures, wishes to change what it is doing; *and* the equilibrium actions of the two firms are consistent with the conjectures that each firm is supposed to hold. In the Cournot and the single-leader von Stackelberg stories, the equilibrium quantities (and prices) were consistent with the firms' conjectures. In the case of Cournot, this is by default; each firm conjectures that the other won't change its quantity, which is consistent with any pair of quantities for the two firms. In the case of von Stackelberg, there is a bit more to this: Firm 2's conjectures about firm 1 (that firm 1 will not change its quantity) hold by default; and firm 1's conjectures about firm 2 hold because of firm 2's conjectures and corresponding reaction. But in the case of two von Stackelberg leaders, there is no equilibrium. The only point at which firms' conjectures about each other are consistent with the situation is where each firm produces $(A - k)/3$. And at that point, both firms, given their conjectures, wish to increase their output.

We will not stress this consistency condition in what follows except in one place. But you should check along the way that the equilibria we describe do give situations where each firm's conjectures about the other are not disconfirmed by the equilibrium activity levels.

Bertrand equilibrium

The two firms are said to have Bertrand conjectures if each believes that the other will not change the price that it is quoting. Now this poses something of a quandary. Suppose the equilibrium price of a good is, say, $10. We typically assume that this means that both firms (in a duopoly) charge $10. Put yourself in the place of one of the two firms and imagine that you (a) have Bertrand conjectures and (b) contemplate lowering your price to $9 (or otherwise taking actions that would cause the market price to fall to $9). What, precisely, does it mean to say that your rival will maintain a price of $10?

Presumably, since the goods in question are undifferentiated, everyone would rather buy from you than from your rival, if you are really selling at $9 and your opponent at $10. So we will assume just this: If, in these circumstances, you contemplate lowering your price to $9, and you anticipate that your rival will hold to a price of $10, then you anticipate that the whole of the market demand at $9 will queue up outside your door clamoring to make a purchase from you. Your opponent, meanwhile, will face a queue without customers. Now, will you be willing to serve all those customers? Perhaps yes and perhaps no — it depends on how many customers are queued and at what point your marginal costs equal $9. But, for the time being, we will assume that for some reason (perhaps legal) you are forced to sell all the demand that comes to your door.

At the same time, if in a given situation the market price is $10, you hold Bertrand conjectures, and you contemplate raising your price, then you contemplate that all your customers will go to your rival, and you make no sales.

Now suppose that you are in an equilibrium situation, where both firms charge the same price, say $10. And suppose that at a price of $10, there is demand of $A - 10$. How is that demand divided between the two firms? This is quite indeterminate. Any number of divisions of market demand between the two firms is consistent with a price of $10. So in looking for a Bertrand equilibrium, we will describe situations in terms of the prices firms are charging and the demand they are serving, where prices and demand served must be consistent with the rules: If the two firms charge unequal prices, the demand served by the low-price firm must equal all of market demand at that price (and the high-price firm gets no sales); and if the two firms charge the same price, total market demand at that price is divided in some arbitrary, but specified, way between the two firms.

Why didn't we need to worry about this in the context of Cournot and von Stackelberg equilibria? That is, why did we simply suppose that the two firms would both wish to charge the market clearing price, so that we could deal in an equilibrium in terms of the two quantity levels of output? For one thing, in any situation where both firms sell strictly positive amounts, they must be selling at the same price, at least in the model under consideration. But still we might worry about an equilibrium where one firm charged a higher price than the other and made no sales; if you wish to be very careful about things, you can go back and reassure yourself that in neither of the previous two cases would such a situation be an equilibrium.[2]

We could next try to construct "reaction functions" just the way we did in the subsection on Cournot conjectures, to find equilibria. But each

---

[2] Once again, for those of you who have seen the Bertrand "story" before and remember it as being less convoluted than this, bear with this convoluted story. This way of doing things will eventually lead you to a better understanding of just what is going on than will direct reference to the less convoluted story that you may have heard.

firm's reaction to a particular "situation" is a bit more complex in this case, since how one reacts to a situation in which the two are charging the identical price may depend on how demand is divided between them. It is easier in this case to try to reason directly about what sort of situation could conceivably be an equilibrium.

An equilibrium will consist of a pair of prices $(\hat{p}_1, \hat{p}_2)$ and a pair of quantities $(\hat{x}_1, \hat{x}_2)$ where:

(a) if $\hat{p}_1 < \hat{p}_2$, then $\hat{x}_1 = A - \hat{p}_1$ and $\hat{x}_2 = 0$

(b) if $\hat{p}_2 < \hat{p}_1$, then $\hat{x}_2 = A - \hat{p}_2$ and $\hat{x}_1 = 0$

(c) if $\hat{p}_1 = \hat{p}_2$, then $\hat{x}_1 + \hat{x}_2 = A - \hat{p}_1$

and, most critically (d) neither firm wishes to change the situation, given that it holds to Bertrand conjectures.

Now we proceed by cases.

(1) *Could there be an equilibrium where the prices are unequal and where the smaller of the two prices is more than k?* No, because in such a situation, the firm charging the higher price is selling nothing and by undercutting the price charged by its rival this firm will capture the entire market, making positive profits as long as it undercuts its rival at a price that still exceeds k.

(2) *Could there be an equilibrium where the prices are unequal and where the smaller of the two prices is less than or equal to k?* No, because in such a situation the firm charging the lower price would wish to raise its price at least a bit. If the high-price firm is charging more than k, then the low-price firm can move from a loss or zero profits (which it incurs by charging a price below or equal to k) to a profit (by charging more than k and a bit less than the other firm), and if the high-price firm is charging k or less, the lower-price firm is charging strictly less than k and so is taking losses, which it can avoid by charging anything above the price charged by the high-price firm.

(3) *Could there be an equilibrium where the prices are equal to each other and equal to something less than k?* No, because then one firm or the other is taking losses (we can't say which one, because we don't know whether both are making positive sales, but one at least is doing so), and that firm would do better to change to a higher price and make zero profits.

(4) *Could there be an equilibrium where the prices are equal to each other and equal to something more than k?* No, because then at least one of the two firms would do better by shaving its price slightly. To see this, note that

one or the other is selling no more than half the market demand at the equilibrium price, so that firm believes that it can more than double its sales by decreasing price slightly. This causes the profit per unit sold to decline, but if it shaves its price only a bit, then the profit per unit won't fall by half, and so total profits will increase.

So the only possibility left is where $\hat{p}_1 = \hat{p}_2 = k$. And any division of market demand between the two firms at those prices is an equilibrium. This is so because each firm makes exactly zero profits in this configuration, which is the best it can do given Bertrand conjectures about its rival. If it lowers its price, it will take a loss on any unit it sells. And if it raises its price, it will make no sales, and hence continue to have zero profit. Even if it could change its share of demand (and we haven't indicated how it might conceivably do that), it has no incentive to do so, since it makes zero profit on each and every unit it might sell.

> *The remainder of this subsection is a bit esoteric, and even readers who religiously read through the small type may wish to avoid it on a first reading.* The analysis given above assumes that a firm must serve any demand that comes to its door. If we modify that assumption, the analysis looks a bit different. To make this precise, however, we have to specify the "mechanics" of the market — what happens if one firm refuses to serve some of the demand that comes to it. The issue here is best understood by considering a case where one firm quotes a price p_1 and the other a price p_2, for $p_1 < p_2$. Then demand at the lower price is $A - p_1$. Suppose that, for whatever reason, firm 1 is only willing to fill $x_1 < A - p_1$ worth of demand. Some of the unsatisfied demand *may* be willing to buy at price p_2. Having been turned away at firm 1, do these consumers get a chance to go to firm 2? And, if so, how much demand turns up at firm 2? If we imagine, for example, that all consumers have identical utility functions and that firm 1 rations its output x_1 equally among all the consumers who show up, then it is "natural" to assume that the demand that moves to firm 2 is $A - p_2 - x_1$, as long as this is positive. (Why is this the natural solution? We won't go into details here, but this makes a good homework problem.) On the other hand, firm 1 might engage in the following rationing scheme: All the consumers who show up are given numbers. Then numbers are drawn randomly; the consumer whose number is drawn first gets to demand as much as he or she wants at p_1. Then a second number is drawn, and so on, until all x_1 units are sold. This sort of rationing scheme leads to the conclusion that firm 2's demand is $(A - p_1 - x_1)(A - p_2)/(A - p_1)$. (Another good homework problem! In fact, here are two good homework problems, since it isn't so natural to assume that this is firm 2's demand if the good in question can be resold.) Moreover, when we analyze the conjectures of each firm about the other, we have to specify conjectures about how much demand each thinks the other will serve at various prices. This is too hard for now, so we will stick to the simple analysis given. But, if you have read this far, do take careful note: To make sense of this story, we had

to begin to be very specific about the "structure" of the marketplace. This, it turns out, will be the key to sorting through the various stories of classic oligopoly.

While we are here, it is a good time to mention another variation on the Bertrand story, which is also too hard for a first pass. This is the *Edgeworth-Bertrand* model, in which firms have Bertrand conjectures about each other (neither will change the price it charges), but each has capacity constraints on the amount of demand it can serve. Firms are assumed to fill all the demand that they can up to their capacity constraints. But there may be unsatisfied demand at some prices because of the capacity constraints. And then we need to specify what becomes of that demand. Does it go to the other firm, and in what quantity? Exactly the sorts of considerations given above intrude.

Another comment to make here is that the assumption that each firm is "forced" to serve all the demand that comes to its door is reasonable in the case we have been considering — constant marginal costs. This is so because no firm will (one expects) ever quote a price below its marginal cost, and so it is willing to serve any demand that does come along. But suppose we tried to redo our analysis in a setting where marginal costs were rising. To be very specific, suppose that we have two identical firms whose marginal costs of production at level x are x^2. (That is, total cost of production of x units is $x^3/3$.) And suppose that the constant A in the demand function is 12. One Bertrand equilibrium, which is analogous to perfect competition, comes where price equals the marginal costs of the two firms. This is where $12 - (x_1 + x_2) = x_1^2 = x_2^2$, or (approximately) $x_1 = x_2 = 2.605$, for a price of 6.789. Note that at this Bertrand equilibrium each firm makes a positive profit, since it has strictly rising marginal costs, and price equals marginal cost at the equilibrium. Note also why this is a Bertrand equilibrium: If either firm raises its price, then it loses all its demand and makes zero profits. (It causes its rival to take substantial losses, but the firms in this story don't care about that.) If it lowers its price just a bit, it can (more than) double its demand. But every additional unit demanded is at a price below the marginal cost for that unit. So profits will go down.

Now consider the situation in which each firm quotes a price of 8, for total demand of four units, or two per firm. (This, it turns out, would be the industry supply if the two firms acted as a single monopoly firm, splitting production efficiently between them.) At this point, each firm has revenue of 16 and costs of 8/3 for a profit of 13.333. Now if either firm raises its price from this point, it gets no demand at all. Whereas if a firm lowers its price a bit, it will (expect to) get a bit more than twice its demand. Ignoring the penny, if it shaves the price by a penny, it doubles its revenues to 32. But its costs shoot up to 21.333, for a net profit of 10.667. So we have another "Bertrand" equilibrium.

Of course, this second equilibrium supposed that a firm must meet all the demand that comes its way at the price it quotes. If the firm could shave its price by a penny from 8 and then only fill the orders it wishes to (up to where its marginal costs equal 8), then it would indeed increase its profits. So our second "Bertrand" equilibrium would collapse if firms could turn away demand. But then our first equilibrium would collapse as well. Recall that there both firms quoted price 6.789. Neither firm will want to lower its price. But suppose that one of the two firms raised its price. The other firm, at a price of 6.789, would not wish to supply more than 2.605 units, since any additional units (at a price of 6.789) would lower its profits. (Marginal cost at 2.605 units is 6.789, recall.) So what demand would face the firm that raises its price? This depends, once again, on the rationing rule that the other firm uses to ration out the 2.605 units that it will sell. But whatever that rationing rule is, as long as the first firm sees some smooth fall in its output as it raises price, it will want to raise price to some extent. Why? Equate the first firm's marginal revenue to marginal cost and reexpress marginal revenue as price times $(1 + 1/\epsilon)$, where ϵ is the elasticity of demand facing the first firm as it raises its price. As long as the elasticity is finite (essentially, as long as its demand falls off smoothly) and marginal costs are nondecreasing, the first firm will raise its price from marginal cost. Most sensible rationing rules, including the two we discussed above, will have demand fall off smoothly. Thus price-equals-marginal-cost won't be a Bertrand equilibrium, when firms can refuse some demand and marginal costs are (strictly) increasing.

So what will be a Bertrand equilibrium? No pair of prices will do in this instance, at least if the firms have the same cost function. For suppose there were a pair of prices and a pair of quantities that would work. One case is that the two prices are the same. Then either that price is at the marginal cost of the two firms, and we saw that this wasn't possible, or it is above the marginal costs of the firms. This isn't possible either, since at least one of the two firms, by cutting price just a bit, can increase its demand discontinuously. As long as price is above marginal cost, profits will increase strictly by such a move. And if the two are quoting different prices, the lower price will have to be the monopoly price or above for one firm, since it acts "as if" it has the entire industry demand curve for itself.[b] But then the firm with the higher price by cutting its price to just below that charged by the firm with the lower price will certainly do better. At this point, it is best that we leave Bertrand competition.

Kinked demand

The last classical model we will look at concerns kinked demand. A version of this is phrased in terms of "price conjectures," and another is phrased in terms of "quantity conjectures." We'll do the latter, as it makes sense a bit more easily.

In this model, the conjectures of each firm about the other depend on the equilibrium attained. Suppose we are in a situation where the two firms are producing, respectively, $\hat{x}_1$ and $\hat{x}_2$. At this point, firm 1 conjectures that firm 2 will continue to produce $\hat{x}_2$ as long as firm 1 produces $\hat{x}_2$ or less. But, firm 1 conjectures, if it attempts to produce an amount x_1 greater than $\hat{x}_2$, then firm 2 will increase its output to match

---

[b] For rigor freaks, this implicitly assumes that the revenue curve in the industry is concave. Can you see the argument if this assumption doesn't hold?

whatever firm 1 produces. And firm 2 has symmetric conjectures about firm 1.

Where do *these* conjectures come from? They are, like all the other conjectures discussed so far, simply supposed. We've so far seen no reasons to support the hypothesis that they are reasonable conjectures. Which isn't to say that they aren't reasonable — each firm may well react in just this fashion. All we are saying is that we have no theoretical grounds to suppose that this will be so.

We note immediately that the consistency condition discussed back in the subsection on two von Stackelberg leaders plays a role here: The only points that are consistent with the firms' conjectures are where $\hat{x}_1 = \hat{x}_2$. This is so because, if $\hat{x}_1 < \hat{x}_2$ (say), then firm 2 conjectures that firm 1 will increase its quantity to $\hat{x}_2$ and symmetrically if $\hat{x}_2 < \hat{x}_1$. Accordingly, we can restrict attention to situations where the two firms pick identical levels of output, and we will use $\hat{x}$ to denote that level.

In this case, reaction functions can be used again. What will the reaction functions look like in this case? Suppose that firm 2 is at output level $\hat{x} = x_2$. Firm 1's problem, then, is to

$$\max_{x_1}(A - x_1 - y_2(x_1, \hat{x}) - k)x_1,$$

where $y_2(x_1, \hat{x}) = \max\{x_1, \hat{x}\}$. (That is, y_2 gives firm 2's supposed response to x_1, which is to produce $x_2 = \hat{x}$ if firm 1 produces $\hat{x}$ or less and to match firm 1's output above $\hat{x}$.) This gives firm 1 a marginal revenue curve that is discontinuous. For $x_1 < x_2$, firm 1's marginal revenue is $A - x_2 - 2x_1$. For $x_1 > x_2$, firm 1's marginal revenue curve is $A - 4x_1$. Firm 1's optimal response is given by the level of x_1 at which marginal revenue equals marginal cost k. This is

$$x_1^*(x_2) = \begin{cases} (A - k - x_2)/2 & \text{if } (A - k - x_2)/2 \le x_2 \text{ (i.e., } x_2 \ge (A - k)/3\text{);} \\ (A - k)/4 & \text{if } (A - k)/4 \ge x_2\text{; and} \\ x_2 & \text{for } (A - k)/4 \le x_2 \le (A - k)/3. \end{cases}$$

We can draw some pictures of this muddle. First, for fixed $\hat{x} = x_2$, firm 1 sees its demand curve as the curve given in figure 10.4. Note well the kink — that is why this is called the theory of the kinked demand curve. The kink falls precisely at $x_1 = x_2$, which is where firm 2's (supposed) behavior changes. This demand curve gives the marginal revenue curve shown. Note the discontinuity in the marginal revenue curve, which falls at the position of the kink. And now we see why we get the funny reaction

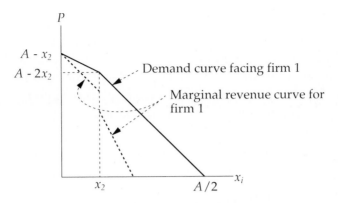

Figure 10.4. Demand and marginal revenue
for the story of kinked demand.

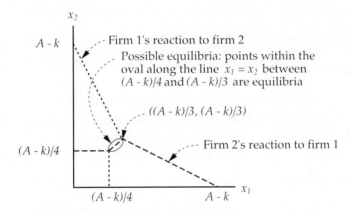

Figure 10.5. The two reaction curves for kinked demand.

curve described above (and drawn in figure 10.5). If x_2 is small enough, then the marginal revenue curve passes through the level k on its "bottom segment." If x_2 is rather large, then the marginal revenue curve passes through the level of k on its "top segment." And for a range of x_2, marginal revenue jumps from above k to below k at its discontinuity point. For those values of x_2, the optimal response of the firm 1 is just to match firm 2's output.

So what are the equilibria? We have also drawn on figure 10.5 the reaction function of firm 2 to firm 1's choice of quantity output. The two intersect at a number of points, namely $x_1 = x_2 (= \hat{x})$ between $(A-k)/4$ and $(A-k)/3$. *Any* of these give an equilibrium. Note that this ranges from the monopoly outcome (total supply is $(A-k)/2$ and price is $(A+k)/2$) down to the Cournot outcome (total supply is $2(A-k)/3$ and price is $A/3 + 2k/3$).

Which of the classic models of duopoly is correct?

We have seen that the models of Cournot, Bertrand, and von Stackelberg all make distinctly different predictions as to what will happen in the duopoly situation we describe. The model of kinked demand makes a number of different predictions, any of which might happen, which widens the set of predictions still further. Which, if any, of these predictions will be borne out by data?

In the end, the answer to this question must be empirical. And it will probably be that none of the models is correct in all cases of real oligopoly. Instead, one may be able to develop propositions such as: Across a set of industries, long-run equilibria more closely resemble the predictions of Cournot, say, the more the industry has the characteristics _____ (fill in the blank). To form a better test of such propositions, one would like to see why, on theoretical grounds, certain characteristics might go well with certain of the classic models.

The sorts of characteristics that might be studied are those concerned with the actual mechanics by which price is set and demand is filled in an industry. The classic models above are quite deficient in this respect. Demand is given, and equilibrium conjectures about out-of-equilibrium responses are specified. But (except for when we discussed rationing in the Bertrand model) no attention is paid to how equilibria are achieved.

To take five extreme cases, suppose that the mechanics of the industry are one of the following:

(a) Two producers work in isolation, preparing the quantity they bring to market. They decide upon these quantities with a foreknowledge of this market structure and with knowledge of the characteristics of demand, but neither side gets to see how much the other is producing. After production is completed, each side brings the quantity it produced to a central market place, where it is handed over to a "state sales commission" that sets price so that the total amount brought to market is just demanded at the set price.

(b) We have the same two producers as above and the same state sales commission, but one producer is able to produce its quantity first. That is, this producer brings to the market a quantity x_1, which the second producer observes. And then the second producer decides on an amount x_2 to produce, knowing that price will be set so that the market clears at total quantity $x_1 + x_2$.

(c) Things work much differently in this case. The two producers independently call the state sales commission and give a price at which each is willing to sell. The state sales commission investigates market demand at those prices, and then calls back the two producers, telling them how much they are obligated to bring to the market. (Or, to take a variation, the state sales commission tells the one quoting a lower price how much it may bring, if it wishes. After the first says how much demand it will service, the state sales commission calls the higher price producer. The state sales commission has a particular rationing scheme it uses in cases where a firm doesn't wish to service all the demand it gets.)

(d) Back to our two producers who produce quantities independently. But now they call the state marketing commission in advance, saying how much they plan to bring. And if one says it will bring more than the other, the second is given permission by the state marketing commission to bring up to the amount being brought by the first.

(e) This one is very complex. The two producers must first install capacity for production. Capacity is costly, coming at a cost of k_1 per unit capacity installed. Capacity is installed by the two simultaneously and independently. Then each sees how much capacity the other installed. And then each calls the state marketing commission and quotes a price at which it is willing to sell. Production is possible up to the level of capacity at an additional marginal cost of k_2 per unit where $k = k_1 + k_2$. No production beyond the level of capacity is possible. If a capacity constraint does bind when prices are named, the state marketing commission rations demand by some system or other. This good is resaleable among consumers, and all consumers are aware of market demand conditions.

In scenario (a), Cournot conjectures make particularly good sense. Each side believes that the other won't change its quantity in the face of a "change" by the one for the simple reason that neither side has the opportunity to change its quantity. In scenario (b), von Stackelberg seems sensible. The second firm (presumably) takes the first firm's quantity supply as given, since it is given, and maximizes its own profits. So it works off its reaction curve. And the first firm, if it understands this, would pick an initial quantity so that it maximizes its profits with the second firm's optimal response coming from that reaction curve. Scenario (c) leads naturally to Bertrand conjectures for the same reason that scenario (a) leads to Cournot. Scenario (d) may remind you of kinked demand, but it isn't quite the same; we have to check that if one firm outproduces the second the second will wish to respond by increasing its output unit for unit. (Any guesses about how this will turn out? Sounds like a good homework problem.) And scenario (e) probably reminds you of nothing you've ever seen before. But, it turns out, it leads fairly naturally to a prediction of Cournot outcomes. Seeing that this is so is fairly difficult.[c]

Do any of these models match the market mechanics of any industry you can think of? Probably not. For one (important) thing, each of them is a story of a one-shot encounter between two firms. Any of them could be complicated by adding, "... and the same thing happens again every month, with the two firms discounting profits at a rate of (say) 10% per year." We will see in chapter 14 that this complication is extraordinarily significant.

The answer to the question posed at the start of this subsection is that no one of the classic models is going to give accurate predictions in every case. Each makes sense (and should give accurate predictions, although this remains an empirical question) if you have in mind a particular detailed mechanism for how the market operates. None will make sense if you have in mind some different mechanisms. You *might* be able to tell whether (or when) one model or another should give a good prediction by looking at the details of the market mechanism. But this will require a theory of how to move from market mechanics to outcomes.

We will use techniques from noncooperative game theory for this purpose. The key to these techniques is that one is very precise about the mechanics of the competitive interaction, saying precisely who moves when, with how much information. By being precise in this fashion, one *sometimes* gets quite sharp predictions. (As we'll see, at other times the predictions are anything but sharp.) We will begin to develop these techniques in chapter 11, and we will return to the classic models of duopoly at the end of chapter 12. But before doing so, we discuss a few further basic ideas from the theory of imperfect competition.

10.2. Bibliographic notes and discussion

The treatment of duopoly with undifferentiated commodities that we have given is adequate for our present purpose of developing the basic tools of microeconomic theory. But this treatment is both a bit unfair to the classical references themselves, which give a much more reasoned explanation of from where the sundry conjectures might come and more than a bit incomplete as a sampling of what is important in the theory of oligopoly and, more generally, imperfect competition. The reader can repair the injustice by reading the classics: Cournot (1838), Bertrand (1883),

---

[c] And if after the next two chapters you wish to see how it works, see Kreps and Scheinkman (1983). Good luck.

von Stackelberg (1934), Hall and Hitch (1939) and Sweezy (1939) (the last two for kinked demand). And, preferably after completing this book, the reader can plunge into the rich theory of imperfect competition quite efficiently by studying Tirole (1988). (By recommending Tirole alone, I do not mean to slight other books. But Tirole gives a comprehensive treatment of most important theoretical issues, with everything done in the most modern style, a style for which the rest of this book is meant to prepare you.)

We will in later chapters return to some of the issues connected with oligopoly and imperfect competition. But these are issues that take many pages to do justice to, so for the most part we do not pursue important variations on the basic models above. To whet your appetite, then, we close with the mention of some of the more important variations.

Oligopoly

We examined only the case of duopoly and, at that, the case of two identical firms. Many oligopolies have more than two firms and/or firms that are not identical; it is obviously germane to extend our models accordingly. Solving for the N–firm symmetric Cournot and Bertrand equilibria, where the firms are identical, demand curves are linear, and production technologies are linear, is an entirely straightforward exercise. (In fact, it is problem 5.) Looking for asymmetric equilibria, which is necessary when firms are not identical, is a bit, but only a bit, harder (cf. problems 6 and 7).

Entry and exit

Why are there only a given number of firms in an oligopoly? Especially when firms in the industry are making profits, we can wonder why the industry doesn't attract entry. In the case of monopoly, one can make a case based on legal restrictions. For oligopolies, similar cases can be made in some instances — only a certain number of firms may be licensed to make a particular product. These licenses may come from the government, say in the production of pharmaceuticals or pesticides or in VHF broadcasting, or they may be granted by a monopoly holder of a patented process.[3]

But more often the explanation is that there are economic (instead of legal) *barriers to entry*. The threat of cut-throat competition by incumbent

---

[3] Why would a patent holder ever license another firm to produce the product on which it holds the patent, instead of producing the product as a monopolist? For one story, see problem 19 of chapter 12.

firms can hold other firms out of the industry. (When spun out into a model, this story becomes a more sophisticated version of story of entry deterrence in monopoly that was caricatured in chapter 9.) There may be technological or "knowledge" barriers to entry; breaking into the business of manufacturing large commercial jet airframes is, to say the least, difficult for a firm that has no experience making jet aircraft. And fixed costs by themselves may prove to be barriers to entry — see problem 8 below.

Taking a more detailed look at an industry, there may be segments, some of which are inhabited by some firms, others inhabited by others. Then the notion of an entry barrier is transformed into the notion of a mobility barrier — something that prevents firm A from moving into the profitable sector of the industry inhabited by firm B. For a normative discussion of entry and mobility barriers, see Porter (1980).[4]

When asking why there are only four or five (or however many) firms in a particular industry, one can think of the industry as static; the focus is on a long-term stationary situation, in which no new firms enter (and no incumbent firms leave). In a sense, these are not theories of entry, but theories of no-entry. A different perspective comes from looking at an industry or a product more dynamically; think of industries that grow and industries that decline. There have been a number of studies (of varying degrees of formality) about entry and exit decisions of firms in such industries, studies of which firms enter at which stage of industry growth, and which depart as the market shrinks away.

Differentiated commodities

In the formal models discussed in this chapter, the duopolists were assumed to be producing and selling undifferentiated commodities. Note especially that it was the undifferentiated character of the product that led to the extreme results of Bertrand competition, since a penny less in price by one firm meant that firm got all the demand.

Some oligopolies produce virtually undifferentiated commodities — producers of industrial chemicals, for example.[5] But in many oligopolies, the products sold are (or are made to seem) different. A Chevrolet and a Ford or a Toyota and a Honda of roughly the same size and character may be similar, but consumers perceive differences between them; if

---

[4] That is, Porter is writing for oligopolists, explaining how to build and maintain entry and mobility barriers.

[5] Even in this case there is some differentiation in the "goods" having to do with relationships between the producer and the client firm. The test of how much differentiation exists is quite simple: How much lower a price would one firm have to charge than all others before it stole virtually the entire market from its rivals?

Toyota charges \$500 less than Honda for a similar car, it may increase its demand at Honda's expense, but some loyal customers will still stick with Honda.

If we just take as given that oligopolists produce differentiated commodities where the differences (and corresponding cross-elasticities of demand) are exogenously imposed, we can redo much of the simple duopoly theory we developed above. (You will do this in problem 9.) But it is even more interesting to consider whether oligopolists will endogenously strive to differentiate their products. The reason to engage in differentiation should be clear: Especially if we believe in the Bertrand model, but in any model where oligopolists "compete," the more they differentiate their goods from one another, the less competition there will be, and the more each can engage in something like monopoly pricing. (See problem 10 for one example.) On the other hand, if your rival has fixed his product in a certain "position" in terms of its attributes, by moving the characteristics of your product closer to his you are providing for yourself a broader market. Starting with Hotelling (1929), there has been great interest in the extent to which oligopolists engage in willful product differentiation and whether the amount of product variety provided is more or less than is socially desirable. Tirole (1988, chap. 7) gives a good survey.

Research and development

Nowhere in this book have we (or, except at the very end, will we) think about the dynamic process of research and development in which new products and production technologies are discovered, developed, and refined. These issues transcend the setting of oligopoly. We can investigate how much R&D will be undertaken in competitive industries and by monopolies, but oligopoly is a particularly fertile field for inquiry into these questions, since the rivalry between oligopolists is meant to provide strong incentives to engage in R&D (incentives that are weaker at best in monopoly, except for the cases where patents reward successful R&D with further monopoly). At the same time, oligopolists have the wherewithal to engage in large scale R&D. As usual, our suggestion is to begin to study these topics with Tirole (1988, chap. 10).

Monopolistic competition

We come in the end to the "other" model of competition between imperfectly competitive firms, the model of *monopolistic competition* as developed by Chamberlin (1933). Most books on intermediate microeconomics (and many principles books) develop this theory in detail, as much detail or more than is given to oligopoly. In comparison with oligopoly, the theory is remarkably

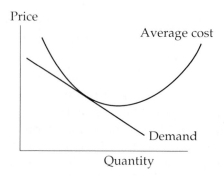

Figure 10.6. Equilibrium in a monopolistically competitive industry.

determinate — it gives simple and clean answers complete with a very interesting picture (figure 10.6). Were it not for the presence of this theory in most lower level texts we would ignore it here altogether. But since many readers will have seen it and wonder how it fits into the general picture being presented here, we will offer a very fast recapitulation and then some criticisms.

The story of monopolistic competition runs as follows: We imagine an industry for a product that can be produced in many different varieties. There are many firms in the industry and many more waiting on the sidelines to enter if entry seems profitable. Each firm produces a particular (unique) variety of the product in question. Each firm's technology is described by a U-shaped average cost curve, given, say, by a fixed cost plus increasing marginal cost technology. If we compute demand curves for each firm by varying the price charged by the firm while holding other prices fixed, each firm faces a downward sloping demand curve. This downward sloping demand curve arises because each firm produces a product that has unique characteristics and so attracts (to some extent) its own clientele.

Each firm believes that it can adjust its price/quantity to be any point along its own demand curve without engendering a change in price for any of its many rivals, so each approaches its own demand curve as would a monopolist; each sets marginal revenue equal to marginal cost, finding the price to set and quantity to sell. The usual justification for this assumption is that if one firm lowers its price all other firms see a very small change in their demand and so will not react at all.

As for entry and exit, if any firm in this industry is making losses, it will leave the industry. And if any firm in this industry is making positive profits, entry to the industry will occur. These entrants all pick their own unique variety of the good to sell, and the entry of any one entrant has negligible effect on the demand curve of any firm already in the industry. But as many entrants enter, the effect is cumulative on industry participants; they see their demand curves shift down and to the left.

Taking this story at face value, what will an equilibrium look like? Every active firm in this industry will be making zero profits; that must be true because firms making negative profits leave, and if firms are making positive profits, entry occurs. If an equilibrium is a situation with no inflow or outflow of firms, the only possibility left is zero profits. This means that the demand curve each firm faces must be tangent to and otherwise below the firm's average cost curve; if the demand curve lies entirely below the average cost curve, the firm will be making losses no matter what it does, whereas if the demand curve is (at any level of quantity) above average costs, the firm can make strictly positive profits at that quantity. *If* in equilibrium firms face downward sloping demand, the only possible picture is that given in figure 10.6. The firm's demand curve is tangent to average cost at a quantity that is less than efficient scale. To speak in jargon, firms are producing (in equilibrium) at a level at which they have *excess capacity*.

Following development of the rudiments of this theory, it is normal to comment on the "efficiency" of this market structure; on the one hand, firms are producing at an inefficient scale (bad), but consumers are getting something for this, namely a wide variety of products (good). The issue of efficiency of a monopolistically competitive industry gets rather complex, and we won't attempt to summarize the debate here. (See Tirole, 1988, chap. 7.) Instead we ask, What industry might this be a model of?

The classic answer given is retailing or service industries. The feature that is meant to differentiate the many shops is in the first place location; each shop is unique in that it alone occupies a particular location in a particular block, and it faces a downward sloping demand curve despite the vast number of shops in the world, because it "really" only competes with shops near to it. Someone living on Second Avenue between 10th and 11th Streets is unlikely to consider a visit to a shop all the way across town, even if that shop across town has the product at a much cheaper price than any of the local shops. The real choice set for this consumer consists of the shops on the corners of Second Avenue and 10th and Second and 11th, and maybe, if it really has good prices, the shop on Third and 10th. Hence each shop, even if it raises its price a bit above that of the competition, will still attract some clientele.

Whether the retailing business approximates the conclusions of monopolistic competition is an empirical question. Retailing in the United States, at least, is usually a very low margin business, which is a point in favor of the theory's implications. But it is worth objecting to the application of the model to shops on various street corners on purely theoretical grounds. (That is, we may have the right conclusions but for the wrong theoretical reasons.) The objection is that what the shop on Second and 10th does cannot be supposed to have negligible effect on how nearby shops fare and what they do. The shop on Second and 11th knows well that its competition is just a block away, and if Second and 10th runs a special on apples, Second and 11th will respond with a special on bananas. Moreover, if the shops on Second Avenue are making profits and a new shop, in response to this, sets up on Second Avenue and 12th, this will significantly affect the demand of the Second Avenue shops (that are near to 12th Street), and it will have little or no effect on the demand at shops across town. This situation is not as described in the model of monopolistic competition; it is a model of local oligopoly with entry.

There is nothing wrong with having a theory of local oligopoly, except that just as oligopoly theory isn't determinant, neither is a theory of local oligopoly. In the story of monopolistic competition, each shop owner believes he can change his prices without response from any competitor. The reason given is that when he changes his prices, none of his competitors see much effect on his own demand. That clearly is wrong for local oligopolists. We could assume in a local oligopoly that all the shop owners have Bertrand conjectures, but (at this point) that is just one assumption out of many that we could make.

Is there an industry that meets the conditions of monopolistic competition? We leave the reader with this question as a challenge. Can you think of an industry in which (a) firms face downward sloping demand, (b) cross-elasticities of demand for any pair of firms are low, and (c) there is free entry? Here is one case to chew on: Consider the lunchtime restaurant trade (or private clubs) in a metropolitan business district. Can you construct a model of consumer demand at a large number of restaurants such that if any restaurant lowers its price it draws a little bit of clientele from each of the other restaurants, and such that a new restaurant entering the business takes a bit away from all incumbents, but doesn't drive any one (or a few) significantly closer to bankruptcy? [d]

References

Bertrand, J. 1883. "Théorie Mathématique de la Richesse Sociale." *Journal des Savants* 499–508.

Chamberlin, E. 1933. *The Theory of Monopolistic Competition*. Cambridge, Mass.: Harvard University Press.

Cournot, A. 1838. *Recherches sur les Principes Mathématiques de la Théorie des Richesses*. English ed., N. Bacon, ed., *Researches into the Mathematical Principles of the Theory of Wealth*. New York: Macmillan, 1897.

Hall, R., and C. Hitch. 1939. "Price Theory and Business Behavior." *Oxford Economic Papers* 2:12–45.

Hart, O. 1985. "Monopolistic Competition in the Spirit of Chamberlin: A General Model." *Review of Economic Studies* 51:63–82.

Hotelling, H. 1929. "Stability in Competition." *Economic Journal* 39:41–57.

Kreps, D., and J. Scheinkman. 1983. "Quantity Precommitment and Bertrand Competition Yield Cournot Outcomes." *Bell Journal of Economics* 14:326–37.

Novshek, W. 1984. "Finding All *n*-Firm Cournot Equilibria." *International Economic Review* 25:61–70.

---

[d] I am grateful to Drew Fudenberg for suggesting this industry as a possibility. If you wish some help in constructing preferences with the required properties and a bit of heavy mathematics won't dissuade you, see Hart (1985), from whom much of this commentary is drawn.

Porter, M. 1980. *Competitive Strategy: Techniques for Analyzing Industries and Competitors.* New York: The Free Press.

Sweezy, P. 1939. "Demand under Conditions of Oligopoly." *Journal of Political Economy* 47:568–73.

Tirole, J. 1988. *The Theory of Industrial Organization.* Cambridge, Mass.: MIT Press.

Von Stackelberg, H. 1934. *Marktform and Gleichgewicht.* Vienna: Julius Springer.

10.3. Problems

■ 1. In the model of a duopoly with undifferentiated commodities, one firm has Cournot conjectures and the second has Bertrand conjectures. Can you find an equilibrium?

■ 2. In the model of kinked demand, the firms' conjectures were such that the only possible equilibria were symmetric. If we change the nature of the firms' conjectures, then perhaps we can find asymmetric equilibria. For both sorts of conjectures described below, find all the pairs $(\hat{x}_1, \hat{x}_2)$ that are equilibria.

(a) At equilibrium $(\hat{x}_1, \hat{x}_2)$, firm 1 believes that firm 2 will continue to produce $\hat{x}_2$ as long as $x_1 < \hat{x}_1$, but that firm 2 will match any increase in firm 1's output (above $\hat{x}_1$) unit for unit, and vice versa. That is, firm 1 believes that firm 2 will produce $\hat{x}_2 + \max\{0, x_1 - \hat{x}_1\}$. Firm 2 holds symmetric conjectures about firm 1.

(b) At equilibrium $(\hat{x}_1, \hat{x}_2)$, firm 1 believes that firm 2 will continue to produce $\hat{x}_2$ as long as firm one produces a level x_1 below $\hat{x}_1$. But firm 2 will increase its production in response to an increase in firm 1's production in an amount that keeps the relative market shares of the two firms the same as in equilibrium. That is, firm 1 believes that firm 2 will produce $\max\{\hat{x}_2, (\hat{x}_2/\hat{x}_1)x_1\}$. Firm 2 holds symmetric conjectures about firm 1.

■ 3. An economy I know has 1,000 identical consumers and two goods. The two goods are phiffle, a nonnarcotic stimulant, and manna, a basic foodstuff. Each consumer has a utility for phiffle and manna of the form $u(x, z) = w(x) + z$, where x is the amount of phiffle consumed and z the amount of manna. Assume that w is strictly concave and continuously differentiable. The function w is concave and satisfies $w'(0) = 100$ and $w'(100) = 1$. The price of manna is always \$1, and each consumer has wealth exceeding \$10,000 which is spent entirely on phiffle and manna.

348   *Chapter ten: Imperfect competition*

(a) What is the shape of the market demand curve for phiffle, for prices between $1 and $100?

Two firms sell phiffle. For some reason, one firm is willing to sell at a price of $2, while the other insists on a price of $3. Moreover, the first firm is willing to sell only 50,000 units of phiffle. The second firm is willing to sell to all comers. Assume that $w'(90) = 2$ and $w'(75) = 3$.

(b) Suppose that the following mechanism is used for the distribution of phiffle. The first firm asks each consumer how much phiffle he wishes to buy at a price of $2. If total orders are less than 50,000, each consumer is given whatever he asks for. Otherwise, phiffle from firm 1 is rationed equally to each person who wants some, up to the amount that the person wants. That is, we divide the 50,000 units equally among all the consumers and ask whether any consumer is getting more than he asked for. If so, those consumers who asked for less are given what they asked for, and the remainder of their share is divided equally among all the consumers who are still rationed, and so on.) After this rationing scheme, consumers can go to the second firm, if they wish, and buy as much (more) phiffle as they would like for $3. What will be the result of this scheme?

(c) Suppose that phiffle is distributed as follows. The first firm asks each consumer how much phiffle she wishes and then distributes the phiffle as follows: A consumer is chosen at random and is given whatever she asks for, up to 50,000 units. Then, if anything remains of the 50,000 units, a second consumer is chosen at random, and so on, until either all consumers have been served or the 50,000 units are exhausted. After this distribution, consumers can purchase phiffle from the other firm, at $3 per unit. What will be the outcome of this distribution system if phiffle cannot be resold?

(d) What will be the outcome of the distribution system in part (c) if phiffle can be resold? (Assume that consumers in this economy are very savvy folks.)

(e) If you like a challenge, think about these three scenarios with the added complication that the economy is populated with a large number of heterogenous consumers. You will need to formulate some of the problem for yourself.

■ 4. Go back to a manufacturing monopoly that produces items at a constant unit cost k, and that must sell these units to retailers who sell the items at zero additional cost (beyond the cost the retailers incur to buy the items from the monopoly). Suppose there are two retailers, and they act according to Cournot conjectures. Demand is (what else) $P = A - Q$.

(a) Assume the monopoly charges retailers according to simple linear prices — at a price the monopoly sets. What is the optimal price for the monopoly to set?

(b) Suppose the monopoly can use a two-part tariff scheme, where it charges each retailer a fixed fee, plus a per unit charge for any units bought. What is the optimal pricing scheme for the monopoly?

(c) Now consider what will happen if the two duopolists compete with Bertrand conjectures.

■ 5. Consider an industry in which N firms all produce an undifferentiated product. Demand for the product is given by $X = A - P$. Each producer is identical, having a constant average cost of k.

(a) Suppose all N producers have Cournot conjectures: Each conjectures that it can change the amount it produces and all its rivals will continue to produce the amounts they are producing. What is the symmetric equilibrium in this case? (An equilibrium is symmetric if all the firms are producing the same amount.) What happens to the equilibrium price as N approaches infinity?

(b) Suppose all N producers have Bertrand conjectures: Each conjectures that it can change the price it charges without any reaction from rivals in the prices they charge. What is the symmetric equilibrium in this case?

(c) Suppose one firm is a Stackelberg leader and all the rest have Cournot conjectures. That is, each of the $N-1$ followers believes that it can change its quantity without any response in quantities from any of the other firms. The one leader understands this and picks its quantity optimally. What equilibria can you find? What happens to price as N goes to infinity?

(d) Suppose the N firms are numbered $1, 2, \ldots, N$, and they have the following sort of conjectures: Firm N has Cournot conjectures. Firm $N-1$ has Cournot conjectures about firms 1 through $N-2$ and believes that firm N works off its Cournot reaction curve. Firm n has Cournot conjectures about firms 1 through $n-1$ and believes that firms $n+1$ through N work off the reaction curves given by their conjectures. What equilibria can you find? What happens to price as N goes to infinity?

(e) Construct a model in the spirit of kinked demand for the setting of an N firm oligopoly.

■ 6. Here is an alternative scheme for finding Cournot equilibria. In our discussion in the chapter, we computed reaction functions for each firm of the form "what quantity x would the firm choose to output if the other firm produced x'?" Suppose instead we answer the question: What quantity x produced by one firm is consistent with X in total from *both* firms? We would find this by looking at the problem

$$\max_{\delta}(A - k - X - \delta)(x + \delta)$$

and finding, for a given X that amount x that has $\delta = 0$ as a solution. Why? Because we are computing here how the firm would choose to vary its output from x if the total output is X when the firm chooses x; when a variation of 0 is optimal, x is consistent with X. Carrying this out (so you will see that it works), the first-order conditions in δ are $A - k - X - x = 2\delta$, which are satisfied at $\delta = 0$ if $A - k - X = x$. That is, $x(X) = A - k - X$ is the production by one firm consistent with X produced by both. At an equilibrium $2x(X) = X$, or $2(A - k - X) = X$, or $2(A - k) = 3X$, or $X = 2(A - k)/3$, which then yields $x = (A - k)/3$, our Cournot equilibrium. (This technique is due to Novshek [1984].)

(a) In part (a) of problem 5, you were asked to find the symmetric equilibrium of an N firm oligopoly where firms have Cournot conjectures. Using the technique just presented, find all the equilibria including any asymmetric ones that may exist.

(b) Now repeat part (a) of this problem but in a setting where the N firms that make up the oligopoly have possibly different unit costs; let k_n be the unit cost of firm n for each n.

■ 7. Suppose that in a duopoly with an undifferentiated product, demand is given by $X = A - P$ and firms have Bertrand conjectures and different unit costs. Specifically, firm 1 has constant average costs of k_1 and firm 2 has constant average costs of k_2, with $k_1 < k_2$. What is (are?) the equilibrium(a)?

■ 8. Suppose an industry produces an undifferentiated product for which market demand is given by $X = A - P$. There are many potential producers for this product, each of whom has a production function of the form: Fixed costs of F must be paid for being in business, and the marginal cost of a unit of production is a constant k. We imagine that firms decide whether to enter the industry under the supposition that, after all the firms that are going to enter do so, competition will be according to the Cournot model. That is, if N firms are in the market each has Cournot conjectures. An equilibrium is achieved with N firms in the industry if each firm, having its Cournot conjectures, does no worse than break even, whereas if another firm entered and made this an $N + 1$ firm Cournot oligopoly, all the firms would lose money. What is the equilibrium in this case? What (if anything) would be the equilibrium if firms had Bertrand conjectures throughout? (Note well: The number of firms is set and then firms compete. The exercise is not that firms charge a price, say, and then other firms can enter assuming firms already in the industry will stick to that price. But as long as we're sketching this alternative, what would be the Cournot and Bertrand equilibria with entry under this alternative scenario?)

■ 9. Suppose two duopolists produce given differentiated goods. The prices that each obtains in equilibrium depends on the quantities output by each (or, alternatively, the equilibrium quantities demanded for each depends on the prices each charges), according to the inverse demand functions

$$p_1 = A - x_1 - bx_2 \quad \text{and} \quad p_2 = A - x_2 - bx_1,$$

for constants A and b. The constant b is restricted to the interval $(-1, 1)$, where $b > 0$ means that the goods in question are "substitutes" and $b < 0$ means they are "complements." (We use quote marks here because we are not working with precise definitions of these terms; cf. chapter 2.)

(a) Give Cournot, von Stackelberg and Bertrand equilibria for this model. If you find the algebra getting a bit too thick, solve for equilibrium values (quantities, prices, profits) for the parameters $A = 10$, $k = 1$ and $b = .9, .5, .1$, and $-.5$. Note that the two firms do better in Bertrand than in Cournot for the case $b < 0$. Can you give an intuitive explanation of this?

(b) In the von Stackelberg equilibrium of part (a), the follower has Cournot conjectures and the leader optimizes given the follower's reaction function. We could equally well imagine a case in which the follower had Bertrand conjectures and the leader optimizes given the reaction function so entailed. This is called the *Bertrand-von Stackelberg* equilibrium. (The von Stackelberg equilibrium in part (a) is then called the *Cournot-von Stackelberg* equilibrium.) Solve for it, at least for the four parameterizations given previously.

(c) In both sorts of von Stackelberg equilibria, the leader has higher profits than if there were no leader at all. Prove that this is so. (It will suffice to demonstrate a weak inequality.)

(d) In Cournot-von Stackelberg for $b > 0$ and Bertrand-von Stackelberg for $b < 0$, the follower has smaller profits than if there is no leader, while for Bertrand for $b > 0$ and Cournot for $b < 0$, the follower has larger profits than if there is no leader. What intuitive explanations can you give for these observations?

This entire problem is the tip of an iceberg that goes by the rubric "strategic substitutes and complements." If you read Tirole (1988) or other treatments of imperfect competition, watch for it under that name.

■ 10. Imagine a duopoly in which firms produce an "identical good" for consumers who live along a 100-mile highway. We imagine (in the spirit of problem 10 in chapter 9) that consumers are distributed uniformly along the highway at a density of ten consumers per mile. Each consumer has reservation price $100 for one unit of the good, but each pays a cost getting to and from the store that must be added to the price of the good when comparing against the reservation price. The good costs each of the two firms $1 per unit to produce. Each firm is allowed to open one store somewhere along the highway. If the firm is located d miles from a consumer, the consumer pays $\$(d/50)^2$ for the round-trip from home to the store and back. The two firms locate their stores (which serves to differentiate their goods in the minds of consumers, if they don't locate one on top of the other) and then they compete with Bertrand conjectures. What is the equilibrium in this case? (We have been a bit imprecise in specifying the model, so be very clear what assumptions you are making. If you like a challenge, consider what would happen if travel costs were linear instead of quadratic. If you do this, be prepared for enormous frustrations.)

Further problems on variations on the classical models of duopoly are given in chapter 12.

Noncooperative game theory

chapter eleven

Modeling competitive situations

Prologue to part III

In part III, you will be introduced to some of the terms and concepts of noncooperative game theory. Note the words "introduce" and "some"; this is far from rigorous and far from comprehensive. But I hope it will serve as enough background for the sorts of applications we will discuss later and will arouse your curiosity sufficiently so that you'll study it further.

Note also at the outset that these chapters will concentrate exclusively on *noncooperative* game theory, and, at that, primarily on equilibrium (or Nash equilibrium) concepts. A lot of game theory, perhaps the bulk of developments from the 1950s and 1960s, concerns so-called cooperative game theory. Recently, however, the emphasis has shifted toward noncooperative game theory — to the point where noncooperative game theory has become a very important tool for microeconomists. Do not be misled by the terminology. It isn't that economists have recently become more interested in uncooperative behavior. Rather, as we will see in great detail in chapter 14, the emphasis recently has been more on explaining how cooperation (and many other forms of aggregate behavior) can emerge from self-interested individual behavior within a given set of "rules," which is the defining characteristic of noncooperative game theory. It is probably best just to regard the terminology as jargon and wait to see what emerges from so-called noncooperative theory. Nevertheless, the jargon is used, so be forewarned that we will not discuss a large chunk of game theory at all. Seek other sources for an introduction to cooperative game theory.

In this chapter, we will look at how competitive situations are conventionally modeled in noncooperative game theory. Two sorts or *forms* of models are used, the so-called *extensive form* game and the *normal* or *strategic* form game. We will describe each of these modeling forms in this chapter and consider some of the basic issues involved in moving from one form to the other. In chapter 12, we will consider solution concepts for the games posed in this chapter, concentrating on *Nash equilibrium* analysis. Then in chapters 13, 14, and 15 we investigate three important types of application of the theory: models of *incomplete information*, *repeated play*, and *bilateral bargaining*.

11.1. Games in extensive form: An example

The story

Consider the following story. As owner-manager of Jokx Toys and Games, you are thinking about introducing a new game called Oligopoly, which will teach children from ages 8 to 12 the basic principles of imperfect competition. You must decide very soon whether to introduce Oligopoly and if you do decide to go ahead, you will have to spend $40,000 to complete design of the game, advertise it, and set up production.

The market for a game like Oligopoly is highly uncertain. You decide to consider two possibilities: The market will either be large, yielding total sales of 20,000 units, or it will be small, with sales totalling 6,000 units. You assess probabilities .4 and .6 for these two possibilities. These figures suppose a wholesale price per unit of $12; raising the price will cause sales to plummet, whereas lowering it will not increase demand appreciably.

Another source of uncertainty is that a competitive firm, Beljeau Games and Toys, is considering the introduction of a game called Reaganomics, which will compete directly with Oligopoly. In fact, if you introduce Oligopoly and Beljeau introduces Reaganomics, the competition that ensues will force each of you to charge only $10 per unit (wholesale) — the overall market, which will be either 20,000 or 6,000 units, will not be enlarged by the fall in price — and you will each get a one-half share of the market.

It will cost you $5 per unit to produce Oligopoly in addition to the $40,000 fixed costs mentioned above. You will be able to produce exactly as many units as you sell (produce to demand).

The situation for Beljeau is somewhat similar. As you sit debating whether to introduce Oligopoly, the managers at Beljeau are debating whether to introduce Reaganomics. The press of getting these games out in time for Christmas means that you cannot wait to see what they do before deciding whether to go ahead with Oligopoly; similarly, they must decide about Reaganomics before learning of your decision on Oligopoly. But they have one advantage — they have commissioned a market survey whose results they will learn before deciding whether to proceed with

Reaganomics, a survey that will tell them without error whether the market will be large or small.

Beljeau will incur a fixed cost of $60,000 if it develops Reaganomics, and a unit cost of $3 per unit (produced to demand). Reaganomics will sell for precisely the same price as Oligopoly — $12 wholesale if only one product is in the market and $10 wholesale if both firms are marketing their (respective) games.

Decision trees

Looking at this problem from your point of view, we can build a *decision tree* that represents the problem you face. The tree is given in figure 11.1. For those of you who have never seen a decision tree before, we offer some words of translation. We start at the left-hand side; the box there with two branches coming out represents the decision that you must make right now whether or not to introduce Oligopoly. Boxes are called *decision* or *choice nodes*. If you choose to introduce Oligopoly, then things will begin to happen to you: You learn the size of the market (large or small), and you learn what Beljeau decided to do (introduce Reaganomics or not). These are things outside your control; from your point of view they are "chance events" (although you may have a pretty good idea what Beljeau will do). So we depict them as *chance nodes*, or branching points in the tree marked by circles. On the other hand, if you don't introduce Oligopoly, from your point of view the problem is over.

This gives us five "branches" in the tree, each one representing a unique sequence of choices by you (Jokx) and outcomes of events that are outside your control. Note in this regard that we put in two chance nodes for Beljeau's choice, so that we have four outcomes following a decision by you to enter the market. Then for each of the five branches, we can

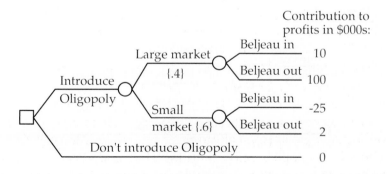

Figure 11.1. The decision tree of Jokx.

evaluate how much contribution to profit you will receive. For example, if you introduce Oligopoly, the market is large, and Beljeau introduces Reaganomics (the topmost branch), you will sell 10,000 units for $10 whole-sale, or $100,000 in revenues, less fixed costs of $40,000 and manufacturing costs of (10,000)($5), or total costs of $90,000, for a $10,000 contribution to profits, and so on. These numbers are written in on figure 11.1 at the end of each branch. Finally, we know the probabilities that the market is large or small, so we put these in on the appropriate branches in the tree.

Could we depict your decision tree in other ways? Figure 11.2 gives two possibilities. In figure 11.2(a) we interchange the two chance nodes, putting Beljeau's decision first and then the size of the market. And in figure 11.2(b) we combine the two chance nodes into one having four possible outcomes. The rule that we must follow in constructing decisions trees is

The fundamental rule of decision trees. *A chance node precedes a choice node in the tree if and only if the uncertainty represented by that chance node resolves*

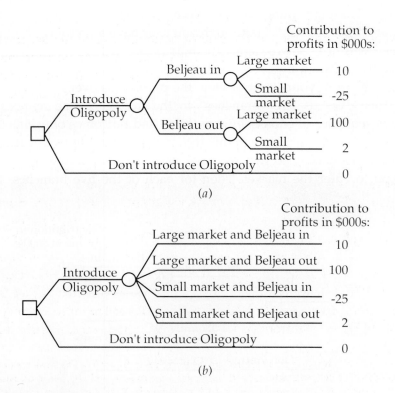

Figure 11.2. Two different representations of Jokx' tree.

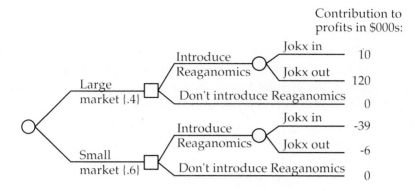

Figure 11.3 The decision tree of Beljeau.

in the mind of the decision maker prior to the time at which the choice must be made.

Since you must decide on Oligopoly before any uncertainty resolves, as long as your choice node comes first, you are living within the strictures of that rule.[a]

As for Beljeau's tree, they will learn the size of the market prior to making their decision, so the chance node for size of market must come first in their tree. And they don't learn about your decision regarding Oligopoly until after their decision, so the chance node for your decision must come after their choice node. This gives the decision tree in figure 11.3, with contributions to profit and probabilities for the market size supplied.

This is a relatively simple example, and we can see the "answer" just by inspecting the decision trees. Look at figure 11.3 first. If the market is large, then Beljeau will make a positive contribution no matter what Jokx does if they go ahead with Reaganomics, so they are pretty sure to do so. Whereas if the market is small, Beljeau is sure to lose money with Reaganomics whatever Jokx does, so they will probably decide not to proceed in this case. This means that in figure 11.1, if the market is large, you (Jokx) can be sure that Beljeau will be in the market, netting you $10,000 if you introduce Oligopoly. Whereas if the market is small, you can be pretty sure that Beljeau will be out of the market, and you will net $2,000 if you introduce Oligopoly. So since you are fairly sure that

---

[a] We haven't supplied probabilities on the branches in figure 11.2, because we don't know probabilities for Beljeau's actions (yet). In general, the rule on probabilities in decision trees is that the probability that goes on any branch must be conditional on any previously resolved event, so we can't even supply probabilities for market size in 11.2(a).

Beljeau will be out if the market is small, you can safely enter the market; you will make a positive contribution no matter what.

Despite this simplicity, we will carry forward with this example. Early in the next chapter we will arrive at the conclusion just stated, and while we already know the answer to this problem, the techniques we will use will help us to see through more complex games.[1]

An extensive form representation

In a *game tree*, we use one tree structure to represent *both* players' decision problems. How could we ever represent both decision problems in a single tree? The obvious problem is that the order of nodes depends on whose perspective we take. Even so, it can be done. Have a look at figure 11.4. This is rather a mess, but if you bear with me, it will become clear.

The game starts with the open circle or *node* near the middle of the page. (The game will always start at the open circle in this sort of picture.) Note that *Jokx* appears besides this open circle, meaning that at this point it is Jokx who must choose what to do. Jokx is limited to two choices that correspond to the two arrows pointing out of this initial node labeled *intro O* (for introduce Oligopoly) and *don't*.

Follow the choice *intro O* by Jokx to a second node depicted by a closed circle. (Open circles will be used to denote only the initial node.[b]) This node is labeled *nature*, meaning that at this point we imagine the

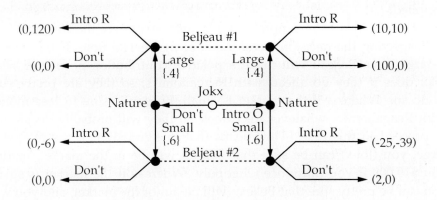

Figure 11.4. The game in extensive form.

---

[1] Problem 1 gives a good example. If you like to work out problems as you read along, now is a good time to do problem 1(a).

[b] Or nodes — see below.

choice of which path to follow is determined by events under the control of neither player. Nature chooses between a *large* market and a *small* one with the probabilities given on the branches. You next come to nodes at which Beljeau must choose between *intro R* (introduce Reaganomics) or *don't*, and at the end of each path through the tree you find a vector of *payoffs*, in this case measured by contributions to profit. Jokx' payoff is first and Beljeau's second. So, for example, if Jokx introduces Oligopoly (move right), the market is small (move down), and Beljeau introduces Reaganomics, you reach the vector $(-25, -39)$, meaning that Jokx loses $25,000 and Beljeau loses $39,000. Similarly, if Jokx introduces Oligopoly, the market is large, and Beljeau doesn't introduce Reaganomics, you reach the vector $(100, 0)$, meaning Jokx has made $100,000 and Beljeau has netted zero.

The one "problem" is that we've put Beljeau's decision after Jokx' decision in the tree. Beljeau, remember, doesn't know what Jokx has done when it must make a decision. We depict this in the picture by the two dashed lines. Take the upper one. This connects Beljeau's two decision nodes in the circumstances (a) Jokx introduces O and the market is large, and (b) Jokx doesn't introduce O and the market is large. Beljeau cannot distinguish between these two circumstances, and so we join these with the interpretation: Whatever Beljeau does at one of the two nodes joined by the dashed line, it must do precisely the same thing at the other. This is called an *information set*; in general, all the nodes in an information set represent circumstances at which some player is called upon to move without knowing which of those circumstances pertain.

Recall that we labeled the initial node *Jokx*, since Jokx moved there, and the second two nodes *nature*, since the moves there were taken by forces outside of players' control. But we didn't label the next set of nodes directly with Beljeau. Instead, we labeled the two dashed lines or information sets, and these labels on dashed lines are meant to imply that at all four of the nodes in the two information sets Beljeau chooses what to do.

Most importantly, note that Beljeau has two information sets labeled *Beljeau #1* and *Beljeau #2*. These correspond to the two different decisions that Beljeau must make: Whether to introduce Reaganomics if the market is large (#1); and whether to introduce Reaganomics if the market is small (#2).

There is, of course, a strong connection between the *extensive form game tree* in figure 11.4 and the two *decision trees* in figures 11.1 and 11.3. In particular, every choice node in the decision tree of a player will correspond to one information set for the player in the game tree. So, just as there are two decision nodes for Beljeau in 11.3, so there are two information sets in 11.4. And just as there is one decision node for Jokx in 11.1, so there is one information set for Jokx in 11.4, where a single node belonging to a player that is not joined to any other by a dashed line is thought of as an information set in its own right.

Why did we put the nodes in the order we did? In many cases, we have a lot of freedom in choosing the order. The only rule that we must follow is that

If someone learns something prior to making a particular decision, where the something learned could be either a move by nature or a move by another player, then the node representing what is learned must precede the node where the decision is taken.

Hence the node(s) for nature must precede Beljeau's nodes. Compare with the rule for decision trees, where the rule is more definitive; there we say that something outside the control of a player, depicted by a chance node, comes before a choice node *if and only if* the player learns the resolution of that chance event before making the decision. For game trees the implication runs only one way: We are allowed to put a "chance node" before a "choice node" if the player who is choosing doesn't learn what happened at the chance node until after the choice must be made; to repair this misordering, we use information sets.

In this particular example, we have three generations of nodes: One for Jokx' decision, one for Beljeau's, and one for nature's. The rule says that in a game tree nature's nodes must precede Beljeau's. But that is the only implication of the rule. Hence besides the order $J \rightarrow n \rightarrow B$ that we used in figure 11.4, it is possible to depict this situation in a game tree with the order $n \rightarrow B \rightarrow J$ and in the order $n \rightarrow J \rightarrow B$. It is probably a good exercise to draw these two "other" orders for the game tree. It hardly needs saying, but the point of this exercise is entirely in getting the information sets drawn correctly.

There is an important point here. In representing the game on a single tree, what we want to do is convey what each party knows whenever it is that party's move, and we want to include all the complete "sequences" of steps that might get us from start to finish. The word "sequence" is in quotes because there is no particular temporal sequence to things — "sets" of events might be better. Actual calendar time matters only insofar as it determines (to some, but not complete, extent) what one party might know when it is time for that party to move. That is, barring prescience, which we will do, one can only know things that happened before. But there is no reason to suppose that one knows everything that happened before — that is hardly descriptive of reality — and it is knowledge and not time that rules what orders of moves can/cannot be used in this sort of tree.

(Once you understand this example, a useful way to test your understanding is to proceed to the problems at the end of the chapter.)

11.2. Games in extensive form: Formalities

The tree representation of a game in figure 11.4 is called a game in *extensive form*. Now that we have an example to bear in mind, we will look at the formal structure of games in extensive form. What follows is formal and mathematical, and the mathematically unsophisticated reader may find it hard to read through. Most of the examples we'll look at will be fairly straightforward, and if you understood the example in the previous section, the formalities to follow are likely to be unnecessary. But it is probably worthwhile to give what follows a try, if not to get all the details (which become fairly obscure toward the end) then at least to get a sense of how one proceeds generally. We will restrict attention in these formalities to finite player, finite action, and finite tree games, with a few comments at the end about extensions to more general settings.

An extensive form representation of a noncooperative game is composed of the following list of items: *a list of players, a game tree, an assignment of decision nodes to players or to nature, lists of actions available at each decision node and a correspondence between immediate successors of each decision node and available actions, information sets, an assignment of payoffs for each player to terminal nodes, and probability assessments over the initial nodes and over the actions at any node that is assigned to nature.* This is a long list and these things are subject to various rules and regulations, so we proceed to develop this list a step at a time.

*(1) There is a finite set of **players**.* We will number the players with arabic numerals, as $1, 2, \ldots, I$, for a game with I players. A typical player will be labeled i. In addition to these players is a "natural force," which we will call *nature*, that acts something like a player. We will refer to nature with the symbol N.

*(2) There is a **game tree**.* This consists of a finite set T and a binary relation $\prec$ on T. A typical element of T is denoted by t and is called a *node*. The binary relation is called *precedence*; and T forms an *arborescence* with $\prec$.

This means that $\prec$ is asymmetric, transitive, and satisfies the following additional property:

If $t \prec t''$ and $t' \prec t''$ and if $t \neq t'$, then either $t \prec t'$ or $t' \prec t$.

To understand what this means, make the following constructions and definitions.

For $t \in T$ write $P(t) = \{t' \in T : t' \prec t\}$ and call $P(t)$ the set of *predecessors* of t.

For $t \in T$ write $S(t) = \{t' \in T : t \prec t'\}$ and call $S(t)$ the set of *successors* of t.

Let W denote the set of nodes in T with no predecessors, or $W := \{t \in T : P(t) = \emptyset\}$. We sometimes call W the set of *initial nodes* of the game tree.

Let Z denote the set of nodes in T with no successors, or $Z := \{t \in T : S(t) = \emptyset\}$. The nodes in Z are called the *terminal nodes* of the game tree.

Let X denote the set of nodes that are not terminal nodes, or $X := T \setminus Z$. These nodes are sometimes referred to as the *decision nodes* of the game for reasons that will become clear in a bit.

Now let us try to make sense of the requirements that $\prec$ is asymmetric and transitive and has the extra property listed above. First, we will translate this extra property into words. What it says is that if two distinct nodes precede a third then one or the other of the two nodes precedes the other one. That is to say, *the set of predecessors of a given node is totally ordered by $\prec$*, where a set is totally ordered by a binary relation if any two distinct elements of the set are ordered in one direction or the other.

Think in terms of the pictures we were drawing in the previous section, where nodes (elements of T) are depicted by circles and arrows point from some nodes to others. We say that $t \prec t'$ if, starting from t, you can find a path of arrows that point from t to some t_1, from t_1 to t_2, from t_2 to t_3, and so on, until t' is reached. Note that the way this has been defined $\prec$ is automatically transitive. Asymmetry of $\prec$ then tells us that there are no cycles in this arrangement of nodes and arrows. And to say that $\prec$ totally orders the set of predecessors of a given node is to rule out the sort of thing shown in figure 11.5(a), where the node labeled x has two predecessors that are unordered by precedence.

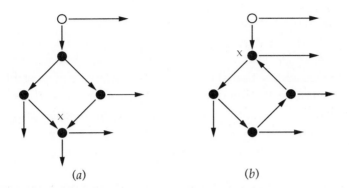

Figure 11.5. Two things that aren't allowed in game trees.
In (a) the node x has two (immediate) predecessors, neither of which
precedes the other. This violates the condition that the predecessors of
any node must be totally ordered by $\prec$. In (b) a cycle starts at x.

To see more formally what this assumption does, consider the following proposition:

Proposition. *For each* $t \in T$ *which is not in* W, *there exists a* **unique** *node*
$p(t) \in T$ *such that* $p(t) \prec t$ *and, if* $t' \prec t$ *and* $t' \neq p(t)$, *then* $t' \prec p(t)$.

We call $p(t)$ the *immediate predecessor* of t. Uniqueness of $p(t)$, if it exists,
is easy to show. If there were two nodes, say t' and t'' that satisfied this
definition, then $t' \prec t''$ and $t'' \prec t'$ would both be required, and this
would contradict asymmetry of $\prec$. As for existence, since $P(t)$ is a finite
set and since it is totally ordered by a transitive and asymmetric $\prec$, there
is some element of $P(t)$ that does not precede any other element of $P(t)$.
(Prove this, if you like little logical puzzles.) This element is $p(t)$.

This is what we get from the assumption that $\prec$ totally orders the
predecessors of any node t: Any node that has predecessors has a unique
immediate predecessor. So if we begin at any node t, either it is an initial
node or it has a unique immediate predecessor $p(t)$. And either $p(t)$ is an
initial node or it has a unique immediate predecessor $p(p(t))$, and so on.
Beginning from t, we can trace back along a *unique* path to some (unique)
initial node. (Remember that T is a finite set, so we have to come to an
initial node eventually if we are to avoid cycles.) This explains why this
sort of structure is called an arborescence or a tree. Think of a point in a
(real) tree. If we go back along the tree's branches from this point toward
the roots of the tree, a single path of branches leads back to the trunk and

thence to the roots. Put the other way around, starting from the roots the tree opens out; it doesn't grow back in on itself.

Note that we have not insisted that our tree T have a single initial node. That is, we allow more than one node to be in W. In figure 11.4, we had a single initial node (the open circle), but we wish to keep available the possibility that the tree T has a number of possible starting points. So, to pursue the botanical metaphor, perhaps we should call T a "grove" instead of a tree. (We will stick to conventional language and use "tree.")

In fact, let us tie together carefully the sort of picture in figure 11.4 and our mathematical construction of a tree. In our pictures, nodes are of three types: open circles, filled-in circles, and vectors of numbers, with arrows pointing from some nodes to others. In these pictures, there is never more than one arrow pointing towards any given node. Open circles are distinguished by the fact that no arrow ever points toward them, i.e., arrows only point out. And vectors of numbers only have a (single) arrow pointing toward them, i.e., no arrows leave them. All nodes that are not vectors of numbers have at least one arrow pointing out from them. And no path that follows arrows is a cycle. With these geometrical conventions, we have that the open circles are the initial nodes (members of W) and vectors of numbers are the terminal nodes (members of Z). One node precedes another if some path from the first along the direction of our arrows leads to the second. The crucial properties are that each node has at most one arrow pointing at it, which corresponds to the assumption that the set of predecessors of a given node are totally ordered by precedence, and the absence of any cycles, which is asymmetry of precedence. (If you have good geometrical intuition, you can see how these properties imply that starting from any node there is a unique path back along the arrows to some node that has no arrow pointing at it.)

This says how we would create the mathematical objects of T and $\prec$ from a picture. To reverse the process, if we had a pair $(T, \prec)$, we would

(a) Draw on a piece of paper a symbol for each element t of T: an open circle if $t \in W$, a set of parentheses (to be filled in later) if $t \in Z$, and a filled-in circle for all other t.

(b) Then for each node t that has at least one predecessor draw an arrow from its unique immediate predecessor $p(t)$ to t. Done!

We will find it useful to have yet another piece of notation. For any node $t \in X$ (any node that is not a terminal node), we write $s(t)$ for the set $\{t' \in T : t = p(t')\}$. That is, $s(t)$ is the set of *immediate successors* of t.

(3) One player (or nature) is assigned to each decision node. This is given formally by a one-to-one function $\iota : X \to \{N, 1, 2, \ldots, I\}$. The interpretation is that at node x player $\iota(x)$ selects what happens next. Note that we allow the possibility that nature makes this selection. If you refer to figure 11.4, you see an example: The initial node of the game (the open circle) is labeled *Jokx*, which means that Jokx moves there. Both successors to the initial node belong to nature, and so ι at each of those nodes would be N. And at each of the four successors to N's two nodes, the move belongs to Beljeau.

*(4) For each $t \in X$, there is a finite set of **available actions** $A(t)$ and a function $\alpha : s(t) \to A(t)$ that is one-to-one and onto.* The idea here is that each arrow or step in the game is given a name, this being the action that is required to move from one node to one of its successors. The requirement that α is a one-to-one and onto function from $s(t)$ to $A(t)$ means that from a given node t there is a correspondence between actions that can be taken and the next node in the game that will be reached. Every action leads to a distinct successor to t, and every successor to t is reached by a distinct action.[c] In terms of figure 11.4, from the node in the left-center of the page following the action *don't* by Jokx, nature has a choice of two actions, *large market* and *small*, which lead to two different nodes (where Beljeau moves).

*(5) The nodes $t \in X$ are partitioned into **information sets** with the following three requirements for any pair t and t' that are in the same information set:*

(a) $t \notin P(t')$ and $t' \notin P(t)$;

(b) $\iota(t) = \iota(t')$; and

(c) $A(t) = A(t')$.

The idea here is that certain subsets of decision nodes are such that the player choosing the action at one of the nodes doesn't know which of those nodes he or she is at. Refer to figure 11.4. All the decision nodes there are partitioned into five information sets. The initial node, belonging to Jokx, is by itself (as a singleton set) an information set. So are its two successors, which belong to nature. (Conventionally, nodes that belong to nature are always singleton information sets, a convention we will follow throughout.) Then there are two nodes in the information set *Beljeau #1* and two in the information set *Beljeau #2*. As shown in this figure, we join

---

[c] If we were being very formal, we would subscript α by t, but we will not be quite that formal.

nodes in a single information set with a dashed line. (Other authors will put all the nodes of a single information set into a "balloon.")

Information sets are meant to model the notion that a player when called upon to move might not know everything that happened "previously" in the game. (We put previously in quotation marks, because, as we noted before, the order of nodes in a game tree needn't necessarily follow temporal order of the moves.) But built into the formal construction that we use are some restrictions to this general notion. First, we require that information sets partition the set of decision nodes. That is, every decision node is in one and only one information set. The point is that if at node t player $\iota(t)$ doesn't know whether he is at t or at some t' (so t' is in the same information set as t), then at t', this player doesn't know that he isn't at t. Now one can imagine circumstances in which a player at one point in a game is so badly confused that he doesn't realize that he isn't at some different point, whereas if he were at that second point, he would realize that he wasn't at the first point. Such circumstances cannot be modeled directly in conventional game theory. (There are ways to model this sort of confusion indirectly within the structures of conventional game theory; see chapter 13 concerning how one models "irrational" behavior.)

Beyond this basic assumption, we make the three further assumptions listed previously. Assumption (a) says that a player remembers at any point in the play of a game whether he moved previously. Assumption (b) says that any two nodes in an information set have the same player moving. This means that a player doesn't confuse a situation in which he is given the choice of action with another situation in which another player has the choice. And assumption (c) says that a player is faced with the same available actions at any two nodes from the same information set; otherwise (the logic goes) the player could look at the sets of available actions and distinguish the two nodes.

In a sense, this construction of information sets and the three assumptions reflect an underlying basic assumption of the model, namely that the structure of the game is understood by the players. Pictures such as figure 11.4 are meant to be available to each player, and each player is smart enough to look at the picture and discern from it all the implications of the structure laid out there. There is more to the three assumptions than this; for example assumption (a) includes the assumption that players remember *that* they moved previously. But it is the underlying basic assumption that plays the largest role in these formal restrictions. Now one may well complain that there are many competitive situations in which players are somewhat ignorant of pieces of the structure of the game. A player, for example, may not know some of the options available in a particular situation. We handle this sort of thing by saying that the player in this case doesn't really have those options. A harder case to domesticate follows: In a given situation, a player believes he does not have certain options. There is another situation that he cannot currently distinguish from the present situation, and thus he currently believes that in this other situation he would not have those options. But in this second situation he would, in fact, know that those options are available, and so he can distinguish between the two. This we can't model directly. (It is hard enough to say. [d]) Or to take a third example, there may be circumstances in which your rival has available options that you don't know she has. This we can't model directly. We will discuss in chapter 13 how we might try to model these things; for now understand that they are things seemingly outside the bounds of our formal models.

We will use H to denote the set of all information sets in a given game, with h a typical information set. That is, H is a partition of X and each h is a subset of X. By virtue of (b) and (c), every node t from a given h has the same assignment of player and the same set of available actions. That is, if $t, t' \in h$, then $\iota(t) = \iota(t')$ and $A(t) = A(t')$. Accordingly, we will abuse notation and write $\iota(h)$ for the player whose turn it is to move at all nodes in h and $A(h)$ for the set of actions available to $\iota(h)$ at any node in h. Finally, for any $x \in X$, we will write $h(x)$ for the information set that contains x.

In addition to the three assumptions above, it is sometimes conventionally required that for t and t' that are in different information sets, $A(t) \cap A(t') = \emptyset$. This assumption is useful to keep notation from getting out of hand and it is without any loss of generality, so we make it whenever convenient.

(6) *An assignment of* **payoffs** *for each player to each terminal node of the game is given.* Formally, a function $u : \{1, 2, \ldots, I\} \times Z \to R$ is given, where $u(i, z)$ is the payoff to player i if the game ends at node z. We sometimes will write this function with the i as a subscript as in $u_i(z)$. In our pictures, we write vectors at each terminal node for the vector of payoffs, with player 1's payoff the first component of the vector, and so on. Insofar as there is or will be any uncertainty in the game, we think of the players as maximizing expected utility, and we think of the payoffs as denominated in units of utility. Insofar as the players pick up bits of payoff as the game

---

[d] Develop a formal model of this situation. The key is to have separate formal objects for the "objective reality" and for a player's subjective perceptions of reality. Information sets formalize subjective perception, but the conditions placed on information sets limit what can be modeled with them.

goes along, all those bits are aggregated into a final outcome and then translated into units of utility by the function u.

(7) A probability distribution ρ is given over the set of initial nodes W, and for each node $t \in X$ with $\iota(t) = N$ a probability distribution ρ_t over $A(t)$ is given. We think of nature as determining which initial node of the game pertains and then, perhaps, moving during the course of the game. Nature's choice of initial node is made according to the probability distribution ρ. If called upon to move during the course of the game, say at node t, the probability that nature takes action $a \in A(t)$ is given by $\rho_t(a)$. In our pictures, we will represent these probabilities by numbers in curly brackets, either at the initial nodes of the game, as in figure 11.7 (a few pages further on), or along the branches leading out of nodes that belong to nature, as in figure 11.4. (When there is a single initial node for the game, as in figure 11.4., we will neglect to put the obvious probability 1 in a curly bracket.)

We make two points about these probabilities. First, it is conventionally assumed that all players share the same assessments over nature's actions. This convention follows from deeply held "religious" beliefs of many game theorists. (Recall our discussion of the Harsanyi doctrine in chapter 3.) Of course one hesitates to criticize another individual's religion, but to my own mind this convention has little basis in philosophy or logic. Accordingly, one might prefer, being more general, to have probability distributions ρ and ρ_t, which are indexed by i, reflecting the possibly different subjective beliefs of each player. For most of this book, we won't consider examples for which this additional structure will be required, and so we follow the conventional assumption except when noted. But in following convention on this point, I do not mean to endorse the dogma that lies behind it.

Second, most treatments of this subject either look at games where W is a singleton set or at games where nature is never assigned to any node. The idea is that if W has more than one element, we could draw in a "super-initial node" that precedes the nodes of W, give nature the move at this super-initial node, and have her pick one of the initial nodes from the original W. Alternatively, in any game where nature is given the move at some node, we could remove that node by having more initial nodes. Both ways of doing things are without loss of generality; with either one (alone), you don't need the other. But we will allow here for both, since sometimes the pictures are neater one way, and sometimes they are neater the other.

That is it. (That's not enough?) That is how, formally, one describes an extensive form game.[2] As noted above, this sort of formalism does put some restrictions on what you can capture, but a lot of things still can be represented. Five things deserve special mention here.

Simultaneous moves

Imagine a game with two players, 1 and 2, who must make their decisions simultaneously. Specifically, player 1 must choose between L and R, whereas player 2 must choose between l and r. Then payoffs are made; for example, if player 1 chooses L and 2 chooses r, player 1 receives 2 and player 2 receives 3. These decisions, because they must be made simultaneously, are each made in ignorance of what the other player is choosing.

We can represent this in an extensive form game as in figure 11.6(a) or as in figure 11.6(b). Note that in (a) we have the node for player 1 coming before the two nodes of player 2, while in (b) we have the node for player 2 coming before the two nodes of player 1. But in each case, we use an information set to record the fact that the player "moving second" moves without knowing what the "first mover" did. Note also the positioning of the payoff vector (2,3) in these two figures; in (a) it comes after the sequence L-r, while in (b) it comes after r-L.

At the risk of beating this to death, note that figures 11.6(a) and (b) are both also consistent with the story. Player 1 chooses between L and R at 9:00 A.M., and player 2 chooses between l and r at 9:10 A.M., but player 2,

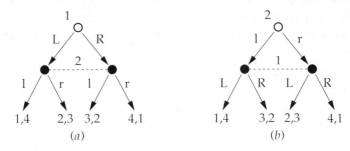

Figure 11.6. Two extensive form representations
of a simultaneous move game.

---

[2] A piece of terminology you might run into is that all the pieces except the last two (except for payoffs and probability assessments for nature) taken together are referred to as an extensive form *game form*.

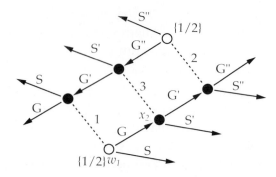

*Figure 11.7. An extensive form game
with a strange order of moves.*

when he chooses, doesn't know what player 1 chose. Insofar as no choices
are simultaneous, it wouldn't hurt to use physical time to determine precedence, but precedence in extensive form games isn't meant necessarily to
convey the temporal sequence of events. As such, there is no problem in
representing even simultaneous choices of action.

Precedence and information sets

Consider the following situation and the game tree in figure 11.7. The
three participants are called 1, 2, and 3. Either 1 or 2 is asked to choose
first, between giving the move to 3 (by choosing G or G″) or ending the
game (by choosing S or S″). If 3 is given the move, she can either end
the game (by choosing S′) or give the move to 2 or to 1 (by choosing G′).
Then, if they get the move, 2 or 1 chooses between two actions (G or S
for 1, and G″ or S″ for 2). The chance that 1 is asked to move first is 1/2.
(Note that we are using multiple initial nodes in this picture.)

The tricky part of this example is that each of the two initial nodes
belongs to an information set for the player who moves there that also includes the other node that belongs to that player. In other words, player 1,
if called upon to move, doesn't know whether she is moving first, because
nature started the game with her on the move, or third, because nature
started the game with 2 on the move, who gave the move to 3, who gave
it to 1 — and similarly for 2. And 3, if given the move, doesn't know
whether 1 moved first or 2 did.

In the game, there is a well-defined order of moves at the level of
nodes: A clear succession of nodes (and actions) leads to each terminal
node. But at the level of information sets, which is the level of what the
players are assumed to know, the order of moves can be uncertain. In

particular, we can say that the initial node labeled w_1 in the tree precedes the node labeled x_2. But the information set to which w_1 belongs, namely 1's information set, cannot be said either to precede or to follow 2's or 3's information set.

For what we will do in this book, there is no need to insist on a precedence order for information sets. But for some theoretical developments such an ordering of information sets is useful. For this reason, there is a specialization of the general notion of an extensive form, due to von Neumann, in which information sets can be ordered — if you ever encounter the term "an extensive form in the sense of von Neumann," it is (probably) to this that the author refers.[3]

Perfect recall

Look next at the tree structures in figure 11.8. Each is peculiar. Figure 11.8(a) is peculiar in that player 1 moves first and then, if she gets to move again, her information set indicates that she forgot what she did. That is, she is assumed to be unable to distinguish between the three sequences of actions $(l, R), (r, L)$, and (r, R). We have no problem with her being unable to distinguish between the second two of these sequences; it is player 2 who chooses between R and L, and it is quite reasonable to suppose that player 2's choice is not revealed to player 1. But how can player 1 fail to distinguish between (l, R) and those other two? If she remembers that she chose l instead of r, she won't be confused.

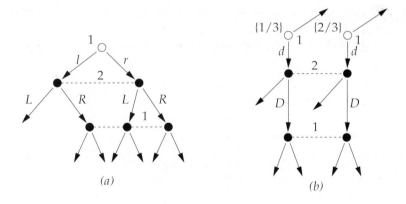

Figure 11.8. Two types of "forgetful" player.

---

[3] To be precise concerning the development of these ideas, von Neumann's extensive form came first and was later generalized to games in which information sets may not be ordered by precedence.

Figure 11.8(b) is interesting in that player 1 is modeled as making her first choice aware of which node nature chose to begin the game. This is indicated by the fact that the two initial nodes are not joined by a dashed line; each as a singleton set is an information set in its own right. But if 1 chooses u (from either starting point) and then 2 chooses D, 1 moves again, and the dashed line indicates that 1 seems to have forgotten what nature did, something she knew previously.

These two examples illustrate that none of the assumptions made so far preclude a player from forgetting certain things as the game progresses. A player is not allowed to forget the fact that she moved previously; assumption (a) concerning information sets precludes this. But a player is permitted, in general, to forget what she did earlier, and she may forget things she knew when moving earlier.

In the analysis of many games, it is useful to assume that the players don't forget these two sorts of things. Accordingly, we say that a game has or satisfies *perfect recall* if players remember what they previously knew and what they previously did.

Here is how this assumption is written formally.

Definition. *Given a game with information sets H, the game is said to satisfy or have* **perfect recall** *if, for any three nodes x, x', and x'' with $\iota(x) = \iota(x') = \iota(x'') = i$ such that $x \prec x'$ and $h(x') = h(x'')$, then*

(a) $P(x'') \cap h(x)$ is a singleton set. We use x^0 to denote the node in this intersection. (The case where $x^0 = x$ is definitely not precluded.)

(b) Let $\{y^0\} = s(x^0) \cap [P(x'') \cup \{x''\}]$ and let $\{y\} = s(x) \cap [P(x') \cup \{x'\}]$. Then $\alpha(y^0) = \alpha(y)$.

Part (a) is, roughly, that players remember everything they knew before. Since x' and x'' are in the same information set, and since x precedes x', there must be some node preceding x'' at which point the player's information was just the same as her information at x. And, from those two points, since she remembers what she did, she must have taken the same action (which is part [b]).

If this definition is mysterious, the reader who is interested in formalism should know that this definition is simpler than the one originally given. The classic reference on games with perfect recall and indeed for the construction of extensive form games is Kuhn (1953). Kuhn does things a bit differently than is done here: In particular, his definition of perfect recall is a bit weaker and even less transparent than our definition. Since Kuhn's definition is what is needed for his theorem (cf. section 11.4), it is certainly the "right" definition mathematically. But because it is a bit harder to understand, we use this stronger rendition. The restriction on information sets — if $x \prec x'$, then $x \notin h(x')$ — is sometimes put as part of the definition of perfect recall instead of being imposed as part of the definition of an extensive form game. It is included here as part of the definition of a game because I know of no useful or interesting examples where it is violated, whereas there are some interesting examples of games that satisfy it but that violate perfect recall as defined here; cf. problem 5. It should be noted, finally, that perfect recall as defined here implies this first restriction on the structure of information sets.

We noted before that, in general, information sets cannot be ordered by precedence. If a game has perfect recall and if we look at two information sets for a single player, however, either every node in one has a predecessor in the other (and not the reverse), or no node in one has a predecessor in the other. In fact, for any game with perfect recall (or even for a game in which some given player i has perfect recall), one can construct from the game tree a *decision tree* for the player where each choice node by the player corresponds to one of the player's information sets and where chance nodes correspond to combinations of actions of other players. The serious reader may find it helpful to give the details of this construction.

Infinitely many players and/or actions

When there are infinitely many players in the game or infinitely many actions (including the possibility of infinitely many initial nodes or moves by nature), then the formal objects given above will not suffice. For example, in some games infinitely many players move simultaneously. Having one move "first," a second move second without knowing what the first did, and so on, will not present a very pleasant looking tree. So, to handle infinities the mathematical notion of an extensive form game must be "tuned up." There is no best or most general way to do the tuning; for special cases, there are specially designed types of extensive games. Aumann (1964) should be consulted by the extremely serious reader.

Rigid and well-specified rules

We noted already that there are certain sorts of confusion that we cannot model with the notion of an extensive form game as described. There are other situations that would be, at the least, hard to model in the fashion given above.

Imagine a situation where two firms are linked by a contractual arrangement; think of the firms as a coal mine and an electric power-generating firm. The contract specifies, for example, that the electric power-generating firm may demand each month not more than X tons of coal at a set price p per ton but the generating firm must pay for at least Y tons of coal for some $Y < X$ even if it doesn't take the coal. Now imagine that demand for electricity falls, so much so that the electric power-generating firm knows that it will not need Y tons of coal. It is willing to pay a price higher than p if it can be released from its obligation to buy at least Y tons. So a meeting is arranged between the two parties to see if they can come to a mutually agreeable renegotiated contract. We are interested in modeling the negotiation process.

Who moves first? Who moves second? What officially signifies that a mutually agreeable deal has been made? In most negotiations these things, which constitute the protocol of negotiations, are not really specified with the precision we require for an extensive form game.

Two options are open to us at this point. One is to forego trying to model the negotiation as an extensive form game and instead use some principle concerning how we think negotiations will conclude. An example of such a principle is: The two will come to an efficient arrangement (one in which it is impossible for both sides to be made better off) that "splits the difference" above the levels of their profits if they have to keep to the original contract. This approach would move us from noncooperative to cooperative game theory, where one looks for general principles on which "deals" will be struck given a description of what players can achieve if they cooperate and if they don't.

Alternatively, we can stick to the "rules" of noncooperative game theory, which are that we have to be very precise about the rules of the game. We might look at the negotiations as a process in which the two make alternating offers with the honor of making the first offer determined by a coin flip. We might look at the negotiations as a process in which the two must simultaneously make offers until they make offers that are compatible (meanwhile living under the strictures of the original contract). In fact, we will study *bargaining protocols* of these sorts in chapter 15. The point for now is that the methodology we are developing requires a very precise and rigidly specified protocol, which in some instances may be quite artificial.[4]

11.3. Games in normal or strategic form

From the example of section 11.1 it should be obvious that some game situations can be represented by a number of different extensive forms. Since all these extensive forms represent the same "game," we might suspect there is another way to represent the game that is a bit clearer about the essence of the situation.

---

[4] We might hope for results that say the precise protocol doesn't matter. If your hopes run in that direction, chapter 15 will be somewhat disillusioning.

What is common to all the different extensive form representations hinted at for Jokx versus Beljeau is that they all represent the same strategic problem for the two sides. Suppose that as owner of Jokx you have decided to take a vacation in Florida. All decisions concerning Oligopoly must be made before you return, and you refuse to ruin your vacation by talking on the phone with the home office. So you decide to leave complete and unambiguous instructions as to what decisions you want taken regarding Oligopoly.

That's pretty easy — you have to decide whether to proceed with Oligopoly or not. You will receive no useful information, so there are really only two possible sets of instructions you might leave:

$s1$: Proceed to market Oligopoly.

$s2$: Don't do this.

What is more interesting is the similar problem for the management of Beljeau. If they are headed off for vacation, the instructions they must leave will concern whether to market Reaganomics or not, contingent on the results of the market survey. There are four sets of instructions they could leave:

$t1$: No matter what the survey says, proceed with Reaganomics.

$t2$: Proceed with Reaganomics if the market will be large, but not if the market will be small.

$t3$: Proceed with Reaganomics if the market will be small, but not if the market will be large.

$t4$: No matter what the survey says, don't proceed with Reaganomics.

Now you may find strategy $t3$ to be fairly silly. (In fact, at the end of section 11.1 we already indicated that $t2$ seems the only sensible thing to do.) We'll worry about choosing among these four *strategies* in the next chapter. For the time being we leave them all, since they represent all the instructions Beljeau could conceivably leave behind before going off on vacation.

Look at the extensive form depicted in figure 11.9. The game depicted there runs as follows. You (Jokx) are heading for Florida, so you select one of your two strategies. Without knowing what you chose (note the information set), Beljeau picks one of their four strategies. And then nature acts to select one of the two market sizes, with payoffs made to each side accordingly. For example, if you pick $s2$, Beljeau picks $t2$, and the market is large, then you are out of the market and Beljeau learns that the market

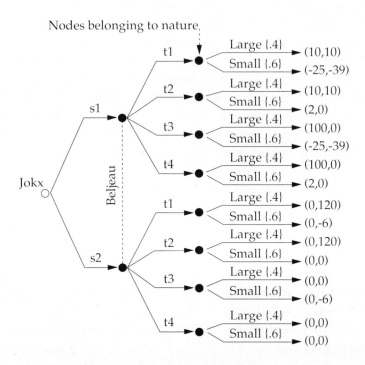

Figure 11.9. Another extensive form representation of Jokx vs. Beljeau.

is large and (according to *t2*) markets Reaganomics. Thus you make $0 and Beljeau makes $120K. Note that we could just as well put Beljeau first and you second, using an information set for you to model the notion that you don't know what strategy Beljeau has selected when you select your own strategy.

One final step, and we have what is known as the *normal or strategic form* of the game. Let's assume that both you and Beljeau are risk neutral — that you evaluate risky prospects according to their expected value. (In general, since endpoints in games are evaluated in terms of the players' von Neumann-Morgenstern utility functions, expected payoffs become expected utilities.) Then if, say, you pick strategy *s1* and Beljeau picks *t2*, you stand a .4 probability of getting a contribution of $10,000 and a .6 probability of a contribution of $2,000. This has an expected value of $5,200. Similarly, for this pair of strategies, Beljeau has an expected value of $4,000.

In figure 11.10 we give what is known as the *normal* or *strategic form* of the game. In this case, because there are two players, this is also sometimes called a *bimatrix* form game. Each row in the table corresponds to one of your two strategies. Each column corresponds to one of Beljeau's four. And in the cells of the matrix, we list your expected contribution and then Beljeau's for the strategy pair corresponding to the cell.

In general, a *normal or strategic form game* is given by: a list of players $i = 1, \ldots, I$; for $i = 1, 2, \ldots, I$, a list of strategies S_i that player i might employ; and for each I-tuple of strategies $(s_1, \ldots, s_I)$, one for each player, the payoff to each player of that combination of strategies, given by functions $u_i : \prod_{j=1}^{I} S_j \to R$. Just the list of players and the lists of their strategies is sometimes called a normal form *game form*.

In moving from an extensive form to the resulting normal form, we undertake the following two-step procedure. First, for each player $i = 1, 2, \ldots, I$, the set of strategies for player i is given by

$$S_i = \prod_{\{h \in H : \iota(h) = i\}} A(h).$$

That is, a strategy s_i for player i specifies precisely which action the player will take in every information set assigned to that player.

Second, for every combination of strategies for the various players, which we will call hereafter a *strategy profile*, one evaluates the expected utility for each player, where one is taking expectation over any randomness in the initial node or in subsequent moves by nature, using the probability distributions ρ and ρ_t that are given as part of the extensive form game.

Consider the extensive form game depicted in figure 11.11. Note that player 1 has two information sets and player 2 has one. At player 1's first information set, she has two moves; she has two as well at her second. According to the formula just given for the strategy space of a player, she should have four strategies, viz., Aa, Ad, Da, and Dd. But if at her first information set she chooses D, there is no reason to consider what she would do at the second; by her own first action the second is precluded. In a sense, Da and Dd are the same strategies for her.

| | | Beljeau's strategy | | |
	t1	t2	t3	t4
s1	-11,-19.4	5.2,4	35,-23.4	41.2,0
s2	0,44.4	0,48	0,-3.6	0,0

(Jokx' strategy)

Figure 11.10. The normal form representation of Jokx vs. Beljeau.

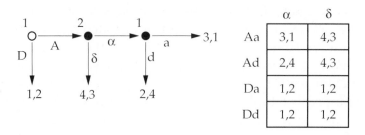

	α	δ
Aa	3,1	4,3
Ad	2,4	4,3
Da	1,2	1,2
Dd	1,2	1,2

Figure 11.11. An extensive form game and its normal form counterpart.

We can see this as well if we look at the normal form of this game, also shown in figure 11.11. We have drawn the normal form with four strategies for player 1. And you will quickly note that the last two rows, corresponding to the strategies Da and Dd, are identical. No matter which strategy player 2 uses, these two strategies for player 1 give identical payoffs to each player.

In general, when two strategies by a single player give every player the same payoff for any combination of strategies by the others, we say that the two strategies are *equivalent*, and we sometimes list "them" only once in the normal form. This applies generally, but it arises most frequently in the sort of case shown in figure 11.11 where earlier actions of a player can render inconsequential her plans at later information sets, because her earlier actions mean that the later information set will not be reached. To be very precise, when we drop equivalent strategies in this fashion, we are creating what is called the *reduced normal form*.

On the other hand, there is no single way to proceed in general from a normal form game to a corresponding extensive form game. In one obvious extensive form the players all choose complete strategies simultaneously, but often other extensive forms could be constructed from a given normal form.[e]

11.4. Mixed strategies and Kuhn's theorem

For reasons that will remain obscure until the next chapter, we consider in this section the possibility that a player might wish to choose her strategy by some random process.

For games in normal form the construction is easy in principle. Take a normal form game with finitely many players, each of whom has available finitely many strategies. Such a game is specified by a list of players

---

[e] In fact, some of the early work in the theory of extensive games took on the question: For a given extensive form game, what other extensive form games are strategically equivalent, in the sense that they give the same (reduced) normal form game? For those of you who are interested, the classic papers to consult are Dalkey (1953) and Thompson (1952).

$\{1, 2, \ldots, I\}$, (finite) sets of strategies S_i for each player, and payoff functions $u_i : \prod_{j=1}^{I} S_j \to R$. Let Σ_i be the set of probability distributions over S_i. An element $\sigma_i \in \Sigma_i$ is called a *mixed strategy* for player i, with the interpretation that if i chooses to play σ_i, then i chooses to take strategy $s_i \in S_i$ with probability $\sigma_i(s_i)$. We write s_i for the "mixed" strategy (element of Σ_i) according to which s_i is done with probability one — these are then called *pure strategies* for player i. It is assumed that players, if they mix, mix independently of one another, so that if players choose the mixed strategy profile $\sigma = (\sigma_1, \ldots, \sigma_I)$, the probability that the pure strategy profile $s = (s_1, \ldots, s_I)$ actually happens is $\prod_{i=1}^{I} \sigma_i(s_i)$. Thus if players use the mixed strategy profile σ, the expected payoff to player i is

$$u_i(\sigma) = \sum_{s = (s_1, \ldots, s_I) \in \prod_{j=1}^{I} S_j} \left[\prod_{j=1}^{I} \sigma_j(s_j) \right] u_i(s).$$

While this is all very simple in principle (and we will have examples in a moment and also in chapter 12), the constructions just given do rely on the fact that there are finitely many players, each of whom has a finite number of (pure) strategies s_i. One must be careful with this sort of definition when there are either uncountably many players or players with uncountably many strategies or both. Consult Aumann (1964) if you wish to see examples of how this is done.

The subject of mixed strategies becomes more interesting when we turn to games in extensive form. Consider the game depicted in figure 11.12(a). In this game, player 1 has two pure strategies and player 2 has

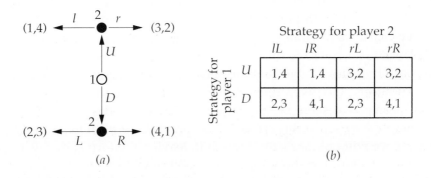

Figure 11.12. *A game in extensive and normal form.*

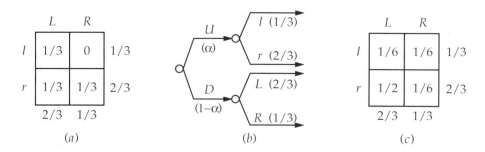

Figure 11.13. Mixed and behaviorally mixed strategies.

four; we can call player 1's two strategies U and D and label player 2's as $lL, lR, rL,$ and rR, where the first letter says what 2 does if 1 chooses U and the second says what 2 does if 1 chooses D. We can then translate this game into the corresponding normal form game shown in figure 11.12(b) and thereby define mixed strategies just as previously; player 1's mixed strategies are probability distributions over her pair of possible pure strategies, whereas 2's are probability distributions over his four strategies.

But there is another way to think about mixed strategies for player 2. Suppose that player 2 chooses to randomize only when necessary. If player 1 chooses U, then 2 randomizes between l and r, whereas if 1 chooses D, then 2 randomizes between L and R. That is to say, instead of randomizing over strategies player 2 randomizes over available actions at each information set.

Every probability distribution over 2's four pure strategies corresponds to this sort of randomization over actions at each information set. For example, suppose that 2 considers the mixed strategy: Play lL with probability 1/3, play rR with probability 1/3, and play rL with probability 1/3. (So lR is played with probability zero.) This is the "same" as: If 1 plays U, play l with probability 1/3 and r with probability 2/3. And if 1 plays D, play L with probability 2/3 and R with probability 1/3. When we say that these two are the same, we mean: For any (mixed) strategy by player 1, whether we think of player 2 randomizing at the outset over his four strategies or we think of player 2 randomizing as needed at information sets, the given two mixed strategies for 2 (of the two different types) lead to the same distribution on outcomes of the game.

How do we know this is true? The "proof" is implicit in figure 11.13(a) and (b); we will talk our way through it, leaving the formal details to you. In figure 11.13(a), we show a joint probability table for player 2's actions at each of his information sets. For example, the lower left box corresponds to the pure strategy rL, and the number 1/3 there is the 1/3 probability that he chooses rL in the mixed strategy listed above. The numbers in the right and bottom margins of the table are the marginal probabilities; the 2/3 along the right margin is the marginal probability that he will choose r. Hence you can see how we derived the "mix-as-you-go" strategy for 2 that corresponds to the listed mixed strategy. Now imagine that we were trying, for some mixed strategy by player 1, to work out the probability distribution over final outcomes. Specifically, suppose that player 1 chooses U with probability α. Then to work out what will happen, it is natural to write down the probability tree in figure 11.13(b), showing first the choice of player 1 and then the choice of player 2. Note well (this is the whole point): The outcome if player 1 chooses U and 2 chooses lL is the same as the outcome if 1 chooses U and 2 chooses lR; if player 1 chooses U, all that matters is the marginal distribution of 2's choice of l versus r. Similarly, if player 1 chooses D, it is only the marginal distribution over L and R that is of consequence.

Suppose that instead of the mixed strategy in 11.13(a), player 2 adopted the mixed strategy shown in 11.13(c). Would it make a difference? Since the margins on l vs. r and on L vs. R in (a) and (c) are the same, it would not, at least insofar as all we care about is the distribution over outcomes, given player 1's choice of strategy. Many mixed strategies for player 2 will give the same mix-as-you-go strategy.

In general, for a given extensive form game, we could recover the strategy sets for the players and define mixed strategies as mixtures over the pure strategies. But, alternatively, we could consider mix-as-you-go strategies, which are more formally referred to as *behaviorally mixed strategies*. For each information set h, we let $\Delta(A(h))$ be the set of probability distributions over the set of actions $A(h)$ that are available at h. And for each player i, a behaviorally mixed strategy for i is an element of $\prod_{h \in H: \iota(h)=i} \Delta(A(h))$. The interpretation is that i, upon reaching an information set h with $\iota(h) = i$, chooses the action to take according to the hth component in this vector of probability distributions.

So we have a choice in how to construct mixed strategies for an extensive form game. Which should we use? At least for games with perfect recall, convenience should be our guide because the choice is without loss of generality. The following result is known as *Kuhn's theorem* (and is first proven in Kuhn [1953]).

Theorem. *For an extensive form game with perfect recall, for every mixed strategy, there is a corresponding behaviorally mixed strategy which is "equivalent." And for every behaviorally mixed strategy, there is at least one (and often many)*

*"equivalent" mixed strategy. "Equivalent" here means "leads to the same distri-
bution of outcomes," if we specify strategies for all the players.*

This is not a trivial result. In particular, it doesn't hold for games without
perfect recall. If you play contract bridge, you will be able to see this by
doing problem 5.

We care about this because in different sorts of games the two different types of mixed strategies are of varying convenience. For simple
games and for certain analytical results, it is often convenient to deal with
strategies mixed in the normal form. For dealing with complex examples,
it is usually more convenient to deal with behaviorally mixed strategies.[f]
So it is nice to know that the two are equivalent concepts (for games with
perfect recall).

11.5. Bibliographic notes

I have tried to be relatively more formal and complete in this chapter
than in others, because I don't know any "next level" textbooks to recommend. The serious reader should instead proceed to the original research
papers on these subjects. References to these were provided in the course
of the chapter. In the other direction, the reader interested in seeing a
slower development of decision trees can consult Holloway (1979), while
a somewhat less formal and annecdotal companion to most of what we will
do on noncooperative game theory is Dixit and Nalebuff (forthcoming).

References

Aumann, R. 1964. "Mixed and Behavior Strategies in Infinite Extensive
    Games." In *Advances in Game Theory*, M. Dresher, L. Shapley, and A.
    Tucker, eds., 627-50. Princeton, N.J.: Princeton University Press.

Dalkey, N. 1953. "Equivalence of Information Patterns and Essentially De-
    terminate Games." In *Contributions to the Theory of Games*, vol. 2, H.
    Kuhn and A. Tucker, eds., 217-45. Princeton, N.J.: Princeton Univer-
    sity Press.

Dixit, A., and B. Nalebuff. Forthcoming. *Thinking Strategically*. New York:
    W. W. Norton.

Holloway, C. 1979. *Decision Making Under Uncertainty: Models and Choices*.
    Englewood Cliffs, N.J.: Prentice-Hall.

---

[f] To prove existence of an equilibrium, the former is more convenient; see the next chapter.
But when we analyze the centipede game with incomplete information in chapter 14, it is
essential that we deal with behaviorally mixed strategies.

Kuhn, H. 1953. "Extensive Games and the Problem of Information." In *Contributions to the Theory of Games*, vol. 2, H. Kuhn and A. Tucker, eds., 193-216. Princeton, N.J.: Princeton University Press.

Thompson, F. 1952. "Equivalence of Games in Extensive Form." The Rand Corporation. Mimeo.

11.6. Problems

Be sure to do problem 4. It will return again and again in the sequel.

■ 1. Let us complicate the story of Jokx and Beljeau enormously by supposing that both Jokx and Beljeau must decide whether to commission market surveys that will reveal the size of the market. For Jokx, this survey will cost $5,000; if they choose to spend this money, Jokx can learn for sure what the market size will be before they have to decide whether to proceed with Oligopoly. And Beljeau (which previously was assumed to have this information coming) now must decide whether to commission a survey; it will cost them $5,000 as well. Both sides must decide whether to commission a survey and then whether to proceed with the respective products without learning what the other has done, both with regard to taking the survey and then to introducing their product.

(a) Draw decision trees for Jokx and Beljeau in this new situation.

(b) Draw a game tree representing the situation for the two. (This is a tedious exercise.)

(c) List all the strategies that each side has. (Depending on what you do with equivalent strategies, they have between six and eight apiece.)

(d) Give the reduced normal form of this game. (Again very tedious.)

■ 2. What are the extensive and strategic forms of the game if, beginning with the variation of problem 1, Beljeau must decide whether to become informed about the size of the market before learning what Jokx does, but if they decide to become informed, they learn whether Jokx chose to become informed or not?

■ 3. Two firms simultaneously produce quantities of a good, which costs them $5 per unit to produce. They can produce any quantity between 0 units and 500 units. (To keep the game finite, assume they must select an integer number of units.) The units produced are then totalled, and a price for them is set that will clear markets where demand for the good is given by $P = \$1000 - 2Q$, where Q is the total quantity supplied. Each firm gets revenue according to the equilibrium price and the amount that it sells. What does an extensive form of this game look like? What does the strategic form of this game look like? How would things change if one firm, say firm A, got to see how much firm B produced before launching production itself?

■ 4. Consider the following game, which we will call the "truth game." There are two players, called 1 and 2, and a game-master. The game-master has a coin that is bent in such a way that, flipped randomly, the coin will come up "heads" 80% of the time. (The bias of this coin is known to both players.) The game-master flips this coin, and the outcome of the coin flip is shown to player 1. Player 1 then makes an announcement to player 2 about the results of the coin flip; player 1 is allowed to say either "heads" or "tails" (and nothing else). Player 2, having heard what player 1 says but not having seen the results of the coin flip then must guess what the result of the coin flip was — either "heads" or "tails." That ends the game. Payoffs are made as follows. For player 2 things are quite simple; player 2 gets $1 if his guess matches the actual results of the coin flip, and he gets $0 otherwise. For player 1 things are more complex. She gets $2 if player 2's guess is that the coin came up "heads", and $0 if player 2 guesses "tails", regardless of how the coin came up. In addition to this, player 1 gets $1 (more) if what she (player 1) says to player 2 matches the results of the coin flip, while she gets $0 more if her message to player 2 is different from the result of the coin flip.

Draw an extensive form representation of this game. Can you draw more than one extensive form representation? Then convert this extensive form representation to a normal form representation. (If you wish to test your intuition, answer: If you were playing this game as player 2, what strategy would you select? If you were player 1, what would you do? Record your reasons, and keep them available; later in the book we will analyze this game according to game-theoretic procedures.)

■ 5. If you read and understood sections 11.2 and 11.4 and if you know the rules of contract bridge, give the details for the following statements. Consider one hand in the game of contract bridge. Viewed as a four-player game, this game has perfect recall. But viewed as a two-player game, it does not. In this respect, viewed as a two-player game, Kuhn's theorem is false. One way to see this is to note that it would be a huge advantage to a partnership that sometimes engaged in psych bidding if they could secretly signal to each other when they were doing so.

chapter twelve

Solution concepts for noncooperative games

Having modeled a situation with either an extensive form or a normal form game, our next objective is to analyze the model in order to make predictions about what will happen in the situation modeled. This chapter concerns the analysis and "solution" of noncooperative games. It is a long and complex chapter, and you should expect it to take a number of readings before it begins to make sense to you (if it ever does).

12.1. Opening remarks

We begin with two opening remarks and an exercise that sets the stage.

The subject population

Any predictions we make about how a game will be played must depend on the characteristics of the individuals playing the game. One would not expect to observe the same behavior from every group of players.

The theories we will present proceed on the presumption that all the players in the game are "rational" (in various senses that we will make more precise as we go along), that each credits their rivals with "rationality," that each believes that all rivals credit their rivals with "rationality," and so forth. Our objective is to predict how people act in gamelike settings, and so one must wonder how useful will be any theory based on such a strong presumption concerning the rationality of the subjects. Some players in some situations might fail to meet this assumption. If you are playing against one of these people, or you suspect that you may be, you would sometimes be foolish to presume that your rival is rational. We will see in chapter 13 an interesting variation on this: If your rival(s) suspect that you are not rational, or even if they suspect that you suspect that they suspect that you aren't rational, then the "rational" actions for you can be quite different than if you ignore this possibility. That is to say, irrational people are out there and their irrationality has a substantial impact in many competitive settings, including an impact on the actions of rational individuals. We would not be developing a useful theory, either positive or normative, if we didn't take the possibility of irrationality into account. We will do this in chapter 13, but for the time being (and with apologies for the delay), we will proceed on the assumption that there isn't significant probability that some player is irrational, or that players think that others might be irrational, and so on.

This is still weaker than the formal assumption upon which some of our arguments will be based, namely that each player is absolutely certain to be rational, each is absolutely certain that all others are rational, each is absolutely certain that all others are certain that all the players are rational, and so on. I would contend (without much argument, presumably) that the ideal conditions of absolute certainty of rationality are never met in the real world. So insofar as the theory we develop depends on this absolute certainty and isn't robust to an "almost certainty," we have a remarkably useless theory. We need to pay attention to how robust our theory is to the slight possibilities that some one or more of the players is irrational, or that one or more suspect that some other(s) might be irrational, and so on. We will have a few things to say along these lines in what follows, but this is a difficult subject that only recently has gotten very much attention.

Some ground rules and cheap-talk

The ground rules in noncooperative game theory are that the description of the game should include all relevant opportunities for the players. That is, if there is the possibility that players can negotiate and form binding agreements, or if there is the possibility that one player can precommit early on to a particular sequence of moves, then this should be reflected in the extensive form and in the list of possible strategies.

One of the hardest things to handle in this regard is the possibility that the players can communicate. We can imagine communication of two different sorts here. One possibility is that players can send signals that involve a significant expenditure of resources. For this sort of communication, we follow the policy of trying to build formally into the model the communication possibilities.[1]

But there is also what is called "cheap-talk" — communication by one or both sides that is costless but which nonetheless might be useful in coordinating actions. Players can often communicate, and when players

---

[1] See especially chapter 17, which is largely given over to this subject.

can engage in cheap-talk, we could not hope to build a model with all the possibilities. How many speeches could one side make? How many replies could a second side make? How many iterations could there be in this speech/counterspeech regime? So it is typical in the analysis of non-cooperative games to omit such communication possibilities from formal models. This doesn't mean that these possibilities won't affect the outcomes of games; they do so in some important ways in various situations. And we will want to note this sort of effect when we can. But once again, our remarks on this point will be very much less than complete. This is another subject which has only recently begun to receive attention, and there is no settled "conventional wisdom" about cheap-talk.

Exercise

The test of the theory we will develop must, in the end, be empirical. A fair bit of experimental work looks at how various subject populations act in different types of "toy games," and (rather less) empirical work has been done on how individuals act in the sorts of real life situations we hope to model and analyze with these tools.

We will not look at this empirical literature, relying instead on your (no doubt razor-sharp) intuition about how people act in competitive situations. To give your intuition a fair test (or, rather, to give the theory a fair test), consider now how you would play a few games. In figure 12.1 are thirteen games in normal form and two games in extensive form, and following in the text are two more games in "verbal form." They are all two-player games, which is something of a simplification, but they cover enough ground for most of the points we will make in this chapter.

In all cases, the rules are that you will play the game once and once only, with no enforceable agreements possible, and with no side-payments between the two players. The numerical units ought to be thought of as in utility terms for the players. But, if you prefer, you can think of these as being "small" monetary payoffs, in pennies or nickels, say. Your rival will be someone very much like yourself — a fellow student, say, or someone who is reading this book just as you are.

Before reading on in this chapter, consider each of these games in turn and answer the following questions:

(a) How would you play as player 1 and as player 2?

(b) What predictions do you make about the play of your opponent? Assess a probability distribution for your opponent's choice of strategy; e.g., in the game in figure 12.1(a), perhaps you assess that your opponent, if

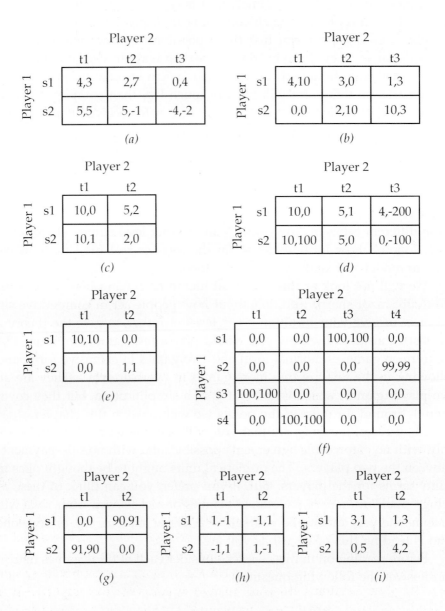

Figure 12.1. Some games.

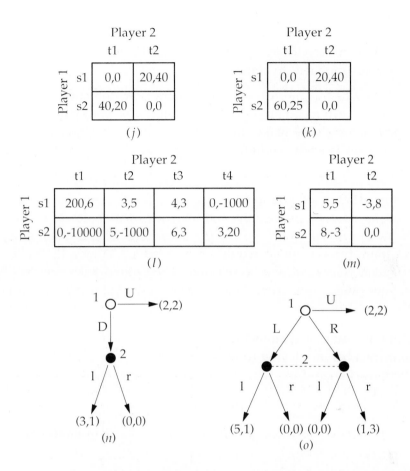

Figure 12.1, continued. Some more games.

choosing between s1 and s2, will choose s1 with probability .1 and s2 with probability .9, while if your opponent takes the role of player 2, he will play t1 with probability .6, t2 with probability .35, and t3 with probability .05. (This is just an example of the sort of assessment you are asked to make; my own assessment for this game would be quite different, as you will see when we get underway.) Of course, your answer to part (b) should have some connection with your answer to part (a). You might wish to write down your assessments and planned strategies for each game, with some notes to yourself about how you came to these assessments. We will discuss each of these games in turn as the chapter progresses, and you might wish to compare your assessments with what the theory will say you "ought" to have done.

As you give these assessments, please take special note of the following two sorts of situations:

Which individual strategies do you think are extremely unlikely for your opponent to choose?

In which games do you think there is an "obvious way to play," by which we mean an outcome (strategies for both players) that you think is very, very likely, and that you think any opponent you might encounter is likely to think very, very likely.

Note that I haven't tried to quantify "extremely" and "very, very" in these questions. That is for you to do.

Insofar as your predictions and/or your own choice of strategy depend on the specification we made concerning who is your rival, you might think through what would change if we changed the population from which your rival will be selected. The ground rules are also apt to affect your predictions. In particular, consider the following two variations for the games in figure 12.1:

(c) How do your predictions change if you can make a cheap-talk speech to your rival before playing (but he can't talk back to you)? How do your predictions change if the two of you can exchange cheap-talk?

The two games in verbal form are:

Divide the cities. Following is a list of eleven cities in the United States: Atlanta, Boston, Chicago, Dallas, Denver, Houston, Los Angeles, New York, Philadelphia, San Francisco, and Seattle. I have assigned to each city a point value from 1 to 100 according to the city's financial and commercial importance and its "quality of life." You will not be told this scale until the game is over, except that I tell you now that New York has the highest score, 100, and Seattle has the least, 1. I do think you will find that my scale is fair. I am going to have you play the following game against a randomly selected student of the Harvard Graduate School of Business Administration.[2] Each of you will be asked to list, simultaneously and without consultation, some subset of these eleven cities. Your list must contain San Francisco, and your opponent's must contain Boston. Then I will give each of you $100 simply for playing the game. And I will add to/subtract from that amount as follows: For every city that appears on one list but not on the other, the person who lists the city will get as many

---

[2] If you are from the Harvard Business School, make it a randomly selected student from the Stanford Graduate School of Business.

dollars as that city has points on my scale. For every city that appears on both lists, I will take from each of you twice as many dollars as the city has points. Finally, if the two of you manage to partition the cities — if each city appears on one and only one list — I will triple your winnings. Which cities will you list?

Divide the letters. Following is a list of eleven letters: A, B, C, D, E, H, L, N, P, S, T. Each has been assigned a point value from 1 to 100 according to some random scheme that I will not tell you, except to say that N has been assigned the highest score of 100 points and T has been assigned 1. I am going to have you play the following game against a randomly selected student of the Harvard Business School. Each of you will be asked to list, simultaneously and without consultation, some subset of these eleven letters. Your list must contain S, and your opponent's must contain B. Then I will give each of you $100 simply for playing the game. And I will add to/subtract from that amount as follows: For every letter that appears on one list but not on the other, the person who lists the letter will get as many dollars as that letter has points on my scale. For every letter that appears on both lists, I will take from each of you twice as many dollars as the letter has points. Finally, if the two of you manage to partition the letters — if each letter appears on one and only one list — I will triple your winnings. Which letters will you list?

12.2. *Dominance and iterated dominance for normal form games*

Let us begin by looking at the normal form of the Jokx-Beljeau game, which is reproduced here as figure 12.2. Does this representation suggest how the game will be played?

| | | Beljeau's strategy | | |
		t1	t2	t3	t4
Jokx' strategy	s1	-11,-19.4	5.2,4	35,-23.4	41.2,0
	s2	0,44.4	0,48	0,-3.6	0,0

Figure 12.2. The normal form representation of Jokx vs. Beljeau.

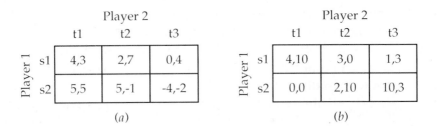

Figure 12.3. Two normal form games that are dominance solvable.

The answer to this question is emphatically yes for Beljeau. If Beljeau anticipates that Jokx will follow strategy s1, then Beljeau's best response is t2. If Beljeau anticipates that Jokx will follow strategy s2, then Beljeau's best response is t2. No matter what Jokx does, *Beljeau's best response is t2*. It stands to reason, then, that we can anticipate t2 from Beljeau.[3]

You may be straining to come to the obvious corollary conclusion, namely that if Jokx understands all this (so Jokx knows that Beljeau will adopt its strategy t2), then Jokx will choose s1. But before doing so, let us analyze the logic being employed a step at a time. We have in this example, for Beljeau, a very strong criterion for assessing what it will do; viz., *its best response to Jokx is independent of what Jokx does*. Whenever a player in a game has a strategy that is so clearly optimal as this, we will assess very high probability that the player will use this strategy, assuming we have correctly modeled the player's situation.

Consider next the game depicted in figure 12.3(a), which is taken from figure 12.1(a). If player 1 plays s1, 2's best response is t2. If player 1 plays s2, 2's best response is t1. So we can't come to the strong sort of conclusion above for player 2. Neither can we come to this sort of conclusion about player 1: s2 is 1's best response to t1 and t2, but s1 is 1's best response to t3. Nonetheless, we can arrive at a "partial" conclusion about player 2: We can conclude that he won't choose t3. This is so because t2 is better than t3 no matter what player 1 does. If player 1 chooses s1, then player 2 gets 7 from t2 and only 4 from t3, while if player 1 chooses s2, player 2 gets –1 from t2 and –2 from t3. We can't say for sure what player 2 *will* do, but we can be pretty sure about something he *won't* do.

We are invoking here the criterion of *strict dominance*. One strategy for a player is said to dominate strictly another if, no matter what other players do, the player in question does strictly better with the first than with the second. When one strategy strictly dominates a second, we will

---

[3] This should come as no surprise: You will recall that we reached this conclusion back when we drew the decision tree of Beljeau.

invariably conclude that the second strategy *will not* be played (or, if it is, we wonder why our model of the situation is incorrect).

Note that our first, very strong criterion (which worked for Beljeau) is an extreme case of strict dominance. It is the case where one strategy for a player strictly dominates all the others. Since by strict dominance we assess zero probability that any of the other strategies will be chosen, we are left concluding that the one strategy that dominates all the others will be chosen with probability one.

Now we take the next step in Jokx–Beljeau, a step we can take as well in figure 12.3(a). If we can predict that Beljeau will choose t2, then Jokx can as well, and Jokx should choose s1. Or in terms of the game in 12.3(a), if player 1 concludes that player 2 will not choose t3, then s2 is better for player 1 than is s1. The only reason player 1 would consider s1 is if she thought there was an appreciable chance that player 2 will play t3. Having concluded that this isn't the case, s2 dominates s1 for the strategies that are "left." And, to go yet another step, if player 2 anticipates that player 1 will anticipate that 2 will not play t3, and if 2 anticipates that player 1 will, therefore, select s2, player 2 then will choose t1 over t2. If we think players will think through the game in this fashion, we predict that the outcome will be s2 and t1. (How did you say you would play this game?)

We have "solved" both the Jokx-Beljeau game and the game in figure 12.3(a) by the criterion of *successive strict dominance*. We eliminate one strategy for one of the players on the basis of strict dominance. In the belief that a rational opponent will figure this out, this may allow us to rule out some of the opponent's strategies on the basis of "dominance," where we only require dominance against strategies not yet eliminated. And this could take us back to further elimination of strategies of the first player, and so on. Sometimes, this will end up with a single cell left, in which case we have figured out how rational opponents will play the game. [a]

Be very careful in noting what is meant by "rational players" here. We presume, and this seems a reasonably safe prediction, that rational players will not play dominated strategies. But when we move from dominance to iterated dominance, we raise the stakes. In a second round of iterated dominance, we are assuming that players assume their opponents won't play dominated strategies. That is, players are presumed to believe that

---

[a] You might wonder if this will be path dependent — if crossing out successively dominated strategies might lead to different results if crossed out in different orders. The answer is no, as long as crossing out is done on the basis of strict dominance, i.e., where you only cross out one strategy if some second strategy is strictly better than the first against every (remaining) choice by one's opponent(s).

their opponents are "rational." And in a third round, players presume that their opponents presume that all *their* opponents are rational. And so on. As the chain gets longer, the presumptions required grow more dubious; and we may feel less happy with predictions based on many rounds of iterated dominance.

Does this require players to be absolutely certain that their opponents are rational? All we need to be fairly sure that players will not play a dominated strategy is a "fair certainty" that players are rational. If, in the game in figure 12.3(a), we assess probability .9 that player 2 is rational (will not play a dominated strategy), then we assess probability .9 or more that player 2 won't play t3. (This just repeats a definition.) But when we move to iterated dominance, other considerations intrude. Suppose that the −4 in the s2-t3 cell of figure 12.3(a) was a −400. Then if player 1 assesses only probability .9 that player 2 is rational, she might choose to play s1 instead of s2. Or make this payoff a −40 and make the 3 in s1-t1 a −30. Suppose that player 2 is rational. Suppose that player 1 assesses probability .99 that player 2 is rational. But suppose that player 2 isn't so sure that player 1 has this high a regard for player 2's rationality. Then player 2 might well consider that player 1 might play s1 to be "safe"; at least player 2 might assess significant probability for this. And player 2 might, therefore, be led to t2 instead of t1.

For a prediction obtained by iterated dominance, there is some robustness in that prediction against the presumption that all players are certainly rational, all are certain that all are rational, and so on (for as many steps as there are steps in the chain of iterated dominations). That is, there is a probability less than one such that if every player believes that others are rational with at least this probability, each believes that each believes this with at least this probability, and so on; then we would still make the prediction that we obtained from iterated dominance. But (a) we might feel less happy with this sort of assessment if the number of iterations is large, and (b) the higher the cost of a "mistake" is, the closer to one must be this probability. We will return to these points near the end of this section.

Now look at the game depicted in figure 12.3(b), which is reproduced from 12.1(b). Can we do anything with dominance here? It would seem not; no one strategy strictly dominates another. But, under the assumption that player 2 is a subjective expected value maximizer, we can rule out t3. Why? Because no matter what probability distribution player 2 assesses for what player 1 will do, one of t1 or t2 (or both) is better than t3. Sometimes t1 is better than t3 (if s1 has probability greater than .3) and sometimes t2 is better (if s1 has probability less than .7). But t3 is never even tied for best of all. And, if we accept this argument and cross out t3 (or, more to the point, if we think that player 1 accepts this argument and crosses out t3), then we can proceed to cross out s2, and thus settle on s1-t1 as the solution.

This is "strict dominance of one strategy by a combination of other strategies." It is more difficult to find in general than strict dominance of one strategy by a second, but it seems legitimate to apply whenever we can. Two remarks about this are in order: If the prizes in the game were in units of millions of dollars, and if player 2 is risk averse, player 2 might prefer the sure $3 million to gambling. But we're assuming that either players are risk neutral or payoffs are in von Neumann-Morgenstern utility units, so this won't be a problem in theory. Secondly, we put the argument above as: Player 2, for any assessment about what player 1 might do, will choose either t1 or t2 as the strategy that maximizes expected utility. One could pose a different argument leading to the same conclusion: If player 2 randomizes by flipping a coin, playing t1 if heads and t2 if tails, then player 2 has a strategy that gives (an expected utility of) 5 if player 1 chooses s1 and 5 if 1 chooses s2, which strictly dominates t3. That is, t3 is dominated by a mixture of t1 and t2. I prefer the first line of argument, but the two come to the same thing.[b]

Now look at the game in figure 12.4(a), reproduced from figure 12.1(c). No strategy strictly dominates another. But s1 *weakly dominates* s2; s1 is as good as s2 against t1 and is better against t2. In general, one strategy for a player weakly dominates a second if against any strategies by the other players the player does as well with the first strategy as with the second,

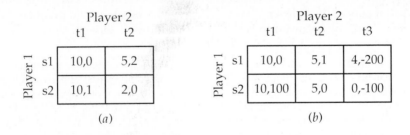

Figure 12.4. Examples of weak dominance.

[b] To be precise, in two-player games the two arguments certainly come to the same thing. In more-than-two-player games, they come to the same thing if a player is allowed to assess that the strategies chosen by his rivals might be correlated. If, however, players in a more-than-two-player game are presumed to assess that rivals' choices of strategy are independently distributed, then my preferred phrasing of the test is stronger. If you know about the separating hyperplane theorem, you can prove all this for yourself.

and against some combination of strategies by the other players, the player does strictly better with the first. Any player who maximizes expected utility and assigns strictly positive probability to every possible strategy combination by others will strictly prefer a weakly dominant strategy to the strategy that it dominates.

Applying weak dominance successively can be problematic, however. Look at figure 12.4(b), reproduced from figure 12.1(d). While s1 weakly dominates s2, it ceases to do so if the strictly dominated strategy t3 is eliminated first; once t3 is eliminated, player 1 is completely indifferent between s1 and s2. Player 2 would certainly like to encourage player 1 to select s2, so perhaps billboards put up by player 2 saying that "s2 is safe" would be in order.[4] [c]

The use of (successive) weak dominance is not as noncontroversial as the use of (successive) strict dominance, in part because of examples such as 12.4(b).[5] Despite such examples, economists tend to use successive weak dominance when they can. And when (as sometimes happens) all strategies except one for each player are eliminated by successive dominance, weak or strict, the game is said to be *dominance solvable*.[6]

> How does weak dominance interact with less-than-complete certainty that the players are rational? — in two ways, depending on who is trying to guess whether his rivals are rational. Suppose that some given player, call him i', has a given strategy s that is weakly dominated. Then if i' is less than completely certain that his opponents are rational, he may not wish to preclude them doing anything at all. That is, his assessment about his rivals' actions puts positive probability on every possibility. In this case s will never maximize i''s expected utility, even weakly, and we have a good argument to conclude that i' won't use s. But this argument presupposes that i' is rational. And if some other player i'' is worried even a bit about the rationality of i', then i'' might not want to count on i' avoiding s. Indeed, since s for i' is

---

[4] It is also in player 1's interest that player 2 thinks that 1 will pick s2, so we might also imagine that player 1 would be renting space on available billboards, to convince player 2 that she will pick s2. But player 2, if he is sceptical, may wonder about this; it is in the interests of player 1 to mislead 2 into thinking that 1 will play s2 even if player 1 fully intends to play s1, since by this means player 1 encourages the play of t1. How would you, as player 2, treat some pregame cheap-talk by player 1 that she fully intends to play s2?

[c] What does this example tell you about path independence and iterated weak dominance?

[5] Remember to review as we go along what you had to say about these games when you did the exercise at the start of this chapter. My experience with student populations, albeit informally tabulated, is that in the game in figure 12.4(b), s2-t1 is the modal response, despite the "logic" of weak domination. Admittedly, this is a very special game. But see below for a more robust example.

[6] Some quite interesting games are dominance solvable. See, for example, the discussion of the Cournot game in section 12.8 and Rubinstein's bargaining game in chapter 15.

only weakly dominated, it seems more likely that a less than fully rational i' might not see this argument. Accordingly, if s must be deleted in some chain of iterated dominance and if others doubt the rationality of i', the chain is more suspicious.

12.3. *Backwards induction in games of complete and perfect information*

So far we've discussed dominance and weak dominance in the context of normal form games. These criteria have important manifestations as well in extensive form games. Consider the extensive form game in figure 12.5(a), reproduced from figure 12.1(n). What predictions did you make about this game?

Most people predict that the outcome of this game will be that player 1 is very likely to choose D and player 2 is likely to respond with l. The argument supporting this prediction runs as follows: If player 1 chooses D, then player 2 is faced with a choice of l, which nets 1, or r, which nets 0. The dominating choice is l, and so we predict that if 1 chooses D, 2 (presuming 2 is rational) will choose l. And if player 1 believes that 2 is rational, 1 will replicate this logic, and she will choose D, which (she expects) will net 3, instead of the 2 she gets from U.

This, it turns out, is an argument equivalent to successive weak domination. In figure 12.5(b), we have the normal form game that corresponds to the extensive form game in figure 12.5(a). In this normal form, l for player 2 weakly dominates r. And once we eliminate r for player 2, D is the dominant choice for player 1. Note that the first step in this progression is weak domination only; if player 1 chooses U, l and r do equally well.

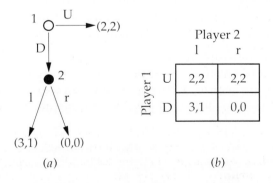

(a)   *(b)*

Figure 12.5. A simple extensive form game and its normal form counterpart.

It is sometimes maintained that the argument for the extensive form game is a bit more convincing than the corresponding argument of weak dominance for the normal form game. The logic for this assertion is that if we think of players 1 and 2 selecting strategies simultaneously and independently, then we might conceivably imagine player 2 choosing r, if he is absolutely certain that player 1 will choose U. But in the extensive form game, player 2 doesn't have this luxury. If he is given the move, player 2 knows that player 1 chose D, and he, therefore, knows that his choice will be of consequence.

Whether you find the two arguments equally compelling or you find the extensive form version more compelling, the connection should be obvious. And we can generalize this substantially. A *game of complete and perfect information* is an extensive form game in which every action node is, by itself, an information set. Think of any such game, and suppose that the tree has only a finite number of nodes. Then we can look at any "next-to-final" node — one whose successors are all terminal nodes. (Since the tree is finite, there must be at least one such. Provide a proof, if you wish.) Whoever has the move at that node, we can quickly decide how the player will act there; he will select whichever of the terminal node successors gives him the highest utility. (What if there is a tie among the terminal successors in terms of his utility? We will ignore this unhappy possibility, which complicates matters without adding much insight.) By weak domination, this player will never adopt a strategy that calls for him to take any other action at this next-to-final node. Now look for any node all of whose successors are either terminal nodes or the next-to-final node we just analyzed. Again, there must be one such. We can now solve the game from this point on (again assuming there are no ties), and so on. Calling any node that we have solved a solved node, as long as there are unsolved nodes, at least one unsolved node has successors that are all either solved or terminal, and we can proceed to solve that node next. Eventually every node in the game will be solved, and we will have a predicted solution for the game.

If the foregoing verbal description was less than completely transparent, you will do well to create and solve an example. Remember the ground rules: Every action node must be, on its own, an information set; there must be (only) finitely many nodes; and ties in payoffs of players are to be avoided. (In case you've forgotten, remember as well that game trees may not have cycles.)

And note how this is just iterated weak dominance, strengthened (if you find it more compelling) because when a player is called upon to move at a given node, he knows that his choice will make a difference.

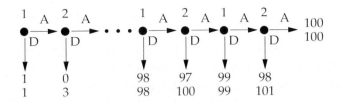

Figure 12.6. Rosenthal's centipede game.

The procedure sketched above is sometimes called backwards induction. One of the first results in game theory was, essentially, that finite games of complete and perfect information are dominance solvable by this backwards induction procedure, at least as long as ties are ruled out.[7] An application of this result will indicate some of the limitations of non-cooperative game theory. The rules of chess make it a finite game of complete and perfect information.[8] Hence we conclude that chess is dominance solvable. Either white has a forced win, or black does, or the game, played optimally, must end in a tie. The game tree for chess is, however, a bit too large for practical application of the backwards induction procedure. So despite the fact that chess must have a "solution," it remains an interesting puzzle how to play the game.[9]

Before departing this subject, one further example may be of interest — the so-called centipede game, popularized by Rosenthal (1981) and depicted in figure 12.6. If we apply backwards induction to this game, we see that at the next-to-final node player 2 will surely choose *D*, taking 101 instead of 100 and leaving player 1 with 98 instead of with 100. Hence at the next-to-next-to-final node player 1 will choose *D*, taking 99 instead of the 98 she would get by choosing *A* and letting 2 choose *D*. This leaves 2 with 99, and so 2 a node earlier chooses *D* and takes 100. And so on — going back up the tree, players 1 and 2 always take *D* instead of *A*, winding up with 1 choosing *D* at the first node in the game for payoffs of one apiece. (Game theorists, like economists, are not the best of linguists. Moving *up* the tree usually means moving in the direction of the tree's roots. Sorry about that.)

Since there are such lovely payoffs out at the end of the tree, this outcome seems rather a shame. More to the point, based on irregularly gathered evidence, it is a poor prediction. Asked to play this game, one

---

[7] The original proof of this result was for two-player zero sum games, where the sum of the two players' payoffs at each terminal node is zero. In this case, ties are irrelevant.

[8] If a particular position recurs three times, the game is drawn.

[9] We will return to the example of chess at the very end of the book.

typically finds even rather sophisticated players moving a fair ways out to the end before one player or the other chooses *D*.

There are two points to make in this regard. First, the prediction that player 1 will choose *D* to start the game is based on *200* rounds of iterated dominance. It is rather hard to believe that players are so sure of their opponent's rationality and their opponent's certainty of theirs, and so on, that we can trust to a prediction so based. Second, suppose that you, as player 2, are absolutely certain that your opponent is rational, and that your opponent is certain that you are, and so on, for as many iterations as this takes. So you are certain that your opponent will begin the game with *D*. And then, *despite all your certainties*, your opponent chooses to start the game with *A*. What do you think then? You have pretty good evidence that your initial hypothesis was wrong. But to justify that your follow-on choice should be *D*, you have to believe ex post that your theory still holds (with very high probability). After all, if your opponent isn't rational, or doesn't think you are, or isn't sure that you think he is, ... then maybe it is better to try *A* and see how far out the tree you can get. And now put yourself in the position of player 1. Just think what havoc you can play in the mind of your opponent by choosing *A*. And look at all those big payoffs (for both of you!) out at the end of the tree. Shouldn't you give *A* a shot?

This is an example to which we will return several times, so for the time being, simply note that many rounds of iterated dominance is sometimes a bit too much to believe. And iterated dominance can be especially unbelievable in extensive form games, where a "wrong prediction" early in the game may lead players to reexamine their faith in the maintained hypothesis that all the players (and especially the one who did the "wrong thing") are rational.

12.4. Nash equilibrium

In the previous two sections, we attempted to predict the outcomes of games by asking the question: What actions by the players can we *rule out*? This may seem a rather indirect way to get at the question of what players will do, and it may leave us well short of a positive prediction. Nonetheless, that question is a model of straightforward logic when compared with what we take on for the next four sections.

Consider the games in figure 12.7, which are reproduced from figure 12.1(e,f,g). Recall the second subsidiary question that you were asked in the exercise at the start of this chapter: In these games, is there an "obvious way to play the game," an outcome that you think is very, very likely, and

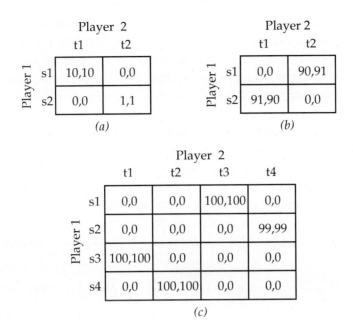

Figure 12.7. Three normal form games.

that (you would expect, with high probability) your rivals would think is very likely?

The typical responses are a definite yes for the game in 12.7(a), namely the outcome s1-t1, a definite no for the game in 12.7(b), and a conditional maybe for the game in 12.7(c). Regarding the last game, the answer I have heard typically runs as follows: If the players are unable to communicate, then s2-t4 seems very likely, although perhaps it is not very, very likely. The reason for this is that players will recognize that it is in their mutual interest to coordinate their actions, and while s2-t4 is not the absolutely best outcome for the two players, it seems the "safest" or "clearest" way to coordinate. If the players can engage in cheap-talk before the game is played, on the other hand, then one of s1-t3 or s3-t1 or s4-t2 is very, very likely to be the outcome, although there is no way to know which until after the cheap-talk is heard. That is, the players will certainly coordinate their actions; their interests are not in the least opposed. And they will use the opportunity of cheap-talk to coordinate on one of the three "best" outcomes.

Looking at the game in figure 12.7(a), and perhaps as well at the game in figure 12.7(c), we are using our intuition to say that there is an "obvious way to play this particular game." On a case-by-case basis, we can explain why these outcomes are "obvious," although what is obvious may depend on context — on whether players can engage in cheap-talk, for example. Even though our intuition may only be engaged on a game-by-game basis, there is a general formal test that we can pose for any candidate "obvious way to play": If this strategy profile is obvious, so that (we expect, with high probability) all the players will figure this out, then it ought to be that players, in their own best interests, carry out their part of this profile. Put differently, what each player is meant to do ought to be a best response to what all the other players are meant to do. This suggests the following formal definition. We pose the definition for the context of a finite player normal form game, where the players are indexed by $i = 1, \ldots, I$, their (respective) available strategy sets are denoted by S_i, and for $s = (s_1, \ldots, s_I) \in \prod_{j=1}^{I} S_j$, $u_i(s)$ is i's payoff if the strategy profile s is played.

Definition. *A strategy profile $\hat{s} = (\hat{s}_1, \ldots, \hat{s}_I)$ is a **Nash equilibrium** if for each player i and $s_i \in S_i$,*

$$u_i(\hat{s}) \geq u_i(\hat{s}_1, \ldots, \hat{s}_{i-1}, s_i, \hat{s}_{i+1}, \ldots, \hat{s}_I).$$

Or, in words, a Nash equilibrium is a strategy profile in which each player's part is as good a response to what the others are meant to do as any other strategy available to that player.

This definition is given for normal form games, but the same basic concept applies to extensive form games — the easiest way to make the translation is to say that a strategy profile for an extensive form game is a Nash equilibrium if it corresponds to a Nash equilibrium as defined above in the corresponding normal form game. This translation hides some interesting facets of equilibria in extensive form games, which we get to only in section 12.7. Until then we will stick for the most part to normal form games.

The contention is that being a Nash equilibrium is a *necessary condition* for an obvious way to play the game, if an obvious way to play the game exists. And, indeed, in the games in figure 12.7(a,c), our candidate "obvious ways to play" are all Nash equilibria. But note carefully that

(a) Being a Nash equilibrium is certainly not sufficient for a strategy profile to be the obvious way to play a given game. In the game in figure 12.7(a), s2-t2 is another Nash equilibrium, and we would hardly call it the obvious way to play this game.

(b) There is no reason to suppose that every game admits an obvious way to play. For example, if players 1 and 2 are unable to communicate, the game in figure 12.7(b) possesses no obvious solution, although it has two Nash equilibria, namely s2-t1 and s1-t2.[10]

In the great majority of the applications of noncooperative game theory to economics, the mode of analysis is equilibrium analysis. And in many of those analyses, the analyst identifies a Nash equilibrium (and sometimes more than one) and proclaims it (them?) as "the solution." I wish to stress that this practice is sloppy at best and probably a good deal worse.[11] We advance the formal concept of a Nash equilibrium in a much narrower spirit: This formal concept is *an* answer to the question: If there is an obvious way to play the game, what properties must that "solution" possess? Given our loose definition of "an obvious way to play the game" — it is something all the players can figure out, and all expect the others can figure out — it is hard to see how some outcome that is not a Nash equilibrium could ever qualify.

But this is a very weak question, and it is clear that having the answer "Nash equilibrium" is pretty thin gruel if what we are after is a way to solve games. All we have is a test of solutions derived by some other means. Some obvious questions arise.

(a) If "Nash equilibrium" is only one answer to this question, what more can be said? Can we sharpen this necessary condition? In this regard, note that a Nash equilibrium can involve weakly dominated strategies. For example, in the game in figure 12.5(b), U-r is a Nash equilibrium, even though l weakly dominates r. Insofar as we believe that players will avoid weakly dominated strategies, we could add to our necessary condition that the "solution" should be a Nash equilibrium in strategies that are undominated, even weakly. Accepting this (although wait until section 12.7 before doing so), is there still more to say?

(b) What are the means by which we are to identify "obvious ways to play a (given) game?"

(c) What would lead one to imagine that a given game admits an "obvious way to play?" This question is closely related to (b) in that if we know

---

[10] In fact, as we will discover momentarily, this game has a third Nash equilibrium, which is also not an obvious way to play.

[11] And, I'm sorry to say, in later chapters I will be somewhat sloppy in just this fashion.

why this sort of solution might exist, we would probably have a good clue to what it might be.

(d) What can one say about games that do not admit a "solution?" And what, if anything, does the notion of Nash equilibrium say concerning such games?

Make no mistake — there are games that, in certain contexts, do not possess "solutions." The game in figure 12.1(j) is a good case in point, at least if played under conditions of no communication. The game in figure 12.1(k) is another. And the game in figure 12.1(l) is especially interesting with regard to question (d) above. In discussing this game with students, I have found that most, cast in the role of player 2, choose t3, and most expect that player 2 will choose t3. Accordingly, most students cast in the role of player 1 choose s2, and most students cast in the role of player 2 expect player 1 to choose s2. But because of those large negative payoffs for player 2 in all the other columns, player 2 must be *very* sure what player 1 is going to do before moving from t3. That is to say, the standards of "very, very sure" are raised when the consequences of being wrong are dire. While I would guess that in eighty percent of the times I have had students play this game, s2-t3 was the outcome, it is still not quite "obvious" enough to qualify as an "obvious way to play the game," given the consequences of being wrong.[12] This game does not admit an obvious way to play.

The point is that this game has Nash equilibria, three of them in fact. One is s1-t1, and a second is s2-t4. The third is an equilibrium in mixed strategies, something which we will introduce in the next section, but for the time being take my word for it: In no Nash equilibrium of this game is t3 played. Indeed, t3 is the only strategy that is unplayed in some Nash equilibrium. So in answer to question (d) above: When the game doesn't admit an "obvious way to play," looking at its Nash equilibria can give precisely the wrong answer. The concept of Nash equilibrium should have no command on our attention when the game doesn't admit of a "solution."[13]

This leaves us with questions (a), (b), and (c). We will get to those questions in a bit, but before doing so, we chase down a bit of esoterica concerning the notion of a Nash equilibrium.

---

[12] And, indeed, my very casual empirical sense is that there is enough play of s1 by player 1 (between ten and twenty percent) to make t3 the optimal strategy for player 2. It is certainly what I would do, playing this game.

[13] For another example, see the end of section 12.6 for a game with a unique Nash equilibrium which, nonetheless, is not what one normally sees when the game is played.

12.5. Equilibria in mixed strategies

Some games don't have Nash equilibria. At least, they don't have equilibria if we stick to the definition given (loosely) above. Consider the games in figure 12.8 reproduced from figure 12.1(h) and (i).[14] In both these games s1-t1 isn't a Nash equilibrium, because if player 1 is choosing s1, then player 2 would wish to move to t2. At s1-t2, player 1 wishes to move to s2. At s2-t2, player 2 takes us back to t1. And at s2-t1, player 1 wishes to shift to s1, which exhausts all the possibilities for a Nash equilibrium in these games.

Despite what was just said, these two games do have Nash equilibria. What was just shown is that no pure strategy profile is a Nash equilibrium. But consider the game of figure 12.8(b), and imagine that player 1 plays s1 with probability .6 and s2 with probability .4. Then player 2, by playing t1, will net expected value 2.6. And playing t2 will net 2.6 for player 2. And playing any mixed strategy will net expected value 2.6. So every strategy by player 2, mixed and pure, is a best response to this strategy by player 1. In particular, one best response is the mixed strategy where player 2 plays t1 with probability .5 and t2 with probability .5. And this strategy causes player 1 to net expected value 2 from s1 and 2 from s2 and 2 from any mixture of s1 and s2. So, in particular, playing s1 with probability .6 and s2 with probability .4 is a best response to player 2's strategy. We have a mixed strategy profile (that is, a mixed strategy for each player) such that each player's strategy is a best response to what the other is playing. Hence we have a Nash equilibrium. Similarly in the game of figure 12.8(a), it is an equilibrium for both players to mix with probability 1/2 for each of their respective strategies.

In these examples, players randomize among all their strategies. So you don't get the wrong idea about this, consider the game in figure 12.1(l).

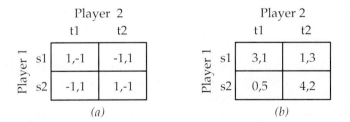

Figure 12.8. Two games with only mixed strategy equilibria.

---

[14] The game in figure 12.8(a) is called "matching pennies," after the children's game.

We have already remarked that this game has two Nash equilibria, s1-t1 and s2-t4. Because these equilibria do not involve any randomization, they are called *pure strategy* equilibria. Now consider the following pair of strategies. Player 1 plays s1 with probability 9000/9001 and s2 with probability 1/9001, and Player 2 plays t1 with probability 1/101 and t2 with probability 100/101. Given player 2's strategy, player 1 nets:

$$(200)(1/101) + (3)(100/101) + (4)(0) + (0)(0) = 500/101 \text{ from s1; and}$$

$$(0)(1/101) + (5)(100/101) + (6)(0) + (3)(0) = 500/101 \text{ from s2.}$$

So player 1 is content to play the mixed strategy. And player 2, against player 1's strategy, nets:

$$(6)(9000/9001) + (-10000)(1/9001) = 44000/9001 \text{ from t1;}$$

$$(5)(9000/9001) + (-1000)(1/9001) = 44000/9001 \text{ from t2;}$$

$$(3)(9000/9001) + (3)(1/9001) = 27003/9001 \text{ from t3; and}$$

$$(-1000)(9000/9001) + (20)(1/9001) = -8,999,980/9001 \text{ from t4.}$$

So player 2 is indifferent between strategies t1 and t2, and strictly prefers these two to t3 and t4. The range of best responses for player 2 (to player 1's strategy), then, is any mixed strategy that puts zero probability on t3 and t4. And our strategy profile has player 2 playing precisely this sort of mixed strategy.

Note that in this sort of equilibrium, the probabilities used by the players to randomize are determined not by their own payoffs but by the payoffs of the other players. If, for example, in figure 12.8(b) we changed the 1 that player 2 gets from s1-t1 to a 2, then the Nash equilibrium would be for player 2 to stick with the .5-.5 randomization and for player 1 to change to playing s1 with probability .75 and s2 with probability .25. The point of randomizing is to keep the other player(s) just indifferent between the strategies that the other player is randomizing among. One randomizes to keep one's rival guessing and not because of any direct benefit to oneself. Put another way, in a mixed strategy Nash equilibrium each player has no *positive* incentive to randomize according to the called-for mixing probabilities; as long as the other player is fulfilling his part of the equilibrium, there are many best responses for the first.

For this reason, many people find the idea of a mixed strategy Nash equilibrium incredible. Are we to believe that individuals faced with real economic decisions decide what to do by flipping a coin? And if we believe that, are we further to believe that individuals will bother to perform just the right randomization, when doing so is not particularly to their advantage? Nothing said so far should be taken to imply that the answer is yes. Remember that being a Nash equilibrium is necessary for "the obvious way to play the game," if an obvious way to play exists. It is in the eyes of the players (or the analyst) whether mixed strategies ever can constitute the obvious way to play the game.

In some cases, it doesn't seem unreasonable to suspect that players use randomized strategies. When playing poker, for example, good players will randomize (bluff) to avoid becoming predictable.[15] In games where one player checks on the other — in cases of auditing or quality inspection, to take two examples — a policy of random checking is often employed.

Still, if you conclude for yourself that mixed strategy equilibria are often not very intuitive and (therefore) not candidates for the "solution" of a given game, you won't get too much of an argument here.

But, in any case, having the notion of mixed equilibrium around is useful in one respect. It gives a rather nice mathematical result:

Proposition. *Every finite player, finite strategy game has at least one Nash equilibrium, if we admit mixed strategy equilibria as well as pure.*

This result can be generalized to classes of games with infinitely many players and/or infinitely many strategies under certain conditions. We won't be concerned with such extensions here.

> The proposition is rather easy to prove if you recall Kakutani's fixed point theorem from chapter 6. Let $i = 1, \ldots, I$ index the players, let S_i be the (pure) strategy space for player i, and let Σ_i be the space of mixed strategies for player i (i.e., Σ_i is the space of probability distributions on S_i). Write $\Sigma = \prod_{i=1}^{I} \Sigma_i$; that is, Σ is the space of mixed strategy profiles.
> For each $\sigma = (\sigma_1, \ldots, \sigma_I) \in \Sigma$, define
>
> $$\phi(\sigma) = \{\hat{\sigma} = (\hat{\sigma}_1, \ldots, \hat{\sigma}_I) \in \Sigma | \hat{\sigma}_i \text{ is a}$$
>
> best response to $(\sigma_1, \ldots, \sigma_{i-1}, \sigma_{i+1}, \ldots, \sigma_I)$ for each $i\}$.
>
> That is, $\phi(\sigma)$ gives the vector correspondence of best responses by the players to σ. We leave as an exercise the proof that ϕ is upper semi-continuous and convex-valued. Then by Kakutani's fixed point theorem, there is some σ

---

[15] There is a counterargument to this: Good players randomly decide when to bluff in order to be unpredictable *in the future*. This is different from the argument in a randomized strategy, where a player randomizes for current purposes only. Put differently, in the last hand of poker you will ever play, will you choose what to do based on the flip of a coin?

such that $\sigma \in \phi(\sigma)$. Which then, by the definition of ϕ, makes σ a Nash equilibrium.

The use of mixed strategies is troubling to much of the laity and even to some game theorists; do we really think that players will choose their actions by rolling dice? Owing to this, there have been attempts to domesticate the concept. The most prevalent is an argument that mixed strategies are an artifice of an unnaturally coarse model of reality. That is, in any real application, each player has many items of personal preference known to himself and unknown by others — things like what side of the bed he got out of, his exact tolerance for risk, etc. One would not wish to build that much detail into a model; the model would become intractable. But that detail is "really" there. And the detail is what determines how an individual chooses between strategies. What maintains the equilibrium is that each player, trying to decide what the other will do, feels that he faces the equilibrium probability distribution over the opponent's (or opponents') strategies. The individual can make a definite choice between the strategies over which he is supposed to randomize based on his personal factors. He can't predict what the other side will do, because he doesn't know the actual values of the other's personal factors. The mathematical results that support this philosophical position are known as *purification theorems*. A classic reference on this subject is Harsanyi (1973); Aumann et al. (1983) is also recommended to the interested reader.

12.6. Why might there be an obvious way to play a given game?

We've said that *if* there is an obvious way to play the game, then it is *necessary* that this is a Nash equilibrium. But we've also said that the only claim that the concept of Nash equilibrium has on our attention is predicated on there being an obvious way to play the game. And we've seen several examples of games without an obvious way to play. So if we think that there is some reason to pay attention to the notion of a Nash equilibrium, we had better give reasons why some games might seem (to the players and to the analyst) to be endowed with a "solution."

We have, of course, seen examples of games that seem to have this sort of solution. The Jokx-Beljeau game and the games in figure 12.7(a) and (c) would be two such, in the case of 12.7(c) depending on what the players can say to one another. Games that are dominance solvable would be another class of games with obvious solutions, at least if the number of rounds of iterated dominance required is not too large: The games in figure 12.3(a) and 12.5 would seem to qualify, although the game in figure 12.6 would not. What is it about these games and others like them?

There is no single answer to this question, and in many cases the answer, such as it is, can only be given informally. This is why the formal notion of a Nash equilibrium is useful; as a necessary condition for any candidate solution, the concept applies no matter what story is believed to be behind the existence of the solution. The formal notion provides a useful test for solutions that others may suggest to you, and it gives us something of a formal language with which to discuss matters. But this utility of the formal concept doesn't mean that one can do without the story about why a game in question does have a solution. So we turn now to some of the stories that are told in the literature.

Preplay negotiation

One means to the existence of an "obvious way to play" is explicit negotiation or cheap-talk among the players, conducted prior to play of the game. If preplay negotiations take place, we cannot guarantee that the players will come to an agreement, nor can we say what agreement will be reached. But, if the players do negotiate and they do reach an agreement, then we would expect the agreed-to action to be "self-enforcing" in the sense that each individual player, expecting the others to carry out their part of the agreement, does not have an incentive to deviate. That is, we will want the agreement to be a Nash equilibrium.

> There is an important caveat to add here. If players can engage in pre-play negotiation, they might be able to move beyond the possibilities suggested by the formal rules of the game, especially if doing so will make everyone better off. We could model this possibility by putting within the formal rules of the game all these possibilities. But some sorts of possibilities are sometimes modeled "indirectly"; the possibilities are not included in the formal model of the game, but the solution concept is changed to reflect their possibility. The most famous of these is Aumann's correlated equilibrium. Aumann (1974) considers what will happen if the players are able to build various sorts of mechanical coordinating devices or employ a disinterested party who will act as a coordinator. For example, consider the two-player game depicted in figure 12.9. This game has a single mixed strategy Nash equilibrium, in which both players have expected payoff 3.75. Now imagine that, via preplay negotiation, the players agree to the following scheme. Some third party will roll a six-sided die. If the die comes up with one or two spots

<table>
<tr><td></td><td></td><td colspan="2" align="center">Player 2</td></tr>
<tr><td></td><td></td><td align="center">t1</td><td align="center">t2</td></tr>
<tr><td rowspan="2">Player 1</td><td>s1</td><td align="center">4,4</td><td align="center">3,5</td></tr>
<tr><td>s2</td><td align="center">5,3</td><td align="center">0,0</td></tr>
</table>

Figure 12.9. A game with a correlated equilibrium.

up, player 1 is told to play s2. If it comes up three through six, this third party tells player 1 to play s1. At the same time, if the die comes up one through four, player 2 is told to play t1, while five or six causes player 2 to be instructed to play t2. Each player is told only what to play and not how many spots came up (precisely). This arrangement is "self-enforcing": If player 1 is told to play s2, she knows that player 2 was told to play t1, and s2 is a best response to t1. While if player 1 is told to play s1, she assesses probability 1/2 that player 2 was instructed to play t1 and 1/2 that player 2 was instructed to play t2. Assuming 2 carries out his instructions, s1 is a best response. A similar argument applies for 2. The point is that the roll of the die and the "intervention" of this third party allow 1 and 2 to correlate their actions in a self-enforcing manner. And in this correlated equilibrium, each player has an expected payoff of 4, which is more than either gets in the unique Nash equilibrium of this game. Can we maintain that the two players can engage in preplay negotiation but they cannot obtain the services of a third party for this purpose? If they can correlate their actions in this fashion, then the range of self-enforcing agreements is larger than the set of Nash equilibria, which presumes independent selection of actions. On all these points, see Aumann (1974). And for even fancier devices of this sort, see Forges (1986) and Myerson (1986).

Convention

Consider the game in figure 12.7(b), played under the following conditions: There is a large population of players who are matched randomly at random times and who at those times must play this game. (Moreover, players are randomly assigned "positions" in the game; a given individual will sometimes be put in the position of player 1 and sometimes in the position of player 2.) The players, when matched, cannot communicate. In this case, it is not hard to imagine that some convention will be developed concerning how to play this game — say, always play s2-t1. This convention is no more likely, on the face of things, than the reverse. By the same token (taking a slightly more complex example), there is no reason why red means stop and green means go on traffic lights. This is convention, and a lot of "good outcomes" on the roads result.

Interesting equilibria "by convention" sometimes are tied to seemingly irrelevant signals or historical summaries. By "seemingly irrelevant" I mean: These things do not affect the range of strategies a player has, or players' payoffs from various strategy profiles. But these things become relevant to the play of the game because convention makes them relevant. Traffic lights are a classic example. Or consider playing the game in figure 12.1(j) in a large population, with random matchings of players, but where the distinguishing labels of player 1 and player 2 are absent, so players cannot use those labels to coordinate. Imagine that each player carries with himself a summary of how well he has fared in the past —

say the sum total of all his winnings in these games. And imagine two different "societies," distinguished by the following two conventions: In the first society, when two players meet, the one who has fared less well in the past is given the edge in this encounter. That is, if player 1 has fared less well in the past, we play s2-t1. (If the players have done precisely as well in the past, convention is silent as to what happens.) In the second society, instead of *noblesse oblige*, the reverse holds: Whichever party has fared better in the past is given the edge. One might argue which is the better society/convention. But both conventions serve at least the purpose of getting players to a Nash equilibrium. (For analysis of this sort of thing, see Rosenthal and Landau [1979].)

Learned behavior

A variation on the convention stories concerns learned behavior. Go back to the game in figure 12.7(b), and consider a pair of players who play this game a number of times. We might not expect them to be able to coordinate their actions on the first round of play or on the second, but it is not hard to imagine that after a few interactions some modus vivendi will spring up between them. (Suppose that the players have constant roles. That is, one individual is always player 1 and the other is player 2. It is then interesting to ask: Given that the difference in payoffs is only 1, versus a loss of 90 if coordination fails, will players tend to stick with one coordinated solution, or will they learn to alternate? Or, put another way, if the 91s were both 1s, we might expect players to learn to alternate. But what about intermediate cases, such as the game in figure 12.1[j]? And what will happen in the game in figure 12.1[k]?)

An early manifestation of learned behavior stories were models of "fictitious play." Imagine two players playing a normal form game with the following decision rules. Begin with any strategy at all. Then, in each round of play, choose whatever strategy is best against the "average play" of your rival in previous rounds. That is, if in one hundred rounds of play your rival has chosen s1 39 times, s2 22 times, s3 16 times, and s4 33 times, then you play whatever is best against the mixed strategy (by your opponent) of (.39, .22, .16, .33). If both players act and "learn" in this fashion, will they settle down to some equilibrium? (If they do, it is clear that this will have to be a Nash equilibrium.) It turns out that this sort of behavior does not necessarily lead to an equilibrium; a famous example of Shapley (1964) establishes this. But one can still wonder to what extent learning by the players can lead them to situations in which each is fairly sure what the others are doing and acting in his own best interests in response reinforces what others think they know about the actions of the first. For one development of this sort of story, especially in the context of extensive form games, see Fudenberg and Kreps (1989).

Although it will make more sense after chapter 14, note that a "problem" with the learned behavior story, insofar as it is meant to apply to a pair of players who play the same game repeatedly, is that the repeated play by itself can enlarge the set of possible Nash equilibria. (If you don't understand this remark, don't panic; wait for chapter 14.) To assume that players play the same game with the same opponents over and over and they thereby "learn" some static Nash equilibrium of the game may require that players are myopic to a certain extent. The story works a bit better if there is a group of individuals who are randomly matched, but then we come to a gray area between learned behavior and convention.

Focal points and principles

The final story we tell about where "solutions" to given games might come from is related to the stories in the previous two subsections. We can introduce this story by returning to the games in figure 12.7(a) and (c). In the game in 12.7(a), it seems clear why s1-t1 is the "solution," even though there is another Nash equilibrium; s1-t1 gives both players the most they can get in this game, and the players can see that this doesn't put their interests in opposition. Even if the players have never spoken and are not allowed to speak, it seems pretty clear that each will realize this (at least, with high probability) and act "accordingly." Note well the quotation marks around accordingly, since it is only accordingly if we make the leap for the two players simultaneously, or rather if we believe that each player, making the leap, simultaneously believes that his opponent is making the corresponding leap.

In 12.7(c), if the players cannot communicate, it is not the optimality of s2-t4 that commends itself, but the "uniqueness" of this mode of coordinating. It just seems likely that each player, looking at this game and thinking about how coordination might be achieved, will see this uniqueness as his best hope (and expect that the other side will see this as well).

Now consider the two verbal games from the first section. Take the game with the eleven cities first. This game has an enormous number of Nash equilibria, even if we restrict attention to pure strategies. Since San Francisco and Boston are preassigned, it has 512 pure strategy equilibria (the 512 partitions of the other nine cities). Moreover, each of these is a strict equilibrium; the players have positive incentive not to deviate in the slightest. Accordingly, you might think that playing this game leads to massive confusion. But it hasn't done so when I've had it played by students from Stanford University. Over eighty percent of the students (who are U.S. nationals or otherwise long-time residents of the U.S.) asked have given the same list of cities, and rarely has anyone's list deviated from this by more than one. For Stanford students, this list is Dallas, Denver, Houston, Los Angeles, Seattle, and San Francisco. It is evident what is going on here; students use an east-west division of the United States to divide the cities. There are eleven cities, so students typically expect that they should get five or six. New York is said to have the highest value and Seattle the lowest, and it is clear to whom these two cities "belong," so it is typically felt that equity considerations should lead the western list to have six. And, rather nicely, the east-west principle leads to just a five-six division.

This doesn't always work. By changing the list of cities, one can make things much less nice. For one thing, when one of the participants in this game (when I've played it with students) is from outside the United States and one is from the U.S., the U.S. resident has worried about how much geography the other student knows. (These worries are only allowed to be expressed after the game is played, since a worry, properly phrased, gives the game away: One student once wondered aloud beforehand whether, since geography was such a tricky thing, whether his rival knew the order of the English alphabet.) Or if one removes Atlanta and Philadelphia from the list and adds Phoenix and San Diego, play becomes much less predictable, even for U.S. residents.

And, of course, the fact that these are cities is crucial. If the game involves not cities but a list of letters, then alphabetical order is the overwhelming choice for division: The list with T always takes S, P, and N, very often L, and almost never H. Again, one can confuse matters easily. Make N (the 100 point letter) the sixth letter in order, and things get touchy. Have one list begin with A and the second with C, and confusion results. Whatever is going on here only goes on in some cases. But, crucially, when it does, players tend to know that it is doing so.

The point is that in many games an equilibrium suggests itself to the players for reasons of symmetry or optimality or some other qualitative principle like those two. Context, the identity of the players, their backgrounds, and other such fuzzy factors play a huge role in this. This is the sense in which this is akin to convention or learned behavior: Although it is learning about "how people think" in general, rather than learning about "how people act conventionally" in a specific situation or "how person X acts in this situation," it is still a manifestation of socially driven expectations and behavior. The equilibria that people sometimes just naturally focus upon are called *focal points* or *focal equilibria*, and we will refer here to the organizing principle (equity, uniqueness, geography, alphabetical order) as the *focal principle*.

Game theorists have not done a good job of formalizing what constitutes a good focal principle, and these ideas remain informal and imprecise. The best (perhaps the only really good) discussion of these ideas can be found in Schelling (1980).

A nonstory

There are stories then, about why a game might possess a "solution" in the sense used here. There could be preplay negotiation; it could be the result of convention or learned behavior; and it could simply be that the solution is focal. At the start of this subsection we added, the game might be dominance solvable, which is a good story, as long as one doesn't need to invoke too many rounds of iterated dominance.

We close this section with a different story, one that is sometimes told and which when heard should be regarded with scepticism. This is the story that strategy profile X is the *only* Nash equilibrium, and so it must be the obvious way to play the game.[16] I contend, however, that uniqueness of the equilibrium alone is not a convincing story.

To see why, consider the following variation on the game in figure 12.7(a). First, change the two 10s both to 100s. Now it seems even more obvious that the "solution" is s1-t1. But add the following complication: Player 1 chooses both a row (either s1 or s2) and a nonnegative integer. That is, player 1's strategy space is $\{s1, s2\} \times \{0, 1, 2, \ldots\}$. Player 2 chooses a column (either t1 or t2) and a nonnegative integer. If player 1 chooses s2 or player 2 chooses t2, payoffs are just as before. But if player 1 chooses s1 and player 2 chooses t1, then whoever named the greater integer gets 101 and the other gets 100. If the integers named are identical, then each gets 99. If you think about this game, you will see that it has only one Nash equilibrium, s2-t2. And even with all this greatest integer stuff, I rather doubt that s2-t2 is the "solution." I would predict, with a fair degree of assurance, that the outcome of the game will be partially described by s1-t1; I have no particular prediction to make about how the greatest integer stuff will resolve. This, then, is a game in which there is no "solution," but where there is a very good and reliable "partial solution," at least to my mind. And this "partial solution" involves outcomes that are part of no Nash equilibrium.

You may be unhappy with this example because of the very strange nature of the game; "name a large integer" is not the stuff of many realistic

---

[16] You will also hear that in a given game profile X is the only refined equilibrium for one of the refinements that will be given in the next section, and hence X must be the obvious way to play the game. Absent any supporting arguments, this is if anything less convincing than the story for plain Nash equilibria.

applications, and the one penny differences are not significant. We can think of this as really two games combined: The first is the game in figure 12.7(a) but with 99s instead of 10s. This game has two Nash equilibria and one quite obvious way to play. And the second is a strange game that is played only if we get the 99s equilibrium in the first game, a game where the stakes are one and two pennies, which has no Nash equilibrium at all, and which clearly has no obvious way to play. If we "decompose" the original game into these two pieces, then there is no reason to think that the presence of this strange second piece affects the reasonableness of playing the 99 equilibrium in the first piece.

Having set up this straw argument, let us demolish it: This is precisely the point. The decomposition of this game into two "pieces" is not something done formally; it is something we did based on intution of how the game will be played. When formal criteria such as the uniqueness of equilibria support one's intuition, or even where the uniqueness of the equilibrium seems intuitively to be a focal principle that is likely to appeal to the particular players in the particular situation, then well and good. The formal criterion *by itself*, however, is inadequate.

In case you are still unhappy, we can make a slightly weaker point with the centipede game of figure 12.6. This game has more than one Nash equilibrium. But every Nash equilibrium of this game leads to the same outcome, namely player 1 playing D at the initial node of the game (proving this is a nice exercise). So if one is inclined to believe that any game with a unique Nash equilibrium *outcome* must have that outcome as obvious, then one believes that the obvious outcome to the centipede game is that player 1 plays D to begin, which we asserted before and continue to assert is not so obvious at all.

12.7. *Refinements of Nash equilibrium*

If being a Nash equilibrium is *a* necessary condition for some strategy profile to be the "obvious way to play" a particular game, perhaps there are other, stronger tests that ought to be passed. For example, we have already remarked on one weakness of the Nash equilibrium concept in section 12.3, namely that a Nash equilibrium can have a player using a weakly dominated strategy. One might wish to say, therefore, that a better necessary condition for a "solution" is that it be a Nash equilibrium with the additional *refinement* that no weakly dominated strategy is played with positive probability. (We will comment on this particular refinement of Nash equilibrium in a moment. For now consider it an example of what we might try to do.)

The general program of requiring more of a "solution" than just that it be a Nash equilibrium is known in the literature as the program of *perfecting* or *refining* Nash equilibrium. The literature on this subject runs in two veins; one can base refinements on arguments that are derived from considerations of the normal form of the game, as in the case of weak dominance, or one can base refinements on extensive form considerations. We have already noted a connection between weak dominance in the normal form and "backwards induction" in extensive form games of complete and perfect information, so you can expect a close connection between these two veins. In this section, we will move back and forth between the two veins, although emphasis will be on the extensive form, on grounds that extensive form considerations are more intuitive.[17] Throughout, when we look at extensive form games, we will consider only games with perfect recall, so that Kuhn's theorem applies.

This is a very long and involved section. I have divided it into numbered subsections, so that it seems less of an endless mass. Certainly try to get through subsections 12.7.1 and 12.7.2. The remainder of this section is increasingly "optional," although some things discussed later in the book (especially in chapters 13 and 17) depend on these later subsections.

I give two final warnings: First, there is no settled conventional wisdom about refinements of Nash equilibrium. Indeed, there is much controversy about which refinements are reasonable and which not. What follows inevitably reflects my personal biases and my own way of viewing Nash equilibrium and noncooperative game theory, a fact that I will attempt to make clear by extensive use of the pronoun *I*. Of course, you get a strong dose of my personal philosophy throughout this book, anyway, but this particular subject is one in which opinions are rather broadly distributed, and my opinions are a bit extreme. Second, to develop fully my philosophy on these things, I need some tools that will be given in the next chapter. Hence in this section I ask a number of questions to which I can, for now, give only cryptic answers. The final section of chapter 13 will provide more satisfactory answers to the questions that are asked but not really answered here.

12.7.1. Weak dominance

We already sketched our first refinement: For games in normal form, look only at Nash equilibria that do not involve the play of weakly dominated strategies. I find this refinement fairly noncontroversial except in

---

[17] My assertion that extensive form considerations are more intuitive is *not* unanimously held.

Player 2
t1   t2

	t1	t2
s1	10,0	5,2
s2	10,11	2,0

Player 1

Figure 12.10. Refining with weak dominance.

very special and extreme examples (such as the game in figure 12.1[d]), and I would be suspicious of any "solution" that involved the play of a weakly dominated strategy.[d]

Since I view this refinement as noncontroversial, it makes a good place to begin to discuss the root of all controversy concerning refinements. Consider the game in figure 12.10. This is a variation on the game in figure 12.1(c), but with player 2's payoff improved in the s2-t1 cell. Just as in the game from 12.1(c), s1 weakly dominates s2, and so the solution by iterated weak dominance is s1-t2. Note that this is a Nash equilibrium. So is s2-t1. But s2-t1 involves the play of a weakly dominated strategy, so we would "refine" it away. Of course, the problem with this is that s2-t1 is better for both players than is s1-t2.

Now with reference to this particular game, I am quite willing to entertain the hypothesis that there is no "solution," especially if the players can't communicate. But suppose the players can engage in preplay negotiation. Shouldn't we then expect them to settle on s2-t1? And doesn't this mean that the weak dominance criterion isn't a good refinement?

The argument against player 1 playing the weakly dominated strategy s2 is that player 1, if she isn't sure that player 2 will play t1, doesn't optimize with s2. If player 1 assesses any probability at all, however small, that player 2 will choose t2, then s1 gives a higher expected utility. But the point of preplay negotiation is that player 2 lays to rest the fears of player 1 on this score. Player 1 is given assurances about player 2's behavior.[18] If there is no preplay communication, one can mount a similar

---

[d] My suspicions would *not* be provoked by equilibria in weakly dominated strategies for certain games with infinitely many strategies. In very natural games with infinitely many strategies, all the Nash equilibria involve weakly dominated strategies. See, for example, the discussion of Bertrand equilibrium in section 12.8. This is something of a mathematical artifact of games with infinitely many strategies; hence it is not cause for serious concern.

[18] But the argument, even with preplay communication, is not as simple as this. Player 2 is as much at risk (or more) at the profile s2-t1: What if player 1 plays s1? So we must also consider whether player 2's fears are laid to rest by preplay communication. To repeat from footnote 4, even if player 1 has every intention of playing s1, she also has every incentive

argument: If s2-t1 is advanced as the "solution," then player 1 is supposed to think that player 2 recognizes this. And if player 2 recognizes this, then player 2 will play t1. Which leads player 1 to dismiss both her fears *and* the argument against playing s2. And once that argument is dismissed, there is nothing wrong with s2-t1 being the solution.

The problem here is one of complete confidence in a "solution" versus being very, very sure, but not certain, that players will see how to play the game and act accordingly. If players are completely certain, then nothing is wrong with playing a weakly dominated strategy. If they are only very, very sure, then they would rationally avoid weakly dominated strategies. So the question comes down to: Is Nash equilibrium appropriate for cases where players are very nearly certain or must it be reserved for cases of complete certainty? If the latter, then the weak-dominance refinement is on weak ground. And even if the former, this refinement is on weak ground in those (perhaps rare) instances with complete certainty.

I prefer to think that there is never complete certainty in the sorts of situations one models with games, and so the appropriate theory is one that involves nearly certain players who still don't rule out entirely any possible action by their opponents. Given this, weak dominance seems a useful refinement of Nash equilibrium.

And, I hasten to add, in the particular example of figure 12.10, my position would be that there is no "obvious solution"; changing the pay-offs from figure 12.1(c) in this manner gives us a game that is hard to play, despite the fact that it has a unique equilibrium in undominated strategies. The usual refrain applies: Nash equilibrium, now refined by weak dominance, is a necessary condition for a "solution" *when one exists*.

The tension just observed is the hallmark of all the literature on refinements. For normal form games, one is concerned with how strategies perform if one's opponents take actions that have "zero" probability in the equilibrium; one has to reason about the *relative* likelihood of things that one feels are not going to happen with any significant probability. In terms of extensive form games, this tension takes the following form: Most refinements that are based on extensive form considerations are keyed to what will happen "out of equilibrium" — that is, at points in the game tree that will not be reached if the equilibrium is played. But how can we reason about what will happen conditional on things that are not meant to happen in the first place? If this question seems cryptic now, keep it

---

to convince player 2 that she will play s2 (so player 2 will respond with t1). If player 2 is intelligently sceptical about what he hears, player 1 may have a hard time reassuring him that she really, truly intends to play s2.

firmly in mind as we continue through this section. It will be a constantly nagging counterpoint to everything that follows.

12.7.2. Subgame perfection (and iterated weak dominance)

Now we move to extensive games. Recall first the game in figure 12.1(n), reproduced (and turned on its side) in figure 12.11(a). In this game are two Nash equilibria: U-r and D-l. Let us be precise about this. First, why is U-r an equilibrium? Because if player 2 is choosing r, then player 1 prefers U to D. And given that player 1 is choosing U, player 2 doesn't care which action he takes. They both give payoff 2, since player 2 won't get the opportunity to move. The profile D-l is also an equilibrium because, if player 2 is choosing l, then player 1 prefers D to U, while if player 1 is choosing D, then player 2 prefers l to r.

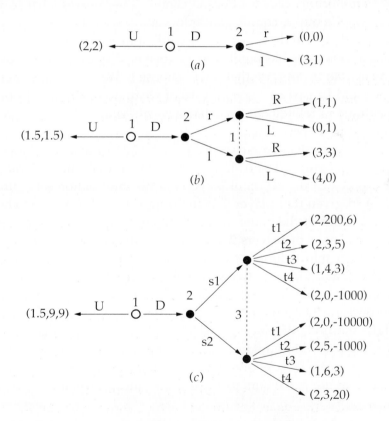

Figure 12.11. Subgame perfection.

This is a good time to make an important observation and set some terminology about Nash equilibria in extensive form games, based on the example of U-r. If player 1 chooses U, then player 2's information set (which is a single node) is not reached. We say that player 2's information set is *out-of-equilibrium* or *off the path of play*. In this case, what player 2 does there is inconsequential to player 2's expected payoff, since there is no chance (given the strategy of the other player) that player 2's choice will matter. To be a bit imprecise, the choice of action of a player at an information set that is off the path of play is unrestricted by the criterion of Nash equilibrium, since that choice cannot affect the payoff of the player who moves there.[e] But the strategy of a player at an out-of-equilibrium information set can affect what other players choose at *in-equilibrium* information sets, since those players, in evaluating the value to them of other strategies they might employ, have to take into account what will happen if they cause a previously out-of-equilibrium information set to be reached. In the U-r equilibrium, player 1 doesn't choose D because of what player 2 does at player 2's out-of-equilibrium information set.

While both U-r and D-l are Nash equilibria, we argued before that U-r is not a very sensible prediction. If player 2 is given the move, it seems reasonable to suppose that 2 will choose l. We saw before that this argument could be cast as a special case of weak dominance, but now let us pose a different refinement for extensive form games that also captures this argument as a special case.

To do so, consider the games in figures 12.11(b) and (c). Note that in the game in figure 12.11(b), U-r-R is a Nash equilibrium. Given that player 1 chooses U, the action of player 2 at his information set is unconstrained. And given that player 2 is choosing r, U and R are best choices for player 1. And in the game in figure 12.11(c), U-s2-t3 is a Nash equilibrium. The actions of players 2 and 3 are unconstrained; given player 1 chooses U, their information sets are off the path of play. And given that they choose s2 and t3, respectively, player 1 prefers U.

I wish to focus on the fact that in each of these games what follows from the decision node of player 2 is a game in its own right. That is to say, take the node of player 2, which we call t, and all its successor nodes, the set $S(t)$. First, node t is an information set as a singleton set. Second, every node that follows t is in an information set that involves only nodes that are successors to t. So if any successor node to t is ever

---

[e] To be precise, this is true of any information set that is off the path of play even if the player who moves there does everything possible to get play to go there. That is, the information set must be off the path of play by virtue of what *others* are doing and not simply because the player in question, at an earlier move, is moving away from that information set.

reached, the player who moves at that node will know that node t had been reached earlier. We make the following definition. Recall that for any given node t, $h(t)$ denotes the information set that contains t.

Definition. *A **proper subgame** of an extensive form game is a node t and all its successors $S(t)$ that have the properties: $h(t) = \{t\}$; and for all $t' \in S(t)$, $h(t') \subseteq S(t)$.*

Suppose we have a "solution" to an extensive form game. We will think of this as a behavior strategy — a prescription of how each player will act at each information set in the game. As always, a "solution" is meant to be a prescription for actions such that every player is very nearly certain that this is how others will act, and every player is nearly certain that others are nearly certain about this. And suppose this game has a proper subgame. Then if the subgame is reached in the course of play, players will be very, very sure what their opponents are doing in the subgame. Because this is a proper subgame, players will be able to evaluate how well they do in the game for the various actions they might take, conditional on the subgame being reached. And it wouldn't be sensible for them to take actions in the subgame which, given what others are doing, give them less expected utility in the subgame than the best they can do. Before moving to examples, we give the formal definition.

Definition. *A **subgame perfect** Nash equilibrium for an extensive form game is a Nash equilibrium for the game that, moreover, gives a Nash equilibrium in every proper subgame of the game.*

As examples, consider the games in figure 12.11. Take 12.11(a) first and the Nash equilibrium U-r. This is not subgame perfect, because in the proper subgame that begins with player 2's node, the choice of r is not "an equilibrium." That is, starting from his node, player 2 gets 1 from l and 0 from r, and so conditional upon getting to this node, 2 prefers l.

Take the game in 12.11(b) and the Nash equilibrium U-r-R. In the subgame that begins with the choice of D by 1, r-R is not a Nash equilibrium. Player 1's choice of R is a best response in the subgame, if we assume that 2 is playing r. But against R, *in the subgame* player 2 prefers l to r. Note well: Player 2 doesn't care about l versus r in the entire game if player 1 begins with U, since then player 2's choice is irrelevant. But if player 2 is put on the move, player 2 knows that his choice is in fact relevant. And given that player 2 is expecting player 1 to play R later on, the better choice is now l. Since r-R is not a Nash equilibrium in the proper subgame beginning with 2's node, U-r-R is not a subgame perfect Nash equilibrium.

And take the game in 12.11(c) and the Nash equilibrium U-s2-t3. In the subgame beginning with player 2's node, s2-t3 is not a Nash equilibrium. And so U-s2-t3 is not subgame perfect.

In games with complete and perfect information, the notion of subgame perfection applies with a vengeance: Since every node is, as a singleton set, an information set, every node begins a proper subgame. It is straightforward to see, for example, that in a finite game of complete and perfect information, if the rollback procedure (i.e., iterated weak dominance) generates no ties, then the strategy profile obtained by rolling back is also the unique subgame perfect equilibrium.

In most applications of game theory to economics, subgame perfection is accepted as an entirely reasonable refinement of Nash equilibrium. More than that, when a given game has a unique subgame perfect equilibrium, it is usually held that this uniqueness is a convincing reason to conclude that this equilibrium is the "solution" of the game. The reader will realize that I most certainly do not ascribe to the second assertion; an example has already been given of a game with a unique Nash equilibrium that, I contend, would almost never be played. And we have an example of a game of complete and perfect information, namely the centipede game, in which I don't find the unique subgame perfect equilibrium to be the obvious solution. But, beyond this, I would contend that there are games for which the outcome is fairly clear, and that outcome, while an equilibrium outcome, is not part of a subgame perfect equilibrium.

The game in figure 12.11(c) is such a game. In case you don't recognize it, the game between 2 and 3 beginning at 2's node is the same as the normal form game in figure 12.1(l). When we examined that normal form game, we concluded (or, rather, I asserted) that it admits no obvious way to play where the standards for an obvious way to play are necessarily very high, since the penalty for being wrong (for player 3 in the game as depicted here) is enormous. My experience with this game, though, leads me to assess a very high probability that player 3 will pick t3 and so, if I were player 1, I would find the choice of U to be fairly obvious. And I would expect most reasonable people put in the role of player 1 would on similar grounds pick U. I comfortably predict that the outcome of this game will be that U is chosen and the game ends.

Notwithstanding this, as we remarked earlier (and you are asked to verify in problem 3), the only Nash equilibria for the subgame involve the play of t1, t2, and t4. If 3 is playing t3 with zero probability, as he must in any equilibrium in the subgame, then 1 will play D. So in every subgame perfect equilibrium of this game (and there are three of them), player 1 chooses D.

What is going on here? The short answer is that application of sub-game perfection requires two things: (1) The game must have a "solution" in all parts of the game tree, including those parts of the game that this solution says are unlikely to be reached. For the game in figure 12.11(c), the outcome U isn't a full solution in this sense, since this outcome doesn't say what will happen if 2 is given the move. (And as I maintained before, I don't find any readily apparent solution to the subgame that starts with player 2's node.) (2) One must assume that players act in a way that max-imizes the payoffs ascribed to them by the model given their conjectures about the actions of their opponents, even in parts of the game that are unlikely to be reached if the "solution" is correct. In out-of-equilibrium subgames, the "solution" is clearly disproved. Yet in applying subgame perfection we are meant to maintain faith in the validity of the "solution" in whatever remains. In games such as the centipede game, this is a bit hard to accept.

Or to give a still shorter answer, with subgame perfection one as-sumes that we can reason with confidence about things that will happen conditional on things that "shouldn't" have happened. This assumption should at least be cause for concern.

These short answers don't nearly do justice to this basic point of the philosophy of refinements. To give a better answer, though, requires a substantial digression, especially for the reader for whom this is the first pass through the common types of Nash equilibrium refinements. Hence we will leave matters of this sort here, to be picked up in the last section of chapter 13.

12.7.3. Sequential equilibrium

Throughout this subsection, we continue to work with extensive form games with perfect recall.

Consider the game depicted in figure 12.12(a).[19] One Nash equilib-rium of the game is player 1 chooses D; player 2 chooses a; player 3 chooses L. Note why this is a Nash equilibrium. Player 1's choice is op-timal given player 2's choice of a and 3's choice of L. Player 3, given 1's choice of D, concludes (when given the move) that she is at the left-hand node in her information set, from which L is optimal. And player 2's choice is optimal because it is irrelevant — given that player 1 is choosing D, player 2's information set (which consists of a single node) is off the path of play.

As we saw above, one has to wonder about choices made off the

---

[19] This example is originally due to Selten (1975).

426 Chapter twelve: Solution concepts for noncooperative games

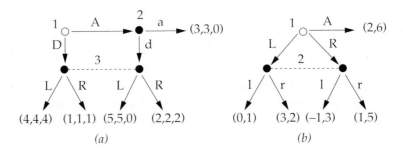

Figure 12.12. Two extensive form games.

path of play. And there is reason to wonder about player 2's choice in this instance. Player 2, if he is given the move and if he maintains the hypothesis that player 3 will choose L, "ought" to choose d. Choosing action a nets 3, while d nets 5 if player 3 chooses L. But if 2 is choosing d instead of a, then player 1 would do better with A than with D. And if player 1 is supposed to choose A and 2 to choose d, then player 3, put on the move, should conclude that she is at the right-hand node in her information set, which leads her to choose R, which then causes 2 to go back to a. (Although now, if 3 is choosing R and 2 is choosing a, player 1 should choose A, and we have a second Nash equilibrium.)

As before, in the equilibrium D-a-L the off-the-path play of a is suspicious. Accordingly, we might try to pose a refinement of Nash equilibrium that eliminates this equilibrium as a potential solution. Subgame perfection as a formal criterion doesn't help us in this game, because the game has no proper subgames. Except for the initial node, only player 2's node is a single-node information set, and one of its successors is joined in an information set to a node that isn't one of its successors. But while subgame perfection doesn't apply, the spirit of subgame perfection seems clear enough here: A player, given the move *and assessing that other players will (subsequently) conform to the equilibrium prescription*, should choose optimally, even if this player is given the move unexpectedly.

Before trying to formalize this into a new refinement of Nash equilibrium, consider the game in figure 12.12(b). Here we have a Nash equilibrium where player 1 chooses A and 2 chooses l. This is an equilibrium: Given 2 is choosing l, 1 prefers A to both L and R, whereas if 1 is choosing A, 2's choice is off the path of play and so unrestricted. But is 2's choice "reasonable?" Once again, the formal criterion of subgame perfection is no help. Since 2's information set contains two nodes, there are no proper subgames with which to work. And there is a technical difficulty in applying the spirit of subgame perfection to 2's choice: We would like to evaluate the ex post expected payoff to 2 of choosing r or l, given that 2 is given the opportunity to move. But we can't evaluate 2's expected payoff ex post because we don't know what odds 2 would assess for being at the left-hand or right-hand node in his information set. We can't use Bayes' rule and player 1's equilibrium strategy to get that ex post assessment, because player 2 assesses zero probability ex ante that he will be given the move by player 1. But surely this shouldn't matter: *No matter what assessment player 2 makes concerning which node he is at in his information set, r is better than l.* (And if player 2 chooses r, then player 1 should choose L.)

The notion of a *sequential equilibrium* is meant to cover these two examples. A sequential equilibrium consists of two pieces. The first piece is, as in any Nash equilibrium, a *strategy profile*, which (thinking in terms of behavior strategies) prescribes for every information set a probability distribution over the actions available. We will use π to denote a typical strategy profile, with π^i denoting the behavior strategy of player i.

The second piece of a sequential equilibrium is a system of *beliefs*, denoted by μ. Beliefs assign to every information set h in the game a probability distribution over the nodes $x \in h$, with the interpretation that these are the beliefs of player $\iota(h)$ about where in his information set he is, given that information set h has been reached. Formally, μ is a function from the set of decision nodes X of the game tree to $[0, 1]$, such that for every information set $h \in H$, $\sum_{x \in h} \mu(x) = 1$.

To take an example, the game in figure 12.12(a) has three information sets. The first, belonging to player 1, has a single node; so 1's beliefs are necessarily that she is at this node with probability one, given that she is given the move. The second, belonging to player 2, also has a single node, so again the only possible beliefs put probability one on that single node. But the third, belonging to player 3, has two nodes, and beliefs for this information set would prescribe the probabilities that player 3 attaches to these two nodes. Or, for the game in figure 12.12(b), it is the two-node information set of player 2 for which beliefs are nontrivial.

Roughly speaking, a *sequential equilibrium* is a profile of strategies π and beliefs μ such that starting from every information set h in the game tree player $\iota(h)$ plays optimally from then on, given that what has transpired previously is given by $\mu(h)$ and what will transpire at subsequent nodes belonging to other players is given by π. This condition is called *sequential rationality*.

To see sequential rationality in action, consider first the game in figure 12.12(a), the strategy profile where player 1 chooses D, 2 chooses a, and 3 chooses L, and the beliefs where player 3 at her information set assesses probability 1 that she is at the left-hand node. (As noted above, the beliefs of players 1 and 2 are trivial.) Player 1's choice is optimal given her trivial beliefs. Player 3's choice is optimal given her beliefs; if she assesses probability one that she is at the left-hand node, then L nets her 4 units while R nets her 1. (Note that 3's choice of L is optimal given any beliefs that assign probability 2/5 or more to her being at the left-hand node.) But player 2's strategy is not sequentially rational; his beliefs are trivially given, and if he maintains the hypothesis that 3 will play L, then he obtains 5 from choosing d and only 3 from choosing a.

And consider the game in figure 12.12(b), the strategy profile where player 1 plays A and player 2 plays l, and beliefs by player 2 that the left-hand node in his information set has (conditional) probability α. It doesn't matter what α is; player 2's choice of l is not sequentially rational. Given α, he nets expected utility $\alpha + 3(1 - \alpha)$ by playing l and $2\alpha + 5(1 - \alpha)$ by playing r. Since the second amount exceeds the first for any α, there is no way that a choice of l by player 2 can be sequentially rational, and so A-l is not the strategy profile part of any sequential equilibrium.

We are looking here at some very simple examples; do not be misled by their simplicity. In some games there are information sets with more than one node and with actions by other players following; in these games both beliefs (about what has happened so far) and the strategy profile (about what will happen in the future) come into play in checking for sequential rationality. For example, in the game in figure 12.13, suppose we specified that player 1 plays L, player 2 plays d, and player 3 plays D. And for player 2 (who is the only player with a nontrivial information set), we specify beliefs that put probability .3 on the topmost node in his information set. Then d is not sequentially rational for 2: If he chooses d, he nets $(.3)(4) + (.7)(2) = 2.6$, while u nets $(.3)[(0)(2) + (1)(8)] + (.7)(1) = 3.1$. Note well how player 3's choice of D affects the second computation; if player 3's part of the strategy profile were to play D with probability .5 and U with probability .5, we would calculate that the consequences of u for player 2 are

$$(.3)[(.5)(2) + (.5)(8)] + (.7)(1) = 2.2,$$

which is less than what 2 expects to get from d, given his beliefs. Thus, with this change in player 3's strategy and holding 2's beliefs fixed, 2's action becomes sequentially rational. On the other hand, if we maintain this change in player 3's strategy and modify 2's beliefs so that he assesses, say, probability .7 that he is at the topmost node in his information set, then (fixing 3's strategy) his choice of d is once again not sequentially rational. (Work this out!)

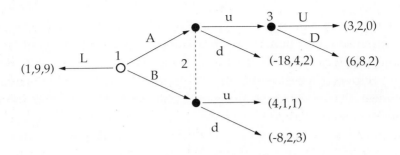

Figure 12.13. An extensive form game.

Sequential rationality is one part of the definition of a sequential equilibrium. In addition, we want beliefs and strategies to make sense together. For example, suppose in the game in figure 12.12(a), player 1 chooses A, player 2 chooses d, and player 3 chooses L. Moreover, player 3's beliefs at her information set are that she is at the left-hand node with probability .95. You can easily check that each player's part of the strategy is sequentially rational. Yet this isn't even a *Nash* equilibrium, let alone any sort of refinement of Nash equilibrium. The problem is that player 3's beliefs are crazy given player 1's and 2's supposed strategies. If the game begins with the play of A followed by d, then player 3 ought to believe given the move that she is at the right-hand node in her information set with probability one. Bayes' rule would certainly tell her this.

At a minimum, we would want to insist that the strategy profile π and the beliefs μ are consistent at the level of Bayes' rule in the following sense: Given the strategy profile π, for any information set h that will be reached with positive probability (if players use the strategies given by π) beliefs at h are computed from the strategies via Bayes' rule.

(In case you are a bit rusty concerning applications of Bayes' rule, let me work an example. Consider the game in figure 12.12(a) and suppose player 1 chooses A with probability 1/3 and D with probability 2/3, and player 2 chooses a with probability 1/4 and d with probability 3/4. Then, in the course of play, we will come to the left-hand node of player 3's information set with (prior) probability 2/3 and the right-hand node with (prior) probability (1/3)(3/4) = 1/4. That is, there is prior probability 11/12 that player 3 will be given the opportunity to move (and 1/12 that the game will end without 3's information set being reached). By applying Bayes' rule, therefore, player 3's beliefs upon being given the move should be that she is at the left-hand node with probability (2/3)/(11/12) = 8/11 and at the right-hand node with probability (1/4)/(11/12) = 3/11.)

But Bayes' rule will not apply to information sets that are not reached with positive probability in the course of play. And it is precisely at such information sets that beliefs are important.[20] So we might want to insist on rather more consistency than just consistency with Bayes' rule when it applies. Suppose, for example, that the game in figure 12.12(a) is modified as follows: Player 4 begins the game, choosing either to end the game (action E) or give player 1 the move (action G), after which the game is just as in 12.12(a). For the strategy profile where 4 chooses E, 1 chooses D, 2 chooses a and 3 chooses R, player 3's information set is not reached with positive probability; player 4, at the start of the game, sees to that. But should we then allow player 3 to have any beliefs at all? Or should 3, given the move, believe that while it is patent that 4 must have chosen G, player 1 is still likely to have picked D, and so her (player 3's) beliefs should put probability one on the left-hand node in her information set?

Let us set some terminology. A behavior strategy profile π is said to be *strictly mixed* if every action at every information set is taken with positive probability. Given a strictly mixed strategy profile π, every information set h will be reached with positive probability, and so Bayes' rule can be used to define a unique (strictly positive) system of beliefs μ that is Bayes' consistent with π.

Definitions. *A strategy profile π and beliefs μ are said to be* **consistent** *in the sense of sequential equilibrium if there is a sequence of strictly mixed strategy profiles $\{\pi_n\}$ such that, for μ_n the strictly positive beliefs that are Bayes' consistent with π_n, the limit of the vector (π_n, μ_n) in n is (π, μ).*[21]

A **sequential equilibrium** *is a strategy profile π and a system of beliefs μ that are consistent with each other in the sense above and that satisfy sequential rationality at every information set.*

The notion of consistency that is given above may look innocuous, if it doesn't look completely mysterious, but it isn't innocuous at all. (It may well be completely mysterious.) Rather a lot of bodies are buried in this definition of consistency. One can try to unearth the bodies, to see what the definition entails, and in the problem set, I give you a few exercises that will help you do this. (See also the discussion at the end of chapter 13.)

The restrictions implicit in this notion of consistency are held by many to be too severe. Insofar as this is so, one can keep sequential rationality and try to find a less restrictive way of tying together strategies and

---

[20] See problem 7.

[21] To those of you who don't know what a limit is, I apologize, but there is no other way to do this.

beliefs. *f* In particular, you will find in the literature an alternative equilibrium notion called *perfect Bayes equilibrium*, which is the conjunction of sequential rationality (for some beliefs) and weaker notions of consistency.[22]

Sequential equilibria are well-behaved:

Proposition. *Every sequential equilibrium is a subgame perfect equilibrium.*

You will be asked to prove this in the problems.

Clearly, since I attacked the "credibility" of subgame perfection in the previous subsection, I must be willing to attack the credibility of sequential equilibrium as well. And indeed I am, although I will hold off on my attack until the next chapter, noting here that the attack when it comes will be an attack on *both* consistency and sequential rationality.

> One reason for attacking the refinements of sequential and subgame perfect equilibrium is easy to give here. Suppose we modify the game in figure 12.12(b) so that player 1's choice of action is done in two stages; first she chooses between A and not A, and if she chooses not A, then she chooses between L and R. This is depicted in figure 12.14. Note that this extensive form is strategically equivalent to the extensive form in figure 12.12(b), in the sense that the two generate the same reduced normal form game. But in this second extensive form, player 1's second decision node does begin a proper subgame. And then, in any subgame perfect equilibrium, player 1 will choose L and player 2 will choose r. That is, in this form of the game, not A-L-r is the unique subgame perfect equilibrium. The same sort of thing is true about sequential equilibrium. If we change the payoff for player 2 in the event of R-r in figure 12.12(b) from 5 to 1, then A-l is a sequential equilibrium

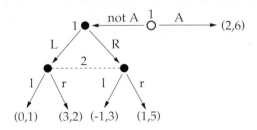

Figure 12.14. A strategically equivalent representation of the game in figure 12.12(b).

---

f However some of the reasons for doubting this notion of consistency are also reasons for doubting sequential rationality. For an argument along these lines, see Kreps and Ramey (1987).

[22] The notion of perfect Bayes equilibrium was developed contemporaneously with sequential equilibrium, but it has only recently been formalized; see Fudenberg and Tirole (1988).

strategy in the game as depicted in figure 12.12(b), but it would not be part of a sequential equilibrium if we broke player 1's choice among A, L, and R into two pieces as in figure 12.14. (Show this.)

It is not considered desirable to be able to change the set of refined equilibria by changing from one extensive form game to another that is strategically equivalent; this is construed as a weakness of the subgame perfection and of sequential equilibrium refinements. But in their defense remember that these refinements are advanced as necessary conditions for a "solution" to the game in question. Sufficiency is not implied by meeting these refined tests, so that meeting a test in one game form but not another (if the games are strategically equivalent) is likely to be an indication that the equilibrium in question is not a good candidate for the "solution" of the given game.

12.7.4. Restrictions on out-of-equilibrium beliefs

Roughly put, a sequential equilibrium adds to the notion of a Nash equilibrium the requirement that actions taken off the path of play must be rationalized by some beliefs about what has happened up to the point where the actions must be taken. This is only a rough paraphrase, because the consistency of beliefs with the strategy profile does restrict somewhat what range of beliefs can be held. But the rough paraphrase captures the "original intent" of this refinement.

What the bare notion of a sequential equilibrium does not capture, however, are various considerations concerning which beliefs are more or less reasonable. The game in figure 12.15, reproduced (and turned on its side) from figure 12.1(o), provides one example of this.[23] Consider the Nash equilibrium where player 1 chooses U and player 2 chooses r. (Check that this is a Nash equilibrium.) We have to wonder whether 2's choice of r is reasonable; after all, this is a choice of action that is off the path of play if player 1 is meant to choose U. Is this choice of action sequentially rational? Yes, if player 2 holds beliefs that he is equally likely to be at either of the two nodes in his information set, then r is better than l.

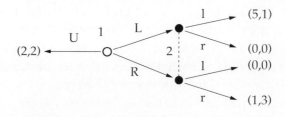

Figure 12.15. An extensive form game.

---

[23] This game is due to Kohlberg and Mertens (1986).

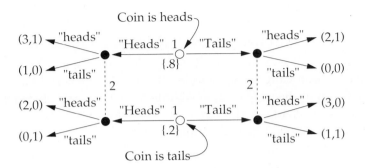

Figure 12.16. *The truth game in extensive form.*

So we come down to the question: Is it reasonable to suppose that 2 will hold beliefs that make r better than l, given that 2 expects that 1 will choose U? The argument against this is quite simple: Player 1 by choosing U can guarantee herself 2. If 1 chooses R, then the best she can do is 1. If she chooses L, on the other hand, she has a chance of obtaining 5. Shouldn't 2 conclude on this basis, if he is given the move, that player 1 must have chosen L, in an attempt to get the 5? If he concludes this, then he should believe that he is at the topmost node of his information set with probability (close to) one, which would mandate a choice of l instead of r. (And if he is going to choose l, then player 1 will shift from U to L.)

What we have done in this example is to reason what a player's beliefs should be at an information set that is off the path of play. In so doing, we see that a particular sequential equilibrium can only be sustained with beliefs that are not so intuitively sensible. The argument in this example can be made pretty sharply. In the game, U strictly dominates R. So it seems ridiculous for player 1 to be supposed to be choosing R, even as an out-of-equilibrium choice.[24] Even if 2 supposes at first that U will be selected, faced with the irrefutable evidence that L or R was selected (namely, being asked to move), 2 ought to conclude that it was L that was chosen after all, which then informs 2's beliefs at his information set.

A somewhat trickier example is given in figure 12.16. This is the "truth game" of problem 4 in chapter 11. (If you did that problem, you can check your answer now.) Consider, in this game, the following Nash equilibrium: Regardless of the result of the coin flip, player 1 says it was "Tails." Player 2 responds "heads" if player 1 says "Tails" and player 2 responds "tails" if player 1 says "Heads."

---

[24] But see subsection 12.7.6 in which a counterargument will be given.

Let's first check that this is a Nash equilibrium. For player 1, given that player 2 will respond to "Tails" with "heads" and to "Heads" with "tails," it is more important to say "Tails" and get the response "heads" than (if the coin flip is in fact Heads) to tell the truth. And for player 2, if player 1 is meant to say "Tails" no matter what the results of the coin flip are, then hearing "Tails" signifies nothing; the chances that the flip was in fact Heads is the same .8 as in the prior. Thus "heads" in response to "Tails" is optimal. While "tails" in response to "Heads" is a best response in the sense that any action taken off the path of play is a best response; since player 1 is meant to say "Tails" there is zero prior probability that player 2 will have to respond to "Heads," and thus all responses to "Heads" are equally good.

As you can imagine by now, we want to think hard about 2's off-the-path response to "Heads"; is it a sensible response? We can ask, for example, whether player 2 might hold any beliefs having heard "Heads" that would make a response of "tails" sequentially rational. That is, have we described the strategy profile part of a sequential equilibrium? The answers to these questions are yes. If player 2, having heard "Heads," believes that the chances the coin was in fact Heads are below .5, then "tails" is the sequentially rational response.[25]

So we are led to ask, Are these beliefs sensible? If player 2 expects player 1 to say "Tails" and player 1 unexpectedly says "Heads," is it sensible for player 2 to infer that there is a 50% or greater chance that the coin flip came up Tails? An argument to say that this is not sensible runs: Player 1 has more incentive to say "Heads" when the coin flip is Heads than when it is Tails, since player 1 gets a unit of payoff for telling the truth. Whatever conjecture player 1 might make about player 2's responses to "Heads" and to "Tails," player 1 seems no less apt to say "Heads" when the flip is Heads than when it is Tails, or to say "Tails" when the flip is Tails instead of when it is Heads. Hence if player 2 hears "Heads," it seems sensible to conclude that it is no less likely that the result of the flip was Heads than in the prior assessment of .8 for Heads. But if 2's beliefs reflect this, if 2 assesses probability .8 or more that the coin was Heads if she hears "Heads" from 1, then we can't sustain a response by him of "tails" to "Heads," and our equilibrium is destroyed.

In both these examples, the mode of analysis takes the following form: An equilibrium is given, with at least some actions taken at information sets that are not reached if the equilibrium is followed. Hence, in the usual fashion, those actions are not constrained by the criterion of Nash

---

[25] And these beliefs are consistent in the sense given in the previous subsection.

equilibrium. Moreover, we can sustain or rationalize those actions for some beliefs by the player who takes the action. But the beliefs necessary to sustain the actions seem unintuitive or unreasonable. One would wish to formalize what makes a system of beliefs unreasonable; certainly one would wish to be more formal than we have. But this can be done. For example,[26]

> We will restrict attention to a particular class of extensive form games, known as *signaling games*. These games have two players called 1 and 2. Nature moves first, selecting one of a number T of possible initial nodes according to a strictly positive probability distribution ρ. Player 1 is informed of nature's choice and sends a signal to player 2 about this; the set of signals available to player 1 is denoted by S. Player 2 then takes an action a in response to this signal, not knowing which $t \in T$ was chosen by nature, drawn from some set A. Player 1's utility is given by $u(t, s, a)$, and player 2's is given by $v(t, s, a)$, both as functions of nature's choice t, 1's signal s, and 2's response a. Note that the truth game is an example of a signaling game, where $T = \{\text{Heads, Tails}\}$, $S = \{\text{"Heads," "Tails"}\}$, and $A = \{\text{"heads," "tails"}\}$.
>
> An equilibrium for a general signaling game consists of (behavior) strategies for players 1 and 2. We use π_1 to denote 1's strategy, where $\pi_1(s; t)$ is interpreted as the probability that player 1 sends message s if nature chooses t. We require that $\sum_{s \in S} \pi_1(s; t) = 1$ for each t. And we use π_2 to denote 2's strategy; $\pi_2(a; s)$ gives the probability that 2 chooses action a having heard signal s, where $\sum_{a \in A} \pi_2(a; s) = 1$ for each s is required.
>
> A signal s is "along the path of play" if $\sum_{t \in T} \rho(t)\pi_1(s; t) > 0$. That is, there is some circumstance in which s is sent by 1. For any such signal s we can use Bayes' rule to compute 2's beliefs about t given 2 hears s. She assesses probability
>
> $$\mu(t|s) = \frac{\rho(t)\pi_1(s; t)}{\sum_{t' \in T} \rho(t')\pi_1(s; t')}.$$

And a pair of strategies (π_1, π_2) is a Nash equilibrium if

(a) For each t, if $\pi_1(s; t) > 0$, then s maximizes $\sum_{a \in A} u(t, s', a)\pi_2(a; s')$ (in s')

(b) For each s that is along the path of play, $\pi_2(a; s) > 0$ implies that a maximizes $\sum_{t \in T} v(t, s, a')\mu(t|s)$ in a', where μ is computed as above from π_1 by Bayes' rule

Moreover, π_1 and π_2 are part of a sequential equilibrium if (a) and (b) above hold and if, moreover, for any s that is not along the path of play, there

---

[26] Read on at your own risk. What follows will be referred to only in optional reading in chapter 17. But if you plan to be an economic theorist of virtually any stripe, you will have some need to be conversant with what follows, at least until fashions in economic theory change.

are some beliefs $\mu(t|s)$ such that (b) holds. Of course, these beliefs must agree with those that are computed by Bayes' rule and are the beliefs part of the sequential equilibrium. (One can verify that the restrictions of consistency do not restrict the off-the-path beliefs.)

Now suppose we have sequential equilibrium strategies π_1 and π_2. (That is, some beliefs off the path rationalize the off-the-path prescriptions of π_2.) We will examine whether the beliefs accompanying these strategies are intuitively sensible.

Suppose for some $t \in T$ and s and $s' \in S$,

$$\min_{a \in A} u(t, s, a) > \max_{a \in A} u(t, s', a).$$

Then we would know that any strategy that involved 1 sending s' if nature picks t is strictly dominated by a strategy where 1 sends s instead. It doesn't matter how 2 responds to s or s'; whatever his (contingent) response, 1 does strictly better with s than with s'. Accordingly, we would wish to restrict 2's beliefs so in the event of s' being sent he doesn't put any weight on t being nature's choice. Why (this logic goes) would 1 send s' if nature picks t, when the strictly dominant s is available? Formally,

*Sequential equilibrium strategies π_1 and π_2 fail the **test of dominated messages** if for some t, s, and s' as above, it is impossible to sustain 2's equilibrium response to s' with beliefs that put zero conditional probability on t given s'.*

(Note that since s' is dominated given t, it can't be that $\pi_1(s';t) > 0$. Hence if s' is along the path of play, beliefs conditional on s' computed by Bayes' rule will put zero probability on t to begin with. This test will be more restrictive than the simple sequential equilibrium test only if s' is off the path.)

This test does not apply to the truth game, since no message is dominated by another, no matter what nature does to start the game.[9] But we can formulate a stronger test that does work for the truth game. Fixing equilibrium strategies π_1 and π_2, for each $t \in T$ let $u^*(t) = \max_{s \in S} \sum_{a \in A} u(t, s, a)\pi_2(a; s)$; that is, $u^*(t)$ gives player 1's conditional expected payoff in the equilibrium, conditional on nature picking t to start the game. Then say that s' is *equilibrium dominated at t* if $u^*(t) > \max_{a \in A} u(t, s', a)$. That is, maybe no alternative signal s dominates s' as before, but the best that can be had by sending s' is dominated by what 1 *gets in the equilibrium*, conditional on t.

*Sequential equilibrium strategies π_1 and π_2 fail the **test of equilibrium domination** if for some t and s' that is equilibrium dominated at t, it is impossible to sustain 2's equilibrium response to s' with beliefs that put zero conditional probability on t given s'.*

The equilibrium where 1 sends the signal "Tails" no matter what she learns about the coin flip fails this test. To see this, note that in this equilibrium, if the coin flip comes up tails, then player 1 will get a payoff of 3 in the equilibrium;

---

[9] However see problem 12.

she says "Tails," which is the truth, and 2 responds with "heads." The best 1 can do if she says "Heads" is 2. So, at this equilibrium, s = "Heads" is equilibrium dominated at t = tails. Hence to pass the test, we have to be able to sustain 2's reaction to s = "Heads" with beliefs that put zero weight on t = tails given "Heads." And this, as we noted in our informal arguments, we cannot do.

For comparison with the literature, you should know that the test of equilibrium domination is referred to in the literature as "the intuitive criterion" on grounds that it is such an intuitive test that it surely must be passed by any reasonable solution. Notwithstanding this bit of editorializing by its inventors, the justification for using the equilibrium domination test in applications is deservedly quite controversial. I will not try to recount the arguments for and against here; instead I give references at the end of this chapter. However, so that you can better consume the literature, it is useful to know at least one further thing (which is also covered in the references given below): The test of equilibrium domination is often further strengthened; when you find mention of *divine* or *universally divine* equilibria, the author is invoking one of these strengthenings.

12.7.5. Trembling-hand perfection

In the previous few subsections we worked with extensive form games. Now we turn back to considerations based on the normal form.

We have stated numerous times that a "solution" to a given game is advanced as a strategy profile in which we and, more to the point, all the players have a lot of confidence as a prediction about how everyone will play. What we haven't done, in any complete or rigorous sense, is to say what explanation might be offered for some player deviating from this solution. One could tell many stories (and we will see a few of them at the end of the next chapter), but the simplest is that players sometimes make mistakes. A player faced with a choice of several actions, one of which he means to play, might through inattention or a slip of the hand (or the pen, or the tongue) take another.

Now if the probability of these mistakes is significant, we wouldn't have that much faith in our "solution" as a nearly certain prediction. But since mistakes do happen, we would probably wish to dismiss predictions that aren't "safe" against the risk of a mistake.

The standard example of an equilibrium in weakly dominated strategies provides the simplest example. Take the game in figure 12.1(c). The profile s2-t1 is a Nash equilibrium; player 1 is happy with s2 as long as there is no chance of t2. But if there is any chance of t2, and in particular if there is some chance, however small, of player 2 playing t2 by mistake, then s2 is not optimal. It may be nearly optimal, but a truly cautious player 1, worried that player 2 might slip, would opt for s1. And player 2, understanding this, responds with t2.

We capture this idea with the following formal definition. Fix an I player normal form game with finitely many strategies for each player. Let S_i be the set of strategies available to player i, for $i = 1, \ldots, I$. Let Σ_i denote the set of mixed strategies available to player i, with typical element σ_i. Let $\sigma = (\sigma_1, \ldots, \sigma_I)$ denote a typical mixed strategy profile. Let $\overline{\Sigma}^i$ denote the set of *strictly mixed* strategies for n — each $\sigma^i \in \overline{\Sigma}^i$ is a mixed strategy that attaches positive probability to each pure strategy in S^i.

Definition. *A Nash equilibrium profile $\sigma = (\sigma^1, \ldots, \sigma^I)$ is **(trembling-hand) perfect (in the Normal form)** if there is for each player i a sequence of strictly mixed strategies $\{\sigma_n^i\}$, such that*

(a) *$\lim_{n \to \infty} \sigma_n^i = \sigma^i$ for each i, and*

(b) *for each i and $n = 1, 2, \ldots$, σ^i is a best response against the profile of strategies*

$$(\sigma_n^1, \ldots, \sigma_n^{i-1}, \sigma_n^{i+1}, \ldots, \sigma_n^I),$$

which we hereafter write as σ_n^{-i}.

The key to this definition is that the σ_n^j must all be strictly mixed. Player i intends to play σ^i, and he assumes that his fellow players intend to play σ^{-i}. But his fellow players, or so the story goes, are susceptible to making mistakes. If they intend to play σ^{-i}, in fact they play σ_n^{-i} for "large" n, a profile in which any combination of actions by i's opponents is possible, but in which i's opponents are "nearly" sure to be playing according to their intentions. (The last assertion follows from [a].) And the equilibrium condition is that what i intends to do (if he doesn't slip) must be a best response against what his opponents actually do (which is [b]), and not simply against what they intend to do (which is the Nash criterion).

We can say lots of things about this definition. First, why is there this limit in n? If players make mistakes, it would seem that we should have functions $\phi^j : \Sigma^j \to \overline{\Sigma}^j$, which give as a function of the intentions of j the actual (mistakes-included) play of j. We want j to be "local" — it shouldn't move too far in translating j's intentions into j's actual actions. But players play against a definite, nonvanishing chance of errors; not against this fancy vanishing sequence. One is queasy, however, to fix ad hoc functions ϕ^j. We are looking for necessary conditions, remember. If in the context of a particular game, we knew something about the precise "technology of errors," then we could sharpen our necessary condition by building into our model this technology. (For an example, read on.) This definition imposes the *minimal* requirement (for our story) that our "solution" can be rationalized by *some* technology of errors, no matter how small we think the possibility of errors is.

Second, we require that each σ^i is optimal against σ_n^{-i} for each n. Although this wasn't made explicit, it is implicit that σ_n^{-i} is made up of independent mixed strategies by i's opponents. This means, in particular, that the chances (and type) of an error by one of i's opponents is independent of errors by other opponents. The assumption of independent errors is conventionally made, but depending on what one thinks of as the reason errors are made, one might wish to allow correlation in errors. Fancy versions of trembling-hand perfection allow for this.

Third, it is implicit in this definition that all the players have the same notions about how their fellow players slip, when those fellow players do slip. That is to say, for each player j a single sequence of strictly mixed strategies σ_n^j is used to form the "test" for the intended σ^i, for each i. One can, once again, think of modifications that would remove this implicit assumption.

Fourth, the definition refers to this as (trembling-hand) perfection. Note the parenthetical modifier. The originator of this concept, Selten (1975), uses the simple name "perfection" without the modifier. But to distinguish from Selten's earlier (1965) concept of subgame perfection, convention has been to use the modifier "trembling-hand," which refers to slips of the hands that act.

Fifth, we motivated this notion by an example of an equilibrium in a weakly dominated strategy. And you should find it easy to prove, for two-player games, that no weakly dominated strategy is ever part of a trembling-hand perfect equilibrium.[h] But trembling-hand perfection doesn't extend to exclude strategies that are excluded by iterated weak dominance. For an example, take the normal form game depicted in figure 12.17(a). Note that Ba for player 1 is weakly dominated by Bb. Having removed Ba, Y weakly dominates X. And if player 2 is playing Y, then player 1 chooses Bb. Nonetheless, A-X is a trembling-hand perfect Nash equilibrium: There is no question that if player 2 is playing a strategy "close" to choosing X for sure, player 1 is doing the best that she can

---

[h] There is an analogous statement for games with more than two players that you can try to dope out on your own. For a hint, go back to the early sections of this chapter and find references to separating hyperplanes.

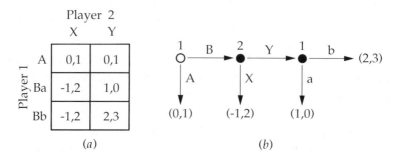

Figure 12.17. A game in normal and extensive form.

with A. And against the strictly mixed strategy where 1 plays A with probability $1 - 2/n$, Ba with probability $1/n$, and Bb with probabilty $1/n$, X for player 2 nets for himself a payoff of $(1)(1 - 2/n) + (2)(1/n) + (2)(1/n) = 1 + 2/n$, while Y nets $(1)(1 - 2/n) + (0)(1/n) + (3)(1/n) = 1 + 1/n$. So X is better. Letting n go to infinity, we pass the test of trembling-hand perfection.

Sixth (and finally), the definition refers to (trembling-hand) perfection (in the normal form), where now you should note the second parenthetical modifier. Consider the extensive form game in figure 12.17(b). This game is an extensive form version of the game in 12.17(a). Note that it is a game of complete and perfect information, so it has a solution by backwards induction, which (of course) is its solution by iterated weak dominance: Bb-Y. This is, of course, the unique subgame perfect equilibrium. Hence we conclude from the previous paragraph that trembling-hand perfection does not imply subgame perfection.

However, think a moment about those mistakes that players are meant to be making. Player 1 has two opportunities to make a mistake, at least in the extensive form game. If either by intent or by mistake player 1 chooses B and 2 replies with Y, then it is clearly a *further* mistake for player 1 to choose a. If we imagine that, whatever player 1 does at the start of the game, she is much more likely to choose b than a if the game gets out that far, then 2 should intend to choose Y, and 1 should intend to choose B. What happened to our previous argument that A-X is trembling-hand perfect? To make that argument, we needed the chances of Ba by mistake to be of the same order of magnitude as Bb by mistake. But if we think that Ba compounds two mistakes and Bb only one, and if (in consequence) we think that Ba must be much less likely than Bb, even if both are very unlikely (because 1 intends to choose A), then we can't sustain the choice of X by 2.

Proceed formally as follows. For any extensive form game, think of constructing a new extensive form game in which every information set of every player in the game belongs to a distinct player; that is, there are as many players in this new normal form game as there are information sets. Letting h denote a typical information set and thus a player in this new extensive form game, in this new extensive form game we let h's payoff function be precisely the payoffs of $\iota(h)$ in the original game. Think of the following story: Player i may "control" more than one information set, but he assigns his decision-making authority at each one to a different agent. These agents of i all have the same payoffs as i, so they act in his interests. But we regard each as an individual player. And then we pass to the normal form of this new extensive form game, which is called the *agent normal form* of the original extensive form game.

And now look for trembling-hand perfect equilibria of the agent normal form game. Since we implicitly assumed in the definition of trembling-hand perfection that players tremble independently, we would, by applying that definition to the agent normal form, be assuming that the various "agents" of a given player tremble independently; and thus in terms of the original extensive form, we are assuming that a mistake at one information set by i does not affect the chances of a mistake at any other. In particular, in terms of the example in figure 12.17(b), even if 1's first agent intends A, Ba by 1's two agents must be much less likely than Bb, because b by 1's second agent is a second mistake.

Selten (1975) reserves the term (trembling-hand) perfect equilibrium for this version of the definition — perfection in the agent-normal form. We follow Selten in this regard and use the second modifier "in the normal form" to denote perfection where one doesn't use the agent-normal form of an extensive form game. You are asked to prove the following in problem 13:

Proposition. *Every (trembling-hand) perfect Nash equilibrium of a given extensive form game is a sequential equilibrium, and hence it is subgame perfect.*

One can also show that every (finite) extensive form game has a trembling-hand perfect equilibrium; indeed, every finite normal form game has an equilibrium that is trembling-hand perfect in the normal form. This is a bit harder to show.[i]

---

[i] And still harder to show, but demonstrating the close connection between normal form and extensive form refinements, for "most" extensive form games "most" of the sequential equilibria are trembling-hand perfect. You'll need to consult Kreps and Wilson (1982) to see what this means precisely.

12.7.6. Proper equilibria and stable sets of equilibria

Reconsider (once again) the game from figure 12.1(o), reproduced in this section as figure 12.15. The equilibrium U-r is, as we noted previously, sequential; it is also trembling-hand perfect. We argued earlier that as a sequential equilibrium it was not too sensible; to support the play of r by 2, 2 must hold beliefs that he is at the node that follows R with probability 1/4 or more. But R is dominated by U for 1 (and L is not). Hence it didn't seem reasonable for 2 to hold these out-of-equilibrium beliefs.

Now that we have a story concerning why one might see off-the-path play, namely such play results from mistakes, we can further investigate this argument. Myerson (1978) presents a strengthening of perfection, called *properness*, which throws doubt on this argument.

Myerson reasons as follows: If player 2 is playing r, then player 1 nets 0 from L and 1 from R. Of course, playing U and getting a payoff of 2 is best of all for 1. But given 2's supposed play of r, the play of L is a "bigger" mistake for player 1 than the play of R, in the sense that it is more costly. If we assume that players are more likely to make smaller mistakes than bigger, it might be reasonable to assume that player 2, put on the move, thinks it at least as likely that 1 erred with R as that 1 erred with L. And, in this case, player 2 optimally responds with r.

I will not give here the precise definition of Myerson's properness. Roughly, it is like trembling-hand perfection, with the addition that one assumes that if one strategy by a given player is a bigger mistake than a second (as measured by expected payoffs at the supposed "solution"), then the first of these strategies is much less likely to be played by mistake. Properness, then, takes the basic notion of trembling-hand perfection and adds to it a notion of which mistakes are more or less likely to be made. Proper equilibria are defined for the normal form of a given game (although one could adapt the definition for the agent normal form). As we see in the example of figure 12.15, there are games solvable by iterated dominance, where equilibria other than the solution so derived are proper.

The mathematically most complex weapon in the arsenal of Nash refinements is Kohlberg and Mertens' (1986) concept of *stability*. Kohlberg and Mertens, noting earlier efforts, including those sketched above, construct the following "wish list" for a solution concept:

(1) Every (finite) game should have a solution.

(2) The solution should be trembling-hand perfect.

(3) The solution should depend only on the reduced normal form of the game. Changing the extensive form should not matter, if no "strategic" changes are thereby entailed.

(4) Players should never be playing (weakly) dominated strategies.

(5) Any solution should survive iterated application of dominance.

They show by example that these requirements cannot possibly be met by any solution concept that prescribes a single strategy profile, and they argue that the appropriate response to this difficulty is to move to a "set-valued" solution concept; that is, a set of strategy profiles comprises a solution. This leads to modification of (2) and (5); (2) is written: Every solution should contain a perfect equilibrium. And (5) becomes: The solution of a game should contain the solution of a game derived by the deletion of dominated strategies in the first game. And they add a sixth requirement:

(6) The solution (which is now a set of strategy profiles) should be topologically connected.

Perfection, as we noted above, fails on requirements (3) and (5). Properness (defined for the normal form) fails (5). Kohlberg and Mertens, by moving to a set-valued solution concept, provide a number of (quite complex) formal definitions that meet various subsets of these desiderata; *stability* is used to denote a concept that meets requirements (1), (3), (4), and (5). Very roughly put, the nature of these definitions is that a "solution" should be stable against a very large class of perturbations to the game; that is, a solution is a set of strategy profiles so that, if one perturbs the game a bit (so that, say, all the players are slightly susceptible to trembling in some manner), then the perturbed game has an equilibrium that is close to some profile in the solution.

I will not attempt to give even a summary formal treatment of this. Consult either the paper by Kohlberg and Mertens (1986) or the book of van Damme (1987). In addition, you can consult Banks and Sobel (1987) or Cho and Kreps (1987) for connections between stability and the sort of refinement posed in 12.7.4, based on restrictions on out-of-equilibrium beliefs.

12.8. Reprise: Classic duopoly

Now that we know all about game theory and Nash equilibria, we can complete our treatment of the classic models of duopoly. We left things in a state of bewilderment concerning the origins of all those different sorts of conjectures and with a suggestion that the "rules" of competition might help us resolve that bewilderment. More specifically, we suggested that, for example, Cournot conjectures made sense in the following sort of situation:

Two producers work in isolation preparing the quantity they bring to market. These quantities are decided upon with a foreknowledge of this market structure and with knowledge of the characteristics of demand, but neither side gets to see how much the other is producing. Each producer brings the quantity it produced to a central marketplace, where it is handed over to a "state sales commission" that sets price so that the total amount brought to market is just demanded at the set price.

The point we made before is that if competition has this sort of structure, then it is sensible to hold to the (Cournot) conjecture that one producer will react to a change in the level of output of its rival by holding fixed its quantity, since the first producer must fix its quantity without seeing precisely what its rival has done.

On the other hand, the following structure of competition was meant to justify von Stackelberg conjectures:

We have the same two producers as above, and the same state sales commission, but one producer is able to produce its quantity first. That is, this producer brings to the market a quantity x_1, which the second producer observes. And then the second producer decides on an amount x_2 to produce, knowing that price will be set so that the market clears at total quantity $x_1 + x_2$.

Now the structure of competition makes it reasonable to suppose that the second producer will take as given the quantity decision of the first producer, since this quantity decision is in fact fixed, and optimize. And the first producer, realizing this, picks its quantity accordingly.

And, on a third hand, we considered the following competitive structure as justifying Bertrand conjectures:

Things work much differently in this case. The two producers, independently, call the state sales commission and give a price at which each is willing to sell. The state sales commission investigates market demand at those prices and then calls the two producers, telling them how much they are obligated to bring to the market.

Now Bertrand conjectures are sensible, because firms must fix their prices simultaneously, without any opportunity to react to what their opponents do.

Of course, each of these three "stories" describes an extensive form game between the two firms. In the first, the first producer selects a quantity, and "then" the second producer selects a quantity without knowing what the first producer has done. We have the extensive form game depicted in figure 12.18(a). (A complication here and in the rest of this section is that each firm has infinitely many actions it can take; infinitely many quantities can be selected in this case. But one can be careful about the formalities and nothing untoward will happen.) The von Stackelberg game is just like the Cournot game, except that the second firm sees the action of the first before picking its quantity; we have the game depicted

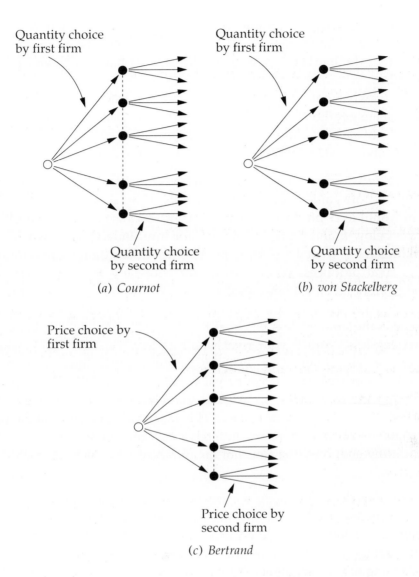

Figure 12.18. The Cournot, von Stackelberg,
and Bertrand extensive form games.

in figure 12.18(b). And the Bertrand game is just like the Cournot game,
except now price is the action chosen by each firm.

Actually, there is one complication in the Bertrand game. In our analysis in chapter 10, we didn't say precisely how demand would be allocated

between the two firms if they charged the same price. To make up a game, we need to specify payoffs for every terminal node, and the firms' payoffs will, in places, depend on how they divide the market when they charge the same price. It is customary, and we will follow custom in this, to assume that the market divides symmetrically — half of demand going to each firm.

Somewhat naturally, we find that the Cournot, Bertrand, and von Stackelberg equilibria (in conjectures) are Nash equilibria of the respective games. In fact, holding to the parameterization of linear demand $P = A - X$ and constant unit costs k, we can say the following:

Concerning Cournot, the Cournot equilibrium is the unique Nash equilibrium, and the game is even dominance solvable. To see this, note that no firm would ever produce more than $A - k$, because to do so would drive prices below k and profits below zero for sure. Indeed, firms would never produce more than $(A - k)/2$, because whatever (nonnegative) amount your rival produces, you are better off with $(A - k)/2$ than with some higher amount. But if your rival will never go above $(A - k)/2$, then you would never produce less than $(A - k)/4$, nor would your rival, since (against any amount less or equal to $(A - k)/2$, $(A - k)/4$ is better than anything less. And if your rival won't go less than $(A - k)/4$, you will never go more than $3(A - k)/8$. (Check my math here.) The same is true for your rival, and if your rival won't go above $3(A - k)/8$, you will never go less than $5(A - k)/16$. And so on, until everything is eliminated except $(A - k)/3$ for both of you. This takes *infinitely* many iterations of dominance, because there are infinitely many other strategies to get rid of. But in the end, only the Cournot quantities of $(A - k)/3$ for each of you survive.[27]

Concerning Bertrand, again we have a unique Nash equilibrium (where each firm charges $P = k$). The argument we gave in chapter 10 is easily adapted to show this. One notices in this regard an extraordinary thing: The strategy of naming the price k is weakly dominated by a strategy of naming any other higher price. Note why this is so. Naming $P = k$ means profits of zero no matter what your opponent does. Naming, say, $P = k + 1$ could mean positive profits, if your opponent names this price or one higher, and $P = k + 1$ can never lead to negative profits. (Of course, it leads to zero profits if your opponent follows the equilibrium strategy of naming $P = k$.) The unique Nash equilibrium involves weakly

---

[27] This argument transcends the specific parameterization we've used. But pressing this argument to its utmost generality is not to my mind very interesting; for reasons to be given in just a bit, I don't find the Cournot game all that interesting.

dominated strategies. This sort of thing sometimes happens with games that have infinitely many strategies, and, if you are unduly concerned about it (now that I've mentioned it), it would be a good idea to prove for yourself that it won't happen if the range of available prices that can be charged is finite — say prices must be in integer multiples of one penny.

Concerning von Stackelberg, there are many Nash equilibria in this game. For example, the second producer could adopt the strategy: Produce $A - k - x_1$ units if $x_1 \neq 0$, and produce $(A - k)/2$ if $x_1 = 0$. One best response for the first producer to this is to set $x_1 = 0$: The first producer makes zero profits, but given the second producer's strategy, it can't do any better. And given that the first producer sets $x_1 = 0$, the second producer's strategy is a best response; what it does for any x_1 that isn't zero is out-of-equilibrium, and it is doing the optimal thing against the chosen x_1. But, if you followed section 12.7, you will see immediately that this Nash equilibrium isn't subgame perfect. In any subgame that begins with a choice of x_1 different from zero, the second producer doesn't optimize by choosing $x_2 = A - k - x_1$. Indeed, the von Stackelberg game is a game of complete and perfect information, and we can use backwards induction to show that the unique equilibrium so obtained (and that is subgame perfect) is the von Stackelberg equilibrium we computed in chapter 10. You should be clear on why this is: In our analysis of von Stackelberg, we assumed that the second firm would react "optimally" to firm 1's choice of quantity, no matter what that quantity was. But this is just an expression of backwards induction (or subgame perfection).

The three "games" given above don't come close to exhausting the possibilities. For example,

Back to our two producers who produce quantities independently. But now they call the state marketing commission in advance, saying how much they plan to bring. And if one says it will bring more than the other, the second is given permission by the state marketing commission to bring up to the amount being brought by the first.

Or how about the following very complex situation.

The two producers must first install capacity for production. Capacity is costly, coming at a cost of $k_1 > 0$ per unit capacity installed. Capacity is installed by the two simultaneously and independently. Then each sees how much capacity the other installed. And then each calls the state marketing commission and quotes a price at which it is willing to sell. Production is possible up to the level of capacity, at an additional marginal cost of $k_2 \geq 0$ per unit. No production *beyond the level of capacity is possible. If a capacity constraint does bind when prices are named, the state marketing commission rations demand by some system or other. This good is resalable among consumers, and all consumers are aware of market demand conditions.*

If you like a challenge, try to find all the subgame perfect equilibria for these two games.[28]

And we can go on from here. We can consider all sorts of variations of these stories including: choices of technologies prior to selection of quantities or of prices; installation of capacity when capacity can only be installed at a finite rate; considerations of how much information to reveal to one's opponent about demand conditions or one's own cost function, if there is initial uncertainty about these things, and so on, and on. Starting in the late 1970s, there was an enormous amount of work of this sort, where the objective was to use these sorts of oligopoly "games" to chase down how competitors would fare in equilibrium under different structural conditions. In all of these, the rivals eventually had to compete, and the model of competition more often than not was one of the three given above. So when you see a paper that says "the firms compete Cournot style," the author usually means that the firms select quantities simultaneously and independently, and price is set so that markets clear. When "firms compete Bertrand style," they name prices simultaneously. When the competition is von Stackelberg, with one leader and (possibly many) followers, the leader chooses quantity first (usually), and then the others react with optimal quantity responses (usually simultaneously if there is more than one follower, although sometimes you'll see one firm pick its quantity, then a second, then a third, and so on). In the problems, you will get a taste of these sorts of game-theoretic models of oligopoly.

So finally we come to the big question of chapter 10: Which of the classic models of duopoly is "correct?" The obvious response at this point is it depends on the details of competition. For real-life oligopolists, therefore, the answer seems to be that none of the models for the structure of competition given above is very realistic, so the classic models explained in this fashion don't give us much guidance. For one thing, firms don't name quantity or price once and for all; they name price or set quantity one day and can reset either the next, reacting perhaps to what their rivals did the previous day. This dynamic character of competition in oligopoly makes an enormous difference to the set of possible equilibria, whether

---

[28] Be forewarned that the second game does give a very nice answer: The unique equilibrium is the Cournot equilibrium for costs $k_1 + k_2$. But showing this is quite difficult. See Kreps and Scheinkman (1983) for the details.

the oligopolists set quantities on a given day, or name prices on a given day, or do some of each. It is to this sort of complication that we turn in chapter 14.

Before leaving this topic again, let me anticipate chapter 14 and offer a word in defense of the classic models of duopoly. The "games" described above are not necessary for the predictions of the classic models to be valid. It suffices for those predictions that rivals have the right sorts of conjectures about their opponents and that an equilibrium is reached. These game-theoretic models say why those sorts of conjectures might be reasonable, but there is nothing to prevent players from holding particular conjectures even if those conjectures are unjustified by the structure of competition. Indeed, we'll see in chapter 14 that adding dynamic considerations to the structure of competition leads us back to having to wave our hands about the origins of the conjectures that players hold. In the end, the test of the classic models must be empirical; this sort of theory may be useful for refining the empirical predictions that we will test, but one shouldn't reject a prediction on grounds that there is reason to doubt the "best" theoretical model one can think of to justify the prediction.

12.9. Bibliographic notes

Many references have been scattered throughout this chapter that I will not repeat here. Some of the basic ideas in this chapter such as dominance, dominance solvability, and Nash equilibrium are covered in many venerated textbooks, and I will not attempt to provide references to those. Other topics that have been covered here are the subject of on-going research, so references I might provide are apt to become dated quite quickly. With those caveats in place, I would recommend the following partial reading list to anyone interested in beginning to pursue these ideas.

For the use of dominance and iterated dominance criteria, begin with Bernheim (1984) and Pearce (1984).

Correlated equilibrium was only mentioned in passing, but the serious student should certainly consult Aumann (1974).

The various rationales for Nash equilibrium are scattered in many places. But Schelling (1980) is an absolute must-read for anyone interested in noncooperative game theory. Schelling is more verbal and less mathematical than most of what you will see in the literature of game theory, but his book bursts with ideas that await higher levels of formalization. As for models of "learned" behavior, my favorite (predictably) is Fudenberg and Kreps (1989).

Concerning refinements of Nash equilibrium, van Damme (1987) presents a unified and up-to-date treatment. The subject was pioneered by Selten (1965, 1975), who defined subgame perfection and (trembling-hand) perfection. Myerson's properness (1978) came next. Sequential equilibrium is analyzed in Kreps and Wilson (1982), stability is developed by Kohlberg and Mertens (1986), and perfect Bayes equilibrium is defined in Fudenberg and Tirole (1988). The literature on formal restrictions on out-of-equilibrium beliefs was begun by McLennan (1985); Banks and Sobel (1987) and Cho and Kreps (1987) present analyses along the lines sketched in 12.7.4. Objections to refinements based on the equilibrium domination are given in Okuno-Fujiwara and Postlewaite (1986).

References

Aumann, R. 1974. "Subjectivity and Correlation in Randomized Strategies." *Journal of Mathematical Economics* 1:67–96.

Aumann, R., Y. Katznelson, R. Radner, R. Rosenthal, and B. Weiss. 1983. "Approximate Purification of Mixed Strategies." *Mathematics of Operations Reseach* 8:327–41.

Banks, J., and J. Sobel. 1987. "Equilibrium Selection in Signaling Games." *Econometrica* 55:647–62.

Bernheim, D. 1984. "Rationalizable Strategic Behavior." *Econometrica* 52:1007–28.

Cho, I-k., and D. Kreps. 1987. "Signaling Games and Stable Equilibria." *Quarterly Journal of Economics* 102:179–221.

Forges, F. 1986. "An Approach to Communication Equilibria." *Econometrica* 54:1375–86.

Fudenberg, D. and D. Kreps. 1989. *A Theory of Learning, Experimentation, and Equilibrium in Games*. Stanford University. Mimeo.

Fudenberg, D., and J. Tirole. 1988. "Perfect Bayesian and Sequential Equilibrium." Massachusetts Institute of Technology. Mimeo.

Harsanyi, J. 1973. "Games with Randomly Disturbed Payoffs: A New Rationale for Mixed-Strategy Equilibrium Points." *International Journal of Game Theory* 2:1–23.

Kohlberg, E., and J.-F. Mertens. 1986. "On the Strategic Stability of Equilibria." *Econometrica* 54:1003–38.

Kreps, D., and G. Ramey. 1987. "Structural Consistency, Consistency, and Sequential Rationality." *Econometrica* 55:1331–48.

Kreps, D., and J. Scheinkman. 1983. "Quantity Precommitment and Bertrand Competition Yield Cournot Outcomes." *Bell Journal of Economics* 14:326–37.

Kreps, D., and R. Wilson. 1982. "Sequential Equilibrium." *Econometrica* 50:863–94.

McLennan, A. 1985. "Justifiable Beliefs in Sequential Equilibrium." *Econometrica* 53:889–904.

Myerson, R. 1978. "Refinements of the Nash Equilibrium Concept." *International Journal of Game Theory* 7:73–80.

———. 1986. "Multistage Games with Communication." *Econometrica* 54:322–58.

Okuno-Fujiwara, M., and A. Postlewaite. 1986. "Forward Induction and Equilibrium Refinements." University of Pennsylvania. Mimeo.

Pearce, D. 1984. "Rationalizable Strategic Behavior and the Problem of Perfection." *Econometrica* 52:1029–50.

Rosenthal, R. 1981. "Games of Perfect Information, Predatory Pricing, and the Chain-store Paradox." *Journal of Economic Theory* 25:92–100.

Rosenthal, R., and H. Landau. 1979. "A Game Theoretic Analysis of Bargaining with Reputations." *Journal of Mathematical Psychology* 20:233–55.

Selten, R. 1965. "Spieltheoretische Behandlung eines Oligopolmodells mit Nachfragetragheit." *Zeitschrift für die gesamte Staatswissenschaft* 121:301–24.

———. 1975. "Re-examination of the Perfectness Concept for Equilibrium Points in Extensive Games." *International Journal of Game Theory* 4:25–55.

Schelling, T. 1980. *The Strategy of Conflict*, 2d ed. Cambridge, Mass.: Harvard University Press.

Shapley, L. 1964. "Some Topics in Two-Person Games." In *Advances in Game Theory*, M. Dresher, L. Shapley, and A. Tucker, eds., 627–50. Princeton, N.J.: Princeton University Press.

Van Damme, E. 1987. *Stability and Perfection of Nash Equilibrium*. Berlin: Springer-Verlag.

12.10. Problems

■ 1. Prove that in any game of complete and perfect information with finitely many nodes, there is always at least one decision node whose immediate successors all are terminal nodes.

■ 2. Prove that if a game is dominance solvable, then the "solution" so determined is a Nash equilibrium. Prove that if a game is dominance solvable using only strict dominance at each step, this solution is the only Nash equilibrium that the game possesses.

■ 3. For the game in figure 12.1(l), we gave in the text two pure and one mixed strategy equilibria. Show that this game possesses no other equilibria, either mixed or pure.

■ 4. Prove that in the centipede game (figure 12.6), every Nash equilibrium begins with player 1 playing D with probability one.

■ 5. A correlated equilibrium for a two-player normal form game can be thought of as a probability distribution over the space of strategy profiles such that for each player and for each of the player's pure strategies (that have positive probability) the strategy is a best-response given the player's opponent chooses according to the conditional distribution on the opponent's strategies, conditional on the strategy for the first player. Find *all* the correlated equilibria for the game in figure 12.9.

■ 6. (a) For the game in figure 12.13, let α be the probability assessed by 2 that he is at the topmost node in his information set, given that he is given the move, and let β be the probability he assesses that player 3 chooses U. For which pairs of α and β is the choice of u by player 2 sequentially rational?

(b) For this game, what is the set of all sequential equilibria?

■ 7. Consider an extensive form game in which no player ever moves more than once along any path through the game tree. (If you wish, take the simple case of a game in which each player has a single information set.) Suppose we have behavior strategies π and beliefs μ that are Bayes' consistent in the sense: Given the strategy profile π, for any information set h that will be reached with positive probability (if players use the strategies given by π) beliefs at h are computed from the strategies via Bayes' rule. Prove: If π is sequentially rational given μ at every information set that is reached with positive probability given π, then π is a Nash equilibrium for the game. Is the requirement that no player ever moves more than once necessary? (Hint: the answer to the last question depends on your precise definition of sequential rationality.)

For the converse, suppose we have a Nash equilibrium π for a given extensive form game. Compute beliefs at information sets that are reached with positive probability given π by Bayes' rule. Show that at these information sets π and the beliefs computed are sequentially rational.

Problems 8 and 9 concern the notion of consistency in sequential equilibria. They are for the pathologically mathematically addicted only.

■ 8. Fix a strategy π for an extensive form game and beliefs μ that are consistent with π in the sense of sequential equilibrium.

(a) In any proper subgame of the game, we can speak of applying Bayes' rule within the subgame at information sets h in the subgame that are reached with positive probability, conditional on the subgame being reached. Prove that μ is consistent with Bayes' rule in every proper subgame, in just this fashion.

(b) Define an *almost-proper subgame* to be an information set h and all the successor nodes to nodes in h, which will be denoted $S(h)$, with the property that if $x \in S(h)$ and $x' \in h(x)$, then $x' \in S(h)$. For an almost-proper subgame whose "root" is h, given a specification of beliefs over nodes in h and a strategy profile π, one can use Bayes' rule to compute beliefs on information sets in $S(h)$ that are reached if π is played, conditional on h being reached according to beliefs μ on h. Show that μ is consistent with Bayes' rule in every almost-proper subgame in this sense.

■ 9. Fix a (finite) extensive form game and a behavior strategy π for the game. For simplicity, consider games without moves by nature. Define a π-*labeling* of the game as a pair of functions $\kappa : A \rightarrow \{0, 1, \ldots\}$ and $\zeta : A \rightarrow (0, \infty)$, where A is the set of actions for the game, such that (a) $\kappa(a) = 0$ if and only if $\pi(a) > 0$ and (b) $\zeta(a) = \pi(a)$ if $\kappa(a) = 0$. (Follow the convention that every action is taken at a single information set in the tree.) Given a π-labeling, define two new functions $\lambda : X \rightarrow \{0, 1, \ldots\}$ and $\xi : X \rightarrow (0, \infty)$, where X is the set of decision nodes, as follows: If x is the initial node, $\lambda(x) = 0$ and $\xi(x) = 1$. (Recall that there is a single initial node, since we've assumed no moves by nature.) Otherwise, $\lambda(x)$ is the sum of all $\kappa(a)$ for actions a that lead from the initial node to x, and $\xi(x)$ is the product of the $\zeta(a)$ for the same sequence of actions. For a given information set h, let $\lambda(h) = \min_{\{x \in h\}} \lambda(x)$. And for a node $x \in h$, let $\mu(x) = 0$ if $\lambda(x) > \lambda(h)$ and let $\mu(x)$ be given by

$$\frac{\xi(x)}{\sum_{\{x' \in h : \lambda(x') = \lambda(h)\}} \xi(x')}$$

if $\lambda(x) = \lambda(h)$.

(a) Prove that for any π-labeling, if we define μ in this fashion, μ is consistent with π in the sense of sequential equilibrium.

(b) (Very hard!) Prove that if μ and π are consistent in the sense of sequential equilibrium, then there is a π-labeling such that μ is obtained by the procedure above from this labeling.

In other words, this labeling procedure characterizes all the beliefs that are consistent with a given π. (If you are very ambitious, you might try to modify things so that moves by nature are allowed.)

■ 10. Prove that every sequential equilibrium is a subgame perfect Nash equilibrium. (If you prove that it is a Nash equilibrium, you are 90% of the way there.)

■ 11. Consider the class of signaling games given in subsection 12.7.4. Prove that any beliefs that are Bayes consistent with a given strategy profile are consistent in the sense of sequential equilibrium. (Don't use problem 9 unless you've proven it.)

■ 12. Consider the truth game of figure 12.16.

(a) The sequential equilibrium in which player 1 always says "Tails" fails the test of equilibrium domination. Find an equilibrium that passes this test.

(b) Write out this game in normal form. Show that the game is dominance solvable, if we allow dominance in mixed strategies. Can you modify the payoffs of the game so that it is not dominance solvable but still equilibrium domination is effective in eliminating a sequential equilibrium?

■ 13. Prove that every trembling-hand perfect equilibrium (for the agent normal form) is sequential. Show by example that the converse is false.

The remaining problems in this chapter concern game-theoretic variations on the classic models of oligopoly. They are primarily about those models and so relate more to material in other chapters, but they could not have been posed until we had covered Nash equilibria and subgame perfection.

■ 14. Prove that in the Bertrand game, if prices must be charged in integer multiples of a penny, then there is always at least one Nash equilibrium in which players do not use weakly dominated strategies.

■ 15. Mr. X and Ms. Y have entered into the following contractual arrangement with D. M. Kreps. Between now and the end of next week, each will install a certain amount of capacity for the manufacture of square based tri-prong slot poiuyts. Then Kreps will assume control of the capacity provided to him and produce and sell poiuyts. Demand for poiuyts is given by the demand function $D = 10 - P$. (To keep matters simple, assume that production takes place for a single period.) The marginal cost of production of poiuyts is zero up to the total level of capacity that Mr. X and Ms. Y install. That is, if Mr. X installs capacity k_x and Ms. Y installs capacity k_y, then Kreps can produce up to $k_x + k_y$ poiuyts and sell them, at zero additional cost. Kreps can, however, produce less if he so chooses.

The contract signed by X, Y, and Kreps calls for Kreps to act in the best interests of X and Y. (He receives a small fixed fee for doing so, which you may ignore.) So that there is no ambiguity about what are the best interests of X and Y, the contract calls for Kreps to set output so that gross profits (= revenue) are maximized. (Kreps, who knows a lot about linear demand systems and zero marginal cost production functions, can be counted on to do this.) These gross profits are split between X and Y in proportion to the capacities they build. That is, if $k_x = 2k_y$, then X receives two-thirds of the gross profits and Y receives one-third.

Capacity is costly for X and Y. Precisely, there is a constant marginal cost of 2 per unit of installed capacity. Hence X's net from the entire arrangement, if he installs k_x, Y installs k_y, and Kreps produces $Q \leq k_x + k_y$, is

$$\frac{k_x}{k_x + k_y}(10 - Q)Q - 2k_x,$$

and similarly for Y.

(a) Suppose that X and Y collude in terms of the capacities they install. That is, k_x and k_y are set to maximize the sum of the net profits of X and Y from this arrangement. (Assume, for the sake of definiteness, that $k_x = k_y$.) What capacities will X and Y install?

(b) (Good luck!) Unhappily, X and Y cannot (or do not) collude. They install capacity levels k_x and k_y "Cournot" style, choosing their capacity levels simultaneously and independently. What is (or are) the equilibrium (or equilibria) in this instance?

(c) If demand is $P = A - Q$ and the marginal cost of capacity is r, can you find any values of A and r such that the total amount of capacity installed in an equilibrium exceeds A?

■ 16. *Since you know all about perfect competition, monopoly, and oligopoly, we can find out how various types of firms might feel about uncertainty concerning the prices of its factors of production and output.* Consider a profit-maximizing firm that produces a single good from several factors. The firm is characterized by a production function $y = f(x_1, \ldots, x_n)$, where y is the level of output obtainable from factor inputs $x_1, \ldots, x_n$. We will use p to denote the price of the output good, and w_i to denote the price of factor input i. When there is uncertainty a priori about these prices, the firm is allowed to choose its production plan *after* any uncertainty in prices resolves.

(a) Suppose that the firm is competitive in all its markets. That is, it takes prices $p, w_1, \ldots, w_n$ as given. Consider two possible price vectors, $(p, w_1, \ldots, w_n)$ and $(p', w_1', \ldots, w_n')$, and let $(p'', w_1'', \ldots, w_n'')$ be the simple average of the two: $p'' = (p + p')/2$, $w_1'' = (w_1 + w_1')/2$, etc. Let π be the firm's level of profits in case of the prices $p, w_1, \ldots$; π' be the firm's profits in case of $p', w_1', \ldots$; and π'' be the firm's profits in case of $p'', w_1'', \ldots$. Show that $\pi'' \leq (\pi + \pi')/2$. (That is, the firm, in terms of expected profits, is risk seeking in the prices it faces.)

(b) Now we suppose that the firm is a monopolist in its product market, but is competitive in all its factor markets. Hence the firm itself determines p, p', etc. Suppose that it makes profits π when facing factor prices $(w_1, \ldots, w_n)$, π' when facing $(w_1', \ldots, w_n')$, and π'' when facing $(w_1'', \ldots, w_n'')$, where $w_i'' = (w_i + w_i')/2$. Can we say that $\pi'' \leq (\pi + \pi')/2$? Provide a proof, if so. If you need to make a further assumption to get this result, state the assumption and say why you need it. If there is no hope of getting this result, indicate why that is.

(c) Finally, consider this question in the context of a von Stackelberg duopoly. Two firms produce an undifferentiated commodity for which demand is given by $P = A - X$, where P is price and X is total supply. Demand is unchanging. Each firm has production technology with a fixed cost F for producing anything at all, and a (constant) variable cost c for producing every unit. Note well that the fixed cost F can be avoided by producing zero. Firm 1 moves first, deciding whether to produce anything and, if it does produce, the amount x_1 that it will supply. Firm 2 sees the decisions of firm 1, and then it decides whether to produce anything at all and, if so, how much. (In cases where firm 2 is indifferent between two courses of action, you may assume that it acts in a way that maximizes the profits of firm 1.) The firms regard the "factor costs" F and c as given to them; their actions do not affect those costs.

Is the result analogous to the result in part (a) of this problem (and in part (b), if it is correct there) correct in this case for firm 1? That is, for all (F, c) and (F', c'), is the firm's average of profits given those two levels of costs at least as large as its level of profits when costs are $((F + F')/2, (c + c')/2)$?

If so, can you conjecture how general the general proposition at work here is? If not, can you succinctly state what went wrong? (One way to do this is to give the "general proposition" in a fashion that applies to those cases [(a) and, perhaps, (b)] where the result is true, and fails to apply in this case.)

■ 17. *Part (a) should be easy. Part (b) will introduce you to how uncertainty might be handled in the classic models. Part (c) foreshadows some developments to come, and you might well miss the point of it now.*

(a) Consider a duopoly where the two firms in question produce an undifferentiated product. Demand for the product is given by $P = A - X$, where X is the total output of the two firms. Each firm has a simple cost function: $TC_i(x_i) = c_i x_i$ where the subscript i refers to the firm, x_i is the firm's output, and c_i is a constant with $0 < c_i < A$. The firms compete Cournot style. What is the equilibrium? Give equilibrium price, levels of output, and profits. (You may assume that $A + c_1 > 2c_2$ and $A + c_2 > 2c_1$ throughout this problem, although if you want a real challenge, try doing the entire problem without this assumption.)

(b) Now suppose that while the two firms are described as above, firm 2 is uncertain about the cost function of firm 1. Specifically, c_1 takes on one of a finite number of values, namely $c_{11}, c_{12}, \ldots, c_{1n}$ with probabilities $p_1, \ldots, p_n$. Firm 2 holds this probability assessment when it chooses its level of output x_2; firm 1 when it chooses x_1 knows the value of c_1 (and is allowed to condition its level of x_1 on c_1). Otherwise, the two engage in Cournot competition. By this we mean: An equilibrium is a quantity $\hat{x}_2$ output by firm 2 and, for each level of firm 1's costs, a quantity $\hat{x}_1(c_1)$, such that firm 2, believing that firm 1's output will be given by the *function* $\hat{x}_1$, maximizes its *expected profits* with output level $\hat{x}_2$, and firm 1, believing that firm 2 will have output $\hat{x}_2$ and knowing that its own costs are given by c_1, would choose to produce $\hat{x}_1(c_1)$.

(c) Suppose the setting is as in (b), but prior to the selection of x_1 and x_2, firm 1 is able to provide irrefutable evidence to firm 2 concerning its cost structure if it chooses to do so. What do you think will happen in this case?

■ 18. Now reconsider problem 17, assuming that the two duopolists produce differentiated commodities. (It will be good enough to assume that demand is given by the demand system in problem 20.) Consider also what happens if the two engage in Bertrand competition in this case.

■ 19. Xyllip is a controlled substance that, by law, can be produced by only two companies, ABC Chemical and XYZ Pharmaceutical. The production of Xyllip for each firm involves combinations of kapitose and legume according to the production function

$$X = k^{1/2}l^{1/2},$$

where X is the level of Xyllip output, k is the level of kapitose input, and l is the level of legume input. (It will be okay to assume that these two firms produce only Xyllip; this isn't really true, but taking into account their other products wouldn't change the answers you'd get.) The two firms are price takers in the markets for kapitose and legume, each of which sell for $1 for purposes of this problem. There are no fixed costs in the production of Xyllip. Demand for Xyllip is given by the demand function $P = 14 - X$.

(a) As a warm-up exercise: ABC and XYZ act as Cournot duopolists in the sale of Xyllip. That is, you can assume that they simultaneously and independently name quantities they will supply to the market, and price is set so that markets clear. What is the equilibrium in the Xyllip market in this case?

A third firm, Kinetiks, has found a way to synthesize a chemical known as Legusude. Kinetiks holds a patent on this process, and it is the only firm capable of producing Legusude. Legusude has only one possible use; it can be used in place of legume in the production of Xyllip. If one uses Legusude instead of legume, the production function for Xyllip is given by

$$X = k^{1/2}L^{1/2},$$

where now L is Legusude input to the production process. We will discuss fixed costs in the manufacture of Xyllip from Legusude (and kapitose) in a moment. The production of Legusude is (for simplicity) very simple; Kinetiks can make as much Legusude as it wishes at zero marginal cost. (There are some fixed costs in the manufacture of Legusude, but you should ignore them throughout.)

Kinetiks has announced that they are willing to supply Legusude to ABC and to XYZ. Kinetiks is not allowed to produce Xyllip, so its only market for selling Legusude is to ABC and XYZ.

To produce Xyllip from Legusude instead of from legume, ABC and/or XYZ must convert their production processes. This is a straightforward operation, but involves a fixed cost incurred by any firm that converts; the fixed cost is $1. If a firm (or both) converts so that it can use Legusude, it retains the option of using legume if the price of legume is below that of Legusude. But even if the firm that has converted uses legume, it must pay the fixed cost.

Imagine the following sequence of events, after Kinetiks has announced its ability to produce Legusude. ABC and XYZ must simultaneously and independently decide whether to convert their production processes so that they can utilize Legusude. This is an irrevocable decision: If a firm decides to convert, it thereafter incurs the fixed cost of $1. The conversion decisions of the two firms are observed by all participants, and then (if either of the firms has decided to convert), Kinetiks announces a price at which it is willing to sell Legusude. There can be no bargaining over price between Kinetiks and ABC and/or XYZ. But, at the same time, Kinetiks is required by law to set a single price and sell as much Legusude at that price as anyone wishes to buy. The price being charged by Kinetiks is observed by all participants, and then ABC and XYZ simultaneously and independently engage in production of Xyllip; that is, once production conditions are known for the two firms, they compete Cournot style.

(b) Give an extensive form "representation" of this game, using the sort of symbolic pictures of figure 12.18.

(c) We are interested in knowing what the subgame perfect equilibria (or, if there is only one, equilibrium) of this game are. To this end, suppose that in stage 1, ABC and XYZ both convert and then Kinetiks announces price q for Legusude. What is the outcome in the final stage of Cournot competition between ABC and XYZ? Given this, what price q should Kinetiks name for Legusude, if both firms have converted?

(d) Repeat step (c) for the case where the game begins with ABC deciding to convert and XYZ deciding not to convert.

(e) What are the subgame perfect equilibria (or equilibrium) of this extensive form game?

(f) Suppose that you are the CEO of Kinetiks. What might you do to change the "rules" of this strategic interaction so that you do better than you do in (e)? You should not answer this question by saying that you should go into the production of Xyllip; that is forbidden. But you should try to invent plausible changes in the rules of the "game" and then investigate their consequences for the profits of Kinetiks.

■ 20. Consider a two-firm industry where each firm has a single output, and the outputs of the two firms are reasonably close substitutes for one another. More precisely, if x_1 is the level of output of firm 1 and x_2 the level of output of firm 2, then the price that firm 1 gets in the market is $p_1 = 10 - x_1 - .5x_2$, while firm 2 gets price $p_2 = 10 - x_2 - .5x_1$.

Firm 2 has a very simple technology in which every unit produced has constant marginal cost 2. Firm 1 will soon have a constant marginal cost technology, but first must choose which technology to install. In fact, firm 1 has a choice of four technologies. The first technology has fixed costs of 12 and a constant marginal cost of 1. The second has fixed costs of 8.1 and a constant marginal cost of 2. For the third, fixed costs are 5 and marginal costs are 3. For the fourth, fixed costs are 2.7 and marginal costs are 4. Firm 1 must select which of these four technologies to install; having done so, the two firms will compete in duopolistic fashion.

(a) Imagine that the sequence of events and competitive variables are: Firm 1 chooses one of the four technologies to install; firm 2 sees which technology firm 1 has chosen; firms 1 and 2 then simultaneously and independently choose output quantities. (That is, they engage in Cournot competition.) What are the Nash equilibria of this game, including the technology selection stage? If you find more than one equilibrium, do you find any one of them particularly persuasive, and why?

(b) Suppose that the sequence of events and competitive variables are: Firm 1 chooses one of the four technologies to install; firm 2 sees which technology firm 1 has chosen; firms 1 and 2 then simultaneously and independently choose prices that they quote. (That is, they engage in Bertrand competition. Please recall that these products are differentiated, so it isn't the case that Bertrand competition must lead to zero profits.) What are the Nash equilibria of this game, including the technology selection stage? If you find more than one equilibrium, do you find any one of them particularly persuasive, and why?

(c) Imagine that the sequence of events and competitive variables are: Firm 1 chooses one of the four technologies to install; firm 2 *does not* see which technology firm 1 has chosen; firms 1 and 2 then simultaneously and independently choose quantities to output. (That is, they engage in Cournot competition.) What are the Nash equilibria of this game, including the technology selection stage? If you find more than one equilibrium, do you find any one of them particularly persuasive, and why?

(d) Suppose that the sequence of events and competitive variables are:

Firm 1 chooses one of the four technologies to install; firm 2 *does not* see which technology firm 1 has chosen; firms 1 and 2 then simultaneously and independently choose prices that they quote. (That is, they engage in Bertrand competition.) What are the Nash equilibria of this game, including the technology selection stage? If you find more than one equilibrium, do you find any one of them particularly persuasive, and why?

Throughout this problem, restrict yourself to pure strategy Nash equilibria only. You will probably find the results a bit surprising. Can you explain what is going on here?

■ 21. Imagine an N firm oligopoly for "nominally differentiated" goods. That is, each of the N firms produces a product that "looks" different from the products of its competitors, but that "really" isn't any different. However, each firm is able to fool some of the buying public. Specifically, each of the N firms (which are identical and have zero marginal cost of production) has a captive market — consumers who will buy only from that firm. The demand generated by each of these capitve markets is given by the demand function $P_n = A - x_n$, where x_n is the amount supplied to this captive market and P_n is the price of the production of firm n. There is also a group of intelligent consumers who realize that the products are really undifferentiated. These consumers are represented by the demand curve $P = A - X/B$, where P is the price of goods sold to these consumers and X is their demand. (If $x_n > A$ or $X/B > A$, then the prices in the respective markets are zero. Prices do not become negative.)

Firms compete Cournot style. Each firm n supplies a total quantity X_n, which is divided between its loyal customers and the customers who are willing to buy from any firm. If we let x_n be the part of X_n that goes to loyal customers, then the price of good n is necessarily $P_n = A - x_n$. The price that goes to the "shoppers" is $P = A - (\sum_n (X_n - x_n))/B$. In an equilibrium, $P_n \geq P$, and if $X_n > x_n$, then $P_n = P$. (That is, a firm can charge a "higher than market" price for its own output, but then it will sell only to its own loyal customers.) By Cournot competition, we mean that each firm n assumes that the other firms will hold fixed their total amounts of output.

(a) For a given vector of output quantities by the firms, $(X_1, \ldots, X_N)$, is there a unique set of equilibrium prices (and a division of the output of each firm) that meets the conditions given above for equilibrium? If so, how do you find those prices? If not, can you characterize all the market equilibria?

(b) Find as many Cournot equilibria as you can for this model, as a function of the parameters N and B. (WARNING: Do not assume that solutions of first-order conditions are necessarily global maxima.)

chapter thirteen

Incomplete information and irrationality

In this chapter we present a methodological innovation, the notion of a *game of incomplete information*, which has been extremely useful in the modeling of all sorts of economic phenomena. As an example of this sort of application, we discuss again the problem of entry deterrence in monopoly. We use games of incomplete information to model situations in which one or more of the players is suspected of being "irrational." And with this tool at our disposal, we return a final time to questions concerning refinements of Nash equilibrium.

13.1. Games of incomplete information

The following story provides an excellent example of what we are after. Imagine two individuals, whom we will call (without much imagination) player 1 and player 2. Player 2 unhappily is something of a bully; he likes to pick fights with cowards. But he is equally averse to picking a fight with someone with courage; he will pick a fight with someone only if he assesses probability .5 or more that this individual is a coward. (He is indifferent between picking and not picking a fight at the assessment .5.) He considers picking a fight with player 1, but he is uncertain whether player 1 is a coward or is brave. He initially assesses probability .8 that player 1 is brave and .2 that player 1 is a coward (these being the only possibilities), and so it seems that he will not pick a fight with this individual.

Before deciding whether to pick a fight with player 1, player 2 gets a signal about player 1's disposition that may be of value, namely what player 1 will have for breakfast. Player 1 will have one of two breakfasts: beer or quiche. If player 1 is brave, then she prefers a breakfast of beer to a breakfast of quiche. If player 1 is a coward, she prefers quiche to beer. So, it might seem, player 2 should observe what player 1 has for breakfast and conclude: If 1 has quiche, she is certainly a coward; pick a fight. But if she has beer, she is certainly brave; avoid a fight. But complicating this is the fact that whether brave or a coward player 1 prefers that player 2 not pick a fight with her, and she cares more about this than she does about the type of breakfast she has. And player 1 realizes that player 2 is lurking at the street corner, watching carefully what player 1 has for breakfast.

We wish to create a game theoretic model of this situation to analyze what player 1 "should" have for breakfast and how player 2 "should" react to this signal. The difficulty we encounter is that player 2 is uncertain about some of the characteristics of player 1: What are player 1's dispositions in terms of a fight? Or, equivalently, what are player 1's preferences concerning breakfast? And we haven't said much about how player 1 regards all this. Does player 1 know that player 2 is uncertain about player 1's tastes? The last line of the previous paragraph seems to indicate that this, at least, is so. But this leads to more questions. For example, does player 1 know precisely what odds player 2 assesses that player 1 is brave?

In answer to these questions, consider the models of this situation given by the games in figures 13.1(a) and 13.1(b). Start with 13.1(a). Here we have modeled the situation as follows. Nature determines whether player 1 is brave or is a coward, with probability .8 that 1 is brave. Player 1 knows her own temperment, and player 1 must choose (perhaps contingent on her temperment) which breakfast to have. Player 2 observes this breakfast choice but not the initial choice of nature and then must decide whether to pick a fight with player 1 or not. Then payoffs are made. Note that player 2's payoffs are designed so that player 2 gets one unit of utility if he picks a fight with a coward or avoids a fight with a brave opponent, and player 2 gets zero if he does the "wrong" thing. Thus, as we said before, player 2 will pick the fight if he assesses probability more than .5 that his opponent is a coward; he avoids the fight if this assessment is below .5; and he is indifferent at the assessment .5. Player 1 gets two units of utility if she avoids the fight, to which is added one unit of utility if she has her preferred breakfast (depending on her disposition, which is determined by nature).

In this model, we have used a move by nature to capture the idea that player 2 is uncertain about the characteristics of player 1. Nature begins the game by selecting those characteristics. This selection of characteristics is known to player 1, and *(please note carefully)* player 1 is aware as well of player 2's initial uncertainty and assessment. Moreover, player 2 is aware of the fact that player 1 is aware of these things, and so on.

Compare this model with the extensive form game in figure 13.1(b). Here are four initial nodes, which we label bo, bp, co, and cp. The first letter in these labels refers to the type of player 1 — either brave or a

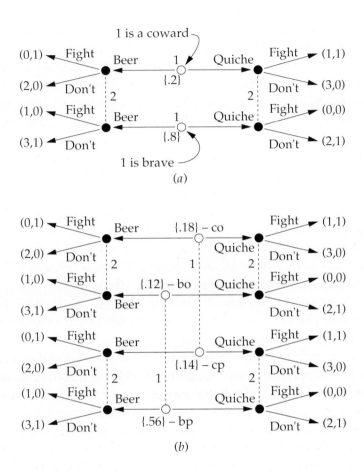

Figure 13.1. *Two versions of the beer-quiche game with incomplete information.*

coward. Now in this game, we have player 1 choosing her breakfast know-ing the first letter of the initial node but not the second. That is, {bo, bp} is one information set for player 1, and {co, cp} is another. And then player 2 chooses whether to pick a fight based on two pieces of information — whether player 1 had beer or quiche for breakfast, and whether the second letter of the initial node is o or p. That is, player 2 has four information sets: {bo-beer, co-beer}; {bp-beer, cp-beer}; {bo-quiche, co-quiche}; and {bp-quiche, cp-quiche}.

This second extensive form game is a model of the following situ-ation. Player 2 has precisely the sorts of doubts that he has in the first model — whether player 1 is brave or a coward. But now player 1 has doubts too. She knows that player 2 is uncertain about her character.

But we have modeled things so that player 1 is unsure about player 2's assessment. Player 1 thinks that player 2 may initially be pessimistic, assessing probability .8 that player 1 is brave (which is, in fact, the situation), or that player 2 may initially be optimistic, assessing probability .4 that player 1 is brave. Player 1 assesses probability .7 that player 1 has the first, pessimistic assessment, and .3 that player 1 has the second, optimistic assessment. The letters o and p in the initial nodes are mnemonics for optimistic and pessimistic. So the initial node bo is: nature begins the game with a brave player 1 and an optimistic player 2. This node, note, has probability .12, obtained as the product of the probability that player 2 is optimistic as assessed by player 1 and the probability that player 1 is brave as assessed by player 2, if player 2 is, in fact, optimistic. Note that in the model player 1 always knows (whenever it is her turn to move) whether the game started at a b-class initial node or a c-class initial node; player 1 always knows her disposition. And player 2, whenever he is called upon to move, knows whether the game started at an o-class initial node or a p-class node; he knows his own initial assessment. Finally, the model "closes" here; player 1 knows what sorts of assessment player 2 might be making, and player 2 knows that player 1 knows this. Player 2 knows the odds that player 1 assigns to the chances that player 2 makes various assessments, and player 1 knows that player 2 knows these odds, and so on.

These are examples of what are called *games of (or with) incomplete information*. These games are used to model situations in which some players have more or less information at the outset than do others. One player will know her own utility function. A second will know what options he has available. A third will have assessments about those two things, and the first two players may have assessments about those assessments. And, if we wanted something really complex, we could imagine that player 3 has an assessment concerning player 2's assessment of player 3's assessment of player 1's utility function. (If you think this is painful to read, imagine having to draw the corresponding extensive form.)

The form of the model is: Nature acts first to determine all these things, and then players' "initial" states of information are set by giving them varying amounts of information about nature's initial choices. These models are not completely general. In particular, they presume:

(a) There is a single, consistent "base model" in the minds of all the players. Everyone agrees on the possible initial states among which nature chose. No player is completely ignorant about something another player knows, although one player may assess very low (conditional) probability to certain states that other players know pertain for sure. (We will see later how you can model your way around this restriction.)

(b) Players agree on the prior distribution on initial states. This is implicit in the model; it is planted when we put at the initial nodes a single probability distribution representing the (unanimous) assessment of how nature starts things off. There is no reason to make this assumption in theory. We could, for example, assume that different players have different priors over nature's initial move, although we would still assume that each player is aware of the priors assessed by all others. (Note well: This isn't to say that each is aware of the posteriors assessed by others. We saw how one player can be unsure what assessment a second player makes, after nature selectively reveals some of what was done in getting the game underway.) But it is conventionally assumed that players have a common prior — more of the religious doctrine about which we spoke in chapter 2 and again in chapter 11.

(c) The model "closes" at a certain point. By this we mean the following. Suppose that player 2 is unaware of some characteristic of player 1. Player 2 will then have a probability assessment over this characteristic. We see in figure 13.1(b) how to model the notion that player 1 is uncertain about player 2's assessment. And we could further complicate the model and have player 2 uncertain about player 1's assessment concerning player 2's assessment. And we could have player 1 uncertain about 2's assessment about 1's assessment about 2's assessment. (Such a model would be quite intractable, so you needn't worry that we will ever look at such a thing.) But, in the end, this chain ends — say with player 1 knowing 2's assessment of 1's assessment of 2's assessment of 1's assessment of 2's assessment of 1's unknown characteristic. In figure 13.1(a) the model closes rather sooner than that; player 2 had an assessment over player 1's character, and player 1 knew 2's assessment. In figure 13.1(b) the model closes a step further along.

This sort of closure is theoretically unnecessary. With some very high-powered mathematics, one can show that an infinite regress of assessments is modelable. But, speaking practically, a model that doesn't close (and quite quickly) would be useless in applications, so the models that people write down and analyze almost always close quickly.

Despite these limitations, this way of modeling situations of incomplete information has proven very powerful in generating insights into behavior in competitive situations. The proof of that pudding will only come in the eating, however, so without too much further ado we proceed to an application of this sort of model.

But before doing so, we make one short remark. The model given in figure 13.1(a) may remind you of a game you have seen earlier; it is the "truth game" described in problem 3 in chapter 11 and discussed and depicted in subsection 12.7.4. The story has changed, but the two games, as extensive form games, are entirely isomorphic. This provides a good opportunity to introduce some conventional language. In the story about the truth game, the randomization by nature (the flipping of the bent coin) was entirely within the game. Because player 1 was told the outcome of the flip and player 2 wasn't, the two players were put on different informational footings. This sort of situation is called, in the literature, a *game with imperfect information*. In contrast, in the beer-quiche story nature is invoked as an external artifice to get the players from some never-relevant point of common information to a "starting point" where one player knows something about which another is uncertain. This sort of situation is conventionally called a *game with incomplete information*. As mathematical models, the two are the same; the different names refer (somewhat vaguely, to my mind) to the sort of story that is being told.

> One further point on this: It is commonplace to regard the truth game as a two-player game, with player 1's expected payoffs computed by averaging over the two possible outcomes of the coin flip. No one ever quibbles with this. But in beer-quiche, things are not so straightforward. Is this a two-player game, or should the two different manifestations of player 1 be treated as different players, so that this is in some sense a three-player game? Making interpersonal comparisons of utility between a cowardly player 1 and a brave player 1, which is what we would do if we took expectations over player 1's disposition, is suspicious at least. For certain game-theoretic considerations this would make a difference; cf. problem 1. There is no set conventional wisdom on this matter; for what little it is worth, my prejudices are to regard this as a three-player game.

13.2. An application: Entry deterrence

To illustrate the uses to which this sort of model has been put in the literature, we briefly consider the problem of entry deterrence by a monopolist that was discussed in section 9.2.[1] This is not meant to be anything like a complete treatment of entry deterrence; consult the relevant papers or, say, Tirole (1988) for that. But, at the same time, to introduce

---

[1] Since there will be both a monopoly firm and an entrant, it is convenient to use personal pronouns of different genders. Hence we will refer to the monopolist as *she* and to the potential entrant as *he*.

the reason for this application we will have to wander a bit far afield of the main subject of this chapter. Your forebearance is, therefore, requested.

To begin, recall the simple story of section 9.2. A monopolist faces demand given by $D(p) = 9 - P$ and has a constant marginal cost production technology with marginal cost of production equal to \$1. The monopolist must also pay a fixed cost of \$2.25. The standard theory of monopoly holds that this monopolist will equate marginal revenue, or $9 - 2X$ at output level X, with marginal cost; this gives $X = 4$, $P = \$5$, and profits of \$13.75.

Despite this, the story goes, we find that this monopolist sets $X = 5$, which leads to $P = \$4$ and profits of \$12.75. When pressed to explain this, the monopolist says:

> A single potential competitor is sitting out there who is considering entry into this market. This competitor has exactly the same production technology as I do. If this entrant believes that I will produce four units, the entrant faces residual demand of $5 - X_2 = P$, which leads the entrant to produce $X_2 = 2$ if he enters, depressing price to \$3, and leaving him with net profits of \$4 $-$ \$2.25 = \$1.75. Hence this competitor will enter. And if he enters, I will make net profits of \$8 $-$ \$2.25 = \$5.75.
>
> But if I produce five units and the entrant believes that I will continue to do this, then the entrant faces residual demand of $4 - X_2$, which leads him to produce $X_2 = 1.5$ if he enters. This pushes price down to \$2.50, giving him a gross profit of \$2.25 (gross of fixed costs), and a net profit of \$0. Hence this entrant will not enter, and I will continue to make profits of \$12.75. So I'm really much better off with my production level of 5.

This, as we noted in chapter 9, is a curious story on several grounds, chief among which is, Why does the potential entrant suppose that, if he enters, the monopolist (now a duopolist) will persist in the quantity that she produces preentry? It is not impossible to tell stories to justify this. One can imagine, for example, a world in which the incumbent monopolist must commit to a certain level of production that is observed by the potential entrant, and the entrant can then decide whether to enter and how much to produce. That is, we imagine a structure of competition like the von Stackelberg extensive form game. But it isn't clear that this is a very realistic model of the details of competition, and so one may wish to look further, particularly at models where the incumbent monopolist and the entrant interact competitively only after the incumbent decides to enter.

This sort of model presents a problem for the story of entry deterrence. If the entrant decides whether to enter or not, the incumbent monopolist sees this, and the two compete, it follows that the postentry competition can be thought of as a proper subgame. And there is no reason (yet) to imagine that the monopolist's preentry pricing or quantity decisions have any effect at all on the entrant's calculations. To take the simplest example once again, imagine the following details of competition: The monopolist, in a first period, exercises however she wishes her monopoly power. The entrant observes this and decides whether to enter. The monopolist observes what the entrant does, and then a second period of production/sales takes place, either in a monopoly (if the entrant chooses not to enter) or in a duopoly (if the entrant does enter). If the entrant does enter, the form of competition in the second period, for the sake of concreteness, is assumed to be Cournot style. The two firms simultaneously and independently choose quantities to supply to the market. (If you have any doubt about it at all, give the extensive form for the game just described.)

The point is that in this game, what happens subsequently if the entrant does enter is a proper subgame. It is a Cournot-style duopoly game, and we know the Cournot equilibrium for this subgame; each firm produces 8/3 units of the good, price is $11/3, and each firm's net profits are approximately $4.86. (You should be working all this out as we go along.)

Now the entire game has many Nash equilibria. For example, it is an equilibrium for the incumbent monopolist to threaten that she will produce 5.01 units in the second period if the entrant enters; this causes the entrant to choose not to enter. Since the entrant doesn't enter, the threat is off the path of play and is okay as part of a Nash equilibrium. But this relies on behavior that is subgame imperfect; the game has a unique subgame perfect equilibrium. If the entrant enters, the incumbent monopolist accommodates herself to this fait accompli and produces 8/3; the entrant nets $4.86; and so the entrant enters. And, going back to the first stage, the incumbent monopolist realizes that nothing she does in the first period will influence this, so she (optimally) chooses to produce four units, knowing that her days as a monopolist are numbered but knowing as well she can do nothing about that.[2]

So how do we resurrect the story of the entry-deterring monopolist? At least three ways are suggested in the literature. First, one can move to a formulation in which the second period is followed by a third, a fourth,

---

[2] If you like irrelevant logical puzzles, try to build a (subgame imperfect) Nash equilibrium for the game in which the incumbent monopolist produces five units in the first period. In this equilibrium, how much will the monopolist necessarily produce in the second period (assuming it is the last)?

ad infinitum, and where profits in different periods are evaluated using discounted present value. This sort of technique, which is the subject of chapter 14, does give us enough leverage to resurrect the story. We leave it to the next chapter to see how.

Second, one can invent ways in which decisions made by the monopolist in the first period affect (physically) what happens in the second. There are a large number of variations on this theme, but the general idea is the same: The incumbent monopolist by something she does in the first period that is observed by the entrant is able to shift around her own second period incentives in a way that makes her "more aggressive" in the second period in the event of entry — aggressive enough so that entry is forestalled. I will not work out an example of this here, but refer you instead to problem 2.

Third (and the point of all this here) is that we can link the two periods by supposing that the potential entrant learns something about the incumbent monopolist from the monopolist's actions in the first period. To illustrate this, we change the numbers around a bit. Suppose that the entrant is uncertain about the marginal cost of the monopolist. The entrant faces a constant marginal cost of 3; the monopolist either has a constant marginal cost of 3 or a marginal cost of only 1. And suppose that the entrant's (and the incumbent's) fixed costs are $3, which is known to both parties.

These numbers are selected so that the entrant will enter if he is sure that she has marginal costs of $3; but he won't enter if he is sure her marginal costs equal $1. Specifically, if the entrant knows that the monopolist has costs of $3, Cournot competition leads each to produce two units, gross profits for each are $4, and so (net of the $3 fixed cost) the entrant makes a $1 profit and will enter. Whereas if the entrant knows that the monopolist has costs of $1, the Cournot equilibrium if the entrant enters will be for the entrant to produce 4/3 and the monopolist to produce 10/3. Price will be 13/3, and the entrant's gross profits will be 16/9 for net profits of $ − 11/9. The entrant doesn't enter.

Suppose the monopolist, in the first period, chooses her single-period optimal level of quantity, as suggested by the standard theory of monopoly. If her costs are 1 per unit, she prices the good at $5. If her costs are 3 per unit, she prices the good at $6. Hence if the entrant anticipates that the monopolist will act in this fashion in the first period, the entrant can learn from the monopolist's first period decisions whether to enter or not. But then the monopolist, if her costs are in fact 3, might wish to price the good at $5 to mislead the entrant into thinking that entry is a bad idea. (This would then be our phenomenon of entry-deterring pricing in the first period.) But then perhaps the entrant would not pay attention to the monopolist's first period decision.

How do we model and analyze this? Needless to say, the appropriate model depends on what (and how much) the incumbent monopolist knows about the uncertainties of the entrant and how much the entrant knows about what the monopolist knows. We can use games of incomplete information to model a number of situations along these lines, of which we will give the simplest example here.

Suppose the entrant assesses probability ρ that the incumbent has marginal costs of $3; suppose the incumbent monopolist knows this; the entrant knows that the monopolist knows this, and so on. Consider the game of incomplete information where Nature first chooses the production function (marginal costs) of the incumbent monopolist, with ρ giving the probability that nature chooses $3, and reveals this to the monopolist. Depending on this, the monopolist chooses her first period levels of output and price. The entrant observes this (but not the monopolist's cost structure) and decides whether to enter. If the entrant enters, the entrant and monopolist play a simultaneous move Cournot "subgame." Since the entrant may be uncertain about what the monopolist's costs are, he may face uncertainty about his profits; we will assume he seeks to maximize the expected level of profits he attains. And since the monopolist will be receiving profits in each of two periods, we have to know how she trades off a dollar today against a dollar tomorrow; we will assume for simplicity that she maximizes the undiscounted sum of her profits. (Accommodating a discount factor would not be difficult.)

We depict this extensive form game symbolically in figure 13.2. Note that we show six information sets for the incumbent — three each for each of her "types." She must decide how much to produce in the first period, how much to produce in the second if the entrant doesn't enter, and how much to produce in the second period if the entrant does enter. (Actually, she has many information sets of the latter two types, as she can condition her second period decisions on her level of output in the first period.) We show two information sets for the entrant: whether to enter or not, and if he enters, how much to produce. This is very deceptive. The entrant has a pair of these information sets for each first-period output decision of the incumbent, and the whole point of the exercise is, How will the first-period output decision of the incumbent affect the decisions taken by the entrant?

We will now undertake to analyze this extensive form game, using as solution concept sequential equilibrium.[a] This analysis will be tough

---

[a] To be very precise, the notion of sequential equilibrium doesn't really apply here, since

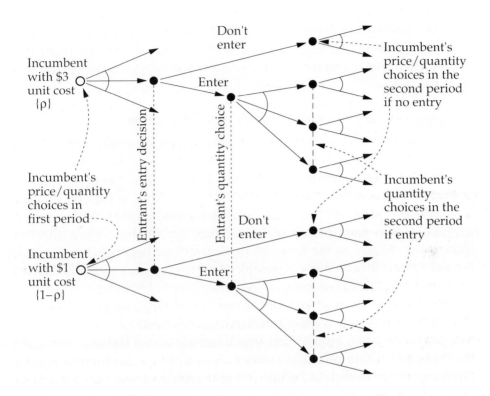

Figure 13.2. An entry deterrence game.

going for many readers; it is the first "serious" problem using noncooperative game theory we've undertaken to examine. We will take things
slowly and in steps, but still this will not be easy to follow. You should
persevere; many recent developments in microeconomics are based on arguments of this sort. If, after struggling with this analysis, you are still
at sea, it may be worthwhile to move immediately to chapter 17 and then
return to this analysis.

    To begin, we note why we use the sequential equilibrium concept.
We have already seen in our discussion of the entry game without incomplete information that we could get "entry deterrence" on the cheap, using
Nash equilibria that are held together by the monopolist's threats to produce very large quantities in the event of entry. To avoid these "threat"
equilibria, we needed to invoke subgame perfection. We are unable to

---

sequential equilibrium is defined for finite game trees only. Our analysis is really only in the
"spirit" of sequential equilibrium.

invoke subgame perfection here; because of the incomplete information, this game has no proper subgames. By using the sequential equilibrium concept, we invoke sequential rationality for the monopolist, which means that she can't threaten to meet entry with an incredibly large amount of output; she must respond optimally to what she supposes the entrant will do if he enters.

Step 1. *The Cournot subgame given the entrant's beliefs*

Of course, the sequential equilibrium notion does more than avoid threats by the monopolist. It also ties the actions of the entrant to his beliefs, after seeing the price/quantity choice of the monopolist in the first round, concerning the monopolist's costs. More precisely, suppose that we write $\mu(p)$ for the beliefs held by the entrant that the incumbent monopolist has marginal cost \$3, as a function of the price p that the monopolist charges in the first round. Given those beliefs, what ensues if the entrant decides to enter is completely fixed by $\mu(p)$ in the fashion of problem 17 in the last chapter.

More precisely, in that problem we asked what would be the outcome of Cournot-style competition between two firms, where the first had marginal costs of c, but the first was uncertain about the marginal costs of the second. In terms of the numbers here, we imagine that the entrant chooses output level $x_e(p)$, while the monopolist chooses $x_m(p, 1)$ if her costs are \$1 and $x_m(p, 3)$ if her costs are \$3. Note that all three of these are taken as functions of p, the price the monopolist charged in the first period, since that may influence the incumbent's beliefs about the monopolist's costs.

In an equilibrium, the monopolist's quantities must be best responses to the entrant's quantity, or

$$x_m(p, 1) = \frac{9 - 1 - x_e(p)}{2} \text{ and } x_m(p, 3) = \frac{9 - 3 - x_e(p)}{2}.$$

(If you aren't sure where these came from, compute the monopolist's profits as a function of her output quantity and optimize.) The entrant's quantity must at the same time be a best response to the (from his perspective) random level of output selected by the monopolist. His expected profits, given his beliefs and given his output level x, are

$$[\mu(p)][(9-3 - x_m(p, 3) - x)x] + [1 - \mu(p)][(9 - 3 - x_m(p, 1) - x)x]$$
$$= (6 - [\mu(p)x_m(p, 3) + (1 - \mu(p))x_m(p, 1)] - x)x,$$

which is maximized at

$$x_e(p) = \frac{6 - [\mu(p)x_m(p,3) + (1 - \mu(p))x_m(p,1)]}{2}.$$

Note well where this expression for his profits comes from; he assesses probability $\mu(p)$ that the monopolist has costs \$3 and so will produce at level $x_m(p,3)$ and probability $1 - \mu(p)$ that she will produce at level $x_m(p,1)$ because her costs are \$1.

This gives us three equations in three unknowns, and if you solve them, you will find that

$$x_e(p) = \frac{2(6 - 3\mu(p) - 4(1 - \mu(p)))}{3} = \frac{2(2 + \mu(p))}{3};$$

$$x_m(p,1) = \frac{6 + 3\mu(p) + 4(1 - \mu(p))}{3} = \frac{10 - \mu(p)}{3}; \text{ and}$$

$$x_m(p,3) = \frac{3 + 3\mu(p) + 4(1 - \mu(p))}{3} = \frac{7 - \mu(p)}{3}.$$

And if you work at the algebra a bit more, you'll find that the profits of the entrant, not including his fixed cost, are $4(2 + \mu(p))^2/9$.

This is an algebraic swamp, but what emerges is sensible: The higher $\mu(p)$ is, the more "optimistic" the entrant is. Higher $\mu(p)$ means he assesses a higher probability that the monopolist has higher costs. This emboldens him; his level of output rises with $\mu(p)$. And this rise in his level of output causes the equilibrium levels of output of the monopolist to fall. All of which raises his expected gross profits.

When seeing this sort of construction for the first time, readers will sometimes latch onto what was just said and conclude that the entrant should "choose to have optimistic beliefs." It should be stressed that players don't choose their beliefs; they have them based on their experiences with life, similar situations, and so on. Players choose their actions optimally given their beliefs, but we don't think of players choosing to be optimistic when being optimistic is to their benefit. Choosing advantageous beliefs would be like choosing to like broccoli this year because the price of broccoli is low.

Let us take stock of where we are. We are looking for sequential equilibria to the extensive form game we have described, a game with which we hope to capture some aspects of entry deterrence. We have shown what will ensue after the monopolist charges price p at the first date, if the entrant, therefore, assesses probability $\mu(p)$ that the entrant has cost $3 and enters. Namely, the entrant and monopolist will act (in equilibrium) in a fashion that leads the entrant to gross profits of $4(2 + \mu(p))^2/9$.

> One skeleton is buried in what was just asserted, which should be ex-humed if not fully explained. In any sequential equilibrium of this game, the beliefs of the entrant at an information set where he is deciding whether to enter will be identical with his beliefs at the subsequent information set if he enters, whether he is supposed to enter or not in equilibrium. This is a con-sequence of the consistency criterion of beliefs and strategies in a sequential equilibrium. Besides, it is fairly sensible. Why should something the entrant does or doesn't do change his beliefs about the costs of the monopolist?

Step 2. The entry decision given the entrant's beliefs

So should the entrant enter, if he believes that the incumbent has costs of $3 with probability $\mu(p)$? He will enter if his expected gross profits are enough to cover his fixed costs of $3. If you compare $4(2 + \mu)^2/9$ with $3, you will find that the critical value of $\mu(p)$ is approximately .598.[b] If the entrant believes that the incumbent monopolist has marginal costs of $3 with probability exceeding .598, he enters. If he assesses probability less than .598, he stays out. (If he assesses precisely .598, he is indifferent between entering and staying out.)

So, with all this as prelude, we can ask, What are the sequential equi-libria of this game? There are, it turns out, many of them. We will not attempt to characterize them all. Instead, we will discuss one set of strate-gies that do not form an equilibrium, and we will give one sequential equilibrium for the case $\rho < .598$ and another sequential equilibrium for the case $\rho > .598$. For now, be content to understand why the nonequilib-rium is not an equilibrium, why the two types of equilibria are equilibria, and what these two equilibria entail for the story of entry deterrence. Later, after completing chapter 17, you will be told to return and conduct a more complete analysis of this problem.

Step 3. A nonequilibrium

No matter what the value of ρ is, it won't be an equilibrium for the monopolist to charge $5 in the first period if her costs are $1 and $6 if her costs are $3. For if she does this, then the entrant will infer that her costs are $3 if she charges $6 and $1 if she charges $5. That is, $\mu(6) = 1$ and $\mu(5) = 0$. These beliefs are forced by Bayes' rule; if the monopolist charges

---

[b] Precisely, $3\sqrt{3}/2 - 2$.

$5 or $6 in the first period, then these observations are along the path of play, and Bayes' rule must be applied.[c]

But given these beliefs, we know that the entrant won't enter if he sees $5 charged in the first period, and he will enter if $6 is charged. Consider the plight of the monopolist if this is the entrant's strategy and she has marginal costs of $3. If she follows the strategy outlined and charges $6, she will net $6 in the first period (net of fixed costs), but then the entrant will enter, and she will make only $1 net in the second period. If, on the other hand, she charges $5 in the first period, mimicking the strategy of the $1 monopolist, her net profits in the first period will fall to $5 in the first period (from $6). But then the entrant will not enter, and she can charge $6 in the second period and make net profits of $6. This is far better than following the strategy outlined, which is, therefore, not part of an equilibrium strategy profile.

Step 4. A pooling equilibrium

Now suppose $\rho < .598$. We claim the following is a sequential equilibrium: The monopolist charges $5 in the first period, no matter what her costs are. The entrant enters if the monopolist charges anything more than $5 in the first period, based on beliefs $\mu(p) = 1$ for $p > \$5$. The entrant does not enter if the monopolist charges anything at or below $5, based on beliefs that $\mu(p) = \rho$ for $p \leq \$5$. (If there is entry, the two play according to the scheme outlined in step 1. If there is no entry, the monopolist charges her monopoly price in the second period.)

Why is this a sequential equilibrium? First note that the entrant is playing optimally given his presumed beliefs. He is entering when he should and staying out when he should, according to the analysis in step 2. Note second that his beliefs are consistent with the supposed equilibrium strategies, at least along the path of play. The only price that is used in the first period is $5 (in these strategies), and since both types of monopolist charge this price, the posterior assessment of the monopolist's type given this price should be the prior. All other prices are off the path, so beliefs can be arbitrary.[d] But they even make some sense: The higher the price the monopolist charges, the greater should be our suspicion that she has high costs. The beliefs we have mandated have this monotonicity character, at least.[3]

---

[c] This is always true in a sequential equilibrium.

[d] They should be consistent in the sense of sequential equilibria, and these are (allowing for the fact that we aren't working with a finite game and so must fudge definitions a bit).

[3] "Aha," the reader is saying, "what was all this stuff about not choosing beliefs? Seems like beliefs are being chosen here!" At the risk of confusing the reader who is not confused,

And finally, the monopolist is optimizing given the entrant's strategy. If the monopolist's costs are $1, she is getting to charge her favorite price in the first period *and* forestall entry. Nothing could be better than that. While if her costs are $3, she would prefer to charge a higher price in the first period, but that will bring on entry. On balance, it is better to accept the smaller profits in the first period and keep the larger profits in the second.

The "intuition" of this equilibrium resides in the last assertion. Because ρ is low, the entrant, if he doesn't learn anything from the first period price charged by the monopoly, will choose to forego entry. Hence the monopolist, if her costs are $3, wishes to hide that fact. And in this equilibrium she hides that fact by charging a $5 price in the first period, just "like" in the story of section 9.2!

This is called a *pooling equilibrium* because the two types of monopolist do the same thing in equilibrium.

Step 5. A screening equilibrium

This pooling equilibrium doesn't work if $\rho > .598$. In this case a pool would be ineffective; entry would not be forestalled at all. And what's the point of the $3 monopolist charging a short-run suboptimal price in the first period if she is going to see entry anyway?

When $\rho > .598$, we assert the following is an equilibrium: If the monopolist has costs $3, she charges $6 in the first period. If she has costs $1, she charges $3.76 (!) in the first period. The entrant enters if the monopolist charges anything above $3.76, based on beliefs $\mu(p) = 1$ for $p > \$3.76$. The entrant stays out if the monopolist charges anything

---

let us be very clear about this. A sequential equilibrium describes what people do and what they believe, both in and out of equilibrium. We aren't saying why they act as they do, although we assume as part of the justification that they all are pretty sure how each will act, and they all choose their actions optimally given their beliefs. Similarly, we aren't saying why they believe what they do (out of equilibrium). We are only seeing whether beliefs and intended actions are in equilibrium, which means that the intended actions are optimal. If we are to have faith in a particular equilibrium, then we need to have some reason to believe that individuals will see the prescribed actions as "obvious ways to play the game," and when we employ sequential equilibria, we essentially are supposing there is reason to think the specified out-of-equilibrium beliefs describe what the players will find the obvious beliefs to have. When we remark, as we did at the end of the previous paragraph, that the beliefs conform to a sensible monotonicity property, we are imposing a *partial* test on the reasonableness of supposed beliefs. But this is a pretty weak test, and if we are going to have faith in this equilibrium, we will need either empirical evidence or some convincing story as to why people will think and act as we are postulating. In this sense, what is demonstrated here is the *possibility* or *coherence* of various sorts of entry deterrence; we would need some other argument to assert that this is what *will* happen.

at or below $3.76, based on beliefs $\mu(p) = 0$ for $p \leq \$3.76$. (If there is entry, the two play according to the scheme outlined in step 1. If there is no entry, the monopolist charges her monopoly price in the second period.)

Why is this an equilibrium? First, the entrant is behaving optimally given his beliefs, according to step 2. And those beliefs make sense given the strategy of the monopolist; a first period price of $6 is a sure indication that the monopolist has costs $3, while a first period price of $3.76 is a sure indication that the monopolist has costs $1. The other prices are off the path of play and so any beliefs will do; the ones we've selected even have the appropriate monotonicity property.

So is the monopolist behaving optimally? Consider first the monopolist if her costs are $1. She would prefer to charge a higher price than $3.76 in the first period, but that would attract entry. We leave to you the task of showing that given the beliefs of the entrant for prices above $3.76 she prefers to keep the entrant out and sacrifice a bit of her first period profits.

The more interesting case is the monopolist if her costs are $3. If she follows the prescriptions above, she makes $6 (net of fixed costs) in the first period and, after entry, $1 (net of fixed costs) in the second. She can only forestall entry by charging a price of $3.76 or less, which forestalls entry completely, and then she would make $6 in the second period. But what does she make if she charges $3.76 in the first period? She makes $.76 per unit on sales of 5.24 units, or $3.98 gross and $.98 net of fixed costs. This is just short of the $1 threshold needed to make forestalling entry worthwhile, and we have an equilibrium. N.B., the level $3.76 is chosen so that, if the monopolist's marginal costs are $3, she just fails to prefer to mimic the low-cost monopoly strategy of charging $3.76 and forestall entry.

Intuitively, in this equilibrium the $1 monopolist to demonstrate convincingly that she has $1 costs must charge a very low price in the first period — a price so low that the $3 monopolist would rather give up the benefits of forestalling entry than take such low profits in the first period. This is called a *screening* equilibrium because the two types of monopolist are screened or separated by their first period actions. Note that in this equilibrium entry occurs whenever it would have had there been complete information about the monopolist's costs. The only thing that incomplete information brings is a better deal for consumers in the first period, if the monopolist has low costs — the low-cost monopolist charges a low price in order to "prove" she has low costs and (thereby) forestall entry that would be forestalled if only she could reveal her cost structure to the potential entrant.[4]

The objective of this example is not to analyze entry deterrence. The model given is frightfully simple, and there is an enormous amount more to the story. The point instead is the form of the model, where we use a game of incomplete information, and then the style of analysis. In particular, note what is presumed by this simple model: The incumbent monopolist is aware of the uncertainty in the mind of the entrant, and (at least in the case $\rho < .598$ and the monopolist's costs are $3) the monopolist uses this uncertainty to her own advantage. If we thought that the monopolist was uncertain what the entrant assessed, we would need a more complex model. We might enrich the model as well by supposing that the monopolist is uncertain about the entrant's fixed or marginal costs: Then the monopolist would be unsure whether the price she charges will deter entry, and she would update her assessment of the entrant's cost structure if the entrant does enter. (And a higher-cost entrant would have a bit of an incentive to enter insofar as this would mislead the monopolist into believing that he is a lower-cost entrant.)

There are other ways we could think of enriching the model. An obvious one is to suppose that the monopolist may be a bit of a dope — unaware of the entrant's uncertainty about her cost structure, or unaware that he will be watching her first period price to uncover that cost structure. Such an unaware monopolist is not fully rational, at least in the sense that she doesn't quite understand the full implications of her actions. So we turn next to the question How would we model "irrationality" of this sort and of others?

13.3. Modeling irrationality

Games of incomplete information can be used to model situations in which one player assesses significant probability that another player is "irrational."

The key comes from identifying what we mean by "irrational." To take the simplest case first, we would call irrational any behavior in the game that flies in the face of the player's own "best interests" as determined by the player's payoffs. For example, consider the extensive form game given in figure 13.3(a). Solved by backwards induction, we see that player 1

---

[4] We will discuss this in chapter 17, but you might think through how things would change if the incumbent monopolist had the ability to reveal at no cost to herself the details of her cost structure.

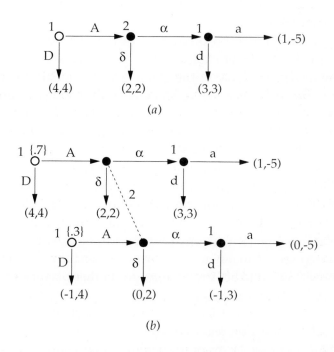

Figure 13.3. Modeling irrationality.

should play d at her final node, hence 2 should play α at his node, and hence player 1 should play D. Suppose, however, that player 2 is concerned that player 1 may for some reason be intending to play Aa. This could be because of inattention on the part of player 1, or because player 1 is malicious, or simply because player 1 has an irrational phobia about the letter d. In particular, suppose that player 2 assesses probability .3 that this player 1's behavior will be to begin with A and, if she gets the opportunity, to continue with a despite 1's (apparent) payoffs.

How do we model this? Consider figure 13.3(b). We have created a game of incomplete information containing two "versions" of the original game, between which nature picks at the outset. In both versions, player 2's payoffs are exactly as in the original game. In the top version, player 1's payoffs are exactly as in the original game. But in the bottom version, player 1 is given payoffs that make the play of Aa a strictly dominant strategy. Notice how we do this: Fixing the strategy Aa for player 1, for each terminal node in the tree, we count the number of information sets of player 1 at which player 1 would have to deviate from the strategy Aa to get us to that terminal node; 1's payoff is set at minus that number.[5] In this way, at any information set possessed by player 1 and given any strategies player 1 supposes her opponents might choose, she will always choose the appropriate part of the fixed strategy (Aa in this case) as a strictly dominant choice.

Of course, there is more to the game in figure 13.3(b) than this. First, nature picks between the two versions with probability .7 and .3. This is intended to model player 2's initial assessment whether player 1 is irrational or not. Player 1, at each of his information sets, knows which version was selected; that is, player 1 "knows" whether she is irrational or not. But player 2 at his information set isn't given this information.

The trick, then, is to model irrational behavior of a particular form by creating uncertainty about the payoffs of the player who might be irrational, where in states in which the player is modeled as irrational we simply make up payoffs that force (by reason of dominance) the player to act in the irrational manner. The player is told his own payoffs, so the player "knows" when to act irrationally. And other players are kept in the dark.[6]

This is how we model irrationality of the form: The player takes a particular course of action regardless of what other players do. Of course, we could have multiple forms of irrationality of this sort for a single player in a single game — if player 2 assessed probability .2 that player 1 irrationally plays Aa, .15 that player 1 irrationally plays Ad, .25 that player 1 irrationally plays D, and .5 that player 1 is "rational," then we would look at a game of incomplete information with four versions of the initial game. In three, player 1 would be given payoffs that force her to play according to the particular behavior being modeled, and in the fourth, player 1 would be given her original payoffs.

At the risk of beating the point to death, let me make a further observation about the nature of irrationality that we are modeling here. In this particular game, a rational player 1 will always pick D. Yet in the preceding paragraph, I spoke of a model where player 2 assesses probability .25 that player 1 irrationally plays D. The distinction here is "rationality"

---

[5] To check your understanding of this rule, consider how it would work if we fixed 1's strategy as Dd. You can check your answer by looking at the bottommost version of the basic game in figure 13.4(c).

[6] A more complicated situation is where there is uncertainty on the part of player 2 about the rationality of player 1, although player 3 does happen to know that player 1 acts rationally. That would be modeled as follows: There is initial uncertainty about player 1's payoffs, as in the example. Player 2 doesn't learn the resolution of that uncertainty and player 1 does, as in the example. And, if we suppose that player 3 knows player 1's "state of mind," player 3 has the uncertainty resolved whenever player 3 has an opportunity to take an action.

is meant to connote behavior that is in accord with the originally given payoffs, taking into account the predicted behavior of one's opponent(s). "Irrationality" connotes, for the time being, behavior that is taken without much thought or introspection. Now in this game it is fairly easy to see that introspection by player 1, given that player 1's payoffs are as originally described, leads to rational play of D. But we can and do want to be able to model situations where player 1 might take action D either because she engages in this sort of thought or because, say, she is averse to the letter A.

Hence, with caveats to be given momentarily, we see how to model the notion that one player assesses positive probability that another player might act in a particular fashion, regardless of what the rationally computed "best interests" of the second player might be. What about other forms of irrationality? Some are easily handled. For example, a player might play to maximize the expected difference between his payoff and that of his rival. It isn't clear that one should call this irrational; perhaps it is better described as play according to a different set of preferences (hence a different set of payoffs). But whatever you choose to call it, this is easily modeled with a game of incomplete information. To take a slightly more complex example, one player might assess positive probability that his opponent plays to maximize the minimum payoff the second player might receive. One could model this in a two-step procedure: First determine what sort of strategy this criterion would lead to; and then enter that into the model "behaviorally," as we have done above. In general, we try to reduce irrationality of any sort to "behavior," so that we can use the sort of model that has been described. In most cases, this will work. (See below for particularly crafty ways to do this.)

The model in figure 13.3(b) implicitly makes other assumptions that should be mentioned. Most importantly, it assumes that player 1 is aware of player 2's uncertainty about player 1's rationality. Player 1, knowing the structure of the game, is aware of the fact that player 2 assesses probability .3 that player 1 will play Aa as a strictly dominant strategy. Player 2 is aware of the fact that player 1 is aware of this, and so on. The model closes with player 2's uncertainty. We can say two things about this:

(a) This knowledge held by player 1 is only conceivably of use to her in the top half of the game in figure 13.3(b). That is, if nature picks the bottom initial node, player 1 will pick Aa no matter what she believes player 2 is doing. So when we say that player 1 is aware of player 2's uncertainties, we could rephrase this as: Player 1, if rational, is aware of 2's uncertainties. The model formally has the irrational type of player 1 knowing this as well, but the knowledge is irrelevant given 1's payoffs.

(b) We could, of course, close the model further down the chain. That is, we could have player 2 uncertain about 1's rationality, with a rational player 1 uncertain about 2's assessment. Precisely the sort of model given in figure 13.1(b) would be employed if we closed the model with: Player 1's assessment concerning player 2's assessment concerning player 1's rationality is known to player 2, etc. The same comment applies here as applied (more generally) in the previous section: On theoretical grounds, we don't need to close the model after any finite number of stages. But on practical grounds, we will always look at models that do so.

Let us now change the payoffs and probabilities in figure 13.3 just a bit to make a couple of final points. Consider first the game in figure 13.4(a). The difference is in player 1's payoff if player 1 chooses A followed by δ by player 2. The payoff 5 in this case means that player 1, playing "rationally" according to the given payoffs, would happily choose A if she thought that player 2 was going to respond with δ with high probability. Of course, if player 2 is sure that player 1 is "rational" and will play d at the final node, then player 2 chooses α. In which case 1 should rationally choose D. So the choice of A by player 1 seems irrational. So perhaps it scares player 2 into δ. In which case the choice of A by 1 isn't irrational, and player 2 shouldn't play δ. But then A is irrational, and so on.

How do we model this mess? By saying that player 2 isn't completely sure at the outset that player 1 is rational, 2 entertains doubts at the start whether player 1 will choose d at the final node. We could, for example, hypothesize that player 2 assesses probability .1 at the outset that player 1 will "irrationally" play Aa, building the model shown in figure 13.4(b), and proceed to analyze this.

The analysis of the game in figure 13.4(b) is a bit complex, and I don't think one can conclude that the "answer" obtained from equilibrium analysis is a clearly obvious way to play this game. But let us pursue this analysis and see if it makes sense in the end.

To begin, note that in any equilibrium, player 1 in the bottom part of the game will choose Aa by strict dominance. So we need only be concerned with the play of player 1 in the top half of the game. Next, note that the game has a pure strategy Nash equilibrium that isn't very plausible: In this equilibrium, player 1 plays Aa in the top half of the game (as well as in the bottom), and player 2 responds with δ. It is clear why player 2 responds with δ; he is going to get −5 if he gives the move to player 1, regardless of which half of the game we are in. And then

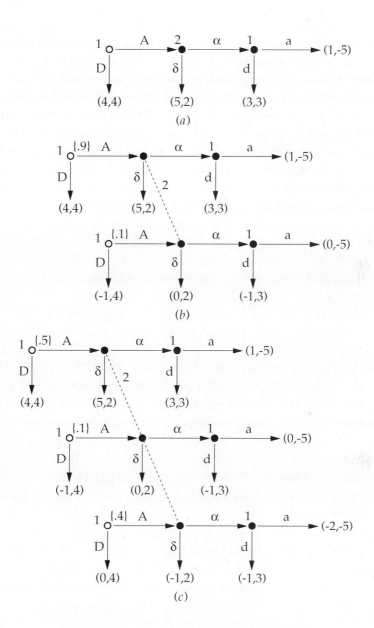

Figure 13.4. Modeling irrationality, continued.

player 1's strategy (in the top half) is optimal; given player 2 will choose δ, A is better than D, and the choice of a over d is irrelevant. But this depends on player 1 choosing a in the top half of the game if given the move, and it is implausible that given the move player 1 would actually do that. Why take 1 when she can have 3? Or, in the language of Nash refinements, the choice of a in the top half of the game isn't sequentially rational. So we hereafter restrict attention to cases where player 1 plays d in the top half of the game (and, of course, a in the bottom half).

Now suppose that player 2, given the move, assesses probability μ that he is in the top part of the game. If he chooses δ, she gets 2 for sure. Whereas if he chooses α, he gets 3 with probability μ and –5 with probability $1-\mu$, for an expected utility of $3\mu-5(1-\mu) = 8\mu-5$. Comparing this with the 2 he gets for sure from δ, player 2 will choose δ for sure if $\mu < 7/8$, he will choose α for sure if $\mu > 7/8$, and he is just indifferent (and can play any mixed strategy at all) if $\mu = 7/8$.

Suppose that the solution of the game is that he plays δ for sure. Then player 1, realizing this, plays A in the top half of the game. This means that player 2 should assess probability .9 that he is in the top half of the game, given the move, which leads him to choose α for sure. This isn't an equilibrium.

Suppose that the solution is that he plays α for sure. Then player 1 will optimally choose D in the top half of the game. But then if player 2 is given the move, he knows he is in the bottom half of the game, and he chooses δ. This isn't an equilibrium either.

So the only possible equilibrium (where 1 plays d in the top half of the game) is where player 2 randomizes between α and δ. For this to be optimal, he must assess probability 7/8 that he is in the top half of the tree, given the move. How can this happen? Suppose player 1 in the top half of the game randomizes between A and D, playing A with probability π. Then Bayes' rule tells us that player 2, given the move, assesses probability $.9\pi/(.9\pi+.1)$ that he is in the top half of the tree. This equals 7/8 if $\pi = 7/9$.

And what would allow a randomized strategy for 1 in the top half of the tree to be optimal? Suppose that 2's strategy at his information set is to play α with probability ϕ and δ with probability $1 - \phi$. Then, in the top half of the tree, player 1 nets 4 for sure if she plays D and 5 with probability $1-\phi$ or 3 with probability ϕ if she plays A. If $\phi = 1/2$, player 1 in the top half is indifferent between A and D.

What we have here is: Assuming 1 plays d in the top half of the tree, there is no possibility of a pure strategy equilibrium. The only possible equilibrium is where player 1 mixes in the top half between A and D just enough so that player 2 is indifferent between α and δ, and player 2 mixes between α and δ so that player 1 is just indifferent between A and D. The appropriate mixing probabilities are computed above. You can decide for yourself whether this qualifies as a "solution." But (always with the reasonable presumption that 1 will play d in the top half of the tree), it is the only possible candidate.

To help build your intuition, note that we get a very intuitive solution if we increase 2's initial assessment that 1 is irrational to .2, or if we decrease the −5s at the rightmost terminal nodes to −10s. With either of these changes, even if player 2 thinks that player 1 will choose A in the top half of the game for sure, player 2 thinks the odds of a bad outcome combined with the severity of that outcome if he picks α are too great; he will pick δ no matter what he thinks the rational sort of player 1 is doing. And then player 1 in the top half of the game clearly wants to give player 2 the opportunity to pick δ.

Let us next pursue a further elaboration on the game of figure 13.3. We have supposed in figure 13.4(b) that player 2 is unsure about the character of player 1 and that player 1 is aware of this (and in the previous analysis tries to take advantage of this). Imagine that player 2 entertains the following more complex initial beliefs: There is probability .1, as before, that player 1 will irrationally choose Aa. Otherwise, player 1 plays according to the payoffs originally given. But there is an additional marginal probability .4 that player 1 is unaware of the fact that player 2 is uncertain of player 1's character. With this .4 probability, player 1 thinks that player 2 thinks the game is precisely as in figure 13.3(a). And with probability .5, player 1 is aware of player 2's uncertainty, including (now) the fact that player 2 entertains three possibilities for player 1: the .1 chance that 1 is irrational, the .4 chance that 1 is "rational but naive," and the .5 chance that 1 is "rational and sophisticated about all this." How would we model this?

One way to model this is to ask, How will the rationally naive player 1 act? This type of player 1 presumably views the situation as given by figure 13.4(a). If we conclude (and for purposes of argument, please so conclude) that player 1, thinking that 13.4(a) describes the game, finds D the obvious action to take, then we can build the sort of model shown in figure 13.4(c), where the topmost version of the initial game represents the possibility that player 1 is rational and sophisticated, the middle version represents the possibility of player 1 irrationally playing Aa, and the bottom version represents the possibility of a rationally naive player 1 — a player who is led by our assignment of payoffs to pick D as a dominant strategy.

This is how one might consider modeling players who are truly ignorant of the situation — who attach zero probability to certain things that other players think are in fact possible. We first look at the world through the eyes of this type of player to try to discern what this player's perspec-

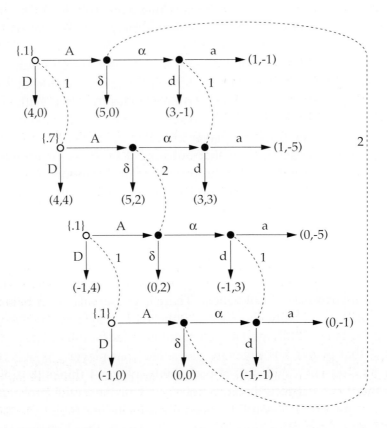

Figure 13.5. An extensive form game of incomplete information.

tive will lead to. And if we can find how that player will act, given his view, we then build that into the larger game in just the way that we build in simpler forms of irrationality.

This two-step (or, rather, multistep) procedure works in a large variety of situations that one wishes to model. But there is another, more complex way to get similar effects, which sometimes permits somewhat more general models. This is to go back to the basic model of games with incomplete information and consider games in which (a) players may have different prior distributions on the set of initial nodes, and (b) those priors may have different supports. That is, one player thinks that certain initial nodes have zero probability, while others think the game might well begin from one of those nodes. Can you see how one would use this sort of model to capture the story just told of the "rational but naive" player 1?

We have looked exclusively at examples where one player is uncertain about the "rationality" of a second, but the second has no questions about the rationality of the first. This is done to keep matters simple. But it is completely unnecessary. One can easily model situations where player 1 is unsure whether player 2 is rational and, at the same time, player 2 is uncertain about the rationality of player 1. To test your ability to disentangle this sort of model, consider the game depicted in figure 13.5 and try to describe just what is being modeled here. (See problem 5 for some more-pointed questions about this game.)

Note that what is called "rational naivety" is another form of irrationality or, at least, limited rationality. It is a type of player who isn't fully clued in to what might be going on — a type of player who isn't aware of all the possibilities entertained by another player.

13.4. *More on refinements: Complete theories*

This entire section is optional. Nothing that follows in the book builds on it, and it may prove to be difficult reading for a first time through the subject.

Consider for a final time the game 12.1(o), which is reproduced here as figure 13.6. What we know about this game is easily summarized: It is dominance solvable. U strictly dominates R, and once R is removed, 1 weakly dominates r, leading to L-l as the solution. This is, of course, a Nash equilibrium. But U-r is also a Nash equilibrium; U-r is even sequential. To support the U-r equilibrium, 2's beliefs at her out-of-equilibrium information set must put weight 1/4 or more on player 1 having picked R instead of L.

Are such beliefs at all plausible? We gave in chapter 12 two arguments, one for and one against.

(1) Against these beliefs was the argument that R is dominated by U while L is not. Put differently, given that 1 has the option U, she has no business at all playing R; she can't possibly do better with R than with U. But there is a reason she might play L, since there is the chance (if 2 responds with l) that she will do better with L than with U. Hence 2 "ought" to conclude, given the move, that L was probably 1's choice, which mandates a response of l.

(2) In favor of these beliefs was Myerson's properness criterion. One begins by taking the perspective that out-of-equilibrium actions are "mistakes" —

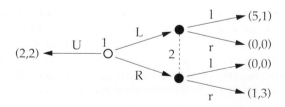

Figure 13.6. An extensive form game.

trembles of the hand. And to this one adds the notion that the relative chance of making a mistake should be related to how severe the mistake will be; players are meant to be more attentive to avoiding mistakes the consequences of which are more substantial. If player 2 is playing r, then L by mistake is a bigger mistake than R by mistake. Hence player 2 should conclude, given the move, that 1 is more likely to have chosen R by mistake. And this leads to r as the rational action. [e]

Now these two arguments are not of equal substance. For one thing, the first argument pins down the answer definitively. If you accept this argument, L-l is the only possible answer. The second argument is more circular, holding that U-r can't be disqualified as a "solution" if it is a solution. That is to say, in the second argument, L is a mistake in the first place only if one accepts the premise that 2 will play r.

I am more interested, though, in a particular strength of the second argument. That strength is that there is a "story" about why one might see a deviation from the supposed solution, a story that is used to guide what is considered a reasonable conjecture out-of-equilibrium. This story is quite explicit: Deviations from a solution are the result of mistakes (the story of the trembling hand), and, moreover, bigger mistakes are less likely than smaller mistakes.

There isn't a similar story for the first argument, but it isn't hard to create one. For example, note that there is a single Nash equilibrium in which player 1 gives the move to player 2: L-l. Suppose that we tell the following story. The players in this game are randomly matched. Most of the players come from a society in which it is "understood" that the solution is what the solution is. But a sprinkling of the players come from other societies, where other "solutions" might prevail. Whenever an out-of-equilibrium action is observed, the most likely explanation, if it fits at all, is that this action was taken by someone from another society in which the game has another conventional solution. If no explanation of this sort can be found, then the next most likely explanation is that the out-of-equilibrium action is the result of a mistaken action.

With this story, since L-l is the only possible "other" conventional solution for this game, when player 2 is put on the move, he assesses as (conditionally) most likely the possibility that this is an action taken by someone from a society where L-l is the convention. But this then destroys the possibility of U-r being a solution, by the argument given.

A different story that one can tell for the first argument is that out-of-equilibrium actions are "tests" of out-of-equilibrium responses. Players are assumed to be extremely certain what will happen if they follow convention in situations where there is conventional wisdom; they are pretty sure as well what happens if they deviate. But, just to check, players sometime experiment with deviations from conventional wisdom. These experiments are not picked haphazardly, however. Players are more likely to experiment with deviations

---

[e] Myerson's notion of properness goes a good deal further than this. It requires that a smaller mistake be asymptotically infinitely more likely than a larger mistake. We don't need quite that much power here.

that have some chance of beating what (they are virtually sure) will happen if they follow conventional wisdom than with deviations that have no chance of doing so. If the solution of this game is U-r, if player 2 believes that player 1 deviates from U on occasion to test the conventional wisdom that 2 will play r, and if player 2 believes that player 1 is more likely to experiment with L than with R, since L holds some possibility of being better than U, then player 2 will not choose r given the move. And then U-r can't be the solution.

What is the point of these stories? In refining the notion of a Nash equilibrium, we are necessarily thinking through what is relatively more likely to have happened (and to happen subsequently) if the "solution" that is proposed is falsified. In any real application, a given "solution" describes what is pretty certain to happen. But it would be foolish (or, at least, heroic) to be completely certain that a given solution applies. There are presumably reasons why "deviations" occur. And if, in a particular context, we understand something about the cause of deviations, we are better able to argue what inferences players will make when confronted with a deviation. This, then, informs the sort of refinement we might be willing to accept.

The term "complete theory" is meant to capture this sort of logic. By this term is meant a theory that rules nothing out a priori; although it may lead to certain things being assessed as very, very unlikely, it nonetheless offers some explanation for why the very unlikely might happen. Trembling-hand perfection is based on the complete theory of mistakes made in the course of play. Alternative complete theories can be built out of stories of randomly matched players from various societies or experimentation by players to check conventional wisdom. [f]

With this as prologue, let us reexamine the logic of subgame perfection and sequential equilibrium. Consider the game in figure 13.7(a), a game of complete and perfect information. By backwards induction, player 1 will choose a at his second node, hence 2 will choose α, and hence 1 will choose A. This is the unique subgame perfect equilibrium. But Da-δ is another Nash equilibrium. This is an equilibrium, moreover, that is fairly "safe" for player 2. What is the argument one would make against it being the solution of this game?

If player 2 subscribes to the theory that deviations from a given solution are most likely to be simple mistakes, and if he further subscribes to the theory (fairly explicit in trembling-hand perfection) that a mistake at one information set has no bearing on the likelihood of subsequent mistakes at subsequent information sets, then, if A is played by 1, he should shrug his shoulders and assume that player 1 will (probably) choose action a given another opportunity to choose, which then rules out δ as a reasonable choice for him.

But let me suggest a different thought process for player 2 that leads to a very different analysis. Suppose that he thinks there is a small chance that his opponent is out to get him — say one chance in one million — but enough chance so this possibility, whenever it is consistent with what he

---

[f] This is the subject of current research, by Suehiro (1989) in the first case and by Fudenberg and Kreps (1989) in the second.

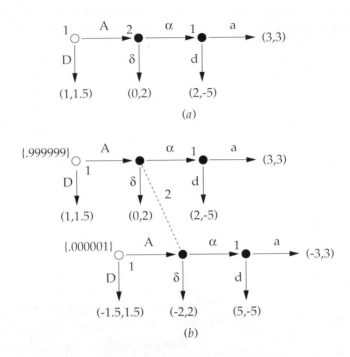

Figure 13.7. Two extensive form games.

observes, is deemed more likely than the chance that his opponent has made an inexplicable error. We can think through the consequences of this sort of thought process by looking at a game of incomplete information, such as the game in figure 13.7(b). Note what we have done here. We've taken the game in figure 13.7(a) and imagined that nature initially selects one of two versions. In the first, player 1's "motivations" are captured by the originally given payoffs. But in the second, which has prior probability .000001, player 1's payoff is simply minus the payoff of player 2; player 1 is "out to get" player 2.

Now suppose that player 2 believes the solution to the game is "probably" that player 1 plays D, player 2 if given the move plays δ, and player 1 if given the move by 2 will intend to play a. This is "probably" the solution in the sense that it is meant to describe 1's actions in the very likely case that player 1 isn't out to get player 2. But if player 1 is out to get player 2 (which is very unlikely), then player 1 will play A and, given the chance, d.

If this is how player 2 views the game, his view passes the equilibrium test of internal consistency. In the first place, if he is given the move by player 1, and if he thinks that the one-in-a-million chance that 1 is out to get him is more likely than the chance that 1 has simply erred, then he will assess substantial a posteriori probability that he faces a malicious player 1. (More precisely, he will assess probability exceeding one-half that the bottom part of the game pertains.) Thus his ex post expectations are that player 1, given the

chance to move again, is now more likely to choose d than a. And so he pru-
dently (and optimally) selects δ. Moreover, assuming player 1 understands
all this, D in the top half and A in the bottom are optimal moves for her.

Of course, the game in figure 13.7(b) possesses another equilibrium. In
this equilibrium, player 1 plays A in both halves of the game, player 2 plays
α, and player 1 plays a in the top half and d in the bottom half. Note why
it is that player 2 is content to play α in this case. Since player 1 is meant to
play A in both halves of the tree, player 2's assessment upon being given the
move is that he is in the top half of the tree with probability .999999. There is
a one-in-a-million chance that, if he plays α, 1 will respond with d. But this
isn't nearly a large enough chance to make δ a better choice.

I do not mean to say that the equilibrium in which 2 plays δ is the
obvious solution. But in this game of incomplete information, one would be
hard pressed to dismiss the 2-plays-δ equilibrium as something unreasonable.
And so, if this sort of model of incomplete information fleshes out the thought
process of player 2 in the game in 13.7(a) concerning where deviations come
from, then I don't think one can so easily dismiss the 2-plays-δ equilibrium
in 13.7(a) on grounds that it is subgame imperfect. It comes down to What
sort of theory does player 2 have about the source of deviations when/if
they occur? The "story" formalized by 13.7(b) is to my mind neither more
nor less outrageous than the story of hands that tremble independently at
different information sets. And while independently trembling hands lead
to refinements such as subgame perfection and sequential equilibrium, other
stories can lead to something less.

The sophisticated reader may object to the argument just given on the
following grounds: The strategy specified at any information set is meant to
be one's prediction about what will happen if that information set is reached.
If an information set is off the path of play, then the strategy specified there
should be conditional on the deviation having occurred. And as long as the
right (conditional) strategy is there, then we can have no grounds for doubting
that players should anticipate the play of this strategy. One cannot maintain
in the analysis of the game of 13.7(a) that the play of action a at 1's second
information set is expected and that player 2 is nonetheless reasonable in the
choice of δ when it is his move.

To this objection I plead guilty, but only on grounds of expositional ease.
What I want to claim is that in the game in figure 13.7(a) it is not so easy to
reject the subgame imperfect equilibrium where player 1 chooses D, 2 chooses
δ, and 1, given the choice again, plays, say, a with probability .1 and d with
probability .9. Rejecting this equilibrium is not so easy because the source
of "deviations" might be an a priori small chance of a malicious player 1;
where the chance that player 1 plays A because she is malicious is nine times
more likely than the chance that player 1 plays A by mistake. (The nine times
then explains the .1 probability, if we consider a still more complex game
of incomplete information in which nature not only gave us a chance of a
malicious player 1 but also a nine times smaller chance of a player 1 who
mistakenly plays A.)

In this sort of theory, subgame perfection and sequential equilibrium
come to grief in the requirement of sequential rationality (or backwards

induction) applied at information sets that follow a deviation from the equilibrium. At least, this is so for the actions of a given player taken subsequent to his own deviation, when one explains the first deviation by the possibility that the player has radically different payoffs from those specified as being likely ex ante.

What precisely do we get as a reasonable refinement concept, if we use this sort of story to explain unlikely deviations from equilibrium play when they occur? I will not attempt to give a precise answer here. For one thing, we are now well past what is reasonable for a first course on this subject and to explore this question fully would take us right to the frontiers of current research and beyond. And more importantly, this question doesn't have an answer that I, at least, find fully satisfactory. But let me give a partial answer for which the intuition is not hard to develop. In any game, any equilibrium outcome that is trembling-hand perfect *in the normal form* will certainly pass if this sort of story is used to explain deviations. Once a player begins to deviate, with this sort of story one can have any ex post beliefs about further deviations by the player. In other words, players tremble at the level of entire strategies, which is just normal form perfection. Of course, perfection in the normal form doesn't imply subgame perfection or sequentiality — that is the whole point. [g]

One needn't stop here, however. One can spin "stories" about the causes or sources of out-of-equilibrium play that rationalize equilibrium outcomes that are not even perfect in the normal form. For example, imagine stories as above, where out-of-equilibrium play is manifestation of very different payoffs for the players (so that sequential rationality out-of-equilibrium is not a tenable requirement), and where one adds the possibility that different players' payoffs are correlated. (Why might this be true? Insofar as players come from similar backgrounds, if one player acts in "irrational" fashion, that could indicate that his or her peers are more likely to do so.) Then if we see one player deviating from the "solution," we might increase the odds that others will not conform to the dictates of sequential rationality. Indeed, if we tell stories (admittedly farfetched) about how players don't necessarily have the best possible information about their own payoffs, so that they look to others' behavior for some indication as to what they should do, then virtually any Nash equilibrium can be rationalized. [h]

Or, without telling stories about small chances that players have radically different payoffs, one can tell different stories that lead to correlated conjectures about out-of-equilibrium play. Recall the stories sketched above that ran: A deviation from expected play is taken as an indication that the player deviating is playing some "other" equilibrium. Needless to say, we

---

[g] I am careful here to say that any equilibrium *outcome* that is trembling-hand perfect in the normal form can be rationalized. In the game in figure 13.7(a), if we are being precise, we would say that what can be rationalized by this story is δ combined with D and a mixture of d and a that puts substantial weight on d. But if we move to the normal form, we don't really distinguish between 1's strategies Da and Dd. So, from the perspective of normal form perfection, it is D-δ that is perfect.

[h] To see these two stories fleshed out, see Fudenberg, Kreps, and Levine (1988) on the subjects of personal types and general elaborations, respectively.

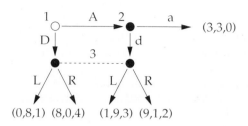

Figure 13.8. An extensive form game.

would expect to see this player continuing to follow the dictates of this other equilibrium, at least until this player gets some indication that his theory of how to play is "wrong." But why should the deviator necessarily be the party with an incorrect theory? In a more-than-two player game, if you see one player deviating from what you suppose is the equilibrium, then perhaps you should entertain the possibility that *your* theory of how people play this game is wrong, and (in consequence) others will play in ways you didn't predict.[i]

It is important in all this that one maintains the hypothesis that players have consensus conjectures concerning the play of others, both in and out of equilibrium. Or, rather, this hypothesis is important if the solution concept to be employed is Nash equilibrium. To take a simple example, consider the game in figure 13.8.

You can quickly verify: No matter what action player 3 takes at her information set, one of players 1 or 2 will choose to give her the move. Hence A-a is not a Nash equilibrium outcome. But if player 1 thinks player 2 will choose a and that player 3 will probably choose L, then 1 prefers A to D. And if player 2 thinks player 1 will choose A and player 3 will probably choose R, then he prefers a. If we allow players to have divergent opinions about what might happen out of equilibrium, we can get "solutions" that aren't even Nash. We saw a related phenomenon in chapter 12, in the example of a game with a single Nash equilibrium that (I assert) is rarely played; "partial solutions" to a given game may be present, and these needn't pass the test of Nash. The point here is that if there is consensus only on what happens along the path of play, then we have only a partial solution, and the Nash criterion is no longer a necessary condition.

So what is the bottom line for refinements of Nash equilibrium? The philosophy espoused here can be paraphrased as: The bottom line is that there is no simple bottom line. In refining Nash equilibria, one is speculating about what is supposed to happen after there is evidence that the going theory is incorrect. Depending on why you (and the players involved) think one sees deviations from a priori likely play and what this portends about future play, one supports or diminishes the relevance of particular formal refinements. Since the appropriate story is apt to be specific to the context (and, especially,

---

[i] See Hillas (1987) and Suehiro (1989).

to depend on why one thinks that there is a "solution" in the first place), it seems fruitless to try to choose among refinements in the abstract.

The usual rejoinder to this philosophy is that the implicit "criticism" is misplaced. The problem is not with the solution concept, but instead with the model of the game that is used. If there are reasons why unexpected actions might be taken, then the thing to do is to include those reasons within the model, using incomplete information. Once these things are modeled directly, we don't need refinements tuned to particular stories of why unexpected actions take place. And then there is no reason not to think that a "universal" solution concept might be available.

I take the main point of the rejoinder to be that the way to understand the effects of various hypothesized causes of unexpected actions is to build more complete models using incomplete information. I fully agree; that is precisely what we've done here. However "completing the model" in an application may well be impractical, and so it may be of practical value to have handy refinements that are well tuned to various sorts of completions. As a practical matter, one may need to select the refinement used with a view towards what has been omitted from the model for reasons of tractability.

13.5. *Bibliographic notes*

The classic paper that introduces the notion of a game of incomplete information is Harsanyi (1967-1968). Harsanyi deals primarily with models where players begin with commonly held priors. This is certainly as befits the author of the so-called Harsanyi doctrine that priors should always be held in common; in fact this is the application for which that doctrine was first formulated. The notion of a game with incomplete information where players have different priors, or even priors that have different supports, is attributed by Harsanyi to Selten, although I do not have a reference I can give. For the question of how to "close" models with incomplete information but with infinite regresses of assessments, the original reference is Mertens and Zamir (1985). A recent paper by Brandenburger and Dekel (1985) may be relatively more accessible. (The word relative is important to stress; this is a very mathematical subject, and no treatment will be accessible unless your math skills are very high.)

I think the best way to get a feel for how models of games of incomplete information are constructed and used is to look at applications. In section 13.2, we discussed the example of entry deterrence, which is an excellent place to begin. See the seminal work of Milgrom and Roberts (1982) on this. Many other applications fall under the general rubric of market signaling; see chapter 17 for references. Problems in mechanism design also use games of incomplete information; see the references given in chapter 18.

The topic of entry deterrence in general is summarized in Tirole (1988).

As for the philosophy of refinements of Nash equilibrium, please understand that this is a highly contentious issue, and the philosophy I've espoused is far from the consensus point of view. The point of view taken here is further developed in Fudenberg and Kreps (1989), Kreps (1989), and Kreps and Ramey (1987). Fudenberg, Kreps, and Levine (1988) develops the appropriate "mathematics" for stories of radically different payoffs with small probability (and the connection to trembling-hand perfection in the normal form), although the results there are couched in somewhat different language. Reny (1988) independently arrives at this conclusion, in language more directly applicable to the problem as posed here. McLennan (1985), Hillas (1987) and, especially from the point of view of complete theories, Suehiro (1989) develop stories about refinements based on the notion that players may have mistaken theories about how to play. Of course, Selten (1975) and Myerson (1978) began this subject with the development of the "deviations-as-trembles" story. Finally, Kohlberg and Mertens (1986) and Mertens (1987) present a very different view of the entire subject.

References

Brandenburger, A., and E. Dekel. 1985. "Hierarchies of Beliefs and Common Knowledge." University of California at Berkeley. Mimeo.

Fudenberg, D. and D. Kreps. 1989. *A Theory of Learning, Experimentation, and Equilibrium in Games.* Stanford University. Mimeo.

Fudenberg, D., D. Kreps, and D. Levine. 1988. "On the Robustness of Equilibrium Refinements." *Journal of Economic Theory* 44:354–80.

Harsanyi, J. 1967–1968. "Games with Incomplete Information Played by Bayesian Players, I, II, and III." *Management Science* 14:159–82, 320–34, 486–503.

Hillas, J. 1987. "Sequential Equilibria and Stable Sets of Beliefs." Stanford University. Mimeo.

Kohlberg, E., and J.-F. Mertens. 1986. "On the Strategic Stability of Equilibria." *Econometrica* 54:1003–38.

Kreps, D. 1989. "Out-of-equilibrium Beliefs and Out-of-equilibrium Behaviour." In *The Economics of Missing Markets, Information, and Games*, F. H. Hahn, ed., 7–45. Oxford: Clarendon Press.

Kreps, D., and G. Ramey. 1987. "Structural Consistency, Consistency, and Sequential Rationality." *Econometrica* 55:1331–48.

McLennan, A. 1985. "Justifiable Beliefs in Sequential Equilibrium." *Econometrica* 53:889–904.

Mertens, J.-F. 1987. "Ordinality in Noncooperative Games." CORE, Université Catholique de Louvain. Mimeo.

Mertens, J.-F., and S. Zamir. 1985. "Formulation of Bayesian Analysis for Games with Incomplete Information." *International Journal of Game Theory* 10:619–32.

Milgrom, P., and J. Roberts. 1982. "Limit Pricing and Entry Under Incomplete Information: An Equilibrium Analysis." *Econometrica* 50:443–59.

Myerson, R. 1978. "Refinements of the Nash Equilibrium Concept." *International Journal of Game Theory* 7:73–80.

Reny, P. 1988. "Backward Induction, Normal Form Perfection, and Explicable Equilibria." University of Western Ontario. Mimeo.

Selten, R. 1975. "Re-examination of the Perfectness Concept for Equilibrium Points in Extensive Games." *International Journal of Game Theory* 4:25–55.

Suehiro, H. 1989. *On "Mistaken Theories" Refinements*. Ph.D. diss., Stanford University.

Tirole, J. 1988. *The Theory of Industrial Organization*. Cambridge, Mass.: MIT Press.

13.6. Problems

■ 1. (a) Consider the version of the beer-quiche game given in figure 13.1(a). What is its normal form, if we think of it as a two-player game?

Parts (b), (c), and (d) to be done precisely require you to know the formal definition of Myerson's proper equilibrium, something we have refrained from giving here. You may wish to find that definition in one of the references given here; alternatively, you can get the gist of this problem using only the informal characterization we gave, which states that a player should be relatively much less likely to make a bad mistake than one that is not so bad.

(b) Following remarks we made in subsection 12.7.4, a "natural" sequential equilibrium for this game is for player 1 to have beer for breakfast whether she is a coward or brave, for player 2 to avoid a fight if he observes 1 having beer for breakfast, and for him to pick a fight if he observes 1 having quiche for breakfast. Using the two-player game normal form you created in part (a) is this equilibrium proper in the sense of Myerson? If we viewed this as a three-player game (the three players being "1 the coward," "1 brave," and 2), would this equilibrium be proper? (To answer this, you will have to consider what the payoffs are to "1 the coward" if nature selects the bottom half of the game to start. Does your choice of payoffs for "1 the coward" in the bottom half matter to the answer?)

(c) Suppose we rescaled the payoffs of player 1 in the top half of the tree only by multiplying each payoff by a factor of 50. That is, the payoffs if 1 is a coward, 1 has quiche, and 2 fights become (50,1). Note that we don't rescale 2's payoffs, and we don't change 1's payoffs in the bottom half of the tree. Does this sort of rescaling change in any way the strategic nature of the game? (There is no right or wrong answer to this question. The quality of your answer turns on how well you defend the position you take and not necessarily on which position you decide to defend.) After completing this rescaling is the equilibrium described in part (b) proper in the sense of Myerson? (To answer this, you have to decide whether you think of this as a two- or as a three-player game.)

(d) Can you find an equilibrium of this game that gives the same outcome as the equilibrium in part 1, such that no matter how we rescale the payoffs of player 1 in either half of the tree, the equilibrium is and remains proper in the sense of Myerson, viewing this as a two-person game? (When you have the answer to this question, you have an important example to carry around in your head if ever you study stability in the sense of Kohlberg and Mertens.)

Problem 2 gives a standard sort of story on entry deterrence based on an action taken by the incumbent monopolist that makes her more aggressive postentry. There are many stories of this sort; for others, see Tirole (1988).

■ 2. Consider an industry with an incumbent monopolist, who is currently producing, and a potential entrant, who might or might not choose to enter.

There is a range of possible production technologies for producing this good, which differ in the level of marginal and fixed costs. Each technology is a constant marginal cost technology with marginal cost somewhere between 1 and 3 per unit. In the technology with marginal cost c (from the range from 1 to 3), fixed costs are $15 - 4c$. That is, lower marginal costs bring with them higher fixed costs. Any firm in this industry may choose whatever technology it wishes to employ, but it can make this choice once only. The choice of technology of any firm is known to all potential and actual competitors.

We imagine that there are two periods of production. In each, demand is given by $D(P) = 9 - P$. In the first period, the incumbent monopolist

is definitely a monopolist. The monopolist begins this period by selecting her production technology and then producing. In the second period,
the entrant decides whether to enter at all. If he does enter, he picks
his production technology. And then the two compete Cournot-style, simultaneously picking quantities. If he does not enter, then the monopolist
retains her monopoly and picks the quantity she wishes to sell. We assume
that the entrant will enter only if he believes he will make positive profits,
and the incumbent monopolist acts in a way that maximizes her sum of
profits in the two periods. (Adding a discount factor only complicates the
arithmetic.)

(a) Suppose there was no threat of entry. What technology would the
monopolist select?

(b) Suppose the monopolist selects the technology you got as the answer
to part (a). Will the entrant enter? If so, with which technology?

(c) If the monopolist, in the first period, picks a technology that discourages
the entrant from entering in the second period, we say that the monopolist
has blockaded entry. Is there a technology the monopolist could pick in the
first period that would blockade entry? If so, what range of technologies
accomplishes this?

(d) Given the threat of entry, what is the optimal course of action for
the monopolist? How does the entrant respond to this? (What solution
concept are you using?)

■ 3. Analyze the game depicted in figure 13.3(b). Assuming this model
describes the situation, do you think you can clearly predict what will
happen?

■ 4. (a) Contrast the analysis of the entry deterrence game in section 13.2
with the analysis of the game in figure 13.4(b). In what senses are the two
games similar? How are they different?

(b) Analyze the game depicted in figure 13.4(c). Assuming this model
describes the situation, do you think you can make any clear prediction
concerning what will happen?

■ 5. Consider the extensive form game depicted in figure 13.5.

(a) Would it make any difference to the analysis of this game if we removed
the information set of player 2 that links the topmost and bottommost
pieces of the tree? If so, what difference? If not, are there information sets
of player 1 that are similar candidates for removal?

(b) Analyze the prior distribution over the four possible initial nodes. Suppose we say that player 1 is "rational" if one of the top two of these initial nodes prevails, and player 2 is "rational" if one of the middle two initial nodes prevails. Is there correlation in the rationality of the two players? Is the correlation positive or negative?

(c) Analyze this game. Assuming this model describes a particular situation, do you think you can clearly predict what will happen?

chapter fourteen

Repeated play: Cooperation and reputation

I begin this chapter with an apology. More than in any other chapter, in this one the text will constantly be shifting between larger and smaller type. The reader who consumes only the larger type should be able to get the flavor of the basic ideas here, but this is a subject that from start to end is best appreciated by seeing at least a bit of how things are done formally and properly. Rather than reserve all the technical material for the back, which would mean repeating a lot of what was said in the front, I have elected to frustrate the nontechnical reader who will often be paging through to find the next group of large type. I hope this frustration will induce some readers to try to consume the entire chapter, which should be possible *if* you understand appendix 2. But to those for whom it doesn't, apologies.

14.1. The prisoners' dilemma

The one game from figure 12.1 that has yet to be discussed is the game in figure 12.1(n), reproduced here as figure 14.1. This game is called the *prisoners' dilemma*. The story that goes with it runs as follows. Two individuals, player 1 and player 2, are being held by the police in separate cells. The police know that the two (together) committed a crime but lack sufficient evidence to convict. So the police offer to each of them separately the following deal: Each is asked to implicate her partner. If neither does so, then each gets no time in jail. If each implicates the other, then each goes to jail for a while. If one implicates the other but is not implicated, the first gets off (and gets a greater share of the loot), while the one implicated goes to jail for a longer period of time. Each player ranks the four possible outcomes: It is best to implicate your associate and not be implicated (so you get the greater share of the loot). Next best

Player 2

		t1	t2
Player 1	s1	5,5	-3,8
	s2	8,-3	0,0

Figure 14.1. The prisoners' dilemma.

is not to implicate and not to be implicated (to avoid jail). Then comes implicating and being implicated (a short jail term). And worst of all is to be implicated while not implicating your associate (a long jail term). If we let s1 and t1 be the "do not implicate" strategies and s2 and t2 be the "implicate" strategies, then the normal form game depicted in figure 14.1 is consistent with this story. (Of course, by giving payoffs we have been much more specific about the relative utilities of the various outcomes). In the sequel, we will refer to the strategies s1 and t1 as *cooperation* (with each other and not with the police), while for s2 and t2, terms synonymous with *noncooperation* will be used.

While the story is fanciful, the basic structure of options and payoffs that characterize this game occur over and over in economics. In this basic structure players can cooperate to greater or to lesser extent. If one player unilaterally decreases the level of her cooperation, she benefits and her rival is made worse off. But if both decrease their level of cooperation equally, both are made worse off. Consider, for example, the case of Cournot duopolists, each (independently) choosing a quantity level to bring to market. Typically, if one firm increases its production (which is a less cooperative strategy), its profits increase, at least for a while, and the profits of its rival decrease. But (past the monopoly level of output) if both firms increase their levels of output, both do worse. We'll get back to this particular economic application in section 14.4.

The analysis of the prisoners' dilemma game using noncooperative game theory seems quite simple: s2 strictly dominates s1, and t2 strictly dominates t1. So the solution by application of one round of strict dominance is s2-t2. Of course, this is also the unique Nash equilibrium. It does seem rather a shame that this happens, because this outcome is quite inefficient. (That is, there is an outcome, namely s1-t1, that is better for both sides.) It may not be surprising that competition of this sort can lead to inefficient outcomes, but you might still wonder how this particular inefficiency can be avoided.

14.2. Repeating games can yield cooperation:
The folk theorem

Imagine that the jail sentence involved is quite short (it was only a petty theft), and the two prisoners will be engaged in this circumstance over and over again. That is, imagine that the players play the game not once but repeatedly, and payoffs are added together. This situation has been the subject of experiments. College sophomores (typically) are matched against one another; instead of playing the game once, they are told that they will play the game many times, with no fixed horizon in view. As long as they don't see a horizon looming, the empirical evidence is that such subjects often cooperate (play s1-t1). The explanation that is typically given for this lack of short-run optimality is that in repeated play there is the long run to worry about as well. If, say, player 1 tries to take advantage of player 2 in the short run by playing s2 instead of s1, player 2 might react to this by subsequently playing t2 instead of t1. Player 1 may feel there is less to gain by optimizing in the short run than to lose in the long run and so chooses to cooperate. If player 2 feels the same way, cooperation ensues. Note well that this is not cooperation borne of altruism or fondness for one's fellow player. This is cooperation arising from a self-interested calculation of the benefits and losses that may accrue from "polite" behavior.

Formal analysis of this point involves what are called repeated games. Imagine two players playing the prisoners' dilemma game over and over again. We could imagine that they play forever and their payoffs for the entire string of games are just the average of the payoffs they get in each stage. That is, if player 1's payoffs in a sequence of rounds are given by $\{u_1(1), u_1(2), u_1(3), \ldots\}$, where the subscript refers to the player's identity and the argument to the round number, then we could assign overall payoff $\lim_{t \to \infty}(1/t)\sum_{i=1}^{t} u_1(i)$ to this sequence.[a] Or we could imagine that they play forever, and they value a stream of payoffs according to the discounted sum of the payoffs. That is, there is some number $\alpha \in (0, 1)$ and the overall value to player 1 of the sequence of payoffs $\{u_1(1), u_1(2), u_1(3), \ldots\}$ is $\sum_{i=1}^{\infty} \alpha^{i-1}u_1(i)$. Or, to take a third possibility, we could imagine that the game is played a finite but indefinite number of times. For example, we could imagine that after each round of play a

---

[a] The very careful reader may wonder what happens if the limit doesn't exist. To avoid this difficulty, formal analysis of this problem is based on the criterion that the stream of rewards $\{u_1(1), u_1(2), u_1(3), \ldots\}$ is better than the stream of rewards $\{u_1'(1), u_1'(2), u_1'(3), \ldots\}$ if $\liminf_t \sum_{i=1}^{t}[u_1(i) - u_1'(i)] > 0$.

roulette wheel is spun. If it comes up 0 or 00 (2 chances in 38) we quit; otherwise we play another round and spin the wheel another time, and so on. Being a bit more general, we let $1 - q$ be the probability that we stop after each round and q be the probability that we continue for at least one more round. Then, the expected value of the sequence of payoffs $\{u_1(1), u_1(2), u_1(3), \ldots\}$ for player 1 is $\sum_{i=1}^{\infty} q^{i-1} u_1(i)$. For $q \in (0, 1)$, assuming players maximize their expected sums of payoffs, this is mathematically equivalent to the formulation with discounting where q takes the place of α. These are all variations of the general notion of a *supergame*, wherein a particular game called the *stage game* is played over and over by two (or more) players. There is a rich literature concerning supergames for both the first and the second two (equivalent) formulations of the problem. We will deal in this chapter primarily with the second two formulations, referring to the sums that give a player's payoff for an entire game as the *expected/discounted value* of the stream of payoffs.

What happens if we go from a one-round prisoners' dilemma to this sort of repeated formulation? Just what we wanted: Cooperation becomes an equilibrium outcome. Suppose that player 1 announces she will play s1 as long as player 2 plays t1. But if ever player 2 plays t2, player 1 will forever after play s2. Player 2, if he believes this, finds it easy to formulate a best response. As long as t1 is played, a payoff of 5 each period will result. This gives a stream of payoffs of 5 extending into the future, which has expected/discounted value $5/(1-q)$. But if player 2 begins with t2 this round, he will get 8 immediately and (at most) 0 forever after. For reasonable values of q (in this case for anything over 3/8), player 2 has no incentive to play t2 in this round. And, a bit of arguing will show, for these values of q player 2 *never* has any incentive to play t2.[b] To have an equilibrium we must also give player 1 the incentive to play the strategy above, but this is easily accomplished. Have player 2 announce that he will play t1 as long as s1 is played, but he will play t2 ever after, if ever player 1 is foolish enough to try s2.

The point is that these two strategies by player 1 and player 2 constitute a Nash equilibrium in the repeated game. Each is a best response to the other. And together they give the cooperative outcome.[c]

There are (at least) four problems with this simple story.

---

[b] The easiest formal proof shows that each strategy is unimprovable in the sense of appendix A2 when played against the other. See the end of the next subsection for a slightly more complex example worked out formally.

[c] These two strategies do not, however, constitute a subgame perfect equilibrium. Starting from the point where one player, say player 1, has just played noncooperatively, player 2 will respond with noncooperation. But according to the strategies given, player 1 will not revert to permanent noncooperation for one round more even though she knows that he is about

(1) Too many equilibrium outcomes

We have produced one Nash equilibrium for this repeated game. But there are many, many others. Suppose, for example, that player 1 announces the following strategy. She will alternate between s1 and s2 as long as player 2 plays t1 all the time. But if ever player 2 deviates and plays t2, player 1 will play s2 forever after. The effect of this is to offer player 2 the choice of getting payoffs of 5 alternating with −3 forever, or (at best) taking one 8 and 0s afterwards. For high enough q, the "cooperative" response is better. This allows us to construct an equilibrium as long as player 2 issues a threat that keeps player 1 honest; e.g., player 2 says that he will play t1 as long as player 1 alternates s1 and s2, but player 2 will play t2 forever after a deviation from this alternating strategy by player 1. Or consider the following pair of strategies: Player 1 says that she will alternate s1 and s2 as long as player 2 does the same, but if ever player 2 deviates, then she will play s2 forever, and the same for player 2. Again, for q close enough to one, we have an equilibrium, where the players get alternating 5s and 0s (or, if they are out of sync, 8s and −3s). Both sides are worse off in this equilibrium than with the first equilibrium we named, but this is nonetheless an equilibrium, as is the situation where both players play s2-t2 all the time.[d]

The problem in the repeated game formulation is a profusion of equilibria. Just what is possible as an equilibrium? We know we couldn't have an equilibrium where player 1 or player 2 came away with less than zero expected value. Why? Because by playing s2 or t2, each can guarantee that she or he will get at least that much. But their opponent can hold them to no more and can threaten to use this as a punishment. So, roughly, any pair of payoffs that is feasible and gives each player more than zero apiece can be sustained in an equilibrium. This statement is completely correct in the infinite horizon, undiscounted formulation. For discounting or a finite but indefinite horizon, we need to amend it slightly. A result where one player is left too close to the value zero cannot be sustained in an equilibrium. Each must have enough stake in maintaining the equilibrium so a one-stage defection (followed forever after by zeros) isn't better than carrying through on the agreement.

---

to play noncooperatively. To make the strategies subgame perfect, amend them as follows: Each player will play cooperatively as long as both have played cooperatively in the past. But if either ever plays noncooperatively, each plays noncooperatively for the rest of the game.

[d] (1) We continue to name strategies that aren't quite subgame perfect, and the technically proficient reader may wish to fix this. (2) We say "for q close enough to one" repeatedly. How close? See problem 1, and see as well the material at the end of this subsection.

This result, which is fairly obvious when you think about it, has been given for general repeated games. Roughly put, the general result says that any feasible expected payoffs can be sustained in an equilibrium as long as each player has expected payoff at least as large as what that player can guarantee for herself even if all the other players gang up on her. The proof of this proposition is really quite simple. Each player is told by the others to stick to the agreement or everyone will gang up on her. Then no single player, acting alone, has any incentive to deviate; the condition necessary for a Nash equilibrium. This result is known as the *folk theorem*, so-called because its statement belongs to the folk literature of game theory; no one has been brash enough to claim it, since it seems to have been well-known long before it appeared in print.

To be precise, suppose we are given an I player normal form game as the stage game, where player i has a finite set S_i of strategies and where the payoff to player i at the strategy profile $(s_1, \ldots, s_I)$ is given by $u_i(s_1, \ldots, s_I)$. Let Σ_i be the space of mixed strategies of player i and define $u_i(\sigma_1, \ldots, \sigma_I)$ to be the expected payoff to player i if players play the mixed strategy profile $(\sigma_1, \ldots, \sigma_I)$. For each player i, define

$$\underline{v}_i = \min_{(\sigma_1, \ldots, \sigma_{i-1}, \sigma_{i+1}, \ldots, \sigma_I)} \max_{s_i} u_i(\sigma_1, \ldots, \sigma_{i-1}, s_i, \sigma_{i+1}, \ldots, \sigma_I).$$

Note carefully how this is defined. We fix the mixed strategies of all the players except i, and we find player i's best response to those. Then we minimize i's payoff over the selection of the strategies of the other players. This is called player i's *minmax* value.

Imagine that the players play this normal form game over and over again, where after each round of play the actions chosen by each are known. Roughly put, the folk theorem states that players can achieve in a Nash equilibrium any feasible payoff that leaves each player at or above her minmax value. This is only rough; making it precise requires the following steps.

(a) It is easy to show that in any Nash equilibrium a player can never do worse than her minmax value. If she plays in each round her best response to whatever her opponents are doing, she does at least this well.

(b) Suppose in an undiscounted, average reward formulation we try to implement payoffs that arise from some pure strategy selection by players and that give each player as much or more than her minmax value. This is easy. Everyone is to play this strategy selection as long as everyone else does. If some one player deviates, everyone plays her part in that player's minmaxing strategy forever after. (For a Nash equilibrium, it is irrelevant what we prescribe if more than one deviates, so make any prescription at all.) Note that there is no reason to believe this is a subgame perfect equilibrium — a matter to which we turn in a bit.

(c) If we attempt to implement payoffs that arise from mixed strategy selections, then we can't tell from observed actions whether there have been deviations. In case we are using an undiscounted, average reward formulation, we can avoid this difficulty by using a pure strategy that "convexifies" with time. If, say, we want a payoff that arises from two-thirds of one pure strategy combination and one-third of another, then we play the first on rounds $3n + 1$ and $3n + 2$ and the second on rounds $3n$, for $n = 1, 2, \ldots$. This is a tiny bit harder to do if the mixing probabilities are irrational, although it is still possible. Note that by this scheme we can get values that result from mixed strategies and also values that arise from correlated mixtures of pure strategies.

(d) If we are using a discounted formulation, we have to worry that a deviation may prove so profitable to a player, relative to what she obtains in equilibrium, that she might deviate even if threatened with minmax punishment. So the statement of the folk theorem becomes: For every feasible payoff above the players' minmax values, there is a value of q (the discount factor or probability of continuing) sufficiently close to one such that for all larger discount factors/probabilities of continuing, this payoff can be implemented in a Nash equilibrium. And we have to worry about convexifying using time, which is harder in this case.

For detailed arguments and precise statements, see the papers cited in section 14.7.

You might worry that ganging up on a deviator can be quite costly for the other players. One player may be able to inflict a terrible punishment on another, but only at tremendous cost to herself. In this case, the first player might not want to carry out the punishment that is threatened. That is, these punishment strategies may not give a subgame perfect Nash equilibrium. Let us give an example. Consider the normal form game in figure 14.2. In this game, player 2 can threaten player 1 that by playing t2 he can hold player 1 to a payoff of (no more than) zero. Hence the following is a Nash equilibrium; player 1 plays s1 all the time. Player 2 plays t1 as long as player 1 plays s1, but moves to t2 if ever player 1 tries s2. The problem is that while player 1 wouldn't want to move to s2 (if q is sufficiently large) if she believes that player 2 will carry out this threat, she may find it hard to believe that he would in fact carry out the threat. After all, player 2 will get no more than -2 by playing t2, while he will

| | | Player 2 | |
		t1	t2
Player 1	s1	5,5	-1,-2
	s2	6,-1	0,-3

Figure 14.2. A bimatrix game.

get at least −1 with t1. So player 1 may play s2 with impunity, on the presumption that player 2 will never carry out the threat to punish her.

It has been shown, however, that the conclusion of the folk theorem holds up if one restricts attention to subgame perfect Nash equilibria.[e] The details are fairly complex and won't be repeated here. But it may be instructive to say how we could get the s1-t1 outcome in the game of figure 14.2 in a perfect equilibrium. Suppose that player 1 and player 2 adopt the following pair of strategies. They begin with s1 and t1 and continue with this unless and until there is a deviation. If either (or both) deviate from this, they play s2 and t2 for one round. If both do this, they go back to s1 and t1. But if either deviates during the "punishment" round, then they have to play s2 and t2 again, and each has to keep this up until they both comply (at which point they can return to s1 and t1). Given that player 2 is playing this strategy, will player 1 ever deviate? The answer is no, at least for high enough q. If play is in the phase where player 1 is supposed to play s1, by changing to s2 she nets 6 instead of 5, but then she'll have to take a 0 instead of a 5 next time. For high q this isn't worth it. And in the punishment phase, player 1 prefers both in the short run and the long to get this phase over with and get back to the cooperative phase. As for player 2, when the two are cooperating, he has no incentive whatsoever to move to t2 and trigger a round (or more) of punishment. The question is, Will he carry out the punishment, which is so costly for him? Given player 1's supposed strategy, the answer is yes; player 2 has a choice of either taking a −3 and then getting back to 5s or getting a −1 and delaying by (at least) one round return to cooperation. For large enough q, it is worth his while to get the punishment phase over with.

> Just to show how it is done, let us derive what is "large enough" q and show formally that this is an equilibrium. In fact, we will show that this equilibrium is subgame perfect, using techniques from appendix 2.
> The proper subgames of this game correspond to the start at each time $t = 1, 2, \ldots$ of that period's stage game, given a history of play up to time stage t, which we write h_t and which is a sequence of $t - 1$ pairs of the form (sx,ty), where x and y are each 1 or 2. Think of play of this game as being at the start of each period in one of two states: ϕ and ψ, where ϕ represents the state where players are to "cooperate" and ψ represents the state where players are "punished." Transitions from period to period of this state depend on the state at the start of the period and play in the period. If at the start of a period the state is ϕ and play that period is s1-t1, then the state is ϕ at the start of the next period. If play in a period begins in state

---

[e] This is subject to some technical restrictions in the case of discounting; see Fudenberg and Maskin (1986).

ψ and play that period is s2-t2, then the state next period is ϕ. In all other cases, next period begins in state ψ.

Note that with this convention, play in period t according to the supposed equilibrium strategies depends only on the current state. Player 1 is supposed to play s1 in state ϕ and s2 in state ψ, and similarly for player 2. As noted already, the state in any period depends only on the state in the previous period and play in that period. So we conclude that play from period t on, according to the presumed strategies, depends on previous history only through the current state. *Thus in checking subgame perfection it suffices to show that each player is using a best response beginning in state ϕ and beginning in state ψ.*

We have four things to check. Is player 1 playing a best response by choosing s1 beginning in state ϕ? Under the equilibrium hypothesis that player 2 conforms to his supposed strategy, if player 1 plays s1 starting in state ϕ and conforms thereafter, the state will stay ϕ forever and player 1 will receive 5 forever, for an expected/present value of $5+5q+5q^2+\ldots = 5/(1-q)$. If, on the other hand, player 1 plays s2 this period *and then goes back to following the strategy assigned to her*, she will net 6 immediately, the state will change to ψ, and she will get (conforming thereafter) 0 next round and (after ϕ is thereby restored) 5s for the rest of the game. The expected/present value is $6+0q+5q^2+5q^3+\ldots = 6+5q^2/(1-q)$. For player 1's strategy in state ϕ to be unimprovable in a single step, it must be that

$$\frac{5}{1-q} \geq 6 + \frac{5q^2}{1-q} \text{ or } q \geq \frac{1}{5}. \tag{ϕ1}$$

Next, is player 1 playing a best response by choosing s2 in state ψ? By conforming, she nets 0 this round and then 5s for the rest of the game. By failing to conform this round but then returning to conformance, she nets −1 this round, 0 next, and then 5s. This is worse than conformance for all q. It seems silly, but for the form of things we'll write down this constraint:

$$q \geq 0. \tag{ψ1}$$

Is player 2 playing a best response by choosing t1 in state ϕ? You should have no problems with this one — conforming always beats deviating for one step and then conforming:

$$q \geq 0. \tag{ϕ2}$$

Is player 2 playing a best response by choosing t2 in state ψ? Conforming forever nets him −3 and then 5s, for an expected/present value of $-3+5q/(1-q)$, while deviating to t1 for one stage and then conforming nets him −1, then −3, and then 5s, for an expected/present value of $(-1)+(-3)q+5q^2/(1-q)$.

If you work through the algebra, you'll find that the constraint on q that ensures that the first is as large as the second is

$$q \geq 1/4. \qquad\qquad (\psi2)$$

As long as all four of these constraints are met, which is to say that as long as $q \geq 1/4$, neither player ever has an incentive to deviate from her prescribed strategy and then return to conformance. *By proposition 4 in appendix 2, any unimprovable strategy is optimal in an infinite horizon, bounded reward, discounted dynamic programming problem. Thus we know then that for these q, neither player ever has an incentive to deviate from the prescribed strategy. That is, we have a subgame perfect equilibrium.*

The key here and in much of the formal literature that looks at the folk theorem with discounting is (1) to construct players' strategies in this fashion, using a small number of "states" that evolve from period to period in relatively simple fashion and that determine what happens from any point on and then (2) to use the theory of dynamic programming and especially the result that unimprovable strategies are optimal to verify that a given strategy profile comprises an equilibrium. We will provide you with further examples of this style of analysis later in this chapter.

(2) Lack of a focal point

Any time there are multiple Nash equilibria, we have to wonder which of them, if any, is the solution. In the story told above, we had one side or the other announcing its strategy and inviting the other to formulate a best response. That is fine if we imagine preplay negotiation between the players, although we might then wonder why one player is able to negotiate from such strength. A good way to interpret the folk theorem, when the players can engage in explicit preplay negotiation, is that it shows how repetition can greatly expand the set of self-enforcing agreements to which the players might come. If the players play the prisoners' dilemma game once (and never meet again, so the game is not embedded into some larger game), then no amount of preplay negotiation will enable them to cooperate. To cooperate, they will need to find some way to form a binding agreement with an enforcement mechanism that is quite outside the game as described. But if this situation is repeated, then there are many self-enforcing agreements they might come to. We don't know which one they will agree to (if any), and we can imagine a rather spirited session of bargaining between them, but we do know that a lot more can (reasonably) be agreed upon.

What if no explicit communication is possible? We said in chapter 12 that the notion of a Nash equilibrium gives a necessary condition for an obvious way to play the game, *if* one exists, without prejudging the existence of an obvious way to play the game. Without preplay communication, we rely on convention, or learned behavior, or a focal point, or something equally vague. Can you see any reason to suppose that any one equilibrium is the obvious/intuitive/focal way to play this game?

In the case of the prisoners' dilemma, which is quite simple and symmetric, principles of symmetry and efficiency point us toward s1-t1 as a likely candidate outcome. In other games, not so symmetric, one might also look for focal points. Or one might try to explain the particular equilibrium one sees as conforming to some social norm or convention. The current state of formal theory is that we know, in general, how repetition allows for the possibility of a wide variety of focal point or conventional equilibria. But we certainly don't have many good formal criteria for picking out any particular one.

(3) Too many out-of-equilibrium threats

The third problem is actually part of the first. Not only is there a profusion of equilibria, but there are many "out of equilibrium" responses that hold them together. In the equilibrium we gave above for the prisoners' dilemma, player 1 told player 2 that if player 2 ever played t2, then player 1 would resort to s2 forever. But, as long as q is fairly large, it is enough for player 1 to threaten player 2 with "If you play t2 in any round, then I will respond with s2 in the next round." (How large does q have to be so that player 2, thinking that player 1 will act in this fashion, will wish to play t1 in every round?) Indeed, player 1 can build this threat into an overall strategy that is very easy to enunciate: "I (player 1) will begin with s1, and in each subsequent round I will do whatever player 2 did in the previous round." This particular strategy for player 1 is known as "tit-for-tat." The point is that a threat never to cooperate will stop player 2 from trying t2, but a tit-for-tat threat, and many others besides, will do so as well as long as q is close enough to 1. Which of these many possible threats will actually occur? It is hard to say, especially when you consider that if the threat works we will never actually see it carried out!

(4) Games with a definite finite horizon

The fourth problem with the repeated game formulation is that it doesn't work when there is a finite and definite horizon. Consider the repeated prisoners' dilemma and imagine playing that game no more than, say, 100 times. That is, if we do reach round 100, there will be no more randomizations to determine if there will be a 101st round. Round 100, if we get there, will definitely be the last.

If we get to round 100, the two players know it will be the last, and so player 1 will play s2 and player 2 t2; there is no longer-term loss to weigh against the short-term gain. Now if we get to round 99, there may be one more round. But we know that both sides will play noncooperatively in round 100, so neither side has the incentive to cooperate in round 99; the short-term gain from noncooperation won't be overcome subsequently, since we will have noncooperation subsequently. Thus we have noncooperation in rounds 99 and 100. So what if we reach round 98? Since we will have noncooperation in rounds 99 and 100 no matter what happens in rounds 1 through 98, it follows that we will have noncooperation in 98, and so on. The entire cooperative scheme unravels from the back. To get cooperation, there must always be a future substantial enough to outweigh immediate considerations.

> If you are very careful about these things, you will note that what we just proved is that there is a unique subgame perfect equilibrium that involves no cooperation. We claim as well a different result: There is no cooperation along the path of play in any Nash equilibrium.
>
> An argument that proves this other result runs as follows. Suppose that in some Nash equilibrium there is cooperation at some stages with positive probability. Let T be the last stage at which this is so; that is, there is zero probability of cooperation along the equilibrium path in stages $T+1, \ldots, 100$. Now examine the incentives of the player who is meant to cooperate along the path of play in stage T. This player will do no better than zero in the remaining stages by following the equilibrium, since her opponent will not cooperate subsequently along the equilibrium path. By acting noncooperatively in stage T and in every subsequent stage, the player does better immediately than if she follows the equilibrium prescription, and she can do no worse than zero subsequently. Hence this player will not cooperate in stage T, a contradiction.

If this sounds vaguely familiar, recall the centipede game from chapter 12. In that game we saw a similar "unravelling from the back." And, indeed, the centipede game is very much like the repeated prisoners' dilemma, except that players take turns moving and the first "noncooperative" action ends the game. Because of these two features (but mostly the first), the centipede game is solvable by backwards induction (i.e., by iterated weak dominance), whereas a slightly more involved argument is needed here. But the same basic idea is at work, and we have the same basic story.

And as with our analysis of the centipede game, the theoretical conclusion that we reach here is not supported either intuitively or empirically.

Play the prisoners' dilemma, say, 100 times, and in most cases (with college sophomores, or with MBA students) you will get "cooperation" for much of the game. Our theoretical analysis of finitely repeated play of the prisoners' dilemma is missing something. We will get back to this (and to what is missing) in section 14.6.

14.3. *Noisy observables*

Note that in our equilibria a defection from cooperation is noticed by the other side immediately and is dealt with summarily. In applications of these ideas, we might be concerned with cases in which one side isn't quite sure what the other is doing. Observable data might indicate that *perhaps* the other side isn't living up to some cooperative arrangement, but the observable data might be less than perfectly conclusive.

One could model this in a number of ways. Imagine, for example, that we played the prisoners' dilemma game above, but with the following "noise" added. The numbers in figure 14.1 give only the means of the payoffs for the players. The actual payoffs are Normally distributed with those means and with standard deviation, say, 5 units. Each side sees both payoffs but not the move chosen by the other side.[f] For example, if player 1 picks s2 and player 2 picks t1 in some round, then in that round player 1 gets a payoff with Normal distribution at mean 8 and standard deviation 5, and player 2's payoff has Normal distribution with mean –3 and standard deviation 5. (The error terms are assumed to independent of one another, both cross-sectionally and serially.)[g]

Suppose you are player 2 playing this game and in the first round you pick t1, get back a payoff of 6.2, and your opponent receives 5.2; in the

---

[f] It is vitally important for what follows that both payoffs are seen, even if this isn't entirely natural. We will say why this is vital below.

[g] A different model of this effect would be to suppose that players work through an intermediary who sometimes fails to follow instructions. That is, imagine that players 1 and 2 on each round send instructions to an intermediary. This intermediary implements the instructions but sometimes does the "wrong" thing; on any given round, the intermediary implements the instructions of a player with probability, say, .8, and with probability .2 takes the "other" action. At the same time, the intermediary may or may not correctly implement the instructions of the other player. Assume that whether the intermediary implements the instructions of a given player is independent of whether he implements the instructions of the second player and independent of what the intermediary does on any other round. And, the key to all this, imagine that players do not see what instructions their rival passes to the intermediary, but only what actions the intermediary takes. This formulation of the problem is of about the same level of technical difficulty of the one we will tackle here, and the reader would do well to see which of the conclusions we derive will work in this somewhat different formulation.

second round you pick t1, get back 4.8, and your opponent receives 3.9; and in the third you pick t1, get back −1.3, and your opponent receives 6.8. (I'll only report your payoff to the level of tenths.) You can't be sure what player 1 has been playing, so you might try maximum likelihood estimation; you would then guess that player 1 has played s1, s1, s2. But these data are not inconsistent with player 1 choosing s1, s1, s1. So should you punish player 1? How stiff should your punishment be? If −1.3 is low enough to trigger punishment, what about −.3? What about 1.3? And should your punishment "fit" the crime — more punishment if you get −1.3 than if you get .3?

You might consider simply "forgiving" player 1 and not engaging in any punishment. But *if* you do this, then player 1 has no incentive to play s1 — she can play s2 every time and blame your string of payoffs on bad luck. At the same time, you don't want your punishment to be triggered too often or to be too harsh. Even if player 1 is playing s1 every time, you will see, by the luck of the draw, some bad payoffs occasionally. If you trigger punishment whenever your payoff is, say, 1 or less and/or if that punishment lasts a long time, then you will be spending a lot of time punishing your opponent (and, presumably, she will spend a lot of time punishing you) and the gains from cooperation/collusion will be lost.

We will give an exact analysis of this problem momentarily (in smaller type), but you should have no difficulty seeing the basic trade-off; too little punishment, triggered only rarely, will give your opponent the incentive to try to get away with the noncooperative strategy. You have to punish often enough and harshly enough so that your opponent is motivated to play s1 instead of s2. But the more often/more harsh is the punishment, the less are the gains from cooperation. And even if you punish in a fashion that leads you to *know* that your opponent is (in her own interests) choosing s1 every time (except when she is punishing), you will have to "punish" in some instances to keep your opponent honest.

Let me make two assertions here (which will be supported in a moment). Recall the third problem listed in the previous section: In the folk theorem there were many threats that could hold together an equilibrium, and we had no reason to choose among them in any fashion. If there are noisy observations, we do have some reason to select one threat over a second; we want our threat (which now will be executed sometimes) to be severe enough to deter the other party from "cheating," but only that severe and no more, because a more severe threat will increase the losses from collusion caused by the inevitable punishments that will be meted.

Second, if we look for equilibria in this setting, and then we vary the level of noise (in terms of the standard deviation of the Normal distributions, say), then we expect to and do find that the higher the noise the less we can get in an equilibrium for both sides. As the noise (standard deviation) rises, it becomes impossible to disentangle what an opponent is doing, and both sides move to play noncooperative strategies (s2 and t2). As the noise falls to zero, we can get closer and closer to the ideal of 5 apiece forever.

We now plunge into a technical analysis of this problem. We will be unable to do full justice to this problem — it sits right at the frontiers of what is known about this form of game — but we can give the technically oriented reader enough of a lead to understand what conclusions the literature comes to. Our analysis comes in two parts: First we look at "trigger equilibria" and then at a more complex form of equilibrium.

Trigger equilibria

To begin, we restrict attention to a very simple form of strategy for each player. We assume that each player begins by playing cooperatively, that is, s1 and t1. And they continue to do so until either of the two payoffs falls to a level at or below some critical *trigger level* T. If in a given round either payoff is less than or equal to T, then for the next N rounds the two play noncooperatively, that is, s2 and t2. After N rounds, whatever happens in those rounds, the two revert to cooperative play, until the next time that a payoff is less or equal to T.

There are two parameters in these strategies, the trigger level T and the length of the punishment phase N. We are interested first in the question *For which values of N and T are the given strategies an equilibrium?*

To answer this question, we begin by computing the expected values to the players of playing these strategies. (Then we will employ the usual dynamic programming technique of seeing whether the strategies are unimprovable.) To be very precise in our technique, we would imagine a state space with $N + 1$ states: $\{\phi, \psi_1, \psi_2, \ldots, \psi_N\}$, where ϕ is the state where the two cooperate and ψ_n is the state where the two are not cooperating and are meant to do so for $N - n + 1$ more periods before returning to cooperation. Then we begin in state ϕ and remain there until the first payoff is seen less or equal to T, at which point we transfer to state ψ_1 and then deterministically through the ψ_n in order, until we get to ψ_N from which we move back to ϕ. We won't try to carry that level of formality around, but the reader should check that what we say can be made this formal.

When cooperating, the two are meant to play s1 and t1. Their immediate rewards are random but have expected values of 5 apiece. What is uncertain is whether they will be cooperating next period or not; if we let $\epsilon_i, i = 1, 2$ be two independent Normal random variables with means zero and standard deviations 5, then the chance that cooperation will continue to reign is

$$\pi_e = \text{Prob}(5 + \epsilon_1 > T, 5 + \epsilon_2 > T),$$

and the chance that noncooperation will take over is $1 - \pi_e$. (We will work in terms of the discounted formulation, so q is a discount factor and not a

$N =$	1	2	3	4
$T = 0$: $v =$	39.59	33.34	29.20	26.26
$T = -1$: $v =$	41.83	36.47	32.70	29.92

Table 14.1. Values for following the given strategies.

chance that the game ends altogether.) We claim, then, that the value to either player of following the strategy given above, assuming her opponent does so as well, is the solution v of the equation

$$v = 5 + q[\pi_e v + (1 - \pi_e)q^N v].$$

Let us explain: The 5 out in front is the immediate expected reward; the q is the discount factor, applied to expected future payoffs. And expected future payoffs are π_e times v, which is the chance that cooperation continues to ensue times the expected value of being in a cooperative phase, plus $(1 - \pi_e)$ times $q^N v$, which is the probability that noncooperation begins times the value starting at a noncooperative phase. This last value requires explanation. For N periods each player receives an expected payoff of zero, and then play reverts to cooperation. Hence the value of cooperation is simply delayed for N periods, hence discounted by q^N.

We can invert this recursion to find

$$v = \frac{5}{1 - q[\pi_e + q^N(1 - \pi_e)]}.$$

Note that as π_e implicitly depends on T, v is a function of T (implicitly) and N (explicitly). Because π_e decreases with T, v is decreasing in T and N (these take some showing); the quicker the trigger or the longer the punishment phase, the lower the value to the players.

In general, we need to compute expected values to the players starting in every possible state, in this case, in the states $\psi_1, \ldots, \psi_N$ as well as in ϕ. But this is easy in this case: The value of starting in ψ_1 is $q^N v$; in ψ_2 is $q^{N-1} v$, and so on.

What sort of values do we get? Consider the parametrization $q = .9$. For $T = 0$ and $T = -1$, and for $N = 1, 2, 3, 4$, the corresponding values of v are given in table 14.1 (rounded to the nearest .01). Note that, as expected, values fall with rising T (quicker to punish) and with rising N (heavier punishment).

Is each strategy unimprovable given the other? The reader may wonder whether this is a useful question to answer. Since the payoffs are now unbounded, we cannot simply plug into our result that unimprovable equals optimal. But the result is valid here. One can replace the actual payoff in any round with its expectation conditional on the actions chosen, and those conditional expectations are bounded. So the question is useful and is equivalent to asking whether each strategy is optimal given the other, that is, whether we have an equilibrium.

We assert that it is clearly optimal to play noncooperatively when in a punishment phase; cooperation returns no more swiftly and one's immediate expected payoff is less, if one plays cooperatively at these times. But there is a real trade-off when cooperation is supposed to be played. By playing noncooperatively, you increase your immediate expected reward (from 5 to 8), and you also increase the chance that you trigger a bout of punishment. Specifically, if you play noncooperatively for one period *and then revert to the strategies prescribed*, your expected payoff is computed as follows. Let

$$\pi_d = \text{Prob}(8 + \epsilon_1 > T, -3 + \epsilon_2 > T).$$

Then π_d is the chance that you will see a payoff that doesn't trigger a punishment phase if you don't cooperate. Your expected payoff is

$$v' = 8 + q[\pi_d v + (1 - \pi_d)q^N v].$$

Note well: This computation assumes you immediately go back to playing according to the strategies prescribed; the only effects your "deviant" play has is to increase your immediate payoff and to change the probabilities that you don't and do trigger punishment. Hence we use v and $q^N v$ for the "continuation" payoffs.

We have an equilibrium, then, if v' as computed above is less or equal to v, since this implies that the strategies are each unimprovable against each other, hence optimal. In table 14.2 we give v and v' for $q = .9$, $T = 0$, and $N = 1, 2, 3, 4$, and we see that we have equilibria for $N = 3$ and 4 but not for $N = 1$ or 2: At a trigger level of $T = 0$, it takes three rounds of punishment to deter players from playing noncooperatively in a presumably cooperative phase.

We can ask now, What is the best combination of N and T? "Best" here has a clear meaning; we are looking at symmetric equilibria, and so we are concerned with finding that pair N and T that gives the highest expected payoff to both players. The scheme for finding the best N and T, at least numerically, is clear: Fix T. For $N = 1$, compute the corresponding values of v and v'. Find whether $v' \leq v$ — whether we have an equilibrium. If not, try $N = 2$, and so on, until you find for the given T the smallest N (hence the best N) that supports an equilibrium. Call this $N(T)$. (You may find that for the given T no N gives an equilibrium.) Do this as you search for the optimal level of T by some numerical procedure.

Table 14.3 provides partial results for such a search, for the case $q = .9$. Each row corresponds to a different level of T. The first column reports T,

$N =$	1	2	3	4
$v =$	39.59	33.34	29.20	26.26
$v' =$	40.99	33.79	29.00	25.61

Table 14.2. Checking for an equilibrium: $T = 0$.

T	$N(T)$	v
2	11	12.76
1	4	23.01
0	3	29.29
-1	3	32.70
-2	3	36.28
-3	3	39.68
-4	3	42.66
-5	3	45.05
-6	4	46.06
-7	5	47.16
-8	6	48.11
-9	10	48.55
-10	20	48.96
-10.1	23	48.99
-10.2	26	49.02
-10.3	34	49.05
-10.33	38	49.06
-10.35	43	49.069
-10.37	52	49.0716
-10.38	67	49.0746

Table 14.3. Finding the efficient trigger equilibrium.

the second $N(T)$, and the third column the expected value v at T and $N(T)$. The search for an N that supported an equilibrium was stopped at $N = 100$, and for values of T outside the range shown (i.e., for $T = 3$ and $T = -10.39$), at $N = 100$ an equilibrium had not been found. Note well: For some values of T no N, no matter how large, will support an equilibrium. This is easiest to see for very small T. As T becomes very small, the chance of triggering punishment is virtually zero, thus there is no penalty for a player to take 8 instead of 5 immediately by playing noncooperatively.

Two things are striking. First, $N(T)$ falls and then rises with falling T. The rise as T gets very small is fairly intuitive. For small T, the chance of triggering punishment is very small, and so it takes a larger and larger punishment to keep players from playing noncooperatively in the cooperative phase. But the fall in $N(T)$ as T falls for large T is a bit surprising. The intuition here is that for large T punishment is likely to be triggered with high probability in either case, so it takes a fair amount of punishment to keep the players cooperating. Put differently, the ratio of the likelihoods of triggering punishment if you cooperate and if you don't is quite high for large T, so the marginal impact on the probability of triggering punishment by playing noncooperatively is quite low. Hence, to keep players honest, punishment must be severe.[h]

---

[h] For readers who think well in terms of relative likelihoods, it may help to note that

The second striking thing is that the value v rises with falling T. (Actually, if we decreased T continuously, it would jump down at values of T where $N(T)$ jumps up by one. But the overall effect is a rise in v with falls in T.) The optimal T is the lowest possible value consistent with equilibrium, which means (although our numbers are too discrete to show this) $N = \infty$.

This is not a fluke result. Given our restriction in this subsection to these sorts of trigger strategy equilibria, one can prove that the efficient equilibrium from this restricted class is the smallest T consistent with equilibrium, which has $N(T) = \infty$. To show this takes very advanced methods; the required methodology (and, once you make a few clever changes in the formulation, the result itself) is found in Abreu, Pearce, and Stacchetti (1989). The technically very adept will find it an interesting exercise to (1) prove what has just been asserted, using their results and (2) show that one can get somewhat better (higher v) results using "trigger equilibria" a bit more sophisticated than the one we've employed here, equilibria where the region of payoffs that triggers punishment is not simply whenever either payoff falls below some single value.

More sophisticated and efficient equilibria

For the parameterization with which we have been working, we've pushed the value of a collusive equilibrium to 49.0746. That is pretty good, especially considering that we know 50 is unattainable. (Why do we know this?) But we can do better still with more sophisticated equilibria.

Consider the following sort of strategy profile parameterized by two numbers, a and b. There are three phases or regimes of play, labeled ϕ, ψ_1, and ψ_2. Phase ϕ is "cooperative"; players choose s1 and t1, respectively, in this phase. Phase ψ_1 is the "punish player 1 and reward player 2" phase, in which player 1 is supposed to play s1 while player 2 plays t2. Note that given these choices player 1 will have an expected immediate payoff of –3 and player 2 a payoff of 8. Phase ψ_2 is symmetric with ψ_1; we reward player 1 and punish 2.

Transitions in the phases from one stage to the next depend on the phase at the start of the stage and the payoffs received by the two players.

Starting a stage in phase ϕ, if player 1 receives more than a and player 2 receives less than a, we transfer to phase ψ_1. (The idea is that player 1 did too well relative to player 2 and must be punished.) If player 1 receives less than a and player 2 receives more, we transfer to ψ_2. Otherwise we remain in phase ϕ.

Starting a stage in phase ψ_1, all that matters is how player 1 does. If she gets more than b, we remain in phase ψ_1. (She did too well and has to be punished again.) If she gets less than b, we go back to stage ϕ.

Starting in phase ψ_2, everything is symmetric with starting in ψ_1.

---

the ratio of the likelihoods of triggering punishment if a player cooperates to if she doesn't approaches zero as $T \to -\infty$ because of properties of the tails of Normal distributions.

Play begins in phase ϕ. With this start and the rules given above, players are always, for every point in the game tree, able to figure out what they are meant to do. This recursive structure specifies, in fairly opaque form, strategies for the two players.

Do these strategies constitute an equilibrium, for a fixed a and b? By now the technology for finding out should be clear to you. First we compute the expected payoffs to the players, starting in phase ϕ, in ψ_1, and in ψ_2, if they follow the strategies described. Let us call these values for player 1 $v(\phi)$, $v(\psi_1)$, and $v(\psi_2)$. These three numbers satisfy three simultaneous equations:

$$v(\phi) = 5 + q[\pi_1 v(\psi_1) + \pi_2 v(\psi_2) + (1 - \pi_1 - \pi_2)v(\phi)],$$

$$v(\psi_1) = -3 + q[\rho v(\phi) + (1 - \rho)v(\psi_1)], \text{ and}$$

$$v(\psi_2) = 8 + q[\mu v(\phi) + (1 - \mu)v(\psi_2)],$$

where π_1 is the probability that if players follow these strategies we transfer from ϕ to ψ_1, and so on. (Note that in the second two equations only two states are involved; given the strategies and transition rules, there is no chance that we transfer from ψ_1 directly to ψ_2 or vice versa.) The transition probabilities are, in the case of π_1 and π_2, products of Normal cumulants, while ρ and μ are simple Normal cumulants. For example,

$$\pi_1 = \text{Prob}(5 + \epsilon_1 > a) \times \text{Prob}(5 + \epsilon_2 \leq a).$$

So, for example, if $a = -9.4$ and $b = -8.2$, you can work out (for $q = .9$) that $v(\phi) = 49.6245$, $v(\psi_1) = 15.6337$, and $v(\psi_2) = 62.5915$.

We check for an equilibrium by checking if each strategy is unimprovable given the other. For player 1, we have to check *Does she prefer s1 to s2 in phase* ϕ? In the now usual fashion, this involves checking whether

$$v(\phi) \geq 8 + q[\pi_1' v(\psi_1) + \pi_2' v(\psi_2) + (1 - \pi_1' - \pi_2')v(\phi)],$$

where π_1' and π_2' are the transition probabilities if player 1 plays s2 instead of s1 while player 2 sticks to t1. For example,

$$\pi_1' = \text{Prob}(8 + \epsilon_1 > a) \times \text{Prob}(-3 + \epsilon_2 \leq a).$$

Does she prefer s2 to s1 in phase ψ_2? This one is trivial — of course she does. (Why of course?) *Does she prefer s1 to s2 in phase* ψ_1? This involves checking whether

$$v(\psi_1) \geq 0 + q[\rho' v(\phi) + (1 - \rho')v(\psi_1)],$$

where $\rho' = \text{Prob}(0 + \epsilon_1 \leq b)$.

For example, if $a = -9.4$ and $b = -8.2$, both tests are passed. (In case you are interested, deviating for one stage in phase ϕ gives 49.597 and deviating for one stage in phase ψ_1 gives 15.61.) Since everything here is symmetric in players 1 and 2, *we do have an equilibrium for $a = -9.4$ and $b = -8.2$, one that is better than the best trigger strategy equilibrium.*

What is going on here? In the trigger strategy equilibria, punishment is very inefficient; one punishes the seeming transgressor (although we know that, in equilibrium, no one has transgressed), but at the same time the seeming transgressed-against is also punished. It is more efficient to punish the seeming transgressor and reward the transgressed-against. You can do this, *if* you are careful to be sure that the seeming transgressor will go along with her punishment.

The equilibrium offered above is certainly not the best one can do. So let me offer a challenge to readers: How much higher can you push the expected value of playing this game for each player in a symmetric equilibrium?

We close with two comments. First, one can, in this exercise, parametrically vary the amount of noise by varying the standard deviation in the noise terms. As that standard deviation rises, any possible gains from this sort of cooperation vanish, since sooner and sooner comes the descent into punishment. And as that standard deviation falls, gains from this sort of cooperation approach those where there is no noise (a theoretical high of $5/.1 = 50$ in this case of $q = .9$), which should be clear since the descent into punishment is pushed further and further into the future. (These things have formal proofs as well.)

Second, we stated at the outset that it was important that both sides saw both payoffs. If each side saw only its own payoff, one imagines that equilibria that support collusion can be constructed, but these equilibria will be quite complex — too complex for us to compute, at least. This is so because one player, receiving a low payoff, may initiate punishment of the other, and the other *will not know* that punishment has begun; she will have to infer that it probably has done so. Put another way, transitions from one phase to another by both players in the clean and crisp fashion of the equilibria above will not be available. It isn't quite clear what will be.

Forgiveness

In all these equilibria, we speak of punishment as if there is some bad behavior to punish. But there is none in equilibrium. There is "punishment," to be sure, when there is noise that makes it impossible to tell whether a bad outcome is due to bad behavior by one's opponent or to bad luck. But in equilibrium both players "know" it wasn't bad behavior. So why punish? Why not "forgive" your opponent and get on with collusive behavior, especially when you know there is nothing really to forgive?

The reason is simple: If you do this, and if your opponent anticipates that you do this, then she *will* engage in bad behavior.[i]

---

[i] Another answer, for those who followed the small type discussion, is that in some

14.4. *Implicit collusion in oligopoly*

The notion that oligopolists collude has been around since the virtual inception of economics. In 1776, Adam Smith (1976, I:144) wrote that "people of the same trade seldom meet together, even for merriment and diversion, but the conversation ends in a conspiracy against the public, or in some contrivance to raise prices."

The theoretical case for how such a conspiracy might be enforced is obvious from developments in the preceding sections. Consider the Cournot game for a duopoly, in which each of two firms simultaneously names a quantity that it will supply to the market. As we saw, the equilibrium in such a situation does not give the firms as much as they could get through collusive action. With collusion, identical firms could each supply half the monopoly quantity, and together they would obtain the monopoly profits. But this isn't an equilibrium; if one side provides half the monopoly quantity, the other side has the incentive to supply more: This lowers overall profits, but raises one's own profits (while lowering the profits of the other side more quickly than one's own are going up). This isn't identical to the prisoners' dilemma game, since there we had a single strictly dominant strategy for each side. But here, as there, we have (in equilibrium) each side taking actions that leave both worse off than if they could collude.

Now imagine that the Cournot game is repeated with profits discounted and summed. A simple application of the folk theorem guarantees (for large-enough discount rate) that we can sustain the collusive outcome. Each side communicates to the other, somehow, its intention to play the strategy: Supply half the monopoly quantity as long as the other side does likewise; revert to the Cournot quantities in the face of any deviation. As long as the discounted present value (or expected value) of half the monopoly profits exceeds the best one can get from a deviation in a single round plus the Cournot profits thereafter, we have an equilibrium in which both sides collude.

In a sense, this is a simple variation on the story of the kinked demand curve. In the story of kinked demand, the response of one firm to the other raising its quantity supplied (or lowering its price) was instantaneous.

---

equilibria, such as the last one discussed, punishment for one player means good times for the other. Rather than call it punishment, we might think of it as compensation for the unwitting victim of circumstance. It isn't the fault of one's rival, but isn't it reasonable that your rival should give something up to help compensate you for your bad luck? Of course, this story doesn't go too well with what is takes to get back to collusion in our example (bad luck by your rival, to balance your own). And it won't help in those cases where punishment of one side necessarily entails a loss for the others, as in the story we tell next.

Here the response is delayed for one round. But as long as the delay isn't too long, which we model mathematically with a discount factor close to one, we get the same outcome, collusion, as a potential equilibrium.

Of course, in the story of the kinked demand curve we had a problem with a multiplicity of "equilibria"; we had no theory about where the status quo point would be. And, although we didn't speak of it at the time (except in problem 10.2), we could have told kinked demand curve stories where the outcomes are not symmetric. Likewise here, the folk theorem tells us that there are many equilibria: Asymmetric equilibria in which one side insists on a share of the market in excess of 50 percent; equilibria in which firms settle on profits less than they get from the most collusive outcome. For two symmetric firms, the "half-the-monopoly-quantity" equilibrium seems a rather strong focal point, but in cases of asymmetric firms, we have no particular theory about which equilibrium will arise, if any.

In a sense, all the classic models of oligopoly can be rooted in the folk theorem. The folk theorem holds that any outcome from the collusive outcome down to the competitive outcome, including all manner of asymmetric outcomes, are outcomes of a Nash equilibrium, if the discount factor is close enough to one. And note well that the fact we (formally) imagine players choosing quantities in a given round is nearly irrelevant. If we imagined them choosing prices, we would have much the same range of possible equilibrium outcomes. Collusion can be sustained if the firms are picking prices. Each firm picks the collusive price, with the implicit threat that it will drop its price precipitously if the other side deviates. And if the firms are picking prices, the same threat to drop prices precipitously will sustain an equilibrium where firms name the Cournot equilibrium prices (and sell the Cournot quantities). Similarly, prices arbitrarily close to Bertrand equilibrium prices can be sustained as an equilibrium (for high-enough discount factor) even if the rivals are simultaneously choosing quantities, although the argument here is a bit complex.[1]

Which of these many equilibria (if any one) is the "solution?" That depends, of course, on how each side imagines the other will react to how each side acts today; it is a matter of equilibrium expectations. This isn't quite the same as the classic story of Cournot, or Bertrand, or von Stackelberg conjectures. But it isn't far removed.

Of course, a model of repeated play is vastly more descriptive of the world of real oligopolists than are the stories we gave at the end of chapter 12, where firms simultaneously pick quantities to output or prices

---

[1] For a general treatment of this problem, see Abreu (1986).

they will charge, *once and for all*. Most oligopolistic competition is played out over time, and the competitors do retain some ability to react to how their opponents act, even if they are not quite as free to react as we might suppose in a repeated game formulation. From this perspective, becoming specific about the "institutional details" of competition does not seem to have paid such large dividends in getting us to definite predictions after all.

Implicit collusion and noise

We can recover some value from the general approach of adding institutional details by adding a second element of realism to our model of oligopolistic competition — noisy observables. Imagine playing the repeated Cournot game with the following variation: Instead of seeing how much the other side puts on the market, all you see is the market clearing price. (Of course, you know how much you put on the market.) No problem so far — if you know your own quantity and the market clearing price, then you know how much your opponent(s) put on the market. You have enough information to detect any defection from the implicit agreement, and, once detected, you can punish that defection. Hence we get collusion as an equilibrium outcome. But now suppose that the demand curve for this product is subject to unobservable noise. Suppose, for example, that demand in period t is $P = A(t) - X$, where X is the total quantity supplied, and $A(t)$ is a constant whose value you don't know; imagine that it has some probability distribution, and the $A(t)$ are independently and identically distributed through time. Then if you put on the market the agreed-upon (equilibrium) quantity and you find a lower than expected market clearing price, it could be because your opponent put more on the market than she was supposed to or because $A(t)$ is lower than its average. Should you punish your opponent? It may not be her fault. But if you never engage in punishment, then your opponent has the incentive to chisel on the deal and put a higher quantity on the market. To keep both sides honest, punishment is called for at least sometimes. Note well: Even punishment of finite duration will cause a dimunition in what can be accomplished collusively because it is sometimes set off by "mistake." But, on the other hand, you cannot go too far in lessening the severity of the punishment, making it of shorter duration, say, or only triggering punishment when prices fall very far. This would encourage each side to chisel somewhat, thereby lessening the gains from collusion.

The following notions are suggested:

(a) It is necessary in any collusive arrangement that each side is able to monitor the actions of others.

(b) Sometimes such monitoring is difficult (or, at least, is costly).

(c) The parties to the agreement have an incentive to chisel on the agreement and blame the results on whatever noise is in the system.

(d) Punishment for implied cheating must, therefore, be imposed, even when the "cheating" is certain to have accidental causes, to prevent chiselling from getting entirely out of hand.

(e) The loss of collusion from the necessary punishment phases must be balanced with the loss of collusion from the chiselling.

(f) The requisite costs of monitoring and punishment increase with the number of participants, hence collusion is more difficult to achieve the more firms there are in the industry.

(g) Collusive schemes work best when they are based on less noisy observables.

These ideas about oligopolistic collusion in noisy environments all predate the sort of formal models we discussed in section 14.3; see, for example, Stigler (1964). But they have recently been addressed with models of the style of section 14.3 in papers by Green and Porter (1984) and Abreu, Pearce, and Stacchetti (1986), among others.

> The reader is left to discover the details of the formal treatments of these ideas from the original papers. But it may be useful for the more technically minded reader to see a sketch of how business of this sort is conducted.
>
> We begin with a sketch of Green and Porter. They deal with an infinite repetition, discounted formulation of the problem with I identical firms producing a homogenous product. In the model they use, price in period t is given by $\theta_t(A - X)$, where θ_t is a random disturbance term and X is total output. They look for equilibria of the following sort: A trigger price P' is set. As long as the equilibrium price stays above P', everyone produces at some level x'. If the equilibrium price falls below P', then a "reversionary" punishment period of set duration ensues: Each firm produces the Cournot quantities for N periods. After these N periods, firms go back to producing x' until the next time they find an equilibrium price below P'. Fix exogenously N and P' and consider the production decision of a given firm. Suppose every other firm produces at level x'. Then for every level x produced by the given firm, we can work out from the distribution of θ_t the distribution of $P(t) = \theta_t(A - (I - 1)x' - x)$. And, therefore, we can find the probability that $P(t)$ will be less than P'. This allows us to compute the expected length of time between reversionary periods. And it allows us to compute as a function of x (and parameters x', P' and N) the discounted profits our single firm will receive if it produces x in the collusive periods instead of x'. Optimizing over x, we find this firm's best

response to everyone else producing x'. We have an equilibrium when the optimal x is equal to x'. The parameters P' and N are fixed throughout the analysis so far; we proceed to vary these parameters to find the "most efficient" equilibrium of this sort — the one that gives all the firms, since they are treated symmetrically in the equilibrium, the highest possible average profits.

The results obtained by Green and Porter are just what we would expect: Lowering P' and/or N, in essence lowering the amount of "punishment," raises the equilibrium value of x'; less punishment means more chiselling. The best equilibrium from the point of view of the firms balances the cost of high P' and/or N, coming from the cost of reversionary periods caused by low values of θ_t, with the benefit in preventing chiselling. As we add more firms (increase I), things get worse; each firm has a smaller impact on $P(t)$, hence is more willing to chisel, and the level of collusion decreases. (With perfect monitoring, there is no theoretical reason why adding firms should lower the amount of collusion.)

Abreu, Pearce, and Stacchetti (1986) pick up this analysis and using techniques from dynamic programming and optimization theory are able to give the structure of symmetric equilibria that give the oligopolists the highest possible expected profits.

We asserted that by adding noisy observables we recovered some value from the general approach of being specific about the institutional details of competition. Why is this? Point (g) above is the key. One expects that oligopolistic firms will tend to collude as much as circumstances permit. At least, they will tend to act more collusively, everything else held equal, when there is less noise than when there is more. And some institutional arrangements for competition are inherently more noisy than others. So we would expect greater levels of collusion in industries where institutions allow for more precise monitoring of rivals.

A classic case of this sort drawn from Sultan (1975) and Porter (1983), concerns the competition between General Electric and Westinghouse in the manufacture and sale of large turbine generators. In 1963, the majority of orders that were placed for these very large pieces of capital equipment were placed (with one of the two firms) after protracted "secret negotiations." An electric utility would negotiate first with GE (say), then with Westinghouse, then with GE again, and so on, without either of the two manufacturers ever being certain what the other was bidding. When an order was placed, there still was no clear indication (to the losing firm) what the winning firm had bid. In this environment, prices were quite low and competition quite severe. GE, however, found a way to "restructure" competition with Westinghouse in a manner that made GE's bids predictable and its winning bids public knowledge. You should consult the original sources to see the extremely clever way in which this was done. But the

essential idea was that GE provided themselves with contractual obligations to reveal this information, with auditing and verification provided
by a public accounting firm. Westinghouse went along with this restruc-
turing and the result was quite successful implicit collusion between the
two firms — collusion so successful that the Antitrust Division of the U.S.
Justice Department stepped in and put a stop to the institutions that supported GE's scheme.

What's wrong with the game theoretic approach?

The discussion above centers on the (in)ability to monitor. But there
is another problem, intuitively similar, to contend with in applications.
What do you monitor? When we have symmetric firms, it seems "obvious" that we should look for symmetric equilibria wherein every firm
acts in the same way.[2] But in an oligopoly of asymmetric firms, it won't
be crystal clear just what is the "rule" each is supposed to follow. (This
is so if we rule out secret negotiations in hotel rooms — something at
which many governments look askance.) When firm A finds that its profits are lower than expected, it must decide whether this is due to (a)
something completely outside the control of A's rivals, (b) an "honest
mistake" by its rivals concerning the nature of the "agreement," or (c)
chiselling by its rivals. Stigler and Green and Porter discuss (a) versus
(c). But (b) versus (c) is at least as important in real life — especially
if one's rivals might chisel and then claim that this was just an honest
mistake.

We have returned to two closely related weaknesses of this approach:
The twin problems of too many equilibria and the selection of one of
them. Compare the model of this section with the Cournot, or Bertrand,
or von Stackelberg model. In the three classic models, a definite prediction
is made about what will happen. One can (and we do) argue that this
definiteness arises speciously. Insofar as the repeated play model is the
right model, the classic models make an ad hoc assumption about rivals'
conjectures, which is virtually equivalent to assuming which equilibrium

---

[2] But even this is too pat an answer. Imagine that Coca Cola and Pepsi are in all respects
identical. (Of course, they aren't.) Should they then collude by each having a presence in
every market in the U.S.? Or should they collude by implicitly segmenting U.S. domestic
markets, with Coke the dominant brand in the South and West and Pepsi strong in the
Northeast and Midwest? Complicating this: Insofar as there are potential entrants, which
scheme is better for preventing entry? Does this inform discussion of how they might collude differently in overseas markets? If you think you've worked out the softdrink business,
consider (and compare with) passenger airlines. Since this is a book on microeconomic theory, we will leave such enticing issues in industrial organization and competitive strategy at
this point in the hope that the tools you are learning here will help you study such questions.

pertains. Unless there is some reason given for the ad hoc assumption, nothing has been gained except perhaps to explain what sort of conjectures lead to certain equilibrium outcomes. (But at least the classic models make predictions definite enough to be refutable.)

A better comparison is with general equilibrium and, in the context of partial equilibrium, with the usual picture of upward sloping supply and downward sloping demand. In the latter class of models, a definite equilibrium prediction is made. In general equilibrium, one mightn't get a single specific prediction. But as noted in chapter 5, with some high-powered math, results are available establishing the "local uniqueness" of equilibria for most economies. In these contexts, then, one is able to do local comparative statics — jiggle this parameter or that a bit, and see how the predicted equilibrium can be expected to react. This adds utility to the model and it gives a handle for testing the model empirically.

Imagine, in contrast, trying to do local comparative statics in a situation where the folk theorem applies. Only if you have an idea how equilibrium expectations move with changes in parameters can you hope to get anywhere. Since the theory is silent on where equilibrium expectations come from, the theory is of limited help (to put it charitably). What is needed is some theory about how and when equilibrium expectations arise, and how they then adapt to changes in the environment.

A second lacuna in the theory is apparent when we examine closely the claim that specifying institutions helps us to understand outcomes, at least in noisy environments. This may be true as far as it goes. (It takes empirical verification before "may be" can be replaced by "is.") But it leaves open the question, Where did the institutions come from? With the benefit of hindsight, we might "predict" that GE and Westinghouse would achieve greater collusion after GE changed the "rules" than before; we might even make this into a legitimate empirical test by looking cross-sectionally at a number of industries. But how do we explain why, suddenly, GE saw how to change the rules to its own benefit? Why weren't those rules changed before? Is it the changed *rules* that led to greater collusion? Or did collusion increase because of the rule *changes*? More generally as we look across industries, do variations in the "rules" reflect uncontrollable environmental differences, or are institutions the result of some conscious or unconscious choices by participants? The answer is almost always going to be that both types of factor intrude. But this leads us to wonder whether there isn't some connection between the chosen parts of the institutional framework and the equilibrium expectations held by individuals. And even if we don't find such a connection, having a theory about how institutions arise and evolve could be more informative than theories of equilibrium within the context of a given set of institutions.

We will not resolve these puzzles at this point. In fact, we won't *resolve* them in this book at all; their full resolutions are over the horizon of economic theory at this point. We will return to them, however, especially in part V and the postscript. For now, we proceed with noncooperative game theory, having noted some fairly substantial limitations and weaknesses.

14.5. Reputation

We have dealt so far with the power of repeated play when two (or more) parties interact repeatedly. Imagine the following alternative story: A monopolist sells a particular product, which it is able to make either high quality or low. Demand for this good depends on its quality: If the good is high quality, demand is $P = 10 - X$. If it is low quality, demand is $P = 4 - X$. The cost of making high-quality goods is \$2 per unit, while low-quality goods cost \$1 per unit to make. Consumers are unable to observe the level of quality when they purchase the good, although they learn shortly afterwards just what they bought.

If we think of this situation as a one-time market, we get the extensive form representation shown in figure 14.3. And we get a very inefficient equilibrium. No matter what strategy consumers will use, the firm is better off making and selling low-quality goods; making high-quality goods won't change consumer buying decisions since consumers don't know the

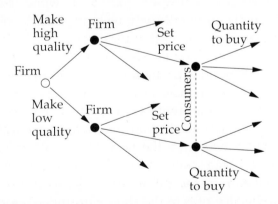

Figure 14.3. A quality choice game.
The firm chooses quality level and sets a price. Consumers purchase knowing the price, but not knowing for sure what quality the firm chose.

quality of the goods. Consumers realize this and anticipate that the firm will produce shoddy goods. So the firm sets price at $2.50 apiece, sells 1.5 units of the good (which it makes low quality) and reaps profits of $2.25.

Now imagine that the firm sells the good not once but repeatedly through time. To be formal, imagine there is a market in this good at the sequence of dates $t = 1, 2, \ldots$. We can imagine that the same consumers continue to buy this good or that there is a fresh batch of consumers each period, as long as we maintain one important assumption: Consumers who might buy at date t are aware of the quality of goods sold previously at dates $t-1, t-2, \ldots, 1$. Finally, the firm seeks to maximize its discounted profits, using discount factor α.

In this new situation, it is still an equilibrium for the firm always to set price at $2.50, make shoddy goods, and sell 1.5 units per period. But there are other, more interesting equilibria as well.

Imagine that the consumers adopt the rule: Assume the firm is producing high-quality goods as long as the goods produced in the previous three periods were all of high quality. Otherwise, assume that the goods produced this period will be shoddy. (For the first three periods, give the firm the benefit of the doubt. Assume the firm is producing high-quality goods unless it has produced shoddy goods previously.) Then the firm by always producing high-quality goods can set a price of $6 each period, sell four units, and realize profits of $16 per period. Of course, the firm could take advantage of consumers in any given period by producing shoddy goods. That would increase the firm's profits from $16 to $20 during that period. But the firm would pay for this subsequently; the most it could make in the next three periods would be $2.25, and if it ever wanted to get back to those $16 profits, it would have to do worse than that. At reasonable values of α the firm will continue to produce high-quality goods. And the consumers' assumption that the firm is producing high-quality goods works out.

There is certainly nothing profound or complex in this. We are simply reinventing in the formal language of game theory the notion of reputation. Our firm can have either a reputation for selling high-quality goods or for selling shoddy merchandise. Consumers form their expectations by looking at recent production by the firm. And, in this case, carrying a reputation for selling high-quality goods is viable as an equilibrium. The value of the reputation in the future is always more than what can be had by taking advantage of it in the short run. Indeed, for α sufficiently close to one, a firm in this situation would want to invest in reputation. It would produce high-quality goods for a few periods even if this cost it money to convince consumers that it produces high-quality goods.

It is crucial here that the firm believes its current actions affect its reputation and, thus, its future demand. If the quality of goods sold at date t never became known to future consumers, or only became known with a substantial lag, then having a reputation for high quality might not be viable as an equilibrium in the sense that a firm with a reputation for high quality would prefer to exploit that reputation in the short run.

This is very much like the construction of the folk theorem, and it suffers from similar problems. First, there are typically many possible "reputational equilibria." It is not hard to imagine complicating the simple story above so that there are many possible levels of quality among which the firm must choose, and it isn't hard to parameterize the problem so that the firm could carry an (equilibrium) reputation for many of those levels. (See problem 3.) It will simply depend on what the consumers anticipate and how they react to the quality levels the firm has previously produced.

Second, given a multiplicity of equilibria, we worry as before about the lack of a focal point.[3]

Third, if there is a fixed and finite horizon, these reputation constructions can collapse. In our simple example, consumers in the last period rationally assume that the firm will end with a run of shoddy goods, no matter what the firm has produced prior to this. Hence in the next-to-last period, the firm has no incentive to produce high-quality goods, and consumers in that period assume as much, and so on, just as before.

Fourth, noisy observables complicate matters. If our firm cannot perfectly control the quality of its output, we run into difficulties. Imagine, for example, that when the firm is trying to produce shoddy goods, each item produced is low quality with probability .9 and high quality with probability .1, independently of the others. Whereas if the firm is trying to produce high-quality goods, each item is high quality with probability .8 and low quality with probability .2. Then if the firm produces and sells four items and two are shoddy and two are high quality, what do consumers do? If they don't sometimes "punish" the firm, the firm will certainly always produce shoddy goods, blaming it all on an incredible string of bad luck. But even if the firm is trying to produce high-quality goods, every so often it will have an unlucky day. Considerations very much like those in the previous sections apply.

You shouldn't imagine from our example that reputation can always do just as much as can be done with the standard model of repeated play. If we imagined that one player played against a sequence of opponents in

---

[3] Although when the party carrying the reputation interacts with a sequence of myopic opponents, there can be quite natural focal points; see Fudenberg and Levine (1988).

the prisoners' dilemma game, and if those opponents had only short-run interests (either because they played only once or because they otherwise weren't concerned with their own reputations), then the fact that the one player carries a reputation will get us nothing. All her opponents will play noncooperatively whatever her reputation is, since noncooperative play in the static prisoners' dilemma is strictly dominant. And so there is no reason for this one player to carry a reputation for acting cooperatively.

This raises the question, Is there a neat characterization of what can be obtained in a reputational equilibrium analogous to the folk theorem? One needs to be a bit more precise about the setting and about what is meant by a reputational equilibrium, but results of this sort have been obtained; see, for example, Fudenberg, Kreps, and Maskin (1989).

This sort of reputation construction is used in many ways in economics. While the reputation sketched above is "beneficial" to both sides, there are other contexts in which one side cultivates a reputation which is harmful to others. A neat example (because it illustrates the limitations of reputation vis à vis the folk theorem) is the following somewhat artificial story concerning market leadership. Imagine a long-lived firm that at a sequence of dates $t = 1, 2, \ldots$ is engaged in duopolistic competition with a sequence of rivals. That is, at date t this firm and a rival compete in a duopoly market; then at date $t + 1$ this firm competes against a new rival. Imagine that at each date t the two firms engage in Cournot style competition. You should think of our standard model of a market for an undifferentiated good with linear demand $P = A - X$ and constant marginal cost c.

If the two firms competed at date t and $t + 1$ and forever into the future (discounting their profits), then the folk theorem shows how with sufficiently high discount factors the two could sustain monopoly profits between themselves. But if one of the two firms competes only at date t, then it isn't concerned with the future when setting its quantity; its only concern is with the quantity that the long-lived firm might set. If in the equilibrium the long-lived firm chooses quantity x_L, then the short-lived (date t) firm will choose its quantity optimally in response, using the response function $x_t^*(x_L) = (A - c - x_L)/2$.[4] So we can never get an equilibrium where the long-lived firm and its rivals share the monopoly profits unless the long-lived firm produces nothing. You can easily confirm that $x_L + x_t^*(x_L) > (A - c)/2$ for $x_L > 0$.

---

[4] In this problem, even if the long-lived firm sets quantity randomly, the same response function works with x_L now the expected value of the long-lived firm's quantity as long as the total quantity supplied is always less or equal to $A - c$.

But now consider the following equilibrium: The long-lived firm produces $(A - c)/2$ in each period, as long as it has produced $(A - c)/2$ in the past. If ever the long-lived firm deviates from this production plan, it will produce $(A - c)/3$ thereafter. The short-lived firms each produce $(A - c)/4$, as long as the long-lived firm in the past has produced $(A - c)/2$. But if ever the long-lived firm produces something other than $(A - c)/2$, the short-lived firms all subsequently produce $(A - c)/3$.

You can check that for a discount factor α that is sufficiently close to one ($\geq 9/17$, if you work it out) this describes an equilibrium. A colorful story goes with this equilibrium. Our long-lived firm has the reputation of being a Stackelberg leader; it sets its quantity at $(A - c)/2$, expecting its rivals to reply with $(A - c)/4$. Of course, in any single period given that it expects its rival to produce $(A - c)/4$, it would prefer (in this round) to set its quantity at $3(A - c)/8$. But if it does this, it loses its reputation for being a Stackelberg leader, after which all its (subsequent) rivals assume it will produce the standard Cournot output $(A - c)/3$, to which they optimally reply with the same level of output. Note two things here. First, in this equilibrium we have the short-lived firms always producing on their short-run optimal reaction function to what the long-lived firm does. This is a quite general property of this sort of equilibrium. Second, the short-lived firms are worse off in this equilibrium than they would be if the long-lived firm couldn't carry a reputation.

A number of simple variations on this story can be played. We can turn it into a story about entry deterrence if we imagine that all the firms involved have fixed costs. For example, consider the parameterization we have used in tales of entry deterrence: Demand is given by $P = 9 - X$, marginal costs are $c = 1$, and fixed costs are \$2.25. And consider the following equilibrium: The long-lived firm produces 5 units, as long as it has produced 5 units in the past. If ever it produces something other than 5 units, it produces 8/3 thereafter. The short-lived firms produce nothing (which we will assume avoids the fixed cost) as long as the long-lived firm has in the past produced 5 units each period, but if ever the long-lived firm deviates from this, short-lived firms subsequently enter and produce 8/3 apiece. You should have no trouble telling the "story" that goes with this equilibrium.

Or consider the original story, but now with noise in the market price as in Green and Porter. This one is left to you as a problem, but try to guess before thinking about it. Should the long-lived firm be "punished" if observed prices are higher than expected or lower? Also left to you is the following very easy exercise. What happens to our basic story if the long-lived and short-lived firms engage in Bertrand style competition?

We will see other, very important applications of this reputation construction in chapter 20.

14.6. Reputation redux: Incomplete information

The details of this section are difficult, and nothing that follows in the book builds on this section. This can be regarded as optional material for a first reading.

One of the deficiencies of the constructions explored so far in this chapter is that they depend heavily on there always being a future that can be used to influence current behavior. It isn't necessary to have infinitely many periods; in the variation where there is always a probability q of at least one more round, there are only finitely many periods before the game ends — but it can't be that players can predict that the game will end by some definite time in the future. For once there is a definite terminus to the game; the sorts of cooperative and reputational equilibria that we've been constructing tend to unravel. Behavior is fixed in the final period, which then fixes it in the penultimate, and so on.[5]

The theory, then, seems to imply that these constructions rely crucially on a horizon that never does loom up. But, as we've noted several times now, this doesn't seem right intuitively. And it certainly isn't right empirically. When students play, say, the prisoners' dilemma twenty times, where it is understood from the start that there will be only twenty rounds, there is usually some cooperation early on.

Or consider the game between players 1 and 2 depicted in figure 14.4. This game goes with the following story. Player 2 is an incumbent monopolist in some market. Player 1 is a potential entrant. First player 1 must decide whether or not to enter player 2's market. If player 1 enters, then player 2 must decide whether to acquiesce to this entry or to fight the entry (with slashed prices, etc.). This game has two Nash equilibria in pure strategies. In the first, player 1 enters and player 2 acquiesces. In the second, player 1 doesn't enter and player 2 fights entry if it comes (which it doesn't). By now you will recognize that only the first of these is subgame perfect, and it is the usual prediction that would be made if player 1 and 2 play this game once.

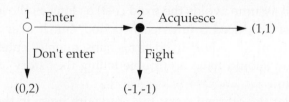

Figure 14.4. The chain-store stage game.

---

[5] Actually, this happens only if there is a single equilibrium in the static stage game. If there are multiple equilibria in the stage game, even with a finite horizon one can construct cooperative or reputational equilibria. See Benoit and Krishna (1985) for details.

But now add the following complication. Player 2 will play this game not once but, say, twenty times in sequence, each time against a different opponent. Each of 2's opponents plays the game once and once only. The order of play is set, and players 1 who play later observe what happened in earlier rounds of play. The story that goes with this is: Player 2 is a chain-store monopolist with twenty stores in as many towns. In each town, there is the threat of entry from a firm that will if it enters be active in that town only. Moreover, there is a set sequence of actions: The entrant in some given town must decide whether to enter or not and the chain store must react to that entry; then in a second given town the entry-reaction decisions must be taken, and so on.

The theory dictates that this complication doesn't really change matters. In the last round, if the entrant enters, the only subgame perfect reaction for the chain store is to acquiesce. But then in round nineteen, the same is true, and so on; the unique subgame perfect equilibrium has every entrant entering in turn and the chain store always acquiescing.

If we string out infinitely many of these stage games, we can get a different equilibrium using a reputation construction as in the previous section. One equilibrium is: No entrant enters as long as the chain store has never acquiesced. Every entrant enters subsequent to the chain store ever acquiescing. The chain store fights any entry, as long as it never previously acquiesced. And the chain store acquiesces if ever, by chance, it had acquiesced previously. You can verify that this equilibrium is subgame perfect. Roughly put, the chain store is willing to fight any entry because, although this is costly in the short run, it is more costly to acquiesce and invite entry from all subsequent entrants.

As with the finitely and infinitely repeated prisoners' dilemma, the theoretical dichotomy between the finite and the infinite repetition versions of the chain store game does not have much intuitive appeal. Indeed, in the original paper on this subject, Selten (1978) finds this dichotomy so counterintuitive that he refers to it as the *chain-store paradox*.

We saw yet another example of the same sort of thing in the centipede game of chapter 12. This game, reproduced here in figure 14.5(a), has a unique subgame perfect equilibrium in which the two players pick D at every node. It has some subgame imperfect equilibria as well, but every Nash equilibrium necessarily begins with player 1 choosing D. Nonetheless, this doesn't seem a very intuitive solution to this game, and this game, played by students and other experimental subjects, certainly doesn't always end with player 1 choosing D at the first opportunity. We say this is another example of the same sort of thing because the argument that the game has a unique subgame perfect equilibrium involves the same sort of unravelling from the back: Player 2 will surely choose D at his last node, so player 1 will surely choose D at the next-to-last node, and so on.

I next present an argument for why this equilibrium seems unintuitive, which I will later tie back to the notion of reputation. The argument involves the incomplete information variation on the basic game depicted in figure 14.5(b). In this game of incomplete information, we suppose that player 1's payoffs are determined by nature. With probability .999 they are as in the

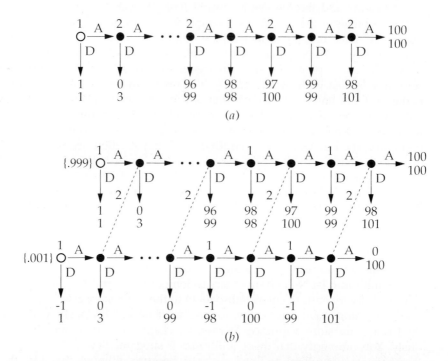

Figure 14.5. The centipede game and a variation.

original centipede game, while with probability .001, these payoffs make playing A until the end of the game a dominant strategy. Think of the following
story. Player 2 assesses, at the outset, a one-in-one-thousand chance that his
opponent overflows with the milk of human kindness and will play A at every opportunity. Player 1 is aware that player 2 entertains this hypothesis,
and player 1 is aware that player 2 doesn't put much store by it. Player 2
only gives it a one-in-one-thousand chance.

It certainly isn't part of an equilibrium in this variation for player 1 to
play D at the outset (and thereafter) in the top half of the game. Why? Because
if player 1 plays this way in the top half of the game, then player 2, given
the move, will believe (by applying Bayes' rule) that he is in the bottom half
of the game. Believing this, he plays A until the last node (when he plays
D) in anticipation that player 1 will play A at each of her nodes. But then
it is in player 1's interests in the top half of the game to play A until the
next-to-last node, beating 2 to the punch by one. Which then causes our logic
to go haywire, as player 2 won't conclude on the basis of A at the first node
that he is in the bottom half of the game.

What does the equilibrium of this game look like? What follows is,
unhappily, not entirely transparent.[j] But I know of no way around this.

---

[j] It is time to remind you that you were specifically warned about this example in

The game has a unique sequential equilibrium, which can be obtained by reasoning back from the last round.[6] First, let me label the nodes 1x, 2x, 3x, ..., 198x, where x is t for top and b for bottom, and where 1x is the last node in the sequence, 2x is the second to last, and so on. Note that at nodes with an odd number for an index player 2 moves, while at even numbered nodes player 1 chooses. (Sorry about that.) Since player 2's information sets contain pairs of nodes $(2n+1)$t and $(2n+1)$b, his actions at these nodes must be the same; we will speak of his move at information set $2n+1$.

Because player 1 chooses A for sure in the bottom half of the tree and there is prior probability .001 that the bottom half prevails, player 2 is never completely surprised to be given the move back if he chooses A. This implies that 2's beliefs at each of his information sets can be computed by Bayes' rule from 1's strategy, whatever that strategy is. We will use μ_{2n+1} to denote the probability 2 assesses that he is in the top half of the tree, given that information set $2n+1$ has been reached. Note that $\mu_{2n+1} \leq .999$ for all n (since player 1 chooses A for sure in the bottom part of the tree).

At information set 1, player 2 chooses D for sure by dominance. Hence at node 2t, player 1 chooses D.

Now move back to information set 3. Player 2 computes: If he plays D, he will get 100. If he plays A, he will get 101 if he is in the bottom half of the tree and 99 if he is in the top half. Letting μ_3 denote his probability assessment that he is in the top half of the tree, he nets expected value $99\mu_3 + 101(1 - \mu_3)$ by playing A, and so he chooses A if $\mu_3 < 1/2$, D if $\mu_3 > 1/2$, and he is indifferent if $\mu_3 = 1/2$.

Now go back to node 4t. Player 1 nets 98 at node 4t by choosing D. If she chooses A, she nets 97 if player 2 follows up with D and 99 if player 2 follows with A. So what she will do depends, in equilibrium, on 2's beliefs at information set 3: If he will believe $\mu_3 < 1/2$, then he will play A, in which case she plays A. If he will believe $\mu_3 > 1/2$, then he will play D, in which case she will play D. If he will believe $\mu_3 = 1/2$ *and* he chooses to randomize exactly 50-50 between A and D, she is indifferent at node 4t.

(a) Since $\mu_3 < 1$, it can't be part of an equilibrium for him to believe $\mu_3 > 1/2$. Because if we suppose these are going to be his beliefs, she will choose D at 4t, and Bayes' rule will give him beliefs of $\mu_3 = 0$, contradicting $\mu_3 > 1/2$.

(b) Could it be that $\mu_3 < 1/2$? This is possible if and only if $\mu_5 < 1/2$ because, if μ_3 is going to be less than 1/2, he will play A at information set 3. Thus she will play A at node 4t. Thus, by Bayes' rule, $\mu_5 = \mu_3$. So if μ_3 is to be less than 1/2, then $\mu_5 < 1/2$ in an equilibrium. Conversely, if $\mu_5 < 1/2$, then Bayes' rule implies that $\mu_3 \leq \mu_5 < 1/2$ and he will play A at information set 3, so she will play A at 4t (and $\mu_3 = \mu_5$).

(c) This leaves the case where $\mu_5 \geq 1/2$. We can't have $\mu_3 < 1/2$, and we can't have $\mu_3 > 1/2$, so we will have to have $\mu_3 = 1/2$. Denote by π_4 the

---

chapter 1.

[6] In fact, the game has a unique Nash equilibrium; this is left as an exercise.

equilibrium probability that 1 chooses A at 4t. Then given π_4 and μ_5, Bayes' rule is used to compute μ_3 as

$$\mu_3 = \frac{\mu_5 \pi_4}{\mu_5 \pi_4 + (1 - \mu_5)}.$$

Since we need $\mu_3 = 1/2$, this gives us $\pi_4 = (1 - \mu_5)/\mu_5$. This tells us a few things. First, at information set 5, player 2 assesses probability $1 - \mu_5 + \pi_4 \mu_5 = 2(1 - \mu_5)$ that player 1 will play A next time. So if $\mu_5 < 3/4$, he definitely wishes to play A at information set 5. If, on the other hand, $\mu_5 > 3/4$, he definitely wishes to play D at information set 5. And he is indifferent if $\mu_5 = 3/4$. (Recall that if $\mu_3 = 1/2$, he has expected payoff of 100 starting from information set 3.) Next, unless $\mu_5 = 1/2$, the only way we will get $\mu_3 = 1/2$ is if $0 < \pi_4 < 1$. This requires that player 1 is indifferent between A and D at node 4t, which in turn requires that player 2 at information set 3 randomizes precisely 50-50 between A and D.

This nails everything down (in terms of μ_5) at nodes 4t and at information set 3 except for the knife-edge case where $\mu_5 = 1/2$. In this case, $\mu_3 = 1/2$ only if player 1 plays A for sure at 4t. And player 1 will play A for sure as long as player 2 chooses A with probability $1/2$ or more at information set 3. So in this knife-edge case, we do have a bit of freedom in what happens.[7]

Now back to information set 5. We already know rather a lot. If $\mu_5 > 3/4$, player 2 will choose D for sure. If $\mu_5 < 3/4$, he will choose A for sure. If $\mu_5 = 3/4$, he is indifferent, and his expected payoff is 99. All of which we use when we ...

... move back to node 6t. The analysis here is a lot like the analysis of 6t, except the role of $\mu_3 = 1/2$ is replaced by $\mu_5 = 3/4$. Essentially, if $\mu_7 < 3/4$, then player 2 is sure to play A at information set 5, so 1 plays A at 6t and $\mu_5 = \mu_7$. If $\mu_7 \geq 3/4$, then the only way to have an equilibrium is to get $\mu_5 = 3/4$ — this determines what player 1 must do at 6t. If $\mu_7 = 3/4$, there is a bit of latitude in what player 2 must do at information set 5; while if $\mu_7 > 3/4$, player 1 must randomize at 6t, which fixes the needed randomization of 2 at information set 5. And when we compute what 1 must do at 6t to get us from $\mu_7 \geq 3/4$ to $\mu_5 = 3/4$, we have begun to ...

... move back to information set 7. If $\mu_7 < 7/8$, player 2 will play A for sure; if $\mu_7 > 7/8$, he will play D for sure; and if $\mu_7 = 7/8$, he is indifferent.

The pattern emerges. The crucial thing on which to focus is that if $\mu_9 < 15/16$, player 2 will definitely play A at information set 9, and so on. In particular, if $\mu_{2n+1} < 1023/1024$ for $n \geq 10$, player 2 will definitely play A at information set $2n + 1$. And then, prior to this, player 1 will play A at node $(2n)$t, for $n > 11$. But $\mu_{2n+1} \leq .999 < 1023/1024$ for every n, since .999

---

[7] In defense of our claim that the game has a unique sequential equilibrium, we later argue that this knife-edge case doesn't happen given the initial conditions specified for the game.

is the prior. For most of the game, until the last 22 or so moves (out of 198), player 1 (in both halves of the game) and player 2 both choose A for sure, which is completely the reverse of what they are meant to do according to subgame perfection in the simple centipede game.

Of course, this is rather complex. The final 22 or so moves involve a complicated dance of mixed strategies that keep player 2 willing to randomize so that player 1 is willing to randomize so that ...; I am not claiming that the precise equilibrium is very intuitive. But, setting aside those final twenty-two moves, the "main effect" does have a good deal of intuition to it.

Player 2 risks one unit of payoff by choosing A instead of D. The potential gains are substantial. If there is a moderate chance of reaping those gains, it would be worthwhile to give A a try. But that isn't all there is to it. Note that the potential gains are on the order of 100. And the chance that player 1 will always play A is only .001. So if player 1 in the top half of the game were always to play D, this wouldn't be a worthwhile investment for player 2. What makes it worthwhile is that it is in the interests of 1 in the top half of the game to convince 2 to keep trying A. Hence it is in 1's interests to play A. And 2, recognizing this, has it in her own interests to play A.

Do not be misled by this argument into thinking that this is simple or straightforward. Exactly the same argument could be made for the original centipede game, and in the original game this argument isn't consistent with any equilibrium. Perhaps the best way to put it is: It is in the interests of both 1 and 2 to play A until near the end of the game. But each one will do so (in equilibrium) only if she believes that she can, on average, beat the other player to the punch. In an equilibrium, their beliefs have to be consistent, and it is inconsistent in the original game for each to think that she will outguess the other. But when we add a little incomplete information about player 1, player 2 can believe that he will "outguess" player 1 because, with small probability, player 1 will permit herself to be outguessed. From this small wedge, we are able to get them both to play A happily until near the end of the game.

How tied is this to the precise specification of incomplete information that we used? Certainly the number of rounds back and forth plays no role at all, once that number gets beyond the twenty-two nodes needed to reach a point where each plays A for sure. If you look over the proof, it doesn't matter whether there are 198 nodes, or 28, or 199,998; except for the last twenty-two, each side plays A with certainty. The size of the probability that 1 is benevolent isn't so important. If we changed the .001 to .0001 (one in ten thousand!), it would take four more pairs of rounds from the back to get to the point where both sides choose A with probability one. The nature of 1's "irrationality" isn't so crucial; the same basic conclusion would be derived if player 2 assesses small probability that player 1 will play A until sometime in the last ten rounds. And it isn't even necessary that 2 have any real doubts about 1's rationality. Imagine a game of incomplete information in which there are three possible initial nodes. The first has probability .998, and player 1 has precisely the payoffs as in the original centipede game. The second has probability .001, and player 1 has precisely the payoffs as in the original game. And the third has probability .001, and player 1 is "benevolent." Moreover, player 2 knows when the first starting point prevails, but is unsure when one of the second two prevails which it is. And player 1 is unsure when one of the first two starting points prevail which it is. In other words, with probability .998 player 1 is "rational" and player 2 is aware of that. But in that event, player 1 isn't sure that player 2 is aware of that; player 1 thinks there is a small chance that player 2 thinks there is a good chance that player 1 is benevolent. Player 1, in this case, will give the move to player 2 to "see" if player 2 is perhaps confused (which player 2 indicates by giving the move back to player 1). And player 2, even if he isn't confused, gives the move back to player 1; the same sort of construction works.

These are very complex games with very complex equilibria. I do not want to suggest that the equilibria are in any sense obvious solutions. Whether people put in the position of having to play these games exhibit behavior that conforms to these equilibria is a nontrivial empirical question. For some initial investigation into this, see Camerer and Weigelt (1988).

At the same time, games like this demonstrate, I think, why the theoretical solution of the original centipede game isn't very intuitive. A one-in-one-thousand chance that one's opponent is generous, or that one's opponent assesses a substantial probability that oneself is benevolent, isn't much of a "change" in the game. Yet it completely changes the theoretical prediction. In any game where such a small change in the formulation can result in such a large change in the theoretical prediction, one will want to be very wary of the theoretical prediction. At the risk of confusing you unnecessarily, we should backreference the discussion of chapter 13 on subgame perfection at this point. The argument there was that if deviations can be attributed to an a priori small chance that players have very different payoffs from those in the model of the game, the motivation behind subgame perfection and sequential rationality might be missing. Here we see something worse: For games with this sort of back and forth structure, such attributions can lead to behavior that is very different from Nash equilibrium behavior in the original game, for reasonably sized perturbations. Let me put it this way: Before we attacked subgame perfection on grounds that it wasn't robust to this sort of perturbation. Now we are attacking the notion of Nash equilibrium, when one has a game like the centipede game where the set of Nash equilibria is not robust to these perturbations.[k]

And to tie this back to reputation and finitely repeated games: In the finitely repeated prisoners' dilemma, suppose one player assesses a small probability that the second will "irrationally" play the strategy of tit-for-tat:

---

[k] There is a theoretical difference between the two points. In our constructions at the end of chapter 13, used to show why a subgame imperfect equilibrium might be reasonable prediction, we can make the small probability that a player is "irrational" as small as we wish (if still strictly positive), and our argument is unaffected. In the construction here, if the probability that player 1 is benevolent is, say, smaller than $1/2^{210}$, then there is a substantial chance that player 1 will play D to start the game. (Put very mathematically, the Nash equilibrium correspondence is upper semi-continuous in these sorts of perturbations, for a fixed extensive form.) But this distinction is not of practical significance. If a $1/1000$ chance of very different payoffs is enough to upset the analysis for a given game, surely the conclusions of the analysis are not altogether trustworthy.

Do to your opponent whatever your opponent did to you on the previous round. In a long-enough (but still finite) repetition of the game, if you think your opponent plays tit-for-tat, you will want to give cooperation a try. And even if your opponent isn't irrational in this fashion, the "rational" thing for her to do is to mimic this sort of behavior to keep cooperation alive. Or, in the chain-store game, imagine that the long-lived player 2 with small probability will fight any entry into any of his markets, even if it is financially costly, because he just doesn't like entrants. A "rational" player 2 would mimic this behavior to convince entrants that he will act in this fashion to keep them from entering. And so entrants, afraid of being fought either because 2 is really irrational or wishes to appear irrational, choose not to enter.

We can think of these effects as "reputation" in the sense that a player will act "irrationally" to keep alive the possibility that she is irrational, if being thought of as irrational will later be to that player's benefit through its influence on how others play. That is, in this sort of situation, players must weigh against the short-run benefits of certain actions the long-run consequences of their actions. I take this short- versus long-run trade-off to be the hallmark of reputation, thus qualifying for this sort of model as an example of the general phenomenon of reputation.

14.7. Bibliographic notes

When structuring a map of the literature on this topic, the following categories are useful. Divide at the broadest level between (I) constructions in the style of sections 14.2 through 14.6, which depend on an infinite horizon, and (II) those that use a bit of incomplete information and so can work in finite horizon models. At the next step, divide between (A) models where two or more players play the game repeatedly and (B) those where one or more of the players are short-lived. Then divide into three: (1) analysis of the average payoff criterion (and more sensitive criteria related to it); (2) analysis of the discounted payoff criterion, for a fixed discount rate less than one; and (3) analysis of the limit set of equilibria in the discounted payoff formulation, as the discount factor goes to one. Finally, we can divide between formulations (a) without and (b) with noisy observables.

On repeated games and the folk theorem with an average payoff criterion and no noise, or category (IA1a), Rubinstein (1979) is a very good place to begin. The seminal references for the case of noise (category [IA1b]) are Radner (1985), Rubinstein (1979), and Rubinstein and Yaari (1983).

When we move to discounted payoffs, most of the action concerns the structure of efficient equilibria. For the analysis without noisy observables (IA2a), consult Abreu (1988). See also Abreu (1986) on applications to Cournot competition, following on the seminal work of Friedman (1971). When noise is added (IA2b), see Abreu, Pearce, and Stacchetti (1989). Green and Porter (1984) and Abreu, Pearce, and Stacchetti (1986) concern noisy observables in repeated Cournot competition. We should also mention the classic, pregame theoretic paper on oligopolistic collusion by Stigler (1964).

The limit set of equilibria as the discount factor goes to one, without noise or category (IA3a), is the subject of the first half of Fudenberg and Maskin (1986). With noise added (category [IA3b]), see Fudenberg, Levine, and Maskin (1989) and Matsushima (1988).

Concerning models where there are short-run players, which we introduced under the rubric of reputation, the basic notion goes back at least as far as Simon (1951), who works with an example that we will discuss in chapter 20. A number of applications have appeared since, but (to my knowledge) the first formalization of a folk theorem for this situation is Fudenberg, Kreps, and Maskin (1989), which covers categories (IB1) and (IB3a). Fudenberg and Levine (1989) concerns category (IB3b).

Concerning cooperation and reputation in finite horizon models, Selten (1978) is the classic reference pointing to the problem, and Rosenthal (1981) contains a very important commentary and prospectus for later theoretical developments.[8] Benoit and Krishna (1985) show how, when the stage game has multiple equilibria, one can make folk-theorem-like constructions even in a finite horizon model. Models using incomplete information were first explored in Kreps, Milgrom, Roberts, and Wilson (1982) (cooperation in the prisoners' dilemma for two long-lived players), and Kreps and Wilson (1982) and Milgrom and Roberts (1982) (entry deterrence in a case with one long-lived player playing against a sequence of opponents). The back half of Fudenberg and Maskin (1986) concerns folk-theorem-like results for this sort of model, when all players are long-lived, while Fudenberg and Levine (1988) contains general analysis of the problem with one long-lived player. Fudenberg and Kreps (1987) concerns models of reputation where one player plays against many opponents simultaneously instead of in sequence. Hart (1985) analyzes the general case of repeated games with one-sided incomplete information and no discounting.

There is a large literature on repeated play of constant-sum games with incomplete information about which we have said nothing. Aumann (1985) provides a survey and introduction.

---

[8] This paper is also the origin of the centipede game.

References

Abreu, D. 1986. "Extremal Equilibria of Oligopolistic Supergames." *Journal of Economic Theory* 39:191–225.

————. 1988. "On the Theory of Infinitely Repeated Games with Discounting." *Econometrica* 56:383–96.

Abreu, D., D. Pearce, and E. Stacchetti. 1986. "Optimal Cartel Equilibria with Imperfect Monitoring." *Journal of Economic Theory* 39:251–69.

————. 1989. "Toward a Theory of Discounted Repeated Games with Imperfect Monitoring." Harvard University. Mimeo. Forthcoming in *Econometrica*.

Aumann, R. 1985. "Repeated Games." In *Issues in Contemporary Microeconomics and Welfare*, G. Feiwel, ed., 209–42. London: Macmillan.

Benoit, J.-P., and V. Krishna. 1985. "Finitely Repeated Games." *Econometrica* 53:905–22.

Camerer, C., and K. Weigelt. 1988. "Experimental Tests of a Sequential Equilibrium Reputation Model." *Econometrica* 56:1–36.

Friedman, J. 1971. "A Noncooperative Equilibrium for Supergames." *Review of Economic Studies* 28:1–12.

Fudenberg, D., and D. Kreps. 1987. "Reputation in the Simultaneous Play of Multiple Opponents." *Review of Economic Studies* 54:541–68.

Fudenberg, D., D. Kreps, and E. Maskin. 1989. "Repeated Games with Long-run and Short-run Players." Massachusetts Institute of Technology. Mimeo.

Fudenberg, D., and D. Levine. 1988. "Reputation and Equilibrium Selection in Games with a Single Patient Player." Massachusetts Institute of Technology. Mimeo. Forthcoming in *Econometrica*.

————. 1989. "Equilibrium Payoffs with Long-run and Short-run Players and Imperfect Public Information." Massachusetts Institute of Technology. Mimeo.

Fudenberg, D., D. Levine, and E. Maskin. 1989. "The Folk Theorem with Imperfect Public Information." Massachusetts Institute of Technology. Mimeo.

Fudenberg, D., and E. Maskin. 1986. "The Folk Theorem in Repeated Games with Discounting or with Incomplete Information." *Econometrica* 54:532–54.

Green, E., and R. Porter. 1984. "Non-cooperative Collusion Under Imperfect Price Information." *Econometrica* 52:975–94.

Hart, S. 1985. "Nonzero Sum Two-person Repeated Games with Incomplete Information." *Mathematics of Operations Research* 10:117–53.

Kreps, D., P. Milgrom, J. Roberts, and R. Wilson. 1982. "Rational Cooperation in the Finitely Repeated Prisoners' Dilemma." *Journal of Economic
Theory* 27:245–52.

Kreps, D., and R. Wilson. 1982. "Reputation and Imperfect Information."
Journal of Economic Theory 27:253–79.

Matsushima, H. 1988. "Efficiency in Repeated Games with Imperfect Monitoring." University of Tsukuba. Mimeo. Forthcoming in *Journal of
Economic Theory*.

Milgrom, P., and J. Roberts. 1982. "Predation, Reputation, and Entry
Deterrence." *Journal of Economic Theory* 27:280–312.

Porter, M. 1983. "General Electric versus Westinghouse in Large Turbine
Generators." In *Cases in Competitive Strategies*, 102–18. New York: Free
Press.

Radner, R. 1985. "Repeated Partnership Games with Imperfect Monitoring
and No Discounting." *Review of Economics Studies* 53:43–58.

Rosenthal, R. 1981. "Games of Perfect Information, Predatory Pricing, and
the Chain-store Paradox." *Journal of Economic Theory* 25:92–100.

Rubinstein, A. 1979. "An Optimal Conviction Policy for Offences that May
Have Been Committed by Accident." In *Applied Game Theory*, S. Brams,
A. Schotter, and G. Schwodiauer, eds. Wurzburg: Physica-Verlag.

Rubinstein, A., and M. Yaari. 1983. "Repeated Insurance Contracts and
Moral Hazard." *Journal of Economic Theory* 30:74–97.

Selten, R. 1978. "The Chain-store Paradox." *Theory and Decision* 9:127–59.

Simon, H. 1951. "A Formal Theory of the Employment Relationship."
Econometrica 19:293–305.

Smith, A. [1776] 1976. *The Wealth of Nations*. Chicago: University of
Chicago Press.

Stigler, G. 1964. "A Theory of Oligopoly." *Journal of Political Economy* 72:44–
61.

Sultan, R. 1975. *Pricing in the Electrical Oligopoly*. Harvard Graduate School
of Business Administration, Division of Research, research report.

14.8. Problems

■ 1. In a number of places in this chapter, I used phrases like "XYZ is an
equilibrium *if q* (the probability of going on to the next round) or α (the
discount factor) is large enough." In this problem, you are asked to puzzle
through, What is large enough?

(a) In the prisoners' dilemma game, we said that as long as $q \geq 3/8$, the threat of any player to meet noncooperation with noncooperation forever would sustain cooperation. Give the calculations that support the 3/8. We also said that for large enough q, it would be enough to threaten to meet noncooperation with one round of noncooperation. To be precise, assume each player adopts the strategy: Play cooperatively unless and until one's opponent plays noncooperatively. Then play noncooperatively for one round. Then go back to playing cooperatively even if your opponent didn't cooperate in the single round of "punishment." And if, by chance or otherwise, a player happens not to cooperate at a time when punishment isn't called for, then the player does not cooperate for the one stage of punishment. For which values of q is this an equilibrium?

(b) In the discussion of Stackelberg leadership arising from reputation (near the end of section 14.5), a "large-enough" α was claimed to be one greater than 9/17. Give calculations that lead to this particular number.

■ 2. In the discussion of noisy observables in section 14.3, we proposed in passing the following sort of model for repeated play of the prisoners' dilemma. Players choose their intended strategies on each round, passing instructions to a referee for implementation. The referee then implements those intentions "noisily": If told to play a noncooperative strategy, the referee plays this strategy with probability .8, but with probability .2, the referee plays cooperatively. If told to play cooperatively, the referee plays cooperatively with probability .8 and noncooperatively with probability .2. Players know what instructions they sent, and at the end of each round the referee's implementation of both strategies are revealed to both players. But players don't know what instructions their opponents sent. Assume that $q = .9$ and that the random ending of the game in any round and the referee's random implementations of strategies are all mutually and serially independent as random variables.

(a) Prove that it is a Nash equilibrium for players always to send instructions to play noncooperatively. What is the expected payoff to the players in this equilibrium?

(b) Suppose players adopt the strategy: Instruct the referee to play cooperatively until either player fails to cooperate (in terms of the implemented strategy) and thereafter instruct the referee to play noncooperatively. Is this an equilibrium? If so, what are the expected payoffs to the players in this equilibrium?

(c) Suppose players adopt the strategy: Instruct the referee to play cooperatively until either player fails to cooperate. Then instruct the referee to play noncooperatively for N periods. Then instruct the referee to play cooperatively again until the next incident of noncooperation. For which N is this an equilibrium? For the smallest such N, what are the expected payoffs to the players in this equilibrium?

(d) Now suppose we have a less capricious referee — one that follows instructions with probability .95. Redo parts (a), (b), and (c).

■ 3. In terms of reputation for quality, imagine that we have a firm that can produce a good at any quality level in the interval $[0, 1]$, where 0 means a good of low quality, and 1 means a good of exceptionally high quality. Demand for the good depends on consumer perceptions of the good's quality. If consumers anticipate that the good is of quality q, their demand is given by $P = 4 + 6q - X$, where X is the quantity demanded. Costs of manufacture depend on the quality level of the good being produced; it costs a constant marginal $2 + 6q^2$ to produce a unit of quality level q. Consider the repeated setting described in section 14.5: In each period, the firm chooses a quality level and price. Consumers see the price but not (until after they have bought) the quality level. But consumers do know the level of qualities the firm has produced previously. Assume the firm discounts profits with a discount factor $\alpha = .9$. For which levels of quality q is there a viable reputational equilibrium, that is, an equilibrium where (along the path) the firm produces in each period at quality level q?

■ 4. Recall our discussion of the prisoners' dilemma game in circumstances where one distinguished player plays a sequence of opponents. Each opponent plays only once, but is able to observe what the one player did earlier. We remarked that in this case even though the one player can carry a reputation, it doesn't help because her opponents, who have no reputation, will always play noncooperatively no matter what she does or what she has done previously. In light of this, suppose we change the rules of the prisoners' dilemma so that first the opponent moves in full view of the distinguished player, and then that player responds. Will reputation help in this case?

■ 5. (a) What would happen to the Stackelberg leadership story at the end of section 14.5 if competition in each period were Bertrand style instead of Cournot style?

(b) What would happen to this story if we added noise as in Green and Porter? That is, firms pick their output quantities, and price is then a random function of the sum of the quantities. This is a very open-ended question, but at least consider: Suppose we try to construct a "trigger price" equilibrium, where if price is observed beyond the trigger, we revert to the standard Cournot equilibrium for a while. Should the trigger be above or below the "average" equilibrium price?

■ 6. Prove that in the variation on the centipede game given in figure 14.5(b) the unique sequential equilibrium described is, in fact, the unique Nash equilibrium. (Hint: Take some presumed Nash equilibrium and suppose information set $2n+1$ [for player 2] is the first unreached information set. Derive an immediate contradiction. Then suppose that node $(2n)$t is the first unreached information set and derive a contradiction that is one degree removed from immediate.)

■ 7. The purpose of this problem is to explore what happens in duopoly when the duopolists are able to use two-part tariffs.

(a) Imagine two commodities — snaffle and manna. A single consumer has a utility function of the form $u(x, z) = x - bx^2 + z$, where x is the amount of snaffle consumed, and z is the amount of manna. The price of manna is always set to be 1. This utility function applies for all levels of snaffle, which just goes to show that too much snaffle can be a bad thing.

Two firms sell snaffle, called Ace Snaffle Vendors (ASV) and United Zeus Snaffle (UZS). Although it won't be relevant until the next part of the problem, both of these firms have a simple production technology; they can produce as much snaffle as they want at a variable unit cost of .1 per unit. In addition, they each face a fixed cost K if they decide to produce any snaffle at all; we don't preclude the possibility that $K = 0$. Each firm charges a two-part tariff for snaffle; if a consumer buys any snaffle from the firm at all, the consumer must pay k_i up front, and in addition the consumer must pay c_i per unit snaffle consumed. Here, $i = 1$ for ASV and $i = 2$ for UZS. (You may assume that both k_i and c_i must be nonnegative.)

Suppose our single consumer faces prices k_1 and c_1 from ASV and k_2 and c_2 from UZS. Snaffle is snaffle — it doesn't matter from whom it comes. Characterize as best you can the demand of the consumer.

(b) There is a large number of identical consumers in this economy — say, 100,000. Suppose the snaffle market operates as follows. First, ASV and UZS must declare (simultaneously and independently) whether they wish to produce any snaffle. If they decide to do so, then they incur the fixed cost K. Each sees whether the other has decided to be active or not, and then the active firm(s) (simultaneously and independently) declares its two-part tariff scheme k_i and c_i. Consumers see those two-part tariffs and then decide whether to order any snaffle at all, and from whom. Consumers do this to maximize their utility. Firms act to maximize their (expected) profits.

We are looking for all the subgame-perfect, pure strategy equilibria of this game. As a function of K, what are they?

(c) Now suppose that this sort of game is repeated indefinitely. (N.B., in each period, firms decide whether to "be in" or not [and thus incur the fixed cost that period]; a firm can be out in one period and in the next.) Consumers discount their utility in each period at discount rate .9 per period. Firms discount their profits at the same rate. For $K = 1$, which of the following describe the outcome of a subgame perfect equilibrium. Support your contentions.

(i) Firms are both active in every period, and each makes half of what a monopoly firm would make.

(ii) Only one firm (UZS, say) is active in every period, and this firm makes what a monopoly firm would make.

(iii) Only one firm (ASV, say) is active in every period, and this firm makes zero profits in each period.

chapter fifteen

Bilateral bargaining

After discussing monopoly, many principles and intermediate microeconomics books move on to the cases of *monopsony* (one buyer and many sellers) and *bilateral monopoly* (one buyer and one seller). The analysis of monopsony is straightforward after monopoly; the monopsonist, taking his supply curve $S(x)$ as given, equates the marginal value of the factor to him with the "marginal factor cost," or $S(x) + xS'(x)$. Then there is a paragraph or two about bilateral monopoly. Being unjust to many fine textbooks, an abridged version of what is typically said follows:

> In cases of *bilateral monopoly*, sharp predictions as to what will happen cannot be offered. An efficient exchange between the buyer and seller may be presumed where the marginal cost to the seller is equated to the marginal value of the factor to the buyer. [Many books will be more sophisticated than this and indicate that inefficient trades may take place, owing to the bargaining process.] But the price at which this exchange takes place is indeterminate. The buyer and the seller will, we can safely assume, not agree to a price where either is worse off than if no exchange at all is made. But in general, many prices will meet that requirement and which one will be agreed to is determined by psychological factors; things that determine the bargaining abilities of the two parties, things that are outside the ken of economic science.

This sort of discussion is not limited to bilateral monopoly; in texts that introduce the Edgeworth box and take it seriously as a model of exchange between two individuals, the contract curve (locus of efficient points) will be identified, and there will be a general presumption that some exchange will take place on the contract curve between the indifference curves through the endowment, but typically no prediction will be offered about which point will be chosen.

In this short chapter we will see a bit of what noncooperative game theory has to offer to this rather dismal state of affairs. One might hope that by being more precise about the protocol of bargaining — the rules by which offers are made and accepted or rejected — we can get some more definite idea about what will be the outcome. We will see that this is a case where institutions matter (according to the theory), and rather more than seems sensible, although the extreme and unintuitive sensitivity to institutional form that we see in the theory may be attributable to the starkness of our models in terms of what players know about each other.

15.1. Simultaneous offers and indeterminacy

To make the problem of bilateral bargaining as simple as possible, consider the following one-dimensional version. Two parties, called 1 and 2, are put into a room and told to negotiate on the simple problem of splitting one dollar. If they can agree on a division (within a specified time period), the division they agree to will be implemented. If they fail to agree, each gets nothing.

In fact, this is no more or less stark than the general bargaining problem of an Edgeworth box, if you think about the original endowment as the "no agreement" point, and splits of the dollar representing points along the contract curve inside the lens defined by the two indifference curves through the endowment point. If we allowed the two parties to split the dollar in ways that leave money on the table — for example, 1 gets fifty cents and 2 gets twenty-five — then we would even have representatives of points inside the lens that are off the contract curve.

What will happen here? To sharpen the question, but not the answer, let us be more specific about the rules of this bargaining "game." Suppose that bargaining is to proceed as follows: The two parties simultaneously and independently name a demand. Ms. 1 says, for example, that she demands seventy-five cents, while Mr. 2 demands fifty cents. If these two demands are compatible (which includes the possibility that they leave money on the table), they are implemented and the game ends. If not, each party, knowing what the other party demanded, decides between *standing firm* on his original demand or *acceding* to the other's demand. These decisions are made simultaneously and independently. If both stand firm, both get nothing and the game is over. If one stands firm and the other accedes, the demand of the first person is implemented. If both accede, each gets his or her part of the other person's original demand, which necessarily leaves money on the table.

What we have done here is to move from an ambiguous description of bargaining to very specific, formal rules of negotiation. You should have no trouble depicting the game just described as an extensive form game, especially if we insist that the first round of demands must be in multiples of a penny (so the game has finitely many strategies for each player). This allows us to analyze bargaining using the tools of noncooperative game theory.

For example, we can ask, What are the possible (Nash) equilibria of the game described? Imagine that 1 is playing the strategy: Demand n cents on the first round and stick to that demand on the second, if there is a second. Player 2's best response to this is to demand $100 - n$ or more on the first round and to accede on the second if he demands more than $100 - n$ on the first. Let us choose one of these for his strategy: He will demand $100 - n$ on the first round, and he will stick to that demand on the second. Then 1's strategy is also a best response to 2's, and we have a Nash equilibrium with the split n to player 1 and $100 - n$ to 2.[a] Since n is completely arbitrary here (it even works if $n = 0$ or 100!), we see that *any* division of the dollar is a possible equilibrium. (We can also construct equilibria where the split isn't achieved until the second round.)

So we have offered a more precise description of the bargaining process, but we have gotten back the basic indeterminacy of the answer. Given the very simple nature of this bargaining protocol, we probably can't say that the result will depend on the players' "relative bargaining abilities." But assuming they play to an equilibrium, the players' equilibrium expectations are all-important.

This is not the only bargaining protocol that leads to this sort of indeterminacy. Some variations with the same basic property include:

(a) Instead of the rules given above, each side simultaneously makes a demand. If demands are compatible, the dollar is split. If not, each side again makes a demand, and so on, for M rounds of demands. If no agreement is reached by the end of M rounds, the game is over and each side gets nothing.

(b) The same as (a), except there is no last round; they can make demands for as long as it takes to reach an agreement. If no agreement is reached, each side gets nothing. Or, instead, at the end of each round, either side can simply quit.

(c) The same as (a), except that after each round one penny is removed from the pot. In the first round, the players bargain to split a dollar; in

---

[a] This equilibrium is not subgame perfect. To make it perfect, add: 1 accedes to 2 if 1 asks for more than n on the first round; 2 accedes to 1 if 2 asks for more than $100 - n$ on the first round and 1 asks for n or less. Do you see why these modifications are needed?

the second round, they bargain to split ninety-nine cents; and so on, until all the money is removed (at which point the game is over).

Under any of the rules given, any split, achieved in the first round, is a Nash equilibrium. You should be able to show that in the originally named protocol or in the protocols given in (a) and (b) above, pure strategy Nash equilibria that result in an agreement are always efficient, and the only pure strategy equilibria that don't result in agreement are very special. Protocol (c) opens other possibilities. Consider, for example, the strategies:

> Demand sixty cents on the first two rounds. If your opponent demands sixty cents on the first two rounds, demand forty-nine cents on the third round. If your opponent does anything else on the first two rounds, demand whatever is left in the pot less one cent until all the money is gone.

You should be able to see that this strategy is a best response against itself, leading to a split of ninety-eight cents (only) on the third round.[b]

15.2. Focal equilibria

If you sat actual players down to play exactly according to the rules given above (one round of demands, then one round of "stand" or "accede"), you would find a large number of pairs playing the equilibrium where the dollar is split fifty-fifty. The symmetry of this equilibrium makes it focal. In a long series of experiments, Alvin Roth and his associates have attempted to see just what makes for a good focal point. This series is summarized in Roth (1983); one of his experiments will be reported here (this one in collaboration with Schoumaker, reported in Roth and Schoumaker [1983]).

To begin, we change the rules a little bit. Instead of bargaining over splitting a dollar, we imagine that the two parties are bargaining over one hundred poker chips. The rules for bargaining are the same: One round of simultaneous demands and, if necessary, one round of simultaneous "stand" or "accede." But prizes are awarded a bit differently. At the start, each party is given a prize that he or she might win. Suppose, for example, that 1 might win $20, and 2 might win $5. Each side knows what the two prizes are, each side knows that the other side knows this,

---

[b] Does this strategy against itself constitute a subgame perfect equilibrium? Why not? How could you modify the pair of strategies so that they give a subgame perfect equilibrum while retaining the basic character of the outcome?

and so on. (In other experiments, Roth tried variations in which one party knew the value of both prizes but one party only knew the value of his own.) Suppose the two agree to split the chips: sixty for 1 and thirty-five for 2, leaving five on the table. Then 1 is given a .6 chance of winning her prize of $20, and 2 is given a .35 chance of winning his prize of $5. In other words, each chip is worth a one percent chance of winning a prize, whatever that prize is. (If no agreement is reached, neither side is given any chance at his or her respective prize.)

Just as in the simple split-the-dollar game, any division of the poker chips is a Nash equilibrium of the game; you should have no trouble adapting the old argument to this new setting. But now a fifty-fifty split is no longer so obviously "focal." Now there are at least two competitors:

(a) Give all the chips to 1, since she has the bigger prize.

(b) Split the chips twenty to 1 and eighty to 2. The virtue of this split is that it gives player 1 an expected prize of $(.2)(\$20) = \$4$ and it gives player 2 an expected prize of $(.8)(\$5) = \$4$. That is, this split equalizes the expected prizes of the two.

In earlier experiments, both the fifty-fifty focal equilibrium and the twenty-eighty focal equilibrium had been observed. (Giving all the chips to 1 was not observed.) So Roth and Schoumaker tried the following experiment. All bargaining was done via a computer, so that players never saw each other. Thus Roth and Schoumaker could "condition" their subjects by having them bargain with computers for a while. Subjects played the bargaining game (via a computer) a number of times. Unbeknownst to them, in the first few rounds their opponent was the computer. For some subjects, the computer was programmed to play the fifty-fifty split. For others, the computer was programmed to play the twenty-eighty split. In this way, some subjects were conditioned to believe that the fifty-fifty split was fair or appropriate, while others were conditioned to believe in the twenty-eighty split. And then conditioned subjects were mixed, with results that you can no doubt anticipate: When two subjects who had been conditioned in compatible fashion were paired, they happily went along with the equilibrium they had been taught. When two subjects were paired, one of whom thought he deserved only twenty chips, while the other was willing to settle for fifty, money was left on the table, at least for a while. And when someone who had been trained to expect eighty was paired with someone who had been conditioned to think that fifty-fifty was right, disagreement outcomes were reached.

This experiment reinforces the notion that the bargaining outcomes depend on individual's expectations as to what the outcomes should be. In fact, it makes this point vividly by showing how those expectations can be manipulated through experience. Insofar as noncooperative game theory is silent (or nearly so) on the subject of where equilibrium expectations come from, it seems that the basic textbook commentary on bilateral monopoly and bargaining had it right.

15.3. *Rubinstein's model*

Before giving up on noncooperative game theory as applied to bargaining, however, let us look at one more bargaining protocol, back in the context of splitting a dollar. Imagine that the two players take turns making offers and counteroffers. Player 1 goes first, say; she proposes a split. Player 2 may accept that split immediately or, after a five second delay, make a counteroffer. Player 1, in response to a counteroffer, may accept immediately or, after a five second delay, make a counter-counteroffer, and so forth.

One further feature is added: Players would rather have the money sooner than later. We suppose that both players discount any money they receive at a rate of, say, 10% per year. So if player 1 obtains n immediately after her first offer, this is worth n to her. If she obtains n after player 2's first counteroffer, this is worth slightly less; it is worth δn, where, by the rules of continuous compounding, $\delta = .999999985$ approximately. If she obtains n on the third round (on her second offer), it is worth only $\delta^2 n$ to her, and so on. The same is true for player 2.

This, you might think, changes very little. Suppose, for example, player 1 plays the strategy: Demand n the first round and refuse to accept any offer or make any offer that gives her less than n. It would seem that 2's best response to this, no matter what n is, is to give in immediately. But this doesn't constitute a subgame perfect equilibrium for, say, $n = 60$. To see why, note first that

$$\frac{40}{\delta} + 60\delta < 100.$$

In case this isn't obvious, we give a proof. Consider the function $f(x) = x/\delta + (100 - x)\delta$. Its derivative is $1/\delta - \delta$ which, for $\delta < 1$ is greater than zero. Now let $n^* = 100\delta/(1 + \delta)$. Note that n^* is a tiny bit less than 50, for the particular δ with which we are working; in particular, $n^* > 40$. As a matter of simple algebra,

$$\frac{n^*}{\delta} + (100 - n^*)\delta = 100.$$

(Do it!) So

$$\frac{40}{\delta} + 60\delta = f(40) < f(n^*) = \frac{n^*}{\delta} + (100 - n^*)\delta = 100.$$

Let ϵ be half the difference between 100 and $40/\delta + 60\delta$. And consider the following strategy by player 2. Refuse to take only 40 on the first round. Offer instead to take $40/\delta + \epsilon$ on the second round. If this offer is accepted, player 2 is better off by $\delta\epsilon$ for having made the offer instead of accepting 40. Will player 1 accept? *If she thinks that by turning this offer down she will net 60 on the third round of offers, player 1 does better to accept player 2's offer.* By accepting player 2's offer, player 1 obtains $\delta(100 - 40/\delta - \epsilon) = \delta(60\delta + \epsilon)$ in units that are discounted back to the start of the game. If she spurns player 2's offer, and if she expects to get 60 when it is again her turn to offer, she nets $60\delta^2$ discounted back to the start of the game. So she is better off accepting 2's offer, and 2 is better off making this offer than to accept 40 only on the first round.

The basic result, with proofs

The only place that 60-40 played a role in this argument came where we stated that $40/\delta + 60\delta < 100$. That will be true of any split where player 1 gets more than $100/(1+\delta)$. And it suggests the following remarkable result:

Proposition 1 (Rubinstein, 1982). *The unique subgame perfect equilibrium in the alternating offers model just given is for the player making the offer always to offer to take $100/(1+\delta)$ for himself and leave $100\delta/(1+\delta)$ for the other party, and for the other party always to accept this offer or any better and to spurn any offer that is worse.*

We have to show that this is a subgame perfect equilibrium and that it is unique. Showing that it is a subgame perfect equilibrium is not difficult. Imagine first that it is your turn to make the offer. If you offer to take $100/(1+\delta)$, your offer will be accepted. There is no reason, then, to offer to take anything less. If you ask for more, you will be turned down, and your rival next time will offer you only $100 - 100/(1 + \delta) = 100\delta/(1 + \delta)$. You are meant to accept this, so from the point where you are making the offer, the strategy described above is unimprovable for you in a single step.

It is more interesting to consider whether your strategy is unimprovable when you are being made an offer. Suppose your rival offers to take n, leaving you with $100 - n$. If you reject this offer and then conform to the equilibrium above, you will get $100/(1 + \delta)$ next time. In current value units, this is worth $100\delta/(1 + \delta)$ to you today. So you should accept whenever $100 - n > 100\delta/(1 + \delta)$, reject when the inequality is strict the other way, and do either when there is equality. But if you work through the algebra, this is precisely the strategy you are meant to be carrying out. We have equality when $n = 100/(1+\delta)$, and we resolve the knife-edge case of equality by having you accept.

Thus we have a subgame perfect equilibrium. The remarkable part of the proposition is that this is the unique subgame perfect equilibrium. We will sketch an argument due to Shaked and Sutton (1984).

Step 1. Let ν be the largest amount that any player can achieve in any subgame perfect equilibrium when the player is making the offer. We claim that $\nu \leq 100/(1 + \delta)$. The proof essentially uses the argument we gave just before the proposition. First, if ν is the largest amount that a player can achieve in any subgame perfect equilibrium when it is his turn to make the offer, then an offer to give a player $\delta\nu + \epsilon$ for any $\epsilon > 0$ is sure to be accepted; the best that a player receiving this offer can do by rejecting it is ν a period later, which nets $\delta\nu$ in current value terms, which is less than the $\delta\nu + \epsilon$ that is offered.

Second, if ν is the largest amount that a player can achieve in any subgame perfect equilibrium when it is his turn to make the offer, it must be achieved by making an acceptable offer on the first round. If the first offer is rejected, then the second player can offer, say, $(\delta\nu + \nu)/2$, which the first player is bound to accept by the argument just given (since $(\delta\nu + \nu)/2 > \delta\nu$). But $(\delta\nu + \nu)/2 < \nu$, and since it is delayed for a period, it is worth $\delta(\delta\nu + \nu)/2$, which is even less.

So ν must be achieved by making an initial offer that is accepted.[c] Suppose $\nu > 100/(1 + \delta)$ and the first player demands ν. The second player can reject this and offer $\delta\nu + \epsilon$, for ϵ equal to half the difference

---

[c] This is a bit sloppy, in that it presumes that the least upper bound on subgame perfect payoffs is achieved in a subgame perfect equilibrium. If we were being careful, we would have ν be the supremum over all subgame perfect equilibrium payoffs and then show that any demand sufficiently close to ν will be rejected if $\nu > 100/(1 + \delta)$.

between 100 and $\delta\nu + (100 - \nu)/\delta$, which is positive if $\nu > 100/(1 + \delta)$. This is sure to be accepted by the first paragraph. And it gives the second player a payoff of $100 - \delta\nu - \epsilon = (100 - \nu)/\delta + \epsilon$ next period, or $100 - \nu + \delta\epsilon$ in present value terms, which is better than the $100 - \nu$ obtained by acceding to the initial demand of the first player. Hence a demand of ν will be rejected if $\nu > 100/(1 + \delta)$, and $\nu > 100/(1 + \delta)$ cannot be a subgame perfect equilibrium payoff for the first player.

Step 2. Given this, any player can be certain that any offer to give more than $100\delta/(1 + \delta)$ will be taken. By rejecting this offer, the best one's rival can do is $100/(1 + \delta)$ starting with her next offer, which is strictly worse than $100\delta/(1 + \delta) + \epsilon$ for any $\epsilon > 0$, however small, immediately.

Step 3. The party to whom the first offer is made can never have a payoff exceeding $100\delta/(1 + \delta)$. For if this party had a payoff exceeding this level, the payoff to the party making the first offer would have to be less than $100/(1 + \delta)$, which contradicts step 2.

Step 4. In equilibrium, any offer to give less than $100\delta/(1 + \delta)$ will certainly be rejected. In fact, the party to whom the first offer is made is assured of a payoff (in present value terms) of at least $100\delta/(1 + \delta)$. If offered less than $100\delta/(1 + \delta)$, one can reject and offer a bit more than $100\delta/(1 + \delta)$ to the other side next time. This is sure to be taken, by step 2. But this means you can be sure to get any amount strictly less than $100/(1 + \delta)$ next time, some one of which will be better than taking something less than $100\delta/(1 + \delta)$ this time.

Step 5. In the unique subgame perfect equilibrium, the party making the first offer proposes to take $100/(1 + \delta)$ and to give $100\delta/(1 + \delta)$, and this is accepted with certainty. No offer to give more can be part of an equilibrium, by step 2. No offer to give less can be part of an equilibrium. It will certainly be rejected by step 4, and then the best one can do, starting from the next period, is less than $100\delta/(1 + \delta)$ (by step 3). This is worse than taking something a bit less than $100/(1 + \delta)$, which is certain to be accepted, by step 2. So the only possible equilibrium offer is $100/(1 + \delta)$. And that must be taken with certainty in any equilibrium: If not, the party making the first offer would do better to offer slightly less than $100/(1 + \delta)$ and be certain of acceptance.

Where, you may ask, did we use subgame perfection? We used it very directly in steps 1 and 2, when we said that an offer would certainly be taken, even if the offer is out of equilibrium, because the person to whom it was made could not do better by rejecting it. If we looked only at Nash equilibria, players' responses to counteroffers that are made out of equilibrium are not bound by "rationality" constraints of this sort.

At the risk of overdoing it, we claim a further result: The equilibrium described above is the only equilibrium that survives iterated elimination of dominated strategies.[1] We will only get the argument started and leave it to you to finish. (a) Suppose player 1 offers to player 2 that he (player 2) may have more than 100δ. Then player 2 is bound to accept; if he rejects, he must wait a period (that is, five seconds) and then the best he could conceivably do is to get the entire dollar, which is worth (in present value terms) no more than 100δ. That is, we can remove from consideration any strategy that includes rejection of such a generous offer. (b) Suppose player 1 offers to player 2 something less than $(100-100\delta)\delta$. Then player 2 should definitely turn this down, because he can, in his turn, offer to player 1 that she take 100δ and be sure to be accepted. This would (next period) leave him with no worse than $(100-100\delta)$, which in present value terms is no worse than $(100-100\delta)\delta$. There is no reason to take less today. Thus we can remove from consideration any strategy that includes acceptance of such a miserly offer. (c) The argument in (b) means that a player can never hope to get more than $100(1-\delta+\delta^2)$. Suppose, then, one player offers something more than $100\delta(1-\delta+\delta^2)$ to his rival. If she turns it down, she can hope to do no better than $100(1-\delta+\delta^2)$ starting next period, which is worse. So she is sure to accept. We can remove strategies that include rejection of such generous (but less generous than in [a]) offers. (d) Now that you know a slightly wider band of offers that are sure to be accepted, return to part (b) and expand the set of offers that are sure to be rejected, and so on. In the end, all strategies that accept less or reject more than $100\delta/(1+\delta)$ are removed, and the equilibrium is forced.

Bargaining over general issues

The result just given extends far beyond splitting a dollar. Imagine two players bargaining over many different commodities or many different clauses in a contract. In general, we might imagine that some abstract set X represents the range of possible agreements. For example, if the two parties are bargaining over how to split a bundle $e \in R^K$ of commodities, then $X = \{(x_1, x_2) \in R^{2K} : x_1 + x_2 \leq e\}$, with the interpretation that the point $x = (x_1, x_2)$ represents an agreement where the first person gets the bundle x_1, the second gets x_2, and $e - x_1 - x_2$ is left on the table. Or we could imagine two parties bargaining over a labor contract, and then the various components of x represent the basic wage rate, the level and nature of overtime wages, the level and nature of health benefits, work rules, and so on.

---

[1] I first heard this argument from Drew Fudenberg.

Each of the two parties derives utility from the various possible splits; we let $u_i(x)$ be the utility that i obtains (immediately) from an agreement on x. If agreement is delayed until time t, i derives net utility $\delta^t u_i(x)$, with u_i normalized so that no agreement gives zero utility. Finally, we imagine alternating offer bargaining; the first player makes an offer (of the form x) at date 0, to which the second player can agree or not. If the second player rejects this offer, then the second party can make a counteroffer after a delay of one period, which the first player accepts or rejects, and so on.

As long as the preferences (utility functions) of the two players are common knowledge between them, this situation is not much more complex than the basic model of splitting one dollar. There is a set of feasible utility imputations, the image of X in R^2 under the vector function (u_1, u_2) (see section 5.1 if you've forgotten about utility imputations), and the two are (essentially) bargaining over which point in the set of feasible utility imputations to select. We will write V for the space of feasible utility imputations, and V^* for the space of feasible utility imputations that are as good as the no-agreement outcome; i.e., $v = (v_1, v_2) \in V^*$ if $v = (u_1(x), u_2(x))$ for some $x \in X$ and $v_1, v_2 \geq 0$.

Assume that V^* is a compact, convex set. Assume that the Pareto frontier of V^* is strictly downward sloping. And assume there is some point v^* in V^* that is strictly better for both players than disagreement. (You may wish to consider more fundamental assumptions that would justify these assumptions.)

Proposition 2. *The (essentially) unique subgame perfect equilibrium of this bargaining game has player 1 offering a point x_1 whenever it is her turn to offer, player 2 offering a point x_2, and both sides accepting the other's offer, where x_1 and x_2 are Pareto efficient agreements satisfying the equations*

$$\delta u_1(x^1) = u_1(x^2) \quad \text{and} \quad \delta u_2(x^2) = u_2(x^1).$$

We have called this an (essentially) unique equilibrium because the utility imputations $v^1 = (u_1(x^1), u_2(x^1))$ and $v^2 = (u_1(x^2), u_2(x^2))$ are unique. But there may be more than one pair of points x^1 and x^2 that give these utility imputations.

The proof is left as an exercise, or see Binmore, Osborne, and Rubinstein (forthcoming). If you take on this exercise, you may find it interesting to consider what happens to the solution as δ goes to one. (Assume the Pareto frontier of V^* is given by a differentiable curve.)

Variations

If it seems remarkable that with these rules we get such definite predictions, let us observe that similar arguments give even more remarkable results. We will give five variations on proposition 1 (so we are back to splitting one dollar), each of which you can prove using the techniques sketched previously.

(1) *Outside options.* Suppose that the bargaining game is just as before, except that player 1 has an outside option. Specifically, she can, after hearing an offer from player 2, choose to accept, to make a counteroffer (after five seconds), or to break off negotiations and take her outside option, which gives her, say, forty-five cents and leaves player 2 with nothing.

Your intuition might be that this strengthens the bargaining position of player 1. But in terms of the theory it does not; the old subgame perfect equilibrium remains the unique subgame perfect equilibrium in this case. (This depends on our choice of δ; in general, it requires that $\delta/(1+\delta) > .45$.)

(2) *Different discount rates.* Suppose that the bargaining game is as above, except that player 1 discounts her payoff at an interest rate of 5% per year, and player 2 discounts his payoff at 15% per year. Then the unique subgame perfect equilibrium gives approximately seventy-five cents to player 1 and twenty-five cents to player 2.

This may not seem entirely unintuitive to you. Player 1 is in a stronger bargaining position because she is more patient. But it may be surprising that, when offers are made every five seconds, the difference in levels of patience should have such dramatic results in terms of the outcome.

(3) *Different speeds of response.* Suppose that the bargaining game is as before (with both parties having the same discount rate), but player 1 can make a counteroffer two seconds after hearing player 2's offer, and player 2 takes six seconds to formulate and make a counteroffer. Then the unique subgame perfect equilibrium gives approximately seventy-five cents to player 1 and twenty-five cents to player 2.

(4) *A variation on different speeds of response.* Suppose that the bargaining game is as before, with two changes: Player 1 can respond two seconds after player 2 makes an offer, and player 2 can respond six seconds after player 1 makes an offer. And acceptance is delayed as much as a counteroffer; e.g., if player 1 makes an offer, player 2 cannot respond in any fashion either to accept or to counteroffer for six seconds. Then the unique subgame perfect equilibrium gives approximately twenty-five cents to player 1 and seventy-five cents to player 2.

(5) *Costs of rejecting offers instead of discounting.* Suppose that the players are bargaining to split $10. In this formulation, they take turns making offers, but there is no discounting. Instead, every time player 1 turns down an offer of player 2, she must pay a fee of $.10, whereas every time player 2 turns down an offer of player 1, he must pay a fee of $.11. Then the unique subgame perfect equilibrium is: If player 1 is making the offer, she proposes to take the entire $10, to which player 2 agrees. If player 2

is making the offer, he offers to take $.10 and to give her $9.90, to which she assents.

Although we didn't say it, in each of these variations, all the subgame perfect equilibria have the initial offer accepted with probability one.

(Readers often find the result for variation (5) astounding, so let us sketch the argument here. Let x be the highest subgame perfect payoff player 2 can get if he makes the first offer. Suppose $x \geq \$.11$. Then if player 1 has the initial offer, she can offer $x - .11 + \epsilon$ to player 2 and be sure it will be accepted, for any $\epsilon > 0$, since if player 2 rejects, the best he can do is $x - .11$. If player 2 proposes, in his turn, to take x and leave player 1 with $\$10 - x$, player 1 will reject the offer, since she can get $\$10.00 - x + .11 - \epsilon$ next time, at a cost of only $.10. This will leave player 2 with $x - .11 + \epsilon$ next time, which is certainly less than x. So there is no way that x can exceed or equal $\$.11$.[d] Suppose $x < .11$. Then player 1, when she has the offer, can be sure of acceptance if she proposes to take the entire $\$10.00$. Hence she will not agree to take anything less than $9.90 when it is 2's turn to offer; better to refuse and then pocket the entire $\$10.00$. The rest of the argument is easy.)

What lies behind these results

If the result that there is a unique subgame perfect equilibrium is surprising, some of the further results listed above are positively astounding. You might make the case that (1) while perhaps a bit counterintuitive is not outlandish. And there is even some sense to (2), although the differences in discount rates seem to lead to quite extraordinary differences in the outcome. But what are we to make of (3), (4), and (5)? The "solution" bounces around an incredible amount for what seem to be insignificant differences in the bargaining protocol. And, in any case, you might wonder why alternating offer bargaining leads to such different results than simultaneous offer bargaining. Is it the alternation per se?

To understand what is driving the basic Rubinstein result and why we get such extraordinary results in the variations above, consider the following very simple form of bargaining over a dollar, in a situation where players discount their payoffs at a rate of, say, 10% per year. Player 1 makes the first proposal and, at the same time she makes her offer, she is able to "lock" her offer for any length of time she desires up to, say, one hundred years. That is, she can say, "I propose to take ninety-five cents and to leave five cents for you. And I hereby disable myself from amending

---

[d] This last step is a little sloppy, and we leave it to the careful reader to make it right.

this generous offer or from accepting any counteroffer you might choose to make for ninety-eight years. What is your response?"

Player 2, faced with this offer, is going to accept (if he doesn't get mad, a sentiment with which we will deal in a bit but ignore for now). If he rejects this offer, he will be unable to do anything for ninety-eight years. And even if after ninety-eight years he gets the entire one dollar, it will be worth far less to him (when discounted) than five cents today.

The point is that player 1 by locking her offer puts the onus entirely on player 2. If player 2 wants a better deal, he must wait; he alone can avoid the waiting period by accepting player 1's offer.

This is what is going on in Rubinstein-style bargaining. Once one party makes an offer, the other party alone can avoid the expense of waiting by accepting. If the offer is insufficiently generous, the respondent may indeed wish to suffer the cost of waiting. But then the party making the offer, in equilibrium, makes an offer just sufficiently generous so that the other party is indifferent between accepting or waiting the necessary length of time and then making an offer that is just sufficiently generous so the first party is indifferent between accepting or waiting.... The uniqueness result is not quite intuitive or obvious, but you should be convinced that what drives these equilibria is that each party when it is making an offer is able to put the onus of waiting entirely on the other side.

With this in mind, consider variations (3) and (4) above. In variation (3), player 1 makes an offer that player 2 can accept or reject immediately. But if player 2 wishes to counteroffer, he must wait six seconds. Player 1, on the other hand, must wait only two seconds before counteroffering. Hence, having heard player 1's offer, if player 2 wishes to counteroffer, he must pay three times the waiting cost that player 1 must pay if she wishes to counteroffer. In variation (4), player 1's offer cannot be accepted by player 2 for six seconds, which is the same length of time it takes player 2 to formulate a counteroffer. So the "waiting cost" to player 2 of counteroffering is not six seconds — he must wait that long anyway — but the two additional seconds it takes player 1 to accept or counter. And the waiting cost incurred by player 1 of rejecting an offer of 2 is the six further seconds it will take 2 to respond in any fashion. Hence in (4), player 1 pays the much heavier waiting cost, and her bargaining position is much weaker.

Alternating offers, per se, are not the key here. This point can be made by considering the model of Perry and Reny (1989). In this variation, players can make offers whenever they wish. That is, at any point in time a player is able to make an offer, even if his opponent is simultaneously making an offer. But there is one limitation: If player 1 makes an offer at time t, then she cannot change the offer she has made for a set small amount of time, say for six seconds. And player 2 cannot change his offer for some given amount of time, say two seconds. Otherwise, when offers are made is entirely up to the players; there is no alternating structure of anything like that. Bargaining terminates when the two offers made are compatible.[e] Payoffs are discounted at given rates which, for the sake of exposition, we take to be identical.

This game doesn't quite have a unique subgame perfect equilibrium, but it comes close. Specifically, every subgame perfect equilibrium gives players payoffs that are approximately seventy-five cents to player 1 and twenty-five cents to player 2. How does this work? Imagine that the very best equilibrium outcome for player 1 gives her appreciably more than seventy-five cents. Look at some equilibrium that supports this outcome. Player 2 can deviate from this equilibrium by proposing slightly better terms for himself at a time when player 1 is either free to move or is just about to become free to move. By doing so, player 2 freezes his own ability to move for two seconds. *Now everything is up to player 1. She can agree to what player 2 has just proposed, or she can counterpropose, but if she counterproposes, she knows that player 2 is unable to respond for two seconds. The cost of waiting those two seconds is entirely on her shoulders; player 2 is committed for this length of time.* This is just the wedge we had before in alternating offers, and it works virtually the same way here, even though there is no set order of moves and simultaneous offers are feasible, in principle. The key to bargaining power here, in Rubinstein's model, and in the other variations given comes from the ability to put the onus of waiting entirely on the other party.

15.4. The experimental evidence about alternating offers

While the logical key to Rubinstein-style results may now be clear, this isn't to say that we believe these results are empirically valid. To take an analogy, we may understand why the unique subgame perfect equilibrium of the centipede game is for the first player to move to end the game, and at the same time we may give little weight to this analytical conclusion as an empirical prediction. We are motivated, therefore, to seek evidence concerning what happens when individuals do bargain in the fashion of alternating offers.

---

[e] There are some mathematical niceties to be observed to make sure that everything is well-defined. And the definition of subgame perfection is not entirely straightforward. We give here a synopsis only. The reader should consult Perry and Reny (1989) for details.

Ochs and Roth (1989) give a survey and some fresh results of their own concerning experiments with alternating offer bargaining. In the papers they survey and in their own experiments, the bargaining protocols used are different from Rubinstein's in one important way: In all the experiments, time horizons are very short — sometimes two, sometimes three, and (very rarely) five rounds of bargaining at most. That is, one player makes an offer, the second may counteroffer, and the first may, perhaps, counter-counteroffer, but that is all. If the third offer is not taken, the game is over and neither side wins anything.

This doesn't compromise the theory much at all; if anything, it makes it a good deal simpler. In finite horizon, alternating offer bargaining, if you accept the complete information bargaining model, backwards induction gives you the answer quite quickly.[2] (See problems 6 and 7.) So it is the predictions of backwards induction in the context of bargaining that are being tested.

Ochs and Roth were led by the data they reported to the conclusion that whatever drives the outcomes in alternating offer bargaining is something more complex than the theoretical considerations provided by backwards induction. In particular, notions of equity intrude: In cases where backwards induction yields a very unequal split, proposals for splits that are so unequal are often rejected, *even though by rejecting the offer the rejecting party is giving up money for sure.*

For example, imagine two rounds of bargaining according to the following rules. Player 1 can propose any split she wishes of $10.00. Player 2 can accept or reject. If player 2 rejects, he can propose any split that he wishes, except that $9.00 of $10.00 is "removed"; he can propose a split of $1.00. (This is like a discount factor of .1.) If player 1 rejects player 2's proposal, the two walk away empty-handed. Backwards induction in this case tells us that player 2, in the event that he is given the opportunity to propose a split, proposes to take $1.00 or $.99, to which player 1 accedes.[3] As player 2 can't possibly do better than $1.00 in the second round, player 1 in the first will propose that she will take $9.00 or perhaps $8.99, which he will accept. But experimental results don't conform to this prediction. In cases where player 1 proposes to take $8.99, player 2 sometimes rejects, presumably on grounds that player 1's "excessive greed" should not be rewarded.

Of course, this sort of consideration puts bargaining in quite a different light from that cast by the theories described above. If player 2 in the

---

[2] The theory of finite horizon, alternating offer bargaining is developed in Stahl (1972).

[3] Because there are "ties" in the game tree and money is not really perfectly divisible, the predictions are not quite sharp.

situation described has some personal notions of what constitutes equity or excessive greed, and if player 1 is unsure what those notions are, then player 1's initial offer will have as much to do with her assessment about player 2's notions as with the amount of money that will be left on the table if player 2 is allowed to counteroffer. Insofar as one player will not know for sure what his rival views as "greed" or "equity," the simple models of complete information that we have analyzed are missing important pieces of the puzzle.

Moving beyond the experimental evidence so far collected, imagine that we stage infinite horizon bargaining experiments where subjects' discount rates are different. How would we go about controlling discount factors in the laboratory? One experimental procedure that could be followed, which gives discount rates .99 and .97 to the two bargainers, is easily described. First (and for reasons to be explained later), rather than have players bargain over some monetary sum directly, we have them bargain over a "unit of probability." If they split this unit with .643 going to player 1 and .324 going to player 2 (which leaves "probability" .033 on the table), then player 1 is given a .643 chance of winning some monetary prize, and player 2 is given a .324 chance of winning some (other) prize. From the point of view of the theory, it doesn't matter what these prizes are or that they are the same, or even that each player knows what prize the other player is going to get; in essence, as long as winning the prize is better than not, players are bargaining over expected utility, and the theory above applies. But to be definite, we will assume that the players know each others' prizes, know that each knows this, and so on. Players negotiate via computer terminals. Player 1 types in an initial offer, which appears on 2's screen. Player 2 can accept 1's offer or can propose a counteroffer. Player 1 can accept 2's counteroffer or can propose a counter-counteroffer, and so on. And to simulate discount rates, instruct players as follows (for example): Player 1 makes the first offer — x_1 for herself, and x_2 for player 2, where $x_1 + x_2 \leq 1$. If player 2 accepts, then player 1 is given an x_1 chance of winning her prize, and player 2 is given an x_2 chance of winning his. Or player 2 can counteroffer, proposing y_2 for himself and y_1 for her, where $y_1 + y_2 \leq 1$. If player 1 accepts this, player 2 is given a $.97y_2$ chance of winning his prize, and player 1 is given a $.99y_1$ chance of winning hers. Or player 1 can counter with z_1 and z_2. If this is accepted, player 1 is given a $.99^2 z_1$ chance of winning her prize, and player 2 is given a $.97^2 z_2$ chance of winning his, and so on. (Of course, if players value the time they spend in the laboratory bargaining, then we have not completely controlled for the costs they expend in back-and-forth bargaining. Perfect experimental controls are not going to be possible.)

If we run the experiment just described, with (say) the prize of player 1 being $20 and the prize of player 2 being $5, the theory predicts that the players will settle on player 1 getting approximately a .75 chance of her prize and player 2 getting a .25 chance of his.[4] If we change the discount factors so that player 1 "discounts" with .97 and player 2 with .99, but we keep the prizes the same, the theory predicts that the agreed-to probabilities will reverse. Since to my knowledge this experiment hasn't been run, it is not possible to say what will result. But my personal conjecture is that the results will not confirm the theory.

Now consider the following elaboration, in the spirit of Roth and Schoumaker (1983). Have the players bargain via computer and exactly as in Roth and Schoumaker (1983) train the parties to expect a particular split. By having players first play against computer programs, train some players to think that a .2–.8 split is the "right" thing to do (where the .8 goes to player 2 because his prize is smaller), and train others to think that a .5–.5 split is what one does in this case. Do this under a number of alternating move protocols, with discount factors varied (but kept close to one). This elaboration is offered to propose the hypothesis that "equilibrium expectations," developed by the conditioning phase, will organize the data of subsequent bargaining much better than will the theoretical predictions based on models of complete information. "Institutional details" concerning who has which discount rate and what is the precise protocol of bargaining will be swamped by expectations as to what one can expect to get and what one expects must be given in order to come to agreement.

15.5. Models with incomplete information

Assuming the conjecture just offered is correct, the theorists' response is clear: Move beyond models of complete information. By moving to models with incomplete information, one hopes that the extreme and unintuitive sensitivity of equilibrium outcomes to "small" changes in the bargaining protocol that we saw above will disappear.

At the same time, a striking feature of the Rubinstein equilibrium is that agreements are always Pareto efficient; in particular, agreement is

---

[4] We have players bargaining over probabilities so that they can have different monetary valuations for the marginal unit over which they bargain. We could as well have had them bargaining over one hundred chips, with different dollar:chip exchange rates. That is, each chip could be worth $.20 to player 1 and $.05 to player 2. But on theoretical grounds, having them bargain over probabilities is cleaner, because attitudes toward risk are not impounded into the experiment. See Roth (1985) on this general point.

immediate. Recall the "abridgement" from standard textbooks with which
we began this chapter and in particular the remark that one might obtain
inefficient trades "because of the bargaining process." We see nothing like
this in the Rubinstein equilibrium; we see no inefficiencies of any sort.
Given the prevalence of labor disputes and other forms of protracted (and,
presumably, wasteful) negotiations in reality, it seems that the Rubinstein
equilibrium is missing something. The theorist's response to this has been
that what is missing is missing from the game that is formulated, where
the preferences of both sides are common knowledge; what is needed to
get delay to agreement and other sorts of inefficiencies is some sort of
incomplete information.

Accordingly, much of the recent literature on bargaining and especially on alternating offer bargaining concerns models with incomplete
information. In these analyses, it has been typical to base the incomplete
information on something tangible about the bargainers. For example, we
might imagine the two parties negotiating on a selling price for some asset, where the value of the asset to the potential buyer is not known to the
seller. If the buyer values the asset highly, he (the buyer) is more impa-
tient to conclude negotiations; this is meant to make the buyer "weaker"
in any negotiations. There has also been some investigation of models
with two-sided incomplete information, where in addition to uncertainty
about the buyer's valuation of the asset the value of the asset to the seller
is unknown to the buyer.

These formulations do not directly address what we see in the experimental literature and what we have conjectured will be found in subsequent experiments. There is no "tangible uncertainty" at work in the Ochs
and Roth experiments. Rather, what seems to be at work are the beliefs of
one player concerning equity and greed and the assessment of the other
player about the beliefs of the first. It is not clear a priori that the forms
of incomplete information that have been investigated so far will speak
adequately to effects driven by these other sorts of considerations. But
any opinions about this are dangerous; this is an area of active and on-
going research, and opinions rendered here will probably be obsolete in
very short order.

In any event, the analysis of bargaining with incomplete information
very quickly becomes very complex (try the last piece of problem 8 and
problem 9 if you want evidence) — a level more complex, for example,
than the analysis of the centipede game in chapter 14. (This is so because
while one has the same back-and-forth structure as in the centipede game,
now what a player can do in his turn, namely make an offer, is a lot richer
than the simple binary choice present in the centipede game.) Hence we

will not pursue this topic further here; the literature awaits the interested reader.

15.6. Bibliographic notes

The development of noncooperative models of bargaining has been one of the most important and active areas in microeconomics and game theory in the past decade. There are far too many important papers to list them all here. Begin with Nash (1950), who notes the basic problem of indeterminacy in simultaneous offer bargaining. And the classic paper on alternating offer bargaining, Rubinstein (1982), should not be missed. But rather than give references beyond these, I suggest that the reader continue with Osborne and Rubinstein (forthcoming), which provides a comprehensive survey of the field, including work on bargaining with incomplete information. Included also in Osborne and Rubinstein is a topic we have not discussed at all — connections between bargaining theory and the "institutional foundations" of Walrasian (price) equilibrium.

For results in bargaining experiments, the cited papers by Ochs and Roth (1989) and Roth (1983) are good places to start.

Given the lack of sharp predictions in simultaneous offer bidding, much attention has been paid to the axiomatic analysis of bargaining. In a typical analysis, one poses a number of desirable properties for a function that will associate to each bargaining problem out of a class of bargaining problems a "solution," and then one sees whether those properties (a) can be satisfied and (b) pin down the "solution." The classic example of this sort of analysis is the Nash bargaining solution, as developed originally by Nash (1953). This form of analysis, which is more in the style of cooperative game theory, is surveyed in Roth (1979).

References

Binmore, K., M. Osborne, and A. Rubinstein. Forthcoming. "Noncooperative Bargaining Models." In *The Handbook of Game Theory*, R. Aumann and S. Hart, eds. Amsterdam: North Holland.

Nash, J. 1950. "The Bargaining Problem." *Econometrica* 18:155–62.

————. 1953. "Two-person Cooperative Games." *Econometrica* 21:128–40.

Ochs, J., and A. Roth. 1989. "An Experimental Study of Sequential Bargaining." *American Economic Review* 79:355–84.

Osborne, M., and A. Rubinstein. Forthcoming. *Bargaining and Markets*. Boston: Academic Press.

Perry, M., and P. Reny. 1989. "Non-cooperative Bargaining without Procedures." University of Western Ontario. Mimeo.

Roth, A. 1979. *Axiomatic Models of Bargaining,* Lecture Notes in Economics and Mathematical Systems no. 170. Berlin: Springer-Verlag.

_____. 1983. "Toward a Theory of Bargaining: An Experimental Study in Economics." *Science* 220:687–91.

_____. 1985. "Laboratory Experimentation in Economics." In *Advances in Economic Theory*, T. Bewley, ed., 269–99. Cambridge: Cambridge University Press.

Roth, A., and F. Schoumaker. 1983. "Expectations and Reputations in Bargaining: An Experimental Study." *American Economic Review* 73:362–72.

Rubinstein, A. 1982. "Perfect Equilibrium in a Bargaining Model." *Econometrica* 50:97–109.

Shaked, A., and J. Sutton. 1984. "Involuntary Unemployment as a Perfect Equilibrium in a Bargaining Model." *Econometrica* 52:1351–64.

Stahl, I. 1972. *Bargaining Theory*. Stockholm: Economics Research Institute.

15.7. Problems

■ 1. Consider two firms, one of which is the sole producer of a factor input that is used solely by the second. The producer of this good is characterized by increasing marginal costs of production for the good in question, and the user obtains decreasing marginal benefit (measured in terms of impact on profits) as it increases the scale of its use of this good. Both firms seek to maximize their profits. (You may assume that the marginal cost to produce the first unit of this good is less than the marginal value to the user of the first unit, and for some large enough amount the marginal cost exceeds the marginal value. You may also assume that marginal cost and marginal benefit functions are continuous.)

We asserted at the start of this chapter that this is a special case of an Edgeworth box. How is it special? (Hint: Your first task is to identify the second good.)

■ 2. Consider the bargaining protocol described in section 15.1 — one round of simultaneous demands, and then (if a deal is not struck in the first round) simultaneous declarations that players stand firm or accede.

(a) Build a subgame perfect, pure strategy equilibrium for this bargaining protocol in which agreement is not reached on the first round, and the equilibrium split is n to player 1 and $100 - n$ to player 2. Be careful in describing the strategies; this isn't hard, but it isn't trivial either.

(b) Show that for any pure strategy equilibrium that results in agreement, no money is left on the table. Show this as well for variations (a) and (b) in section 15.1. Describe the pure strategy equilibria that leave money on the table (if any exist). Are the equilibria you describe subgame perfect?

(c) Build a subgame perfect equilibrium for this bargaining protocol in which money is left on the table and there is agreement with positive probability. (This will involve mixed strategies, according to part [b].)

■ 3. (a) Provide a proof of proposition 2. Before doing this, you might wish to explore part (c).

(b) Suppose that the Pareto frontier of V^* is differentiable. What happens to the equilibrium in proposition 2 as δ approaches 1? (What happens if the frontier of V^* is not differentiable?)

(c) In the context of proposition 2, suppose that V^* is the unit square. That is, $V^* = \{(v_1, v_2) : 0 \le v_1 \le 1 \text{ and } 0 \le v_2 \le 1\}$. What are the subgame perfect equilibria for alternating offer bargaining in this case?

■ 4. For each of the five variations on the basic Rubinstein model outlined in section 5.3, show that there is a unique subgame perfect equilibrium that gives the outcomes claimed. (You were given quite a good start on variation [5]!)

■ 5. Suppose we have the basic Rubinstein model, except that for reasons of feasibility, the only splits of \$1 that can be proposed are those that involve integer multiples of \$.01. Suppose that $\delta = .9999$. What happens to proposition 1?

■ 6. Take the simple Rubinstein alternating offer structure where both players have the same discount factor per bargaining period. Imagine, though, that there are only two rounds of bargaining. Player 1 makes an offer, which 2 can accept or reject. If player 2 rejects player 1's original offer, he can make a counteroffer, which player 1 can accept or reject. What is (are?) the subgame perfect equilibrium of this game?

■ 7. Redo problem 6, but assuming that precisely N rounds of bargaining are permitted. What is the limit of the equilibrium outcome as N approaches infinity? Repeat this exercise for each of the five variations on the basic Rubinstein model outlined in section 5.3.

■ 8. Suppose we have one-sided bargaining. Player 1, say, proposes a split which player 2 can accept or reject. If player 2 rejects, player 1 can propose another split for 2's consideration, and so on, until an agreement is reached. Each time player 1 makes an offer, the prizes eventually achieved are discounted by δ, for some $\delta < 1$.

What is (are?) the subgame perfect equilibrium of this game? Do you believe this as an empirical prediction? (A real challenge: Build a model of this sort of bargaining, where player 2 has an "equity threshold"; he won't take any offer below this threshold, and player 1 is unsure what 2's threshold is.)

■ 9. Consider the following incomplete information variation on the Rubinstein model. Two players are bargaining over splitting $10.00. They take turns making offers, with discount factor $\delta = .999999$ applied every time an offer is rejected. Player 1 seeks to maximize her expected payoff. There is incomplete information about player 2. Player 1 assesses probability π that player 2 seeks to maximize his expected payoff, and she assesses probability $1 - \pi$ that he will ask for $8.00 precisely every time he is able to offer, and he will resolutely turn down any offer that leaves him with less than $8.00.

(a) Construct a sequential equilibrium for this bargaining game for the case $\pi = .2$. (This is hard, but not impossible.)

(b) Construct a sequential equilibrium for this bargaining game for the case $\pi = .8$. (This is harder.)

(c) Construct a sequential equilibrium for every possible value of π (and, in particular, for π very close to one). (Good luck!)

part IV

Topics in information economics

chapter sixteen

Moral hazard and incentives

Prologue to part IV

We turn now to the subject of *information economics*. Information economics is a broad subject with many variations and subtopics, and we will not do anything close to full justice to it here. In this chapter, we consider the problem of *moral hazard*, where one party to a transaction may undertake certain actions that (a) affect the other party's valuation of the transaction but that (b) the second party cannot monitor/enforce perfectly. A classic example here is fire insurance, where the insuree may or may not exhibit sufficient care while storing flammable materials. The "solution" to a problem of moral hazard is the use of *incentives* — structuring the transaction so that the party who undertakes the actions will, in his own best interests, take actions that the second party would (relatively) prefer. For example, fire insurance is often only partial insurance so that the insuree has a financial interest in preventing a fire.

In chapter 17 we look at problems of *adverse selection* where one party to a transaction knows things pertaining to the transaction that are relevant to but unknown by the second party. Here a classic example is life insurance, where the insuree may know things about the state of her health that are unknown by the insurer. The "solution" to problems of adverse selection is *market signaling*, where the party in possession of superior information signals what she knows through her actions. For example, an insurance company may offer life insurance on better terms if the insuree is willing to accept very limited benefits for the first two or three years the policy is in effect, on the presumption that someone who suffers from ill health and is about to die (or has substantial probability of dying) is unwilling to accept those limited benefits.

Whenever there are informational problems of these or other sorts it is natural to ask, What is the best contract that can be devised? We will investigate optimal incentives design in a simple setting in this chapter, but a more general attack on *optimal contract and mechanism design* stressing cases of adverse selection, which makes use of the *revelation principle*, will be given in chapter 18.

These three topics are all important, but they do not even begin to exhaust the important category of models and concepts from information economics. Particularly noticeable by their absence are models of *optimal search* and *coordination failures*, where parties desirous of making a particular exchange must search for potential trading partners and where the need for search discourages certain otherwise beneficial trading activity, and models of *rational expectations*, where some parties have information that would be useful to others, information that is conveyed at least in part by equilibrium prices themselves.

All these situations and others as well fall under the broad rubric of *information economics* because in each case the driving factor is the lack of information on the part of some market participants, whether about what others are doing, or what others know, or where the best trading opportunities are to be found. This feature was ignored in part II of the book (with a very few exceptions, notably in the analysis of price discrimination). Now this feature becomes the center of attention.

16.1. Introduction

As noted above, this chapter concerns transactions taken under conditions of *moral hazard* or, as it is sometimes called, *hidden action*.[1] We have already introduced one example: In the fire insurance business, an insurance company would want the insuree to store flammable materials carefully, keep quality fire extinguishers on hand, etc. To take other examples: If I lease a car from you that I return to you in three years, you want me to have it serviced regularly, to drive it carefully (no redlining), and so forth. If you hire me to do a particular arduous job, you want me to work hard at the tasks that are set for me.

In each of these examples, it is possible to monitor and enforce levels of care, or servicing, or effort. Insurance companies will send out inspectors, and some insurance contracts provide that no benefits will be paid if it can be shown that the insurer did not provide sufficient "due care."

---

[1] The terms of information economics, such as moral hazard, adverse selection, hidden action, hidden information, signaling, screening, and so on, are used somewhat differently by different authors, so you must keep your eyes open when you see any of these terms in a book or article. For example, we just equated moral hazard with hidden action; you will read elsewhere that there is a serious distinction between them. (My own opinion is that there is a distinction, but it is hardly serious.) I do not wish to subject you to a precise categorization, largely on the grounds that very interesting problems mix more than one form, and then how would we call them? As a consumer of the literature, you should pay less attention to these labels and more to the "rules of the game" the author specifies — who knows what when, who does what when.

A car lease contract may require that routine maintenance is performed. If I am working for you, you might hire monitors to observe my level of effort.

But in each case, perfect monitoring and enforcement may be impossible, and hence the transaction might be structured so that the party taking the action has relatively greater *incentive* to act in a way the second party prefers. The insurance company may only insure up to 90% of the building. If the leased car is sold after the lease period, the contract may call for the party that leased the car to get a share of the proceeds from the sale.[2] And you might tie my compensation to some observable measure of how hard I work.

From the point of view of providing incentives, we would like to structure the transaction so that the party who is taking the "hidden action" bears fully the consequences of his actions. The insurance company may refuse to give insurance; instead of leasing the car, you may simply sell it to me; you may pay me as a function of the output I produce, using (for example) a piece-rate system, where I am paid a set amount for each piece of output I produce. But in each of these cases there may be "inefficiencies" in such a contractual form: A company owning a warehouse, if closely held by a few individuals, may be less able to bear the risk of having the warehouse burn down than is an insurance company with many shareholders. A leasing arrangement may produce tax savings relative to a direct sale, owing to pecularities in the tax system.[3] Piece-rate systems may be infeasible because the work involved is machine paced, or because the quality of worksmanship as well as quantity may be important, or because the piece-rate system may subject the worker to risks that the worker is less well equipped to bear than is the firm for which he works. So a balance must be struck between providing incentives and exploiting all the other advantages of trade in a particular setting.

16.2. *Effort incentives: A simple example*

All these words and vague generalities may be a bit hard to parse, so let us turn to an illustrative example. Imagine a situation in which one party, called the *principal*, hires a second party, called the *agent*, to perform some task. The agent is drawn from a large population of similar

---

[2] You *don't* see this in most car lease contracts in the United States, largely because leasing is motivated by tax considerations, and such a contract would void the tax savings.

[3] You may wonder why such a tax system would be created, but that is well beyond the scope of this book.

agents and is willing to undertake this task as long as his net utility from performing the task is at least as large as he can get at his next best opportunity; we refer to this level of utility as the agent's *reservation level of utility*. The agent, if and when he is hired, must then decide whether to work hard or not on this particular job. Hard work is not to this particular agent's taste, and so, all other things equal, he would prefer not to work hard. Whether this agent works hard or not determines the value to the principal of having this agent work. If the agent is not going to work hard, then the principal will get very little from the deal — so little that it is not worth her while to pay the agent his reservation wage (a wage high enough so that combined with not working hard the agent's net utility exceeds his reservation level of utility). But if the agent does work hard, then the principal will get enough out of the transaction to make it worthwhile for both sides.

Specifically, suppose that the agent's reservation level of utility is (completely arbitrarily, as the scale doesn't mean anything) 9. The agent derives utility from how much he is paid, w, and how hard he works, a. The level of a can be "hard" or "high," which we denote $a = 5$, or it can be "not hard" or "low," denoted by $a = 0$. The agent's overall (von Neumann-Morgenstern) utility from w and a is given by

$$U(w, a) = \sqrt{w} - a.$$

If the agent works hard, the accomplished task is worth \$270 to the principal. And if the agent doesn't work hard, the task will be worth only \$70 to the principal.

To get the agent to work at a low level of effort, the principal must offer the agent wages high enough so that $\sqrt{w} \geq 9$, or $w \geq \$81$. Since the job, if done with low effort, is worth only \$70 to the principal, there will be no deal of this sort.

But if the agent can be persuaded to expend high effort, then the principal must offer the agent wages high enough so that $\sqrt{w} - 5 \geq 9$, or $\sqrt{w} \geq 14$, or $w \geq \$196$. Since the principal values the job done with a high level of effort at \$270, this is a worthwhile deal for her. She should try to arrange this.

How? Perhaps she should write a contract that offers the agent \$197 (be generous!) for performing the task, and trust that the agent will indeed work hard. Trust is nice and can work (although we might try to think why it does), but the title of this chapter is "moral hazard," so we assume this won't work. If the principal offers this agent a fixed fee contract, we assume that the agent will take the money, put in low effort, and leave the principal paying $197 for a task that is worth to her only $70.

Another possibility is to offer a contract that calls for the agent's pay to depend on how much effort he puts in. The contract might read something like "I (the principal) agree to pay the agent $197 if he works hard, and $25 (say) if he doesn't." If this contract is enforceable, then the agent will optimally work hard — doing so gives him a utility of (slightly more than) 9, while taking the contract and not working hard would net $\sqrt{25} - 0 = 5$, which is less than his reservation utility level.

But is this contract enforceable? Suppose the agent signs it, doesn't work hard, and then claims that he did work hard. The principal will need some tangible evidence that he didn't work hard, evidence that will stand up in some legal proceeding. It may be that no tangible evidence exists, or even that the principal is unable to see any conclusive evidence about how hard the agent worked. (This may seem a bit strange to you, because the principal's valuation of the task depends on how hard the agent worked. But, in a bit, we'll see why there might be no conclusive evidence.) There may be conclusive evidence, but not evidence that a court of law, or whoever is going to enforce this contract, would accept as evidence. Or it may be that court costs are too high to make one side wish to enforce such a contract. For any of these reasons, writing this sort of contract might not work.

We could have the principal monitor the agent's efforts, with a contract that gives the principal the right to fire the agent (at a low level of severance pay) if he doesn't work hard. Of course, the principal might still have to go to the courts to justify a termination, so the problems just mentioned might still be present. And there will be some cost of monitoring the agent; the principal, presumably, has better things to do with her time. The principal, if her time is especially valuable, might think of hiring some third party to monitor the agent. But then she'll have to pay this monitor, and she might be concerned that the monitor and the agent will collude against her; the agent might offer the monitor a bribe if the monitor will say that the agent did indeed work hard. Finally, the agent mightn't sign any such contract, fearing that the principal will fire him just before the task is completed. (In chapter 20, we'll consider how the principal's concern for her reputation among workers in general might reassure this particular worker on this count.)

Even if the principal cannot tie the worker's wage directly to his level of effort, the principal might be able to find some indirect measure of effort to which wages can be tied in a contract that will stand up in court. To give an example of this, we have to be a bit more specific about what this agent is doing. We suppose that the agent is a salesman, who will be representing the principal to a particular client. There are three possible outcomes to this interaction: The client can place no order with the principal; the client can place an order that is worth a (gross) $100 with the principal; or the client can place an order that is worth a (gross) $400 with the principal. The agent's level of effort affects the odds of each of these three outcomes. If the agent works hard at making the sale, then a $400 sale results with probability .6, a $100 sale with probability .3, and no sale with probability .1. If the agent doesn't work hard, there is a $400 sale with probability .1, a $100 sale with probability .3, and no sale with probability .6. The size of the sale is observable, and (we assume) the agent's wages can be made contingent upon this variable.

The principal is risk neutral. Note, in particular, where the $70 and $270 figures came from; these are the expected gross profits from the sale, for low- and high-effort levels, respectively. Note also that, unless the principal can observe the effort level of the agent directly, the data received (size of the order placed, if any) do not tell conclusively what level of effort was put in. A $400 sale indicates that a high level of effort was more likely, but it isn't conclusive.

Case 1. A risk neutral agent

Now imagine that the agent is also risk neutral. (Note well: This isn't what we assumed above, and we'll get back to our earlier assumptions in a bit.) By this we mean that the agent's utility function is $u(w, a) = w - a$. For the duration of this case, we assume that the agent's reservation level of utility is 81, and high and low effort correspond to $a = 25$ and $a = 0$, respectively. With these new numbers, the same problem as we had before presents itself: The principal would be willing to hire the agent and pay him a bit more than $106 if hard work could be guaranteed. This would leave the principal with a net profit of $270 - $106 = $164. But the principal would be unwilling to expend the $81 it would take to get the agent to work if the agent puts in low effort. And she would certainly be unhappy if she hired the agent for $106 and then he put in low effort.

But now there is a simple solution. Offer the agent the following contingent contract: "If you make no sale, you pay me $164. If you make a small sale (worth $100 gross), you only pay me $64. And if you make a large sale, you will be paid $400 - $164 = $236. The agent, offered this, can choose one of the following three courses of action:

(a) Turn down the contract, and get reservation utility level 81.

(b) Take the contract and put in a low level of effort. This will net expected utility

$$(.1)(236) + (.3)(-64) + (.6)(-164) - 0 = -94.$$

(c) Take the contract and work hard. This will net expected utility

$$(.6)(236) + (.3)(-64) + (.1)(-164) - 25 = 81.$$

The agent is just indifferent between options (a) and (c), and if the principal sweetens the contract just a bit, the agent will prefer (c). The principal is quite happy with this. The agent, in his own interests now, will work hard. Indeed, the principal's net from the sale net of the payment to the agent is $164 (less any sweetening) *with certainty*!

What our principal has done is to get the agent to internalize the effect of his effort decision. The agent now bears fully the cost of putting in less than a high level of effort.

Case 2. A risk averse agent

Now go back to the original formulation, where the agent's utility function is $u(w, a) = \sqrt{w} - a$, his reservation utility level is 9, and $a = 5$ for high effort and $a = 0$ for low. If we could write a contract contingent on the effort level of the agent, then the best contract for the principal to write is one in which the agent gets $196 (plus a bit, perhaps) if he works hard and some low amount (such as $0) if he doesn't. This leaves the principal with an expected net profit of $270 - $196 = $74.

But we assume that the principal can only make the agent's wages contingent on the (gross) size of the sale. In case 1, we could still find a contract that would make the principal as well off as if she could write a contract contingent on actual effort level. But in this case we cannot. Two countervailing forces are at work in this case:

(a) In this case, where the principal is risk neutral and the agent is risk averse, the most "efficient" arrangement is one in which the agent's wage is certain. Why? *In general, if one party to a transaction is risk averse and the other is risk neutral, then it is efficient for the risk neutral party to bear all the risks.* In the somewhat different context of syndicate theory in chapter 5, you saw this proved formally. The same formal techniques work here. So instead of subjecting you for a second time to the formal proof, let us give the intuition: If the principal pays the agent a random wage, then the agent evaluates the wage according to his expected utility. Being risk averse, if the wage is at all risky the agent values it at less than its expected value. But the principal, being risk neutral, values the cost of the wages paid at their expected value. If we imagine that the agent's wages had expected value $\bar{w}$, then the principal would see this as an outflow from her pocket equivalent to $\bar{w}$, but the agent would see this as an inflow to his pocket of something less than $\bar{w}$ as long as there is any risk at all.

(b) On the other hand, if we give the agent a riskless wage, the agent has no incentive to work hard. And if the agent doesn't work hard, the principal doesn't want to enter the transaction.

To induce the agent to work hard, we will have to give up some of the efficiency that is obtained by putting all the risk on the principal. The question is, How can we do this as efficiently as possible?

To answer this, suppose that we form a contract in which the agent is paid $\$x_0^2$ if no sale is obtained, $\$x_1^2$ if the small sale is made, and $\$x_2^2$ if the large sale is made. I am squaring the values so that when I apply the agent's utility function his utility in each contingency will be $x_i - a$, for $i = 0, 1, 2$. Hence, offered this contract, the agent has three choices:

(a) Refuse the contract, and get reservation utility 9

(b) Take the contract and put in a low level of effort, for an expected utility of

$$(.6)x_0 + (.3)x_1 + (.1)x_2$$

(c) Take the contract and put in a high level of effort, for an expected utility of

$$(.1)x_0 + (.3)x_1 + (.6)x_2 - 5$$

Assume for the moment that we wish to write the best possible contract (from the point of view of the principal) subject to the constraints that the agent will take the contract and put in a high level of effort. Then we wish to

$$\text{minimize} \quad (.1)x_0^2 + (.3)x_1^2 + (.6)x_2^2$$

subject to

$$(.1)x_0 + (.3)x_1 + (.6)x_2 - 5 \geq 9$$

and

$$(.1)x_0 + (.3)x_1 + (.6)x_2 - 5 \geq (.6)x_0 + (.3)x_1 + (.1)x_2.$$

That is, we wish to minimize the expected wage (since we are taking the perspective of the principal) subject to two constraints; the first is that the agent should sign on the dotted line, and the second is that the agent should then choose to put in the high level of effort. (We should add constraints that the x_i must all be nonnegative, but I'll proceed without them and add them in later if necessary.) These two constraints have names: The first is often called the *individual rationality* or *participation* constraint, and the second is called the *incentive* constraint.

You should have no difficulty solving this constrained optimization problem. To spare you all that needless effort, let us simply give the solution here: $x_0 = 5.42857, x_1 = 14, x_2 = 15.42857$. Both constraints bind at the optimum, which is fairly intuitive: The principal doesn't want to pay the agent any more than necessary to get him to work, and she doesn't want to put any more risk on the agent than is necessary to get the agent to work hard, because it is costly to her to put risk on the agent. Thus we have the following as the optimal contract, if our objective is to get the agent to take the job and to put in high effort:

If no sale is made, wages are $5.42857^2 = \$29.46$

If a \$100 sale is made, wages are $14^2 = \$196$

If a \$400 sale is made, wages are $15.42857^2 = \$238.0407$

The expected wage bill is $(.1)(29.46) + (.3)(196) + (.6)(238.0407) = \$204.56$, which leaves the principal with an expected profit of $270 - 204.56 = \$65.44$.

Compare this with the "first best" contract — the contract where the principal gives the agent a flat wage of \$196 and relies on trust or the compulsion of a monitoring scheme to ensure that the agent puts in a high level of effort. To give the agent the right incentives, we had to have him bear some of the risk by rewarding him in case of the outcome that is more likely if he puts in greater effort. This cost the principal an expected \$8.56.

16.3. *Finitely many actions and outcomes*

A general formulation

The technique just used generalizes very nicely to a class of principal-agent problems. We imagine an agent who may agree to undertake a task for a principal, and who then chooses an *action* a to take out of some finite set $A = \{a_1, \ldots, a_N\}$. The action choice by the agent is not observed by the principal; instead the principal sees an imperfect signal of what the agent did. We model this by saying that the principal (and the agent) observe a *signal* s that is drawn from a finite set $S = \{s_1, \ldots, s_M\}$. If the agent chooses action a_n, the probability that signal s_m is produced is π_{nm}, where $\sum_{m=1}^{M} \pi_{nm} = 1$ for each n. The principal is unable to write a contract that makes the agent's compensation directly dependent on a; the best she (the principal) can do is to make his compensation a function of s.

Note carefully that we refer to the agent's choice of *action* instead of his choice of *effort*. We do not preclude the interpretation of a as a level of effort, and in a later subsection we will specialize to a case that has that interpretation quite naturally. But for now we don't rule out other interpretations.

Both for ease of exposition and for some of the results we later give, we make our first assumption:

Assumption 1. *The probability* $\pi_{nm} > 0$ *for all* n *and* m.

In words, every outcome is possible under every action.

The agent's utility depends on the wages he receives, denoted by w, and the action he takes, denoted by a. His preferences over lotteries concerning his income obey the von Neumann-Morgenstern axioms, and $U(w, a) = u(w) - d(a)$ is his von Neumann-Morgenstern utility function. Note carefully that we assume that $U(w, a)$ is *additively separable* into a piece that depends on wages, $u(w)$, and a piece that depends on the action selected, $-d(a)$. (The letter d here is a mnemonic for disutility.) We assume that the agent has a reservation utility level u_0. And we add the following innocuous assumption.

Assumption 2. *The function* u *is strictly increasing, continuously differentiable, and concave.*

Concavity of u is just risk aversion for our agent (in terms of lotteries over his wages). We don't preclude that u is linear.

The principal cares about the action chosen by the agent and about the wages she pays to him. Specifically, we suppose that $B(a)$ for some function B gives the gross benefits to the principal of hiring the agent if the agent chooses action a, and the principal's net benefit is $B(a)$ less the expected wages she must pay.

> This formulation is far from general. We are assuming that the principal is risk neutral, and we assume a very special form of utility function for the agent. Much of what follows can be extended somewhat to encompass more general formulations. In particular, Grossman and Hart (1983), from whom a lot of what follows is taken, assume throughout that the agent's utility function takes the somewhat more general form $U(w, a) = f(a)u(w) - d(a)$ for a strictly positive function f. You will be asked to look at more general formulations in the problems.

Solving the basic problem

The basic problem is to find the optimal incentive scheme for the principal to offer the agent. To solve this problem, we proceed as follows.

Step 1: For each $a_n \in A$, what is the cheapest way to induce the agent to take the job and choose action a_n? Cheapest here is measured in terms of the expected wages that must be paid. Following the pattern of our example from the previous section, we solve this problem by solving a constrained maximization problem.

The variables in this maximization problem are the levels of "wage-utility" the agent is given as a function of the signal s. That is, we take variables x_m for $m = 1, \ldots, M$, where if $w(s_m)$ is the wage paid to the agent if the signal is s_m, then

$$x_m = u(w(s_m)).$$

We assume the $u(\cdot)$ is a strictly increasing and continuous function, and we let v be the inverse of u; that is, $v(z) = w$ if $u(w) = z$. Thus the wage paid to the agent if signal s_m is produced, as a function of the variable x_m, is just

$$w(s_m) = v(x_m).$$

Thus, as a function of the variables $\{x_1, \ldots, x_M\}$, the expected wages the principal must pay if the agent takes action a_n is

$$\sum_{m=1}^{M} \pi_{nm} v(x_m).$$

If the agent is offered wages as a function of signal as given by $v(x_m)$, what constraints must be met to be sure that he will select action a_n? We first must be sure that in choosing a_n the agent achieves at least his reservation level of utility,

$$\sum_{m=1}^{M} \pi_{nm} x_m - d(a_n) \geq u_0.$$

Note two things here. First, the expected utility of wages to the agent is $\sum_{m=1}^{M} \pi_{nm} u(v(x_m))$, which since v is the inverse of u is just $\sum_{m=1}^{M} \pi_{nm} x_m$. Second, we have a weak inequality, which means that if the constraint is binding the agent is indifferent between taking the job or not. It is standard to work with weak inequalities, presuming that the agent, if indifferent, will resolve ties in the interests of the principal. (See the later subsection on game theoretic connections.)

We must be sure that choosing a_n is better than choosing some other action n'. This is modeled by imposing the constraints

$$\sum_{m=1}^{M} \pi_{nm} x_m - d(a_n) \geq \sum_{m=1}^{M} \pi_{n'm} x_m - d(a_{n'}), \ n' = 1, \ldots, N.$$

The two comments made in the previous paragraph apply here as well. Note that we have included the constraint for $n' = n$, although it is satisfied trivially.

There may also be constraints on the level of wages that can be paid. A standard constraint of this sort is that wages may be constrained to be nonnegative. For example, this was implicit in our example, since the agent's square-root utility function is not defined for negative wages. In such cases we would add constraints such as $x_m \geq v(0)$. We will not carry constraints such as this along in our formulation, although at one point we will comment on the effect that such a constraint might have.

So we have step 1: For each action a_n

$$\text{minimize } \sum_{m=1}^{M} \pi_{nm} v(x_m)$$

$$\text{subject to } \sum_{m=1}^{M} \pi_{nm} x_m - d(a_n) \geq u_0, \text{ and}$$

$$\sum_{m=1}^{M} \pi_{nm} x_m - d(a_n) \geq \sum_{m=1}^{M} \pi_{n'm} x_m - d(a_{n'}), \ n' = 1, \ldots, N.$$

Call the value of this problem (that is, the value of the objective function at the optimal solution) $C(a_n)$. This is the *minimal expected cost of inducing the agent to select action* a_n. We will use the label (Cn) for this problem, a mnemonic for cost of action number n. The first constraint is called the *participation* constraint, and the other constraints are called the *relative incentive* constraints.

> For readers who know about such things: Because u is concave, v is convex, and this is a well-behaved mathematical programming problem. We are minimizing a convex function subject to linear constraints, so that satisfaction of the first-order equations and the complementary slackness conditions (and the problem constraints) is necessary and sufficient for a solution. General convex programming algorithms can be employed to solve this problem numerically.
>
> For a given a_n, there may be no solution at all on grounds that the set of values (x_m) that meet all the constraints is empty; examples are easy to construct. In this case we would say that $C(a_n) = +\infty$. Note that $C(a_n)$ is finite for at least one n. If we set $x_m \equiv u_0 + \min_n d(a_n)$, then the constraints are all satisfied for the problem (Cn^*) where n^* is the index of the effort level that has minimal disutility. In fact, for cases where u is concave this is the solution to (Cn^*), a result that you should find easy to prove following chapter 5 or from the first-order equations. (See later.)
>
> The problem of nonexistence of any solution to the constraints is the only sort of problem concerning existence of a solution to (Cn) that may arise: If there is some set of variables (x_m), which meets all the constraints, then there is an optimal solution. You are asked to show this in problem 9; hints as to how to prove this are given there. It is worth noting that this result depends crucially on the assumption that $\pi_{nm} > 0$ for all n and m; see problem 7.

Step 2. For which $a \in A$ is $B(a) - C(a)$ maximized? This is a simple maximization problem.

> Since we know that $C(a_{n*})$ is finite where n^* is as before, and since each $C(a_n)$ is either finite or equal to $+\infty$, there is always a solution to the principal's overall problem.
>
> If we wish to be very careful about this, we have to wonder what happens if $B(a) < C(a)$ for all a. Is it viable for the principal to refuse to hire the agent at all or, rather, for the principal to make a wage offer that the agent is sure to turn down? If so, what are the consequences for the gross benefits of the principal? We will not be tidy about this possibility but instead implicitly assume that some level of effort a can be implemented at a cost sufficiently low to make it worth the principal's while to do so.

The key to this technique is the way that it takes the problem in steps. First we find the minimum cost way to induce action a for each $a \in A$, and then we choose the optimal a by comparing benefits and costs.

Basic results and analysis

Within the context of this somewhat general formulation, we can obtain a result along the lines sketched in the previous section.

To set a benchmark, consider the solution to the problem *if* it is possible to specify (and enforce the choice of) the action in the contract. From results in chapter 5, since the agent is risk averse (possibly risk neutral) and the principal is risk neutral, the cheapest method of guaranteeing the agent a given level of utility is with a fixed payment. (If the agent is risk neutral over some range, other schemes may be equally cheap, but none will be cheaper.) So the cheapest way to get the agent to accept a contract that *specifies* action choice a_n is to offer to pay him

$$C^0(a_n) \equiv v(u_0 + d(a_n)).$$

To be very formal about this, this is obtained from the solution of the problem

$$\text{minimize } \sum_{m=1}^{M} \pi_{nm} v(x_m) \text{ subject to } \sum_{m=1}^{M} \pi_{nm} x_m - d(a_n) \geq u_0.$$

This is the "same" as the problem (Cn) except that the relative incentive constraints are missing. We don't need them because the contract, by assumption, can specify which action is taken. Since the problem is just like (Cn) but with some constraints eliminated, it is evident that $C^0(a_n) \leq C(a_n)$ for all n. We can go on to

$$\text{maximize } B(a_n) - C^0(a_n);$$

the effort level that solves this problem is called the *first-best level of effort*.

We are supposing, however, that the principal can't write an enforceable contract that specifies the first-best or any other level of effort. As in the example of the previous section, we obtain the following result:

Proposition 1. *If the agent is strictly risk averse, $C^0(a_n) < C(a_n)$ for any action a_n that is more onerous than some other action; i.e., such that $d(a_n) > min_{a'} d(a')$.*

The proof is fairly simple. If the agent is strictly risk averse, then the unique efficient risk-sharing arrangement is for the principal to bear all the risk; the agent gets a sure wage. But if the agent is given a wage that is independent of the signal, he will choose the least onerous action.[4]

We next address the question *Is the participation constraint binding at the optimal solution?* The answer is (a qualified) yes. In fact, for any effort level a_n such that the constraints defining (Cn) can be satisfied, in the solution of (Cn) the participation constraint is binding (with qualifications). To see why, suppose that (x_m) is a solution of (Cn) such that $\sum_{m=1}^{M} \pi_{nm} x_m - d(a_n) = u' > u_0$. Consider the alternative incentive scheme given by $x_m' = x_m - u' + u_0$. This clearly satisfies the participation constraint (with equality!), and since we decrease each x_m by the same amount, satisfaction of the relative incentive constraints is guaranteed. But if v is strictly increasing, this lowers the cost to the principal, which contradicts the assumption that (x_m) is a solution of (Cn). Nothing very mysterious is going on here. We simply are taking the same amount of wage-utility away from the agent at every outcome, which doesn't affect his relative incentives at all.

> What is the qualification? Suppose there were constraints on the variables x_m such as $x_m \geq u(0)$. Then we could not be sure that x_m', which is x_m less some amount, would continue to satisfy such constraints. In fact, it is easy to construct examples where, because of the presence of constraints such as $x_m \geq u(0)$, the participation constraint does not bind. To be sure that this problem doesn't appear, we need to be sure that we are always able to lower the utility levels received by the agent; essentially, u should have range that is unbounded below. (If the domain of u is all of R, this will hold automatically since u is concave. So this qualification pertains to cases where the domain of u is itself bounded below.)

As a final piece of basic analysis, we turn to the first-order conditions (and complementary slackness conditions) of the problem (Cn). Our reason for interest in these conditions is straightforward. As we noted before (in the small type), assumption 2 implies that satisfaction of the first-order and complementary slackness conditions of (Cn) is necessary and sufficient for an optimal solution of (Cn).

Letting λ be the multiplier on the participation constraint and $\eta_{n'}$ be the multiplier on the relative incentive constraint for action $a_{n'}$, the

---

[4] In the previous section we had something of a converse to this proposition, namely that if the agent is risk neutral, then $\max_a B(a) - C^0(a) = \max_a B(a) - C(a)$; the principal can achieve her first-best outcome. We don't obtain that result in this general formulation; it must await a specialization to be given in the next subsection.

first-order condition for x_m is

$$v'(x_m) = \lambda + \sum_{n'=1}^{N} \eta_{n'} \left(1 - \frac{\pi_{n'm}}{\pi_{nm}} \right).$$

(This is after some algebraic manipulation, which you should replicate.) This has a very clean and intuitive explanation. Recall that the multipliers must all be nonnegative and, from the complementary slackness conditions, $\eta_{n'}$ will be strictly positive only if the relative incentive constraint on action $a_{n'}$ is binding. Note that since v is convex, v' is an increasing function. Thus a larger right-hand side in the first-order condition means a larger value of x_m. With these preliminary observations, think of the scheme (x_m) as follows:

(a) A "base payment" (measured in utility) is made to the agent, given by the equation $v'(x_m) = \lambda$. If none of the relative incentive constraints bind, then this is the first-order equation, and we have the result that x_m is constant in the outcome m.[a] This is not surprising; we are just rediscovering the result from chapter 5 that when there are no incentive problems the optimal arrangement gives the risk-averse agent a constant wage.

(b) But when there are binding relative incentive constraints, the wages of the agent are not constant. Specifically, if $\eta_{n'} > 0$, then the right-hand side, and hence the agent's wages, are increased at outcomes m such that $\pi_{n'm}/\pi_{nm} < 1$ and they are decreased at outcomes m such that $\pi_{n'm}/\pi_{nm} > 1$. When $\pi_{n'm}/\pi_{nm} < 1$, outcome m is less likely if the agent takes action n' than if he takes the desired action n. So this does indeed seem a good time to pay him more to get him to choose n over n'. And the agent is "penalized" if the outcome is an s_m such that $\pi_{n'm}/\pi_{nm} > 1$, an outcome that is more likely under the action choice n' than under the desired n.

That, pretty much, is all there is to it. Of course, the levels of the "basic marginal utility wage" λ and the relative effort multipliers $\eta_{n'}$ all must be determined, and they must work together in a fashion that causes all the initial constraints and the complementary slackness conditions to be met. But the essential idea is simple: At the optimum, you reward the agent if the outcome is relatively more likely if he took the desired action,

---

[a] To be precise, it is constant if u is strictly concave, hence v is strictly convex, and hence v' is strictly increasing.

and you penalize him if the outcome is relatively less likely, relative to the actions that bind in the relative incentive constraints.

The formulation: A special case

We next make use of a special case of the formulation given above. To begin, we imagine that the signals s_m are levels of gross profit accruing to the principal, exactly as in the example of the previous section. In this case $B(a_n) = \sum_{m=1}^{M} \pi_{nm} s_m$.

With this specialization, we can give the converse to the proposition from the previous subsection:

Proposition 2. *For a risk neutral agent,* $\max_a B(a) - C^0(a) = \max_a B(a) - C(a)$. *In fact, if* a^* *achieves the maximum in* $\max_a B(a) - C^0(a)$, *one scheme that implements this action is for the principal to pay the agent* $s_m - B(a^*) + C^0(a^*)$ *if the gross profits are* s_m, *so the principal receives* $B(a^*) - C^0(a^*)$ *for sure and the agent bears all the risk.*

We will not go through the proof of this result except to note the intuition: If the agent is risk neutral, efficient risk sharing between the principal and agent is consistent with the agent bearing all the risk. And by having the agent bear all the risk, we have him bearing entirely the consequences of his action choice. It is as if the principal "sold the venture" to the agent, who is now sole proprietor and is working for himself, and who now chooses the optimal action in his own sole and best interests. [b]

To continue our specialization, we further imagine that the actions are levels of effort that the agent might select, ordered in terms of increasing disutility. That is,

$$d(a_1) < d(a_2) < \ldots < d(a_N).$$

In this case, there is no reason to carry around the extra baggage of the function d; we can use a_n for the disutility of effort choice n, so that $U(w, a) = u(w) - a$, and the condition becomes $a_1 < a_2 < \ldots < a_N$.

Finally, we imagine that higher (i.e., more onerous) levels of effort result in higher gross profits for the principal. To write this assumption, we assume that the gross profit levels s_m have been arranged in increasing

---

[b] Perhaps now is the time to ask, Why couldn't we give this proposition before we specialized to this case? If the answer isn't obvious, consider what would happen in the previous subsection if the number of signals, M, was one.

order: $s_1 < s_2 < \ldots < s_M$.[c] To assume that higher levels of effort lead to higher profits, we might simply assume that $\sum_{m=1}^{M} \pi_{nm} s_m$ is increasing in n. But usually something more stringent is assumed, namely that an increase in effort results in a higher probability of higher levels of profit. Formally:

Assumption 3. *For all pairs n and n' such that $n' > n$ and for all $m = 1, \ldots, M$,*

$$\sum_{i=m}^{M} \pi_{ni} \leq \sum_{i=m}^{M} \pi_{n'i}$$

with for each n and n' a strict inequality for at least one m.

For those who know the terminology, assumption 3 states that increased effort results in a first-order stochastic increase in the levels of gross profits. Although it may not be immediately evident to you, this does imply that $\sum_{m=1}^{M} \pi_{nm} s_m$ is increasing in n. (See problem 10.)

We motivate the analysis to come by asking the following question:

Is the wage paid, or equivalently the wage-utility level x_m, nondecreasing with increases in the level of gross profits?

Since the principal will wish to reward the agent for higher levels of effort, and since higher levels of effort "go with" higher levels of profit, it may seem natural to suppose that the answer will be yes. But the answer is no in general. An easy-to-comprehend example where it fails runs as follows.

There are three possible levels of gross profit, $1, $2, and $10,000, and two possible effort levels, $a_1 = 1$ and $a_2 = 2$. (Remember that we identify an effort level with its disutility in this specialized formulation.) If the agent chooses effort level a_1, the outcomes are $1 gross profit with probability .5, $2 gross profit with probability .3, and $10,000 gross profit with probability .2. If the agent chooses effort level a_2, the outcomes have probabilities .4, .1 and .5, respectively. Note that as promised, higher effort leads to higher probabilities of better outcomes in precisely the sense of assumption 3.

We leave it to you to flesh out this example so that the agent has a strictly concave utility function for wages u and a reservation utility level u_0 such that the solution to the principal's problem is to provide the agent

---

[c] The use of strict inequalities here may trouble the very picky reader. In essence, we are assuming that the *only* information upon which contracts can be written is the level of gross profits.

with incentives to choose a_2. This shouldn't be hard to do. Expected gross profits if the agent chooses a_1 are \$2,001.50, while they are \$5,000.60 if he chooses a_2. This gives the principal a strong reason to create incentives for a_2.

When you do this, the multiplier on the relative incentive constraint for choosing a_2 instead of a_1 will necessarily be strictly positive. Why? Because if it isn't, in the first-order conditions we will get a flat wage payment to the agent, and we know that this will cause him to choose a_1. (Go slowly here. I'm skipping steps to force you to think this through.) So the three first-order equations will be

$$v'(x_1) = \lambda + \eta(1 - (.5/.4)) = \lambda - .25\eta$$
$$v'(x_2) = \lambda + \eta(1 - (.3/.1)) = \lambda - 2\eta, \text{ and}$$
$$v'(x_3) = \lambda + \eta(1 - (.2/.5)) = \lambda + .6\eta,$$

where x_1 is the wage-utility level corresponding to \$1 gross profits, x_2 corresponds to \$2, and x_3 corresponds to \$10,000, λ is the multiplier on the participation constraint, and η is the multiplier on the binding relative incentive constraint. The point, simply, is that if $\eta > 0$, which it must be, then $x_1 > x_2$.

There should be no mystery why this is. While higher effort shifts upwards the probability of higher gross profits in the sense of assumption 3, the ratio of the probability of the *outcomes* under a_2 to their probability under a_1 goes down and then up. Evidently, to get an affirmative answer to the question posed above, we need something stronger than assumption 3.[d] We seemingly need

Assumption 4. The monotone-likelihood ratio property. *For any two effort levels a_n and $a_{n'}$ such that $n < n'$, and for any two gross-profit outcomes s_m and $s_{m'}$ such that $m < m'$, the relative likelihood of the better outcome under the higher effort level to the lower is at least as large as this likelihood ratio for the lower outcome. Or, in symbols,*

$$\frac{\pi_{n'm'}}{\pi_{nm'}} \geq \frac{\pi_{n'm}}{\pi_{nm}}.$$

---

[d] You should verify that assumption 4, which follows immediately, is indeed strictly stronger than assumption 3. In fact, if you know about first-order stochastic dominance, you might wish to ponder the connections between that property and assumption 4.

Is assumption 4 enough to get an affirmative answer to our motivating question? It is certainly moving us in the right direction, but even this it is not enough. To see why, go back to the first-order equations for (Cn), for the effort level a_n that the principal optimally chooses to implement. *Insofar as the only binding relative incentive constraints are for effort levels less than* a_n, *we are okay.* Because v is convex, the sign of $x_m - x_{m'}$ for $m < m'$ is the same as the sign of $v'(x_m) - v'(x_{m'})$. But from the first-order conditions,

$$v'(x_m) - v'(x_{m'}) = \sum_{n'=1}^{N} \eta_{n'} \left[\frac{\pi_{n'm'}}{\pi_{nm'}} - \frac{\pi_{n'm}}{\pi_{nm}} \right].$$

As long as $n' < n$, assumption 4 says that the sign of each term in the brackets is nonpositive, hence (since multipliers are all nonnegative) the sum is nonpositive, which is just what we want.

But if $\eta_{n'}$ is positive for some $n' > n$, then we may be sunk; now the monotone likelihood ratio property runs the wrong way.

It may seem incredible to you that, in any problem (Cn), the relative incentive constraints for greater levels of effort than the one desired will be binding. Or rather, it may seem incredible that this would hold in the problem (Cn) for the a_n that is optimal for the principal. After all, if the agent wants to choose a higher level of effort, why would the principal ever wish to stop him from doing so? There is a reason why. It is true that the principal benefits from higher levels of effort by the agent in terms of the function $B(a)$. But for a given wage schedule, there are also costs that the principal incurs: Insofar as higher wages are paid for better outcomes, by expending more effort the agent increases his expected wages. It is possible to construct examples where there are three levels of effort, a_1, a_2, and a_3, the monotone likelihood ratio property holds, the middle level of effort is optimal, and, in the problem $(C2)$ *both* relative incentive constraints bind in a way that gives optimal wages that are not nondecreasing in gross profits.[e] The details of this example are not illuminating; if you wish to see them, consult Grossman and Hart (1983, example 1).

What is needed in addition to assumption 4 is an assumption that implies that the only binding relative incentive constraints in (Cn) for the optimal effort level a_n are constraints corresponding to levels of effort lower than a_n. We proceed to develop one condition, which Grossman

---

[e] Test your understanding of this by answering the following question before reading further. Why is it impossible, in this case, that only the relative incentive constraint for a_3 binds in $(C2)$?

and Hart attribute to unpublished work by J. Mirrlees. (This condition will play a role in later analysis as well, which is the excuse for not shifting to the smaller type size just yet.)

Assumption 5. *If a_n, $a_{n'}$, and $a_{n''}$ are effort levels such that $a_{n'} = \beta a_n + (1 - \beta)a_{n''}$, then for each $m = 1, \ldots, M$,*

$$\sum_{i=m}^{M} \pi_{n'i} \geq \beta \sum_{i=m}^{M} \pi_{ni} + (1 - \beta) \sum_{i=m}^{M} \pi_{n''i}.$$

This is called the *concavity of the distribution function condition.* To aid in making comparisons with the literature and, in particular, with the treatment in Grossman and Hart (1983), recall that here we are identifying the effort level a_n with its disutility. To interpret this assumption (and for later purposes of notation), let $\Pi_m(a_n) = \sum_{i=m}^{M} \pi_{ni}$. That is, $\Pi_m(a_n)$ is the probability of seeing a gross profit level at least as large as s_m if effort level a_n is taken. Then, roughly, the assumption says that increases in effort (as measured by their disutility) have decreasing marginal impact on the probabilities of better outcomes. You can see this most easily if you think of $a_n, a_{n'}$, and $a_{n''}$ such that $a_n - a_{n'} = a_{n'} - a_{n''} > 0$. This gives $\beta = 1/2$ in the assumption. Then the increase in disutility in moving from the lowest level of effort $a_{n''}$ to the intermediate level $a_{n'}$ is the same as the increase in moving from $a_{n'}$ to a_n. And according to the assumption, for each m, $\Pi_m(a_{n'}) - \Pi_m(a_{n''}) \geq \Pi_m(a_n) - \Pi_m(a_{n'})$.

What does this assumption do for us?

Proposition 3. *If assumptions 1, 2, 4, and 5 all hold and u is strictly concave, then the optimal wage-incentive scheme for the principal has wages that are nondecreasing functions of the level of gross profits.*

The proof of this proposition is a bit much for one's first pass through this subject, so we relegate most of the details to smaller type. But before switching type size, we record the first step along the way, which we will need in the next section. We first give a piece of notation. For any fixed wage-incentive scheme (w_m), let $U(a_n)$ be the overall expected utility of the agent under this scheme if he chooses effort level a_n. That is,

$$U(a_n) = \sum_{m=1}^{M} \pi_{nm} u(w_m) - a_n.$$

Lemma. *Fix a wage-incentive system that is nondecreasing in the gross profit of the firm. (That is, $w_1 \leq w_2 \leq \cdots \leq w_M$.) If assumption 5 holds, $U(a)$ is a concave function of a.*[5]

Note carefully: This is true of *any* nondecreasing wage-incentive system. As you will see in the proof, it doesn't depend at all on an assumption 4 or even on an assumption 3. And all that is required from assumption 2 is that u is nondecreasing.

Proof of the lemma. Write x_m for $u(w_m)$. If the function u is nondecreasing (which is assumed), then so is the sequence x_m. Write $\delta_1 = x_1$ and, for $m = 2, \ldots, M$, let $\delta_m = x_m - x_{m-1}$. Note that $\delta_m \geq 0$ for all $m \geq 2$. Then

$$\sum_{m=1}^{M} \pi_{nm} u(w_m) = \sum_{m=1}^{M} \pi_{nm} x_m = \sum_{m=1}^{M} \left[\pi_{nm} \sum_{j=1}^{m} \delta_j \right]$$

$$= \sum_{m=1}^{M} \left[\delta_m \sum_{i=m}^{M} \pi_{ni} \right] = \delta_1 + \sum_{m=2}^{M} \delta_m \Pi_m(a_n).$$

The first, second, and fourth equalities are just a matter of rewriting; it is the third equality that may not be immediately obvious. But if you consider the matter carefully, you will see that this is correct. Hence

$$U(a_n) = \delta_1 + \sum_{m=2}^{M} \delta_m \Pi_m(a_n) - a_n.$$

This is the sum of a constant, nonnegative weightings of concave functions of a_n, and a linear function of a_n. Hence it is concave in a_n.

With this lemma in hand, we can proceed to a second lemma. To set up for this, consider, for each $n = 1, 2, \ldots, N$, the problem

$$\text{minimize} \quad \sum_{m=1}^{M} \pi_{nm} v(x_m)$$

$$\text{subject to} \quad \sum_{m=1}^{M} \pi_{nm} x_m - d(a_n) \geq u_0, \text{ and}$$

$$\sum_{m=1}^{M} \pi_{nm} x_m - d(a_n) \geq \sum_{m=1}^{M} \pi_{n'm} x_m - d(a_{n'}), \ n' = 1, \ldots, n-1.$$

---

[5] The notion of a concave function on a discrete domain may be a bit mysterious to you, but the idea is that if $a' = \beta a + (1 - \beta)a''$ for a, a', and a'' all in the domain of U and $\beta \in [0, 1]$, then $\beta U(a) + (1 - \beta)U(a'') \leq U(a')$.

To see the difference between this and (Cn), look closely at the range of n' in the third line. This problem is just the same as (Cn), except that the relative incentive constraints for effort levels greater than n are missing. We will call this problem $(C^{\star}n)$.

Lemma. *If assumptions 1, 2, and 4 hold and u is strictly concave, then any solution (x_m) of $(C^{\star}n)$ is nondecreasing: $x_1 \leq x_2 \leq \ldots \leq x_M$. If, in addition, assumption 5 holds, then any solution of $(C^{\star}n)$ is a solution of (Cn).*

Proof. A necessary condition for a solution of $(C^{\star}n)$ is the first-order conditions. If u is strictly concave, the values of the x_m at any solution are strictly increasing in the right-hand sides of the first-order equations. And in $(C^{\star}n)$, as long as assumption 4 holds, those right-hand sides are nondecreasing in m. The last assertion follows because, by construction, in $(C^{\star}n)$ we only have relative incentive constraints for effort levels less than the one being implemented. This gives the first assertion of the lemma.

For the second assertion, we consider cases. For $n = 1$, strict concavity of u ensures that the solution of both $(C^{\star}n)$ and (Cn) is a constant wage set equal to reservation wage of the agent. For $n \geq 2$, we know that the solution to $(C^{\star}n)$ involves a nonconstant wage, because at a constant wage a_1 would be chosen. From the first-order conditions this implies that at least one of the relative incentive constraints must have a positive multiplier, which by complementary slackness implies that this constraint must be binding. Let n' be the binding constraint, which of course has $n' < n$. Fix the wage-incentive scheme that solves $(C^{\star}n)$, and consider, as in the previous lemma, $U(a)$ as a function of a for $j = 1, \ldots, N$, at this wage-incentive scheme. By the first assertion of this lemma combined with the previous lemma, $U(\cdot)$ is concave in a. By construction, $U(a_n) = U(a_{n'})$ (and these are at least as large as $U(a_j)$ for every $j \leq n$). But then the concavity of $U(a)$ in a for all a implies that $U(a_j) \leq U(a_n)$ for all $j > n$. To see this, suppose that $U(a_j) > U(a_n)$ for some $j > n$. Since a_n is a strict convex combination of a_j and $a_{n'}$, we would know that $U(a_n)$ must be at least the corresponding strict convex combination of $U(a_j)$ and $U(a_{n'})$, which would contradict $U(a_{n'}) = U(a_n) < U(a_j)$.

Thus we know that at the optimal solution of $(C^{\star}n)$, $U(a_j) \leq U(a_n)$ for all $j > n$. But this says that the solution of $(C^{\star}n)$ solves the additional constraints imposed in (Cn), and so it is a solution of (Cn). This completes the proof.

Proof of Proposition 3. Suppose that the optimal solution of the principal's problem corresponds to implementation of effort choice a_n. Then the solution of $(C^{\star}n)$, which is a solution of (Cn), is nondecreasing. Strict concavity of u implies that the solution of (Cn) is unique. (If there are two solutions, take a convex combination of them. All the constraints continue to be met and since v is strictly convex, the expected wage paid at the convex combination is less.) That gives the result.

One can go on to examine conditions under which the optimal wage-incentive schedule is convex or concave as a function of gross profits. Grossman and Hart (1983, proposition 9) give a result along these lines.

A further specialization: The case of two outcomes

Instead of pursuing this, we turn to a different sort of question. So far we have been concerned primarily with properties of the optimal incentive wages. The results we have derived have concerned solution of the subproblem (Cn) without any real use or mention of the larger problem of choosing an effort level to implement. You might wonder what can be said about the level of effort that the principal optimally chooses. An intuitive case might be made that the principal would always choose to implement a level of effort less than or equal to the first-best level, since risk-sharing between the agent and principal entails shielding the (risk-averse) agent from some of the consequences of his effort in terms of profits, while he bears fully its disutility. (If you are sceptical about this "intuition," don't worry; scepticism is appropriate.)

We will examine this issue in a very special setting. As in the previous subsection, we hold to the story of the action choice being effort measured along a one-dimensional scale of disutility, and we continue to assume that the only signal received about what effort the agent chose is the gross profit received. But we further specialize by assuming that gross profits can take on only two possible levels: s_1 and $s_2 > s_1$. In words, we imagine that the agent's efforts result in either *failure* or *success* of some venture, and profit depends solely on whether the venture succeeds.

In this setting, our assumptions translate as follows: Assumption 1 simply says that both success and failure are possible outcomes at any level of effort; assumption 2 is not changed or reinterpreted; assumption 3 is that higher levels of effort lead to increased chances of success, and this implies, with no further restrictions, that assumption 4 holds. That is, the monotone likelihood ratio property is redundant in this special situation, given assumption 3. Finally, assumption 5 states simply that the probability of a success is a concave function of the effort level.

Given assumption 3, we do not require assumption 5 in this case to obtain the result that the optimal wage incentive scheme is nondecreasing in effort if u is strictly concave. To see why, note that with two outcomes the only way one can fail to have a nondecreasing wage-incentive schedule is if failure is rewarded more than success. But given assumption 3, for any such wage-incentive schedule the agent will choose the lowest level of effort. And we know that (for strictly concave u) a better way to implement the lowest level of effort is to have constant wages.

Hence, with assumption 3 alone, we can think of wages in this case as being of a particularly simple form. The agent has a base wage, denoted by b_1, to which is added a bonus $b_2 \geq 0$ in the event of a successful outcome.

If we write $\sigma = b_2/(s_2 - s_1)$ the agents wages are b_1 and $b_1 + \sigma(s_2 - s_1)$, or a base wage plus a "share" of any extra gross profits accruing from a success. We know that $\sigma \geq 0$, and we know that $\sigma > 0$ if the principal wishes to implement any effort level above the minimal level possible (why?). We can also bound σ from above.

Proposition 4. *If u is strictly concave, then $\sigma < 1$ at the optimal wage-incentive schedule.*

The idea here is that if $\sigma \geq 1$, then the principal prefers that the outcome is failure, ex post. This can never be part of an overall optimal scheme. The proof is surprisingly difficult and is omitted here. See Grossman and Hart (1983, proposition 4), who gave the result generalized suitably to cases with more than two outcomes.

Now we return to the question with which we began. Can one say anything in general about how the effort level the principal chooses to implement compares with the first-best effort level? An example will illustrate the difficulties.

Example, part 1: There are two outcomes and two possible effort levels. Effort level $a_1 = 0$ gives a .9 probability of failure and .1 of success, while effort level $a_2 = .1$ gives probabilities .85 and .15, respectively. The agent has utility function $U(w, a) = \ln(w) - a$. The reservation utility level is 0. Success is worth \$10 to the principal, and failure is worth \$0.

It is immediate that to implement effort level a_1, the principal should pay a constant wage of \$1, which nets her \$0; the \$1 gross expected profit just goes to pay the agent's wages.

If the principal could write a contract that specified (in enforceable fashion) effort level a_2, the optimal contract would give the agent wages of $e^{0.1} = \$1.105$ regardless of action, for an expected net profit of \$1.50 − \$1.105 = \$.395. Hence the first-best effort level is a_2.

But to implement the first-best level of effort, the principal must pay the agent higher wages in case of success than in case of failure. It is easy to work out the optimal wage-incentive contract. In the problem (C2), both the participation and the sole relative-incentive constraints must bind. (Why?) These are two linear equations in two unknowns and solving them gives wages of \$.8187 if the outcome is failure and \$6.04965 in case of success. (You should do the arithmetic if you are at all unsure where these numbers come from.) This has an expected cost (in terms of wages) of \$1.6034, which means that the principal's net profit from implementing

a_2 is a *loss* of \$.1034. Hence the principal chooses to implement a_1 with a flat \$1 wage.

Example, part 2: Now we add a third possible effort level, $a_3 = 2.27$, which gives a .99 chance of success. Note that assumption 5 is satisfied in this case.

First we look at what the principal could make if she could write an enforceable contract that specified a_3. The optimal wages in such a contract would pay $e^{2.27} = \$9.6794$ regardless of outcome, for a net to the principal of \$9.90 - \$9.6794 = \$.2206. Hence the first-best effort level remains a_2.

(Although it isn't germane, we can ask whether the addition of this third action changes the cost of implementing a_2. If a_2 can be implemented, it must be at wages where the participation and relative-incentive constraint for a_1 bind. (Why?) So we know that the wages must be as in part 1 of this example, and the only thing to check is whether, at these wages, a_2 is better than a_3 for the agent. (What would happen if a_3 turned out better than a_2 at these wages? What would $C(a_2)$ be in that case?) In fact, this does work out — at the wages computed in step 1, actions a_1 and a_2 give the agent expected utility of 0, while a_3 gives him an expected utility of $-.49$.)

What does it cost to implement a_3? When solving the subproblem (C3), we know that the participation constraint must bind. We also have two relative-incentive constraints and only two unknowns. So, unless there is a coincidence, one of those two relative-incentive constraints will bind and the other will be slack. (Why can't they both be slack at the solution of [C3]?) If you try each possibility in turn, you will find that it is the relative-incentive constraint for a_2 that binds, giving wages of \$.7501 if the outcome is failure and \$9.9327 if the outcome is success. This costs the principal an expected \$9.8409 in wages, for a net profit of \$.0591. Hence this is the solution when there are three possible effort levels.

This covers all the possibilities. In the case of only two effort levels, the principal chooses an effort level lower than the first-best. With the third added, she chooses to implement an effort level that is higher than the first-best. (You should have little problem creating an example where she chooses the first-best level itself.) All that remains is to see why this is happening.

The basic idea is that in our example effort level a_2, while first-best, gives very weak statistical evidence against the hypothesis that the effort level chosen was a_1. Relative to what one gains from implementing a_2 in terms of gross profits, the cost of separating a_2 from a_1 is substantial. Effort level a_3, on the other hand, gives a very different statistical pattern of outcomes, and so it is not so costly to separate from the others, relative to what is gained in gross profits.

To drive this point home, imagine that a_3 ensured success. (This violates assumption 1 and so is only for purposes of discussion.) Then we could get incentive schemes that implement a_3 with costs arbitrarily close to the first-best cost of a_3. We would do this with dire threats in case the outcome is a failure — wages very close to zero. The agent can avoid the threat by choosing a_3, if a_3 ensures success. But threats of this sort are terrible in case the agent contemplates any action that has a nonzero chance of failure, since $\ln(w) \to -\infty$ as $w \to 0$. For more on this point, see problem 7.

Connecting to game theory

The analysis that we have conducted has not been couched in game theoretic terms, but it is easy enough to do so. The "game" that is being played can be thought of as follows: The principal offers a contract to an agent, who then either accepts or rejects the contract and, if he accepts it, chooses an action to take. The space of contracts that the principal may offer is limited exactly as we have postulated; the payoff of the agent if he rejects the contract is his reservation level of utility; and the payoffs to both principal and agent are computed in obvious fashion.

The solution concept we have been using, at least for the game just described, is subgame perfect Nash equilibrium. Note where we use the subgame perfection: We assume that the agent accepts the contract and chooses his action optimally *given* the contract. We could easily construct subgame imperfect equilibria where the agent threatens to reject any contract that doesn't give him some amount more than his reservation level of utility. (Or he could threaten to accept such a contract but then take an action that, while suboptimal for him, is disastrous for the principal.) We have implicitly ruled out such threats.

It sometimes troubles readers that in our equilibria the agent is indifferent between many courses of action, and we assume he chooses the one we or, rather, the principal desires. But this is standard fare for this form of analysis. Thinking of this as a game, it is the continuous action space for the principal that forces this in our solutions. If, for example, we tried to require that the principal offer a contract that makes acceptance strictly better than rejection, there would be no optimal contract at all: At any contract where the participation constraint doesn't bind, we can design a better contract where it still doesn't bind. And there would be no subgame perfect equilibrium of our game. If the agent used the strategy of rejecting contracts that gave him precisely his reservation utility, the principal's better response (assuming she gets positive net profits at the optimal scheme) would be to sweeten the contract just a bit, so the agent isn't indifferent. But there is no optimal amount of sweetener to put in; there is no single best response. The only way we get equilibrium is to assume that ties are broken in a fashion that favors the first mover.[f] This is a "problem" with the style of analysis we use that you should learn to live with, because it is pervasive in the literature.

16.4. Continuous actions: The first-order approach

If you consult the early literature on the principal-agent model, you will find models that assume that both the possible signals and the possible actions or effort levels are not finite in number. The typical model will say that the agent can choose any effort level drawn from some interval $[a_0, a_1]$ and that the range of possible gross profit levels is R or some appropriate subinterval.

Some technical difficulties arise if there are infinitely many possible signals or outcomes. These are especially associated with assumption 1: You can't say that every outcome has positive probability when there are uncountably many. The important part of assumption 1, though, is that likelihood ratios are uniformly bounded and bounded away from zero, for any two actions, as we vary the signals. These are technical difficulties, and while there is some economic intuition to them (see problem 8), we will not pursue them here.

We should, however, discuss the technical difficulties that arise when actions or effort levels are chosen from some interval. To fix matters, we use the model of two possible outcomes, success and failure, and an action choice that bears the interpretation of "effort." Effort is chosen from an interval $[a_0, a_1]$ where effort is measured on the scale of disutility; i.e., $U(w, a) = u(w) - a$ for some function u satisfying assumption 2. If effort level a is chosen, then the probability of a successful outcome is $\pi(a)$, where $\pi(\cdot)$ is a strictly increasing function.

How are we to construct the subproblem analogous to (Cn) in this

---

[f] Or, to be very precise, this is so in cases where the first mover has a rich enough strategy space so that she could, at vanishing cost, "enforce" the choice she wants.

case? If we want to discover the minimal cost of implementing a^*, we would seem to want to solve

$$\text{minimize } (1 - \pi(a^*))v(x_f) + \pi(a^*)v(x_s)$$
$$\text{subject to } (1 - \pi(a^*))x_f + \pi(a^*)x_s - a^* \geq u_0$$
$$\text{and } (1 - \pi(a^*))x_f + \pi(a^*)x_s - a^* \geq$$
$$(1 - \pi(a))x_f + \pi(a)x_s - a \text{ for all } a \in [a_0, a_1],$$

where the decision variables x_f and x_s are the utility wage levels contingent on failure and success, respectively.

The last "constraint," which is really an infinite number of constraints, is a killer to handle analytically. So in much of the early literature the following reasoning was employed. The last "constraint" can be recast as: The function

$$U(a) = (1 - \pi(a))x_f + \pi(a)x_s - a$$

should be maximized at $a = a^*$. The maximand of this function, assuming that it doesn't fall at one of the endpoints of $[a_0, a_1]$, can be found from the first-order condition $U'(a) = 0$ or

$$\pi'(a)[x_s - x_f] = 1.$$

So simply substitute this first-order condition into the subproblem formulation in place of the last constraint. That is, rewrite the problem of implementing a^* at minimal expected cost as

$$\text{minimize } (1 - \pi(a^*))v(x_f) + \pi(a^*)v(x_s)$$
$$\text{subject to } (1 - \pi(a^*))x_f + \pi(a^*)x_s - a^* \geq u_0$$
$$\text{and } \pi'(a^*)[x_s - x_f] = 1.$$

Fixing a^*, this gives us two equations in two unknowns (assuming both constraints bind), and we are virtually home free.

Or are we? Is it legitimate to replace the infinite set of relative-incentive constraints with a single "first-order constraint?" In general, it is not. But one can give conditions under which this approach does work. Suppose assumption 5 holds. In this context, this is just a statement that $\pi(\cdot)$ is a concave function. Then for any nondecreasing wage-incentive scheme (that is, any scheme that pays at least as much for success as for failure), we know from earlier analysis that the agent's expected utility function $U(a)$ as defined above is concave. If $\pi(\cdot)$ is assumed to be differentiable, then $U(\cdot)$ is also differentiable. And we then know that solution of the first-order condition is necessary and sufficient for an optimum, at least off the boundary. Moreover, in this two-outcome case, it is easy to argue from first principles that the optimal incentive-wage system is nondecreasing. So we know indeed that this approach is valid in this case *if assumption 5 holds*. But if assumption 5 doesn't hold, then one doesn't always obtain the optimal solution by this process. In particular, a scheme designed to satisfy the participation and first-order constraints may not satisfy all the relative-incentive constraints; i.e., it may not even be a feasible solution to the original problem.

When you read in the literature about the first-order approach to the principal-agent problem and about problems in that approach, it is this to which reference is being made.

Let us harvest at least one simple result from this first-order approach. Assume that $\pi(\cdot)$ is concave, so the approach is valid, and assume that $\pi(\cdot)$ is continuously differentiable. Consider the problem of implementing effort level a. The first-order constraint is

$$\pi'(a)[x_s - x_f] = 1 \ \text{ or } \ x_s - x_f = \frac{1}{\pi'(a)}.$$

Substituting this into the participation constraint, we obtain the solution

$$x_f(a) = u_0 + a - \frac{\pi(a)}{\pi'(a)} \ \text{ and } \ x_s(a) = u_0 + a + \frac{1 - \pi(a)}{\pi'(a)}.$$

Hence the expected level of wages that must be paid to implement a is

$$C(a) = (1 - \pi(a))v(x_f(a)) + \pi(a)v(x_s(a)).$$

Note well: This doesn't apply to $C(a_0)$; by the (I hope by now) obvious argument, to implement the lowest level of effort the principal should pay constant wages of $v(u_0 + a_0)$, which gives $C(a_0) = v(u_0 + a_0)$. We have:

Proposition 5. *Assume that u is strictly concave and that assumptions 1 through 5 all hold.*

(a) The function $x_f(a)$ is nonincreasing in a.

(b) The function $x_s(a)$ is nondecreasing in a.

(c) The function $C(a)$ is increasing in a.

(d) All of these functions are continuous for $a > a_0$. At $a = a_0$ they jump as follows: x_f jumps down; x_s and C jump up.

We leave the proof to you, with the following hints. For (a) and (b), take the derivatives of these functions, being careful about the value a_0. For (c), use parts (a) and (b), the fact that $(1 - \pi(a))x_f(a) + \pi(a)x_s(a) = u_0 + a$, and the convexity of v. (Draw a picture of v, and locate the points $x_s(a)$ and $x_f(a)$ for two values of a.) Continuity of all these functions for $a > a_0$ follows from the fact that they are made up of continuous functions. The jump discontinuities rely on the fact that $\pi'(a_0) > 0$, which follows from concavity of π and assumption 3.

An economically interesting part of this lemma is the upward jump in C at a_0. Since $B(a)$ is a continuous function of a, we will not tend to find optimal incentive schemes that implement a "small" amount of effort relative to the lowest possible level. A discrete cost must be paid to get the agent to do anything above the minimum, and that discrete cost must be "covered" by a discrete increase in benefits, which in turn requires a discrete step-up in the amount of effort chosen by the agent.

Since you will see it in many papers on the subject, let us close here with the formulation in the case where the set of outcomes is an interval $[s_0, s_1]$ from R. (To follow precisely what comes next, you need to know about Lagrangians for problems with infinitely many decision variables. But even if you don't know about such rarified optimization theory, you may get the basic idea by reading on.) We assume that as a function of a the distribution of outcomes is given by the cumulative distribution function $\Phi(s; a)$, which is assumed to have a continuous density function $\phi(s; a)$. We write $x(s)$ for the wage-utility if the outcome is s. Then for a fixed incentive scheme given by $x(\cdot)$, the utility to the agent of expending effort a is

$$\int_{s_0}^{s_1} x(s)\phi(s; a)ds - a,$$

so the first-order condition that a^* is optimal is

$$\int_{s_0}^{s_1} x(s)\phi_a(s; a)ds = 1,$$

where $\phi_a(s; a)$ means the partial derivative of $\phi(s, a)$ with respect to a. The subproblem with this first-order constraint put in place of the relative incentive constraints is

$$\text{minimize} \int_{s_0}^{s_1} v(x(s))\phi(s;a)ds$$

$$\text{subject to} \int_{s_0}^{s_1} x(s)\phi(s;a)ds - a \geq u_0$$

$$\text{and} \int_{s_0}^{s_1} x(s)\phi_a(s;a)ds = 1.$$

Letting λ be the multiplier on the participation constraint and η the multiplier on the first-order constraint, the entire problem has "first-order condition"

$$v'(x(s)) = \lambda + \eta\left(\frac{\phi_a(s;a)}{\phi(s;a)}\right).$$

(When and if you see this in other places, you may see the left-hand side written as $1/u'(w(s))$, where the decision variable is the wages paid if the gross profit level is s. Of course, by the formula for the derivative of the inverse of a function, these come to the same thing.)

Our remarks about when the first-order approach is valid in the case of two signals carries over to this situation. If the appropriate analogue of assumption 5 holds, then the agent's objective function is concave for any nondecreasing wage-incentive scheme, and the agent's optimal response is characterized by the first-order condition. Moreover, in the spirit of our analysis in the previous section, one can show that the optimal wage-incentive scheme will be nondecreasing if, in addition to the analogue of assumption 5, the appropriate analogue of the monotone likelihood ratio property holds.

From this "first-order equation" one can obtain a number of interesting results. In particular, watch out for the so-called Holmstrom informativeness condition (Holmstrom, 1979; Shavell, 1979), which concerns when information will be used in an optimal incentive scheme.

16.5. Bibliographic notes and variations

The story developed in sections 16.2, 3, and 4 is the basic *principal-agent* problem, the starting point of the literature on incentives. We have dealt primarily with the problem in the context of labor contracts, where the notion is to induce an effort-averse worker to choose a desired level of effort. But other contexts have been explored. These ideas appear in the realm of public finance; one issue that is explored there is the design of an income tax that maximizes net tax revenue (or maximizes some particular social welfare functional), recognizing that workers may work less if the marginal tax rate is high. These ideas also appear in the realm of insurance markets where moral hazard is a problem. In each of these cases, there are reasons why it is not desirable to have the "agent" fully internalize the consequences of his actions: In the context explored in this chapter and in the context of hazard insurance, to share risk efficiently; and to promote equity or provide public goods in the context of public finance. The hallmark of these models is the trade-off between having the agent bear fully the consequences of his actions and obtaining the "other" sort of desirable end.

J. Mirrlees (1975) has made many of the significant contributions to the development of this theory, but his contributions are largely unpublished. The treatment given here relies heavily on Grossman and Hart (1983), and you would do well to see also Holmstrom (1979), Shavell (1979), Rogerson (1985), and Jewitt (1988) for related developments of the basic model.

A very large number of variations and elaborations on the basic model have been analyzed, some of which lead to results that cast quite a different light on the entire picture. We cannot hope here to give a complete survey, but we can offer a quick overview of a few interesting variations. (The references that are supplied are convenient and very far from exhaustive.) You may think of these variations as following (or combining) four basic lines: Incentive problems where the action choice is not interpreted as simple effort; problems where more than one agent and or principal is present; problems where time plays a significant role (the principal and agent deal not once but repeatedly and, perhaps, interactively); and problems concerning incentives when "agents" interact in imperfectly competitive environments.

Incentives to take appropriate decisions

The effort-aversion story we have given is not all that palatable in many contexts. When we think of providing incentives for managers, for example, it is not that the managers are necessarily effort averse, but that they tend to bend their efforts in directions that the principal might not particularly desire. (For the perspective of a sociologist on this, see J. Baron [1988].) This has led researchers to look into different sorts of formulations of the moral hazard problem, where incentives are designed to motivate agents to work according to the desires of the principal. Included here are studies of situations in which the agent will before taking an action receive some information that will be useful in making the decision. (Cases where the agent *already* possesses the information prior to the stage where he must accept or reject the contract are another variation, but this blends together material from this chapter and the next two.)

The general "technology" of section 16.3 can be adapted to analyze such situations. In essence, one specializes not with the story of effort aversion that we analyzed in some detail but with some other special structure.

There is a large variety of models of this sort in the literature, and any list is bound to be woefully incomplete. Moreover, many of these variations are set up to interact with factors that arise in multiperson or multiperiod situations to be discussed in a moment. A short list would include: Incentives for managers to invest capital fruitfully instead of in perks (Grossman and Hart, 1982); incentives to invest in human capital (Holmstrom and Ricart i Costa, 1986); incentives to obtain information about and invest in risky assets (Lambert, 1986); incentives issues in defense contracting (Baron and Besanko, 1987); incentives issues in regulated industries (Baron, 1989); incentives to obtain and use information in general (Demski and Sappington, 1987).

Multiple agents and multiple principals

Suppose that the principal in section 16.2 had not one but two salesmen going after different sales. Suppose that the reason one can't be sure what size sale will be made given the level of effort is that a competitive product might be better. Insofar as this competitive product affects the outcome to both salesmen, one would expect the outcomes that they achieve to be correlated. If one makes a large sale, then it is more likely that the competitive product is not so good. This increases the odds that the other will make a large sale, if he puts in the effort. In such a case, the principal might do well to structure the incentives so that the payment to one salesman depends on the outcome achieved by the other. For example, the principal might give them base wages, commissions on their own levels of sales, and a special bonus to the top salesman of the month/year. Or the principal might use an incentive scheme that is purely ordinal: So much for the agent who does the best, so much for the agent who comes in second, and so on. The literature on *tournaments* is about this sort of comparative incentives system.

More generally, when the random factors that affect the measured "performance" of one agent are correlated with factors that affect the measured performance of others, it can make sense to engage in relative performance evaluation. Analyses include Baiman and Demski (1980), Green and Stokey (1983), Holmstrom (1982b), Lazear and Rosen (1981), Mookherjee (1984), and Nalebuff and Stiglitz (1983). An issue that arises is whether agents will play the desired equilibrium when there is relative performance evaluation; see Demski and Sappington (1984) and Ma, Moore, and Turnbull (1988).[6]

For an example along these lines, see problem 3.

In the literature on tournaments and relative performance evaluation, it is usually assumed that each agent has a project on which he works, and for each project there is some (imperfect) indication of how hard the agent worked. A different situation arises when there is group production; a number of individuals all contribute to a single project, with a single signal produced of how hard they (collectively) worked. This leads in turn to questions concerning internal versus external monitoring and incentives and to questions about task design and work-group composition. (Do you put all the hardworkers in one group or do you spread them among several groups?) For models along these lines, see Holmstrom (1982b), McAfee and McMillan (1986), and Lazear (1989). In a variation each agent has his own project, but can devote some time and effort to helping fellow agents. The principal in such a case may wish to provide incentives that promote helping efforts. See, for example, Itoh (1988).

A different sort of multiperson variation concerns situations where one agent works simultaneously for many different principals. Think, for example, of a consultant who is kept on retainer or a salesman who sells products for many different companies. In this case there would be competition among the principals to get the agent to devote relatively more time and effort to their interests at the expense of the interests of the other principals. See Bernheim and Whinston (1986).

Multiperiod incentives

When the relationship between the principal and agent is of longer duration, then opportunities may appear to improve the incentives given to agents. Radner (1985) suggests that with many independent signals of how hard an agent is working one can use the law of large numbers to provide first-best incentives. Fudenberg, Holmstrom, and Milgrom (1988) provide further analysis of this and argue that the result is due more to the ability to spread risk through time in a multiperiod setting.

The models we analyzed suggested that optimal incentive schemes will in general be very complex, depending on the very fine structure of the environment. This is not a prediction that is verified empirically; incentive schemes in practice are usually quite simple. One explanation might be

---

[6] If the question here seems cryptic, wait until chapter 18.

that our models assume the principal has very precise information about the (distribution of) consequences of the agent's actions; if the details of the situation are somewhat hazy (which, presumably, one could model with incomplete information), then incentive schemes that are more robust to changes in the fine structure of the model might be more likely to be employed. A second explanation is offered by Holmstrom and Milgrom (1987). Within the context of a multiperiod, stationary environment, they show that optimal incentives will be "linear" in an appropriate sense. In essense, the idea is that the agent's ability to change his actions through time as consequences are realized gives him a great deal of control over the overall outcome. This, in turn, gives the agent the ability to manipulate any incentive scheme that depends on the fine details of an outcome; to avoid this, the principal chooses an incentive scheme that depends coarsely and simply on the overall outcome.

In the models so far discussed, the characteristics of the agent and the various tasks were held fixed and were assumed to be known to both the principal and the agent. But in many applications of interest, the difficulty of a particular task is not known a priori. In multiperiod contexts this complication multiplies. The principal observes what outcomes the agent obtains in early periods to try to gauge the difficulty of the task. If the agent does well early on, the principal will come to believe that the task is relatively easy, and she will, therefore, lower the incentive wages she is willing to pay. An agent who knows this is going to happen will in response tend to underperform early on to make the principal think that the job is relatively difficult. The principal, in equilibrium, is not deceived by this, but still in equilibrium the agent will hold back early on, so as not to convince the principal that the task is very easy. In general, the principal would benefit if, ex ante, she could commit to an incentive system that will not change as results unfold. But when she cannot so commit, this sort of *ratchet effect* complicates both the incentive system she puts in place and the agent's response to that system. For discussion and analysis, see Gibbons (1987) and Laffont and Tirole (1988).

The other side of this coin finds the principal unsure, a priori, how much ability the agent has. We imagine that the measured outcome of an agent compounds the agent's effort and some exogenous noise, as in this chapter, but also the agent's ability. Moreover, we imagine that the principal is willing to pay relatively more for a more able agent. (Think of there being a competitive market for labor services, although see the next paragraph.) Then insofar as a high level of output from an agent early on is taken as (partial) evidence that the agent is more able, the agent has a relatively greater personal incentive to work hard earlier; the principal, in response, may have less need to provide for immediate direct incentives. An early model along these lines is provided by Holmstrom (1982a).

Continuing along these lines, the question how an agent's immediate output affects the evaluation of the agent and his subsequent opportunities and pay has been the subject of much analysis. The general question of career concerns and its effect on incentive structures is investigated by Holmstrom (1982a). Milgrom (1988) and Milgrom and Roberts (1989) explore the incentives for workers to exert influence on their superiors and the consequences (in terms of optimal incentive structures) for organizational design. Another subject of interest is the existence of so-called internal labor markets, where employees of one firm rise within the firm; that is, workers join the firm primarily at low level "ports of entry" and then progress through the ranks. See Gibbons (1985) and MacLeod and Malcolmson (1988) for two analyses.

Incentives for agents who interact

Imagine a duopoly in which the firms compete in, say, Cournot fashion. Suppose that one firm is managed by its owner, but the second firm has a manager who is distinct from the owner. The owner of this second firm wishes to provide an incentive contract for her manager that will leave her (the principal) with as much net profit as possible. Beyond the sorts of issues that we considered, a new issue intrudes here: How will the incentive scheme employed for the manager of the second firm affect the production decisions of the owner-manager of the first firm? If, to take a simple example, the owner of the second firm could give her manager a contract where he only made money if he chose the von Stackelberg level of output, and if the owner-manager of the first firm knows this, then the owner-manager of the first firm will not respond (in equilibrium) as aggressively as if the second firm also had an owner-manager.

In general, when one provides incentives to an agent who interacts with others in a gamelike situation, the incentives provided can affect both what the agent and others do. This can significantly complicate the problem of designing incentives. See problem 2 for an example, and see Fershtman and Judd (1987) and Maksimovic (1986) for analyses.

Contextual applications

In the literatures of academic accounting, finance, operations, and marketing one can find many interesting applications of incentive theory. These applications are especially interesting because the models are often created with very specific institutions in mind. Some of the papers cited above are drawn from these literatures, and I will not attempt here to list others. But in looking for applications and variations, one should consult not only the economics journals but also journals such as the *Journal of Accounting Research*. Your attention is called in particular to one contextual application — the effect of the tax code on incentives, as studied in Scholes and Wolfson (forthcoming).

It would be easy to go on for pages more, listing interesting variations on the basic story given in this chapter. And a book of quite substantial length could be written giving details. Not having that much space, we suspend discussion here, although you will quickly realize that most of the remainder of the book deals in varying levels of formality with the problem of incentives to do one thing or another.

References

Baiman, S., and J. Demski. 1980. "Economically Optimal Performance Evaluation and Control Systems." *Supplement to the Journal of Accounting Research* 18:184–220.

Baron, D. 1989. "Design of Regulatory Mechanisms and Institutions." In *Handbook of Industrial Organization*, R. Schmalensee and R. Willig, eds. Amsterdam: North Holland.

Baron, D., and D. Besanko. 1987. "Monitoring, Moral Hazard, Asymmetric Information, and Risk Sharing in Procurement Contracting." *Rand Journal of Economics* 18:509–32.

Baron, J. 1988. "The Employment Relation as a Social Relation." *Journal of Japanese and International Economies* 2:492–525.

Bernheim, D., and M. Whinston. 1986. "Common Agency." *Econometrica* 54:923–42.

Demski, J., and D. Sappington. 1984. "Optimal Incentive Contracts with Multiple Agents." *Journal of Economic Theory* 33:152–71.

————. 1987. "Delegated Expertise." *Journal of Accounting Research* 25:68–79.

Fershtman, C., and K. Judd. 1987. "Equilibrium Managerial Incentives in Oligopoly." *American Economic Review* 77:927–40.

Fudenberg, D., B. Holmstrom, and P. Milgrom. 1988. "Short-term and Long-term Agency Relationships." Yale University. Mimeo. Forthcoming in *Journal of Economic Theory*.

Gibbons, R. 1985. "Incentives in Internal Labor Markets." In *Essays on Labor Markets and Internal Organizations*, Ph.D. diss., Stanford University.

————. 1987. "Piece-rate Incentive Schemes." *Journal of Labor Economics* 5:413–29.

Green, J., and N. Stokey. 1983. "A Comparison of Tournaments and Contracts." *Journal of Political Economy* 91:349–64.

Grossman, S., and O. Hart. 1982. "Corporate Financial Structure and Managerial Incentives." In *The Economics of Information and Uncertainty*, J. McCall, ed., 107–40. Chicago: University of Chicago Press.

————. 1983. "An Analysis of the Principal-Agent Problem." *Econometrica* 51:7–45.

Holmstrom, B. 1979. "Moral Hazard and Observability." *Bell Journal of Economics* 10:74–91.

————. 1982a. "Managerial Incentive Problems — A Dynamic Perspective." In *Essays in Economics and Management in Honor of Lars Wahlbeck*. Helsinki: Swedish School of Economics.

————. 1982b. "Moral Hazard in Teams." *Bell Journal of Economics* 13:324–40.

Holmstrom, B., and P. Milgrom. 1987. "Aggregation and Linearity in the Provision of Intertemporal Incentives." *Econometrica* 55:303–28.

Holmstrom, B., and J. Ricart i Costa. 1986. "Managerial Incentives and Capital Management." *Quarterly Journal of Economics* 101:835–60.

Itoh, H. 1988. "On Incentives to Help in Multi-Agent Situations." University of California at San Diego. Mimeo.

Jewitt, I. 1988. "Justifying the First-Order Approach to Principal Agent Problems." *Econometrica* 56:1177–90.

Laffont, J.-J., and J. Tirole. 1988. "The Dynamics of Incentive Contracts." *Econometrica* 56:1153–76.

Lambert, R. 1986. "Executive Effort and the Selection of Risky Projects." *Rand Journal of Economics* 16:77–88.

Lazear, E. 1989. "Pay Equality and Industrial Politics." *Journal of Political Economy* 97:561–80.

Lazear, E., and S. Rosen. 1981. "Rank-Order Tournaments as Optimum Labor Contracts." *Journal of Political Economy* 89:841–64.

Ma, C., J. Moore, and S. Turnbull. 1988. "Stopping Agents from Cheating." *Journal of Economic Theory* 46:355–72.

MacLeod, W., and J. Malcolmson. 1988. "Reputation and Hierarchy in Dynamic Models of Employment." *Journal of Political Economy* 96:832–54.

Maksimovic, V. 1986. *Optimal Capital Structure in Oligopolies*. Ph.D. diss., Harvard University.

McAfee, R., and J. McMillan. 1986. "Optimal Contracts for Teams." University of California at San Diego. Mimeo.

Milgrom, P. 1988. "Employment Contracts, Influence Activities, and Efficient Organization Design." *Journal of Political Economy* 96:42–60.

Milgrom, P., and J. Roberts. 1989. "An Economic Approach to Influence Activities in Organizations." *American Journal of Sociology* 94:154–79.

Mirrlees, J. 1975. "The Theory of Moral Hazard and Unobservable Behavior, Part I." Nuffield College, Oxford. Mimeo.

Mookherjee, D. 1984. "Optimal Incentive Schemes with Many Agents." *Review of Economic Studies* 51:433–46.

Nalebuff, B., and J. Stiglitz. 1983. "Prizes and Incentives: Towards a General Theory of Compensation and Competition." *Bell Journal of Economics* 13:21–43.

Radner, R. 1985. "Repeated Principal-Agent Games with Discounting." *Econometrica* 53:1173–98.

Rogerson, W. 1985. "The First-Order Approach to Principal-Agent Problems." *Econometrica* 53:1357–68.

Scholes, M., and M. Wolfson. Forthcoming. *Taxes and Business Strategy: A Global Planning Approach*. Englewood-Cliffs, N.J.: Prentice-Hall.

Shavell, S. 1979. "Risk Sharing and Incentives in the Principal and Agent Relationship." *Bell Journal of Economics* 10:55–73.

16.6. Problems

■ 1. To test your understanding of the model in section 16.2 consider the following reparameterization. The reservation utility level of the agent is only 3. A high level of effort gives $a = 3$, while a low level gives $a = 0$. (Thus, if we can contract contingent on the level of effort, we would have to pay \$9 for a low level of effort and \$36 for high.) A high level of effort gives no sale with probability .2, a \$100 sale with probability .4, and a \$400 sale with probability .4. For a low level of effort, the three probabilities are .4, .4, and .2.

(a) What is the optimal way to induce the agent to put in a low level of effort, if you can contract contingent on the size of the sale (only)?

(b) What is the optimal way to induce the agent to put in a high level of effort?

(c) What is the optimal contract (if you are a risk neutral principal) to offer this agent?

■ 2. *The point of this problem is "incentives meet duopoly theory."* Consider a simple duopoly problem, with two firms that are identical except in one important sense. The two produce an undifferentiated good, the (total) demand for which is given by the demand curve $P = A - X$, where P is price and X is total quantity produced. The two compete as Cournot competitors; each names a quantity supplied, simultaneously and independently of the other, and market price is set so that demand equals the sum of the two supplies. Both firms have zero marginal costs of production. (So far, completely standard.)

One firm is owner managed. The quantity decision for this firm is made by the owner, who retains any profits. This owner is risk neutral.

The second firm is not managed by its owner. The owner of the second firm has hired a manager and has given this manager a contract wherein the compensation paid to the manager is a linear function of the profits the firm shows, π, and the quantity that the firm sells, x_2. Specifically, this contract calls for the manager to be paid $\alpha\pi + \beta x_2$, where α and β are given constants. The owner retains any profits made by the firm, net of pay to the manager. Note well that the manager makes the quantity decision and not the owner, and the manager does so to maximize *her* compensation and not the net profits of the owner.

(a) What, in this case (for given α and β), is the Cournot equilibrium in the market? What (as a function of α and β) are the profits of the first firm, the manager's compensation, and the net profits (to the owner) of the second firm?

(b) The owner of the second firm is interested in designing the "optimal" contract for her manager. The contract must, in equilibrium, provide the manager with a reservation level of income Y. Other than that, the owner can choose any *linear* contract she wishes; α and β are chosen to maximize her net (after compensation) profits. The owner-manager of the first firm and the manager of the second firm will behave in Cournot fashion after this contract is chosen. If you are worried about such things, the owner-manager of the first firm will know the contract terms under which the manager of the second firm operates. What is that optimal contract? (Hint: Draw pictures!)

(c) Suppose now that both firms are managed by managers distinct from owners, both managers are paid according to contracts that have compensation linear in profits and sales quantity, and both managers have a reservation level of compensation that must be met. The two owners simultaneously and independently set the terms for their managers' (respective) contracts. What will be the equilibrium in this game?

(d) We can imagine, in (c), many possible ways this game is played. Here are two extremes.

In the first, the two owners simultaneously name contract terms for their managers. Those terms are named publicly, so each manager sees the terms offered to the other. The two managers then decide whether to take the contract offered. They do so if, in the subsequent round of quantity setting, they will get their reservation level of compensation. Then the managers set quantities. If only one manager signs, the other firm (the one without a manager) is out of the market, and the one with a manager acts as a (compensation-maximizing) monopolist.

In the second extensive form, the two owners simultaneously name contract terms, and the two managers either sign or not and choose quantities without knowing what is going on at the other firm. If the manager at a firm doesn't sign, then that firm cannot produce.

We're only looking for (subgame) perfect equilibria. Then does the formulation matter? In particular, which (if either) of these formulations have you assumed in your answer to part (c)?

■ 3. *In this problem, we will deal with incentives for multiple agents.* You are a manager in charge of two workers. Each worker is asked to perform a particular task, and each can either work hard at the task or loaf. The value to you of each task will be either $10 or $0. The value is determined in part by how hard the worker works, but there are also some random factors not within the control of the worker. The following data apply:

If the worker works hard, there is a .7 probability that the value to you will be $10 and a .3 chance that the value will be $0. If the worker loafs, these probabilities reverse, so that there is a .3 chance of a $10 outcome and a .7 chance of a $0 outcome.

Moreover, there is correlation between the outcomes of the two tasks:

• If both workers work hard, then there is .6 joint probability that each will produce a $10 outcome

• If both loaf, there is a .2 joint probability that each will produce a $10 outcome

- If one loafs and the other works, there is a .25 joint probability that each will produce a $10 outcome

(Start by putting together joint probability tables from the data above.)

Each worker has a utility function that depends on the amount of money received and the amount of effort expended. The form of the utility function is

$$U(w, a) = \sqrt{w} - a,$$

where w is the amount of money received, and $a = 0$ for loafing and $a = .8$ for working hard. The two workers have the same utility function, and each has a reservation utility level of 1. The worker's expected utility must be 1 to get the worker to take the job.

You as the employer are risk neutral. You seek to maximize your net profit from these two workers.

(a) Suppose that you could at zero cost monitor the efforts of the two workers. Would you want to make them work hard, or is it better to have them loaf? What payments would you offer them?

(b) Suppose that you cannot monitor the efforts of the two workers. You can, however, sign a contract of the form: I agree to pay $X if the task you perform has value $10 to me, and $Y if the task has value $0. Subject to the constraints that the worker must be willing to sign, and the worker, seeing what is being paid, will choose how hard to work, what is the best contract of this form for you? (The worker will resolve all ties in his utility in your favor.)

Now suppose that you cannot monitor the two, but you can offer them more complex contracts, of the following form: I agree to pay $X if both of you produce a $10 outcome for me, $Y if you produce a $10 outcome and your fellow worker produces $0, $Z if you produce $0 and your fellow worker produces a $10 outcome, and $W if you both produce $0.

(c) What contracts of this form are optimal if you want to induce both workers to loaf?

(d) Suppose that you wish to offer contracts that will induce both to work hard. Imagine that this means you must meet the following constraints: Each worker must be induced to take the contract; each worker, assuming that his fellow worker is going to work hard, must be induced to work hard. What is the optimal contract to offer in this case?

(e) You are worried that the contract offered in (d) might induce the following behavior: Each worker will loaf. You would feel less worried about this possibility if you knew that each one, given the other was loafing, would prefer to work hard. If you add this constraint to part (d), is the old solution still valid? If not, what is the new solution?

(f) Can you do better to induce one worker to loaf and the other to work hard? How well do you do in this case?

■ 4. I am trying to decide on the scale of investment that I will make in a particular project. The returns on my investment will depend on the scale of the investment and one environmental variable that will either be S or F. Right now, I think that the probability of S is .7. But out there is someone who could, with some effort, refine that assessment. This individual can run a test that will give one of two outcomes s or f, each with probability .5. If the test gives outcome s, then the posterior probability of S is .9, while if the outcome of the test is f, then the posterior probability of S is .5.

If I hire this individual, I can't observe whether she has run the test or, if she has, what outcome she actually got. She can report to me the outcome, but I will have to take her word for the fact that she ran the test and reported truthfully what the test result was. If she is indifferent between two reports or between running the test or not, she will resolve ties in the way that is most favorable to me.

I can pay this individual depending on her report and on the ultimate outcome S or F of the environmental variable.

Her von Neumann-Morgenstern utility function is given by

$$\sqrt{\text{Dollar payment to her}} - f(\text{effort}),$$

where $f(\text{no effort}) = 0$ and $f(\text{run the test}) = f > 0$. She has a reservation expected utility level of f'.

My utility takes the form

Expected Gross Benefits(my investment decision, true state)
− Expected payment to her.

I need some help in deciding whether to hire this person and, if I hire her, how to structure the payments I make to her. Help me. Write a (maximum) two-page memo to me outlining what I should do and why.

Please note that you don't have enough data to tell me whether to hire, or what contract to give her exactly. All that is desired is an outline of how I should go about solving the problem (justifying your suggested method of solution).

■ 5. Consider an individual who owns a warehouse that is subject to a fire danger. Suppose that the warehouse, if it burns at all, suffers damage that has a uniform distribution over the range from $10,000 to $190,000. The owner of this warehouse can take precautions against the event of fire — for simplicity, we imagine that the owner can either "take care" or "be negligent." The owner's decision whether to take care or be negligent affects the probability whether there is a fire at all: If she takes care, the probability a fire occurs π_1, while if she is negligent, the probability of a fire is $\pi_2 > \pi_1$. The extent of damage is independent of the action the owner takes, if there is a fire.

The owner's preferences are described by a von Neumann-Morgenstern utility function U that depends on the level of damages incurred in a fire (if any) and the actions she takes to prevent a fire. We write her utility function as $U(K - L - E)$ where K is some constant, L is the size of her loss, if any, and $E = 0$ if she is negligent and $E = \$10,000$ if she takes care. Note that if there is no fire, her utility will be $U(K - E)$. Assume that U is concave.

This individual has the opportunity to insure against her loss by fire. A typical insurance contract will take the following form: The owner pays a premium P up front; if the owner sustains a loss of size L, then the contract specifies an amount $\alpha(L)$ that is returned to the owner. In this case, the owner's utility is $U(K - L + \alpha(L) - E - P)$ if she has a fire with loss at level L and $U(K - E - P)$ if she has no fire. (We implicitly assume that $\alpha(0) = 0$.)

The insurance companies with which she might deal are all regulated by government authorities, and they are required to offer insurance at premiums that on average will net zero profit. That is, the premium P must be set to equal the expected payout on the insurance policy. (If you want to make the problem more realistic, you can change this. Assume instead that the insurance company is regulated so that some fixed small percentage of the premium it charges is taken as profit. This will, however, make some of the answers obtained below less clean than in the formulation we gave.) The owner can deal with at most one of these insurance companies.

(a) Suppose that insurance companies are compelled to offer complete coverage: $\alpha(L) = L$. What will be the results in terms of the insurance policy that is offered and the level of care the warehouse owner will take?

(b) Suppose insurance companies can offer insurance that insures only a portion of the loss incurred: $\alpha(L) = \gamma L$ for some $\gamma < 1$. Show by means of a numerical example that this might make the warehouse owner better off than if the insurance companies were compelled to offer full coverage.

(c) Suppose insurance companies can offer insurance that insures the full loss but with a deductible: $\alpha(L) = \max\{L - D, 0\}$ for some fixed deductible D. Show by means of a numerical example that this might make the warehouse owner better off than if the insurance companies were compelled to offer full coverage.

(d) Consider the problem of designing an insurance policy of the sort given above (where there is a fixed premium and a payment given back to the owner in the event of a fire in an amount that depends on the losses sustained) that is "optimal" in the sense that it makes the warehouse owner as well off as possible, given the regulatory constraint that the insurance company must break even on average. How would you go about finding this optimal policy? Can you say anything about the function $\alpha(L)$ at the optimal policy? For example, does $\alpha(L)$ rise with L?

(e) Suppose that the size of the loss sustained by the warehouse owner, given there is a fire, depends on the care she did or didn't take. More specifically, suppose that she is more likely to sustain a larger loss, given she has a fire at all, if she is negligent than if she takes due care. How does this affect your answers to part (d)?

■ 6. Consider the basic problem of section 16.3, but in a situation where the agent's utility function $U(w, a)$ is not necessarily additively separable. We assume that for each fixed a, $w \to U(w, a)$ is continuous, strictly increasing, and concave. Reformulate the method of solution of the basic problem in this case. (About the only thing to do here is decide on what you will make your decision variables and then write things down. Don't look for great mysteries or complications.)

The next three problems concern assumption 1. Problem 7 is relatively easy, and everyone should try it. Problem 8 is a bit more difficult. Problem 9 involves a fairly high level of skill at mathematical analysis.

■ 7. Suppose that we have a two-action, two-outcome principal-agent problem. The outcomes are denoted s_1 and s_2 and represent gross profits to the principal with $s_2 > s_1$. The two actions are effort levels, denoted a_1

and a_2, with $a_1 < a_2$. The agent's utility function is of the form $U(w, a) = -e^{-w} - a$, where a denotes effort and w is the wage payment. The first effort level results in outcome s_1 with probability .1 and s_2 with probability .9. The second effort level results in outcome s_2 with certainty. Show that it is possible, with a contract that depends on gross profit levels only, to implement the action choice a_2 at an expected wage payment that is arbitrarily close to the cost of implementing a_2 in a contract that can specify the action choice. (Note well: We don't constrain the wage payments to be nonnegative.)

■ 8. Suppose that we have a two-action, principal-agent problem where the range of possible outcomes is the entire real line R. As in problem 7, outcomes are gross profit levels. The agent's utility function is precisely as in problem 7. If the agent takes action a_1, the level of gross profits is Normally distributed with mean μ_1 and standard deviation $\sigma > 0$, whereas action a_2 gives gross profits that are Normally distributed with mean μ_2 and standard deviation σ for $\mu_2 > \mu_1$. Show that it is possible with a contract that depends on only gross profit levels to implement the action choice a_2 at an expected wage payment that is arbitrarily close to the cost of implementing a_2 in a contract that can specify the action choice.

■ 9. Prove that if assumptions 1 and 2 hold and if there is any set of decision variables (x_m) that satisfies the constraints of the problem (Cn) for given n, then the problem (Cn) has a (finite) solution. (Hints: To prove this, consider separately the case where u is linear and where it is not. When u is linear, think of the problem as a linear programming problem. The only way we could fail to find a finite solution is if we found an infinite ray along which the objective function decreased indefinitely. But from the participation constraint, we know that $\sum_{m=1}^{M} \pi_{nm} v(x_m)$ is bounded below by $a_m + u_0$. If, on the other hand, u is not linear, but concave, you can show that any unbounded sequence of solutions (x_m^k) of the participation constraint (where k indexes the sequence) must have an objective function value that diverges to $+\infty$. Hence you can restrict attention to bounded sequences of solutions of the constraints.)

■ 10. Prove that if assumption 3 holds, then $\sum_{m=1}^{M} \pi_{nm} s_m$ is increasing in n. (Hint: Read the proof of the first lemma after assumption 5. The key step is the interchange of the order of addition right near the start. If you understand that step, you'll see how to prove this.)

■ 11. Consider the second part of the example in the subsection of section 16.3 on the two-outcome case. What would happen if a_3 turned out better than a_2 at these wages? (Can you change the numbers so that this is so?) What would $C(a_2)$ be in that case?

■ 12. Prove proposition 5.

■ 13. Return to the finite action, finite outcome formulation of section 16.3 in the specialization where a is effort and the signals s are levels of gross profits. Assume that assumptions 1, 2, and 4 all hold and that u is strictly concave. An alternative to assumption 5 is: There are two probability distributions $(\pi_1^1, \ldots, \pi_M^1)$ and $(\pi_1^2, \ldots, \pi_M^2)$ such that for every action a_n there is a number $\alpha_n \in [0,1]$ with $\pi_{nm} = \alpha_n \pi_m^1 + (1 - \alpha_n)\pi_m^2$. (Assume that α_n is increasing in n. What conditions must hold between π^1 and π^2 so that assumption 4 is guaranteed?) Show that this alternative with assumptions 1, 2, and 4, is sufficient to show that the optimal wage-incentive scheme is nondecreasing in gross profits. (Hint: Do *not* try to prove that the only binding relative incentive constraints will be those of index lower than the effort level that is being implemented.)

chapter seventeen

Adverse selection and market signaling

Imagine an economy in which the currency consists of gold coins. The holder of a coin is able to shave a bit of gold from it in a way that is undetectable without careful measurement; the gold so obtained can then be used to produce new coins. Imagine that some of the coins have been shaved in this fashion, while others have not. Then someone taking a coin in trade for goods will assess positive probability that the coin being given her has been shaved, and thus less will be given for it than if it was certain not to be shaved. The holder of an unshaved coin will therefore withhold the coin from trade; only shaved coins will circulate. This unhappy situation is known as Gresham's law — bad money drives out good.

17.1. *Akerlof's model of lemons*

Gresham's law has had more recent expression in Akerlof (1970). (See problem 12 after you finish this section, however.) In Akerlof's context, Gresham's law is rephrased as "Bad used cars drive out good." It works as follows.

Suppose there are two types of used cars: peaches and lemons. A peach, if it is known to be a peach, is worth $3,000 to a buyer and $2,500 to a seller. (We will assume the supply of cars is fixed and the supply of possible buyers is infinite, so that the equilibrium price in the peach market will be $3,000.) A lemon, on the other hand, is worth $2,000 to a buyer and $1,000 to a seller. There are twice as many lemons as peaches.

If buyers and sellers both had the ability to look at a car and see whether it was a peach or a lemon, there would be no problem: Peaches would sell for $3,000 and lemons for $2,000.

Or if neither buyer nor seller knew whether a particular car was a peach or a lemon, we would have no problem (at least, assuming risk neutrality, which we will to avoid complications): A seller, thinking she has a peach with probability 1/3 and a lemon with probability 2/3, has a car that (in expectation) is worth $1,500. A buyer, thinking that the car might be a peach with probability 1/3 and a lemon with probability 2/3, thinks that the car is worth on average $2,333.33. Assuming an inelastic supply of cars and perfectly elastic demand, the market clears at $2,333.33.

Unhappily, it isn't like this with used cars. The seller, having lived with the car for quite a while, knows whether it is a peach or a lemon. Buyers typically can't tell. If we make the extreme assumption that buyers can't tell at all, then the peach market breaks down. To see this, begin by assuming that cars are offered for sale at any price above $1,000. All the lemons will be offered for sale. But only if the price is above $2,500 will any peaches appear on the market. Hence at prices below $2,500 and above $1,000, rational buyers will assume that the car must be a lemon. Why else would the seller be selling? Given this, the buyers conclude that the car is worth only $2,000. And at prices above $2,500, the car has a 2/3 chance of being a lemon, hence is worth $2,333.33. *There is no demand at prices above $2,000*, because (a) above $2,333.33, there is no demand whatsoever — no buyer is willing to pay that much — and (b) below $2,500 there is only demand starting at $2,000, since buyers assume that they must be getting a lemon. So we get as equilibrium: Only lemons are put on the market, at a price of $2,000. Further gains from trade are theoretically possible (between the owners of peaches and buyers), but these gains cannot in fact be realized, because buyers can't be sure that they aren't getting a lemon.

Note that if there were two peaches to every lemon, the story wouldn't be so grim. Then, as long as cars reach the market in these proportions, a buyer is willing to pay $2,666.67. And that is enough to induce owners of peaches to sell; we get the market clearing at this price, with all the cars for sale. (What does the demand curve look like in this case? What does the supply curve look like? Are there other market clearing prices? See problem 1.) Owners of peaches are not pleased about those lemon owners; without them, peach owners would be getting an extra $333.33 for their peaches. But at least peaches can be sold.

This is a highly stylized example of Akerlof's market for lemons. It illustrates the problem of *adverse selection*. Assume a particular good comes in many different qualities. If in a transaction one side but not the other knows the quality in advance, the other side must worry that it will get an adverse selection out of the entire population. The classic example of this is in life/health insurance. If premiums are set at actuarially fair rates for the population as a whole, insurance may be a bad deal for healthy people, who then will refuse to buy. Only the sick and dying will sign up. And premium rates must then be set to reflect this.

The problem noted above becomes worse the greater the number of qualities of cars and the smaller the "valuation gaps," the differences between what a car is worth to a buyer and a seller, assuming they have the same information. Imagine, for example, that the quality spectrum of used cars runs from real peaches, worth $2,900 to sellers and $3,000 to buyers, down to real lemons, worth $1,900 to sellers and $2,000 to buyers. Between the two extremes are cars of every quality level, always worth $100 more to buyers than to sellers. Suppose that the distribution of quality levels is uniform between these two extremes. To be very specific, suppose there are 10,001 cars, one of which is worth $1,900.00 to its owner and $2,000.00 to buyers, a second worth $1,900.01 to its owner and $2,000.01 to buyers, and so on. What will be the equilibrium then? (Continue to assume inelastic supply and elastic demand at every level of quality.)

Let us draw the supply curve first. At price $p = \$1,900$ there is one car offered for sale; at $p = \$1,901$ there are 101 cars offered, and so on. At $p = \$2,900$, all 10,001 cars are offered for sale, and that is all that is offered at any higher price. If we smooth out supply over the small discrete bumps, we get the supply curve shown in figure 17.1(a).

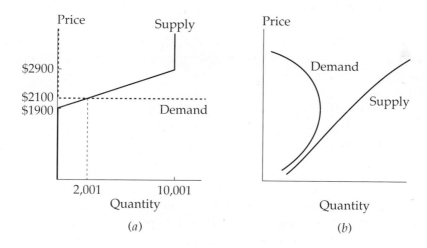

Figure 17.1. Supply and demand with adverse selection.
In (a), we have supply and demand for the second version of the lemons market. In (b), we depict the sad situation of upward sloping demand and a market that shuts down completely.

As for demand, at a price p between \$3,000 and \$2,000, buyers assume that only sellers who value their own cars at p or less are willing to sell. Hence a car being sold at price p has a quality level that makes it worth between \$2,000 and \$$(p + 100)$ to buyers, with each value in this range equally likely. Therefore, the average car being sold is worth \$$(2000 + p + 100)/2$. If p exceeds \$2,100, this average value is something less than p, *and there is no demand*. If p is less than \$2,100, this average value exceeds p, and there is infinite demand. At $p = \$2,100$ (plus or minus a penny) the average car offered for sale is worth \$2,100, and buyers are indifferent between buying and not. So we get the demand curve shown in figure 17.1(a) — no demand at prices exceeding \$2,100, perfectly elastic demand at $p = \$2,100$. The market equilibrium is where supply and demand cross, or $p = \$2,100$, at which only 2,001 of the 10,001 cars change hands. (And if the \$100 difference in valuations between buyers and sellers is \$50 instead, then the equilibrium price is $p = \$2,000$, and only 1,001 of the cars change hands.)

Let us do this one more time (just to pound it into your brain), at one level greater generality. We imagine that some item (a durable good, or some service) comes in one of N quality levels, $q^1, q^2, \ldots, q^N$, arranged in ascending order. The supply of quality n depends on the price p and is given by an upward sloping supply function $s^n(p)$. Demand depends on price p and the average quality in the market, which by the assumptions we've made can be computed as

$$q^{\text{avg}}(p) = \frac{\sum_n q^n s^n(p)}{\sum_n s^n(p)}.$$

Let $D(p, q^{\text{avg}})$ be this demand function, which we will assume is decreasing in p and increasing in q^{avg}. Hence market demand at a price p is obtained, at least if buyers anticipate where supply will come from, as $D(p, q^{\text{avg}}(p))$. To find the slope of market demand we compute

$$\frac{dD}{dp} = \frac{\partial D}{\partial p} + \frac{\partial D}{\partial q} \times \frac{dq^{\text{avg}}(p)}{dp}.$$

The first term on the right-hand side is negative. The second is a positive term, times $dq^{\text{avg}}(p)/dp$, which may be positive; average quality supplied may be increasing in price. Hence it is possible if the second term is large enough that demand has positive slope for some levels of price. And, therefore, it is even possible that we get the sort of picture in figure 17.1(b), where the only intersection between demand and supply is at zero; the market shuts down, even though gains from trade are possible.

17.2. Signaling quality

In spite of the lemons problem, used car markets and life/health insurance markets and all manner of markets subject to adverse selection do function. Why?[1] Often it is because the side to the transaction that has the superior information will do something that indicates the quality of the good being sold. With used cars, the seller may offer a partial warranty or may get the car checked by an independent mechanic.[2] In insurance, medical checkups are sometimes required. Another ploy in the realm of life insurance concerns "golden age" insurance, which is often marketed with the come-on that no one will be turned down. These policies often contain an important bit of fine print: "Benefits are greatly reduced for the first two years." That is, the insurance company is betting that if the buyer knows that he is going to die, it will probably happen quickly. The key to such signals is that the sellers of higher quality, or buyers in the case of insurance, to distinguish themselves from sellers of lower quality are willing to take actions the sellers of lower quality do not find worthwhile.

One can think of adverse selection as a special case of moral hazard and market signals as a special case of incentive schemes. We want the individual to self-identify as having a used car that is a lemon or a peach; as being gravely ill or not; and so on. But there is moral hazard in such self-identification; the seller of a used car cannot be trusted to represent honestly the quality of the car for sale unless provided with some incentive for doing so. The incentive could be relatively direct; the seller will be tossed in jail if he has egregiously misrepresented the quality of the car sold. Or it could be more indirect, as in the sort of market signals just described; the individual could be asked to give a six-month warranty if he says that the car is a peach. The point is that such an "incentive

---

[1] We saw one possible answer in chapter 14 — reputation. But in this chapter, we consider cases where the informed party isn't able to make use of a reputation, say because this is a one-time transaction. We could also use reputation indirectly, through recourse to a market intermediary such as a reputable used car dealer. But that takes us to topics we will discuss in chapter 20.

[2] Since the buyer can't be sure how independent this mechanic is, in the used car market in the United States it is often the buyer who will provide the mechanic and the money for this. But the signal is still being provided by the seller, insofar as she allows the buyer's mechanic to investigate the car. By way of contrast, in other countries "inspection companies" are so well known and credible that it is customary for the seller to provide a report from one of them. Remember this example when we discuss trilateral governance in chapter 20.

contract" (I will pay you $X if you don't give me a warranty and $Y >
$X if you do) gives the party with private information the incentive to
self-identify honestly, and the moral hazard problem of self-identification
is defeated.

The two classic models of this in the literature are Spence's (1974)
job market signaling model and Rothschild and Stiglitz's (1976) model of
an insurance market. While cast in different settings, the two seem at
first to be about the same problem. But their analyses come to different
conclusions. We will use the Spence setting to illustrate their two analyses
(and further variations): [3]

We imagine a population of workers, some of high innate ability, some
of low. We will use t to denote the level of ability, with $t = 2$ for high
ability and $t = 1$ for low. The numbers of high- and low-ability workers
are equal. There are also firms that will (eventually) hire the workers;
these firms operate in a competitive labor market and so will be making
zero profits (when all the dust settles) out of their workers.

The key ingredient comes next: Before going to work, workers seek
education that enhances their productivity. Specifically, each worker
chooses a level of education e from some set, say $[0, 16]$, for the number of years in school. [4] A worker of type t with education level e is
worth precisely te to a firm. Note that for every level of education, a
more able worker is worth twice as much as a less able worker. Firms,
when they hire a worker, are unable to tell whether the worker is able or
not. But they do get to see the worker's c.v., and they thereby learn how
many years the worker went to school. Hence they can make wage offers
contingent on the number of years that the worker went to school.

What do the workers want out of all this? They want higher wages,
to be sure. But they also dislike education. And the less able dislike
education even more than do the more able. Specifically, workers seek
to maximize a utility function of wages and education, which we will
write as $u_t(w, e)$, where w is the wage rate, e the education level, and t
the worker's type. We assume that u_t is strictly increasing in w, strictly
decreasing in e, and strictly concave. And we make the following very
important assumption: Take any point (e, w) and consider the two indifference curves of high- and low-ability workers through that point. (Refer
to figure 17.2, noting that the monotonicity and concavity assumptions
we made concerning the functions u_t give us strictly convex indiffer-

---

[3] In the problems, you will be given some leads on how these two stories are told in the
case of insurance markets.

[4] We allow any number between 0 and 16 to keep the pictures relatively simple. A treatment where education levels came only in discrete numbers would not be very different.

curves and the direction of increasing preference as depicted.) *We assume that the indifference curve of the low-ability worker is always more steeply sloped* (as in figure 17.2). That is, to compensate a worker for a given increase in education requires a greater increase in wages for a low-ability worker than for a high-ability worker. Both sorts of worker dislike education, but low-ability workers dislike education relatively more (measured in terms of wage compensation). This assumption is crucial for what follows because it implies that a more able worker finds it relatively cheaper (in terms of utility) to obtain a higher level of education, which then can be used to distinguish more able workers from those of lower ability. The assumption is known informally as the *single-crossing property*.[5] Utility functions of the form $u_t(w,e) = f(w) - k_t g(e)$, for f an increasing and concave function, g an increasing and strictly convex function, and the k_t positive constants with $k_2 < k_1$ constitute an example.

What would happen if the ability level of an employee were observable? Then a high-ability worker with education level e would be paid $2e$, and a low-ability worker with education level e' would be paid e'. As in figure 17.3, high- and low-ability workers will pick education levels that maximize their utility, given these wages.

But we are interested here in cases where ability level is not directly observable. Consider the following two stories: *job market signaling* and then *worker self-selection facing a menu of contracts*.

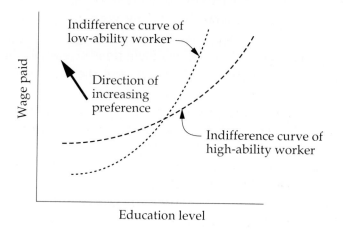

Figure 17.2. *Worker indifference curves in wages-education level space.*

---

[5] It is usually formulated with a bit more precision than we have done here, and you will be given the chance to provide a more precise formulation in the problems.

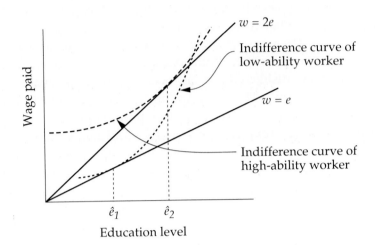

Figure 17.3. The full information equilibrium.
If ability is observable, high-ability workers will select education level $\hat{e}_2$
and be paid $2\hat{e}_2$, and low-ability workers will select $\hat{e}_1$ and be paid $\hat{e}_1$.

Spence's story: Job market signaling

Suppose that workers move first in the following sense. With no
guarantees except that they expect the market mechanism to work when
the time comes, workers choose how many years to go to school. They
do so anticipating some wage function $w(e)$ that gives wages for every
level of education. After they spend their time in school, they present
themselves to a competitive labor market, and the firms in that market
bid for their services.

*Formally, an equilibrium in the sense of Spence consists of (a) an anticipated
wage function $w(\cdot)$ that gives the wages $w(e)$ that workers anticipate will be
paid to anyone obtaining this education level e, for every e, and (b) probability
distributions π_t on the set of education levels for each type of worker $t = 1, 2$
such that the following two conditions are met:*

*(1) For each type t of worker and education level e, $\pi_t(e) > 0$ only if $u_t(w(e), e)$
achieves the maximum value of $u_t(w(e'), e')$ over all e'.*

(2) For each education level e such that $\pi_1(e) + \pi_2(e) > 0$,

$$w(e) = \frac{.5\pi_1(e)}{.5\pi_1(e) + .5\pi_2(e)}e + \frac{.5\pi_2(e)}{.5\pi_1(e) + .5\pi_2(e)}2e. \qquad (\clubsuit)$$

This has the following interpretation: $\pi_t(e)$ gives the proportion of type t workers who select education level e in equilibrium.[a] Then condition (1) is a *self-selection condition*: Based on the wages that workers anticipate, they only select education levels that with the corresponding wage levels maximize their utility. And condition (2) says that at education levels picked in equilibrium the wages paid are appropriate in a competitive labor market for a worker offering that education level. This comes about because the two fractions on the right-hand side of (♣) are the conditional probabilities that the worker is of low and high ability, respectively, obtained by Bayes rule.[6] Hence the right-hand side of (♣) is the conditional expected value of a worker presenting education level e, and (it is assumed) competition among firms pushes the worker's wage to that level.

In the definition of an equilibrium just given, we allow workers of a given type to choose more than one level of education. But we will restrict attention here to equilibria in which all the workers of a given type choose the same level of education:

In the first type of equilibrium, workers of the two types are **separated**; *this is called a* **separating equilibrium**. *All the workers of type $t = 1$ choose an education level e_1, and all the workers of type $t = 2$ choose an education level $e_2 \neq e_1$. Firms, seeing education level e_1, know that the worker is of type 1, and pay a wage e_1. And if they see education level e_2, they offer a wage of $2e_2$, because they correctly assume that worker is of type 2.*

In the second type of equilibrium, workers all **pool** *at a single education level; this is called a* **pooling** *equilibrium. All the workers choose some education level e^*, at which point wages are $1.5e^*$.*

In addition to these pooling and separating equilibria, there are other types, which you will explore in problem 2.

---

[a] If we wanted to be fancy, we would permit general probability distributions, replacing (1) with a statement about e in the support of the distribution and turning (2) into the appropriate statement about conditional probabilities. But this generality would be wasted. If you start with a general formulation, you can prove in this setting, with strictly concave u_t that no type would ever select more than a finite number of education levels; see problem 2.

[6] To be pedantic: $.5\pi_1(e)$ is the joint probability that a worker is of low ability and he chooses education level e obtained as the product of the marginal probability that a worker is of low ability, $.5$, and the conditional probability that a worker chooses education level e given he has low ability, $\pi_1(e)$. Hence $.5\pi_1(e) + .5\pi_2(e)$ is the marginal probability that a worker chooses education level e. And, by the rules of conditional probability, $.5\pi_1(e)/[.5\pi_1(e) + .5\pi_2(e)]$ is the conditional probability that a worker is of low ability given he chooses education level e.

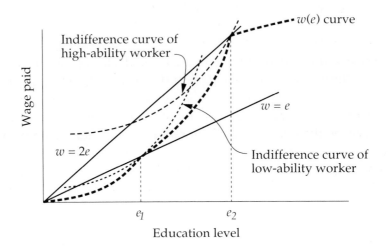

Figure 17.4. A separating equilibrium.
In this picture and in all others to follow, the heavy dashed curve indicates the workers' conjectures about what wages they will receive at every given level of education.

Return to the description of a separating equilibrium. For this to be an equilibrium, we need that workers, anticipating all this, are content to be separated in this fashion. That is, a worker of type 1 would rather choose the wage-education pair $(w = e_1, e = e_1)$ than $(w = 2e_2, e = e_2)$, and vice versa for workers of type 2. You'll see just such a situation in figure 17.4.

In this figure, note carefully the heavy dashed curve. This represents the function $w(e)$, workers' conjectures about the wages they will receive as a function of the level of education they select. Note that this function must lie everywhere at or below the indifference curves of the workers at points that the workers select; this is the self-selection condition. Condition (2) for an equilibrium pins down the $w(e)$ curve at the two levels of education selected, as shown.

This does not restrict the curve $w(e)$ at points e that are not selected in equilibrium. What restrictions might we wish to place on $w(e)$ at such points? For now, consider the following three possibilities:

(a) No restrictions whatsoever are placed on $w(e)$ at points e that are not selected in equilibrium. (We require throughout that $w(e)$ is nonnegative for every value of e; that is, the institution of slavery is not part of our economy.)

(b) We require that $e \leq w(e) \leq 2e$ for all e.

(c) We require (b) and, in addition, that $w(e)/e$ is nondecreasing.

What might motivate us to assume (b) or (c)? We reason as follows. A worker who chooses education level e is worth either e or $2e$ to a firm. The worker cannot possibly be worth more than $2e$ or less than e. Now if firms are unsure of the worker's level of ability, firms cannot be certain which of e or $2e$ is correct. And so, depending on their assessments for the chances that the worker is worth e or $2e$, they might be willing to bid anywhere between these two levels. But they would never pay more than $2e$, and the forces of competition between firms mean that they could never get away with paying less than e. Workers anticipate all this, so they anticipate that $e \leq w(e) \leq 2e$. As for (c), take this a step further and imagine that workers conjecture that firms will assess that a worker who chooses education level e will be of low ability with probability $\alpha(e)$. Assuming firms are risk neutral (which we do) and that they share assessments, competition amongst them would lead them to bid $w(e) = \alpha(e)e + (1 - \alpha(e))2e$. (Note that this is just another way of giving our justification for [b].) And now (c) can be translated as: $\alpha(e)$ is nonincreasing. Or firms' conjectures as to the ability of a worker do not give a higher probability for a lower-ability worker if the worker obtains more education.

At the risk of (re)stating the obvious, let us rephrase the equilibrium condition (2) in these terms. *We require that firms' assessments given by $\alpha(e)$ are confirmed at education levels that workers do select in equilibrium.* Or, in symbols,

$$\alpha(e) = \frac{.5\pi_1(e)}{.5\pi_1(e) + .5\pi_2(e)}.$$

If we imagine a stable population with new workers coming along and presenting themselves for employment each year, and if we imagine that the equilibrium distribution of workers' abilities and education levels is stable, then we would be saying that firms, based on their experience, know that distribution. What we do not restrict, or restrict only minimally, are the conjectures of firms at education level choices that are not chosen and, therefore, at which the firms have no experience.

> You may be thinking that we shouldn't speak directly about the firms' conjectures concerning the ability of a worker who chooses a nonequilibrium level of education. The function $w(e)$ represents the workers' conjectures about the wages they will be paid. Hence, at least, we should speak of

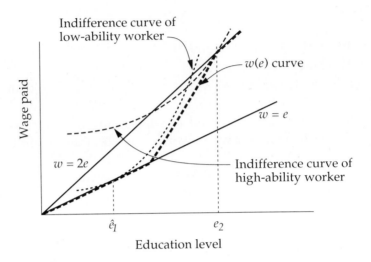

Figure 17.5. Another separating equilibrium.

the workers' conjectures concerning the firms' assessments about the ability of a worker who chooses a nonequilibrium level of education. And then, by having a single $w(e)$ function, we have implicitly assumed that all the workers have the same conjectures about the firms' assessments, and this conjecture holds that all the firms will have the same assessments. Are these assumptions of coincident conjectures and assessments necessary? If you are very careful, you should be able to see that much of what we will say does not depend on this, although we will hold to this implicit assumption to keep the exposition simple. You may also wonder why we have not introduced game-theoretic terminology for all of this. We will do so in the next section, but there are reasons to put this off for a while.

Note that the function $w(e)$ in figure 17.4 does not satisfy (b) or (c), although it does satisfy one somewhat obvious condition, namely that it is nondecreasing. In figure 17.5 we give a second separating equilibrium in which $w(e)$ does satisfy (b).

Note in figure 17.5 the point chosen by the low-ability workers, denoted by $\hat{e}_1$. This, as drawn, is the point along the ray $w = e$ that low ability workers like most; notice that their indifference curve through this point is tangent to $w = e$. In contrast, in figure 17.4, low-ability workers get less utility than they would get from $(w = \hat{e}_1, e = \hat{e}_1)$. We use $\hat{e}_1$

throughout this chapter to denote this particular point of tangency, and we have the following result:

Proposition 1. *In any separating equilibrium for which the function $w(e)$ satisfies (b), low-ability workers choose precisely $\hat{e}_1$ and get the corresponding wages. In any equilibrium (separating or not) for which the function $w(e)$ satisfies (b), low-ability workers get at least the utility that they get from $(w = \hat{e}_1, e = \hat{e}_1)$.*

You should have no problems at all seeing why this is true. Or, rather, you should have no problems with the first part of this proposition. The second part may be a tiny bit harder.

Pictures of pooling equilibria are relatively easy to draw. In a pooling equilibrium, recall, we assume that all the workers choose a single education level $e^\star$. As before, firms' beliefs, seeing $e^\star$, must be confirmed. Since we have supposed that the numbers of high- and low-ability workers in the population are equal, and since (in this equilibrium) all workers choose $e^\star$, we see that in terms of the notation above $\alpha(e^\star) = .5$, and $w(e^\star) = 1.5e^\star$. An equilibrium of this sort is given in figure 17.6. Note that the function $w(e)$ in this case satisfies (c). Note also that the function $w(e)$ has a kink at the pooling point. This is necessary; without a kink, we couldn't have $w(e)$ underneath both types' indifference curves and touching those curves at the pooling point.

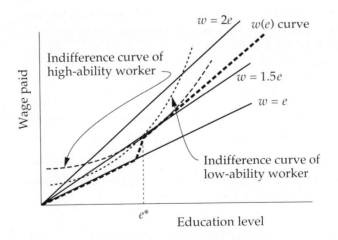

Figure 17.6. A pooling equilibrium.

As you can see (and imagine), there are a lot of equilibria here. Is there any reason to suspect that one is more plausible than another? We will get back to this question, but before doing so we look at another way to tell the basic story of market signaling.

The story of Rothschild and Stiglitz: Worker self-selection from a menu of contracts

In the story just told, workers choose education levels in anticipation of offers from the firm, and (we assume) those anticipations are correct, at least for the education levels actually selected. Let's turn this around and suppose that the firms move first. Specifically, suppose that firms offer to workers a number of "contracts" of the form (w, e) before workers go off to school. Workers consider the menu of contracts on offer, sign the one they like best, and then go off to school, content in the knowledge of what wage they will get once school is done (assuming they complete the number of years of schooling for which they have contracted). This story may seem a bit lame in the context of education level choices. If you find it so, think instead of insurance markets, the context with which Rothschild and Stiglitz deal explicitly. Insurance companies are willing to insure one's life in any of a number of ways, with different premiums, death benefits, exclusions, and so on. A customer shops for the policy best suited to himself, given both his preferences and, what is important here, the knowledge he has about his prospects for a long and healthy life.

An equilibrium in the sense of Rothschild and Stiglitz consists of (a) a menu of contracts, a set of pairs $\{(w^1, e^1), (w^2, e^2), \ldots, (w^k, e^k)\}$ for some finite integer k [b] and (b) a selection rule by which workers are "assigned" to contracts or, for each type t, a probability distribution π_t over $\{1, 2, \ldots, k\}$, that satisfy three conditions:

(1) Each type of worker is assigned only to contracts that are best for that worker among all the contracts in the menu. In symbols, $\pi_t(j) > 0$ only if $u_t(w^j, e^j)$ achieves the maximum of $u_t(w^{j'}, e^{j'})$ for $j' = 1, \ldots, k$.

(2) Each contract in the menu to which workers are assigned at least breaks even on average. (Otherwise, firms offering that contract would withdraw the contract.) In symbols, for each $j = 1, \ldots, k$, if $\pi_1(j) + \pi_2(j) > 0$, then

$$w^j \leq \frac{.5\pi_1(j)}{.5\pi_1(j) + .5\pi_2(j)} e^j + \frac{.5\pi_2(j)}{.5\pi_1(j) + .5\pi_2(j)} 2e^j.$$

---

[b] We assume that the menu of contracts offered is finite mostly for expositional convenience.

(3) No contract can be created that if offered in addition to those in the menu would make strictly positive profits for the firm offering it, assuming that workers choose among contracts in a manner consistent with rule (1) above.

We won't try to write (3) out formally — it makes a good exercise if you are fascinated by symbol manipulation. [c]

This change in formulation has dramatic effects. To begin the analysis, we assert something common to the Spence formulation:

Proposition 2. *In an equilibrium, any contract that is taken up by workers must earn precisely zero expected profits per worker.*

The proof of this is a little tricky.[7] A natural argument to try runs as follows: Suppose that (w', e') is offered, is taken by some workers, and earns an expected profit of size ϵ per worker who took it. Then have some firm offer $(w' + \epsilon/2, e')$. This new contract will attract all the workers who previously were attracted by (w', e') and will still return a profit of $\epsilon/2$, contradicting condition (3) of an equilibrium. The trouble with this argument is that the new contract may attract others besides those who previously took (w', e'), and those others may render this contract unprofitable.

Only a sketch of the correct proof will be given, with details left for the reader to fill in. First, the argument just given works if the contract (w', e') attracts only low-ability workers. Then if $(w' + \epsilon/2, e')$ manages to attract any high-ability workers, it is even more profitable. So the hard case is where (w', e') attracts some high-ability workers. At this point, wait to read through the proof of proposition 3, which shows how to break a pooling equilibrium. The key to that argument is that it is possible to devise a contract $(w' + \epsilon/2, e' + \delta)$, for $\delta > 0$ that is more attractive to high-ability workers than is (w', e') but is less attractive to low-ability workers. Hence if a firm offers this contract, it will attract all the high-ability workers who previously chose (w', e'), leaving the low-ability workers at (w', e') (or somewhere else). If (w', e') made profits ϵ per worker, then this new contract makes profits exceeding $\epsilon/2$ per worker.

---

[c] And if you do try to write this out formally, you will run up against the following question: Should we insist that the contract earn nonpositive profits for every assignment consistent with (1), or just that it make nonpositive profits for some assignment consistent with (1)? It won't matter to the theory which you choose, as long as you are careful about the arguments that follow.

[7] In Spence's formulation, it is true by fiat.

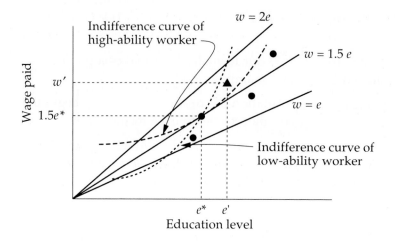

Figure 17.7. Destroying a pooling equilibrium.

Now we give a result that distinguishes this model from that of Spence:

Proposition 3. *It is impossible that an equilibrium is a pooling equilibrium.*

The argument runs as follows: Consider figure 17.7, and the pooling equilibrium depicted. Suppose the firms are offering a menu of contracts that causes all the workers to choose $(1.5e^\star, e^\star)$ as shown. In this figure, the filled-in dots are the menu of contracts that we suppose are offered. We have added a few contracts to the menu besides $(1.5e^\star, e^\star)$, although they are irrelevant, since (in our pooling equilibrium) the contract $(1.5e^\star, e^\star)$ is best for all types of worker.

From this position, any one of the firms can offer the contract (w', e') that is shown as a filled-in triangle. Saying in words what the picture shows: This is a contract that has slightly higher wages and education levels than $(1.5e^\star, e^\star)$, where the increased wages more than compensate a high-ability worker but don't compensate a low-ability worker relative to the pooling contract. Since this contract is added to the contracts already in the menu, it will only attract the high-ability workers; all the low-ability workers prefer the $e^\star$ offer. But if all the high-ability workers flock to (w', e'), and none of the low-ability workers do so, each worker who chooses (w', e') will be worth $2e'$ to the firm that makes this offer. The firm makes a profit, and we can't have an equilibrium.

The same sort of argument can be used to establish

Proposition 4. *It is impossible, in equilibrium, that any contract (w, e) is taken by positive fractions of the high- and low-ability workers both. Or, in other words, the only possible equilibria are separating equilibria.*

The details are left to you; a picture very much like figure 17.7 is the key. Next we establish

Proposition 5. *There is a single candidate for a separating equilibrium. In this candidate equilibrium, low-ability workers choose the contract $(\hat{e}_1, \hat{e}_1)$, where $\hat{e}_1$ is defined as before, and ... (to be continued)*

Why must this be so? Because if low-ability workers are separated and are choosing any other contract, a firm could add to the menu of contracts a contract $(w = \hat{e}_1 - \delta, e = \hat{e}_1)$ for $\delta > 0$ small enough so that low-ability workers prefer this to the contract they are choosing in the supposed equilibrium. But then for any $\delta > 0$, this contract must be profitable.

Fixing $\hat{e}_1$ at this value, define the education level $\hat{f}_1$ to be that level of education such that low-ability workers are indifferent between $(w = \hat{e}_1, e = \hat{e}_1)$ and $(w = 2\hat{f}_1, e = \hat{f}_1)$. Figure 17.8 shows this point. And let $\hat{f}_2$ solve the problem: Maximize $u_2(2e, e)$ subject to $e \geq \hat{f}_1$. That is, $\hat{f}_2$ is the

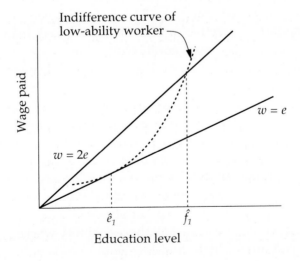

Figure 17.8. Determination of $\hat{f}_1$.

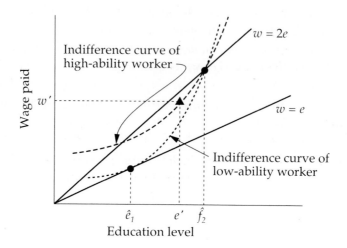

Figure 17.9. A separating equilibrium.

education level that high-ability workers would choose if they could have any point along the ray $w = 2e$ for $e \geq \hat{f}_1$.

Proposition 5, continued. ... *and (in the single candidate separating equilibrium) high-ability workers get* $(w = 2\hat{f}_2, e = \hat{f}_2)$.

Why? Because if they are separated at any other contract, some firm could come along and offer a contract $(w = 2\hat{f}_2 - \delta, e = \hat{f}_2)$ that for δ sufficiently small would be more attractive to high-ability workers than the contract they are taking at the supposed equilibrium. Since $\hat{f}_2 \geq \hat{f}_1$, this contract is less appealing than $(w = \hat{e}_1, e = \hat{e}_1)$ for the low-ability workers. Hence this contract will attract precisely the high-ability workers. And thus for any $\delta > 0$, this contract is strictly profitable.

Consider figure 17.9. We have there depicted the proposed separating equilibrium in a case where $\hat{f}_2 = \hat{f}_1$. It may be helpful to say why no firm would try to break this equilibrium by offering a contract in a position such as (w', e') that is shown, with w' a bit less than $2e'$ and e' a bit less than $\hat{f}_1$. This contract, added to the menu, would certainly attract high-ability workers. And every high-ability worker attracted would be profitable at this wage. But it would *also* attract all the low-ability workers. And in this population, if you attract high- and low-ability workers in proportion to the population, you have to pay less than 1.5 of the education level they pick to make a profit.

Now consider figure 17.10. This is just like figure 17.9, except that the indifference curve of the high-ability workers through the point ($w = 2\hat{f}_2, e = \hat{f}_2$) dips below the line $w = 1.5e$. In this case, a firm could offer a contract such as (w', e') as shown, below the line $w = 1.5e$, but still above the high-ability worker's indifference curve. This would break the equilibrium, because even though it attracts all the workers, high-ability and low-, it is still profitable.

In figure 17.10, then, there can be no equilibrium at all. Any sort of pooling is inconsistent with equilibrium. And the only possible separating equilibrium can also be broken. In contrast, although we won't go through all the details, in situations such as figure 17.9 (or situations where $\hat{f}_2 > \hat{f}_1$), the candidate separating equilibrium is an equilibrium. Summarizing all this:

Proposition 6. *In the formulation of Rothschild and Stiglitz, there is at most one equilibrium. In the candidate equilibrium, low-ability workers choose ($w = \hat{e}_1, e = \hat{e}_1$) and high-ability workers choose the education level $\hat{f}_2$ such that ($w = 2\hat{f}_2, e = \hat{f}_2$) is their most preferred point along the ray $w = 2e$ for $e \geq \hat{f}_1$. If the indifference curve for high-ability workers through the point ($w = 2\hat{f}_2, e = \hat{f}_2$) dips below the pooling line $w = 1.5e$, then there is no equilibrium at all. If this indifference curve stays above (or just touches) the pooling line, then this single candidate equilibrium is an equilibrium.*

Quite a difference from Spence's model, where there were many possible equilibria!

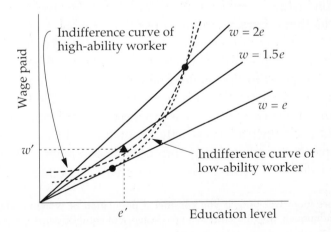

Figure 17.10. No equilibrium at all.

The stories of Riley and Wilson

In many markets where signaling takes place, such as insurance, it seems natural to suppose that the uninformed parties put a menu of offers "on the table" from which informed parties must choose. So the conclusion of the Rothschild and Stiglitz analysis, namely that there may be no equilibrium at all, is rather troubling.[d] A number of authors have suggested that the "flaw" in the analysis lies in the notion of equilibrium proposed by Rothschild and Stiglitz. In particular, it is implicit in the equilibrium notion that if a new contract is added to the menu, nothing further (concerning the menu) changes. In place of this, one might imagine that firms already offering contracts would react in one way or another, possibly rendering previously profitable deviations unprofitable and restoring particular equilibria.

Two of the original treatments of this are due to Riley (1979) and Wilson (1977). Riley advances the notion of a *reactive* equilibrium, in which, to destroy a proposed equilibrium, it must be possible to add a contract to the menu that will be strictly profitable and that will not become strictly unprofitable if other firms are allowed to *add* still more contracts to the menu.[8] In this sort of scheme, our argument for why there are no pooling equilibria stands up; we broke a pooling equilibrium by adding a contract that attracted high-ability workers only, given that the pooling contract remained to attract low-ability workers. There is no way to make this pool-breaking contract strictly unprofitable as long as the old pooling contract remains, because as long as that old pooling contract is present, only high-ability workers would ever consider taking the new contract. But you are much more at risk when adding a contract that attempts to break a separating equilibrium by pooling high- and low-ability workers. For in this case, still another contract can be added that siphons from your contract the high-ability workers, leaving you (the original defector) with only low-ability workers. Hence, Riley concludes, reactive equilibria always exist, and they correspond to the single candidate separating equilibrium.

Wilson, on the other hand, proposes a notion called an *anticipatory* equilibrium. In this case, to break a proposed equilibrium it must be possible to add a contract that is strictly profitable and that doesn't become strictly unprofitable when (now) unprofitable contracts from the original menu are *withdrawn*. Now if you try to break a pooling equilibrium by

---

[d] It becomes more troubling if you consider a population of workers whose education levels are continuously distributed. Then nonexistence of equilibrium is the "usual" state of affairs; cf. Riley (1979).

[8] The discussion given here is a bit rough. Consult the literature to get more precise statements of these results.

skimming the high-ability workers, you are at risk; the pooling contract that you destroy becomes unprofitable because after your addition it attracts only low-ability workers. But if it is withdrawn, all these low-ability workers may flock to your contract. On the other hand, if you break a separating equilibrium with a pooling contract, you are not at risk; because you have created a contract that attracts all the workers, you don't care if other, now unused contracts are withdrawn. So, Wilson concludes, anticipatory equilibria always exist; sometimes there is more than one; and pooling is possible as an equilibrium outcome.

How do we sort between Rothschild and Stiglitz, Riley, and Wilson? This clearly depends on what you think are reasonable assumptions in a given market concerning firms' abilities to add or withdraw contracts from what is offered to the public. Think in terms of an insurance market that is regulated by some regulatory authority. If you think that firms cannot withdraw contracts because (say) the regulatory authority forbids this, then Riley's equilibrium concept seems the more reasonable. If you think that the regulatory authorities permit the firms to withdraw unprofitable contracts and are very tough on adding contracts that potentially affect the profitability of others, then Wilson's notion seems quite reasonable. As for Rothschild and Stiglitz, think of regulators who call for firms to register simultaneously and independently the contracts they wish to offer, with no room to add or subtract subsequently. (Do any of these sound particularly realistic to you? If not, see the discussion in section 17.4.)

17.3. *Signaling and game theory*

If you paid attention to part III of this book, you should have no difficulty guessing where the preceding paragraph is taking us. We can try to sort through the different equilibrium concepts by sorting through details of the market institutions. Perhaps by specifying precise "rules of the game" we can see when one equilibrium notion or another is more relevant.

Spence's model in game theoretic terms

It is easy to distinguish between Spence on the one hand and Rothschild and Stiglitz on the other. For Spence's story, consider the following extensive form game with incomplete information. A worker's abilities are determined by nature and are revealed to the worker. That is, this is a game of incomplete information about the worker's level of ability. The worker, based on this, determines how much education to obtain. The level of education obtained, but not the worker's abilities, is observed by a number of firms, who then bid in Bertrand fashion for the worker's services. [e]

The Nash equilibria of this game are precisely the equilibria of Spence if we do not add any restrictions to $w(e)$ beyond the basic (equilibrium) restriction that $w(e)$ must be "correct" for levels of education that are chosen in equilibrium by the worker. Firms' responses to other choices of e are out-of-equilibrium responses, since the worker wasn't supposed to pick those levels of e, and (as you will recall) the Nash equilibrium criterion doesn't restrict out-of-equilibrium responses. We restrict those responses by refining the Nash concept. Subgame perfection isn't much use in this case; this game of incomplete information has no proper subgames. But the notion of sequential equilibrium is quite helpful. For example, if we require that the equilibrium is sequential, then we get precisely restriction (b) on the $w(e)$ function; at every level of education, including those that are out-of-equilibrium, each firm must have out-of-equilibrium beliefs $\alpha(e)$ that the worker is low ability, and must bid accordingly. [f] And restrictions such as (c) that $\alpha(e)/e$ must be nonincreasing are straightforward restrictions on beliefs; restriction (c), for example, says that the probability assessed by a firm that a worker is of high ability is nondecreasing in the level of education the worker chooses.

In fact, high-powered restrictions on out-of-equilibrium beliefs are very powerful in this sort of application. Let us pose here three increasingly stiffer restrictions, and then see where they lead:

(1) The equilibrium should be sequential.

(2) Suppose a type t of worker and education levels e and e' are such that $u_t(e,e) > u_t(2e',e')$. Then in any Nash equilibrium, it must be possible to sustain the equilibrium outcome with beliefs that put probability zero on education level e' being selected by type t.

(3) Fix a sequential equilibrium, and let u_t^* be the equilibrium level of utility achieved in this equilibrium by a worker of type t. Suppose that for some type t and education level e', $u_t(2e',e') < u_t^*$. Then it must be possible to sustain the given equilibrium outcome with beliefs that put probability zero on education level e' being selected by type t.

---

[e] By having the firms bid in Bertrand fashion, we are guaranteed that in any equilibrium the worker will be paid his conditional expected value, conditional on the level of education he selects. This is true in any Nash equilibrium for education levels that are selected with positive probability in the equilibrium, and it is true in any sequential equilibrium for any education level at all, where we compute conditional expected values using the firms' beliefs.

[f] The fact that the firms all have the same out-of-equilibrium beliefs derives from the consistency requirement of a sequential equilibrium. If we dropped this for something weaker, the "answers" would not change much, but the analysis would be a bit trickier.

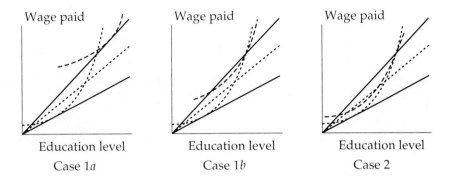

Figure 17.11. Three cases for market signaling.

Requirement (1) is entirely straightforward. The motivation behind (2) runs as follows: Fix t, e, and e' as postulated. In *any* sequential equilibrium a type t worker is guaranteed utility level at least $u_t(e, e)$ if he picks education level e. If he picks e', the best he could conceivably do is $u_t(2e', e')$. So if he anticipates sequentially rational responses by employers at all levels of education, he has no business whatsoever in picking education level e'; he is guaranteed a better outcome if he picks e. Employers should be able to figure this out and, therefore, assess probability zero that the choice of education level e' comes from t. Requirement (2) is that the equilibrium can be sustained with beliefs so restricted.

Requirement (3) takes (2) another step. There the test is, Is the best that type t can do if he chooses e' worse than what he gets *in equilibrium*? If so, requirement (3) is that employers should be able to assess probability zero that e' comes from t.

Note well: Requirement (2) is something like elimination of dominated strategies, where we require that a strategy be dominated by another only at sequentially rational responses by firms. Requirement (3) is stronger; it is of the category of elimination of strategies that are *equilibrium dominated* (cf. subsection 12.7.4). Taking the extra step from (2) to (3) is controversial; see the brief discussion and references given in chapter 12.

What are the consequences of these requirements? Recall from our discussion above that $\hat{e}_1$ is the level of education that maximizes u_1 along the ray $w = e$; $\hat{f}_1$ is the level of education such that $u_1(\hat{e}_1, \hat{e}_1) = u_1(2\hat{f}_1, \hat{f}_1)$; and $\hat{f}_2$ is the education level most preferred by the type two workers along the ray $w = 2e$ for $e > \hat{f}_1$. (See figure 17.8.) We distinguish between two cases: In case 1 the high-ability worker's indifference curve through $(w = 2\hat{f}_2, e = \hat{f}_2)$ stays above the pooling line $w = 1.5e$; and in case 2 the high-ability worker's indifference curve through this point passes below the pooling line. Case 1 can be divided into two subcases: Case 1a, where $\hat{f}_2 > \hat{f}_1$; and case 1b, where $\hat{f}_2 = \hat{f}_1$. In figure 17.11, we depict all three cases for purposes of comparison.

Proposition 7. *For market signaling formulated as a game in which workers choose education levels and then firms bid in Bertrand-like fashion:*

(a) If we insist on our equilibrium being sequential (requirement [1]), then in any separating equilibrium the low-ability workers select education level $\hat{e}_1$. More generally, in any sequential equilibrium, low-ability workers obtain utility at least equal to $u_1(\hat{e}_1, \hat{e}_1)$.

(b) If we insist in addition that requirement (2) is met, then the only possible separating equilibrium has high-ability workers choosing education level $\hat{f}_2$. In general, in any sequential equilibrium that meets requirement (2), high-ability workers must obtain utility at least equal to $u_2(2\hat{f}_2, \hat{f}_2)$. And in case 1, the separating equilibrium is the only possible sequential equilibrium that meets requirement (2), separating or not.

(c) The only sequential equilibrium that meets requirement (3) is the separating equilibrium in which low-ability workers choose $\hat{e}_1$ and high-ability workers choose $\hat{f}_2$.

Let us sketch the proof. If the equilibrium is sequential, then wages in response to any education level e cannot be less than e or more than $2e$. Hence if low-ability workers choose $\hat{e}_1$, they are assured of utility $u_1(\hat{e}_1, \hat{e}_1)$. This implies (a) immediately.

For part (b), consider any education level $e' > \hat{f}_1$. By the definition of $\hat{f}_1$, $u_1(\hat{e}_1, \hat{e}_1) > u_2(2e', e')$. Hence if requirement (2) is imposed, we must be able to sustain the equilibrium with beliefs that education levels $e' > \hat{f}_1$ are certainly from high-ability workers, which means they command wages $2e'$. Hence for any $e' > \hat{e}_1$, a high-ability worker is sure to get utility $u_2(2e', e')$. In any equilibrium, a high-ability worker need never accept utility less than $\sup\{u_2(2e', e') : e' > \hat{f}_1\}$, which implies that he must get utility at least equal to $u_2(2\hat{f}_2, \hat{f}_2)$. This is the second part of (b). (You may need to think a bit about this step.) In any separating equilibrium, a high-ability worker can't separate at a level of education less than $\hat{f}_1$ (Why not?), and so we have the first part of (b).

The third part of (b) is the hardest and is left to the virtuous reader with the following hint: We know that at any equilibrium outcome, low-ability workers sit on an indifference curve on or above their curve through $(\hat{e}_1, \hat{e}_1)$. Consider separately the case where they sit along the indifference curve through $(\hat{e}_1, \hat{e}_1)$ (in which case apply the second part of [b]) and the case where they sit above this curve, in which case (we assert and you must show) they must all be part of a single pool, which leads to a contradiction.

As for (c), the key is to show that any pooling at all in equilibrium will not meet requirement (3). Consider figure 17.12 and the point shown with the dot. Imagine that both high- and low-ability workers pooled at that point. Then, in the equilibrium, low-ability workers must obtain the utility level that parameterizes the indifference curve through that point. Consider education levels between the points $\hat{g}_1$ and $\hat{g}_2$ shown in the figure. At any education level $g > \hat{g}_1$, the low-ability worker cannot do better than he does at his equilibrium level of utility, even if wages $2g$ are paid. So by requirement (3), we must be able to sustain this equilibrium with beliefs that attribute no chance to education levels $g > \hat{g}_1$ coming from low-ability workers. Hence wages $2g$ will be paid for such education levels. And then a high-ability

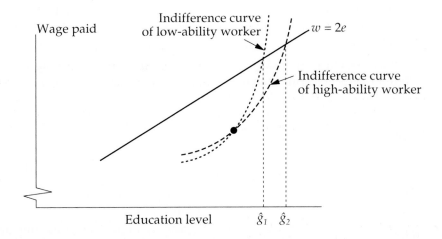

Figure 17.12. *Breaking a pooling equilibrium with requirement (3).*

worker would rather choose some such g that is less than $\hat{g}_2$ than stick to the supposed pool. Done.

Rothschild and Stiglitz and game theory

Rothschild and Stiglitz, on the other hand, can be understood as an analysis of the following alternative extensive form game. Firms simultaneously and independently name contracts (in wage-education space, in our example) that they are willing to honor. Then the worker responds by taking one of the contracts (or refusing them all).[9] The equilibria of Rothschild and Stiglitz correspond to pure strategy, subgame perfect Nash equilibria of this game. In particular, when there are no Rothschild and Stiglitz equilibria, this game has no pure strategy, subgame perfect Nash equilibria.[9]

Further variations

For Riley and for Wilson, we might imagine game forms of the following sorts. For Riley, firms simultaneously and independently propose

---

[9] By invoking subgame perfection, we can and hereafter do assume that the worker chooses the contract that he likes best from those that are offered. We can use subgame perfection here because Nature's move can be put in after the firms offer their contracts, and at that point Nature's move starts a proper subgame.

[9] The game always admits Nash equilibria, in mixed strategies if there are no pure strategy equilibria. (The existence result behind this claim is not trivial.) Whether one believes that the mixed strategy equilibria have any particular relevance is another matter.

contracts. The set of contracts offered are made public. Then firms are given the opportunity to add contracts. If anyone adds a contract, firms are given a further opportunity to add, and so on, until no firm adds any contracts. And then workers choose their preferred contracts. (What if firms add contracts perpetually? I will leave this question hanging for now.) For Wilson, imagine that firms simultaneously and independently propose contracts. These contracts are made public. And then firms are allowed to remove contracts from the offer set. After one or more rounds of removals, workers choose.

The game form proposed for Riley is incompletely specified, because we haven't said how the game ends if firms keep adding contracts. And, in any case, this game form admits too many Nash equilibria. Consider, for example, an equilibrium where firms initially offer to pay workers much less than they are worth. We would imagine a single firm breaking this equilibrium by offering slightly better terms and getting all the workers. But now firms can respond, and they might be supposed to respond in a way that leaves all the firms making zero profits. In which case no firm would have a positive incentive to deviate from the first, positive profits situation. In a sense, we have "implicit collusion" among the firms, supported by supergamelike threats of reaction. (On this point and others concerning this game form and its relation to Riley's reactive equilibrium, see Engers and Fernandez [1987].)

We leave it to you to connect the game form advanced for Wilson's equilibrium notion to that notion; you will (clearly) have to study Wilson's paper first.

> To close this discussion, we mention yet another game form that with high-powered refinements of Nash equilibrium leads to a strong result. Imagine a three-stage game constructed as follows. Firms make offers, just as in Rothschild and Stiglitz. Workers choose their education levels and queue for jobs at the firms whose offers they wish to take. But then firms can renege; having seen which other contracts were offered and which choices were made, firms can decide not to honor offers they made initially. Hellwig (1986) studies this game form and obtains results that can be paraphrased roughly as: If one looks for *stable equilibrium* outcomes in the sense of Kohlberg and Mertens (1986), then Wilson-style equilibria are selected.

17.4. Bibliographic notes and discussion

Several messages can be obtained from the preceding analyses. First, "lemons problems" can exist in markets where one party to a transaction has available information that a second party lacks.

Second, these problems may be ameliorated through market signaling or self-selection by the side having the private information. If the informed side takes the active role as in Spence's analysis, this is known as *market signaling*. If the side without information proposes a menu of contracts among which the informed side selects, this is conventionally called *market screening*. The "instrument" used to send this signal should have the property that it is relatively cheaper for "higher quality" parties to convey; i.e., something analogous to the single-crossing property should hold. Higher quality parties are "usually" adversely affected by the presence of lower quality parties; either the higher quality parties are pooled in with lower quality parties, to their detriment, or they must invest in signals beyond the point that they would if there were no informational asymmetry to distinguish themselves from their lower quality peers. (I put "usually" in quotes here because this result must be made precise. It is a substantial challenge, but you might wish to try your hand at turning this vague assertion into a precise result.)

The range of applications for this sort of signaling or screening is quite large. Besides education as a signal (Spence, 1974) and signaling in insurance (Rothschild and Stiglitz, 1976), a partial list of applications is: a manufacturer offers warranties as a signal that the goods in question are of high quality (Grossman, 1981); a plaintiff demands a high pretrial settlement as a signal that her case is particularly strong (Reinganum and Wilde, 1986; Sobel, forthcoming); a bargainer, to signal relative bargaining strength, rejects the other side's offer (Rubinstein, 1985) or delays making his own offer (Admati and Perry, 1987); and a monopolist, to signal low costs and so to forestall entry by potential rivals, charges a low price before entry occurs (Milgrom and Roberts, 1982). You may recall this last application from chapter 13. Lest you think you've seen the whole story, there is much more to entry deterrence as signaling than the simple analysis in chapter 13 conveys. In particular, Milgrom and Roberts show how the incumbent monopolist could engage in entry deterring pricing that is completely ineffective in deterring entry. You may also recognize the beer-quiche example of chapter 13 as another example of signaling.

The relationships between the early models of market signaling and game theory have been developed only recently. Stiglitz and Weiss (forthcoming) should be consulted concerning the basic differences between signaling and screening models. Work on signaling models (i.e., on Spence-style models) stressing restrictions on out-of-equilibrium beliefs can be found in Banks and Sobel (1987), Cho and Kreps (1987), and Cho and Sobel (1988) among others. Less work has been done on connecting screening models to game theory, although Engers and Fernandez (1987) and Hellwig (1986) can be consulted for some initial work.

The topic of market signaling fans out in many directions from the very simple and basic model that has been discussed here. In the first place, one might think of looking at models with more than two types of employee. This sort of extension is relatively straightforward, and most of the references given above do this. More interesting are applications where more than one signal is available (see Engers [1987] for screening models; and see Cho and Sobel [1988] for signaling models), or where the "quality" being signaled is multidimensional (Quinzii and Rochet, 1985), or where signals are noisy so that the act of signaling by itself is a superior signal (Hillas, 1987).

An important variation that we have not touched upon concerns signaling models where the signals are costless to send. That is, participants can engage in "cheap talk" — things costless to say, but not at all inconsequential to the equilibria that can be attained. See Crawford and Sobel (1982) and Farrell (1988) on this topic. And throughout this chapter we have been concerned with the signaling of private information. One can also analyze the signaling of previously taken actions, or even the signaling of actions intended in the future. (See, for example, Wolinsky [1983] or Ben-Porath and Dekel [1989].)

An issue less theoretical and more "practical" concerns the impact of repeated play in the oligopolistic sense on equilibria in the context of screening. That is, if we imagine insurance companies that offer potential clients a menu of contracts, and we think that these companies might engage in some form of implicit collusion, then the discussion of Rothschild and Stiglitz versus Riley versus Wilson might be turned on its head. Perhaps the companies collude and offer a menu of contracts that is best for them as a cartel, held together by a threat of reversion to cut-throat competition. This leads one to ask, If the insurance business is not competitive but instead is a monopoly (or a cartel), what menu of contracts will be offered? (And if the insurance business is regulated, what then?) With this as a lead-in we move on to chapter 18.

References

Admati, A., and M. Perry. 1987. "Strategic Delay in Bargaining." *Review of Economic Studies* 54:345–64.

Akerlof, G. 1970. "The Market for Lemons: Quality Uncertainty and the Market Mechanism." *Quarterly Journal of Economics* 89:488–500.

Banks, J., and J. Sobel. 1987. "Equilibrium Selection in Signaling Games." *Econometrica* 55:647–62.

Ben-Porath, E., and E. Dekel. 1989. "Coordination and the Potential for Self-Sacrifice." University of California at Berkeley. Mimeo.

Cho, I-k., and D. Kreps. 1987. "Signaling Games and Stable Equilibria." *Quarterly Journal of Economics* 102:179–221.

Cho, I-k., and J. Sobel. 1988. "Strategic Stability and Uniqueness in Signaling Games." University of Chicago. Mimeo.

Crawford, V., and J. Sobel. 1982. "Strategic Information Transmission." *Econometrica* 50:1431–51.

Engers, M. 1987. "Signaling with Many Signals." *Econometrica* 55:663–74.

Engers, M., and L. Fernandez. 1987. "Market Equilibrium with Hidden Knowledge and Self-selection." *Econometrica* 55:425–40.

Farrell, J. 1988. "Meaning and Credibility in Cheap-talk Games." in *Mathematical Models in Economics*, M. Dempster, ed. Oxford: Oxford University Press.

Grossman, S. 1981. "The Role of Warranties and Private Disclosure about Product Quality." *Journal of Law and Economics* 24:461–83.

Hellwig, M. 1986. "Some Recent Developments in the Theory of Competition in Markets with Adverse Selection." University of Bonn. Mimeo.

Hillas, J. 1987. *Contributions to the Theory of Market Screening.* Ph.D. diss., Stanford University.

Kohlberg, E., and J.-F. Mertens. 1986. "On the Strategic Stability of Equilibria." *Econometrica* 54:1003–38.

Milgrom, P., and J. Roberts. 1982. "Limit Pricing and Entry under Incomplete Information: An Equilibrium Analysis." *Econometrica* 50:443–59.

Quinzii, M., and J.-C. Rochet. 1985. "Multidimensional Signalling." *Journal of Mathematical Economics* 14:261–84.

Reinganum, J., and L. Wilde. 1986. "Settlement, Litigation, and the Allocation of Litigation Costs." *Rand Journal of Economics* 17:557–66.

Riley, J. 1979. "Informational Equilibrium." *Econometrica* 47:331–59.

Rothschild, M., and J. Stiglitz. 1976. "Equilibrium in Competitive Insurance Markets: An Essay on the Economics of Imperfect Information." *Quarterly Journal of Economics* 80:629–49.

Rubinstein, A. 1985. "A Bargaining Model with Incomplete Information about Time Preferences." *Econometrica* 53:1151–72.

Sobel, J. Forthcoming. "An Analysis of Discovery Rules." *Law and Contemporary Problems*.

Spence, A. M. 1974. *Market Signaling.* Cambridge, Mass.: Harvard University Press.

Stiglitz, J., and A. Weiss. Forthcoming. "Sorting Out the Differences Between Screening and Signaling Models." In *Oxford Essays in Mathematical Economics*, M. Bachrach, ed. Oxford: Oxford University Press.

Wilson, C. 1977. "A Model of Insurance Markets with Incomplete Information." *Journal of Economic Theory* 16:167–207.

Wolinsky, A. 1983. "Prices as Signals of Product Quality." *Review of Economic Studies* 50:647–58.

17.5. Problems

■ 1. Recall the lemons problem at the start of the chapter. Some used cars are peaches, worth $3,000 to buyers and $2,500 to sellers, and some are lemons, worth $2,000 to buyers and $1,000 to sellers. There is a fixed supply of cars and unlimited demand. Suppose there are twice as many peaches as lemons. Assume buyers can't tell the quality of a given car, while sellers can. What do the supply and demand curves look like? In the text, we asserted that markets clear at $2,666.67. Are there other market clearing prices?

■ 2. Consider the model of job market signaling explored in section 17.2. More specifically, consider the mode of analysis that is attributed to Spence, where workers choose education levels in anticipation of the wages they will receive. We explored in section 17.2 both separating and pooling equilibria, where we assumed that each type of worker chooses one and only one level of education in equilibrium.

(a) Are there any separating equilibrium where one type (or both) chooses more than one level of education? By a separating equilibrium we mean that if one type chooses a given education level with positive probability, then the other type does not.

(b) Is there any pooling equilibrium where both types choose more than one level of education? By a pooling equilibrium we mean that every education level chosen by one type with positive probability is chosen by the other type with positive probability.

(c) A hybrid equilibrium is one in which some education levels are chosen by one type only and others are chosen by both types. Are there any hybrid equilibria? If so, how many different "types" of them can you construct?

(d) What is the maximum number of education levels that a low-ability worker can choose with positive probability in any equilibrium? What is the maximum number of education levels that a high-ability worker can choose with positive probability in any equilibrium? Justify your answers.

■ 3. (a) Complete the proof of proposition 2.

(b) Prove proposition 4.

■ 4. (a) Consider the model of job market signaling explored in section 17.2, but with one modification: Education is completely worthless in terms of increasing worker productivity. That is, a low-ability worker is worth v_1 to a firm and a high-ability worker is worth v_2, regardless of how much education either has. We assume that $v_1 < v_2$. Otherwise, things are as in section 17.2; workers like higher wages and dislike education, their indifference curves have the "single-crossing property," and so on. Recount the conclusions of Spence and then of Rothschild and Stiglitz in this modified formulation.

(b) In the modified formulation, it is clear that any education obtained is socially wasteful; it doesn't improve productivity and it lessens the utility of the worker. Put another way, if workers obtain any education at all in equilibrium, they are clearly being overeducated from the point of view of enhanced productivity by society. Presumably you showed in part (a), therefore, that equilibria in this setting can result in "too much" education, and separating equilibria must do so. In the original setting of section 17.2 do similar conclusions apply? Is it the case that there is never, in equilibrium, "too little" education? In other words, comment on the following assertion: "The model of education as a signal due to Spence and to Rothschild and Stiglitz shows that people overinvest in education, when education is used to signal ability."

■ 5. Recall that we gave a very imprecise formulation of the single-crossing property. Suppose that the utility functions $u_t(w, e)$ are concave, monotonic in the right directions, and have derivatives of all orders. Can you give a more precise formalization of the single-crossing property that uses appropriate partial derivatives of the u_t?

■ 6. A quite abstract formulation of the single-crossing property can be given for the following setting: The worker is one of a finite number of types, indexed by $t = 1, 2, \ldots, T$. The worker can choose education levels e from some interval, say $[0, \infty)$, and firms can pay wages w drawn from some interval, say $[0, \infty)$. We let $u_t(w, e)$ denote the utility obtained by a worker of type t from wages w and education level e. Then if, for some type of worker $t = 1, 2, \ldots, T$, $u_t(w, e) \geq u_t(w', e')$ for $e > e'$, then for all $t' = t + 1, t + 2, \ldots, T$, $u_{t'}(w, e) > u_{t'}(w', e')$. In words, if a type t prefers (weakly) the package (w, e) to (w', e'), and the preferred package has higher education, then all types t' with higher index strictly prefer the package (w, e).

Suppose we have a formulation of job market signaling as in Spence's story with finitely many types of workers as in the preceding paragraph. Suppose that we find an equilibrium. Assume that in this equilibrium workers conjecture that for each education level they might select, the wage that they will receive is nonrandom. (You saw no examples with random wages, so this last line may confuse you. If so, ignore it.) Assume the formulation of single-crossing just given and prove the following: If a type t worker obtains education level e with positive probability in the equilibrium, and a type t' obtains e', then $t' > t$ implies $e' \geq e$.

■ 7. Consider the following game form representation of worker selection from a menu of contracts. The number of firms is finite. (Two will be enough.) Firms simultaneously and independently name contracts (pairs (w, e)); with each firm limited to a finite number of contracts. (If you wish, assume each firm can name no more than four contracts.) The contracts tentatively offered are announced, and then firms simultaneously and independently decide whether they wish to withdraw some of the contracts they offered initially. The new set of tentatively offered contracts is announced, and if any contracts were removed, firms are again given the opportunity to remove contracts. And so on, until either no contracts are left or, in a given round, no contracts are removed. (Since there are finitely many firms and finitely many contracts, this process must terminate.) Workers then self-select from among the contracts (if any) that are left. Otherwise, things are just as in the models of this chapter.

What can you say about the subgame perfect equilibria of this game? Can you give a precise characterization? If not, can you give partial characterizations? Can you describe at least one equilibrium? (There are many proper subgames here, and you may find things easier if you look for Nash equilibria where workers play sequentially rational strategies. That is, don't worry about subgame perfection for the firms.)

■ 8. Besides education as a signal, the other classic application of these ideas is the insurance market. The following simple story is usually told. Imagine an individual who is subject to a random loss. Specifically, the individual may have Y_1 with which to consume, and she may have only $Y_2 < Y_1$. This individual is strictly risk averse, with von Neumann-Morgenstern utility function U defined on the amounts of money she has to consume. There is a probability π_i that the individual will have income Y_2 only (and a probability $1 - \pi_i$ that she will have income Y_1), where the subscript i stands for either H or L, mnemonics for high and low risk. We have $\pi_H > \pi_L$. The individual knows whether she is a high- or low-risk individual.

Several insurance companies offer insurance against the bad outcome for this consumer. An insurance contract is very simple: It specifies amounts y_1 and y_2 that the individual is left with if she would otherwise be consuming Y_1 or Y_2. That is, you can think of $y_1 = Y_1 - P$, where P is the insurance premium, and $y_2 = Y_2 - P + B$, where B is a benefit paid in case the individual would otherwise be left with only Y_2. The insurance companies are competitive and risk neutral. This implies that contracts that are offered and taken in equilibrium on average break even, or $\pi(Y_2 - y_2) + (1 - \pi)(Y_1 - y_1) = 0$, where π is the chance that the consumer would otherwise be left with Y_2. The insurance companies do not know what type the consumer is, but have equilibrium conjectures based on the type of contract that the consumer proposes or takes. Insurance firms begin with the prior assessment that the consumer is high risk with probability $1/2$.

Adapt first Spence and then Rothschild and Stiglitz to this setting.

The key is to get the right "picture," and we will give you some assistance here. Think of the "commodity space" (replacing (w, e) space) as the space of pairs (y_1, y_2) where y_1 is the amount of money the consumer has to use in the contingency where she would otherwise have Y_1 and y_2 is her wealth in the contingency where she would otherwise have Y_2. Begin by locating the consumer's endowment (Y_1, Y_2). Then draw in indifference curves for the consumer in this space. Note carefully, the indifference curves are different if the consumer is high-risk or low-. It is useful to compute the slope of the consumer's indifference curve at a point (y_1, y_2) where $y_1 = y_2$. Finally, find the locus of zero-profit contracts (y_1, y_2) for the insurance firm if it knows that it is dealing with a high-risk client, with a low-risk client, and with a client who is high-risk with probability $1/2$. (Our offer of this assistance is not entirely altruistic. If you get stuck, or you succumb to laziness, the answer can be found at the start of the next chapter.)

■ 9. In a particular population, everyone runs the risk of losing $1,000 randomly. Each person's random event (which determines whether the person loses the $1,000 or not) is independent of everyone else's, and the chance that any single individual will lose the $1,000 depends on the individual; 90% of the population will lose the $1,000 with probability .1, while the other 10% will lose the $1,000 with probability .6. Each individual know's her own probability of loss, but no one knows the probability of loss of anyone else. Everyone in this population has the same von Neumann-Morgenstern utility function for this particular gamble, (either lose $1,000 or lose $0), given by $u(x) = 1 - e^{-\lambda x}$, where x is the net of this gamble.

A regulated insurance company stands ready to offer insurance for this gamble. If an individual pays a premium P, then the individual is insured against the loss of $1,000. In terms of the net, the individual trades a gamble where the two possible prizes are $x = 0$ and $x = -1,000$ for a sure thing where $x = -P$. Because this insurance company is regulated, it must set the premium so that its expected net profit is zero.

(a) If $\lambda = .002$, is there a pooling equilibrium for this economy? If $\lambda = .0005$, is there a pooling equilibrium? For what values of λ is there a pooling equilibrium? (Answer the last question only if you have access to a computer or a programmable calculator.) As part of your answer to this, you must say what constitutes a pooling equilibrium.

(b) Suppose $\lambda = .001$, and individuals can undergo an examination that with some chance of error identifies whether the individual has a chance of .1 of losing the $1,000 or a chance of .6. Specifically, this exam has two outcomes: H (for high risk) and L. If the individual is the sort who will lose the $1,000 with probability .1, then this test gives the outcome L with probability p and the outcome H with probability $1 - p$. If the individual will lose the $1,000 with probability .6 then the outcomes are H with probability p and L with probability $1 - p$. It costs $10 to administer this test. The regulatory body says that the insurance company must charge any consumer who wants the test a nonrefundable $10 (consumers may only take the test once), and the company must then break even on each and every contract that it offers. (That is, one contract may not be allowed to cross-subsidize another.) The insurance company may make the premium dependent on the the results of the test if taken. Will this economy admit a screening equilibrium? What is the nature of that equilibrium? For what values of p will such an equilibrium exist?

Note: In both halves of this problem, do not assume competition among insurance companies. The single insurance company is subject to regulation, as noted above. If you want to think about it, you might consider what would happen if there was a competitive insurance industry.

■ 10. Return to section 13.2 and the story of entry deterrence told there. If you didn't understand the equilibria that were described then, you should go back to them now. (Can you now find all the equilibria?)

In the game theoretic analysis of the Spence model given here, we saw that pooling equilibria are destroyed if we employ equilibrium dominance criteria. This is not true in the pooling equilibrium we sketched in section 13.2. Why not? (Hint: When you summarize your answer, begin with the following line: "In the model of this chapter, if there is a pool, the high-ability worker suffers for it. But....")

■ 11. *We have now discussed problems of adverse selection and problems of moral hazard. In this problem, you may try your hand at a situation with both at the same time. If you find this problem too hard, wait until the end of the next chapter, when you should find it very easy.* Consider a situation just like the salesman problem in section 16.2, with one additional fillip. Specifically, the salesman will be of either high or low ability. To be exact: You are going to hire a salesman to try to make a particular sale for you. You are risk neutral in all this. He is risk averse, with von Neumann-Morgenstern utility function $\sqrt{x} - a$, where x is the amount you pay him, and a is an index of the level of effort he exerts. He is either of good ability or of bad ability, each with probability .5. In parts (a) and (b) you will know his level of ability; in later parts you will not. He will exert either a high level of effort or a low, and you will be unable to observe which. (Note: Good and bad pertain to ability, and high and low pertain to effort.) Regardless of his level of ability, he has reservation utility level 5. And if he puts in a high level of effort, a in his utility function is 1; $a = 0$ for a low level of effort.

He either will make the sale or he won't. The sale, gross of your payment to him, will net you $100 if he makes it. The chances that he makes the sale depend both on his level of ability and on his level of effort. Specifically:

If he is good and gives high effort, he makes the sale with probability .9.

If he is good and gives low effort, he makes the sale with probability .6.

If he is bad and gives high effort, he makes the sale with probability .5.

If he is bad and gives low effort, he makes the sale with probability .3.

(This is a world in which ability counts more than effort.)

Although it doesn't make much sense in the context I have outlined, assume that you are only allowed to deal with one salesman. You may offer him a contract, which he will either accept or reject; if he rejects, you net zero. Any time that the salesman is indifferent, he will elect the option that is more favorable to you. (That is, you don't have to worry about ties.)

(a) Suppose you are able to observe his ability, and you find that the salesman you are dealing with has bad ability. What, from your point of view, is the optimal contract to offer him? Will he give high or low effort under this contract? What will be your profits?

(b) Suppose you are able to observe his ability, and you find that the salesman you are dealing with has good ability. What, from your point of view, is the optimal contract to offer to him? Will he give high or low effort under this contract? What will be your profits?

(c) Now suppose that you are unable to observe the ability of the salesman you are dealing with. If you offer him a choice from the contracts you identified in parts (a) and (b), what will be the outcome for you? Why is this? Be very clear and explicit as to what you expect to happen in this case.

(d) You are unable to observe the ability of the salesman that you are dealing with, and you may either offer him a pair of contracts from which he can choose, or a single contract, that he may elect to take or not. (If you offer a pair of contracts, he can refuse employment altogether as well, although remember that when he is indifferent, he is presumed to do what is in your interests.) I want you to produce an offer to him that does better than offering him the pair of contracts from parts (a) and (b). Say what the contract(s) is (are), and what will be the outcome of your offer. You should produce the best contract(s) you can — ideally, you should devise the optimal contract(s) to offer him, and you should prove that this is the optimal offering.

■ 12. At the start of this chapter we used Gresham's law to motivate Akerlof's lemons model and problems of adverse selection. But this motivation is not entirely appropriate, at least for the way we described Gresham's law. Why not? How can you make Gresham's law appropriate? (For the second question, begin your answer with "Suppose some of the people in this economy are pathologically honest....")

chapter eighteen

The revelation principle and mechanism design

In chapter 16, we saw how to design optimal incentive contracts for a principal who wishes to get a single agent to take some action. We hinted there, both in the text and in the problems, at techniques for the design of optimal contracts when the agent possesses private information and when there are multiple agents.

In this chapter, we look at a grab bag of situations in which these techniques are employed. The specific applications that we will examine, insurance contracts when there is adverse selection (and, more generally, optimal nonlinear pricing), optimal procurement, and elicitation of preferences for the provision of a public good, are all interesting in their own right, and we carry through the first level of analysis for all. But the point of this chapter is the general mode of analysis that is employed and, in particular, the progression from contracts designed for a single party to the revelation principle and contracts and mechanisms designed for many parties.

18.1. *Optimal contracts designed for a single party*

At the end of the last chapter, we asked what would happen in an insurance setting with adverse selection if the insurance industry instead of being competitive is either a monopoly or is cartelized so effectively that it acts like a monopoly. In chapter 8 (problem 4), we posed the problem of finding an optimal nonlinear pricing scheme in the context of a manufacturing monopolist selling to retail monopolists. In this section we see how to solve these two problems.

Profit-maximizing insurance contracts with adverse selection

To begin, we develop a context within which the question of profit-maximizing insurance can be studied.[1] Imagine an individual who will

---

[1] This analysis is taken from Stiglitz (1977).

receive an uncertain amount of money with which to consume. Specifically, the individual may receive the amount Y_1, or she may receive only $Y_2 < Y_1$. Which of these two prevails is determined at a later date. This individual is strictly risk averse, with strictly increasing and strictly concave von Neumann-Morgenstern utility function U defined on the amounts of money she has to consume. There is a probability π_i that the individual will have endowment Y_2 only and a probability $1 - \pi_i$ that she will have endowment Y_1, where the subscript i stands for either H or L, mnemonics for high and low risk. We assume $\pi_H > \pi_L$. The individual knows whether she is a high- or low-risk individual.

Because she is subject to endowment risk and she is risk averse, this consumer might seek to insure herself against a low level of endowment. In essence, she will give up some of her endowment in the high-endowment state of nature in return for more in the low-endowment state. Suppose there is a single insurance company with which the consumer can deal. An insurance contract between the insurance company and the consumer specifies two numbers, y_1 and y_2, where y_k is the total resources left to the consumer if her endowment is Y_k, for $k = 1, 2$. You can think of $y_1 = Y_1 - P$, where P is the insurance premium, and $y_2 = Y_2 - P + B$, where B is a benefit paid if the individual would otherwise be left with only Y_2. The insurance company, then, will have "profits" $Y_1 - y_1$ in the high-endowment state and $Y_2 - y_2$ in the low-endowment state; we put "profits" in quotes because one or the other of these quantities will presumably be negative. (In fact, it is reasonable to presume that $Y_2 - y_2$ will be negative; the insurance company pays out in the low-endowment state.) The insurance company does not know whether the consumer is high or low risk and begins with the prior assessment that the consumer is high risk with probability ρ. What sort of contract(s) will the insurance company offer to this consumer in order to make the largest possible expected profit?

It may help to draw some pictures of this situation. The "commodity space" for the consumer is the set of all pairs (y_1, y_2), with the interpretation that y_1 is the amount the consumer has to spend in the state of nature where she would (without the benefit of insurance) consume Y_1, and y_2 is the amount she has to spend in the state of nature where her initial endowment is Y_2. We can draw indifference curves for the consumer in (y_1, y_2) space; these are curves of the form $(1 - \pi_i)U(y_1) + \pi_i U(y_2) = k$ for constant k where π_i is the consumer's probability of having a low level of endowment. In figure 18.1 we draw the indifference curve of a high-risk consumer through the endowment point (Y_1, Y_2).

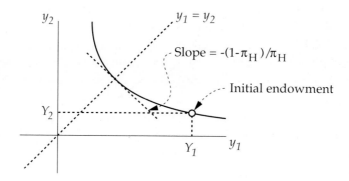

Figure 18.1. A high-risk consumer's indifference curve.

Fix the constant k, and think of the curve as determining y_2 as a function of y_1. That is, define a function $y_2(y_1)$ by the implicit relation

$$(1 - \pi_i)U(y_1) + \pi_i U(y_2(y_1)) = k.$$

Letting V be the inverse of U, this is

$$y_2(y_1) = V\left(\frac{k - (1 - \pi_i)U(y_1)}{\pi_i}\right).$$

(We should be worried whether $[k - (1 - \pi_i)U(y_1)]/\pi_i$ is in the domain of V, but we'll simply proceed on the assumption that it is, and we leave it to you to clean up the details.) Hence

$$\frac{dy_2}{dy_1} = -V'\left(\frac{k - (1 - \pi_i)U(y_1)}{\pi_i}\right)\left(\frac{1 - \pi_i}{\pi_i}\right)U'(y_1), \quad \text{or}$$

$$\frac{dy_2}{dy_1} = -V'(U(y_2))\left(\frac{1 - \pi_i}{\pi_i}\right)U'(y_1) \quad \text{for} \quad y_2 = V\left(\frac{k - (1 - \pi_i)U(y_1)}{\pi_i}\right).$$

This looks like (and is) a mess, but from it we can harvest two facts that are useful in drawing pictures.

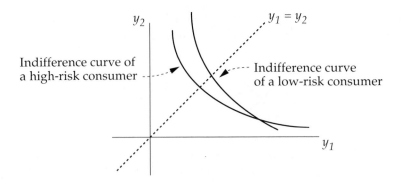

Figure 18.2. A pair of indifference curves, one for each type.

(1) If $y_2(y_1) = y_1$, then the slope of the indifference curve through (y_1, y_2) equals $-(1 - \pi_i)/\pi_i$. (This follows because $V'(U(x)) = 1/U'(x)$.)

Consider superimposing indifference curves of the consumer for the two cases where the consumer is high and low risk. In particular, consider the indifference curves of the consumer through some point (y_1, y_2). *(2) The indifference curve of the low-risk consumer is steeper than that of the high-risk consumer.* Put differently, if we start from a point (y_1, y_2) and decrease y_1 by a little bit, it takes a smaller increase in y_2 to compensate the high-risk consumer than to compensate the low-risk consumer. The intuition for this should be clear; the high-risk consumer has a greater chance of having the low-endowment state prevail, hence additional income in that state is worth more to her. We also see this algebraically, since the slopes are the same except for the scale factors $(1 - \pi_i)/\pi_i$; this factor is lower for the high-risk consumer than for the low-risk.

Indeed, we have something stronger, namely that the ratio of the slopes of the indifference curves through any point is independent of the point. But we won't need this stronger result. All we need is the "single-crossing" condition for any pair of indifference curves, one for a high-risk consumer and one for a low-, with the crossing as shown in figure 18.2.

Consider next iso-expected profit lines for the firm. Suppose the firm sells a contract to the consumer that leaves the consumer at the point (y_1, y_2). The firm is left with profits $Y_1 - y_1$ in the high-endowment state and $Y_2 - y_2$ in the low-endowment state, hence the firm's expected profits are $(1 - \pi)(Y_1 - y_1) + \pi(Y_2 - y_2)$, where π is the firm's overall assessment as

to how likely it is that the consumer will have a low level of endowment.
Iso-expected profit lines for the firm are given by

$$(1 - \pi)(Y_1 - y_1) + \pi(Y_2 - y_2) = k'$$

for some constant k', and a bit of algebra shows that the slope of these
(viewed with y_2 on the ordinate and y_1 on the abscissa) is $-(1 - \pi)/\pi$.

Suppose that the firm knows it is dealing with a high-risk consumer,
so it assesses $\pi = \pi_H$. What contract does it wish to offer to the consumer
in order to maximize its expected profits? The picture is as in figure
18.3. The consumer isn't going to settle for any contract that leaves her
worse off than at her endowment point. So the firm is constrained to offer
her a contract in the shaded area, if it wishes to do business. Its highest
expected profits are at the point along her indifference curve where $y_2 = y_1$.
(We have discovered yet again the fact, first discovered in chapter 5, that
efficient risk sharing between a risk-averse and a risk-neutral party shifts
all the risk onto the risk-neutral party.)

Similarly, if the firm knows it is dealing with a low-risk consumer, it
offers the contract with $y_2 = y_1$ along the low-risk consumer's indifference

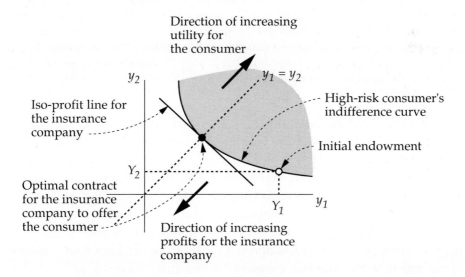

Figure 18.3. *The optimal contract to offer a high-risk consumer.*

curve through the endowment point. Since the low-risk consumer has indifference curves that are more steeply sloped, this will be at a point that is "higher up" the line $y_2 = y_1$ than is the point for high-risk consumers. (Put differently, this is because the low-risk consumer is less willing to buy "expensive" insurance.)

Either from the picture or algebraically, it is straightforward to prove the following further result:

Lemma. *Suppose the firm offers a contract (y_1, y_2) that is accepted by some type of consumer. If we change that contract in a way that keeps the utility of this type of consumer constant and we move in the direction of full insurance, $y_1 = y_2$, then the expected profits of the insurance firm (from this type of consumer accepting the contract) increase.*

In other words, in figure 18.3, not only is the highest level of expected profits for the firm along the high-risk consumer's indifference curve to be found along the line $y_1 = y_2$, but expected profits are increasing on each side as the contract is moved along this indifference curve towards this line.

> All this, it should be noted, has been done with the implicit assumption that the firm can make a take-it-or-leave-it offer to the consumer. The firm offers to trade some pair (y_1, y_2) for the consumer's initial endowment or, equivalently, the firm says that it will charge a premium $Y_1 - y_1$ in exchange for a guarantee that the consumer will have y_1 to consume when times are tough. It is possible, though, that the insurance company cannot make offers of this sort; perhaps it must name a premium P and a low-endowment state payout B, and the consumer can choose how much of this insurance to buy. We leave it to you to discover how this would change the story we are telling. We will continue under the hypothesis that the firm is able to make take-it-or-leave-it offers.

We come back to the question with which we began. The insurance company can't tell whether the consumer is high risk or low. What should it do in this case? It clearly won't do to offer the optimal contracts for the two types of consumer and expect the consumer to select the one that is "right" for her. If the firm does this, the consumer, whether high risk or low, is going to choose the contract optimally designed for the low-risk consumer, since this gives a higher level of income in both states. The insurance firm could offer the optimal contract for the high-risk consumer alone, but then the low-risk consumer will refuse to buy.

Or consider the scheme depicted in figure 18.4. We have in mind that the firm offers the two contracts shown as the heavy dot and square

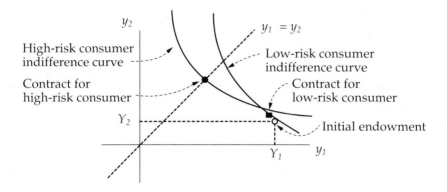

Figure 18.4. A possible pair of contracts.

and allows the consumer to pick one. The contract depicted by a dot represents complete insurance; the square represents only partial insurance. We have also drawn in the indifference curves of the high-risk consumer through the dot and low-risk consumer through the square. From this you can see that given a choice between the dot, the square, or no contract at all (the open circle) the high-risk consumer will choose the dot, and the low-risk consumer will choose the square. In this arrangement, the firm provides complete insurance to the high-risk consumer, although on somewhat better terms for the consumer than if the firm knew it was dealing with the high-risk consumer. It provides partial insurance for the low-risk consumer as well. Perhaps some scheme of this sort is optimal for the firm.

We can solve the firm's problem analytically as follows. We imagine that the firm offers two contracts, (y_1^H, y_2^H) and (y_1^L, y_2^L). The contract (y_1^H, y_2^H) is intended for the high-risk consumer and the contract (y_1^L, y_2^L) for the low-. If we assume that the consumer chooses the contract intended for her, the firm's expected profits are

$$\rho[(1 - \pi_H)(Y_1 - y_1^H) + \pi_H(Y_2 - y_2^H)] + (1 - \rho)[(1 - \pi_L)(Y_1 - y_1^L) + \pi_L(Y_2 - y_2^L)].$$

This is what the firm seeks to maximize. But we have to make sure that the consumer picks the contract that is intended for her. There are four constraints to add: The high-risk consumer must prefer (y_1^H, y_2^H) to her endowment (Y_1, Y_2). The high-risk consumer must prefer (y_1^H, y_2^H) to (y_1^L, y_2^L). The low-risk consumer must prefer (y_1^L, y_2^L) to her endowment (Y_1, Y_2).

And the low-risk consumer must prefer (y_1^L, y_2^L) to (y_1^H, y_2^H). In order, these four constraints are:

$$(1 - \pi_H)U(y_1^H) + \pi_H U(y_2^H) \geq (1 - \pi_H)U(Y_1) + \pi_H U(Y_2); \qquad (PH)$$

$$(1 - \pi_H)U(y_1^H) + \pi_H U(y_2^H) \geq (1 - \pi_H)U(y_1^L) + \pi_H U(y_2^L); \qquad (IH)$$

$$(1 - \pi_L)U(y_1^L) + \pi_L U(y_2^L) \geq (1 - \pi_L)U(Y_1) + \pi_L U(Y_2); \qquad (PL)$$

$$(1 - \pi_L)U(y_1^L) + \pi_L U(y_2^L) \geq (1 - \pi_L)U(y_1^H) + \pi_L U(y_2^H). \qquad (IL)$$

The names given to the four constraints are mnemonics for: The Participation constraint for the High-risk type; the Incentive constraint for the High-risk type; and similar names for the Low-risk types.

So we have the problem: Choose the four variables y_1^H, y_2^H, y_1^L, and y_2^L to maximize the objective function shown, subject to these four constraints.

You may be a bit queasy about this formulation on three grounds. The first two are: We seem to be assuming that the firm offers different contracts for the two types of consumer. Why can't the firm choose to pool the two types by offering a single contract? And we seem to be assuming that the firm serves both types. Is it possible that the firm will wish to offer a contract that only one type and not the other will accept, leaving the other type uninsured? The formulation given allows for each of these two possibilities. We have not precluded finding a solution where $y_1^H = y_1^L$ and $y_2^H = y_2^L$. If this turns out to be the solution, the two types are pooled. And we haven't precluded finding a solution where $(y_1^H, y_2^H) = (Y_1, Y_2)$ or where $(y_1^L, y_2^L) = (Y_1, Y_2)$. In the first of these cases, the firm is "offering" the high-risk consumer her original endowment, which is equivalent to leaving this type to fend for herself. If we find a solution where the second case prevails, it is the low-risk consumer who is not being given any insurance at all.[2]

The third reason for unease is more substantial. We have blithely assumed that the optimal "mechanism" for the insurance firm to use is to offer the consumer a menu of two contracts, one intended for the consumer if she is low risk, and one intended for her if she is high risk. Perhaps some more complex scheme for marketing insurance will make more profits for the firm.

If the consumer anticipates all the things the firm will do in marketing insurance, and if she responds to these things rationally, then our menu of two contracts is without loss of generality. The argument runs as follows:

---

[2] See the remarks in the next subsection on mixed moral hazard and adverse selection problems for another way to do this.

Whatever scheme the insurance company plans to adopt, it will end with the consumer taking some contract or another. A contract will be taken by the low-risk consumer, and a contract will be taken by the high.[a] These contracts could be the same, they could be different, and either or both could be the endowment point. Now for the crux of the argument. *If the consumer anticipates all this, she must prefer the low-risk contract to the high-risk contract if she is low risk and she must prefer the high-risk contract to the low-risk contract if she is high risk.* The reason is that if she is, say, high risk, and she prefers the low-risk contract to the high-risk contract, she could obtain the low-risk contract simply by mimicking the actions that she would take if she were low risk. The insurance company can't tell the difference. Moreover, the contract that she winds up with must be as good as the endowment point for her, as long as she retains the right to say no. So any marketing scheme, however complex, comes down to the final contracts that the consumer might have, and the firm can do no better than to offer the menu of these contracts at the outset and let the consumer choose.

We stress the proviso that the consumer must rationally anticipate the marketing scheme the firm will employ. The firm might do better than to offer a menu *if* the consumer does not anticipate all the things the firm will do along the way through some scheme. The consumer might not anticipate that certain options will be made available to her if she makes certain choices early on; we will return to this in a couple of subsections when we discuss the credibility problem facing the insurance firm at the optimal contract. The consumer might be misled into thinking that certain options will be offered to her that will not appear, and so on. Without meaning to cast aspersions at the honorable profession of marketing, it sometimes seems that marketing schemes are devised to confound the consumer. *A confoundable consumer might be confounded by a complex marketing mechanism and not by a simple choice from a menu.* Insofar as this is so, the maximization problem above may not find the optimal scheme for the insurance company. But we assume as part of the basis for this form (and most other forms) of economic analysis that consumers are not confoundable. The consumer can work through the choices she will be offered, and she responds optimally. Given this, the two-choice menu scheme (one for

---

[a] We should be careful here. Perhaps the marketing mechanism employed by the insurance company will result in a random assignment of contracts to the consumer; the consumer, if she is high risk, gets contract A with some probability, contract B with some other, and so on. We will ignore mechanisms with random outcomes here, for the reason that they are never optimal in this setting, but a more careful analysis would allow for them and then derive the fact that they are never optimal.

each of the two types of consumer) will give the optimal scheme for the insurance firm.

Having settled the relevance of the constrained optimization problem given, we could dive into the problem algebraically, looking at first-order equations and complementary slackness conditions. Instead, we will argue graphically.

> But before moving to graphical analysis, a remark is in order about trying algebra. The problem is a bit easier to analyze if we first make a change of variables. Let the decision variables be $u_k^H = U(y_k^H)$ and $u_k^L = U(y_k^L)$, for $k = 1, 2$. Then the objective function becomes
>
> $$\rho[(1 - \pi_H)(Y_1 - V(u_1^H)) + \pi_H(Y_2 - V(u_2^H))]$$
> $$+ (1 - \rho)[(1 - \pi_L)(Y_1 - V(u_1^L)) + \pi_L(Y_2 - V(u_2^L))],$$
>
> where V is the inverse of U. Note that if U is concave, V is convex, so $-V$ is concave, and we will be seeking to maximize a concave function of our variables. And the four constraints become linear; for example, (IH) becomes
>
> $$(1 - \pi_H)u_1^H + \pi_H u_2^H \geq (1 - \pi_H)u_1^L + \pi_H u_2^L.$$
>
> Note that since, with this change of variables, the objective function (to be maximized) is concave and the constraints are linear, we know that solution of the first-order and complementary slackness conditions (together with feasibility) are necessary and sufficient for a solution. The main advantage of this change of variables, though, is that the algebra is usually simpler. In particular, if you are diligent, you may wish to replicate the graphical analysis to follow algebraically, using the first-order and complementary slackness conditions. Having linear constraints will be a blessing in this activity.

Proposition 1. *At the solution of this problem, the constraints (PL) and (IH) will be binding, and the high-risk contract will be a full-insurance contract; i.e.,* $y_1^H = y_2^H$.

The proof of this result will be given in a number of steps. Throughout, we imagine that $\{(y_1^H, y_2^H), (y_1^L, y_2^L)\}$ is a solution of the problem. Whenever we draw pictures, we use an open circle for the endowment point, a filled in circle for (y_1^H, y_2^H), and a filled in square for (y_1^L, y_2^L).

Step 1. Consider figure 18.5(a). We have drawn there the low-risk contract (y_1^L, y_2^L), and through this point we have drawn in indifference curves for the high- and low-risk types of consumer. *The high-risk contract* (y_1^H, y_2^H) *lies within the shaded "wedge."*

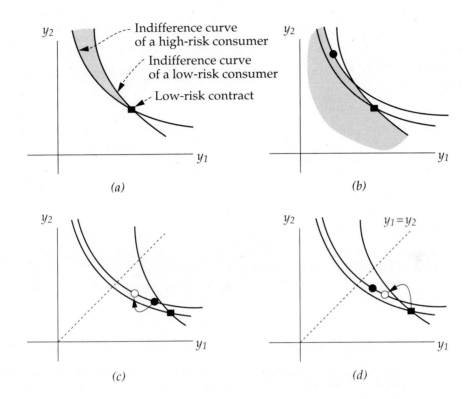

Figure 18.5, part 1. Graphical analysis of profit-maximizing insurance.
In (a), we show the "wedge" relative to (y_1^L, y_2^L) within which (y_1^H, y_2^H)
must lie. In (b) we show the region in which (Y_1, Y_2) must lie relative
to (y_1^L, y_2^L) and (y_1^H, y_2^H). In (c) moving (y_1^H, y_2^H) to the point (Y_1, Y_2)
improves expected profits while maintaining feasibility; in (d) the same
is true for (y_1^L, y_2^L).

This follows immediately from the constraints (IH) and (IL). To satisfy (IH), (y_1^H, y_2^H) must lie on or above the high-risk indifference curve
through (y_1^L, y_2^L). To satisfy (IL), (y_1^H, y_2^H) must lie on or below the low-risk
indifference curve through (y_1^L, y_2^L). The intersection of these two regions
defines the wedge.

*Step 2. The constraint (PL) binds. In particular, (Y_1, Y_2) must lie along the
low-risk indifference curve through (y_1^L, y_2^L) to the right of (y_1^L, y_2^L).*

To see this, consider figure 18.5(b). We have drawn there (y_1^L, y_2^L),
(y_1^H, y_2^H), and indifference curves for both types through (y_1^L, y_2^L) and for
the high-risk type through (y_1^H, y_2^H). We note first that (Y_1, Y_2) must lie in
the shaded region of 18.5(b) in order to satisfy (PH) and (PL). Also, it is

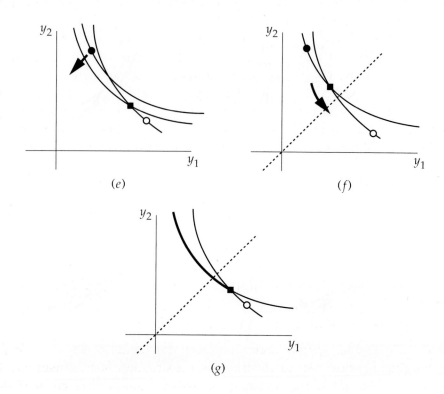

Figure 18.5, part 2. Graphical analysis of profit-maximizing insurance.
Thus (Y_1, Y_2) must lie as shown in (e). But in (e) there is the problem that
(IH) doesn't bind, and movement of (y_1^H, y_2^H) in the direction indicated
improves profits. In (f) is a situation where (y_1^L, y_2^L) involves overinsurance, in which case movement in the direction indicated improves profits. And in (g), the portion of the high-risk indifference curve through
(y_1^H, y_2^H) lying to the left of (y_1^H, y_2^H) is feasible, and full insurance is the
point that maximizes expected profits.

impossible that both (PL) and (PH) are slack, for if this were the case, we
could lower the payments made in the two contracts somewhat without
affecting feasibility (taking care so that (IH) and (IL) continue to hold),
which would certainly increase the firm's expected profits. Hence (Y_1, Y_2)
must lie along the boundary between the shaded and unshaded regions
in figure 18.5(b).

Suppose (Y_1, Y_2) lies to the left of (y_1^H, y_2^H), necessarily along the high-
risk indifference curve through (y_1^H, y_2^H), as in figure 18.5(c). Then all the

constraints continue to be satisfied if we move (y_1^H, y_2^H) to the point (Y_1, Y_2), and profits increase because $Y_1 > Y_2$.

Suppose (Y_1, Y_2) lies at or to the right of (y_1^H, y_2^H) and to the left of (y_1^L, y_2^L). One case is shown in figure 18.5(d). We claim that if we move (y_1^L, y_2^L) to the point (Y_1, Y_2), expected profits increase and all the constraints continue to be satisfied. To see that expected profits increase, note that this shift involves movement along the low-risk indifference curve in the direction of full insurance (since $Y_1 > Y_2$) and (in the case depicted) a lowering of both payments. You can see by inspection that the constraints all continue to hold.

Hence (Y_1, Y_2) must lie along the low-risk indifference curve through (y_1^L, y_2^L) to the right of (y_1^L, y_2^L).

Step 3. The constraint (IH) must bind. By steps 1 and 2, the picture must be as in figure 18.5(e). But if (IH) doesn't bind, as is depicted in figure 18.5(e), then movement of (y_1^H, y_2^H) in any direction down and to the left, staying within the wedge, doesn't compromise feasibility and improves expected profits. The key is the positioning of (Y_1, Y_2), which implies that as long as (y_1^H, y_2^H) stays within the wedge, (PH) is maintained.

Step 4. The contract (y_1^L, y_2^L) does not involve overinsurance; that is, $y_1^L \geq y_2^L$. To see this, consider figure 18.5(f), where a situation of overinsurance is depicted. If (y_1^L, y_2^L) is moved along the low-risk indifference curve in the direction of the arrow, towards full insurance, feasibility is maintained (the constraints on y^H are actually loosened), and expected profits increase by the lemma.

Step 5. The contract (y_1^H, y_2^H) involves full insurance. By steps 1 through 4, the picture must be as in figure 18.5(g), where (y_1^H, y_2^H) lies along the high-risk indifference curve to the left of (y_1^L, y_2^L) and the full-insurance line lies on or to the left of (y_1^L, y_2^L). All points along the high-risk indifference curve to the left of (y_1^L, y_2^L) maintain feasibility and, by the lemma, we know that full insurance maximizes expected profits along this curve.

From the proposition, we see that the problem is essentially one di-mensional. Consider figure 18.6. The high-risk contract (y_1^H, y_2^H) must involve full insurance and must lie between the high-risk and low-risk indifference curves through the endowment. Once the location of (y_1^H, y_2^H) is selected, we know that (IH) and (PL) must be binding, so the location of (y_1^L, y_2^L) is forced to be at the intersection of the high-risk indifference curve through (y_1^H, y_2^H) and the low-risk indifference curve through (Y_1, Y_2). When we put (y_1^H, y_2^H) at the first-best location for a high-risk consumer, we are forced to put $(y_1^L, y_2^L) = (Y_1, Y_2)$. Essentially, this involves first-

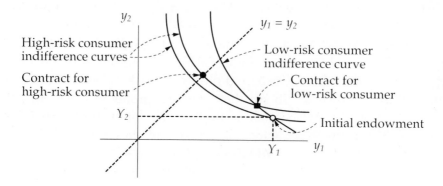

Figure 18.6. The picture for profit-maximizing insurance.

best insurance for a high-risk consumer and no insurance for a low-risk consumer. When we put (y_1^H, y_2^H) at the first-best location for a low-risk consumer, $(y_1^L, y_2^L) = (y_1^H, y_2^H)$ is forced. This corresponds to full insurance for both types, at terms that are best (from the perspective of the firm) for low-risk types. Otherwise, we get full insurance for high-risk types and partial insurance for low-risk types. Note that the only possibility of pooling is at $(y_1^L, y_2^L) = (y_1^H, y_2^H)$ and both equal to the first-best contract for low-risk types.

Now think of varying ρ parametrically, beginning with $\rho = 1$ (the consumer is sure to be the high-risk type) and decreasing ρ to zero. When $\rho = 1$, it is clear that the optimum is to provide first-best insurance for the high-risk consumer. When $\rho = 0$, it is clear that the optimum is to provide first-best insurance for the low-risk consumer. It can be shown that as ρ decreases, the contract (y_1^H, y_2^H) moves up the full-insurance line. So all that remains to be answered is the question, For $\rho \in (0, 1)$ (that is, there is strictly positive probability that the consumer is either type), can we get one of the "corner" solutions, or do we necessarily get one of the interior solutions? This question is of particular interest for the case ρ near 0. As we noted above, in this context we will have a pooling contract only at terms that involve complete insurance at the first-best contract for the low-risk types. If we knew that, for any $\rho > 0$, this is not the profit-maximizing contract (i.e., it is optimal only for $\rho = 0$), we would know that pooling does not occur. With this as a teaser, the analysis is left to you.

Variations, extensions, and complications

Besides being of independent interest, the analysis just completed illustrates how to formulate the problem of designing an optimal contract for a single party in a situation where the party has private information. The party is presented with a menu of options, one option for every possible piece of private information that the party might possess, where the items on the menu are constrained so that for each piece of private information the party self-selects the item on the menu that is intended for "her." In the literature, you will find reference to various *types* of party, as in "the low-risk type" or "the high-risk type"; each piece of private information that the party might possess corresponds to a different type.

In the analysis above, the criterion maximized was profit of the insurance company. But one needn't restrict to profits. If we think of the insurance company as being regulated, then the regulatory body might wish to maximize some sort of weighted sum of the consumer's expected utilities. Or, taking shareholders into account, we might consider maximizing some criterion that puts positive weight on the firm's profits. (If the firm is regulated so that it must achieve some minimal return on its capital, we could include that as a constraint.)

Another variation concerns problems that combine moral hazard with adverse selection. Suppose the party for whom the contract is to be designed must take an action that affects the welfare of the party designing the contract. Suppose this action is taken under circumstances of moral hazard; i.e., the contract cannot (enforceably) specify what action the party will take. For example, in life insurance, the insuree might take better or worse care of herself, affecting the odds of early demise, and the insurance company cannot enforceably include in an insurance policy rules about the insuree's diet or exercise regime. The insurance company would then wish to design a menu contract that not only caused the insuree to identify herself on the basis of her health, but that also provided her with an incentive to take care of herself. A combination of techniques from this chapter and chapter 16 can be employed. Suppose there are T types of consumer, indexed by $t = 1, \ldots, T$, and each type of consumer can take any action a from some finite set A. Imagine some selection of one action for each type, a function $\alpha : \{1, \ldots, T\} \rightarrow A$. We can ask, Can the firm design a menu of contracts, $c_1, \ldots, c_T$, such that a consumer of type t will select contract c_t and then choose action $\alpha(t)$? If so, what is the optimal (say, profit-maximizing) menu of contracts that implements α in this sense? This is a more complex problem only in that there are more constraints. For each type t, we have one constraint less than there are pairs $(t', a') \in \{1, \ldots, T\} \times A$. If the individual is of type t, she must prefer to choose the contract option c_t and take action $\alpha(t)$ to choosing any other $c_{t'}$ and taking action a', for any $t' \neq t$ or $a' \neq \alpha(t)$. Problem 11 of the previous chapter is attacked in this manner.

In essence, we did something along these lines in the example of this section. The actions available to the insuree were to choose a contract or to refuse all the contracts offered, and the (PH) and (PL) constraints were there to ensure that the agent took the desired action, namely signing a contract. (The option of choosing a contract but then not signing leaves the consumer at her endowment point.) We noted that we could mimic the option of not signing by including a contract that specified that the consumer would remain at her endowment; alternatively, we could use a structure of the sort just described, where we would find in turn the optimal expected profits given that both types sign, that the high-risk signs but not the low, that the low-risk signs but not the high, and that neither sign.

As we noted in the specific case of insurance contracts, our formulation assumes that the party designing the contract can make a take-it-or-leave-it offer to the second party. Because of the possibility of resale or purchase from multiple vendors, the seller of a particular good or service may be unable to make this sort of offer.

For example, imagine that insurance companies are very effectively cartelized (thus motivating our attention to profit-maximizing contracts). Imagine that the equilibrium has the low-risk consumer obtaining only partial insurance. We might then imagine that the high-risk consumer purchases partial insurance from a number of different firms, getting terms better than those she can get by buying complete insurance from one firm. (This is a good exercise for graphical analysis. Consider figure 18.6. If insurance policies are written to specify a premium and a payment in the low-endowment state, and the high-risk consumer buys two insurance policies of the sort intended for the low-risk consumer, what will be her levels of consumption? How does she feel about this combination vis à vis the full insurance contract that is intended for her? How do the insurance companies feel about this?) If the consumer can do this, it will wreak havoc with the insurance firms' supposedly profit-maximizing contracts. So insurance companies might put into their policies clauses about not being able to insure the same risk with two different carriers.[3]

In general, these sorts of considerations can restrict the menus that a firm can offer. Analysis along the lines we have indicated is possible, but it is often harder.

A final "generalization," and one that is immensely complicated, involves contract design by an informed party. Imagine a situation in which

---

[3] If you know about the insurance business and, in particular, moral hazard problems associated with full or even overinsurance, you will see another reason for insurance companies to write such clauses into their policies.

a government agency wishes to procure some items from a manufacturer. The government agency may not know the cost structure facing the firm as well as the firm does, and so it may design a menu of contracts from which the firm is to choose. If the firm is a higher cost firm, it chooses a contract with a greater amount of cost sharing, say, while a lower cost firm might choose a contract with less cost sharing but a higher unit price. It is easy to imagine, in this case, that the government possesses information not held by the firm, say about the engineering costs that the particular item entails. Depending on what the government knows, the menu of contracts that would be optimal for the government to offer might change. But then the firm, seeing what menu it is offered, might learn something about what the government knows. In designing the menu of options to offer the firm, the government must decide how "inscrutable" it should be. This involves thinking through what inferences the firm will make as a function of the menu of options the firm is offered, and how those inferences will affect what options the firm chooses given its own private information.

This variation on the basic puzzle falls under the rubric of "mechanism design by an informed principal." It is a good deal more complicated than what we have described above, and we leave it to you to read about in the literature.

The problem of credibility

One complication of (or caveat to) the basic story given above should be noted especially well. Suppose that in our example the insurance company offers two contracts, one with complete insurance intended for the consumer if she is high risk and one with partial insurance intended for her if she is low risk. Suppose she takes the low-risk insurance contract. Since this is a partial insurance contract, there remain gains from trade between the insurance company and the insuree. Why doesn't the insurance company turn around and offer a full-insurance contract that makes higher expected profits for it and leaves the consumer no worse off?

The answer is immediate. *If* the insuree anticipates that this is what the insurance company will do, the insuree, whether high-risk or low-, will choose the contract designed for the low-risk consumer, in anticipation of a further offer of a complete insurance contract (necessarily at better terms than the high-risk consumer is initially offered). The insurance company would do a good deal worse than with the original separating contracts.

While immediate, this answer is also a bit too glib on two grounds. First, it assumes that the consumer anticipates the further offering of full insurance if she elects the partial insurance "intended" for a low-risk consumer. If the consumer doesn't anticipate that this offer will be made (or, as much to the point, if the firm believes that the consumer won't anticipate this), then the company will expect to have higher profits if it offers insurance in this two-stage manner. You should recall at this point the previous discussion about why it is that our formulation of the firm's problem, where the firm offers a single menu of contracts, may not give us the profit-maximizing marketing scheme for the firm to use. In particular, for a consumer who might not see all the options coming to her in a multistage scheme, our formulation would not necessarily find the profit-maximizing marketing scheme.

In addition, (and the main point of this subsection), even if the consumer does foresee all the options that will be made available (as a function of her earlier choices), we have to wonder whether the firm can constrain itself from offering full insurance to a customer who chooses partial insurance from one of our supposedly optimal menu contracts. Ex post, if partial insurance is selected, the firm knows that the consumer is low risk. It knows that it can make more profits by making a further offer. But it is supposed to have the ability to refrain from acting on this information. If it cannot commit not to act on this information, and if the consumer anticipates this, then the consumer anticipates a further offer if she takes the low-risk partial insurance contract. And the firm, anticipating ex ante that it will act in this way (that is, anticipating its inability to refrain later from a further offer), will not wish to try to separate the consumer types. (But see the small type following.)

We don't mean to suggest by this that the analysis given before is wrong. We simply wish to stress that our analysis depends on the firm's ability to make and stick with a particular set of offers. One reason why the firm may have this ability is that it may be involved in this sort of situation repeatedly, so it has a reputation to protect.[4]

> Alternatively, we may wish to consider what happens in optimal contract design where the party designing the contract cannot forebear from renegotiating the contract ex post, after the party with private information has taken some action or made some selection. The analysis of this is tricky, because if precise assumptions are made about opportunities to renegotiate contracts, then one can be led to the conclusion that the insurance firm will offer the optimal separating menu at the last possible instant, just before the time at which the consumer's endowment is realized and after all opportunities for renegotiation have passed. This can be complicated in one of two ways: First,

---

[4] Or, in the spirit of our discussion in chapter 9, it may offer to consumers "most favored policyholder" contracts, where any offer made to any policyholder must be made available to all others. (This is relegated to a footnote because it gets a bit ahead of the story, to the next subsection where we discuss an insurance firm insuring many consumers simultaneously.)

there may be no "last instant" at all. This, for example, could come about if the time at which the risk is realized (or not) is random; a loss may be incurred at any moment, but if it doesn't happen now, it may happen later. (If it makes sense to you, consider a formulation where the time at which the consumer sustains a loss is random, with positive probability that the time never comes [the loss is never sustained], and conditional on a loss occurring, the time is exponentially distributed.) Second, we could consider a situation in which the loss situation is repeated. The consumer is either high or low risk in each of several periods (i.e., her type doesn't change), but conditional on her type, she stands to suffer a loss in income in each period independently of losses in other periods. For analysis (in a different context) along the second line, see Laffont and Tirole (1988).

Contracts designed for noninteracting parties: Optimal nonlinear prices

In the example, we were careful to speak of the (single) consumer, stressing the idea that this story was about the design of a contract for a single consumer whose type was unknown to the insurance company. Of course, insurance companies deal not with a single individual but with many individuals of varying types. So we can suppose the insurance company is extending insurance to many consumers, each of whom is subject to endowment risk of the sort we indicated. What sort of contracts should the firm offer in this case to maximize its expected profits?

To answer this question we need to ask two more. Can the firm tell which of the consumers is high risk and which is low? And, if it can, is it able to act on that information in the sense that it can offer a different contract or menu of contracts to each individual according to the individual's type? If the answers to both questions are yes, then the solution is just as in chapter 9: Offer a first-best (profit-maximizing) contract for each individual to each individual on a take-it-or-leave-it basis. But if the answer to either question is no, either because (say, on legal grounds) the insurance company is barred from "discriminating" in its offers or because it can't tell the characteristics of the individual, then the sort of analysis performed above becomes appropriate.

An important caveat should be made here. In the case of insurance, it seems reasonable to imagine that the choice of a contract from a menu by one insuree is unaffected by choices made by other insurees.[5] This is

---

[5] Actually, this is not so reasonable if there is risk that the insurance company will default on its obligations. Buying earthquake insurance from a firm that has a large amount of money at risk in the event of an earthquake may be somewhat less desirable than buying the same insurance from a company that does not have a large stake in this particular segment of the business.

crucial to our mode of analysis. As we analyze what choice one consumer will make from a given menu, we don't want to be forced to consider the choices others are making. This isn't to say that the objective function must be constructed separately for each individual consumer; perhaps it can be (if, for example, the firm wishes to maximize the sum of its expected profits), and then the analysis will be identical to that of the first subsection of this section. But even if the firm's objective function has as argument the entire array of consumer choices (which it would, for example, if the firm had a nonlinear cost structure for the provision of insurance), as long as the self-selection constraints can be constructed "individually," the basic techniques used in this section can be applied.

We can imagine other applications, in contrast, where the choices and actions made by one contractee affect how others in a similar position will fare. We move to such applications in the next section.

But before doing so, we note that the style of analysis in this section is precisely what we want for standard problems of optimal nonlinear pricing. Recall the example of chapter 9: A manufacturing monopolist is selling wholesale to retail monopolists. Different retail monopolists face different demand curves, and so, ideally, the manufacturer would like to make different take-it-or-leave-it offers to the retailers. But if the monopolist is constrained by law from doing this, or if the monopolist is unable to do this because she is unable to tell which demand curve faces a particular retailer, then the methods employed here would be used. For each "type" of retailer, where "type" corresponds to the demand curve the retailer faces, the monopolist designs a specific contract. These contracts are constrained so that each type of retailer prefers the contract designed for him to the contracts intended for other types. Subject to those constraints, the manufacturer designs a profit-maximizing menu and lets the retailers self-identify. In case you didn't do problem 4 of chapter 9 before, you get another chance here; it is repeated as problem 1.

18.2. Optimal contracts for interacting parties

Things get more interesting when we try to design optimal contracts for parties whose actions and choices interact. The examples that appear in the literature tend to involve a lot of mathematics. The mathematics isn't (usually) especially deep or complex, but it can get in the way of understanding the basic issues. So we will only go through the analysis of a toy problem that illustrates many of the important conceptual issues, leaving you to read elsewhere about more realistic applications.

A toy problem

Imagine that some party must procure one hundred units of a particular item. We will call this party "the government," and you may think of a government that is seeking to procure one hundred jet fighter planes (although we will work with a formulation that assumes these hundred units are perfectly divisible). Two firms could supply these units. We index the firms by $i = 1, 2$. Each firm has a simple linear cost structure — constant marginal cost c_i and no fixed costs. But, and this is the complicating feature, the value of c_i for each i can be either 1 or 2, each equally likely. The values of c_1 and c_2 are statistically independent. While each firm i knows its own cost, neither the government nor the other firm knows the costs of the firm i. Instead, both the government and the other firm believe that c_i is either 1 or 2 with probability $1/2$ apiece.

We assume throughout that the government is able to propose contracts to the two firms to which they must respond on a take-it-or-leave-it basis. And we assume that they will respond favorably whenever it is (weakly) in their interest to do so.

If the government knew the costs of the two firms, its procurement problem would be easily solved. It would propose to buy from either firm if they have the same unit costs (or split its order between them) and to buy from the lower-cost firm if one firm has unit cost 1 and the other has cost 2. Since the government makes take-it-or-leave-it offers, it need never pay more than the unit costs of the firm, which means that it pays 100 with probability three-quarters and 200 with probability one-quarter, for an expected cost of 125.

But since the government doesn't know the unit costs of the firm, it can't do this. Suppose it tries the following scheme: The firms are asked voluntarily to reveal their costs. If both firms name the same cost, the government will split the order between the two, paying the named cost. If one firm names lower costs, the government will buy from the firm naming the lower cost, at that cost. In response to this, if firms are restricted to naming either 1 or 2 as their cost, they will name 2 regardless of what their cost is. When a firm's cost is 2, there is no point to naming a cost of 1; this will result in a loss of either 50 (if the other firm names a cost of 1) or 100 (if the other firm names 2). And when the firm's cost is 1, it makes zero profits if it says its costs are 1 while, if it names 2 and the other firm names 2 (which the other firm is bound to do with probability at least $1/2$), then the first firm makes 50. So both firms will name 2 for sure, and the government's costs will be 200.

Clearly, the government needs to provide firms with an incentive for revealing that their cost is 1 when it is 1. Consider the scheme: If both firms name 2, the order is split and the government pays 2 per unit. If both name 1, the order is split and the government pays $x > 1$ per unit. If one names 1 and the other names 2, the order goes to the firm that named 1, and the government pays $y > 1$ per unit. What must x and y be in order to get the firms to reveal truthfully their costs? Assume that firm 1 believes that firm 2 will truthfully reveal its costs. (Assume $x, y \leq 2$ so this is valid.) Then if firm 1's costs are 1, it can name 2 and have profits of 50 with probability 1/2. Or it can name 1 and have profits of $50(x - 1)$ with probability 1/2 (if the other firm's costs are 1) and $100(y - 1)$ with probability 1/2 (if the other firm's costs are 2). Assuming the firms try to maximize their expected profits, firm 1 truthfully reveals a cost of 1 if

$$\frac{1}{2}50(x - 1) + \frac{1}{2}100(y - 1) \geq 25.$$

Or, rather, it is a Nash equilibrium between the two firms to truthfully reveal their costs in this case. Let us proceed under the assumption that firms truthfully reveal their costs. Then the government's expected costs are

$$100[\frac{1}{4}x + \frac{1}{2}y + \frac{1}{4}2].$$

That is, with probability 1/4, the government pays x per unit, with probability 1/2, it pays y per unit, and with probability 1/4, it pays 2 per unit. The truth-inducing constraint can be written $25x + 50y \geq 100$, and the government's objective function is to minimize $25x + 50y + 50$, so it is evident that any selection of x and y that satisfies the constraint with equality gives minimum expected cost to the government, and that expected cost is 150.

Suppose the government chooses $x = 2$ and $y = 1$. Is truth-telling the only Nash equilibrium? Suppose firm 2 reports costs of 2 regardless of what its costs are. If firm 1 reports costs of 2 when its costs are in fact 1, then it is sure to make 50. (It gets half the order for sure, and it is paid 2 per unit when its costs are 1.) If it reports costs of 1 when its costs are 1, it gets the entire order but makes nothing. (It has reported 1, its rival has reported 2, and so it is paid precisely its costs.) Of course, when its costs are 2 it will name 2 as its costs. Hence if firm 2 always reports costs of 2, then it is a best response for firm 1 always to report costs of 2. It is a Nash equilibrium for both firms always to report costs of 2, and at this Nash equilibrium, each firm has expected profits of 25. By comparison, at the Nash equilibrium where both firms always tell the truth, each has expected profits of 12.5. If we believe that firms will find their way to Nash equilibria that are better for both of them, then $x = 2$ and $y = 1$ doesn't seem so good. At least, the goverment is risking the possibility that the firms find a Nash equilibrium that is better for both of them and worse for the government.

To avoid this, we clearly want to make y as large as possible. So consider setting $x = 0$ and $y = 2$. (It is assumed that x and y are constrained to be nonnegative. Note that $x = 0$ is bad enough; the firms are told by the government that if each reports low costs, each gets to provide half the order *for free*.) If $x = 0$ and $y = 2$, and if firm 2 always reports costs of 2, then firm 1, when its costs are 1, nets 50 for sure by reporting costs of 2, and 100 for sure by reporting costs of 1. Hence we would not have the problem of an equilibrium where both firms report 2 regardless of their costs. But now something worse comes along. Suppose one firm adopts the strategy of always reporting that its costs are 1. The other firm, in response, can never do better than to report costs of 2; if it reports costs of 1, it will have to produce half the output and it will be paid nothing. And if the second firm always reports costs of 2, then among the first firm's best responses is always to report costs of 1; this gives it 2 per unit regardless of its costs. We have a second Nash equilibrium with an expected cost to the government of 200.

So y is too high. Try $y = 1.9$ and $x = .2$. Now we're in business. If a firm's costs are 2, it will not report 1, no matter what it thinks the other firm is doing. If it reports 1, it will be saddled with some of the output, and it won't recover its costs. While if a firm's costs are 1, it must assume that its rival will report 2 when its costs are 2. If it thinks its rival will truthfully report 1 when its costs are 1, then it is indifferent between reporting 1 or 2. If it thinks its rival will report 2 when its costs are 1, then it strictly prefers to report costs of 1; reporting 2 nets 50, while reporting 1 nets 90. If we sweeten the pot just a bit, making $y = 1.91$ and $x = .21$, then the unique Nash equilibrium between the two firms, given the *mechanism* the government has imposed, is to reveal costs truthfully. And the government's expected cost of procurement is 150.50. (The extra .50 is the result of sweetening the pot.)

It is possible, though, to continue to quibble about this scheme. Suppose that firm 1 gets it into its head that firm 2 will always report a cost of 1, even though this is not Nash behavior. If firm 1's costs are 1, then reporting the truth means that firm 1 will sustain a loss (it gets half the order and is paid less than its costs). So firm 1, if it is convinced that firm 2 will always report a cost of 1, prefers to name costs of 2 (or to refuse to participate altogether).

Consider the following scheme. The government announces that if both firms claim that their costs are 2, the order will be split between them, and each will be paid 2 per unit. If both claim that their costs are 1, the order will be split between them and each will be paid 1.01. And if one claims that its costs are 1 and the other claims its costs are 2, then the one claiming costs of 1 will get the entire order and will be paid 1.51 per unit. And each firm will be given .01 for participating at all.

Suppose firm 1 has costs of 2. Then no matter what it thinks firm 2 will do, it is better to name 2 than to name 1, and the .01 participation bonus means that it is better to name 2 than to refuse to participate. Suppose firm 1 has costs of 1. If firm 2 names costs of 1, it is better for firm 1 to name a cost of 1 (and make .01 on each of fifty units) than to name a cost of 2 and make nothing. If firm 2 names costs of 2, it is better for firm 1 to name a cost of 1 than a cost of 2; naming 2 will net 1.00 on each of fifty units, while naming 1 will net .51 on each of one hundred units. That is, against this scheme, truth-telling is a strictly dominant strategy for each of the firms. Note that this costs the government $(1/4)101 + (1/2)151 + (1/4)200 + .02 = 150.77$. Moreover, by making the sweeteners (the extra .01's) vanishingly small, the cost falls to 150.

Let us summarize where we are. We found a scheme in which truth-telling is a Nash equilibrium, costing the government an expected 150. But this scheme has multiple Nash equilibria for the two firms, one of which is better for both firms than is truth-telling. So we modified the scheme in a way that makes truth-telling the unique Nash equilibrium. But truth-telling isn't, in this case, a dominant strategy. So we modified the scheme again, so that truth-telling becomes a dominant strategy for each firm. And still, except for "sweeteners" that can be made arbitrarily small, the expected cost to the government is 150.

Optimal direct revelation mechanisms

In the foregoing analysis, we made two special assumptions about the *mechanism* the government employs to award the contract. First, we made a qualitative assumption that the government would ask the firms to name their costs, with the contract amounts and corresponding payments depending on the pair of named costs. Second, we assumed that the contract amounts and corresponding payments took a particular form. The contract quantities are split if the firms name the same price, and the entire contract is given to the firm naming the lower price. If both name 2, each is paid 2 per unit. If one names 1 and the other 2, the one naming 1 is paid y per unit. And if both name 1, both are paid x per unit.

If we look at different schemes, either of the same general qualitative structure but with different sorts of quantity assignments and payments, or of a completely different form, perhaps we can find one that will lower the government's expected costs below 150. Over the next two subsections we will see that this can't be done, subject to some qualifications. In this section, we keep to the general qualitative form used previously, varying the parameterization. In the next section, we argue that *any* general mechanism is "equivalent" in terms of outcomes to some mechanism of the qualitative form of this section. The second step, which is called the *revelation principle*, gives this chapter its name.

We begin with a definition of the "general qualitative structure" of the mechanisms discussed in the previous subsection. A *direct revelation mechanism* is any mechanism of the following sort. For each of the four pairs mn such that $m = 1, 2$ and $n = 1, 2$, there is given a four-tuple $(x_{mn}^1, x_{mn}^2, t_{mn}^1, t_{mn}^2) \in R_+^4$ such that $x_{mn}^1 + x_{mn}^2 \geq 100$. (By R_+^4, we mean the nonnegative orthant in R^4.) The two firms, who already know their true costs, are given the opportunity to participate. If they elect to do so, they simultaneously and independently announce whether their costs are 1 or 2. (This is what gives a direct revelation mechanism its name.) Letting m be the announcement of firm 1 and n the announcement of firm 2, the four-tuple $(x_{mn}^1, x_{mn}^2, t_{mn}^1, t_{mn}^2)$ corresponding to their announcement mn determines their responsibilities: Firm i must produce x_{mn}^i units of the item, for which it receives a payment of t_{mn}^i. Note that if c^i is the true marginal cost of firm i, then the firm's net profits are $t_{mn}^i - c^i x_{mn}^i$.

Note carefully that we have allowed firms the option of refusing to participate at the stage after they know their true costs but before they have learned what the other firm announces. In effect, we are supposing that the government can compel the firms to produce according to the "rules" of the mechanism if they agree to participate at the point indicated. We can think of at least two other possibilities: (a) The government cannot compel the firms to carry out the dictates of the mechanism at any time; firms need only carry through with the dictates of the mechanism if they continue not to expect a loss; (b) the government can propose this mechanism to the two firms before they know their costs, and they are compelled to carry through with the mechanism if they agree at that point.

In restricting the t^i to be nonnegative, we are making a further assumption, namely that the government cannot compel the firm to make a payment to the government. You may feel that this is in the spirit of but a poor substitute for (a); if the idea is that the government cannot compel the firm to take a loss ex post, then (a) and not our nonnegativity constraint would seem appropriate. We continue our analysis under the assumptions that the firm can be compelled to take a loss if it agrees to participate after it learns its own cost but cannot be compelled to make a monetary payment to the government, bearing in mind that perhaps the sign of the t^i should be unrestricted or that (a) or (b) should be assumed.

Now we ask the following question.

Suppose the government restricts attention to direct revelation mechanisms with the property that agreeing to participate and then truthfully revealing costs constitutes a Nash equilibrium for the two firms in the corresponding game of incomplete information between them. What is the lowest expected payment that government must make to the firms using such a mechanism?

You may wonder why we are asking (and answering) this question. If so, suspend your wonder for the time being.

This question can be turned into a linear programming problem. A linear programming problem is a constrained maximization problem with linear objective function and linear constraints. Such problems are very easily solved numerically, using a variety of methods, the most prominent of which are variations on the *simplex algorithm*. If you don't know about linear programming, you should learn; Luenberger (1984) gives an accessible treatment. In any event, in all the optimization problems that follow in this chapter, we will announce answers. This may seem a bit like magic if you don't know about linear programming, but in fact we are simply reporting solutions obtained by the simplex algorithm. (Trying to solve the problems given below by hand with Lagrange multipliers is *not* recommended.)

To begin, we consider what is required if participation and truthtelling are to be a Nash equilibrium for a given direct revelation mechanism. For each of the two firms, we have four constraints. For firm 1 they are:

(P1-1) If firm 2 participates and tells the truth, and if firm 1's costs are 1, then firm 1 is willing to participate in the mechanism and tell the truth instead of refusing to participate,

$$\frac{1}{2}[t_{11}^1 - 1x_{11}^1] + \frac{1}{2}[t_{12}^1 - 1x_{12}^1] \geq 0.$$

(P1-2) If firm 2 participates and tells the truth, and if firm 1's costs are 2, then firm 1 is willing to participate in the mechanism and tell the truth rather than refusing to participate,

$$\frac{1}{2}[t_{21}^1 - 2x_{21}^1] + \frac{1}{2}[t_{22}^1 - 2x_{22}^1] \geq 0.$$

(I1-1) If firm 2 participates and tells the truth, and if firm 1's costs are 1, then firm 1 is willing to participate in the mechanism and tell the truth instead of participating and falsely claiming that its costs are 2,

$$\frac{1}{2}[t^1_{11} - 1x^1_{11}] + \frac{1}{2}[t^1_{12} - 1x^1_{12}] \geq \frac{1}{2}[t^1_{21} - 1x^1_{21}] + \frac{1}{2}[t^1_{22} - 1x^1_{22}].$$

(I1-2) If firm 2 participates and tells the truth, and if firm 1's costs are 2, then firm 1 is willing to participate in the mechanism and tell the truth instead of participating and falsely claiming that its costs are 1,

$$\frac{1}{2}[t^1_{21} - 2x^1_{21}] + \frac{1}{2}[t^1_{22} - 2x^1_{22}] \geq \frac{1}{2}[t^1_{11} - 2x^1_{11}] + \frac{1}{2}[t^1_{12} - 2x^1_{12}].$$

If you go through each of these four constraints carefully, you will be able to make sense of them. Take *(I1-2)*, a mnemonic for the Incentive constraint for firm *1* when its costs are 2. On the left-hand side we have the expected profits of this firm if it participates, truthfully says that its costs are 2, and the other firm participates and tells the truth. This is the appropriately weighted average of its profits if the other firm's costs are 1 (and are so revealed) and if the other firm's costs are 2. On the right-hand side we have the expected profits of this firm when its costs are 2 if it participates and falsely maintains that its costs are only 1. Note that on both sides, the production quantity the firm is assigned is premultiplied by 2, since these are the true costs of the firm in this case.

There are four similar constraints for firm 2. We also have nonnegativity constraints (by assumption) on all the variables and four constraints that say that the government obtains its 100 units, constraints such as

$$x^1_{11} + x^2_{11} \geq 100.$$

The set of direct relevation mechanisms, specified by the sixteen variables x^i_{mn} and t^i_{mn} for $i, m, n = 1, 2$, that satisfy all these constraints is precisely the set of direct relevation mechanisms for which participation and truth-telling is a Nash equilibrium. So to answer the question that has been posed, we wish to minimize

$$\frac{1}{4}[t^1_{11} + t^2_{11}] + \frac{1}{4}[t^1_{21} + t^2_{21}] + \frac{1}{4}[t^1_{12} + t^2_{12}] + \frac{1}{4}[t^1_{22} + t^2_{22}],$$

which is the expected amount the government pays out in a given mechanism, subject to all the constraints so far given.

We asked the computer to solve this linear programming problem (minimize the objective function subject to all the constraints above), and it gave back: $x_{11}^1 = x_{12}^1 = x_{21}^2 = x_{22}^2 = 100$, $t_{12}^1 = t_{21}^2 = t_{22}^2 = 200$, and all other variables equal to zero. That is, firm 1 is assigned all the production if it announces costs of 1; otherwise firm 2 is assigned to produce all 100 units. Firm 1 is paid 200 if it announces its costs are 1 and firm 2 announces costs of 2, and firm 2 is paid 200 if firm 1 announces that its costs are 2. This costs the government an expected 150.

As we know from our earlier discussion, this is not the only way to induce truth-telling as a Nash equilibrium in a direct revelation game. Another way is to set $x_{11}^1 = x_{11}^2 = x_{22}^1 = x_{22}^2 = 50, x_{12}^1 = x_{21}^2 = 100, t_{11}^1 = t_{11}^2 = 50$, $t_{22}^2 = t_{22}^2 = 100$, $t_{12}^1 = t_{21}^2 = 150$, and all other variables equal to zero. (This corresponds to paying 1 per unit when both firms name costs of 1, 2 per unit when both name costs of 2, and 1.5 per unit to the firm that names 1 if one names 1 and the other 2.) We will wish to refer to this particular scheme later on, so we give it a name; this will hereafter be referred to as the *nice* direct revelation scheme. The solution given in the previous paragraph is much more "extreme"; it has many more zero elements. In general, linear programming will tend to produce extreme solutions of this sort. But the point is not so much the solution produced as it is the value of the solution: There are many direct relevation schemes for which participation and truth-telling give a Nash equilibrium in this situation and which cost the government an expected 150. But there is *no* scheme for which participation and truth-telling is a Nash equilibrium that produces a lower expected cost; this is what we learned by solving the constrained optimization problem using linear programming.

In the formulation above, we have limited attention to direct revelation mechanisms where, for each pair of reports mn by the two firms, a single four-tuple $(x_{mn}^1, x_{mn}^2, t_{mn}^1, t_{mn}^2)$ is implemented. For later purposes, we need to generalize this a bit and consider direct revelation mechanisms where, for each pair mn, there is a probability distribution μ_{mn} over such four-tuples. The idea is that firms report their costs, and then a lottery over four-tuples is conducted, with distribution given by μ_{mn} for the reported pair mn. The outcome of this lottery is then implemented.

In the context of this problem, allowing for random direct relevation mechanisms doesn't change anything. Since the government and firms are risk neutral and the firms have linear production technologies, replacing any lottery μ_{mn} by the four-tuple that is its mathematical expectation doesn't affect any party's expected profits. Hence the best the government can do (in terms of minimum expected costs) with a random direct revelation mechanism (which induces participation and truth-telling as a Nash equilibrium) is the best it can do with a nonrandom mechanism, and that is expected costs of 150.

We will return to this basic formulation in a bit, but before doing so we consider three alternative formulations, based on different notions of which constraints bind on the government in designing a direct revelation mechanism.

(a) Imagine that the government cannot compel a firm to produce if the firm would, by producing, sustain a loss. In other words, firms are allowed to refuse to participate after they learn their assignments and monetary transfers. We assume that firms, if indifferent between participating or not, will agree to participate. (This is the usual problem of weak versus strict inequalities in this sort of analysis.)

Suppose the government restricts attention to direct revelation mechanisms with the property that truthfully revealing costs and then, ex post, agreeing to participate constitutes a Nash equilibrium in the game with incomplete information between the two firms. What is the lowest expected payment that government must make to the firms in such mechanisms?

We already know the answer to this question; the lowest expected payment will be 150. We know that this is the answer by the following chain of logic: (1) The lowest expected payment under these constraints will be no lower than the lowest expected payment if a firm can be compelled to produce if it agrees to participate once it knows its own costs but not those of its rival. This is so because in any scheme where the firms will always agree to participate ex post, they will surely agree at the earlier stage. Mechanisms that meet the test of this question meet the test of the earlier question, and the minimum cost under the earlier constraints was found to be 150. Hence 150 is a lower bound on what can be achieved under these tighter restrictions. (2) In the nice[b] direct revelation scheme, which has expected costs to the government of 150, these extra constraints are met.

Even though we know the answer to this question, it is instructive to see how we would modify our constrained optimization problem to encompass this changed formulation. It is easy. In place of the four participation constraints we had before, we now have eight. A typical one of these is

$$t_{21}^1 - 2x_{21}^1 \geq 0, \qquad (P1\text{-}21)$$

which expresses the constraint that if firm 1's costs are 2 and firm 2's costs are 1, then firm 1 is willing to undertake the assigned production level x_{21}^1, based on a comparison of what the government will pay and what this level of production will cost.[c] If we drop the four old participation constraints in

---

[b] Go back six paragraphs if you don't know what nice means in this context.

[c] If you write down the corresponding constraint for firm 1 when its costs are 2 and those of its rival are 2, and you compare these two constraints with the constraint (P1-2) from before, you will see why this formulation is theoretically more restrictive than the earlier formulation.

favor of these eight "ex post" participation constraints, we can again feed the problem to a linear programming algorithm. When we did this, the linear programming algorithm used didn't come up with the nice direct relevation mechanism but instead suggested the following mechanism. Everything depends on what firm 1 reports. If firm 1 reports that its costs are 1, then we pay it 100 and tell it to produce one hundred units. (We pay nothing to firm 2.) But if firm 1 reports costs of 2, we pay it nothing, we pay 200 to firm 2, and we assign firm 2 production of all one hundred units.

(b) Going in the other direction, suppose the government can approach the firms with a mechanism before they learn their costs. Firms agree whether to participate based on their initial assessments of what their costs will be, and once they agree to participate, they are compelled to complete any assignments made in exchange for compensation agreed to ex ante as part of the mechanism originally proposed. In this case, we would replace the four original participation constraints with two "ex ante" participation constraints. The constraint for firm 1 would read

$$\frac{1}{4}[t_{11}^1 - 1x_{11}^1] + \frac{1}{4}[t_{12}^1 - 1x_{12}^1] + \frac{1}{4}[t_{21}^1 - 2x_{21}^1] + \frac{1}{4}[t_{22}^1 - 2x_{22}^2] \geq 0.$$

We can ask

What is the lowest expected cost to the government if it can employ a direct revelation mechanism where truth-telling is a Nash equilibrium and where participation constraints are as just above?

If we look for a solution to this formulation, we find that costs to the government can be driven down to the first-best level of 125. One scheme that does this is: Firm 1 produces all one hundred units if it names costs of 1 or if firm 2 names costs of 2. Only if firm 1 says its costs are 2 and firm 2 says its costs are 1 does firm 2 get to produce. Firm 2 is paid 100 if it says its costs are 1 and firm 1 says its costs are 2; note that this induces truth-telling on the part of firm 2, since to claim costs of 2 means firm 2 is shut out entirely, but to claim costs of 1 when its costs are in fact 2 means it may lose money (if firm 1 claims costs of 2). Firm 1 is paid 250 if it claims costs of 1 and firm 2 claims costs of 2, and it is paid 150 if it claims costs of 2 and firm 2 claims costs of 2. Otherwise firm 1 is paid nothing. Why does this induce truth-telling by firm 1? If its costs are 1, by claiming costs of 1 it knows it will produce one hundred units and it will get 250 with probability 1/2. If it claims costs of 2, it will produce one hundred units with probability 1/2 and receive 150 with probability 1/2. Telling the truth is just as good as lying. But if its costs are 2, telling the truth means a loss of 25 (with probability 1/2 it will be told to produce one hundred, costing 200, and it gets back 150), while lying means a loss of 75 (it will be told to produce one hundred, costing 200, for sure, and it gets 250 with probability 1/2).

Variations (a) and (b) turn on when the firm is allowed to decide whether to participate or, more precisely, when the firm is no longer allowed to opt out of a mechanism earlier agreed to. Can the firms be approached before they learn their true costs and then be compelled to continue if they agreed ex ante? Can they only be approached after they learn their true costs, or compelled to continue only after they learn those costs? Or do firms always retain the right to opt out? In the literature you will find reference to *ex ante*, *interim*, and *ex post* implementation, referring (roughly) to variations (b), the original formulation, and variation (a), respectively.

(c) As noted earlier, we have constrained the government to make nonnegative payments to the firm. We might wonder what can be achieved (say, in our original formulation) if we allow the t^i_{mn} to be negative. This change, in this case, doesn't amount to much. The minimum cost remains 150, and in fact the computer returned the same solution as we obtained for the original formulation. (However this variation will become interesting in problem 8.)

The revelation principle

We now know that the government cannot do any better than an expected cost of 150 by using a direct revelation mechanism that induces participation and truth-telling as a Nash equilibrium. Can it do better with some more complex sort of mechanism?

The *revelation principle* says that it cannot, subject to some important caveats. Truth-telling in a direct revelation mechanism (which induces truth-telling) mimics every possible *equilibrium outcome* in every possible mechanism, however complex.

The revelation principle is one of those things that is obvious once you understand it but somewhat cumbersome to explain. We try here to strike a balance between excessive formality and verbal arm waving, but the appropriate level of formality is highly subjective, and if, after reading about this here, you don't find the basic idea rather transparent, then you should seek a different treatment.

To begin, we have to say what we mean by a general mechanism. We have in mind some "game form" that the government will design and in which it asks the two firms to participate. We think of this general mechanism as a finite extensive form tree for the two firms, possibly incorporating moves by nature.[d][e] At the end of each branch of the tree is a four-tuple of the sort in the previous section. The government designs and presents this game tree to the two firms and asks if they would like to play. (We assume that each firm knows its costs but not those of its rival when faced with the decision whether to participate; variations in the spirit

---

[d] The government is presumed able to conduct any needed randizations objectively and credibly.

[e] We assume that the game tree prescribed is one of perfect recall and the two firms are capable of playing the game tree as it is designed.

of those in the previous section are straightforward.) If both agree, then they play the game, and the four-tuple at the end of the branch they play determines what each is asked to produce and how much each is paid.

Because the government is allowed to present any finite game tree at all (with the sorts of endpoints we've described) for its mechanism, this formalism encompasses many mechanisms one can imagine.[f]

In the context we have set, for every general mechanism of this sort there is a corresponding game of incomplete information for the two firms. Each firm begins with private information about its costs; think of four possible initial nodes. Append to each of these initial nodes a copy of the mechanism, and at each endpoint use the four-tuple specified by the mechanism with the costs of the firms as specified by the initial node to compute payoffs for the players. Right at the start of the game, give each player the option to decline to participate, with payoff zero for each if either declines.[g] Information sets are used to mimic the idea that the firms know their own costs but not the costs of the other firm while playing this game.

An example may help clarify. Imagine the following simple mechanism. The government goes to firm 1 and offers to firm 1 the opportunity to produce the hundred units for a payment of 100. If firm 1 declines, the government goes to firm 2 and offers firm 2 the opportunity to produce the hundred units for a payment of 150. If firm 2 declines, the government goes back to firm 1 and offers it the opportunity to produce the hundred units for a payment of 200. And if firm 1 refuses, the rules specify that firms 1 and 2 each produce 50 at a payment of 10 for each firm.

We depict this mechanism in figure 18.7(a). At the end of each endpoint is a four-tuple, which gives in order the production quantity assigned to firm 1 and then to firm 2, and then the payments made to the firms.

---

[f] Certain relatively free-form bargaining schemes may not be reducible to a definite game tree, and you may wish to consider how what we will say here applies to such situations. In this regard, note especially our later comments about games so complex that it is inappropriate to assume that players will play a Nash equilibrium.

[g] If one firm accepts and the other declines, why is the payoff zero for the accepting firm? Why doesn't the government continue to conduct business with the firm that accepts? We could specify something more interesting for cases where one firm accepts and the other declines, but whatever is specified will be irrelevant to what follows, because we assume that both firms anticipate that the other will accept. You might worry that this will preclude mechanisms that are intended to ignore one firm entirely. But we can construct mechanisms where one firm or the other gets nothing and does nothing at the end of each branch; such a mechanism would be as if the government decided to deal with the other firm only, and the first firm in this mechanism would be indifferent between accepting and rejecting. Hence the revelation principle encompasses mechanisms where the government sets out to deal with one firm only.

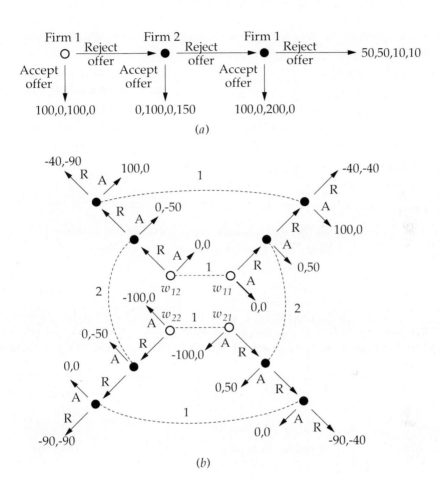

Figure 18.7. *A complex mechanism and the
corresponding game of incomplete information.*

In (a), a complex mechanism is depicted. The endpoints give firm 1's
production quantity, then 2's quantity, then 1's income, and then 2's
income. In (b), we show the corresponding game of incomplete information between the players, although we have left off the diagram the
opportunity to opt out at the start of the game. The four initial nodes in
the game tree are labeled w_{mn} where m is the actual costs of firm 1 and
n is the actual costs of firm 2. We have supressed the initial probability
distribution, which is 1/4 on each of the four initial nodes. Endpoints
are evaluated in terms of firm 1's profits and then firm 2's profits.

Then in figure 18.7(b), we construct the associated game of incomplete information.[6] Here the endpoints are evaluated using the firms' costs as determined by the initial node in the game tree.

The revelation principle. Consider any mechanism of the sort described above, the associated game of incomplete information between the two firms, and any Nash equilibrium of this game in which both firms agree to participate. The expected costs to the government and the assignment of production levels and payments to the firms in this equilibrium, viewed as a function of their costs, can be precisely obtained by participation and truth-telling in a direct revelation game for which participation and truth-telling give a Nash equilibrium.

The proof runs along the following lines. Take the mechanism, associated game, and Nash equilibrium. Think of the equilibrium strategies for the two firms as being given in the following form: Firm 1 follows (possibly mixed) strategy σ_1^1 in the mechanism tree if its costs are 1, while if its costs are 2, it follows strategy σ_2^1; similar notation is used for firm 2.

Now construct a (possibly random) direct revelation game as follows. Take each of the four possible pairs of costs in turn. For the pair corresponding to the costs m for firm 1 and n for firm 2, construct the probability distribution over outcomes in the mechanism tree that results from firm 1 playing σ_m^1 and firm 2 playing σ_n^2. This gives a probability distribution over four-tuples, which in the direct revelation game is μ_{mn}.

The claim is that in this direct revelation game, truth-telling and participation is a Nash equilibrium that induces the same outcomes as the Nash equilibrium in the original game. The reason is simple (but hard to say). Suppose, by way of contradiction, that firm 1 strictly prefers in the direct revelation game to report costs of 2 when its costs are 1. By construction if firm 1's costs are 1, then the distribution over outcomes of claiming costs of 1 in the direct revelation game against truth-telling by firm 2 is precisely the same as the distribution over outcomes of playing σ_1^1 against firm 2's strategy in the original game, and the distribution over outcomes of claiming costs of 2 in the direct revelation game against truth-telling by firm 2 is precisely the same as the distribution of outcomes from playing σ_2^1 against firm 2's strategy in the original game. If firm 1, when its costs are 1, prefers to claim costs of 2 in the direct revelation game, then it must prefer to play σ_2^1 when its costs are 1 in the original game. But since we suppose that we began with a Nash equilibrium in the original game, this is impossible.

---

[6] To keep the figure from becoming too complex, we have left off the initial option not to participate.

If that didn't penetrate, try putting it this way: In the original game, a firm can always act as if its costs were "the other" value. The statement that we have a Nash equilibrium means that it has no positive incentive to do this. Our direct revelation game is constructed essentially as follows. The two firms simultaneously and independently report their costs to some disinterested third party. This third party then implements in the original general mechanism what the firms would have done in the original equilibrium as a function of the costs they report. That is, if firm 1 reports costs m and firm 2 reports n, the third party implements play of σ_m^1 against play of σ_n^2. Since a firm would not choose in the original game to act as if its costs were other than what they are, so the firm would not wish to have the third party "misplay" on its behalf.

Similar arguments ensure that firms will participate in the direct revelation game. If a firm prefers in the direct revelation game not to participate (against truth-telling by its opponent), then it would prefer not to participate in the original game (against its opponent's strategy). But the hypothesis of the revelation principle is that the firms choose to participate in the original game.

We employed the revelation principle, albeit in somewhat degenerate form, in section 18.1, when we asserted that to find the optimal marketing strategy for the insurance firm, it suffices to look for the optimal menu of contracts to offer, with the choice of contract from the menu left to the consumer. Think of implementing this choice as follows: The insurance company says that contract A will be given to any consumer who reveals that she is high risk, and B will be given to any consumer who reveals she is low risk; then the consumer is told to state which she is. Anything that can be achieved by a complex marketing scheme, the revelation principle asserts, can be asserted by this simple direct revelation mechanism. This isn't precisely the same as having the consumer choose directly between A and B, which is what we imagine when we think of a menu of choices from which the consumer chooses. But in a one-person problem, it comes down to the same thing.

A sometimes heard paraphrase of the revelation principle (adapted to this context) is: Anything that the government can achieve with a general mechanism can be achieved by a direct revelation mechanism where truth-telling is a Nash equilibrium. This, like many paraphrases, is too broad. The antecedent in the paraphrase should be: Anything that the government can achieve in a Nash equilibrium between the two firms in a general mechanism.... Getting the antecedent right is important on at least two grounds, both having to do with the revelance of Nash analysis in general mechanisms.

In the first place, the government might be able to devise a mechanism so complex that the firms do not see their way to a Nash equilibrium in it, and their behavior may then give the government lower expected costs than it gets in a truth-telling equilibrium of a direct revelation game. (In the one-person case of section 18.1, this is just the problem of the insurance-buying consumer who is not completely aware of all the choices she will be offered. Rational maximization in a one-person choice problem is "Nash equilibrium analysis" if we think of the choice problem as a one-person game.) Of course, unless we have a theory about how the firms will act in the face of mechanisms so complex that they don't see their way to a Nash equilibrium, it will be hard to see how the government can evaluate such mechanisms. This isn't to say that interesting theories of this sort can't be devised. But such theories are not very well developed at present.

The second objection relates to chapter 14. We can imagine contexts in which the two firms interact repeatedly. Think of the firms as being, say, Boeing and Airbus, and the hundred units being commercial aircraft. Although perhaps not descriptive of the current relations between Boeing and Airbus, we can imagine that the firms are engaged in implicit collusion, sustained by the usual sort of folk theorem construction. If this is so, it is not entirely reasonable to suppose that the firms in one particular encounter will behave according to the dictates of Nash equilibrium in that encounter. We might anticipate two implicitly collusive firms maintaining that each has costs of 2, even if one or the other has costs of 1, and even if it is to the short-run advantage of the firm with costs of 1 to so state, because the short-run advantage must be weighed against long-run considerations of future encounters between the firms. In such a situation, the party designing the mechanism might do well to think about how to design a mechanism that *reduces* the firm's abilities to collude, for example, by adding noise to the outcome. Direct revelation mechanisms may be more or less conducive to collusion between the firms; insofar as direct revelation supports collusion, the government may do better with a more complex mechanism.

One should be clear about the uses to which the revelation principle is put. It can be thought of as a statement about *how* actually to implement contracts. But it may be better to use it with greater circumspection as a tool of analysis for finding the limits of *what* outcomes can be implemented, without reference to how best to implement a particular outcome.[7]

We can make this point in another way. In some contexts of direct revelation, there will be situations ex post where the party in the role of

---

[7] And, in the literature, this is primarily how it is used.

the government knows that it can obtain further gains from trade from one or more of the parties who participated. We already saw an example in the context of insurance with adverse selection, where the insurance company knows ex post that it can improve its profits and the welfare of the consumer, if the consumer self-identifies as being low-risk. As we said before, the insurance company must be able to restrain itself from renegotiating with a consumer who identifies herself as being low-risk. Similarly, in many applications of the revelation principle, the party in the role of mechanism designer must be able to commit credibly to no subsequent (re)negotiation once it learns the types of the parties with which it is dealing. As a matter of practical implementation, the ability to make such a credible commitment may be greater if the optimal mechanism is implemented by some scheme other than direct revelation, because more complex mechanisms may give less information (on which to base renegotiation) to the party designing the mechanism. So, to repeat, the revelation principle can be useful for saying what is the range of (conceivably) implementable outcomes, without being taken quite seriously as a statement of how to implement a given outcome.

What do we know, then, about our problem of the government procuring the one hundred units? The best that it can do (in terms of minimizing its costs) with truth-telling in a direct revelation mechanism is to get costs down to 150. If it can do better with some fancy mechanism, then this will have to be a mechanism that so confuses the two firms that they don't play to a Nash equilibrium. In any mechanism where they play to a Nash equilibrium, the expected payments to them can be no less than 150.

Multiple equilibria and dominant strategy implementation

To continue on the theme of *how* to implement a particular outcome, we note once more that in many direct revelation mechanisms truth-telling is a Nash equilibrium that costs the government 150 in expectation, and some are "better" than others. Recall that we described a direct revelation mechanism in which truth-telling was a Nash equilibrium (with expected costs of 150), but another Nash equilibrium (involving some lying) was better for both firms and worse for the government. And we described a direct revelation mechanism in which truth-telling was the only Nash equilibrium (with expected costs of 150), but where a firm would deviate from truth-telling if it thought its rival was playing a non-Nash strategy. Best of all the mechanisms we constructed was the *nice*[8] mechanism, in which truth-telling was a dominant strategy for each of the firms.

---

[8] See footnote b if you've forgotten what this means.

More generally, when one designs a mechanism, either a direct revelation mechanism in which truth-telling is a Nash equilibrium or something more general, it is natural to worry whether there are other Nash equilibria (with outcomes that are not so good for the mechanism designer), or whether the participants in the mechanism will find their way to the Nash equilibrium. Everything else held equal, it seems natural to prefer a mechanism in which the equilibrium the designer wishes is the only Nash equilibrium or, at least, in which all the equilibria are no worse for the designer than the one being aimed for. Moreover, the mechanism designer might worry that the players won't settle on an equilibrium at all, for example, because the environment is too complex for players to find their way to an equilibrium.

These worries are ameliorated if the desired behavior constitutes a dominant strategy for all the players in the mechanism that is designed. If the desired behavior is a strictly dominant strategy for each player, then it is of course the unique Nash equilibrium. And more: In cases where it may be unreasonable to expect players to find their way to a Nash equilibrium, it may be reasonable to expect them to recognize (and play) a dominant strategy. Even if the strategies are not strictly dominant (so there may be other equilibria in weakly dominated strategies), the mechanism designer may feel relatively secure in a prediction that players will settle on strategies that are dominant.

These considerations motivate the notion of a *dominant strategy mechanism*, a mechanism (of the general sort described in the previous subsection) in which each participant, for each possible value of her private information, has one course of action that dominates all others, no matter what other participants in the mechanism do. Suppose the government, in our example, thought that it would like to see what its expected costs would be if it insisted on the "safety" of a dominant strategy mechanism for the two firms. How could it proceed to conduct an analysis?

Of course, we already know the bottom-line answer for the problem we have been analyzing. The government can construct a direct revelation mechanism, the nice mechanism, in which truth-telling is a dominant strategy for each firm and the expected costs to the government are 150. In this case there is no loss from insisting on a dominant strategy mechanism. But if we hadn't stumbled upon the nice mechanism, could we have come to this conclusion analytically?

We could have done so, in two steps. First, we can consider direct revelation mechanisms in which truth-telling (and participation) is a dominant strategy for both firms. We ask, For which direct revelation mechanisms (x^i_{mn}, t^i_{mn}) is participation and truth-telling a dominant strategy?

There are more constraints than before, but all the constraints are simple. For firm 1, we have four participation and four incentive constraints. The participation constraints are: For each of the four pairs of its actual cost and the cost reported by its rival, it must not sustain a loss by reporting its true cost. For example,

$$t_{21}^1 - 2x_{21}^1 \geq 0$$

is the constraint that firm 1 must not sustain a loss when it truthfully reports its costs are 2 and firm 2 (truthfully or not) reports costs of 1. The incentive constraints are: For each of the four pairs of its actual cost and the cost reported by its rival, the firm must prefer truth-telling to lying about its own cost. So, for example,

$$t_{21}^1 - 2x_{21}^1 \geq t_{11}^1 - 2x_{11}^1$$

expresses the constraint that firm 1, when its costs are 2 (note the cost premultiplying the production quantity it is allocated) and when its rival reports costs of 1, prefers to report truthfully that its costs are 2 rather than misrepresenting its costs as 1. If we satisfy all eight of these constraints for firm 1 and all eight for firm 2, we have a direct revelation mechanism in which participation and truth-telling are dominant.[h] (We are only requiring weak dominance. To be really safe, the government might wish for strict dominance, in which case we could sharpen the constraints by adding a few pennies difference in the right direction in each.)

The government, then, can solve the problem of minimizing its expected costs of

$$\frac{1}{4}[t_{11}^1 + t_{11}^2] + \frac{1}{4}[t_{21}^1 + t_{21}^2] + \frac{1}{4}[t_{12}^1 + t_{12}^2] + \frac{1}{4}[t_{22}^1 + t_{22}^2]$$

subject to the constraints above that ensure that the mechanism has truth-telling as a dominant strategy. (We impose any appropriate nonnegativity constraints, and we insist on $x_{mn}^1 + x_{mn}^2 \geq 100$, so the government is sure to get its hundred units.) Once again we have a linear programming problem, and we can go to the computer to find a solution. When we did this, the computer returned a minimum cost to the government of 150 (which, given

---

[h] Compare the participation constraints with those we imposed when we considered cases in which the firms could opt out of the mechanism ex post. In a direct revelation mechanism, where ex post opting out means opting out after all the players' types become common knowledge, the two are the same.

that we know about the nice mechanism, is hardly a surprise), and it gave the mechanism: $x_{11}^2 = x_{12}^2 = x_{22}^1 = x_{12}^1 = 100$, $t_{12}^1 = t_{22}^1 = 200$, $t_{11}^2 = t_{21}^2 = 100$, and everything else equal to zero. In words, firm 2 makes all the hundred units if it reports costs of 1, for which it is paid 100. If firm 2 reports costs of 2, firm 1 is given the assignment to make the hundred units and is paid 200. (If it isn't evident, go through the steps to show that this mechanism does indeed have truth-telling and participation as a dominant strategy for each firm.)

Can the government do better with some more complex dominant strategy mechanism? Of course, since we already know that 150 is the best we can do in any Nash equilibrium for any complex mechanism, we know that the answer is no. But for problems where the answer isn't apparent, we give the following general result.

The revelation principle for dominant strategy mechanisms. *The outcome of any dominant strategy mechanism can be achieved in a direct revelation mechanism for which truth-telling and participation is a dominant strategy.*

The proof is left as an exercise. If you understood the proof of our first revelation principle, this one should be easy.

General discussion

We have couched our discussion in terms of our simple toy problem, but it should be apparent that what we have said about direct revelation mechanisms, the revelation principle, and the revelation principle for dominant strategy mechanisms generalizes considerably.

The problem we have tackled can be stated roughly as: *Which mechanism among all possible mechanisms is optimal for achieving some given end?* Again roughly, we tackled this question in a two-step attack. First, we restricted attention to "direct revelation mechanisms," and specifically to truth-telling behavior in direct revelation mechanisms. Then via a revelation principle, we were able to show that restricting attention from "all possible mechanisms" to "direct revelation mechanisms" was without loss of generality. Consider each of these two steps in turn.

The problem of finding an optimal direct-revelation mechanism in which truth-telling is a Nash equilibrium or is a dominant strategy equilibrium is a fairly simple mathematical programming problem, because the conditions that "truth-telling is Nash" and "truth-telling is dominant" are expressible as a set of inequalities. This continues to hold in problems more general than our toy problem, although our toy problem was special in two ways that made the problem we looked at especially simple:

(1) In our toy problem, each of the firms had only a finite number of types (i.e., costs). Many applications in the literature deal with a continuum of types (e.g., the firms' levels of costs can be any number within some closed interval); and one will have to find ways of analyzing the problem algebraically instead of numerically.

(2) The linearity of the cost structures in our toy problem meant that all the constraints were linear. If instead the firms had nonlinear cost functions, we would be doubly cursed. For one thing, we couldn't apply linear programming. For another, even if the cost function is convex, if we wrote the incentive constraints, we would be putting a convex function on both sides of the inequality, which means that, viewed as an optimization problem, what we would have would not necessarily be well behaved.[i]

In the toy problem, we discovered that it costs the government no more to have a mechanism in which truth-telling is dominant than to have one in which truth-telling constitutes a Nash equilibrium. You might wonder whether this is a fluke or the tip of some general result. It is, so to speak, both. If the firms have three possible costs and if those costs are not independently distributed, then it can be costly for the government to insist on dominant strategy implementation. (If you have access to a linear programming package, you can verify this in problem 8.) Hence the result we obtained is somewhat special. On the other hand, there are general classes of problems for which dominant strategy implementation costs no more than Nash implementation; this is so, for example, for a range of optimal auction design problems (see Bulow and Roberts, forthcoming.) A general analysis of this question is given by Mookherjee and Reichelstein (1989b).

Now we turn to the second part of our general attack: the demonstration that we can restrict attention to truth-telling in a direct revelation game, to see which outcomes can be "implemented" in general mechanisms.

The term *outcome* as used here in general means the selection of some state of affairs as a function of the private information held by parties for

---

[i] The reader may wish to consider whether, in the spirit of the analysis of chapter 16, we could employ some substitution of variables to make the constraints linear, even if the objective function is nonlinear.

whom the mechanism is to be designed. An outcome in this sense is something more than just the expected costs to the government; an outcome specifies how much each firm produces and what transfer is made to the firm as a function of the firms' costs. In our toy problem, and in many problems of *optimal* mechanism design, all that matters to the mechanism designer about the implemented outcome is some one-dimensional measure of goodness, such as expected cost. But in other applications, such as the one in the next section, we would want to look at the implementability of outcomes in the more general sense.

The term "implementable" is put in quotes because it can take on a number of different meanings, such as:

(1) There is some mechanism with a Nash equilibrium (in the associated game of incomplete information) which gives this outcome.

(2) There is some mechanism for which all the Nash equilibria give this outcome.

(3) There is a mechanism for which there is a unique Nash equilibrium, and this Nash equilibrium gives this outcome.

(4) There is a mechanism in which the outcome arises from the play of dominant strategies.

Each of these is progressively stronger,[j] and each is presumably progressively more desirable for the mechanism designer, in order to have faith in the participants finding their way to the desired outcome. To repeat what we said before, if a mechanism admits several Nash equilibria, some of which are worse for the designer (and, more importantly, better for the participants) than is the equilibrium that is desired, then one worries that the participants will find their way to the wrong equilibrium. And even if the equilibrium is unique, one might worry whether the participants have the sophistication needed to find the equilibrium strategies (or that they have sufficient faith in their fellow participants' sophistication, so that they are happy to carry out their part of the equilibrium). If the desired outcome is the product of dominant strategy choices by the participants, then the mechanism designer can (presumably) have the greatest faith in the mechanism she has designed.

These four possibilities are far from exhaustive. You can probably think of other variations on this general theme, and you will find most of those variations somewhere in the literature.

---

[j] To be precise, in (4) we must worry about other equilibria in weakly dominated strategies, so (4) isn't quite stronger than (3).

We have seen two revelation principles, which claim that anything that can be implemented in the sense of (1) or (4) can be implemented in the corresponding sense in the form of truth-telling in direct revelation games. These results are true in substantial generality.

We have not seen revelation principles corresponding to (2) and (3) as the notion of implementation. In general, the correspondence between truth-telling in direct revelation games and outcomes of general mechanisms breaks down when the solution concept is adapted from (2) or (3). But it is possible to augment a direct revelation game, adding signals that the participants send (beyond a declaration of type), and then to obtain "augmented revelation principles" that speak to implementation in the sense of (2) and (3). That is, for any outcome that is implementable in the sense of, say, (2) in a general mechanism, there is an augmented direct revelation mechanism for which truth-telling is a Nash equilibrium that gives this outcome, and all other Nash equilibria give this outcome. The observation that this is possible is made in Ma, Moore, and Turnbull (1988), and the corresponding general "augmented revelation principles" are given by Mookherjee and Reichelstein (1989a).

> Some outcomes cannot be implemented in the sense of (2), but there are mechanisms such that every subgame perfect Nash equilibrium for the mechanism gives this outcome, even though some subgame imperfect equilibria give other outcomes. And for outcomes that cannot be implemented in the sense of (2), there are mechanisms such that all the Nash equilibria that involve the play of no dominated strategy give this outcome, even though other Nash equilibria involving dominated strategies give other outcomes. That is, we can implement more (in the rough sense of [2]) if we look not at Nash equilibria but at some suitable refinement of Nash. For developments along these lines, see Moore and Repullo (1988) and Palfrey and Srivastava (1987).

All of the extensions and elaborations on optimal contract design that were described in section 18.1 can be undertaken in this more general and complex context. In particular, mixtures of adverse selection and moral hazard are possible. We might imagine, for example, that our two firms' costs are not determined entirely endogenously but result as well from R&D and investment decisions made by the firms. Then the government, besides buying its hundred units, might seek to put in place a mechanism that induces firms to invest optimally in plant and in R&D, where "optimality" means "that make the government's costs as low as possible." In principle, one can use the revelation principle to tackle such problems; in practice, they become rather complex. See Laffont and Tirole (1987) for an example.

18.3. The pivot mechanism

In the literature are a number of applications of the general ideas just given to the design of optimal mechanisms that deserve your attention. In particular, the analysis of optimal auction design is especially rich and well developed; references will be supplied at the end of this chapter.

Rather than pursue one of these, we look at a different sort of problem in mechanism design that uses some of the notions of the previous section. Instead of looking for an "optimal" mechanism, according to the interests of some individual who (presumably) is designing the mechanism with her own interests in mind, we will look at a classic example of mechanism design where the objective is to satisfy a set of criteria.

Consider the following story. Several farmers live on the banks of a stream. (Some live on one side, some on the other.) The number of farmers is I, and we index them by $i = 1, 2, \ldots, I$. They consider building a bridge over the stream that will permit them all to cross back and forth. There is only one place where the bridge can be constructed, and the bridge will cost K to construct. Each farmer attaches some value to having the bridge constructed, but none is quite sure what value the others attach to it. If they construct the bridge, the funds to do so will have to come from their own pockets.

These farmers must decide whether or not to build this bridge. We take it as given that if the bridge is built, each farmer will pay K/I, his pro rata share of the costs of building the bridge. But in addition to this, the farmers are willing to consider transfers among themselves; we write t^i for the amount of money *taken* from farmer i, above and beyond the K/I that is collected if the bridge is to be built. We do not preclude $t^i < 0$, which means that a subsidy is paid to farmer i.

Farmer i's utility depends on whether the bridge is built and on any monetary transfer t^i that is made to or from him. We suppose that each farmer i attaches some monetary value to the bridge, u^i, and that farmer i's utility is linear in money and in this valuation. That is, farmer i's utility depends on (a) whether the bridge is built, (b) the building tax K/I that he pays if it is built, and (c) any further tax or subsidy, t^i; this utility is given by

$$\text{Farmer } i\text{'s utility } = \begin{cases} u^i - K/I - t^i & \text{if the bridge is built, and} \\ -t^i & \text{if the bridge isn't built.} \end{cases}$$

Note that we permit transfers even if the bridge isn't built. We assume that farmers may dislike having this bridge built; i.e., $u^i < 0$ is possible.

In fact, we assume that u^i could be any real number whatsoever; no value is precluded.

It will be expositionally convenient to work with the farmer's valuation of the bridge, *net* of his contribution for building it, or $v^i = u^i - K/I$. Note that with this substitution, farmer i's utility is $v^i - t^i$ if the bridge is built.

The farmers meet together one evening to try to decide whether to build the bridge and what taxes and subsidies to enforce beyond the pro rata contribution to building it. One farmer suggests majority rule and no transfers: Put building the bridge to a vote, and if a majority vote to build the bridge, then everyone pays only his contribution K/I; if a majority vote against, no transfers are made at all. If this plan is adopted, farmers will vote for the bridge if and only if their net personal valuation v^i exceeds 0. But there are several objections to this. One farmer observes that some farmers may really want this bridge, and if most farmers don't care that much (i.e., if $u^i < K/I$ for many farmers), then the bridge won't be built, even though general social welfare would be improved if it were built. Another objects that he doesn't want this bridge much at all, in fact he positively dislikes it, and yet he may be assessed with a building fee of K/I. What justice is there in that?

So someone suggests that farmers "subscribe" to the bridge. Everyone will write his name and a pledge (an amount of money) on a piece of paper and toss it into a hat. After all the pledges are collected, they will be added together. Negative pledges are allowed; farmers in this way demand compensation for having the bridge built. If the sum of the pledges exceeds 0, the bridge will be built, and every farmer must contribute the amount of his pledge (plus his share K/I). If the pledges amount to less than 0, then the bridge isn't built and no transfers will be made. What to do with the surplus, if more than zero is pledged? One farmer suggests that this surplus be divided equally among all the farmers. Another suggests that it be divided proportionally (in proportion to original pledges) among those farmers who pledged positive amounts. Still another suggests that it might be a good thing to collect the excess and burn it. (This last suggestion is met with some incredulity.)

Thinking about this mechanism, the farmers recognize some difficulties. Imagine a farmer who values the bridge at a net amount v^i. How much should he pledge? If he believes that it will take a pledge of v^i or more to get the bridge built, then he is willing to pledge precisely v^i. He certainly would never wish to pledge more than this, since he will be stuck with a pledge that is greater than the net value of the bridge to him. On the other hand, if he believes that a pledge of less than v^i will do, then he wishes to shade his pledge down from v^i and "free-ride" on the pledges of his fellow farmers. In general, he won't be sure which of these two circumstances pertains, but as long as he assesses positive probability for the second, his optimal bid will be something less than v^i. Hence the total pledges will be less than $\sum_i v^i$, and the bridge may not be built when it should be. In any case, another farmer objects that figuring out how to behave in this mechanism is too hard for simple country bumpkins, and all sorts of bad outcomes may result.

After much discussion, the farmers decide that they wish to find some mechanism for deciding whether to build the bridge and what taxes to assess that has the following properties:

(a) The bridge will be built if and only if it is socially efficient to do so; that is, if and only if $\sum_i v^i \geq 0$.

(b) No farmer should have to waste his time doing complicated analysis of how to behave in the mechanism. In particular, no farmer should have to spend time trying to assess what his fellow farmers will do. Put another way, the optimal actions of each farmer in the mechanism (as a function of the farmer's private valuation v^i) should dominate any other actions the farmer might take, no matter what his fellow farmers do.

(c) The mechanism, if played optimally by a farmer, should never be so injurious to the welfare of the farmer that he would prefer that the decision to build or not to build is taken by decree. That is, farmer i should not wind up with utility less than $\min\{v^i, 0\}$.

(d) Since no outsider is willing to put up money to permit the mechanism to function, the taxes collected (less any subsidies, and not including the building tax K/I per farmer, if the bridge is built) must be nonnegative.

One can certainly quibble (a), (b), and (c) (and later we will have a very large quibble with [a], in particular), but let us accept them and see where they lead.

We translate (b) as saying that the farmers want a dominant strategy mechanism. They wish to design a general mechanism in which each farmer, as a function of his personal valuation v^i, has a dominant strategy to play. With this, we appeal to the revelation principle for dominant strategy mechanisms: Anything we can do with a general dominant strategy mechanism can be done with a direct revelation mechanism in which truth-telling is a dominant strategy. So we can restrict attention to direct revelation mechanisms.

In this context a direct revelation mechanism takes the form: Each farmer is asked to reveal his personal valuation v^i. We put hats on variables to distinguish what farmers reveal from their true valuations; that is, $\hat{v}^i$ is what farmer i reveals. As a function of the vector of revealed valuations $\hat{v} = (\hat{v}^1, \ldots, \hat{v}^I)$, a decision is made whether to build the bridge or not, and taxes on each farmer are determined. We write $\alpha(\hat{v})$ for the decision whether to build the bridge, where $\alpha(\hat{v}) = 1$ means that the bridge is built and $\alpha(\hat{v}) = 0$ means it is not. (In a more general treatment of these issues, we might let $\alpha(\hat{v})$ take on any value in the interval $[0, 1]$, interpreting this as the probability that the bridge will be built. But given the farmers' requirement [a], we know what α must be, and this doesn't entail randomized decisions whether to build the bridge.) And we write $t^i(\hat{v})$ for the tax imposed on farmer i. (More generally, we could permit random taxes, but as farmers are risk neutral, this would add nothing to the story except horrid notation.)

It will be handy to have the following pieces of notation. We let $\hat{v}^{-i} = (\hat{v}_1, \ldots, \hat{v}_{i-1}, \hat{v}_{i+1}, \ldots, \hat{v}_I)$. That is, $\hat{v}^{-i}$ is the vector of reported valuations for all the farmers except for i. We sometimes write $t^i(\hat{v})$ as $t^i(\hat{v}^i, \hat{v}^{-i})$; i.e., we put i's valuation as the first argument. Finally, we write $\hat{\Sigma}$ for $\sum_{j=1}^{I} \hat{v}^j$ and $\hat{\Sigma}^{-i}$ for $\sum_{j \neq i} \hat{v}^j$. That is, $\hat{\Sigma}$ is the sum of all the announced valuations, and $\hat{\Sigma}^{-i}$ is the sum of all the announced valuations save i's.

We are looking for a direct revelation mechanism in which truth-telling is a dominant strategy and in which the bridge is built if and only if $\sum_i v^i \geq 0$. The latter restriction, combined with the notion that truth-telling will be dominant tells us what the function α must be:

$$\alpha(\hat{v}) = \begin{cases} 1, & \text{if } \hat{\Sigma} \geq 0, \text{ and} \\ 0, & \text{if } \hat{\Sigma} < 0. \end{cases} \tag{1}$$

Furthermore, we have the following results:

Lemma 1. *The taxes paid by farmer i must take the form*

$$t^i(\hat{v}^i, \hat{v}^{-i}) = \begin{cases} \bar{t}^i(\hat{v}^{-i}), & \text{if } \hat{\Sigma} \geq 0, \text{ and} \\ \underline{t}^i(\hat{v}^{-i}), & \text{if } \hat{\Sigma} < 0, \end{cases} \tag{2}$$

for $\bar{t}^i$ and $\underline{t}^i$ functions of $\hat{v}^{-i}$.

The idea is that what a farmer pays in taxes cannot depend on what he himself reveals as his valuation, except insofar as this revelation changes the decision whether or not to build the bridge. To see why this is so, suppose v^i and w^i, two valuations for i, and $\hat{v}^{-i}$ are such that $v^i + \hat{\Sigma}^{-i} > 0$, $w^i + \hat{\Sigma}^{-i} > 0$, and $t^i(v^i, \hat{v}^{-i}) > t^i(w^i, \hat{v}^{-i})$. In words, if the other farmers are announcing $\hat{v}^{-i}$, then whether i announces v^i or w^i, the bridge will be built. But announcing v^i (when the others are announcing $\hat{v}^{-i}$) results in higher taxes than does announcing w^i. In such circumstances, the mechanism doesn't have truth-telling as a dominant strategy; farmer i, if his valuation is v^i, would prefer to misrepresent his valuation as w^i (if his fellow farmers announce $\hat{v}^{-i}$). This establishes the first part of the proposition: For $\hat{v}$ such that $\hat{\Sigma} \geq 0$, $t^i(\hat{v})$ depends only on $\hat{v}^{-i}$. A similar argument gives the other half.

Lemma 2.

$$\bar{t}^i(\hat{v}^{-i}) - \underline{t}^i(\hat{v}^{-i}) = -\hat{\Sigma}^{-i}. \tag{3}$$

To prove this, fix $\hat{v}^{-i}$ and consider the case where $v^i = -\hat{\Sigma}^{-i}$. If farmer i truthfully reveals v^i when the others reveal $\hat{v}^{-i}$, then farmer i must prefer revealing v^i to revealing $v^i - \epsilon$ for $\epsilon > 0$. But, in these circumstances, revealing v^i means the bridge will be built and revealing $v^i - \epsilon$ means that the bridge won't be built. So by revealing v^i, farmer i nets $v^i - \bar{t}^i(\hat{v}^{-i})$, while revealing $v^i - \epsilon$ nets $-\underline{t}^i(\hat{v}^{-i})$. The former must be at least as large as the latter, so

$$v^i = -\hat{\Sigma}^{-i} \geq \bar{t}^i(\hat{v}^{-i}) - \underline{t}^i(\hat{v}^{-i}).$$

Now consider the case where $v^i = -\epsilon - \hat{\Sigma}^{-i}$ for $\epsilon > 0$. Truthful revelation of v^i causes the bridge not to be built, giving farmer i utility $-\underline{t}^i(\hat{v}^{-i})$. Falsely revealing $v^i + \epsilon$ causes the bridge to be built, and farmer i has utility $v^i - \bar{t}^i(\hat{v}^{-i})$. Since the former must be at least as large as the latter (to support truth-telling),

$$v^i = -\epsilon - \hat{\Sigma}^{-i} \leq \bar{t}^i(\hat{v}^{-i}) - \underline{t}^i(\hat{v}^{-i}).$$

This is true for arbitrary $\epsilon > 0$, so by letting $\epsilon \to 0$,

$$-\hat{\Sigma}^{-i} \leq \bar{t}^i(\hat{v}^{-i}) - \underline{t}^i(\hat{v}^{-i}).$$

Together with the next to last inequality, this gives the desired result.

Lemma 3.

$$\underline{t}^i(\hat{v}^{-i}) \leq \begin{cases} \hat{\Sigma}^{-i}, & \text{if } \hat{\Sigma}^{-i} \geq 0, \text{ and} \\ 0, & \text{if } \hat{\Sigma}^{-i} < 0. \end{cases} \tag{4}$$

Consider first the case where $\hat{\Sigma}^{-i} \geq 0$. Suppose $v^i = 0$. By truthfully reporting v^i, farmer i causes the bridge to be built. His utility in this case is $v^i - \bar{t}^i(\hat{v}^{-i}) = 0 - [\underline{t}^i(\hat{v}^{-i}) - \hat{\Sigma}^{-i}]$. Since (c)[9] entails that farmer i is no worse off for having revealed the truth than 0 (in utility), we have $-[\underline{t}^i(\hat{v}^{-i}) - \hat{\Sigma}^{-i}] \geq 0$ or $\underline{t}^i(\hat{v}^{-i}) \leq \hat{\Sigma}^{-i}$. Consider next the case where $\hat{\Sigma}^{-i} < 0$. Again suppose $v^i = 0$. By truthfully revealing v^i, farmer i causes the bridge not to be built. Hence he nets $-\underline{t}^i(\hat{v}^{-i})$. Since he must be no worse off than 0 by so doing, we have $-\underline{t}^i(\hat{v}^{-i}) \geq 0$, or $\underline{t}^i(\hat{v}^{-i}) \leq 0$.

Lemma 4.

$$\underline{t}^i(\hat{v}^{-i}) = \begin{cases} \hat{\Sigma}^{-i}, & \text{if } \hat{\Sigma}^{-i} \geq 0, \text{ and} \\ 0, & \text{if } \hat{\Sigma}^{-i} < 0. \end{cases} \tag{5}$$

In other words, inequality (4) must be an equation.

To see this, we note first that from lemmas 1 and 2, (d) rendered in symbols is

$$\sum_i \underline{t}^i(\hat{v}^{-i}) \geq 0 \text{ if } \hat{\Sigma} < 0, \text{ and} \tag{d1}$$

$$\sum_{n=1}^{N} \bar{t}^i(\hat{v}^{-i}) = \sum_i [\underline{t}^i(\hat{v}^{-i}) - \hat{\Sigma}^{-i}] \geq 0 \text{ if } \hat{\Sigma} \geq 0. \tag{d2}$$

Suppose, then, that for some i and $\hat{v}^{-i}$ such that $\hat{\Sigma}^{-i} \geq 0$ we had a strict inequality in (4). That is, $\underline{t}^i(\hat{v}^{-i}) < \hat{\Sigma}^{-i}$. Choose v^i to be sufficiently large so that $\hat{\Sigma}^{-i'} > 0$ for all i' and so that $\hat{\Sigma} > 0$. The bridge will be built, and by lemmas 1 and 2, farmer i' pays

$$\bar{t}^{i'}(\hat{v}^{-i'}) = \underline{t}^{i'}(\hat{v}^{-i'}) - \hat{\Sigma}^{-i'}.$$

By lemma 3, each such term is nonpositive and, by the supposition, the term for i is strictly negative. Hence the sum of all the payments is strictly negative, contradicting (d2).

Similarly, suppose that for i and $\hat{v}^{-i}$ such that $\hat{\Sigma}^{-i} < 0$, we had $\underline{t}^i(\hat{v}^{-i}) < 0$. We can choose v^i sufficiently small so that $\hat{\Sigma}^{-i'} < 0$ for all i'

---

[9] In case you forgot, (c) says that, in general, a farmer should do no worse than $\min\{v^i, 0\}$ by reporting the truth.

and $\hat{\Sigma} < 0$. Arguing along the lines just given, we obtain a violation of (d1).

We now put all the pieces together and provide a converse.

Proposition 2. *There is only one direct revelation mechanism for which (a) through (d) hold, namely the direct revelation mechanism defined by (1), (2), (3), and (5). This mechanism is alternatively defined by (1) and*

$$
t^i(\hat{v}) = \begin{cases} 0, & \text{if } \hat{\Sigma} \geq 0 \text{ and } \hat{\Sigma}^{-i} \geq 0, \\ 0, & \text{if } \hat{\Sigma} < 0 \text{ and } \hat{\Sigma}^{-i} < 0, \\ \hat{\Sigma}^{-i}, & \text{if } \hat{\Sigma} < 0 \text{ and } \hat{\Sigma}^{-i} \geq 0, \text{ and} \\ -\hat{\Sigma}^{-i}, & \text{if } \hat{\Sigma} \geq 0 \text{ and } \hat{\Sigma}^{-i} < 0. \end{cases}
\tag{6}
$$

Proof.   The lemmas establish that this is the only possible candidate. Showing that (6) is equivalent to (2), (3), and (5) is a matter of simple bookkeeping. We see from (6) that $t^i(v) \geq 0$ in all cases, so (d) is obvious. So all that remains is to show that the mechanism defined by (1) and (6) satisfies (b) and (c). We will do half of this, leaving the other half for homework.

Suppose that, for some i and $\hat{v}^{-i}$, $\hat{\Sigma}^{-i} \geq 0$ and $v^i + \hat{\Sigma}^{-i} \geq 0$. If i tells the truth, the mechanism calls for the bridge to be built and for i to pay no tax. The only way that i can change the outcome is to report (falsely) a valuation $\hat{v}^i$ less than $-\hat{\Sigma}^{-i}$. Then the bridge won't be built, and i will pay a tax of $\hat{\Sigma}^{-i}$. Reporting truthfully, then, leaves i with utility v^i, and a misrepresentation sufficient to change the outcome leaves i with utility equal to $-\hat{\Sigma}^{-i}$. Since we assume in this case that $v^i + \hat{\Sigma}^{-i} \geq 0$, $v^i \geq -\hat{\Sigma}^{-i}$. Thus, telling the truth is a best reply; also, i ends up with utility v^i, so (c) holds in this case.

Suppose that, for some i and $\hat{v}^{-i}$, $\hat{\Sigma}^{-i} < 0$ and $v^i + \hat{\Sigma}^{-i} \geq 0$. The bridge will be built if i reports truthfully, and he will pay a tax of $-\hat{\Sigma}^{-i}$, which gives i utility $v^i + \hat{\Sigma}^{-i} \geq 0$. So (c) holds. Moreover, the only way that i can change the outcome (and his utility) is by reporting a valuation $\hat{v}^i < -\hat{\Sigma}^{-i}$. But if he does this, $\hat{\Sigma}^{-i} < 0$ and $\hat{\Sigma} < 0$, which means that there is no transfer, and i winds up with utility 0. So misrepresenting is not beneficial.

(The other two cases are left for you.)

This particular mechanism is called the *pivot mechanism* because a tax is paid by farmer i only if his valuation v^i is pivotal, that is, only if his valuation changes the decision from what it would be if he reported zero.

Moreover, when i's valuation is pivotal, i is taxed an amount that is just equal to the "social distress" his pivotal valuation causes; i.e., if he causes the bridge to be built when it otherwise wouldn't be, he pays $-\hat{\Sigma}^{-i}$, which is the monetary "cost" to the rest of the farmers of the bridge; and if he causes the bridge not to be built when it otherwise would be, he pays $\hat{\Sigma}^{-i}$, the monetary benefit to the other farmers of the bridge.

This mechanism satisfies our four criteria, and in fact it is the only mechanism that does this, so if we accept the four as desirable, we have come upon quite a nice result. Condition (a), however, seems especially suspect. The justification for it is that we wish to achieve a "social optimum," which in this society where utility is linear in money means maximizing the sum of individual utilities. But the mechanism doesn't achieve a social optimum if there are any pivotal individuals, because it produces a positive net collection of taxes. Note well: The transfers are all nonnegative, and they are all zero only if there are no pivotal individuals.

This raises the question, If there are pivotal individuals, so a net surplus of funds is collected, what happens with that surplus? Unthoughtful answers are to give it back to the farmers, or to hold it for the next project to come along, or to use it to throw a dance. If the surplus is used in any fashion that gives utility to the farmers, and if the farmers anticipate this, then the direct revelation mechanism isn't what we described. We would have to include in the farmer's utilities the value they attach to the uses to which the surplus is put. But our uniqueness result is that the only mechanism that will achieve the four required properties is the one described. This means that if we wish to achieve (a) through (d), we must find a use for the surplus that is of no benefit (or detriment) to our farmers. The surplus must be burned, or mailed off to aid some other lucky group of individuals about whom none of our farmers cares in the least. (And our farmers can't anticipate that any such largesse may result in a reciprocal gift coming to them. It is probably safest to burn any surplus.)

Condition (a), then, can be attacked on the grounds that it doesn't guarantee that a social optimum is reached. The decision whether to build the bridge will be done "optimally," but at a waste of other social resources, if there are any pivotal individuals.

We can put this another way. Condition (a) would imply that a social optimum is reached *if* it were joined to the following modification of (d): The sum of taxes and transfers, not including the taxes collected to build the bridge if the bridge is built, totals zero precisely. This condition is known in the literature as the *balanced budget condition*, and what we know from our analysis is that it is impossible to satisfy this together with (a), (b), and (c). In fact, one can show that the balanced budget condition is inconsistent with (a) and (b) alone. It is impossible to achieve a Pareto optimal outcome in this closed society with a dominant strategy mechanism.

18.4. *The Gibbard-Satterthwaite theorem*

One way to view the results of the previous section is that asking for a dominant strategy mechanism may be asking too much. We close by alerting you to another result that reinforces this message (or which, at least, implies that asking for a dominant strategy mechanism is asking for rather a lot).

Recall Arrow's impossibility theorem from chapter 5. The setting is one with a finite number I of individuals, and a finite number of possible social outcomes. We let X be the set of social outcomes. Each individual has preferences $\succ_i$ defined on X that are asymmetric and negatively transitive.

In Arrow's theorem, we were concerned with aggregation of the array of society's preferences $(\succ_1, \ldots, \succ_I)$ into a social ordering $\succ^*$ on X. The story before was that members of society attempted to design some social choice rule that would take the array of preferences $(\succ_1, \ldots, \succ_I)$ and transform them in desirable fashion into society's preferences. We saw that a few, seemingly quite desirable properties for the social choice rule, forces social choice to be dictatorial, which doesn't seem very desirable.

One thing unexplained was how, even if we had found a nice social choice rule, we were going to work out what the preferences of each member of society were. Perhaps the preferences of individual i would be obvious. But it seems more likely that at some point individual i would have to volunteer what she liked and didn't like. And even if we had a nice social choice rule, we might worry that individual i would misrepresent her preferences in an attempt to get social preferences more to her liking.

So we can approach the matter as one of mechanism design. Suppose we had a desirable social choice rule. In fact, we'll make things easier on ourselves: Suppose we had a desirable social choice *function* ϕ that associates with every array of individual preferences $(\succ_1, \ldots, \succ_I)$ some outcome $\phi(\succ_1, \ldots, \succ_I) = x \in X$, which is the outcome that is implemented. All we want to know is whether the given ϕ can be implemented "reliably" by some mechanism, where what we mean by reliable implementation is that if individual preferences are given by $(\succ_1, \ldots, \succ_I)$, then the mechanism (which involves actions of some sort by the members of society, each of whom knows her own preferences) has *dominant strategies* for members of society that lead to the outcome $\phi(\succ_1, \ldots, \succ_I)$. By the revelation principle for dominant strategy mechanisms, we can turn this into the following question:

Given ϕ, is there a direct revelation mechanism, where each individual is called upon to reveal her preferences over X, which has truth-telling as a dominant strategy and which results in the outcome $\phi(\succ_1, \ldots, \succ_I)$ when preferences are $(\succ_1, \ldots, \succ_I)$?

The Gibbard-Satterthwaite theorem. *If the domain of ϕ is the space of all I-tuples of preferences over X, if the range of ϕ has at least three elements, and if ϕ can be implemented by a dominant strategy mechanism, then ϕ must be dictatorial; there is some i such that $\phi(\succ_1, \ldots, \succ_I)$ is one of the $\succ_i$-most preferred elements of X.*

For elegant proofs, see Schmeidler and Sonnenschein (1978) and Barbera (1983).

You may find the conjunction of the Gibbard-Satterthwaite theorem and proposition 2 (on the pivot mechanism) a bit jarring. The pivot mechanism implements a particular social choice function with dominant strategy mechanism, yet that social choice function is hardly dictatorial. As we noted in the previous section, the social choice function of the pivot mechanism is not efficient. But the Gibbard-Satterthwaite theorem says nothing about efficiency of the social choice function. So how are these reconciled?

They reconcile because the Gibbard-Satterthwaite theorem requires that domain of the social choice function is the set of *all* possible I-tuples of preferences over the social outcome. In the farmers and bridge story, preferences over social outcomes come from a very restrictive domain. Preferences are "quasi-linear" in the decision whether to build the bridge and the transfer received by a farmer, and farmers don't care at all about the transfers their neighbors receive. If we allowed farmers to have all manner of preferences over the full social outcome, proposition 2 would crumble, as the Gibbard-Satterthwaite theorem says it must.

18.5. Bibliographic notes

The general subject of optimal contract and mechanism design covers many different categories in the literature. In this chapter, we have limited attention to contract design when adverse selection (or hidden information) is the issue; compare with chapter 16, where we studied some basic results in optimal contract design in situations of moral hazard. (Although we didn't discuss it except in passing in chapter 16, issues related to implementation of particular sets of actions for interacting agents arises there, just as in this chapter. If you did problem 3 in chapter 16, you at least got a taste of this.) And while we have looked at problems that involve only moral hazard or only adverse selection, problems that mix the two can be tackled by a mixture of the methods we have explored.

At the same time, the techniques discussed in this chapter are used to study optimal contracts and problems in social choice, where the objective is to see which social choice rules can be implemented in particular environments. (Sections 18.3 and 18.4 gave two examples of the latter sort of activity.) Finally, there is a wide range of applications of these techniques.

Sending you out into the literature, therefore, is a formidable task. It is hard to know where to begin, and once a list is started, it is harder to know where to stop. So we make very limited suggestions.

(1) A neat application of optimal contract design for a single party is found in Baron and Myerson (1982), where they study how to regulate a monopolist whose costs are unknown to the regulatory body. We did nothing at all with the problem of mechanism design by an informed party; on this topic, Myerson (1983) is seminal.

(2) The issues tackled with the toy problem of section 18.2 are especially well developed in the domain of optimal auction design. Myerson (1981) is seminal, McAfee and McMillan (1987) and Milgrom (1987, 1989) give very nice, up-to-date surveys, and Bulow and Roberts (forthcoming) is recommended for the way in which they reduce auction design to a classical problem in price theory.

(3) For an analysis of a problem of optimal mechanism design that mixes adverse selection and moral hazard, see Laffont and Tirole (1987).

(4) On the general topics of sections 18.3 and 18.4, Green and Laffont (1979) is a good place to begin. The introduction to Moore and Repullo (1988) provides an excellent summary of recent developments concerning mechanism design in the context of general social choice.

References

Barbera, S. 1983. "Strategy-proof and Pivotal Voters: A Direct Proof of the Gibbard-Satterthwaite Theorem." *International Economic Review* 24:413–18.

Baron, D., and R. Myerson. 1982. "Regulating a Monopolist with Unknown Costs." *Econometrica* 50:911–30.

Bulow, J., and D. Roberts. Forthcoming. "The Simple Economics of Optimal Auctions." *Journal of Political Economics* 97.

Crémer, J., and R. McLean. 1988. "Full Extraction of the Surplus in Bayesian and Dominant Strategy Auctions." *Econometrica* 56:1247–58.

Green, J., and J.-J. Laffont. 1979. *Incentives in Public Decision Making*. Amsterdam: North Holland.

Laffont, J.-J., and J. Tirole. 1987. "Auctioning Incentive Contracts." *Journal of Political Economy* 95:921–37.

————. 1988. "The Dynamics of Incentive Contracts." *Econometrica* 56:1153–76.

Luenberger, D. 1984. *Linear and Nonlinear Programming,* 2d edition. Reading, Mass.: Addison-Wesley.

Ma, C., J. Moore, and S. Turnbull. 1988. "Stopping Agents from Cheating." *Journal of Economic Theory* 46:355–72.

McAfee, R. P., and J. McMillan. 1987. "Auctions and Bidding." *Journal of Economic Literature* 25:699–754.

Milgrom, P. 1987. "Auction Theory." In *Advances in Economic Theory, Fifth World Congress,* T. Bewley, ed., 1–32. Cambridge: Cambridge University Press.

———. 1989. "Auctions and Bidding: A Primer." *Journal of Economic Perspectives* 3:3–22.

Mookherjee, D., and S. Reichelstein. 1989a. "Implementation via Augmented Revelation Mechanisms." Stanford University. Mimeo.
———. 1989b. "Dominant Strategy Implementation of Bayesian Incentive Compatible Allocation Rules." Stanford University. Mimeo.
Moore, J., and R. Repullo. 1988. "Subgame Perfect Implementation." *Econometrica* 56:1191–220.

Myerson, R. 1981. "Optimal Auction Design." *Mathematics of Operations Research* 6:58–73.

———. 1983. "Mechanism Design by an Informed Principal." *Econometrica* 51:1767–98.

Palfrey, T., and S. Srivastava. 1987. "Mechanism Design with Incomplete Information: A Solution to the Implementation Problem." Carnegie-Mellon University. Mimeo.

Schmeidler, D., and H. Sonnenschein, H. 1978. "Two Proofs of the Gibbard-Satterthwaite Theorem on the Possibility of a Strategy-Proof Social Choice Function." In *Decision Theory and Social Ethics,* H. Gottinger and W. Leinfellner, eds. Dordrecht, Holland: D. Reidel Publishing.

Stiglitz, J. 1977. "Monopoly, Nonlinear Pricing, and Imperfect Information: The Insurance Market." *Review of Economic Studies* 44:407–30.

18.6. Problems

■ 1. Recall that in chapter 9, we considered a large manufacturing monopolist selling to individual retailing monopolists. Recall that in one parameterization of the problem, there were ten retailers, three of whom faced demand of the form $p = 12 - 9x$, five of whom faced demand of the form $p = 12 - 6x$, and two who faced demand of the form $p = 12 - 2x$. Costs of production and sales were zero. The retailers are price-takers in their dealings with the manufacturing monopolist.

(a) Assume that the manufacturer can tailor a take-it-or-leave-it offer for each individual retailer, of any form desired. To maximize her profits, what should the manufacturer do?

(b) Suppose the manufacturer is compelled by law to make identical offers to all ten retailers, but she can otherwise make take-it-or-leave-it offers, offers with menus where retailers are restricted to taking only one item from the menu, and so on. What is the best the manufacturer can do in this instance?

■ 2. Consider the problem of designing an optimal insurance contract as discussed in section 18.1. Prove that it is never optimal to offer consumers a "random contract," where by a random contract we mean one in which the amount the consumer is left with, y_1 or y_2, is random beyond the randomness caused by the initial endowment risk. (You should assume that any additional randomness has the same distribution for high- and low-risk consumers.) Compare this with problem 12 in chapter 3.

■ 3. In the optimal menu of insurance contracts offered to the consumer in section 18.1, if $\rho > 0$ is it ever optimal to pool the two types of consumer? If $\rho < 1$ is it ever optimal to offer only full insurance to high-risk consumers, leaving low-risk consumers uncovered?

■ 4. Suppose that the insurance company of section 18.1 was (for some reason) constrained to offer a single insurance policy. That is, menus are not permitted. What will the optimal (profit-maximizing) insurance policy look like? In particular, will it involve full insurance? (Hint: If you did problem 3, you should have a good start on this. If you need a bit of inspiration, go back to the analysis in chapter 9 of the manufacturer selling to retailers under the constraint that all the retailers had to be made the same single take-it-or-leave-it offer.)

■ 5. Suppose, in the context of the menu of insurance policies depicted in figure 18.6, a number of (cartelized) firms were offering the menu shown, and consumers could buy the policies from different firms simultaneously. We imagine the policies being in the form of a premium that is paid at the outset and, if the low-endowment state prevails, a payment that is made from the firm to the insuree. Hence buying two of the same contract would double both the premium and the contingent payments. (Don't worry about the time value of money or the fact that the premium must be paid before the insuree's endowment is realized.) What would a high-risk consumer do in this case? What would a low-risk consumer do? How does this affect the profits of the insurance firms? (How would similar considerations affect the answers you gave to problem 5 in chapter 16?)

■ 6. Consider the toy problem of section 18.2. Imagine that the government institutes the following procedure: The two firms are asked to bid (simultaneously and independently) on the prices they will charge. They may not name a price greater than 4 or less than zero. (Of course, each knows its own unit cost when it does this.) If they name the same price, the order is split between them. If they name a different price, the order is given entirely to the firm naming the lower price. In both cases, the firm is paid per unit what it bids.

(a) If we construct from this mechanism the corresponding game (between the firms) of incomplete information, does the game have a pure strategy Nash equilibrium?

(b) If not, can you find a symmetric mixed strategy equilibrium?

(c) If you find any equilibrium, what is the corresponding direct revelation mechanism?

■ 7. Suppose we modify problem 6 in two ways. First suppose that the firms have costs of 1, 2, or 3, with each level of cost equally likely, and with the cost levels of the two firms independent of one another. (Each firm knows its own cost but not the costs of its rival.) Suppose the government solicits bids from the firms. If they bid the same amount, the order is split; if one firm bids less, it is given the entire order. And (the second change) a firm is paid not what it bid but what the other firm bid.

(a) If we construct from this mechanism the corresponding game of incomplete information, does this game have a pure strategy Nash equilibrium? Does it have more than one? If there is more than one, is there any reason to think that one equilibrium is more tenable than the others?

(b) For the equilibria you find in (a) construct the corresponding direct revelation games.

(This sort of auction, where the winning bidder is rewarded according to the bid made by the "second" best bid, is called a Vickrey auction. Almost any treatment of auction theory will tell you how to analyze this sort of auction, if you can't figure it out for yourself.)

■ 8. *(Do this problem only if you have access to a linear programming package on a computer. Do not attempt to do it by hand.)* Consider a problem similar to the toy problem of section 18.2. The government must procure one hundred units of some good. The good can be procured from two firms. Each firm has a linear cost technology with costs that are private information. Each firm's costs are either 1, 2, or 3 per unit produced. The marginal probabilities of each of the three costs prevailing at one of the firms are all $1/3$. But the costs are not statistically independent. The probability that both firms have costs of 1 is $1/6$, as is the probability that both have costs of 2 and the probability that both have costs of 3. The probability that firm 1 has costs of 1 and firm 2 has costs of 2 is $1/12$, as is the probability of all the other nonequal cost combinations.

If the government knew the costs of the two firms, it could get its hundred units at a cost of 100 with probability $1/2$, at a cost of 200 with probability $1/3$, and at a cost of 300 with probability $1/6$, for a total expected cost of 166.67. But, we suppose, the government doesn't know the costs of the two firms. In addition, we suppose that all that one firm knows about the costs of its rival is the value of its own costs. That is, firm 1 might know that its costs are 2, which means that it assesses probabilities $1/4$ that its rival's costs are 1, $1/2$ that its rival's costs are 2, and $1/4$ that its rival's costs are 3.

(a) Suppose the government seeks to find the best it can do (in terms of minimizing expected costs) in a Nash equilibrium of some mechanism. Firms must agree to participate after they learn their own costs, but then they are constrained to continue to participate. The government is not allowed to extract money from the firms; i.e., the transfers t^i must be nonnegative. What is the best the government can do?

(b) Suppose we remove from (a) the constraint that transfers must be non-negative. What is the best the government can do? (If you find the answer striking, see Cremer and McLean [1988].)

(c) Suppose the government seeks to find the best it can do (in terms of minimizing expected costs in a dominant strategy mechanism). What is the mimimum expected payment the government must make?

■ 9. Consider the mechanism depicted in figure 18.7(a). What are the Nash equilibria associated with this mechanism (that involve participation by both firms)? For one of those Nash equilibria, design the corresponding direct revelation mechanism and verify that participation and truth-telling is a Nash equilibrium in the corresponding direct revelation game.

■ 10. Finish the proof of proposition 2.

■ 11. In the context of the pivot mechanism, show that (a), (b), and the balanced budget condition are incompatible.

part V

Firms and transactions

chapter nineteen

Theories of the firm

In this last part of the book, we take a brief look at firms (and, implicitly, other sorts of economic institutions). Our purpose is two-fold. Needless to say, firms are important parts of most capitalist economies, and a better understanding of what they do and why they exist is important to any conception of the economy. At the same time, discussion of the current state of theorizing about firms gives us an excellent vehicle for exploring some of the weaknesses of the methods with which we have been concerned in the second half of this book and, in the end, with the methods that we have used throughout. In a sense, this part of the book and especially the postscript that follows serve as denouement. We take stock of the limits of the tools that formal microeconomic theory provides.

The plot is as follows: We begin in this chapter with models of the firm that have the firm as the unit of analysis when they become formal. The classic theory of the firm as a profit-maximizing production possibilities set (a wonderful subject for animation) is the starting point, and we begin by attacking the notion that profit maximization is what a firm does or ought to do. We then very briefly discuss so-called *managerial models of the firm*, where the firm is conceived of as a production possibilities set that doesn't (necessarily) maximize profits but pursues some other goal that reflects the interests of managers: maximization of sales revenue, or of capital, or of the probability of a "satisfactory" level of profits. Finally we consider a very different conception of the firm, due to Nelson and Winter (1982). In this approach, firms are dynamic entities, which at a given point of time, are described by a production *routine* and which evolve according to environmental factors through patterns of *search* and *imitation*, looking for better (but in no sense optimal) routines.

Although the firm is the unit of analysis in all these models, each is grounded in some finer conception of what goes on within the firm, and each is amenable to (some) finer-grained analysis. In chapter 20, we explore a general paradigm for finer-grained analysis, known as *transaction cost economics*, where the unit of analysis is the individual transaction. In this theory, firms are not entities, things of the rough category of the consumer; instead firms are institutions, in the rough category of the market.

Firms are places in which exchanges take place between individuals, exchanges that could take place in markets, but which are more efficiently
consummated within a firm.

In this theory, the line between firms and markets is rather fuzzy, but
what line there is is drawn along the dimension of the frequency of interaction, the relative permanence of certain legal and market relationships,
and the extent to which parties to a transaction are "tied" to one another.
The methods of part III and, in particular, chapter 14 seem natural for an
explanation of such relationships. At the same time, firms both respond
to and call up an array of informationally complex transactions, the stuff
of part IV. So it seems natural to attack some of the basic notions of chapter 20 with those techniques as well. But the complexity of transactions
within a firm and the inherent indeterminateness of equilibrium in situations of repeated interaction call into question both the standard models
of individual dynamic choice and the relevance of equilibrium analysis,
where every individual is well aware of the role she has to play. In the
postscript, we will see that this presents both a weakness in the current
state of formal theory and an opportunity for the development of new
methods.

19.1. The firm as a profit-maximizing entity

In neoclassical theory, the firm is described by a production possibilities set, and it is assumed to choose the (feasible) production plan that
maximizes profits. For the time being, we will accept the notion that those
who control the firm know the production possibilities of the firm, and we
will consider why the firm would seek to maximize its profits.

Some typically cited reasons are:

(1) It is a good positive model of how firms act.

This may well be the case, but if it is to be believed, we'll need either
some empirical evidence or some more fundamental theoretical analysis
that leads to this conclusion. An example of the latter might be:

*(2) Firms that profit maximize will drive out firms that don't by a process of
natural selection.*

"Natural selection" of this sort might work, but just the bald assertion
that this is so is hardly convincing. Some sort of detailed model of the
natural selection process is needed. We will return to this in section 19.3.

But for now we adopt a cynical demeanor and press on for other possible rationales for profit maximization.

(3) If the managers of the firm don't maximize profits, then the firm will be taken over by some corporate raider (who can make money by maximizing profits), and the managers will be fired. Since managers don't want to be fired, they maximize profits.

At least two things are missing from this argument. First, it requires that one have faith in the takeover mechanism; that is, we must believe (or be convinced) that firms that don't maximize profits will be taken over. Second, it ignores the unhappy possibility that in order to avoid being taken over, the incumbent management of a firm will pursue any number of strategies whose aim is to avoid a takeover, to the detriment of profits. At least in the United States, the financial press is filled with notions such as: "green mail," where incumbent management buys off a corporate raider (with shareholders' money, presumably) to defeat a takeover attempt; "poison-pill provisions," where incumbent management adopts policies that are solely intended to forestall raiders; and "golden parachutes," where incumbent management provides itself with employment contracts that transfer a lot of wealth to themselves and away from the firm in the event that the firm is taken over and they are discharged, thus (simultaneously) lessening the profits of the firm in the event of a takeover and lowering the incentives of incumbent management to avoid a takeover.

Formal analysis of the takeover mechanism as a form of discipline on incumbent management has been an area of very active research in microeconomic theory over the past few years. We will not review this literature here, except to give the basic observation that provided the starting point for many recent developments. This basic observation addresses the point that takeover targets will be those firms from which the raider can expect to extract profits for *herself*, which don't necessarily coincide with firms whose current management is not pursuing maximal profits.

Imagine that a firm is being poorly run to the extent that a share of its profits is worth only $10. A raider comes along, and it is known by all and sundry that this raider will, if she succeeds in taking over the firm, adopt all manner of improvements in the running of the firm, enough so that a share in the profits of the firm will be worth $20. To take over the firm, she must buy up a majority of the stock. But can she do so successfully? If it is known that she will succeed, then an individual holding a share of stock knows that the stock will become worth $20. This individual would, in consequence, refuse to tender (sell) his shares to the raider at anything less than $20. But if this raider must pay $20 per share, she is making nothing for herself by taking over the firm, and if there are costs to attempting a takeover (the costs of finding the target, registering the tender offer, lining up capital with which to accomplish the takeover), she will not even try. She must be compensated if she succeeds, to persuade her to try.

How might she be compensated? She might take her compensation in the form of perks: an overly generous salary for herself, a corporate jet, a corporate retreat in the Bahamas; these are hardly profit maximizing. She might benefit by diluting the value of the shares, once she takes control: If, for example, she owns a competing firm, she might be able to sell some of the assets of the firm taken over to her original firm at less than their full value. This doesn't sound like profit maximization, per se, nor is it clear that targets possessing such assets include all poorly run firms. She could benefit if she already holds a significant fraction of the shares of the firm (valued, until she shows her hand, at something less than $20 per share); she benefits to the extent that the shares she purchased (quietly) at $10 or so per share will become worth $20 if she succeeds. This story hangs together rather well, as long as the raider has an opportunity to accumulate quietly a number of shares large enough so that the improvement in their value covers the costs of the takeover. But then raids that will result in minor improvements only will not pay for themselves, and while grossly mismanaged firms may be takeover targets, firms that are not so poorly managed will not be targets, and profit maximization will not be achieved by the discipline of takeovers.

We will not attempt a formal presentation of any of these ideas or those that follow them in the literature; a reference will be provided at the end of the chapter. For our purposes, the point is that justification (3) may not be entirely erroneous, but it requires a good deal of study if it is to be believed, and those analyses that have been performed do not provide unambiguous support of the justification.

(4) (a) Profit maximization is in the best interests of shareholders of the firm. (b) Shareholders can and do create incentive schemes for managers that force managers to do what is best for the shareholders. So we conclude that managers maximize profits.

The second part of this argument, that shareholders are able to (and do) give managers the incentives to do *whatever* it is that shareholders want, is somewhat dubious; this should be clear from our study of incentives in part IV. At least, it should be clear that assertion (b) requires some very substantial justification itself.

Be that as it may, we take this opportunity to attack (a). Suppose that managers are just good-hearted people who will automatically do whatever is in the best interests of the firms' shareholders. Should they select whatever production plan maximizes the firms' profits?

The notion that shareholders necessarily want the managers of their firms to maximize profits is a long-standing component of the folklore of capitalism. But it is incorrect folklore, if the firm has market power[1] and if its shareholders participate, even indirectly, in the markets that are affected by the operations of the firm. Consider four shareholders of XYZ, Inc., which has market power both in output and factor markets.

Shareholder 1 is a consumer of the output of XYZ. If XYZ has and uses its market power in the output markets to push up its profits, it does so at the expense of its customers, who must pay more for what they buy. If shareholder 1 consumes a lot of the output of XYZ and owns a relatively small fraction of its shares, she can be hurt by XYZ's exercise of market power (in the pursuit of profits) more than she is helped by the distribution of those profits to shareholders.

Shareholder 2 sells factor inputs to XYZ. If XYZ exploits its market power in the factor markets to maximize profits, it may increase the dividends that shareholder 2 receives. But it may hurt shareholder 2 more by driving down the price for the factor that 2 sells.

Shareholder 3, having taken a course in portfolio management and having been convinced that diversification of her investments is the wise course of action, holds shares in many companies, some of which compete with XYZ, some of which buy from XYZ, some of which sell to XYZ. As XYZ exercises its market power, it may hurt any of those other companies (and it may help them, although hurting them is the important possibility here), and thus make 3 worse off.

Shareholder 4 buys nothing from XYZ, sells nothing to XYZ, consumes none of the factor inputs of XYZ, and holds only shares of XYZ. But this shareholder does happen to consume a good that is complementary to one of XYZ's factor inputs for some consumers (but not for XYZ itself or for shareholder number 4). Then as XYZ holds down the price of its factor inputs (in its pursuit of profits, on behalf of shareholder 4 and others), it indirectly increases demand for the factor from other sources, which increases demand for the complementary good, which bids up the

---

[1] Recall that if a firm can affect by its actions the prices it faces, it is said to have market power. If the firm doesn't have any effect on the prices it faces, it is said to be a price-taker or a competitive firm.

price of the complementary good, which makes poor shareholder 4 worse off.

What, then, could conceivably be the basis for this bit of capitalist folklore? Imagine that the firm is competitive. Its actions do not affect the price of any good. Now consider a shareholder in the company. Imagine that this shareholder is a consumer just as in chapter 2, who is seeking to maximize utility, subject to a budget constraint. Some of the consumer's wealth comes from the dividends the firm pays, and so the consumer is better off the more wealth she has, hence the consumer is better off the greater are the dividends paid by the firm. Moreover, higher dividends equals greater wealth is the *only* impact that the firm's decisions have on the consumer, since the firm is competitive. In particular, because the firm doesn't affect any prices, it has no impact on the profits made by other firms,[a] and thus it doesn't indirectly affect the consumer's wealth adversely. Hence, in this case, the consumer is unambiguously better off when the firm maximizes profits.[2] What goes wrong in the four cases above is that when the firm is not competitive, the effect it has on prices can undo the beneficial effects of greater wealth for the consumer/shareholder.

We can repose this point in the context of the model of general equilibrium with firms developed in chapter 8. Recall that consumer i's problem there was to maximize utility of consumption subject to a budget constraint which took the form

$$p \cdot x \leq p \cdot e^i + \sum_{j=1}^{J} s^{ij} p \cdot z^j,$$

where p gives equilibrium prices, x is the consumer's consumption bundle, e^i is i's endowment, s^{ij} is i's share of the profits of firm j, and z^j is the production plan of firm j. It is clear that consumer i is better off if $p \cdot z^j$ is raised (as long as $s^{ij} \geq 0$) and p doesn't change: The budget constraint loosens. But if p changes with changes in z^j, then no clear statements can be made.

We could make clear statements (or, rather, relatively clear statements) if we knew that any change in the prices faced by consumer i was "small" relative to the change in i's income generated by increased profits for firm j. Consider, for example, a case where the only price firm j affects is the price of its own output. If consumer i is a shareholder in firm j who consumes

---

[a] Nonprice externalities are also ruled out.

[2] We should have said earlier: We have in mind a world in which all profits are paid out in dividends. This isn't a realistic assumption; firms retain part of their profits in reality. This brings on multiperiod complications, for which see the discussion following.

little of firm j's output, then perhaps we can be sure that she will prefer an increase in the profits of firm j.

One must be careful with this argument. While consumer/shareholder i may not consume much of the output of firm j, neither may she hold many shares of firm j. Very roughly put, we need to know that her "share" of the output of firm j is very much smaller than her share of j's equity. Insofar as consumers can easily hold well-diversified portfolios (and the theory of finance teaches that well-diversified portfolios may well be optimal choices), it isn't clear how the comparison will run. For an exact analysis of all this, see Hart (1979).

We take this opportunity to add a further thought: Once we pass from a one-period, no-uncertainty world, into the world of uncertainty and many periods of economic activity, it isn't even clear what the term "profit maximization" means. The firm will hold some assets through time, and it could increase short-run profits by selling off those assets. In the interests of long-run profit maximization, we surely don't expect it to do so. The firm may be able to influence overall price levels by, for example, triggering inflation. Profits are usually measured in dollar amounts, so do we expect a firm to trigger or increase inflation, insofar as it is able, so that it will make more dollars and hence greater overall profits? How do we compare dollars earned in one state of nature against dollars earned in another? The usual pat answer to all these questions is: The firm should maximize the value of current shareholder's equity. There is a large literature concerning why this might be so (and what it means), which comes down to: This makes sense (once again) only if the firm is a price-taker, where being a price-taker in this context entails many more conditions. (For a survey of this literature, see Kreps [1987].)

All this isn't to say that firms with market power don't maximize profits, only that "because it is in the interests of shareholders" is a poor excuse indeed.

19.2. The firm as a maximizing entity

If a firm doesn't maximize profits, what might it do? Suppose we continue to take the point of view that the managers of the firm are aware of all of its production possibilities, but they do not choose a production plan to achieve maximal profits. Instead they choose in order to advance some other (personal) agenda.

What might that agenda be? To know this, we must consider, however informally, the objectives of those who control the firm. Think of managers who are distinct from shareholders. Of course, shareholders (working, one presumes, through the board of directors, which is another class of individuals whose interests and incentives must be analyzed) will attempt to provide managers with incentives to act on behalf of shareholders. So that there is no ambiguity about what is in the interest of shareholders, imagine that the firm is competitive; shareholders would wish the managers to maximize profits. Accordingly, we can imagine that managers are given incentives to maximize profits though stock option plans, bonuses tied to the profits the firm earns, and so on.

Even so, managers are motivated by things other than their salaries.[3] Managers like prestige, and it is sometimes held that the prestige a manager is accorded by her peers derives from the size of her organization measured in terms of gross sales or in terms of capital. (By what measures, for example, are the "Fortune 500" ranked?) Of course, the single-minded pursuit of ever-increasing sales or physical plant and equipment will shortly drive a firm into bankruptcy. But we might imagine a manager whose objective is to maximize some combination of profits and sales and capital; or one who seeks to maximize sales or capital subject to a minimum profit constraint.

And when there is uncertainty about profits, managers must worry about the chances of profits so low that shareholders become angry and displace them. A manager, liking her position of power and prestige, may well become conservative in the actions she takes, so as not to lose her position in some risky venture that holds out excellent prospects for profits in expectation, but that at the same time holds out some chances of losses or even worse.

Managerial theories of the firm begin with discussions of the sort above, and move from such informal discussions to models of firms in which the firm chooses a production plan, say, to maximize sales subject to a profit constraint, or to maximize capital subject to a profit constraint, or to maximize the probability that profits stay above some critical level. This sort of theory is not much in vogue these days, but it presents a first variation on the neoclassical model of the firm — firms as maximizing entities with well-defined production possibilities sets.

A variation on managerial theories of the firm (and a variation that is somewhat more in vogue at the current time) is the notion of the worker-managed firm. In this sort of model, the firm is run "in the interests of" its workers; the production plan is selected in order to maximize the size of the wage bill the firm pays, or the average compensation per worker. As with managerial theories, the firm's production possibilities are assumed known to some decision maker, who then selects whatever production plan that maximizes a well-defined objective function.

---

[3] And it is worth observing here that it is far from clear that managerial compensation provides managers with the incentive to maximize profits. Excellent empirical work has been conducted on the structure of managerial compensation packages; see, for example, Antle and Smith (1986) and Gibbons and Murphy (1989).

19.3. The firm as a behavioral entity

To go one step further away from the neoclassical model, we can imagine treating the firm as an entity that acts in a particular fashion, but which doesn't (necessarily) act in a way that can be described as maximizing anything at all. This sort of model is especially relevant in a dynamic setting, since most interesting behavioral patterns are dynamic.

To set the scene, imagine an industry in which there are a large number of firms; six to be precise. Each of these firms hires capital and labor to produce an undifferentiated product. Demand for this product is given by the demand function $X = 100 - P$, where P is the price of the good in question and X is the industry level of supply. Because there are so many firms in the industry, firms are price-takers. In any event, the prices of capital and labor are unaffected by any decisions taken by this industry; for convenience we imagine that these prices are both one.

Production in this economy occurs in each of a sequence of periods: $t = 0, 1, \ldots$. In period t, the production function of firm i depends on two parameters α_t^i and β_t^i and is given by

$$y_i = \left(\min \left(\frac{K}{\alpha_t^i}, \frac{L}{1 - \alpha_t^i} \right) \right)^{\beta_t^i}.$$

Besides the costs of the two factor inputs, each firm also has fixed costs of 100 per period.

Both α_t^i and β_t^i change with time. Specifically, suppose that $\alpha_t^i = .8\alpha_{t-1}^i + .05 + \epsilon_t^i$, where ϵ_t^i is a random variable that is uniformly distributed over the interval $(0, .1)$. And $\beta_t^i = .94\beta_{t-1}^i + .02 + \delta_t + \gamma_t^i$, where δ_t and γ_t^i are uniformly distributed over the interval $(0, .01)$. It is assumed that the ϵ_t^i, γ_t^i, and δ_t are all independent of each other. Note that α_t^i will be independent across firms, whereas the β_t^i will be correlated across different firms because of the common shock term δ_t.

(You should be able to convince yourself that if we begin with $\alpha_0^i \in (0, 1)$ and a $\beta_0^i \in (0, 1)$, then α_t^i and β_t^i for every t will live in the interval $(0, 1)$. The sequences of parameters will look something like "random walks on a rubber band"; they will drift slowly, with enough pull towards .5 so that they never drift too far away from that level. In table 19.1, you will see "typical" sequences of $\{\alpha_t^i\}$ and $\{\beta_t^i\}$ for $i = 1, \ldots, 6$, beginning with $\alpha_0^i = .37, .38, \ldots, .42$ and $\beta_0^i = .5$ for all i, generated by Monte Carlo simulation.)

We have in this example an industry in which the production functions of the firms are uncertain and move through time. Note that there

	PERIOD 1			PERIOD 4	
FIRM	ALPHA	BETA	FIRM	ALPHA	BETA
1	.422308	.50068	1	.476185	.495287
2	.371998	.50521	2	.398806	.502979
3	.452288	.501514	3	.408959	.497389
4	.458984	.501289	4	.45912	.511639
5	.416701	.500184	5	.456818	.508136
6	.433592	.500652	6	.492404	.498119

	PERIOD 2			PERIOD 5	
FIRM	ALPHA	BETA	FIRM	ALPHA	BETA
1	.466295	.495808	1	.525771	.491632
2	.41925	.501068	2	.403722	.497977
3	.439777	.496075	3	.397327	.495878
4	.478998	.504609	4	.457687	.509075
5	.422759	.499498	5	.417736	.502173
6	.491228	.49901	6	.450174	.48946

	PERIOD 3			PERIOD 6	
FIRM	ALPHA	BETA	FIRM	ALPHA	BETA
1	.522857	.494829	1	.500224	.494885
2	.395073	.500286	2	.405354	.496073
3	.421801	.499734	3	.455182	.4957
4	.447678	.507847	4	.510295	.510537
5	.467395	.504796	5	.476586	.497293
6	.45029	.494539	6	.473573	.493652

Table 19.1. Sequences of $\{\alpha_t^i, \beta_t^i\}$ for $i = 1, \ldots, 6$ and $t = 1, \ldots, 6$.

is a "common component" to this uncertainty and an "idiosyncratic component." How would a neoclassical economist handle this sort of uncertainty? It depends on what the firms are presumed to know about their production functions. We might imagine that the firms know at each date t just what their production functions are. Then we can imagine that firms, acting as price-takers, set their output quantities to maximize profits. The supply function of any individual firm, if firms are price-takers, is given by $x^i(P; \alpha_t^i, \beta_t^i) = (P\beta_t^i)^{\beta_t^i/(1-\beta_t^i)}$.[b] Note that α_t^i doesn't enter into this at all, owing to the nature of the production function and the fact that (we assume) prices of capital and labor are always equal. In a more complex

---

[b] You might wonder how it is that firms know the equilibrium price when they set their output quantities. If this bothers you, you might think in terms of a Cournot-style model, where firms take as given the equilibrium production levels of their rivals.

example, say where the prices of capital and labor were different, α_t^i would enter into the firm's supply function. [c]

In terms of our example of a six-firm industry, and the set of parameter values given in table 19.2, this would give the corresponding "equilibrium" shown in table 19.2. We'll say where these parameters come from in a bit.

One might object to this story about the firm knowing precisely the parameters of its production function. We might suppose that the firm only learns the values of α_t^i and β_t^i after it produces in period t. In this case, we could move (within the neoclassical tradition) to a model in which firms pick their production plans with a view towards, say, maximizing their expected levels of profits, given whatever information they happen to have available when production decisions must be made. This gets very complicated very quickly, and so we won't try to work out what the equilibrium would look like.

Instead, we move next to a general critique of the neoclassical approach to the problem, following the more general critique of the neoclassical approach by Nelson and Winter (1982). [4]

Nelson and Winter contend that it is unlikely the firm would even be aware of the "distribution" of its possible production function. What the

FIRM	ALPHA	BETA	CAPITAL	LABOR	OUTPUT	PROFITS
1	.53197	.49805	85.58	75.30	12.56	$62.14
2	.50980	.50038	84.76	81.50	12.92	$66.01
3	.51384	.49318	77.21	73.05	11.85	$54.42
4	.55856	.49935	91.52	72.33	12.76	$64.28
5	.50430	.49807	81.15	79.77	12.56	$62.17
6	.52309	.49168	76.99	70.19	11.64	$52.16

price: $25.72

Table 19.2. Theoretical equilibrium values for given α^i and β^i.

---

[c] We haven't said anything about what firms know about each other's production functions. In this example, what firm i knows about the values of α_t^j and β_t^j turns out to be irrelevant on two grounds: The nature of firm j's production function is such that its supply function doesn't depend on α_t^j; the supply of firm j does depend on β_t^j, but the price-taking assumption implies that firm i will be able to "react" to equilibrium prices, and so doesn't need to know about j's supply function. If we had an underlying model of imperfect competition, where, say, the firms had Cournot conjectures about each other, then we would need to say what each firm knows about the other firm's β^j s.

[4] What follows is a very quick summary of the arguments of Nelson and Winter. Consult their book for a fuller account.

firm "knows" (in quotes, because no single entity has this knowledge) is the pattern of productive activities that it has been able to follow in the past, its *routine*. The model given would have the firm changing the amounts of capital and labor from period to period, with changes in the two parameters. This is unlikely to happen in reality. Firms will change their production routines only infrequently. Costs are involved in shifting production routines, both in terms of hiring/discharge costs, and also (and more fundamentally) in getting members of the organization to adapt what they do. Nelson and Winter present an image of the firm as a "truce" among various employees, suppliers, and so on, wherein the conflicting interests of those parties are reconciled. While Nelson and Winter do not delve formally into the mechanics of the truce, they do note that insofar as what a firm does at any point in time is the result of such a truce, and insofar as truces, once made, are relatively hard to rearrange, firms' routines will not jump around in response to relatively minor changes in their opportunities, technology, and so on.

This is not to say that firms never change what they do. But they change relatively less frequently than the neoclassical model would predict.[5] Firms change in response to a perception that making a change represents substantial gains. When they do change, moreover, they do not necessarily "optimize" in any exact sense. They search somewhat haphazardly for ways in which to change, and (especially) they tend to imitate the actions of those rivals that they think are doing better. (Think of all the manufacturing firms in the United States that have attempted to imitate "Japanese manufacturing techniques" over the past decade without a very clear understanding of why or how those techniques work.) Indeed, the patterns of search and/or imitation that a firm chooses to employ is itself a matter of organizational routine; if one method of search has proven fruitful in the past, then it is apt to be the method relied upon at the present, and it will continue to be relied upon until the firm feels the need to change its search/imitation routine.

In place, then, of the neoclassical pair of concepts, the *opportunity set* and *profit-maximization criterion*, Nelson and Winter offer a different pair of organizing concepts: the short-run production *routine* and the longer-run process of *search* for a better routine. They then take this pair as characterizing the single firm and embed firms in an environment where the firms will act, interact, and change according to the behavioral models posed

---

[5] A true-blue believer in the neoclassical model would object that one can build into a neoclassical model the costs, if any, of adjusting the levels of factor inputs. That is, the problem is not with the neoclassical model, but with an overly simple specification of it in this context. We will deal with this objection in a bit.

and the overall environmental equilibrium. The objective is to see how the observed behavior of firms and the overall environmental equilibrium evolve together.

To take a very simple example, suppose in a six-firm industry that each firm acts as follows. Each begins with a routine that describes how much capital and labor is hired. Fixing the capital and labor quantity choices by firms, the firms' different production functions yield levels of output for each firm, and hence a market (equilibrium) price for the firms and profits for each firm. In each period, firms' profits are reported publicly, and these serve as the cue for firms to change their routines: When a firm's profits are more than 15% below the industry average, the firm searches for a new pattern of production. This search is conducted in two parts: The searching firm engages in "introspection," to see whether to adjust its capital to labor ratio. And it imitates more successful rivals in setting its level of capital input.

Specifically, a firm that is searching adopts the level of capital employed by its most profitable rival. Note that firms may be making "mistakes" by so doing; the firm being imitated may be profitable because its scale parameter β_t^j is relatively high or even because it has found a profitable (for it) capital/labor ratio. Firms recognize that they should not look to other firms for the right capital/labor ratio for themselves, so they do not engage in imitation here; instead, if a firm decides to search (i.e., if its profits are more than 15% below the industry average), it draws a noisy signal λ of the "optimal" capital proportion α_t^i. Specifically, $\lambda = \rho \alpha_t^i$, where ρ has uniform distribution from .9 to 1.1. If λ is more than 5% away from the ratio the firm is currently using, the firm adopts the ratio given by λ; otherwise it stays with its old capital/labor ratio. (The rationale for this bit of the model is that changing ratios is costly, and firms will not undertake to make a small change.) After each period's price and profits are realized, firms decide whether to search as above. If they decide to do so, they carry out the search in time for next period's production. Parameters for production for the following period evolve according to the random process specified above, firms set their levels of inputs, and so on.

What will happen in this industry? Will firms evolve to a position where their behavior approximates the behavior of profit-maximizing, competitive firms? The system of behavior described above is fairly simple to describe, yet it seems too complex to answer even these simple questions analytically. We can, however, simulate the system. A Monte Carlo simulator for this system was built, where firms were started off "knowing" the correct capital/labor ratios and producing at the theoretically

PERIOD 98

FIRM	ALPHA	BETA	PROFITS	SCALE	RATIO
1	.530549	.499526	173.835	110.003	.539757
2	.519665	.495387	160.707	126.692	.468657
3	.529616	.490394	156.749	118.087	.502806
4	.511884	.50331	180.407	124.876	.475472
5	.500778	.494868	180.98	132.596	.494924
6	.522573	.495059	158.708	108.484	.547317

PERIOD 99

FIRM	ALPHA	BETA	PROFITS	SCALE	RATIO
1	.507066	.499206	172.128	110.003	.539757
2	.545456	.496198	161.179	126.692	.468657
3	.527188	.492893	170.285	118.087	.502806
4	.518491	.503433	186.755	124.876	.475472
5	.456039	.497635	182.573	132.596	.494924
6	.528068	.489151	158.599	108.484	.547317

PERIOD 100

FIRM	ALPHA	BETA	PROFITS	SCALE	RATIO
1	.531965	.498054	172.694	110.003	.539757
2	.509804	.500375	174.758	126.692	.468657
3	.513837	.493177	168.342	118.087	.502806
4	.558562	.499345	156.798	124.876	.475472
5	.504303	.49807	187.03	132.596	.494924
6	.523086	.491682	154.07	108.484	.547317

Table 19.3. Results from a simulation.

correct scale for the starting values in table 19.1, and then 100 periods were simulated. The results of periods 98, 99, and 100 are given in table 19.3. In the first two columns we list the firms' production parameters α_t^i and β_t^i; in the third column, the firms' levels of profits; in the fourth column, the total amount of capital and labor the firms hired; and in the fifth column, the proportion of total capital and labor that is capital. Note that a firm that "knows" its production function would want the first and last columns to be equal. And if the firms conform to the neoclassical model and know their production functions, they would be producing at a total scale (column 4) of approximately 156.25. More precisely, for the values of period 100, the theoretical equilibrium values are given in table 19.2.

In the three periods represented in table 19.3, no firm engaged in search, so no firm modified its production routine. Nonetheless, levels of profits bounce around as the firms' production parameters move. In the one hundred periods simulated, fifty-one searches were conducted.

What do we learn from this simulation? This is a very simple model, built for exposition and not to conform to any realistic model of how firms operate, so the appropriate answer must be "nothing about the real world." Nonetheless, we can learn something about the model we have built. The most striking thing about the ending values are that firms are producing at a scale significantly below the scale they would use according to the neoclassical model based on the hypothesis that they know their production functions. And, in consequence, they are making higher profits than they would according to the neoclassical model.[6] This particular simulation was run several times, and for 1,000 periods, and the scales observed in period 100 are not atypical of where firms wound up after 1,000 periods.

Can you see why this is happening? We'll give the answer in the next paragraph, but if you like to play detective, this is a good chance. The model we have described here is very seriously flawed, and the flaw, while obvious after the fact, illustrates my own lack of experience with this sort of model. Can you see where I screwed up?

Think about the evolution of the capital levels firms employ. A firm either keeps its level of capital or it copies the level employed by one of its rivals. I began the simulation with six different levels of capital, and when the first firm began to search only five were left, and so on. In the situation described in table 19.3, only two of the original six capital levels are left, and (it is relatively easy to prove rigorously) eventually only one level of capital will remain. Moreover, I began the model with six levels of capital appropriate for αs of .37, .38, .39, .4, .41, and .42, which is significantly lower than the long-run levels of α we see (which roam around in the neighborhood of .5). Hence I started the industry off in a "capital-poor" state, and I imposed dynamics for capital that ensured the industry could never escape; capital levels can never rise above the largest initial level of capital (around 65) or get any smaller than the smallest initial level of capital (around 59). Without some external source of "mutation" in capital levels that would allow a firm to experiment with a larger level of capital (and discover how profitable this can be), there is no way for the firms in this industry to attain the neoclassical scale of 156.25 once they realize that capital/labor ratios should be approximately one-to-one.

---

[6] Be careful here: The profits of firm i are high because the other firms are producing at a relatively small scale. Given the scales used by the other firms and given the price-taking assumption, a firm that knows its production function would make much higher profits by increasing its scale from the values in table 19.3.

This is a very simple and flawed example of the mode of analysis adopted by Nelson and Winter. Their book should be consulted for more complete, better-analyzed, and (needless to say) much better models. But the basic constructions in this model and the use (in the end) of a simulation model to see how things evolve is typical of their general plan. It would be very useful to complement their simulations with analytical analysis, but even in the simple model given above, you can see how hard analytical analysis would be.[7]

We can tie this mode of analysis to an idea from section 19.1. Recall that one of the alleged reasons for believing that firms act as if they maximize profits is that in an evolutionary sense profit-maximizing firms ·will come to dominate the industry at least insofar as there is initially a "mix" of firm types, and profit-maximizing firms survive longer and grow larger. Presumably, one would build a model where firms behaved differently — some coming closer to profit maximization in their routine and in their search behavior, and some further. And one would wish to build into the model a stronger tie from period to period. For example, one could naturally model capital as a durable good, subject to depreciation, and have firms accumulate capital out of retained earnings. That way, more profitable firms would have higher earnings and, in accordance with the story we are attempting to provide, more profitable firms would grow more quickly and dominate less profitable firms. The point is that with such an elaborated model we could either give a decent burial to the story that "competition" leads to dominance by profit-maximizing firms or we could provide a setting in which the story is theoretically consistent. Some work along these lines has been done by Nelson and Winter, but a lot more remains.

This is a very new mode of analysis in economics, and it is clearly one that deserves further development in building models, running simulations, doing more exact analysis, and developing procedures for calibrating and testing models. Certainly, the sort of behavioral patterns that are naturally built into these models are more realistic than those in simple neoclassical models. A true believer in the neoclassical model would have a ready retort to all this, which would run something like: "One can accommodate within the neoclassical framework all manner of adjustment costs, search costs, and so on. The behavioral models of Nelson and Winter are entirely ad hoc. The right way to do business is to stick with the standard

---

[7] Actually, the simple model we have given is amenable to straightforward analysis, but only because it is so badly flawed.

model of maximizing behavior, complicating the environment." But to accommodate all these things within a neoclassical framework is at least an awesome undertaking and probably impossible. If we are unable to analyze these models, then it is difficult at least to see how managers can truly optimize dynamically in the vastly complex problems they are set. In any event, the notion of a single manager deciding on a production plan for the entire firm does not seem very descriptive of the way firms make decisions.[8] And we still don't have any good reason to believe in profit maximization as being descriptive of what firms pursue. Any of these would be sufficient grounds to push research in the direction of models of the sort described above. Put all together, they make the case fairly compelling: *If* profit maximization is a good model, then a demonstration of that fact (along these lines) should be feasible.

19.4. Firms in the category of markets

So we have firms first as profit-maximizing entities, and then as _____ (fill in the blank) maximizing entities, and then characterized behaviorally. In each case, the firm is an entity. In the justification for the sort of "inertial" behavior seen in the simulation model, in the justifications for some of the criteria that replaced profit maximization, and even in the justifications that are made for profit maximization, we see reference to the actors within the firm: managers and raiders in section 19.1, managers (and their objectives) in section 19.2, and the "truce" within a firm in section 19.3. But these are largely informal arguments. (The literature on takeovers is quite formal, and it fits into the category to which we are now coming.) When it comes down to modeling the firm formally, all these models take the firm and its behavior as the unit of analysis.

This leaves a very different way of modeling the firm to be explored, namely the firm as an arena within which the conflicting interests of managers, workers, capitalists, customers, and so on are met and resolved. But this raises the question: Why should a firm have advantages or disadvantages relative to any other "marketplace?" To address this question, and to address generally the notion of the firm (and other organizations) as marketlike entities, we turn in chapter 20 to the topic of transaction cost economics.

---

[8] This isn't to say that such a model isn't a good reduced form for what does go on in a firm. But one would like either empirical or theoretical confirmation of this.

19.5. *Bibliographic notes*

For a survey of the theoretical work on profit maximization as an "appropriate" criterion for managers (in the sense that it is in the interests of shareholders), see Kreps (1987). For managerial theories of the firm, see Baumol (1959) and Williamson (1964). There has been quite a lot of analysis on the takeover mechanism as a restraining influence on managers; an introductory survey is provided in Schleifer and Vishny (1988). Needless to say, Nelson and Winter (1982) is highly recommended. To my own tastes, they are unduly harsh concerning the neoclassical traditions. (My reasons are given in chapter 1 and don't need reiterating here.) But the positive aspects of their research program deserve a lot of attention.

References

Antle, R., and A. Smith. 1986. "An Empirical Investigation of the Relative Performance Evaluation of Corporate Executives." *Journal of Accounting Research* 24:1–39.

Baumol, W. 1959. *Business Behavior, Value and Growth.* New York: Macmillan.

Gibbons, R., and K. Murphy. 1989. "Relative Performance Evaluation for Chief Executive Officers." Massachusetts Institute of Technology. Mimeo.

Hart, O. 1979. "On Shareholder Unanimity in Large Stock Market Economies." *Econometrica* 47:1057–83.

Kreps, D. 1987. "Three Essays on Capital Markets." *Revista Espanola de Economía* 4:111–45.

Nelson, R., and S. Winter. 1982. *An Evolutionary Theory of Economic Change.* Cambridge, Mass.: Belknap/Harvard University Press.

Schleifer, A., and R. Vishny. 1988. "Value Maximization and the Acquisition Process." *Journal of Economic Perspectives* 2:7–20.

Williamson, O. 1964. *The Economics of Discretionary Behavior: Managerial Objectives in a Theory of the Firm.* Englewood Cliffs, N.J.: Prentice-Hall.

19.6 *Problems*

■ 1. Consider an industry in which firms produce an undifferentiated commodity for which demand is given by $X = 100 - P$. A number of firms produce the item in question, all of whom have production function

$$Y = \left(\min \left(\frac{K}{\alpha}, \frac{L}{1-\alpha} \right) \right)^{1/2},$$

where Y is the level of output and α is some constant from $(0,1)$, K is the amount of capital employed, and L is the amount of labor employed. The prices of capital and labor are fixed at \$1 throughout. All firms have fixed costs of \$16.

(a) Suppose precisely six firms are in this industry, all of which maximize profits taking prices as given. What is the equilibrium in this case?

(b) Suppose there is free entry into this industry, with all of the firms having the production function given above. What is the equilibrium in this case?

■ 2. (a) Suppose that firms in this industry maximize their sales revenue, taking prices as given, subject to constraint that profits must be nonnegative. What is the equilibrium in this industry if there are precisely six firms?

(b) What would be the equilibrium if three of the six firms were profit maximizers and three maximized revenue?

(c) Now suppose that all firms are revenue maximizers, taking prices as given, subject to a zero-profit constraint. Why is it difficult to contemplate an equilibrium in a case where there is free entry?

■ 3. Suppose that the industry has six firms, each of which seeks to maximize its use of capital, subject to a zero-profit constraint. (Firms continue to be price-takers.) What is the equilibrium in this case?

■ 4. To repair the model that was discussed and simulated in section 19.3, one thing that comes to mind is to have firms that are imitating the capital levels of other firms "over-do" the imitation. That is, if firm i is imitating the level of capital of firm j, firm i chooses capital that is, say, three percent higher than the level of capital of j (on the grounds that firm j is doing so well that firm i should do even more of whatever it is that firm j is doing). This is not much better (in fact, it's worse) than the model discussed in section 19.3. Why?

■ 5. Give suggestions how the model in section 19.3 might be repaired. If you have access to a computer and know how to construct Monte Carlo simulations, you might wish to try out your suggestions.

chapter twenty

Transaction cost economics and the firm

This chapter continues the discussion initiated in chapter 19 about models of the firm, with consideration given to models where the firm is something more like a market than a consumer. That is, we think of the firm as an institution within which transactions between individuals take place — an alternative to transactions that take place in a market. To make sense of this, we have to see how a transaction placed within the context of a firm is different from the "same" transaction placed within a market, which is the subject of *transaction cost economics*.

This chapter also continues to prepare for our critique of the methods that have been developed throughout the book. To accomplish this second purpose, we take things in somewhat roundabout fashion. To begin, we recount the theory of transaction cost economics as told by Williamson (1985).[1] This recounting will seem more verbal and less mathematical than topics discussed earlier in the book, and after laying out the theory along the lines of Williamson (1985), we go back and see how we can match pieces of that theory with things we did earlier.

20.1. Transaction cost economics and firms

Transaction costs

When undertaking a transaction, parties to the transaction must incur several sorts of costs. *Ex ante costs* are incurred before the transaction takes place. If the transaction is to be governed by a written contract, the contract must be drafted. Whether governed by a contract or simply by verbal commitments, the terms of the transaction must be negotiated. *Ex post costs* are incurred in consummating and safeguarding the deal that was originally struck.

---

[1] The rendition given here is not precisely as in Williamson (1985) in emphasis or, in some minor respects, in organization. And the rendition here is not nearly as rich in examples and elaborations as is the work being abridged.

In some cases these costs are negligible. But in other cases they can be quite substantial. Insofar as transactions can be arranged in different ways (making use of different legal and social institutions, providing more or less detail in a contract, reserving rights to the transacting parties in one fashion or another), these different ways will have distinct costs. The basic notion of transaction costs economics is that *transactions tend to be "placed" in a way that maximizes the net benefits they provide, including the costs of the transaction*. In particular, a transaction whose (transaction) costs outweigh the benefits of completion will not be undertaken at all.

To get a better fix on these costs, it is helpful to look at factors that give rise to them. Williamson compiles a list of these factors in two parts: factors pertaining to the individuals who undertake the transaction, and factors specific to the particular transaction.

Human factors

Human beings are *boundedly rational* and *opportunistic*. Bounded rationality is important because, in the first place, it means that it will be costly for individuals to contemplate and contract for every contingency that might arise over the course of the transaction; this adds to the ex ante cost of drafting the contract. These costs may be so high that the individuals fail to provide for the contingency in the contract or fail to undertake the contemplation necessary to foresee the contingency. And there may be contingencies that the individuals cannot foresee at all.[2] Contingencies that are not provided for ex ante may add to ex post costs, since parties to the transaction may be required to negotiate further whenever such contingencies arise. And, insofar as it is understood that some contingencies are not foreseen or provided for ex ante, the parties may build into the original contract specific means by which the contract will be amended as required. These "means" or *governance structures* bring on costs of administration and the like.

To say that individuals are *opportunistic* means that they are self-interested with guile. If it will further his own weal, an opportunistic individual will break any of the commandments. Note well the conditional *if* here. Institutions can be sometimes arranged so that when an individual gives his "word of honor," then it will not be in his interests to go back on that word to extract some short-term gain. (Think back to chapter 14 or see below if it isn't obvious to you how this can happen.)

---

[2] We will distinguish between contingencies that are unforeseeable and those that could be foreseen but that are not foreseen because of the costs of contemplation. From a theoretical point of view, these two categories could be combined by saying that the cost of foreseeing the first sort is infinite.

To distinguish simple self-interest from opportunism, think of a completely honest individual who would never break her word or misrepresent what she knows, but who still seeks to maximize her own welfare. This is self-interest, as compared to an opportunistic individual who would break his word or engage in misrepresentation under the right circumstances. Moreover, our use of the term "opportunism" is stretched to mean that it is opportunistic to refuse to divulge information that you hold and another lacks when the other person asks you to give up that information. That is, if you are selling a used car whose quality you know and a buyer asks you what the quality is, even to withhold this information would be opportunistic behavior. [a]

Classify individuals according to a three-by-three scheme, where the first dimension is the individual's degree of rationality and the second is the individual's self-interest orientation.

For degree of rationality, our three categories are complete rationality, bounded rationality, and behavioral. A completely rational individual has the ability to foresee everything that might happen and to evaluate and optimally choose among available courses of action, all in the blink of an eye and at no cost. A boundedly rational individual attempts to maximize but finds it costly to do so and, unable to anticipate all contingencies and aware of this inability, provides ex ante for the (almost inevitable) time ex post when an unforeseen contingency will arise. A behavioral individual acts according to some specified behavioral pattern that doesn't (except by coincidence) correspond to the maximization of any specific utility or welfare function.

For the individual's self-interest orientation, to the opportunist and the completely honest but self-interested individuals discussed, add the utopian, someone who has a sense of the social good and seeks to maximize it.

Various pieces of economic theory can be thought of as concerning societies comprising one of the nine classes of individuals so created. If the individuals in a society are behavioral, then their self-interest orientation is irrelevant once their behavior is specified, since (by definition) they don't act out of self-interest at all.[3] Also irrelevant to such individu-

---

[a] This stretches the notion of opportunism very far indeed, far beyond its most "natural" usage. To amplify, suppose A owns a piece of land on which is buried some treasure. A doesn't know where the treasure is, and it is too expensive to dig up the entire plot to find it. B knows where the treasure is, however, and with that knowledge it would be worthwhile for B (or, if A had the knowledge, for A) to dig. According to this definition of opportunism, it would be opportunistic of B to refuse to tell A where the treasure is, if A asks.

[3] While correct as stated, this is a bit misleading. Reasonable models of behavior will reflect the self-interest orientation that is supposed of the individual. For example, firms

als is all of orthodox economic theory, which is based on consumers who maximize. Evolutionary theories, such as in Nelson and Winter, but applied to the actions of consumers instead of the actions of firms, would seem to be appropriate to the economic analysis of a society of such individuals.

Most economic theory concerns completely rational individuals. If they are utopian in their interest orientation, then one employs *team theory*, in which (it is assumed) all individuals have the same utility function (which can be thought of as social welfare). They may not have common information, which makes the subject interesting, but they all act in a way that anticipates perfectly what their fellows will do contingent on the information their fellows possess, and they act to maximize some single criterion of overall welfare.[4]

Completely rational individuals who are self-interested but without guile populate the economies of general equilibrium. There is no mention of deceit or of private information. Since self-interested individuals who are not opportunistic will not withhold pertinent information, and since each side to the transaction is completely rational and so anticipates the possibly pertinent information that the other side possesses, there will be no pertinent private information at all (after a round of questions and honest answers). In undertaking a transaction, therefore, parties know just what they are getting, and any allowance for future contingencies is complete and completely understood by all.[b]

Completely rational and opportunistic individuals populate the models of moral hazard and incentives and adverse selection and market signaling; i.e., the stuff of part IV. One is able to work through how others will act and react given appropriate incentives. And one is able to work through the distribution of qualities that will be brought to market, or the distribution of qualities that accompanies some given signal or other, or the appropriate (equilibrium) action to take when faced with a menu of contracts. But the incentives that are put in place (either to take a particular action or to send a particular signal) must respect the ability of the individuals to lie, cheat, and steal if so doing would be beneficial.

---

in the simulation model of section 19.3 are "behavioral," but their behavior is tied to their "self-interest" as measured by relative profitability. Similarly, we could imagine a model of individual behavior where the individual responds to prompts that are tied to her "self-interest" such as her levels of consumption of various goods relative to those of her neighbors, and so on.

[4] For an exposition of team theory, see Marshak and Radner (1972).

[b] In general equilibrium, different firms are allowed to have different production functions. So, as a matter of the formal theory, the fact that one firm can undertake a particular production plan that another cannot is *not* based on proprietary information held by the first.

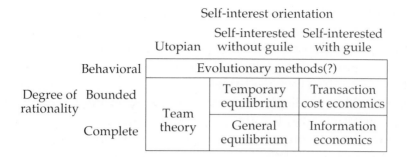

Figure 20.1. Matching economic theories to types of individuals.

This leaves boundedly rational individuals. For boundedly rational individuals who are utopian, some pieces of team theory (Marshak and Radner, 1972) apply. For boundedly rational individuals who are self-interested but without guile, the literature of *temporary equilibrium* applies. (See Grandmont [1988].) And, finally, boundedly rational individuals who are self-interested with guile populate the world of transaction cost economics.

Figure 20.1 (loosely adapted from Williamson [1985, fig. 2-1]) presents all this schematically. (The question mark attached to evolutionary methods records the relative lack of work along these lines. The usefulness of evolutionary methods for exploring these categories seems clear, but more evidence is desirable.)

Qualities of transactions

Bounded rationality and opportunism don't come to much when the sort of transaction that is contemplated is something like an exchange of apples for oranges or for money. At least, this is so if we imagine that the buyer of the apples/oranges is sufficiently well versed in these matters to be able to tell the quality of a piece of fruit upon quick inspection. It is the conjunction of the human factors discussed above and various aspects of the specific transaction that lead to significant transaction costs. Williamson identifies three aspects or qualities of a transaction that bear on the level and nature of transaction costs: *asset specificity, extent of uncertainty,* and *frequency.*

A transaction has high levels of *asset specificity* if as the trade develops one side or the other or both becomes more tied to and in the "power" of the other side. A simple example is a company that makes glass bottles locating a plant adjacent to a bottler. Before the bottle maker puts his plant next to the bottler, each side can (potentially) deal with many alternate traders. If there is negotiation between bottle manufacturer and bottler before any plants are built, we would expect (if there are many of each type) that the deal struck will reflect other opportunities that each side has. The technology of the two production processes is such that there are efficiency gains if the two locate side by side, and we expect the two to divide, according to some bargaining scheme, the efficiency gains that come from side-by-side plants. Note well that in ex ante negotiations, if a bottler doesn't like the deal that a specific bottle manufacturer proposes, she can (typically) turn to many other bottle manufacturers. But once the bottle manufacturer puts his plant next to the bottler and the bottler puts her bottling lines next to the bottle manufacturing plant, each side has specific assets at risk. Now each side has a degree of monopoly power against the other; opportunism has scope to operate. The bottler, for ex- ample, might tell the bottle manufacturer that despite the contract signed earlier she wants a lower price per bottle. The bottle manufacturer, held up in this fashion, doesn't have any as-good alternative trading partners. So, anticipating this possibility, the bottle manufacturer (and, for that mat- ter, the bottler) may expend resources to negotiate a very rigid contract ex ante and to have the ability to enforce that contract ex post. Or, to take a slightly less oportunistic example, the bottler and bottle manufacturer may not foresee, ex ante, the impact that plastics will have on their two industries. But the two will have to adapt their transactions as the tech- nology for plastic containers develops, and their proximity will mean that each is somewhat a captive of the other in any ex post (re)negotiations.[5]

In the story above, asset specificity is at work on both sides of the transaction. There will also be cases in which asset specificity binds only or mainly on one side. To take an example, consider the plight of the graduate student. After a year or two of study, the student has invested enormously in assets that are specific to the department at which she studies, such as meeting specific requirements, passing specific exams, and so on. Some of this may be transferable to another department, but much is not. The department, on the other hand, has much less invested in the particular student. (When the student proceeds to the dissertation stage, this balance is redressed to some extent.) What began as an exchange in which each party had many alternative trading partners becomes one in which one side has much more at risk. In such cases, relatively more resources will be expended in the form of transaction costs to safeguard the individual student from being exploited by professors and administrators; e.g., formal structures are set up by which the student can appeal unjust

---

[5] For this to be an example of asset specificity, it is important that the old assets put in place earlier are not rendered completely obsolete by the new technology.

decisions to department chairpersons, deans, and the like; and both within the university and in the courts the burden of proof rests more on the university than on the student.[c]

The second quality of a transaction that bears on its costs is the extent of *uncertainty* in the transaction. This goes hand in hand with bounded rationality. Indeed, uncertainty is the major complexity that gives rise to bounded rationality. Note that uncertainty here is defined very broadly. It includes uncertainty about contingencies that can be anticipated, insofar as it is costly to anticipate them or to include provisions for dealing with them within a contract. It includes uncertainty about contingencies the nature of which can only roughly (or not even roughly) be divined ex ante. And it includes uncertainty of the sort where one party has information that the other lacks.

Finally, there is the *frequency* of the transaction. This aspect of the transaction does not bear on the absolute magnitude of its costs, as with the previous two aspects, but rather on the relative costs of various means for dealing with the transaction. When a transaction between two parties recurs frequently, the two parties can construct special governance structures for the transaction, even if these special structures are costly, since the cost of the structure can be amortized over many transactions. But when the transaction is a one-time-only transaction or recurs only infrequently, then it is generally more costly to put into place specialized mechanisms for this particular transaction and relatively less costly to make use of "general purpose" governance structures, which are, perhaps, less than ideally tuned to the specific transaction.

Classifying transactions by governance provisions

Transaction cost economics lays great stress when classifying different forms of transaction on the way in which the terms of the transaction are adapted to circumstances as they arise. These features of a transaction are called the *terms of governance*. Terms of governance can be explicitly and rigidly specified within a contract that governs a transaction, for example, an explicit and formalized procedure for arbitration, as in major league baseball. Or the terms of governance can be implicit, arising from common practice and law. For example, ownership of an asset generally

---

[c] In relations between the courts and universities, private universities are usually allowed to pursue consistent, so-called "dean's justice," where the decision of the dean is without serious appeal on procedural grounds. The notion is that if the university follows this practice consistently, then the student should know of it at the inception of the relationship, and the courts have no reason to interfere in a private transaction. Of course, this leaves the question why students would ever trust to dean's justice, a point we will return to in the next section.

confers upon the owner the right to command the use of that asset, within limits. Hence, when a bottler purchases from a bottle manufacturer the bottle manufacturing plant and simultaneously hires the manufacturer to staff the facility, the bottler has different "rights" under law than if she simply contracts to buy bottles from a manufacturer who owns the bottle manufacturing plant. The "contract" between the two explicitly specifies ownership of the assets, and the pattern of ownership together with the law implicitly specifies the resulting governance provisions.

Williamson (1985, chap. 3) gives the following classification scheme:

Transactions within the framework of *classical contracting* are those in which the terms of the transaction are completely specified ex ante. This includes the textbook exchange of apples for oranges, but goes beyond this to include any contract where adaptation beyond the explicit terms of the contract is not expected. For example, a complex purchase and sale agreement for a given piece of real estate would be included within this category.[6] Such P&S agreements typically include very specific clauses pertaining to liquidated damages: Party 1 receives such and such if party 2 fails to perform in such and such a manner. This sort of explicit, ex ante provision for nonperformance is typical of classical contracts whenever nonperformance is an issue. Of course, enforcement of the contract remains a problem; one can rely upon bonded third parties, who act with very little discretion (such as escrow agents), and in the end (and often with this sort of contract, from the beginning) the courts are called in to adjudicate disputes.

As third parties who act with discretion are added, we move into the realm of *neoclassical contracting* or *trilateral relationships*. The contract no longer says what damages are due for various sorts of breach or, more generally, what sort of adaptation will be made in various contingencies, but instead prescribes a third party who will determine appropriate damages/adaptation, according, perhaps, to some specified procedure. For example, in arbitration one sometimes sees a scheme in which both parties to the dispute submit their "claims" between which the arbiter is compelled to choose; the arbiter may not propose a compromise.

---

[6] A difficulty in providing illustrative examples in this chapter is that social customs often decide the form that a transaction takes. Real estate transactions, for example, are conducted quite differently in different states of the United States, and it is easy to envisage a society in which the form of real estate transactions is trilateral (see below), with the lending authority taking the role of the adjudicating third party. The examples that are used throughout this chapter are drawn from customs and practices that are prevalent in the United States, and they may not be descriptive of other countries. The obvious challenge in such cases is to explain in terms of the theory why there are differences. In general, cross-society comparisons of institutional practices is a very fertile field for empirical tests of the theory described here.

When the two parties to the transaction have no formal agreement about how the arrangement will be adapted to circumstances but instead rely upon their own ability to work things out as they go along, we have a *bilateral relationship*. Successful bilateral relationships remind one of co-operation in the repeated game version of the prisoners' dilemma: Each side is willing to cooperate with the other in order to preserve cooperation. (This connection will be developed more fully in the next section.)

Just as many sorts of trilateral arrangements can be made, so there are many forms of bilateral contracting. One extreme form deserves special attention. In a *hierarchical transaction* one of the two parties retains, by law or by custom, most of the authority to determine how the contract will be fulfilled. The second party will retain some explicit rights, such as to abrogate the contract, perhaps at some specified cost. And certain rights are implicitly retained under law. But up to such limits, the first party or *hierarchical superior* determines how matters will proceed. The chief example of this form, and the reason for its importance, is the classic labor contract: A worker earns his wages by carrying out the demands of his boss, retaining (in economies where slavery and indenture are illegal) the right to quit the job if these demands become too onerous or distasteful (cf. Simon, 1951).

When one party to the transaction takes command of the assets of the second, effectively internalizing the transaction, we have a *unified governance structure*. Here the focus is on the fact that "ownership" connotes control according to common practice. Note that where slavery and indenture are illegal, one party cannot buy the human capital of a second party; employment of a worker by a firm is not a transaction with a unified governance structure, but is instead a hierarchical transaction (if not some other form of transaction).

Matching transactions to governance structures

What sort of governance structure will minimize transaction costs in specific instances? Williamson advances the following scheme: Transactions are classified according to the specificity of the assets involved (from nonspecific through intermediate specificity to highly specific) and the frequency of the transaction (from occasional to frequent).

If assets are nonspecific, then there is no need for any fancy form of governance, since there is no need for complex, long-term contracts. Even if the relationship between the two parties is enduring, the relationship can be governed by a sequence of short-term contracts, since competition from the marketplace will prevent either individual from taking too great an advantage of the other. Classical contracting, then, goes with nonspecific assets. It is when assets become more specific that the fancier forms come into play, if at all.

Two caveats to this assertion should be offered. First, this presumes that the extent to which the two parties face competition in the relationship is unchanging with time. We can imagine a situation in which A has a lot of competition initially for B, but that competition disappears through time, even though no physical specific assets are put in place. To keep the simple conclusion just given while accommodating such a case, we would need to expand the definition of specific asset to include "market power."

Second, we earlier mentioned a purchase and sale agreement for the purchase of real estate as an example of classical contracting. But when buying and selling real estate, the parties involved commit quite significant specific assets to the transaction, namely their opportunity to find in timely fashion an alternative partner should the current deal go awry. What keeps this within the domain of classical contracting is that the transaction is one with which there is a lot of experience. A real estate lawyer may be required to explain to you all the contingencies for which you must make allowance, but the extent of those contingencies is fairly well known; "boilerplate" contract forms can often be used. From the point of view of the match being developed here, what goes wrong in this case is that we do not have a third axis for "uncertainty" or "complexity." The usual real estate transaction may be very occasional (for the parties involved) and may involve substantial specific assets (for a short period of time), but the range of possible contingencies is well known; it is not complex in the relevant sense. (Or, alternatively, you can think of this as a case in which the extent of rationality is substantial, at least if the parties take the prudent course of action and employ specialists to help draft the contract.) Hence this sort of transaction can be handled by a classical contract.

Similar qualifications can be made to almost every piece of the match between transactions and governance structures that we lay out. We will refrain hereafter from making these qualifications, but be clear that this is a very simplistic scheme. It gives general tendencies and it should be qualified in many ways.

When assets are moderately specific, relational contracting (i.e., trilateral, bilateral, hierarchical) comes to the fore. It is the pattern of the frequency of the transaction that plays the principal role in determining which relational-contracting form is best.[7] If the given transaction between the two parties is repeated between them frequently, then full bilateral contracting can work well. If one party of the two engages in this sort of transaction relatively frequently (and the second party engages in

---

[7] For frequency of the transaction, you should have in mind the frequency of the specific transaction or of transactions of a roughly similar nature. Anticipating what will come later, if two parties never repeat a precise transaction but frequently repeat transactions sufficiently similar to one another so that parties can carry an overall reputation for behavior, then we would essentially have a case of frequent transactions.

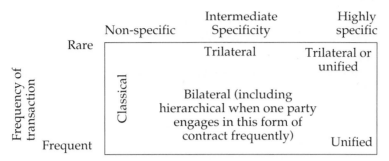

Figure 20.2. *Matching governance structures to characteristics of the specific transaction.*

the transaction with less frequency), then we may be able to get by with a bilateral form that gives most of the discretion to the first party; i.e., a hierarchical form may be appropriate.[8] But as the frequency of the transaction for either of the two parties decreases, bilateral forms in general begin to suffer, and it may become necessary to enlist the aid of a third party who can act in an adjudicary role.

When assets become very specific to the transaction, the costs of relational contracting rise: Each party has more at risk, and so must engage in more and more pretransaction planning, during-transaction monitoring, and posttransaction enforcement. A point is reached, then, where the costs of relational contracting become quite high, and the parties consider, if the laws permit, a unified governance structure, where one party buys out the other and takes full command of and responsibility for the transaction.

All these considerations lead to the picture in figure 20.2, adapted with minor modifications from Williamson (1985, fig. 3-2).

Firms and markets

The connection from the theory just developed to the theory of the firm is relatively straightforward. A firm corresponds to unified governance; a firm is a legal entity that commands an array of assets and in whose name various transactions are consummated (with other firms and with individuals).[9]

---

[8] We will see one reason why in the next section.

[9] We will not be very precise here about the differences between corporations, proprietorships, partnerships, and so on. These differences can be significant, but for a first cut at the theory they are best ignored.

Why does this make a firm into something in the category of a market? After all, the preceding sentence has firms acting in markets, playing the sort of role that is played by the individual consumer. Think of it in terms of the following example: Party A and party B wish to undertake an exchange. Party A will supply expertise concerning the design of some product, and B will supply expertise in manufacturing the product. This transaction requires certain tools — computers to aid in the design, and industrial lathes and various jigs to produce the product. We could imagine A owning the computers and B owning the lathe and jigs, in which case we would think of the exchange between them as a market-mediated exchange. Alternatively, we can imagine (say, because once B owns the jigs, he doesn't need many of the design capabilities of A) that A owns the computers, the lathes, and the jigs; she then controls a firm, which employs B for his labor services. The exchange of labor services for money is a firm-mediated transaction; as distinct from (say) the market-mediated exchange of a product design for money where B continues to own the lathes and jigs, or the market-mediated exchange where A obtains from B finished pieces produced according to plans given to B by A, which A then sells to the consumer. If A controls all the assets and employs B, it isn't important at a first level of analysis whether A owns the assets directly or controls the assets through some form of corporation; it is A's control of the assets that changes the nature of the transaction.[10]

In this example, if the design and/or the production technique is proprietary then perhaps the most important asset of all will be the design or the technique or both. And ownership of this asset is the most complex thing of all. If A owns all the physical capital and also the right to block others from using the design, so she controls the production amounts, and if B supplies labor services and is disbarred from taking the knowledge he acquires about the production technique to form another firm or to some competitor, then we have a very clean case of a firm (controlled by A) employing B's labor services. An equally clean case would be where B owns all the physical capital and the design, and he has the right to employ another designer who can modify A's original design, while A is barred from using the design or a modification of it. Now imagine a case where the two work across a market interface, with A owning the computer and B the machine tools. Who owns the design? Who controls the amount produced of the good? (If B purchases the design from A, then presumably B. But if B acts as a subcontractor to A, then A has this control.) Who controls the ability to modify the design? (If A sells "turn-key" jigs, then this could be A; if A sells the details of the design outright, then perhaps both have this right, depending on the details

---

[10] The legal form of A's control may have important consequences for legal responsibilities, taxes, and the like and, at a second level of analysis, these considerations would enter into the calculus of transaction cost economics.

of the contract between them.) Even a very simple exchange like this one can become quite complex very quickly.

Inefficiencies in unified governance

This example suggests a question that brings to bear the final piece of theory that will be recounted from Williamson: What are the relative *inefficiencies* of unified governance? When telling the tale of figure 20.2, it was asserted that we move to unified governance when the level of specialized assets is high, presumably because the costs of consummating, monitoring, and enforcing the transaction at arms length, given the amount at risk and the relative infrequency of the transaction, become prohibitive. But if one avoids these costs through unified governance, then why not use unified governance exclusively?[11]

As our example of A and B points out, the move to unified governance doesn't avoid transactions all together; instead it changes the nature of the exchange that must be made. In place of an exchange of plans for money or finished pieces for money, we have an exchange of labor services for money. This new exchange comes with an array of transaction costs itself, and it is the *relative* costliness of the various sorts of transaction that determines which form of governance we use. Note well: We see some cases of our prototypical transaction in which B buys plans from A in the market (A is an independent industrial designer), cases where A buys pieces from B (B is a subcontractor), cases where A holds all the equipment and buys labor services from B (the typical machine shop), and cases where B holds all the equipment and buys labor input from A (automobile manufacturers who employ designers). Of course, real-world examples will usually involve more than two individuals and so will be vastly more complex than the simple example we have given, but in each case you should expect to see how the relative costs and benefits of various patterns of exchange determine which pattern of exchange is used.

So what are the costs attendant to unified governance? Williamson points to the differences in what he calls *high-powered* market incentives and *low-powered* internal incentives. That is, with a full market inter-face between A and B, B faces strong incentives to produce efficiently, to care for his lathe, and so on. There are many things that dull these

---

[11] A related question can be asked at a more macroeconomic level. As there are such things as market power and externalities in the world, we know that a market economy will not necessarily reach a Pareto-efficient outcome. Doesn't this make a centrally planned and run economy superior? What can the market do that a centralized economy cannot? What are the inefficiencies in centralization? These questions, which have answers somewhat similar to the answers we will give for unified governance of a single transaction, are known as the Lange-Lerner controversy in the literature.

incentives when A owns all the assets and employs B. Williamson's list (1985, chap. 6), which is longer and more detailed than we can give here, but a selection follows. If A buys out B's assets and employs B, then A is unable to match such strong incentives in the employment contract she gives to B. She has a difficult time monitoring the effort B expends, and she has an especially difficult time seeing *how* B expends whatever effort he does expend. For example, A may give B a piece-rate contract, which gives B strong incentives to produce parts but very weak incentives to maintain what are now A's lathe and jigs. If B has private information about how hard a particular task is, A may have a difficult time wresting that information from him. It might be imagined that any incentives the market can provide, A can provide for B as well. But there are measurement problems in this case. If B is responsible for maintaining the lathe in good condition and if his contract gives him a financial incentive to do so, the cost of inspecting the lathe must be borne by the two parties. If B's contract incorporates some measure of the profitability of the entire enterprise, B must be concerned that A will manipulate the accounting system to B's detriment. On a more humane note, if A and B form a long-term employer-employee relationship, then A may "forgive" B if certain bad outcomes occur. But this removes the hard edge of market incentives that B would face in an arms-length, market-mediated transaction.[12]

20.2. *Mathematical models of transaction cost economics*

The preceding discussion, while (I hope) clear, does not conform to the style adopted throughout the book. By now you are probably used to seeing ideas exposited with models that begin with consumers who have specific utility functions, living in a particular (highly stylized) environment, who go on to maximize their way to whatever they can get. How much of Williamson's story can be cast in such terms?[13]

---

[12] There is another side to this last point. Sociologists are usually aghast at the way economists predicate most behavior on base self-interest, and they are quick to point out that in a "good" organization workers internalize the interests of the organization and act at least in part for it. Presumably, the social forces that lead boss A to forgive and protect subordinate B also lead subordinate B to act against his own narrow interests and in favor of the interests of A. Forgiveness may be a cost of unified governance (or any form of long-term relationship), but it may accompany substantial benefits.

[13] Why should we attempt to recast Williamson's story in this fashion? The maintained hypothesis throughout this book is that formal mathematical modeling promotes comprehension and clarity of thought, and it is especially valuable for checking the internal consistency of the stories told.

Williamson locates transaction cost economics in the domain of individuals who are boundedly rational and opportunistic. After part IV (and even part III), you should have no problem with opportunism. But all the consumers we have analyzed in this book have been "rational," at least in the sense that their choice behavior has conformed to the basic models of chapters 2, 3, and (when there were dynamics) 4. How are we to model boundedly rational behavior? What does boundedly rational behavior mean?

As noted in part I, there are no generally accepted answers to these questions. There has been some movement towards developing theories of boundedly rational behavior, but nothing yet has taken center stage as the standard model. In retelling pieces of the preceding story in terms familiar from earlier parts of this book, we must rely on models of individual behavior that are rational in all the standard ways. In effect, we are pushing the theory of transaction cost economics into the domain of individuals who are unboundedly rational and opportunistic. It is important to think through how this colors the analysis and, as importantly or more so, what is missed by this.

With all this as prologue, we mention (in varying degrees of detail) a few of the pieces of the grand scheme of the previous section that have been scrutinized in more mathematical terms.

Incomplete contracts and ownership

Grossman and Hart (1986) analyze a variation on the basic story of the designer A and craftsman B. Their focus is on who should own which assets. The story runs roughly as follows: A and B must, in a two-period model, decide how much to invest in their particular assets, A in a computer system that will aid the design and B in a lathe and jigs. We let a_A and a_B be these levels of investment. The investment levels are chosen, and then further decisions q_A and q_B must be taken. The benefit to party X (X = A or B) depends on the initial decision a_X that X takes as well as the two subsequent decisions and is given by a function $V_X(a_X, q_A, q_B)$.[d]

The crucial assumptions made in the analysis are:

(1) At the outset, before the decisions a_X are taken, the two parties can negotiate over ownership of the two types of assets. This is done in a competitive market. Ownership of an asset gives its owner the right to choose q_X. So, for example, if B sells his assets to A, then in the second period A chooses both q_A and q_B.

---

[d] Grossman and Hart use a particular functional form for V_X. As we won't attempt to reproduce their analysis but only to relate the form of their story, we won't go into these details.

(2) Irrespective of who owns the assets, party X must choose a_X. Think of a_X as a maintenance decision, made in an earlier period while the assets were being used.

(3) Payments made for the exchange of ownership rights to the assets cannot be made contingent on the a_X, q_X, or the values of V_X.

(4) Binding contracts concerning the levels of the a_X cannot be written.

(5) Binding contracts concerning the levels of the q_X can be written, but only after the a_X decisions have been made. It is assumed that efficient levels of the q_X will be chosen. If each party retains ownership of his own asset, then the gains from choosing efficient levels of the q_X (over the levels of benefits obtained if the q_X are chosen noncooperatively) are split 50-50 between the two, coming from some (unmodeled) bargaining process.

   Assumptions 3, 4, and 5 drive the model and deserve comment. Assumption 4 corresponds to a standard story of moral hazard with no observability at all. This also explains why it is that the prices charged for ownership rights cannot depend on the a_X. It is further assumed that the V_X are not observable or, if observable, cannot be made the basis of an enforceable contract. (The latter possibility can arise if the levels of the V_X cannot be verified to a standard required by a court of law or some other third party who would be called in to adjudicate any disputes.) As for the q_X, the notion is that q_X comprises a lot of detail about what to do with asset X, depending on contingencies that ex ante cannot be foreseen, or that are too expensive to foresee, or that are foreseen but too expensive or (because of problems of verifiability) impossible to provide for contractually. Ex post binding contracts concerning the q_X can be made, however, since once the contingencies have been realized, a simple, single decision is taken.

   When Grossman and Hart turned to analysis, they assumed that the two individuals are well aware ex ante what levels of q_X will be chosen (depending on the pattern of ownership rights). That is, there is no uncertainty about the level of q_X in the model. Why is it infeasible to contract over the levels of the q_X in the first period, but feasible to specify these levels contractually in the second period? Grossman and Hart suggested a model in which q_X is an overall level of investment or effort, which must be directed in particular ways ex post, and one cannot specify ex ante which of the many ways investment or effort should be allocated because of an inability to foresee later contingencies. But then why not write a contract giving the overall level of investment or effort in the first period?

A consistent story is that while an enforceable contract *can* be written concerning the precise allocation of investment or effort (so much to task 1, so much to 2, and so on), one cannot write an enforceable contract on the overall level (so much effort to be distributed in a manner later to be determined). And, in the first period, a detailed contingent contract is either impossible or too expensive to write.

Because ownership confers the right to choose the q_X, different patterns of ownership yield different initial decisions concerning the a_X. If A sells her assets to B, she can anticipate that q_A and q_B will be chosen with B's interests in mind, and this will affect her choice of a_A. A similar story results if A owns the assets. And if each party owns his own asset, then the a_X decisions are made with a view towards strengthening the bargaining position of each, in the bargaining envisioned in (5). Grossman and Hart show how different parameterizations of the model lead to different patterns of ownership being optimal; in effect, they give cases where it is optimal for A to buy out B, for B to buy out A, and for the two to maintain an arms-length, market-based relationship.

This model gives a mathematical look into several of the aspects of transaction cost economics crucial to theories of the firm. The opportunism of individuals is represented by the choices of the a_X. Asset specificity is captured by the fact that each side is locked into a relationship with the other once we move past the stage of choosing the a_X. Governance ex post is determined by ownership; the contract is "filled out" in the second period according to who owns the assets. If we make a rough identity between ownership of assets, unified governance, and firms, then we have a theory that, depending on the particular circumstances, specifies what is the transactionally efficient scope of the firm or firms.

The importance of bargaining costs

Milgrom and Roberts (forthcoming) offer an important commentary on the basic scheme of transaction cost economics. Specifically, they reinforce the importance of the human factors to the story, and they suggest that emphasis in the context of market-mediated transactions should be placed on *short-run bargaining costs*. Their argument runs as follows: Imagine two parties to a transaction are fully rational (in particular, they can foresee all future contingencies and how those contingencies will be met, even if a contract doesn't specify these things) and are able to execute binding short-term contracts. Assume as well that the parties are risk neutral, so that any redistribution of wealth between them has only distributional consequences; there are no income effects.

In general, if the two parties undertake a long-term transaction and do not write (for whatever reason) a long-term contract covering all contingencies, they will have to engage in bargaining and renegotiation as events unfold. In general, bargaining can be costly; time is taken, and (although we didn't see this in the simple settings of chapter 15) in cases where parties have private information, inefficient outcomes can result. It is clear, therefore, that bargaining costs are an important part of transaction costs.

Milgrom and Roberts argue that in this context bargaining costs are the *only* part of transaction costs. Even if there is high asset specificity, much uncertainty, and any specification of frequency, if short-term bargaining costs are zero, all transaction costs will be zero; the parties will reach efficient arrangements as time unfolds. What does it mean for short-term bargaining costs to be zero? That binding contracts governing short-run actions can be made at zero cost, and these contracts always result in short-run efficient actions (holding fixed subsequent actions).

Consult Milgrom and Roberts (forthcoming) for the formal argument, but a sketch is easy to give. In the final stage of any transaction, the assumptions guarantee that an efficient arrangement will be reached. Move back to the penultimate stage. Because the two parties are farsighted, they know what arrangements will arise in the final period, and they know those arrangements will be efficient. Because they are risk neutral, any redistribution of wealth that will take place in the final round of arrangements can be "undone" at the current stage.[e] Applying the no-bargaining-costs assumption again, they achieve an efficient arrangement concerning the penultimate round of actions, and so on. They can work back to the start of the transaction, and their short-term agreements will guarantee efficient actions all the way along.

All of Milgrom and Roberts' assumptions play a role in this argument, but two deserve special highlighting. The assumption that the two parties are rational (in particular, farsighted) is crucial, and it reinforces the importance Williamson attaches to human factors. The assumption that enforceable short-term contracts can be reached is crucial. Compare the conclusion reached by Milgrom and Roberts with that reached by Grossman and Hart. Grossman and Hart had rational, farsighted individuals. But in their story, these individuals cannot sign a binding agreement concerning the initial round of decisions a_X. As both Grossman and Hart and Milgrom and Roberts noted, if the a_X could be made the subject of a

---

[e] If they discount, they would seemingly have to discount at the same rates or have available simple loan contracts between themselves so that they could take advantage of any efficient trading of wealth across time.

binding contract, then (in their setting) the ownership of the assets would be irrelevant.

Having put bargaining costs into the spotlight, Milgrom and Roberts went on to study the costs of bargaining and their sources. In so doing, they made use of the formal literature on bargaining — what we discussed in chapter 15, what we omitted (i.e., bargaining with incomplete information) — and also work on "bargaining via particular mechanisms," such as auctions. And they discussed how both asset specificity and measurement problems play a role in bargaining costs. [14]

Chapter 14 and figure 20.2

A third way we can set the discussion of the first section to mathematics is to interpret figure 20.2 using the theory of repeated play from chapter 14. We saw in chapter 14 that cooperative behavior can arise in situations of repeated interaction where each side to the transaction cooperates because each has a stake in the future sufficient to outweigh any gains that could be obtained by acting opportunistically in the short run. The theory of chapter 14 suggests the following:

(a) Each side must have a stake in a maintained relationship. Or, more accurately, if one party is at risk from opportunistic behavior by the second, then the second must be at risk in the future if he engages in opportunism. Moreover, if the short-run gains for the second party from opportunism are quite large, the current value of the long-run gains from a continued relationship must be large as well. Either the relationship must be repeated fairly frequently (so that, effectively, the discount factor is close to one), or the value of the continuing relationship must be high.

(b) It is enough that the party who puts the other party at risk repeats the transaction fairly frequently, has a substantial amount at stake in the execution of any single transaction, and has her performance observed by potential future trading partners. Then this party's behavior can be tied to her reputation for behaving in a particular way.

(c) The noisier the environment, the less well such constructions work.

(d) There are many possible "equilibria" in repeated interactions, so that definite predictions can become difficult.

Figure 20.2, at least in one respect, appears to fit well with this theory. As the frequency of the transaction is lowered, the nature of relational

---

[14] They went on to study the sources of "bargaining costs" in unified governance, to which we will come in a bit.

contracting passes from bilateral and hierarchical to trilateral. This can be explained in some cases very naturally and directly from (a) and (b) above.[15] Think, for example, in terms of the sale of securities. An individual seller of securities may sell with sufficient frequency to particular buyers (or a particular community of buyers) so that no intermediation is necessary. An example might be AT&T directly marketing its securities to its shareholders (although even here there is some intermediation). But in most cases a third party, an *exchange*, is brought into the picture; the exchange provides certain guarantees that facilitate trade. For example, in futures contracts, the exchange acts as guarantor that the contract will be made good. The exchange polices the trades that take place, monitoring the actions of professional traders, and the exchange (often) offers arbitration services when disputes arise. For this the exchange is paid some sum of money. It is the stream of those payments (or, rather, the amount by which this stream exceeds the direct costs of the service) that gives the exchange an incentive to police trades made in its name, at least as long as investors monitor the reputation of the exchange and are willing to take their business elsewhere if the exchange doesn't fulfill its part of the bargain.[16]

Another example of the applicability of (a) and (b) to the study of governance of transactions is given by Simon (1951). He considers the basic labor exchange relationship and, in particular, the fact that the employer is typically a hierarchical superior in this relationship. That is, the employer specifies what tasks the worker will undertake as those tasks arise, subject only to some general "rules" and to the worker's right to quit. Discretion is reserved largely to the employer, and so the reputational glue that holds this together (that allows the worker to trust the employer) is the general reputation of the employer.

---

[15] Other explanations can be given as well. For example, the lower the frequency, the more the cost of a specialized institution must be amortized over a single transaction, and hence the greater the incentive to move to some form of "general purpose" trilateral relationship. See Milgrom and Roberts (forthcoming) for a detailed development of this argument.

[16] Reputation is not the full story here. (1) Informational efficiency plays a role. Because many trades take place on the exchange, the exchange is able to centralize information about the traders — who is honest and who is not. Even if individual investors can obtain information about one another and deal with each other with sufficient frequency that bilateral relationships are possible, the relatively lower costs of the information for the exchange may still push the transaction from bilateral to trilateral form. (2) Securities trading is really a good deal more complex than a simple exchange between two individuals. Typically, each individual has an agent, a broker, who executes the trade for the individual. As individuals deal relatively infrequently with their brokers, and brokers deal with each other constantly, the possibility of collusion between the brokers against the interests of the individuals is quite high. Hence the exchange has a role to play in monitoring the actions of brokers.

Point (c) fits very neatly into the commentary that accompanies figure 20.2 as well. Quoting from Williamson, successful bilateral relationships are found in cases where the conditions to which parties adapt are "exogenous, germane, and easily verifiable ... and ... consequences must be confidently related thereto" (Williamson, 1985, 77). In other words, it must be clear to each party that circumstances call for an adaptation, and the nature of the required adaptation must also be clear.

Consider in this context the trilateral relationship between a publicly held firm, investors, and external auditors. The firm, to raise capital provides investors with information about its financial health. Since a good deal of moral hazard is associated with the provision of this information, a third party, an auditor, is brought in to bless the reported information (or not). These auditing firms are well paid for their services, as long as they maintain a reputation for giving honest audits. The question is, On what is this reputation pegged? Because each audit engagement is unique and because the number of decisions an audit firm must make is very large, if each audit was tailored to very specific circumstances, it would be quite difficult to decide ex post whether an audit firm was diligent and honest in what it did. Accordingly, when the quality of an audit is questioned, what is important is whether the auditing firm followed well-established guidelines (in the United States called Generally Accepted Auditing Standards) that are set by the industry, even if following those guidelines does not provide the most informative audit possible in the particular circumstance. Moreover, auditors provide very coarse signals of the information they receive. In most cases, they say only that the information provided by the firm is "basically okay" by giving an "unqualified" positive opinion. By having fixed procedures and very coarse reports, it is possible to check ex post whether the auditing firm did what it is supposed to, and so it is possible to maintain a useful reputation as an independent third party.

> It is worth noting that chapter 14 doesn't apply precisely to this story. Chapter 14 concerns simple repeated game situations where one party (or both) plays the same game over and over. In most applications, a transaction is never repeated precisely. But you shouldn't have a hard time seeing how the theory in chapter 14 adapts to cases in which the sequence of "repeated transactions" is really a sequence of similar but not precisely identical transactions. As long as one can find some rule that can be applied (in observable fashion) to the sequence of similar transactions, reputation and folk-theorem style constructions can be made to work.

While the theory of chapter 14 helps us to understand parts of figure 20.2, it does not explain all of that figure. In particular, for very high levels of asset specificity, figure 20.2 calls for unified governance. How do we explain this? (1) Perhaps it has something to do with the requirement that the value of a continued relationship must rise with increases in the short-run inducements to act opportunistically. With higher levels of asset specificity, short-run inducements can certainly be higher. (2) As assets become more specific, losses from the loss of cooperation increase. Insofar as there are noisy observables, so that relational contracting will require some periods of "noncooperation," we might expect to find a move towards unified governance as the cost of those periods increases.[f] (3) There is also intuitive appeal to the notion that "strategic risk aversion" plays a role here. Parties to a relational contract may be afraid of finding an inappropriate trading partner, of a relation gone permanently sour, or of long periods of time spent sorting out how the benefits of cooperation will be divided; higher levels of asset specificity mean an increase in the cost of such things, and thus an increase of the overall costs of a relational transaction. Some of these things can be found in chapter 14, but others play no role there; it remains to refine the theory of repeated interaction to encompass the missing effects.

Firms and reputation

Firms have no role to play in the previous subsection, but it is not difficult to provide one for them. In all the constructions of chapter 14, at least one party must be long lived. There are long-lived individuals for whom these constructions can work, but the reach of these constructions is lengthened considerably if we allow firms to carry reputations. A stylized model of the basic idea runs as follows. We imagine a sequence of pairs of individuals who play the game in figure 20.3. That is, at date t, for $t = 1, 2, \ldots$, an individual A_t plays this game against B_t. Note that the unique Nash equilibrium has B choosing x', which gives both sides a payoff of 0.

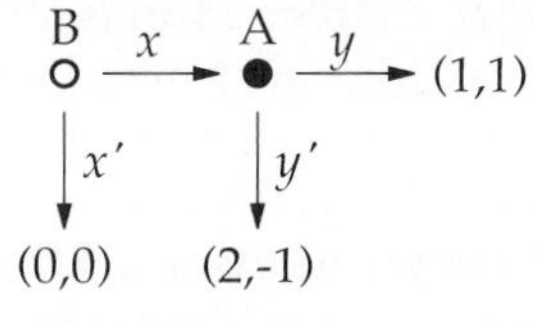

$$
\begin{array}{ccc}
\overset{\text{B}}{\circ} & \xrightarrow{\ x\ } & \overset{\text{A}}{\bullet} \xrightarrow{\ y\ } (1,1) \\
\big\downarrow x' & & \big\downarrow y' \\
(0,0) & & (2,-1)
\end{array}
$$

Figure 20.3. *An extensive form game.*
In this game, the payoff to player A is listed first and that of B is listed second.

---

[f] Note that these factors would bind relatively less strongly on the third party to a trilateral arrangement, and so we do not completely lose this form of governance for highly specific assets and low frequency.

If we had one player A playing a sequence of Bs, and if this A discounted her payoffs with a discount factor close to one, in the spirit of chapter 14 we could construct an equilibrium in which B_t always chooses action x and A chooses action y, giving both sides a payoff of 1: A chooses y because if ever she chooses y', all subsequent Bs choose x'. In effect, A maintains a reputation for choosing y.

But if each A_t plays only once, this construction will not work, and the mutually beneficial transaction x followed by y cannot be supported (owing to A_t's opportunism and inability to guarantee that she won't select y').

We can get back the reputation construction if we imagine that each A_t lives and consumes for two periods. In period t, A_t plays the game shown in figure 20.3 against B_t. In period $t+1$, A_t retires and lives off her savings. Assume that A_t's utility is given by $c_t + .95c_{t+1}$, where c_k is A_t's level of consumption of the numeraire good in period k $(k = t, t+1)$.

Suppose then that a "firm" is formed by A_1, called *Honest A, Inc.* This firm carries a reputation with the B_ts as follows: B_t is willing to trust A_t (that is, play x) if A_t owns Honest A, and no previous A_s who owned Honest A ever chose y' when trusted by B_s. That is, if some A_s ever chooses y' instead of y given the chance, and if this A_s owns Honest A, then the reputation of Honest A is irretrievably besmirched.

If the B_ts act in this fashion, each A_t has a positive incentive to purchase Honest A from A_{t-1} if the reputation of Honest A is still good. Suppose the purchase price of Honest A is 10 as long as its reputation is good. Will A_t purchase this firm from A_{t-1}? If A_t believes she can sell the firm to A_{t+1} for \$10 as long as she doesn't hurt its reputation, the answer is yes. Her choices are:

(1) Don't purchase the firm from A_{t-1}. Then B_t will choose x', and A_t will obtain 0 in each of periods t and $t+1$, for a discounted payoff of 0.[17]

(2) Purchase the firm, and then, when B_t chooses x, choose y'. This gives $2 - 10$ in period t (the payoff from the game less the purchase price) and 0 in period $t+1$ (her ownership rights are worthless, since she sullied the reputation of the firm), for a discounted payoff of -8.

(3) Purchase the firm, and then, when B_t chooses x, choose y. This gives $1 - 10$ in period t and then 10 in period $t+1$, the latter being the proceeds from selling the firm to A_{t+1}. This gives a discounted payoff of .5.

---

[17] We do not include in these computations the utility A_t derives from any endowment she might have. Since we have assumed a linear utility function, this is okay. We should assume that A_t has endowment of at least 10 in period t, so she can afford to buy Honest A from A_{t-1}.

Hence (3) is best for A_t, given the posited behavior by A_{t+1} (a willingess to buy) and B_t (a willingness to choose x). This in turn justifies the presumed strategies of A_{t+1} and B_t; we have a Nash equilibrium.

There is nothing complicated here. This is just like the reputation constructions of chapter 14, except that Honest A carries the reputation, and each owner of this "firm" is willing to preserve that reputation in order to recoup the cost of buying the reputation. If Grossman and Hart's story revolved around the notion of a firm as the owner of capital, here the firm is something less tangible; it comprises only its reputational capital. The key is that the individual who makes decisions in the name of the firm has a stake in the consequences for the firm's reputation of those decisions, obtained here by tying the decision maker's second period consumption to the capitalized value of the firm's reputation.[9]

Even by the standards of stylized models in this book, this model is extraordinarily stylized. It should certainly come as no surprise that firms and other organizations carry reputations, or even that for some firms their reputation is as valuable an asset as they have. (Public accounting firms and investment banks come to mind immediately.) These reputations enable all manner of transactions to take place that without the force of reputation would either require extraordinarily complex contracts or would become impossible. Return to the example of the "contract" between a graduate student and the department in which she studies. The contract, such as it is, specifies almost nothing except governance procedures. New students are given a handbook of requirements (subject to change more or less without notice) and instructions how to appeal to the department chairperson and/or the dean. The specific details of a student's program, advisor, financial aid, and so on, are all determined by the parties as time passes and contingencies arise, with the bulk of discretion given to the faculty of the department and sundry deans and administrators. Students can appeal capricious behavior on the part of

---

[9] We don't provide any problems at the end of this chapter, but if we did, one would be: In fact, this setting permits a few things not altogether possible in chapter 14. Suppose, for example, there is noise in the observable action of A. That is, suppose that A may intend to choose y, but there is some chance that by a slip of the hand, y' is observed instead. Can you construct an equilibrium of the following form? If some A_t is observed to choose y', then the value of the firm owned by A_t falls to zero. But A_{t+1} is then able to form a new Honest A, which starts with a fresh reputation. The value of the reputation of this firm doesn't start at 10 immediately, but it grows to 10 as long as its owners are never observed choosing y'. Can you construct an equilibrium where each A_t intends to choose y and each B_t chooses x, if the probability of "y' by mistake" is small? For which patterns in the growth of the value of Honest A is this sort of behavior sustained in an equilibrium? Must the value of Honest A's reputation fall to zero if A_t is observed choosing y'? And what happens if A_{t+1} has the ability to slip some money surreptitiously to A_t?

professors to the department chairperson and capricious behavior on the part of the department chairperson to the dean, but why would a student ever trust the dean? The student trusts in a combination of goodwill and concern for the department's and university's reputation with prospective future students. The stylized model shows how this sort of reputation works in equilibrium, at least as long as retired faculty and administrators continue to take pleasure in the distinction of their old department or university.

The question naturally arises whether reputation really adheres to the individual manager or to the firm. Common sense suggests that the answer is some of both. The stylized model shows how, in an extreme case where the manager (party A_t) is so short lived that reputation cannot adhere to her, reputation adhering to the firm can work instead. But this model, because of its simple structure, misses important pieces of this story. In particular, it may be informationally efficient for reputation to adhere to the organization and not to the individual. It is easier to keep in mind that Honda produces excellent cars than to keep in mind the names of all the engineers and mechanics who together make the cars with the Honda logo. Although more difficult to tell mathematically (because it involves a formal specification of information processing costs or some other model where consumers are not hyperrational), firms and other organizations provide an efficient means for enlisting the power of reputation in promoting transactions.

> Of course, there is a potentially substantial free-rider problem here. Engineer Yamazaki may have to work quite hard to provide his portion of the excellent design of a Honda. He bears all the costs of this effort, yet would (probably) see only a tiny dimunition in the reputation of Honda if he slacked off. So the force of Honda's reputation in keeping him hard at work is probably quite low. But this free-rider problem is met by peer-group and supervisory pressure. (If you are unhappy that there are no problems at the end of this chapter, you could try to flesh this out into a full-fledged model.)

Ex ante versus ex post incentives

Turning to Williamson's discussion of the inefficiencies of unified governance, we note two sorts of contributions.

A major piece of Williamson's discussion concerns the inability of a hierarchical superior to match market incentives because the hierarchical superior retains the ability to "reset" the terms of a contract, an ability that she will enlist in her own interests ex post. The problem is that the knowledge that this is how she will behave ex post prevents otherwise sharp-edged incentives from being put in place ex ante. The problem is an inability to commit a priori to a particular incentive scheme and/or intervention rule.

We have seen this theme (the inability to commit) in several places in the book, and we will not go into much detail here. But, to refresh your memory, recall our discussion of the ratchet effect. We imagine a principal, an agent, and a task the difficulty of which is unknown to the principal. This task must be performed twice (say), and (we suppose) the principal cannot commit to a two-period incentive scheme. If in the first period the principal learns from the agent's performance precisely how difficult the task is, then she will use this information in designing second period incentives. Hence it will be in the interests of the agent to make the task look harder than it really is in the first period. Note that the root of this problem is the principal's inability to commit to a two-period incentive contract. If the principal could commit at the outset to a compensation package (and to refrain from manipulating the accounts, intervening whenever she wishes to ex post, forgiving unlucky agents, and so on), then she can (theoretically) match high-powered market incentives.

We can take these ideas a step further with an analysis of influence costs. In a unified governance structure, the authority to make decisions is centralized, and individuals affected by these decisions will wish to influence the central authority to whatever extent is possible. If the central authority can be corrupted, attempts will be made to corrupt her. If activities intended to corrupt the central authority take time away from more productive activities, this is a cost of unified governance. These costs increase if the corruption causes the central authority to make decisions that are inefficient. Of course, corruption across a market interface is not unheard of, but the more centralized the authority, the greater will be the level of energy devoted to corrupting activities.

It might seem that this depends on a corruptable centralized authority. But even an "uncorruptable" central authority may be amenable to influence. Insofar as the central authority lacks information relevant for making decisions and looks to subordinates (or to their performances) for this information, then those subordinates will attempt to influence the central authority by manipulating this information. The central authority may well be aware of these attempts at manipulation, but the only way to stop them entirely is to shut off the flow of information, which may be far from optimal. In equilibrium, even with an uncorruptable central authority, wasteful influence activities may go on. See Holmstrom (1982), Holmstrom and Ricart i Costa (1986), Milgrom and Roberts (1988), and Tirole (1986) for formal models.

20.3. Bibliographic notes

Repeated reference has been made to Williamson (1985) as the basic source of transaction cost economics; this is an important summary statement of the subject that should be read by all. While Williamson's contributions have been many and important (not the least of which is the unified treatment of the subject in his book), the subject really originates with Coase (1937). Chandler (1977) and Klein, Crawford, and Alchian (1978) provide other important perspectives.

As for the more mathematical analyses of section 20.2, besides the already referenced Grossman and Hart (1986), Holmstrom (1982), Holmstrom and Ricart i Costa (1986), Milgrom and Roberts (1988, forthcoming), Simon (1951), and Tirole (1986), see Kreps (forthcoming) for the notion of a firm as the carrier of a reputation that passes from one generation of owners to the next and Wilson (1983) on the role and nature of reputation in auditing. For a survey of other work along these lines, see Holmstrom and Tirole (1989).

References

Chandler, A. 1977. *The Visible Hand*. Cambridge, Mass.: Harvard University Press.

Coase, R. 1937. "The Nature of the Firm." *Economica* n.s. 4:386–405..

Grandmont, J.-M., ed. 1988. *Temporary Equilibrium*. Boston: Academic Press.

Grossman, S., and O. Hart. 1986. "The Costs and Benefits of Ownership: A Theory of Vertical and Lateral Integration." *Journal of Political Economy* 94:691–719.

Holmstrom, B. 1982. "Managerial Incentive Problems — A Dynamic Perspective." In *Essays in Economics and Management in Honor of Lars Wahlbeck*. Helsinki: Swedish School of Economics.

Holmstrom, B., and J. Ricart i Costa. 1986. "Managerial Incentives and Capital Management." *Quarterly Journal of Economics* 101:835–60.

Holmstrom, B., and J. Tirole. 1989. "The Theory of the Firm." In *Handbook of Industrial Organization*, R. Schmalensee and R. Willig, eds. Amsterdam: North Holland.

Klein, B., R. Crawford, and A. Alchian. 1978. "Vertical Integration, Appropriable Rents, and the Competitive Contracting Process." *Journal of Law and Economics* 21:297–326.

Kreps, D. Forthcoming. "Corporate Culture and Economic Theory." In *Positive Perspectives on Political Economy*, J. Alt and K. Shepsle, eds. Cambridge: Cambridge University Press.

Marshak, J., and R. Radner. 1972. *The Theory of Teams.* New Haven, Conn.: Yale University Press.

Milgrom, P., and J. Roberts. 1988. "An Economic Approach to Influence Activities in Organizations." *American Journal of Sociology* 94:S154–79.

————. Forthcoming. "Bargaining Costs, Influence Costs, and the Organization of Economic Activity." In *Positive Perspectives on Political Economy*, J. Alt and K. Shepsle, eds. Cambridge: Cambridge University Press.

Simon, H. 1951. "A Formal Model of the Employment Relationship." *Econometrica* 19:293–305.

Tirole, J. 1986. "Hierarchies and Bureaucracies." *Journal of Law, Economics, and Organization* 2:181–214.

Williamson, O. 1985. *The Economic Institutions of Capitalism.* New York: Free Press.

Wilson, R. 1983. "Auditing: Perspectives from Multi-Person Decision Theory." *Accounting Review* 58:305–18.

postscript

As we compare transaction cost economics in section 20.1 with the more mathematical attempts at theorizing related in section 20.2, several pieces missing from the mathematical analysis spring to mind:

(1) Williamson (1985) stresses bounded rationality and, especially, the inability of individuals to foresee all future contingencies and how they will be met. The argument of Milgrom and Roberts (forthcoming) shows just how important this can be.

(2) We rely on folk-theorem constructions to motivate relational contracting. But as we saw in chapter 14 such constructions alone do not give particularly sharp predictions. There are many plausible equilibria in repeated games situations, and the theory doesn't give us much of a handle on which will be adopted. And if we cannot pin down which equilibrium will be adopted (or, rather, if we cannot think why some specific equilibrium will be adopted by the participants), then there is no particular reason to restrict attention to equilibrium outcomes. We certainly have a problem if we try to analyze how the equilibrium will shift with small changes in the environment. (In fact, Nelson and Winter [1982] have suggested that small changes in the environment will be met with no change at all in the equilibrium. Similar predictions are made in the literature of sociology and social psychology. See, for example, Hannan and Freeman [1984] and Stinchcombe [1965])

(3) A similar problem confronts us if we think of parties bargaining (in the short run) in a situation where each has a degree of monopoly power over the other. We saw in chapter 14 that one can get quite specific predictions from bargaining models with certain types of bargaining institutions, but the predictions seemed intuitively to be too sharp, intuition that is verified in experiments. Individuals may bargain to consistent and definite outcomes in certain situations, but the extant formal theory doesn't seem to be of much use in predicting what those outcomes will be or how they will change with small changes in the environment.

(4) Earlier in the book, we complained that a weakness of game theory was that it took institutions (the rules of the game) as given exogenously, without explaining where the institutions come from. We can view transaction cost economics as giving us a bit of a lead on this, insofar as we

maintain the hypothesis that institutions will be created with a general
view toward minimizing transaction costs (or, more precisely, with a view
towards maximizing the net benefits of transactions). But important pieces
of transaction cost economics depend on the society in which the transaction is embedded — on the framework of laws and customs, in particular.

In various places in this book, I have advanced the notion that the
solution to the problem of multiple equilibria, pointed to in (3) and (4),
lies in the individual's strategic expectations and social and normative
environment. This thought is certainly not original to me; the heart of
Schelling (1980) is predicated on this; it is evident from much of the experimental work in bargaining, such as Roth and Schoumaker (1983)[1]; and
it can be found in the literature of sociology (Granovetter, 1985; Parsons,
1954). But when one approaches the problem of strategic expectations
with the choice-theoretic orientation of traditional microeconomics, a barrier is hit: Many things *can* be an equilibrium, if we arrange everyone's a
priori expectations correctly. There are no limits to the individual's processing power. There are no theoretical reasons to expect players to pick
a simple equilibrium. (We don't even have a generally accepted formal
definition of the term "simple.") For example, we can imagine repeated
game equilibria in which play at date n depends on the n^n th digit of an
octal expansion of π; players in our models can anticipate that this is how
their fellow players will behave, and then they respond in kind.

To my mind, all the items listed above are tied together, and their resolution will come only with better models of boundedly rational choice; in
particular, boundedly rational choice in dynamic settings, where individuals do not have the incredible powers of foresight that they are granted in
the standard models. Instead, individuals learn (or think they do) somewhat imperfectly from past experience about what will happen in the
future. It is this retrospection that forms strategic expectations, and, moreover, it is experiences from the past that (imperfectly) guide the evolution
of institutions.

The game of chess provides an interesting example. Played by the sort
of individuals who populate the economies of this book, a chess match
would be a boring affair; the players would come on stage, look at each
other, and agree to whatever (forced) outcome the game happens to have.
Of course, because of the complexity of the game, no one knows what
outcome is forced. And so players are guided by experience and (very
occasionally) by experimentation: This or that variation or gambit seems

---

[1] See also Roth (1985).

to work in this or that way, where the evidence is that this is how things have worked in the past. But no player can be completely sure how a particular move will work, and it is especially exciting when grandmasters suddenly return in a match to "well-known" variations and try to find advantage where none is thought to exist.

From the point of view of this book, chess is a dangerous example to mention. Only the simplest of endgame situations fit nicely into the sort of equilibrium analysis we have used here. If the economic environment is as continuously complex as chess, then we would seem to have wasted a lot of time studying equilibrium techniques. But (of course) the implicit assertion is that economic situations are not in all respects so complex that equilibrium analysis is irrelevant. Pieces of the economic environment, parts of the greater "game" each economic actor plays, are amenable to the form of analysis we have used. The problem comes in applying the forms of analysis we have used for larger chunks of the game each actor faces; especially chunks that involve long stretches of time and much uncertainty. Moreover, we may have a good intuitive feel for when equilibrium analysis is useful (on small pieces), but our feel depends on there being (roughly) common strategic expectations about how to behave in a particular situation, and we have much less handle on how to model where those strategic expectations come from or how they change. The techniques we have are useful in some contexts, but they are potentially dangerous in others, and even when they are useful, we don't have the complete story why. It remains to develop the tools necessary for the bigger picture and to place the smaller picture properly in that bigger picture.

These observations are also hardly original to me. A long list of economists and social scientists have expressed this view both earlier and with greater eloquence than I. The difficulty, also generally recognized, is in finding acceptable tools, which I take to be models of boundedly rational behavior (and especially models that stress retrospection).

There has recently been an upsurge in interest in formal models of bounded rationality, but since no one of the models advanced is yet emerging as a "winner," I will not go into details.[2] So I close simply, with the cautions expressed above and with the hope that in subsequent editions of this book (if any appear), this postscript will be gone, and the material on dynamic choice, game theory, and firms and other institutions will look quite different and will be more satisfactory.

---

[2] Since I have my own entries in the sweepstakes, I am probably too biased to give a good survey anyway.

References

Granovetter, M. 1985. "Economic Action and Social Structure: A Theory of Embeddedness." *American Journal of Sociology* 91:481-510.

Hannan, M., and J. Freeman. 1984. "Structural Inertia and Organizational Change." *American Sociological Review* 49:194-64.

Milgrom, P., and J. Roberts. Forthcoming. "Bargaining Costs, Influence Costs, and the Organization of Economic Activity." In *Positive Perspectives on Political Economy*, J. Alt and K. Shepsle, eds. Cambridge: Cambridge University Press.

Nelson, R., and S. Winter. 1982. *An Evolutionary Theory of Economic Change.* Cambridge, Mass.: Belknap/Harvard University Press.

Parsons, T. 1954. *Essays in Sociological Theory.* Glencoe, Ill.: Free Press.

Schelling, T. 1980. *The Strategy of Conflict,* 2d ed.. Cambridge, Mass.: Harvard University Press.

Stinchcombe, A. 1965. "Social Structure and Organizations." In *Handbook of Organizations*, J. March, ed., 153-93. Chicago: Rand McNally.

Roth, A. 1985. "Toward a Focal-point Theory of Bargaining." In *Game-theoretic Models of Bargaining*, A. Roth, ed., 259-68. Cambridge: Cambridge University Press.

Roth, A., and F. Schoumaker. 1983. "Expectations and Reputations in Bargaining: An Experimental Study." *American Economic Review* 73:362-72.

Williamson, O. 1985. *The Economic Institutions of Capitalism.* New York: Free Press.

appendix one

Constrained optimization

The aim of this appendix is to give you a bare working knowledge of how to solve problems of the form

$$\text{maximize } f(x)$$

$$\text{subject to } g_i(x) \le c_i \text{ for } i = 1, \ldots, n$$

for functions $f, g_1, g_2, \ldots, g_n$ whose domain is R^k for some integer k and whose range is R, and for constants $c_1, c_2, \ldots, c_n$. The mathematical theory of optimization with inequality constraints concerns all the things discussed here, and this discussion won't get you within shouting distance of that theory. So while this appendix will tell you enough to make it through the applications in the book, you should engage in further rigorous study of this material; two recommendations are made at the end of the appendix.

We'll proceed as follows. First, in cookbook fashion, the recipe for finding solutions to this sort of problem will be given. Then an example will be worked to illustrate the recipe. And then, by looking at the simplest possible example we'll try to give some intuition for the recipe.

A1.1. A recipe for solving problems

We want to solve

$$\text{maximize } f(x)$$

$$\text{subject to } g_i(x) \le c_i \text{ for } i = 1, \ldots, n.$$

Here, mechanically, is what to do.

Step 1. *Form the Lagrangian.*

For each of the n constraints, create a *multiplier* — this is a real variable. The multiplier for the constraint $g_i(x) \leq c_i$ will be denoted by λ_i. Then the Lagrangian is the function

$$f(x) - \sum_{i=1}^{n} \lambda_i g_i(x).$$

(In some books the term for the ith constraint is $\lambda_i(g_i(x) - c_i)$. It will make no difference for the form of the recipe that I'm giving you here.) This should be thought of as a function of $k + n$ variables, namely the k components of x and the n λs. We'll write $L(x, \lambda)$ for this function, where λ should be thought of as the vector $(\lambda_1, \ldots, \lambda_n)$.

Step 2. Write out the first-order conditions for the x_js.

The first-order condition for the variable x_j $(j = 1, \ldots, k)$ is that $\partial L / \partial x_j = 0$, or, expanded,

$$\frac{\partial f}{\partial x_j} - \sum_{i=1}^{n} \lambda_i \frac{\partial g_i}{\partial x_j} = 0.$$

Step 3. Write the n constraints.

Not much to do here: The ith constraint is

$$g_i(x) \leq c_i.$$

Step 4. Write the inequality constraints for the multipliers.

This is purely according to recipe; the multipliers must all be nonnegative, or

$$\lambda_i \geq 0.$$

Step 5. Write the complementary slackness conditions.

There are n of these — one for each constraint. The ith complementary slackness condition is that

$$\lambda_i(c_i - g_i(x)) = 0.$$

Stare at this one for a moment. In step 3 we required that $g_i(x) \leq c_i$, or $c_i - g_i(x) \geq 0$. In step 4 we required that $\lambda_i \geq 0$. Hence the product $\lambda_i(c_i - g_i(x))$ is nonnegative. Now, in this step, we require in addition that the product be zero. That is, we require that if the ith constraint does not bind (that is, if $c_i > g_i(x)$), the ith multiplier must be zero. And if the ith multiplier is positive, the ith constraint must be an equality (that is, the ith constraint must bind). Note that we don't preclude the possibility that the multiplier is zero and also that the ith constraint binds; both terms in the product could be zero.

Step 6. *Mix all the above ingredients.*

Look for a solution in x and λ to the first-order conditions, the two types of inequality constraints, and the complementary slackness conditions. When and if you find one, it is the solution to your problem.

That's it. That is the recipe for finding the solution to constrained optimization problems. For reasons alluded to below (that are properly explained in good books on optimization and nonlinear programming), this recipe will produce a solution to most of the constrained optimization problems in this book. In following this recipe, it is crucial that you get the "signs" right; this recipe works: (a) if the problem is a maximization problem; (b) if the constraints are stated in the form of $g_i(x) \leq c_i$; (c) you are careful to write the Lagrangian precisely as above (note the minus sign in front of the sum term); and (d) you remember that the multipliers must be nonnegative.

How do you make the recipe work in variations? If you are asked to minimize $f(x)$, then that is the same as maximizing $-f(x)$. If you are asked to satisfy a constraint $g_i(x) \geq c_i$, rewrite it as $-g_i(x) \leq -c_i$. If you are asked to satisfy an equality constraint $g_i(x) = c_i$, write it as two constraints $g_i(x) \leq c_i$, and $g_i(x) \geq c_i$, and then you'll have two multipliers for these two constraints. Once you get used to adapting this basic recipe to these sorts of variations, you'll see how to shortcut these steps. For example, you can handle equality constraints with a single multiplier if you don't constrain that multiplier to be nonnegative and if you replace the corresponding complementary slackness condition with the condition that the constraint must hold as an equality. But until you are used to such variations the basic recipe can be adapted, as long as you're careful about it.

A1.2. *The recipe at work: An example*

That is a pretty amazing recipe. It will work, and in just a bit I'll try to explain what it is doing and why it will work, but first let's do an example and see it in action.

A consumer consumes two commodities, wheat and candy. If w is the amount of wheat this individual consumes and c is the amount of candy (in some units that are well specified and that we won't bother with), then the consumer's utility is given by the utility function $u(w, c) = 3 \log(w) + 2 \log(c + 2)$. The consumer seeks to maximize the utility he gets from his consumption of wheat and candy, subject to four constraints. The amounts of wheat and candy consumed must both be nonnegative. The consumer has \$10 to spend, and the price of wheat and the price of candy are each \$1 per unit. A unit of wheat contains 150 calories and a unit of candy 200 calories, and the consumer is constrained to eat no more than 1550 calories.

Mathematically, the consumer's problem is to pick w and c to solve the following problem:

$$\max 3 \log(w) + 2 \log(2 + c)$$

$$\text{subject to } c \geq 0$$
$$w \geq 0$$
$$w + c \leq 10, \text{ and}$$
$$150w + 200c \leq 1550.$$

(This mathematical formulation should be obvious to you. But in case it is not: The third constraint is the budget constraint, and the fourth is the calorie constraint.)

Now to apply the recipe from the cookbook, we rewrite the first two constraints in the form needed for our recipe: $-w \leq 0$ and $-c \leq 0$. Then we

1. *Form the Lagrangian.*

I'll use μ_w for the multiplier on the constraint $-w \leq 0$, μ_c for $-c \leq 0$, λ for $w + c \leq 10$, and ν for $150w + 200c \leq 1550$, so the Lagrangian is

$$3 \log(w) + 2 \log(2 + c) - \lambda(w + c) - \nu(150w + 200c) + \mu_w w + \mu_c c.$$

(Note that the last term is $-\mu_c(-c)$, which comes to $\mu_c c$.)

2. *Write the first-order conditions for w and c.*

They are

$$\frac{3}{w} - \lambda - 150\nu + \mu_w = 0, \text{ and}$$

$$\frac{2}{2 + c} - \lambda - 200\nu + \mu_c = 0.$$

3. *Write the four constraints.*

We've already done this, so I won't repeat it here.

4. *Constrain all the multipliers to be nonnegative.*

$$\lambda \geq 0, \nu \geq 0, \mu_w \geq 0, \text{ and } \mu_c \geq 0.$$

5. *Write the four complementary slackness conditions.*

These are

$$\mu_w w = 0, \mu_c c = 0, \lambda(10 - w - c) = 0, \text{ and } \nu(1550 - 150w - 200c) = 0.$$

6. *Look for a solution (in w, c, and the four multipliers) to all the equations and inequalities above.*

The way this is done, typically, is by trial and error, working with the complementary slackness conditions (hereafter, CSCs). What the CSCs tell you is that either one thing or another *equals* zero. For example, $\mu_w w = 0$ means that either μ_w or w is zero. Could it be w? If $w = 0$, then the first of the first-order conditions won't be solved, since that has a $3/w$ in it. So μ_w will have to be zero, and we can disregard it in all that follows.

Next, what about $\mu_c c = 0$? Is it possible that $c = 0$? If this happens, then the second first-order condition reads $1 - \lambda - 200\nu + \mu_c = 0$. So either

$\lambda > 0$ or $\nu > 0$ or both. (Otherwise, the left-hand side of the equation just given will be at least 1; remember that multipliers are always nonnegative in this recipe.) Now by complementary slackness, the only way that λ can be positive is if $w + c = 10$, and since we're hypothesizing that $c = 0$, this will mean $w = 10$. That's not bad, since then the diet constraint is met easily: $150 \cdot 10 + 200 \cdot 0 < 1550$. But then ν will have to be zero. (Why? complementary slackness again.) And then the FOCs (first-order conditions), with $w = 10$ and $c = 0$ inserted, will read

$$.3 - \lambda = 0 \text{ and } 1 - \lambda + \mu_c = 0.$$

The first tells us that $\lambda = .3$. But then the second won't work, because μ_c will have to be $-.7$, and negative multipliers aren't allowed. So (summing up what we know so far), if $c = 0$, then λ can't be positive. But then ν will have to be positive (if $c = 0$), and that is even worse; complementary slackness says that the only way $\nu > 0$ is if $150w + 200c = 1550$, and this together with $c = 0$ gives $w = 31/3 > 10$, and the budget constraint is violated. So, we conclude $c = 0$ won't be a solution and $\mu_c = 0$ will have to hold.

Now look again at the first FOC: $3/w - \lambda - 150\nu = 0$. I've taken the liberty of getting rid of the μ_w, since we know there won't be a solution with $\mu_w \neq 0$. Since $3/w > 0$ for any positive w, one or both of λ and ν must be positive. (A similar conclusion would have emerged if we had looked at the second FOC.) So we have three cases left to try: $\lambda > 0$ (alone), $\nu > 0$ (alone), or both. Take $\lambda > 0$ and $\nu = 0$ first. Then (complementary slackness, one more time) $w + c = 10$. The FOCs become $3/w - \lambda = 0$ and $2/(2 + c) - \lambda = 0$. That is three equations in three unknowns, and we can solve $\lambda = 3/w = 3/(10 - c)$, which substituted into the second FOC is $2/(2 + c) = 3/(10 - c)$, or $(2 + c)/2 = (10 - c)/3$, or $3(2 + c) = 2(10 - c)$, or $6 + 3c = 20 - 2c$, or $5c = 14$, or $c = 14/5$, which then gives $w = 10 - 14/5 = 36/5$, and (if anyone cares) $\lambda = 15/36 = 5/12$.

Bingo! We have an answer! Or do we? The FOCs are solved. The multipliers are nonnegative. The CSCs hold. But we have to go back and check the original constraints. And, when we look at the calorie constraint ... disaster: $(36/5)(150) + (14/5)(200) = 1640$. Oh well.

Let me try $\lambda = 0$ and $\nu > 0$ next. Then by the CSC, $150w + 200c = 1550$. In addition, the FOCs now read $3/w - 150\nu = 0$ and $2/(2 + c) - 200\nu = 0$. That is three equations in three unknowns, and we can solve. First write the two FOCs as $3/w = 150\nu$ and $2/(2 + c) = 200\nu$. Then we can eliminate ν, since $3/(150w) = \nu = 2/(200(2 + c))$. Rewrite this equation as $150w/3 = 200(2 + c)/2$, or $50w = 200 + 100c$. Multiply both sides by 3, to get $150w = 600 + 300c$, and then use this and the first equation to eliminate w, or $600 + 300c + 200c = 1550$, or $c = 950/500 = 1.9$. This gives $w = 4 + 3.8 = 7.8$. Which is nice, because this means this solution meets the budget constraint. It hits the calorie constraint on the nose (since it was designed to do so). It solves the FOCs (if we figure out what ν must be) and the CSCs. But we still need to check that the value of ν that comes out of the FOCs is nonnegative. And it is: $\nu = 1/(50w) = 1/390 = .00256410\ldots$. Let me summarize this solution:

$$w = 7.8, c = 1.9, \nu = .00256410\ldots,$$

with $\lambda = \mu_w = \mu_c = 0$.

There is actually one more thing to try, namely $\lambda > 0$ and $\nu > 0$. I'll leave it to you to show that this doesn't work with a few hints. First, if both multipliers are to be positive, then complementary slackness says that both constraints must be satisfied with equality, or $w + c = 10$ and $150w + 200c = 1550$. That is two equations in two unknowns, and you can solve for w and c directly. Then with these two values for w and c, the two FOCs become two equations in two unknowns, those unknowns being λ and ν. And you can solve those. And when you do, one of the two multipliers will turn out to be negative — no solution there. (For those readers who have seen this all before and are reading along only to review this, you know that the solution lies where the calorie constraint and not the budget constraint binds. So you should be able to tell before doing the algebra which of the two multipliers will turn out to be negative at the point where both constraints bind.)

We've solved the problem, and in a moment I'll try to give you some intuition about just why this recipe works. But before doing so, I want to make two comments about the problem. First, if we had used a little common sense, we could have saved a bit of work. This is a very typical consumer budgeting problem, with the not-so-typical addition of a calorie constraint. Nonetheless, we can draw the shape of the feasible set of wheat-candy pairs as in figure A1.

The line b-b is the budget constraint line, and c-c is the calorie constraint line, so the shaded quadrilateral is the set of feasible consumption pairs. Now this consumer is locally insatiable; his utility increases if we increase either his wheat consumption or his candy consumption or both, so the only possible places an answer could be found would be at one of the points marked x, y, and z, or on the line segment xy, or the segment yz. Each of these corresponds to a particular set of binding constraints, and

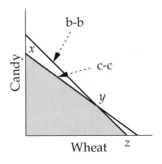

Figure A1. The feasible set of wheat-candy pairs in the example.

so a particular set of (possibly) nonnegative multipliers, according to complementary slackness. In this particular case, the picture won't cut down a lot on the algebra needed to find the solution, but in other applications, knowing how to draw this sort of figure and relate it to sets of binding constraints (and nonnegative multipliers) can be a substantial help. (Imagine, for example, that I added a third constraint on the amount of cholesterol that the consumer can take in. Then knowing which pairs of constraints can simultaneously bind can be a big help.)

Second, one thing we didn't do is compute the consumer's utility at the optimal solution given above. It is

$$3 \log(7.8) + 2 \log(2 + 1.9) = 8.88432431\ldots$$

Now let me suppose that this particular consumer, having been something of a success at his diet, is allowed by his doctor to increase his caloric intake by one calorie to 1,551 per day. If we go back and solve the problem, we find that the new optimal levels of wheat and candy are $c = 951/500 = 1.902$ and $w = 1951/250 = 7.804$. This, in turn, gives him utility $3 \log(7.804) + 2 \log(2 + 1.902) = 8.88688776\ldots$. So the additional utility that he gets from one extra calorie is $.00256345\ldots$, or, to the third significant decimal place, *the value of the multiplier ν*. An amazing coincidence? No — read on.

A1.3. Intuition

The intuition behind this recipe is most easily communicated in the special case where $k = 1$; that is, where the vector x is one-dimensional. Of course, this special case hides some of the subtleties. But if you see why things work in this special case, then it shouldn't be too hard to imagine that it will work in general — the principles are exactly the same — and you should be able to consult a book on optimization and nonlinear programming to see this done more carefully and in greater generality.

Moreover, I'm going to make a number of assumptions that in total mean that the problem we're trying to solve is "well behaved." To be precise, I'm going to assume that the problem we're trying to solve is

$$\max f(x) \text{ subject to } g_1(x) \le c_1 \text{ and } g_2(x) \le c_2.$$

I'm going to assume throughout that the three functions given are differentiable everywhere, that the set of x satisfying the two constraints is a finite union of disjoint intervals, that there is no point x at which both constraints bind simultaneously, and that if $g_i(x) = c_i$ at some point x, then the derivative of g_i at this point is either strictly positive or strictly negative. (If you are reviewing this material after encountering it previously, you may recognize that I have just assumed the great-granddaddy of all constraint qualifications.)

A review of unconstrained optimization

But before we take on this problem in constrained optimization, we review unconstrained optimization. Suppose that the problem was to maximize $f(x)$ without any constraints at all. Then (this is the part you're supposed to know) you find the optimum by setting the derivative of f to zero. This is called the *first-order condition*, and it is a necessary condition for finding a maximum value of f. Why? Because if at a point x^0 the derivative of f is positive, then by increasing x a bit from x^0 you'll get a bigger value of f. And if the derivative of f is negative at x^0, then f gets bigger if you decrease x a bit from x^0.

You may also recall that finding all the points where $f' = 0$ generates all candidates for the optimum, but there is generally no guarantee that any solution of this FOC is even locally a maximum. These solutions, called *critical points*, could be minima. Or they could be points like the point 0 in the function x^3, which are neither local minima nor maxima. To know that we have a local maximum, we check the second-order condition: If f is twice continuously differentiable and $f'' < 0$ at a point where $f' = 0$, then that point is a local maximum. (Why? If you know how to create Taylor's series expansions, you should be able to see why the condition $f'' < 0$ is sufficient for a local maximum. Note that $f'' \le 0$ is necessary for this, but that if $f'' = 0$, we need to look at higher order derivatives, assuming f has them.)

And even if we have a local maximum, there is no guarantee in general that it is a global max. This is, however, guaranteed if f is concave. Then any local maximum is a global maximum. Why? Suppose the function f is concave. That is, $f(ax + (1-a)y) \geq af(x) + (1-a)f(y)$ for all x, y and $0 \leq a \leq 1$. Then if x isn't a global max, there is some value y with $f(y) > f(x)$. But then $f(ax + (1-a)y) \geq af(x) + (1-a)f(y) > f(x)$ for all a greater than zero and less than one. But this says that x isn't a local max, since for a arbitrarily close to (and less than) one, $ax + (1-a)y$ is arbitrarily close to x. Moreover, if f is concave, any solution of $f' = 0$ is automatically a local and hence a global max. (If you never knew this before, just take my word for it.) So if f is concave, we know that satisfaction of the FOC is necessary and sufficient for a global maximum.

Drawing pictures

Now back to our simple example of constrained optimization: maximize $f(x)$ subject to $g_1(x) \leq c_1$ and $g_2(x) \leq c_2$. Recall that we assumed that the set of x satisfying the two constraints is a finite union of disjoint intervals. In particular, assume that the set of x satisfying the two constraints is a union of three intervals, the middle one of which we will call I. That is, the feasible set is like the shaded region in figure A2. Now what sort of conditions must hold at some point x^* in the interval I, if x^* is to be a candidate solution for the maximizing value of x? (The fact that I is the middle of the three intervals is completely irrelevant to what follows.)

Consider first a case where x^* is in the interior of I, as in figure A3(a). Then, just as in the case of unconstrained maximization, it had better be that $f'(x^*) = 0$. Why? Because at such an x^*, we can move up a bit and

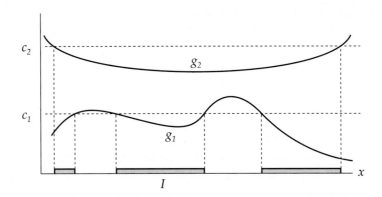

Figure A2. The feasible set.

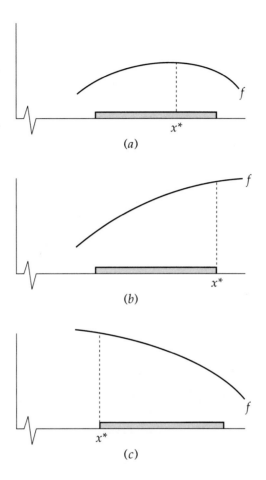

Figure A3. Possible locations of the optimal solution.
In (a), the solution, x^* is in the interior of a feasible interval. In (b), it is
at a right-hand endpoint, and in (c) it is at a left-hand endpoint.

down a bit and not violate either constraint (that is, stay inside of I). This
means that if x^* is going to be optimal, it has to be as good as values just
above and just below it, and, as before, this implies that f cannot have a
strictly positive or negative derivative at x^*.

Now suppose that x^* is up against the right-hand side of I, as in
figure A3(b). Now x^* could be the optimal value of x even if $f'(x^*) > 0$;

we can increase the value of f by moving up a bit further, but this will violate one of the constraints.

And in figure A3(c) we see the other "boundary" possibility. If x^* is up against the left-hand side of the interval I, then $f'(x^*)$ could be negative and still x^* is a candidate for the optimum.

The FOCs, the CSCs, and the preceding pictures

Now we relate these three pictures to the FOCs and the CSCs. Let λ_i be the multiplier on the constraint $g_i(x) \leq c_i$ for $i = 1, 2$. Then the Lagrangian is $f(x) - \lambda_1 g_1(x) - \lambda_2 g_2(x)$, and the FOC is

$$f'(x) - \lambda_1 g_1'(x) - \lambda_2 g_2'(x) = 0.$$

Case a. Suppose we find a solution x^* to the FOC, the CSCs (and the constraints, including the nonnegativity constraints on the multipliers), such that neither constraint binds at x^*. That is, x^* is in the interior of an interval such as I, as in figure A3(a). Since x^* is in the interior of I, the CSCs mandate that $\lambda_1 = \lambda_2 = 0$, and the FOC will read that $f'(x^*) = 0$. Precisely what we said we'd want in such a case.

Case b. Suppose that x^* is a solution to all the equations and constraints, the first constraint binds at x^* (and the second is slack; recall our assumptions), and $g_1'(x^*) > 0$. Then x^* must be on the right-hand side of an interval such as I, as in figure A3(b). Why? Because since $g_1'(x^*) > 0$, increasing a bit past x^* will cause the constraint $g_1(x) \leq c_1$ to be violated, while decreasing a bit will cause this constraint to go slack (and since the other constraint is slack by assumption, it won't be a problem, for small decreases in x, at least). Now the CSC allows λ_1 to be nonnegative; $\lambda_2 = 0$ must hold, however. Hence the FOC is now

$$f'(x^*) - \lambda_1 g_1'(x^*) = 0.$$

Since λ_1 is constrained to be nonnegative and $g_1'(x^*) > 0$ by assumption, the FOC reads that $f'(x^*) \geq 0$, which is precisely what we want for a candidate solution at the right-hand side of an interval; cf. figure A3(b).

Case c. Suppose the first constraint binds at x^*, the second is slack, and $g_1'(x^*) < 0$. Then by logic just as above, x^* will have to be on the left-hand side of an interval like I, complementary slackness will say that the FOC simplifies to $f'(x^*) - \lambda_1 g_1'(x^*) = 0$, and since $\lambda_1 \geq 0$ and $g_1'(x^*) < 0$, we have that $f'(x^*) \leq 0$, or just what we want for figure A3(c).

A few words about the coincidence in the example

About that coincidence, notice that in case b, in the solution to the
FOC we'll find that $\lambda_1 = f'(x^*)/g'_1(x^*)$. Now suppose we increase the
right-hand side of the constraint $g_1(x) \leq c_1$ by just a bit — say, to $c_1 + \epsilon$.
This is going to lengthen the interval I by a bit; the interval gets longer by
approximately $\epsilon/g'_1(x^*)$. A picture may help you see this. In figure A4, we
have a more detailed look at the situation in case b. On the bottom set of
axes we've plotted g_1, and you'll see that the right-hand side of the interval
I is determined by the solution of $g_1(x) = c_1$. When we increase c_1 by ϵ,
we can push over the right-hand side, and to a first-order approximation,
the right-hand side moves up by $\epsilon/g'_1(x^*)$. But then on the top set of axes,
we see that loosening the constraint by this amount allows the function f
to rise a bit more; it rises by approximately the amount $f'(x^*) \times (\epsilon/g'_1(x^*))$,
which is $\lambda_1\epsilon$. That is, the rate of increase in the objective function value
at our "candidate solution" per unit increase in the right-hand side of

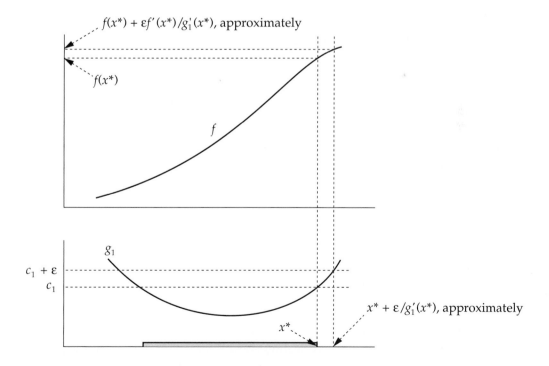

Figure A4. Explaining the coincidence.

the binding constraint is precisely the value of the multiplier on that constraint. This isn't special to case b; you could draw a similar picture for case c. (It might be a useful exercise to do so.) And this isn't anything special to the case of one dimension either, as long as the problem you're looking at is well behaved.

Some general comments

All this talk proves nothing. It is meant to indicate how the CSCs work — by modifying the FOCs in the "natural" way when you are at a point that is up against a constraint. The pictures are harder to draw when you move from one-dimensional to multidimensional problems, and I won't try to draw them here, but the same basic principles apply; complementary slackness says that a multiplier can be strictly positive only when a constraint binds, and then that multiplier is used to allow the objective function f to increase in directions that owing to the binding constraint(s) are infeasible.

Finally, you'll note that everything discussed in this section on intuition (after the review of unconstrained optimization) was about producing candidate solutions. Just as in unconstrained optimization, you might wonder what guarantee you have that a solution to all the equations and inequalities is really globally (or even locally) optimal. Accompanying theory about things analogous to the second-order conditions in unconstrained optimization gives you sufficient conditions for a candidate solution to be locally optimal. From this I happily spare you. And a theory analogous to the result in unconstrained optimization about concave f ensures that any candidate solution is in fact globally optimal. That theory is actually fairly simple, but I'll spare you that as well. However, I will assure you that for purposes of the problems in this book, at least until we get to oligopoly, any candidate solution is in fact a global optimum. And I'll even tell you how to watch for the exceptions in general: Watch for problems where the objective function f is not concave and/or the set of solutions of the constraints is not convex.

A1.4. Bibliographic notes

The cookbook recipe and very brief intuitive remarks presented here are certainly no substitution for learning properly about constrained optimization. Because constrained optimization plays such an important role in economic theory, the serious student of economics should study (either independently or in a course on mathematical methods) this subject. At a minimum, you should know about the FOCs and CSCs as necessary conditions for an optimum and so-called *constraint qualifications, second-order conditions*, sufficiency of the FOCs and CSCs in *convex problems*, and problems with quasi-convex or -concave objective functions. Any number of books provide treatments of this material; Mangasarian (1969) covers much of the nuts and bolts, although this book doesn't explain why the multipliers are partial derivatives of the value function. Luenberger (1984) does discuss this and provides much of what one needs for convex problems but doesn't discuss quasi-convexity. Luenberger also provides an excellent treatment of linear programming and numerical methods for solving constrained and unconstrained programming problems.

References

Luenberger, D. 1984. *Linear and Nonlinear Programming*, 2d ed. Reading, Mass.: Addison-Wesley.

Mangasarian, O. 1969. *Nonlinear Programming*. New York: McGraw-Hill.

A1.5. Problems

■ 1. What is the solution to the dieting consumer's problem if his calorie constraint is 1,650 calories? If his calorie constraint is 550 calories? If his calorie constraint is 1,600 calories?

■ 2. Suppose that our consumer also has a problem with his cholesterol levels. Each unit of wheat supplies 10 unit of cholesterol, whereas each unit of candy supplies 100. The consumer has been told by his doctor to limit his cholesterol intake to no more than 260 units per day. What is the optimal solution to the consumer's problem now, with this additional constraint (with a calorie constraint of 1,550 calories per day)? Be sure to compute the value of the multipliers. Then work through the solution if the consumer (a) is allowed 261 units of cholesterol per day, 1,550 calories per day, and has $10 to spend; (b) is allowed 260 units of cholesterol per day, 1,551 calories per day, and has $10 to spend; and (c) is allowed 260 units of cholesterol per day, 1,550 calories per day, and has $10.10 to spend. In terms of the coincidence we observed before, what happens in this case?

■ 3. I've assured you that for most of the problems you encounter in this book, when you have one candidate solution, you will know that you have a global optimum. A part of this assurance may be provided by the following fact: If, in the general problem with which this appendix began, the function f is strictly concave, and the functions g_i are all convex, then the problem necessarily has at most a single solution. Prove this.

appendix two

Dynamic programming

For the solving of all manner of dynamic choice problems, an important technique is *dynamic programming*. In this appendix you will be briefly introduced to the techniques and basic results. All readers should go through the material in the first two sections, which concerns finite horizon problems. The material in the rest of this appendix is only used in optional (small type) parts of the book (mostly in chapter 14), and so can be regarded as optional as well. But the techniques of infinite horizon dynamic programming are becoming more pervasive in economics generally, and many of you will find that you have to learn this stuff some day. In case you find the treatment here too cryptic (which is quite possible, given the small amount of space devoted to the subject here), references to more expansive treatments are provided at the end of this appendix.

A2.1. An example with a finite horizon

We begin with an example of finite horizon dynamic programming. (This is problem 3[a] from chapter 4.)

A consumer lives for three periods denoted by $t = 0, 1, 2$ and consumes artichoke and broccoli each day. We let a_t be the amount of artichoke consumed on day t, and we let b_t be the amount of broccoli. This consumer has preferences over lotteries on consumption bundles (where a consumption bundle is a six-tuple $(a_0, b_0, a_1, b_1, a_2, b_2)$) that satisfy the von Neumann-Morgenstern axioms and that are represented by the von Neumann-Morgenstern utility function

$$U(a_0, b_0, a_1, b_1, a_2, b_2) = (a_0 b_0)^{.25} + .9(a_1 b_1)^{.25} + .8(a_2 b_2)^{.25}.$$

This consumer can buy artichoke and broccoli in the marketplace each day. Because both vegetables spoil rapidly, what he buys on any given day is his consumption for that day. (He is constrained to consume nonnegative amounts of each vegetable.) The price of artichoke is $1 per unit on each and every day. The price of broccoli is more complex: It begins as $1 per unit of broccoli at $t = 0$. But at $t = 1$, it is either $1.10 or it is $.90, each of these being equally likely. And at $t = 2$, the price of broccoli is again random and depends on the price the day before: If the price was $1.10 at $t = 1$, then it is either $1.20 or $1.00, with each equally likely. If the price was $.90 at $t = 1$, then at $t = 2$ it is either $.98 or $.80, each equally likely. At date $t = 0$, the consumer has no information (beyond what is given above) about subsequent prices of broccoli. At date $t = 1$, he knows the current price of broccoli and no more. At date $t = 2$, he knows the current price.

This consumer has $300 to spend on artichoke and broccoli over the three days, which he can divide any way he wishes. Any money he doesn't spend on a given day sits in his pocket where it earns zero interest.

This is a fairly complex problem, because the consumer has a large number of decisions to make. He must decide how much artichoke and broccoli to consume at $t = 0$ (and, implicitly, how much of his $300 to save); given the price of broccoli at $t = 1$ he must decide how much of what remains of his $300 to save and how much to spend immediately on artichoke and broccoli, and he must decide how much to spend on artichoke and broccoli at $t = 2$, given prices at $t = 2$. Even if we assume that any money unspent at $t = 0$ and $t = 1$ is saved (which is certainly a reasonable assumption) and that all remaining money will be spent on broccoli or artichoke at $t = 2$ (also reasonable), this gives us two variables for $t = 0$, four variables for $t = 1$ (two vegetable amounts in each of two contingencies), and four variables for $t = 2$ (one vegetable amount in each of four contingencies). Rather than try to optimize over all ten variables at once, we will approach the problem in steps.

Step 1. Find contingent optimal decisions for $t = 2$. To begin, imagine that the consumer arrives at time $t = 2$ with z remaining to be spent. This consumer must decide how to allocate that z between artichoke and broccoli. Because his utility function U is additively separable over time periods, this decision can be made without reference to the earlier consumption decisions the consumer made. The consumer will solve the problem

$$\text{Given } z, \text{ maximize } .8(a_2 b_2)^{.25}$$
$$\text{subject to } a_2 + p_b b_2 \leq z,$$

where p_b is the current price of broccoli. This is a simple maximization problem, and if you go through the algebra, you'll find the solution

$$a_2 = \frac{z}{2} \quad \text{and} \quad b_2 = \frac{z}{2p_b}.$$

That is, the expenditures on the two types of vegetables are the same.[1]

From this we are able to compute the value of the objective function as a function of z for each of the four possible prices of broccoli. Substituting the optimal values of a_2 and b_2, the optimal value of $.8(a_2 b_2)^{.25}$ is

$$.8\left[\frac{z}{2}\right]^{.5}\left[\frac{1}{p_b}\right]^{.25},$$

which is (approximately) $.54048z^{.5}$ if $p_b = 1.2$, $.56569z^{.5}$ if $p_b = 1$, $.56855z^{.5}$ if $p_b = .98$, and $.59814z^{.5}$ if $p_b = .8$.[2]

We have determined the optimal *contingent* decisions at time $t = 2$, so-called because these decisions are contingent on two things: The price that prevails for broccoli, and the amount of money left to buy vegetables at $t = 2$.

Step 2. Find the optimal contingent decisions for $t = 1$. Now we step back to decisions that are made at $t = 1$. Imagine that the consumer has y left to spend at this point. He must divide this between immediate consumption of artichoke and broccoli and money left for $t = 2$. *From step 1, we know how much, on average, money left for $t = 2$ will be worth, assuming the consumer purchases vegetables optimally at date $t = 2$. Hence we can use that value in determining what decisions to make at $t = 1$.*

Let us illustrate: Suppose the price of broccoli is $\$.90$, so that next period the price will be either $\$.98$ or $\$.80$, each equally likely. The consumer must divide his y between artichoke, broccoli, and money left for $t = 2$. If we let a_1, b_1, and z be these three amounts, the expected utility

---

[1] If you have never worked with this sort of utility function before, and this solution seems remarkable to you, you should definitely do the algebra leading to this conclusion. This sort of utility function, which is part of the Cobb-Douglas family of utility functions, is much used in examples in economics. In fact, you might find it helpful to solve the problem $\max a^\alpha b^\beta c^\gamma$ subject to $p_a a + p_b b + p_c c \leq y$. Also try maximizing $\alpha \ln(a) + \beta \ln(b) + \gamma \ln(c)$ subject to the same constraint.

[2] These are, of course, indirect utility functions, and you should think of them as such if it helps your understanding.

for the consumer of the decision (a_1, b_1, z) (for periods $t = 1$ and $t = 2$ together) is

$$.9(a_1 b_1)^{.25} + [.5(.56855 z^{.5}) + .5(.59814 z^{.5})].$$

This is the crucial step, so let us take this slowly. The first term in the expression is the utility derived from the amounts of vegetable consumed immediately; and the second term (everything within the square brackets) is the expected utility derived from saving z until next period. The two .5s are the probabilities of the two different prices next time, and the terms inside the parentheses are the utilities derived from z in each of the two contingencies. So at $t = 1$, if the price of broccoli is \$.90, the consumer will pick (a_1, b_1, z) to maximize the function just displayed, subject to the constraint that

$$a_1 + .9 b_1 + z \leq y.$$

Similarly, if the price of broccoli is \$1.10, so the possible prices of broccoli next period are \$1.20 and \$1.00, the consumer will (at $t = 1$, if he has y with which to consume) solve

max $.9(a_1 b_1)^{.25} + [.5(.54048 z^{.5}) + .5(.56569 z^{.5})]$ subject to $a_1 + 1.1 b_1 + z \leq y$.

You are certainly capable of solving these two problems, although it may take a fair bit of scribbling on some scratch paper. We will give a trick for solving these two problems in the next paragraph (in small type), but this trick (while it employs dynamic programming in a perverse way) will probably confuse you more than help if you are seeing dynamic programming for the first time. So let us be clear that the key step to dynamic programming is what you have just seen and not what will follow in small type. The key step is that we solved the period $t = 2$ problem as a function of z and the price of broccoli, and then took the value of the optimal solution (as a function of z and the possible prices of broccoli) and employed it in determining what to do at date $t = 1$. Because we have already found the optimal way to spend z at $t = 2$, we don't need to include that explicitly in our $t = 1$ problems; we only need the optimal values as a function of z. We proceed to solve the two optimization problems posed above, by hook or by crook, which then gives us optimal value functions for consuming from $t = 1$ on to the end as a function of y and the price of broccoli at $t = 1$; after the small type we will use these value functions to solve the $t = 0$ problem facing the consumer. For the record, if you solve the two optimization problems given above, you get the following answers:

If the price of broccoli is $.90, set $a_1 = .27822y$, $b_1 = .30914y$, and $z = .44355y$, which gives expected utility equal to $.87590y^{1/2}$.

If the price of broccoli is $1.10, set $a_1 = .27899y$, $b_1 = .25363y$, and $z = .44201y$, which gives expected utility equal to $.83190y^{1/2}$.

How did we get these answers? The trick we employed was to look at the $t = 1$ problem in two pieces. Fix a division of the total resources y between immediate consumption and future consumption, say $y - z$ for now and z for later. Optimally divide the $y - z$ between immediate broccoli and artichoke. This is a simple problem; it shouldn't take you long to see (if you don't alreay know) that half of $y - z$ will be spent on each of the two vegetables, leading to $a_1 = (y - z)/2$ and $b_1 = (y - z)/(2p_b)$. This means that $y - z$ allocated for current consumption yields immediate utility

$$.9[(y - z)^2/(4p_b)]^{.25} = .9[1/p_b]^{.25}[(y - z)/2]^{.5}.$$

All this is for a fixed division of y into immediate and future consumption: We optimize the split by maximizing

$$.9[1/p_b]^{.25}[(y - z)/2]^{.5} + k(p_b)z^{.5},$$

where $k(p_b)$ is a constant which we take from whichever of the two objective functions we are working with; .58334 for $p_b = .90$ and .55308 for $p_b = 1.10$. If you do the algebra, you'll find these to be particularly simple optimization problems, leading to the answers we gave above.

Step 3. Find the optimal decisions for $t = 0$. Finally we get to $t = 0$. If we let a_0 be the amount of artichoke the consumer buys immediately, b_0 the amount of broccoli, and y the amount he saves, *and if we assume that, contingent on the price of broccoli at $t = 1$, the consumer proceeds optimally with the y that is in his pocket*, he will have expected utility

$$(a_0 b_0)^{.25} + [.5(.87590y^{.5}) + .5(.83190y^{.5})].$$

Once again, this is the sum of the immediate utility of consumption and the expected value provided by having y in hand beginning next period, where we average over the two possible prices. This objective function must be maximized subject to the constraint

$$a_0 + b_0 + y \leq 300,$$

and if you carry out the maximization, you will find that the solution is

$$a_0 = b_0 = 61.02 \text{ and } y = 177.96.$$

Now that we know the optimal value of y, we can reconstruct the optimal levels of consumption at time 1, depending on the price of broccoli. For example, if the price of broccoli at $t = 1$ is \$1.10, set

$$a_1 = (.27899)(177.96) = 49.65, b_1 = (.25362)(177.96) = 45.14, \text{ and}$$
$$z = (.44202)(177.96) = 78.66.$$

And with this, you can work out how to consume at date $t = 2$, depending on the price of broccoli.

A2.2. Finite horizon dynamic programming

We hope that the intuition behind this solution technique is fairly clear. We compute the optimal thing to do at the last date, contingent on conditions that apply. This gives us the expected value of carrying forward any amount of money from date $t = 1$ and then proceeding optimally, which we use to compute the optimal thing to do at $t = 1$, contingent on conditions then applying. And this gives us the expected value of carrying forward any amount of money from date $t = 0$ and then proceeding optimally, which we use to compute the optimal thing to do at time $t = 0$.

This technique works in all manner of problems besides consumption-savings problems. Here is another typical (and somewhat simpler) example. You are searching for employment. You have four interviews lined up today, and for reasons we will not go into, you will definitely take one of the four jobs. You know (given your sterling credentials) that each firm with which you interview will offer you a job; what is unclear is the wage they will offer. We let w_t be the wage offered by firm t, for $t = 1, 2, 3, 4$. You interview at each firm in turn, and at the end of the interview the firm offers you a wage. *If you refuse the job when it is offered, you cannot go back to it.* You must decide on the spot whether to take a particular job. Wage offers are all uniformly distributed on the interval $[0, 10]$ and are statistically independent of each other. You wish to maximize the expected wage you will be paid.

This is an example of an optimal stopping problem, so called because the sole decision you make is whether to "stop" the process or continue at each stage. It is used in modeling job search, searching for the lowest price at which to buy a good, searching for the highest quality individual among those being interviewed, deciding when to harvest a crop, and so on. The assumption that you are unable to recall a previous offer is, perhaps, a bit unnatural in the context we've described, and you might think of a somewhat more complex model where, if you refuse a job offer, you can later go back to it, but then there is a chance it will have been filled by someone else. (See problem 3.) Or you can think of a situation in which you must pay a cost every time you interview at another firm, but you can always go back to the best offer made so far. (See problems 1 and 2.)

We solve this problem using the same sort of technique we used in the previous section, by going to the last period and then working through to the first. If you haven't taken a job by the time you will interview at firm 4, you will be forced to take their offer. This gives you an expected wage of 5.

Hence when you hear the offer at firm 3, your decision is simple. If you are offered a wage below 5, you do better to continue on to firm 4, which gives you an expected wage of 5. But if you are offered a wage above 5, you do better to take this.

What, then, is your expected wage from following an optimal strategy at firms 3 and 4, given you didn't take a job at either firm 1 or firm 2? It is

$$\int_0^{10} \max\{w, 5\}(.1)dw.$$

This is obtained by averaging over all the possible values of w_3 the expected wages you will receive by acting optimally: If $w_3 < 5$, then your expected wage is 5 (because you continue on to firm 4), while if $w_3 \geq 5$, your expected wage is w_3.[3] If we evaluate this integral, we get

$$\int_0^{10} \max\{w, 5\}(.1)dw = \int_0^5 \max\{w, 5\}(.1)dw + \int_5^{10} \max\{w, 5\}(.1)dw$$

$$= \int_0^5 5(.1)dw + \int_5^{10} w(.1)dw = \frac{1}{2}5 + \frac{.1w^2}{2}\Big|_5^{10} = 2.5 + 3.75 = 6.25.$$

---

[3] The density of a uniform distribution on $[0, 10]$ is .1 for all $w \in [0, 10]$.

That is, if you turn down the jobs offered at firms 1 and 2 and proceed optimally, your expected wage will be 6.25.

So now it is clear what you should do upon hearing job offer 2. If this offer exceeds 6.25, take it. If it falls below 6.25, turn it down and take your chances with firms 3 and 4. And so proceeding optimally beginning with firm 2 gives you an expected wage of

$$\int_0^{10} \max\{w, 6.25\}(.1)dw = \int_0^{6.25} \max\{w, 6.25\}(.1)dw + \int_{6.25}^{10} \max\{w, 6.25\}(.1)dw$$

$$= \int_0^{6.25} 6.25(.1)dw + \int_{6.25}^{10} w(.1)dw$$

$$= \frac{5}{8}6.25 + \frac{.1w^2}{2}\Big|_{6.25}^{10} = 3.90625 + 3.046875 = 6.953125.$$

And now it is clear what you should do upon hearing job offer 1. If this offer exceeds 6.953125, take it. If it is less, then turn it down and take your chances with jobs 2, 3, and 4. (What is the expected wage you garner by following the optimal strategy in this case? If you work through the math, you should find that it is approximately 7.4173.)

Once again, the idea is that we solve the problem from the back. We work out what the optimal strategy and optimal value are starting from each time until the end recursively, where the optimal value starting at $t+1$ is used to find the optimal strategy and optimal value starting at time t. We are using the basic principle that

If a strategy is optimal for each point in time at that point of time, given that an optimal strategy will be used thereafter, then the strategy is optimal.

This is known as the *principle of optimality*, or as *Bellman's principle of optimality*, or as *the discrete maximum principle*.

Underpinning this principle is the following simple bit of mathematics. Suppose we wish to maximize a function of two variables, $f(x, y)$. For each x, we can find that value of y that maximizes $f(x, y)$ holding x fixed; and then we can find the overall maximum by optimizing over x. That is, first compute $f^*(x) = \max_y f(x, y)$, then maximize f^* over x. In symbols,

$$\max_{x,y} f(x, y) = \max_x [f^*(x)] = \max_x [\max_y f(x, y)]. \qquad (\star)$$

If we were being very precise about this, we'd worry about whether those maxima are achieved[a] and we'd worry, as in our first application, about how to handle constraints on the variables x and y. But the basic idea is conveyed by $(\star)$.

> There is nothing in $(\star)$ about the decision concerning y being made "after" the decision concerning x; equation $(\star)$ is phrased for a general two-variable optimization problem. So it is with dynamic programming. Most applications, and certainly most applications in economics, involve decisions made through time. In such cases, it is natural to work from later dates back to earlier dates. This is especially true in applications with uncertainty that resolves through time, because then later decisions are conditioned on more information. But from the point of view of the optimization theory being employed in dynamic programming, this isn't necessary. If, for example, there was no uncertainty in our artichoke and broccoli problem, then there would be nothing to prevent us from first finding the optimal way to split z between artichoke and broccoli at $t = 1$, then computing the optimal way to split y between artichoke and broccoli at $t = 0$ and funds for consumption at time $t = 1$, and then computing the optimal way to split the entire \$300 between the two types of vegetable at $t = 2$ and funds for consumption at $t = 0$ and $t = 1$. It might not be natural to think of the problem this way, but the optimization would go through just the same.

> We will, for the remainder of this appendix, speak in terms of decisions made through time and the use of dynamic programming to solve such optimization problems. But you should not be misled into thinking that to employ dynamic programming it is necessary that decisions have this sort of temporal ordering.

Things that link the past, the present, and the future

A difference between the consumption-savings problem of the previous section and the job-taking problem described in this section is that in the consumption-savings problem, when we analyze decisions made at later dates, we analyze those decisions depending on the level of money in the consumer's pocket (z or y) and the current price of broccoli. The amount of money in the consumer's pocket is a variable that links past decisions with present opportunities, and it links the present decision with future opportunities, and thus future values. The price of broccoli at any point in time determines (in part) current opportunities. But it also is used to "predict" future broccoli prices, and so it provides a further link between the past and present on one hand and the future on the other.

In general dynamic programming problems, the opportunities the decision maker has now and will have in the future depend on previous decisions made. And when there is uncertainty about the future, data

---

[a] Is $(\star)$ correct if we replace the *max*s with *sup*s?

from the past and present are useful in predicting the future. These links must be included in the analysis; optimal decisions and values must be computed contingent on whatever links are pertinent.

In this regard, note two things about the formulation of the consumption-savings problem used in the previous section.

(1) In general, one of the things that can link past with present and future is that past decisions can affect the preferences one has over current decisions. It is not hard to imagine an individual whose preferences mandate that excessive artichoke at $t = 0$ lessens the utility derived from artichoke at $t = 1$ and $t = 2$. The preferences that we specified did not have this property; because utility is additively separable through time, the marginal rates of substitution of broccoli for artichoke at any time beyond a given date are independent of consumption up to that date.

What would happen if we had preferences where the levels of consumption at one date affected the marginal rates of substitution at later dates? Then in solving for the optimal way to spend z at date $t = 2$, we would have to condition on past consumption levels. That is, we would compute "values of optimally continuing" as a function of z and the price of broccoli, as before, and also as a function of the vector (a_0, b_0, a_1, b_1). Depending on the exact specification of the consumer's preferences, we might be able to get away with something less than conditioning on the entire vector of past consumption. For example, if all that matters (in terms of previous consumption) to preferences for consumption at date t and beyond is the sum total consumption of artichoke, then we could condition our date 2 decisions on $a_0 + a_1$ and our date 1 decision on a_0 only.

In most applications in economics, preferences are assumed to be additively separable in just the fashion we've assumed here. (Additive separability is a bit more than is needed, but it is convenient parametrically.) The point to understand here is that this is a matter of analytical convenience and not necessity. In theory, one can use dynamic programming without additive separability as long as all the "links" between past, present, and future are properly taken into account. (For most applications, though, additive separability is a practical necessity, because otherwise the analysis becomes intractable.)

(2) Imagine that we reformulated the consumption-savings problem so that it has four time periods, and so that at $t = 0$, the price of broccoli is $1; at $t = 1$, it is either $1.10 or $.90; at $t = 2$, it is either $1.20, $1.00, or $.80; and at $t = 3$, it is $1.30, $1.10, $.90, or $.70. Imagine sitting at time $t = 2$ with a broccoli price of $1.20 and y in the consumer's pocket to spend

immediately or to save for period 3. The expected utility of funds saved depends on the future price of broccoli, and so the decision taken at $t = 2$ depends on the best current assessment of that future price.

It is easy to imagine a formulation of the evolution of the price of broccoli where the only relevant data for predicting future prices of broccoli is the current price of broccoli. For example, we can imagine a model where the price of broccoli rises or falls by a \$.10 in each period, with each of those two changes equally likely. In this case, the decision made at time $t = 2$ would depend on the current price of broccoli in two ways: This price determines what bundles of current vegetable are affordable, and it determines the distribution of the value of money set aside for future consumption.

But it is also possible to imagine formulations where best assessment that can be made at time $t = 2$ about the price of broccoli at time $t = 3$ depends on both the current price of broccoli and the price in the previous period. (Suppose broccoli takes two periods to harvest, and farmers who planted at time $t = 1$ determined how much to plant in part by looking at the prevailing price of broccoli.) In this case, in deciding how to split y at time $t = 2$ between current and future consumption, we have to condition the decision on the previous price of broccoli, as well as the current price, insofar as the previous price helps us to assess future prices.

If we had such a formulation, there would be no problem theoretically in using dynamic programming. Decisions made at $t = 2$ would be conditioned on previous prices of broccoli, as well as on current prices and the amount of money the consumer possesses.

As a practical matter, however, this increases the complexity of the problem by increasing the "number" of contingent problems that must be solved for $t = 2$. The analytical practicalities lead economists to formulate models in which the past is useful for predicting the future in particular low-dimensional ways. That is (if you know the terminology), models usually assume that there are low-dimensional statistics of the past that are sufficient for predicting the future, and these low-dimensional sufficient statistics become "state variables" or links in the dynamic programming formulations. Indeed, in many formulations it is assumed that current prices are sufficient for predicting the future; the fancy way of saying this is that *Markovian* assumptions are made.

A2.3. *An example with an infinite horizon*

While two examples certainly don't constitute a general theory, the two examples given will probably give you enough lead on how to use dynamic programming in finite horizon problems. A bit more complex is the use of dynamic programming techniques for infinite horizon problems. That is, we imagine a formulation in which there is no "last decision" from which we can begin our analysis; at each point in time there are always many more decisions to come. We look at a specific example in this section; the general theory is discussed in the next.

Consider the following variation on the consumption-savings problem of section A2.1. (This is problem 3[b] from chapter 4.) The consumer now consumes at times $t = 0, 1, 2, \ldots$. At each date, he consumes both artichoke and broccoli. His utility function, defined for an infinite stream of consumption $(a_0, b_0, a_1, b_1, \ldots)$ is

$$U(a_0, b_0, a_1, b_1, \ldots) = \sum_{t=0}^{\infty} (.95)^t (a_t b_t)^{.25}.$$

This consumer starts with wealth $1,000, which he can spend on vegetables or can deposit in his local bank. Any funds deposited at the bank earn interest at a rate of 2% per period, so that $1 deposited at time t turns into $1.02 at time $t + 1$.

The price of artichoke is fixed at $1. The price of broccoli is random. It begins at $1. Then, in each period, it either increases or decreases. Being very specific, if the price of broccoli at date t is p_t, then

$$p_{t+1} = \begin{cases} 1.1 p_t & \text{with probability .5, and} \\ .9 p_t & \text{with probability .5.} \end{cases}$$

The consumer wishes to manage his initial wealth $1,000 in a way that maximizes his expected utility. How should he do this?

We will "solve" this problem by using the following recipe.

Step 1. Guess what strategy our consumer should follow in this problem. Call your guess the candidate strategy.

Step 2. For the candidate strategy, compute the expected discounted utility the consumer will obtain if he follows this strategy as a function of his current level of wealth and the current price of broccoli.

*Step 3. Having computed the value of following the candidate strategy, ask the question, Can the consumer do any better by a strategy that is completely arbitrary at the start and then conforms forever after to the candidate strategy? If the answer is no, the candidate strategy is said to be **unimprovable**, where we should really say that it is unimprovable **in a single step**. If the strategy is not* *unimprovable, then it is not optimal. And, for a wide range of infinite horizon problems (including this problem), unimprovable strategies are optimal.*

This recipe is not, to be sure, very transparent, and you shouldn't despair that you don't understand it until after you've seen it worked out on an example (which happens momentarily). But it is probably sufficiently comprehensible so that you can see that it isn't really a recipe for solving the problem directly. If you have a guess what the solution is, this recipe allows you to check whether your candidate strategy is in fact optimal.

Now try this recipe out on our problem.

Step 1. Guess what strategy our consumer should follow in this problem. We guess that the strategy will take the following form: In each period the consumer spends a constant fraction of his wealth on current consumption, spending half that amount on artichoke and half on broccoli, with the rest of his wealth going into savings. We don't know what the fraction is, so for the time being we make it a variable, namely k.

Where did this guess come from? Since the solution to this problem is not original to this book, the accurate but not very useful answer is that it appears in the literature. But if it hadn't, some techniques lead to this guess; techniques that we will explore at the end of the next section. For now, assume that this guess is the result of brilliant inspiration.

Step 2. For the candidate strategy, compute the expected discounted utility the consumer will obtain if he follows this strategy as a function of his current level of wealth and the current price of broccoli. We perform this computation as follows: Let us write $v(y, p)$ for the value to the consumer of following the strategy just described if his initial wealth is y and the price of broccoli begins at p. (The initial conditions we are given are $y = 1,000$ and $p = 1$, but we take a slightly more general approach here.) And, to make the equations a bit prettier, let us write $\hat{k}$ for $1 - k$. Then $v(y, p)$ satisfies the functional equation

$$v(y, p) = \left[\frac{ky}{2} \frac{ky}{2p} \right]^{.25} + .95 \left[.5v(1.02\hat{k}y, 1.1p) + .5v(1.02\hat{k}y, .9p) \right].$$

This comes from the following considerations. If the guessed-at strategy is followed, and if we begin with initial conditions (y, p), then the strategy calls for setting immediate consumption of artichoke equal to $ky/2$ and immediate consumption of broccoli equal to $ky/(2p)$. The immediate utility from this is just the first term on the right-hand side. This strategy also means that $\hat{k}y$ will go into the bank, and so $1.02\hat{k}y$ will come out next period. The price of broccoli next period will be either $1.1p$ or $.9p$, each equally likely, and since the strategy we are following looks the same starting next period (as a function of the then initial conditions) as it does now, the value of following the strategy, discounted back to next time, is either $v(1.02\hat{k}y, 1.1p)$ or $v(1.02\hat{k}y, .9p)$, with each of these equally likely. The second term on the right-hand side is thus the expected value of the utility of future consumption (if we follow this strategy), where the extra .95 discounts this expected value back to the current period.

This is a pretty miserable looking functional equation, but now for the next bit of magic: If the guessed at strategy is followed, then $v(y, p)$ will have the form $Ky^{.5}/p^{.25}$ for some constant K. How do we know this? Think of it this way: If the consumer's initial wealth is doubled, then the strategy calls for him to eat precisely twice as much artichoke and broccoli this period, and his wealth next period will be precisely twice what it otherwise would have been, so in the next period he doubles his consumption, and so on. Given the consumer's utility function, this means that his utility goes up by the factor of $2^{.5}$. Similarly, if the price of broccoli were doubled, the consumer would spend the same amount of money on artichoke and broccoli in each period, but he would get half the broccoli he would have had otherwise, which, given his utility function, means his utility decreases by the multiplicative factor $1/2^{.25}$. (These are loose verbal arguments but they contain the germ of a formal proof; you are asked to provide a rigorous proof in problem 5.)

Once we know that this is the form of $v(y, p)$, we can substitute into the functional equation we had before, and we get the equation

$$K\frac{y^{.5}}{p^{.25}} = \left[\frac{ky}{2}\frac{ky}{2p}\right]^{.25} + .95\left[.5K\frac{[1.02\hat{k}y]^{.5}}{[1.1p]^{.25}} + .5K\frac{[1.02\hat{k}y]^{.5}}{[.9p]^{.25}}\right].$$

This doesn't look too much prettier, but looks are deceiving: It has its virtues. For one thing, the term $y^{.5}/p^{.25}$ can be factored out of both sides, leaving an equation in the variables K and k. (Recall that $\hat{k} = 1 - k$, so $\hat{k}$ is not another variable.) Taking that equation, a bit of fairly simple algebra will allow you to isolate K on one side of the equation; we obtain (approximately)

$$K = \frac{(k/2)^{.5}}{1 - .96096132\hat{k}^{.5}}. \qquad (\clubsuit)$$

Note what we've done: We considered a strategy of a particular form, parameterized by k, the fraction of wealth that is used for current consumption. Because of the simple nature of the strategy, we are able to prove (or, more precisely, you will prove for homework) that the expected utility of using that strategy has a particular functional form, up to a second parameter K. We could also find a functional equation of the expected utility of using the strategy, and from this we are able to find what value K takes as a function of parameter k.

It may be worth noting that this function, given by (♣) behaves rather well at the two extreme values of k, namely $k = 0$ and $k = 1$. If $k = 0$, then the consumer always invests all of his wealth and never has anything to eat. Of course, this leads to $K = 0$; if you never eat, you never get any utility. And if $k = 1$, then $\hat{k} = 0$, and $K = (1/2)^{.5}$; our consumer spends his entire endowment on initial consumption and, of course, this gives him utility $(y/2)^{.5}(1/p)^{.25}$.

One thing we can do immediately is to answer the question, Of all the strategies of the form of our guess, which value of k gives the highest lifetime utility? That is, which value of k gives the highest value of K? Taking the derivative of the function giving K in terms of k doesn't look particularly appealing, so we approach this problem numerically. Up to six decimal points, the K is maximized at $k^* = .076553$, for a value of $K^* = 2.55565129$. Note well: This doesn't show that the candidate strategy for k^* is the optimal strategy overall. All we've shown so far is that among strategies of this special type, k^* is best. (Indeed, it is only now that we have truly completed step 1. Until now we guessed at the form of the optimal solution. Now at last we have a single candidate strategy.)

But now we show that the strategy with k^* is optimal.

*Step 3. Having computed the value of following the candidate strategy, ask the question, Can the consumer do any better by a strategy that is completely arbitrary at the start and then conforms forever after to the candidate strategy? If the answer is no, the candidate strategy is said to be **unimprovable**, where we should really say that it is unimprovable **in a single step**. If the candidate strategy is not unimprovable, it is not optimal. And for a wide range of infinite horizon problems (including this problem), unimprovable strategies are optimal.*

The last line is the punchline, so please read it again. If the candidate strategy passes the test that it cannot be improved upon in a single step, then it is optimal. This isn't true for every problem in dynamic programming; but sufficient conditions will be supplied below, and for the time being you can rest content in the knowledge that this problem meets those conditions. If our strategy passes the unimprovability test, then we've got a winner.

Suppose, then, that the consumer begins with wealth y, when the price of broccoli is p. The immediate decisions to make are how much to spend on artichoke, how much on broccoli, and how much to save. Let a be the amount of artichoke consumed immediately, b the amount of broccoli, and z the amount saved. Then the utility the consumer obtains from these three immediate decisions *followed by conformance to our candidate solution* is

$$(ab)^{.25} + .95\left[.5K^* \frac{(1.02z)^{.5}}{(1.1p)^{.25}} + .5K^* \frac{(1.02z)^{.5}}{(.9p)^{.25}}\right].$$

This is the sum of the utility of immediate consumption and the expected utility from future consumption, discounted back to the current period. Note carefully that the candidate solution is buried in second term through the multiplicative factor K^*. More generally, what we have inside the brackets in the second term is the expected value of the value of the candidate solution, which we computed in step 2, averaged over the possible initial conditions beginning next period, given current conditions and current decisions. We wish to maximize this expression subject to the budget constraint $a+pb+z \leq y$, and we hope that the solution to this optimization problem is

$$a = k^*y/2, b = k^*y/(2p), \text{ and } z = (1 - k^*)y.$$

And, sure enough, if you plug in $K^* = 2.55565912$, the optimal solution has $a = .076553y/2$, and so on. Up to the limits of our computational ability, the candidate strategy is unimprovable in a single step. (And if we ground through the problem algebraically, we would find that the precise candidate solution is unimprovable.) Hence, by the test of step 3, our candidate solution is optimal.

A2.4. Stationary Markov decision problems

This is all very nice, but you may wonder why this test works, and how we might pose all this a bit more generally. (Also left in limbo is the question of how we ever managed to guess at the nature of the solution.) We will not give proofs, but by developing the theory just applied in greater generality, we can at least give the basic intuition.

Formulation of the general problem

We imagine a decision maker who must take an action α_t at each of a countable number of dates, $t = 0, 1, 2, \ldots$. A current "state of affairs" prevails at each time t, denoted by the variable θ_t.[b] The state θ_t serves three functions. First, it determines which actions are feasible at the current date; we write $A(\theta_t)$ as the set of actions feasible at time t as a function of the state θ_t. Second, together with the chosen action, it determines a reward that the decision maker receives at time t; we write $r(\theta_t, \alpha_t)$ for this reward. Third, it serves as a sufficient statistic of all history prior to date t for predicting the values of future state variables. If the decision maker takes action α_t at time t, the probability that the next state is θ_{t+1} (given all information available up to time t) is $\pi(\theta_{t+1}|\theta_t, \alpha_t)$.

The decision maker's problem is to select actions at each time as a function of past history to maximize the expected discounted sum of rewards he receives; that is, he seeks to maximize the expectation of

$$\sum_{t=0}^{\infty} \gamma^t r(\theta_t, \alpha_t),$$

where future states (and, therefore, future actions) are random. We assume that $\gamma \in [0, 1)$.

This sort of problem is called a *stationary Markov decision problem*. The modifier "Markov" is used because the current state is a sufficient statistic for predicting future states (given the current action). The modifier "stationary" is used because the problem facing the decision maker looks the same (contingent on the state) at each time t.

Our consumption-savings problem fits into this general framework (with one bit of shoehorning). Think of $\alpha_t = (a_t, b_t, z_t)$, where a_t is the amount of artichoke consumed at time t, b_t is the amount of broccoli consumed, and z_t is the amount of money saved for next period. For the state variable, think of $\theta_t = (y_t, p_t)$, where y_t is the amount of money available at the start of period t and p_t is the current price of broccoli. Then:

(1) $A(\theta_t) = \{(a_t, b_t, z_t) : a_t + p_t b_t + z_t \leq y_t,\ a_t, b_t, y_t \geq 0\}$; these are just the usual budget and nonnegativity constraints;

(2) $r(\theta_t, \alpha_t) = (a_t b_t)^{.25}$ for $\alpha_t = (a_t, b_t, z_t)$; that is, the immediate reward in any period is the utility of consumption in that period; and

---

[b] For reasons of analytical tractability, we assume that there are at most countably many possible values of θ_t. We won't explain why this assumption is made, except to say that we don't want the mathematical results we will announce in a bit to be incorrect, and without this technical condition one must worry about the measurability of some of the functions we define. It is possible to do without this assumption and, as we will note later, we must do without it to accommodate the example of the previous section, but then we would have to make a larger number of technical assumptions in footnotes similar to this one.

(3) $\theta_{t+1} = (y_{t+1}, p_{t+1})$ is determined by $\theta_t = (y_t, p_t)$ and $\alpha_t = (a_t, b_t, z_t)$ as follows: $y_{t+1} = 1.02 z_t$ with certainty, and p_{t+1} has probability distribution (conditional on p_t) given by

$$p_{t+1} = \begin{cases} 1.1 p_t & \text{with probability .5, and} \\ .9 p_t & \text{with probability .5.} \end{cases}$$

Finally, $\gamma = .95$.[c]

Strategies and value functions

A *strategy* for the Markov decision problem is a rule for choosing actions at each time t as a function of all the information available at time t, namely all previously taken actions and the present and all previous states. We write σ as a symbolic representation of a strategy, which is really quite a complex animal. Each strategy for choosing actions together with an initial state θ_0 leads to a probability distribution over the sequence of rewards the decision maker will receive, and so for each strategy σ we can (in theory) compute a function that gives the expected discounted sum of rewards the decision maker will receive by following σ as a function of the initial state θ_0. We denote this expected value by $v(\theta_0, \sigma)$.[d]

In general, it will be very hard to compute the expected value of following a strategy. But for some strategies the computation is not so difficult. The strategy σ is said to be *stationary* if the action prescribed by σ at time t when the current state is θ_t depends *only* on θ_t. The "only" here has two parts to it: The action chosen doesn't depend on the current date *per se*, and it doesn't depend on anything that happened prior to time t.

For a stationary strategy σ, we can build a *recursive equation* for the value function associated with using σ. We will write this equation and then explain it. One piece of notation is needed: When σ is a stationary strategy, we write $\sigma(\theta)$ for the action prescribed by σ when the state is θ. Then the recursive equation is

$$v(\theta_0, \sigma) = r(\theta_0, \sigma(\theta_0)) + \gamma \sum_{\theta} v(\theta, \sigma) \pi(\theta | \theta_0, \sigma(\theta_0)).$$

---

[c] There is one problem with this. The range of possible values of θ_t is uncountable, because there are uncountably many savings decisions that can be made. For this reason, the results we announce don't quite apply to our problem. Or, to be more precise, the results are correct, but it takes a bit more on the technical side to be sure that this is so.

[d] Some technical restrictions are needed to be sure the integrals that define this expectation are well defined. If r is bounded above or below, then the integrals are well defined, although values of minus or plus infinity, respectively, are not precluded.

Note that this is a recursive equation because the unknown function v appears on both sides. This equation arises as follows: If the intial state is θ_0 and the decision maker employs σ, then he takes action $\sigma(\theta_0)$ initially, giving immediate reward $r(\theta_0, \sigma(\theta_0))$. Moreover, the state at time $t = 1$ is θ with probability $\pi(\theta|\theta_0, \sigma(\theta_0))$. Starting next period, if the state is θ, the discounted sum of all rewards from next period on, discounted back to $t = 1$, is just $v(\theta, \sigma)$; this is so because σ is stationary. So the discounted expected value of all future rewards from using σ, discounted back to the present time $t = 0$, is $\gamma \sum_{\theta} v(\theta, \sigma) \pi(\theta|\theta_0, \sigma(\theta_0))$. The recursive equation, then, says that the value of following σ is the sum of the current reward and the discounted sum of all future rewards. With this recursive equation and a bit of luck or skill, we may be able to find $v(\theta, \sigma)$ (as we did in the example).

Having this recursive solution and being able to solve it are two different things, of course. Moreover, we can't be sure that every solution of the recursive equation is, in fact, the value function v. For example, if r is bounded, then $v \equiv +\infty$ and $v \equiv -\infty$ are both solutions of this equation. In the theory of dynamic programming, characterizations of solutions are given for particular special cases. A sample of typical results is

Proposition 1. (a) *Suppose r is a bounded function. Then $v(\cdot, \sigma)$ is the unique bounded solution of the recursive equation.* [e]
(b) *If r is bounded below, then $v(\cdot, \sigma)$ is the smallest solution of the recursive equation that is bounded below. If r is bounded above, then $v(\cdot, \sigma)$ is the greatest solution of the recursive equation that is bounded above.*
(c) *Suppose the range of possible states is a finite set Θ. Let Π be the $\Theta \times \Theta$ matrix whose θ, θ' term is $\pi(\theta'|\theta, \sigma(\theta))$. Then $v(\cdot, \sigma)$ is the vector $r(\sigma(\cdot), \cdot) \cdot (I - \gamma \Pi)^{-1}$, where I is the appropriately sized identity matrix. (Part of this statement is the assertion that the matrix $(I - \gamma \Pi)$ is in fact invertible.)* [f]

The optimal value function, optimal strategies, and Bellman's equation

For every conceivable strategy σ, stationary or not, we can compute $v(\cdot, \sigma)$, the expected value of using σ, considered as a function of the initial state. The *optimal value function* is then defined as

$$f(\theta) = \sup_{\sigma} v(\theta, \sigma),$$

---

[e] We remind the careful reader that $\gamma < 1$ is assumed throughout. In treatments of dynamic programming where this restriction on γ is removed (a) would not hold.

[f] If the notion of the inverse of an infinite dimensional matrix is not too much for you to stomach, part (c) generalizes to countable state spaces as long as r is bounded.

where the *supremum* is taken over all conceivable strategies σ. And strategy σ is *optimal* if $f(\theta) = v(\sigma, \theta)$ for all θ. Moreover, we have the following recursive equation for f.

Proposition 2. *The optimal value function f satisfies the recursive equation*

$$f(\theta_0) = \sup_{\alpha \in A(\theta_0)} \left[r(\theta_0, \alpha) + \gamma \sum_{\theta} f(\theta) \pi(\theta | \theta_0, \alpha) \right].$$

This is known as *Bellman's equation* or the *optimality equation*. The idea it expresses is that the optimal value is obtained if one takes the best possible action in the first period and then employs an optimal strategy. It takes a proof (and, in fact, it requires some technical conditions, conditions similar to those that guarantee all the expectations that make up value functions are well-defined). But it should not be so hard to believe.

Conserving strategies

Suppose we could find a strategy σ that attained the supremum in Bellman's equation for every state θ. That is, for all θ_0, σ satisfies

$$f(\theta_0) = r(\theta_0, \sigma(\theta_0)) + \gamma \sum_{\theta} f(\theta) \pi(\theta | \theta_0, \sigma(\theta_0)).$$

Such a strategy is called *conserving*, because it conserves the optimal value; if you use this strategy for one stage and then follow an optimal strategy (which gives you value f), you will get the optimal value.

Proposition 3. *(a) Any optimal strategy σ is conserving.*

(b) If r is bounded above, then any conserving strategy is optimal.

In other words, being a conserving strategy is equivalent to being optimal for a wide range of problems, including all those where r is bounded.

> The qualification is necessary, as the following simple example demonstrates: Suppose $\Theta = \{0, 1, 2, \ldots\}$, $A(\theta) = \{\theta + 1, 0\}$ for $\theta > 0$, and $A(0) = \{0\}$. Transitions from one state to the next are very simple; you go with certainty to the state that has the same label as the action you select. That is, from state $\theta > 0$ you can choose to go either to $\theta + 1$ or to 0. Once you get to state 0, you never get out. Rewards are given by

$$r(\theta, \alpha) = \begin{cases} 0 & \text{if } \alpha = \theta + 1, \text{ and} \\ (1/\gamma)^{\theta} & \text{if } \alpha = 0, \end{cases}$$

if $\theta > 0$, and $r(0,0) = 0$. That is, if you choose to make a transition to state 0 from $\theta > 0$, you receive a reward whose size grows with θ in a way that just offsets the discount rate. In all other cases, you get zero reward. You can show that in this case $f(n) = 1/\gamma^n$; if you start at $t = 0$ in state $\theta = n$, then as long as you make the transition to state 0 sometime, you get $1/\gamma^n$ (in present value terms). But then one conserving strategy is $\sigma(\theta) = \theta + 1$; always put off making the transition. It is conserving, because there is never any hurry to make the transition to 0, as long as you do it. The problem is that with this particular conserving strategy you never make the transition to 0, so you never accrue any reward.

Once you have digested this example, consider a simple variation in which the reward of moving from θ to 0 is $(1/\gamma)^\theta - 1$. In this case, things get better and better the longer you delay the transition to state 0. But if you never make the transition, you never get a positive reward. What is f in this case? Which strategies are conserving? Which strategies are optimal?

The intuition behind proposition 3(b) can now be seen. If r is bounded above, then the value of rewards accrued in the distant future must vanish (because of the discount factor). So "conserving" the optimal value does not mean putting off an ever bigger prize, and (one can prove) conserving strategies are optimal.

In what ways is the notion of a conserving strategy useful? To apply this notion, you have to know the optimal value function f. In most problems, you will not know what f is, and so as a means of finding a specific optimal strategy, this concept isn't useful. (In a few cases you can determine what f is from first principles. And you can sometimes "compute" f by approximating an infinite horizon problem with infinite horizon problems; this is called *value iteration* in the literature.)

But there is another way to use the notion of a conserving strategy. Suppose you can argue from first principles and assumptions made that a conserving strategy exists. For example, if each $A(\theta)$ is finite, then there must be a conserving strategy, since then the supremum is automatically a maximum. Then if r is bounded above, you know that an optimal strategy *exists*, which is not otherwise guaranteed.[9]

Sometimes you can argue from first principles that f takes a particular form. And then you can get a lead on what an optimal strategy must look like. A particular example of this is our consumption-savings problem. Recall the argument we employed to show that, for our candidate strategy σ, $v(\cdot, \sigma)$ takes the form $Ky^{.5}/p^{.25}$ for some constant K. By a similar argument it can be shown that the optimal value function f takes the form $Ly^{.5}/p^{.25}$ for some L. It may be helpful to see a bit of the argument sketched. (You are asked to give the complete argument in problem 5.) Take any y and p and any strategy σ that is

---

[9] For example, see the variation sketched three paragraphs ago.

feasible starting at (y, p). Consider starting the problem with λy and p for $\lambda > 0$, and consider modifying σ so that the consumer simply scales up (or down) all consumption and savings decisions by the constant λ. This strategy will be feasible starting at $(\lambda y, p)$. And it will deliver utility $\lambda^{.5}v(\sigma, (y, p))$. Hence $f((\lambda y, p)) \geq \lambda^{.5}v(\sigma, (y, p))$ for all σ. Since σ is arbitrary here, $f((\lambda y, p)) \geq \lambda^{.5}f((y, p))$. And since λ can be replaced by $1/\lambda$ and y by λy in this inequality, we see that $f((\lambda y, p)) = \lambda^{.5}f((y, p))$. By a similar argument, $f((y, \lambda p)) = f((y, p))/\lambda^{.25}$. If you work at it, you will see that these two equations establish that f takes the form we indicated. (Hint: Let $L = f(1, 1)$.)

Knowing that f takes the form $Ly^{.5}/p^{.25}$ is extremely helpful in one way. Once we know this, we can work out the form of any conserving strategy from Bellman's equation. It should come as no surprise to learn that if f takes this form, then conserving strategies must be of the form of our candidate solution. Spend a constant fraction of y on current consumption and save the rest, and divide current spending half each on artichoke and broccoli. We don't know, of course, the constant k of y that is spent on current consumption until we know what L is. But we know that the optimal strategy, since it is conserving, must take this form. And then we can proceed to the next bit of technique.[h]

Unimprovable strategies

The strategy σ is said to be *unimprovable* if it satisfies Bellman's equation with $v(\cdot, \sigma)$ in place of f; i.e., if for all θ_0,

$$v(\theta_0, \sigma) = \sup_{\alpha \in A(\theta_0)} \left[r(\theta_0, \alpha) + \gamma \sum_{\theta} v(\theta, \sigma)\pi(\theta|\theta_0, \alpha) \right],$$

or, equivalently, if $\sigma(\theta_0)$ achieves the supremum in the expression on the right-hand side for every θ_0. As noted in the previous section, a more apt description of this property is "unimprovability in a single step."

Proposition 4. *(a) Any optimal strategy σ is unimprovable.*

(b) If r is bounded below, then any unimprovable strategy is optimal.

Here is the canonical example to show why you need to assume that rewards are bounded below. Let $\Theta = \{1, 2, 3, \ldots\}$ and let $A(\theta) = \{C, F\}$. No

---

[h] Perhaps you wish to object: In the problem of the previous section, r wasn't bounded above. But this objection doesn't hold water. We are using here the result that every optimal strategy is conserving; once we characterize the nature of all conserving strategies, we a fortiori have characterized the nature of any optimal strategy.

matter what action you take in state θ, transition on the next step is to $\theta + 1$ with probability one. But there is a difference in the two actions: $r(\theta, F) = 0$ while $r(\theta, C) = -(1/\gamma)^\theta$. That is, F is free, and C is costly. Of course, the optimal strategy is always to choose F, yielding $f = 0$. But consider the abysmal strategy σ that always chooses C. This gives a total discounted cost $v(\theta, \sigma) = -\infty$. The point is that σ is unimprovable. If you choose F for one period and then revert back to σ, your expected value will continue to be $-\infty$. The only way to do better than σ is to deviate from it at all but a finite number of periods (and the best thing is to deviate from it all the time); since unimprovability only checks one-step deviations, σ passes the test of unimprovability.

From this example, you may be able to see the intuition behind proposition 4(b). If a strategy is unimprovable in a single step, then (one can show by induction) it is unimprovable if you change it over any finite time horizon. It can be suboptimal, then, only if it is "bad" in the arbitrarily far distant future. But if rewards are bounded below (and we are discounting with a discount factor strictly less than one), no strategy can be that bad in the arbitrarily far distant future. Hence unimprovability over any finite horizon implies optimality.

In the previous section we saw how useful proposition 4 can be.

A2.5. *Bibliographic notes and discussion*

For the purposes of this book, the functional equation for $v(\cdot, \sigma)$ and proposition 4(b) are what matters. And when we wish to use these two, r will be bounded and Θ will be finite so there will be no difficulties encountered at all.

But the theory of dynamic programming, which is used more and more in economics, goes far beyond the little we've mentioned here. And complementary to the theory of dynamic programming, which envisions decisions made at discrete points in time, is control theory, where the decision maker is continually choosing actions. We recommend the following for further reading: Howard (1960) is an excellent introduction to the subject. Ross (1983) is perhaps one level deeper. Whittle (1982) is authoritative. Stokey and Lucas (1989) is another complete treatment that is expecially useful because it is devoted to applications in economic theory.

References

Howard, R. 1960. *Dynamic Programming and Markov Processes.* Cambridge, Mass.: MIT Press.

Ross, S. 1983. *Introduction to Stochastic Dynamic Programming.* Boston: Academic Press.

Stokey, N.; and Lucas, R. 1989. *Recursive Methods in Economic Dynamics.* Cambridge, Mass.: Harvard University Press.

Whittle, P. 1982. *Optimization Over Time*, vols. I, II. New York: John Wiley and Sons.

A2.5. Problems

■ 1. In the problem of section A2.3, suppose that you can interview up to 4 firms, where each will offer you a wage uniformly distributed on the interval $[0, 10]$. Every time you interview, though, you pay a fee of $1. What is the optimal strategy to follow if you must take an offer when made, as in section A2.3? What is the optimal strategy to follow if you can always go back to previous offers?

■ 2. Now consider problem 1, but in the case where you can interview infinitely many firms at a cost of $1 per firm.

■ 3. In the problem of section A2.3, suppose that if you turn down a job, you can later make (costless) inquiries to see if it is still available, but there is a probability that the job will already have been filled. Because this is a difficult problem, consider the case where there are only three possible jobs. And suppose that if you turn down job 1, there is a .5 probability that it will be filled when you hear the offer made at job 2, and a .75 chance that it will be filled when you hear the offer made at job 3; and if you turn down job 2, there is a .5 probability that it will be filled when you hear the offer made at job 3. What is the optimal strategy to follow? (Hint: Suppose you are offered a wage of 5 at job 1 and 6 at job 2. Do you make inquiries about the availability of the job at firm 1? You may wish to do so, if not for 5 and 6, then for other numbers where job 1 pays less than job 2, and you won't have the answer until you understand why this is.)

■ 4. (a) Consider the following problem. You are driving down a long line of parking spaces, looking for a place to park your car. Think of potential parking spaces at locations $-100, -99, -98, \ldots, -1, 0, 1, 2, \ldots$. You are currently at location -100, which is unoccupied, and you are considering whether to park there. If you decide not to park there, you will drive a bit further and see whether location -99 is occupied or not; if it is, you must proceed to -98; and if not, you must decide whether to park there or try your luck with -98, and so on. You cannot circle back to empty parking spots; U-turns are strictly forbidden. Each spot is occupied with another car with probability $\alpha < 1$, and whether a spot is occupied is independent of the occupancy of any and all other slots. You know the value of α. Your objective is to park as close as possible to location 0. More specifically, if you park in location n, then the cost to you is $|n|$, and you seek to minimize the expected cost you incur. You are able to see only the occupancy status of one spot at a time. What should you do? What is the expected cost to you?

(b) Suppose that when you are at spot n, you can see the occupancy status of spot n and the next five spots ahead. What should you do? What is the expected cost to you?

(c) Suppose that you don't know the value of α. Being very specific, suppose $\alpha = .9$ or $\alpha = .7$, with each of these two values being equally likely. (If you know the terminology, this makes the occupancy status of the spots exchangeable instead of being independent.) What should you do? What is the expected cost to you? (Use the formulation where you cannot see ahead. A numerically derived solution is quite adequate. An important first step is to decide on what links the "past" to the "future" in this problem.

■ 5. (a) Give a rigorous proof of the assertion that if in the consumption savings problem of section A2.3 you spend constant and equal fractions of your wealth on artichoke and broccoli (and save the rest), then your discounted expected utility takes the form $Ky^{.5}/p^{.25}$, where y is your current wealth and p is the current price of broccoli.

(b) Give a rigorous proof of the assertion that the optimal value function f in this context takes the form $Ly^{.5}/p^{.25}$.

■ 6. Suppose in the consumption-savings problem of section A2.3 the price of broccoli is constant (and equal, say, to 2), but now there are two ways to save. You can put your savings in a bank, where $1 put in today returns $1.02 tomorrow. Or you can invest in a risky asset that for every $1 invested on one day returns either $1.07 or $.99 the following day, with each of these values equally likely. (The return on the risky asset is independent from one day to the next.) What is the optimal strategy to follow in this case?

■ 7. Consider the variation on the example given following proposition 3. Are there any conserving strategies in this case? Are there any optimal strategies?

index

Absolute risk aversion, Anscombe and Aumann theory of, 109

Actor, in microeconomic theory, 3–4

Actuarial fairness, demand for insurance and, 92

Actuarial unfairness, demand for insurance and, 92, 97n.j

Acyclicity of preferences, 22

"Adding up" constraint, syndicate theory and, 169–74

Additive across states representation, 102

Additivity, finite actions and outcomes and, 586

Adverse selection, 577; Akerlof's model of lemons, 625–29; human factors in transaction cost economics, 746–47; optimal contract design and, 703; profit-maximizing insurance contracts and, 661–74; signaling quality and, 629–45; worker self-selection from menu of contracts, 638–44

Agent normal form game, trembling-hand perfection and, 441

Agents: effort incentives and, 579–80; incentives for interaction, 613; multiple, 610–11; reservation level of utility and, 580; risk averse, 583–85; risk neutral, 582–83

Aggregate demand, 62–63 consumer choice models and, 4–5; correspondence, defined, 210; existence and Walrasian equilibrium, 207–208, 209–210; fixed point theorem and, 212–13; monopoly and, 299; upper semicontinuity of, 210–211 Walras' law, 41n.8

Akerlof's model of lemons, 625–69

Algebra, in profit-maximization insurance contracts, 670

Allais paradox, 116; framing and, 118

Alternating offer bargaining: bibliographic notes, 570; in bilateral bargaining, 564–65; experimental evidence about, 565–68

Anscombe and Aumann theory, 103–

110; Ellsberg paradox, 117–18; normative applications of, 121

Anticipatory equilibrium: game theory and, 649–50; model for market signaling, 644–45

Arbitrage opportunity, 94

Arborescence, in extensive form game trees, 363; uniqueness in, 365–66

Archimedean axiom: limits of, 81; probability distributions, 75–76

Arrow-Debreu contingent claim theory: bibliographic notes, 224; general equilibrium theory and, 217–20

Arrow's impossibility theorem, Gibbard-Satterthwaite theorem and, 712–13

Arrow's possibility theorem, 164; absence of dictator and, 177–78; bibliographic notes on, 181; Borda rule, 176; independence of irrelevant alternatives, 177; interpersonal comparisons of preference intensity, 180–81; major-